EMPLOYMENT DISCRIMINATION LAW

CASES AND MATERIALS ON EQUALITY IN THE WORKPLACE

Ninth Edition

■ ■ ■

Maria L. Ontiveros
Professor of Law
University of San Francisco School of Law

Roberto L. Corrada
Mulligan Burleson Chair in Modern Learning and Professor of Law
University of Denver, Sturm College of Law

Michael Selmi
Samuel Tyler Research Professor of Law
The George Washington University Law School

Melissa Hart
Professor of Law
University of Colorado Law School

for

THE LABOR LAW GROUP

AMERICAN CASEBOOK SERIES®

444 Cedar Street, Suite 700
St. Paul, MN 55101
1-877-888-1330

Printed in the United States of America

ISBN: 978-1-63459-747-0

For Paul, Henry, and Clara, and in memory of my parents.

M.L.O.

For Amelia and Maximo.

R.L.C.

For Fiona and Seamus.

M.S.

For Kevin, Talia, and Noah.

M.H.

FOREWORD

The Labor Law Group had its origins in the desire of scholars to produce quality casebooks for instruction in labor and employment law. Over the course of its existence, the hallmarks of the Group have been collaborative efforts among scholars, informed by skilled practitioners, under a cooperative nonprofit trust in which royalties from past work finance future meetings and projects.

At the 1946 meeting of the Association of American Law Schools, Professor W. Willard Wirtz delivered a compelling paper criticizing the labor law coursebooks then available. His remarks so impressed those present that the Labor Law Roundtable of the Association organized a general conference on the teaching of labor law to be held in Ann Arbor in 1947. The late Professor Robert E. Mathews served as coordinator for the Ann Arbor meeting, and several conferees agreed to exchange proposals for sections of a new coursebook that would facilitate training exemplary practitioners of labor law. Beginning in 1948, a preliminary mimeographed version was used in seventeen schools; each user supplied comments and suggestions for change. In 1953, a hardcover version was published under the title *Labor Relations and the Law*. The thirty-one "cooperating editors" were so convinced of the value of multicampus collaboration that they gave up any individual claims to royalties. Instead, those royalties were paid to a trust fund to be used to develop and "provide the best possible materials" for training students in labor law and labor relations. The Declaration of Trust memorializing this agreement was executed November 4, 1953, and remains the Group's charter.

The founding committee's hope that the initial collaboration would bear fruit has been fulfilled. Under Professor Mathews's continuing leadership, the Group's members produced *Readings on Labor Law* in 1955 and *The Employment Relation and the Law* in 1957, edited by Robert Mathews and Benjamin Aaron. A second edition of *Labor Relations and the Law* appeared in 1960, with Benjamin Aaron and Donald H. Wollett as coeditors of the book and cochairs of the Group, and a third edition was published in 1965, with Jerre S. Williams at the helm.

In June 1969 the Group, now chaired by William P. Murphy, sponsored a conference to reexamine the labor law curriculum. Practitioners and full-time teachers, including nonmembers as well as members of the Group, attended the meeting, held at the University of Colorado. In meetings that followed the conference, the Group decided to reshape its work substantially. It restructured itself into ten task forces, each assigned a unit of no more than two hundred pages on a discrete topic such as employment discrimination or union-member relations. An individual teacher could then choose two or three of these units as the material around which to build a particular course. This multiunit approach dominated the Group's work throughout much of the 1970s under Professor Murphy and his successor as chair, Herbert L. Sherman, Jr.

As the 1970s progressed and teachers refined their views about what topics to include and how to address them, some units were dropped from the series while others increased in scope and length. Under Professor Sherman's leadership, the Group planned a new series of six enlarged books to cover the full range of topics taught by labor and employment law teachers. Professor James E. Jones, Jr., was elected chair in 1978, and he shepherded to completion the promised set of six full-size, independent casebooks. The Group continued to reevaluate its work and eventually decided that it was time to convene another conference of law teachers.

In 1984 the Group, now chaired by Robert Covington, sponsored another general conference to discuss developments in the substance and teaching of labor and employment law, this time in Park City, Utah. Those discussions and a subsequent working session led to the conclusion that the Group should devote principal attention to three new conventional length coursebooks, one devoted to employment discrimination, one to union-management relations, and one to the individual employment relationship. In addition, work was planned on more abbreviated coursebooks to serve as successors to the Group's earlier works covering public employment bargaining and labor arbitration.

In 1989, with Alvin Goldman as chair, the Group met in Breckenridge, Colorado, to assess its most recent efforts and develop plans for the future. In addition to outlining new coursebook projects, the Group discussed ways to assist teachers of labor and employment law in their efforts to expand conceptual horizons and perspectives. In pursuit of the latter goals it cosponsored, in 1992, a conference held at the University of Toronto Faculty of Law at which legal and nonlegal specialists examined alternative models of corporate governance and their impact on workers.

When Robert J. Rabin became chair in 1996, the Group and a number of invited guests met in Tucson, Arizona, to celebrate the imminent fiftieth anniversary of the Group. The topics of discussion included the impact of the global economy and of changing forms of representation on the teaching of labor and employment law, and the impact of new technologies of electronic publishing on the preparation of teaching materials. The Group honored three of its members who had been present at the creation of the Group, Willard Wirtz, Ben Aaron, and Clyde Summers. The Group next met in Scottsdale, Arizona, in December 1999, to discuss the production of materials that would more effectively bring emerging issues of labor and employment law into the classroom. Among the issues discussed were integration of international and comparative materials into the labor and employment curriculum and the pedagogical uses of the World Wide Web.

Laura J. Cooper became chair of the Group in July 2001. In June 2003, the Group met in Alton, Ontario, Canada. The focus there was on "labor law on the edge"—looking at doctrinal synergies between workplace law and other legal and social-science disciplines—and "workers on the edge"—exploring the legal issues of highly compensated technology workers, vulnerable immigrant employees, and unionized manufacturing employees threatened by foreign competition. The Group also heard a report from its study of the status of the teaching of labor and employment law in the nation's law schools and discussed the implications of the study for the Group's future projects. Members of the Group began work on the casebook on international labor law at this meeting. During Professor Cooper's term, the Group also finished its popular reader *Labor Law Stories*, which examines the stories behind many of the most important American labor law cases.

In July 2005, Kenneth G. Dau-Schmidt became the chair of the Labor Law Group. Shortly after his election, the Group held a meeting in Chicago with nationally recognized practitioners to discuss how best to teach students about the practice of labor law in the new global economy of the information age. The outline that resulted from this meeting served as the basis for *Labor Law in the Contemporary Workplace*. Following the Chicago meeting, the Group met several times to work on new editions of its books and develop new projects: June 2006 in Saratoga Springs, New York; June 2007 in St. Charles, Illinois; and June 2010 in Arrowhead, California. Group projects that grew out of or benefited from these meetings include *International Labor Law: Cases and Materials on Workers' Rights in the Global Economy* and *A Concise Hornbook on Employment Law*. The Group also hosted: a November 2007 symposium on the problems of low-wage workers, the proceedings of which were published in the *Minnesota Law Review*; a February 2009 symposium on the American Law Institute's Proposed Restatement of Employment Law, the proceedings of which were published in the *Employee Rights and Employment Policy Journal*; and a November 2010 symposium on labor and employment law policies under the Obama administration, the proceedings of which were published in the *Indiana Law Journal*.

Marion Crain became chair of the Group at the beginning of 2011. That same year, the Group sponsored a one-day conference on the crisis confronting public-sector employment, the proceedings of which were published in the *ABA Journal of Labor and Employment Law*. In 2011 the Group also hosted a meeting of experts in Chicago to consider the ongoing Restatement of Employment Law project. In June 2012, the Group met in Asheville, North Carolina, and approved the formation of an editorial policy committee charged with establishing policies to ensure that the Group's products continue to reflect its tradition of close collaboration and high standards. The Asheville meeting served as the genesis for a labor arbitrator training workshop for academics in Chicago in December 2012. In February 2013, the Group cosponsored a symposium at the University of California-Irvine School of Law on alternatives to the Wagner Act and employment law models of workplace protection. The proceedings of the conference, called "Re-imagining Labor Law: Building Worker Collectivities After the NLRA," will be published in the *UC Irvine Law Review*. In June 2014, the Group met in Ithaca, New York and conducted a lively educational program.

Steve Befort and Melissa Hart became Co-Chairs of the Group at the beginning of 2015. In that year, Group members voted to approve a partnership between the Group and the Chicago-Kent Law School to oversee the publication of the Employee Rights and Employment Policy Journal. As of the date of this publication, Group members are working on one new casebook and three new casebook editions.

At any one time, roughly twenty-five to thirty members are actively engaged in the Group's work; this has proven to be a practical size, given the challenges of communication and logistics. Coordination and editorial review of the projects are the responsibility of the executive committee, whose members are the successor trustees of the Group. Governance is by consensus; votes are taken only to elect trustees and to determine whom to invite to join the Group. Since 1953, more than eighty persons have worked on Group projects; in keeping with the original agreement, none has ever received anything more than reimbursement of expenses.

The Labor Law Group currently has eight books in print. West has published *Public Sector Employment: Cases and Materials* (Second Edition) by Martin H. Malin, Ann C. Hodges, and Joseph E. Slater; *Principles of Employment Law* by Peggie R. Smith, Ann C. Hodges, Susan J. Stabile, and Rafael Gely; *Labor Law in the Contemporary Workplace* (Second edition) by Kenneth G. Dau-Schmidt, Martin H. Malin, Roberto L. Corrada, Christopher David Ruiz Cameron, and Catherine L. Fisk (Second Edition); *International Labor Law: Cases and Materials on Workers' Rights in the Global Economy* by James Atleson, Lance Compa, Kerry Rittich, Calvin William Sharpe, and Marley S. Weiss; *Employment*

Discrimination Law: Cases and Materials on Equality in the Workplace (Ninth Edition) by Maria L. Ontiveros, Roberto L. Corrado, Michael L. Selmi, and Melissa Hart; *ADR in the Workplace* (Third Edition) by Laura J. Cooper, Dennis R. Nolan, Richard A. Bales, and Stephen F. Befort, and *Legal Protection for the Individual Employee* (Fifth Edition) by Kenneth G. Dau-Schmidt, Matthew W. Finkin and Robert N. Covington. Foundation Press has published the Group's eighth book, *Labor Law Stories*, edited by Laura J. Cooper and Catherine L. Fisk.

Employment Discrimination Law: Cases and Materials on Equality in the Workplace is the ninth edition of the Labor Law Group's casebook on employment discrimination.

Maria L. Ontiveros is Professor of Law at the University of San Francisco School of Law. She has earned degrees from the University of California, Harvard Law School, Cornell University, and Stanford Law School. Her research interests focus on workplace issues affecting women of color and organizing immigrant workers. Professor Ontiveros has been a member of the Labor Law Group since 1998 and was a co-author of the eighth edition of *Employment Discrimination Law*, as well as the supplements.

Roberto L. Corrada holds the Mulligan Burleson Chair in Modern Learning and is a Professor of Law at the University of Denver Sturm College of Law. He earned his undergraduate degree from the George Washington University and his law degree from the Catholic University of America's Columbus School of Law. His scholarship and teaching interests include labor and employment discrimination law, administrative law, the scholarship of teaching and learning, contracts, and LatCrit theory. He has been a member of the Labor Law Group since 2000 and was a co-author of the eighth edition of *Employment Discrimination Law*.

Michael Selmi is the Samuel Tyler Research Professor at George Washington University Law School where he teaches employment discrimination and employment law. He has published widely in those areas, and prior to entering teaching, he litigated employment discrimination cases with the U.S. Department of Justice and the Lawyers' Committee for Civil Rights. He graduated from Harvard Law School and clerked for Chief Judge James Browning of the U.S. Court of Appeals for the Ninth Circuit. Professor Selmi has been a member of the Labor Law Group since 2006 and joined the Employment Discrimination Law casebook with its eighth edition.

Melissa Hart is a Professor of Law at the University of Colorado School of Law where she has been teaching Employment Discrimination, Civil Procedure and Legal Ethics since 2001. Her research has focused on class action litigation of discrimination claims, and the role of subjective judgment in employment decisionmaking and its implication for both litigation and compliance efforts. Before teaching, Professor Hart was a lawyer at the U.S. Department of Justice and a law clerk for Judge Guido Calabresi on the U.S. Court of Appeals for the Second Circuit and Justice John Paul Stevens on the U.S. Supreme Court. Professor Hart has been a member of the Labor Law Group since 2009.

PREFACE

This is the ninth edition of the Labor Law Group's casebook on employment discrimination law, which was first published in 1971 under the title *Discrimination in Employment: Unit Three of Labor Relations and Social Problems.* Beginning with the sixth edition, a new title, *Employment Discrimination Law: Cases and Materials on Equality in the Workplace*, was adopted, reflecting the maturation, since the publication of the first edition, of employment discrimination law as a critical tool in the broader goal of implementing equality in society.

Like prior editions, this edition focuses primarily on the federal statutory protections against discrimination in employment, and, when appropriate, the role of constitutional provisions and state laws on workplace equality are also explored. Cases dealing with discrimination on the basis of race, color, religion, sex, and national origin, that arise under Title VII of the Civil Rights Act of 1964, as amended, form the foundation of any study of employment discrimination law. Other federal statutes studied include § 1981, the Equal Pay Act (EPA), the Age Discrimination in Employment Act (ADEA), the Americans with Disabilities Act (ADA), and the Family and Medical Leave Act (FMLA), and we have added material on sexual orientation and identity discrimination, primarily under Title VII to reflect evolving changes in the law.

The eighth edition represented a substantial revision and reorganization of the prior edition, and the ninth edition has continued in a similar but less revisionist fashion. There are updated introductory material, notes, and questions, including examination of important new statutes, recent doctrinal developments in judicial decisions, and significant scholarship in the field of employment discrimination. We have also combined what used to be Chapter 7 (Discrimination Because of Sex) and Chapter 11 (Sex-Based Wage Discrimination), into a single chapter on Sex Discrimination, now Chapter 7. Users of the prior edition will find much that is familiar, but we have reorganized material, trimmed down our treatment of some subjects, and added much that is new. Following is a summary of the organization of the book, highlighting some of these changes:

Part I consists of two chapters that form an introduction to the topic of the law on status discrimination in the workplace. Chapter 1 is an essay on the historical and contemporary significance of race in American society—as the impetus for the Civil Rights Act of 1964 and as a focus of continuing debates about the meanings of "discrimination" and "equality."

These concepts frame much of the doctrinal development in the law and continue to challenge and sometimes confound legislators, judges, lawyers, and scholars alike, and we have chosen to frame our book with a brief exploration of the debates about how these theories might shape our laws.

The second chapter begins with a brief survey of the major federal laws that prohibit discrimination in employment and examines the statutory procedures and enforcement schemes, as well as the statutory definitions of protected individuals or groups and covered entities. Union liability for employment discrimination, which had been a separate chapter in the seventh edition, is now in Chapter 2 in the section on covered entities. The section on procedure includes the Supreme Court's 2007 *Ledbetter v. Goodyear Tire & Rubber Co.* case and a discussion of the Lilly Ledbetter Fair Pay Act of 2009. The topic of remedies was moved into Chapter 2 in the eighth edition, with the goal that it can easily be covered at the beginning of the course as a foundation for understanding the potential benefits, as well as the limitations, of legal solutions to workplace inequality.

Part II, Theories of Discrimination and Analytical Paradigms, forms the core of the book. With a primary focus on Title VII of the Civil Rights Act of 1964 and its 1991 amendments, Chapters 3 and 4 cover the basic theories of discrimination (or meanings of equality), the analytical paradigms for bringing disparate treatment and disparate impact claims, and available defenses. In the eighth edition, we moved the cases and materials on statistical evidence into Chapter 3 on disparate treatment, which has an expanded treatment of pattern-or-practice (systemic disparate treatment) cases. In addition, the chapter provides substantially revised materials on mixed-motive cases in the aftermath of the Civil Rights Act of 1991, as well as an in-depth treatment of the impact of *Desert Palace v. Costa* on litigation strategies in individual disparate treatment cases. With the ninth edition, Chapter 3 offers yet another completely restructured section on retaliation claims, highlighting the new Supreme Court opinion in *Nassar* and court of appeals cases.

Chapter 4 examines disparate impact in a reorganized chapter (again reorganized in the eighth edition) that begins with the landmark 1971 Supreme Court case of *Griggs v. Duke Power Co.*, considered a high-water mark of civil rights law, and concludes with the 2009 *Ricci v. DeStefano* opinion, a case that goes to the heart of questions about the contemporary contours of workplace racial equality and the meaning of discrimination. The journey from *Griggs*, to the Civil Rights Act of 1991 that codified *Griggs*, to *Ricci* is traced in this chapter through the developments of disparate impact doctrine, the increasingly sophisticated methods of proof, and the changing evidentiary burdens and analytical frameworks intended to get at the effects of unintentional discrimination.

Chapter 5 provides a basis for comparing constitutional and statutory approaches to equality in the workplace through materials on equal protection doctrine and § 1981, which have their source in Reconstruction-era reforms. These civil rights laws and constitutional protections offer significant rights, remedies, and procedures that are quite different from Title VII, the ADA, and the ADEA. Chapter 6, which was new in the eighth edition, features three scenarios from three different types of workplaces—a restaurant, a law office, and a construction site—that offer students an opportunity to apply the analytical frameworks and evidentiary rules covered in Chapters 3, 4, and 5 to fact patterns that have the complexity typical of cases they might handle in law practice. We have called this new chapter an "underview," because we believe it will give students a perspective from the ground up of how doctrine and theory shape the sometimes difficult, but very concrete, questions employment lawyers have to address for their clients.

Part III provides coverage of discrimination on the basis of specific categories: sex and sex-based wage discrimination (Chapter 7), pregnancy and family responsibilities (Chapter 8), sexual orientation, gender expression, and gender identity (Chapter 9), harassment (Chapter 10), religion (12), national origin (Chapter 12), age (Chapter 13), and disability (Chapter 14).

Chapter 7 reorganizes the chapter on sex discrimination and now includes the wage-discrimination material in a trimmed down version. The Supreme Court's *Oncale v. Sundowner Offshore Services* same-sex harassment case has been moved into this chapter to address the question of what "sex" means in the statutory prohibition of sex discrimination. The section on sex-based dress, grooming, and appearance requirements includes the Ninth Circuit opinion and dissents in *Jespersen v. Harrah's Operating Co.* and highlights recent scholarship on the topic. Chapter 8 features material on family responsibilities discrimination (FRD) claims as part of its coverage of pregnancy discrimination and care-giving responsibilities. Chapter 9 is substantially revised in this edition to recognize the changing law on employment discrimination and harassment on the basis of sexual orientation, gender expression, and gender identity. The chapter includes examination of state law developments in workplace rights for gay, lesbian, bisexual, and transgender individuals, and federal case law and EEOC rulings that either transcend or reinforce the boundaries of the categories of sex and gender. Chapter 10 examines new developments in sexual harassment law. The chapter concludes where it starts, with a discussion of harassment on the basis of race and ethnicity; harassment claims on the basis of religion, national origin, age, and disability are treated separately in the chapters that cover those protected statuses.

Chapter 11 on religion includes new cases and materials that capture the often intractable clash between the public world of work and commerce and the private domain of religious belief and practice, with Title VII doctrine attempting to achieve a principled balance between the two that is informed by First Amendment values. As the materials in this chapter illustrate, enforcing Title VII antidiscrimination law protecting all workers' religious (or nonreligious) beliefs and accommodating some aspects of religious practice for some workers presents a challenge for employers and employees.

Chapter 12 on national origin begins with an exploration of the sometimes elusive concept of what it means to discriminate on the basis of "national origin." The relationship between claims brought under Title VII and the Immigration Reform and Control Act is covered, and the chapter features new cases on English-only rules.

Chapter 13 explores significant doctrinal developments under the Age Discrimination in Employment Act of 1967 (ADEA), including the Supreme Court's disparate treatment case, *Gross v. FBL Financial Services*, as well as its disparate impact cases, *Smith v. City of Jackson* and *Meacham v. Knolls Atomic Power Laboratory*.

Chapter 14 covers the most recent comprehensive federal civil rights law, the Americans with Disabilities Act of 1990 (ADA) and the ADA Amendments Act of 2008 (ADAAA), along with the Genetic Information Nondiscrimination Act of 2009 (GINA). Disability law is a rapidly growing field, and the chapter emphasizes the difficult questions presented when courts grapple with the meaning of discrimination and the duty to make reasonable accommodations under the statute. This chapter also briefly examines the Supreme Court cases that led to passage of the ADAAA and its potential significance in expanding the meaning of "disability." Coverage of the topic of disability law here is necessarily somewhat limited, and the materials in this chapter are intended to serve as an introduction to a more comprehensive treatment of the subject in other courses.

Part IV, Implementing Equality, presents a single chapter that is essentially a bookend to Chapter 1. The major portion of Chapter 15 examines the legality of affirmative action as a remedy under federal employment discrimination statutes, but materials on the legality of affirmative action under the Constitution are included for comparative purposes. In this edition, the chapter materials have been edited to focus more on Title VII and private employer affirmative action, but the new edition includes coverage of new Supreme Court decisions in *Schuette* and *Fisher*. Throughout the chapter, the debates about what affirmative action means and how and whether it is necessary, achievable, or even constitutional are reflected in the cases, authors' notes and questions, and excerpts from scholars.

Part V, Alternative Dispute Resolution, consists of Chapter 16, which examines new developments in the law covering arbitration of statutory claims of employment discrimination. This chapter highlights the legal consequences of predispute and postdispute arbitration agreements in which employees waive their rights to bring federal discrimination claims in court.

Like prior editions, this edition features diverse contemporary scholarship drawn from critical race theory, feminist legal theory, history, social science, and law and economics, among other disciplines. Our goal has been to offer a number of different perspectives on the social and historical context in which employment discrimination law has developed. At various points we have included international and comparative materials to suggest alternative perspectives on the problems of discrimination in employment. The approach we have taken focuses on the ideals of equality of opportunity and fairness to individuals as the motivating purposes of civil rights legislation in general and employment discrimination statutes in particular. The extensive materials framing the cases are designed to prepare students thoroughly for practice in this rapidly changing field of law.

A word about our editing conventions: The cases and excerpted materials have been edited, sometimes extensively, to suit the requirements of space and our pedagogical purposes. In general, deleted material is indicated by ellipses, and original footnote numbers have been retained. Citations in cases, however, have sometimes been omitted without ellipses or parenthetical explanation, unless the context required clarification. Citations in some cases have been altered for clarity or to conform to Bluebook style.

Our goal has been to produce a casebook that is a readable and teachable introduction to the law of employment discrimination; inevitably, we have produced a book that reflects our own teaching and research interests and strengths. We hope that somewhere between our desires and our abilities we have struck a balance that will suit the needs of many of our colleagues and their students.

MARIA L. ONTIVEROS
San Francisco, Ca.

MICHAEL SELMI
Washington, D.C.

ROBERTO L. CORRADA
Denver, Co.

MELISSA HART
Boulder, Co.

December 2015

ACKNOWLEDGMENTS

We would like to acknowledge a number of people who have made important contributions to our work on this edition.

At the University of San Francisco School of Law, excellent research assistance was provided by reference librarians Lee Ryan and John Shafer, as well as Jenica Maldonado who helped research a variety of topics. In addition to her co-authors past and present, Maria also thanks her colleague Michelle Travis for discussion about disability discrimination, and Professors Christopher Cameron and Juan Perea who have helped push her thinking on issues relating to discrimination based on national origin.

Roberto Corrada thanks a number of people who contributed to the writing and preparation of this edition. Mostly, Roberto thanks Professor Michael Selmi who graciously took on the completely thankless task of pulling the entire book together, making suggestions on all of the chapters and coordinating the efforts of all the coauthors. Roberto benefitted from discussions with his other co-authors, Professors Melissa Hart and Maria Ontiveros, and also from conversations with his colleagues, Professors Nancy Ehrenreich, Beto Juarez, Martin Katz, Nantiya Ruan, and Catherine Smith. Roberto also thanks Professors Charles Sullivan, Rick Bales, and Angela Onwuachi Willig, whose insights into employment discrimination law have proven invaluable. Roberto thanks members of CELF (Colorado Employment Law Forum), including (not mentioned already) Professors Rachel Arnow-Richman, Scott Moss, Helen Norton, and Raja Raghunath, for their support. Excellent research assistance was provided by Jonathan Eddy. Roberto's work on the book was facilitated by summer research support provided by the University of Denver Sturm College of Law. For Theresa Corrada, Roberto's spouse, who practices in the employment law area in Denver, thanks for your love, friendship, support and many conversations about the theory and practice of employment discrimination law. For Amelia Corrada, Roberto's daughter, thanks for your love, your joy, and your support of Mom's and Dad's work. Finally, Roberto notes that he is always inspired by the memory of his son Maximo (1996–2009).

At George Washington University Law School helpful research assistance has been provided by Lesley Fredin, Ryan Green, Kyle Herrig, Evan Sheets, and on the 9th Edition by Paulina Starostka and Sylvia Tsakos. Librarian extraordinaire Leslie Lee provided terrific assistance on this and many other projects. Mike has greatly appreciated the opportunity to collaborate with his co-authors and the support of the Labor Law Group.

As with every academic project undertaken at the University of Colorado Law School, this work could not have been completed without the extraordinary efforts of Jane Thompson, the CU Law Library's Assistant Director for Faculty Services. Melissa is grateful to Dean Phil Weiser for supporting her work; to Roberto, Maria, and Mike for the opportunity to collaborate on this project and the many good conversations it generated; and to her husband, Kevin Traskos, for his insights and his patience. Special thanks are due to Talia (12) and Noah (10) for all the times they shut the office door.

The authors of the ninth edition want to acknowledge those who laid the pedagogical foundations in earlier editions of this book. The sixth and seventh editions of this book bear the distinctive stamp of Robert Belton, Professor at Vanderbilt University Law School, a pioneer in the field of civil rights litigation whose vision of workplace equality shaped those editions. A stalwart of the earlier editions is James E. Jones, Jr., Professor Emeritus at the University of Wisconsin Law School. Professor Jones was an author on each edition published between 1971 and 1987, as well as a 1990 supplement to the 1987 edition. Other editors of previous editions include Dianne Avery, Robert N. Covington, and the late Aaron A. Caghan and William P. Murphy. We are indebted to their work.

Finally, collectively, we want to thank the Labor Law Group for supporting our meetings over several years of work on this edition and for making it possible for us to contribute to its mission of producing classroom materials for labor and employment law. This edition of *Employment Discrimination Law* has benefited from numerous collegial exchanges with members of the Labor Law Group, our colleagues throughout the academy, and, especially, our students.

MARIA L. ONTIVEROS

ROBERTO L. CORRADA

MICHAEL SELMI

MELISSA HART

THE LABOR LAW GROUP

Executive Committee

Stephen Befort
Co-Chair
University of Minnesota

Melissa Hart
Co-Chair
University of Colorado-Boulder

Richard A. Bales
Ohio Northern University

Marion Crain
Washington University-St. Louis

Cynthia Estlund
New York University

Jeffrey Hirsch
University of North Carolina

Kerry Rittich
University of Toronto

Peggie R. Smith
Washington University-St. Louis

Editorial Policy Committee

Members

Steven D. Anderman
University of Essex

Harry W. Arthurs
York University (Emeritus)

James B. Atleson
State University of New York-Buffalo (Emeritus)

Dianne Avery
State University of New York-Buffalo

Richard A. Bales
Ohio Northern University

Stephen Befort
University of Minnesota

Adele Blackett
McGill University

Dr. Roger Blanpain
Institut voor Arbeidsrecht

Christopher David Ruiz Cameron
Southwestern Law School

Lance Compa
Cornell University

Laura Cooper
University of Minnesota

Roberto L. Corrada
University of Denver

Robert N. Covington
Vanderbilt University (Emeritus)

Marion G. Crain
Washington University-St. Louis

Kenneth G. Dau-Schmidt
Indiana University-Bloomington

John E. Dunsford
St. Louis University (Emeritus)

Cynthia Estlund
New York University

Matthew Finkin
University of Illinois

Catherine L. Fisk
University of California-Irvine

Joel W. Friedman
Tulane University

Ruben Garcia
University of Nevada-Las Vegas

Rafael Gely
University of Missouri

Julius G. Getman
University of Texas (Emeritus)

Alvin L. Goldman
University of Kentucky (Emeritus)

Joseph R. Grodin
University of California-Hastings (Emeritus)

Melissa Hart
University of Colorado-Boulder

Jeffrey Hirsch
University of North Carolina

Ann C. Hodges
University of Richmond

Alan Hyde
Rutgers University-Newark

Pauline T. Kim
Washington University-St. Louis

Tom Kohler
Boston College

Brian A. Langille
University of Toronto

Orly Lobel
University of San Diego

Deborah Malamud
New York University

Martin H. Malin
Illinois Institute of Technology, Chicago-Kent College of Law

Mordehai Mironi
University of Haifa

Robert B. Moberly
University of Arkansas

Charles J. Morris
Southern Methodist University (Emeritus)

Cynthia Nance
University of Arkansas-Fayetteville

Dennis R. Nolan
University of South Carolina (Emeritus)

Maria L. Ontiveros
University of San Francisco

Angela Onwuachi-Willig
University of Iowa

Nicole Buonocore Porter
University of Toledo

Robert J. Rabin
Syracuse University (Emeritus)

Kerry Rittich
University of Toronto

Alvaro Santos
Georgetown University

George Schatzki
Arizona State University (Emeritus)

Michael Selmi
George Washington University

Calvin W. Sharpe
Case Western Reserve University

Eileen Silverstein
University of Connecticut (Emerita)

Joseph E. Slater
University of Toledo

Sara Slinn
York University

Peggie R. Smith
Washington University-St. Louis

Susan J. Stabile
University of St. Thomas

Katherine V. W. Stone
University of California-Los Angeles

Lea S. VanderVelde
University of Iowa

June Weisberger
University of Wisconsin-Madison (Emerita)

Marley Weiss
University of Maryland

Michael Wishnie
Yale University

Noah Zatz
University of California-Los Angeles

Affiliated Practitioners

Founding Trustees

SUMMARY OF CONTENTS

FOREWORD v

PREFACE xi

ACKNOWLEDGMENTS xvii

THE LABOR LAW GROUP xix

TABLE OF CASES xli

PART 1. INTRODUCTION

Chapter 1. Race and the Development of Laws Prohibiting Discrimination in Employment: A Brief Overview 3

Chapter 2. Laws Prohibiting Discrimination in Employment: An Overview 11
A. Introduction 11
B. Survey of Major Federal Laws on Employment Discrimination 11
C. Enforcement Schemes 20
D. Coverage Under Laws Prohibiting Discrimination in Employment 42
E. Remedies 68

PART 2. THEORIES OF DISCRIMINATION AND ANALYTICAL PARADIGMS

Chapter 3. Disparate Treatment 95
A. Introduction: The Meaning and Theories of "Discrimination" 95
B. Disparate Treatment Claims 97
C. Retaliation 161
D. Statistical Evidence and Pattern-or-Practice Cases 207

Chapter 4. Disparate Impact 245
A. Introduction 245
B. The Theory of Disparate Impact 246
C. The Civil Rights Act of 1991 and Contemporary Disparate Impact Doctrine 270
D. Remedying the Disparate Impact of Selection Procedures 284

Chapter 5. Equal Protection and the Reconstruction Civil Rights Acts 303
A. Introduction: The Legacy of the Reconstruction-Era Reforms 303
B. Equal Protection: The Fifth and Fourteenth Amendments 306
C. The Civil Rights Act of 1866, 42 U.S.C. § 1981 321

Chapter 6. Evidentiary Frameworks for Status Discrimination: An Underview **339**

PART 3. SPECIFIC CATEGORIES OF DISCRIMINATION

Chapter 7. Discrimination Because of Sex **349**
A. Introduction and Historical Overview 349
B. What Is Discrimination "Because of Sex"? 355
C. Sex-Based Wage Discrimination 375
D. The Bona Fide Occupational Qualification Defense to Sex Discrimination 391
E. Sex-Based Dress, Grooming, and Appearance Requirements 414
F. Systemic Claims and the Glass Ceiling 434

Chapter 8. Discrimination Because of Pregnancy and Family Responsibilities **441**
A. Introduction and Historical Overview 441
B. The Pregnancy Discrimination Act 443
C. Discrimination Against Caregivers 468

Chapter 9. Discrimination Because of Sexual Orientation, Gender Expression, and Gender Identity **491**
A. Introduction 491
B. Definitions 492
C. The Applicability of Title VII to Discrimination Against LGBT Employees 495
D. Sources of Employment Rights for LGBT Individuals Beyond Title VII 526

Chapter 10. Harassment **535**
A. Introduction 535
B. Harassment Because of Sex 536
C. Employer Liability for Discriminatory Harassment 568
D. Harassment Because of Race 618

Chapter 11. Discrimination Because of Religion **629**
A. Introduction: Statutory Overview 629
B. The Meaning of "Religion" 632
C. The Religious Entity Exemptions 636
D. Establishing a Prima Facie Case 641
E. Reasonable Accommodation and Undue Hardship 650
F. Claims Against Government Employers 672

Chapter 12. Discrimination Because of National Origin **685**
A. Introduction 685
B. The Meaning of "National Origin" 688
C. Citizenship and Immigration Status 702
D. National Origin Discrimination Based on Language and Accent 712

Chapter 13. Discrimination Because of Age **743**
A. Introduction 743
B. Disparate Treatment 744
C. Separations, Waivers, and Reductions-in-Force 782
D. Disparate Impact 798

Chapter 14. Discrimination Because of Disability **809**
A. Introduction 809
B. The Meaning of "Discrimination" Under the ADA 815
C. The Meaning of "Disability" 840
D. Qualifications, Direct Threat, and Undue Hardship 853
E. Medical Inquiries, Medical Examinations, and Medical Benefits 871

PART 4. IMPLEMENTING EQUALITY

Chapter 15. Affirmative Action **881**
A. Introduction 881
B. The Evolution of Affirmative Action as a Remedy 886
C. Affirmative Action Under Federal Antidiscrimination Statutes 888

PART 5. ALTERNATIVE DISPUTE RESOLUTION

Chapter 16. Arbitration of Employment Discrimination Claims **931**
A. Introduction 931
B. Arbitration of Employment Discrimination Claims in Nonunion Workplaces 933
C. Arbitration of Employment Discrimination Claims in Unionized Workplaces 961

INDEX 965

TABLE OF CONTENTS

FOREWORD ... v
PREFACE ... xi
ACKNOWLEDGMENTS ... xvii
THE LABOR LAW GROUP ... xix
TABLE OF CASES ... xli

PART 1. INTRODUCTION

Chapter 1. Race and the Development of Laws Prohibiting Discrimination in Employment: A Brief Overview ... 3

Chapter 2. Laws Prohibiting Discrimination in Employment: An Overview ... 11
A. Introduction ... 11
B. Survey of Major Federal Laws on Employment Discrimination ... 11
Note: The Eleventh Amendment as a Bar to Civil Claims for Damages Against States ... 16
Notes: Other Remedies for Employment Discrimination ... 19
C. Enforcement Schemes ... 20
1. Administrative Exhaustion ... 22
Ledbetter v. Goodyear Tire & Rubber Co., Inc. ... 27
Notes and Questions ... 35
2. Judicial Enforcement ... 40
D. Coverage Under Laws Prohibiting Discrimination in Employment ... 42
1. The Meaning of "Race" and "Color" ... 43
St. Francis College v. Al-Khazraji ... 44
Notes and Questions ... 46
Notes: Intersectionality ... 49
2. Who Is an "Employee"? ... 52
Clackamas Gastroenterology Associates v. Wells ... 52
Notes and Questions ... 55
3. The Meaning of "Employer" ... 57
4. The Meaning of an "Employment Practice" ... 60
Note: Extraterritorial Application of Discrimination Laws ... 60
5. Union Liability for Discrimination ... 61
a. The Duty of Fair Representation ... 61
b. Union Liability for Discrimination as an "Employer" and as a "Labor Organization" ... 62
Notes and Questions ... 65
E. Remedies ... 68
1. Basic Remedial Principles ... 69

2. Reinstatement 71
3. Back Pay 73
4. Front Pay 76
5. Compensatory and Punitive Damages 77
6. Liquidated Damages 83
7. Taxation of Awards 84
8. Attorney's Fees 85
   a. Entitlement to Fees 85
   b. Standards for an Award of Fees 88
   Note: Insuring Against Employment Discrimination Claims 90

PART 2. THEORIES OF DISCRIMINATION AND ANALYTICAL PARADIGMS

Chapter 3. Disparate Treatment 95
A. Introduction: The Meaning and Theories of "Discrimination" 95
   Questions 97
B. Disparate Treatment Claims 97
   1. Foundations 99
      McDonnell Douglas Corp. v. Green 99
      Notes and Questions 102
      St. Mary's Honor Center v. Hicks 110
      Notes and Questions 116
      Note: The Perjurious Client and a Lawyer's Ethical Obligations 125
      Note: The Same-Actor Defense 126
      Note: "Reverse Discrimination" Claims 127
      Note: Discrimination and Critical Race Theory 128
   2. Mixed-Motive Cases and the Civil Rights Act of 1991 133
      Price Waterhouse v. Hopkins 133
      Notes and Questions 141
      Desert Palace, Inc. v. Costa 144
      Notes and Questions 150
   3. Multiple Decisionmakers and the "Cat's Paw" Theory 154
      Staub v. Proctor Hospital 154
      Notes and Questions 160
C. Retaliation 161
   1. Introduction 161
   2. Who Is Protected from Retaliation? 163
      a. Protection Against Direct Retaliation 163
      b. Protection Against Indirect (3rd Party) Retaliation 163
         Thompson v. North American Stainless 163
         Notes and Questions 167
   3. Analytical Framework for Retaliation Claims 168
      a. Analytical Framework 168

b. The Prima Facie Requirement of a "Materially Adverse Action" ... 169
Burlington Northern & Santa Fe Railway v. White ... 169
Notes and Questions ... 179
c. The Prima Facie Requirement of a "Causal Link" ... 182
Clark County School District v. Breeden ... 182
Notes and Questions ... 184
4. Scope of Statutorily Protected Activity ... 186
a. The Participation Clause ... 187
Notes and Questions ... 189
b. The Opposition Clause ... 191
Crawford v. Metropolitan Government ... 191
Notes and Questions ... 196
Clark County School District v. Breeden ... 198
Notes and Questions ... 200
5. The Ultimate Burden in Retaliation Cases: "But-For" Causation ... 200
University of Texas Southwestern Medical Center v. Nassar ... 200
Notes and Questions ... 206
D. Statistical Evidence and Pattern-or-Practice Cases ... 207
Teamsters v. United States ... 208
Hazelwood School District v. United States ... 212
Notes and Questions ... 217
Wal-Mart Stores, Inc. v. Dukes ... 228
Notes and Questions ... 242

Chapter 4. Disparate Impact ... 245
A. Introduction ... 245
B. The Theory of Disparate Impact ... 246
1. Objective Criteria ... 246
Griggs v. Duke Power Co. ... 246
Notes and Questions ... 252
Note: The Legitimacy of the Disparate Impact Theory ... 259
2. Griggs Revisited ... 261
Wards Cove Packing Co. v. Atonio ... 261
Notes and Questions ... 268
C. The Civil Rights Act of 1991 and Contemporary Disparate Impact Doctrine ... 270
Lanning v. Southeastern Pennsylvania Transportation Authority (Lanning I) ... 270
Lanning v. Southeastern Pennsylvania Transportation Authority (Lanning II) ... 275
Notes and Questions ... 279
D. Remedying the Disparate Impact of Selection Procedures ... 284
Ricci v. DeStefano ... 284
Notes and Questions ... 300

Chapter 5. Equal Protection and the Reconstruction Civil Rights Acts **303**
A. Introduction: The Legacy of the Reconstruction-Era Reforms 303
B. Equal Protection: The Fifth and Fourteenth Amendments 306
Washington v. Davis 307
Notes and Questions 313
Note: The Analytical Framework and the Burden of Proof in Equal Protection Cases 318
C. The Civil Rights Act of 1866, 42 U.S.C. § 1981 321
1. Theory of Liability 322
General Building Contractors Association v. Pennsylvania 322
Notes and Questions 326
2. Section 1981 Remedies and Procedural Requirements 331
Jones v. R. R. Donnelley & Sons 331
Notes and Questions 335

Chapter 6. Evidentiary Frameworks for Status Discrimination: An Underview **339**
Questions 345

PART 3. SPECIFIC CATEGORIES OF DISCRIMINATION

Chapter 7. Discrimination Because of Sex **349**
A. Introduction and Historical Overview 349
B. What Is Discrimination "Because of Sex"? 355
City of Los Angeles Department of Water & Power v. Manhart 356
Notes and Questions 360
Price Waterhouse v. Hopkins 361
Notes and Questions 366
Oncale v. Sundowner Offshore Services, Inc. 369
Notes and Questions 372
C. Sex-Based Wage Discrimination 375
1. The Equal Pay Act 378
2. The Bennett Amendment to Title VII 386
Notes and Questions 389
D. The Bona Fide Occupational Qualification Defense to Sex Discrimination 391
International Union, United Automobile Workers v. Johnson Controls 396
Notes and Questions 405
E. Sex-Based Dress, Grooming, and Appearance Requirements 414
Jespersen v. Harrah's Operating Company, Inc. 416
Notes and Questions 428
F. Systemic Claims and the Glass Ceiling 434

And Bostock v. Clayton County online

Chapter 8. Discrimination Because of Pregnancy and Family Responsibilities **441**
A. Introduction and Historical Overview 441
B. The Pregnancy Discrimination Act 443
1. The Meaning of "Discrimination on the Basis of Pregnancy" 447
Young v. United Parcel Services 448
Notes and Questions 456
Note on the Scope of "Related Medical Conditions" Under the PDA 464
C. Discrimination Against Caregivers 468
1. Family Responsibilities Discrimination 470
Chadwick v. Wellpoint, Inc. 470
Notes and Questions 476
2. The Family and Medical Leave Act 479
Notes and Questions 481

Chapter 9. Discrimination Because of Sexual Orientation, Gender Expression, and Gender Identity **491**
A. Introduction 491
B. Definitions 492
C. The Applicability of Title VII to Discrimination Against LGBT Employees 495
1. Discrimination on the Basis of Sexual Orientation 495
Baldwin v. Foxx 496
Notes and Questions 501
2. Discrimination on the Basis of Gender Identity 505
Smith v. City of Salem, Ohio 506
Notes and Questions 512
3. Sexual Harassment of Sexual Minorities 515
Rene v. MGM Grand Hotel, Inc. 515
Notes and Questions 522
D. Sources of Employment Rights for LGBT Individuals Beyond Title VII 526
1. Federal Legislative Reform Proposals 526
2. Existing Federal and State Protections 527
Notes and Questions 529

Chapter 10. Harassment **535**
A. Introduction 535
B. Harassment Because of Sex 536
1. Estimating the Prevalence and Costs of Workplace Sexual Harassment 536
2. The Two Theories of Sexual Harassment: Quid Pro Quo and Hostile Work Environment 537
a. Quid Pro Quo Sexual Harassment: The Prima Facie Case 539
b. Hostile Work Environment: The Prima Facie Case 540
Harris v. Forklift Systems, Inc. 542

Notes and Questions ... 546
Note: The Impact of Oncale on Sexual Harassment Law ... 558
Note: Claims Arising out of Paramour Preferential Treatment and the Termination of Consensual Sexual Relationships ... 563
Note: Alternative Theories of Liability for Sexual Harassment ... 566
C. Employer Liability for Discriminatory Harassment ... 568
1. Vicarious Liability: Harassment by Supervisors ... 570
Burlington Industries, Inc. v. Ellerth ... 570
Vance v. Ball State University ... 579
Notes and Questions ... 589
Pennsylvania State Police v. Suders ... 604
Notes and Questions ... 609
2. Liability for Negligence: Harassment by Co-Workers and Nonemployees ... 612
Notes and Questions ... 614
Note: Timely Filing of Harassment Charges—The Morgan Case ... 616
D. Harassment Because of Race ... 618
Harris v. International Paper Co. ... 618
Notes and Questions ... 621

Chapter 11. Discrimination Because of Religion ... 629
A. Introduction: Statutory Overview ... 629
B. The Meaning of "Religion" ... 632
Notes and Questions ... 634
C. The Religious Entity Exemptions ... 636
Questions ... 638
Note: The "Ministerial Exception" to Title VII Discrimination Claims Against Religious Institutions ... 639
D. Establishing a Prima Facie Case ... 641
EEOC v. Abercrombie & Fitch Stores, Inc. ... 641
Notes and Questions ... 645
Note: The Bona Fide Occupational Qualification Defense ... 648
E. Reasonable Accommodation and Undue Hardship ... 650
Trans World Airlines, Inc. v. Hardison ... 650
Ansonia Board of Education v. Philbrook ... 657
Notes and Questions ... 661
Note: Unions, Religious Discrimination Claims, and the Charity Substitution Rule ... 666
Note: Religious Freedom and Laws Prohibiting Discrimination on the Basis of Sexual Orientation and Gender Identity ... 668
Note: Harassment Because of Religion ... 669
Note: Disparate Impact Religious Discrimination Claims Under Title VII ... 671

F. Claims Against Government Employers 672
Brown v. Polk County, Iowa 672
Notes and Questions 680

Chapter 12. Discrimination Because of National Origin 685
A. Introduction 685
B. The Meaning of "National Origin" 688
Dawavendewa v. Salt River Project Agricultural Improvement & Power Dist. 689
Notes and Questions 693
Notes: Native Americans 697
Note: National Origin and the Bona Fide Occupational Qualification Defense 699
Note: Harassment Because of National Origin 700
C. Citizenship and Immigration Status 702
1. Citizenship Requirements 702
Espinoza v. Farah Manufacturing Company, Inc. 702
Notes and Questions 707
2. Undocumented Workers and Title VII 710
D. National Origin Discrimination Based on Language and Accent 712
1. English Proficiency as a Job Requirement 713
2. English-Only Requirement for Bilingual Employees 713
Pacheco v. New York Presbyterian Hospital 713
EEOC v. Sephora U.S.A., LLC 722
Notes and Questions 728
3. Accent Discrimination as National Origin Discrimination 732
In re Rodriguez 732
Notes and Questions 737

Chapter 13. Discrimination Because of Age 743
A. Introduction 743
Note: ADEA Claims Against States 744
B. Disparate Treatment 744
Gross v. FBL Financial Services, Inc. 746
Notes and Questions 753
Hazen Paper Co. v. Biggins 754
Notes and Questions 757
Sperling v. Hoffmann-La Roche, Inc. 759
Notes and Questions 764
Note: Kentucky Retirement Systems v. EEOC 768
Note: O'Connor v. Consolidated Coin Caterers Corp. 773
Note: Sex-Plus-Age Claims 775
Note: Employee Benefits 779
Note: Hostile Work Environment Claims Under the ADEA 780
Note: The Bona Fide Occupational Qualification Defense 781

C. Separations, Waivers, and Reductions-in-Force ... 782
Oubre v. Entergy Operations, Inc. ... 783
Notes and Questions ... 786
Note: Reduction-in-Force or Downsizing Cases ... 791
D. Disparate Impact ... 798
Smith v. City of Jackson, Mississippi ... 798
Notes and Questions ... 805

Chapter 14. Discrimination Because of Disability ... 809
A. Introduction ... 809
Notes and Questions ... 814
B. The Meaning of "Discrimination" Under the ADA ... 815
Raytheon, Co. v. Hernandez ... 816
US Airways, Inc. v. Barnett ... 822
Notes and Questions ... 831
Huber v. Wal-Mart Stores, Inc. ... 832
Notes and Questions ... 835
Note: Association Discrimination ... 836
Note: Hostile Work Environment Claims Under the ADA and the Rehabilitation Act ... 839
C. The Meaning of "Disability" ... 840
Mazzeo v. Color Resolutions Int'l, LLC ... 847
Notes and Questions ... 851
D. Qualifications, Direct Threat, and Undue Hardship ... 853
1. Essential Functions and Qualification Standards ... 853
2. Qualification Standards and the Direct Threat Defense ... 856
Notes and Questions ... 858
Note: Threats to a Worker's Own Health or Safety ... 860
Notes and Questions ... 862
3. Reasonable Accommodation and Undue Hardship ... 863
Vande Zande v. Wisconsin Department of Admin. ... 863
Notes and Questions ... 868
E. Medical Inquiries, Medical Examinations, and Medical Benefits ... 871
1. Medical Inquiries and Examinations Under the ADA ... 871
Notes and Questions ... 874
2. Medical Benefits Under the ADA ... 875
Notes and Questions ... 878

PART 4. IMPLEMENTING EQUALITY

Chapter 15. Affirmative Action ... 881
A. Introduction ... 881
B. The Evolution of Affirmative Action as a Remedy ... 886
C. Affirmative Action Under Federal Antidiscrimination Statutes ... 888
1. Affirmative Action as Remedy for Present and Past Discrimination ... 888

a. Title VII ... 888
United Steelworkers of America v. Weber ... 888
Notes and Questions ... 894
Johnson v. Transportation Agency of Santa Clara County ... 896
Notes and Questions ... 908
Note: Affirmative Action and the Civil Rights Act of 1991 ... 912
b. Equal Protection Clause ... 913
Notes and Questions ... 917
2. Affirmative Action to Increase Diversity ... 921
Notes and Questions ... 924
Note: Diversity and Title VII ... 925

PART 5. ALTERNATIVE DISPUTE RESOLUTION

Chapter 16. Arbitration of Employment Discrimination Claims ... 931
A. Introduction ... 931
B. Arbitration of Employment Discrimination Claims in Nonunion Workplaces ... 933
1. Arbitrability ... 933
Circuit City Stores, Inc. v. Adams ... 933
Notes and Questions ... 939
2. The Arbitration Agreement ... 943
a. Contract Formation ... 943
Circuit City Stores, Inc. v. Najd ... 943
Notes and Questions ... 945
Circuit City Stores, Inc. v. Adams ... 947
Notes and Questions ... 951
b. Due Process and the Terms of the Arbitral Contract ... 952
Notes and Questions ... 953
3. The Arbitral Result ... 957
Cole v. Burns International Security Services ... 957
Notes and Questions ... 959
C. Arbitration of Employment Discrimination Claims in Unionized Workplaces ... 961

INDEX ... 965

TABLE OF CASES

The principal cases are in bold type.

---

14 Penn Plaza LLC v. Pyett 66, 945, 963
A. H. Phillips, Inc. v. Walling 379
Abbott v. Crown Motor Co...... 192, 735
Abdu-Brisson v. Delta Air Lines ... 745, 774
Abrahmson v. William Patterson College of New Jersey 603
Abrams v. Baylor College of Medicine 649
Abrams v. Department of Public Safety 143
Adams v. Philip Morris, Inc. 790
Adams v. Wal-Mart Stores, Inc...... 106
Adamson v. Multi Community Diversified Services, Inc. 774
Adarand Constructors, Inc. v. Pena 15, 306, 883, 914, 916, 917, 918, 919
Agent Orange Product Liability Litigation, In re 720
Akins v. Texas 310, 311
Akouri v. Florida Dept. of Transportation 734
Alabama v. United States 207
Alalade v. AWS Assistance Corp. 599
Albemarle Paper Co. v. Moody 69, 70, 178, 254, 255, 267, 890
Albertson's, Inc. v. Kirkingburg 842, 844
Alcaraz v. Avnet, Inc. 954
Alden v. Maine 17, 19
Aldrich v. Randolph Cent. School Dist. 384
Alexander v. Gardner-Denver Co. 24, 65, 95, 962, 963
Alexander v. Louisiana 212, 311
Ali v. National Bank of Pakistan 49
Ali v. Southeast Neighborhood House 635
Allen v. Baltimore County, Md. 873
Allen v. City of Chicago. 281
Allen v. Gold Country Casino 698
Allison v. Citgo Petroleum Corp. 82
Almond v. Unified Sch. Dist. #501 ... 38
Altman v. Minnesota Department of Corrections 669
Altman v. New York City Dept. of Educ. 738
Alvarado v. City of San Jose 634
Alvarez v. Des Moines Bolt Supply, Inc. 596, 598
Alyeska Pipeline Service Co. v. Wilderness Society 85
Aman v. Cort Furniture Rental Corp. 623, 624
Ambat v. City and County of San Francisco 413
Amerada Hess Corp. v. Director, Div. of Taxation, New Jersey Dept. of Treasury 561
American Exp. Co. v. Italian Colors Restaurant 954
Amini v. Oberlin College 735
Amirmokri v. Baltimore Gas & Elec. Co. 700
Amro v. Boeing Co., No. 97–3049 ... 734
Anderson v. Baxter Healthcare Corp. 116, 760, 765
Anderson v. City of Bessemer 98
Anderson v. Conboy 329, 330
Anderson v. State University of New York 18
Ang v. Procter & Gamble Co. 733, 734, 736
Annis v. County of Westchester 318, 319
Ansonia Board of Education v. Philbrook 657
Antonio v. Sygma Network, Inc...... 126
Aramburu v. Boeing Co. 330
Arbaugh v. Y & H Corp. 57
Arizona Governing Committee for Tax Deferred Annuity and Deferred Compensation Plans v. Norris 360, 404
Arizona v. United States 687
Arizonans for Official English v. Arizona 731
Arlington Heights, Village of v. Metropolitan Housing Development Corp. 314, 315, 316, 326
Armendariz v. Foundation Health Psychcare Services, Inc. 944, 947, 948, 950
Armindo v. Padlocker, Inc. 457
Armstrong v. Index Journal Co. 197
Arnett v. Aspin 374, 775
Arrieta-Colon v. Wal-Mart P.R., Inc. 603, 839

Articles of Banned Hazardous Substances, United States v....... 720
Arvin-Thornton v. Philip Morris Prods., Inc. 664
Aryain v. Wal-Mart Stores Texas LP 180
Asad v. Continental Airlines.......... 406
Ash v. Tyson Foods, Inc.... 82, 143, 623
Ashcroft v. Iqbal 42
Association of Mexican-American Educators v. California............... 688
AT&T Corp. v. Hulteen 443, 445, 446
AT&T Mobility v. Concepcion 956
Atlantic Richfield Co. v. District of Columbia Commission on Human Rights............................. 433
Atonio v. Wards Cove 269
Aulicino v. New York City Dept. of Homeless Services 108
Avitia v. Metropolitan Club of Chicago, Inc.................................. 76
B.K.B. v. Maui Police Dept............. 555
Back v. Hastings on Hudson Union Free School Dist................. 472, 477
Backus v. Baptist Medical Center... 402
Bailey v. Henderson 373, 561
Baker v. Home Depot 665
Baker v. Silver Oak Senior Living Management Co......................... 754
Baldwin County Welcome Center v. Brown 41
Baldwin v. Foxx........... 491, **496**, 528
Balint v. Carson City, Nevada 661
Balmer v. HCA, Inc. 87
Bank of New England, N. A., United States v. 157
Banks v. Service America Corp...... 662
Barker v. Riverside County Office of Educ... 839
Barnes v. City of Cincinnati..... 89, 513
Barnes v. Costle............................. 538
Barnes v. GenCorp Inc. 793, 796
Barnowe v. Kaiser Foundation Health Plan of the Northwest................ 461
Barrett v. Applied Radiant Energy Corp. 598
Barth v. Gelb.......................... 832, 868
Bay v. Times Mirror Magazines, Inc... 764
Bayma v. Smith Barney, Harris Upham & Co............................... 950
Bazemore v. Friday 32, 221, 223
Beadle v. Hillsborough County Sheriff's Dept. 661
Beaird v. Seagate Tech., Inc........... 795
Beard v. Flying J., Inc. 595
Beatty Safway Scaffold, Inc. v. B.H. Skrable.. 944
Beauford v. Father Flanagan's Boys' Home 877
Beck v. UFCW Local 99 62
Beckel v. Wal-Mart Assocs. 618
Beck-Wilson v. Principi.................. 381
Beith v. Nitrogen Products, Inc...... 762
Belfi v. Prendergast 390
Bell Atlantic v. Twombly 42
Bellamy v. Mason's Stores, Inc....... 634
Bence v. Detroit Health Corp. 381
Bennett v. Coors Brewing Co. 787, 789
Bennun v. Rutgers State University 47
Bergerson v. New York State Office of Mental Health, Central New York Psychiatric Center................ 70
Berke v. Ohio Dept. of Public Welfare.............................. 732, 734
Berkley v. Dillard's, Inc. 940
Berman v. Orkin Exterminating Co. 168
Bernier v. Morningstar, Inc............ 615
Berry v. Department of Social Services 680
Berry v. Stevinson Chevrolet 173
Betances v. Prestige Decorating & Wallcovering, Inc........................ 715
Betts v. Costco Wholesale Corp...... 552
Bhatia v. Chevron USA, Inc. 649
Bhaya v. Westinghouse Elec. Corp.. 83
Bhella v. England........................... 734
Bibby v. Philadelphia Coca Cola Bottling Co......................... 500, 515
Biggins v. Hazen Paper 758, 759
Bill Johnson's Restaurants, Inc. v. NLRB 174
Billings v. Town of Grafton............ 180
Black v. Snyder 639
Blair v. Scott Specialty Gases 954
Blake v. Baltimore County, Md...... 873
Bledsoe v. Palm Beach County Soil & Water Conservation District....... 815
Blistein v. St. John's College 795
Blizzard v. Marion Tech. College 105, 122
Blum v. Stenson 89
BMW of North America, Inc. v. Gore... 81
Board of Educ. for School Dist. of Philadelphia, United States v. 673, 674
Board of Regents of University of State of New York v. Tomanio.... 333

Board of Trustees of University of Alabama v. Garrett 16, 17, 307, 814
Bobo v. ITT, Continental Baking Co. 330
Bobo v. UPS 107
Boerne, City of v. Flores 482, 681, 682
Bollard v. California Province of the Society of Jesus 558
Bollenbach v. Board of Education of Monroe-Woodbury Central School District 649
Bolling v. Sharpe 15, 314
Bonilla v. Oakland Scavenger Co. ... 65
Booker v. Brown & Williamson Tobacco Co. 186
Borkowski v. Valley Cent. School Dist. 827, 868
Bornstad v. Sun Company Inc. 760
Boston Chapter, NAACP, Inc. v. Beecher 257
Boutros v. Canton Regional Transit Authority 319
Bowen v. Missouri Dept. of Social Services 626
Bowman v. Shawnee State University 562
Boy Scouts of America v. Dale 533
Boy Scouts of America v. Wyman 533
Boyer-Liberto v. Fontainebleau Corp. 550, 589
Bradley v. Pizzaco of Nebraska, Inc. 51
Bradley v. Widnall 184
Bradwell v. Illinois 353, 441, 483
Brady v. Office of the Sergeant at Arms 108
Brady v. Thurston Motor Lines, Inc. 74
Bragdon v. Abbott 857
Branco v. Norwest Bank Minnesota, N.A. 956
Branham v. Snow 858
Breda v. Wolf Camera & Video 613
Brener v. Diagnostic Center Hospital 659
Brennan v. Metropolitan Opera Ass'n 525, 526
Brennan, United States v. 919
Brewster v. City of Poughkeepsie 715, 716, 720
Bridenbaugh v. O'Bannon 636
Bridge v. Phoenix Bond & Indemnity Co. 749
Bridgeforth v. Jewell 181
Brinkley v. Harbour Recreation Club 384
Briscoe v. City of New Haven 300
Brocklehurst v. PPG Industries, Inc. 793
Brooks v. City of San Mateo 549
Brooks v. Woodline Motor Freight, Inc. 75
Brown v. Advocate South Suburban Hosp. 180
Brown v. Board of Education 3, 5, 252, 305, 307
Brown v. City of Tucson 168
Brown v. General Services Administration 314, 337, 683
Brown v. Henderson 373, 560
Brown v. J. Kaz, Inc. 327
Brown v. Nucor Corp. 627
Brown v. Parkchester South Condominiums 38
Brown v. Pena 634
Brown v. Perry 597
Brown v. Polk County, Iowa 643, 645, 663, **672**
Brown v. Scott Paper Worldwide Co. 601
Brown v. Sessoms 336
Brown v. Unified School Dist. 501 335
Bruso v. United Airlines, Inc. 76
Bryant v. Bell Atlantic Maryland, Inc. 25
Bryant v. Jones 610
Bryson v. Chicago State University 590
Buckhannon Board & Care Home, Inc. v. West Virginia Department of Health & Human Resources 86
Buckley v. Reynolds Metals Co. 74, 77
Buckley v. Valeo 917
Bundy v. Jackson 538
Buntin v. Breathitt County Bd. of Educ. 380, 381
Burch v. Coca-Cola Co. 874
Burke, United States v. 84
Burks v. Wisconsin Dept. of Transp. 107
Burlington, City of v. Dague 89
Burlington Industries, Inc. v. Ellerth 174, 193, 194, 197, 540, **570**, 579, 581, 585, 588, 590, 592, 605, 608, 612
Burlington Northern and Santa Fe Ry. Co. v. White 164, 165, **169**, 716
Burnell v. Gates Rubber Co. 206
Burnett v. Tyco Corp. 550
Burns v. McGregor Electronic Industries, Inc. 556

Burns v. Southern Pac. Transp. Co. 676
Burstein v. Entel, Inc. 151
Burwell v. Eastern Air Lines, Inc. 401
Burwell v. Hobby Lobby Stores, Inc. 681
Butler v. Davis Automotive Industries 59
Butler v. Home Depot, Inc. 434
Cain v. Blackwell 616
Calero-Cerezo v. United States Dept. of Justice 184
Califano v. Yamasaki 231, 239
California Federal Savings and Loan Association v. Guerra 403
Calloway v. Gimbel Bros. 635
Cannatta v. Catholic Diocese of Austin 641
Carey v. 24 Hour Fitness, USA, Inc. 946
Carino v. University of Oklahoma 732, 738
Carnegie Center Associates, In re 459, 795
Carney v. Martin Luther Home, Inc. 488
Carolene Products Co., United States v. 811, 915
Carpenter v. Boeing 221, 269
Carr v. Allison Gas Turbine Div. 548
Carr v. Reno 867
Carroll v. Talman Federal Savings & Loan Ass'n of Chicago 426
Carter v. Countrywide Credit 955
Casiano v. AT&T, Corp. 597
Castaneda v. Partida 215, 216, 218, 370
Castellano v. City of New York 877
Catlett v. Missouri State Highway Commission 74
CBOCS West, Inc. v. Humphries 162
Centola v. Potter 499
Cerros v. Steel Tech., Inc. 603, 623, 700
Chadwick v. Wellpoint, Inc. 470
Chalmers v. Tulon Co. of Richmond 662
Chalout v. Interstate Brands Corp. 594
Chambers v. Omaha Girls Club, Inc. 374, 406, 408
Chambers v. Trettco, Inc. 604
Chance v. Board of Examiners 307
Chandler v. Roudebush 40
Chapter 7 Trustee v. Gate Gourmet, Inc. 180
Chatman v. Gentle Dental Center of Waltham 567
Chavez v. Hydril Co. 713
Chellen v. John Pickle Co. 707
Chen-Oster v. Goldman, Sachs & Co. 434
Chevron U.S.A., Inc. v. Echazabal 860, 861, 862
Chiano v. Dimension Molding Corporation 760
Chicago, United States v. 257
Childress v. City of Richmond 553
Chin v. Port Auth. of New York & New Jersey 74
Choudhury v. Polytechnic Institute of New York 161, 162
Christiansburg Garment Co. v. EEOC 87, 153
Chrysler Motors Corp. v. International Union Allied Indus. Workers of America 601
Cianci v. Pettibone Corp. 774
Cilecek v. Inova Health System Services 52
Circuit City Stores, Inc. v. Adams 933, 944, **947**
Circuit City Stores, Inc. v. Ahmed 944
Circuit City Stores, Inc. v. Mantor 953
Circuit City Stores, Inc. v. Najd 943
Citigroup Global Markets, Inc. v. Bacon 960
Civil Rights Cases 305
Clackamas Gastroenterology Associates v. Wells 52, 55, 56
CL-Alexanders Laing & Cruickshank v. Goldfeld 720
Clark County School District v. Breeden 182, 195, **198**, 551, 602
Clark v. DaimlerChrysler Corp. 953
Clark v. United Parcel Service, Inc. 594
Clarke v. Securities Industry Ass'n 166
Cleburne, Tex., City of v. Cleburne Living Center 16, 306, 914
Cleveland v. Policy Management Systems Corp. 855
Clover v. Total System Services, Inc. 190
Coalition to Defend Affirmative Action v. Regents of the University of Michigan 920
Coburn v. Pan American World Airways, Inc. 794, 795
Coghlan v. American Seafoods Co. 126
Cohen v. Wedbush, Noble, Cooke, Inc. 950

Cole v. Burns International Security Services 949, 952, **957**, 960
Cole v. Chandler 602
Coleman v. B-G Maintenance Management of Colorado, Inc. ... 374
Coleman v. Court of Appeals of Maryland 18, 485
Coleman v. Donahoe.............. 107, 945
Coleman v. Quaker Oats Co........... 121
Collings v. Longview Fibre Co. 873
Comedy Club Inc. v. Improv. West Assocs. 960
Committee for Public Education v. Nyquist 631
Commodore Home Systems, Inc. v. Superior Court of San Bernardino County 949
Community for Creative Non-Violence v. Reid.................................... 53, 54
Community Schools v. Seattle School District No. 1...................... 922, 923
Compston v. Borden, Inc. 669
Connecticut Nat. Bank v. Germain 148
Connecticut v. Teal............... 252, 258, 259, 265
Conner v. Schrader-Bridgeport International, Inc....................... 561
Conroy v. New York State Dept. of Correctional Services................. 873
Consolidated Rail Corp. v. Darrone 812
Cook v. IPC International Corp..... 160
Cook v. Rhode Island Dept. of Mental Health, Retardation, and Hospitals 852
Cooke v. Stefani Management Services, Inc. 600
Cooley v. DaimlerChrysler Corp.... 465
Cooper v. Asplundh Tree Expert Co... 77
Cooper v. City of North Olmsted.... 185
Cooper v. Federal Reserve Bank of Richmond 232
Cooper v. General Dynamics.......... 630
Cooper v. Oak Rubber Co....... 663, 665
Cooper v. University of Texas at Dallas 219
Corcoran v. Shoney's Colonial, Inc... 597
Corning Glass Works v. Brennan...................................... 381
Corporation of the Presiding Bishop v. Amos 637, 638
Cosme v. Salvation Army 717
Cota v. Tucson Police Dept............. 730
Cotran v. Rollins Hudig Hall International, Inc....................... 602
Crady v. Liberty Nat. Bank and Trust Co. of Indiana 576
Craft v. Metromedia, Inc. 415
Craig v. Boren 482
Craig v. M & O Agencies, Inc. 591, 598
Craig v. Y&Y Snacks, Inc. 75
Cravens v. Blue Cross and Blue Shield of Kansas City.................. 835
Crawford v. BNSF Ry. Co.............. 593
Crawford v. Medina General Hosp. 780
Crawford v. Metropolitan Government **191**, 594
Cremin v. Merrill Lynch Pierce Fenner & Smith, Inc. 438
Crist v. Focus Homes, Inc.............. 615
Crone v. United Parcel Service, Inc. 375
Cross v. Alabama 568
Croushorn v. Board of Trustees of University of Tennessee............. 187
Cruz v. Coach Stores, Inc........ 197, 622
Cruzan v. Special School Dist. No. 1 514
Cullen v. Indiana University Board of Trustees 380
Culver v. Gorman & Co. 189
Cummins v. Parker Seal Co. 631
Curay-Cramer v. Ursuline Acad. ... 639
Czekalski v. Peters......................... 106
Dailey v. Societe Generale 75
Dale v. Chicago Tribune Co. 727
Danco, Inc. v. Wal-Mart Stores, Inc. 626
Daniels v. Pipefitters' Association Local Union No. 597.................... 335
Darnell v. City of Jasper............ 72, 74
Daubert v. Merrell Dow Pharmaceuticals, Inc.......... 226, 720, 727
Davis v. Bombardier Transp. Holdings, Inc................................. 38
Davis v. City of Dallas 273
Davis v. Coastal International Security, Inc............................... 372
Davis v. Construction Materials 76
Davis v. Monsanto Chemical Co..... 546
Davis v. Nordstrom, Inc.................. 946
Davis v. Passman........................... 314
Davis v. Target Stores Div. of Dayton Hudson Corp................................ 86
Davis v. Team Electric Co. 375
Dawavendewa v. Salt River Project Agricultural Improvement & Power Dist. **689**
Dawson v. Bumble & Bumble........ 424, 499, 504

Dearth v. Collins 601
DeCintio v. Westchester County Medical Center 206, 563
DeClue v. Central Illinois Light Co. 375
Dediol v. Best Chevrolet, Inc. 669, 780
Deffenbaugh-Williams v. Wal-Mart Stores, Inc. 501
Degraffenreid v. General Motors 51
DeHart v. Horn 634
Delaware State College v. Ricks 29
Den Hartog v. Wasatch Academy 837, 838
Densberger v. United Technologies Corp. 720
Dercach v. Indiana Dept. of Revenue 713
DeSantis v. Pacific Tel. & Tel. Co., Inc. 495, 500, 526
Desert Palace, Inc. v. Costa 98, **144**, 424, 748
Desiderio v. National Ass'n of Securities Dealers 941
Deters v. Equifax Credit Information Services, Inc. 600
Dewey v. Reynolds Metals Co. 630
Dewitt v. Proctor Hosp. 837, 838
Diamond v. Colonial Life & Accident Ins. Co. 151
Diaz v. Fort Wayne Foundry Corp. 485
Diaz v. Pan American World Airways, Inc. 409, 726
Diaz v. Swift-Eckrich, Inc. 624
Dick v. Phone Directories Co. 525
Dille v. Council of Energy Resource Tribes 698
Dimino v. New York City Transit Authority 462
Discover Bank v. Superior Court ... 957
Doctor's Associates, Inc. v. Casarotto 950
Dodge v. Giant Food, Inc. 415
Doe v. Belleville 370, 372
Doe v. C.A.R.S. Protection Plus, Inc. 467
Doe v. City of Belleville 424, 522
Doe v. Oberweiss Dairy 548
Doebele v. Sprint/United Management Co. 119
Doerhoff v. McDonnell Douglas Corp. 796
Dollar v. Smithway Motor Xpress, Inc. 75
Dominguez-Curry v. Nevada Transp. Dept. 142
Donald v. Sybra, Inc. 207
Donnellon v. Fruehauf Corp. 72
Dothard v. Rawlinson 257, 393, 400, 407, 862
Douglas v. DynMcDermott Petroleum Operations Co. 196
Dowd v. United Steelworkers of America 63
Drum v. Leeson Elec. Corp. 384
Duane v. GEICO 330
Dukes v. Wal-Mart Stores, Inc. 243, 436, 554
Duncan v. Children's National Medical Center 406
Duncan v. General Motors Corp. 549
Duncan v. Walker 453
Dunn v. Washington County Hosp. 615
Ebbert v. DaimlerChrysler Corp. 41
Eckles v. Consolidated Rail Corp. 72
Edelman v. Lynchburg College 21, 24
EEOC v. Abercrombie & Fitch Stores, Inc. **641**, 643, 647
EEOC v. Aetna Ins. Co. 382
EEOC v. Alamo Rent-A-Car, LLC 644
EEOC v. Aldi, Inc. 644
EEOC v. Amego, Inc. 858
EEOC v. American National Bank 218
EEOC v. Arabian American Oil Co. 60
EEOC v. Board of Regents of the University of Wisconsin System ... 19
EEOC v. Boeing Co. 126
EEOC v. Boh Bros. Const. Co., LLC 523, 594
EEOC v. Catholic University of America 640
EEOC v. Central Wholesalers, Inc. 552, 625
EEOC v. Chemsico, Inc. 643, 644, 645
EEOC v. Children's Hosp. Medical Center 963
EEOC v. Clay Printing Co. 755
EEOC v. CNA Ins. Co. 877
EEOC v. Commercial Office Products Co. 26
EEOC v. CRST Van Expedited, Inc. 587
EEOC v. Exxon Mobil Corp. 407
EEOC v. Firestone Fibers & Textiles Co. 665
EEOC v. Ford Motor Co. 854
EEOC v. Freeman 282
EEOC v. Fremont Christian School 639
EEOC v. Harbert-Yeargin, Inc. 372

EEOC v. Houston Funding II, Ltd. 465
EEOC v. Humiston-Keeling, Inc. 834, 835
EEOC v. Ilona of Hungary, Inc. 646, 665
EEOC v. Indiana Bell Telephone 614
EEOC v. Ithaca Indus., Inc. 631, 662
EEOC v. Johnson & Higgins, Inc. 56
EEOC v. Kallir, Philips, Ross, Inc. 71, 72
EEOC v. Kamehameha Schools/Bishop Estate 648
EEOC v. Kaplan Higher Educ. Corp. 282
EEOC v. Local 350, Plumbers & Pipefitters 767
EEOC v. Luce, Forward, Hamilton & Scripps 941
EEOC v. Management Hospitality of Racine, Inc. 594
EEOC v. Mercy Health Center 412
EEOC v. Mitsubishi Motor Manufacturing 554
EEOC v. New Breed Logistics 600
EEOC v. Oak-Rite Mfg. Corp. 664
EEOC v. Peoplemark 282
EEOC v. Pipefitters Ass'n Local Union 597 66
EEOC v. Premier Operator Services 721
EEOC v. Prevo's Family Market, Inc. 859
EEOC v. Propak Logistics, Inc. 41, 86
EEOC v. PVNF, LLC 552
EEOC v. READS, Inc. 646
EEOC v. Resources for Human Development, Inc. 852
EEOC v. Sage Realty Corp. 422
EEOC v. Sambo's of Georgia 671
EEOC v. Sears, Roebuck & Co. 224, 225
EEOC v. Sephora USA, LLC 718, 719, **722**
EEOC v. Staten Island Savings Bank 877
EEOC v. Synchro-Start Prods., Inc. 713, 721
EEOC v. Technocrest Sys., Inc. 707
EEOC v. Tortilleria 710
EEOC v. Townley Engineering & Mfg. Co. 501
EEOC v. Trans State Airlines 48
EEOC v. United Parcel Service, Inc. 465, 671
EEOC v. University of Chicago Hospitals 109
EEOC v. V & J Foods, Inc. 593
EEOC v. Waffle House 42, 940, 941, 942, 952
EEOC v. Wyoming 756
Egbuna v. Time-Life Libraries, Inc. 710, 711
Egelston v. State University College at Geneseo 22
El v. Southeastern Pennsylvania Transp. Authority (SEPTA) 281
Electrical Workers v. NLRB 65
Ellerth v. Burlington Industries 566
Ellis v. Costco Wholesale Corp. 434
Ellison v. Brady 516, 551, 556
Elnashar v. Speedway SuperAmerica, LLC 109
Elsensohn v. St. Tammany Parish Sheriff's Office 488
Employment Division, Department of Human Resources of Oregon v. Smith 641, 675, 680, 681
Emporium Capwell Co. v. Western Addition Community Organization 66, 67
Emswiler v. Great Eastern Resort Corp. 381
Englehardt v. S.P. Richards Co. 58
Engquist v. Oregon Dept. of Agriculture 307
Enriquez v. Honeywell, Inc. 693
Ensley-Gaines v. Runyon 452
Erie County Retirees Ass'n v. County of Erie 780
Escobar-Noble v. Luxury Hotels International of Puerto Rico, Inc. 953
Eshelman v. Agere Systems, Inc. 76
Espinoza v. Farah Manufacturing Company, Inc. 329, 330, 691, **702**, 734
Etienne v. Spanish Lake Truck & Casino Plaza 142
Etsitty v. Utah Transit Auth. 514
Evance v. Trumann Health Services, LLC 107
Evans v. Jeff D. 85
Everson v. Michigan Dept. of Corrections 413
Exxon Co., U.S.A. v. Sofec, Inc. 158
Fagan v. National Cash Register Co. 416
Fallon v. Illinois 389
Fantini v. Salem State Coll. 59
Faraca v. Clements 59
Farafaras v. Citizens Bank & Trust 552
Faragher v. City of Boca Raton 174, 175, 193, 197, 199, 578, 579, 585, 588, 589, 594, 596, 605
Farrar v. Hobby 86, 153

Federal Express Corp. v. Holowecki 21, 25, 748
Federation of African American Contractors v. City of Oakland 336
Feingold v. New York 184
Fernandez v. Wynn Oil Co. 411
Ferris v. Delta Air Lines, Inc. 549, 558, 614
Fesel v. Masonic Home of Delaware, Inc. 412
Fierro v. Saks Fifth Avenue 724
Filar v. Board of Educ. of City of Chicago 745, 793
Filipovic v. K & R Express Sys., Inc. 185
Finnegan v. Trans World Airlines, Inc. 767
Firebird Soc. of New Haven, Inc. v. New Haven Bd. of Fire Commissioners 295
Firefighters Local Union 1784 v. Stotts 72
Firefighters v. Cleveland 297, 903, 904
Firefighters' Institute for Racial Equality v. City of St. Louis 257, 299
First Options of Chicago, Inc. v. Kaplan 946, 957
Fisher v. University of Texas at Austin 923
Fisher v. Vassar Coll. 374
Fite v. First Tennessee Production Credit Ass'n 74
Fitzpatrick v. Bitzer 18
Fitzpatrick v. City of Atlanta 407
Flaherty v. Gas Research Institute 576
Flowers v. Southern Regional Physician Services, Inc. 839
Floyd v. Amite County School Dist. 498
Fogg v. Gonzales 151
Foley v. University of Houston System 59
Folkerson v. Circus Circus Enterprises, Inc. 615
Fonseca v. Sysco Food Services of Arizona, Inc. 738
Forbus v. Sears Roebuck & Co. 789
Ford Motor Co. v. EEOC 75
Ford Motor Co. v. Huffman 62, 65
Ford v. Schering-Plough Corp. 875, 877
Forrest v. Brinker International Payroll Co. 373, 566
Fountain v. Safeway Stores, Inc. 420
Fowler v. Rhode Island 646
Fowler v. UPMC Shadyside 42
Fox v. General Motors Corp. 839
Fox v. Vice 87
Fragante v. City & County of Honolulu 733, 736, 737, 738, 739
Frank v. United Airlines, Inc. 419, 425, 432
Franklin v. Local 2 of the Sheet Metal Workers International Ass'n 281
Franks v. Bowman Transportation Co. 69, 70, 72, 655
Frazee v. Illinois Department of Employment Security 633
Frazier v. Delco Electronics Corp 617
Fredenburg v. Contra Costa County Dept. of Health Services 856
Frederick v. Sprint/United Management Co. 593, 599
Freeman v. Dal-Tile Corp. 615
Friedman v. Southern California Permanente Medical Group 634
Frontiero v. Richardson 444
Fullilove v. Klutznik 916, 917
Furnco Construction Corp. v. Waters 103, 115, 128, 267, 454, 892
Gallagher v. C.H. Robinson Worldwide, Inc. 566, 594
Galloway v. General Motors Services Parts Operations 373
Garcetti v. Cebbalos 336
Garcia v. Gloor 713, 716, 717
Garcia v. Spun Steak Co. 713, 716, 722, 728
Garcia-Ayala v. Lederle Parenterals, Inc. 825
Gardner v. Morris 813
Garrett v. Hewlett-Packard Co. 121
Gaston County v. United States 248
Gates v. Caterpillar, Inc. 107
Gawley v. Indiana University 598
Gay Law Students Assn. v. Pacific Tel. & Tel. Co. 531
Geary v. Visitation of the Blessed Virgin Mary Parish School 639
Gebin v. Mineta 708
Geiger v. Tower Auto. 753
Geller v. Markham 764
General Bldg. Contractors Ass'n v. Pennsylvania 321, **322**
General Dynamics Land Systems, Inc. v. Cline 21, 748, 775
General Electric Co. v. Gilbert 22, 443, 454, 541
General Telephone Co. of Northwest v. EEOC 231
General Telephone Co. of Southwest v. Falcon 231, 232, 233, 235

George v. Leavitt 122
Georgia v. Rachel........................... 323
Gerdom v. Continental Airlines, Inc.............................. 419, 725, 726
Ghosh v. Getto 734
Gibson v. Arkansas Department of Correction.................................... 19
Gibson v. Neighborhood Health Clinics, Inc................................... 946
Gilbert v. St. Rita's Professional Services, LLC 488
Gilmer v. Interstate/Johnson Lane Corp. 935, 938, 947, 949, 958, 963
Givhan v. Western Line Consol. School Dist. 138
Glenn v. Brumby 513
Goesaert v. Cleary 483
Goff v. Continental Oil Co. 162
Goins v. West Group....................... 514
Golden Eagle Ins. Co. v. Foremost Ins. Co. 944
Gomez-Perez v. Potter 162, 715
Gomillion v. Lightfoot.................... 315
Gonzales v. O Centro Espirita Beneficente................................. 681
Gonzalez v. Connecticut 318
Gonzalez v. Salvation Army 726
Gonzalo v. All Island Transportation 718
Good v. U.S. West Communications, Inc.. 776
Goodman v. Lukens Steel Co.. 63, 331
Gordon v. Shafer Contracting Co.. 594
Graham v. Long Island R.R. 107
Graham v. Richardson................... 330
Graham-Humphreys v. Memphis Brooks Museum of Art, Inc........... 38
Grano v. Department of Development of Columbus 821
Gratz v. Bollinger 921
Green Tree Financial Corp.-Alabama v. Randolph 954
Green v. American Federation of Teachers/Illinois Federation of Teachers Local 604 961
Green v. Franklin Nat. Bank of Minneapolis........................ 198, 613
Green v. McDonnell Douglas Corp. 102, 103
Green v. Missouri Pac. R.R. 257
Greene v. Safeway Stores, Inc. 745, 774
Gregory v. Georgia Dept. of Human Resources 25
Gregory v. Litton Sys., Inc. 257
Grendel's Den, Inc. v. Larkin........... 88
Griffin v. Kraft General Foods, Inc. 787
Griffin v. Prince William Health System 855
Griffith v. City of Des Moines......... 150
Griffiths, In re 708
Griggs v. Duke Power Co. 6, 96, 234, 245, **246**, 253, 255, 273, 309, 325, 388, 436, 541, 704, 706, 798, 887, 892
Griggs v. National R.R. Passenger Corp., Inc. 566
Groesch v. City of Springfield........... 38
Grosjean v. First Energy Corp. 105, 774
Gross v. FBL Financial Services, Inc. 154, 201, 204, 205, 327, 743, 745, **746**, 753
Grutter v. Bollinger 294, 306, 883, 921
Guardians Ass'n of New York City Police Dept., Inc. v. Civil Service Commission of City of New York 257
Gudenkauf v. Stauffer Communications, Inc. 154, 487
Guimares v. Supervalu, Inc. 160
Gulf Oil v. Copp Paving Co. 937
Gulino v. Board of Educ. of City School Dist. of City of New York 282
Gulino v. New York State Educ. Dept.. 256
Gunther v. Iowa State Men's Reformatory.............................. 396
Gutchen v. Board of Governors of Rhode Island.............................. 780
Gutierrez v. Municipal Court 729
Hackett v. McGuire Bros., Inc. 165
Hall Street Assocs. v. Mattel, Inc. 959, 960
Hall v. BNSF Ry. Co. 497, 502
Hall v. Bodine Elec. Co. 593
Hall v. Missouri Highway & Transp. Commission 777
Hall v. Nalco.................................. 466
Halliburton Co., In re 951
Halligan v. Piper Jaffray, Inc. 960
Hamilton v. Geithner...................... 184
Hamm v. Weyauwega Milk Prods., Inc. 523
Hamner v. St. Vincent Hosp. and Health Care Center, Inc............. 200
Hampel v. Food Ingredients Specialties, Inc. 603
Hans v. Louisiana 17
Harlston v. McDonnell Douglas Corp... 576
Harmar v. United Airlines, Inc. 181

Harrell v. Donahue 72
Harris v. Forklift Systems, Inc. 176, 199, **542**, 559, 700, 701, 702, 719, 780
Harris v. International Paper Co. **618**
Harrison v. Westinghouse Savannah River Co., United States ex rel. 157
Harriss v. Pan American World Airways, Inc. 406
Harsco Corp. v. Renner 600
Hartley v. Wisconsin Bell, Inc. 774
Harvender v. Norton Co. 488
Harvey v. City of New Bern Police Department 41
Hasham v. California State Board of Equalization 738
Haskins v. Prudential Ins. Co. of America 946
Haskins v. United States Dept. of Army 98
Haugerud v. Amery School Dist. 594
Hawkins v. Anheuser-Busch, Inc. 180, 614
Hawkins v. Holloway 568
Hayden v. County of Nassau 715
Hazelwood School District v. United States **212**, 218, 263, 900
Hazen Paper Co. v. Biggins 83, 120, 744, 749, **754**, 761, 763, 765, 766, 778, 800, 801, 804, 820, 821
Healey v. Southwood Psychiatric Hospital 407
Heller v. Columbia Edgewater Country Club 500, 504
Helm v. Kansas 593
Hemi Group, LLC v. City of New York 158
Hendricks-Robinson v. Excel Corp. 825
Hennick v. Schwans Sales Enterprises, Inc. 380
Henry v. Lennox Industries, Inc. 74
Henry v. Milwaukee County 407
Henschel v. Clare County Road Commission 854
Hensley v. Eckerhart 88
Henson v. Dundee 538, 546
Hensworth v. Quotesmith.com, Inc. 143
Hernandez v. Hughes Missile Systems Co. 818
Hernandez v. New York 695, 716, 734
Hernandez-Miranda v. Empresas Diaz Masso, Inc. 78
Herrera v. Lufkin Indus., Inc. 623
Herx v. Diocese of Fort Wayne-South Bend, Inc. 466
Hesse v. Dolgencorp of New York, Inc. 461
Hicks v. Gates Rubber Co. 50, 625
Higgins v. New Balance Athletic Shoe, Inc. 522
Hilao v. Estate of Marcos 231
Hilburn v. Murata Electronics North America, Inc. 849
Hill v. American General Finance, Inc. 594
Hill v. John Chezik Imports 41
Hill v. Lockheed Martin Logistics Management, Inc. 151, 776
Hinds v. Sprint/United Management Co. 110
Hines v. Grand Casino of Louisiana 699
Hishon v. King & Spalding 54, 134, 174, 660
Hitchcock v. Angel Corps, Inc. 121
Hocevar v. Purdue Frederick Co. ... 548
Hochstadt v. Worcester Foundation for Experimental Biology 162, 187, 197
Hoffman Plastic Compounds, Inc. v. National Labor Relations Board 711
Hoffman-La Roche, Inc. v. Zeltwanger 567
Hogan v. Bangor & Aroostook R.R. 78
Holcomb v. Iona Coll. 498
Hollander v. American Cyanide Co. 796
Holloway v. Arthur Andersen & Co. 510
Holly D. v. California Institute of Technology 591
Holly v. Clairson Industries, LLC 849
Holman v. Indiana 560
Holt v. JTM Industries, Inc. 168
Hopwood v. Texas 921
Horner v. Mary Institute 86
Hosanna-Tabor Evangelical Lutheran Church & School v EEOC ... 640, 641
Hostetler v. Quality Dining, Inc. 549
Houston v. Sidley & Austin 41
Howard v. National Cash Register Co. 701
Howe v. Haslam 531
Howley v. Town of Stratford 550
Hoyt v. Florida 483
Huber v. Wal-Mart Stores, Inc. **832**, 836
Hudson v. Reno 76, 78
Hughes v. Derwinski 184

Humenny v. Genex Corp. 733
Hundertmark v. Florida Dept. of Transp. 385
Hurd v. Hodge 323, 326
Hutchins v. International Brotherhood of Teamsters 380
Iadimarco v. Runyon 127
Imaging Bus. Machines, LLC v. BancTec, Inc. 851
ING Financial Partners v. Johansen 940
Ingle v. Circuit City Stores, Inc. 951, 953, 954
Inglis v. Buena Vista University 390
Insignia Residential Corp. v. Ashton 567
International Association of Machinists & Aerospace Workers, Lodge 751 v. Boeing Co. 668
International Union, United Automobile Workers v. Johnson Controls **396**, 406, 461, 649, 700, 862
Isaacs v. Felder Services, LLC 501
Isabel v. City of Memphis 281, 301
Jackman v. Fifth Judicial Dist. Dept. of Correctional Services 106
Jackson v. Birmingham Bd. of Educ. 162, 171
Jacobs v. North Carolina Administrative Office of the Courts 851
James v. City of Costa Mesa 875
Jansen v. Packaging Corp. of America 566
Jaramillo v. Colorado Judicial Dept. 119, 123
Jarrell v. Eastern Airlines 431
Jarvis v. Potter 858
Jefferies v. Harris County Community Action Association 50, 391, 775
Jefferson v. California Dept. of Youth Authority 567
Jefferson v. Hackney 311
Jeffries v. Chicago Transit Authority 41
Jenkins v. New York City Transit Authority 671
Jennings v. New York State Office of Mental Health 412
Jenson v. Eveleth Taconite Co. 553, 554
Jespersen v. Harrah's Operating Company, Inc. **416**
Jett v. Dallas Independent School District 336
Jin v. Metropolitan Life Ins. 591
Jock v. Sterling Jewelers Inc. 961
Johal v. Little Lady Foods, Inc. 794
Johnson v. Circuit City Stores, Inc. 941
Johnson v. Crown Enterprises, Inc. 335
Johnson v. Kroger Co. 121, 142
Johnson v. Martin 321
Johnson v. Oregon 855
Johnson v. Palma 66
Johnson v. Railway Express Agency, Inc. 69, 70, 322, 331
Johnson v. Riverside Healthcare System, LP 624, 626
Johnson v. Shalala 109
Johnson v. Transportation Agency of Santa Clara County 297, 370, **896**, 909
Johnson v. University of Pittsburgh 514
Johnson v. Wells Fargo Home Mortgage, Inc. 961
Johnson v. Zema Systems Corp. 127
Jolley v. Phillips Educ. Group of Central Florida, Inc. 461
Jones v. Alfred H. Mayer Co. 322, 325
Jones v. City of Boston 257, 282
Jones v. Clinton 568
Jones v. Dillard's, Inc. 38
Jones v. Madison Service Corp. 41
Jones v. R. R. Donnelley & Son **331**
Jones v. Robinson Property Group 142
Jones v. TEK Industries, Inc. 643
Jones v. UPS Ground Freight 624
Jones v. Walgreen Co. 206
Kania v. Archdiocese of Philadelphia 718, 721, 726
Kanzler v. Renner 566
Kapche v. Holder 73
Kaplan v. Multimedia Entertainment, Inc. 181
Kassner v. 2nd Ave. Delicatessen Inc. 780
Kasten v. Saint-Gobain Performance Plastics Corp. 167, 185
Kastl v. Maricopa County Community College Dist. 514
Kastor v. Cash Express of Tennessee, LLC 488
Kawaauhau v. Geiger 157
Keener v. Department of Army 88
Keith v. County of Oakland 869
Kellogg v. Union Pac. R.R. Co. 835
Kelly v. Drexel University 777
Kendrick v. Penske Transp. Services, Inc. 119, 120
Kennedy v. St. Joseph's Ministries, Inc. 669

Kentucky Retirement Systems v. EEOC 768
Kern v. Dynalectron Corp. 649
Keyes v. School Dist. No.1 311
Kidd v. Mando American Corp 108
Killinger v. Samford University 637
Kim v. Nash Finch Co. 78
Kimel v. Florida Board of Regents 16, 17, 307, 385, 744
King v. General Elec. Co. 743
Knott v. Missouri Pac. R. Co. 420, 422
Knowles v. Citicorp Mortgage, Inc. 20
Knussman v. Maryland 478
Knutson v. Schwan's Home Service, Inc. 855
Kocak v. Community Health Partners of Ohio, Inc. 462
Koch v. Lightning Transp., LLC 447
Kocsis v. Multi-Care Management, Inc. 576
Kodish v. United Air Lines 330
Kolodziej v. Smith 636
Kolstad v. American Dental Association 80, 599, 600
Koren v. Ohio Bell Telephone Co. 504
Kotcher v. Rosa & Sullivan Appliance Center, Inc. 577
Kouba v. Allstate Insurance Co. 383
Kovacevich v. Kent State 18
Kramer v. Union Free School Dist. No. 15 914
Kramer v. Wasatch County Sherrif's Office 568
Krauel v. Iowa Methodist Medical Center 465, 878
Kresko v. Rulli 556
Kristian v. Comcast Corp. 953
Kucharski v. CORT Furniture Rental 457
Kumho Tire Co. v. Carmichael 225
Kunin v. Sears Roebuck & Co. 613
Kyles v. J.K. Guardian Security Services 56
Lack v. Wal-Mart Stores, Inc. 560
Ladd v. Grand Trunk Western R.R. 552
Ladik v. Wal-Mart Stores, Inc. 436
Laffey v. Northwest Airlines 381
Lam v. University of Hawai'i 51, 374, 775
Lamonica v. Safe Hurricane Shutters, Inc. 712
Lander v. Lujan 76
Landgraf v. USI Film Products 145
Landrau-Romero v. Banco Popular De Puerto Rico 623
Langon v. Department of Health & Human Services 867
Lanning v. Southeastern Pennsylvania Transp. Authority 275, 353
Lanning v. Southeastern Pennsylvania Transp. Authority (SEPTA) 270, 275
Lapka v. Chertoff 181
Larimer v. International Business Machines Corp. 837
Laster v. City of Kalamazoo 109, 168, 611
Laughlin v. Metropolitan Washington Airports Authority 187, 196
Lautermilch v. Findlay City School 375
Lavin-McEleny v. Marist College 379
Law v. United States Postal Service 867
Lawrence v. CNF Transp., Inc. 381
Lawrence v. Texas 530, 532, 534
Laxton v. Gap, Inc. 120, 460
LeBlanc v. Great American Ins. Co. 795
Ledbetter v. Goodyear Tire & Rubber Co., Inc. 27, 36, 37, 240, 390, 953
Leibowitz v. Cornell University 754
Leitgen v. Franciscan Skemp Healthcare, Inc. 189
Lemon v. Kurtzman 638
Lewis v. Aetna Life Ins. Co. 875
Lewis v. City of Chicago, Illinois ... 258, 953
Lewis v. Heartland Inns of America, LLC 415
Lewis v. St. Cloud State University 105
Liao v. Tennessee Valley Authority 909
Lincoln County v. Luning 19
Lindsey v. Prive Corp. 779
Lipsett v. University of Puerto Rico 618, 619
Lisdahl v. Mayo Foundation 611
Little v. Windermere Relocation, Inc. 549, 558
Little v. Wuerl 637
Local 53, Asbestos Workers v. Vogler 257
Lochren v. County of Suffolk 462
Lockard v. Pizza Hut, Inc. 615
Lockridge v. Board of Trustees of University of Arkansas 103
Loeffler v. Frank 75
Loftin-Boggs v. City of Meridian ... 556
Lomack v. City of Newark 925

Long v. First Union Corp. 715, 718, 719, 721, 726
Long v. Sears Roebuck & Co. 788
Lopez v. Four Dee, Inc. 488
Lopez v. River Oaks Imaging & Diagnostic Group, Inc. 512
Lorance v. AT&T Technologies, Inc. 29
Los Angeles Department of Water & Power, City of v. Manhart 70, 99, 138, 203, 227, **356**, 365, 382, 499, 541
Loudermilk v. Best Pallet Co. 207
Love v. Pullman Co. 24, 26
Love v. Reed 634
Love v. Wal-Mart Stores, Inc. 436
Loving v. Virginia 914
Lowery v. Circuit City Stores, Inc. 82
Lucas v. Jerusalem Cafe 712
Luce v. Dalton 777, 778
Lucero v. Nettle Creek School Corp. 180, 181
Lujan v. National Wildlife Federation 166
LULAC, United States v. 318
Lust v. Sealy, Inc. 473
Lutkewitte v. Gonzales 590, 591
Lyes v. City of Riviera Beach, Fla. ... 58
Lyles v. District of Columbia 615
Lynch v. Freeman 375
Maalik v. International Union of Elevator Constructors, Local 2 67
Mabra v. United Food & Commercial Workers 327
Mach Mining, LLC v. EEOC 39
Machinchick v. PB Power, Inc. 151
Macias v. Excel Bldg. Services LLC 951
Mack v. Otis Elevator Co. 581, 586
Macklin v. Mendenhall 556
Madel v. FCI Marketing, Inc. 743
Magana v. Northern Mariana Islands 330
Makovi v. Sherwin-Williams Co. ... 567
Maksimovic v. Tsogalis 566
Maldonado v. City of Altus 716, 717
Maldonado v. U.S. Bank 460
Malik v. Carrier Corp. 602
Malnak v. Yogi 634
Manatt v. Bank of America, NA 626
Manessis v. New York City Dept. of Transp. 737
Mangold v. California Public Utilities Commission 89
Mann v. Frank 644
Mantolete v. Bolger 869
Mararri v. WCI Steel, Inc. 874
Maraschiello v. City of Buffalo Police Dept. 302
Markham v. Geller 755
Marriage Cases, In re 531
Marshall v. American Hospital Association 460
Marshall v. Dallas Independent School Dist. 379
Martens v. Smith Barney Inc. 438
Martin v. Local 1513, IAMAW 66
Martin v. New York State Dept. of Correctional Services 200
Martin v. Wilks 895
Martini v. Federal Nat. Mortg. Ass'n 40
Massachusetts v. Feeney 316
Massachusetts, Commonwealth of v. Bull HN Information Systems, Inc. 790
Mastro v. Potomac Elec. Power Co. 128
Mathis v. Phillips Chevrolet, Inc. 766
Matima v. Celli 197
Mattson v. Caterpillar, Inc. 189
Matvia v. Bald Head Island Management, Inc. 590, 598
Mauro, Estate of v. Borgess Medical Center 859
Maxfield v. Sinclair International 74
Mayer v. Nextel W. Corp. 745
Maynard v. Pneumatic Prods. Corp. 26
Mayor of Philadelphia v. Educational Equality League 210
Mazzeo v. Color Resolutions International, LLC 847
McCallum v. Archstone Communities, LLC 460
McCann v. Tillman 623
McCaskill v. SCI Management Corp. 956
McClain v. Lufkin Industries, Inc. 259
McClure v. Salvation Army 640
McCormick v. Kmart Distribution Center 604
McCoy v. City of Shreveport 180
McCullough v. University of Arkansas for Medical Sciences 168, 602
McCurdy v. Arkansas State Police 599
McDaniel v. Essex International, Inc. 631
McDaniel v. Mississippi Baptist Medical Center 874
McDonald v. Santa Fe Trail Transportation Co. 44, 106, 328, 892

McDonald v. Wise 601
McDonnell Douglas Corp. v. Green 24, 40, 96, 98, **99**, 108, 115, 139, 173, 210, 226, 255, 327, 448, 449, 624, 715, 735, 745, 748, 757, 818, 820
McElwee v. County of Orange........ 848
McGinest v. GTE Service Corp. 151, 622, 626
McIntosh v. Jones Truck Lines, Inc. 72
McKeever v. Ironworkers' Dist. Council.. 767
McKenna v. City of Philadelphia ... 160
McKennon v. Nashville Banner Publishing Co. 73, 196, 743
McKenzie v. Benton........................ 858
McKenzie v. Illinois Dept. of Transportation 185, 186
McLaughlin v. Richland Shoe 83
McNeil v. Aguilos 730, 731
McWilliams v. Fairfax County Board of Supervisors............................ 370
Meacham v. Knolls Atomic Power Laboratory.................................. 806
Mead Corp., United States v. 588
Medina v. Income Support Div., State of New Mexico 525
Medina-Munoz v. R.J. Reynolds Tobacco Co. 117
Meeks v. Computer Associates International 390
Mejia v. New York Sheraton Hotel 737
Meloff v. New York Life Ins. Co. 602
Mendelsohn v. Sprint/United Management Co. 124
Mendoza v. Borden, Inc. 546, 548, 562
Meng v. Ipanema Shoe Corp. 737, 738
Merillat v. Metal Spinners, Inc. 794
Meritor Savings Bank, FSB v. Vinson..........140, 516, 518, 535, 539, 540, 541, 545, 546, 547, 559, 568, 569, 577, 604, 607, 622, 669, 700, 839
Meriwether v. Caraustar Packaging Co. 550, 613
Metoyer v. Chassman 327
Metz v. Transit Mix, Inc. 755, 757, 765
Meyer v. Holley 203
Meyers, United States v. 634
Michas v. Health Cost Controls of Illinois.. 794
Mickelson v. New York Life Ins. Co. 180
Mickey v. Zeidler Tool & Die Co. ... 168, 184
Millbrook v. IBP, Inc. 123
Miller v. Department of Corrections 563
Miller v. Kenworth of Dothan, Inc. 700
Miller v. Maxwell's International Inc. 58
Milton v. Scrivner, Inc. 72
Miranda v. Arizona 606
Mississippi Dept. of Public Safety, United States v. 19
Missouri v. Jenkins 88
Mitchell v. Data General Corp. 794, 795
Mitchell v. Jefferson County Board of Educ. 380, 390
Mitchell v. OsAir, Inc. 73
Mitchell v. Robert DeMario Jewelry, Inc. 175, 179
Mitchell v. Vanderbilt University 745
Mitsubishi Motors Corp. v. Soler Chrysler-Plymouth, Inc. 939, 952, 958
Mohasco Corp. v. Silver 26
Momah v. Dominguez 734
Monell v. Department of Social Services of City of New York 321
Monteagudo v. Asociacion de Empleados del Estado Libre Asociado de P.R. 598
Montero v. Agco Corp. 594, 598
Montes v. Vail Clinic, Inc. 716, 717, 719
Moon v. Secretary, United States Dept. of Labor 813
Moore v. City of Philadelphia 180
Morales v. Human Rights Division 730
Morgan v. Swanson 337
Morgan v. United Parcel Service of America, Inc. 223
Moring v. Arkansas Dept. of Correction 558
Morris v. City of Colorado Springs 549
Morrison v. Circuit City Stores, Inc. 952, 955
Morrissey v. Boston Five Cents Savings Bank 791
Morton v. Mancari 692
Moses v. American Nonwovens, Inc. 858, 862
Moss v. Southern Ry. Co. 186
Mt. Healthy City School Board of Educ. v. Doyle 140, 145

Mulhall v. Advance Sec., Inc. 379, 385
Muller v. Oregon 405, 441, 483
Mumfrey v. CVS Pharmacy, Inc. ... 184
Muriithi v. Shuttle Exp., Inc. 955
Murnane v. American Airlines, Inc. 781
Murphy Oil USA, Inc. 954
Murphy v. United Parcel Service, Inc. 842
Murray v. City of Onawa 86
Muzzy v. Cahillane Motors, Inc. 551
Myers v. Central Florida Investments, Inc. 566
NAACP v. North Hudson Regional Fire & Rescue 282
Nanda v. Board of Trustees of University of Illinois 18
Nashville Gas Co. v. Satty 660
National Credit Union Admin. v. First Nat. Bank & Trust Co. 167
National Railroad Passenger Corporation v. Morgan..... 27, 28, 37, 60, 616, 617
Nationwide Mut. Ins. Co. v. Darden 53, 54, 55
Navarro v. Pfizer Corp. 486
Nelson v. University of Texas at Dallas 19
Nevada Department of Human Resources v. Hibbs 16, 18, 306, 385, 443, 472, 473, 475, 482, 484, 485
New York City Transit Authority v. Beazer 257, 263
New York Gaslight Club, Inc. v. Carey 26, 88
New York State Ass'n of Retarded Children, Inc. v. Carey 89
Newman v. Piggie Park Enters., Inc. 85
Newport News Shipbuilding & Dry Dock Co. v. EEOC 444, 453, 464
Newsday, Inc. v. Long Island Typographical Union 601
Nghiem v. NEC Electronics, Inc. ... 940
Nichols v. Azteca Restaurant Enterprises, Inc. 422, 430, 495, 500, 519, 520, 523
Nichols v. Frank 539, 540, 565
Nicholson v. Hyannis Air Service, Inc. 107
Nicol v. Imagematrix, Inc. 461
Nino v. Jewelry Exch., Inc. 951
Niswander v. Cincinnati Ins. Co. ... 196
NLRB v. Catholic Bishop of Chicago 680
NLRB v. Gullet Gin Co. 75
NLRB v. Scrivener 175
NLRB v. United Ins. Co. of America 55
Noel v. New York State Office of Mental Health Central New York Psychiatric Center 75
Norbuta v. Loctite Corp. 735
Norman-Bloodsaw v. Lawrence Berkeley Lab 871, 875
Norris v. Sysco Corp 154
Noviello v. Boston 581
Noyes v. Kelley Servs 670
O'Connor v. Consolidated Coin Caterers Corp. 105, 745, 748, 773, 774
O'Gilvie v. United States 84
O'Neal v. Ferguson Const. Co. 184
O'Regan v. Arbitration Forums, Inc. 777
O'Shea v. Yellow Technology Services, Inc. 373, 623
Oberg v. Allied Van Lines, Inc. 788
Obergefell v. Hodges 491, 504, 530
Oblix, Inc. v. Winiecki 946
Occidental Life Insurance Co. v. EEOC 41
Ocheltree v. Scollon Prods., Inc. 561
Odima v. Westin Tucson Hotel 688
Officers for Justice v. Civil Service Commission 912
Ogden v. All-State Career School 556
Oglebay Norton Co. v. Jenson 554
Okruhlik v. University of Arkansas ex rel. May 18
Oncale v. Sundowner Offshore Services, Inc. 175, 178, **369**, 500, 515, 517, 518, 519, 521, 551, 558, 719
Ondricko v. MGM Grand Detroit, LLC 121
Opalinski v. Robert Half Int'l Inc. 956
Opuku-Boateng v. State of California 662
Organized Village of Kake v. Egan 692
Osborne v. Baxter Healthcare Corp. 857
Oscar Mayer & Co. v. Evans 743
Oubre v. Entergy Operations, Inc. **783**
Oxford Health Plans LLC v. Sutter 956
Oxman v. WLS–TV 795, 796
Pacheco v. Mineta 25
Pacheco v. New York Presbyterian Hospital **713**
PacifiCare Health Systems v. Book 956

Pacourek v. Inland Steel Co. 461
Paladino v. Avnet Computer Technologies, Inc. 954
Palmer v. Circuit Court of Cook County Ill. 863
Palmer v. Shultz 222
Palomares v. Second Federal Sav. and Loan Ass'n of Chicago 476
Panis v. Mission Hills Bank 375
Papa v. Katy Indus., Inc. 58
Paradise, United States v. 916, 919
Parents Involved in Community Schools v. Seattle School District No. 1 5
Parker v. Baltimore & O. R. Co. 128
Parker v. Metropolitan Life Ins. Co. 877, 878
Parrott v. District of Columbia 662
Passananti v. Cook County 373, 561
Passantino v. Johnson & Johnson Consumer Prods., Inc. 600
Patane v. Clark 168, 181
Patrick v. LeFevre 646
Patterson v. American Tobacco Co. 72
Patterson v. McLean Credit Union 162, 319, 322, 326, 327, 332, 335
Pejic v. Hughes Helicopters, Inc. ... 691
Penn v. Ryan's Family Steak Houses 946
Pennsylvania State Police v. Suders 108, 174, 176, 592, **604**, 609
Pennsylvania v. Delaware Valley Citizens' Council for Clean Air 89
Penry v. Federal Home Loan Bank of Topeka 562
Pension Benefit Guaranty Corp. v. LTV Corp. 500
Peralta v. Chromium Plating & Polishing Corp. 406
Perdue v. Kenny A. ex rel. Winn 89
Perez v. Texas Dept. of Criminal Justice 107
Perkins v. Lake County Dept. of Utilities 691
Perry v. McGinnis 320
Personnel Administrator of Massachusetts v. Feeney ... 315, 316, 317, 318, 326
Peters v. City of Shreveport 379
Peterson v. Wilmur Communications, Inc. 635
Petit v. City of Chicago 925
Pettway v. American Cast Iron Pipe Co. 74, 188
Phelps v. Hamilton 87
Phelps v. Yale Sec., Inc. 110
Philbrook v. Ansonia Board of Education 645
Phillips v. Martin Marietta Corp. 374, 393, 399, 468, 477, 705, 706, 707
Phipps v. Wal-Mart Stores, Inc. 243, 436
Pickering v. Board of Education 677
Pime v. Loyola University of Chicago 648
Pink v. Modoc Indian Health Project, Inc. 698
Piva v. Xerox Corp. 74
Pivirotto v. Innovative Systems, Inc. 105
Plessy v. Ferguson 3, 305
Plotke v. White 119
Pokorny v. Quixtar, Inc. 953
Poland v. Chertoff 109
Pollard v. E.I. du Pont de Nemours & Co. 77, 78
Ponte v. Steelcase Inc. 548
Porter v. Erie Foods Int'l, Inc. 626
Porter v. Natsios 74
Powell v. Yellow Book USA, Inc. 670
Prado v. L. Luria & Son, Inc. 717, 726
Prandini v. National Tea Co. 85
Prebilich-Holland v. Gaylord Entertainment Co. 460
Preston v. Wisconsin Health Fund 563
Prevot v. Phillips Petrol. Co. 951
Prewitt v. United States Postal Service 869
Price v. Northern States Power Co. 382
Price Waterhouse v. Hopkins 99, **133**, 144, 145, 149, 171, 203, 361, 424, 477, 496, 498, 501, 508, 509, 511, 519, 676, 746
Price, United States v. 324
Proud v. Stone 126
Prowel v. Wise Business Forms, Inc. 524
Public Employees Retirement System v. Betts 779, 788
Pugh v. Locke 394
Pullman-Standard v. Swint 97
Quantock v. Shared Marketing Services, Inc. 550
Quiles-Quiles v. Henderson 839
Raad v. Fairbanks North Star Borough School District 738
Rabidue v. Osceola Refining Co. ... 618, 619
Rachid v. Jack in the Box, Inc. 151
Racicot v. Wal-Mart Stores, Inc. 780
Radue v. Kimberly-Clark Corp. 142

Ragone v. Atlantic Video at Manhattan Center 952
Ragsdale v. Wolverine World Wide, Inc. 479
Ramirez v. Baush & Lomb 184
Ramos v. Lamm 89
Ramos-Santiago v. United Parcel Serv. 960
Randolph v. Ohio Dept. of Youth Services 616
Rasimas v. Michigan Dept. of Mental Health 74
Ray v. Henderson 60
Raytheon Co. v. Hernandez 449, **816**
Redd v. New York Div. of Parole.... 562
Reeb v. Economic Opportunity Atlanta, Inc. 38
Reed v. Reed 483
Reeves v. C.H. Robinson Worldwide, Inc. 373
Reeves v. Jewel Food Stores, Inc. 869
Reeves v. Sanderson Plumbing Products, Inc. 97, 117, 119, 120, 148, 177, 475, 745, 748
Reeves v. Swift Transp. Co. 452
Regents of the University of California v. Bakke....5, 886, 904, 905, 914, 915
Reid v. Kraft General Foods, Inc. 635
Reid v. Memphis Pub. Co. 631
Reine v. Honeywell Intern. Inc. 560
Reinhold v. Virginia 590, 592
Rene v. MGM Grand Hotel, Inc. 422, 430, 495, **515**
Rent-A-Center, West, Inc. v. Jackson 952
Resources v. Smith 635
Reyes v. Pharma Chemie, Inc. 721
Reyes-Gaona v. North Carolina Growers Ass'n 61
Rhodes v. Illinois Dept. of Transp. 586
Ricci v. DeStefano 6, **284**
Rice v. Cayetano 697
Richards v. CH2M Hill, Inc. 949
Richmond v. Oneok, Inc. 184
Richmond, City of v. J.A. Croson Co. 290, 883, 916, 917, 918
Riordan v. Kempiners 624
Rivera v. Baccarat 725, 737
Rivers v. Roadway Express, Inc. 335
Rizzo v. Children's World Learning Centers, Inc. 858, 863
Roach v. Dresser Indus. Valve & Instrument Division 691
Robbins v. Jefferson County School Dist. 197
Roberts v. Texaco, Inc. 91
Robino v. Iranon 413
Robinson v. Jacksonville Shipyards, Inc. 556
Robinson v. Lorillard Corp. 24
Robinson v. Metro-North Commuter Railroad Co. 82
Robinson v. Runyon 735
Robinson v. Shell Oil Co. 56, 163, 173, 176, 767
Rochon v. Gonzales 173, 175
Rodgers v. Fisher Body Div., General Motors Corp. 79
Rodriguez de Quijas v. Shearson/American Express, Inc. 957
Rodriguez v. Chicago 663
Rodriguez, In re **732**
Rodriguez-Hernandez v. Miranda-Velez 615
Roe v. Cheyenne Mountain Conference Resort, Inc. 875
Roeben v. BG Excelsior Ltd. Partnership 745
Rogers v. American Airlines, Inc. 433
Rogers v. EEOC 535, 700
Rogers v. Missouri Pac. R. Co. 149
Rojo v. Kliger 567
Roman v. Cornell University 716, 717, 719, 724, 726
Romer v. Evans 530, 532
Rosario-Torres v. Hernandez-Colon 72
Rosenfeld v. Department of Army 963
Ross v. Douglas County, Nebraska 626
Ross v. Kansas Commission on Civil Rights 186
Rosser v. Laborers' International Union 187
Rowan v. Lockheed Martin Energy Systems 153
Rummery v. Illinois Bell Telephone Co. 226
Runyon v. McCrary 44, 322, 325, 330
Rupert v. PPG Indus., Inc. 789
Rush v. McDonald's Corp. 25
Russell v. McKinney Hosp. Venture 745
Russello v. United States 172
Ryduchowski v. Port Authority of New York and New Jersey 382
Safeco Ins. Co. of America v. Burr 749

Sagana v. Tenorio 330
Sail'er Inn, Inc. v. Kirby 395
Saks v. Franklin Covey Co..... 466, 878
Sanchez v. Denver Public School ... 184
Sanchez v. Nitro-Lift Technologies, LLC 86, 953
Sanchez-Rodriguez v. AT&T Mobility Puerto Rico, Inc. 665
Sanders v. Southwestern Bell Co. 142
Sandoval v. American Bldg. Maintenance Industries, Inc. 613
Sangamon County Sheriff's Department v. Illinois Human Rights Commission 604
Santiago v. Stryker Corp. 49
Santiago-Ramos v. Centennial P.R. Wireless Corp. 473
Santiero v. Denny's Restaurant Store 592
Sauers v. Salt Lake County 58
Sayger v. Riceland Foods, Inc. ... 72, 79
Scaria v. Rubin 727
Schiano v. Quality Payroll Systems, Inc. 550
Schiltz v. Burlington Northern R.R. 774
Schlagenhauf v. Holder 552
Schleier, Commissioner v. 84
Schmedding v. Tnemec Company, Inc. 523
Schoffstall v. Henderson 552
School Board of Nassau County v. Arline 857
Schroer v. Billington 512
Schuette v. Coalition to Defend Affirmative Action 920
Schuster v. Derocili 567
Schweiker v. Wilson 914
Schwenk v. Hartford 496
Science Applications Int'l Corp, United States v. 157
Scobey v. Nucor Steel-Ark. 479
Scott v. City of New York 88
Scott v. Family Dollar Stores 243
Scott v. Omega Protein, Inc. 708
Seeger, United States v. 633
Selenke v. Medical Imaging of Colorado 168
Sellers v. Delgado Community College 74
Seminole Tribe of Florida v. Florida 17
Sempier v. Johnson & Higgins 774
Serapion v. Martinez Odell & Calabria 52
Serednyj v. Beverly Healthcare, LLC 452, 460
Setser v. Novack Inv. Co. 162
Shager v. Upjohn Co. 156, 577
Shahar v. Bowers 636
Shankle v. B-G Maintenance Management of Colorado 954
Shapolia v. Los Alamos National Laboratory 647, 670
Shaver v. Independent Stave Co. ... 839
Shaw v. Hunt 918
Shazor v. Professional Transit Management, Ltd. 374
Shearson/American Exp., Inc. v. McMahon 958
Sheehan v. Donlen Corp. 461, 473
Sheet Metal Workers v. EEOC 903, 905, 916
Shell v. Smith 854
Shepherd v. Comptroller of Public Accounts of Texas 550
Sheppard v. Riverview Nursing Center 153
Sherbert v. Verner 680
Sherman v. American Cyanamid Co. 776
Shirley v. Chrysler First, Inc. 186
Showalter v. University of Pittsburgh Medical Center 774
Siler-Khodr v. University of Texas Health Science Center San Antonio 18, 385
Silk v. City of Chicago 839
Silverman v. Board of Educ. of City of Chicago 180
Silverman v. City of New York 319
Simmons v. Sykes Enterprises, Inc. 160
Simon v. Eastern Kentucky Welfare Rights Organization 877
Simonton v. Runyon 499, 504, 515
Simpson v. Beaver Dam Community Hospitals, Inc. 122
Simpson v. Ernst & Young 52
Sims v. Mulcahy 320
Singletary v. Missouri Dept. of Corrections 19
Sischo-Nownejad v. Merced Community College Dist. 780
Skidmore v. Precision Printing & Pkg., Inc. 595
Skidmore v. Swift & Co. 22, 55, 463, 501, 588
Slaughter-House Cases 305
Slayton v. Ohio Dept. of Youth Services 616
Sledge v. J.P. Stevens & Co. 56
Smith v. Chrysler Corp. 122, 735
Smith v. City of Des Moines 274
Smith v. City of Jackson, Miss 383, 743, 749, 752, **798**

Smith v. City of Salem, Ohio.... 424, 496, **506**
Smith v. Diffee Ford-Lincoln-Mercury, Inc. 486
Smith v. First Union National Bank 550
Smith v. Midland Brake, Inc. 834
Smith v. Pyro Mining Co. 646, 662
Smith v. Riceland Foods 184
Smith v. Sheahan 550
Smith v. Wade 79
SmithKline Beecham Corp. v. Abbott Labs. 321
Sobel v. Yeshiva University 221
Soberal-Perez v. Heckler 715
Solomon v. Vilsack 855
Soltani v. Western & Southern Life Ins. Co. 953
Somoza v. University of Denver..... 180
Soroka v. Dayton Hudson Corp...... 531
Sosa v. Alvarez-Machain 158
Soto v. State Industries Products, Inc. 946
Soto-Fonalledas v. Ritz-Carlton San Juan Hotel Spa & Casino 941
Southland Corp. v. Keating............ 938
Sowell v. Alumina Ceramics, Inc. 380
Sparrow v. Piedmont Health Systems Agency, Inc. 190
Spence v. Maryland Cas. Co. 780
Sperling v. Hoffmann-La Roche, Inc. **759**
Spivey v. Beverly Enterprises, Inc. 452
Sprague v. Thorn Americas, Inc. 379, 389
Springer v. Convergys Customer Management Group, Inc. 123
Sprint/United Management Co. v. Mendelsohn 123
Sprogis v. United Air Lines, Inc. 365, 374
Spurlock v. United Airlines, Inc. 272, 273
St. Francis College v. Al-Khazraji **44**, 305, 328, 693
St. Mary's Honor Center v. Hicks... **110**, 125, 126, 182, 319, 745
Stafford Unified School Dist. v. Redding 337
Standard v. A.B.E.L. Servs., Inc. ... 796
State Dept. of Health Services v. Superior Court 604
State Farm Mutual Automobile Insurance Co. v. Campbell 81
Staub v. Proctor Hospital **154**
Steele v. Louisville & Nashville Railroad 61
Steiner v. Showboat Operating Co. 560
Stella v. Mineta 105
Stender v. Lucky Stores, Inc. 434
Stephens v. Erickson 180
Stewart v. City of Houston 407
Stewart v. Rise, Inc. 546, 700
Stirlen v. Supercuts, Inc. 947
Stolt-Nielsen S.A. v. AnimalFeeds Int'l Corp. 956, 960
Stone v. Autoliv ASP, Inc. 795
Stormans, Inc. v. Selecky 663
Strag v. Board of Trustees, Craven Community College 381
Strauder v. West Virginia 310
Strauss v. Horton 531
Sturgill v. United Parcel Service, Inc. 644, 665
Suarez v. Pueblo International, Inc. 781
Succar v. Dade County School Board 565
Sugarman v. Dougall 708
Suggs v. Servicemaster Educ. Food Management 77, 78
Sutton v. United Air Lines, Inc. 840, 848
Swackhammer v. Sprint/United Management Co. 120
Swanks v. Washington Metropolitan Area Transit Authority 856
Swann v. Charlotte-Mecklenburg Board of Educ. 316
Swenson v. Potter 613
Syverson v. International Business Machines Corp. 787
T.I.M.E.-D.C. Inc., United States v. 236
Tabor v. Hilti, Inc. 259
Tademy v. Union Pac. Corp. 627
Tagatz v. Marquette University 671
Takahashi v. Fish & Game Commission 330
Tate v. Farmland Industries, Inc. 480
Tatum v. Arkansas Dept. of Health 611
Taxman v. Board of Education of Township of Piscataway 924
Taylor v. Cardiology Clinic, Inc. 40
Taylor v. City of Shreveport 815
Taylor v. Principal Financial Group, Inc. 869
Taylor v. Solis 598
Taylor v. Teletype Corp. 73
Taylor v. White 385
Teamsters Local Union No. 117 v. Washington Dept. of Corrections 413

Teamsters v. United States 70, 95, 103, 104, **208**, 215, 217, 218, 226, 236, 237, 242, 245, 260, 655, 820, 890, 900, 901
Templet v. Hard Rock Const. Co.... 460
Tenge v. Phillips Modern Ag Co. ... 563
Terminix Cos. v. Dobson 935, 936, 938
Terry v. Ashcroft 719
Terry v. Laurel Oaks Behavioral Health Center, Inc. 598
Terveer v. Billington 504
Texas Dept. of Community Affairs v. Burdine 98, 103, 112, 114, 115, 128, 152, 326, 450, 454, 745, 801, 820
Texas v. Lesage 320
Thaddeus-X v. Blatter 735
Thelusma v. New York City Board of Educ. 738, 739
Thomas v. Choctaw Management/Services Enterprise 698
Thomas v. Cooper Lighting, Inc..... 184
Thomas v. Eastman Kodak Co....... 475
Thomas v. L'Eggs Products, Inc..... 566
Thomas v. Review Board 675
Thompson v. North American Stainless **163**, 165, 488
Thomure v. Phillips Furniture Company 760
Thorn v. Amalgamated Transit Union 66
Thornton, Estate of v. Caldor......... 681
Tice v. Centre Area Transp. Authority 873
Ticknor v. Choice Hotels Int'l, Inc. 947, 950
Ticor Title Ins. Co. v. Brown 237
Tillman v. Macy's, Inc. 940, 946
Tillman v. Wheaton-Haven Recreation Ass'n 324
Tinder v. Pinkerton Sec. 946
Toledo v. Nobel-Sysco, Inc...... 635, 664
Tomanovich v. City of Indianapolis 206
Tooley v. Martin-Marietta Corp.... 666, 667
Torres v. Pisano 622
Torres v. Wisconsin Department of Health & Social Services 412
Townsend v. Benjamin Enterprises, Inc. 190
Toyota Motor Manufacturing, Kentucky, Inc. v. Williams 842, 848
Trafficante v. Metropolitan Life Ins. Co. 165, 166
Trainor v. HEI Hospitality, LLC 74
Trans World Airlines, Inc. v. Hardison **650**, 661, 667, 831
Trans World Airlines, Inc. v. Thurston 400, 449
Traxler v. Multnomah Cnty............. 77
Trent v. Valley Electric Assn. Inc. 199
Troupe v. May Department Stores 457
Truax v. Raich 16
Trujillo v. PacifiCorp 838
TRW Inc. v. Andrews 453
Tung v. Texaco Inc. 789
Turic v. Holland Hospitality, Inc. 467
Turley v. ISG Lackawanna, Inc...... 626
Turlington v. Atlanta Gas Light Co. 86
Turnbull v. Topeka State Hosp. 616
TWA, Inc. v. Thurston 83
Tyler v. Bethlehem Steel Corp. 743
Tyler v. Union Oil Co. 795
Tyndall v. National Education Centers, Inc. 867
U.S. Airways, Inc. v. Barnett 72, 661, **822**, 835
Uddin v. City of New York 181
Ulane v. Eastern Airlines, Inc. 505, 510, 512, 526
Union Pacific Railroad Employment Practices Litigation, In re 465
United Air Lines, Inc. v. Evans 29, 31
United Air Lines, Inc. v. McMann 779
United Brotherhood of Carpenters & Joiners of America v. Anderson 329
United States Postal Service Board of Governors v. Aikens 97, 98, 113, 121, 148
United Steelworkers of America v. Weber 259, **888**, 894, 900, 901, 904
University and Community College System of Nevada v. Farmer 384
University of Texas Southwestern Medical Center v. Nassar **200**
Urbano v. Continental Airlines, Inc. 452
Usery v. Tamiami Trail Tours, Inc. 781
Utley v. Goldman Sachs & Co. 963
Vaca v. Sipes 62, 961
Vacco v. Quill 318
Vajdl v. Mesabi Academy of KidsPeace, Inc. 616
Van Voorhis v. Hillsborough County 142

Vance v. Ball State University 182, **579**, 603
Vance v. Boyd Mississippi, Inc....... 699
Vande Zande v. Wisconsin Department of Admin............. **863**
Varner v. Illinois State University...................................... 18
Varnum v. Brien............................ 531
Vasquez v. County of Los Angeles....................................... 106
Vaughn v. Vilsack.......................... 168
Vega v. Hempstead Union Free School District............................ 320
Velasquez v. Goldwater Memorial Hosp.................................. 715, 716
Velazquez v. Chardon...................... 73
Velazquez-Perez v. Developers Diversified Realty Corp. 589
Velez v. Novartis Pharmaceuticals Corp. 91
Velez v. Thermo King de Puerto Rico, Inc...................................... 753
Velez-Rivera v. Agosto-Alicea 320
Venters v. City of Delphi....... 142, 647, 670, 682
Vetter v. Farmland Indus. 663
Vickers v. Fairfield Medical Center... 524
Vigars v. Valley Christian Center of Dublin, Cal......................... 637, 639
Villiarimo v. Aloha Island Air, Inc... 122
Virginia, United States v. 306, 482, 483, 914, 919
Vivian v. Madison.......................... 601
Vulcan Pioneers, Inc. v. New Jersey Dept. of Civil Service 299
Wachovia Bank, N.A. v. Schmidt... 173
Wachovia Sec., LLC v. Brand......... 961
Walden v. Centers for Disease Control & Prevention................. 634
Walker v. Abbott Labs.................... 328
Walker v. Mortham 104
Walker v. Ryan's Family Steak Houses....................................... 946
Walker v. Secretary of Treasury, IRS.. 49
Walker v. United Parcel Service, Inc.. 40
Wallace Corp. v. NLRB 62
Wallace v. Methodist Hosp. System................................ 143, 461
Wal-Mart Stores, Inc. v. Dukes 83, **228**, 366, 434
Walters v. Metropolitan Educational Enterprises, Inc............................ 57
Walz v. Ameriprise Financial, Inc... 869
Wang v. Phoenix Satellite TV US, Inc. 56
Ward v. Int'l Paper Co. 110
Wards Cove Packing Co. v. Atonio 245, 259, **261**, 273, 752, 802, 803, 805, 820, 883
Warren, Mich., City of, United States v. 282
Wasek v. Arrow Energy Servs. Inc. 180
Washington v. Davis...........**307**, 314, 315, 316, 908
Washington v. Illinois Dept. of Revenue 175
Washington v. Norton.................... 181
Washington, County of v. Gunther 382, 387
Wathen v. General Elec. Co............ 601
Watson v. Blue Circle, Inc. 618
Watson v. Fort Worth Bank and Trust 234, 235, 241, 242, 258, 260, 263, 264, 265, 266, 267, 268, 436, 803, 805
Watt v. New York Botanical Garden 737
Watts v. Kroger Co......................... 597
Weahkee v. Perry........................... 691
Weaver v. Amoco Prod. Co................ 70
Weaving v. City of Hillsboro........... 851
Weber v. Battista 181
Weber v. Roadway Exp., Inc. 664
Weberg v. Franks........................... 320
Wedow v. City of Kansas City, Mo. 180
Weeks v. Baker & McKenzie 91
Weeks v. Southern Bell Tel. & Tel. Co. 403
Wells v. SCI Management, L.P. 106
Welsh v. United States................... 633
Wernsing v. Dept. of Human Services.............................. 383, 384
West v. Gibson 78, 178
West v. Tyson Foods, Inc. 600
Western Air Lines, Inc. v. Criswell...................... 396, 400, 401, 407, 756, 781, 782
Westmoreland v. Prince George's County 51
Weyers v. Lear Operations Corp............................ 581, 603, 781
Whidbee v. Garzarelli Food Specialties, Inc. 59, 498, 622
Whitaker v. Bosch Braking Systems...................................... 487
White v. Baxter Healthcare Corp................................... 106, 151
White v. Burlington Northern & Santa Fe R. Co........................... 178

White v. Westinghouse Electric Co. ... 755
Whitney v. California ... 679
Whitten v. Fred's, Inc. ... 581, 587
Whittlesey v. Union Carbide ... 791
Wilko v. Swan ... 957
Williams v. Bell ... 538
Williams v. Cigna Financial Advisors, Inc. ... 959, 960
Williams v. General Motors, Corp. ... 562, 755, 795
Williams v. New York City Housing Authority ... 529
Williams v. Owens-Illinois, Inc. ... 498
Williams v. Saxbe ... 538
Williams v. Vitro Services Corp. ... 126
Williams v. W.D. Sports, N.M., Inc. ... 184
Williams v. Wal-Mart Stores, Inc. ... 501
Williamson v. A.G. Edwards & Sons, Inc. ... 505
Willingham v. Macon Tel. Pub. Co. ... 415, 729
Wilson v. Garcia ... 333
Wilson v. National Labor Relations Board ... 668
Wilson v. Southwest Airlines ... 408, 410
Wilson v. U.S. West Communications ... 663
Windsor, United States v. ... 530
Winspear v. Community Development, Inc. ... 670
Wisconsin v. Yoder ... 633
Wittenburg v. American Express Financal Advisors, Inc. ... 776
Wolak v. Spucci ... 555
Wolf v. J.I. Case Co. ... 200
Woods v. Graphic Communications ... 62, 66
Woodson v. Scott Paper Co. ... 188
Worcester v. State of Georgia ... 692
Wright v. Murray Guard, Inc. ... 152
Wright v. Rockefeller ... 310
Wrightson v. Pizza Hut of America ... 370
Wygant v. Jackson Board of Education ... 254, 290, 883, 896, 905, 906, 907, 915, 916, 918, 926
Yancey v. Weyerhauser Co. ... 75
Yanowitz v. L'Oreal USA, Inc. ... 432
Yellow Freight System, Inc. v. Donnelly ... 40
Yick Wo v. Hopkins ... 311, 315
York v. American Tel. & Tel. Co. ... 66
Young v. Crystal Evangelical Free Church ... 681
Young v. Southwestern Sav. and Loan Ass'n ... 636
Young v. United Parcel Service, Inc. ... 448, 501
Young, Ex Parte ... 19
Yuknis v. First Student, Inc. ... 553
Zambrano-Lamhaouhi v. New York City Board of Education ... 477
Zann Kwan v. Andalex Group LLC ... 184, 185
Zimmerman v. Oregon Dept. of Justice ... 815
Zipes v. Trans World Airlines, Inc. ... 38

EMPLOYMENT DISCRIMINATION LAW

CASES AND MATERIALS ON EQUALITY IN THE WORKPLACE

Ninth Edition

PART 1

INTRODUCTION

■ ■ ■

CHAPTER 1

RACE AND THE DEVELOPMENT OF LAWS PROHIBITING DISCRIMINATION IN EMPLOYMENT: A BRIEF OVERVIEW

■ ■ ■

Federal employment discrimination law in the United States today offers protection to employees on the basis of many protected categories—race, color, national origin, sex, religion, age, and disability. For many years, Congress has also considered adding sexual orientation and gender identity to this list but has yet to take any action. However, many state antidiscrimination statutes cover these and other protected categories as well. This book explores all of these legal protections, but the central role of race in the development of national prohibitions against discrimination serves as our starting point. The history of antidiscrimination law is grounded in the long struggle to eliminate and redress rampant mistreatment of African Americans. Moreover, many of the most entrenched policy debates in antidiscrimination law—questions about the meaning of equality and the definition and pervasiveness of discrimination—have centered on race even as they have expanded to encompass other protected traits.

National laws aimed at prohibiting discrimination first emerged in efforts to protect the rights of newly freed slaves in the wake of the Civil War. The Reconstruction-era Congress sought to guarantee the rights of African Americans with both constitutional amendments—the Thirteenth, Fourteenth, and Fifteenth Amendments to the Constitution—and civil rights statutes—including the Civil Rights Act of 1866, which guaranteed all U.S. citizens the same property and contract rights previously afforded only white citizens. These early efforts were brought to a halt by, among other things, a series of Supreme Court decisions interpreting the post-Civil War enactments so as to render them substantially meaningless. Perhaps the most infamous of these decisions was *Plessy v. Ferguson*, 163 U.S. 537, 16 S.Ct. 1138, 41 L.Ed.256 (1896), which legitimized racial segregation. (Chapter 5 discusses this history in greater detail.)

More than half a century later, in *Brown v. Board of Education*, 347 U.S. 483, 74 S.Ct. 686, 98 L.Ed.873 (1954), the Supreme Court rejected *Plessy*'s "separate but equal" doctrine and enunciated a fundamental principle of racial equality. The decision did little, standing alone, to eradicate the legacy of decades of racial discrimination. The *Brown* decision, however, focused public attention on racial inequalities and galvanized civil rights leaders and communities to action. The years between the Court's decision in *Brown* and the passage of the 1964 Civil Rights Act saw Rosa Parks refuse to give up her seat on the bus, sparking the Montgomery Bus Boycott; "sit-ins" at segregated lunch counters and other nonviolent forms of protest; the 1961 Freedom Rides and subsequent voter registration drives throughout the South; the "March on Washington for Jobs and Freedom" led by Reverend Martin Luther King, Jr. in 1963; and countless other citizen-led protests against race discrimination and systemic inequality. These public protests, together with the succession of Vice President Lyndon Johnson to the presidency following the assassination of President John F. Kennedy on November 22, 1963, were critical to the passage of the Civil Rights Act of 1964. *See generally* Nancy MacLean, Freedom Is Not Enough: The Opening of the American Workplace (2006); Charles Whalen & Barbara Whalen, The Longest Debate: A Legislative History of the 1964 Civil Rights Act (1985). For a documentary film series on the continuing significance of racial discrimination in the aftermath of *Brown*, *see* Eyes on the Prize: America's Civil Rights Years (1954–65).

The enactment of Title VII of the Civil Rights Act of 1964, 42 U.S.C. § 2000e *et seq.*, was the major turning point in the development of a national policy on discrimination in employment. Title VII prohibits employers (as defined in the Act), employment agencies, and labor organizations from discriminating against applicants and employees on the basis of race, color, sex, religion, and national origin. Title VII is only one of several titles in the Civil Rights Act of 1964; other titles deal with discrimination in public accommodations, education, voting, and federally assisted programs. While the Civil Rights Act of 1964 is the most comprehensive of the federal statutes that provide individuals with a remedy for unlawful discrimination, the United States now has a number of laws, federal executive orders, and regulations prohibiting discrimination in employment because of race, color, sex, religion, age, disability, and national origin. Section B of Chapter 2 provides a survey of the major federal laws prohibiting discrimination in employment.

The most blatant and overt discriminatory employment practices that were commonplace at the time Congress enacted Title VII are fairly unusual today. We have now arrived at a point in our effort to remedy discrimination in employment—as well as in other contexts such as public accommodations and housing—when most would agree that progress has been made in implementing a national commitment to the principle of equality. Nevertheless, we continue to disagree about the meaning of "equality" and the nature of "discrimination" as a social, moral, and political problem; we also disagree about the extent to which discrimination on the basis of race (as well as other protected characteristics) continues to shape employment decisions.

At least two theories of equality have emerged since *Brown v. Board of Education* and the Civil Rights Act of 1964. *See generally* Robert Belton, *Discrimination and Affirmative Action: An Analysis of Competing Theories of Equality and* Weber, 59 N.C.L.Rev. 531 (1981); Julia Lamber, *Discretionary Decisionmaking: The Application of Title VII's Disparate Impact Theory*, 1985 U.Ill.L.Rev. 869.

One theory of equality is *equal treatment*: It embraces the notion of "color-blind" or "sex-blind" decisionmaking. Under this view of equality, an employee's race, color, religion, sex, national origin, age, or disability should not be a factor in any way in an employment decision. As Chief Justice John Roberts, one proponent of this vision of equality, wrote in 2007, "The way to stop discrimination on the basis of race is to stop discriminating on the basis of race." Parents Involved in Community Schools v. Seattle School District No. 1, 551 U.S. 701, 748, 127 S.Ct. 2738, 2768, 168 L.Ed.2d. 508 (2007). A strict application of this view of equal treatment would prohibit consideration of statutorily protected criteria in all circumstances, including an affirmative action program intended to mitigate the continuing effects of discrimination.

A second conception of equality is *equal opportunity*. This view of equality starts from the premise that formal equality—equality on paper—is meaningless so long as pervasive inequality is a social reality. Those who support equal opportunity criticize equal treatment as an inadequate conception of equality because it fails to account for the continuing impact of discrimination. Justice Harry Blackmun famously articulated this view of equality in his separate opinion in *Regents of the University of California v. Bakke*, 438 U.S. 265, 407, 98 S.Ct. 2733, 2807, 57 L.Ed.2d 750 (1978), where he wrote: "In order to get beyond racism, we must first take account of race. There is no other way. And in order to treat some persons equally, we must treat them differently. We cannot—we dare not—let the Equal Protection Clause perpetuate racial supremacy." According to this view of equality, it is sometimes appropriate (and may be necessary) for employers to consider the race or sex of employees in order to remedy continuing effects of race or sex discrimination. Similarly, statutes that require some accommodation of unique circumstances—like the Americans with Disabilities Act (discussed in Chapter 14) and the Family and Medical Leave Act (discussed in Chapter 8)—embody this vision of equality.

Both theories—equal treatment and equal opportunity—find support in federal antidiscrimination statutes and judicial decisions. In particular, equal treatment is associated with claims for "disparate treatment" under Title VII. *See* 42 U.S.C. § 2000e–2(a)(1) (providing that it is an "unlawful employment practice" to discriminate against an individual "because of such individual's race, color, religion, sex, or national origin."). Equal opportunity is often associated with the "disparate impact" provisions of the law. *See* 42 U.S.C. § 2000e–2(k) (prohibiting neutral employer practices that adversely impact a protected class and cannot be justified by business necessity). *See also* 42 U.S.C. § 2000e–2(a)(2) (it is an unlawful employment practice for an employer to "limit, segregate, or classify his employees or applicants for employment in any way which would *deprive or tend to deprive* any individual of employment opportunity or otherwise *adversely affect* his status as an employee, because of such individual's race, color, religion, sex, or national origin.") (emphasis added); Griggs v. Duke Power Co., 401 U.S. 424, 429–30, 91 S.Ct. 849, 852–53, 28 L.Ed.2d 158 (1971) (finding that the legislative purpose of Title VII was to achieve equality of employment "opportunities" and to remove "barriers" to such equality). The development of these two theories of discrimination is the focus of Chapters 3 and 4. In recent years, however, the argument that the two theories are in irreconcilable tension has gained traction, most prominently in the 2009 decision in *Ricci v. DeStefano*, 557 U.S. 557, 129 S.Ct. 2658, 174 L.Ed.2d 490, in which the Supreme Court held that an employer seeking to comply with disparate impact obligations may face liability for disparate treatment. (*Ricci* is reproduced in Chapter 4). Can discrimination law embody both equal treatment and equal opportunity? If not, which vision of equality should prevail?

The election of Barack Obama as President in 2008, highlighted a dramatic division in perceptions of the continuing significance of race and race discrimination in the United States. Following the election, many commentators asserted that the election of an African-American President proved that the nation was a "post-racial" society in which we could officially declare race discrimination a problem of the past and look for other explanations for inequalities. *See, e.g.,* Sumi Cho, *Post-Racialism*, 94 Iowa L.Rev. 1589, 1593 (2009) (describing post-racialism as a "retreat from race-based remedies on the basis that the racial eras of the past have been and should be transcended"). Others argued that race was still a prominent dividing line in our society, that the election of an African-American President could not erase the inequalities that continue to affect African Americans at work, in schools, and in public life, and that continued discrimination is responsible for these continuing inequalities. For a discussion of these issues see Roy L. Brooks, Racial Justice in the Age of Obama (2009).

What accounts for these different perspectives? One explanation may come from differing perceptions of what constitutes "discrimination." Some people understand workplace race and sex discrimination as pervasive and often structural, arising out of organizational practices and norms. *See, e.g.*, Susan Sturm, *Second Generation Employment Discrimination: A Structural Approach*, 101 Colum.L.Rev. 458, 459 (2001). Others see discrimination as implicit or unconscious. *See, e.g.*, Tristin K. Green & Alexandra Kalev, *Discrimination-Reducing Measures at the Relational Level*, 59 Hastings L.J. 1435 (2008) (noting "a shift in the nature of discrimination from mostly egregious exclusion to decisions contaminated by unconscious biases"); Anthony G. Greenwald & Linda Hamilton Krieger, *Implicit Bias: Scientific Foundations*, 94 Cal.L.Rev. 945 (2006) (discussing theories behind and results of the Implicit Association Test (IAT)). Still others consider racial discrimination, for example, to be an unusual deviation from a norm of "colorblindness," which occurs through discrete, overt acts of animus-based conduct, such as racial epithets. *See* Russell K. Robinson, *Perceptual Segregation*, 108 Colum.L.Rev. 1093, 1126–27 (2008) (describing and criticizing this perspective).

There are also wide gaps in perspective between racial groups as to the continued significance of race discrimination. As the authors of one survey of U.S. workers concluded, "race is the most significant determinant in how people perceive and experience discrimination in the workplace, as well as what they believe employers should do to address such incidents and attitudes." K.A. Dixon, Duke Storen & Carl E. Van Horn, A Workplace Divided: How Americans View Discrimination and Race on the Job 1 (2002. In describing what he calls "perceptual segregation"—the racial divide in how Americans view the problem of discrimination—Professor Russell Robinson points to, among other evidence, the following empirical information:

> Half of the African American respondents [in a 2002 Rutgers University survey] said that "African-Americans are treated unfairly in the workplace," while just 10% of white respondents agreed with that statement. Thirteen percent of nonblack people of color shared this perception. Almost half (46%) of the African Americans surveyed said their employer awarded promotions in a manner unfair to African Americans, compared to 6% of whites, and 12% of nonblack people of color. * * * Just 28% of African Americans said that they had personally been treated unfairly at work because of race. [But] 55% of black employees said that they knew of instances in the last year in which a coworker believed they [sic] suffered racial discrimination. A mere 13% of whites, and 21% of nonblack people of color, reported similar awareness. * * *
>
> * * * Eight-one percent of blacks [in a 2003 Gallup poll] reported that blacks still lack equal job opportunities (43% of

whites agreed), and 52% of blacks called for the enactment of new civil rights laws (20% of whites agreed).

Robinson, *supra*, at 1107–10 (citations omitted). *See also* Pat Chew & Robert E. Kelley, *Myth of the Color-Blind Judge: An Empirical Analysis of Racial Harassment Cases,* 86 Wash. U. L. Rev. 1117, 1156–63 (2009) (examining the meaning of research showing that a judge's race is likely to have an impact on his or her perceptions of the significance of racial harassment); David Benjamin Oppenheimer, *Understanding Affirmative Action*, 23 Hastings Const.L.Q. 921, 946–73 (1996) (describing national surveys over the past fifty years of racial stereotypes about blacks held by white Americans that "support the view that overt racism has lost favor socially, but racist attitudes lie close beneath the surface of our society," *id.* at 947). These disparities in perception have been reaffirmed more recently. Writing in the Washington Post, Michael Fletcher stated, "A series of surveys in recent years about Americans' perceptions of the very existence of racism and racial disparities in our society shows that white people believe the problem of racial bias against blacks has effectively faded as a national issue." Michael A. Fletcher, *Whites Think Discrimination Against Whites A Bigger Problem than Bias Against Whites*, Wash. Post, Oct. 8, 2014, at A3. He notes that a recent poll conducted by the Pew Research Center found that 16% of whites believe there is still "a lot of discrimination" compared to 56% of African Americans. *Id.*

In fact, there is considerable evidence of continuing workplace inequality along both race and gender lines. *See, e.g.,* Marianne Bertrand & Sendhil Mullainathan, *Are Emily and Greg More Employable Than Lakisha and Jamal? A Field Experiment on Labor Market Discrimination*, 94 Am.Econ.Rev. 991 (2004) (describing a field study showing significant discriminatory response by employers to job candidates with African-American sounding names and otherwise identical credentials); Laura Guiliano, David I. Levine & Jonathan Leonard, *Manager Race and the Race of New Hires,* 27 J.Lab.Econ. 589 (2009) (showing relationships between the race of managers and the race of new employees); Michael Selmi & Sonia Weil, *Can All Women Be Pharmacists? A Critique of Hannah Rosin's* The End of Men, 93 Boston Univ. L. Rev. 852 (2013) (documenting continued gender discrimination); Anne Lawton, *The Meritocracy Myth and the Illusion of Equal Employment Opportunity*, 85 Minn.L.Rev. 587, 600–01 (2000) (describing studies that show both race and gender disparities, particularly in more highly paid, prestigious fields). But while empirical evidence demonstrates workplace inequality, it does not explain the reasons for continuing disparities. Are they explained by divergences in qualifications? By the lingering effects of historical discrimination? Or by current discrimination? How can and should the law respond to these disparities? It may be that "[w]hat really matters, and what ought to matter to law, is whether people are treated worse because of their race—or other protected characteristic, such as sex—in the real world. * * * [T]he focus should not be on attitudes or sympathies, but traditionally on actionable discrimination." Amy L. Wax, *The Discriminating Mind: Find It, Prove It, 40 Conn.L.Rev. 979, 985 (2008).* The challenge for courts, legislatures, lawyers, and scholars is to articulate not just theories of discrimination and equality, but how unlawful discrimination can be proven (or not), and if discrimination is proven, how it can be effectively remedied. These issues are central to this casebook.

As you read the cases and materials that follow, consider how these questions—what is equality?, what is discrimination?—shape legislative texts and judicial interpretations of them. Did the enacting legislatures of Title VII and other antidiscrimination statutes have in mind particular definitions of these concepts? How have courts defined and redefined these central concepts over time? How have these understandings shaped the legal doctrines of employment discrimination law? How might different definitions of "equality" and "discrimination" change the meaning and scope of employment discrimination law?

CHAPTER 2

LAWS PROHIBITING DISCRIMINATION IN EMPLOYMENT: AN OVERVIEW

■ ■ ■

A. INTRODUCTION

The United States has a number of laws, federal executive orders, and regulations prohibiting discrimination in employment in the public and private sectors because of race, color, sex, religion, national origin, age, disability, status as a veteran, and, most recently, genetic makeup. Even before the enactment of Title VII of the Civil Rights Act of 1964, some states had adopted laws prohibiting discrimination in employment, but many of these earlier state laws were limited to discrimination because of race, creed, color, or national origin. Since Title VII became law, most states and many municipalities have enacted laws prohibiting discrimination in employment. Some of these state laws provide broader coverage than analogous federal laws, and many of the local and state laws prohibit discrimination based on sexual orientation and/or identity.

The purpose of this chapter is to provide an overview of laws prohibiting discrimination in employment. Section B is a brief survey of federal statutes, constitutional provisions, and executive orders that prohibit discrimination in employment. Section C presents a broad overview of the administrative and judicial enforcement schemes of the major federal laws on employment discrimination. Section D identifies and briefly discusses some of the major issues of coverage that are not clearly defined in federal statutory law. These issues include identifying the individuals and groups who are protected from unlawful discrimination in the workplace (focusing on the meaning of "race" and "color"), determining who is an "employee" and who is an "employer" for purposes of Title VII, defining an "unlawful employment *practice*," and describing how labor organizations can be liable for discrimination. Section E provides an overview of the remedies available to employees under the federal laws on employment discrimination.

B. SURVEY OF MAJOR FEDERAL LAWS ON EMPLOYMENT DISCRIMINATION

The following is a survey of major federal laws on employment discrimination. We have grouped the statutes consistent with their primacy in the area of employment discrimination law, which is primarily statutory in nature. Three statutes generate the vast majority of employment discrimination cases and claims: Title VII, the Age Discrimination in Employment Act ("ADEA") and the Americans With Disabilities Act ("the ADA"). Another important statute was passed during Reconstruction and is known as Section 1981—all of these statutes, and others are briefly discussed below, and more extensively within subsequent chapters.

1. *Statutes.*

a. *Title VII of the Civil Rights Act of 1964*: Title VII, 42 U.S.C. § 2000e *et seq.*, is the statute that generates the most litigation and makes it unlawful for public and private employers, labor organizations, and employment agencies to discriminate against applicants and employees on the basis of their race, color, sex, religion, and national origin. Among the more significant amendments to Title VII are the 1972 amendments extending coverage to federal, state, and local government employers; the 1978 amendment providing that discrimination because of pregnancy is sex discrimination; and the 1991 amendments providing for compensatory and punitive damages, and jury trials in Title VII cases (discussed separately below). The pervasive influence of Title VII's jurisprudence is manifest throughout each of the chapters that follow.

b. *The Civil Rights Act of 1991*: Congress enacted the Civil Rights Act of 1991, Pub. L. No. 102–166, 105 Stat. 1071 (1991) (codified in scattered sections of 2 U.S.C., 16 U.S.C., 29 U.S.C., and in 42 U.S.C. §§ 2000e, 1981, 12111), to overturn or modify a series of employment discrimination decisions that the Supreme Court issued during some of its previous Terms. Although the 1991 Civil Rights Act is technically an Amendment to Title VII, it is often identified as a free-standing statute because it altered significantly the remedial structure of the statute, in addition to overturning Supreme Court decisions that were seen to have "weakened the scope and effectiveness of Federal civil rights protections." Pub. L. No. 102–166, § 2(2). As part of the 1991 Act, Congress also provided for jury trials and compensatory and punitive damages; before the Act, cases were tried before a judge and only equitable remedies were available.

c. *The Age Discrimination in Employment Act of 1967*: The Age Discrimination in Employment Act (ADEA), 29 U.S.C. § 621 *et seq.*, prohibits discrimination on the basis of age against applicants and employees who are forty years of age or older. The ADEA is covered in Chapter 13.

d. *Title I of the Americans with Disabilities Act of 1990*: Congress enacted the Americans with Disabilities Act of 1990 (ADA), 42 U.S.C. § 12111 *et seq.*, for the purpose of eliminating discrimination against qualified individuals with disabilities. In addition to covering employment discrimination, this comprehensive statute prohibits discrimination against individuals with disabilities in public accommodations, services provided by state and municipal governments, public and private transportation, and telecommunications. Title I of the ADA prohibits discrimination in employment against qualified individuals with a disability who, with or without reasonable accommodation, can perform the essential functions of the job. Significant amendments to the ADA, known as the ADA Amendments Act of 2008 (Pub. L. No. 110–325, 122 Stat. 3553), went into effect in 2009. Discrimination in employment on the basis of disabilities is covered in Chapter 14.

e. *The Equal Pay Act of 1963*: The Equal Pay Act (EPA), 29 U.S.C. § 206(d), which was enacted as an amendment to the Fair Labor Standards Act, proscribes sex-based wage discrimination in employment. The Equal Pay Act is explored in Chapter 7 but it historically has not generated a substantial amount of litigation for reasons that will be explained in Chapter 7.

f. *Family and Medical Leave Act of 1993*: Congress passed the Family and Medical Leave Act (FMLA) in an effort "to balance the demands of the workplace with the needs of families, to promote the stability and economic security of families, and to promote national interests in preserving family integrity." FMLA § 2601(b)(1), 29 U.S.C. § 2601(b)(1). The FMLA entitles eligible employees to take up to twelve weeks of unpaid leave "for medical reasons, for the birth or adoption of a child, and for the care of a child, spouse, or parent who has a serious health condition." *Id.* at § 2601(b)(2), 29 U.S.C. § 2601(b)(2). The FMLA is covered in Chapter 8.

g. *The Rehabilitation Act of 1973*: Prior to the enactment of the Americans with Disabilities Act of 1990, 42 U.S.C. § 12111 (ADA), the Rehabilitation Act of 1973, 29 U.S.C. §§ 791, 793, 794, was the principal federal statute prohibiting employment discrimination against persons with disabilities. The Rehabilitation Act (known generally as the "Rehab Act") prohibits the federal government, federal contractors, and federal grantees from discriminating against individuals with disabilities who are otherwise qualified to perform the work. 29 U.S.C. § 791 (federal government); *id.* § 793 (federal contractors); *id.* § 794 (entities receiving federal funds). Employment discrimination on the basis of disabilities and the relationship between the Rehabilitation Act and the ADA are explored in Chapter 14 but for the most part there is little substantive difference between the two statutes.

h. *The Immigration Reform and Control Act of 1986*: The Immigration Reform and Control Act of 1986 (IRCA), 8 U.S.C. § 1324B, prohibits discrimination in employment on the basis of national origin and citizenship. There is an overlap between Title VII and IRCA because both statutes prohibit discrimination in employment on the basis of an individual's national origin. IRCA is covered briefly in Chapter 12.

i. *The Genetic Information Nondiscrimination Act of 2008*: On May 21, 2008, President Bush signed the Genetic Information Nondiscrimination Act of 2008 (GINA), Pub. L. No. 110–223. The Act prohibits discrimination by employers and insurers on the basis of genetic information about potentially inheritable diseases and health conditions. Information about the risks of developing certain genetically linked diseases has become available in part because of research findings from the Human Genome Project. Before the Act was passed, many potentially high risk individuals have refused to have genetic testing because of their concerns that they would be denied health insurance or jobs if the tests were positive for certain genes. In addition, many employees who were subjected to routine medical screening in the workplace were concerned about whether employers would obtain genetic information about health risks and use this as a basis for discharge. GINA is discussed in the notes to Chapter 14, which covers the Americans with Disabilities Act (ADA).

j. *The Reconstruction Era Civil Rights Legislation*: Congress enacted a number of civil rights statutes after the Civil War to enforce the rights embodied in the Thirteenth, Fourteenth, and Fifteenth Amendments. Of these statutes, the two most significant for employment discrimination law are 42 U.S.C. §§ 1981 and 1983. Section 1981 now codified, as amended, as 42 U.S.C. § 1981 provides that "[a]ll persons within the jurisdiction of the United States shall have the same right * * * to make and enforce contracts * * * as is enjoyed by white citizens," which has been construed to prohibit intentional discrimination based on race and national origin. Section 1981 is discussed in Chapter 5. The other Reconstruction era statute is known as Section 1983, codified at 42 U.S.C. § 1983. Section 1983, unlike § 1981, is not a source of substantive rights, but it provides individuals a cause of action for the deprivation of substantive rights guaranteed under the Constitution and occasionally other federal laws. Section 1983 is often implicated when federal employees sue for a violation of their constitutional and has generated a complicated body of law that is typically covered in a course on federal courts or complex litigation. The statute is briefly discussed in Chapter 5.

k. *The Congressional Accountability Act of 1995*: As a result of the Congressional Accountability Act (CAA), Pub. L. No. 104–1, 109 Stat. 3 (1995) (codified at 2 U.S.C. §§ 1301–1438, and in scattered sections of 2 U.S.C., 5 U.S.C., 29 U.S.C., 40 U.S.C., and 42 U.S.C.), eleven civil rights and labor laws, including Title VII, the ADA, the ADEA, and the Rehabilitation Act, are applicable to the legislative branch of the federal government. 2 U.S.C. § 1302. The CAA also establishes remedies and procedures for aggrieved employees to seek relief from violations of these laws. During the discussions about the CAA, Congress contemplated covering the judiciary but opted instead to include a statutory directing the federal Judicial Conference to study and report to Congress on the propriety of applying the laws to the judiciary. The Judicial Conference ultimately concluded, "in light of current judicial branch policies, * * * legislation is neither necessary nor advisable in order to provide judicial branch employees with protections comparable to those provided to legislative branch employees." Study of Judicial Branch Coverage Pursuant to the Congressional Accountability Act of 1995, at 2.

1. *Presidential Executive Orders*: Beginning with Executive Order 8802 issued by President Roosevelt in 1941, 3 C.F.R. § 234 (1941), every president has issued or affirmed an executive order prohibiting discrimination in employment by private employers who contract with the federal government to perform work above a specified dollar amount. In 1965, President Johnson issued Executive Order 11,246, 3 C.F.R. § 339 (1965). Originally limited to prohibiting discrimination by federal contractors on the basis of race, color, national origin, or religion, Executive Order 11,246 was amended by Executive Order 11,375 in 1967 to include sex discrimination, 3 C.F.R. § 684 (1967). Executive Order 11,246, as amended, is implemented by Revised Order No. 4, 41 C.F.R. § 60 (1999), and enforced by the Office of Federal Contract Compliance Programs in the Department of Labor.

In 1969, President Nixon issued Executive Order 11,478, prohibiting discrimination in federal employment on the basis of race, color, religion, sex, or national origin. 34 Fed.Reg. 12,985 (1969). President Carter amended Executive Order 11,478 in 1978 to add handicap and age to its categories of prohibited discrimination. Exec. Order No. 12,106, 44 Fed.Reg. 1053 (1978). Executive Order 11,478 was again amended in 1998 when President Clinton added sexual orientation as a prohibited basis for discrimination in federal employment. Exec. Order No. 13,087, 3 C.F.R. § 191 (1998), *reprinted as amended in* 42 U.S.C. § 2000e (2000).

2. *The United States Constitution*:

a. *The Fifth Amendment*: The Due Process Clause of the Fifth Amendment is a constitutional provision that prohibits federal employers from, *inter alia*, engaging in discrimination in employment. Unlike the Fourteenth Amendment, the Fifth Amendment does not have an express clause on equal protection, but the Supreme Court has construed its Due Process Clause as embodying an equal protection component making it akin to the Fourteenth Amendment but for federal employees. *See, e.g.*, Bolling v. Sharpe, 347 U.S. 497, 499–500, 74 S.Ct. 693, 694–95, 98 L.Ed.884 (1954); Adarand Constructors, Inc. v. Pena, 515 U.S. 200, 115 S.Ct. 2097, 132 L.Ed.2d 158 (1995) (describing the Court's history of applying identical equal protection standards to state and federal action).

b. *The Fourteenth Amendment*: The Due Process and Equal Protection Clauses of the Fourteenth Amendment provide public employees some protections against employment discrimination by state and local government employers. For example, state and municipal employees can use the Fourteenth Amendment to challenge governmental classifications or intentional disparate treatment on the basis of race, sex, alienage, or national origin, but the level of protection is not the same for all classifications. For example, classifications based on race, alienage, or national origin are subject to strict scrutiny, City of Cleburne, Tex. v. Cleburne Living Ctr., 473 U.S. 432, 440, 105 S.Ct. 3249, 3254, 87 L.Ed.2d 313 (1985), whereas classifications based on sex are subject to "heightened scrutiny," Nev. Dep't of Hum. Res. v. Hibbs, 538 U.S. 721, 728, 123 S.Ct. 1972, 1978, 155 L.Ed.2d 953 (2003). Lawful resident aliens have long been entitled to protection under the equal protection clauses of the Constitution. *See* Truax v. Raich, 239 U.S. 33, 36 S.Ct. 7, 60 L.Ed.131 (1915). On the other hand, because classifications based on age and disability are not "suspect," they are subject to rational basis review under equal protection analysis. *See* Kimel v. Fla. Bd. of Regents, 528 U.S. 62, 83, 120 S.Ct. 631, 646, 145 L.Ed.2d 522 (2000) (age); Bd. of Trs. of Univ. of Ala. v. Garrett, 531 U.S. 356, 367, 121 S.Ct. 955, 964, 148 L.Ed.2d 866 (2001) (disability). Equal protection analysis is covered in Chapter 5.

c. *The First Amendment*: The First Amendment protects public employees against religious discrimination by their governmental employers. Both the Free Exercise and the Establishment Clauses of the First Amendment have been relied upon to regulate discrimination because of religion in the workplace. Public and private employers also have relied upon the free speech provision in the First Amendment as a defense to workplace harassment claims. The role of the First Amendment in employment discrimination law is discussed in Chapters 10 (harassment) and 12 (religion).

The Constitution does not provide a cause of action to government employees; rather employees typically sue under Section 1983 for a violation of their constitutional rights.

NOTE: THE ELEVENTH AMENDMENT AS A BAR TO CIVIL CLAIMS FOR DAMAGES AGAINST STATES

The Eleventh Amendment to the Constitution of the United States provides:

> The Judicial power of the United States shall not be construed to extend to any suit in law or equity, commenced or prosecuted against one of the United States by Citizens of another State, or by Citizens or Subjects of any Foreign State.

U.S. Const. amend. XI. The Supreme Court has held that the Eleventh Amendment bars a citizen from bringing suit against a state in federal court. Hans v. Louisiana, 134 U.S. 1, 10 S.Ct. 504, 33 L.Ed.842 (1890). The Court has recognized several exceptions to the Eleventh Amendment: (1) a state may waive its immunity and consent to suit in federal court, and (2) Congress can abrogate a state's Eleventh Amendment immunity without the state's consent as long as Congress does so pursuant to its power to enforce, by appropriate legislation, the substantive provisions of the Fourteenth Amendment. In *Seminole Tribe of Florida v. Florida*, 517 U.S. 44, 116 S.Ct. 1114, 134 L.Ed.2d 252 (1996), and *Alden v. Maine*, 527 U.S. 706, 119 S.Ct. 2240, 144 L.Ed.2d 636 (1999), the Court held that the Eleventh Amendment bars civil actions for damages brought by private parties under federal laws unless Congress, in enacting the legislation, has both (1) unequivocally expressed its intent to abrogate a state's Eleventh Amendment immunity, and (2) acted pursuant to a valid exercise of power granted to Congress by the Constitution. Congress can abrogate a state's Eleventh Amendment immunity by means of its enforcement authority under § 5 of the Fourteenth Amendment, but it cannot do so under its Article I Commerce Clause power. *Seminole Tribe*, 517 U.S. at 55, 116 S.Ct. at 1123. Following the Court's decisions in *Seminole Tribe* and *Alden*, states regularly raised the Eleventh Amendment defense, namely challenging whether Congress had the constitutional authority to abrogate their Eleventh Amendment immunity. The following material briefly reviews the case law, which has now largely been settled.

ADEA: In *Kimel v. Florida Board of Regents*, 528 U.S. 62, 120 S.Ct. 631, 145 L.Ed.2d 522 (2000), the overarching issue was whether the Eleventh Amendment bars suits for monetary damages brought in federal courts by state employees against nonconsenting states for violations of the ADEA. In a 5–4 decision authored by Justice O'Connor, the Court ruled that the Eleventh Amendment bars such suits because Congress exceeded its authority under § 5 of the Fourteenth Amendment. The Court held that the substantive mandate the ADEA imposes on state governments is disproportionate to any unconstitutional conduct that conceivably could be targeted by the ADEA because age, unlike race, is not a suspect classification and a state may discriminate on the basis of age without offending the Fourteenth Amendment if the age classification is rationally related to a legitimate state interest. The Court found little in the legislative history of the ADEA to confirm that age discrimination was a widespread problem that demanded what the Court termed "the strong remedy" of the ADEA.

ADA: In *Board of Trustees of University of Alabama v. Garrett*, 531 U.S. 356, 121 S.Ct. 955, 148 L.Ed.2d 866 (2001), in another 5–4 decision this time authored by Chief Justice Rehnquist, the Court held that private ADA suits for employment discrimination brought against nonconsenting states in federal court for money damages are barred by the Eleventh Amendment. Among other reasons, the Court found that the legislative history of the ADA failed to support an identifiable history of irrational employment discrimination against the disabled. The reasoning of the Court in *Garrett* paralleled, in substantial part, the reasoning of the Court in *Kimel*.

Family and Medical Leave Act: In *Nevada Department of Human Resources v. Hibbs,* 538 U.S. 721, 123 S.Ct. 1972, 155 L.Ed.2d 953 (2003), the Court held that a private party's suit seeking damages under the Family and Medical Leave Act of 1993 (FMLA), 29 U.S.C. § 2612 (2000), is not barred by the Eleventh Amendment. The FMLA and *Hibbs* are covered in Chapter 8. More recently, the Supreme Court invalidated the self-care provision of the FMLA, which allows employees to take leave for their own serious health condition, as applied to state employers. *See* Coleman v. Court of Appeals of Maryland, 132 S.Ct. 1327, 182 L.Ed.2d 296 (2012).

Equal Pay Act: Of the eight cases the Court remanded to lower courts for reconsideration in light of *Kimel*, two were Equal Pay Act cases in which the court of appeals rejected the Eleventh Amendment immunity defense in cases brought by private citizens seeking, *inter alia*, monetary damages: Varner v. Ill. State Univ., 150 F.3d 706 (7th Cir.1998), *vacated and remanded*, 528 U.S. 1110, 120 S.Ct. 928, 145 L.Ed.2d 806 (2000); and Anderson v. State Univ. of N.Y., 169 F.3d 117 (2d Cir.1999), *vacated and remanded*, 528 U.S. 1111, 120 S.Ct. 929, 145 L.Ed.2d 807 (2000). On remand, the Seventh Circuit reaffirmed its earlier decision that the Eleventh Amendment does not bar EPA claims against states. Varner v. Ill. State Univ., 226 F.3d 927 (7th Cir.2000). The court held that, in contrast to the ADEA, the EPA is not aimed at the kind of discrimination that receives only rational basis review. Rather, under the Constitution, gender-based discrimination to which the EPA is directed is subject to an exceedingly more rigorous standard of review—heightened scrutiny—than is true of age discrimination. Other courts that have considered the issue post-*Kimel* have also held that Congress validly abrogated states' immunity in private EPA claims. *See, e.g.*, Siler-Khodr v. Univ. of Tex. Health Sci. Ctr. San Antonio, 261 F.3d 542, 550 (5th Cir.2001) (collecting cases); Kovacevich v. Kent State, 224 F.3d 806 (6th Cir.2000).

Title VII: In *Fitzpatrick v. Bitzer*, 427 U.S. 445, 96 S.Ct. 2666, 49 L.Ed.2d 614 (1976), the Court held that the Eleventh Amendment does not immunize a state from liability for back pay and attorney's fees awards in a Title VII employment discrimination case. *Fitzpatrick* was decided before *Kimel* and *Garrett*. Subsequent to *Kimel* and *Garrett*, the lower courts have continued to rely upon *Fitzpatrick* to hold that the Eleventh Amendment does not bar private suits against states for monetary damages. *See, e.g.*, Nanda v. Bd. of Trs. of Univ. of Ill., 303 F.3d 817 (7th Cir.2002); Okruhlik v. Univ. of Ark., Bd. of Trs., 255 F.3d 615, 622 (8th Cir.2001) (collecting cases). The Supreme Court's decision in *Hibbs* offers strong support that Congress acted constitutionally in abrogating states' Eleventh Amendment immunity in Title VII. In discussing the history of states in limiting employment opportunities of women, the Court in *Hibbs* stated that "Congress responded to this history of discrimination by abrogating States' sovereign immunity in Title VII * * *, and we sustained this abrogation in *Fitzpatrick*." *Hibbs,* 538 U.S. at 730, 123 S.Ct. at 1978.

Section 1981: The courts are unanimous in holding that states cannot be sued in federal court for monetary damages under § 1981 because Congress did not unmistakably express its intent in the legislation to waive states' Eleventh Amendment immunity. *See* Singletary v. Mo. Dep't of Corrs., 423 F.3d 886, 890 (8th Cir.2005) (collecting cases).

Discrimination Claims Brought by the Federal Government: Although individuals are barred by the Eleventh Amendment from suing states for damages for employment discrimination under the ADEA and the ADA, when the federal government, including the EEOC, prosecutes such cases in federal court, states are not immune from monetary damages, even when damages are sought on behalf of individuals. *See, e.g.*, United States v. Miss. Dep't of Pub. Safety, 321 F.3d 495 (5th Cir.2003) (citing Supreme Court authority); EEOC v. Bd. of Regents of the Univ. of Wis. Sys., 288 F.3d 296 (7th Cir.2002). In *EEOC v. Board of Regents*, the Seventh Circuit relied upon *Alden v. Maine*, 527 U.S. 706, 755, 119 S.Ct. 2240, 2267, 144 L.Ed.2d 636 (1999), in which the Supreme Court said that "[in] ratifying the Constitution, the States consented to suits brought by other States or by the Federal Government." Also in *Garrett*, the Court recognized that, even though private suits against states under the ADA are barred by the Eleventh Amendment, the ADA can nevertheless be enforced by the United States in actions for damages. 531 U.S. 356, 374 n.9, 121 S.Ct. 955, 968 n.9.

The Ex Parte Young *Exception to the Eleventh Amendment*: The Supreme Court has endorsed an important exception to the rule that the Eleventh Amendment bars private suits against states for damages in federal courts. In *Ex Parte Young*, 209 U.S. 123, 28 S.Ct. 441, 52 L.Ed.714 (1908), the Supreme Court held that when a state official acts in violation of the Constitution or federal law, he is acting *ultra vires* and is no longer entitled to the state's immunity from suit. The *Ex Parte Young* doctrine allows civil actions against state officials for prospective injunctive relief but it does not allow monetary damages. In *Gibson v. Arkansas Department of Correction*, 265 F.3d 718 (8th Cir.2001), the court held that a private party may sue a state official for prospective injunctive relief under the ADA by relying on the *Ex Parte Young* doctrine. *See also* Nelson v. Univ. of Tex., 535 F.3d 318, 322 (5th Cir.2008) (collecting cases).

Local Governments: The Eleventh Amendment immunity does not extend to local government units such as cities and counties. Lincoln County v. Luning, 133 U.S. 529, 10 S.Ct. 363, 33 L.Ed.766 (1890).

NOTES: OTHER REMEDIES FOR EMPLOYMENT DISCRIMINATION

1. *State and Local Laws*: Most states and a number of municipalities have laws prohibiting discrimination in employment. State laws frequently extend discrimination protection to categories not covered under federal laws. For example, many states and municipalities prohibit discrimination in employment because of marital status, sexual orientation, gender identity, or

physical appearance. A current listing of state legislation can be found at *https://www.aclu.org/map/non-discrimination-laws-state-state-information-map*.

2. *Labor Relations Laws*: The Supreme Court has construed the National Labor Relations Act, 29 U.S.C. § 151 *et seq*., and the Railway Labor Act, 45 U.S.C. § 151 *et seq*., to impose on labor organizations the obligation to represent the interests of all members of the appropriate bargaining unit fairly and without regard to race, sex, religion, or national origin. This obligation is referred to as the duty of fair representation (DFR). The duty of fair representation, as well as union liability for discrimination under civil rights laws such as Title VII or § 1981, is covered in Section D.5 of this chapter.

3. *Veterans' Rights*: Veterans are not only protected from employment discrimination on the basis of their former military status, but they are also provided certain job preferences because of their military service or training. The Uniformed Services Employment and Reemployment Rights Act of 1994 (USERRA), 38 U.S.C. §§ 4301–07, strengthens, replaces, and overhauls the earlier Veterans' Reemployment Rights Act. Courts interpreting USERRA frequently borrow from Title VII jurisprudence. *See* Knowles v. Citicorp Mortgage, Inc., 142 F.3d 1082 (8th Cir.1998). Section 712 of Title VII, 42 U.S.C. § 2000e–11, provides that nothing in Title VII is to be "construed to repeal or modify any Federal, State, territorial, or local law creating special rights or preference for veterans."

C. ENFORCEMENT SCHEMES

Because there is no administrative enforcement scheme for employment discrimination claims based upon § 1981 or the Constitution, plaintiffs bringing such claims are not required to exhaust administrative remedies before filing suit. Section 1981 and constitutional claims (brought pursuant to section 1983) are filed directly in the appropriate state or federal court, subject to the applicable statute of limitations. On the other hand, employment discrimination claims brought under Title VII, the ADEA, and the ADA are subject to both administrative processes and adjudication in civil court. Thus, exhaustion of administrative remedies is a prerequisite to a lawsuit brought under these statutes. Administrative resolution of employment discrimination charges is primarily the responsibility of the Equal Employment Opportunity Commission.

The Equal Employment Opportunity Commission: Congress established the Equal Employment Opportunity Commission (EEOC) to enforce Title VII. Initially, the EEOC had authority only to investigate charges of unlawful discrimination and if the EEOC found reasonable cause to believe that a charge was true, it could attempt to resolve the charge through "informal methods of conference, conciliation, and persuasion." Title VII, § 706(b), 42 U.S.C. § 2000e–5(b). Because Congress declined to provide the EEOC with the "cease and desist" authority given to some other federal agencies, such as the National Labor Relations Board, NLRA § 10(c), the EEOC initially was characterized as a "poor enfeebled thing." Michael I. Sovern, Legal Restraints on Racial Discrimination in Employment 205 (1966).

Since 1965, when the Act first became applicable, several reforms have strengthened the EEOC's enforcement authority. In 1972, the Act was amended to give the EEOC the authority to seek judicial enforcement of Title VII. 42 U.S.C. § 2000e–5(f). The EEOC has also been designated as the primary enforcement agency and has the major enforcement responsibility for Title VII, the ADEA, the ADA, and the Equal Pay Act. In addition, the EEOC has responsibility for employment discrimination enforcement in the federal sector.

The EEOC has statutory authority to promulgate procedural regulations to enforce Title VII, 42 U.S.C. § 2000e–12, and the ADA, 42 U.S.C. § 12116. Those regulations are found at 29 C.F.R. § 1601 (Title VII), and 29 C.F.R. § 1630 (ADA). The EEOC also has promulgated procedural regulations for ADEA claims, 29 C.F.R. § 1626, federal sector employment discrimination claims, 29 C.F.R. § 1614, and other statutes over which it has administrative enforcement responsibility. The EEOC typically does not follow the formal rulemaking proceedings dictated by the Administrative Procedure Act ("APA"), and there has long been a question of what level of deference EEOC procedural regulations should be afforded. The Supreme Court has repeatedly declined to resolve this issue instead holding that the EEOC's regulations were either plainly correct or plainly incorrect, thus affording no need for deference. *See* Edelman v. Lynchburg Coll., 535 U.S. 106, 114, 122 S.Ct. 1145, 1150, 152 L.Ed.2d 188, 199 (2002) ("[T]here is no reason to resolve any question of deference here. We find the EEOC rule not only a reasonable one, but the position we would adopt even if there were no formal rule and we were interpreting the statute from scratch."); Gen. Dynamics Land Sys., Inc. v. Cline, 540 U.S. 581, 600, 124 S.Ct. 1236, 1248, 157 L.Ed.2d 1094, 1113 (2004) (concluding that there was no need for deference where the "[EEOC] is clearly wrong"). More recently, the Supreme Court afforded deference to the EEOC's interpretation of one of its own regulations regarding what constitutes a charge. *See* Fed. Express Corp. v. Holowecki, 522 U.S.389, 128 S.Ct. 1147, 170 L.Ed.2d 10 (2008). Although the Court has declined to define a specific level of deference, there is little question that the Court weighs the EEOC's regulations and interpretations as part of its statutory analysis. Several Justices have urged the Court to afford more formal deference to EEOC regulations, even when they are not issued through formal rulemaking. *See, e.g.*, Edelman v. Lynchburg College, 535 U.S. at 119, 122 S.Ct. at 1153, 152

L.Ed.2d at 201 (Thomas, J., concurring) ("I concur because I read the Court's opinion to hold that the EEOC possessed the authority to promulgate this procedural regulation, and that the regulation is reasonable, not proscribed by statute, and issued in conformity with the APA."); *id.* at 122–23, 122 S.Ct. at 1155, 152 L.Ed.2d at 203 (Scalia, J., concurring) ("I think the EEOC's regulation is entitled to *Chevron* deference.").

In addition to procedural regulations, the EEOC has issued *Guidelines* on, for example, claims based on discrimination because of sex, religion, national origin, and harassment, and on employment selection procedures. Unlike the procedural regulations, the *Guidelines* are the EEOC's substantive interpretations of the statutes. The Supreme Court has held that the level of deference it will accord to the EEOC's *Guidelines* "will depend upon the thoroughness evident in its consideration, the validity of its reasoning, its consistency with earlier and later pronouncements, and all those factors which give it power to persuade." Gen. Elec. Co. v. Gilbert, 429 U.S. 125, 142, 97 S.Ct. 401, 411, 50 L.Ed.2d 343 (1976) (quoting Skidmore v. Swift & Co., 323 U.S. 134, 140, 65 S.Ct. 161, 89 L.Ed.124 (1944)).

The 2008 Amendments to the ADA provided the EEOC with authority to issue regulations interpreting the Act. After Notice and Comment, the final regulations were published in 2011. *See* ADA Regulations, 29 C.F.R. parts 1630, 1640, 1641.

1. ADMINISTRATIVE EXHAUSTION

As one judge has observed, Title VII is "rife with procedural requirements which are sufficiently labyrinthine to baffle the most experienced lawyer, yet its enforcement mechanisms are usually triggered by laymen." Egelston v. State Univ. Coll. at Geneseo, 535 F.2d 752, 754 (2d Cir.1976). What follows is a brief overview of the administrative process followed by a more detailed outline of the administrative requirements that plaintiffs must satisfy prior to filing a civil action under Title VII and the ADA. There are some differences with the procedural requirements for ADEA claims, which will be discussed where applicable below.

Claims filed by private employees under Title VII, the ADA or the ADEA must first be filed with the EEOC. The filing is known as a "charge of discrimination" and the time for filing such claims depends on whether the individual first files with an appropriate state agency. If the individual files with a state agency, generally at the same time the claim is filed with the EEOC, she must file the claim within 300 days from the date the discriminatory act occurred (how that time is calculated is discussed below), whereas if the claim is not filed with a state agency, the claim must be filed within 180 days. The longer filing deadline for state agencies was designed to preserve state interests and provide the state agency with sufficient time to initially process the complaints. The current reality is that most complaints are filed directly with the EEOC, except in certain jurisdictions, and are simultaneously filed with the state when the employee checks a box on the charge form, which satisfies the requirement for the longer filing deadline. Only one agency (federal or state) will review the charge, and that is most commonly the EEOC.

Once a charge of discrimination is filed, the responsible agency will often seek to resolve the charge informally, and if that fails, the agency conducts an investigation. It is also possible that conciliation efforts will begin after the investigation commences. After conducting an investigation, the agency will make a determination as to whether it believes discrimination occurred. If the agency decides discrimination was the underlying cause of the challenged action, it will issue a "cause" determination explaining its basis for the decision and inviting the employer into settlement talks. If, however, the agency determines discrimination was not involved, the agency will issue a "no cause" determination, and, at the same time, will issue the employee a "Notice of Right to Sue."

If the agency issues a cause determination, and the charge is not settled, then the EEOC will typically file a federal lawsuit on behalf of the employee. The employee has an absolute right to intervene in that lawsuit, and many employees choose to do so. In addition, the charging party, as the person who files the claim is known, has a right to request a Notice of Right to Sue any time after 180 days have elapsed from the date the charge was filed. Often times the charging party will request the Notice of Right to Sue before an investigation has commenced or has been completed, but the EEOC must issue the notice upon request once the 180 days have passed.

Once the charging party obtains a Notice of Right to Sue, either by request or after a cause determination, she can file a civil action in federal or state court within 90 days of receiving the notice. A right-to-sue notice functions as the party's ticket to filing a federal complaint, and it is a prerequisite to suit. A more detailed discussion of the procedural requirements follows. This is where there is a slight difference with the ADEA: in addition to the 90-day rule following the right to sue notice, a charging party may also proceed to file a court action 60 days after the charge was initially filed and does not need to wait for a right-to-sue notice.

a. *Basic requirements for Title VII and ADA claims*: An individual seeking relief from unlawful employment discrimination under Title VII or the ADA may not file a civil suit until she has first exhausted administrative remedies before the EEOC. 42 U.S.C. § 2000e–5. *See* Love v. Pullman Co., 404 U.S. 522, 523, 92 S.Ct. 616, 617, 30 L.Ed.2d 679 (1972). The ADA adopts the same administrative exhaustion requirement applicable to Title VII claims. 42 U.S.C. § 12117. An individual (or the aggrieved or charging party) must satisfy two statutory requirements in order to bring a civil action: she must (1) timely file a charge with the EEOC, and (2) timely file a complaint in federal court within ninety days of receipt of the right-to-sue notice from the EEOC. McDonnell Douglas Corp. v. Green, 411 U.S. 792, 798, 93 S.Ct. 1817, 1822, 36 L.Ed.2d 668 (1973); Alexander v. Gardner-Denver Co., 415 U.S. 36, 47, 94 S.Ct. 1011, 1019, 39 L.Ed.2d 147 (1974). The administrative exhaustion requirement is covered in this section. The timely filing requirement is covered in the next section on judicial enforcement.

To satisfy the administrative filing requirement under Title VII § 706(e)(1), 42 U.S.C. § 2000e–5(e)(1), an aggrieved party must file a charge with the EEOC "within one hundred and eighty days after the alleged unlawful employment practice occurred" or "within three hundred days after the alleged unlawful employment practice occurred" if the aggrieved party has "initially instituted proceedings with a State or local agency with authority to grant or seek relief." Most states now have equivalent state agencies so the general filing deadline is 300 days, with some exceptions (for example, in the *Ledbetter* case below, the charge arose in Alabama which does not have an equivalent state agency).

As to the second statutory filing requirement, Title VII § 706(f)(1), 42 U.S.C. § 2000e–5(f)(1), provides that an aggrieved person has ninety days within which to file a civil action after receipt of notice-of-right-to-sue from the EEOC. If these two filing requirements have been satisfied, a federal or state court has jurisdiction to hear and decide the case even though the EEOC has not complied with or completed all of its statutory obligations under Title VII, such as making a reasonable cause determination or attempting conciliation, *see, e.g.*, Robinson v. Lorillard Corp., 444 F.2d 791 (4th Cir.), *cert. dismissed*, 404 U.S. 1006, 92 S.Ct. 573, 30 L.Ed.2d 655 (1971).

Section 706(b) of Title VII, 42 U.S.C. § 2000e–(5)(b), provides that a charge filed with the EEOC "shall be in writing under oath or affirmation." An EEOC regulation states that "a charge is sufficient when the [EEOC] receives from the person making the charge a written statement sufficiently precise to identify the parties and to describe generally the action or practices complained of." 29 C.F.R. § 1601.12(b). The regulation further provides that "[a] charge may be amended to cure technical defects or omissions, including the failure to verify the charge. * * * Such amendments * * * shall relate back to the date the charge was first received." *Id.*, In *Edelman v. Lynchburg College*, 535 U.S. 106, 122 S.Ct. 1145, 152 L.Ed.2d 188 (2002), the Supreme Court resolved a circuit split over whether an unverified EEOC intake questionnaire that is timely filed but not verified within the 180- or 300-day filing period constitutes a timely filed charge. *Edelman* upheld an EEOC regulation permitting a timely filed unverified charge to be verified after the expiration of the charge-filing period. The regulation provides that the verification of a charge relates back to a timely filed unverified charge, which the Court determined was a reasonable interpretation of the Title VII filing requirements.

Most charges are filed without the assistance of counsel and have limited information. The scope of the charge, however, will later define the permissible causes of action if a complaint is filed in court. More specifically, a plaintiff's judicial complaint is confined to the scope of the administrative investigation that can reasonably be expected to flow out of the charge. *See* Bryant v. Bell Atl. Med., Inc., 288 F.3d 124, 132 (4th Cir.2002). The question courts address is what causes of action could be expected "to grow out of the charge of discrimination" from a reasonable investigation. Gregory v. Ga. Dep't of Hum. Res., 355 F.3d 1277, 1280 (11th Cir.2004) (per curiam). As a result, courts may dismiss certain causes of action if they were not sufficiently related to the original charge. *See, e.g.*, Pacheco v. Mineta, 448 F.3d 783, 792 (5th Cir.2006) (finding that disparate impact claim was not within scope of charge that alleged disparate treatment); *Bryant*, 288 F.3d at 132 (dismissing retaliation claim); Rush v. McDonald's Corp., 966 F.2d 1104, 1111 (7th Cir.1992) (holding that racial harassment claim fell outside scope of charge that mentioned termination).

The ADEA provides that "[n]o civil action may be commenced by an individual under [the ADEA] until 60 days after a charge alleging unlawful discrimination has been filed with the [EEOC], 29 U.S.C. § 626(d), but the statute does not define the meaning of a "charge." In *Federal Express Corp. v. Holowecki,* 522 U.S. 389, 128 S.Ct. 1147, 170 L.Ed.2d 10 (2008), the Supreme Court held that "the [EEOC] acted within its authority in formulating the rule that a filing is deemed a charge if the document reasonably can be construed to request agency action and appropriate relief on the employee's behalf * * * ." 128 S.Ct. at 1159. The Court found that a completed "Intake Questionnaire" that was filed with the EEOC along with a detailed affidavit indicating the respondent's desire to obtain relief for age discrimination was sufficient to constitute a "charge," and this ruling should be equally applicable to the other statutes for which the EEOC has authority.

b. *Deferral or nondeferral jurisdiction and timely filing*: As noted previously, the time requirement for filing an EEOC charge depends upon whether the claim arises in a deferral or nondeferral jurisdiction. A deferral jurisdiction has a state or local agency that is authorized "to grant or seek relief" from employment discrimination or "to institute criminal proceedings" against such practices. Title VII, § 706(c), 42 U.S.C. § 2000e–5(c). A nondeferral jurisdiction is one which does not satisfy the requirements of § 706(c), 42 U.S.C. § 2000e–5(c). The EEOC determines which jurisdictions qualify as deferral jurisdictions, and today, most states have properly authorized deferral agencies. *See* 29 C.F.R. §§ 1601.70–1601.75. In a deferral jurisdiction, the charge must be filed with the EEOC within 300 days after the alleged unlawful employment practice has occurred, but the charge may not be filed with the EEOC before the expiration of 60 days after proceedings have been commenced under state or local law, unless such proceedings have been terminated earlier. Title VII §§ 706(c), 706(e), 42 U.S.C. §§ 2000e–5(c),–5(e). With respect to claims arising in nondeferral jurisdictions, Title VII provides that a charge shall be filed within 180 days after the alleged unlawful employment practice has occurred. In *New York Gaslight Club, Inc. v. Carey*, 447 U.S. 54, 65, 100 S.Ct. 2024, 2031–32, 64 L.Ed.2d 723 (1980), the Supreme Court held that, in deferral jurisdictions, "initial resort to state and local remedies is mandated." The EEOC cannot proceed with a charge if that charge should have been filed with a state or local agency in the first instance. The EEOC may, however, refer the charge to a state or local agency on behalf of a charging party, defer its own action on the charge, and then assume jurisdiction over the charge when appropriate deference to the state or local agency has been satisfied. *See* Love v. Pullman Co., 404 U.S. 522, 92 S.Ct. 616, 30 L.Ed.2d 679 (1972).

In *Mohasco Corp. v. Silver*, 447 U.S. 807, 100 S.Ct. 2486, 65 L.Ed.2d 532 (1980), the Supreme Court had ruled that, in a deferral jurisdiction, a charge that was initially filed with the EEOC had to be filed within 240 days of the alleged discriminatory event so as to afford the state 60 days to process the complaint. *See* Title VII, §§ 706(c), (e)(1), 42 U.S.C. §§ 2000e–5(c), (e)(1). By entering into worksharing agreements, however, the EEOC and the various deferral jurisdictions have eliminated some of the procedural hurdles that charging parties previously faced. *See* Title VII, § 709(b), 42 U.S.C. § 2000e–8(b). The worksharing agreements render the filing with one agency the equivalent to filing with both, and typically provide for a waiver of the 60-day investigation period, which effectively terminates the state's exclusive jurisdiction over the claim. *See* EEOC v. Com. Off. Prods. Co., 486 U.S. 107, 125, 108 S.Ct. 1666, 1676, 100 L.Ed.2d 96 (1988) (upholding EEOC interpretation that waiver pursuant to worksharing agreement terminates state proceeding). As a result of the worksharing agreements, the general deadline for filing a charge with the EEOC in deferral jurisdictions is 300 days. *See* Maynard v. Pneumatic Prods. Corp., 256 F.3d 1259 (11th Cir.2001) (explaining the process).

c. *The timely filing requirement*: Section 706(e)(1) of Title VII, 42 U.S.C. § 2000e–5(e)(1), requires the timely filing of a charge with the

EEOC within either 180 days or 300 days "after the alleged unlawful employment practice occurred * * * ." The question when an "alleged unlawful practice has occurred" so as to trigger the running of the 180- or 300-day filing requirement has been a contentious issue in many cases. The issue most frequently arises in cases in which a plaintiff relies upon a series of alleged adverse employment actions, some of which occurred within and some of which occurred outside of the 180- or 300-day period. The case that follows is the Supreme Court's latest treatment of the issue.

LEDBETTER V. GOODYEAR TIRE & RUBBER CO., INC.

Supreme Court of the United States, 2007.
550 U.S. 618, 127 S.Ct. 2162, 167 L.Ed.2d 982.

JUSTICE ALITO delivered the opinion of the Court.

This case calls upon us to apply established precedent in a slightly different context. We have previously held that the time for filing a charge of employment discrimination with the Equal Employment Opportunity Commission (EEOC) begins when the discriminatory act occurs. We have explained that this rule applies to any "[d]iscrete ac[t]" of discrimination, including discrimination in "termination, failure to promote, denial of transfer, [and] refusal to hire." *National Railroad Passenger Corporation v. Morgan,* 536 U.S. 101, 114, 122 S.Ct. 2061, 153 L.Ed.2d 106 (2002). Because a pay-setting decision is a "discrete act," it follows that the period for filing an EEOC charge begins when the act occurs. Petitioner, having abandoned her claim under the Equal Pay Act, asks us to deviate from our prior decisions in order to permit her to assert her claim under Title VII. Petitioner also contends that discrimination in pay is different from other types of employment discrimination and thus should be governed by a different rule. But because a pay-setting decision is a discrete act that occurs at a particular point in time, these arguments must be rejected. We therefore affirm the judgment of the Court of Appeals.

I

Petitioner Lilly Ledbetter (Ledbetter) worked for respondent Goodyear Tire and Rubber Company (Goodyear) at its Gadsden, Alabama, plant from 1979 until 1998. During much of this time, salaried employees at the plant were given or denied raises based on their supervisors' evaluation of their performance. In March 1998, Ledbetter submitted a questionnaire to the EEOC alleging certain acts of sex discrimination, and in July of that year she filed a formal EEOC charge. After taking early retirement in November 1998, Ledbetter commenced this action, in which she asserted, among other claims, a Title VII pay discrimination claim and a claim under the Equal Pay Act of 1963 (EPA), 29 U.S.C. § 206(d).

The District Court granted summary judgment in favor of Goodyear on several of Ledbetter's claims, including her Equal Pay Act claim, but allowed others, including her Title VII pay discrimination claim, to proceed to trial. In support of this latter claim, Ledbetter introduced evidence that during the course of her employment several supervisors had given her poor evaluations because of her sex, that as a result of these evaluations her pay was not increased as much as it would have been if she had been evaluated fairly, and that these past pay decisions continued to affect the amount of her pay throughout her employment. Toward the end of her time with Goodyear, she was being paid significantly less than any of her male colleagues. Goodyear maintained that the evaluations had been nondiscriminatory, but the jury found for Ledbetter and awarded her backpay and damages.

On appeal, Goodyear contended that Ledbetter's pay discrimination claim was time barred with respect to all pay decisions made prior to September 26, 1997—that is, 180 days before the filing of her EEOC questionnaire. And Goodyear argued that no discriminatory act relating to Ledbetter's pay occurred after that date.

The Court of Appeals for the Eleventh Circuit reversed, holding that a Title VII pay discrimination claim cannot be based on any pay decision that occurred prior to the last pay decision that affected the employee's pay during the EEOC charging period. The Court of Appeals then concluded that there was insufficient evidence to prove that Goodyear had acted with discriminatory intent in making the only two pay decisions that occurred within that time span, namely, a decision made in 1997 to deny Ledbetter a raise and a similar decision made in 1998. [Ledbetter did not challenge the ruling on the sufficiency of the evidence.]

* * *

II

Title VII of the Civil Rights Act of 1964 makes it an "unlawful employment practice" to discriminate "against any individual with respect to his compensation * * * because of such individual's * * * sex." 42 U.S.C. § 2000e–2(a)(1). An individual wishing to challenge an employment practice under this provision must first file a charge with the EEOC. § 2000e–5(e)(1). Such a charge must be filed within a specified period (either 180 or 300 days, depending on the State) "after the alleged unlawful employment practice occurred," *ibid.*, and if the employee does not submit a timely EEOC charge, the employee may not challenge that practice in court, § 2000e–5(f)(1).

In addressing the issue whether an EEOC charge was filed on time, we have stressed the need to identify with care the specific employment practice that is at issue. [*National Railroad Passenger Corp. v. Morgan,*

536 U.S. 101, 110–11, 122 S.Ct. 2061, 153 L.Ed.2d 106 (2002).] Ledbetter points to two different employment practices as possible candidates. Primarily, she urges us to focus on the paychecks that were issued to her during the EEOC charging period (the 180-day period preceding the filing of her EEOC questionnaire), each of which, she contends, was a separate act of discrimination. Alternatively, Ledbetter directs us to the 1998 decision denying her a raise, and she argues that this decision was "unlawful because it carried forward intentionally discriminatory disparities from prior years." Both of these arguments fail because they would require us in effect to jettison the defining element of the legal claim on which her Title VII recovery was based.

Ledbetter asserted disparate treatment, the central element of which is discriminatory intent. However, Ledbetter does not assert that the relevant Goodyear decisionmakers acted with actual discriminatory intent either when they issued her checks during the EEOC charging period or when they denied her a raise in 1998. Rather, she argues that the paychecks were unlawful because they would have been larger if she had been evaluated in a nondiscriminatory manner *prior to* the EEOC charging period. Similarly, she maintains that the 1998 decision was unlawful because it "carried forward" the effects of prior, uncharged discrimination decisions. In essence, she suggests that it is sufficient that discriminatory acts that occurred prior to the charging period had continuing effects during that period. * * * This argument is squarely foreclosed by our precedents.

In *United Air Lines, Inc. v. Evans,* 431 U.S. 553, 97 S.Ct. 1885, 52 L.Ed.2d 571 (1977), we rejected an argument that is basically the same as Ledbetter's. * * *

We agreed with Evans that the airline's "seniority system [did] indeed have a continuing impact on her pay and fringe benefits," *id.,* at 558, 97 S.Ct. 1885, but we noted that "the critical question [was] whether any present *violation* exist[ed]." *Ibid.* (emphasis in original). We concluded that the continuing effects of the precharging period discrimination did not make out a present violation. * * * [As the *Evans* Court wrote:] "A discriminatory act which is not made the basis for a timely charge * * * is merely an unfortunate event in history which has no present legal consequences." *Ibid.* It would be difficult to speak to the point more directly.

[The discussion of *Delaware State College v. Ricks,* 449 U.S. 250, 101 S.Ct. 498, 66 L.Ed.2d 431 (1980), where the Court held that in a tenure denial case the charging period begins when the decision is communicated, rather than when it becomes effective, has been omitted.]

This same approach dictated the outcome in *Lorance v. AT&T Technologies, Inc.,* 490 U.S. 900, 109 S.Ct. 2261, 104 L.Ed.2d 961 (1989), which grew out of a change in the way in which seniority was calculated under a collective-bargaining agreement. Before 1979, all employees at the plant in question accrued seniority based simply on years of employment at the plant. In 1979, a new agreement made seniority for workers in the more highly paid (and traditionally male) position of "tester" depend on time spent in that position alone and not in other positions in the plant. Several years later, when female testers were laid off due to low seniority as calculated under the new provision, they filed an EEOC charge alleging that the 1979 scheme had been adopted with discriminatory intent * * * .

We held that the plaintiffs' EEOC charge was not timely because it was not filed within the specified period after the adoption in 1979 of the new seniority rule. We noted that the plaintiffs had not alleged that the new seniority rule treated men and women differently or that the rule had been applied in a discriminatory manner. Rather, their complaint was that the rule was adopted originally with discriminatory intent. And as in *Evans* and *Ricks,* we held that the EEOC charging period ran from the time when the discrete act of alleged intentional discrimination occurred, not from the date when the effects of this practice were felt. * * *[2]

Our most recent decision in this area confirms this understanding. In *Morgan,* we explained that the statutory term "employment practice" generally refers to "a discrete act or single 'occurrence' " that takes place at a particular point in time. We pointed to "termination, failure to promote, denial of transfer, [and] refusal to hire" as examples of such "discrete" acts, and we held that a Title VII plaintiff "can only file a charge to cover discrete acts that 'occurred' within the appropriate time period."

The instruction provided by *Evans, Ricks, Lorance,* and *Morgan* is clear. The EEOC charging period is triggered when a discrete unlawful practice takes place. A new violation does not occur, and a new charging period does not commence, upon the occurrence of subsequent nondiscriminatory acts that entail adverse effects resulting from the past discrimination. But of course, if an employer engages in a series of acts each of which is intentionally discriminatory, then a fresh violation takes place when each act is committed.

Ledbetter's arguments here—that the paychecks that she received during the charging period and the 1998 raise denial each violated Title

[2] After *Lorance,* Congress amended Title VII to cover the specific situation involved in that case. See 42 U.S.C. § 2000e–5(e)(2) (allowing for Title VII liability arising from an intentionally discriminatory seniority system both at the time of its adoption and at the time of its application). The dissent attaches great significance to this amendment, suggesting that it shows that *Lorance* was wrongly reasoned as an initial matter. * * * For present purposes, what is most important about the amendment in question is that it applied only to the adoption of a discriminatory seniority system, not to other types of employment discrimination. * * *

VII and triggered a new EEOC charging period—cannot be reconciled with *Evans, Ricks, Lorance,* and *Morgan*. Ledbetter, as noted, makes no claim that intentionally discriminatory conduct occurred during the charging period or that discriminatory decisions that occurred prior to that period were not communicated to her. Instead, she argues simply that Goodyear's conduct during the charging period gave present effect to discriminatory conduct outside of that period. But current effects alone cannot breathe life into prior, uncharged discrimination; as we held in *Evans,* such effects in themselves have "no present legal consequences." 431 U.S. at 558, 97 S.Ct. 1885. Ledbetter should have filed an EEOC charge within 180 days after each allegedly discriminatory pay decision was made and communicated to her. She did not do so, and the paychecks that were issued to her during the 180 days prior to the filing of her EEOC charge do not provide a basis for overcoming that prior failure.

* * *

Certainly, the 180-day EEOC charging deadline is short by any measure, * * * . This short deadline reflects Congress' strong preference for the prompt resolution of employment discrimination allegations through voluntary conciliation and cooperation.

A disparate-treatment claim comprises two elements: an employment practice, and discriminatory intent. Nothing in Title VII supports treating the intent element of Ledbetter's claim any differently from the employment practice element. If anything, concerns regarding stale claims weigh more heavily with respect to proof of the intent associated with employment practices than with the practices themselves. For example, in a case such as this in which the plaintiff's claim concerns the denial of raises, the employer's challenged acts (the decisions not to increase the employee's pay at the times in question) will almost always be documented and will typically not even be in dispute. By contrast, the employer's intent is almost always disputed, and evidence relating to intent may fade quickly with time. In most disparate-treatment cases, much if not all of the evidence of intent is circumstantial. Thus, the critical issue in a case involving a long-past performance evaluation will often be whether the evaluation was so far off the mark that a sufficient inference of discriminatory intent can be drawn. This can be a subtle determination, and the passage of time may seriously diminish the ability of the parties and the factfinder to reconstruct what actually happened.[4]

[4] * * * [T]his case illustrates the problems created by tardy lawsuits. Ledbetter's claims of sex discrimination turned principally on the misconduct of a single Goodyear supervisor, who, Ledbetter testified, retaliated against her when she rejected his sexual advances during the early 1980's, and did so again in the mid-1990's when he falsified deficiency reports about her work. His misconduct, Ledbetter argues, was "a principal basis for [her] performance evaluation in 1997." Yet, by the time of trial, this supervisor had died and therefore could not testify. A timely charge might have permitted his evidence to be weighed contemporaneously.

Ledbetter contends that employers would be protected by the equitable doctrine of laches, but Congress plainly did not think that laches was sufficient in this context. Indeed, Congress took a diametrically different approach, including in Title VII a provision allowing only a few months in most cases to file a charge with the EEOC.

* * * We therefore reject the suggestion that an employment practice committed with no improper purpose and no discriminatory intent is rendered unlawful nonetheless because it gives some effect to an intentional discriminatory act that occurred outside the charging period. Ledbetter's claim is, for this reason, untimely.

III

A

In advancing her two theories Ledbetter does not seriously contest the logic of *Evans, Ricks, Lorance,* and *Morgan* as set out above, but rather argues that our decision in *Bazemore v. Friday,* 478 U.S. 385, 106 S.Ct. 3000, 92 L.Ed.2d 315 (1986) *(per curiam),* requires different treatment of her claim because it relates to pay. Ledbetter focuses specifically on our statement that "[e]ach week's paycheck that delivers less to a black than to a similarly situated white is a wrong actionable under Title VII." *Id.,* at 395, 106 S.Ct. 3000. She argues that in *Bazemore* we adopted a "paycheck accrual rule" under which each paycheck, even if not accompanied by discriminatory intent, triggers a new EEOC charging period during which the complainant may properly challenge any prior discriminatory conduct that impacted the amount of that paycheck, no matter how long ago the discrimination occurred. * * *

Bazemore concerned a disparate-treatment pay claim brought against the North Carolina Agricultural Extension Service (Service). Service employees were originally segregated into "a white branch" and "a 'Negro branch,'" with the latter receiving less pay, but in 1965 the two branches were merged. After Title VII was extended to public employees in 1972, black employees brought suit claiming that pay disparities attributable to the old dual pay scale persisted. The Court of Appeals rejected this claim, which it interpreted to be that the "'discriminatory difference in salaries should have been affirmatively eliminated.'" *Id.,* at 395, 106 S.Ct. 3000.

This Court reversed in a *per curiam* opinion, but all of the Members of the Court joined Justice Brennan's separate opinion [concurring in part]. Justice Brennan wrote:

> The error of the Court of Appeals with respect to salary disparities created prior to 1972 and perpetuated thereafter is too obvious to warrant extended discussion: that the Extension Service discriminated with respect to salaries *prior* to the time it

> was covered by Title VII does not excuse perpetuating that discrimination *after* the Extension Service became covered by Title VII. To hold otherwise would have the effect of exempting from liability those employers who were historically the greatest offenders of the rights of blacks. A pattern or practice that would have constituted a violation of Title VII, but for the fact that the statute had not yet become effective, became a violation upon Title VII's effective date * * * .

Id. at 395, 106 S.Ct. 3000 (emphasis in original).

Far from adopting the approach that Ledbetter advances here, this passage made a point that was "too obvious to warrant extended discussion"; namely, that when an employer adopts a facially discriminatory pay structure that puts some employees on a lower scale because of race, the employer engages in intentional discrimination whenever it issues a check to one of these disfavored employees. An employer that adopts and intentionally retains such a pay structure can surely be regarded as intending to discriminate on the basis of race as long as the structure is used.

* * *

The sentence in Justice Brennan's opinion on which Ledbetter chiefly relies comes directly after the passage quoted above, and makes a similarly obvious point: "Each week's paycheck that delivers less to a black than to a similarly situated white is a wrong actionable under Title VII, regardless of the fact that this pattern was begun prior to the effective date of Title VII." *Id.* at 395, 106 S.Ct. 3000.

In other words, a freestanding violation may always be charged within its own charging period regardless of its connection to other violations. We repeated this same point more recently in *Morgan* * * * . Neither of these opinions stands for the proposition that an action not comprising an employment practice and alleged discriminatory intent is separately chargeable, just because it is related to some past act of discrimination.

* * *

Because Ledbetter has not adduced evidence that Goodyear initially adopted its performance-based pay system in order to discriminate on the basis of sex or that it later applied this system to her within the charging period with any discriminatory animus, *Bazemore* is of no help to her. Rather, all Ledbetter has alleged is that Goodyear's agents discriminated against her individually in the past and that this discrimination reduced the amount of later paychecks. Because Ledbetter did not file timely EEOC charges relating to her employer's discriminatory pay decisions in the past, she cannot maintain a suit based on that past discrimination at this time.

B

The dissent also argues that pay claims are different. Its principal argument is that a pay discrimination claim is like a hostile work environment claim because both types of claims are " 'based on the cumulative effect of individual acts,' " but this analogy overlooks the critical conceptual distinction between these two types of claims. And although the dissent relies heavily on *Morgan,* the dissent's argument is fundamentally inconsistent with *Morgan's* reasoning.

Morgan distinguished between "discrete" acts of discrimination and a hostile work environment. A discrete act of discrimination is an act that in itself "constitutes a separate actionable 'unlawful employment practice' " and that is temporally distinct. As examples we identified "termination, failure to promote, denial of transfer, or refusal to hire." A hostile work environment, on the other hand, typically comprises a succession of harassing acts, each of which "may not be actionable on its own." * * * In other words, the actionable wrong is the environment, not the individual acts that, taken together, create the environment.

Contrary to the dissent's assertion, what Ledbetter alleged was not a single wrong consisting of a succession of acts. Instead, she alleged a series of discrete discriminatory acts (arguing that payment of each paycheck constituted a separate violation of Title VII), each of which *was* independently identifiable and actionable, and *Morgan* is perfectly clear that when an employee alleges "serial violations," *i.e.,* a series of actionable wrongs, a timely EEOC charge must be filed with respect to each discrete alleged violation.

* * * [I]t should also be noted that the dissent is coy as to whether it would apply the same rule to all pay discrimination claims or whether it would limit the rule to cases like Ledbetter's, in which multiple discriminatory pay decisions are alleged. The dissent relies on the fact that Ledbetter was allegedly subjected to a series of discriminatory pay decisions over a period of time, and the dissent suggests that she did not realize for some time that she had been victimized. But not all pay cases share these characteristics.

If, as seems likely, the dissent would apply the same rule in all pay cases, then, if a single discriminatory pay decision made 20 years ago continued to affect an employee's pay today, the dissent would presumably hold that the employee could file a timely EEOC charge today. And the dissent would presumably allow this even if the employee had full knowledge of all the circumstances relating to the 20-year-old decision at the time it was made. * * * We refuse to take that approach.

IV

* * *

Ledbetter, finally, makes a variety of policy arguments in favor of giving the alleged victims of pay discrimination more time before they are required to file a charge with the EEOC. Among other things, she claims that pay discrimination is harder to detect than other forms of employment discrimination.

* * *

Ledbetter's policy arguments for giving special treatment to pay claims find no support in the statute and are inconsistent with our precedents. We apply the statute as written, and this means that any unlawful employment practice, including those involving compensation, must be presented to the EEOC within the period prescribed by statute.

* * *

[JUSTICE GINSBURG dissented in an opinion joined by JUSTICES STEVENS, SOUTER, and BREYER.]

NOTES AND QUESTIONS

1. *Lilly Ledbetter's Litigation Strategy*: Professor Selmi has commented on three aspects of the *Ledbetter* litigation that may have affected the outcome:

> Three aspects of [the] factual background [of the case] are important to understanding the way the case unfolded in the Supreme Court. First, Ms. Ledbetter's case was largely an accidental pay claim. Most of her case was a standard disparate treatment claim focusing on her poor annual reviews, some of which she attributed to retaliation because she had declined to go out with one of her supervisors (who was deceased by the time of the trial). It seems likely that the jury's $3 million punitive damage award was related to the disparate treatment she experienced throughout her career, as opposed to the more isolated pay claim, although it also appears that the evidence may not have clearly differentiated between the two claims. Second, only her pay claim had a timing issue. Her age and sex claims turned on her transfer to the technology engineer position, and those claims were clearly timely, as was probably true of her Equal Pay Act claim. Her Title VII pay claim was problematic because Ledbetter was unable to establish any discrimination relating to a pay decision that was made within 180 days of her EEOC charge, and even if the focus was on the pay checks she received during the statute of limitations, it would have been difficult to justify such a large award. Finally, and of perhaps greatest importance for how the case was resolved in the Supreme

> Court, Ledbetter never explained why she delayed in filing her pay claim—why it took her so long to complain about her salary, particularly since her salary increases were based on annual performance reviews. In fact, in the opinions and briefs, no one appears to have offered any explanation for the delayed filing, which I will suggest was a glaring, and perhaps damning, omission.

Michael Selmi, *The Supreme Court's 2006–2007 Term Employment Law Cases: A Quiet But Revealing Term,* 11 Emp.Rts. & Emp. Pol'y J. 219, 225 (2007). Would you agree? What could account for Ledbetter's delay in filing a charge of pay discrimination?

2. *A Discovery Rule*: Is it true, as Ledbetter claimed, "that pay discrimination is harder to detect than other forms of employment discrimination"? *Ledbetter,* 550 U.S. at 642, 127 S.Ct. at 2177. Justice Ginsburg noted in her dissent that Goodyear kept information about employee compensation confidential and that "it is not unusual * * * for management to decline to publish employee pay levels, or for employees to keep private their own salaries." *Id.* at 649–50, 127 S.Ct. at 2181. Would a discovery rule be appropriate in pay discrimination cases in light of the barriers—particularly in the private sector—to learning about pay disparities? Professor Selmi observed that

> Ledbetter might have argued that the time to file a claim began when the employee knew, or should have known, of the discrimination. After all, the strongest reason to have a different rule for pay decisions is that the plaintiff typically will not know that the pay decision is discriminatory until some time after the decision is made.

Selmi, *supra* Note 1, at 236. In a note in *Ledbetter,* the Court stated: "We have previously declined to address whether Title VII suits are amenable to a discovery rule. Because Ledbetter does not argue that such a rule would change the outcome in her case, we have no occasion to address this issue." *Ledbetter,* 550 U.S. at 642 n.10, 127 S.Ct. at 2177 n.10. Would a discovery rule have helped Ledbetter? Why or why not?

3. *Reasons for Delay in Filing Charges*: Assuming that Ledbetter could have learned of Goodyear's gender-based pay disparities at the time the annual salary decisions were announced, could other reasons explain her—or anyone's—reluctance to file an EEOC charge of discrimination? Justice Ginsburg noted in her dissent:

> The problem of concealed pay discrimination is particularly acute where the disparity arises not because the female employee is flatly denied a raise but because male counterparts are given larger raises. Having received a pay increase, the female employee is unlikely to discern at once that she has experienced an adverse employment decision. She may have little reason even to suspect discrimination until a pattern develops incrementally and she

> ultimately becomes aware of the disparity. Even if an employee suspects that the reason for a comparatively low raise is not performance but sex (or another protected ground), the amount involved may seem too small, or the employer's intent too ambiguous, to make the issue immediately actionable—or winnable.

Ledbetter, 550 U.S. at 651. Consider the insights offered by Professors Brake and Grossman:

> Title VII's requirements for reporting and challenging discrimination reveal a view of "employee initiative"—how employees perceive and respond to discrimination—that is contrary to the way these processes actually take place. The law's timely filing and reporting doctrines take as their worthy claimant a person who quickly and accurately perceives discrimination and responds by promptly challenging it, undeterred by the social costs of complaining or the prospect of retaliation. Many employees do not measure up to these expectations—they consistently "name," "blame," and "claim" less well than courts expect—and are thus unable to invoke the law's substantive protections.

Deborah L. Brake & Joanna L. Grossman, *The Failure of Title VII as a Rights-Claiming System,* 86 N.C. L. Rev. 859, 863 (2008). Did Ledbetter lose because she was not a "worthy claimant"?

4. *"Discrete" Versus "Continuing" Acts*: In *National Railroad Passenger Corp. v. Morgan*, 536 U.S. 101, 122 S.Ct. 2061, 153 L.Ed.2d 106 (2002), the Supreme Court considered how to define the filing period for a hostile environment harassment case. By definition, a hostile environment claim, which is discussed further in **Chapter 10**, requires the plaintiff to demonstrate that there was a pattern of harassing conduct, and the Court held that a charge was timely filed so long as one of the acts that formed the pattern occurred within three hundred days before the date the charge was filed. As reflected in the *Ledbetter* decision, the Court in *Morgan* also distinguished harassment cases from "discrete" acts and determined that the pay decision at issue in *Ledbetter* was a discrete rather than a continuing act.

5. *The Legislative Response—The Lilly Ledbetter Fair Pay Act of 2009*: The *Ledbetter* decision provoked an immediate public reaction with editorials in major newspapers and widespread calls for legislation. The Supreme Court's decision was handed down on May 29, 2007, with Justice Ginsburg's dissent concluding with the statement that "the ball is in Congress' court." *Ledbetter,* 550 U.S. at 661. Congress responded quickly, and on January 29, 2009, the Lilly Ledbetter Fair Pay Act became the first bill President Obama signed into law. *See* The Lilly Ledbetter Fair Pay Act, Pub. L. No. 111–2, 123 Stat. 5 (2009), amending sections 42 U.S.C. §§ 2000e–5, 2000e–16, 2000a, 29 U.S.C. §§ 626, 633a, and 794a. The Act repudiates the Court's decision and amends Title VII so that "an unlawful employment practice occurs, with respect to discrimination in compensation in violation of this title, when a discriminatory compensation decision or other practice is adopted, when an

individual becomes subject to a discriminatory compensation decision or other practice, or when an individual is affected by application of a discriminatory compensation decision or other practice, including each time wages, benefits, or other compensation is paid, resulting in whole or in part from such a decision or other practice." *Id.* Consistent with Title VII more broadly, an employee may seek back pay for up to two years prior to the filing of a charge. To date, the statute has been interpreted by a few courts and generally courts have limited the statute to claims alleging unequal pay. *See* Davis v. Bombardier Transp. Holdings, Inc., 794 F.3d 266 (2d Cir.2015) (rejecting application of statute to a discriminatory demotion decision despite its pay implications); Almond v. Unified Sch. Dist. #501, 665 F.3d 1174 (10th Cir.2011) (confining the statute to a claim of unequal pay and rejecting its application to a discriminatory pay decision). The Seventh Circuit, however, has applied the Ledbetter statute to a race discrimination challenge to a seniority accrual system. See Groesch v. City of Springfield, 635 F.3d 1020 (7th Cir.2011).

6. *Timely Filing and Equitable Considerations*: In *Zipes v. Trans World Airlines, Inc.*, 455 U.S. 385, 102 S.Ct. 1127, 71 L.Ed.2d 234 (1982), the Supreme Court held that "filing a timely charge of discrimination with the EEOC is not a jurisdictional prerequisite to suit in federal court, but a requirement that, like a statute of limitations, is subject to waiver, estoppel, and equitable tolling." *Id.* at 393, 102 S.Ct. at 1132. Courts, however, apply these principles only in limited circumstances: "The federal courts sparingly bestow equitable tolling. Typically, equitable tolling applies only when a litigant's failure to meet a legally-mandated deadline unavoidably arose from circumstances beyond that litigant's control." Graham-Humphreys v. Memphis Brooks Museum of Art, Inc., 209 F.3d 552, 560–61 (6th Cir.2000) (citations omitted). Courts have, for example, found that mental disability can toll the filing deadline. *See* Brown v. Parkchester S. Condos., 287 F.3d 58, 60 (2d Cir.2002). Estoppel may be raised where an employer affirmatively misleads a claimant or intentionally prevents a claimant from filing a charge with the EEOC in a timely fashion. For example, in *Reeb v. Economic Opportunity Atlanta, Inc.*, 516 F.2d 924 (5th Cir.1975), the employer told the plaintiff that she was being terminated because the company did not have the funds to continue her position. More than six months later, the plaintiff learned that her job had not been eliminated but that the position had been filled by a male who was allegedly less qualified. The district court dismissed the plaintiff's complaint on the ground that she had not satisfied the filing requirements. The Fifth Circuit reversed, holding that the statutory period for filing "does not begin to run until the facts which would support a cause of action are apparent or should be apparent to a person with a reasonably prudent regard for his rights." *Id.* at 930; *see also* Jones v. Dillard's, Inc., 331 F.3d 1259 (11th Cir.2003) (following *Reeb* and discussing cases).

7. *Exhaustion Requirement in ADEA Actions*: Unlike Title VII and the ADA, which generally requires exhaustion of administrative remedies before the EEOC, the ADEA provides two separate avenues for relief to employees

who claim they have been the victims of unlawful employment discrimination. First, federal employees may file an administrative complaint pursuant to the rules and regulations that the ADEA authorizes the EEOC to promulgate. 29 U.S.C. § 633a(b). Second, an employee or applicant may bring a civil action for legal and equitable relief after filing a charge with the EEOC and waiting sixty days, or within ninety days following the issuance of a right-to-sue notice. 29 U.S.C. § 633a(d). Importantly, an ADEA plaintiff does not have to wait for a right-to-sue notice before he or she files a court action.

8. *Administrative Exhaustion for Federal Employees*: The procedures required for exhaustion of administrative remedies in employment discrimination cases against federal employers are generally more complex than in other cases. One of the main reasons for the complexity is that federal employees have a broad range of job protections. Most federal employees are protected from political patronage under the merit system. They are also protected from discrimination on the basis of race, color, religion, sex, national origin, age, and disability. The Office of Personnel Management (OPM), the Merit Systems Protection Board (MSPB), and the EEOC have overlapping jurisdiction for job protection for federal sector employees. The administrative exhaustion requirement for federal employees is explored in detail in John P. Stimson, *Unscrambling Federal Merit Protection*, 150 Mil.L.Rev. 165 (1995). Briefly, the process works like this: The federal employee must first exhaust the procedures required by the particular federal agency where the charge arose. The second step involves an appeal to the EEOC, at the conclusion of which the charging party may elect to continue to pursue administrative relief or to file a civil action. If the complainant elects to pursue a civil action under Title VII or the ADA, the time period for filing the action depends on the type of charges before the EEOC. ADEA claimants have more "flexibility" than Title VII or ADA claimants in the administrative exhaustion process. Different exhaustion issues arise in a "mixed" case, which is a claim involving allegations of both a general civil service violation and unlawful employment discrimination.

9. *The Conciliation Requirement*: Under the terms of Title VII, the EEOC is required to seek to conciliate a charge of discrimination after it renders a cause finding. When conciliation failed, a number of employers sought to dismiss the subsequent court action under the theory that the EEOC had failed to engage in good faith settlement negotiations. The EEOC had long argued that its conciliation efforts were not subject to judicial review. In *Mach Mining, LLC v. EEOC*, 135 S.Ct. 1645, 191 L.Ed.2d 607 (2015), the Supreme Court recently addressed the issue and arrived at a compromise position. The Supreme Court held that the EEOC's mandatory duty to conciliate was subject to judicial review but a narrow and deferential form of review. The Court went so far as to note that a sworn affidavit from the EEOC that it had engaged in good faith negotiations "will usually suffice" to satisfy its statutory obligations. *Id.* at 1656.

2. JUDICIAL ENFORCEMENT

Section 706(f)(1) of Title VII, 42 U.S.C. § 2000e–5(f)(1), provides that if the EEOC dismisses a charge, or if, within 180 days of the filing of the charge, the EEOC (or the Attorney General in a case involving a governmental employee) has not filed a civil action or entered into a conciliation agreement, the EEOC must notify the aggrieved party who may then file a civil action within ninety days of receiving such notice. This notice is known as the "right-to-sue letter." The Supreme Court has interpreted the phrase "civil action" in Title VII, § 706(f), 42 U.S.C. § 2000e–5(f), to mean a trial *de novo*, so that the EEOC's administrative determination has no binding effect in a judicial proceeding. *See* Chandler v. Roudebush, 425 U.S. 840, 844–45, 96 S.Ct. 1949, 1952, 48 L.Ed.2d 416 (1976) (federal employees); McDonnell Douglas Corp. v. Green, 411 U.S. 792, 798–99, 93 S.Ct. 1817, 1822, 36 L.Ed.2d 668 (1973) (private employees). Both federal and state courts of competent jurisdiction are authorized to exercise jurisdiction over Title VII and ADA claims. *See* Yellow Freight System, Inc. v. Donnelly, 494 U.S. 820, 821, 110 S.Ct. 1566, 1567, 108 L.Ed.2d 834 (1990).

a. *Timely filing in court*: Receipt of the right-to-sue letter triggers the beginning of the ninety days within which an aggrieved party must file a civil action in state or federal court. This statutory notice requirement has raised a number of issues. When the EEOC determines that it will likely be unable to process a charge within the 180-day period, a long-standing regulation authorizes sending out a right-to-sue letter prior to the expiration of the 180 days. 29 C.F.R. § 1601.28(a)(2). The courts are divided on the validity of this regulation. Some courts have upheld the regulation on the ground that the practice is not expressly prohibited under Title VII or that it protects aggrieved parties when the EEOC, a perpetually underfunded agency, clearly will not be able to investigate a charge within the 180-day period. *See, e.g.*, Walker v. United Parcel Serv., 240 F.3d 1268, 1276–77 (10th Cir.2001). Other courts have held that the regulation is invalid on the ground that it undermines the congressional goal of achieving nonadversarial resolution of employment discrimination claims or, alternatively, that the practice will inundate the federal courts with frivolous discrimination lawsuits. *See, e.g.*, Martini v. Fed. Nat'l Mtg. Ass'n (Fannie Mae), 178 F.3d 1336 (D.C.Cir.1999) (invalidating the regulation and discussing the circuit split). For a recent case invalidating the regulation and collecting cases see Taylor v. Cardiology Clinic, Inc., No. 4:14–Cv–0046, 2015 WL 770439 at *X (W.D. Va. Feb. 24, 2015).

The courts have adopted different rules on when the 90-day filing period begins to run after the EEOC sends the notice-of-right-to-sue letter. For example, the Seventh Circuit has adopted an actual notice rule, but the rule does not apply to a plaintiff who fails to receive actual notice through her own fault. *See* Houston v. Sidley & Austin, 185 F.3d 837 (7th Cir.1999). In *Harvey v. City of New Bern Police Department*, 813 F.2d 652 (4th Cir.1987), the Fourth Circuit expressly rejected the Seventh Circuit's rule and adopted instead a "reasonable short time" rule within which a plaintiff must pick up the right-to-sue notice after receiving notice from the Post Office that a letter is waiting for her. In *Ebbert v. DaimlerChrysler Corp.*, 319 F.3d 103 (3d Cir.2003), the court held that oral notice from the EEOC may trigger the 90-day filing rule if it is equivalent to written notice from the EEOC. If an attorney has been designated as the agent of the plaintiff to receive the EEOC notice, the 90-day period begins to run when the attorney receives the notice. *See* Jones v. Madison Serv. Corp., 744 F.2d 1309, 1313–14 (7th Cir.1984).

The 90-day rule is not jurisdictional, *Hill v. John Chezik Imports*, 869 F.2d 1122 (8th Cir.1989), and the Supreme Court has stated that equitable tolling may be justified where the notice from the EEOC is inadequate, where a motion for appointment of counsel is pending, where the court has led the plaintiff to believe all statutory requirements for bringing suit have been satisfied, or where the defendant's misconduct has "lulled the plaintiff into inaction." Baldwin County Welcome Ctr. v. Brown, 466 U.S. 147, 151, 104 S.Ct. 1723, 1725–26, 80 L.Ed.2d 196 (1984).

The doctrine of laches may bar suit if an aggrieved party unreasonably delays requesting the right-to-sue notice or the notice is returned to the EEOC because the plaintiff failed to provide the EEOC with a current address and the defendant is prejudiced by the plaintiff's conduct. *See, e.g.*, Jeffries v. Chicago Transit Auth., 770 F.2d 676 (7th Cir.1985) (laches bar suit where plaintiff filed complaint in court more than ten years after filing the charge with the EEOC), *cert. denied*, 475 U.S. 1050, 106 S.Ct. 1273, 89 L.Ed.2d 581 (1986). The EEOC is not subject to the same timely filing requirements as private parties, but in *Occidental Life Insurance Co. v. EEOC*, 432 U.S. 355, 97 S.Ct. 2447, 53 L.Ed.2d 402 (1977), the Supreme Court held that suits filed by the EEOC may be dismissed under the laches doctrine. *See, e.g.*, EEOC v. Propak Logistics, Inc., 746 F.3d 145 (4th Cir.2014) (upholding award of attorney's fees against EEOC in part based on a laches defense).

b. *What constitutes a complaint?*: In *Baldwin County Welcome Center v. Brown*, 466 U.S. 147, 104 S.Ct. 1723, 80 L.Ed.2d 196 (1984) (per curiam), a pro se litigant filed his right-to-sue letter in the district court because he had difficulty obtaining an attorney to represent him. The plaintiff argued that the filing of the right-to-sue letter tolled the running of the 90-day filing period. The Court disagreed, holding that the filing of the notice of right-to-sue does not toll the running of the 90-day filing requirement because the statutory notice, standing alone, fails to satisfy Rule 8(a) of the Federal Rules of Civil Procedure. Under Rule 8(a), a complaint must state the basis of jurisdiction, set forth a short, plain statement of the facts, and a prayer for relief. Because a right-to-sue letter does not contain a statement of the factual basis of the claim, it cannot qualify as a complaint under Rule 8(a). *Id.* at 149, 104 S.Ct. at 1723.

In *Ashcroft v. Iqbal*, 556 U.S. 662, 129 S.Ct. 1937, 173 L.Ed.2d 868 (2009), the Supreme Court held that conclusory allegations in a complaint are not entitled to an assumption of truth and therefore should not be considered in deciding whether the plaintiff has adequately stated a claim for relief. *Id.* at 679, 129 S.Ct. at 1950. The *Iqbal* opinion concluded that "[t]hreadbare recitals of elements of a cause of action, supported by mere conclusory statements, do not suffice," instead, the district court should only consider "well-pleaded factual allegations." *Id. See also* Bell Atlantic v. Twombly, 550 U.S. 544, 554–60, 127 S.Ct. 1955, 1964–67, 167 L.Ed.2d 929 (2007). Neither *Aschcroft* nor *Twombly* were employment discrimination cases, but they reflect a more stringent interpretation of the pleading standards under the Federal Rules of Civil Procedure, which may have an effect on many civil cases, including employment discrimination claims. *See, e.g.*, Fowler v. UPMC Shadyside, 578 F.3d 203, 209–11 (3d Cir.2009) (discussing effect of *Ashcroft* and *Twombly* on the standard of pleading in employment discrimination cases). The Supreme Court cases have sparked a lively literature on their effect on employment discrimination cases. For a sampling see Charles A. Sullivan, *Plausibly Pleading Employment Discrimination*, 52 Wm. & Mary L. Rev. 1613 (2011); Suja Thomas, *Oddball Iqbal & Twombly and Employment Discrimination*, 2011 U. Ill. L. Rev. 215 (2011); Michael J. Zimmer, *Title VII's Last Hurrah: Can Discrimination Be Plausibly Pled?* 2014 U. Chi. L. F. 19.

c. *Suits by the EEOC and the Attorney General*: The EEOC has authority to bring civil actions in its own name. Title VII § 706, 42 U.S.C. § 2000e–5. The Court affirmed the authority of the EEOC to bring suits in its own name, independent of the rights or the actions or inactions of alleged discriminatees, in *EEOC v. Waffle House*, 534 U.S. 279, 122 S.Ct. 754, 151 L.Ed.2d 755 (2002), which is discussed in Chapter 16. Also, the Attorney General is authorized to bring civil actions against governmental employers who are covered by the relevant statutory scheme. Title VII, § 707, 42 U.S.C. § 2000e–6.

D. COVERAGE UNDER LAWS PROHIBITING DISCRIMINATION IN EMPLOYMENT

A fundamental policy objective of laws prohibiting discrimination in employment is to make "equality" a reality in the workplace. To accomplish this objective, the basic mandate of these laws is to make it unlawful for employers, employment agencies, and labor organizations to discriminate against applicants and employees because of such individuals' race, color, religion, sex, national origin, age, or disability. Because Congress left undefined many key terms in these statutes, a recurring issue in employment discrimination law is how to define the boundaries of each category or status that is protected under federal employment discrimination statutes. Of course, determining whether an individual is protected under the Age Discrimination in Employment Act is rarely, if ever, an issue because the protected class is defined as individuals forty years of age and over. The meaning of race, sex, or disability, unlike chronological age, is not as readily ascertained. How these terms are defined is important for several reasons, for example, identifying those who are the beneficiaries of these laws, complying with statutory record-keeping requirements, and collecting and analyzing statistical data as evidence in employment discrimination cases. In addition, Congress failed to provide a meaningful definition of employer, perhaps the most important entity that is subject to the basic mandate of these laws.

The following materials briefly explore some recurring issues regarding coverage of the antidiscrimination laws that arise because of the absence of statutory definitions of several key terms. First, by focusing on the meaning of "race" and "color," we begin to grapple with the problem of identifying the individuals or groups who are protected from unlawful employment discrimination. (The meaning of "sex" is discussed in Chapters 7, 8, 9, and 10; "religion" in Chapter 11; "national origin" in Chapter 12; and "disability" in Chapter 14.) Next, we briefly explore the problem of defining "employee" and the related issue of distinguishing between "employer" and "employee." Another issue is whether an employer's "agent" can be held individually liable for the unlawful employment decisions he makes for his "employer." We then explore the meaning of employment "practice," because unless plaintiff's claim falls within the meaning of "terms, conditions, or privileges of employment" that practice is not unlawful. Finally, we briefly examine the role of private-sector unions as statutory representatives of employees and the circumstances under which unions can be held liable for employment discrimination in their capacities as either "employers" or "labor organizations." A key term that also is not defined in federal statutes, other than the ADA, is *discrimination*. The problem of defining the meaning of discrimination is pervasive throughout most of the remaining chapters in this book.

1. THE MEANING OF "RACE" AND "COLOR"

The primary reason Congress enacted Title VII was to provide a remedy for African Americans who have been the victims of racial discrimination in employment. The statutory term Congress selected in order to achieve this objective, however, is race-neutral; the term is just plain "race." But what is "race"? And who should decide who belongs to which "race"? In *McDonald v. Santa Fe Trail Transportation Co.*, 427 U.S. 273, 96 S.Ct. 2574, 49 L.Ed.2d 493 (1976), the Supreme Court held that whites as well as blacks are protected from racial discrimination under Title VII and § 1981, even though § 1981 refers to "white citizens." The Supreme Court's most comprehensive exploration of the meaning of the term "race" in employment discrimination law is found in the following decision, which arose under § 1981.

ST. FRANCIS COLLEGE V. AL-KHAZRAJI

Supreme Court of the United States, 1987.
481 U.S. 604, 107 S.Ct. 2022, 95 L.Ed.2d 582.

JUSTICE WHITE delivered the opinion of the Court.

[The issue in *Al-Khazraji* was whether the plaintiff, a citizen of the United States who was born in Iraq, could bring a race discrimination claim under § 1981.]

Although § 1981 does not itself use the word "race," the Court has construed the section to forbid all "racial" discrimination in the making of private as well as public contracts. Runyon v. McCrary, 427 U.S. 160, 168, 174–175, 96 S.Ct. 2586, 49 L.Ed.2d 415 (1976). * * *

Petitioners contend that respondent is a Caucasian and cannot allege the kind of discrimination § 1981 forbids. Concededly, *McDonald v. Santa Fe Trail Transportation Co.*, 427 U.S. 273, 96 S.Ct. 2574, 49 L.Ed.2d 493 (1976), held that white persons could maintain a § 1981 suit; but that suit involved alleged discrimination against a white person in favor of a black, and petitioner submits that the section does not encompass claims of discrimination by one Caucasian against another. * * *

Petitioner's submission rests on the assumption that all those who might be deemed Caucasians today were thought to be of the same race when § 1981 became law in the 19th century; and it may be that a variety of ethnic groups, including Arabs, are now considered to be within the Caucasian race.[4] The understanding of "race" in the 19th century,

[4] There is a common popular understanding that there are three major human races—Caucasoid, Mongoloid, and Negroid. Many modern biologists and anthropologists, however, criticize racial classifications as arbitrary and of little use in understanding the variability of human beings. It is said that genetically homogeneous populations do not exist and traits are not discontinuous between populations; therefore, a population can only be described in terms of relative frequencies of various traits. Clear-cut categories do not exist. The particular traits which have generally been chosen to characterize races have been criticized as having little biological significance. It has been found that differences between individuals of the same race are often greater than the differences between the "average" individuals of different races. These observations and others have led some, but not all, scientists to conclude that racial classifications are for the most part sociopolitical, rather than biological, in nature.

however, was different. Plainly, all those who might be deemed Caucasian today were not thought to be of the same race at the time § 1981 became law.

In the middle years of the 19th century, dictionaries commonly referred to race as a "continued series of descendants from a parent who is called the *stock*," N. Webster, An American Dictionary of the English Language 666 (New York 1830) (emphasis in original), "the lineage of a family," 2 N. Webster, A Dictionary of the English Language 411 (New Haven 1841), or "descendants of a common ancestor," J. Donald, Chambers' Etymological Dictionary of the English Language 415 (London 1871). * * * It was not until the 20th century that dictionaries began referring to the Caucasian, Mongolian, and Negro races, 8 The Century Dictionary and Cyclopedia 4926 (1911), or to race as involving divisions of mankind based upon different physical characteristics. Webster's Collegiate Dictionary 794 (3d ed. 1916). * * *

Encyclopedias of the 19th century also described race in terms of ethnic groups, which is a narrower concept of race than petitioners urge. Encyclopedia Americana in 1858, for example, referred to various races such as Finns, vol. 5, p. 123, Gypsies, 6 *id.*, at 123, Basques, 1 *id.*, at 602, and Hebrews, 6 *id.*, at 209. The 1863 version of the New American Cyclopaedia divided the Arabs into a number of subsidiary races, vol. 1, p. 739; represented the Hebrews as of the Semitic race, 9 *id.*, at 27, and identified numerous other groups as constituting races, including Swedes, 15 *id.*, at 216, Norwegians, 12 *id.*, at 410, Germans, 8 *id.*, at 200, Greeks, 8 *id.*, at 438, Finns, 7 *id.*, at 513, Italians, 9 *id.*, at 644–645 (referring to mixture of different races), Spanish, 14 *id.*, at 804, Mongolians, 11 *id.*, at 651, Russians, 14 *id.*, at 226, and the like. The Ninth edition of the Encyclopedia Britannica also referred to Arabs, vol. 2, p. 245 (1878), Jews, 13 *id.*, at 685 (1881), and other ethnic groups such as Germans, 10 *id.*, at 473 (1879), Hungarians, 12 *id.*, at 365 (1880), and Greeks, 11 *id.*, at 83 (1880), as separate races.

These dictionary and encyclopedic sources are somewhat diverse, but it is clear that they do not support the claim that for the purposes of § 1981, Arabs, Englishmen, Germans, and certain other ethnic groups are to be considered a single race. We would expect the legislative history of § 1981 to reflect this common understanding, which it surely does. The debates are replete with references to the Scandinavian races, Cong. Globe, 39th Cong., 1st Sess., 499 (1866) (remarks of Sen. Cowan), as well as the Chinese, *id.*, at 523 (remarks of Sen. Davis), Latin, *id.*, at 238 (remarks of Rep. Kasson during debate of home rule for the District of Columbia), Spanish, *id.*, at 251 (remarks of Sen. Davis during debate of District of Columbia suffrage), and Anglo-Saxon races, *id.*, at 542 (remarks of Rep. Dawson). Jews, *ibid.*, Mexicans, *see ibid.* (remarks of Rep. Dawson), blacks, *passim*, and Mongolians, *id.*, at 498 (remarks of

Sen. Cowan), were similarly categorized. Gypsies were referred to as a race. *ibid.* (remarks of Sen. Cowan). * * *

The history of the 1870 Act reflects similar understanding of what groups Congress intended to protect from intentional discrimination. It is clear, for example, that the civil rights sections of the 1870 Act provided protection for immigrant groups such as the Chinese. This view was expressed in the Senate. Cong. Globe, 41st Cong., 2d Sess., 1536, 3658, 3808 (1870). In the House, Representative Bingham described § 16 of the Act, part of the authority for § 1981, as declaring "that the States shall not hereafter discriminate against the immigrant from China and in favor of the immigrant from Prussia, nor against the immigrant from France and in favor of the immigrant from Ireland."

Based on the history of § 1981, we have little trouble in concluding that Congress intended to protect from discrimination identifiable classes of persons who are subjected to intentional discrimination solely because of their ancestry or ethnic characteristics. Such discrimination is racial discrimination that Congress intended § 1981 to forbid, whether or not it would be classified as racial in terms of modern scientific theory. The Court of Appeals was thus quite right in holding that § 1981, "at a minimum," reaches discrimination against an individual "because he or she is genetically part of an ethnically and physiognomically distinctive subgrouping of homo sapiens." It is clear from our holding, however, that a distinctive physiognomy is not essential to qualify for § 1981 protection.

* * *

NOTES AND QUESTIONS

1. Should the *Al-Khazraji* definition of "race" apply equally to claims brought under § 1981 and Title VII? For example, should a Jewish employee be allowed to allege race discrimination in a Title VII claim solely on the ground that she is Jewish?

2. Do the terms "race" and "ethnicity" refer to natural or socially constructed categories, or a combination of both? Consider the following perspective:

> [W]hat constitutes a race and how one recognizes a racial difference are culturally determined. Whether two individuals regard themselves as of the same or of different races depends not on the degree of similarity of their genetic material but on whether history, tradition, and personal training and experiences have brought them to regard themselves as belonging to the same group or to different groups. Since all human beings are of one species and since all populations tend to merge when they exist in contact, group differentiation will be based on cultural behavior and not on genetic difference.

James C. King, The Biology of Race 156–57 (1981). For further discussion of race as being socially constructed, *see* Michael Omi & Howard Winnant, Racial Formation in the United States: From the 1960s to the 1990s (2d ed. 1994); Ian F. Haney Lopez, *The Social Construction of Race: Some Observations on Illusion, Fabrication, and Choice*, 29 Harv.C.R.–C.L.L.Rev. 1 (1994). Describing race as a social construction does not diminish its social importance. As Professor Alex Johnson has noted, "Quite the contrary, race is an intractable force in American society touching every facet of day-to-day American life—often affecting where one goes to school, the job opportunities presented, who one marries, where one lives, the health care one receives, and even where one is interred following death. Race, in other words, continues to matter in our society, whether its definitional base is scientific or not." Alex M. Johnson, Jr., *The Re-Emergence of Race as a Biological Category: The Societal Implications—Reaffirmation of Race*, 94 Iowa L.Rev. 1547, 1562–63 (2009) (citations omitted).

3. Should an employer be permitted to challenge a plaintiff's characterization of his own racial identity? This has clear implications for the affirmative action debate **(see** Chapter 15). Consider the following: In 1975, twin brothers, Paul and Philip Malone, took a civil service competitive exam for jobs with the fire department in Boston, Massachusetts. The Malone brothers were fair-haired and light-skinned, and they had Caucasian features; moreover, they listed their race as "white" on their initial job applications. They both performed poorly on the 1975 exam and were denied employment. In 1977, they took the civil service exam again, but this time they identified their race as "black." At the time of the second exam, Boston had agreed to a court-ordered affirmative action plan in order to increase the number of blacks in the fire department, and the Malones wanted to benefit from this affirmative action plan. With the scores the Malones received in 1977, they would not have qualified if they were treated as white candidates, but based on their self-identification as black, they could be hired under the affirmative action program. What factors should be relevant in deciding whether the Malones are white or black: (1) visual observations of their features; (2) appropriate documentation, such as birth certificates, which establish ancestry; or (3) evidence that they or their families hold themselves out to be black and are considered to be black in their community? The Malones' evidence that they are "black" consisted of a questionable and inconclusive photograph of a woman alleged to be the Malones' maternal great grandmother and the Malones' claim that they had been told that she was black. Other evidence, however, showed that Malone family members had consistently held themselves out as white for three generations. Should the Malones have been denied employment on the basis of "racial fraud"? The Malones' case is discussed in the Luther Wright, Jr., Note, *Who's Black, Who's White, and Who Cares: Reconceptualizing the United States's Definition of Race and Racial Classifications*, 48 Vand.L.Rev. 513 (1995).

4. In *Bennun v. Rutgers State University*, 941 F.2d 154 (3d Cir.1991), the plaintiff claimed that he had been discriminated against because he was

Hispanic. In an affidavit, the plaintiff asserted "that his father was a Sephardic Jew who, like all Sephardic Jews, traced his lineage to those Jews who were expelled from Spain during the Spanish Inquisition." *Id.* at 172. The district court, however, based its finding that the plaintiff was Hispanic on the following facts: the plaintiff was born in Argentina, he believed that he was Hispanic, he had adopted Spanish cultural traditions, and he spoke Spanish at home. The court of appeals rejected the defendant's argument that the plaintiff was not Hispanic because the district court judge, based on his opportunity to observe the plaintiff's "appearance, speech and mannerisms," had ruled in favor of the plaintiff on the issue. *Id.* at 173. On the issue of how plaintiff's status as a protected class member should be determined under Title VII, the Third Circuit said:

> We think unlawful discrimination must be based on [the plaintiff's] objective appearance to others, not his subjective feeling about his own ethnicity. Discrimination stems from a reliance on immaterial outward appearances that stereotype an individual with imagined, usually undesirable, characteristics thought to be common to members of the group that shares these superficial traits. It results in a stubborn refusal to judge a person on his merits as a human being. Our various statutes against discrimination express the policy that this refusal to judge people who belong to various, particularly disadvantaged, groups is too costly to be tolerated in a society committed to equal individual liberty and opportunity.

Id. Do you agree with the standard adopted by Third Circuit in *Bennun*? Under *Bennun,* is it irrelevant what race the plaintiff considers himself to be? In *EEOC v. Trans State Airlines*, 462 F.3d 987, 992 (8th Cir.2006), the plaintiff argued that his name, Mohammed Hussein, was so connected with "being Muslim and Arab" that he should be permitted to proceed on a Title VII claim of discrimination on the basis of race or national origin even though he was not an Arab. The court rejected his argument, noting that it was based on the premise that the defendant's agent would have necessarily engaged in "inaccurate stereotyping." *Id.*

An important study that sought to measure labor market discrimination based on names demonstrated that those with names associated with whites received 50% more call back interviews than those with names that are associated with African Americans. *See* Marianne Bertrand & Sedhil Mullainathan, *Are Emily and Greg More Employable than Lakisha & Jamal? A Field Experiment on Labor Market Discrimination*, 94 Am.Econ.Rev. 991 (2004). The authors made their name selections based on birth certificate data and submitted resumes to employers that varied only by the names on the resume. The authors also found that an African-American sounding name largely nullified the effect of a higher quality resume. For an argument that an individual should be able to pursue a claim if they are treated as if they are African American see Angela Onwuachi-Willig & Mario L. Barnes, *By Any Other Name?: On Being "Regarded As" Black, and Why Title VII Should Apply Even If Lakisha & Jamal Are White*, 2005 Wis.L.Rev. 1283. *See also*

Camille Gear Rich, *Elective Race: Recognizing Race Discrimination in an Era of Self-Identification*, 102 Geo. L.J. 1501 (2014).

5. *The Meaning of "Color"*: Title VII also prohibits discrimination on the basis of "color." Title VII, § 703(a), 42 U.S.C. § 2000e–2(a). How is "color" different from "race"? Consider the following case: Employees in the Internal Revenue Service (IRS) office in which the plaintiff works are predominantly black. The plaintiff is a light-skinned black person; her supervisor is a dark-skinned black person. Plaintiff sues the IRS under Title VII and § 1981 alleging that her supervisor treats her differently because of her light complexion. Should her claim be treated as an allegation of discrimination based on "race" or based on "color?" *See* Walker v. Sec'y of the Treas., IRS, 713 F.Supp. 403 (N.D.Ga.1989). *See also* Santiago v. Stryker Corp., 10 F.Supp.2d 93, 97 (D.P.R.1998) (Puerto Rican plaintiff alleged that he was discriminated against based on his skin color because person who received job, although Puerto Rican, was white); Ali v. National Bank of Pakistan, 508 F.Supp. 611 (S.D.N.Y.1981) (plaintiff, a light-skinned individual, whose origins are in Punjab, brought an action under Title VII alleging discrimination on the basis of "color" by other dark-skinned individuals who also were from India).

6. In her article, *Shades of Brown: The Law of Skin Color*, 49 Duke L.J. 1487 (2000), Professor Trina Jones argued that because "antidiscrimination efforts have focused primarily on race, the courts have largely ignored discrimination within racial classifications on the basis of skin color," and that " 'colorism' is a present reality" that "will assume increasing significance in the future." *Id.* at 1487. She further argued that "color hierarchy in the U.S. is relatively easy to define at its extremes"—whites at the top and blacks at the bottom. *Id.* at 1555. A fundamental question she raised is whether "there [is] a danger that one segment of the race may move forward while another segment is left behind." *Id.* at 1554. What are the implications of her arguments for the multiracial-categorization movement?

NOTES: INTERSECTIONALITY

1. Intersectionality theory posits that individuals have multiple identities that are not addressed by legal doctrines based solely on a single identity or status. For example, in a well-known article on the multi-dimensionality of "Black women," Professor Kimberlé Crenshaw criticized the judicial developments under Title VII for requiring "Black women" to seek relief based on either race or sex but not both. Kimberlé Crenshaw, *Demarginalizing the Intersection of Race and Sex: A Black Feminist Critique of Antidiscrimination Doctrine, Feminist Theory and Antiracist Politics*, 1989 U.Chi. Legal F. 139. She argued that black women should be recognized as a separate protected class under the statute because the discrimination that black women experience is different in kind and degree from the discrimination faced by white women or black men. Professor Crenshaw observed that

> in race discrimination cases, discrimination tends to be viewed in terms of sex- or class-privileged Blacks; in sex discrimination cases, the focus is on race and class-privileged women.
>
> This focus on the most privileged group members marginalizes those who are multiply-burdened and obscures claims that cannot be understood as resulting from discrete sources of discrimination. I suggest further that this focus on otherwise-privileged group members creates a distorted analysis of racism and sexism because the operative conceptions of race and sex become grounded in experiences that actually represent only a subset of a much more complex phenomenon.

Id. at 140.

2. Several courts have been willing to embrace intersectionality theory in Title VII cases. One of the leading cases is *Jefferies v. Harris County Community Action Association*, 615 F.2d 1025 (5th Cir.1980), a Title VII employment discrimination case brought by a black female. The issue in *Jefferies* was whether the district court erred in refusing to recognize a protected subclass of black females. The district court viewed the plaintiff as having membership in two separate protected classes: race and sex. First, viewing the plaintiff as a member of the black race, the court rejected her race discrimination claim because a black male had been given the at-issue job. Then, viewing the plaintiff as a female, the district court found that statistical evidence showed no discrimination against women. The court of appeals reversed, holding that the plaintiff's claim should have been evaluated on the basis of her status as a *black female*.

> We agree with Jefferies that the district court improperly failed to address her claim of discrimination on the basis of both race and sex. The essence of Jefferies' argument is that an employer should not escape from liability for discrimination against black females by a showing that it does not discriminate against blacks and that it does not discriminate against females. We agree that discrimination against black females can exist even in the absence of discrimination against black men or white women.
>
> * * * In the absence of a clear expression by Congress that it did not intend to provide protection against discrimination directed especially toward black women as a class separate and distinct from the class of women and the class of blacks, we cannot condone a result which leaves black women without a viable Title VII remedy.

Id. at 1032.

The *Jefferies* court implicitly recognized that black women throughout American history have worked in subservient roles and have been subjected to adverse conditions that have not been imposed upon either black men or white women. *See id.* at 1034. The Tenth Circuit followed *Jefferies* in *Hicks v. Gates Rubber Co.*, 833 F.2d 1406 (10th Cir.1987).

In *Degraffenreid v. General Motors*, 413 F.Supp. 142 (E.D.Mo.1976), *aff'd in part, rev'd in part on other grounds*, 558 F.2d 480 (8th Cir.1977), the district court declined to recognize black women as a protected subclass. The court reasoned that to do so would create a "super-remedy," which would give black women additional avenues of relief not envisioned by the drafters of Title VII. The court argued that "[t]he prospect of the creation of new classes of protected minorities, governed only by the mathematical principles of permutation and combination, raises the prospect of opening the hackneyed Pandora's box." *Id.* at 145. On appeal, the Eighth Circuit did not reach the intersectionality issue; nevertheless, Judge Bright stated, in dicta, "[w]e do not subscribe entirely to the district court's reasoning in rejecting [plaintiffs'] claims of race and sex discrimination under Title VII." *DeGraffenreid*, 558 F.2d at 484. What is your view on whether recognizing black women as a separate subgroup protected under employment discrimination laws destabilizes or undermines the traditional categories of "race" and "sex"? *See also* Westmoreland v. Prince George's County, 876 F. Supp. 2d 594, 604 (D. Md. 2012) ("The Court joins the evolving body of authority and concludes that intersectional claims based on sex and race are generally cognizable under Title VII" in a case involving an African-American female alleging discrimination in the fire department).

3. Should the courts recognize a subclass of Asian women under the intersectionality theory? Relying on *Jefferies*, the Ninth Circuit in *Lam v. University of Hawai'i*, 40 F.3d 1551, 1562 (9th Cir.1994), held yes, because "[l]ike other subclasses under Title VII, Asian women are subject to a set of stereotypes and assumptions shared neither by Asian men nor by white women," and they may be targeted for discrimination even in the absence of discrimination against Asian men or white women.

4. Should black men be recognized as a subgroup that is separate and distinct from black women and white men? Consider the following: In *Bradley v. Pizzaco of Nebraska, Inc.*, 7 F.3d 795 (8th Cir.1993), a black male sued his employer, claiming that he was discharged from his job delivering pizzas for failure to comply with the employer's no-beard policy. The evidence showed that plaintiff suffers from psuedofolliculitis barbae (PFB), a skin condition affecting approximately 50 percent of black males, half of whom cannot shave because of the condition. As a general rule, white males do not suffer from the same medical condition. For arguments why black men should be recognized as a separate subclass protected by Title VII, *see* Floyd D. Weatherspoon, *Remedying Employment Discrimination Against African-American Males: Stereotypical Biases Engender a Case of Race Plus Sex Discrimination*, 36 Washburn L.J. 23 (1996); Note, *Invisible Man: Black and Male Under Title VII*, 104 Harv.L.Rev. 749 (1991).

5. There is an extensive body of scholarly literature on intersectionality theory in discrimination law that challenges the traditional binary racial paradigm in the discourse on race and sex. *See, e.g.*, Regina Austin, *Sapphire Bound!*, 1989 Wis.L.Rev. 539; Mary Eaton, *At the Intersection of Gender and Sexual Orientation: Toward Lesbian*

Jurisprudence, 3 S.Cal.Rev.L. & Women's Stud. 183 (1994); Trina Grillo, *Anti-Essentialism and Intersectionality: Tools to Dismantle the Master's House*, 10 Berkeley Women's L.J. 16 (1995); Darren Leonard Hutchinson, *Identity Crisis: "Intersectionality," "Multidimenstionality," and the Development of an Adequate Theory of Subordination*, 6 Mich. J. Race & L. 285 (2001); Jennifer C. Nash, *"Home Truths" On Intersectionality*, 23 Yale J. L. & Feminism 445 (2011); Judy Scales-Trent, *Black Women and the Constitution: Finding Our Place, Asserting Our Rights*, 24 Harv.C.R.–C.L.L.Rev. 9 (1989). Some of the more recent scholarship has expanded to other areas of interest. See, e.g., Shahar F. Aziz, *Coercive Assimilation: The Perils of Muslim Women's Identity Performance in the Workplace*, 20 Mich. J. Race & L. 1 (2014); Jourdan Day, *Closing the Loophole—Why Intersectional Claims Are Needed to Address Discrimination Against Older Women*, 75 Ohio St. L.J. 447 (2014); Leticia Saucedo, Intersectionality, *Multidimensionality, Latino Immigrant Workers and Title VII*, 67 SMU L. Rev. 257 (2014).

2. WHO IS AN "EMPLOYEE"?

Whether a plaintiff is an "employee" generally is not an issue in the majority of employment discrimination cases, but it is now being raised more frequently. For example, a number of cases have addressed the issue of whether partners or other professionals are employees under laws prohibiting discrimination. *See, e.g.*, Serapion v. Martinez Odell & Calabria, 119 F.3d 982 (1st Cir.1997) (holding that a former law partner who brought a sex discrimination claim was found to be a proprietor, not an "employee," under Title VII); Cilecek v. Inova Health Sys. Servs., 115 F.3d 256 (4th Cir.1997) (holding that a doctor who contracted to perform medical services at hospital emergency room was not an "employee" under Title VII but an independent contractor); Simpson v. Ernst & Young, 100 F.3d 436 (6th Cir.1996) (holding that an accountant, who had title of partner but lacked authority usually associated with partnership status, was an "employee" under the ADEA). Lower courts adopted different tests to determine whether an individual was an employee under federal laws prohibiting discrimination in employment. In the following case, the Supreme Court granted certiorari to resolve a circuit split on the appropriate test to determine whether an individual is an "employee" under federal antidiscrimination statutes.

CLACKAMAS GASTROENTEROLOGY ASSOCIATES V. WELLS

Supreme Court of the United States, 2003.
538 U.S. 440, 123 S.Ct. 1673, 155 L.Ed.2d 615.

JUSTICE STEVENS delivered the opinion of the Court.

The Americans with Disabilities Act of 1990 (ADA or Act), 104 Stat. 327, as amended, 42 U.S.C. § 12101 *et seq.*, like other federal antidiscrimination legislation, is inapplicable to very small businesses.

Under the ADA an "employer" is not covered unless its workforce includes "15 or more employees for each working day in each of 20 or more calendar weeks in the current or preceding calendar year." § 12111(5). The question in this case is whether four physicians actively engaged in medical practice as shareholders and directors of a professional corporation should be counted as "employees."

I

Petitioner, Clackamas Gastroenterology Associates, P. C., is a medical clinic in Oregon. It employed respondent, Deborah Anne Wells, as a bookkeeper from 1986 until 1997. After her termination, she brought this action against the clinic alleging unlawful discrimination on the basis of disability under Title I of the ADA. Petitioner denied that it was covered by the Act and moved for summary judgment, asserting that it did not have 15 or more employees for the 20 weeks required by the statute. It is undisputed that the accuracy of that assertion depends on whether the four physician-shareholders who own the professional corporation and constitute its board of directors are counted as employees.

* * *

II

"We have often been asked to construe the meaning of 'employee' where the statute containing the term does not helpfully define it." *Nationwide Mut. Ins. Co. v. Darden,* 503 U.S. 318, 322, 112 S.Ct. 1344, 117 L.Ed.2d 581 (1992). The definition of the term in the ADA simply states that an "employee" is "an individual employed by an employer." 42 U.S.C. § 12111(4). That surely qualifies as a mere "nominal definition" that is "completely circular and explains nothing." *Darden,* 503 U.S., at 323, 112 S.Ct. 1344. As we explained in *Darden,* our cases construing similar language give us guidance on how best to fill the gap in the statutory text.

In *Darden* we were faced with the question whether an insurance salesman was an independent contractor or an "employee" covered by the Employee Retirement Income Security Act of 1974 (ERISA). Because ERISA's definition of "employee" was "completely circular," 503 U.S., at 323, 112 S.Ct. 1344, we followed the same general approach that we had previously used in deciding whether a sculptor was an "employee" within the meaning of the Copyright Act of 1976, see Community for Creative Non-Violence v. Reid, 490 U.S. 730 (1989), and we adopted a common-law test for determining who qualifies as an "employee" under ERISA.[5]

---

[5] *Darden* described the common-law test for determining whether a hired party is an employee as follows:

> " '[W]e consider the hiring party's right to control the manner and means by which the product is accomplished. Among the other factors relevant to this inquiry are the

Quoting *Reid,* 490 U.S., at 739–740, 109 S.Ct. 2166, we explained that " 'when Congress has used the term "employee" without defining it, we have concluded that Congress intended to describe the conventional master-servant relationship as understood by common-law agency doctrine.' " *Darden,* 503 U.S., at 322–323, 112 S.Ct. 1344.

Rather than looking to the common law, petitioner argues that courts should determine whether a shareholder-director of a professional corporation is an "employee" by asking whether the shareholder-director is, in reality, a "partner." * * * The question whether a shareholder-director is an employee, however, cannot be answered by asking whether the shareholder-director appears to be the functional equivalent of a partner. Today there are partnerships that include hundreds of members, some of whom may well qualify as "employees" because control is concentrated in a small number of managing partners. Cf. *Hishon v. King & Spalding,* 467 U.S. 69, 80, n.2, 104 S.Ct. 2229, 81 L.Ed.2d 59 (1984) (Powell, J., concurring) ("[A]n employer may not evade the strictures of Title VII simply by labeling its employees as 'partners' ") * * *. Thus, asking whether shareholder-directors are partners—rather than asking whether they are employees—simply begs the question.

* * * [T]he common law's definition of the master-servant relationship does provide helpful guidance. At common law the relevant factors defining the master-servant relationship focus on the master's control over the servant. The general definition of the term "servant" in the Restatement (Second) of Agency § 2(2) (1958), for example, refers to a person whose work is "controlled or is subject to the right to control by the master." See also *id.,* § 220(1) ("A servant is a person employed to perform services in the affairs of another and who with respect to the physical conduct in the performance of the services is subject to the other's control or right to control"). In addition, the Restatement's more specific definition of the term "servant" lists factors to be considered when distinguishing between servants and independent contractors, the first of which is "the extent of control" that one may exercise over the details of the work of the other. *Id.,* § 220(2)(a). We think that the common-law

skill required; the source of the instrumentalities and tools; the location of the work; the duration of the relationship between the parties; whether the hiring party has the right to assign additional projects to the hired party; the extent of the hired party's discretion over when and how long to work; the method of payment; the hired party's role in hiring and paying assistants; whether the work is part of the regular business of the hiring party; whether the hiring party is in business; the provision of employee benefits; and the tax treatment of the hired party.' " 503 U.S., at 323–324, 112 S.Ct. 1344 (quoting *Community for Creative Non-Violence v. Reid,* 490 U.S. 730, 751–752, 109 S.Ct. 2166, 104 L.Ed.2d 811 (1989), and citing Restatement (Second) of Agency § 220(2) (1958)).

These particular factors are not directly applicable to this case because we are not faced with drawing a line between independent contractors and employees. Rather, our inquiry is whether a shareholder-director is an employee or, alternatively, the kind of person that the common law would consider an employer.

element of control is the principal guidepost that should be followed in this case.

This is the position that is advocated by the Equal Employment Opportunity Commission (EEOC), the agency that has special enforcement responsibilities under the ADA and other federal statutes containing similar threshold issues for determining coverage. * * *

We are persuaded by the EEOC's focus on the common-law touchstone of control, see *Skidmore v. Swift & Co.,* 323 U.S. 134, 140, 65 S.Ct. 161, 89 L.Ed.124 (1944) * * * .

As the EEOC's standard reflects, an employer is the person, or group of persons, who owns and manages the enterprise. The employer can hire and fire employees, can assign tasks to employees and supervise their performance, and can decide how the profits and losses of the business are to be distributed. The mere fact that a person has a particular title—such as partner, director, or vice president—should not necessarily be used to determine whether he or she is an employee or a proprietor. Nor should the mere existence of a document styled "employment agreement" lead inexorably to the conclusion that either party is an employee. Rather, as was true in applying common law rules to the independent-contractor-versus-employee issue confronted in *Darden,* the answer to whether a shareholder-director is an employee depends on " 'all of the incidents of the relationship * * * with no one factor being decisive.' " 503 U.S., at 324, 112 S.Ct. 1344 (quoting *NLRB v. United Ins. Co. of America,* 390 U.S. 254, 258, 88 S.Ct. 988, 19 L.Ed.2d 1083 (1968)).

[The dissenting opinion of JUSTICE GINSBURG joined by JUSTICE BREYER has been omitted.]

NOTES AND QUESTIONS

1. The Court remanded *Clackamas* for reconsideration of whether the four physicians were employees under the ADA in light of the right-to-control test because the evidentiary record in the case would be dispositive on the question of whether the plaintiff or the defendant could prevail on the "employee" issue. *See Clackamas*, 538 U.S. at 451, 123 S.Ct. at 1681.

2. Although *Clackamas* was an ADA case, the Court specifically noted that the disagreement in the lower courts on the proper test for determining who is an "employee" extended to cases arising under Title VII and the ADEA. *Clackamas*, 538 U.S. at 444 n.3, 123 S.Ct. at 1677 n.3.

3. *Clackamas* specifically noted that the meaning of the term "employee" is important on two coverage issues. The first issue is whether an individual is an "employee" who may invoke the statutory protections afforded to persons claiming unlawful employment discrimination. The second issue is who is an "employee" for purposes of determining whether an employer satisfies the 15- or 20-employee threshold for coverage of the

relevant antidiscrimination statute. *Clackamas*, 538 U.S. at 447 n.6, 123 S.Ct. at 1679 n.6.

4. In *Robinson v. Shell Oil Co.*, 519 U.S. 337, 117 S.Ct. 843, 136 L.Ed.2d 808 (1997), the Court held that the term "employee" under Title VII covers a former employee who claims that his former employer retaliated against him because he had filed a charge of racial discrimination with the EEOC.

5. Should medical interns and residents in graduate medical training programs be considered "employees" under the *Clackmas* test? Should a member of the board of directors of a corporation, who continues to work as a full-time officer and manager of the corporation, be considered an employee protected under the ADEA? *See* EEOC v. Johnson & Higgins, Inc. 91 F.3d 1529 (2d Cir.1996). More recently, the question of whether unpaid interns are protected by antidiscrimination laws has generated considerable controversy. Courts have often held that unpaid interns are not employees protected by antidiscrimination laws, a conclusion that was recently affirmed under New York State law. *See* Wang v. Phoenix Satellite TV US, Inc., 976 F. Supp.2d 527 (S.D.N.Y. 2013). The *Wang* case received widespread attention, in part because of the sharp rise of unpaid internships, and a number of jurisdictions, including New York, have passed statutory protections for unpaid interns. *See* Cindy S. Minniti & Mark S. Goldstein, *New York State Becomes the Fourth Jurisdiction to Protect Unpaid Interns from Employment Discrimination*, Forbes Magazine, July 28, 2014.

6. Public interest groups and the EEOC may use "testers" who pose as job applicants to determine whether employers engage in discriminatory hiring practices or to gather evidence of discriminatory employment practices. This practice is sometimes called auditing. For example, a black tester and a white tester, both with similar qualifications, are sent at different times to apply for a job for which an employer may be seeking applicants. As a general rule, neither has the intent to accept a job offer if one is made by the employer. The treatment that each tester receives is then compared to evaluate whether the white tester applicant received more favorable treatment than the black tester applicant. Should the black tester have standing to sue if he received less favorable treatment from the employer than the white tester? The courts of appeals are divided on the issue. In *Kyles v. J.K. Guardian Security Services*, 222 F.3d 289, 298 (7th Cir.2000) (collecting cases), the Seventh Circuit held that testers who experience discrimination as job applicants have standing to sue under Title VII. The court held, however, that testers do not have standing under § 1981 because the requisite intent to "make or enforce a contract" is nonexistent. The Fourth Circuit, in *Sledge v. J.P. Stevens & Co.*, 585 F.2d 625 (4th Cir.1978), held testers do not have standing because they have suffered no cognizable injury as they are not seriously interested in the jobs for which they applied. The EEOC has issued a Policy Guidance supporting the right of testers to sue. *See Kyles*, 222 F.3d at 299 (discussing the EEOC Policy Guidance on testers); EEOC, Enforcement Guidance: Whether "Testers" Can

File Charges and Litigate Claims of Employment Discrimination, EEOC Notice No. 915.002 (May 22, 1996), available at *www.eeoc.gov/policy/docs/damages.html.* Which do you think is the better view?

3. THE MEANING OF "EMPLOYER"

Title VII defines the term "employer" as, *inter alia,* "a person engaged in an industry affecting commerce who has fifteen or more employees for each working day in each of twenty or more calendar weeks in the current or preceding calendar year." Title VII § 701(b), 42 U.S.C. 2000e(b). "Employer" is similarly defined in the ADA, ADA § 101(5)(A), and the ADEA, 29 U.S.C. § 630(b), except that the threshold number of employees under the ADEA is twenty rather than fifteen. Does *Clackamas* help define the meaning of "employer"?

In *Walters v. Metropolitan Educational Enterprises, Inc.*, 519 U.S. 202, 117 S.Ct. 660, 136 L.Ed.2d 644 (1997), the Supreme Court addressed the issue whether Title VII's jurisdictional definition of "employer" is satisfied when an employer maintains fifteen or more employees on its payroll for the requisite number of weeks even though fewer than fifteen employees report to work or are on paid leave on each day of such week. In a unanimous decision, the Supreme Court adopted the "payroll" method, which relies on the "ultimate touchstone," i.e., "whether the employer has an employment relationship with the individual on the day in question." *Walters,* 519 U.S. at 211, 117 S.Ct. at 666, 663.

Subsequently, in *Arbaugh v. Y & H Corp.*, 546 U.S. 500, 126 S.Ct. 1235, 163 L.Ed.2d 1097 (2006), the Supreme Court held that the fifteen-employee threshold for Title VII claims was not an issue that fell within the court's subject matter jurisdiction but instead related to the plaintiff's claim for relief. The issue arose because the defendant, for reasons that were never disclosed, did not assert that it had fewer than fifteen employees until after the jury had rendered a verdict for the plaintiff (whether the defendant had fewer than fifteen employees turned on the status of several of its drivers). The district court reluctantly dismissed the case for lack of subject matter jurisdiction, but the Supreme Court unanimously reversed that determination, holding that "when Congress does not rank a statutory limitation on coverage as jurisdictional, courts should treat the restriction as nonjurisdictional in character. * * * [T]he threshold number of employees for application of Title VII is an element of a plaintiff's claim for relief, not a jurisdictional issue." *Id.* at 516, 126 S.Ct. at 1245, 163 L.Ed.2d at 1110. It is worth noting that there is no minimum number of employees required for coverage under § 1981; therefore, even very small employers can be sued under that statute.

Single employer: The courts have not adopted a uniform test for deciding whether a small employer with fewer than fifteen (or twenty) employees, and its larger parent company or other affiliates with fifteen (or twenty) or more employees constitute a single employer. *See* Lyes v. City of Riviera Beach, Fla., 166 F.3d 1332 (11th Cir.1999). Most of the courts deciding the issue have adopted the common law "integrated employer" test, which was initially adopted by, the National Labor Relations Board to decide employer coverage under the National Labor Relations Act. The factors the courts consider under the "integrated employer" test include (1) interrelation of operations, (2) common management, (3) common ownership, (4) and centralized control of labor relations and personnel. *See* Papa v. Katy Indus., Inc., 166 F.3d 937, 940–41 (7th Cir.1999) (collecting cases), *cert. denied*, 528 U.S. 1019, 120 S.Ct. 526, 145 L.Ed.2d 408 (1999). In *Papa*, the Seventh Circuit rejected the "integrated employer" test and, instead, focused on the policy for exempting smaller employers from coverage of laws prohibiting discrimination in employment. The relevant inquiry under the Seventh Circuit test asks: (1) whether a parent company would be liable for the subsidiary employer's debts, torts, or contract breaches under the traditional standards for "piercing the corporate veil"; (2) whether the enterprise split itself into smaller companies, "each with fewer than the statutory minimum of employees, for the express purpose of avoiding liability under the discrimination laws"; and (3) whether "the parent company might have directed the discriminatory act, practice, or policy of which the employee of its subsidiary was complaining." *Id.* at 940–41. *See also* Englehardt v. S.P. Richards Co., 472 F.3d 1, 5 (1st Cir 2006) (focusing on whether the company was structured so as to avoid the application of labor laws and finding that the defendant was not an integrated employer).

Individual Liability of Agents of Employers: Under Title VII, the ADEA, and the ADA, the term "employer" is statutorily defined to include "any agent" of the employer. Title VII § 701(b), 42 U.S.C. § 2000e–(b); ADEA § 630(b), 29 U.S.C. § 630(b); ADA § 101(5)(A), 42 U.S.C. 12111(5)(A). Courts generally define the term "agent" as a supervisory employee who has the authority to make personnel decisions regarding hiring or firing employees or to otherwise set the terms and conditions of employment for applicants and employees. *See* Sauers v. Salt Lake County, 1 F.3d 1122, 1125 (10th Cir.1993). The statutes are silent on whether "agents" of "employers" are liable in their individual capacity for any unlawful discriminatory employment decisions that they make, but courts have uniformly held that individual employees cannot be held liable under the antidiscrimination statutes.

The Ninth Circuit's decision in *Miller v. Maxwell's International Inc.*, 991 F.2d 583 (1993), is one of the leading cases holding that agents are not liable in their individual capacity. In *Miller v. Maxwell's*, the court held that imposing individual liability on agents is inappropriate. The court reasoned that Congress expressed its intent to impose liability only on employers because (1) the term "agent" was included in these statutes only to incorporate respondeat superior liability; (2) the employee limitation in the definition of an employer (fifteen or more employees under Title VII and the ADA, and twenty or more employees under the ADEA) indicates congressional intent not to subject small businesses to the costs of defending employment discrimination claims and makes it "inconceivable that Congress intended to allow civil liability to run against individual employees," *id.* at 587; and (3) the statutory language of the amendments to Title VII in the Civil Rights Act of 1991 indicates that compensatory and punitive damages can be awarded only against employers and not their agents. *See also* Fantini v. Salem State Coll., 557 F.3d 22, 28–31 (1st Cir.2009) (following *Miller* and discussing cases).

Individual liability under § 1981 has been addressed in only a few cases. One of the leading cases holding that agents of employers are liable in their individual capacities is *Faraca v. Clements*, 506 F.2d 956 (5th Cir.1975) (holding the director of a state agency personally liable for discriminatory action even though the employer was immune from liability). *See also* Foley v. Univ. of Houston Sys., 355 F.3d 333, 338 n.7 (5th Cir.2003) (citing cases); Whidbee v. Garzarelli Food Specialties, Inc., 223 F.3d 62, 75 (2d Cir.2000) (individual liability permitted when there is some personal involvement or affirmative link to the individual and the discriminatory behavior).

Temporary Employees and Employers: Who is the "employer" of "employees" when individuals are leased out by one company to work on a temporary basis for another company? In its *Enforcement Guidance: The Application of EEO Laws to Contingent Workers Placed by Temporary Employment Agencies and Other Staffing Firms*, EEOC Notice No. 915.002 (Dec. 3, 1997), available at *http://www.eeoc.gov/policy/docs/conting.html*, the EEOC warns employers using individuals hired and paid by a staffing firm that the workers "typically qualify as 'employees' of the staffing firm, the client to whom they are assigned, or both." The Fourth Circuit recently applied what is known as "the joint-employer doctrine" to a Title VII claim to hold that both the staffing agency and the company that contracted with the agency were liable for a harassment claim. *See* Butler v. Davis Automotive Indus., 793 F.3d 404 (4th Cir.2015). The joint employer doctrine is employed in other areas, particularly labor law, and is generally premised on whether a party has sufficient control over the workplace and the employee to be held liable. *Id.* at 414–15. For a discussion of the issue see Daniel P. O'Gorman, *Paying for the Sins of Their Clients: The EEOC's Position That Staffing Firms Can Be Liable When Their Clients Terminate an Assigned Employee for a Discriminatory Reason*, 112 Penn.St.L.Rev. 425 (2007).

4. THE MEANING OF AN "EMPLOYMENT PRACTICE"

A threshold issue in employment discrimination cases is whether the plaintiff is seeking relief from an "unlawful employment *practice*" or an adverse employment *practice*. To be actionable the "practice" must fall within the statutory phrase, "compensation, terms, conditions, or privileges of employment." *See, e.g.*, Title VII § 703(a)(1), 42 U.S.C § 2000e–2(a)(1); ADEA § 4(a)(1), 29 U.S.C. § 623(a)(1); *see also* ADA § 102(a), 42 U.S.C. § 12112(a). Like the term "discriminate," Congress did not define the phrase "compensation, terms, conditions, or privileges of employment." If the "practice" of an employer does not fall within the meaning of "compensation, terms, conditions, or privileges of employment," then arguably that "practice" is not unlawful even if the employer was motivated by discriminatory intent in taking the action. The Supreme Court has defined the term *practice* to include discrete acts and acts that are continuing in nature. Nat'l R.R. Passenger Corp. v. Morgan, 536 U.S. 101, 111, 122 S.Ct. 2061, 2071, 153 L.Ed.2d 106 (2002) ("[w]e have repeatedly interpreted the term 'practice' to apply to a discrete act or single 'occurrence,' even when it has a connection to other acts.").

Some of the most obvious employment practices that fall within the statutory phrase "compensation, terms, conditions, or privileges of employment" are terminations, failures to promote, denials of transfer, or refusals to hire. *See Morgan, id.* at 113, 122 S.Ct. at 2972. Although courts have held that not every employment or personnel decision an employer makes is a "practice," they disagree on the test for deciding which practices of employers do or do not come within the statutory phrase. *See, e.g.*, Ray v. Henderson, 217 F.3d 1234, 1240–42 (9th Cir.2000) (discussing various tests). In recent years, the issue has taken on greatest importance in the context of retaliation claims and claims alleging sexual harassment, and we will accordingly defer further discussion to those specific contexts.

NOTE: EXTRATERRITORIAL APPLICATION OF DISCRIMINATION LAWS

In *EEOC v. Arabian American Oil Co.*, 499 U.S. 244, 111 S.Ct. 1227, 113 L.Ed.2d 274 (1991), the Supreme Court held that Title VII does not apply extraterritorially. Congress overruled that decision in § 109 of the Civil Rights Act of 1991; thus, Title VII and the ADA, like the ADEA, now apply extraterritorially to individuals who are citizens of the United States employed by a covered U.S. employer in a foreign country. *See* Title VII, § 701(f), 42 U.S.C. § 2000e(f). For a discussion of some of the issues that arise in applying employment discrimination laws to United States employers who do business in foreign countries, see Kathy Roberts, *Correcting Culture: Extraterritoriality and U.S. Employment Discrimination Laws*, 24 Hofstra

Lab. & Emp.L.J. 295 (2007); Meredith Poznanski Cook, Note, *The Extraterritorial Application of Title VII: Does the Foreign Compulsion Defense Work?*, 20 Suffolk Transnat'l L.Rev. 133 (1996). For a discussion of some of the problems of applying the extraterritorial provisions to foreign individuals who apply in foreign countries for jobs in the United States, see Reyes-Gaona v. N.C. Growers Ass'n, 250 F.3d 861 (4th Cir.2001); Ruhe C. Wadud, Note, *Allowing Employers to Discriminate in the Hiring Process Under the Age Discrimination in Employment Act: The Case of* Reyes-Gaona, 27 N.C.J. Int'l L. & Com.Reg. 335 (2001).

5. UNION LIABILITY FOR DISCRIMINATION

a. The Duty of Fair Representation

Union liability for unlawful discrimination under Title VII is integrally related to the duties imposed on unions under the federal labor laws and the role that unions play in collective bargaining and grievance arbitration. Long before Title VII was enacted, the Supreme Court recognized that the Railway Labor Act (RLA), 45 U.S.C. § 151 et seq., bars labor unions from engaging in invidious discrimination on the basis of race when they act in their role as statutory representative. In *Steele v. Louisville & Nashville Railroad*, 323 U.S. 192, 65 S.Ct. 226, 89 L.Ed.173 (1944), a railway union that was the exclusive representative for a bargaining unit of locomotive firemen excluded black firemen from membership in the union and bargained with the railroad to restrict the employment and promotion of black workers. Without limiting the union's right to restrict its membership on the basis of race, the Supreme Court held that the union violated the duty of fair representation by discriminating against the black firemen in its bargaining demands with the employer. The Court held:

> [T]he language of the [Railway Labor] Act * * * expresses the aim of Congress to impose on the bargaining representative of a craft or class of employees the duty to exercise fairly the power conferred upon it in behalf of all those for whom it acts, without hostile discrimination against them.
>
> This does not mean that the statutory representative of a craft is barred from making contracts which may have unfavorable effects on some of the members of the craft represented. Variations in the terms of the contract based on differences relevant to the authorized purposes of the contract in conditions to which they are to be applied, such as differences in seniority, the type of work performed, the competence and skill with which it is performed, are within the scope of the bargaining representation of a craft, all of whose members are not identical in their interest or merit. Without attempting to

> mark the allowable limits of differences in the terms of contracts based on differences of conditions to which they apply, it is enough for present purposes to say that the statutory power to represent a craft and to make contracts as to wages, hours and working conditions does not include the authority to make among members of the craft discriminations not based on such relevant differences. Here the discriminations based on race alone are obviously irrelevant and invidious. Congress plainly did not undertake to authorize the bargaining representative to make such discriminations.

Id. at 202–03, 65 S.Ct. at 232.

The same day that the *Steele* case was decided, the Supreme Court determined that the duty of fair representation should also be read into the National Labor Relations Act (NLRA), 29 U.S.C. § 151 et seq., because the duty derives from the union's status as the exclusive bargaining agent for all employees in the bargaining unit. *See* Wallace Corp. v. NLRB, 323 U.S. 248, 65 S.Ct. 238, 89 L.Ed.216 (1944). Subsequently, in *Ford Motor Co. v. Huffman*, 345 U.S. 330, 73 S.Ct. 681, 97 L.Ed.1048 (1953), the Court made clear that labor organizations have a wide range of reasonableness in their choice of bargaining positions in representing a diverse membership. In *Vaca v. Sipes*, 386 U.S. 171, 87 S.Ct. 903, 17 L.Ed.2d 842 (1967), the Supreme Court held that the duty of fair representation does not give individual employees an "absolute right" to have their grievances arbitrated, but requires only that a union process the grievances of employees in a manner that is not arbitrary, discriminatory, or in bad faith. For example, the Ninth Circuit held that a union's "intentional and knowing failure to file grievances on behalf of [a black member] concerning racial harassment" is a "primary violation" of its duty of fair representation. Woods v. Graphic Communications, 925 F.2d 1195, 1203 (9th Cir.1991). A labor organization that discriminates in handling grievances on the basis of a federally protected status such as race or sex can also be found liable under Title VII, as discussed in the next section. *See, e.g.*, Beck v. UFCW Local 99, 506 F.3d 874 (9th Cir.2007).

b. Union Liability for Discrimination as an "Employer" and as a "Labor Organization"

A union is subject to liability under federal antidiscrimination laws in two capacities: as an "employer" and as a "labor organization." When Title VII was enacted in 1964, labor organizations that operated a hiring hall or had 100 or more members were covered by the Act. As a result of the 1972 amendments, Title VII now covers any "labor organization" that has fifteen or more members or operates a hiring hall. Title VII, § 701(e), 42 U.S.C. § 2000e(e). Title I of the Americans with Disabilities Act of 1990

(ADA) covers the same labor organizations as Title VII, whereas the Age Discrimination in Employment Act (ADEA) covers any "labor organization" that maintains a hiring hall or has twenty-five or more members, 29 U.S.C. § 630(e).

A union's obligations to its own employees under Title VII, the ADEA, and the ADA are the same as any other "employer" covered by those statutes. For example, a labor organization can be sued for discrimination under Title VII in its capacity as an "employer" if it meets the jurisdictional requirements of a Title VII employer, i.e., if it has "fifteen or more employees for each working day in each of twenty or more calendar weeks in the current or preceding year." Title VII, § 701(b), 42 U.S.C. § 2000e(b). One court has noted the irony that "[m]any labor organizations have fewer than 14 employees but thousands of members." Dowd v. United Steelworkers of Am., 253 F.3d 1093, 1099–1100 (8th Cir.2001).

A union's liability in its capacity as a "labor organization" for discrimination on the basis of race, color, religion, sex, or national origin is covered by §§ 703(c) and 703(d) of Title VII. Section 4(c) of the ADEA, 29 U.S.C. § 623(c), which prohibits age discrimination by labor organizations, is analogous to § 703(c) of Title VII. The ADA prohibits disability discrimination by "covered entities," which include labor organizations. *See* 42 U.S.C. §§ 12111(2), 12112(a). Labor organizations are also prohibited from retaliating against a "member" or "applicant for membership" for opposing unlawful discriminatory practices or participating in investigations or proceedings under the federal discrimination laws. *See* Title VII, § 704(a), 42 U.S.C. § 2000e–3(a); ADEA, § 4(d), 29 U.S.C. § 623(d).

The Supreme Court addressed the meaning of § 703(c)(1) of Title VII in *Goodman v. Lukens Steel Co.,* 482 U.S. 656, 107 S.Ct. 2617, 96 L.Ed.2d 572 (1987). In *Goodman,* employees of a steel company sued their employer and unions for race discrimination under Title VII. Although the collective-bargaining agreement expressly prohibited racial discrimination, the employer had discriminated by discharging black probationary employees and the unions involved had refused to file grievances based on these discharges. Moreover, the unions had ignored grievances about racial harassment and refused to include claims of racial discrimination in grievances about other contract issues. In the majority opinion, Justice White wrote:

> The Unions submit that the only basis for any liability in this case under Title VII is § 703(c)(3), which provides that a Union may not "cause or attempt to cause an employer to discriminate against an individual in violation of this section," * * * . We need not differ with the Unions on the reach of

§ 703(c)(3), for § 703(c)(1) makes it an unlawful practice for a Union to "exclude or to expel from its membership, *or otherwise to discriminate against*, any individual because of his race, color, religion, sex, or national origin." (Emphasis added.) Both courts below found that the Unions had indeed discriminated on the basis of race by the way in which they represented the workers, and the Court of Appeals expressly held that "[t]he deliberate choice not to process grievances also violated § 703(c)(1) of Title VII." The plain language of the statute supports this conclusion.

* * *

As we understand it, there was no suggestion below that the Unions held any racial animus against or denigrated blacks generally. Rather, it was held that a collective-bargaining agent could not, without violating Title VII * * *, follow a policy of refusing to file grievable racial discrimination claims however strong they might be and however sure the agent was that the employer was discriminating against blacks. The Unions, in effect, categorized racial grievances as unworthy of pursuit and, while pursuing thousands of other legitimate grievances, ignored racial discrimination claims on behalf of blacks, knowing that the employer was discriminating in violation of the contract. Such conduct, the courts below concluded, intentionally discriminated against blacks seeking a remedy for disparate treatment based on their race and violated [Title VII]. As the District Court said: "A union which intentionally avoids asserting discrimination claims, either so as not to antagonize the employer and thus improve its chances of success on other issues, or in deference to the perceived desires of its white membership, is liable under [Title VII], regardless of whether, as a subjective matter, its leaders were favorably disposed toward minorities."

Id. at 667–69, 107 S.Ct. at 2624–25.

Justice Powell's dissent in *Goodman*, joined by Justices Scalia and O'Connor, disagreed with the majority's interpretation of § 703(c)(1) and included the following observations on a union's obligations under Title VII:

Section 703(c), the provision of Title VII governing suits against unions, does not suggest that the union has a duty to take affirmative steps to remedy employer discrimination. Section 703(c)(1) makes it unlawful for a union "to exclude or to expel from its membership, or otherwise to discriminate against, any individual because of his race, color, religion, sex, or national origin." This subsection parallels § 703(a)(1), that applies to employers. This parallelism, and the reference to union membership, indicate that § 703(c)(1) prohibits direct discrimination by a union against its members; it does not impose upon a union an obligation to remedy discrimination by the *employer*. Moreover, § 703(c)(3) specifically addresses the union's interaction with the employer, by outlawing efforts by the union "to cause or attempt to cause an employer to discriminate against an individual in violation of this section." * * * [T]he language of § 703(c)(3) is taken *in haec verba* from § 8(b)(2) of the National Labor Relations Act (NLRA), 29 U.S.C. § 158(b)(2). That provision of the NLRA has been held not to impose liability for passive acquiescence in wrongdoing by the employer. Indeed, well before the enactment of Title VII, the Court held that even encouraging or inducing employer discrimination is not sufficient to incur liability under § 8(b)(2) [of the NLRA]. Electrical Workers v. NLRB, 341 U.S. 694, 703, 71 S.Ct. 954, 959, 95 L.Ed.1299 (1951).

* * * A union, unlike an employer, is a democratically controlled institution directed by the will of its constituents, subject to the duty of fair representation. Like other representative entities, unions must balance the competing claims of its constituents. A union must make difficult choices among goals such as eliminating racial discrimination in the workplace, removing health and safety hazards, providing better insurance and pension benefits, and increasing wages. The Court has recognized that "[t]he complete satisfaction of all who are represented is hardly to be expected." Ford Motor Co. v. Huffman, 345 U.S. 330, 338, 73 S.Ct. 681, 686, 97 L.Ed.1048 (1953). For these reasons unions are afforded broad discretion in the handling of grievances. Union members' suits against their unions may deplete union treasuries, and may induce unions to process frivolous claims and resist fair settlement offers. The employee is not without a remedy, because union members may file Title VII actions directly against their employers. Alexander v. Gardner-Denver Co., 415 U.S. 36, 94 S.Ct. 1011, 39 L.Ed.2d 147 (1974). I therefore would hold that Title VII imposes on unions no affirmative duty to remedy discrimination by the employer.

Id. at 687–89, 107 S.Ct. at 2635–36.

NOTES AND QUESTIONS

1. *Acquiescence*: Before *Goodman*, some courts had ruled that a union could be liable under Title VII for "acquiescing" in an employer's racially discriminatory conduct. *See, e.g.*, Bonilla v. Oakland Scavenger Co., 697 F.2d

1297, 1304 (9th Cir.1982). What exactly is "acquiescence"? After *Goodman*, one court held that "[m]ere inaction does not constitute acquiescence." Rather, "[a]cquiescence requires: 1) knowledge that prohibited discrimination may have occurred, and 2) a decision not to assert the discrimination claim." York v. American Tel. & Tel. Co., 95 F.3d 948, 956–57 (10th Cir.1996). "Liability by way of acquiescence" has been rejected by several courts of appeals since *Goodman*. *See, e.g.*, EEOC v. Pipefitters Assoc. Local 597, 334 F.3d 656 (7th Cir.2003); Martin v. Local 1513, IAMAW, 859 F.2d 581, 584 (8th Cir.1988). *See also* Johnson v. Palma, 931 F.2d 203, 209 (2d Cir.1991) (ruling that "the refusal to proceed with [a] grievance process because of a company policy amounts to more than mere passivity"). For a post-*Goodman* case approving the acquiescence theory, see *Woods v. Graphic Communications*, 925 F.2d 1195, 1200 (9th Cir.1991). What are the policy arguments for and against recognition of an acquiescence theory of union liability in discrimination cases? At a minimum, does a union have an affirmative obligation to investigate any complaints of unlawful discrimination that are brought by members of the bargaining unit? *See* Thorn v. Amalgamated Transit Union, 305 F.3d 826, 832 (8th Cir.2002) ("[N]owhere in [Title VII] do we find language imposing upon unions an affirmative duty to investigate and take steps to remedy employer discrimination.").

2. In *14 Penn Plaza LLC v. Pyett*, 556 U.S. 247, 129 S.Ct. 1456, 173 L.Ed.2d 398 (2009), the Supreme Court called into question the continued vitality of the *Alexander v. Garner-Denver* case, which Justice Powell cited as a rationale for his dissent in *Goodman*. *Pyett*, which is covered in Chapter 16, held that "a collective-bargaining agreement that clearly and unmistakably requires union members to arbitrate ADEA claims is enforceable as a matter of federal law." *Id.* at 274, 129 S.Ct. at 1474. Such an agreement would constitute a waiver of the rights of individuals in the bargaining unit to pursue judicial relief for unlawful discrimination. Does this doctrinal development significantly undercut Justice Powell's dissent in *Goodman* and give additional support to the majority's holding? Does it suggest that unions that agree to such a waiver in a collective bargaining agreement should have an affirmative duty to take aggressive steps to investigate and remedy employer discrimination?

3. *Title VII and the NLRA's Exclusivity Principle*: In *Emporium Capwell Co. v. Western Addition Community Organization*, 420 U.S. 50, 95 S.Ct. 977, 43 L.Ed.2d 12 (1975), two black employees were discharged for engaging in picketing and boycott activities in protest of their employer's racially discriminatory practices. Previously, a group of black employees had presented a list of grievances, including claims of racial discrimination, to the union representatives, and the company and union had agreed to "look into the matter" of discrimination and see what needed to be done. A local civil rights association filed charges with the National Labor Relations Board (NLRB) on behalf of the discharged employees claiming that the employer had interfered with the employees' rights under § 7 of the NLRA to engage in

concerted activity "for the purpose of collective bargaining or other mutual aid or protection." 29 U.S.C. § 157. The NLRB found that the employees' conduct was not protected under the NLRA because they were, in effect, attempting to bargain directly with their employer on the issue of racial discrimination. The Board held that such bargaining circumvented the efforts to remedy discrimination undertaken by their union, which had the statutory authority under § 9(a) of the NLRA to act as the exclusive representative of all the employees in the bargaining unit. 29 U.S.C. § 159(a).

The Supreme Court upheld the Board's findings and conclusions. In response to the argument that the "unique status" of racial discrimination should permit an exception to the exclusivity principle, Justice Marshall wrote for the Court:

> Plainly, national labor policy embodies the principles of nondiscrimination as a matter of highest priority, and it is a commonplace that we must construe the NLRA in light of the broad national labor policy of which it is a part. These general principles do not aid respondent, however, as it is far from clear that separate bargaining is necessary to help eliminate discrimination. Indeed, as the facts of this litigation demonstrate, the proposed remedy might have just the opposite effect. The collective-bargaining agreement involved here prohibited without qualification all manner of invidious discrimination and made any claimed violation a grievable issue. The grievance procedure is directed precisely at determining whether discrimination has occurred. That orderly determination, if affirmative, could lead to an arbitral award enforceable in court. Nor is there any reason to believe that the processing of grievances is inherently limited to the correction of individual cases of discrimination. Quite apart from the essentially contractual question of whether the Union could grieve against a "pattern or practice" it deems inconsistent with the nondiscrimination clause of the contract, one would hardly expect an employer to continue in effect an employment practice that routinely results in adverse arbitral decisions.

Emporium Capwell, 420 U.S. at 66–67, 95 S.Ct. at 986–87.

4. *Union Liability for Discrimination in Apprenticeship and Training Programs—§ 703(d)*: A black female "helper" sued a union of elevator workers under Title VII for its failure to do anything in response to her complaints that white male master mechanics discriminated against her when they refused to provide her with on-the-job training she needed for a mechanic's permit. The Court of Appeals for the Seventh Circuit ruled that the union was not liable under Title VII for the discriminatory actions of the company's line employees, but was liable for its own "decision to do nothing in response [to her complaints], a passivity that led it to grant mechanics' credentials (and thus higher pay) to many of its members while holding back [the plaintiff] because of race and sex." Maalik v. International Union of Elevator

Constructors, Local 2, 437 F.3d 650, 653 (7th Cir.2006). Only if the union "did everything that was reasonable under the circumstances," could it be found liable, and "turning a blind eye to members' or employees' discrimination is not reasonable" because the union "has tools (from fines to expulsion) and decided not to use them." *Id.* Is the union's responsibility for nondiscrimination in training programs under § 703(d) of Title VII different from its responsibilities as a bargaining agent under § 703(c)(1) as interpreted by *Goodman*?

5. How do the duty of fair representation and the principles of majority rule and exclusivity affect the responsibility unions should bear for unlawful discrimination in the workplace? Can the processes of collective bargaining and grievance arbitration offer employees fairer, quicker, and more creative solutions to discriminatory employment practices than Title VII? Or than self-help? In light of the limits that *Emporium Capwell* imposes on minority groups in a unionized workplace, what role can or should a union play in ensuring that all members of a particular bargaining unit work in an environment free from unlawful discrimination? Is it enough that the union does not violate its duty of fair representation or one of the federal or state antidiscrimination statutes? Or should unions be expected (if not legally required) to play a more active role in promoting nondiscrimination policies—to "provide voice and muscle to enforce workers' public law rights"? Robert J. Rabin, *The Role of Unions in the Rights-Based Workplace*, 25 U.S.F.L.Rev. 169, 171 (1991). For that matter, are unions capable of adapting to the new demands that are placed on them by an increasingly diverse workforce? *See generally* Marion Crain, *Colorblind Unionism*, 49 UCLA L.Rev. 1313 (2002); Marion Crain & Ken Matheny, *Labor's Identity Crisis*, 89 Cal.L.Rev. 1767 (2001); Ruben J. Garcia, *New Voices at Work: Race and Gender Identity Caucuses in the U.S. Labor Movement*, 54 Hastings L.J. 79 (2002); Molly S. McUsic & Michael Selmi, *Postmodern Unions: Identity Politics in the Workplace*, 82 Iowa L.Rev. 1339 (1997).

E. REMEDIES

Two separate but related issues are involved in every employment discrimination case. The first concerns substantive liability: whether a defendant has discriminated against an individual or a class of individuals in violation of the applicable law. The second involves a determination of the appropriate forms of relief to redress the substantive violation: for example, whether a proven victim of unlawful employment discrimination is entitled to reinstatement, promotion, back pay, front pay, preliminary injunctions, or attorney's fees. Anyone involved with employment discrimination cases must be as familiar with the law on relief as they are with the law on substantive liability. For a comprehensive treatment of remedies (except for attorney's fees), see Robert Belton, Remedies in Employment Discrimination Law (1992) (hereinafter Belton, Remedies).

Statutory Provisions: Each of the federal statutes covered in these materials, except § 1981, has a specific provision on relief. Section 706(g)(1) of Title VII, 42 U.S.C. § 2000e–5(g)(1), provides that upon a finding of unlawful discrimination, a "court may enjoin the [defendant] from engaging in [the] unlawful employment practice, and order such affirmative action as may be appropriate, which may include, but is not limited to, reinstatement or hiring of employees, with or without back pay * * *, or any other equitable relief as the court deems appropriate." Section 107 of the ADA, 42 U.S.C. § 12117, provides that the same forms of relief available under Title VII are also available under the ADA (subject to a "good faith" defense on accommodation claims). The Rehabilitation Act incorporates the remedies available under § 706(g) of Title VII with respect to claims against the federal government and federal grantees. 29 U.S.C. §§ 791, 794. The Civil Rights Act of 1991 provides for limited compensatory and punitive damages under Title VII, the ADA, and the Rehabilitation Act. 42 U.S.C. § 1981a(a)(1)–(2). The ADEA incorporates many of the remedial schemes of the Fair Labor Standards Act of 1938, 29 U.S.C. § 201. Like the FLSA, § 626(b) of the ADEA, 29 U.S.C. § 626(b), provides for "such legal or equitable relief as may be appropriate to effectuate the purposes" of the ADEA, "including judgments compelling employment, reinstatement or promotion." The ADEA also incorporates the FLSA provisions that permit awards of liquidated damages (double the back wages owed), which are recoverable only for willful violations. *See* 29 U.S.C. § 216(b). The Equal Pay Act, which is an amendment to the FLSA, provides for both legal and equitable relief, including reinstatement, promotion, and "the payment of wages lost and an additional equal amount as liquidated damages." *Id.* The Equal Pay Act, like the ADEA, permits recovery of liquidated damages only for willful violations. Section 1981 does not have a specific provision on relief, but in *Johnson v. Railway Express Agency, Inc.*, 421 U.S. 454, 460, 95 S.Ct. 1716, 1720, 44 L.Ed.2d 295 (1975), the Supreme Court held that legal and equitable relief, including compensatory and punitive damages, can be recovered under § 1981.

1. BASIC REMEDIAL PRINCIPLES

Prior to the Civil Rights Act of 1991, which amended Title VII to provide for punitive and compensatory damages, statutory relief available under Title VII was limited to back pay and other "equitable" remedies. Before 1991, the Supreme Court enunciated the two basic remedial principles governing employment discrimination cases—make-whole and rightful place relief (equitable relief)—in the leading cases of *Albemarle Paper Co. v. Moody*, 422 U.S. 405, 95 S.Ct. 2362, 45 L.Ed.2d 280 (1975), and *Franks v. Bowman Transportation Co.*, 424 U.S. 747, 96 S.Ct. 1251, 47 L.Ed.2d 444 (1976). *Moody* and *Franks* limited a trial court's discretion to deny relief upon finding a Title VII violation because the statutory prohibition of employment discrimination is designed to serve two purposes: deterrence and compensation. The deterrence principle is effectuated by the *rightful place theory of relief* enunciated in *Franks*. Under this theory, a court is to award successful plaintiffs the "terms, conditions, or privileges" of employment they would have had with the defendant but for unlawful employment discrimination. The compensatory principle is effectuated by the *make-whole theory of relief* enunciated in *Moody*. Under this theory, successful plaintiffs are entitled to monetary compensation to remedy the economic harm they have suffered in the past or may suffer in the future as a consequence of the defendant's unlawful employment discrimination. *See generally* Robert Belton, *Harnessing Discretionary Justice in the Employment Discrimination Cases: The* Moody *and* Franks *Standards*, 44 Ohio St.L.J. 571 (1983).

Moody and *Franks* established a rebuttable presumption, known as the "presumptive entitlement" rule, which allows victims of unlawful employment discrimination to be awarded whatever remedies are necessary to achieve rightful place and make-whole relief. In *City of Los Angeles Department of Water & Power v. Manhart*, 435 U.S. 702, 719, 98 S.Ct. 1370, 1381, 55 L.Ed.2d 657 (1978), the Supreme Court stated that the presumption is "seldom overcome." Moreover, trial courts must make findings of fact to justify the denial of complete make-whole and rightful place relief. *See Moody*, 422 U.S. at 421 n.14, 95 S.Ct. at 2372 n.14 ("It is necessary * * * that if a district court does decline to award backpay, it carefully articulate its reasons."); *see also* Bergerson v. New York State Office of Mental Health, Cent. New York Psychiatric Ctr., 652 F.3d 277, 287 (2d Cir.2011) (vacating a district's court's decision to exclude remedial back pay where compensatory damages were awarded, holding that each remedy requires a separate inquest with careful articulation if award is denied); Weaver v. Amoco Prod. Co., 66 F.3d 85 (5th Cir.1995) (vacating a district court's award of front pay and remanding for review of the remedy where district court failed to articulate its reasons for concluding that reinstatement was not feasible). Under *Moody* and *Franks*, in the remedial phase of a discrimination trial, the plaintiff has a relatively light burden of establishing her "presumptive entitlement" to a particular form of relief such as back pay or reinstatement. Once the plaintiff has met her burden, the defendant has the heavier burden of proof, i.e., the burdens of persuasion and production, to demonstrate that the plaintiff should get no relief or only limited relief. *See Teamsters v. United States*, 431 U.S. 324, 361–62, 97 S.Ct. 1843, 52 L.Ed.2d 396 (1977) (citing *Franks*, 424 U.S. at 773 n.32, 96 S.Ct. at 1268 n.32).

Compensatory and punitive damages have been available in § 1981 employment discrimination cases since the Supreme Court decided *Johnson v. Railway Express Agency, Inc.*, 421 U.S. 454, 95 S.Ct. 1716, 44

L.Ed.2d 295 (1975). The Civil Rights Act of 1991 now makes compensatory and punitive damages available under Title VII and the ADA but only in disparate treatment cases not involving mixed-motive claims. 42 U.S.C. § 1981a, §§ 703(m) and 706(g)(2)(b) of Title VII, 42 U.S.C. §§ 2000e–2(m), and 2000e–5(g)(2)(b). The expansion of monetary relief in the 1991 Act was, in substantial part, Congress's response to the argument that it was patently unfair to deny the right to recover compensatory and punitive damages for claims of sex or disability discrimination when such damages are recoverable in race discrimination claims brought under § 1981. The Civil Rights Act of 1991, however, places caps on the amounts that can be awarded as compensatory and punitive damages, depending upon the size of the employer's workforce. Until the 1991 Act, all relief available under Title VII was considered equitable in nature, so jury trials were not possible. Under the 1991 Act, however, whenever "a complaining party seeks compensatory or punitive damages[,] * * * any party may demand a trial by jury." 42 U.S.C. § 1981a(c). Compensatory and punitive damages are discussed further in Section E.5, *infra*.

2. REINSTATEMENT

A reinstatement order in a discharge case (or instatement in a refusal to hire case) is an affirmative injunction directing the defendant to re-employ (or employ) the plaintiff in the job or position that she had or would have had but for the discriminatory conduct of the employer. District Judge Weinfeld's discussion of the reinstatement remedy has been quoted frequently:

> Like the other remedies available under Title VII, reinstatement is not mandatory upon a finding that an employee has been discriminatorily discharged, but is an equitable remedy whose appropriateness depends upon the discretion of the court in the light of the facts of each individual case. However, since the purpose of reinstatement is to make the plaintiff whole for the injury she has suffered, it, like back pay, should be denied only for reasons which, if applied generally, would not frustrate the central statutory purposes of eradicating discrimination throughout the economy and making persons whole for injuries suffered through past discrimination.

EEOC v. Kallir, Philips, Ross, Inc., 420 F.Supp. 919, 926 (S.D.N.Y.1976), *aff'd*, 559 F.2d 1203 (2d Cir.1977).

Reinstatement serves several objectives: (1) it recreates the employment relationship as it would have existed but for unlawful employment discrimination; (2) it prevents future economic loss to the plaintiff; (3) it allows an employer to demonstrate good faith compliance with the law to other employees; and (4) it prevents the employer from trying to get rid of employees, at any cost, who assert their rights under laws prohibiting discrimination in employment. *See* Darnell v. City of Jasper, 730 F.2d 653, 655–56 (11th Cir.1984); Belton, Remedies § 7.4 (collecting cases). Reinstatement is particularly appropriate in retaliatory discharge cases. Donnellon v. Fruehauf Corp., 794 F.2d 598, 602 (11th Cir.1986).

Reinstatement may be denied if the employer is able to prove special or exceptional circumstances. *See* Rosario-Torres v. Hernandez-Colon, 889 F.2d 314, 323–24 (1st Cir.1989). The two situations in which courts have deemed it appropriate to deny reinstatement are: (1) when an "innocent employee" currently occupies the at-issue job and should not be bumped, and (2) when hostility or animosity between the plaintiff and employer would make an amicable and productive working relationship impossible.

The "innocent employee" rule is based, in substantial part, on the potentially unsettling "domino" effect that bumping might have on employees who had no role in the employer's discriminatory conduct. *See* Patterson v. Am. Tobacco Co., 535 F.2d 257 (4th Cir.1976). The Supreme Court has endorsed the innocent victim doctrine. *See* Franks v. Bowman Transp. Co., 424 U.S. 747, 96 S.Ct. 1251, 47 L.Ed.2d 444 (1976); Firefighters Local Union 1784 v. Stotts, 467 U.S. 561, 104 S.Ct. 2576, 81 L.Ed.2d 483 (1984). The "no-bumping" rule may also apply if bumping would require the employer to violate a seniority provision of a collective bargaining agreement. *See e.g.*, Milton v. Scrivner, Inc., 53 F.3d 1118, 1125 (10th Cir.1995) ("reasonable accommodation" under the ADA cannot defeat seniority rights under a collective bargaining agreement); Eckles v. Consol. Rail Corp., 94 F.3d 1041, 1047–48 (7th Cir.1996) (collecting cases upholding the same rule under the Rehabilitation Act), *cert. denied*, 520 U.S. 1146, 117 S.Ct. 1318, 137 L.Ed.2d 480 (1997). *See also* U.S. Airways, Inc. v. Barnett, 535 U.S. 391, 393, 122 S.Ct. 1516, 152 L.Ed.2d 589 (2002) ("[T]o show that a requested accommodation conflicts with the rules of a seniority provision is ordinarily to show that the accommodation is not 'reasonable.' "); Harrell v. Donahue, 638 F.3d 975, 982 (8th Cir.2011) (stating the same in case involving religious accommodation).

Evidence of hostility or animosity between the plaintiff and the employer that would make it impossible for them to have a harmonious working relationship may be sufficient to rebut the presumption that the plaintiff is entitled to reinstatement. *See* EEOC v. Kallir, Philips, Ross, 420 F.Supp. at 926–27 (S.D.N.Y.1976) (leading case); McIntosh v. Jones Truck Lines, Inc., 767 F.2d 433 (8th Cir.1985) (reinstatement denied where hostility between parties occurred prior to suit); Sayger v. Riceland Foods, Inc., 735 F.3d 1025, 1034–35 (8th Cir.2013) (finding no abuse of discretion in lower court's denial of reinstatement where plaintiff expressed concern over future retaliation if reinstatement were granted).

But see Taylor v. Teletype Corp., 648 F.2d 1129, 1139 (8th Cir.1981) (rejecting employer's argument that reinstatement must be set aside because of hostility engendered by the filing of discrimination case). For an analysis of available remedies in discrimination cases involving workplace hostility, see Susan K. Grebeldinger, *The Role of Workplace Hostility in Determining Prospective Remedies for Employment Discrimination: A Call for Greater Judicial Discretion in Awarding Front Pay*, 1996 U. Ill. L. Rev. 319 (1996). Front pay is discussed below.

Congress has legislatively overruled the presumptive reinstatement rule in mixed-motive cases in which the defendant proves the "same decision" defense. Title VII, § § 703(m), 706(g)(2)(B), 42 U.S.C. §§ 2000e–2(m), –5(g)(2)(B). And, in *McKennon v. Nashville Banner*, 513 U.S. 352, 115 S.Ct. 879, 130 L.Ed.2d 852 (1995), which was covered earlier in Chapter 2, the Supreme Court endorsed a strong presumption against reinstatement in after-acquired evidence cases when the employer proves that the later-acquired legitimate nondiscriminatory reason is of such severity that it justifies a decision in favor of the employer. *See also* Kapche v. Holder, 677 F.3d 454, 464 (D.C. 2012) (Citing *McKennon* and affirming lower court's denial of reinstatement sought pursuant to the Rehabilitation Act, where after-acquired evidence had been shown).

Reinstatement and monetary damages are the forms of relief that courts have ordered most frequently in employment discrimination cases. The courts, however, have been willing to consider and order a wider range of remedies when necessary to effectuate the rightful place and make-whole principles of *Moody* and *Franks*. In some instances, declaratory relief might be the only remedy that would be appropriate. *See* Mitchell v. OsAir, Inc., 629 F.Supp. 636 (N.D.Ohio 1986) (the court found discrimination, but also found plaintiff had been discharged for lawful reasons). "[D]eclaratory relief simply declares the rights of the parties or expresses the court's opinion on a question of law without any party having to do anything," and in employment discrimination cases this form of relief "is likely to provide no more than a statement which says that the defendant violated plaintiff's rights * * * because of * * * race or sex." Belton, Remedies § 8.2.

3. BACK PAY

The theory of back pay, based upon the *Moody* make-whole principle, is to compensate victims of unlawful employment discrimination for the economic losses they have suffered from the date of the occurrence of the discriminatory act to the date of the entry of judgment on liability or until the date the plaintiff finds comparable employment. As a general rule, the beginning date is the date of the occurrence of the discriminatory act, e.g., discharge, refusal to hire, or failure to promote. *See* Velazquez v. Chardon, 736 F.2d 831 (1st Cir.1984). Back pay cannot extend to more than two years prior to the filing of a charge with the EEOC. *See, e.g.*, Title VII, § 706(g), 42 U.S.C. § 2000e–5(g). The ending date varies depending upon the circumstances of the particular case, but the general rule is that it is the date of the entry of judgment on liability. *See* Henry v. Lennox Indus., Inc., 768 F.2d 746 (6th Cir.1985). Other potential cut-off dates include the date on which the plaintiff's income from a new job exceeds the income she would have received "but for" the discrimination, *see* Darnell v. City of Jasper, 730 F.2d 653 (11th Cir.1984); the date the plaintiff removed herself from the labor market, *see* Brady v. Thurston Motor Lines, Inc., 753 F.2d 1269 (4th Cir.1985); or the date of normal retirement, *see* Fite v. First Tenn. Prod. Credit Ass'n, 861 F.2d 884 (6th Cir.1988). Back pay may not be awarded in mixed motive cases if the defendant carries its burden of proof in showing that the same decision would have been made despite the discrimination. *See* Porter v. Natsios, 414 F.3d 13 (D.C. Cir.2005).

The elements used in computing back pay include but are not limited to wages, salary, bonuses, commissions, raises, and fringe benefits, e.g., sick pay, vacation pay, pension benefits, health benefits, stock purchase benefits, and bonuses (including the cost of the missed Christmas turkey or ham). *See* Pettway v. Am. Cast Iron Pipe Co. 494 F.2d 211 (5th Cir.1974); Rasimas v. Mich. Dep't of Mental Health, 714 F.2d 614 (6th Cir.1983); Catlett v. Mo. State Highway Comm'n, 627 F.Supp. 1015 (W.D.Mo.1985), *aff'd in part, rev'd in part*, 828 F.2d 1260 (8th Cir.1987); Buckley v. Reynolds Metals Co., 690 F.Supp. 211 (D.C.N.Y.1988) (dental and vision insurance); Chin v. Port Auth. of New York & New Jersey, 685 F.3d 135, 141 (2d Cir.2012).

Title VII and the ADA impose on victims of discrimination a statutory duty to mitigate damages: "Interim earnings or amounts earnable with reasonable diligence by the person or persons discriminated against shall operate to reduce the back pay otherwise allowable." 42 U.S.C. § 2000e–5(g); 42 U.S.C. § 12117(a). The courts have also read a duty to mitigate damages into the ADEA, the Equal Pay Act, and § 1981. *See, e.g.*, Maxfield v. Sinclair Int'l, 766 F.2d 788, 793–95 (3d Cir.1985) (ADEA); Trainor v. HEI Hospitality, LLC, 699 F.3d 19 (1st Cir.2012) (ADEA); Piva v. Xerox Corp., 654 F.2d 591, 598–99 (9th Cir.1981) (Equal Pay Act). The failure to mitigate damages is an affirmative defense on which the employer bears the burden of proof—both the burden of the production of evidence and the burden of persuasion. Generally, the plaintiff's duty to mitigate is not an onerous burden; the plaintiff is required only to try to find a "substantially equivalent" position or to use "reasonable diligence" to try to find a job that is the same or substantially equivalent in responsibilities, working conditions, and status to the job discriminatorily denied. Success in the plaintiff's efforts to find another position is not essential. Sellers v.

Delgado Cmty. Coll., 839 F.2d 1132, 1138 (5th Cir.1988). Moreover, the courts have held that the plaintiff is required only to make a good faith reasonable effort. *See e.g.*, Dollar v. Smithway Motor Xpress, Inc., 710 F.3d 798, 808 (8th Cir.2013);Yancey v. Weyerhauser Co., 277 F.3d 1021 (8th Cir.2002); Brooks v. Woodline Motor Freight, Inc., 852 F.2d 1061 (8th Cir.1988).

Suppose an employer has denied jobs to several female applicants and there is a strong basis for believing that the employer did so solely because they are female. Later the employer offers the women jobs, but does not include compensation for the economic loss they suffered between the date they were first rejected and the date they received the job offers. Should the women be required to accept the job offers pursuant to the duty to mitigate damages? *Ford Motor Co. v. EEOC*, 458 U.S. 219, 102 S.Ct. 3057, 73 L.Ed.2d 721 (1982), held that, absent special circumstances, an offer of employment to a rejected applicant tolls the accrual of back pay if the employer makes an unconditional offer of the job denied, even if the offer does not include all the relief that the plaintiff is entitled to receive.

Are defendants entitled to a set-off for income that plaintiffs receive from collateral sources? Some of the most obvious collateral sources are social security, unemployment compensation, welfare benefits, and disability income. Some courts hold that benefits received from a source collateral to the discriminatory conduct of the employer may not be used to reduce back pay awards. *See, e.g.*, Craig v. Y&Y Snacks, Inc., 721 F.2d 77 (3d Cir.1983); *see also* NLRB v. Gullet Gin Co., 340 U.S. 361, 364, 71 S.Ct. 337, 339, 95 L.Ed.337 (1951) (back pay award under the National Labor Relations Act not to be reduced by amount received under unemployment benefits). Others hold that district courts have discretion to set off collateral source income against a back pay award. *See, e.g.*, Noel v. New York State Office of Mental Health Cent. New York Psychiatric Ctr., 697 F.3d 209, 212 n. 1 (2d Cir.2012) (questioning state's authority to deduct hypothetical social security contribution from employee's back pay award); Dailey v. Societe Generale, 108 F.3d 451 (2d Cir.1997). For a discussion of the problem of applying the collateral source doctrine to front pay, see Eric Pearson, Note, *Collateral Benefits and Front Pay: A Rule of No Offset Encourages Agency Recoupment*, 69 U.Chi. L.Rev. 1957 (2002).

Prejudgment interest is intended to compensate the plaintiff for the loss of an opportunity to invest her wages at the going rate of interest. The Supreme Court has recognized the consensus view that trial courts have discretion to award prejudgment interest as part of back pay in Title VII lawsuits against private employers. *See* Loeffler v. Frank, 486 U.S. 549, 558–59, 108 S.Ct. 1967, 1970–71, 100 L.Ed.2d 459 (1988). Several courts, relying on *Moody*'s make-whole theory, have adopted a strong presumption in favor of prejudgment interest. *See, e.g.*, Eshelman v. Agere Sys., Inc., 554 F.3d 426, 440 (3d Cir.2009); Davis v. Constr. Materials, 558 F.Supp. 697 (N.D.Ala.), *aff'd*, 720 F.2d 1293 (11th Cir.1983). The courts have not adopted a uniform standard for determining the rate of prejudgment interest. For a list of prejudgment rates used by various courts, *see* Belton, Remedies § 15.11 (1998 Supplement). Postjudgment interest, however, is now mandatory under federal law, 28 U.S.C. § 1961 (1986), and the rate of interest is tied to federal interest rates. Congress amended Title VII, § 717, 42 U.S.C. § 2000e–16, to make the federal government subject to the same interest rates as are applied to nonpublic parties.

4. FRONT PAY

Although reinstatement has traditionally been the preferred remedy in employment discrimination cases, there are times when reinstatement is not feasible, either because the employer has no open position or because employer relations with the employee have become too strained to make reinstatement workable. In these circumstances, courts often award a monetary amount to compensate for lost future wages, what is known as front pay. *See, e.g.*, Avitia v. Metro. Club of Chi., 49 F.3d 1219, 1232 (7th Cir.1995); Bruso v. United Airlines, Inc., 239 F.3d 848, 862 (7th Cir.2001). The courts have adopted a variety of definitions of front pay. For example, the Seventh Circuit has defined front pay as "the difference (after proper discounting to present value) between what the plaintiff would have earned in the future had he been reinstated at the time of trial and what he would have earned in the future in his next best employment." *Avitia*, 49 F.3d at 1231. In *Lander v. Lujan*, 888 F.2d 153, 159 (D.C.Cir.1989), then-Judge Ruth Bader Ginsburg, concurring in a Title VII case, referred to an award of front pay as "rightful place" relief because it avoids any unfairness resulting from "bumping" an incumbent out of a position when a court orders the employer to promote the plaintiff immediately.

Even though none of the federal statutes prohibiting employment discrimination specify front pay as a remedy, the overwhelming weight of judicial opinion is that front pay can be awarded under Title VII, ADEA, ADA, the Rehabilitation Act, and § 1981. *See* Belton, Remedies § 10.3 (collecting cases). For example, prior to the Civil Rights Act of 1991, many courts found the statutory authority to award front pay—as an alternative to reinstatement—in the catchall phrase in § 706(g)(1) of Title VII: "any other equitable *relief* the court deems appropriate." *See* Hudson v. Reno, 130 F.3d 1193, 1203 & n. 6 (6th Cir.1997). Front pay generally is not awarded in an Equal Pay Act case because back pay and an injunction to equalize the wages of males and females usually provides adequate relief. Plaintiffs generally are not entitled to both front pay and reinstatement because this would provide a windfall to the plaintiff. *See* Traxler v. Multnomah Cnty., 596 F.3d 1007, 1012 (9th Cir.2010) ("As a practical matter, front pay is awarded * * * only if the court determines that reinstatement is inappropriate."); Suggs v. Servicemaster Educ. Food Mgmt., 72 F.3d 1228, 1234–35 (6th Cir.1996).

The elements used to determine the amount of front pay are generally the same as those used in determining back pay. *See* Buckley v. Reynolds Metals Co., 690 F.Supp. 211 (S.D.N.Y.1988) (using wages, and pension, health, and life insurance benefits to determine front pay). *See* Section 3, *supra*. The amount awarded as front pay is not included in calculating liquidated damages in ADEA cases because front pay does not fall within the meaning of "amounts owing" under § 216(b) of the Fair Labor Standards Act. *See* Cooper v. Asplundh Tree Expert Co., 836 F.2d 1544, 1556–57 (10th Cir.1988).

In *Pollard v. E.I. du Pont de Nemours & Co.*, 532 U.S. 843, 121 S.Ct. 1946, 150 L.Ed.2d 62 (2001), the Supreme Court upheld the authority of lower courts to award front pay under § 706(g) of Title VII:

> Although courts have defined "front pay" in numerous ways, front pay is simply money awarded for lost compensation during the period between judgment and reinstatement or in lieu of reinstatement.
>
> * * *
>
> * * * [T]he original language of § 706(g) authorizing backpay awards was modeled after the same language in the NLRA. This provision in the NLRA has been construed to allow awards of backpay up to the date of reinstatement, even if reinstatement occurred after the judgment. Accordingly, backpay awards made for the period between the date of judgment and the date of reinstatement, which today we call front pay awards under Title VII, were authorized under § 706(g).
>
> As to front pay awards that are made in lieu of reinstatement, we construe § 706(g) as authorizing these awards as well. We see no logical difference between front pay awards made when there eventually is reinstatement and those made when there is not.

Id. at 846, 853, 121 S.Ct. at 1948, 1952. Under the Civil Rights Act of 1991, front pay cannot be awarded in mixed-motive cases. Title VII, § 706(g)(2)(B)(ii), 42 U.S.C. § 2000e–5(g)(2)(B)(ii).

5. COMPENSATORY AND PUNITIVE DAMAGES

The Caps on Compensatory and Punitive Damages Under the Civil Rights Act of 1991: Compensatory and punitive damages for disparate treatment claims under Title VII were first authorized in the Civil Rights Act of 1991. Compensatory and punitive damages are now recoverable under Title VII in addition to the traditional Title VII remedies, like front pay and back pay. 42 U.S.C. § 1981a(a)(1) (2006). Compensatory and punitive damages, however, are subject to the following caps:

—Employers with more than 14 but fewer than 101 employees: $50,000.

—More than 100 but fewer than 201: $100,000.

—More than 200 but fewer than 501: $200,000.

—More than 500: $300,000.

See 42 U.S.C. § 1981a(b)(3). *But see,* Hernandez-Miranda v. Empresas Diaz Masso, Inc., 651 F.3d 167, 176 (1st Cir.2011) (holding that defendant bears the burden of presenting evidence when seeking to impose a cap). Juries are not to be informed of the caps on damages, but a court must reduce the amounts awarded as compensatory and punitive damages if the jury's award exceeds the statutory caps. *See, e.g.*, Hudson v. Reno, 130 F.3d 1193, 1198–1201 (6th Cir.1997), *abrogated on other grounds*, 121 S.Ct. 1946 (2001); Hernandez-Miranda v. Empresas Diaz Masso, Inc., 651 F.3d 167, 173 (1st Cir.2011). For a discussion of the merits of this approach, see Rebecca Hollander Blumoff & Matthew Bodie, *The Effects of Jury Ignorance About Damages Caps: The Case of the 1991 Civil Rights Act,* 90 Iowa L.Rev. 1361 (2005). The courts uniformly hold that the caps apply to the aggregate of all claims brought by a single plaintiff and not to each individual claim on which the plaintiff prevails, *Hudson*, 130 F.3d at 1200; that is, the total of both compensatory and punitive damages cannot exceed the caps for each plaintiff. *See* Hernandez-Miranda, 651 F.3d at 172; Suggs v. Servicemaster Educ. Food Mgmt., 72 F.3d 1228 (6th Cir.1996); Hogan v. Bangor & Aroostook R.R., 61 F.3d 1034, 1037 (1st Cir.1995). The statutory caps on compensatory and punitive damages under the Civil Rights Act of 1991, however, are not applicable to claims brought under § 1981, even if the § 1981 claim is joined with a claim that would be subject to the caps. *See* Kim v. Nash Finch Co., 123 F.3d 1046, 1067 (8th Cir.1997).

In addition to limiting damages by caps, the Civil Rights Act of 1991 exempts federal, state, and local government agencies from awards of punitive damages. 42 U.S.C. § 1981a(a)(1) (2006). The EEOC has been found to have the authority under the Civil Rights Act of 1991 to require federal agencies to pay compensatory damages. *See* West v. Gibson, 527 U.S. 212, 119 S.Ct. 1906, 144 L.Ed.2d 196 (1999). The section of the Act imposing caps on compensatory and punitive damages also provides that a complaining party may recover compensatory and punitive damages under Title VII only if it "cannot recover under § 1981." *Id.* Legislative history suggests that this provision was included only to prevent double recovery. *See* 137 Cong. Rec. H9526–27 (daily ed. Nov. 7, 1991) (statement of Rep. Edwards) ("While these plaintiffs may proceed under both sections, they, of course, cannot recover double damages for the same harm arising under the same facts and circumstances.") Most courts have found that plaintiffs can receive compensatory and punitive damages under Title VII unless such damages are *actually* available to them under § 1981. *See, e.g.*, Sayger v. Riceland Foods, Inc., 735 F.3d 1025, 1034 (8th Cir.2013).

Compensatory Damages: Compensatory damages are defined under the Civil Rights Act of 1991 to include "future pecuniary losses, emotional pain, suffering, inconvenience, mental anguish, loss of enjoyment of life, and other nonpecuniary losses." 42 U.S.C. § 1981a(b)(3). The EEOC has issued a policy statement that the following are recoverable as compensatory damages: injury to professional standing, injury to character and reputation, injury to credit standing, loss of health, and aggravation of preexisting emotional difficulties if further deterioration is caused by the employer's conduct (e.g., victim of incest who brings a sexual harassment claim). *EEOC Enforcement Guidance: Compensatory and Punitive Damages Available Under Section 102 of the Civil Rights Act of 1991*, available at *http://www.eeoc.gov/policy/docs/damages.html* (July 6, 2000).

Punitive Damages: The Civil Rights Act of 1991 provides that punitive damages may be recovered against a defendant (other than any government agency or political subdivision) if the plaintiff proves that the defendant engaged in an unlawful employment practice "with malice or with reckless indifference to the federally protected rights" of the plaintiff. 42 U.S.C. § 1981a(b)(1). This is essentially the same standard adopted by the Supreme Court in § 1983 litigation in *Smith v. Wade*, 461 U.S. 30, 55, 103 S.Ct. 1625, 1640, 75 L.Ed.2d 632 (1983) ("reckless or callous indifference to the federally protected rights of others"). Conduct more egregious than intentional discrimination is required to support an award of punitive damages, but the courts have generally rejected a standard requiring a showing of "extraordinarily egregious" conduct. Factors to be considered in determining the amount of punitive damages include the nature and the severity of the discriminatory conduct, the duration and frequency of the conduct, and the financial status of the employer. *See EEOC Enforcement Guidance: Compensatory and Punitive Damages Available Under Section 102 of the Civil Rights Act of 1991*, available at *www.eeoc.gov/policy/docs/damages.html* (July 6, 2000) (collecting cases brought under § 1981). Evidence about a defendant's net worth is highly relevant on the issue of the amount to be awarded as punitive damages. *See* Rodgers v. Fisher Body Div., GMC, 739 F.2d 1102 (6th Cir.1984). *See also*, Jill Wieber Lens, *Procedural Due Process and*

Predictable Punitive Damage Awards, 2012 B.Y.U. L. Rev. 1, 49 (2012) (discussing the idea of pegging damage awards to defendant's wealth).

With respect to punitive damages, questions arose quickly after the 1991 Civil Rights Act about the proper standard to apply in employment discrimination cases. In *Kolstad v. American Dental Association,* 527 U.S. 526, 119 S.Ct. 2118, 144 L.Ed.2d 494 (1999), the Supreme Court resolved a conflict between the circuits on the burden a plaintiff must carry to prove malice or recklessness. The Court granted certiorari to address the issue of "the circumstances under which a jury may consider a request for punitive damages under § 1981a(b)(1)." *Id.* at 533, 119 S.Ct. at 2123. The Court construed the statutory structure as requiring two separate standards for recovery of compensatory and punitive damages:

> The very structure of § 1981a suggests a congressional intent to authorize punitive awards in only a subset of cases involving intentional discrimination. Section 1981a(a)(1) limits compensatory and punitive awards to instances of intentional discrimination, while § 1981a(b)(1) requires plaintiffs to make an additional "demonstrat[ion]" of their eligibility for punitive damages. Congress plainly sought to impose two standards of liability—one for establishing a right to compensatory damages and another, higher standard that a plaintiff must satisfy to qualify for a punitive award.

Id. at 534, 119 S.Ct. at 2124.

Having concluded that Congress intended to impose a higher standard for an award of punitive damages in statutory employment discrimination cases, the Court then set out to define what that standard should be. The Court squarely rejected the lower court's standard that punitive damages can be awarded only upon a showing of egregious conduct. Egregious conduct may be "evidence of the requisite mental state, [but] § 1981a does not limit plaintiffs to this form of evidence, and the section does not require a showing of egregious or outrageous discrimination independent of the employer's state of mind." *Id.*, 119 S.Ct. at 2124. Based upon its reading of congressional intent, the Court held that the statutory standards of "malice" or "reckless indifference to federally protected rights of an aggrieved individual" require proof that an employer had "guilty" knowledge that it "may be acting in violation of federal law," rather than proof that the employer was aware that it was "engaging in unlawful discrimination." *Id.* at 535, 119 S.Ct. at 2124. The Court variously characterized the terms "malice" or "reckless indifference" as imposing an obligation on a plaintiff to prove that the employer's conduct was not only the result of intentional discrimination, but also was "motivated by evil motive or intent or callous indifference to rights of others," or showed a "subjective consciousness of a risk of injury or illegality," or showed "knowledge of falsity or reckless disregard of the truth." *Id.,* 119 S.Ct. at 2125.

The Court then attempted to shed light on the types of situations in which a plaintiff proves intentional discrimination but where the requisite malice or reckless indifference may not be present:

> In some instances, the employer may simply be unaware of the relevant prohibition. There will be cases, moreover, in which the employer discriminates with the distinct belief that its discrimination is lawful. The underlying theory of discrimination may be novel or otherwise poorly recognized, or an employer may reasonably believe that its discrimination satisfied the bona fide occupational qualification defense or other statutory exception to liability.

Id. at 536–37, 119 S.Ct. at 2125.

The Supreme Court has held that there are substantive and procedural constitutional limitations on punitive awards that state courts can award because the Constitution provides an upper limit on punitive damages so that a person has "fair notice not only of the conduct that will subject him to punishment but also the severity of the penalty that * * * may be imposed." BMW of North America, Inc. v. Gore, 517 U.S. 559, 574 116 S.Ct. 1589, 134 L.Ed.2d 809 (1996). *Gore* instructs courts reviewing punitive damages awards to consider three guideposts: (1) reprehensibility of defendant's conduct; (2) the disparity between the actual and potential harm suffered by the plaintiff and the punitive damages award; and (3) the difference between the punitive damages awarded by the jury and the civil penalties authorized or imposed in comparable cases. 517 U.S. at 575, 116 S.Ct. at 1598–99. Later, in *State Farm Mutual Automobile Insurance Co. v. Campbell*, 538 U.S. 408, 123 S.Ct. 1513, 155 L.Ed.2d 585 (2003), the Court explained that "in practice, few awards exceeding a single-digit ratio between punitive and compensatory damages, to a significant degree, will satisfy due process," though it emphasized that the precise award must be based on the facts and circumstances of each case. *Id.* at 425, 123 S.Ct. at 1524. Due process concerns regarding the extremity of a punitive damages award should not materialize under Title VII where compensatory and punitive damages are capped by statute. For a further discussion on the issues surrounding punitive damages in employment discrimination claims, see Sandra F. Sperino, *Direct Employer Liability for Punitive Damages*, 97 Iowa L. Rev. Bull. 24 (2012).

The Requirement of Employer Vicarious Liability for an Award of Punitive Damages: The more controversial and difficult holding in *Kolstad* is Part II, where the majority of the Court reached out to decide an issue not presented for review in the granting of certiorari. The Court held that, in addition to proving malice or reckless indifference under its newly crafted test for punitive damages, there must be some basis for imputing liability to the employer for the award. Observing that "[i]n express terms, Congress has directed federal courts to interpret Title VII based on agency principles," the Court cited the following provisions of the Restatement (Second) of Agency:

> "Punitive damages can properly be awarded against a master or other principal because of an act by the agent, if but only if:
>
> "(a) the principal authorized the doing and manner of the act, or
>
> "(b) the agent was unfit and the principal was reckless in employing him, or
>
> "(c) the agent was employed in a managerial capacity and was acting in the scope of employment, or
>
> "(d) the principal or a managerial agent of the principal ratified or approved the act."

Id. at 542–43, 119 S.Ct. at 2128 (quoting Restatement (Second) of Agency § 217(C)(1957)). The Court observed that the Restatement (Second) of Agency contemplates employer liability for punitive damages where an employee is serving in a "managerial capacity" and is "acting in the scope of employment." Whether an employee is employed in a managerial capacity is a "fact-intensive inquiry," which requires a court to " 'review the type of authority that the employer has given to the employee, the amount of discretion the employee has in what is done and how it is accomplished.' " *Id.* at 548, 119 S.Ct. at 2128 (citation omitted). *See also,* Lowery v. Circuit City Stores, Inc., 206 F.3d 431, 443 (4th Cir.2000) (suggesting a series a questions that are relevant in assessing the evidence to determine whether the employer is liable for punitive damages); Ash v. Tyson Foods, Inc., 664 F.3d 883, 904 (11th Cir.2011) (citing *Kolstad* and precluding punitive damages where employer had shown good faith in complying with anti-discrimination laws).

The Availability of Compensatory and Punitive Damages in Class Actions: Prior to 2011, the courts were split on whether compensatory and punitive damages could be recovered in class actions brought under Rule 23(b)(2) of the Federal Rules of Civil Procedure. In *Allison v. Citgo Petroleum Corp.*, 151 F.3d 402 (5th Cir.1998), the court denied class certification where the predominant relief plaintiffs sought was compensatory and punitive damages. The court ruled that "monetary relief may be obtained in a * * * class action so long as the predominant relief sought is injunctive or declaratory." *Id.* at 411. In contrast, the Second Circuit had reached the opposite result in *Robinson v. Metro-North Commuter Railroad Co.,* 267 F.3d 147 (2dCir.2001). In 2011, the Supreme Court held that monetary relief could generally not be granted in cases involving class actions certified under F.R.C.P. 23(b)(2). *See,* Wal-Mart Stores, Inc. v. Dukes, 131 S. Ct. 2541, 2557, 180 L. Ed. 2d 374 (2011) (holding that monetary relief not incidental to injunctive or declaratory relief shall not be granted in certain class action proceedings). For a critical discussion of *Dukes, see* Suzette M. Malveaux, *How Goliath Won: The Future Implications of Dukes v. Wal-Mart,* 106 Nw. U.L. Rev. Colloquy 34, 45 (2011).

6. LIQUIDATED DAMAGES

Liquidated damages under the Equal Pay Act and the ADEA are an additional amount awarded to the plaintiff that is equal to the back pay award. 29 U.S.C. §§ 216(b), 626(b). The term "liquidated damages" has a different meaning here than in contract law. Under the ADEA (and the FLSA) liquidated damages simply means double (unpaid wages) damages, and are viewed as a substitute for punitive damages. In contracts, of course, liquidated damages refers to contractual attempts by parties to fix damages prior to breach. Contract liquidated damages must reasonably approximate actual damages while ADEA liquidated damages are calculated on the basis of actual damages but are intended to enhance them to deter violations of the statute. *See, e.g.,.* TWA, Inc. v. Thurston, 469 U.S. 111, 125–26, 105 S.Ct. 613, 624, 83 L.Ed.2d 523 (1985) (discussing the legislative history of the liquidated damages provision of the ADEA). Set-offs should be made before liquidated damages are determined. *See* Bhaya v. Westinghouse Elec. Corp., 624 F.Supp. 921 (E.D.Pa.1985), *vacated & remanded on other grounds,* 832 F.2d 258 (3d Cir.1987).

Liquidated damages are recoverable in ADEA cases if the evidence supports a finding of a willful violation. 29 U.S.C. § 626(b). In *Trans World Airlines v. Thurston,* 469 U.S. 111, 105 S.Ct. 613, 83 L.Ed.2d 523 (1985), the Supreme Court resolved a conflict between the circuits on the standard of willfulness. The Court adopted a test requiring proof that the employer "knew or showed reckless disregard" whether the conduct was prohibited by the ADEA standard. *Id.* at 126, 105 S.Ct. at 624. This standard of willfulness was not met in *Thurston* because the policy at issue—the employer's refusal to permit flight engineers who reached the age of sixty to bump other flight engineers with less seniority in order to avoid layoff—was adopted after consultation with counsel. In a later case, *McLaughlin v. Richland Shoe,* 486 U.S. 128, 108 S.Ct. 1677, 100 L.Ed.2d 115 (1988), the Court held that even if an employer acted unreasonably, but not recklessly, in determining its statutory obligation, such conduct would not be "willful" under the *Thurston* standard. *Thurston* involved an ADEA challenge to a policy that was discriminatory on its face, but the lower courts had adopted differing standards of willfulness in ADEA disparate treatment cases. In *Hazen Paper Co. v. Biggins,* 507 U.S. 604,

113 S.Ct. 1701, 123 L.Ed.2d 338 (1993), reproduced in Chapter 14, the Supreme Court, in a unanimous decision, resolved the split in the circuits and held that the *Thurston* standard applies in disparate treatment ADEA cases.

7. TAXATION OF AWARDS

Monetary awards that are recoverable under the *Moody* make-whole theory of relief include back pay, front pay, compensatory damages, punitive damages, liquidated damages, and prejudgment and postjudgment interest. Which of these items of monetary recovery should be subject to taxation under federal and state income tax laws has become an important and complex subject in employment discrimination law. The Supreme Court's decision in *United States v. Burke*, 504 U.S. 229, 112 S.Ct. 1867, 119 L.Ed.2d 34 (1992), was a major decision that ushered in the movement toward taxation of damages in employment discrimination law. In *Burke*, the Supreme Court held that back pay awards under Title VII are not excludable from taxable income because Title VII, prior to the Civil Rights Act of 1991, provided only for back pay and other equitable relief, not a "tort-type personal injury" recovery that would be excludable from gross income under the Internal Revenue Code. The decision in *Burke* arose in a Title VII case that was settled before 1991. In the Civil Rights Act of 1991, Congress amended Title VII, the ADA, and the Rehabilitation Act to allow compensatory and punitive damages.

Following *Burke*, the Internal Revenue Service first issued a ruling that provided that all the damages received under Title VII after the 1991 Act were excludable from gross income, but the Service later rescinded that ruling. In 1995, in *Commissioner v. Schleier*, 515 U.S. 323, 115 S.Ct. 2159, 132 L.Ed.2d 294, the Supreme Court held that neither back pay nor liquidated damages recovered under the ADEA were excludable from gross income. And in *O'Gilvie v. United States*, 519 U.S. 79, 117 S.Ct. 452, 136 L.Ed.2d 454 (1996), the Court held that punitive damages received in a tort action for personal injuries were not excludable from taxable gross income.

The Small Business Job Protection Act of 1996, Pub. L. No. 104–188, § 1605, 110 Stat. 1755, 1838 (codified at 26 U.S.C. § 104(a)), amended the Internal Revenue Code to provide that all punitive damages are taxable and that damages for emotional distress are excludable only if recovered for physical sickness or physical injury. The post-*Burke* developments in tax law make it clear that most monetary awards recovered in employment discrimination cases are to be treated as taxable income. These monetary awards, whether received as a result of a judicial order or through a settlement, pose significant compliance problems for the recipients and potential ethical problems for their attorneys. For a discussion of some of these problems, *see* Laura A. Quigley, *IRS Nips at*

Damages Awards; Attorneys Confront Conflicts, Nat'l L.J., Mar. 17, 1997, at B8; Douglas A. Kahn, *Compensatory and Punitive Damages for a Personal Injury: To Tax or Not to Tax?*, 2 Fla.Tax Rev. 327 (1994). *See also* Robert W. Wood, Taxation of Damage Awards and Settlement Payments, ch.3 (2d ed.1998).

Attorney's fees, as discussed in the next section, are recoverable under substantially all of the federal statutes prohibiting discrimination in employment. Suppose the parties to an employment discrimination lawsuit decide to settle the case and the employer is willing to agree to a handsome recovery, but is willing to issue only a single check in the amount of $500,000 to cover both the plaintiff's monetary recovery and attorney's fees. You represent the plaintiff in this situation. Do you envision any ethical problems in simultaneously negotiating a settlement on behalf of your client and the amount of your attorney's fees? The Third Circuit, in *Prandini v. National Tea Co.*, 557 F.2d 1015 (3d Cir.1977), was one of the first circuits to adopt an ironclad rule barring fee negotiation until after the settlement of the merits of a case. In *Evans v. Jeff D.*, 475 U.S. 717, 106 S.Ct. 1531, 89 L.Ed.2d 747 (1986), the Supreme Court rejected the *Prandini* rule, unanimously approving the simultaneous negotiation of attorney's fees and the plaintiff's recovery.

8. ATTORNEY'S FEES

a. Entitlement to Fees

Traditionally, all parties involved in litigation in the United States are obligated to bear their own costs and attorney's fees. This is the so-called American no-fee rule. The American courts, particularly the federal courts, have carved out certain exceptions to the no-fee rule. One of the exceptions is the "private attorney general" rule. This exception empowers courts to impose the costs of litigation and attorney's fees on the losing party in litigation that is deemed to vindicate important public policy. *See, e.g.*, Newman v. Piggie Park Enters., Inc., 390 U.S. 400, 88 S.Ct. 964, 19 L.Ed.2d 1263 (1968). In *Alyeska Pipeline Service Co. v. Wilderness Society*, 421 U.S. 240, 95 S.Ct. 1612, 44 L.Ed.2d 141 (1975), the Supreme Court limited the application of the private attorney general doctrine to cases in which Congress has specifically enacted a statutory fee-shifting provision. A fee-shifting statute empowers a court to require one party to pay the other party's attorney's fees or attorney's fees and costs.

All of the major federal statutes prohibiting discrimination in employment have fee-shifting provisions. For example, § 706(k) of Title VII provides: "In any action or proceeding under [Title VII] the court, in its discretion, may allow the prevailing party, other than the [EEOC] or the United States, a reasonable attorney's fee (including expert fees) as part of the costs * * * ." 42 U.S.C. § 2000e–5(k). The ADA, § 107, 42 U.S.C. § 12117, incorporates the fee-shifting provision of Title VII. Fees and costs for claims brought under § 1981 and the Fourteenth Amendment Equal Protection Clause are recoverable under the Civil Rights Attorney's Fees Awards Act of 1976, 42 U.S.C. § 1988. Fees can be awarded to a "prevailing plaintiff" or a "prevailing defendant" under Title VII, § 1981, or the ADA. But only "prevailing plaintiffs" are entitled to benefit from the fee-shifting provision in Equal Pay Act cases because the statute on fees provides that a court "shall * * * allow a reasonable attorney's fee to be paid by the defendant, and costs of the action." 29 U.S.C. § 216(b). *See* Horner v. Mary Inst., 613 F.2d 706 (8th Cir.1980). The ADEA incorporated the Fair Labor Standards Act provision on fees (the same statutory provision as is applicable in Equal Pay Act cases), but some courts have allowed prevailing defendants to recover fees and costs in ADEA cases only where the district court finds that the plaintiff litigated the case in bad faith. *See, e.g.*, Turlington v. Atlanta Gas Light Co., 135 F.3d 1428, 1437 (11th Cir.1998) (citing other circuits that permit recovery of fees only under the bad faith rule); Sanchez v. Nitro-Lift Technologies, L.L.C., 12–7046, 2014 WL 3882543 (10th Cir.Aug. 8, 2014) (citing *Turlington*, stating the same). *but see* E.E.O.C. v. Propak Logistics, Inc., 746 F.3d 145, 151 (4th Cir.2014) (stating that mere unreasonableness on part of plaintiff is sufficient, and that bad faith is not required); Davis v. Target Stores Div. of Dayton Hudson Corp., 87 F.Supp.2d 492, 494–95 (D.Md.2000) (discussing disagreement in lower courts about a bad faith prerequisite).

Clearly, determining who is a "prevailing party" is a key to the award of fees. The Supreme Court in *Farrar v. Hobby,* 506 U.S. 103, 111–12, 113 S.Ct. 566, 573, 121 L.Ed.2d (1992), stated that, "a plaintiff 'prevails' when actual relief on the merits of his claim materially alters the legal relationship between the parties by modifying the defendant's behavior in a way that directly benefits the plaintiff." Courts have found parties to be prevailing under the *Farrar* standard when the plaintiff has earned more than mere nominal damages or the relief awarded has an important impact on statutory rights. *See, e.g.,* Murray v. City of Onawa, 323 F.3d 616 (8th Cir.2003). In *Buckhannon Board & Care Home, Inc. v. West Virginia Department of Health & Human Resources*, 532 U.S. 598, 121 S.Ct. 1835, 149 L.Ed.2d 855 (2001), a case brought under the Fair Housing Amendments Act of 1988 and the ADA, the Court held that the term "prevailing party" requires that a plaintiff obtain a judgment or similar form of judicial relief, such as a court-ordered consent decree, as a predicate for attorney's fees.

Recovery of attorney's fees by a prevailing plaintiff is hardly controversial, but for a time courts struggled with the issue of attorney's fee awards in cases where the defendant was the prevailing party. The

Supreme Court finally addressed the issue in *Christiansburg Garment Co. v. EEOC*, 434 U.S. 412, 98 S.Ct. 694, 54 L.Ed.2d 648 (1978). Citing *Moody*, the Court acknowledged: "It can thus be taken as established * * * that under § 706(k) of Title VII a prevailing *plaintiff* ordinarily is to be awarded attorney's fees in all but special circumstances." *Id.* at 417, 98 S.Ct. at 698. Nevertheless, the Court agreed that, because " 'policy considerations which support the award of fees to a prevailing plaintiff are not present in the case of a prevailing defendant[,]' [a] successful defendant seeking counsel fees under § 706(k) must rely on quite different equitable considerations." *Id.* at 418–19, 98 S.Ct. at 699 (citation omitted). As a result, the Court stated,

> a plaintiff should not be assessed his opponent's attorney's fees unless a court finds that his claim was frivolous, unreasonable, or groundless, or that the plaintiff continued to litigate after it clearly became so. And, needless to say, if a plaintiff is found to have brought or continued such a claim in *bad faith*, there will be an even stronger basis for charging him with the attorney's fees incurred by the defense.

Id. at 422, 98 S.Ct. at 701.

It appears that *Christiansburg* establishes a strong, but rebuttable, presumption in favor of awards of attorney's fees for prevailing plaintiffs and a corresponding rebuttable presumption against awards of attorney's fees for prevailing defendants. In *Balmer v. HCA, Inc.*, 423 F.3d 606, 615–16 (6th Cir.2005), the Sixth Circuit followed two other circuits in setting out several factors for determining whether fees should be awarded to a prevailing defendant: (1) whether the plaintiff had enough evidence for a prima facie case, (2) whether the defendant offered to settle, and (3) whether the case was dismissed by the trial court or proceeded to trial. The court reversed a defendant fee award where one out of three claims was not frivolous, claiming that defendant fee awards were warranted only in the most "egregious" circumstances. *Id.* at 616–17. This Sixth Circuit decision was abrogated however by the Supreme Court in *Fox v. Vice*, 131 S. Ct. 2205, 180 L. Ed. 2d 45 (2011). In *Fox*, the court held that a defendant can recover attorneys' fees incurred due to frivolous claims brought by the plaintiff. *Id* at 2214–15. In disagreeing with the result in *Balmer*, however, the court went on to say that: "fee-shifting to recompense a defendant * * * is *not* all-or-nothing[,] [a] defendant need not show that every claim in a complaint is frivolous to qualify for fees." (emphasis added) *Id* at 2214. Additionally, the court stated that "the presence of reasonable allegations in a suit does not immunize the plaintiff against paying for the fees that his frivolous claims imposed." *Id.* There have been only a few cases in which courts have found special circumstances sufficient to deny fees to prevailing plaintiffs. *See, e.g.*, Phelps v. Hamilton, 120 F.3d 1126 (10th Cir.1997).

b. Standards for an Award of Fees

Calculating a Reasonable Fee: Prior to *Hensley v. Eckerhart*, 461 U.S. 424, 103 S.Ct. 1933, 76 L.Ed.2d 40 (1983), the courts had adopted various standards for determining what constitutes a reasonable fee. *See Hensley*, 461 U.S. at 429–34, 103 S.Ct. at 1937–40. *Hensley* endorsed the "lodestar" method that is now the predominant method for calculating a reasonable fee. The Court explained:

> The most useful starting point for determining the amount of a reasonable fee is the number of hours reasonably expended on the litigation multiplied by a reasonable hourly rate. This calculation provides an objective basis on which to make an initial estimate of the value of a lawyer's services. The party seeking an award of fees should submit evidence supporting the hours worked and rates claimed. Where the documentation of hours is inadequate, the district court may reduce the award accordingly.

Id. at 433, 103 S.Ct. at 1939.

1. *Reasonable Number of Hours*: The first step under the lodestar approach is to ascertain the number of hours "reasonably expended." Under *Hensley*, excessive, redundant, or otherwise unnecessary hours should be excluded from the calculation. 461 U.S. at 434, 103 S.Ct. at 1939–40. *Hensley* thus requires fees claimants to exercise billing judgment. Billing judgment requires the fees claimant to exclude hours that would be unreasonable to bill to paying clients. Time spent in administrative proceedings before the EEOC are compensable because exhaustion of administrative procedures is required. *See* New York Gaslight Club, Inc. v. Carey, 447 U.S. 54, 100 S.Ct. 2024, 64 L.Ed.2d 723 (1980). Reasonable hours also includes time spent by law clerks and paralegals even though their time is compensated at a lower hourly rate than the time spent by an attorney. *See* Mo. v. Jenkins, 491 U.S. 274, 109 S.Ct. 2463, 105 L.Ed.2d 229 (1989).

Suppose an attorney who represented a prevailing party requested an unreasonable hourly rate, billed the client for hours spent on other services, and agreed to split the fee with the client. Should a fee be allowed? Are there other sanctions that would be appropriate? *See* Keener v. Dep't of Army, 136 F.R.D. 140, 150–51 (M.D.Tenn.1991) (imposing Rule 11 sanctions, Fed.R.Civ.P. 11, on attorney for double-billing in action to recover fees in Title VII case), *aff'd in unpublished opinion*, 956 F.2d 269 (6th Cir.1992) (table). Some courts have held that fees will be denied to a prevailing party if contemporaneous time records are not kept. *See* Scott v. City of New York, 626 F.3d 130, 132 (2d Cir.2010) (citing *Carey,* enforcing strict requirement in FLSA case); Grendel's Den, Inc. v. Larkin, 749 F.2d 945, 952 (1st Cir.1984) (applying Civil Rights Attorney's Fees

Award Act); N.Y. State Ass'n of Retarded Children, Inc. v. Carey, 711 F.2d 1136, 1147 (2d Cir.1983) (same); Ramos v. Lamm, 713 F.2d 546, 553 (10th Cir.1983) (same), *overruled on other grounds sub nom.* Penn. v. Del. Valley Citizens' Council for Clean Air, 483 U.S. 711, 725, 107 S.Ct. 3078, 97 L.Ed.2d 585 (1987) .

2. *Reasonable Hourly Rate*: Unlike attorneys with major law firms, many public interest attorneys, small practitioners, legal services attorneys, and some civil rights attorneys do not have established hourly billing rates. What standard should determine the reasonable hourly rate for this category of attorney? In *Blum v. Stenson*, 465 U.S. 886, 104 S.Ct. 1541, 79 L.Ed.2d 891 (1984), the Supreme Court adopted the prevailing market rate standard. The "prevailing market rate" is broadly defined as "those [rates] prevailing in the community for similar services by lawyers of reasonably comparable skill, experience and reputation." *Id.* at 896, 104 S.Ct. at 1547. The prevailing market rate is applicable regardless of whether the plaintiff is represented by private or nonprofit counsel. *See also* Perdue v. Kenny A. ex rel. Winn, 559 U.S. 542, 551, 130 S. Ct. 1662, 1672, 176 L. Ed. 2d 494 (2010) (reiterating application of the market rate standard).

3. *Enhancement to the Lodestar*: In *City of Burlington v. Dague*, 505 U.S. 557, 562, 112 S.Ct. 2638, 2641, 120 L.Ed.2d 449 (1992), a Clean Water Act case, the Court held that the lodestar method has "become the guiding light of our fee-shifting jurisprudence," establishing a "strong presumption" that this method yields a "reasonable" fee. Whether a lodestar amount should be increased because of a contingency or risk-of-loss factor was not ultimately decided until *Dague*. Lower courts prior to *Dague* had often used a contingency factor or risk multiplier to enhance the lodestar on the ground that many lawyers who represent civil rights claimants risk not getting a fee at all because civil rights plaintiffs simply do not have the resources to pay fees. If the plaintiff prevailed on the merits, then the attorney would petition for fees; otherwise the attorney was not paid. Earlier Supreme Court cases tended to support an upward adjustment based upon the contingency factor, but in *Dague*, a majority of the Court held that contingency enhancement is never appropriate. *Id.* at 566, 112 S.Ct. at 2643. Despite *Dague*'s ruling and general applicability to all federal fee-shifting statutes, some courts have awarded a contingency premium in cases where there is a pendent state law claim. *See, e.g.,* Mangold v. Cal. Pub. Utility Comm'n, 67 F.3d 1470 (9th Cir.1995). Other reasons, like extraordinary results in a controversial case, may likewise support a lodestar enhancement. *See, e.g.,* Barnes v. City of Cincinnati, 401 F.3d 729 (6th Cir.2005) (prevailing plaintiff was a pre-operative transsexual police officer). The case is discussed, *infra,* Chapter 9.

For a comprehensive treatment of attorney's fees under fee-shifting statutes, *see, e.g.*, Yelena Zaslavskaya, *Reasonable Hourly Rate*

Determination: Overview of Recent Decisions, 10 Loy. Mar. L.J. 67 (2011); Mary Frances Derfner & Arthur Wolf, Court Awarded Attorney Fees (1997) (3 vols.); Alba Conte, Attorney Fee Awards (2d ed.1993); Martin A. Schwartz & John E. Kirklin, 2 Section 1983 Litigation: Claims, Defenses and Fees (1991).

Taxation of Fee Awards: Is a plaintiff who recovers both damages and attorney's fees in an employment discrimination case required to include both the damages and the fees in gross income for income tax purposes if the attorney must also report his attorney's fees in his gross income? If so, is this double taxation of attorney's fees good public policy? This problem was persuasively illustrated in a New York Times article. The plaintiff, a police officer brought a sex discrimination and sexual harassment case. She was eventually awarded $300,000, attorney's fees of $850,000, and costs in the amount of $100,000. Under the law, she was responsible for paying income taxes on both her award and the attorney's fees award, which combined is over $1 million dollars. Her attorney said that the plaintiff "loses every penny of the award * * * plus she will end up owing the Internal Revenue Service $99,000." Adam Liptak, *Tax Bill Exceeds Award to Officer in Sex Bias Suit*, N.Y. Times, Aug. 11, 2002, at A 12. *See also* Gregg Polsky, *The Contingent Attorney's Fee Tax Trap: Ethical, Fiduciary Duty, and Malpractice Implications,* 23 Va. Tax Rev. 615 (2004). To address this type of situation, Congress passed the Civil Rights Tax Relief Act as part of the American Jobs Creation Act of 2004. Pub. L. No. 108–357, § 1(a), 118 Stat. 1418 (2004). The new tax law allows plaintiffs in computing adjusted gross income to deduct "attorney fees and costs paid by, or on behalf of, the taxpayer in connection with any action involving a claim of unlawful discrimination." I.R.C., 26 U.S.C. § 62(a)(20) (2008). Although the plaintiff must still report on his tax return any attorney's fee award considered to be income, the amount is fully deductible, even when the Alternative Minimum Tax (AMT) applies. The attorney, of course, must still report the attorney's fees she receives as income. *See generally* Michael K. Hulley, Jr., *Taking Your Lump Sum or Just Taking Your Lumps? The Negative Tax Consequences in Employment Dispute Recoveries and Congress's Role in Fashioning A Remedy*, 2012 Mich. St. L. Rev. 171 (2012).

NOTE: INSURING AGAINST EMPLOYMENT DISCRIMINATION CLAIMS

Employers commonly obtain insurance to protect themselves against the numerous claims that might be made against them that arise in the course of doing business. The more traditional of these insurance policies are directors and officers (D & O) policies and comprehensive general liability (CGL) policies. Employers, concerned about liability for their employment decisions, including liability for unlawful employment discrimination, increasingly have begun to seek more effective insurance coverage against these claims because of the mixed results in coverage under the more traditional D & O and CGL policies. The move toward insurance against employment discrimination claims is fueled not only by the growing number of statutory and common law claims now available to applicants and employees, but also by the headline-grabbing, multimillion dollar verdicts and settlements in employment discrimination cases. For example, in *Velez v. Novartis Pharm. Corp.*, 04 CIV 09194 CM, 2010 WL 4877852 (S.D.N.Y. Nov. 30, 2010), a New York district court certified a class of over 6,000 female sales associates, each claiming gender discrimination against a large pharmaceutical corporation. To avoid the significant risk involved with moving forward with litigation, which had already consumed seven years, defendant corporation settled the suit for $250 million. *Id.* Additionally, in *Weeks v. Baker & McKenzie*, 74 Cal.Rptr.2d 510 (Cal.Ct.App.1998), a California court affirmed a multi-million dollar award in a sexual harassment case. Likewise, Texaco settled a race discrimination claim reported to be worth about $176 million, *see* Roberts v. Texaco, Inc., 979 F.Supp. 185, 191 n.6 (S.D.N.Y.1997) . Also, attorney's fees in successful employment discrimination cases can be substantial. *See, e.g.*, Darryl Van Duch, *Merrill Deal Paves Way for New ADR*, Nat'l L.J., May 18, 1998, at B1, B4 (noting multimillion dollar payments for legal fees provided in settlements of class action employment discrimination suits). *See also* Richard A. Bales & Julie McGhghy, *Insuring Title VII Violations,* 27 S.Ill.U.L.J. 71 (2002).

A newer type of insurance available to defendants is called Employment Practices Liability Insurance (EPLI). EPLI policies are specifically drafted to cover employment discrimination claims. For a comprehensive treatment of insurance coverage of employment discrimination claims under traditional policies and EPLI policies, see Janet R. Davis, Gary L. Gassman, *The Ins and Outs of Employment Practices Liability Insurance Coverage and Claims*, Brief, Winter 2013, at 22; Francis J. Mootz, III, *Insurance Coverage of Employment Discrimination Claims*, 52 U.Miami L.Rev. 1 (1997).

As a matter of policy, should defendants be permitted to obtain insurance for employment discrimination claims? If so, should they be allowed to insure against all types of claims, e.g., disparate impact (nonintentional) and disparate treatment (intentional) claims, including, for example, claims of sexual harassment and retaliation? What about employment discrimination claims based upon the Equal Protection Clause or the Religion Clauses of the U.S. Constitution? Should employers be allowed to insure against all types of monetary remedies, e.g., punitive damages or liquidated damages that are punitive in nature? Can such insurance coverage introduce an additional overseer (the insurance carrier) with a stake in curbing violations of antidiscrimination laws? Consider also that insurance is but one form of risk management that prudent employers use to protect their profit margins in a competitive economy. *See generally* Nancy H. Van der Veer, Comment, *Employment Practices Liability*

Insurance: Are EPLI Policies a License to Discriminate? Or Are They a Necessary Reality Check for Employers?, 12 Conn.Ins.L.J. 173 (2006).

PART 2

THEORIES OF DISCRIMINATION AND ANALYTICAL PARADIGMS

■ ■ ■

CHAPTER 3

DISPARATE TREATMENT

■ ■ ■

A. INTRODUCTION: THE MEANING AND THEORIES OF "DISCRIMINATION"

In this chapter we begin an in-depth study of employment discrimination law by first examining the meaning and theories of discrimination. The two major theories of discrimination are disparate treatment and disparate impact. The disparate treatment theory is covered in this chapter. The disparate impact theory is covered in Chapter 4.

Although federal laws prohibit discrimination in employment because of specific characteristics, federal laws, except for the Americans with Disabilities Act, do not provide a statutory definition of "discriminate." An often-quoted interpretive memorandum entered into the Congressional Record by Senators Case and Clark, the Republican and Democratic floor managers of Title VII in the Senate, states that

> [t]o discriminate is to make a distinction, to make a difference in treatment or favor, and those distinctions or differences in treatment or favor which are prohibited by section 704 are those which are based on any five of the forbidden criteria: race, color, religion, sex, and national origin. Any other criterion or qualification for employment is not affected by this title.

110 Cong.Rec. 7213 (1964). Senator McClellan, concerned that Title VII would become a "dragnet, a catchall," that would reach far beyond the purposes of the statute, proposed an amendment to Title VII that would limit its scope to adverse employment actions based "solely" on race, color, religion, sex, or national origin. *Id.* at 13,837 (1964). However, the Senate rejected the McClellan proposal. *Id.* at 13,838. A similar amendment was rejected by the House of Representatives. 110 Cong.Rec. 2728 (1964). Ultimately, Congress left the responsibility for defining discrimination to the federal courts. *Cf.* Alexander v. Gardner-Denver, 415 U.S. 36, 44, 94 S.Ct. 1011, 1017, 39 L.Ed.2d 147 (1974) ("final responsibility for enforcement of Title VII is vested with federal courts"). After more than a decade of judicial developments under Title VII, the Supreme Court in *Teamsters v. United States*, 431 U.S. 324, 335 n.15, 97 S.Ct. 1843, 1854 n.15, 52 L.Ed.2d 396 (1977), summarized the two basic theories of

discrimination on which much of the jurisprudence of employment discrimination law is based—disparate treatment and disparate impact:

> "Disparate treatment" * * * is the most easily understood type of discrimination. The employer simply treats some people less favorably than others because of their race, color, sex, religion or national origin. Proof of discriminatory motive is critical, although it can in some situations be inferred from the mere fact of differences in treatment. Undoubtedly disparate treatment was the most obvious evil Congress had in mind when it enacted Title VII. *See, e.g.*, 110 Cong. Rec. 13088 (1964) (remarks of Sen. Humphrey) ("What the bill does * * * is simply make it an illegal practice to use race as a factor in denying employment. It provides that men and women shall be employed on the basis of their qualifications, not as Catholic citizens, not as Protestant citizens, not as Jewish citizens, not as colored citizens, but as citizens of the United States").
>
> Claims of disparate treatment may be distinguished from disparate impact claims. The latter involves employment practices that are facially neutral in their treatment of different groups but in fact fall more harshly on one group than another and cannot be justified by business necessity. Proof of discriminatory motive * * * is not required under a disparate impact theory.

The disparate treatment theory is based on judicial construction of § 703(a)(1) of Title VII, 42 U.S.C. § 2000e–2(a)(1). McDonnell Douglas Corp. v. Green, 411 U.S. 792, 93 S.Ct. 1817, 36 L.Ed.2d 668 (1973). The disparate impact theory, which is grounded in the landmark Supreme Court case of *Griggs v. Duke Power Co.*, 401 U.S. 424, 91 S.Ct. 849, 28 L.Ed.2d 158 (1971), is based on judicial construction of § 703(a)(2) of Title VII, 42 U.S.C. § 2000e–2(a)(2). A major difference between the two theories is that discriminatory intent is the key element in a disparate treatment claim, while intent is not an element in a disparate impact claim. Most employment discrimination cases are brought under the disparate treatment theory, which is the focus of this chapter and, indeed, most of the materials in this book.

The two basic theories of discrimination originated in cases arising under Title VII, and both theories are not applicable to all of the laws prohibiting discrimination in employment. For example, the disparate impact theory is not applicable in employment discrimination claims based on the Equal Protection Clause of the Fourteenth Amendment or the Civil Rights Act of 1866, 42 U.S.C. § 1981. *See* Chapter 5. The disparate impact theory, however, is available under the Age Discrimination in Employment Act and the Americans with Disabilities

Act. The Americans with Disabilities Act of 1990 (ADA), § 102(b), 42 U.S.C. § 12112(b), includes an additional theory of discrimination. The ADA defines the term, "discriminate," *inter alia,* as "not making reasonable accommodations to the known physical and mental limitations of an otherwise qualified individual with a disability who is an applicant or employee." ADA, § 102(b)(5)(A), 42 U.S.C. § 12112(b)(5)(A). There is a similar, though not identical, accommodation requirement with claims of religious discrimination, a discussion we will defer until Chapter 11.

QUESTIONS

As you read and study the cases and other materials in this and subsequent chapters, consider the following questions:

1. What are the implications of the two basic theories of discrimination—disparate treatment and disparate impact—for achieving "equality" in the workplace? And what would equality in the workplace look like?

2. The two theories of discrimination parallel the two conceptions of equality discussed in Chapter 1. Can the goals of equal treatment and equal opportunity be reconciled or accommodated or do they embrace different visions of equality?

3. To what extent do the experiences and views of judges (and your own experiences and views) influence the rules and doctrines that they (or you) are willing to adopt in interpreting the laws prohibiting discrimination?

B. DISPARATE TREATMENT CLAIMS

When a plaintiff seeks relief in an employment discrimination case under the disparate treatment theory, the critical issue the factfinder must decide is whether the plaintiff has proven that she has suffered an adverse employment practice based upon unlawful discrimination. As the Supreme Court has said, "[t]he ultimate question in every discrimination case involving a claim of disparate treatment is whether the plaintiff was the victim of intentional discrimination." Reeves v. Sanderson Plumbing Prod., Inc., 530 U.S. 133, 153, 120 S.Ct. 2097, 2111, 147 L.Ed.2d 105 (2000). In *United States Postal Service Board of Governors v. Aikens*, 460 U.S. 711, 103 S.Ct. 1478, 1482, 75 L.Ed.2d 403 (1983), the Court said that the "factual inquiry" in an employment discrimination case based on the disparate treatment theory is whether the defendant was "treating 'some people less favorably than others because of their race, color, religion, sex or national origin.'" *Id.* at 715, 103 S.Ct. at 1482 (citations omitted). Intentional discrimination is an issue of fact to be decided by the factfinder, Pullman-Standard v. Swint, 456 U.S. 273, 287–88, 102 S.Ct. 1781, 1789, 72 L.Ed.2d 66 (1982), and the factfinder's determination will be set aside on appeal only if it is clearly erroneous, Anderson v. City of Bessemer, 470 U.S. 564, 573, 105 S.Ct. 1504, 1511, 84 L.Ed.2d 518 (1985).

Proving intentional discrimination can be difficult, particularly in those cases in which a plaintiff must rely upon circumstantial evidence as opposed to the far less common direct evidence. The law is well settled that a plaintiff may prove a claim of unlawful employment discrimination by direct or circumstantial evidence. *See, e.g.*, United States Postal Serv. Bd. of Governors v. Aikens, 460 U.S. at 714 n.3, 103 S.Ct. at 1481 n.3; Desert Palace, Inc. v. Costa, 539 U.S. 90, 94, 123 S.Ct. 2148, 2154, 156 L.Ed.2d 84 (2003) (the conventional rule in civil litigation allows a plaintiff in an employment discrimination case to prove a case of intentional discrimination by direct or circumstantial evidence).

With this in mind, we begin the study of the disparate treatment theory of discrimination with the leading case of *McDonnell Douglas Corp. v. Green*, 411 U.S. 792, 93 S.Ct. 1817, 36 L.Ed.2d 668 (1973). Plaintiffs in the overwhelming majority of individual, non-class-action disparate treatment cases must rely solely on circumstantial evidence. The purpose of the *McDonnell Douglas* framework, discussed shortly, is to assist the factfinder in deciding the "elusive factual question of intentional discrimination" when a plaintiff uses circumstantial evidence to prove intentional discrimination under the disparate treatment theory. Texas Dep't of Comty. Affairs v. Burdine, 450 U.S. 248, 255, n.8, 101 S.Ct. 1089, 1094 n.8, 67 L.Ed.2d 207 (1981).

The *McDonnell Douglas* evidentiary and analytical approach assumes that a single motive—either a lawful motive or an unlawful motive, but not both—is the reason for the challenged employment action. In the classic *McDonnell Douglas* paradigm, the plaintiff, relying upon circumstantial evidence, tries to prove that an unlawful discriminatory reason, rather than the lawful reason articulated by the employer, is the real or true reason for the employer's decision. The employer, on the other hand, seeks to convince the factfinder that its decision was based on a legitimate, nondiscriminatory reason. *See* Haskins v. Dep't of Army, 808 F.2d 1192, 1197 (6th Cir.1987). Over time, however, different factual paradigms emerged, and we will later discuss what is known as a "mixed motives" case, where discriminatory and nondiscriminatory reasons both played a role in the employer's decision.

This chapter explores the disparate treatment theory through three factual and analytical schemes: (1) single-motive or pretext cases, (2) mixed- or dual-motive cases, and (3) pattern-or-practice cases. The materials in Section B.2. of this chapter explore a set of issues on proving discriminatory intent by circumstantial or direct evidence. At the time the complaint is filed, a plaintiff is not required to specify which of these proof and analytical schemes she intends to rely upon, but at some point during the trial the district court must determine which evidentiary scheme is appropriate in order to decide the merits of the case or to instruct the jury, if it is a jury trial. Price Waterhouse v. Hopkins, 490 U.S. 228, 247 n.12, 109 S.Ct. 1775, 1789 n.12, 104 L.Ed.2d 268 (1989).

Although the vast majority of cases brought under the disparate treatment theory involve individual claims of discrimination that are pursued through the various proof structures discussed in this chapter, there is another form of disparate treatment that merits special mention. A classic case of disparate treatment involves a statute that is facially discriminatory—a statute that treats a protected group, most commonly gender or age, differently on the face of the statute. For example, one well-known case involved a pension system that required women to pay more into the system than men, ostensibly because they were likely to outlive men. *See* Los Angeles Dep't of Water & Power v. Manhart, 435 U.S. 702, 98 S.Ct. 1370, 55 L.Ed.2d 657 (1978). When the statute is facially discriminatory, the employer has limited defenses, and these will be explored in Chapter 7.

1. FOUNDATIONS

MCDONNELL DOUGLAS CORP. V. GREEN

Supreme Court of the United States, 1973.
411 U.S. 792, 93 S.Ct. 1817, 36 L.Ed.2d 668.

JUSTICE POWELL delivered the opinion of the Court.

The case before us raises significant questions as to the proper order and nature of proof in actions under Title VII of the Civil Rights Act of 1964.

Petitioner, McDonnell Douglas Corp., is an aerospace and aircraft manufacturer headquartered in St. Louis, Missouri, where it employs over 30,000 people. Respondent, a black citizen of St. Louis, worked for petitioner as a mechanic and laboratory technician from 1956 until August 28, 1964 when he was laid off in the course of a general reduction in petitioner's work force.

Respondent, a long-time activist in the civil rights movement, protested vigorously that his discharge and the general hiring practices of petitioner were racially motivated. As part of this protest, respondent and other members of the Congress on Racial Equality illegally stalled their cars on the main roads leading to petitioner's plant for the purpose of blocking access to it at the time of the morning shift change. * * *

On July 2, 1965, a "lock-in" took place wherein a chain and padlock were placed on the front door of a building to prevent the occupants, certain of petitioner's employees, from leaving. Though respondent apparently knew beforehand of the "lock-in," the full extent of his involvement remains uncertain.

Some three weeks following the "lock-in," on July 25, 1965, petitioner publicly advertised for qualified mechanics, respondent's trade, and respondent promptly applied for re-employment. Petitioner turned down respondent, basing its rejection on respondent's participation in the "stall-in" and "lock-in." Shortly thereafter, respondent filed a formal complaint with the Equal Employment Opportunity Commission, claiming that petitioner had refused to rehire him because of his race and persistent involvement in the civil rights movement, in violation of § 703(a)(1) * * * of [Title VII].

[The District Court ruled against respondent, but the Court of Appeals reversed.]

* * *

II

The critical issue before us concerns the order and allocation of proof in a private, non-class action challenging employment discrimination. * * * The language of Title VII makes plain the purpose of Congress to assure equality of employment opportunities and to eliminate those discriminatory practices and devices which have fostered racially stratified job environments to the disadvantage of minority citizens. * * *

* * * The broad overriding interest, shared by employers, employees, and the consumer, is efficient and trustworthy workmanship assured through fair and racially neutral employment and personnel decisions. In the implementation of such decisions, it is abundantly clear that Title VII tolerates no racial discrimination, subtle or otherwise.

In this case respondent, the complainant below, charges that he was denied employment "because of his involvement in civil rights activities" and "because of his race and color." Petitioner denied discrimination of any kind, asserting that its failure to re-employ respondent was based upon and justified by his participation in the unlawful conduct against it. Thus, the issue at the trial on remand is framed by those opposing factual contentions. * * *

The complainant in a Title VII trial must carry the initial burden under the statute of establishing a prima facie case of racial discrimination. This may be done by showing (i) that he belongs to a racial minority; (ii) that he applied and was qualified for a job for which the employer was seeking applicants; (iii) that, despite his qualifications, he was rejected; and (iv) that, after his rejection, the position remained open and the employer continued to seek applicants from persons of complainant's qualifications. In the instant case, we agree with the Court of Appeals that respondent proved a prima facie case. Petitioner sought mechanics, respondent's trade, and continued to do so after respondent's rejection. Petitioner, moreover, does not dispute respondent's qualifications and acknowledges that his past work performance in petitioner's employ was "satisfactory."

The burden then must shift to the employer to articulate some legitimate, nondiscriminatory reason for the employee's rejection. We need not attempt in the instant case to detail every matter which fairly could be recognized as a reasonable basis for a refusal to hire. Here petitioner has assigned respondent's participation in unlawful conduct against it as the cause for his rejection. We think that this suffices to discharge petitioner's burden of proof at this stage and to meet respondent's prima facie case of discrimination.

The Court of Appeals intimated, however, that petitioner's stated reason for refusing to rehire respondent was a "subjective" rather than objective criterion which "carr[ies] little weight in rebutting charges of discrimination." This was among the statements which caused the dissenting judge to read the opinion as taking "the position that such unlawful acts as Green committed against McDonnell would not legally entitle McDonnell to refuse to hire him, even though no racial motivation was involved * * * ." Regardless of whether this was the intended import of the opinion, we think the court below seriously underestimated the rebuttal weight to which petitioner's reasons were entitled. Respondent admittedly had taken part in a carefully planned "stall-in," designed to tie up access to and egress from petitioner's plant at a peak traffic hour. Nothing in Title VII compels an employer to absolve and rehire one who has engaged in such deliberate, unlawful activity against it. * * *

Petitioner's reason for rejection thus suffices to meet the prima facie case, but the inquiry must not end here. While Title VII does not, without more, compel rehiring of respondent, neither does it permit petitioner to use respondent's conduct as a pretext for the sort of discrimination prohibited by § 703(a)(1). On remand, respondent must * * * be afforded a fair opportunity to show that petitioner's stated reason for respondent's rejection was in fact pretext. Especially relevant to such a showing would be evidence that white employees involved in acts against petitioner of comparable seriousness to the "stall-in" were nevertheless retained or rehired. Petitioner may justifiably refuse to rehire one who was engaged in unlawful, disruptive acts against it, but only if this criterion is applied alike to members of all races.

Other evidence that may be relevant to any showing of pretext includes facts as to the petitioner's treatment of respondent during his prior term of employment; petitioner's reaction, if any, to respondent's legitimate civil rights activities; and petitioner's general policy and practice with respect to minority employment. On the latter point, statistics as to petitioner's employment policy and practice may be helpful to a determination of whether petitioner's refusal to rehire respondent in this case conformed to a general pattern of discrimination against blacks. In short, on the retrial respondent must be given a full and fair opportunity to demonstrate by competent evidence that the presumptively valid reasons for his rejection were in fact a cover-up for a racially discriminatory decision.

* * *

III

In sum, respondent should have been allowed to pursue his claim under § 703(a)(1). If the evidence on retrial is substantially in accord with that before us in this case, we think that respondent carried his burden of establishing a prima facie case of racial discrimination and that petitioner successfully rebutted that case. But this does not end the matter. On retrial, respondent must be afforded a fair opportunity to demonstrate that petitioner's assigned reason for refusing to re-employ was a pretext or discriminatory in its application. If the District Judge so finds, he must order a prompt and appropriate remedy. In the absence of such a finding, petitioner's refusal to rehire must stand.

NOTES AND QUESTIONS

1. Although it is now widely accepted that the disparate treatment theory of discrimination is based on a construction of § 703(a)(1), the Supreme Court has never clearly tied its prima facie case doctrine or order and allocation of proof to specific statutory language. The genesis of the prima facie case and the burden-allocation rules probably originated in the Eighth Circuit's decision in *McDonnell Douglas*. In its original decision, the Eighth Circuit stated,

> When a black man demonstrates that he possesses the qualifications to fill a job opening and that he was denied the job, we think he presents a prima facie case of racial discrimination and that the burden passes to the employer to demonstrate a substantial relationship between the reasons offered for denying employment and the requirements of the job. * * *
>
> * * * [R]emand is required because the district court did not use the correct standard in determining whether McDonnell's refusal to rehire Green was racially motivated. If McDonnell can demonstrate that Green's participation in the "stall-in" in some objective way reflects adversely upon job performance, McDonnell's refusal to rehire Green will be justified.

Green v. McDonnell Douglas Corp., 463 F.2d 337, 344 (8th Cir.1972), *remanded on other grounds*, 411 U.S. 792, 93 S.Ct. 1817, 36 L.Ed.2d 668 (1973). In a footnote, the Eighth Circuit observed that "the reasons advanced by McDonnell for refusing to hire Green may be found to be pretextual, particularly since McDonnell advanced the unsupported charge that Green had 'actively cooperated' in the 'lock-in.' " *Id.* at 344 n.6. For an account of the story behind Percy Green's lawsuit against McDonnell Douglas and its aftermath, see David Benjamin Oppenheimer, *The Story of* Green v. McDonnell Douglas, *in* Employment Discrimination Stories 13 (Joel Wm. Friedman, ed. 2006).

2. The Supreme Court elaborated upon the rationale for the *McDonnell Douglas* analytical framework in *Teamsters v. United States*, 431 U.S. 324, 358 n.44, 97 S.Ct. 1843, 1866 n.44, 52 L.Ed.2d 396 (1977):

> The *McDonnell Douglas* case involved an individual complainant seeking to prove one instance of unlawful discrimination. An employer's isolated decision to reject an applicant who belongs to a racial minority does not show that the rejection was racially based. Although the *McDonnell Douglas* formula does not require direct evidence of discrimination, it does demand that the alleged discriminatee demonstrate at least that his rejection did not result from the two most common legitimate reasons on which an employer might rely to reject a job applicant: an absolute or relative lack of qualifications or the absence of a vacancy in the job sought. Elimination of these two reasons for the refusal to hire is sufficient, absent other explanation, to create an inference that the decision was a discriminatory one.

Is the Court suggesting that employers are rational economic actors? *See also* Furnco Const. Corp. v. Waters, 438 U.S. 567, 98 S.Ct. 2943, 57 L.Ed.2d 957 (1978) (noting that the prima facie case eliminates the two most common reasons someone does not get a job while introducing a third common reason, race, gender, etc.). In addition, in the *Furnco* case, the Supreme Court cautioned that the *McDonnell Douglas* framework of analysis "was never intended to be rigid, mechanized, or ritualistic," but is rather "merely a sensible, orderly way to evaluate the evidence in light of common experience as it bears on the critical question of discrimination." *Furnco*, 438 U.S. at 577, 98 S.Ct at 2949.

3. *Elements of a Prima Facie Case*: Even though the Supreme Court has stated in *Burdine* that "the burden of establishing a prima facie case of disparate treatment is not onerous," Texas Dep't of Comm. Affairs v. Burdine, 450 U.S. 248, 252, 101 S.Ct. 1089, 1095, 67 L.Ed.2d 207 (1981), difficult questions frequently arise regarding whether the plaintiff has established a prima facie case. Proving membership in a protected class is probably the easiest element to establish.

a. *The application element*: As a general rule, the failure of a plaintiff to apply formally for a job is fatal to establishing a prima facie case of a discriminatory refusal to hire. *See, e.g.*, Lockridge v. Bd. of Trs. of Univ. of Ark., 315 F.3d 1005 (8th Cir.2003) (en banc). There are, however, some circumstances in which the failure to apply for a position may be excused.

The dissenting opinion in *Lockridge* set out some of those reasons: "where the employer has no formal application process, where the employee is unaware of the opportunity, or where the employer's employment promotions policy is 'informal and subjective,' and 'vague or secretive,' " or where the plaintiff has "made every reasonable attempt to convey his interest in the job to the employer," or "the employer has failed to establish a clear personnel procedure for promotions." *Id.* at 1013 (Heaney, J., dissenting) (citations omitted).

The futile gesture doctrine: The futile gesture doctrine may also excuse a plaintiff's failure to apply. For example, if an employer has a reputation for refusing to employ members of a protected group, the failure to apply may be excused. The futile gesture doctrine is grounded in *Teamsters v. United States*, 431 U.S. 324, 365–66, 97 S.Ct. 1843, 1870, 52 L.Ed.2d 396 (1977), where the Court said:

> If an employer should announce his policy of discrimination by a sign reading "Whites Only" on the hiring-office door, his victims would not be limited to the few who ignored the sign and subjected themselves to personal rebuffs. The same message can be communicated to potential applicants more subtly but just as clearly by an employer's actual practices by his consistent discriminatory treatment of actual applicants, by the manner in which he publicizes vacancies, his recruitment techniques, his responses to casual or tentative inquiries, and even by the racial or ethnic composition of that part of his work force from which he has discriminatorily excluded members of [protected] groups. When a person's desire for a job is not translated into a formal application solely because of his unwillingness to engage in a futile gesture he is as much of a victim of discrimination as is he who goes through the motion of submitting an application.

b. *The qualification element*: Very often the most critical factual issue in an employment discrimination case is whether the plaintiff is qualified for the job at issue. However, in the initial stages of proof, most courts require only that the plaintiff establish that she satisfies the minimum qualifications for the position. *See, e.g.*, Walker v. Mortham, 158 F.3d 1177, 1193 (11th Cir.1998) (holding that the trial court erred in "imposing as part of the prima facie case a requirement that [a] plaintiff establish that the successful applicant for his or her coveted position was less than or equally qualified to hold the position."). Ultimately, a plaintiff's relative qualifications are most relevant to pretext analysis if an employer satisfies its evidentiary burden of production by simply stating that the person selected had qualifications superior to the plaintiff's, an issue discussed further below.

c. *Must the employment opportunity be awarded to a person outside of plaintiff's protected class?* The fourth prong of the *McDonnell Douglas* prima facie case provides that in a failure to hire case, the plaintiff needs to put on evidence that "after [plaintiff's] rejection, the position remained open and the employer continued to seek applicants from persons of complainant's qualifications." This element was designed to ensure that a job was available, and it has been applied in the context of promotions and even discharges to ensure that a position remained available. A question naturally arose how courts should assess a situation in which the person who received the job, or promotion, was a member of the plaintiff's protected class. For example, would a woman who was not hired for a particular job be precluded from claiming sex discrimination if another woman ultimately was hired for the job at issue?

Although lower courts initially divided over the issue, the Supreme Court resolved the question in the context of an age discrimination claim by holding that a person is not precluded from pursuing a discrimination claim simply because the person who received the contested job was a member of the same protected group. *See* O'Connor v. Consol. Coin Caterers Corp., 517 U.S. 308, 116 S.Ct. 1307, 134 L.Ed.2d 433 (1996). In a unanimous decision, the Court in *O'Connor* held that "[t]he fact that one person in the protected class has lost out to another person in the protected class is * * * irrelevant, so long as he has lost *because of* [his status as a protected class member]," and evidence that a "plaintiff was replaced by someone outside the protected class is not a proper element of the *McDonnell Douglas* prima facie case." 517 U.S. at 312, 116 S.Ct. at 1310. Most of the courts of appeals have applied the *O'Connor* rule to employment discrimination cases other than age discrimination cases. *See* Stella v. Mineta, 284 F.3d 135, 145–46 (D.C.Cir.2002) (collecting cases); Pivirotto v. Innovative Sys., Inc., 191 F.3d 344, 355 (3d Cir.1999) (applying the *O'Connor* rule to race and sex cases).

Even though a plaintiff is generally not precluded from bringing a claim when the at-issue job is ultimately filled by a person from the same protected class, it can be quite difficult to establish discrimination in this situation, and courts have struggled with how to weigh this fact. The question has been explored most extensively in the age discrimination context, in part because the statute protects employees who are in a wide age spectrum. Relying on language from the *O'Connor* case, several courts require the plaintiff to establish that a person "substantially younger" than the plaintiff received the job or promotion in order to establish a prima facie case. *See, e.g.*, Lewis v. St. Cloud State Univ., 467 F.3d 1133, 1137 (8th Cir.2006) (holding that a plaintiff had failed to establish a "prima facie case of age discrimination since his permanent replacement was only two-and-a-half years younger."). After surveying the case law, one court concluded, "The overwhelming body of cases in most circuits has held that age differences of less than ten years are not significant enough to make out [a] * * * prima facie case." Grosjean v. First Energy Corp., 349 F.3d 332, 338 (6th Cir.2003) (citations omitted); *see also* Blizzard v. Marion Tech. College, 698 F.3d 275, 284 (6th Cir.2012) ("[W]hile an age difference of ten or more years is generally considered significant . . . replacement of the employee by a person who is six to ten years her junior must be considered on a case-by-case basis."). Several courts, however, treat the age difference as a factor to be considered by the jury. *See* Blizzard v.

Marion Tech. College, 698 F.3d 275, 284 (6th Cir.2012) (noting that a six-and-a-half year age difference was "sufficient to create an issue of material fact at the summary judgment stage"). How do you think the issue should be weighed in the context of race, national origin or gender?

d. *Similarly situated comparators*: Although *McDonnell Douglas* lists three elements to the prima facie case, many circuit courts have added a fourth element. These courts require, as part of the prima facie case, that the plaintiff establish that "a similarly situated person outside the protected class was treated better." Adams v. Wal-Mart Stores, Inc., 324 F.3d 935, 939 (7th Cir.2003); Jackman v. Fifth Judicial Dist. Dept. of Corr. Servs., 728 F.3d 800, 804 (8th Cir.2013) (age discrimination case plaintiff must establish that she was "treated differently than similarly situated employees who were not members of her protected class."). This element first arose in a discriminatory discharge case in which two white employees and one black employee were jointly charged with stealing property that belonged to a customer of the employer. The employer discharged the two white employees involved but retained the black employee. The discharged employees sued the employer under Title VII and § 1981 for a discriminatory discharge on the basis of race. *See* McDonald v. Santa Fe Trail Transp. Co., 427 U.S. 273, 96 S.Ct. 2574, 49 L.Ed.2d 493 (1976). The Court in *Santa Fe* adopted a "comparable seriousness" standard as a critical element in disciplinary discharge cases:

> [P]recise equivalence in culpability between employees is not the ultimate question: as we indicated in *McDonnell Douglas*, an allegation that other "employees involved in acts against [the employer] of *comparable seriousness* * * * were nevertheless retained * * * " is adequate to plead an inferential case that the employer's reliance on his discharged employee's misconduct as grounds for terminating him was merely a pretext.

427 U.S. at 283 n.11, 96 S.Ct. at 2580 n.11 (citation omitted). That language has since been transformed into a critical fourth element of the prima facie case in many circuits, and one that frequently poses significant problems at the summary judgment stage. It has also has been extended to all of the other employment contexts with the important exception of the hiring stage where the plaintiff will generally not have access to comparable individuals. *See, e.g.*, White v. Baxter Healthcare Corp., 533 F.3d 381 (6th Cir.2008) (promotion); Vasquez v. County of L.A., 349 F.3d 634 (9th Cir.2003) (transfer).

Rather than creating a fourth element of the prima facie case, several courts have held that establishing a "similarly situated" comparator is one means of proving discrimination, but is not a required element of proof. *See* Wells v. SCI Mgmt., L.P., 469 F.3d 697, 701 (8th Cir.2006) (defining the similarly situated comparator as providing "facts that give rise to an inference of discrimination" and noting that proving similarly situated individuals were treated differently is a typical means of proof). The D.C. Circuit has expressly rejected the requirement. *See* Czekalski v. Peters, 475

F.3d 360, 365–66 (D.C.Cir.2007). As will be discussed shortly, proving that a similarly situated individual was treated differently is the most common means of establishing the ultimate question of discrimination, and the Circuit Court of Appeals for the District of Columbia specifically held that the issue was only relevant with respect to the ultimate question of discrimination rather than at the prima facie stage. *Id. See also* Nicholson v. Hyannis Air Serv., Inc., 580 F.3d 1116 (9th Cir.2009) (holding that subjective criteria should not be considered as part of the prima facie case but instead are relevant to the ultimate question of discrimination).

Lower courts have also struggled to define what constitutes a "similarly situated" comparator and have arrived at varying standards. A common standard is that developed in the Seventh Circuit: "In order for an individual to be similarly situated to the plaintiff, the plaintiff must show that the individual is directly comparable to her in all material respects." Burks v. Wis. Dep't of Transp., 464 F.3d 744, 751 (7th Cir.2006). The court went on to note that this required the same supervisor, the same job duties, experience, performance, and whatever other relevant factors were at issue. *Id.* However the court later emphasized that similarly situated employees "need not be identical in every conceivable way" and that the inquiry "should not devolve into a mechanical, one-to-one mapping between employees." Coleman v. Donahoe, 667 F.3d 835, 846–47 (7th Cir.2012). The Fifth Circuit has defined similarly situated as "nearly identical." Perez v. Tex. Dep't of Crim. Justice, 395 F.3d 206, 213 (5th Cir.2004). Other formulations of the "similarly situated" test include "reasonably close resemblance of the facts and circumstances of the plaintiff's and comparator's cases, rather than showing they are identical," with "reasonableness" defined as the "touchstone" of the court's inquiry. Graham v. Long Island R.R., 230 F.3d 34, 40 (2d Cir.2000). *See also* Bobo v. UPS, 665 F.3d 741, 751 (6th Cir.2012) (noting that a plaintiff "is not required to demonstrate an exact correlation between himself and other similarly situated" individuals and that while similarly situated comparators may have to have dealt with the same supervisor, the criterion is not an "inflexible requirement.").

Problems arise when no similarly situated individual can be identified. For example, in one case the employee was fired for abusing the company's computer and internet policy while on suspension, and the court rejected the various comparators the plaintiff put forward because none of them had committed his or her workplace infraction while on suspension and none was found to have lied about having access to the internet system. *See* Gates v. Caterpillar, Inc., 513 F.3d 680 (7th Cir.2008); *see also* Evance v. Trumann Health Servs., LLC, 719 F.3d 673, 678 (8th Cir.2013) (granting summary judgment to the employer because employer had failed to identify "other employees who were not Pentecostal, female, or disabled [who] were accused of the exact or similar behavior as she was.") As the court in the *Gates* case pointed out, the question of the similarly situated comparator as part of the prima facie case often dovetails with the pretext inquiry, given that the primary means of proving pretext is to show that someone outside of the protected group was treated better than the plaintiff. This issue is discussed further below. For two scholarly explorations regarding the use of evidence of comparators at either the prima facie or pretext stage of a *McDonnell Douglas* case, see Suzanne B. Goldberg, *Discrimination By Comparison*, 120 Yale L.J. 728 (2011) and Charles A. Sullivan, *The Phoenix from the* Ash: *Proving Discrimination by Comparators*, 60 Ala.L.Rev. 191 (2008).

4. *McDonnell Douglas* was a refusal to hire case, but the Supreme Court admonished lower courts that "[t]he facts necessarily will vary in Title VII cases, and the specification * * * of the prima facie proof [in hiring cases] is not necessarily applicable in every respect to differing factual situations." 411 U.S. at 802 n.13, 93 S.Ct. at 1824 n.13. The following examples illustrate how the lower courts have adapted the *McDonnell Douglas* framework to other kinds of employment discrimination claims:

a. *Promotions*: For all intents and purposes, promotion cases proceed the same as hiring claims. The plaintiff must establish that she was qualified for the promotion, was rejected despite being qualified, and another applicant outside the protected class was promoted. *See* Kidd v. Mando Am. Corp., 731 F.3d 1196, 1202, 1204–05 (11th Cir.2013); Aulicino v. N.Y.C. Dep't of Homeless Servs., 580 F.3d 73, 80 (2d Cir.2009).

b. *Demotions*: At the time of the plaintiff's demotion, the plaintiff must establish that she was performing her job at a level that met the employer's legitimate expectations; after the demotion, the employer replaced the plaintiff with someone of comparable qualifications. *See* Brady v. Office of the Sergeant at Arms, 520 F.3d 490, 493 n.1 (D.C.Cir.2008) (describing prima facie case in demotion claim and equating issue to the standard for a discharge); Kidd v. Mando Am. Corp., 731 F.3d 1196, 1202–04 (11th Cir.2013) (applying *McDonnell Douglas* framework to a demotion claim). The *Hicks* case, reproduced below, is also a case involving a demotion.

c. *Discharges*: The vast majority of discrimination claims involve terminations or discharges, and this is an area where establishing that a similarly situated person was treated differently proves particularly significant. Two other situations are unique to discharge claims and merit additional discussion.

i. Constructive discharges: Under the doctrine of constructive discharge, an employer engages in unlawful employment discrimination when an employee involuntarily resigns in order to escape intolerable working conditions that she was subjected to because of her race, sex, national origin, or religion. In *Pennsylvania State Police v. Suders,* 542 U.S. 129, 124 S.Ct. 2342, 159 L.Ed.2d 204 (2004), the Supreme Court recognized that the constructive discharge doctrine applies in Title VII cases and adopted an objective standard for determining whether a "constructive discharge" has occurred. The Court stated:

> Under the constructive discharge doctrine, an employee's reasonable decision to resign because of unendurable working

> conditions is assimilated to a formal discharge for remedial purposes. The inquiry is objective: Did working conditions become so intolerable that a reasonable person in the employee's position would have felt compelled to resign?
>
> The constructive discharge concept originated in the labor-law field in the 1930's; the National Labor Relations Board (NLRB) developed the doctrine to address situations in which employers coerced employees to resign, often by creating intolerable working conditions, in retaliation for employees' engagement in collective activities. * * * By 1964, the year Title VII was enacted, the doctrine was solidly established in the federal courts.
>
> The Courts of Appeals have recognized constructive discharge claims in a wide range of Title VII cases. And the Equal Employment Opportunity Commission * * * has stated: An employer "is responsible for a constructive discharge in the same manner that it is responsible for the outright discriminatory discharge of a charging party." EEOC Compliance Manual 612:9(a) (2002).
>
> Although this Court has not had occasion earlier to hold that a claim for constructive discharge lies under Title VII, we have recognized constructive discharge in the labor-law context. * * * Furthermore, we have stated that "Title VII is violated by either explicit or constructive alterations in the terms or conditions of employment." * * * We agree with the lower courts and the EEOC that Title VII encompasses employer liability for a constructive discharge.

Id. at 141–43, 124 S.Ct. at 2351–52 (citations omitted).

A constructive discharge may also arise when an employee resigns in lieu of being fired. *See, e.g.*, Laster v. City of Kalamazoo, 746 F.3d 714, 727–28 (6th Cir.2014); EEOC v. Univ. of Chi. Hosps., 276 F.3d 326, 331–32 (7th Cir.2002) ("When an employer acts in a manner so as to have communicated to a reasonable employee that she will be terminated, and the plaintiff employee resigns, the employer's conduct may amount to constructive discharge."). In addition to proving that working conditions were intolerable, several courts require the plaintiff to establish that the employer created the intolerable conditions with the intent to cause the employee to resign. *See, e.g.*, Elnashar v. Speedway SuperAmerica, LLC, 484 F.3d 1046, 1058 (8th Cir.2007) (requiring plaintiff to prove employer's intent); Johnson v. Shalala, 991 F.2d 126, 131 (4th Cir.1993) ("The standard for constructive discharge requires a plaintiff to show both intolerable working conditions and a deliberate effort by the employer to force the employee to quit."). Other courts, however, have specifically declined to require proof of the employer's intent to force an employee to resign. *See, e.g.*, Poland v. Chertoff, 494 F.3d 1174, 1186 (9th Cir.2007) (citing cases).

ii. *Reductions-in-force (RIFs)*: Discrimination claims often arise after employers engage in reductions-in-force or mass layoffs, and these claims are particularly prominent among age discrimination plaintiffs. Often the cases are class actions, rather than individual claims, but individual claims also arise and courts have crafted particular principles to analyze these cases, including requiring "some additional evidence that age was a factor in the employer's action." Ward v. Int'l Paper Co., 509 F.3d 457, 461 (8th Cir.2007); *see also* Phelps v. Yale Sec., Inc., 986 F.3d 1020, 1023 (6th Cir.1993) (requiring evidence that the "employer singled out the plaintiff for discharge for impermissible reasons"). Why do you think courts have created these principles to evaluate claims that arise in the context of reductions-in-force? Often this element can be established by demonstrating that similarly situated, younger employees, or employees outside of the protected class, were retained. *See, e.g.*, Hinds v. Sprint/United Mgmt. Co., 523 F.3d 1187, 1196 (10th Cir.2008).

5. Suppose the factfinder disbelieves the employer's evidence offered as a legitimate, nondiscriminatory reason or, worse yet, believes that the employer actually lied with respect to its rebuttal evidence. Should the plaintiff be entitled to a judgment in her favor on that ground alone? Consider this question as you read the following case:

ST. MARY'S HONOR CENTER V. HICKS

Supreme Court of the United States, 1993.
509 U.S. 502, 113 S.Ct. 2742, 125 L.Ed.2d 407.

JUSTICE SCALIA delivered the opinion of the Court.

We granted certiorari to determine whether, in a suit against an employer alleging intentional racial discrimination in violation of § 703(a)(1) of Title VII of the Civil Rights Act of 1964, the trier of fact's rejection of the employer's asserted reasons for its actions mandates a finding for the plaintiff.

I

Petitioner St. Mary's Honor Center (St. Mary's) is a halfway house operated by the Missouri Department of Corrections and Human Resources (MDCHR). Respondent Melvin Hicks, a black man, was hired as a correctional officer at St. Mary's in August 1978 and was promoted to shift commander, one of six supervisory positions, in February 1980.

In 1983 MDCHR conducted an investigation of the administration of St. Mary's, which resulted in extensive supervisory changes in January 1984. Respondent retained his position, but John Powell became the new chief of custody (respondent's immediate supervisor) and petitioner Steve Long the new superintendent. Prior to these personnel changes respondent had enjoyed a satisfactory employment record, but soon thereafter became the subject of repeated, and increasingly severe, disciplinary actions. He was suspended for five days for violations of institutional rules by his subordinates on March 3, 1984. He received a letter of reprimand for alleged failure to conduct an adequate investigation of a brawl between inmates that occurred during his shift on March 21. He was later demoted from shift commander to correctional officer for his failure to ensure that his subordinates entered their use of a St. Mary's vehicle into the official log book on March 19, 1984. Finally, on June 7, 1984, he was discharged for threatening Powell during an exchange of heated words on April 19.

* * *

II

* * * Petitioners do not challenge the District Court's finding that respondent satisfied the minimal requirements of * * * a [*McDonnell Douglas*] prima facie case * * *. Respondent does not challenge the District Court's finding that petitioners sustained their burden of production by introducing evidence of two legitimate, nondiscriminatory reasons for their actions: the severity and the accumulation of rules violations committed by respondent. * * *

The District Court, acting as trier of fact in this bench trial, found that the reasons petitioners gave were not the real reasons for respondent's demotion and discharge. It found that respondent was the only supervisor disciplined for violations committed by his subordinates; that similar and even more serious violations committed by respondent's coworkers were either disregarded or treated more leniently; and that Powell manufactured the final verbal confrontation in order to provoke respondent into threatening him. It nonetheless held that respondent had failed to carry his ultimate burden of proving that *his race* was the determining factor in petitioners' decision first to demote and then to dismiss him. In short, the District Court concluded that "although [respondent] has proven the existence of a crusade to terminate him, he has not proven that the crusade was racially rather than personally motivated."

The Court of Appeals set this determination aside on the ground that "[o]nce [respondent] proved all of [petitioners'] proffered reasons for the adverse employment actions to be pretextual, [respondent] was entitled to judgment as a matter of law." The Court of Appeals reasoned:

> Because all of defendants' proffered reasons were discredited, defendants were in a position of having offered no legitimate reason for their actions. In other words, defendants were in no better position than if they had remained silent, offering no rebuttal to an established inference that they had unlawfully discriminated against plaintiff on the basis of his race.

That is not so. By producing *evidence* (whether ultimately persuasive or not) of nondiscriminatory reasons, petitioners sustained their burden of production, and thus placed themselves in a "better position than if they had remained silent."

* * *

If * * * the defendant has succeeded in carrying its burden of production, the *McDonnell Douglas* framework—with its presumptions and burdens—is no longer relevant. To resurrect it later, after the trier of fact has determined that what was "produced" to meet the burden of production is not credible, flies in the face of our holding in *Burdine* that to rebut the presumption "[t]he defendant need not persuade the court that it was actually motivated by the proffered reasons." 450 U.S. at 254, 101 S.Ct. at 1094. The presumption, having fulfilled its role of forcing the defendant to come forward with some response, simply drops out of the picture. The defendant's "production" (whatever its persuasive effect) having been made, the trier of fact proceeds to decide the ultimate question: whether plaintiff has proven "that the defendant intentionally discriminated against [him]" because of his race. *Id.* at 253, 101 S.Ct. at 1093. The factfinder's disbelief of the reasons put forward by the defendant (particularly if disbelief is accompanied by a suspicion of mendacity) may, together with the elements of the prima facie case, suffice to show intentional discrimination. Thus, rejection of the defendant's proffered reasons will *permit* the trier of fact to infer the ultimate fact of intentional discrimination, and the Court of Appeals was correct when it noted that, upon such rejection, "[n]o additional proof of discrimination is *required*," (emphasis added). But the Court of Appeals' holding that rejection of the defendant's proffered reasons *compels* judgment for the plaintiff disregards the fundamental principle of Rule 301 that a presumption does not shift the burden of proof, and ignores our repeated admonition that the Title VII plaintiff at all times bears the "ultimate burden of persuasion."

III

Only one unfamiliar with our case-law will be upset by the dissent's alarum that we are today setting aside "settled precedent," "two decades of stable law in this Court," "a framework carefully crafted in precedents as old as 20 years," which "Congress is [aware]" of and has implicitly approved. * * * We mean to answer the dissent's accusations in detail, by examining our cases, but at the outset it is worth noting the utter implausibility that we would ever have held what the dissent says we held.

* * *

The principal case on which the dissent relies is *Burdine*. While there are some statements in that opinion that could be read to support the dissent's position, all but one of them bear a meaning consistent with our interpretation, and the one exception is simply incompatible with other language in the case. *Burdine* describes the situation that obtains after the employer has met its burden of adducing a nondiscriminatory reason as follows: "Third, should the defendant carry this burden, the plaintiff must then have an opportunity to prove by a preponderance of the evidence that the legitimate reasons offered by the defendant were not its true reasons, but were a pretext for discrimination." 450 U.S. at 253, 101 S.Ct. at 1093. The dissent takes this to mean that if the plaintiff proves the asserted reason to be *false*, the plaintiff wins. But a reason cannot be proved to be "a pretext *for discrimination*" unless it is shown *both* that the reason was false, *and* that discrimination was the real reason. *Burdine*'s later allusions to proving or demonstrating simply "pretext," are reasonably understood to refer to the previously described pretext, *i.e.*, "pretext for discrimination."

[The Court's dissection of *Burdine* is omitted.]

[W]hatever doubt *Burdine* might have created was eliminated by [*United States Postal Serv. Bd. of Governors v. Aikens*, 460 U.S. 711, 103 S.Ct. 1478, 75 L.Ed.2d 403 (1983)]. There we said, in language that cannot reasonably be mistaken, that "the ultimate question [is] discrimination *vel non*." 460 U.S. at 714, 103 S.Ct. at 1481. Once the defendant "responds to the plaintiff's proof by offering evidence of the reason for the plaintiff's rejection, the factfinder must then decide" *not* (as the dissent would have it) whether that evidence is credible, but "whether the rejection was discriminatory within the meaning of Title VII." *Id.* at 714–15, 103 S.Ct. at 1481. * * * It is not enough, in other words, to *dis*believe the employer; the factfinder must *believe* the plaintiff's explanation of intentional discrimination. * * *

IV

We turn, finally, to the dire practical consequences that the respondents and the dissent claim our decision today will produce. What appears to trouble the dissent more than anything is that, in its view, our rule is adopted "for the benefit of employers who have been found to have given false evidence in a court of law," whom we "favo[r]" by "exempting them from responsibility for lies." As we shall explain, our rule in no way gives special favor to those employers whose evidence is disbelieved. But initially we must point out that there is no justification for assuming (as the dissent repeatedly does) that those employers whose evidence is disbelieved are perjurers and liars. * * * To say that the company which in good faith introduces such testimony, or even the testifying employee himself, becomes a liar and a perjurer when the testimony is not believed, is nothing short of absurd.

Undoubtedly some employers (or at least their employees) will be lying. But even if we could readily identify these perjurers, what an extraordinary notion, that we "exempt them from responsibility for their lies" unless we enter Title VII judgments for the plaintiffs! Title VII is not a cause of action for perjury; we have other civil and criminal remedies for that. * * *

The dissent repeatedly raises a procedural objection that is impressive only to one who mistakes the basic nature of the *McDonnell Douglas* procedure. It asserts that "the Court now holds that the further inquiry [*i.e.*, the inquiry that follows the employer's response to the prima facie case] is wide open, not limited at all by the scope of the employer's proffered explanation." The plaintiff cannot be expected to refute "reasons not articulated by the employer, but discerned in the record by the factfinder." * * * These statements imply that the employer's "proffered explanation," his "stated reasons," his "articulated reasons," somehow exist *apart from the record*—in some pleading, or perhaps in some formal, nontestimonial statement made on behalf of the defendant to the factfinder. ("Your honor, pursuant to *McDonnell Douglas* the defendant hereby formally asserts, as *its* reason for the dismissal at issue here, incompetence of the employee.") Of course it does not work like that. The reasons the defendant sets forth are set forth "through the introduction of admissible evidence." *Burdine*, 450 U.S. at 255, 101 S.Ct. at 1094. In other words, the defendant's "articulated reasons" *themselves* are to be found "lurking in the record." It thus makes no sense to contemplate "the employer who is caught in a lie, but succeeds in *injecting* into the trial an *unarticulated* reason for its actions." There is a "lurking-in-the-record" problem, but it exists not for us but for the dissent. *If*, after the employer has met its preliminary burden, the plaintiff need not prove discrimination (and therefore need not disprove *all* other reasons suggested, no matter how vaguely, in the record) there must be some device for determining which particular portions of the record represent "articulated reasons" set forth with sufficient clarity to satisfy *McDonnell Douglas*—since it is only *that* evidence which the plaintiff must refute. But of course our *McDonnell Douglas* framework makes no provision for such a determination, which would have to be made not at the close of the trial but *in medias res*, since otherwise the plaintiff would not know what evidence to offer. It makes no sense.

* * *

Finally, respondent argues that it "would be particularly ill-advised" for us to come forth with the holding we pronounce today "just as Congress has provided a right to jury trials in Title VII" cases. We think quite the opposite is true. Clarity regarding the requisite elements of proof becomes all the more important when a jury must be instructed concerning them, and when detailed factual findings by the trial court will not be available upon review.

* * *

JUSTICE SOUTER, with whom JUSTICE WHITE, JUSTICE BLACKMUN, and JUSTICE STEVENS join, dissenting.

Twenty years ago, in *McDonnell Douglas Corp. v. Green*, 411 U.S. 792, 93 S.Ct. 1817, 36 L.Ed.2d 668 (1973), this Court unanimously prescribed a "sensible, orderly way to evaluate the evidence" in a Title VII disparate-treatment case, giving both plaintiff and defendant fair opportunities to litigate "in light of common experience as it bears on the critical question of discrimination." Furnco Constr. Corp. v. Waters, 438 U.S. 567, 577, 98 S.Ct. 2943, 2949 (1978). We have repeatedly reaffirmed and refined the *McDonnell Douglas* framework, most notably in *Texas Dept. of Community Affairs v. Burdine*, 450 U.S. 248, 101 S.Ct. 1089, 67 L.Ed.2d 207 (1981), another unanimous opinion. But today, after two decades of stable law in this Court and only relatively recent disruption in some of the Circuits, the Court abandons this practical framework together with its central purpose, which is "to sharpen the inquiry into the elusive factual question of intentional discrimination." *Id.* at 255 n.8, 101 S.Ct. at 1095 n.8. Ignoring language to the contrary in both *McDonnell Douglas* and *Burdine*, the Court holds that, once a Title VII plaintiff succeeds in showing at trial that the defendant has come forward with pretextual reasons for its actions in response to a prima facie showing of discrimination, the factfinder still may proceed to roam the record, searching for some nondiscriminatory explanation that the defendant has not raised and that the plaintiff has had no fair opportunity to disprove. Because the majority departs from settled precedent in substituting a scheme of proof for disparate-treatment actions that promises to be unfair and unworkable, I respectfully dissent.

* * *

The majority's scheme greatly disfavors Title VII plaintiffs without the good luck to have direct evidence of discriminatory intent. * * * [U]nder the majority's scheme, a victim of discrimination lacking direct evidence will now be saddled with the tremendous disadvantage of having to confront, not the defined task of proving the employer's stated reasons to be false, but the amorphous requirement of disproving all possible nondiscriminatory reasons that a factfinder might find lurking in the record. In the Court's own words, the plaintiff must "disprove *all* other reasons suggested, no matter how vaguely, in the record."

While the Court appears to acknowledge that a plaintiff will have the task of disproving even vaguely suggested reasons, and while it recognizes the need for "[c]larity regarding the requisite elements of proof," it nonetheless gives conflicting signals about the scope of its holding in this case. In one passage, the Court states that although proof of the falsity of the employer's proffered reasons does not "compe[l] judgment for the plaintiff," such evidence, without more, "will permit the trier of fact to infer the ultimate fact of intentional discrimination." The same view is implicit in the Court's decision to remand this case, keeping Hicks's chance of winning a judgment alive although he has done no more (in addition to proving his prima facie case) than show that the reasons proffered by St. Mary's are unworthy of credence. But other language in the Court's opinion supports a more extreme conclusion, that proof of the falsity of the employer's articulated reasons will not even be sufficient to sustain judgment for the plaintiff. For example, the Court twice states that the plaintiff must show "*both* that the reason was false, *and* that discrimination was the real reason." * * * This "pretext-plus" approach would turn *Burdine* on its head, and it would result in summary judgment for the employer in the many cases where the plaintiff has no evidence beyond that required to prove a prima facie case and to show that the employer's articulated reasons are unworthy of credence.

* * *

Because I see no reason why Title VII interpretation should be driven by concern for employers who are too ashamed to be honest in court, at the expense of victims of discrimination who do not happen to have direct evidence of discriminatory intent, I respectfully dissent.

NOTES AND QUESTIONS

1. The *Hicks* case provides a good illustration of how the *McDonnell Douglas* proof structure operates. You should plot out the various steps: (1) plaintiff's evidence of his prima facie case, (2) defendant's articulated "legitimate, nondiscriminatory" reason(s), and (3) plaintiff's evidence to establish pretext. You should also be able to identify the arguments of the parties, and how and why the arguments differed.

2. Prior to *Hicks*, the federal courts of appeals were divided on what a plaintiff had to prove to demonstrate pretext. The split developed primarily over whether *Burdine* required that the plaintiff prove *only* that the defendant's proffered legitimate, nondiscriminatory reason(s) was not credible or, *in addition*, that the defendant was actually motivated by discrimination. The circuits thus adopted at least three theories on the issue: "pretext only," "pretext-maybe", and "pretext-plus." *See* Anderson v. Baxter Healthcare Corp., 13 F.3d 1120, 1122–23 (7th Cir.1994).

a. *Pretext-only*: Under the pretext-only rule, if the plaintiff convinced the factfinder that the employer's proffered reasons were not credible or not the real reasons for the adverse employment decision, she was automatically entitled to a judgment in her favor. This was the position adopted by the Court of Appeals in *Hicks* but ultimately rejected by the Supreme Court.

b. *Pretext-maybe*: The pretext-maybe rule holds that the prima facie case combined with sufficient evidence for a reasonable factfinder to reject the employer's evidence of a legitimate, nondiscriminatory reason permits, but does not require, the factfinder to find that the employer's decision was based on a discriminatory or unlawful motive. This is the position that was adopted by the Supreme Court in *Hicks*.

c. *Pretext-plus*: Courts that adopted the pretext-plus rule required evidence sufficient to undermine the credibility of the employer's justifications and some *additional* evidence that the employer's *real reason* was motivated by discriminatory intent. Jurisdictions adopting a pretext-plus standard supported the rule on the ground that laws prohibiting discrimination in employment do not prohibit poor business judgment, arbitrary behavior, or discrimination not based on a prohibited criterion. Thus, under pretext-plus, employers that made decisions motivated by considerations not otherwise prohibited by law could conceal their reasons without violating employment discrimination laws. *See, e.g.*, Medina-Munoz v. R.J. Reynolds Tobacco Co., 896 F.2d 5, 9 (1st Cir.1990) ("In the final round of shifting burdens, it is up to plaintiff, unassisted by the original presumption, to show that the employer's stated reason 'was but a pretext for [unlawful discrimination].' To achieve this plateau, a * * * plaintiff must do more than simply refute or cast doubt on the company's rationale for the adverse action. The plaintiff must also show a discriminatory animus based on [an unlawful reason].").

3. The federal courts were initially split on what *Hicks* meant, and several courts required plaintiffs to offer proof beyond pretext—"pretext plus"—in order to survive summary judgment. The Supreme Court sought to clarify the standard of proof in *Reeves v. Sanderson Plumbing Products, Inc.*, 530 U.S. 133, 120 S.Ct. 2097, 147 L.Ed.2d (2000), an age discrimination case in which the Fifth Circuit had required the plaintiff to produce additional evidence beyond what was offered to prove pretext in order to survive summary judgment. In a unanimous decision, the Supreme Court reversed. Much of the opinion simply reiterates the main points of *Hicks*, but the Court also sought to emphasize the importance of proving pretext:

> [T]he Court of Appeals misconceived the evidentiary burden borne by plaintiffs who attempt to prove intentional discrimination through indirect evidence. This much is evident from our decision in St. Mary's Honor Center. There we held that the factfinder's rejection of the employer's legitimate, nondiscriminatory reason for its action does not compel judgment for the plaintiff. * * * In reaching this conclusion, however, we reasoned that it is

permissible for the trier of fact to infer the ultimate fact of discrimination from the falsity of the employer's explanation. * * *

Proof that the defendant's explanation is unworthy of credence is simply one form of circumstantial evidence that is probative of intentional discrimination, and it may be quite persuasive. * * * In appropriate circumstances, the trier of fact can reasonably infer from the falsity of the explanation that the employer is dissembling to cover up a discriminatory purpose. * * * Moreover, once the employer's justification has been eliminated, discrimination may well be the most likely alternative explanation, especially since the employer is in the best position to put forth the actual reason for its decision. * * * Thus, a plaintiff's prima facie case, combined with sufficient evidence to find that the employer's asserted justification is false, may permit the trier of fact to conclude that the employer unlawfully discriminated.

This is not to say that such a showing by the plaintiff will always be adequate to sustain a jury's finding of liability. Certainly there will be instances where, although the plaintiff has established a prima facie case and set forth sufficient evidence to reject the defendant's explanation, no rational factfinder could conclude that the action was discriminatory. For instance, an employer would be entitled to judgment as a matter of law if the record conclusively revealed some other, nondiscriminatory reason for the employer's decision, or if the plaintiff created only a weak issue of fact as to whether the employer's reason was untrue and there was abundant and uncontroverted independent evidence that no discrimination had occurred. * * *

Whether judgment as a matter of law is appropriate in any particular case will depend on a number of factors. Those include the strength of the plaintiff's prima facie case, the probative value of the proof that the employer's explanation is false, and any other evidence that supports the employer's case and that properly may be considered on a motion for judgment as a matter of law. For purposes of this case, we need not—and could not—resolve all of the circumstances in which such factors would entitle an employer to judgment as a matter of law. It suffices to say that, because a prima facie case and sufficient evidence to reject the employer's explanation may permit a finding of liability, the Court of Appeals erred in proceeding from the premise that a plaintiff must always introduce additional, independent evidence of discrimination.

Id. at 148–49, 120 S.Ct. at 2108–09. Does *Reeves* resolve the conflicting interpretations of pretext in *Hicks*, i.e., pretext-plus and pretext-only? If so, is pretext-plus no longer relevant after *Reeves*? Does it really matter if pretext-plus is dead or alive in view of the fact that the ultimate finding of intentional discrimination is to be made on the "record as a whole"?

4. Although the pretext-plus standard has now been firmly rejected by the Supreme Court, federal courts continue to grapple with the question of the meaning of pretext and, more specifically, whether plaintiffs have offered sufficient evidence to reach a jury. One court has summarized the state of the law as:

> Since a plaintiff utilizing the *McDonnell Douglas* framework normally cannot provide direct evidence of discrimination, a pretext argument provides a method of satisfying this burden by allowing the factfinder "to infer the ultimate fact of discrimination from the falsity of the employer's explanation." Reeves v. Sanderson Plumbing Prods., Inc., 530 U.S. 133, 147, 120 S. Ct. 2097, 147 L. Ed. 2d 105 (2000). A plaintiff shows pretext by demonstrating "such weaknesses, implausibilities, inconsistencies, incoherencies, or contradictions in the employer's proffered legitimate reasons for its action that a reasonable factfinder could rationally find them unworthy of credence" and hence infer that the employer did not act for the asserted nondiscriminatory reasons. Plotke [v. White], 405 F.3d 1092, 1102 (10th Cir.2005).
>
> One typical method for a plaintiff to prove pretext is by providing direct "evidence that the defendant's stated reason for the adverse employment action was false." Kendrick v. Penske Transp. Servs., Inc., 220 F.3d 1220, 1230 (10th Cir.2000). Another common method is a differential treatment argument, in which the plaintiff demonstrates that the employer "treated [the plaintiff] differently from other similarly-situated employees who violated work rules of comparable seriousness" in order to show that the employer failed to follow typical company practice in its treatment of the plaintiff. *Id.* * * *
>
> However the plaintiff may choose to demonstrate pretext, we have definitively rejected a "pretext plus" standard; in order to survive summary judgment, a plaintiff generally need not provide affirmative evidence of discrimination beyond the prima facie case and evidence that the employer's proffered explanation is pretextual. Jaramillo v. Colo. Judicial Dep't, 427 F.3d 1303, 1312 (10th Cir.2005); see also Doebele v. Sprint/United Mgmt. Co., 342 F.3d 1117, 1135–36 (10th Cir.2003) ("The plaintiff need not show both that the defendant's reasons were a pretext *and* that the real reason was discrimination—the fact of pretext alone may allow the inference of discrimination."). * * *
>
> However, it is not *always* permissible for the factfinder to infer discrimination from evidence that the employer's explanation is unworthy of belief. "[I]f the record conclusively revealed some other, nondiscriminatory reason for the employer's [adverse employment] decision, or if the plaintiff created only a weak issue of fact as to whether the employer's reason was untrue and there was abundant

and uncontroverted independent evidence that no discrimination had occurred," the fact that the employer's explanation was unworthy of belief would no longer be sufficient to create an inference of discrimination. *Reeves*, 530 U.S. at 148. The same reasoning applies to a plaintiff's attempts to show pretext through evidence of differential treatment; if the employer's differential treatment of similarly-situated employees is "trivial or accidental or explained by a nondiscriminatory motive," such treatment is insufficient to create an inference of discrimination. *Kendrick*, 220 F.3d at 1232.

This exception to the general rule against "pretext plus" makes sense because the falsity of an employer's proffered explanation, or the existence of differential treatment, defeats summary judgment only if it could reasonably lead the trier of fact to infer a discriminatory motive; where the evidence of pretext supports only nondiscriminatory motives, such an inference is logically precluded and summary judgment for the employer is appropriate. * * *

Swackhammer v. Sprint/United Mgmt., 493 F.3d 1160, 1168–70 (10th Cir.2007). The Fifth Circuit has stated the issue slightly differently by defining the circumstances when summary judgment might be appropriate: "The 'rare' instances in which a showing of pretext is insufficient to establish discrimination are (1) when the record conclusively reveals some other nondiscriminatory reason for the employer's decision or (2) when the plaintiff creates only a weak issue of fact as to whether the employee's reason was untrue and there was abundant and uncontroverted evidence that no discrimination occurred." Laxton v. Gap, Inc., 333 F.3d 572, 578 (5th Cir.2003).

5. *The "Legitimate, Nondiscriminatory Reason" Defense*: *McDonnell Douglas* imposes an obligation on the employer to introduce evidence of a "legitimate, nondiscriminatory reason" to rebut a plaintiff's prima facie case in circumstantial evidence cases.

a. Is there a substantive difference between the terms "legitimate" and "nondiscriminatory"? In *Hazen Paper Co. v. Biggins*, 507 U.S. 604, 612, 113 S.Ct. 1701, 1707, 123 L.Ed.2d 338 (1993), an age discrimination case reproduced in Chapter 13, the Supreme Court interpreted "legitimate" to mean no more than "nondiscriminatory" when it held that firing the plaintiff to prevent his pension plan from vesting was a legitimate, nondiscriminatory reason. In other words, the reason does not have to be a good reason—it might even violate a statute like ERISA which protects pensions—it need only be nondiscriminatory in the sense that it does not violate the discrimination statute that is at issue. How does this apply in the *Hicks* case?

b. What are some of the more obvious "legitimate, nondiscriminatory" reasons an employer could "articulate" that would readily satisfy the defense in a discharge case? In a refusal to hire case? In a failure to promote case? A reduction-in-force is generally treated as a legitimate nondiscriminatory reason. *See* Coleman v. Quaker Oats Co., 232 F.3d 1271, 1282 (9th Cir.2000).

c. What if the employer's "legitimate, nondiscriminatory reason" is that it does not know why the person was not hired. Should that suffice? How should a court evaluate such a response?

6. The courts generally have held that the *McDonnell Douglas* analytic scheme is not a three-step "judicial minuet" of procedure—plaintiff's evidence of a prima facie case, and the sufficiency of the prima facie case is often decided on a motion for summary judgment. However, once a case proceeds to the next stage and the defendant has produced evidence of a legitimate, nondiscriminatory reason, the evidentiary sufficiency of the prima facie case is no longer at issue. In *United States Postal Service Board of Governors v. Aikens*, 460 U.S. 711, 715, 103 S.Ct. 1478, 1482, 75 L.Ed.2d 403 (1983), the Court held that "[w]here the defendant has done everything that would be required of him if the plaintiff had properly made out a *prima facie* case, whether the plaintiff really did is no longer relevant," and that the "district court has before it all the evidence it needs to decide whether 'the defendant intentionally discriminated against the plaintiff.' "

7. *Pretext and the Honest Belief Defense*: Pretext analysis generally involves an assessment of the totality of the evidence presented by the parties to decide whether it is more probable than not that discrimination was the explanation for the contested employment decision. *McDonnell Douglas* equates a finding of pretext with "a cover-up for a racially discriminatory decision." As noted previously, the most common way to show pretext is to demonstrate that similarly situated individuals in a different class received more favorable treatment. But that is not the only means of proving prextext. In *Johnson v. Kroger Co.*, 319 F.3d 858, 866–87 (6th Cir.2003), the court held that a plaintiff can show pretext to refute an employer's evidence of a legitimate, nondiscriminatory reason in three ways: the proffered reason "(1) has no basis in fact; (2) did not actually motivate the defendant's challenged conduct; or (3) was insufficient to warrant the challenged conduct." Weaknesses, implausibilities, or contradictions in the employer's proffered legitimate reason for its adverse action may be sufficient to allow a reasonable factfinder to find them unworthy of credence. *See* Garrett v. Hewlett-Packard Co., 305 F.3d 1210, 1217 (10th Cir.2002). Similarly, a decision that is inconsistent with an employer's prior conduct may establish pretext (Ondricko v. MGM Grand Detroit, LLC, 689 F.3d 642, 651 (6th Cir.2012)) as may shifting explanations for the employer's action. *See* Hitchcock v. Angel Corps, Inc., 718 F.3d 733, 738 (7th Cir.2013).

One issue on which courts unanimously agree is that an employer's good-faith, mistaken belief in the correctness of its employment decision is not the equivalent of pretext. If, for example, an employer fires an employee for being late to work, but the employee is able to demonstrate that he was, in fact, on time, that by itself will not constitute pretext. This principle has come to be known as "the honest belief rule," some variation of which has been adopted in all circuits. The varying perspectives are set out in the Sixth Circuit's decision in *Smith v. Chrysler Corp.*, 155 F.3d 799 (6th Cir.1998):

> * * * [The "honest belief" rule] * * * provides that so long as the employer honestly believed in the proffered reason given for its employment action, the employee cannot establish pretext even if the employer's reason is ultimately found to be mistaken, foolish, trivial, or baseless. The rationale behind the rule is that the focus of a discrimination suit is on the intent of the employer. If the employer honestly, albeit mistakenly, believes in the non-discriminatory reason it relied upon in making its employment decision, then the employer arguably lacks the necessary discriminatory intent. * * *
>
> In deciding whether an employer reasonably relied on the particularized facts then before it, we do not require that the decisional process used by the employer be optimal or that it left no stone unturned. Rather, the key inquiry is whether the employer made a reasonably informed and considered decision before taking an adverse employment action. Although courts should resist attempting to micro-manage the process used by employers in making their employment decisions, neither should they blindly assume that an employer's description of its reasons is honest. When the employee is able to produce sufficient evidence to establish that the employer failed to make a reasonably informed and considered decision before taking its adverse employment action, thereby making its decisional process "unworthy of credence," then any reliance placed by the employer in such a process cannot be said to be honestly held.

Id. at 806–08. *See also* Simpson v. Beaver Dam Cmty., Hosps., Inc., 780 F.3d 784 (7th Cir.2015) (the focus is on the "honesty, not the accuracy" of the decision); Villiarimo v. Aloha Island Air, Inc., 281 F.3d 1054, 1063 (9th Cir.2002) ("[C]ourts only require that an employer honestly believed its reasons, even if its reason is foolish or trivial or even baseless."). What would you identify as the rationale for the honest belief defense? Under what circumstances might the fact that the employer made a mistake be relevant to the pretext analysis? One court has noted, "[A]n employer's action may be justified by a reasonable belief in the validity of the reason given even though that reason may turn out to be false. Of course, the fact that a proferred reason is objectively false may undermine an employer's honest belief in that reason, but this is not always so." George v. Leavitt, 407 F.3d 405, 415 (D.C.Cir.2005) (citations omitted). An employee may overcome the employer's showing of honest believe by "put[ting] forth evidence which demonstrates that the employer did not honestly believe in the proffered non-discriminatory reason for its adverse employment action." Blizzard v. Marion Tech. College, 698 F.3d 275, 286 (6th Cir.2012).

8. Suppose an employer's rebuttal to a prima facie case is that a plaintiff was denied an employment opportunity because it was awarded to a better qualified candidate. How might the plaintiff raise a triable issue of intentional discrimination for pretext analysis? In *Millbrook v. IBP, Inc.*, 280 F.3d 1169 (7th Cir.2002), the court cautioned that

> " * * * a plaintiff's own opinions about her work performance or qualifications do not sufficiently cast doubt on the legitimacy of her employer's proffered reasons for its employment actions." Similarly * * * mere "submission of materials from a co-worker or supervisor indicating that an employee's performance is satisfactory does not * * * create a material issue of fact." A plaintiff's contention that he is the better candidate for a vacancy constitutes nothing but the employee's own opinion as to his qualifications. This cannot create an issue of material fact because "[a]n employee's perception of his own performance * * * cannot tell a reasonable factfinder something about what the employer believed about the employee's abilities." "And without proof of a lie [as to what the employer believed] no inference of discriminatory motive can be drawn."

Id. at 1181 (citations omitted). Even when the plaintiff's qualifications are objectively superior to another candidate's, courts have been reluctant to allow a case to go forward solely based on the fact that the plaintiff was the better qualified candidate. For example, in *Springer v. Convergys Customer Management Group, Inc.*, 509 F.3d 1344 (11th Cir.2007), the court held that it was insufficient to argue that the plaintiff was the better qualified candidate and instead required that "[a] plaintiff must show not merely that the defendant's employment decision was mistaken but that [it was] in fact motivated by race." *Id.* at 1349. The Tenth Circuit has stated, "[M]inor differences between a plaintiff's qualifications and those of a successful applicant are not sufficient to show pretext. To show pretext, the disparity in qualifications must be overwhelming." Jaramillo v. Colo. Judicial Dep't., 427 F.3d 1303, 1309 (10th Cir.2005). What is it that a court might be concerned about when it comes to determining who is the most qualified? What evidence do you think a plaintiff could or should offer?

9. *"Me Too" Evidence*: An issue that arises in many trials is whether evidence of discrimination against other employees within the company can be admitted in a trial brought by an individual plaintiff. The Supreme Court addressed this question in the context of an age discrimination lawsuit where the plaintiff sought to introduce testimony of five employees regarding their alleged discriminatory treatment. The district court had excluded the evidence because the employees were not "similarly situated" to the plaintiff. The court of appeals reversed because it believed the district court had invoked a *per se* rule that always required the exclusion of such evidence. A unanimous Supreme Court vacated the judgment, holding that "evidence of discrimination by other supervisors" is neither automatically excluded nor automatically admissible, but instead must meet the relevance test generally applicable to evidentiary issues. *See* Sprint/United Mgmt. Co. v. Mendelsohn,

522 U.S. 379, 128 S.Ct. 1140, 170 L.Ed.2d 1 (2008). Because the court of appeals had concluded on its own that the evidence was relevant, the Supreme Court vacated the judgment and remanded so the district court could determine whether the evidence was relevant. How should the district court make this determination? What factors should the court take into account? On remand the District Court reaffirmed its decision to exclude the evidence, a decision that was upheld on appeal. *See* Mendelsohn v. Sprint/United Mgt. Co., 402 Fed. Appx. 337 (10th Cir.2010).

10. Given that the *McDonnell Douglas* framework was created in 1973, in one of the Supreme Court's earliest decisions interpreting Title VII, one might wonder whether its use of presumptions still makes sense. If courts did not follow the *McDonnell Douglas* framework, how would discrimination be proved? Professor Deborah Calloway has argued,

> In enacting Title VII, Congress was primarily concerned with bringing an end to disparate treatment, the most basic form of discrimination. * * * Because direct evidence of discrimination is rarely available, Title VII's success in rooting out disparate treatment has been due, in large measure, to methods of proof based on the assumption that, absent explanation, adverse treatment of statutorily protected groups is more likely than not the result of discrimination. * * *
>
> * * * With its decision in [*Hicks*] the Court joined academics, judges, and a growing segment of the American population that has come to believe that discrimination no longer exists. Under this view, the failure of African Americans, women, and other groups protected by Title VII to achieve equal employment opportunities results not from discrimination, but rather from inadequate motivation or deficient personal and work skills. * * * [T]he Court both questioned the continued prevalence of discrimination and invited lower court judges and juries to do the same. * * * Juries, drawn from a society that believes discrimination has been eliminated, may also view alleged discrimination with skepticism.

Deborah A. Calloway, St. Mary's Honor Center v. Hicks: *Questioning the Basic Assumption*, 26 Conn.L.Rev. 997, 997–98 (1994). Professor Calloway continued,

> *Hicks* is significant, not for its narrow legal holding, but for the attitude underlying that holding * * * [T]his is about what evidence is sufficient to meet the plaintiff's burden of persuasion on discriminatory intent. What evidence makes it "more likely than not" that the defendant discriminated? The answer depends on one's belief about the prevalence of discrimination.

Id. at 1008–09. How would you evaluate Professor Calloway's criticism of *Hicks*?

NOTE: THE PERJURIOUS CLIENT AND A LAWYER'S ETHICAL OBLIGATIONS

Recall that in *Hicks* the Supreme Court said that the term "pretext" provides "no justification for assuming * * * that those employers whose evidence is disbelieved are perjurers and liars," and "[t]o say that the company which in good faith introduces such testimony, or even the testifying employee himself, becomes a liar and a perjurer when the testimony is not believed, is nothing short of absurd." 509 U.S. at 520–21, 113 S.Ct. at 2742. A witness commits perjury if (a) he testifies under oath about a material fact; (b) his testimony is false; (c) he knows it is false; and (d) his testimony is voluntary and intentional and not the result of confusion, mistake, or faulty memory. *See* 18 U.S.C. § 1621 (2002). Even though there are federal and state laws on perjury, prosecution for perjury typically occupies a low priority for prosecutors because of lack of adequate resources.

A perjurious client can be a problem for an attorney who must ethically and effectively discharge the responsibilities owed to the client, colleagues, the public, the courts, and to himself or herself. The difficulties arise because of two competing imperatives in the ABA Model Rules of Professional Conduct and Disciplinary Rules. Model Rule 3.3 (Candor Toward the Tribunal) provides that a lawyer shall not knowingly "offer evidence that the lawyer knows to be false." Model Rule 3.4(b) states that a lawyer must not "counsel or assist a witness to testify falsely." Model Rule 1.6 (Confidentiality of Information) provides for client confidentiality. Model Rule 3.3 and almost all jurisdictions provide that the rule against false testimony trumps Model Rule 1.6 on confidentiality. Model Code DR 7–102(A)(4) provides that a lawyer must not "knowingly use perjured testimony or false evidence," and Model Code DR 7–102(A)(6) states that a lawyer must not "participate in the creation or preservation of evidence when he knows or it is obvious that the evidence is false."

Another source of concern is procedural. Under Rule 11 of the Federal Rules of Civil Procedure, every pleading, written motion, and similar court document submitted to a federal court by a represented party must be signed by an attorney of record in his or her own name. The signature on the document is deemed to certify that the attorney has made a reasonable inquiry into the facts and that all the allegations or factual assertions are either supported by evidence or likely to be supported by evidence after further investigation or discovery. Denials of fact must be either warranted by the evidence or identified as being reasonably based on a lack of information or belief. Violations of Rule 11 can subject the signing attorney, as well as law firms and parties, to sanctions, including payment of attorney's fees resulting from the violation.

To what extent does *Hicks* compound the legal and ethical difficulties an attorney faces with a perjurious client or witness in employment litigation? What is the extent of an attorney's ethical obligation to ensure that his client is truthful in testifying or presenting other kinds of evidence? On remand, the defendants in *Hicks* changed their strategy. As the court of appeals explained: "[D]efendants' counsel now abandons the rule violations explanation (even though Long himself does not) and astutely embraces 'personal animosity' as the justification for defendants' actions. Defendants now argue that Powell's personal animosity toward plaintiff is 'the lawful reason for [plaintiff's] discharge.' " Hicks v. St. Mary's Honor Ctr., 90 F.3d 285, 291 (8th Cir.1996). As a result of the changed theory, the appellate court summarily affirmed judgment for the defendant. *Id.* Do these events on remand suggest any ethical or legal issues?

NOTE: THE SAME-ACTOR DEFENSE

In some situations, the person who initially hires an employee is also the person who later discharges her. If the plaintiff is able to establish a prima facie case of employment discrimination based upon circumstantial evidence, what weight, if any, should be given to the fact that the same individual both hired and fired the plaintiff? A majority of the circuit courts have endorsed what is generally referred to as the same-actor inference (also known as the same supervisor, same decision-maker or common actor inference or defense). *See, e.g.*, Antonio v. Sygma Network, Inc., 458 F.3d 1177, 1883 (10th Cir.2006) (cataloging cases). Courts adopting the same-actor defense hold that, where the same supervisor both hired and fired an employee and the period between the hiring and firing is relatively short, the employer is entitled to an inference that the discharge was not motivated by discriminatory animus. For a discussion of the issue, see Anna Laurie Bryant & Richard Bales, *Using the Same-Actor "Inference" in Employment Discrimination Cases*, 1999 Utah L. Rev. 255.

The Court of Appeals for the Fourth Circuit was the first court to endorse the same-actor defense in *Proud v. Stone*, 945 F.2d 796 (4th Cir.1991). The court reasoned that "[i]t hardly makes sense to hire workers from a group one dislikes (thereby incurring the psychological costs of associating with them), only to fire them once they are on the job." *Id.* at 797. A number of courts have determined that same actor evidence is a matter for the jury to consider in relation to the ultimate question of discrimination. *See* Williams v. Vitro Servs. Corp., 144 F.3d 1438, 1443 (11th Cir.1998) ("[I]t is the province of the jury rather than the court * * * to determine whether the inference generated by the 'same actor' evidence is strong enough to outweigh a plaintiff's evidence of pretext."). Other courts have staked out a middle ground by determining that the same-actor inference "is neither a mandatory presumption * * * nor a mere possible conclusion for the jury to draw on * * * . Rather it is a 'strong inference' that a court must take into account on a summary judgment motion." Coghlan v. Am. Seafoods Co., 413 F.3d 1090, 1098 (9th Cir.2005). *See also* EEOC v. Boeing Co., 577 F.3d 1044 (9th Cir.2009) (evaluating weight of evidence supporting same-actor inference). In the original case *Proud v. Stone,* the court focused on the "relatively short" period between the hiring and firing but the courts have applied the same-actor defense to intervals up to three years or more. *See* Coghlan, 413 F.3d at

1098 (three years between hiring and termination not a bar to same-actor inference).

An implicit assumption in the same-actor defense is that discriminatory animus, if it exists, manifests itself in all aspects of the employment relationship from initial hire through termination and all other terms and conditions of employment. Is the assumption flawed? Professor Linda Krieger argued that the same-actor defense is problematic because "[c]ognitive forms of intergroup bias will not operate consistently, even in the same decision maker," because expression of intergroup bias "will vary, according to the specific situation in which the decision maker finds himself." Linda Hamilton Krieger, *Civil Rights Perestroika: Intergroup Relations After Affirmative Action*, 86 Cal.L.Rev. 1251, 1314–16, (1998). Could intergroup bias vary by the identity of the protected class of the plaintiff and the decisionmaker—whether, for example, it is, race, gender, national origin, or age? The Seventh Circuit in *Johnson v. Zema Systems Corp.*, 170 F.3d 734 (7th Cir.1999), observed:

> The psychological assumption underlying the same-actor inference may not hold true on the facts of the particular case. For example, a manager might hire a person of a certain race expecting [him] not to rise to a position in the company where daily contact with the manager would be necessary. Or an employer might hire an employee of a certain gender expecting that person to act, or dress, or talk in a way the employer deems acceptable for that gender and then fire that employee if she fails to comply with the employer's gender stereotype. Similarly, if an employee were the first African-American hired, an employer might be unaware of his own stereotypical views of African-Americans at the time of hiring. If the employer subsequently discovers he does not wish to work with African-Americans and fires the newly hired employee for this reason, the employee would still have a claim of racial discrimination despite the same-actor inference.

Id. at 745.

NOTE: "REVERSE DISCRIMINATION" CLAIMS

Should the *McDonnell Douglas* analytic scheme be modified for white or male plaintiffs who claim discrimination? Does the fact that white males in particular, as a group, have not suffered the history of discrimination experienced by either blacks or women provide an adequate rationale for heightened evidentiary and procedural burdens in "reverse discrimination" challenges? In *Iadimarco v. Runyon*, 190 F.3d 151 (3d Cir.1999), the Third Circuit considered a discrimination claim brought by a white male employee who alleged he had been denied a promotion because of the employer's desire to promote a "diverse" candidate. In evaluating Iadimarco's claim, the court reviewed the range of approaches courts have taken to "reverse discrimination" claims:

> [C]ourts have struggled in attempting to apply the *McDonnell Douglas* burden-shifting framework to Title VII suits by White plaintiffs, and no universally accepted statement of the appropriate standard has emerged. The confusion arises from the wording of the very first prong of the *McDonnell Douglas* test. Obviously, a White plaintiff can not establish "membership in a minority group" in the same way a Black plaintiff can. In an effort to cram the "reverse discrimination" cases into the *McDonnell Douglas* framework, most courts of appeals that have considered the issue require white plaintiffs to present evidence of "background circumstances" that establish that the defendant is "that unusual employer who discriminates against the majority," *Parker v. Baltimore & O. R. Co.*, 652 F.2d 1012, 1017 (D.C.Cir.1981), instead of showing minority group status. * * * However, application and interpretation of the test has often proven difficult.
>
> The prima facie case under *McDonnell Douglas* merely states "the basic allocation of burdens and order of presentation of proof [under] Title VII * * * ." *Burdine*, 450 U.S. at 252, 101 S.Ct. 1089. It raises an inference of discrimination only because we presume these acts, if otherwise unexplained in the context of the prongs of the *McDonnell Douglas* prima facie case, are more likely than not based on the consideration of impermissible factors. See Furnco Const. Corp. v. Waters, 438 U.S. 567, 577, 98 S.Ct. 2943, 57 L.Ed.2d 957 (1978). However, "[t]he central focus of the inquiry * * * is always whether the employer is treating some people less favorably than others because of their race, color, religion, sex, or national origin." *Id.* (internal quotation marks omitted).
>
> Accordingly, rather than require "background circumstances" about the uniqueness of the defendant employer, a plaintiff who brings a "reverse discrimination" suit under Title VII should be able to establish a prima facie case in the absence of direct evidence of discrimination by presenting sufficient evidence to allow a reasonable fact finder to conclude (given the totality of the circumstances) that the defendant treated plaintiff "less favorably than others because of [his] race, color, religion, sex, or national origin." *Furnco*, 438 U.S. at 577, 98 S.Ct. 2943.

Id. at 158–61. What kinds of evidence should a "reverse discrimination" plaintiff be required to present in order to satisfy his prima facie case? To prove pretext? If evidence of background circumstances are required as part of the plaintiff's prima facie case, what sorts of evidence would suffice? *See* Mastro v. Potomac Elec. Power Co., 447 F.3d 843, 852–53 (D.C. Cir.2006).

NOTE: DISCRIMINATION AND CRITICAL RACE THEORY

Writing at the beginning of the twentieth century, William E. B. DuBois, a distinguished African-American scholar, asserted that the problem of the twentieth century is "the problem of the color line." W. E. B. DuBois, The Souls of Black Folk 1 (Candace Press 1996) (1903). The problem of how to eradicate racial discrimination or to remedy "the problem of the color line" remains one of the thorniest issues in American society. The civil rights movements of the 1950s and 1960s and the civil rights legislation of the 1960s, including the Civil Rights Act of 1964, brought about important social reforms. The legal system and traditional liberal discourse and scholarship on civil rights played important roles in producing the civil rights reforms of the 1960s and 1970s. *See generally* Robert Belton, *Title VII of the Civil Rights Act of 1964: A Decade of Private Enforcement and Judicial Development*, 20 St. Louis U.L.J. 225, 304–05 (1976). The dominant discourse on civil rights, however, also undermined the transformative potential of the civil rights movement. The introduction to a collection of essays on critical race theory notes:

> The law's incorporation of what several authors * * * call "formal equality" (prohibitions against explicit racial exclusion, like "white only" signs) marks a decidedly progressive movement in U.S. political and social history. However, the fact that civil rights advocates met with some success in the nation's courts and legislatures ought not obscure the role that the American legal order played in the deradicalization of racial liberation movements. Along with the suppression of explicit white racism (the widely celebrated aim of civil rights reform), the dominant legal conception of racism as a discrete and identifiable act of "prejudice based on skin color" placed virtually the entire range of everyday social practices—social practices developed and maintained throughout the period of formal American apartheid—beyond the scope of critical examination or remediation.
>
> * * * From its inception, mainstream legal thinking in the U.S. has been characterized by a curiously constricted understanding of race and power. Within this cramped conception of racial domination, the evil of racism exists when—and only when—one can point to specific, discrete acts of racial discrimination, which is in turn narrowly defined as decision-making based on the irrational and irrelevant attribute of race. Given this essentially negative, indeed, dismissive view of racial identity and its social meanings, it was not surprising that mainstream legal thought came to embrace the idea of "color-blindness" as the dominant moral compass of social enlightenment about race.

Introduction to Critical Race Theory: The Key Writing That Formed the Movement xiv–xv (Kimberlé Crenshaw et al., eds.1995).

Critical race theory emerged in the wake of concerns about the slow and cyclical nature of racial remediation over the course of many decades, the liberal and conservative discourse about the degree to which racial discrimination continued to exist in American life, and the fact that most of the scholarship on civil rights considered to be significant was written by a small group of white male professors of constitutional law who worked at elite law schools. *See, e.g.*, Richard Delgado, *The Imperial Scholar: Reflections on a Review of Civil Rights Literature*, 132 U.Pa.L.Rev. 561 (1984).

Kimberlé Crenshaw, a critical race scholar, articulated some of the basic tenets of critical race theory:

> While no determinative definition of the work is yet possible, one can generally say that [critical race scholarship] focuses on the relationship between law and racial subordination in American society. It shares with liberal race critique a view that law has provided an area for challenging white supremacy. Critical race theory goes beyond the liberal critiques, however, in that it exposes the facets of law and legal discourse that create racial categories and legitimate racial subordination.
>
> Other broad themes common to critical race theory include the view that racism is endemic to, rather than a deviation from American norms. This developing literature reflects a common skepticism toward dominant claims of meritocracy, neutrality, objectivity, and color blindness. Critical race theory embraces a contextualized historical analysis of racial hierarchy as part of its challenge to the presumptive legitimacy of societal institutions.

Kimberlé Crenshaw, *A Black Feminist Critique of Antidiscrimination Law and Politics, in* Politics of Law: A Progressive Critique 195, 213–14 (David Kairys ed.1990).

Professor Richard Delgado, a prolific critical race scholar, offers this view of critical race theory ("CRT"):

> CRT begins with a number of basic insights. One is that racism is normal, not aberrant in American society. Because racism is an ingrained feature of our landscape, it looks ordinary and natural to persons in the culture. Formal equality—rules and laws that insist on treating blacks and whites (for example) alike—can thus remedy only the most extreme and shocking forms of injustice, the ones that stand out. It can do little about the business-as-usual forms of racism that people of color confront every day and that account for much misery, alienation, and despair.

Introduction, Critical Race Theory: The Cutting Edge xvi (Richard Delgado & Jean Stefancic eds.2000).

In a book assessing more than a decade of critical race jurisprudence, the editors argue that

> CRT [rejects] at least three entrenched, mainstream beliefs about racial injustice. * * * The first * * * is that "blindness" to race will eliminate racism. * * * Critical race theorists have challenged this belief, asserting instead that self-conscious racial identities can

> be and have been the source of individual fulfillment, collective strength, and incisive policymaking.
>
> The second * * * is that racism is a matter of individuals, not systems. The goal of antidiscrimination law, as understood historically and currently by courts, was to search for perpetrators and victims: perpetrators could be identified through "bad" acts and intentions, while victims were (only) those who could meet shifting, and increasingly elusive, burdens of proof. Instead, critical race theorists have located racism and its everyday operation in the very structures within which the guilty and the innocent were to be identified * * * .
>
> The third is that one can fight racism without paying attention to sexism, homophobia, economic exploitation, and other forms of oppression or injustice. From the beginning, CRT has been dedicated to antiracist social transformation through an antisubordination analysis that would be "intersectional" or "multidimensional," taking into account the complex layers of individual and group identity that help to construct social and legal positions.

Francisco Valdes, Jerome McCristal Culp & Angela P. Harris, *Introduction: Battles Waged, Won, and Lost: Critical Race Theory at the Turn of the Millennium, in* Crossroads, Directions, and a New Critical Race Theory 1–2 (Francisco Valdes et al. eds., 2002).

One of the major issues of concern to critical race scholars is the role of intent in antidiscrimination law. Critical race scholar, Professor Charles R. Lawrence, III, drew upon both psychoanalytic theory and cognitive psychology in his highly influential article, *The Id, the Ego, and Equal Protection: Reckoning with Unconscious Racism*, 39 Stan.L.Rev. 317 (1987), to expose some of the critical fault lines in the intent theory. Professor Lawrence argued that the Equal Protection Clause, embodying a theory that "seeks to remove racial prejudice from governmental decisionmaking[,] must acknowledge and incorporate * * * unconscious motivation." *Id.* at 327. He wrote:

> There are two explanations for the unconscious nature of our racially discriminatory beliefs and ideas. First, Freudian theory states that the human mind defends itself against discomfort or guilt by denying or refusing to recognize those ideas, wishes, and beliefs that conflict with what the individual has learned is good or right. While our historical experience has made racism an integral part of our culture, our society has more recently embraced an ideal that rejects racism as immoral. When an individual experiences conflict between racist ideas and the societal ethic that condemns those ideas, the mind excludes his racism from consciousness.

> Second, the theory of cognitive psychology states that culture—including for example, the media and an individual's parents, peers, and authority figures—transmits certain beliefs and preferences. Because these beliefs are so much a part of the culture, they are not experienced as explicit lessons. Instead, they seem part of the individual's rational ordering of her perceptions of the world. The individual is unaware, for example, that the ubiquitous presence of a cultural stereotype has influenced her perceptions that blacks are lazy or unintelligent. * * * These tacit understandings, because they have never been articulated, are less likely to be experienced at a conscious level.

Id. at 322–23.

Professor Russell Robinson has emphasized the differences that exist between African-Americans and whites—what he refers to as "outsiders" and "insiders"—on their perceptions of discrimination. Russell K. Robinson, *Perceptual Segregation*, 108 Colum.L.Rev. 1093 (2008). Robinson explores the many studies that document the perceptual gulf and also emphasizes the different experiences groups have that contribute to their perceptions of what constitutes discrimination. He also notes that the insider perspective is frequently represented in judicial proceedings: "[A]ntidiscrimination adjudications are biased in the sense that they tend to align with white and male perspectives rather than outsider perspectives * * *. The upshot of this insider bias is that outsiders are likely to perceive discrimination adjudications as inaccurate, and also inconsistent with their lived experiences." *Id.* at 1155.

Much of the critical race scholarship in the early days focused almost exclusively on the black/white paradigm in race discourse. Over time, however, other historically subordinated groups began to develop a body of scholarship that was responsive to their own analyses of traditional liberal civil rights discourse. For example, Latina/o Critical Theory (LatCrit) endeavors to address the ways in which Latinas/os have been racialized in the United States. *See, e.g.*, Symposium, *LatCrit Theory: Naming and Launching a New Discourse of Critical Legal Scholarship*, 2 Harv.Latino LRev. 177 (1997). Some of the central concerns of LatCrits are issues regarding immigration, nativism, language rights, and transnational identities. Critical race feminist scholars combine feminism with critical race theory to challenge liberal theories of racism and civil rights by focusing on the persistence and pervasiveness of racial discrimination. *See, e.g.*, Critical Race Feminism (Adrien Katherine Wing ed.1997). Critical race feminist scholars set out to expose racism in judicial rulings by arguing that women of color may suffer intersectional or multidimensional discrimination that is different from harms inflicted on white women or black men. Asian American scholars also began to explore issues of race and ethnicity, such as the myth of the "model minority," from a different perspective. *See, e.g.*, Robert Chang, *Toward an Asian American Legal Scholarship: Critical Race Theory, Post-Structuralism, and Narrative Space*, 81 Cal.L.Rev. 1243 (1993). Critical race theory has generated another new category of legal scholarship known as "critical white studies" which focuses on white supremacy and white privilege as a social organizing principle. *See, e.g.*, Critical White Studies: Looking Behind the Mirror (Richard Delgado & Jean Stefancic eds. 1997).

2. MIXED-MOTIVE CASES AND THE CIVIL RIGHTS ACT OF 1991

A mixed-motive case is one in which the employer relies upon both a legitimate, nondiscriminatory reason and an unlawful, discriminatory reason at the moment it makes an adverse employment decision, and both the legitimate and illegitimate reasons are motivating factors in that decision.

PRICE WATERHOUSE V. HOPKINS

Supreme Court of the United States, 1989.
490 U.S. 228, 109 S.Ct. 1775, 104 L.Ed.2d 268.

JUSTICE BRENNAN announced the judgment of the Court and delivered an opinion, in which JUSTICE MARSHALL, JUSTICE BLACKMUN, and JUSTICE STEVENS join.

Ann Hopkins was a senior manager in an office of Price Waterhouse when she was proposed for partnership in 1982. She was neither offered nor denied admission to the partnership; instead, her candidacy was held for reconsideration the following year. When the partners in her office later refused to repropose her for partnership, she sued Price Waterhouse under Title VII of the Civil Rights Act of 1964, as amended, 42 U. S. C. § 2000e *et seq.*, charging that the firm had discriminated against her on the basis of sex in its decisions regarding partnership. Judge Gesell in the Federal District Court for the District of Columbia ruled in her favor on the question of liability, and the Court of Appeals for the District of Columbia Circuit affirmed. We granted certiorari to resolve a conflict among the Courts of Appeals concerning the respective burdens of proof of a defendant and plaintiff in a suit under Title VII when it has been shown that an employment decision resulted from a mixture of legitimate and illegitimate motives.

I

At Price Waterhouse, a nationwide professional accounting partnership, a senior manager becomes a candidate for partnership when the partners in her local office submit her name as a candidate. All of the other partners in the firm are then invited to submit written comments on each candidate—either on a "long" or a "short" form, depending on the partner's degree of exposure to the candidate. Not every partner in the firm submits comments on every candidate. After reviewing the comments and interviewing the partners who submitted them, the firm's

Admissions Committee makes a recommendation to the Policy Board. This recommendation will be either that the firm accept the candidate for partnership, put her application on "hold," or deny her the promotion outright. The Policy Board then decides whether to submit the candidate's name to the entire partnership for a vote, to "hold" her candidacy, or to reject her. * * * Price Waterhouse places no limit on the number of persons whom it will admit to the partnership in any given year.

Ann Hopkins had worked at Price Waterhouse's Office of Government Services in Washington, D.C., for five years when the partners in that office proposed her as a candidate for partnership. Of the 662 partners at the firm at that time, 7 were women. Of the 88 persons proposed for partnership that year, only 1—Hopkins—was a woman. Forty-seven of these candidates were admitted to the partnership, 21 were rejected, and 20—including Hopkins—were "held" for reconsideration the following year.[1] Thirteen of the 32 partners who had submitted comments on Hopkins supported her bid for partnership. Three partners recommended that her candidacy be placed on hold, eight stated that they did not have an informed opinion about her, and eight recommended that she be denied partnership.

In a jointly prepared statement supporting her candidacy, the partners in Hopkins' office showcased her successful 2-year effort to secure a $25 million contract with the Department of State, labeling it "an outstanding performance" and one that Hopkins carried out "virtually at the partner level." Despite Price Waterhouse's attempt at trial to minimize her contribution to this project, Judge Gesell specifically found that Hopkins had "played a key role in Price Waterhouse's successful effort to win a multi-million dollar contract with the Department of State." Indeed, he went on, "[n]one of the other partnership candidates at Price Waterhouse that year had a comparable record in terms of successfully securing major contracts for the partnership."

The partners in Hopkins' office praised her character as well as her accomplishments, describing her * * * as "an outstanding professional" who had a "deft touch," a "strong character, independence and integrity." Clients appear to have agreed with these assessments. At trial, one official from the State Department described her as "extremely

---

[1] Before the time for reconsideration came, two of the partners in Hopkins' office withdrew their support for her, and the office informed her that she would not be reconsidered for partnership. Hopkins then resigned. Price Waterhouse does not challenge the Court of Appeals' conclusion that the refusal to repropose her for partnership amounted to a constructive discharge. * * * We are concerned today only with Price Waterhouse's decision to place Hopkins' candidacy on hold. Decisions pertaining to advancement to partnership are, of course, subject to challenge under Title VII. Hishon v. King & Spalding, 467 U.S. 69, 104 S.Ct. 2229, 81 L.Ed.2d 59 (1984).

competent, intelligent," "strong and forthright, very productive, energetic and creative." * * *

On too many occasions, however, Hopkins' aggressiveness apparently spilled over into abrasiveness. Staff members seem to have borne the brunt of Hopkins' brusqueness. Long before her bid for partnership, partners evaluating her work had counseled her to improve her relations with staff members. Although later evaluations indicate an improvement, Hopkins' perceived shortcomings in this important area eventually doomed her bid for partnership. Virtually all of the partners' negative remarks about Hopkins—even those of partners supporting her—had to do with her "inter-personal skills." Both "[s]upporters and opponents of her candidacy," stressed Judge Gesell, "indicated that she was sometimes overly aggressive, unduly harsh, difficult to work with and impatient with staff."

There were clear signs, though, that some of the partners reacted negatively to Hopkins' personality because she was a woman. One partner described her as "macho"; another suggested that she "overcompensated for being a woman"; a third advised her to take "a course at charm school". Several partners criticized her use of profanity; in response, one partner suggested that those partners objected to her swearing only "because it's a lady using foul language." Another supporter explained that Hopkins "ha[d] matured from a tough-talking somewhat masculine hard-nosed mgr to an authoritative, formidable, but much more appealing lady ptr candidate." But it was the man who, as Judge Gesell found, bore responsibility for explaining to Hopkins the reasons for the Policy Board's decision to place her candidacy on hold who delivered the *coup de grace*: in order to improve her chances for partnership, Thomas Beyer advised, Hopkins should "walk more femininely, talk more femininely, dress more femininely, wear make-up, have her hair styled, and wear jewelry."

Dr. Susan Fiske, a social psychologist and Associate Professor of Psychology at Carnegie-Mellon University, testified at trial that the partnership selection process at Price Waterhouse was likely influenced by sex stereotyping. Her testimony focused not only on the overtly sex-based comments of partners but also on gender-neutral remarks, made by partners who knew Hopkins only slightly, that were intensely critical of her. One partner, for example, baldly stated that Hopkins was "universally disliked" by staff, and another described her as "consistently annoying and irritating"; yet these were people who had had very little contact with Hopkins. According to Fiske, Hopkins' uniqueness (as the only woman in the pool of candidates) and the subjectivity of the evaluations made it likely that sharply critical remarks such as these were the product of sex stereotyping—although Fiske admitted that she could not say with certainty whether any particular comment was the result of stereotyping. * * *

Judge Gesell found that Price Waterhouse legitimately emphasized interpersonal skills in its partnership decisions, and also found that the firm had not fabricated its complaints about Hopkins' interpersonal skills as a pretext for discrimination. Moreover, he concluded, the firm did not give decisive emphasis to such traits only because Hopkins was a woman; although there were male candidates who lacked these skills but who were admitted to partnership, the judge found that these candidates possessed other, positive traits that Hopkins lacked.

The judge went on to decide, however, that some of the partners' remarks about Hopkins stemmed from an impermissibly cabined view of the proper behavior of women, and that Price Waterhouse had done nothing to disavow reliance on such comments. He held that Price Waterhouse had unlawfully discriminated against Hopkins on the basis of sex by consciously giving credence and effect to partners' comments that resulted from sex stereotyping. Noting that Price Waterhouse could avoid equitable relief by proving by clear and convincing evidence that it would have placed Hopkins' candidacy on hold even absent this discrimination, the judge decided that the firm had not carried this heavy burden.

The Court of Appeals affirmed the District Court's ultimate conclusion, but departed from its analysis in one particular: it held that even if a plaintiff proves that discrimination played a role in an employment decision, the defendant will not be found liable if it proves, by clear and convincing evidence, that it would have made the same decision in the absence of discrimination. Under this approach, an employer is not deemed to have violated Title VII if it proves that it would have made the same decision in the absence of an impermissible motive, whereas under the District Court's approach, the employer's proof in that respect only avoids equitable relief. We decide today that the Court of Appeals had the better approach, but that both courts erred in requiring the employer to make its proof by clear and convincing evidence.

II

The specification of the standard of causation under Title VII is a decision about the kind of conduct that violates that statute. * * *

A

In passing Title VII, Congress made the simple but momentous announcement that sex, race, religion, and national origin are not relevant to the selection, evaluation, or compensation of employees. Yet, the statute does not purport to limit the other qualities and characteristics that employers *may* take into account in making employment decisions. The converse, therefore, of "for cause" legislation,

Title VII eliminates certain bases for distinguishing among employees while otherwise preserving employers' freedom of choice. This balance between employee rights and employer prerogatives turns out to be decisive in the case before us.

Congress' intent to forbid employers to take gender into account in making employment decisions appears on the face of the statute. In now-familiar language, the statute forbids an employer to "fail or refuse to hire or to discharge any individual, or otherwise to discriminate with respect to his compensation, terms, conditions, or privileges of employment," * * * *because of* such individual's * * * sex." 42 U. S. C. §§ 2000e–2(a)(1), (2) (emphasis added). We take these words to mean that gender must be irrelevant to employment decisions. To construe the words "because of" as colloquial shorthand for "but-for causation," as does Price Waterhouse, is to misunderstand them.

* * * The critical inquiry, the one commanded by the words of § 703(a)(1), is whether gender was a factor in the employment decision *at the moment it was made*. Moreover, since we know that the words "because of" do not mean "*solely* because of," we also know that Title VII meant to condemn even those decisions based on a mixture of legitimate and illegitimate considerations. When, therefore, an employer considers both gender and legitimate factors at the time of making a decision, that decision was "because of" sex and the other, legitimate considerations—even if we may say later, in the context of litigation, that the decision would have been the same if gender had not been taken into account.

* * * To say that an employer may not take gender into account is not, however, the end of the matter, for that describes only one aspect of Title VII. The other important aspect of the statute is its preservation of an employer's remaining freedom of choice. We conclude that the preservation of this freedom means that an employer shall not be liable if it can prove that, even if it had not taken gender into account, it would have come to the same decision regarding a particular person. * * *

* * * The central point is this: while an employer may not take gender into account in making an employment decision (except in those very narrow circumstances in which gender is a BFOQ), it is free to decide against a woman for other reasons. We think these principles require that, once a plaintiff in a Title VII case shows that gender played a motivating part in an employment decision, the defendant may avoid a finding of liability only by proving that it would have made the same decision even if it had not allowed gender to play such a role. This balance of burdens is the direct result of Title VII's balance of rights. * * *

C

In saying that gender played a motivating part in an employment decision, we mean that, if we asked the employer at the moment of the decision what its reasons were and if we received a truthful response, one of those reasons would be that the applicant or employee was a woman. In the specific context of sex stereotyping, an employer who acts on the basis of a belief that a woman cannot be aggressive, or that she must not be, has acted on the basis of gender.

* * * As for the legal relevance of sex stereotyping, we are beyond the day when an employer could evaluate employees by assuming or insisting that they matched the stereotype associated with their group, for "[i]n forbidding employers to discriminate against individuals because of their sex, Congress intended to strike at the entire spectrum of disparate treatment of men and women resulting from sex stereotypes." *Los Angeles Dept. of Water and Power* v. *Manhart*, 435 U.S. 702, 707, n. 13 (1978). An employer who objects to aggressiveness in women but whose positions require this trait places women in an intolerable and impermissible catch 22: out of a job if they behave aggressively and out of a job if they do not. Title VII lifts women out of this bind.

Remarks at work that are based on sex stereotypes do not inevitably prove that gender played a part in a particular employment decision. The plaintiff must show that the employer actually relied on her gender in making its decision. In making this showing, stereotyped remarks can certainly be *evidence* that gender played a part. In any event, the stereotyping in this case did not simply consist of stray remarks. On the contrary, Hopkins proved that Price Waterhouse invited partners to submit comments; that some of the comments stemmed from sex stereotypes; that an important part of the Policy Board's decision on Hopkins was an assessment of the submitted comments; and that Price Waterhouse in no way disclaimed reliance on the sex-linked evaluations. This is not, as Price Waterhouse suggests, "discrimination in the air"; rather, it is, as Hopkins puts it, "discrimination brought to ground and visited upon" an employee. * * *

As to the employer's proof, in most cases, the employer should be able to present some objective evidence as to its probable decision in the absence of an impermissible motive. Moreover, proving "that the same decision would have been justified * * * is not the same as proving that the same decision would have been made." *Givhan*, 439 U.S., at 416. An employer may not, in other words, prevail in a mixed-motives case by offering a legitimate and sufficient reason for its decision if that reason did not motivate it at the time of the decision. Finally, an employer may not meet its burden in such a case by merely showing that at the time of the decision it was motivated only in part by a legitimate reason. The very premise of a mixed-motives case is that a legitimate reason was present, and indeed, in this case, Price Waterhouse already has made this showing by convincing Judge Gesell that Hopkins' interpersonal problems were a legitimate concern. The employer instead must show that its legitimate reason, standing alone, would have induced it to make the same decision.

III

The courts below held that an employer who has allowed a discriminatory impulse to play a motivating part in an employment decision must prove by clear and convincing evidence that it would have made the same decision in the absence of discrimination. We are persuaded that the better rule is that the employer must make this showing by a preponderance of the evidence.

Conventional rules of civil litigation generally apply in Title VII cases * * * and one of these rules is that parties to civil litigation need only prove their case by a preponderance of the evidence. * * *

[The concurring opinion of JUSTICE WHITE is omitted].

JUSTICE O'CONNOR, concurring in the judgment.

I agree with the plurality that, on the facts presented in this case, the burden of persuasion should shift to the employer to demonstrate by a preponderance of the evidence that it would have reached the same decision concerning Ann Hopkins' candidacy absent consideration of her gender. I further agree that this burden shift is properly part of the liability phase of the litigation. I thus concur in the judgment of the Court. My disagreement stems from the plurality's conclusions concerning the substantive requirement of causation under the statute and its broad statements regarding the applicability of the allocation of the burden of proof applied in this case. * * *

II

* * * [T]he facts of this case, and a growing number like it * * *, convince me that the evidentiary standard I propose is necessary to make real the promise of *McDonnell Douglas* that "[i]n the implementation of [employment] decisions, it is abundantly clear that Title VII tolerates no * * * discrimination, subtle or otherwise." 411 U.S., at 801. In this case, the District Court found that a number of the evaluations of Ann Hopkins submitted by partners in the firm overtly referred to her failure to conform to certain gender stereotypes as a factor militating against her election to the partnership. The District Court further found that these evaluations were given "great weight" by the decisionmakers at Price Waterhouse. * * * As the Court of Appeals characterized it, Ann Hopkins proved that Price Waterhouse "permitt[ed] stereotypical attitudes towards women to play a significant, though unquantifiable, role in its decision not to invite her to become a partner."

At this point Ann Hopkins had taken her proof as far as it could go. She had proved discriminatory input into the decisional process, and had proved that participants in the process considered her failure to conform to the stereotypes credited by a number of the decisionmakers had been a substantial factor in the decision. It is as if Ann Hopkins were sitting in the hall outside the room where partnership decisions were being made. As the partners filed in to consider her candidacy, she heard several of them make sexist remarks in discussing her suitability for partnership. As the decisionmakers exited the room, she was *told* by one of those privy to the decisionmaking process that her gender was a major reason for the rejection of her partnership bid. * * * [O]ne would be hard pressed to think of a situation where it would be more appropriate to require the defendant to show that its decision would have been justified by wholly legitimate concerns.

Moreover, there is mounting evidence in the decisions of the lower courts that respondent here is not alone in her inability to pinpoint discrimination as the precise cause of her injury, despite having shown that it played a significant role in the decisional process. * * * Particularly in the context of the professional world, where decisions are often made by collegial bodies on the basis of largely subjective criteria, requiring the plaintiff to prove that *any* one factor was the definitive cause of the decisionmakers' action may be tantamount to declaring Title VII inapplicable to such decisions. * * *

In my view, in order to justify shifting the burden on the issue of causation to the defendant, a disparate treatment plaintiff must show by direct evidence that an illegitimate criterion was a substantial factor in the decision. * * * As an evidentiary matter, where a plaintiff has made this type of strong showing of illicit motivation, the factfinder is entitled to presume that the employer's discriminatory animus made a difference to the outcome, absent proof to the contrary from the employer. Where a disparate treatment plaintiff has made such a showing, the burden then rests with the employer to convince the trier of fact that it is more likely than not that the decision would have been the same absent consideration of the illegitimate factor. The employer need not isolate the sole cause for the decision; rather it must demonstrate that with the illegitimate factor removed from the calculus, sufficient business reasons would have induced it to take the same employment action. This evidentiary scheme essentially requires the employer to place the employee in the same position he or she would have occupied absent discrimination. Cf. *Mt. Healthy City Bd. of Ed.* v. *Doyle*, 429 U.S. 274, 286 (1977). If the employer fails to carry this burden, the factfinder is justified in concluding that the decision was made "because of" consideration of the illegitimate factor and the substantive standard for liability under the statute is satisfied.

Thus, stray remarks in the workplace, while perhaps probative of sexual harassment, see *Meritor Savings Bank* v. *Vinson*, 477 U.S. 57, 63–69 (1986), cannot justify requiring the employer to prove that its hiring or promotion decisions were based on legitimate criteria. Nor can statements by nondecisionmakers, or statements by decisionmakers unrelated to the decisional process itself, suffice to satisfy the plaintiff's burden in this regard. In addition, in my view testimony such as Dr. Fiske's in this case, standing alone, would not justify shifting the burden of persuasion to the employer. Race and gender always "play a role" in an employment decision in the benign sense that these are human characteristics of which decisionmakers are aware and about which they may comment in a perfectly neutral and nondiscriminatory fashion. For example, in the context of this case, a mere reference to "a lady candidate" might show that gender "played a role" in the decision, but by no means could support a rational factfinder's inference that the decision was made "because of" sex. What is required is what Ann Hopkins showed here: direct evidence that decisionmakers placed substantial negative reliance on an illegitimate criterion in reaching their decision.

* * *

[The dissenting opinion of JUSTICE KENNEDY, with whom THE CHIEF JUSTICE and JUSTICE SCALIA joined, is omitted.]

NOTES AND QUESTIONS

1. The *Price Waterhouse* case was significant in two respects. First, and foremost, the Supreme Court plurality recognized what has come to be known as the "mixed-motives" evidentiary framework and burdens of proof for litigating Title VII claims in which both legitimate and illegitimate motives played a role in an employer's adverse employment decision. Second, the Court acknowledged the role that sex stereotyping can play in limiting women's employment opportunities and permitted the plaintiff, Ann Hopkins, to use evidence of sex stereotyping in the employer's decisionmaking process to support her discrimination claim. We defer more detailed discussion of sex stereotyping to Chapter 7, but it is worth briefly exploring here how sex stereotyping operated in this case. For example, was an expert witness necessary to explain the influence of sex stereotyping in the accounting firm's decision not to promote Hopkins? How would you characterize the stereotyping at issue in this case? What was the employer's legitimate motive(s) in failing to promote Hopkins? For an account of Ann Hopkins' litigation against *Price Waterhouse*, see Cynthia Estlund, *The Story of* Price Waterhouse v. Hopkins, in Employment Discrimination Stories 66 (Joel Wm. Friedman ed., 2006).

2. Many academics have been drawn to the mixed-motives theory because they contend that it better represents how workplace decisions are actually made. Professor Charles Sullivan, for example, has noted: "[F]rom a commonsense perspective, almost all cases involving any discrimination at all are likely to be *Price Waterhouse* cases, not *McDonnell Burdine* ones, in the sense that the employer will have both good reasons and bad ones for its

decisions." Charles A. Sullivan, *Accounting for* Price Waterhouse*: Proving Disparate Treatment Under Title VII,* 56 Brooklyn L. Rev. 1107, 1162 (1991).

3. Justice O'Connor's concurring opinion in *Price Waterhouse* proved especially influential, and most lower courts adopted her position that the mixed-motives theory was only appropriate in cases that involved direct evidence of discrimination. This requirement necessitated that courts define direct evidence, and courts have struggled to provide a clear and helpful definition. In its most stringent form, direct evidence is akin to an admission or confession of liability. *See* Radue v. Kimberly-Clark Corp., 219 F.3d 612, 616 (7th Cir.2000) ("Direct evidence essentially requires an admission by the decision-maker that his actions were based upon the prohibited animus."). Another widely used definition is "evidence of discrimination that does not require a factfinder to draw any inferences in order to conclude that the challenged employment action was motivated at least in part by prejudice against members of the protected group." Johnson v. Kroger Co., 319 F.3d 858, 865 (6th Cir.2003); *see also* Sanders v. Sw. Bell Co., 544 F.3d 1101, 1105 (10th Cir.2008) ("Direct evidence is evidence from which the trier of fact may conclude, without inference, that the employment action was, undertaken because of the employer's protected status.").

These definitions are not always easy to apply in particular circumstances. Perhaps the most common form of direct evidence is when the employer expressly denies an individual a job because of a statutorily prohibited motive. For example, in *Jones v. Robinson Prop. Group*, 427 F.3d 987, 993 (5th Cir.2005), the court found a casino manager's statements that "good old white boys didn't want blacks touching their cards" and that he was not supposed "to hire too many blacks in the poker room" constituted direct evidence of race-based animus. *See also* Etienne v. Spanish Lake Truck & Casino Plaza, 778 F.3d 473, 476 (5th Cir.2015) (statement that plaintiff was "too black to do various tasks at the casino" constituted direct evidence.) Likewise, some courts have recognized that remarks to the effect that "I won't hire you because you are a woman," or "I'm firing you because you are not a Christian," or "I'm reassigning you because you are black," are compelling examples of direct evidence of discriminatory animus. *See* Venters v. City of Delphi, 123 F.3d 956, 973 (7th Cir.1997). *See also* Van Voorhis v. Hillsborough County, 512 F.3d 1296, 1300 (11th Cir.2008) (manager's statement that he "didn't want to hire any old pilots" constituted direct evidence of age-based animus); Dominguez-Curry v. Nev. Transp. Dep't, 424 F.3d 1027, 1038 (9th Cir.2005) (manager's statements that "women have no business in construction," that "women should only be in subservient positions" and that he "would never work for a woman" treated as direct evidence sex-based animus).

In 2006, the Supreme Court addressed the implications of a case in which a manager referred to an African-American employee as "boy." In an unpublished opinion, the Eleventh Circuit had held that use of the term "boy" alone, without a racial indicator (such as in "black boy"), was not evidence of discriminatory intent. In a unanimous and short per curiam opinion, the

Supreme Court reversed, holding instead that "[a]lthough it is true the disputed word will not always be evidence of racial animus, it does not follow that the term, standing alone, is always benign. The speaker's meaning may depend on various factors including context, inflection, tone of voice, local custom, and historical usage." Ash v. Tyson Foods, Inc., 546 U.S. 454, 456, 126 S.Ct. 1195, 1197, 163 L.Ed.2d 1053, 1057 (2006).

4. *The Stray Remarks Doctrine*: Justice O'Connor's concurrence in *Price Waterhouse* distinguished "stray remarks" from direct evidence, and lower courts have adopted the "stray remarks" terminology to determine when statements by employers and their agents constitute direct or circumstantial evidence of discriminatory intent. In other words, comments that do not indicate discriminatory animus are typically classified as stray remarks, and they do not constitute direct evidence of the speaker's state of mind. Several courts have adopted a four-part test to determine whether epithets, stereotyping evidence, or other evidence or remarks made by supervisors should be treated as direct evidence or, alternatively, as stray remarks. The Fifth Circuit explained the factors to be considered:

> [F]or comments in the workplace to provide sufficient evidence of discrimination, they must be 1) related [to the protected class of persons of which the plaintiff is a member]; 2) proximate in time to the terminations; 3) made by an individual with authority over the employment decision at issue; and 4) related to the employment decision at issue. Where [c]omments[ ] are vague and remote in time [they] are insufficient to establish discrimination. In contrast, specific comments made over a lengthy period of time are sufficient.

Wallace v. Methodist Hosp. Sys., 271 F.3d 212, 222 (5th Cir.2001) (internal citations omitted). *See also* Hensworth v. Quotesmith.com, Inc., 476 F.3d 487, 491 (7th Cir.2007) ("[A] particular remark can provide an inference of discrimination when the remark was (1) made by the decision maker, (2) around the time of decision, and (3) in reference to the adverse employment action.")

Statements and other comments found to be stray remarks may still constitute circumstantial evidence that is probative of the ultimate fact of intentional discrimination. *See, e.g.,* Abrams v. Dept. of Pub. Safety, 764 F.3d 244, 253 (2nd Cir.2014) (comments that a candidate did not "fit in" were not direct evidence of racial discrimination but may create an inference of discrimination depending on the circumstances).

5. *The Civil Rights Act of 1991*: Congress altered the *Price Waterhouse* mixed-motive proof structure as part of its comprehensive amendments to Title VII through a statute known as the Civil Rights Act of 1991. Specifically, § 107(m) provides that "an unlawful employment practice is established when the complaining party demonstrates that race, color, religion, sex, or national origin was a motivating factor for any employment practice, even though other factors also motivated the practice." Title VII, § 703(m), 42 U.S.C. § 2000e–2(m). As a result, any time a plaintiff is able to

prove that an impermissible factor "was a motivating factor" she is entitled to a judgment in her favor. A new remedial section was also added to Title VII to provide that if an employee succeeds in proving discrimination was "a motivating factor" for an employment decision, and the employer demonstrates that it would have made the same decision without the impermissible factor, the court is not permitted to award damages or order certain forms of injunctive relief such as reinstatement, hiring, promotion, or backpay, but is limited to ordering declaratory and injunctive relief, attorney's fees, and costs. *See* Title VII, § 706(g)(2)(B), 42 U.S.C. § 2000e–5(g)(2)(B). As a result of these changes, a plaintiff who establishes a mixed-motive claim is entitled to judgment on liability, with the employer then having the opportunity to prove it would have made the same decision absent the impermissible factor as a way of limiting its damages. A question remained, however, whether Justice O'Connor's view in *Price Watherhouse* that mixed-motive claims could only be pursued in cases involving direct evidence of discriminatory intent was consistent with the new statutory requirements under the Civil Rights Act of 1991.

DESERT PALACE, INC. V. COSTA

Supreme Court of the United States, 2003.
539 U.S. 90, 123 S.Ct. 2148, 156 L.Ed.2d 84.

JUSTICE THOMAS delivered the opinion of the Court.

The question before us in this case is whether a plaintiff must present direct evidence of discrimination in order to obtain a mixed-motive instruction under Title VII of the Civil Rights Act of 1964, as amended by the Civil Rights Act of 1991 (1991 Act). We hold that direct evidence is not required.

I

A

Since 1964, Title VII has made it an "unlawful employment practice for an employer * * * to discriminate against any individual * * * , *because of* such individual's race, color, religion, sex, or national origin." 78 Stat. 255, 42 U.S.C. § 2000e–2(a)(1) (emphasis added). In *Price Waterhouse v. Hopkins,* 490 U.S. 228, 109 S.Ct. 1775, 104 L.Ed.2d 268 (1989), the Court considered whether an employment decision is made "because of" sex in a "mixed-motive" case, *i.e.,* where both legitimate and illegitimate reasons motivated the decision. The Court concluded that, under § 2000e–2(a)(1), an employer could "avoid a finding of liability * * * by proving that it would have made the same decision even if it had not allowed gender to play such a role." *Id.,* at 244, 109 S.Ct. 1775; see *id.,* at 261, 109 S.Ct. 1775, n. (White, J., concurring in judgment); *id.,* at 261, 109 S.Ct. 1775 (O'CONNOR, J., concurring in judgment). The Court was divided, however, over the predicate question of when the burden of proof may be shifted to an employer to prove the affirmative defense.

Justice Brennan, writing for a plurality of four Justices, would have held that "when a plaintiff * * * proves that her gender played a *motivating* part in an employment decision, the defendant may avoid a finding of liability only by proving by a preponderance of the evidence that it would have made the same decision even if it had not taken the plaintiff's gender into account." *Id.,* at 258, 109 S.Ct. 1775 (emphasis added). The plurality did not, however, "suggest a limitation on the possible ways of proving that [gender] stereotyping played a motivating role in an employment decision." *Id.,* at 251–252, 109 S.Ct. 1775.

Justice White and Justice O'Connor both concurred in the judgment. Justice White would have held that the case was governed by *Mt. Healthy City Bd. of Ed. v. Doyle,* 429 U.S. 274, 97 S.Ct. 568, 50 L.Ed.2d 471 (1977), and would have shifted the burden to the employer only when a plaintiff "show[ed] that the unlawful motive was a *substantial* factor in the adverse employment action." *Price Waterhouse, supra,* at 259, 109 S.Ct. 1775. Justice O'Connor, like Justice White, would have required the plaintiff to show that an illegitimate consideration was a "substantial factor" in the employment decision. 490 U.S., at 276, 109 S.Ct. 1775. But, under Justice O'Connor's view, "the burden on the issue of causation" would shift to the employer only where "a disparate treatment plaintiff [could] show by *direct evidence* that an illegitimate criterion was a substantial factor in the decision." *Ibid.* (emphasis added).

Two years after *Price Waterhouse,* Congress passed the 1991 Act "in large part [as] a response to a series of decisions of this Court interpreting the Civil Rights Acts of 1866 and 1964." *Landgraf v. USI Film Products,* 511 U.S. 244, 250, 114 S.Ct. 1483, 128 L.Ed.2d 229 (1994). In particular, § 107 of the 1991 Act, which is at issue in this case, "respond[ed]" to *Price Waterhouse* by "setting forth standards applicable in 'mixed motive' cases" in two new statutory provisions.[1] 511 U.S., at 251, 114 S.Ct. 1483. The first establishes an alternative for proving that an "unlawful employment practice" has occurred:

> Except as otherwise provided in this subchapter, an unlawful employment practice is established when the complaining party demonstrates that race, color, religion, sex, or national origin was a motivating factor for any employment practice, even though other factors also motivated the practice.

42 U.S.C. § 2000e–2(m). The second provides that, with respect to "a claim in which an individual proves a violation under section 2000e–2(m)," the employer has a limited affirmative defense that does not

[1] This case does not require us to decide when, if ever, § 107 applies outside of the mixed-motive context.

absolve it of liability, but restricts the remedies available to a plaintiff. The available remedies include only declaratory relief, certain types of injunctive relief, and attorney's fees and costs. 42 U.S.C. § 2000e–5(g)(2)(B). In order to avail itself of the affirmative defense, the employer must "demonstrat[e] that [it] would have taken the same action in the absence of the impermissible motivating factor." *Ibid.*

Since the passage of the 1991 Act, the Courts of Appeals have divided over whether a plaintiff must prove by direct evidence that an impermissible consideration was a "motivating factor" in an adverse employment action. See 42 U.S.C. § 2000e–2(m). Relying primarily on Justice O'Connor's concurrence in *Price Waterhouse,* a number of courts have held that direct evidence is required to establish liability under § 2000e–2(m). [Citations omitted.] In the decision below, however, the Ninth Circuit concluded otherwise.

B

Petitioner Desert Palace, Inc. * * * employed respondent Catharina Costa as a warehouse worker and heavy equipment operator. Respondent was the only woman in this job and in her local Teamsters bargaining unit.

Respondent experienced a number of problems with management and her co-workers that led to an escalating series of disciplinary sanctions, including informal rebukes, a denial of privileges, and suspension. Petitioner finally terminated respondent after she was involved in a physical altercation in a warehouse elevator with fellow Teamsters member Herbert Gerber. Petitioner disciplined both employees because the facts surrounding the incident were in dispute, but Gerber, who had a clean disciplinary record, received only a 5-day suspension.

Respondent subsequently filed this lawsuit against petitioner in the United States District Court for the District of Nevada, asserting claims of sex discrimination and sexual harassment under Title VII. The District Court dismissed the sexual harassment claim, but allowed the claim for sex discrimination to go to the jury. At trial, respondent presented evidence that (1) she was singled out for "intense 'stalking'" by one of her supervisors, (2) she received harsher discipline than men for the same conduct, (3) she was treated less favorably than men in the assignment of overtime, and (4) supervisors repeatedly "stack[ed]" her disciplinary record and "frequently used or tolerated" sex-based slurs against her.

Based on this evidence, the District Court denied petitioner's motion for judgment as a matter of law, and submitted the case to the jury with instructions, two of which are relevant here. First, without objection from petitioner, the District Court instructed the jury that the plaintiff has the burden of proving * * * by a preponderance of the evidence that she "suffered adverse work conditions" and "that her sex was a motivating factor in any such work conditions imposed upon her."

Second, the District Court gave the jury the following mixed-motive instruction:

> "You have heard evidence that the defendant's treatment of the plaintiff was motivated by the plaintiff's sex and also by other lawful reasons. If you find that the plaintiff's sex was a motivating factor in the defendant's treatment of the plaintiff, the plaintiff is entitled to your verdict, even if you find that the defendant's conduct was also motivated by a lawful reason.
>
> "However, if you find that the defendant's treatment of the plaintiff was motivated by both gender and lawful reasons, you must decide whether the plaintiff is entitled to damages. The plaintiff is entitled to damages unless the defendant proves by a preponderance of the evidence that the defendant would have treated plaintiff similarly even if the plaintiff's gender had played no role in the employment decision."

Petitioner unsuccessfully objected to this instruction, claiming that respondent had failed to adduce "direct evidence" that sex was a motivating factor in her dismissal or in any of the other adverse employment actions taken against her. The jury rendered a verdict for respondent, awarding backpay, compensatory damages, and punitive damages. The District Court denied petitioner's renewed motion for judgment as a matter of law.

The Court of Appeals initially vacated and remanded, holding that the District Court had erred in giving the mixed-motive instruction * * * .

The Court of Appeals reinstated the District Court's judgment after rehearing the case en banc. The en banc court saw no need to decide whether Justice O'Connor's concurrence in *Price Waterhouse* controlled because it concluded that Justice O'Connor's references to "direct evidence" had been "wholly abrogated" by the 1991 Act. * * * Accordingly, the court concluded that a "plaintiff * * * may establish a violation through a preponderance of evidence (whether direct or circumstantial) that a protected characteristic played 'a motivating factor.'" Based on that standard, the Court of Appeals held that respondent's evidence was sufficient to warrant a mixed-motive instruction and that a reasonable jury could have found that respondent's sex was a "motivating factor in her treatment." * * *

II

This case provides us with the first opportunity to consider the effects of the 1991 Act on jury instructions in mixed-motive cases. Specifically, we must decide whether a plaintiff must present direct evidence of discrimination in order to obtain a mixed-motive instruction under 42 U.S.C. § 2000e–2(m). Petitioner's argument on this point proceeds in three steps: (1) Justice O'Connor's opinion is the holding of *Price Waterhouse;* (2) Justice O'Connor's *Price Waterhouse* opinion requires direct evidence of discrimination before a mixed-motive instruction can be given; and (3) the 1991 Act does nothing to abrogate that holding. Like the Court of Appeals, we see no need to address which of the opinions in *Price Waterhouse* is controlling: the third step of petitioner's argument is flawed, primarily because it is inconsistent with the text of § 2000e–2(m).

Our precedents make clear that the starting point for our analysis is the statutory text. See *Connecticut Nat. Bank v. Germain,* 503 U.S. 249, 253–254, 112 S.Ct. 1146, 117 L.Ed.2d 391 (1992). And where, as here, the words of the statute are unambiguous, the " 'judicial inquiry is complete.' " *Id.,* at 254, 112 S.Ct. 1146. Section 2000e–2(m) unambiguously states that a plaintiff need only "demonstrat[e]" that an employer used a forbidden consideration with respect to "any employment practice." On its face, the statute does not mention, much less require, that a plaintiff make a heightened showing through direct evidence. Indeed, petitioner concedes as much.

Moreover, Congress explicitly defined the term "demonstrates" in the 1991 Act, leaving little doubt that no special evidentiary showing is required. Title VII defines the term " 'demonstrates' " as to "mee[t] the burdens of production and persuasion." § 2000e(m). If Congress intended the term " 'demonstrates' " to require that the "burdens of production and persuasion" be met by direct evidence or some other heightened showing, it could have made that intent clear by including language to that effect in § 2000e(m). * * *

In addition, Title VII's silence with respect to the type of evidence required in mixed-motive cases also suggests that we should not depart from the "[c]onventional rul[e] of civil litigation [that] generally appl[ies] in Title VII cases." That rule requires a plaintiff to prove his case "by a preponderance of the evidence," using "direct or circumstantial evidence," *Postal Service Bd. of Governors v. Aikens,* 460 U.S. 711, 714, n. 3, 103 S.Ct. 1478, 75 L.Ed.2d 403 (1983). We have often acknowledged the utility of circumstantial evidence in discrimination cases. For instance, in *Reeves v. Sanderson Plumbing Products, Inc.,* 530 U.S. 133, 120 S.Ct. 2097, 147 L.Ed.2d 105 (2000), we recognized that evidence that a defendant's explanation for an employment practice is "unworthy of credence" is "one form of *circumstantial evidence* that is probative of intentional discrimination." *Id.,* at 147, 120 S.Ct. 2097 (emphasis added). The reason for treating circumstantial and direct evidence alike is both clear and deep-rooted: "Circumstantial evidence is not only sufficient, but may also be more certain, satisfying and persuasive than direct evidence."

Rogers v. Missouri Pacific R. Co., 352 U.S. 500, 508, n. 17, 77 S.Ct. 443, 1 L.Ed.2d 493 (1957).

* * *

Finally, the use of the term "demonstrates" in other provisions of Title VII tends to show further that § 2000e–2(m) does not incorporate a direct evidence requirement. See, *e.g.,* 42 U.S.C. §§ 2000e–2(k)(1)(A)(i), 2000e–5(g)(2)(B). For instance, § 2000e–5(g)(2)(B) requires an employer to "demonstrat[e] that [it] would have taken the same action in the absence of the impermissible motivating factor" in order to take advantage of the partial affirmative defense. Due to the similarity in structure between that provision and § 2000e–2(m), it would be logical to assume that the term "demonstrates" would carry the same meaning with respect to both provisions. * * * Absent some congressional indication to the contrary, we decline to give the same term in the same Act a different meaning depending on whether the rights of the plaintiff or the defendant are at issue. * * *

For the reasons stated above, we agree with the Court of Appeals that no heightened showing is required under § 2000e–2(m).

* * *

In order to obtain an instruction under § 2000e–2(m), a plaintiff need only present sufficient evidence for a reasonable jury to conclude, by a preponderance of the evidence, that "race, color, religion, sex, or national origin was a motivating factor for any employment practice." Because direct evidence of discrimination is not required in mixed-motive cases, the Court of Appeals correctly concluded that the District Court did not abuse its discretion in giving a mixed-motive instruction to the jury. Accordingly, the judgment of the Court of Appeals is affirmed.

JUSTICE O'CONNOR, concurring.

I join the Court's opinion. In my view, prior to the Civil Rights Act of 1991, the evidentiary rule we developed to shift the burden of persuasion in mixed-motive cases was appropriately applied only where a disparate treatment plaintiff "demonstrated by direct evidence that an illegitimate factor played a substantial role" in an adverse employment decision. *Price Waterhouse v. Hopkins,* 490 U.S. 228, 275, 109 S.Ct. 1775, 104 L.Ed.2d 268 (1989) (O'CONNOR, J., concurring in judgment). This showing triggered "the deterrent purpose of the statute" and permitted a reasonable factfinder to conclude that "absent further explanation, the employer's discriminatory motivation 'caused' the employment decision." *Id.,* at 265, 109 S.Ct. 1775 (O'CONNOR, J., concurring in judgment).

As the Court's opinion explains, in the Civil Rights Act of 1991, Congress codified a new evidentiary rule for mixed-motive cases arising under Title VII. I therefore agree with the Court that the District Court did not abuse its discretion in giving a mixed-motive instruction to the jury.

NOTES AND QUESTIONS

1. The Court's opinion in *Costa* made clear that cases relying on circumstantial evidence can also be tried under a mixed-motives framework, thus rejecting Justice O'Connor's position from *Price Waterhouse* that a mixed-motive evidentiary framework requires direct evidence. While the decision was both unanimous and short, it raised a number of interesting and important questions. (Note that in cases and commentary *Desert Palace v. Costa* is referred to as either *Desert Palace* or *Costa*; we will use the shorter title *Costa* in these notes.)

2. Perhaps the most interesting question after *Costa* is whether all Title VII discrimination cases should now be treated as mixed-motive cases, and if so, what that might mean for litigants' burdens in proving or defending discrimination claims. Immediately after *Costa* was decided, a number of commentators suggested that the *McDonnell Douglas* proof structure should no longer be relevant in discrimination claims and that all cases should now be treated as mixed-motive cases. Professor William Corbett, for example, suggested that the *McDonnell Douglas* proof structure was no longer necessary because cases involving pretext analysis are based on the problematic assumption that the challenged adverse employment decision has only a single motive. "Once a defendant produces evidence of a legitimate, nondiscriminatory reason, the case has at least two motives at issue, and pretext analysis, with its higher standard of causation, is irrelevant." William R. Corbett, *McDonnell Douglas, 1973–2003: May You Rest in Peace?* 6 U.Pa.J.Lab. & Emp.L. 199, 213 (2003). Several courts shared this sentiment and suggested that to survive summary judgment, a plaintiff need only offer evidence sufficient to demonstrate that discrimination was a motivating factor in the adverse employment decision. Other courts did not see any shift in the law, in part because in *Costa* the Supreme Court never mentioned *McDonnell Douglas*, and they believed it would be highly unusual for the Court to change the landscape of employment discrimination law *sub silentio*. How do you explain note 1 in *Costa*? Does the note imply anything about whether *McDonnell Douglas* survives *Costa*?

One appellate court has summarized the various approaches courts have adopted in the wake of the *Costa* decision:

> Since *Desert Palace,* the federal courts of appeals have, without much, if any, consideration of the issue, developed widely differing approaches to the question of how to analyze summary judgment challenges in Title VII mixed-motive cases. * * * The Eighth Circuit has explicitly held that the *McDonnell Douglas/Burdine* burden-shifting framework applies to the summary judgment analysis of mixed-motive claims after *Desert Palace. See* Griffith v. City of Des Moines, 387 F.3d 733, 736 (8th Cir.2004). The Eleventh Circuit

seems to have joined the Eighth Circuit in this regard. *See* Burstein v. Entel, Inc., 137 Fed. Appx. 205, 209 n.8 (11th Cir.2005) (unpublished) * * * .

The Fifth Circuit, in contrast, has adopted a "modified *McDonnell Douglas*" approach, under which a plaintiff in a mixed-motive case can rebut the defendant's legitimate non-discriminatory reason not only through evidence of pretext (the traditional *McDonnell Douglas/Burdine* burden), but also with evidence that the defendant's proffered reason is only one of the reasons for its conduct (the mixed-motive alternative). *See* Machinchick v. PB Power, Inc., 398 F.3d 345, 352 (5th Cir.2005); Rachid v. Jack in the Box, Inc., 376 F.3d 305, 312 (5th Cir.2004).

Adopting a sort of middle ground between these two positions are the Fourth and Ninth Circuits which permit a mixed-motive plaintiff to avoid a defendant's motion for summary judgment by proceeding either under the "pretext framework" of the traditional *McDonnell Douglas/Burdine* analysis or by "presenting direct or circumstantial evidence that raises a genuine issue of material fact as to whether an impermissible factor such as race motivated[, at least in part,] the adverse employment decision." Diamond v. Colonial Life & Accident Ins. Co., 416 F.3d 310, 318 (4th Cir.2005); *see Hill* [v. Lockheed Martin Logistics Mgmt., Inc., 354 F.3d 277, 284–85 (4th Cir.2004)]; McGinest v. GTE Serv. Corp., 360 F.3d 1103, 1122 (9th Cir.2004). The D.C. Circuit appears to have recently joined this middle ground approach. *See* Fogg v. Gonzales, 492 F.3d 447, 451 & n* (D.C. Cir.2007) (indicating that "a plaintiff can establish an unlawful employment practice by showing that 'discrimination or retaliation played a "motivating part" or was a 'substantial factor" in the employment decision' " but noting that a "plaintiff may also, of course, use evidence of pretext and the *McDonnell Douglas* framework to prove a mixed-motive case").

White v. Baxter Healthcare Corp., 533 F.3d 381, 398–99 (6th Cir.2008). The Sixth Circuit went on to consider what the appropriate standard should be. It explained:

This case now presents us with the opportunity to finally clarify how Title VII mixed-motive claims should be analyzed at the summary judgment stage. We do so by holding that the *McDonnell Douglas/Burdine* burden-shifting framework does *not* apply to the summary judgment analysis of Title VII mixed-motive claims. We likewise hold that to survive a defendant's motion for summary judgment, a Title VII plaintiff asserting a mixed-motive claim need only produce evidence sufficient to convince a jury that: (1) the defendant took an adverse employment action against the plaintiff; and (2) "race, color, religion, sex, or national origin was *a* motivating factor" for the defendant's adverse employment action. 42 U.S.C.

§ 2000e–2(m) (emphasis added). * * * This burden of producing some evidence in support of a mixed-motive claim is not onerous and should preclude sending the case to the jury only where the record is devoid of evidence that could reasonably be construed to support the plaintiff's claim. * * *

Our refusal to extend the application of the *McDonnell Douglas/Burdine* framework to our summary judgment analysis of Title VII mixed-motive claims is based upon a careful consideration of the Supreme Court's opinions in those cases. In *Burdine,* the Court explained that the purpose of the "McDonnell *Douglas* division of intermediate evidentiary burdens" is "to bring litigants and the court expeditiously and fairly to [the] ultimate question" of whether the defendant intentionally discriminated against the plaintiff. Burdine, 450 U.S. at 253. In single-motive Title VII cases, the *McDonnell Douglas* shifting burdens of production effectively accomplish this task by "smok[ing] out the single, ultimate reason for the adverse employment decision." Wright [v. Murray Guard, Inc., 455 F.3d 702, 720 (6th Cir.2006)] (Moore, J, concurring). * * * [T]he pretext requirement is designed to test whether the defendant's allegedly legitimate reason was the real motivation for its actions. Such a narrowing of the actual reasons for the adverse employment action is necessary to determine whether there is sufficient evidence to proceed to trial in a single-motive discrimination case because the plaintiff in such a case must prove that the defendant's discriminatory animus, and not some legitimate business concern, was the ultimate reason for the adverse employment action.

However, this elimination of possible legitimate reasons for the defendant's action is not needed when assessing whether trial is warranted in the mixed-motive context. In mixed-motive cases, a plaintiff can win simply by showing that the defendant's consideration of a protected characteristic "was *a* motivating factor for any employment practice, *even though other factors also motivated the practice.*" 42 U.S.C. § 2000e–2(m) (emphasis added). In order to reach a jury, the plaintiff is not required to eliminate or rebut all the possible legitimate motivations of the defendant as long as the plaintiff can demonstrate that an illegitimate discriminatory animus factored into the defendant's decision to take the adverse employment action. * * * The only question that a court need ask in determining whether the plaintiff is entitled to submit his claim to a jury in such cases is whether the plaintiff has presented "sufficient evidence for a reasonable jury to conclude, by a preponderance of the evidence, that 'race, color, religion, sex, or national origin was a motivating factor for' " the defendant's adverse employment decision.

Id. at 400–01. How would you classify the Sixth Circuit's approach when compared to that of other circuits? What do you think should be the proper standard based on the Court's decision in *Costa*? In addition, should a plaintiff have to choose a method of proof or can the case simply proceed as a mixed-motive claim regardless of the nature of the plaintiff's and defendant's evidence on motive?

3. What are the advantages and disadvantages for plaintiffs and defendants if a case is decided as a mixed-motive case? Recall that, in the Civil Rights Act of 1991, in § 703(m) of Title VII, Congress overturned *Price Waterhouse*, but only to a limited extent. In § 706(g)(2)(B) of Title VII, 42 U.S.C. § 2000e–5(g)(2)(B), Congress limited plaintiffs to injunctive relief and attorneys' fees if the employer prevails on its same-decision defense. As a result, although the mixed-motive theory proves beneficial to plaintiffs on summary judgment, it is less beneficial on the ultimate question of discrimination. How does this dichotomy affect how a plaintiff might want to proceed?

4. Even though the Supreme Court repudiated the notion that the mixed-motive proof structure could only be invoked in cases involving direct evidence of discriminatory intent, the distinction between direct and circumstantial evidence remains relevant. When a plaintiff offers direct evidence of discrimination, the case avoids the *McDonnell Douglas* burden-shifting proof structures and moves directly into the remedial phase to determine whether the employer would have made the same decision absent the discriminatory motive. *See, e.g.*, Rowan v. Lockheed Martin Energy Sys., 360 F.3d 544, 546 (6th Cir.2004) ("If plaintiffs can establish direct evidence of discrimination, they then need not go through the *McDonnell Douglas* burden-shifting analysis."). This is consistent with the notion, discussed earlier, that direct evidence is often treated as akin to an admission of unlawful motive, and implies that, although the mixed-motive framework is not limited to cases involving direct evidence, such cases will proceed under the mixed-motive burdens of proof.

5. The general rule on attorney's fees in employment discrimination cases is that a prevailing plaintiff should recover attorney's fees unless special circumstances would render such an award unjust. *See* Christiansburg Garment Co. v. EEOC, 434 U.S. 412, 98 S.Ct. 694, 54 L.Ed.2d 648 (1978), discussed in Chapter 2. Although the Civil Rights Act of 1991 permits courts to award attorney's fees when the plaintiff recovers only injunctive relief, it is often difficult in such cases to determine what the appropriate attorney's fee award might be. Relying on the Supreme Court's decision in *Farrar v. Hobby*, 506 U.S. 103, 113 S.Ct. 566, 121 L.Ed.2d 494 (1992), the majority of the courts of appeals that have addressed the issue have adopted a proportionality rule on awards of fees in Title VII mixed-motive cases. *See, e.g.*, Sheppard v. Riverview Nursing Ctr., 88 F.3d 1332 (4th Cir.1996). In *Farrar*, the Supreme Court held that attorney's fees should be awarded to prevailing plaintiffs who have received some relief on the merits of their claims, but that the reasonableness of the fee award should be

proportional to the success of the claims. The court in *Sheppard* stated that the *Farrar* proportionality rule was "designed to prevent a situation in which a client receives a pyrrhic victory and the lawyers take a pot of gold." *Id.* at 1338. The *Sheppard* rule appears to be that *Farrar* should be applied in mixed-motive cases to deny prevailing plaintiffs all but a nominal fee award simply because a prevailing plaintiff in a Title VII mixed-motive case cannot recover monetary damages or obtain certain forms of injunctive relief, such as reinstatement, hiring, promotion, or backpay. *See* Title VII, § 706(g)(2)(B)(ii); 42 U.S.C. § 2000e–5(g)(2)(B)(ii). The majority of the courts of appeals have followed *Sheppard. See, e.g.*, Norris v. Sysco Corp., 191 F.3d 1043 (9th Cir.1999); *but see* Gudenkauf v. Stauffer Commc'ns, Inc., 158 F.3d 1074 (10th Cir.1998) (holding that attorney's fees should ordinarily be awarded to prevailing plaintiffs in mixed-motive cases in all but special circumstances).

6. The Supreme Court has held that the mixed-motive framework is not available for claims brought under the Age Discrimination Act, and instead, under that statute, plaintiffs must prove that age was the but-for cause of the challenged action. *See* Gross v. FBL Fin. Servs., Inc., 557 U.S.167, 129 S.Ct. 2343, 174 L.Ed.2d 119 (2009). The *Gross* case is reproduced in Chapter 13.

3. MULTIPLE DECISIONMAKERS AND THE "CAT'S PAW" THEORY

Just as an employment decision might be based on multiple motives, such decisions can also be the product of multiple decisionmakers. When multiple decisionmakers are involved, it can be difficult to determine whether the decision is the product of a discriminatory motive, and courts are frequently called on to evaluate the decisionmaking process. One particular fact pattern has generated extensive case law: when the ultimate decisionmaker was not aware that an employee—who was involved in the decisionmaking process at some point—had an unlawful discriminatory motive. This circumstance has been termed subordinate bias liability, or more poetically, the "cat's paw theory." The next case addresses that situation under a statute that prohibits discrimination against uniformed services personnel.

STAUB V. PROCTOR HOSPITAL

Supreme Court of the United States, 2011.
562 U.S. 411, 131 S.Ct. 1186, 179 L.Ed.2d 144.

JUSTICE SCALIA delivered the opinion of the Court.

We consider the circumstances under which an employer may be held liable for employment discrimination based on the discriminatory animus of an employee who influenced, but did not make, the ultimate employment decision.

I

Petitioner Vincent Staub worked as an angiography technician for respondent Proctor Hospital until 2004, when he was fired. Staub and Proctor hotly dispute the facts surrounding the firing, but because a jury found for Staub * * *, we describe the facts viewed in the light most favorable to him.

While employed by Proctor, Staub was a member of the United States Army Reserve, which required him to attend drill one weekend per month and to train full time for two to three weeks a year. Both Janice Mulally, Staub's immediate supervisor, and Michael Korenchuk, Mulally's supervisor, were hostile to Staub's military obligations. Mulally scheduled Staub for additional shifts without notice so that he would "pa[y] back the department for everyone else having to bend over backwards to cover [his] schedule for the Reserves." 560 F.3d 647, 652 (CA7 2009). She also informed Staub's co-worker, Leslie Sweborg, that Staub's "military duty had been a strain on th[e] department," and asked Sweborg to help her "get rid of him." *Ibid.* Korenchuk referred to Staub's military obligations as "a b[u]nch of smoking and joking and [a] waste of taxpayers['] money." *Ibid.* He was also aware that Mulally was "out to get" Staub. *Ibid.*

In January 2004, Mulally issued Staub a "Corrective Action" disciplinary warning for purportedly violating a company rule requiring him to stay in his work area whenever he was not working with a patient. The Corrective Action included a directive requiring Staub to report to Mulally or Korenchuk "when [he] ha[d] no patients and [the angio] cases [we]re complete[d]." *Id.*, at 653. * * *

On April 2, 2004, Angie Day, Staub's co-worker, complained to Linda Buck, Proctor's vice president of human resources, and Garrett McGowan, Proctor's chief operating officer, about Staub's frequent unavailability and abruptness. McGowan directed Korenchuk and Buck to create a plan that would solve Staub's "availability problems." *Id.*, at 654. But three weeks later, before they had time to do so, Korenchuk informed Buck that Staub had left his desk without informing a supervisor, in violation of the January Corrective Action. Staub now contends this accusation was false: he had left Korenchuk a voice-mail notification that he was leaving his desk. Buck relied on Korenchuk's accusation, however, and after reviewing Staub's personnel file, she decided to fire him. The termination notice stated that Staub had ignored the directive issued in the January 2004 Corrective Action. * * *

Staub sued Proctor under the Uniformed Services Employment and Reemployment Rights Act of 1994, 38 U.S.C. § 4301 *et seq.*, claiming that his discharge was motivated by hostility to his obligations as a military reservist. His contention was not that Buck had any such hostility but that Mulally and Korenchuk did, and that their actions influenced Buck's ultimate employment decision. A jury found that Staub's "military status was a motivating factor in [Proctor's] decision to discharge him," and awarded $57,640 in damages.

The Seventh Circuit reversed, holding that Proctor was entitled to judgment as a matter of law. The court observed that Staub had brought a "cat's paw case," meaning that he sought to hold his employer liable for the animus of a supervisor who was not charged with making the ultimate employment decision.[1] It explained that under Seventh Circuit precedent, a "cat's paw" case could not succeed unless the nondecisionmaker exercised such "singular influence" over the decisionmaker that the decision to terminate was the product of "blind reliance." * * * Because the undisputed evidence established that Buck was not wholly dependent on the advice of Korenchuk and Mulally, the court held that Proctor was entitled to judgment.

II

The Uniformed Services Employment and Reemployment Rights Act (USERRA) provides in relevant part as follows:

> "A person who is a member of . . . or has an obligation to perform service in a uniformed service shall not be denied initial employment, reemployment, retention in employment, promotion, or any benefit of employment by an employer on the basis of that membership, . . . or obligation." 38 U.S.C. § 4311(a).

It elaborates further:

> "An employer shall be considered to have engaged in actions prohibited . . . under subsection (a), if the person's membership . . . is a motivating factor in the employer's action, unless the employer can prove that the action would have been taken in the absence of such membership." § 4311(c).

The statute is very similar to Title VII, which prohibits employment discrimination "because of . . . race, color, religion, sex, or national origin" and states that such discrimination is established when one of those factors "was a motivating factor for any employment practice, even though other factors also motivated the practice." 42 U.S.C. §§ 2000e–2(a), (m).

---

[1] The term "cat's paw" derives from a fable conceived by Aesop, put into verse by La Fontaine in 1679, and injected into United States employment discrimination law by Posner in 1990. See *Shager* v. *Upjohn Co.*, 913 F.2d 398, 405 (CA7). In the fable, a monkey induces a cat by flattery to extract roasting chestnuts from the fire. After the cat has done so, burning its paws in the process, the monkey makes off with the chestnuts and leaves the cat with nothing. A coda to the fable (relevant only marginally, if at all, to employment law) observes that the cat is similar to princes who, flattered by the king, perform services on the king's behalf and receive no reward.

The central difficulty in this case is construing the phrase "motivating factor in the employer's action." When the company official who makes the decision to take an adverse employment action is personally acting out of hostility to the employee's membership in or obligation to a uniformed service, a motivating factor obviously exists. The problem we confront arises when that official has no discriminatory animus but is influenced by previous company action that is the product of a like animus in someone else.

In approaching this question, we start from the premise that when Congress creates a federal tort it adopts the background of general tort law. Intentional torts such as this, "as distinguished from negligent or reckless torts, . . . generally require that the actor intend 'the *consequences*' of an act, not simply 'the act itself.' " *Kawaauhau* v. *Geiger*, 523 U.S. 57, 61–62, 118 S. Ct. 974, 140 L. Ed. 2d 90 (1998).

Staub contends that the fact that an unfavorable entry on the plaintiff's personnel record was caused to be put there, with discriminatory animus, by Mulally and Korenchuk, suffices to establish the tort, even if Mulally and Korenchuk did not intend to cause his dismissal. But discrimination was no part of Buck's reason for the dismissal; and while Korenchuk and Mulally acted with discriminatory animus, the act they committed—the mere making of the reports—was not a denial of "initial employment, reemployment, retention in employment, promotion, or any benefit of employment," as liability under USERRA requires. If dismissal was not the object of Mulally's and Korenchuk's reports, it may have been their result, or even their foreseeable consequence, but that is not enough to render Mulally or Korenchuk responsible.

Here, however, Staub is seeking to hold liable not Mulally and Korenchuk, but their employer. Perhaps, therefore, the discriminatory motive of one of the employer's agents (Mulally or Korenchuk) can be aggregated with the act of another agent (Buck) to impose liability on Proctor. Again we consult general principles of law, agency law, which form the background against which federal tort laws are enacted. Here, however, the answer is not so clear. The Restatement of Agency suggests that the malicious mental state of one agent cannot generally be combined with the harmful action of another agent to hold the principal liable for a tort that requires both. See Restatement (Second) Agency § 275, Illustration 4 (1958). Some of the cases involving federal torts apply that rule. See *United States* v. *Science Applications Int'l Corp.*, 626 F.3d 1257, 1273–1276 (CADC 2010) * * * But another case involving a federal tort, and one involving a federal crime, hold to the contrary. See *United States ex rel. Harrison* v. *Westinghouse Savannah River Co.*, 352 F.3d 908, 918–919 (CA4 2003); *United States* v. *Bank of New England, N. A.*, 821 F.2d 844, 856 (CA1 1987). Ultimately, we think it unnecessary in this case to decide what the background rule of agency law may be, since the former line of authority is suggested by the governing text, which requires that discrimination be "a motivating factor" in the adverse action. When a decision to fire is made with no unlawful animus on the part of the firing agent, but partly on the basis of a report prompted (unbeknownst to that agent) by discrimination, discrimination might perhaps be called a "factor" or a "causal factor" in the decision; but it seems to us a considerable stretch to call it "a motivating factor."

Proctor, on the other hand, contends that the employer is not liable unless the *de facto* decisionmaker (the technical decisionmaker or the agent for whom he is the "cat's paw") is motivated by discriminatory animus. This avoids the aggregation of animus and adverse action, but it seems to us not the only application of general tort law that can do so. Animus and responsibility for the adverse action can both be attributed to the earlier agent (here, Staub's supervisors) if the adverse action is the intended consequence of that agent's discriminatory conduct. So long as the agent intends, for discriminatory reasons, that the adverse action occur, he has the scienter required to be liable under USERRA. And it is axiomatic under tort law that the exercise of judgment by the decisionmaker does not prevent the earlier agent's action (and hence the earlier agent's discriminatory animus) from being the proximate cause of the harm. Proximate cause requires only "some direct relation between the injury asserted and the injurious conduct alleged," and excludes only those "link[s] that are too remote, purely contingent, or indirect." *Hemi Group, LLC* v. *City of New York*, 559 U.S. 1, ___, 130 S. Ct. 983, 175 L. Ed. 2d 943, 951 (2010). We do not think that the ultimate decisionmaker's exercise of judgment automatically renders the link to the supervisor's bias "remote" or "purely contingent." The decisionmaker's exercise of judgment is *also* a proximate cause of the employment decision, but it is common for injuries to have multiple proximate causes. See *Sosa* v. *Alvarez-Machain*, 542 U.S. 692, 704, 124 S. Ct. 2739, 159 L. Ed. 2d 718 (2004). Nor can the ultimate decisionmaker's judgment be deemed a superseding cause of the harm. A cause can be thought "superseding" only if it is a "cause of independent origin that was not foreseeable." *Exxon Co., U.S.A.* v. *Sofec, Inc.*, 517 U.S. 830, 837, 116 S. Ct. 1813, 135 L. Ed. 2d 113 (1996).

Moreover, the approach urged upon us by Proctor gives an unlikely meaning to a provision designed to prevent employer discrimination. An employer's authority to reward, punish, or dismiss is often allocated among multiple agents. The one who makes the ultimate decision does so on the basis of performance assessments by other supervisors. Proctor's view would have the improbable consequence that if an employer isolates a personnel official from an employee's supervisors, vests the decision to take adverse employment actions in that official, and asks that official to review the employee's personnel file before taking the adverse action, then the employer will be effectively shielded from discriminatory acts and recommendations of supervisors that were *designed and intended* to produce the adverse action. That seems to us an implausible meaning of the text, and one that is not compelled by its words.

Proctor suggests that even if the decisionmaker's mere exercise of independent judgment does not suffice to negate the effect of the prior discrimination, at least the decisionmaker's independent investigation (and rejection) of the employee's allegations of discriminatory animus ought to do so. We decline to adopt such a hard-and-fast rule. As we have already acknowledged, the requirement that the biased supervisor's action be a causal factor of the ultimate employment action incorporates the traditional tort-law concept of proximate cause. Thus, if the employer's investigation results in an adverse action for reasons unrelated to the supervisor's original biased action, then the employer will not be liable. But the supervisor's biased report may remain a causal factor if the independent investigation takes it into account without determining that the adverse action was, apart from the supervisor's recommendation, entirely justified. * * *

We therefore hold that if a supervisor performs an act motivated by antimilitary animus that is *intended* by the supervisor to cause an adverse employment action, and if that act is a proximate cause of the ultimate employment action, then the employer is liable under USERRA.

III

Applying our analysis to the facts of this case, it is clear that the Seventh Circuit's judgment must be reversed. Both Mulally and Korenchuk were acting within the scope of their employment when they took the actions that allegedly caused Buck to fire Staub. * * * As the Seventh Circuit recognized, there was evidence that Mulally's and Korenchuk's actions were motivated by hostility toward Staub's military obligations. There was also evidence that Mulally's and Korenchuk's actions were causal factors underlying Buck's decision to fire Staub. Buck's termination notice expressly stated that Staub was terminated because he had "ignored" the directive in the Corrective Action. Finally, there was evidence that both Mulally and Korenchuk had the specific intent to cause Staub to be terminated. Mulally stated she was trying to "get rid of" Staub, and Korenchuk was aware that Mulally was "out to get" Staub. Moreover, Korenchuk informed Buck, Proctor's personnel officer responsible for terminating employees, of Staub's alleged noncompliance with Mulally's Corrective Action, and Buck fired Staub immediately thereafter; a reasonable jury could infer that Korenchuk intended that Staub be fired. The Seventh Circuit therefore erred in holding that Proctor was entitled to judgment as a matter of law.

* * *

The judgment of the Seventh Circuit is reversed, and the case is remanded for further proceedings consistent with this opinion.

JUSTICE KAGAN took no part in the consideration or decision of this case.

The concurring opinion of JUSTICE ALITO, joined by JUSTICE THOMAS, is omitted.

NOTES AND QUESTIONS

1. How would you characterize the Supreme Court's decision? Where did the Court come down in the debate over subordinate liability? Was this a victory for plaintiffs?

2. Based on the decision, do you think the Court would apply the same standard to a Title VII claim? To date, the answer has been an unqualified yes, and courts have often applied the *Staub* case without any analysis. *See* Guimares v. Supervalu, Inc., 674 F.3d 962, 972 (8th Cir.2012) (applying to Title VII); McKenna v. City of Philadelphia, 649 F.3d 171 (3rd Cir.2011) (applying to Title VII case with little discussion). Judge Posner has written an entertaining exegesis of the cat's paw theory, with an apology for its confusing nature. *See* Cook v. IPC Int'l Corp., 673 F.3d 625, 627–29 (7th Cir.2012). Whether the *Staub* standard applies in the age discrimination context seems a more difficult question. One court recently applied the standard in a modified fashion by requiring "but-for" rather than proximate causation regarding the role the subordinate played. *See* Simmons v. Sykes Enterprises, Inc., 647 F.3d 943 (10th Cir.2012). Based on the limited early sampling, the subordinate liability cases have proved difficult to establish but the reasons seem to turn on the particular facts of the cases rather than the standard the Supreme Court adopted.

The issue relating to subordinate bias or the "cat's paw" gained momentum over the last five or six years. Does it surprise you that the Supreme Court had not addressed the issue previously? And what do you think might account for the lengthy delay in having the issue resolved by the Supreme Court? The prior sections set forth the manner in which courts analyze cases involving individual cases of disparate treatment. Amidst the complexity of proof structures and evidentiary issues, it is easy to lose sight of the fact that they are all designed to aid the factfinder in determining whether discrimination occurred, which is the ultimate question in the cases. The various evidentiary issues—the same actor inference, the honest belief rule, the search for similarly situated comparators—are all related to how courts define discrimination, particularly when the plaintiff proffers circumstantial evidence to prove her claim. Now that you have worked through the material, you should reconsider why courts have crafted the elaborate proof structures, what purpose the *McDonnell Douglas* structure, for example, continues to serve, or why courts persist in distinguishing between mixed-motive and single-motive cases? What is it about employment discrimination cases that require these methods of proof and various evidentiary doctrines? After having read the material, how would you say courts define discrimination?

Several scholars have embarked on ambitious examinations of the Court's proof structures. *See, e.g.,* Martin J. Katz, *Reclaiming McDonnell Douglas*, 83 Notre Dame L.Rev. 109 (2007) (defending utility of the *McDonnell Douglas* structure but arguing that it should not be mandatory); Martin J. Katz, *Unifying Disparate Treatment (Really)*, 59 Hastings L.J. 643 (2008) (proposing a single unified framework for Title VII cases); Michael J. Zimmer, *A Chain of Inferences Proving Discrimination*, 79 U.Colo.L.Rev. 1243 (2008) (emphasizing the need for a chain of inferences to reach conclusion of discrimination).

C. RETALIATION

1. INTRODUCTION

Effective enforcement of laws prohibiting discrimination in employment depends greatly on evidence provided by those discriminated against and the testimony of witnesses. The simple fact is that such critical evidence and testimony will never appear if individuals discriminated against and witnesses are not protected against retaliation. *See* Deborah L. Brake, *Retaliation,* 90 Minn.L.Rev. 18, 20 (2005) ("To a large extent, the effectiveness and very legitimacy of discrimination law, turns on people's ability to raise concerns about discrimination without fear of retaliation."). Protection against retaliation is also an integral part of the right to equality:

> [A]n employee who is punished for seeking administrative or judicial relief, regardless of the merits of his initial claim, has failed to secure that right to equal treatment which constitutes the fundamental promise of [laws prohibiting discrimination in employment]. When a complainant experiences retaliation for the assertion of a claim to even-handed treatment, he remains under a handicap not faced by his colleagues.

Choudhury v. Polytec. Inst. of N.Y., 735 F.2d 38, 43 (2d Cir.1984).

Title VII and the ADEA contain almost identical provisions that make it an unlawful employment practice to discriminate against any individual because that individual has *opposed* any practice made unlawful under these statutes or because he has *participated* in any manner in proceedings to enforce these statutes. Title VII, § 704(a), 42 U.S.C. § 2000e–3(a); ADEA, § 4(d), 29 U.S.C. § 623(d). The ADA, § 503(a), 42 U.S.C. § 12203(a), also prohibits retaliation because of an individual's "opposition" to unlawful practices or "participation" in enforcement proceedings. In addition, § 503(b) of the ADA, 42 U.S.C. § 12203(b), makes it unlawful to "coerce, intimidate, threaten, or interfere" with any individual based on the exercise of rights under the ADA, or because an individual has "aided or encouraged any other individual in the exercise or enjoyment of" rights provided under the ADA. Protection from retaliation in Equal Pay Act cases is provided in the Fair Labor Standards Act, 29 U.S.C. § 215(a)(3). The Supreme Court has held that retaliation protection extends to Title IX claims, Jackson v. Birmingham Bd. of Educ., 544 U.S. 167, 125 S.Ct. 1497, 161 L.Ed.2d 361 (2005), and to federal-sector age discrimination claims, Gomez-Perez v. Potter, 553 U.S. 474, 128 S.Ct. 1931, 170 L.Ed.2d 887 (2008).

Prior to the Supreme Court's decision in *Patterson v. McLean Credit Union*, 491 U.S. 164, 109 S.Ct. 2363, 105 L.Ed.2d 132 (1989), the lower courts were uniform in holding that retaliation claims were cognizable under § 1981, even absent specific statutory authorization. *See, e.g.*, Choudhury v. Polytech. Inst. of N.Y., 735 F.2d 38 (2d Cir.1984); Goff v. Cont'l Oil Co., 678 F.2d 593 (5th Cir.1982); Setser v. Novack Inv. Co., 638 F.2d 1137 (8th Cir.), *modified on other grounds*, 657 F.2d 962 (1981) (en banc). In *Patterson*, the Supreme Court held that racial harassment claims cannot be brought under § 1981, but Congress overturned *Patterson* in the Civil Rights Act of 1991. Since that time, the lower courts—relying on the 1991 Act—have recognized that retaliation claims are actionable under § 1981. *See* CBOCS West, Inc. v. Humphries, 553 U.S. 442, 128 S.Ct. 1951, 1957, 170 L.Ed.2d 864 (2008) (noting that federal courts have consistently found § 1981 retaliation claims actionable since the 1991 amendments).

Legislative history on both the scope and extent of protection under the participation and opposition clauses is practically nonexistent. Thus, the federal judiciary has played a significant role in the development of the law on retaliation. *See, e.g.*, Hochstadt v. Worcester Found. for Experimental Biology, 545 F.2d 222, 230 (1st Cir.1976). The recent litigation history of the retaliation claim has revealed its importance in discrimination law. In the period from FY 2003 to FY 2013, retaliation charges filed with the EEOC each year grew from 27.9 percent (22,690) to 41 percent (38,539) of all charges filed with the Commission. EEOC Charge Statistics: *http://www.eeoc.gov/eeoc/statistics/enforcement/retaliation.cfm*. Retaliation complaints now comprise more than one-third of all charges filed with the EEOC in any category. Empirical studies show that retaliation may be experienced in as many as 50 to 60 percent of all cases in which discrimination is reported. *See* B. Glenn George, *Revenge*, 83 Tul.L.Rev. 439, 442 & n.6 (2008) (citing various studies).

2. WHO IS PROTECTED FROM RETALIATION?

a. Protection Against Direct Retaliation

Section 704(a) of Title VII specifically covers "employees" and "applicants for employment." 42 U.S.C. § 2000e–3(a). Are former employees covered? In *Robinson v. Shell Oil Co.*, 519 U.S. 337, 117 S.Ct. 843, 136 L.Ed.2d 808 (1997), the Supreme Court resolved a split in the circuits on this question. Shell Oil had discharged Robinson, the plaintiff, in 1991. Robinson then filed a charge of racial discrimination with the EEOC claiming that his termination was racially motivated. While the charge was pending before the EEOC, Robinson applied for a position with Metropolitan Life Insurance Co. Metropolitan had indicated to Robinson that it would hire him contingent upon a favorable employment reference from Shell. Shell, using Metropolitan's reference form, rated Robinson as "poor" in all areas. Robinson then filed a second charge with the EEOC against Shell Oil alleging that Shell Oil had given him a negative job reference in retaliation for his having filed the first charge with the EEOC. The Fourth Circuit held that former employees are not within the class protected from retaliation because the plain language of § 704(a) applies only to "employees" and "applicants for employment." A unanimous Supreme Court reversed. The Court held that although the language of § 704(a) is ambiguous, former employees are protected from retaliatory conduct.

• Employees
• Applicants
• former Emplees

b. Protection Against Indirect (3rd Party) Retaliation

THOMPSON V. NORTH AMERICAN STAINLESS

Supreme Court of the United States, 2011.
562 U.S. 170, 131 S.Ct. 863, 178 L.Ed.2d 694.

fiance filed claim, so fired husband, so husband files retaliation for fiance filing charge

JUSTICE SCALIA delivered the opinion of the Court.

Until 2003, both petitioner Eric Thompson and his fiancée, Miriam Regalado, were employees of respondent North American Stainless (NAS). In February 2003, the Equal Employment Opportunity Commission (EEOC) notified NAS that Regalado had filed a charge alleging sex discrimination. Three weeks later, NAS fired Thompson.

Thompson then filed a charge with the EEOC. After conciliation efforts proved unsuccessful, he sued NAS * * * claiming that NAS had fired him in order to retaliate against Regalado for filing her charge with the EEOC. The District Court granted summary judgment to NAS, concluding that Title VII "does not permit third party retaliation claims." After a panel of the Sixth Circuit reversed the District Court, the Sixth Circuit granted rehearing en banc and affirmed by a 10-to-6 vote. The court reasoned that because Thompson * * * "is not included in the class

D.Ct. → NAS

of persons for whom Congress created a retaliation cause of action." We granted certiorari.

I.

Title VII provides that "[i]t shall be an unlawful employment practice for an employer to discriminate against any of his employees . . . because he has made a charge" under Title VII. 42 U.S.C. § 2000e–3(a). The statute permits "a person claiming to be aggrieved" to file a charge with the EEOC alleging that the employer committed an unlawful employment practice, and, if the EEOC declines to sue the employer, it permits a civil action to "be brought . . . by the person claiming to be aggrieved . . . by the alleged unlawful employment practice." § 2000e–5(b), (f)(1).

It is undisputed that Regalado's filing of a charge with the EEOC was protected conduct under Title VII. In the procedural posture of this case, we are also required to assume that NAS fired Thompson in order to retaliate against Regalado for filing a charge of discrimination. This case therefore presents two questions: First, did NAS's firing of Thompson constitute unlawful retaliation? And second, if it did, does Title VII grant Thompson a cause of action?

II.

With regard to the first question, we have little difficulty concluding that if the facts alleged by Thompson are true, then NAS's firing of Thompson violated Title VII. In *Burlington N. & S. F. R. Co.* v. *White*, 548 U.S. 53, 126 S. Ct. 2405, 165 L. Ed. 2d 345 (2006), we held that Title VII's antiretaliation provision must be construed to cover a broad range of employer conduct. We reached that conclusion by contrasting the text of Title VII's antiretaliation provision with its substantive antidiscrimination provision * * * "[T]he antiretaliation provision, unlike the substantive provision, is not limited to discriminatory actions that affect the terms and conditions of employment." *Id.*, at 64, 126 S. Ct. 2405, 165 L. Ed. 2d 345. Rather, Title VII's antiretaliation provision prohibits any employer action that "well might have dissuaded a reasonable worker from making or supporting a charge of discrimination." *Id.*, at 68, 126 S. Ct. 2405, 165 L. Ed. 2d 345.

We think it obvious that a reasonable worker might be dissuaded from engaging in protected activity if she knew that her fiance would be fired. Indeed, NAS does not dispute that Thompson's firing meets the standard set forth in *Burlington*. NAS raises the concern, however, that prohibiting reprisals against third parties will lead to difficult line-drawing problems concerning the types of relationships entitled to protection. Perhaps retaliating against an employee by firing his fiancée would dissuade the employee from engaging in protected activity, but what about firing an employee's girlfriend, close friend, or trusted co-worker? Applying the *Burlington* standard to third-party reprisals, NAS argues, will place the employer at risk any time it fires any employee who happens to have a connection to a different employee who filed a charge with the EEOC.

Although we acknowledge the force of this point, we do not think it justifies a categorical rule that third-party reprisals do not violate Title VII. As explained above, we adopted a broad standard in *Burlington* because Title VII's antiretaliation provision is worded broadly. We think there is no textual basis for making an exception to it for third-party reprisals, and a preference for clear rules cannot justify departing from statutory text.

We must also decline to identify a fixed class of relationships for which third-party reprisals are unlawful. We expect that firing a close family member will almost always meet the *Burlington* standard, and inflicting a milder reprisal on a mere acquaintance will almost never do so, but beyond that we are reluctant to generalize. As we explained in *Burlington*, 548 U.S., at 69, 126 S. Ct. 2405, 165 L. Ed. 2d 345, "the significance of any given act of retaliation will often depend upon the particular circumstances." Given the broad statutory text and the variety of workplace contexts in which retaliation may occur, Title VII's antiretaliation provision is simply not reducible to a comprehensive set of clear rules. We emphasize, however, that "the provision's standard for judging harm must be objective," so as to "avoi[d] the uncertainties and unfair discrepancies that can plague a judicial effort to determine a plaintiff's unusual subjective feelings." *Id.*, at 68–69, 126 S. Ct. 2405, 165 L. Ed. 2d 345.

III.

The more difficult question in this case is whether Thompson may sue NAS for its alleged violation of Title VII. The statute provides that "a civil action may be brought . . . by the person claiming to be aggrieved." 42 U.S.C. § 2000e–5(f)(1). The Sixth Circuit concluded that this provision was merely a reiteration of the requirement that the plaintiff have Article III standing. 567 F.3d at 808, n. 1. We do not understand how that can be. * * *

We have suggested in dictum that the Title VII aggrievement requirement conferred a right to sue on all who satisfied Article III standing. *Trafficante* v. *Metropolitan Life Ins. Co.*, 409 U.S. 205, 93 S. Ct. 364, 34 L. Ed. 2d 415 (1972), involved the "person aggrieved" provision of Title VIII (the Fair Housing Act) rather than Title VII. In deciding the case, however, we relied upon, and cited with approval, a Third Circuit opinion involving Title VII, which, we said, "concluded that the words used showed 'a congressional intention to define standing as broadly as is permitted by Article III of the Constitution.' " *Id.*, at 209, 93 S. Ct. 364, 34 L. Ed. 2d 415 (quoting *Hackett* v. *McGuire Bros., Inc.*, 445 F.2d 442, 446

(1971)). We think that dictum regarding Title VII was too expansive. Indeed, the *Trafficante* opinion did not adhere to it in expressing its Title VIII holding that residents of an apartment complex could sue the owner for his racial discrimination against prospective tenants. The opinion said that the "person aggrieved" of Title VIII was coextensive with Article III "*insofar as tenants of the same housing unit that is charged with discrimination are concerned.*" 409 U.S., at 209, 93 S. Ct. 364, 34 L. Ed. 2d 415 (emphasis added).In any event, it is Title VII rather than Title VIII that is before us here, and as to that we are surely not bound by the *Trafficante* dictum.

We now find that this dictum was ill-considered, and we decline to follow it. If any person injured in the Article III sense by a Title VII violation could sue, absurd consequences would follow. For example, a shareholder would be able to sue a company for firing a valuable employee for racially discriminatory reasons, so long as he could show that the value of his stock decreased as a consequence. At oral argument Thompson acknowledged that such a suit would not lie, Tr. of Oral Arg. 5–6. We agree, and therefore conclude that the term "aggrieved" must be construed more narrowly than the outer boundaries of Article III.

At the other extreme from the position that "person aggrieved" means anyone with Article III standing, NAS argues that it is a term of art that refers only to the employee who engaged in the protected activity. We know of no other context in which the words carry this artificially narrow meaning, and if that is what Congress intended it would more naturally have said "person claiming to have been discriminated against" rather than "person claiming to be aggrieved." We see no basis in text or prior practice for limiting the latter phrase to the person who was the subject of unlawful retaliation. * * *

In our view there is a common usage of the term "person aggrieved" that avoids the extremity of equating it with Article III and yet is fully consistent with our application of the term in *Trafficante.* The Administrative Procedure Act, 5 U.S.C. § 551 *et seq.*, authorizes suit to challenge a federal agency by any "person . . . adversely affected or aggrieved . . . within the meaning of a relevant statute." § 702. We have held that this language establishes a regime under which a plaintiff may not sue unless he "falls within the 'zone of interests' sought to be protected by the statutory provision whose violation forms the legal basis for his complaint." *Lujan* v. *National Wildlife Federation*, 497 U.S. 871, 883, 110 S. Ct. 3177, 111 L. Ed. 2d 695 (1990). We have described the "zone of interests" test as denying a right of review "if the plaintiff's interests are so marginally related to or inconsistent with the purposes implicit in the statute that it cannot reasonably be assumed that Congress intended to permit the suit." *Clarke* v. *Securities Industry Assn.*, 479 U.S. 388, 399–400, 107 S. Ct. 750, 93 L. Ed. 2d 757 (1987). We hold that the term "aggrieved" in Title VII incorporates this test, enabling suit by any plaintiff with an interest "arguably [sought] to be protected by the statutes," *National Credit Union Admin.* v. *First Nat. Bank & Trust Co.*, 522 U.S. 479, 495, 118 S. Ct. 927, 140 L. Ed. 2d 1 (1998), while excluding plaintiffs who might technically be injured in an Article III sense but whose interests are unrelated to the statutory prohibitions in Title VII.

Applying that test here, we conclude that Thompson falls within the zone of interests protected by Title VII. Thompson was an employee of NAS, and the purpose of Title VII is to protect employees from their employers' unlawful actions. Moreover, accepting the facts as alleged, Thompson is not an accidental victim of the retaliation—collateral damage, so to speak, of the employer's unlawful act. To the contrary, injuring him was the employer's intended means of harming Regalado. Hurting him was the unlawful act by which the employer punished her. In those circumstances, we think Thompson well within the zone of interests sought to be protected by Title VII. He is a person aggrieved with standing to sue.

* * *

The judgment of the Sixth Circuit is reversed, and the case is remanded for further proceedings consistent with this opinion.

NOTES AND QUESTIONS

1. The Court acknowledged a concern with defining when third-party reprisal is sufficiently connected to a plaintiff's Title VII complaint to fall within the scope of the statute, but declined to draw any definitive line. A spouse is within the boundary, but what about a close friend? Does the formality of the connection between a Title VII plaintiff and a third party retaliated against by an employer matter? Should it?

2. The Court rejects Article III standing as the test for whether someone is sufficiently aggrieved to sue for retaliation. Instead, the Court invokes the "zone of interest" test that it applies in determining whether someone aggrieved by administrative agency action may sue. Is it clear after *Thompson* what types of claims fall within this test and which do not? In the *Thompson* case the Court seemed to believe that an employer's *intentional* action against the aggrieved party was important in making the determination. Does the intentional action inquiry help with the standing determination in third party cases?

3. The *Thompson* case continues in the Court's recent protective stance towards retaliation claims. The same term the Court issued another potentially far-reaching decision under the Fair Labor Standards Act when it held that an oral complaint was sufficient to trigger the protections of that statute's retaliation provision. *See* Kasten v. Saint-Gobain Performance Plastics Corp., 563 U.S.1, 131 S.Ct 1325, 179 L.Ed.2d 379 (2011). Although

the case involved the FLSA, the Court relied on several Title VII cases and pointed favorably towards a similar position adopted by the EEOC in its compliance manual, suggesting that, as has generally been the case, oral complaints are protected under Title VII.

3. ANALYTICAL FRAMEWORK FOR RETALIATION CLAIMS

a. Analytical Framework

Courts have adjusted the burden-shifting scheme of *McDonnell Douglas v. Green* for retaliation claims. First, the plaintiff must establish a prima facie case of retaliation. The plaintiff must prove (1) that she was engaged in statutorily protected activity; (2) that she suffered a materially adverse action at the hands of the employer; and (3) that a causal link exists between the protected activity and the adverse action. *See, e.g.*, McCullough v. Univ of Ark for Med Sci., 559 F.3d 855, 864 (8th Cir.2009). Some courts separately list a fourth element—that the defendant has knowledge of the protected activity, whereas others include this evidence as part of the first element, or implicitly, as part of the plaintiff's evidence of causation. *Compare* Mickey v. Zeidler Tool & Die Co., 516 F.3d 516, 523 (6th Cir.2008) (listing a requirement of employer knowledge as the fourth element of the prima facie case), *with* Patane v. Clark, 508 F.3d 106, 115 (2d Cir.2007) (articulating the first of three elements as requiring the plaintiff "to show * * * she participated in a protected activity known to the defendant").

The prima facie case establishes a rebuttable presumption of unlawful retaliatory motive. Assuming the plaintiff establishes a prima facie case, the burden then shifts to the employer to rebut the presumption of unlawful retaliation by articulating a legitimate, nondiscriminatory reason for the adverse action it took against the plaintiff. The plaintiff then has the ultimate burden of proving pretext, i.e., that the adverse action was motivated by retaliatory animus. *See, e.g.*, Laster v. City of Kalamazoo, 746 F.3d 714, 730 (6th Cir.2014) (Title VII); Vaughn v. Vilsack 715 F.3d 1001, 1006 (7th Cir.2013) (Title VII); Berman v. Orkin Exterm'g Co., 160 F.3d 697, 701–02 (11th Cir.1998) (Title VII); Holt v. JTM Indus., Inc., 89 F.3d 1224, 1225–26 (5th Cir.1996) (ADEA). There is currently some debate over whether the *McDonnell Douglas* burden shifting analysis applies to ADA claims. *Compare* Brown v. City of Tucson, 336 F.3d 1181, 1188–93 (9th Cir.2003) (no Title VII burden shifting because Fair Housing Act more applicable to the ADA) *with* Selenke v. Med. Imaging of Colo., 248 F.3d 1249, 1264 (10th Cir.2006) (applying Title VII burden-shifting and pretext analysis to decide ADA retaliation claim).

b. The Prima Facie Requirement of a "Materially Adverse Action"

BURLINGTON NORTHERN & SANTA FE RAILWAY V. WHITE

Supreme Court of the United States, 2006.
548 U.S. 53, 126 S.Ct. 2405, 165 L.Ed.2d 345.

JUSTICE BREYER delivered the opinion of the Court.

Title VII of the Civil Rights Act of 1964 forbids employment discrimination against "any individual" based on that individual's "race, color, religion, sex, or national origin." * * * A separate section of the Act—its anti-retaliation provision—forbids an employer from "discriminating against" an employee or job applicant because that individual "opposed any practice' made unlawful by Title VII or "made a charge, testified, assisted, or participated in" a Title VII proceeding or investigation.

The Courts of Appeals have come to different conclusions about the scope of the Act's anti-retaliation provision, particularly the reach of its phrase "discriminate against." Does that provision confine actionable retaliation to activity that affects the terms and conditions of employment? And how harmful must the adverse actions be to fall within its scope?

We conclude that the anti-retaliation provision does not confine the actions and harms it forbids to those that are related to employment or occur at the workplace. We also conclude that the provision covers those (and only those) employer actions that would have been materially adverse to a reasonable employee or job applicant. In the present context that means that the employer's actions must be harmful to the point that they could well dissuade a reasonable worker from making or supporting a charge of discrimination.

I

A

This case arises out of actions that supervisors at petitioner Burlington Northern & Santa Fe Railway Company took against respondent Sheila White, the only woman working in the Maintenance of Way department at Burlington's Tennessee Yard. In June 1997, Burlington's roadmaster, Marvin Brown, interviewed White and expressed interest in her previous experience operating forklifts. Burlington hired White as a "track laborer," a job that involves removing and replacing track components, transporting track material, cutting brush, and clearing litter and cargo spillage from the right-of-way. Soon after White arrived on the job, a co-worker who had previously operated the forklift chose to assume other responsibilities. Brown immediately assigned White to operate the forklift. While she also performed some of the other track laborer tasks, operating the forklift was White's primary responsibility.

In September 1997, White complained to Burlington officials that her immediate supervisor, Bill Joiner, had repeatedly told her that women should not be working in the Maintenance of Way department. Joiner, White said, had also made insulting and inappropriate remarks to her in front of her male colleagues. After an internal investigation, Burlington suspended Joiner for 10 days and ordered him to attend a sexual-harassment training session.

On September 26, Brown told White about Joiner's discipline. At the same time, he told White that he was removing her from forklift duty and assigning her to perform only standard track laborer tasks. Brown explained that the reassignment reflected co-worker's complaints that, in fairness, a " 'more senior man' " should have the "less arduous and cleaner job" of forklift operator. * * *

On October 10, White filed a complaint with the Equal Employment Opportunity Commission (EEOC or Commission). She claimed that the reassignment of her duties amounted to unlawful gender-based discrimination and retaliation for her having earlier complained about Joiner. In early December, White filed a second retaliation charge with the Commission, claiming that Brown had placed her under surveillance and was monitoring her daily activities. That charge was mailed to Brown on December 8.

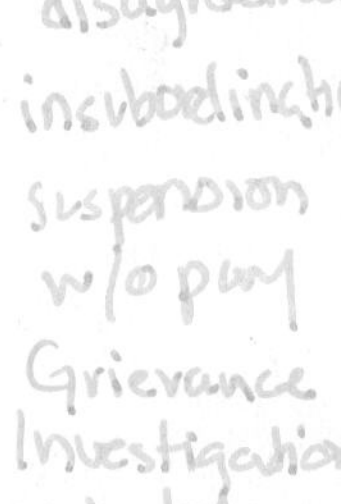

A few days later, White and her immediate supervisor, Percy Sharkey, disagreed about which truck should transport White from one location to another. The specific facts of the disagreement are in dispute, but the upshot is that Sharkey told Brown later that afternoon that White had been insubordinate. Brown immediately suspended White without pay. White invoked internal grievance procedures. Those procedures led Burlington to conclude that White had not been insubordinate. Burlington reinstated White to her position and awarded her backpay for the 37 days she was suspended. White filed an additional retaliation charge with the EEOC based on the suspension.

B

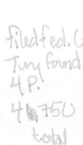

After exhausting administrative remedies, White filed this Title VII action against Burlington in federal court. As relevant here, she claimed that Burlington's actions—(1) changing her job responsibilities, and (2) suspending her for 37 days without pay—amounted to unlawful retaliation in violation of Title VII. * * * A jury found in White's favor on both of these claims. It awarded her $43,500 in compensatory damages, including $3,250 in medical expenses. * * *

Initially, a divided Sixth Circuit panel reversed the judgment and found in Burlington's favor on the retaliation claims. * * * The full Court of Appeals vacated the panel's decision, however, and heard the matter en banc. The court then affirmed the District Court's judgment in White's favor on both retaliation claims. While all members of the en banc court voted to uphold the District Court's judgment, they differed as to the proper standard to apply. * * *

II

Title VII's anti-retaliation provision forbids employer actions that "discriminate against" an employee (or job applicant) because he has "opposed" a practice that Title VII forbids or has "made a charge, testified, assisted, or participated in" a Title VII "investigation, proceeding, or hearing." § 2000e–3(a). No one doubts that the term "discriminate against" refers to distinctions or differences in treatment that injure protected individuals. *See* Jackson v. Birmingham Bd. of Ed., 544 U.S. 167, 174, 125 S.Ct. 1497, 161 L.Ed.2d 361 (2005); Price Waterhouse v. Hopkins, 490 U.S. 228, 244, 109 S.Ct. 1775, 104 L.Ed.2d 268 (1989) (plurality opinion); *see also* 4 Oxford English Dictionary 758 (2d ed. 1989) (def. 3b). But different Circuits have come to different conclusions about whether the challenged action has to be employment or workplace related and about how harmful that action must be to constitute retaliation.

* * *

We granted certiorari to resolve this disagreement. To do so requires us to decide whether Title VII's anti-retaliation provision forbids only those employer actions and resulting harms that are related to employment or the workplace. And we must characterize how harmful an act of retaliatory discrimination must be in order to fall within the provision's scope.

A

Petitioner and the Solicitor General both argue that the Sixth Circuit is correct to require a link between the challenged retaliatory action and the terms, conditions, or status of employment. They note that Title VII's substantive anti-discrimination provision protects an individual only from employment-related discrimination. They add that the anti-retaliation provision should be read *in pari materia* with the anti-discrimination provision. And they conclude that the employer actions prohibited by the anti-retaliation provision should similarly be limited to conduct that "affects the employee's 'compensation, terms, conditions, or privileges of employment.' " * * *

We cannot agree. The language of the substantive provision differs from that of the anti-retaliation provision in important ways. Section

703(a) sets forth Title VII's core anti-discrimination provision in the following terms:

> "It shall be an unlawful employment practice for an employer—
>
> "(1) *to fail or refuse to hire or to discharge* any individual, or otherwise to discriminate against any individual *with respect to his compensation, terms, conditions, or privileges of employment,* because of such individual's race, color, religion, sex, or national origin; or
>
> "(2) to limit, segregate, or classify his employees or applicants for employment in any way *which would deprive or tend to deprive any individual of employment opportunities or otherwise adversely affect his status as an employee,* because of such individual's race, color, religion, sex, or national origin." § 2000e–2(a) (emphasis added).

Section 704(a) sets forth Title VII's anti-retaliation provision in the following terms:

> It shall be an unlawful employment practice for an employer *to discriminate against* any of his employees or applicants for employment * * * because he has opposed any practice made an unlawful employment practice by this subchapter, or because he has made a charge, testified, assisted, or participated in any manner in an investigation, proceeding, or hearing under this subchapter.

§ 2000e–3(a) (emphasis added).

The underscored words in the substantive provision—"hire," "discharge," "compensation, terms, conditions, or privileges of employment," "employment opportunities," and "status as an employee"—explicitly limit the scope of that provision to actions that affect employment or alter the conditions of the workplace. No such limiting words appear in the anti-retaliation provision. Given these linguistic differences, the question here is not whether identical or similar words should be read in pari materia to mean the same thing. Rather, the question is whether Congress intended its different words to make a legal difference. We normally presume that, where words differ as they differ here, " 'Congress acts intentionally and purposely in the disparate inclusion or exclusion.' " Russello v. United States, 464 U.S. 16, 23, 104 S.Ct. 296, 78 L.Ed.2d 17 (1983).

There is strong reason to believe that Congress intended the differences that its language suggests, for the two provisions differ not only in language but in purpose as well. The anti-discrimination provision seeks a workplace where individuals are not discriminated against because of their racial, ethnic, religious, or gender-based status. *See* McDonnell Douglas Corp. v. Green, 411 U.S. 792, 800–01, 93 S.Ct. 1817, 36 L.Ed.2d 668 (1973). The anti-retaliation provision seeks to secure that primary objective by preventing an employer from interfering (through retaliation) with an employee's efforts to secure or advance enforcement of the Act's basic guarantees. The substantive provision seeks to prevent injury to individuals based on who they are, i.e., their status. The anti-retaliation provision seeks to prevent harm to individuals based on what they do, i.e., their conduct.

To secure the first objective, Congress did not need to prohibit anything other than employment-related discrimination. The substantive provision's basic objective of "equality of employment opportunities" and the elimination of practices that tend to bring about "stratified job environments," *id.*, at 800, 93 S.Ct. 1817, 36 L.Ed.2d 668, would be achieved were all employment-related discrimination miraculously eliminated.

But one cannot secure the second objective by focusing only upon employer actions and harm that concern employment and the workplace. Were all such actions and harms eliminated, the anti-retaliation provision's objective would *not* be achieved. An employer can effectively retaliate against an employee by taking actions not directly related to his employment or by causing him harm outside the workplace. See, e.g., Rochon v. Gonzales, 438 F.3d at 1213 (FBI retaliation against employee "took the form of the FBI's refusal, contrary to policy, to investigate death threats a federal prisoner made against [the agent] and his wife"); Berry v. Stevinson Chevrolet, 74 F.3d 980, 984, 986 (CA10 1996) (finding actionable retaliation where employer filed false criminal charges against former employee who complained about discrimination). A provision limited to employment-related actions would not deter the many forms that effective retaliation can take. Hence, such a limited construction would fail to fully achieve the anti-retaliation provision's "primary purpose," namely, "maintaining unfettered access to statutory remedial mechanisms." Robinson v. Shell Oil Co., 519 U.S. 337, 346, 117 S.Ct. 843, 136 L.Ed.2d 808 (1997).

Thus, purpose reinforces what language already indicates, namely, that the anti-retaliation provision, unlike the substantive provision, is not limited to discriminatory actions that affect the terms and conditions of employment. *Cf.* Wachovia Bank, N.A. v. Schmidt, 546 U.S. 303, 126 S.Ct. 941, 163 L.Ed.2d 797, 811 (2006) (rejecting statutory construction that would "treat venue and subject-matter jurisdiction prescriptions as *in pari materia*" because doing so would "overlook the discrete offices of those concepts").

Our precedent does not compel a contrary conclusion. Indeed, we have found no case in this Court that offers petitioner or the United States significant support. *Burlington Industries, Inc. v. Ellerth,* 524 U.S. 742, 118 S.Ct. 2257, 141 L.Ed.2d 633 (1998), as petitioner notes, speaks of a Title VII requirement that violations involve "tangible employment action" such as "hiring, firing, failing to promote, reassignment with significantly different responsibilities, or a decision causing a significant change in benefits." Id., at 761, 118 S.Ct. 2257, 141 L.Ed.2d 633. But *Ellerth* does so only to "identify a class of [hostile work environment] cases" in which an employer should be held vicariously liable (without an affirmative defense) for the acts of supervisors. *Id.*, at 760, 118 S.Ct. 2257, 141 L.Ed.2d 633; *see also* Pennsylvania State Police v. Suders, 542 U.S. 129, 143, 124 S.Ct. 2342, 159 L.Ed.2d 204 (2004) (explaining holdings in *Ellerth* and Faragher v. City of Boca Raton, 524 U.S. 775, 118 S.Ct. 2275, 141 L.Ed.2d 662 (1998), as dividing hostile work environment claims into two categories, one in which the employer is strictly liable because a tangible employment action is taken and one in which the employer can make an affirmative defense). *Ellerth* did not discuss the scope of the general anti-discrimination provision. *See* 524 U.S., at 761, 118 S.Ct. 2257, 141 L.Ed.2d 633 (using "concept of a tangible employment action [that] appears in numerous cases in the Courts of Appeals" only "for resolution of the vicarious liability issue"). And *Ellerth* did not mention Title VII's anti-retaliation provision at all. * * *

Finally, we do not accept the petitioner's and Solicitor General's view that it is "anomalous" to read the statute to provide broader protection for victims of retaliation than for those whom Title VII primarily seeks to protect, namely, victims of race-based, ethnic-based, religion-based, or gender-based discrimination. * * * Congress has provided similar kinds of protection from retaliation in comparable statutes without any judicial suggestion that those provisions are limited to the conduct prohibited by the primary substantive provisions. The National Labor Relations Act, to which this Court has "drawn analogies * * * in other Title VII contexts," Hishon v. King & Spalding, 467 U.S. 69, 76, n.8, 104 S.Ct. 2229, 81 L.Ed.2d 59 (1984), provides an illustrative example. Compare 29 U.S.C. § 158(a)(3) (substantive provision prohibiting employer "discrimination in regard to * * * any term or condition of employment to encourage or discourage membership in any labor organization") with § 158(a)(4) (retaliation provision making it unlawful for an employer to "discharge or otherwise discriminate against an employee because he has filed charges or given testimony under this subchapter"); *see also* Bill Johnson's Restaurants, Inc. v. NLRB, 461 U.S. 731, 740, 103 S.Ct. 2161, 76 L.Ed.2d 277 (1983) (construing anti-retaliation provision to "prohibit a wide variety of employer conduct that is intended to restrain, or that has the likely effect of restraining, employees in the exercise of protected activities," including the retaliatory filing of a lawsuit against an employee); NLRB v. Scrivener, 405 U.S. 117, 121–22, 92 S.Ct. 798, 31 L.Ed.2d 79 (1972) (purpose of the anti-retaliation provision is to ensure that employees are " 'completely free from coercion against reporting' " unlawful practices).

In any event, as we have explained, differences in the purpose of the two provisions remove any perceived "anomaly," for they justify this difference of interpretation. * * * Title VII depends for its enforcement upon the cooperation of employees who are willing to file complaints and act as witnesses. "Plainly, effective enforcement could thus only be expected if employees felt free to approach officials with their grievances." Mitchell v. Robert DeMario Jewelry, Inc., 361 U.S. 288, 292, 80 S.Ct. 332, 4 L.Ed.2d 323 (1960). Interpreting the anti-retaliation provision to provide broad protection from retaliation helps assure the cooperation upon which accomplishment of the Act's primary objective depends.

For these reasons, we conclude that Title VII's substantive provision and its anti-retaliation provision are not coterminous. The scope of the anti-retaliation provision extends beyond workplace-related or employment-related retaliatory acts and harm. We therefore reject the standards applied in the Courts of Appeals that have treated the anti-retaliation provision as forbidding the same conduct prohibited by the anti-discrimination provision and that have limited actionable retaliation to so-called "ultimate employment decisions."

* * *

B

The anti-retaliation provision protects an individual not from all retaliation, but from retaliation that produces an injury or harm. As we have explained, the Courts of Appeals have used differing language to describe the level of seriousness to which this harm must rise before it becomes actionable retaliation. We agree with the formulation set forth by the Seventh and the District of Columbia Circuits. In our view, a plaintiff must show that a reasonable employee would have found the challenged action materially adverse, "which in this context means it well might have 'dissuaded a reasonable worker from making or supporting a charge of discrimination.' " *Rochon*, 438 F.3d at 1219 (quoting *Washington*, 420 F.3d at 662).

We speak of *material* adversity because we believe it is important to separate significant from trivial harms. Title VII, we have said, does not set forth "a general civility code for the American workplace." Oncale v. Sundowner Offshore Services, Inc., 523 U.S. 75, 80, 118 S.Ct. 998, 140 L.Ed.2d 201 (1998); *see Faragher*, 524 U.S., at 788, 118 S.Ct. 2275, 141 L.Ed.2d 662 (judicial standards for sexual harassment must "filter out complaints attacking 'the ordinary tribulations of the workplace, such as the sporadic use of abusive language, gender-related jokes, and occasional teasing' "). An employee's decision to report discriminatory behavior cannot immunize that employee from those petty slights or minor annoyances that often take place at work and that all employees experience. See 1 B. Lindemann & P. Grossman, Employment Discrimination Law 669 (3d ed. 1996) (noting that "courts have held that personality conflicts at work that generate antipathy" and " 'snubbing' by supervisors and co-workers" are not actionable under § 704(a)). The anti-retaliation provision seeks to prevent employer interference with "unfettered access" to Title VII's remedial mechanisms. *Robinson*, 519 U.S., at 346, 117 S.Ct. 843, 136 L.Ed.2d 808. It does so by prohibiting employer actions that are likely "to deter victims of discrimination from complaining to the EEOC," the courts, and their employers. *Ibid.* And normally petty slights, minor annoyances, and simple lack of good manners will not create such deterrence. *See* 2 EEOC 1998 Manual § 8, p.8–13.

We refer to reactions of a *reasonable* employee because we believe that the provision's standard for judging harm must be objective. An objective standard is judicially administrable. It avoids the uncertainties and unfair discrepancies that can plague a judicial effort to determine a plaintiff's unusual subjective feelings. We have emphasized the need for objective standards in other Title VII contexts, and those same concerns animate our decision here. *See, e.g., Suders,* 542 U.S., at 141, 124 S.Ct. 2342, 159 L.Ed.2d 204 (constructive discharge doctrine); Harris v. Forklift Systems, Inc., 510 U.S. 17, 21, 114 S.Ct. 367, 126 L.Ed.2d 295 (1993) (hostile work environment doctrine).

We phrase the standard in general terms because the significance of any given act of retaliation will often depend upon the particular circumstances. Context matters. "The real social impact of workplace behavior often depends on a constellation of surrounding circumstances, expectations, and relationships which are not fully captured by a simple recitation of the words used or the physical acts performed." *Oncale*, supra, at 81–82, 118 S.Ct. 998, 140 L.Ed.2d 201. A schedule change in an employee's work schedule may make little difference to many workers, but may matter enormously to a young mother with school age children. *Cf., e.g., Washington,* supra, at 662 (finding flex-time schedule critical to employee with disabled child). A supervisor's refusal to invite an employee to lunch is normally trivial, a nonactionable petty slight. But to retaliate by excluding an employee from a weekly training lunch that contributes significantly to the employee's professional advancement might well deter a reasonable employee from complaining about discrimination. See 2 EEOC 1998 Manual § 8, p.8–14. Hence, a legal standard that speaks in general terms rather than specific prohibited acts is preferable, for an "act that would be immaterial in some situations is material in others." *Washington,* supra, at 661.

Finally, we note that contrary to the claim of the concurrence, this standard does not require a reviewing court or jury to consider "the nature of the discrimination that led to the filing of the charge." * * * Rather, the standard is tied to the challenged retaliatory act, not the underlying conduct that forms the basis of the Title VII complaint. By focusing on the materiality of the challenged action and the perspective of a reasonable person in the plaintiff's position, we believe this standard will screen out trivial conduct while effectively capturing those acts that are likely to dissuade employees from complaining or assisting in complaints about discrimination.

III

Applying this standard to the facts of this case, we believe that there was a sufficient evidentiary basis to support the jury's verdict on White's retaliation claim. See Reeves v. Sanderson Plumbing Products, Inc., 530 U.S. 133, 150–51, 120 S.Ct. 2097, 147 L.Ed.2d 105 (2000). The jury found that two of Burlington's actions amounted to retaliation: the reassignment of White from forklift duty to standard track laborer tasks and the 37-day suspension without pay.

Burlington does not question the jury's determination that the motivation for these acts was retaliatory. But it does question the statutory significance of the harm these acts caused. The District Court instructed the jury to determine whether respondent "suffered a materially adverse change in the terms or conditions of her employment," * * * and the Sixth Circuit upheld the jury's finding based on that same stringent interpretation of the anti-retaliation provision (the interpretation that limits § 704 to the same employment-related conduct forbidden by § 703). Our holding today makes clear that the jury was not required to find that the challenged actions were related to the terms or conditions of employment. And insofar as the jury also found that the actions were "materially adverse," its findings are adequately supported.

First, Burlington argues that a reassignment of duties cannot constitute retaliatory discrimination where, as here, both the former and present duties fall within the same job description. * * * We do not see why that is so. Almost every job category involves some responsibilities and duties that are less desirable than others. Common sense suggests that one good way to discourage an employee such as White from bringing discrimination charges would be to insist that she spend more time performing the more arduous duties and less time performing those that are easier or more agreeable. That is presumably why the EEOC has consistently found "retaliatory work assignments" to be a classic and "widely recognized" example of "forbidden retaliation." 2 EEOC 1991

Manual § 614.7, pp.614–31 to 614–32; *see also* 1972 Reference Manual § 495.2 (noting Commission decision involving an employer's ordering an employee "to do an unpleasant work assignment in retaliation" for filing racial discrimination complaint); EEOC Dec. No. 74–77, 1974 EEOC LEXIS 2, 1974 WL 3847, *4 (Jan. 18, 1974) ("Employers have been enjoined" under Title VII "from imposing unpleasant work assignments upon an employee for filing charges").

To be sure, reassignment of job duties is not automatically actionable. Whether a particular reassignment is materially adverse depends upon the circumstances of the particular case, and "should be judged from the perspective of a reasonable person in the plaintiff's position, considering 'all the circumstances.' " *Oncale*, 523 U.S., at 81, 118 S.Ct. 998, 140 L.Ed.2d 201. But here, the jury had before it considerable evidence that the track labor duties were "by all accounts more arduous and dirtier"; that the "forklift operator position required more qualifications, which is an indication of prestige"; and that "the forklift operator position was objectively considered a better job and the male employees resented White for occupying it." 364 F.3d at 803 (internal quotation marks omitted). Based on this record, a jury could reasonably conclude that the reassignment of responsibilities would have been materially adverse to a reasonable employee.

Second, Burlington argues that the 37-day suspension without pay lacked statutory significance because Burlington ultimately reinstated White with backpay. Burlington says that "it defies reason to believe that Congress would have considered a rescinded investigatory suspension with full back pay" to be unlawful, particularly because Title VII, throughout much of its history, provided no relief in an equitable action for victims in White's position. * * *

We do not find Burlington's last mentioned reference to the nature of Title VII's remedies convincing. After all, throughout its history, Title VII has provided for injunctions to "bar like discrimination in the future," Albemarle Paper Co. v. Moody, 422 U.S. 405, 418, 95 S.Ct. 2362, 45 L.Ed.2d 280 (1975) (internal quotation marks omitted), an important form of relief. * * * And we have no reason to believe that a court could not have issued an injunction where an employer suspended an employee for retaliatory purposes, even if that employer later provided backpay. In any event, Congress amended Title VII in 1991 to permit victims of intentional discrimination to recover compensatory (as White received here) and punitive damages, concluding that the additional remedies were necessary to " 'help make victims whole.' " West v. Gibson, 527 U.S. 212, 219, 119 S.Ct. 1906, 144 L.Ed.2d 196 (1999) (quoting H.R.Rep.No. 102–40, pt.1, pp.64–65 (1991)); *see* 42 U.S.C. §§ 1981a(a)(1), (b). We would undermine the significance of that congressional judgment were we to conclude that employers could avoid liability in these circumstances.

Neither do we find convincing any claim of insufficient evidence. White did receive backpay. But White and her family had to live for 37 days without income. They did not know during that time whether or when White could return to work. Many reasonable employees would find a month without a paycheck to be a serious hardship. And White described to the jury the physical and emotional hardship that 37 days of having "no income, no money" in fact caused. 1 Tr. 154 ("That was the worst Christmas I had out of my life. No income, no money, and that made all of us feel bad. * * * I got very depressed"). Indeed, she obtained medical treatment for her emotional distress. A reasonable employee facing the choice between retaining her job (and paycheck) and filing a discrimination complaint might well choose the former. That is to say, an indefinite suspension without pay could well act as a deterrent, even if the suspended employee eventually received backpay. *Cf.* Mitchell, 361 U.S., at 292, 80 S.Ct. 332, 4 L.Ed.2d 323 ("It needs no argument to show that fear of economic retaliation might often operate to induce aggrieved employees quietly to accept substandard conditions"). Thus, the jury's conclusion that the 37-day suspension without pay was materially adverse was a reasonable one.

IV

For these reasons, the judgment of the Court of Appeals is affirmed. * * *

[The opinion of JUSTICE ALITO, concurring in the judgment, is omitted.]

NOTES AND QUESTIONS

1. *Materially Adverse*: Unlike Title VII, under which discrimination claims can be brought any time prohibited discrimination affects terms and conditions of employment, *Burlington Northern* requires that for retaliation to be actionable the employer's actions must be "materially adverse," defined as including those employer actions which "well might have dissuaded a reasonable worker from making or supporting a charge of discrimination." Does the imposition of a threshold of substantial harm for retaliation have a basis in the language of Title VII? For a good account of the circuit court split before *Burlington Northern*, see Brian A. Riddell & Richard A. Bales, *Adverse Employment Action in Retaliation Cases,* 34 U.Balt.L.R. 313 (2005). For a discussion of the materially adverse requirement in *Burlington* and the cases decided in its aftermath, see Deborah L. Brake & Joanna L. Grossman, *The Failure of Title VII as a Rights Claiming System*, 86 N.C.L.Rev. 859, 906–13 (2008).

2. *Summary Judgment*: In his concurring opinion in *Burlington*, Justice Alito made the argument that the majority's expansive rule for retaliation claims will make it harder to "weed out" unmeritorious claims at

the summary judgment stage. Do you agree? Even if this is the case, what is the harm of allowing juries to make these determinations?

3. Burlington's *Impact*: What type of activity qualifies as a materially adverse action under the Supreme Court's standard? *Burlington* has had the most impact on claims brought in circuits that had previously required a higher threshold of harm involving an "ultimate employment decision." *See, e.g.,* McCoy v. City of Shreveport, 492 F.3d 551 (5th Cir.2007) (holding, before *Burlington,* that simply being placed on administrative leave would not have qualified as materially adverse, but that, after *Burlington,* being placed on paid administrative leave in the right circumstances could qualify as materially adverse); Wedow v. City of Kansas City, Mo., 442 F.3d 661, 675 (8th Cir.2006) (finding sufficient evidence to uphold jury verdict that denial of on-the-job training due to failure to assign special shifts and out-of-class promotions was materially adverse). Workplace harassment in response to Title VII complaints can be materially adverse under the *Burlington* standard, whereas previously retaliatory harassment had to meet the Title VII standard for "severe or pervasive" harassment. *See* Moore v. City of Phila., 461 F.3d 331 (3d Cir.2006). *See also* Hawkins v. Anheuser-Busch, 517 F.3d 321, 347 (6th Cir.2008) (concluding that "*Burlington Northern* made clear [that] the tests for harassment and retaliation are not coterminous").

Generally, retaliation that only amounts to "petty slights, minor annoyances, and simple lack of good manners" is not sufficient. Under that rubric, a transfer to a position of equal prestige and an undesirable but routine assignment do not qualify. *See* Aryain v. Wal-Mart Stores Tex. LP, 543 F.3d 473, 485–86 (5th Cir.2008). Being subjected to rude and hostile behavior from co-workers during meetings and derogatory emails, along with acts targeted at committees or departments but not employees individually, do not qualify as materially adverse. *See, e.g.,* Brown v. Advocate S. Suburban Hosp., 700 F.3d 1101 (7th Cir.2012); Somoza v. Univ. of Denver, 513 F.3d 1206, 1214–16 (10th Cir.2007); Mickelson v. N.Y. Life Ins. Co., 460 F.3d 1304, 1318 (10th Cir.2006). However, recommending retaliatory transfers can meet the *Burlington* standard even if there is no corresponding loss of pay. *See, e.g.,* Chapter 7 Tr. v. Gate Gourmet, Inc., 683 F.3d 1249 (11th Cir.2012) (failure to give pregnant employee light-duty job, as required by company policy); Wasek v. Arrow Energy Servs. Inc., 682 F.3d 463 (6th Cir.2012) (banning employee from work in a particular state); Billings v. Town of Grafton, 515 F.3d 39, 52–54 (1st Cir.2008) (finding that transfer objectively resulted in a loss of prestige). *But see* Silverman v. Bd. of Educ., 637 F.3d 729 (7th Cir.2011) (rehiring into different, more difficult position, not materially adverse); Lucero v. Nettle Creek Sch. Corp, 566 F.3d 720, 728–30 (7th Cir.2009) (finding no materially adverse action where teacher was reassigned from teaching twelfth grade students to seventh grade and such reassignment would not reasonably deter teachers from complaining about discrimination); Stephens v. Erickson, 569 F.3d 779, 791 (7th Cir.2009) (finding that a reassignment without "a significant alteration to the employee's duties" is not materially adverse). Also, an increase—but not a complete change—in undesirable case assignments is not sufficiently adverse even if the change results in lower performance ratings that disqualify the employee from a merit bonus. *See* Lapka v. Chertoff, 517 F.3d 974, 986 (7th Cir.2008). However, lowering an employee performance evaluation can be materially adverse if the result is employee failing to receive a cash award she has earned in the prior three years. *See* Weber v. Battista, 494 F.3d 179 (D.C. Cir.2007). *But see* Bridgeforth v. Jewell, 721 F.3d 661 (D.C. Cir.2013) ("failure to nominate for time-off awards does not qualify as the type of objective, tangible harm akin to 'firing' or a 'significant change in benefits' that is obviously materially adverse").

The filing of formal disciplinary charges where such charges are entered into the employee's permanent file can qualify as materially adverse. *See, e.g.,* Uddin v. City of N.Y., 316 Fed.Appx. 4, at *5–6 (2d Cir.2008). Merely placing an employee on a performance plan or issuing a disciplinary letter, however, has been found not to qualify under the new Supreme Court standard. *See* Kaplan v. Multimedia Entm't, Inc., No. 03–CV–085C(F), 2008 WL 686774, at *6 (W.D.N.Y. Mar. 10, 2008) (performance plan); Wash. v. Norton, No. 3:04CV104, 2007 WL 1417290, at *4 (N.D.W.Va. May 11, 2007) (discipline letter). A supervisory conspiracy to force the complaining employee to quit her job, however, is sufficiently adverse. *See* Patane v. Clark, 508 F.3d 106, 115–16 (2d Cir.2007).

Should an employer be able to defend against a finding that its conduct toward one employee constituted a materially adverse action by showing that later complaints about discrimination have indeed been filed by other employees? For example, if an employee filed a claim for both discrimination and retaliation, could the employer argue that subsequent discrimination claims—or even testimony by other employees supporting the original complaint—show that the alleged retaliatory conduct had no chilling effect? Can an employer prevail on a motion for summary judgment by admitting the alleged retaliatory conduct occurred and presenting evidence that employee complaints of discrimination continued nevertheless? *See Lucero*, 566 F.3d at 729 ("Lucero submitted affidavits from colleagues that state that Lucero's reassignment has dissuaded other discrimination charges. However, the same individuals that filed the affidavits have been involved in making and supporting discrimination charges on Lucero's behalf since the reassignment, demonstrating that they were not in fact dissuaded.").

4. *Retaliatory Litigation*: Suppose that a plaintiff makes defamatory and untrue statements about the employer in a Title VII charge filed with the EEOC. If the employer brings a common law action for defamation in state court, would this constitute unlawful retaliation under the participation clause? Before *Burlington,* some courts had held that a Title VII retaliation claim could be based on a defamation action that is filed in bad faith, motivated by retaliatory animus. *See* Harmar v. United Airlines, Inc., No. 95–C–7665, 1996 WL 199734, at *1 (N.D.Ill.1996) (collecting cases). How should this issue be resolved after *Burlington*? *See generally* Adam J. Berstein, Note, *Retaliatory Litigation Conduct After* Burlington Northern &

Santa Fe Railway Company v. White, 42 Colum.J.L. & Soc.Probs. 91, 107–09 (2008) (discussing post-*Burlington* retaliatory lawsuits). What factors would be relevant in determining whether the employer has satisfied the good faith standard in filing the defamation suit? Recall that, in *St. Mary's Honor Center v. Hicks*, 509 U.S. 502, 521, 113 S.Ct. 2742, 2754, 125 L.Ed.2d 407 (1993), reproduced in Section B.1 of this chapter, Justice Scalia said that "Title VII is not a cause of action for perjury; we have other civil and criminal remedies for that."

5. *Employer Liability*: How should *Burlington* affect an employer's liability for retaliatory conduct engaged in by its agents? Recently, the Supreme Court was given the opportunity to answer a question left open in *Burlington* regarding who can qualify as a "supervisor." *Vance v. Ball State Univ.*, 133 S. Ct. 2434, 2443, 186 L. Ed. 2d 565 (2013). The majority concluded that an employer may be liable for an employee's unlawful harassment only when the employer has empowered that employee to take "tangible employment actions against the victim." *Id.* The court described tangible employment action as the ability for one employee to inflict a significant change in employment status over another, such as "hiring, firing, failing to promote, reassignment with significantly different responsibilities, or a decision causing a significant change in benefits." *Id.* Although the *Vance* decision does appear to limit employer liability to some degree, the majority emphasized the fact that a failure to show supervisor retaliation would not preclude liability where the employer has failed to respond to complaints, does not monitor the workplace, or discourages complaints. *Id.* at 2453.

c. The Prima Facie Requirement of a "Causal Link"

CLARK COUNTY SCHOOL DISTRICT V. BREEDEN

Supreme Court of the United States, 2001.
532 U.S. 268, 121 S.Ct. 1508, 149 L.Ed.2d 509.

PER CURIAM.

[In the first part of the *Breeden* decision, reproduced below, the Court dealt with the respondent's claim that she was fired for complaining about sexual harassment. The Court held that, as a matter of law, the respondent, Breeden, could not have reasonably believed that the incident she reported to her supervisors was sexual harassment.]

* * * [R]espondent also claimed that she was punished for filing charges against petitioner with the Nevada Equal Rights Commission and the Equal Employment Opportunity Commission (EEOC) and for filing the present suit. Respondent filed her lawsuit on April 1, 1997; on April 10, 1997, respondent's supervisor, Assistant Superintendent Rice, "mentioned to Allin Chandler, Executive Director of plaintiff's union, that she was contemplating transferring plaintiff to the position of Director of Professional Development Education," and this transfer was "carried

through" in May. In order to show, as her defense against summary judgment required, the existence of a causal connection between her protected activities and the transfer, respondent "relied wholly on the temporal proximity of the filing of her complaint on April 1, 1997 and Rice's statement to plaintiff's union representative on April 10, 1997 that she was considering transferring plaintiff to the [new] position." The District Court, however, found that respondent did not serve petitioner with the summons and complaint until April 11, 1997, one day after Rice had made the statement, and Rice filed an affidavit stating that she did not become aware of the lawsuit until after April 11, a claim that respondent did not challenge. Hence, the court concluded, respondent "had not shown that any causal connection exists between her protected activities and the adverse employment decision." *Id.*, at 21.

The Court of Appeals reversed, relying on two facts: The EEOC had issued a right-to-sue letter to respondent three months before Rice announced she was contemplating the transfer, and the actual transfer occurred one month after Rice learned of respondent's suit. The latter fact is immaterial in light of the fact that petitioner concededly was contemplating the transfer before it learned of the suit. Employers need not suspend previously planned transfers upon discovering that a Title VII suit has been filed, and their proceeding along lines previously contemplated, though not yet definitively determined, is no evidence whatever of causality.

As for the right-to-sue letter: Respondent did not rely on that letter in the District Court and did not mention it in her opening brief on appeal. Her demonstration of causality all along had rested upon the connection between the transfer and the filing of her lawsuit—to which connection the letter was irrelevant. When, however, petitioner's answering brief in the Court of Appeals demonstrated conclusively the lack of causation between the filing of respondent's lawsuit and Rice's decision, respondent mentioned the letter for the first time in her reply brief. The Ninth Circuit's opinion did not adopt respondent's utterly implausible suggestion that the EEOC's issuance of a right-to-sue letter—an action in which the employee takes no part—is a protected activity of the employee, see 42 U.S.C. § 2000e–3(a). Rather, the opinion suggests that the letter provided petitioner with its first notice of respondent's charge before the EEOC, and hence allowed the inference that the transfer proposal made three months later was petitioner's reaction to the charge. This will not do.

First, there is no indication that Rice even knew about the right-to-sue letter when she proposed transferring respondent. And second, if one presumes she knew about it, one must also presume that she (or her predecessor) knew *almost two years earlier* about the protected action (filing of the EEOC complaint) that the letter supposedly disclosed. (The complaint had been filed on August 23, 1995, and both Title VII and its implementing regulations require that an employer be given notice within 10 days of filing, 42 U.S.C. § 2000e–5(b), (e)(1); 29 CFR § 1601.14 (2000).) The cases that accept mere temporal proximity between an employer's knowledge of protected activity and an adverse employment action as sufficient evidence of causality to establish a prima facie case uniformly hold that the temporal proximity must be "very close," *Neal v. Ferguson Constr. Co.*, 237 F.3d 1248, 1253 (CA10 2001). See *e.g., Richmond v. Oneok, Inc.*, 120 F.3d 205, 209 (CA10 1997) (3-month period insufficient); *Hughes v. Derwinski*, 967 F.2d 1168, 1174–75 (CA7 1992) (4-month period insufficient). Action taken (as here) 20 months later suggests, by itself, no causality at all.

NOTES AND QUESTIONS

1. *Plaintiff's Burden of Proof in the Prima Facie Case*: The causal link between the employee's protected activity and the employer's materially adverse action has in the past been established by showing that the protected conduct and the adverse action are not unrelated. This can be accomplished at the prima facie stage by showing a temporal proximity between the employee's protected action and an employer's retaliatory conduct, even though it might be questioned whether a temporal link meets the but-for causation standard. *See* Zann Kwan v. Andalex Grp. LLC, 737 F.3d 834, 845 (2d Cir.2013) (employee's dismissal three weeks after complaint was sufficiently short enough for a *prima facie* showing of causation). An employer's proven lack of knowledge that the employee engaged in protected activity, however, has been found to be fatal to a *prima facie* showing of causation despite any temporal link. *See, e.g.,* Sanchez v. Denver Pub. Sch., 164 F.3d 527, 533–34 (10th Cir.1998); Smith v. Riceland Foods, 151 F.3d 813, 818 (8th Cir.1998).

2. *The Role of Temporal Proximity*: There is an apparent split in the federal circuits regarding whether temporal proximity alone is sufficient to establish a causal link in retaliation cases. Some courts hold that temporal proximity alone is sufficient. *See, e.g.,* Ramirez v. Baush & Lomb, 546 Fed. Appx. 829, 832 (11th Cir.2013); Hamilton v. Geithner, 666 F.3d 1344, 1357–58 (D.C. Cir.2012); Williams v. W.D. Sports, N.M., Inc., 497 F.3d 1079, 1091–92 (10th Cir.2007); Thomas v. Cooper Lighting, Inc., 506 F.3d 1361, 1364 (11th Cir.2007); Calero-Cerezo v. U.S. Dep't of Justice, 355 F.3d 6, 25–26 (1st Cir.2004); Feingold v. N.Y., 366 F.3d 138, 156–57 (2d Cir.2004). Other courts require that temporal proximity be combined with some other evidence of retaliation even to survive summary judgment. *See, e.g.,* Mumfrey v. CVS Pharmacy, Inc., 719 F.3d 392, 405 (5th Cir.2013); Bradley v. Widnall, 232 F.3d 626, 633 (8th Cir.2000). In a Sixth Circuit case, *Mickey v. Zeidler Tool & Die Co.*, 516 F.3d 516, 523 (6th Cir.2008), the court examined the conflict between "recent case law [that] presents as settled the proposition that temporal proximity alone may not establish a causal connection" and cases

that recognize that temporal proximity may be sufficient in some circumstances. The court reconciled the conflicting positions with this rationale:

> Where an adverse employment action occurs very close in time after an employer learns of a protected activity, such temporal proximity between the events is significant enough to constitute evidence of a causal connection for the purposes of satisfying *a prima facie case* of retaliation. But where some time elapses between when the employer learns of a protected activity and the subsequent adverse employment action, the employee must couple temporal proximity with other evidence of retaliatory conduct to establish causality. * * *
>
> The reason for this distinction is simple: if an employer immediately retaliates against an employee upon learning of his protected activity, the employee would be unable to couple temporal proximity with any such other evidence of retaliation because the two actions happened consecutively, and little other than the protected activity could motivate the retaliation. Thus, employers who retaliate swiftly and immediately upon learning of protected activity would ironically have a stronger defense than those who delay in taking adverse retaliatory action.

Id. at 525 (emphasis added). The court in *Mickey* opined that "one could read the Supreme Court [in *Breeden*] as having accepted that temporal proximity may be sufficient in a narrow set of cases." *Id.* at 524. Even if temporal proximity is not sufficient by itself to prove overall "but-for" causation, should temporal proximity be enough to show causal connection as part of a prima facie case of retaliation? *See* Troy B. Daniels & Richard Bales, *Plus at Pretext: Resolving the Split Regarding the Sufficiency of Temporal Proximity Evidence in Title VII Retaliation Cases,* 44 Gonzaga L.Rev. 493 (2008/09) (arguing temporal proximity alone should be enough to make out a prima facie case). Should a showing of temporal proximity allow the claim to survive summary judgment? *See* Kasten v. Saint-Gobain Performance Plastics Corp., 703 F.3d 966, 974 (7th Cir.2012) ("We have explained that mere temporal proximity between the filing of the charge of discrimination and the action alleged to have been taken in retaliation for that filing will rarely be sufficient in and of itself to create a triable issue") (internal quotations omitted). *But see* Zann Kwan, 737 F.3d at 845 (holding that three-week period from complaint to termination is sufficient to make a prima facie showing of causation indirectly through temporal proximity).

As the temporal distance between the protected activity and the adverse employment action increases the less likely it is that the causal element can be established. *See, e.g.*, Filipovic v. K & R Express Sys., Inc., 176 F.3d 390, 398–99 (7th Cir.1999) (four-month delay is a "substantial time lapse"); McKenzie v. Ill. Dep't of Transp., 92 F.3d 473, 485 (7th Cir.1996); Cooper v. City of N. Olmsted, 795 F.2d 1265, 1272 (6th Cir.1986) (fact that plaintiff was discharged four months after filing a discrimination claim was "insufficient to support an inference of retaliation"). But the fact that a substantial period of time has elapsed between the protected conduct and the adverse employment action will not necessarily defeat a finding of causation:

> Our research reveals that other cases which permit claims of retaliation after * * * long periods of time each involve additional circumstances which raised suspicion about the legitimacy of the employer's acts. *See, e.g.*, Moss v. Southern Ry. Co., 1986 WL 10510 (N.D.Ga.1986) (one-year time span between expression and retaliation did not defeat plaintiff's claim where termination was disproportionately severe for minor error); Ross v. Kansas Comm'n on Civil Rights, 1985 WL 17574 (D.Kan.1985) (one-year time span did not defeat plaintiff's claim in light of plaintiff's prior outstanding job performance); Shirley v. Chrysler First, Inc., 970 F.2d 39 (5th Cir.1992) (plaintiff's verdict affirmed, despite fourteen-month time span between expression and retaliation, where retaliation occurred two months after the EEOC dismissed the complaint).

McKenzie, 92 F.3d at 485.

4. SCOPE OF STATUTORILY PROTECTED ACTIVITY

Two kinds of activities are protected under the anti-retaliation provisions of Title VII. The *participation clause* prohibits retaliation because an individual "has made a charge, testified, assisted, or participated in any manner in an investigation, proceeding, or hearing" to enforce laws prohibiting discrimination in employment. Title VII, § 704(a), 42 U.S.C. § 2000e–3(a). The *opposition clause* prohibits retaliation because an employee or applicant "has opposed any practice made an unlawful employment practice" by Title VII. *Id.* The Sixth Circuit in *Booker v. Brown & Williamson Tobacco Co.*, 879 F.2d 1304 (6th Cir.1989), discussed the rationale for the distinction between the two clauses:

> The distinction between employee activities protected by the participation clause and those protected by the opposition clause is significant because federal courts generally have granted less protection for opposition than participation in enforcement proceedings. The "exceptionally broad protection" of the participation clause extends to persons who have "participated in any manner" in Title VII proceedings. Protection is not lost if the employee is wrong on the merits of the charge, nor is protection lost if the contents of the charge are malicious and defamatory as well as wrong. Thus, once the activity in question is found to be within the scope of the participation clause, the employee is generally protected from retaliation. However, the fact an

> employee files a complaint or a charge does not create any right on the part of the employee "to miss work, fail to perform assigned work, or leave work without notice," unless absence from work is necessitated by proceedings that occur subsequent to the filing of a complaint or charge. Still, while the absence may be excused, the employee is generally required to provide notice to his employer that the reason for his absence is a proceeding recognized by [Title VII].
>
> On the other hand, " 'the opposition clause' does not protect all 'opposition' activity." Courts are required "to balance the purpose of [Title VII] to protect persons engaging reasonably in activities opposing * * * discrimination, against Congress' equally manifest desire not to tie the hands of employers in the objective selection and control of personnel * * *. The requirements of the job and the tolerable limits of conduct in a particular setting must be explored." Hochstadt v. Worcester Found. for Experimental Biology, 545 F.2d 222, 231 (1st Cir.1976). "There may arise instances where the employee's conduct in protest of an unlawful employment practice so interferes with the performance of his job that it renders him ineffective in the position for which he was employed. In such a case, his conduct, or form of opposition, is not covered * * *." Rosser v. Laborers' Int'l Union, 616 F.2d 221, 223 (5th Cir.), *cert. denied*, 449 U.S. 886, 101 S.Ct. 241, 66 L.Ed.2d 112 (1980). An employee is not protected when he violates legitimate rules and orders of his employer, disrupts the employment environment, or interferes with the attainment of his employer's goals.

Id. at 1312.

Although the participation clause covers a narrower range of activities than the opposition clause covers, it provides greater protection to those activities. The courts, however, have not always clearly delineated "whether a particular claim is cognizable under the 'participation' or the 'opposition' clause." Laughlin v. Metro. Wash. Airports Auth., 952 F.Supp. 1129, 1133 n. 9 (E.D.Va.1997) (quoting Croushorn v. Bd. of Trs. of Univ. of Tenn., 518 F.Supp. 9, 22 n.8 (M.D.Tenn.1980)). As one court noted, the opposition clause is "often relied upon in cases in which application of the 'participation' clause to the employee's conduct is considered dubious." *Croushorn*, 518 F.Supp. at 24.

a. The Participation Clause

The courts have broadly construed the protection afforded employees by the participation clause of § 704(a). The paradigm case in which such protection is extended is the filing of a charge with the EEOC. *See, e.g.*,

Woodson v. Scott Paper Co., 109 F.3d 913, 920 (3d Cir.1997). The types of activities covered by the participation clause have been described as follows:

> An employee who files charges with the EEOC or with a similar state agency is protected by § 704(a) from employer retaliation. * * *
>
> In addition * * * § 704(a) also protects employees who participate in a Title VII investigation, proceeding, or hearing on their own behalf or on behalf of another. An employee is protected if the employee encourages co-workers to enforce their Title VII rights, refuses to sign an inaccurate affidavit on behalf of the employer, testifies on behalf of a co-worker, aids the state or federal investigating authority, participates in a conciliation meeting on behalf of a co-worker, submits affidavits on behalf of co-workers to the EEOC, or submits nonconfidential documentary evidence to an agency investigating a discrimination complaint. An employer is liable for retaliation if the employer promulgates a rule prohibiting employees from cooperating in Title VII investigations without prior supervisory approval, coercively interviews employees under circumstances that could render their testimony involuntary, or fails to prevent harassment of an employee by co-workers who give the employer notice that they intend to engage in harassment of the employee.

R. Bales, *A New Standard for Title VII Opposition Cases: Fitting the Personnel Manager Double Standard into a Cognizable Framework*, 35 S.Tex.L.Rev. 95, 104–05 (1994) (citing cases).

The participation clause protects employees and applicants from retaliation regardless of the underlying merits of the claim. The leading case on this point is the Fifth Circuit's decision in *Pettway v. American Cast Iron Pipe Co.*, 411 F.2d 998 (5th Cir.1969). In *Pettway*, Peter Wrenn, one of a group of black employees who had previously filed a charge with the EEOC, sent a letter to the EEOC complaining about the racially discriminatory practices of the employer. The letter suggested that a company official had bribed an EEOC official in order to influence that official to make a no-cause finding on the prior charge that the black employees had filed. The employer discharged Wrenn after the EEOC sent it a copy of his letter. The employer's ground for discharge was that Wrenn had made malicious and untrue statements about the employer in his letter to the EEOC. The Fifth Circuit, in *Pettway*, held that "where, disregarding the malicious material contained in a charge (or * * * other communication with EEOC sufficient for EEOC purposes, or in a proceeding before EEOC) the charge otherwise satisfies the liberal requirements of a charge, the charging party is exercising a protected right under [Title VII]." *Id.* at 1007. The court found that Wrenn's letter was protected conduct under Title VII, even if a trial court agreed that Wrenn's letter contained misstatements and potentially libelous statements. *But see* Mattson v. Caterpillar, Inc., 359 F.3d 885, 889–92 (7th Cir.2004) (distinguishing *Pettway* and holding that a Title VII complaint that is "not only unreasonable and meritless, but also motivated by bad faith" is not protected under the participation clause, *id.* at 892). *See also* Leitgen v. Franciscan Skemp Healthcare, Inc., 630 F.3d 668, 674 (7th Cir.2011) (holding that because female physician had a good-faith belief that her employer's compensation system discriminated against women, her Title VII retaliation claim could stand). The court in *Pettway* left open the possibility that the employer could seek relief for damage to its reputation in state court on a state cause of action for libel if malice could be proven. *Id.* at 1007 n.22. ("We in no way imply that an employer is preempted by Section 704(a) from vindicating his reputation through resort to a civil action for malicious defamation."). Is this sufficient to protect EEOC processes? Wouldn't the threat of a potential defamation case by an employer against an employee be enough to deter the employee from filing a libelous charge with the EEOC?

NOTES AND QUESTIONS

1. Should an employee be protected under the participation clause for simply mentioning Title VII or the EEOC in the context of alleging potential discrimination? Is an employer likely to react just as strongly at the mention of a Title VII charge as at the actual filing of such a charge? *Cf.* Culver v. Gorman & Co., 416 F.3d 540 (7th Cir.2005) (employer admitting for summary judgment purposes that mention of filing a Title VII charge with the EEOC is enough to allege retaliation).

2. Warren and Clover, two employees at two different companies, were each asked questions pursuant to internal investigations regarding sexual harassment complaints filed against other workers at their respective workplaces, and in both cases the employees lied in response to questions. In the first case, Warren falsely responded that she had seen a co-worker engage in sexually harassing activity. In the second case, Clover falsely stated her reasons for being late to the investigational interrogation. Warren's employer was conducting an internal investigation pursuant to a strictly internal complaint, with no EEOC involvement whatsoever. Clover's employer, however, was conducting an investigation because it had received notice that a charge had been filed with the EEOC. When both Warren and Clover were terminated for lying, they each filed retaliation claims alleging that they had been fired for their participation in internal investigations regarding Title VII claims. At the time of their terminations, however, neither Warren nor Clover knew that Title VII charges had been filed. Does the participation clause protect either employee?

The Eleventh Circuit ruled against Warren in the first case, maintaining that the participation clause "protects proceedings and activities which occur in conjunction with or after the filing of a formal charge with the EEOC; it does not include participating in an employer's internal, in-house investigation, conducted apart from a formal charge with the EEOC." EEOC v. Total Sys. Servs., Inc., 221 F.3d 1171, 1174 (11th Cir.2000); *see also* Townsend v. Benjamin Enterprises, Inc., 679 F.3d 41 (2d Cir.2012) (holding that the participation clause does not extend to investigations that are "purely internal" where no formal EEOC charges have been filed). The court, however, ruled in favor of Clover in the second case, stating that "[b]ecause the information the employer gathers as part of its investigation in response to the notice of discrimination will be utilized by the EEOC, it follows that an employee who participates in the employer's process of gathering such information is participating, in some manner, in the EEOC's investigation." Clover v. Total Sys. Servs., Inc., 176 F.3d 1346, 1353 (11th Cir.1999). Would Warren nonetheless be protected under the opposition clause after the *Crawford* case, set out below, or is his conduct not "purposive" enough? Does it matter that he lied about the occurrence of discriminatory activity?

3. Because of the risk of defamation suits brought by individuals against their former employers, many employers have adopted "no comment" policies in order to reduce their chances of being sued. Under a "no comment" policy, a referring employer refuses to disclose to prospective employers any information other than the employee's dates of employment and the positions he held. *See generally* Markita D. Cooper, *Job Reference Immunity Statutes: Prevalent But Irrelevant,* 11 Cornell J.L. & Pub.Pol'y 1 (2001); Robert S. Adler & Ellen R. Peirce, *Encouraging Employers to Abandon Their "No Comment" Policies Regarding Job References: A Reform Proposal*, 53 Wash. & Lee L.Rev. 1381 (1996). Suppose an employer, Zerkon, has adopted a "no comment" policy. A female employee of Zerkon is discharged and files a charge of discrimination with the EEOC claiming the discharge occurred because of sex. The charge is served on Zerkon by the EEOC, so the employer is aware she has filed the charge. The employee then seeks a job with Alpha which informs her that she will be hired if Zerkon gives a full accounting of her prior employment. Alpha calls Zerkon for a job reference, but the only information Zerkon provides is the dates of her employment and the jobs she held. Does she have a claim for retaliation against Zerkon for not providing more information? *See* Sparrow v. Piedmont Health Sys. Agency, Inc., 593 F.Supp. 1107 (M.D.N.C.1984).

b. The Opposition Clause

CRAWFORD V. METROPOLITAN GOVERNMENT

Supreme Court of the United States, 2009.
555 U.S. 271, 129 S.Ct. 846, 172 L.Ed.2d 650.

JUSTICE SOUTER delivered the opinion of the Court.

* * *

I

In 2002, respondent Metropolitan Government of Nashville * * * (Metro) began looking into rumors of sexual harassment by the Metro School District's employee relations director, Gene Hughes. When Veronica Frazier, a Metro human resources officer, asked petitioner Vicky Crawford, a 30-year Metro employee, whether she had witnessed "inappropriate behavior" on the part of Hughes, Crawford described several instances of sexually harassing behavior: once, Hughes had answered her greeting, " 'Hey Dr. Hughes, what's up?,' " by grabbing his crotch and saying " '[Y]ou know what's up' "; he had repeatedly " 'put his crotch up to [her] window' "; and on one occasion he had entered her office and " 'grabbed her head and pulled it to his crotc[h]' " Two other employees also reported being sexually harassed by Hughes. Although Metro took no action against Hughes, it did fire Crawford and the two other accusers soon after finishing the investigation, saying in Crawford's case that it was for embezzlement. Crawford claimed Metro was retaliating for her report of Hughes's behavior and filed a charge of a Title VII violation with the Equal Employment Opportunity Commission (EEOC), followed by this suit in the United States District Court for the Middle District of Tennessee.

The Title VII antiretaliation provision has two clauses, making it "an unlawful employment practice for an employer to discriminate against any of his employees * * * [1] because he has opposed any practice made an unlawful employment practice by this subchapter, or [2] because he has made a charge, testified, assisted, or participated in any manner in an investigation, proceeding, or hearing under this subchapter." 42 U.S.C. § 2000e–3(a). The one is known as the "opposition clause," the other as the "participation clause," and Crawford accused Metro of violating both.

The District Court granted summary judgment for Metro. It held that Crawford could not satisfy the opposition clause because she had not "instigated or initiated any complaint," but had "merely answered questions by investigators in an already-pending internal investigation, initiated by someone else." It concluded that her claim also failed under the participation clause, which Sixth Circuit precedent confined to protecting " 'an employee's participation in an employer's internal investigation—where that investigation occurs pursuant to a pending EEOC charge' " (not the case here). (emphasis omitted) (quoting *Abbott* v. *Crown Motor Co.*, 348 F.3d 537, 543 (CA6 2003)).

The Court of Appeals affirmed on the same grounds * * *. Because the Sixth Circuit's decision conflicts with those of other Circuits, particularly as to the opposition clause, we granted Crawford's petition for certiorari. We now reverse and remand for further proceedings.

II

opp. clause

The opposition clause makes it "unlawful * * * for an employer to discriminate against any * * * employe[e] * * * because he has opposed any practice made * * * unlawful * * * by this subchapter." § 2000e–3(a). The term "oppose," being left undefined by the statute, carries its ordinary meaning, "to resist or antagonize * * * ; to contend against; to confront; resist; withstand," Webster's New International Dictionary 1710 (2d ed. 1958). Although these actions entail varying expenditures of energy, "RESIST frequently implies more active striving than OPPOSE."

The statement Crawford says she gave to Frazier is thus covered by the opposition clause, as an ostensibly disapproving account of sexually obnoxious behavior toward her by a fellow employee, an answer she says antagonized her employer to the point of sacking her on a false pretense. Crawford's description of the louche goings-on would certainly qualify in the minds of reasonable jurors as "resist[ant]" or "antagoni[stic]" to Hughes's treatment, if for no other reason than the point argued by the Government and explained by an EEOC guideline: "When an employee communicates to her employer a belief that the employer has engaged in * * * a form of employment discrimination, that communication" virtually always "constitutes the employee's *opposition* to the activity." It is true that one can imagine exceptions, like an employee's description of a supervisor's racist joke as hilarious, but these will be eccentric cases, and this is not one of them.

* * *

"Oppose" goes beyond "active, consistent" behavior in ordinary discourse, where we would naturally use the word to speak of someone who has taken no action at all to advance a position beyond disclosing it. Countless people were known to "oppose" slavery before Emancipation, or are said to "oppose" capital punishment today, without writing public letters, taking to the streets, or resisting the government. And we would call it "opposition" if an employee took a stand against an employer's discriminatory practices not by "instigating" action, but by standing pat, say, by refusing to follow a supervisor's order to fire a junior worker for discriminatory reasons. There is, then, no reason to doubt that a person can "oppose" by responding to someone else's question just as surely as by provoking the discussion, and nothing in the statute requires a freakish rule protecting an employee who reports discrimination on her own initiative but not one who reports the same discrimination in the same words when her boss asks a question.

Metro * * * [argues] that the lower the bar for retaliation claims, the less likely it is that employers will look into what may be happening outside the executive suite. As they see it, if retaliation is an easy charge when things go bad for an employee who responded to enquiries, employers will avoid the headache by refusing to raise questions about possible discrimination.

The argument is unconvincing, for we think it underestimates the incentive to enquire that follows from our decisions in *Burlington Industries, Inc. v. Ellerth*, 524 U.S. 742, 118 S.Ct. 2257, 141 L.Ed.2d 633, and *Faragher v. Boca Raton*, 524 U.S. 775, 118 S.Ct. 2275, L.Ed.2d 662 (1998). *Ellerth* and *Faragher* hold "[a]n employer * * * subject to vicarious liability to a victimized employee for an actionable hostile environment created by a supervisor with . . . authority over the employee." *Ellerth, supra*, at 765; *Faragher, supra*, at 807. * * * Although there is no affirmative defense if the hostile environment "culminates in a tangible employment action" against the employee, *Ellerth*, 524 U.S. at 765, an employer does have a defense "[w]hen no tangible employment action is taken" if it "exercised reasonable care to prevent and correct promptly any" discriminatory conduct and "the plaintiff employee unreasonably failed to take advantage of any preventive or corrective opportunities provided by the employer or to avoid harm otherwise, *ibid.*" Employers are thus subject to a strong inducement to ferret out and put a stop to any discriminatory activity in their operations as a way to break the circuit of imputed liability. The possibility that an employer might someday want to fire someone who might charge discrimination traceable to an internal investigation does not strike us as likely to diminish the attraction of an *Ellerth-Faragher* affirmative defense.

That aside, * * * [i]f it were clear law that an employee who reported discrimination in answering an employer's questions could be penalized with no remedy, prudent employees would have a good reason to keep quiet about Title VII offenses against themselves or against others. This is no imaginary horrible given the documented indications that "[f]ear of retaliation is the leading reason why people stay silent instead of voicing their concerns about bias and discrimination." Brake, *Retaliation*, 90 Minn. L. Rev. 18, 20 (2005) * * * . The appeals court's rule would thus create a real dilemma for any knowledgeable employee in a hostile work environment if the boss took steps to assure a defense under our cases. If the employee reported discrimination in response to the enquiries, the employer might well be free to penalize her for speaking up. But if she kept quiet about the discrimination and later filed a Title VII claim, the employer might well escape liability, arguing that it "exercised reasonable care to prevent and correct [any discrimination] promptly" but "the plaintiff employee unreasonably failed to take advantage of . . . preventive or corrective opportunities provided by the employer." *Ellerth, supra,* at 765. Nothing in the statute's text or our precedent supports this catch-22.

Because Crawford's conduct is covered by the opposition clause, we do not reach her argument that the Sixth Circuit misread the participation clause as well. But that does not mean the end of this case, for Metro's motion for summary judgment raised several defenses to the retaliation charge besides the scope of the two clauses; the District Court never reached these others owing to its ruling on the elements of retaliation, and they remain open on remand.

JUSTICE ALITO, with whom JUSTICE THOMAS joins, concurring in the judgment.

* * *

* * * I * * * agree with the Court's primary reasoning, which is based on "the point argued by the Government and explained by an EEOC guideline: 'When an employee communicates to her employer a belief that the employer has engaged in * * * a form of employment discrimination, that communication' virtually always 'constitutes the employee's *opposition* to the activity.' " I write separately to emphasize my understanding that the Court's holding does not and should not extend beyond employees who testify in internal investigations or engage in analogous purposive conduct.

As the Court concludes, the term "oppose" does not denote conduct that necessarily rises to the level required by the Sixth Circuit—*i.e.,* conduct that is " 'consistent' " and "instigated or initiated" by the employee. The primary definitions of the term "oppose" do, however, require conduct that is active and purposive. For example, the first three definitions of the term in the dictionary upon which the Court principally relies are as follows:

> "1. to act against or provide resistance to; combat. 2. to stand in the way of; hinder; obstruct. 3. to set as an opponent or adversary." Random Dict. 1359 (2d ed. 1987).

* * * [I]n dicta, the Court notes that the fourth listed definition in the Random House Dictionary of the English Language goes further, defining "oppose" to mean " 'to be hostile or adverse to, *as in opinion.*' " Thus, this definition embraces silent opposition.

While this is certainly *an* accepted usage of the term "oppose," the term is not always used in this sense, and it is questionable whether silent opposition is covered by the opposition clause. It is noteworthy that all of the other conduct protected by this provision—making a charge, testifying, or assisting or participating in an investigation, proceeding, or hearing—requires active and purposive conduct. " 'That several items in a list share an attribute counsels in favor of interpreting the other items as possessing that attribute as well.' "

An interpretation of the opposition clause that protects conduct that is not active and purposive would have important practical implications. It would open the door to retaliation claims by employees who never expressed a word of opposition to their employers. To be sure, in many cases, such employees would not be able to show that management was aware of their opposition and thus would not be able to show that their opposition caused the adverse actions at issue. But in other cases, such employees might well be able to create a genuine factual issue on the question of causation. Suppose, for example, that an employee alleges that he or she expressed opposition while informally chatting with a co-worker at the proverbial water cooler or in a workplace telephone conversation that was overheard by a co-worker. Or suppose that an employee alleges that such a conversation occurred after work at a restaurant or tavern frequented by co-workers or at a neighborhood picnic attended by a friend or relative of a supervisor.

Some courts hold that an employee asserting a retaliation claim can prove causation simply by showing that the adverse employment action occurred within a short time after the protected conduct. See, *e.g., Clark County School Dist.* v. *Breeden,* 532 U.S. 268, 273, 121 S.Ct. 1508, 149 L.Ed.2d 509 (2001) (*per curiam*) (noting that some cases "accept mere temporal proximity between an employer's knowledge of protected activity and an adverse employment action as sufficient evidence of causality to establish a prima facie case"). As a result, an employee claiming retaliation may be able to establish causation simply by showing that, within some time period prior to the adverse action, the employer, by some indirect means, became aware of the views that the employee had expressed. Where the protected conduct consisted of a private conversation, application of this rule would be especially problematic because of uncertainty regarding the point in time when the employer became aware of the employee's private expressions of disapproval.

The number of retaliation claims filed with the EEOC has proliferated in recent years. See U.S. Equal Employment Opportunity Commission, Charge Statistics: FY 1997 Through FY 2015, *http://www.eeoc.gov/eeoc/statistics/enforcement/retaliation.cfm.* Retaliation charges have nearly doubled—to almost 40,000—between 1999 and 2015. An expansive interpretation of protected opposition conduct would likely cause this trend to accelerate.

The question whether the opposition clause shields employees who do not communicate their views to their employers through purposive conduct is not before us in this case; the answer to that question is far from clear; and I do not understand the Court's holding to reach that issue here. For present purposes, it is enough to hold that the opposition clause does protect an employee, like petitioner, who testifies about unlawful conduct in an internal investigation.

NOTES AND QUESTIONS

1. The Court in *Crawford* seems to suggest that silent opposition to unlawful discrimination can sometimes be protected. The Court describes as "opposition" the situation where an employee—in silent protest—disregards "a supervisor's order to fire a junior worker for discriminatory reasons." The Court's example is one where causation is obvious, isn't it? Justice Alito's concurrence suggests that the Court's decision reaches silent opposition that is in no way communicated, or intended to be communicated, directly by the employee—a sort of strict liability standard, if you will. Do you agree the majority intended to go that far? The concurrence cites retaliation cases in which causation is inferred by the timing of the employer's adverse action. But do those cases apply to witnesses? In other words, if an employee files a charge or, as here, complains internally of discrimination, and the employer fires a completely different employee soon after, will that second employee be able to support a retaliation claim merely by saying she was in "silent opposition" to the employer's discrimination against the first employee? Does that make sense without more proof? At oral argument in *Crawford*, Justice Scalia remarked that he would have an issue if the Court's reading meant silent opposition would be protected, but Justice Scalia did not join Justice Alito's concurrence. Why is that? Is it possible Justice Scalia agreed to join the majority only if some of the "silent opposition" language in the majority opinion were scaled back? Do you think it might have been?

2. Misappropriation or unauthorized copying and distribution of an employer's documents, particularly confidential documents, is not protected activity under the opposition clause, even if the employee's intent is to substantiate her own claim of unlawful employment discrimination or to assist her co-worker in a claim of employment discrimination. *See* McKennon v. Nashville Banner, 513 U.S. 352, 115 S.Ct. 879, 130 L.Ed.2d 852 (1995), which was discussed in Chapter 2. *See also* Niswander v. Cincinnati Ins. Co. 529 F.3d 714, 727 (6th Cir.2008) (holding that employee's disclosing employer's confidential, proprietary documents in her possession to her attorney during discovery was not protected opposition conduct); Laughlin v. Metro. Wash. Airports Auth.,149 F.3d 253, 260 (4th Cir.1998) (holding that employee who "breached her employer's trust by copying confidential material and sending it to an outside party" was not engaged in protected oppositional activity); Douglas v. DynMcDermott Petrol. Ops. Co., 144 F.3d 364, 376 (5th Cir.1998) (holding "as a matter of law that conduct that breaches the ethical duties of the legal profession is unprotected under Title VII"). Conduct is not necessarily protected under the opposition clause simply because it is not otherwise unlawful:

> Congress certainly did not mean to grant sanctuary to employees to engage in political activity for women's liberation on company time, and an employee does not enjoy immunity from discharge for misconduct merely by claiming that at all times she was defending the rights of her sex by "opposing" discriminatory practices. An employer remains entitled to loyalty and cooperativeness from employees:
>
> "Management prerogatives * * * are to be left undisturbed to the greatest extent possible. Internal affairs * * * must not be interfered with except to the limited extent that correction is required in discrimination practices."

Hochstadt v. Worcester Found. for Experimental Biology, 545 F.2d 222, 230 (1st Cir.1976) (citation omitted). *See also* Matima v. Celli, 228 F.3d 68, 79 (2d Cir.2000); Robbins v. Jefferson County School Dist., 186 F.3d 1253, 1260 (10th Cir.1999). In *Armstrong v. Index Journal Co.*, 647 F.2d 441 (4th Cir.1981), the court stated that the opposition clause "was not intended to immunize insubordinate, disruptive or nonproductive behavior at work. * * * An employer must retain the power to discipline and discharge disobedient employees." *Id.* at 448. *See, e.g.*, Cruz v. Coach Stores, Inc., 202 F.3d 560, 566 (2d Cir.2000) (superseded on other grounds) (holding that an employee who was fired because she slapped her alleged harasser—purportedly in opposition to conduct that would be unlawful under Title VII—was not engaged in protected opposition activity when she had "many options for resisting"). For a discussion of a broad range of issues posed by the opposition clause, *see* Edward C. Walterscheid, *A Question of Retaliation: Opposition Conduct as Protected Expression Under Title VII of the Civil Rights Act of 1964*, 29 B.C.L.Rev. 391 (1988).

3. *Crawford* discusses the Supreme Court's companion cases of *Burlington Industries, Inc. v. Ellerth*, 524 U.S. 742, 118 S.Ct. 2257, 141 L.Ed.2d 633 (1998), and *Faragher v. City of Boca Raton* 524 U.S. 775, 118 S.Ct. 2275, 141 L.Ed.2d 662 (1998), reproduced in Chapter 10, which resolved the conflict among the circuits over the appropriate standard for employer liability in cases of actionable hostile work environment created by supervisory employees. *Ellerth* and *Faragher* involved sexual harassment claims, but, as will be discussed in Chapter 10, these employer liability rules also apply in hostile work environment claims based on other protected statuses as well, such as race, religion, national origin, age, and disability. The Court in *Crawford* briefly described the *Ellerth/Faragher* employer liability rule to emphasize that these cases create significant incentives for employers to initiate prompt and thorough internal investigations when employees complain about a hostile work environment. It also creates incentives to have open and effective complaint procedures. These internal procedures and investigations ostensibly place more employees—like Crawford—in the position of "opposing" employer practices through filing internal complaints or through responding to questions during internal investigatory interviews, either as witnesses or victims of the allegedly

harassing conduct. If the employer takes an adverse employment action against the employee who speaks up about alleged workplace harassment, he or she has a potential *Crawford* retaliation claim. Did the *Ellerth* and *Faragher* employer liability rules compel the result in the *Crawford* case? Would *Crawford* have been decided differently if the incentives provided to employers by *Ellerth* and *Faragher* did not exist?

Although the U.S. Supreme Court in *Crawford* expansively interprets the word "oppose" in Title VII's opposition clause, not all opposition is protected. The opposition must be of an "employment practice made unlawful by [Title VII]." 42 U.S.C. § 2000e–3(a) (2008). Of course, laypersons are unlikely to know exactly what is made unlawful by Title VII and, accordingly, courts have found that it is enough for legal protection that an employee had a "reasonable and good faith belief" that the opposed practice violated Title VII. *See, e.g.,* Green v. Franklin Nat. Bank of Minneapolis, 459 F.3d 903, 914 (8th Cir.2006) (when raising a retaliation claim "a plaintiff need not establish the conduct which [he or] she opposed was in fact discriminatory but rather must demonstrate a good faith, reasonable belief that the underlying conduct violated the law") (internal quotations omitted).

But, what does it mean for someone to have such a reasonable and good faith belief? Consider the following U.S. Supreme Court decision:

CLARK COUNTY SCHOOL DISTRICT V. BREEDEN

Supreme Court of the United States, 2001.
532 U.S. 268, 121 S.Ct. 1508, 149 L.Ed.2d 509.

PER CURIAM.

On October 21, 1994, respondent's male supervisor met with respondent and another male employee to review the psychological evaluation reports of four job applicants. The report for one of the applicants disclosed that the applicant had once commented to a co-worker, "I hear making love to you is like making love to the Grand Canyon." At the meeting respondent's supervisor read the comment aloud, looked at respondent and stated, "I don't know what that means." The other employee then said, "Well, I'll tell you later," and both men chuckled. Respondent later complained about the comment to the offending employee, to Assistant Superintendent George Ann Rice, the employee's supervisor, and to another assistant superintendent of petitioner. Her first claim of retaliation asserts that she was punished for these complaints.

The Court of Appeals for the Ninth Circuit has applied § 2000e–3(a) to protect employee "opposition" not just to practices that are actually "made * * * unlawful" by Title VII, but also to practices that the employee could reasonably believe were unlawful. * * * *Trent v. Valley Electric Assn. Inc.*, 41 F.3d 524, 526 (CA9 1994). We have no occasion to rule on the propriety of this interpretation, because even assuming it is correct, no one could reasonably believe that the incident recounted above violated Title VII.

Title VII forbids actions taken on the basis of sex that "discriminate against any individual with respect to his compensation, terms, conditions, or privileges of employment." 42 U.S.C. § 2000e–2(a)(1). Just three Terms ago, we reiterated, what was plain from our previous decisions, that sexual harassment is actionable under Title VII only if it is "so 'severe or pervasive' as to 'alter the conditions of [the victim's] employment and create an abusive working environment.'" *Faragher v. Boca Raton*, 524 U.S. 775, 786, 141 L. Ed. 2d 662, 118 S. Ct. 2275 (1998) * * *. Workplace conduct is not measured in isolation; instead, "whether an environment is sufficiently hostile or abusive" must be judged "by 'looking at all the circumstances,' including the 'frequency of the discriminatory conduct; its severity; whether it is physically threatening or humiliating, or a mere offensive utterance; and whether it unreasonably interferes with an employee's work performance.'" *Faragher v. Boca Raton*, 524 U.S. at 787–88 (quoting *Harris v. Forklift Systems, Inc.*, 510 U.S. 17, 23, 126 L. Ed. 2d 295, 114 S. Ct. 367 (1993)). Hence, "[a] recurring point in [our] opinions is that simple teasing, offhand comments, and isolated incidents (unless extremely serious) will not amount to discriminatory changes in the 'terms and conditions of employment.'" *Faragher v. Boca Raton, supra*, at 788. * * *

No reasonable person could have believed that the single incident recounted above violated Title VII's standard. The ordinary terms and conditions of respondent's job required her to review the sexually explicit statement in the course of screening job applicants. Her co-workers who participated in the hiring process were subject to the same requirement, and indeed, in the District Court respondent "conceded that it did not bother or upset her" to read the statement in the file. Her supervisor's comment, made at a meeting to review the application, that he did not know what the statement meant; her co-worker's responding comment; and the chuckling of both are at worst an "isolated inciden[t]" that cannot remotely be considered "extremely serious," as our cases require, *Faragher v. Boca Raton*, 524 U.S. at 788. The holding of the Court of Appeals to the contrary must be reversed.

* * *

NOTES AND QUESTIONS

1. Should it make a difference whether the mistaken belief is one of law or fact? *See* Wolf v. J.I. Case Co., 617 F.Supp. 858 (E.D.Wis.1985) (finding retaliation claim survives summary judgment even though plaintiff was mistaken about legal applicability of the ADEA to employees abroad; mistaken belief of law was not unreasonable or in bad faith). Which kind of mistaken belief was at issue in *Breeden*? Does the Court presume that reasonably prudent persons will be aware of Supreme Court caselaw and be presumed to know it where the law is clear? For example, can an employee have a "reasonable belief" that Title VII prohibits discrimination based on sexual orientation when courts have consistently ruled that an individual's sexual orientation is not a protected status under Title VII? *Compare* Martin v. N.Y. State Dep't of Corr. Servs., 224 F. Supp.2d 434, 448 (N.D.N.Y.2002) (yes), *with* Hamner v. St. Vincent Hosp. & Health Care Ctr., Inc., 224 F.3d 701, 706–07 (7th Cir.2000) (no).

2. Does *Breeden* effectively narrow the protection afforded by the opposition clause? Even if, after *Crawford,* "opposition" has a fairly broad meaning, does it much matter if employees, under *Breeden,* must accurately predict how a court will view the underlying claim? *See* Deborah Brake, *Retaliation,* 90 Minn.L.Rev. 18, 76–102 (2005) (criticizing *Breeden* and arguing that the "reasonable belief" doctrine limits the scope of discrimination law and limits its progressive potential); Deborah L. Brake & Johanna L. Grossman, *The Failure of Title VII as a Rights Claiming System*, 86 N.C.L.Rev. 859, 913–33 (2008) (criticizing *Breeden* and analyzing post-*Breeden* caselaw developments on the "reasonable belief" doctrine).

5. THE ULTIMATE BURDEN IN RETALIATION CASES: "BUT-FOR" CAUSATION

UNIVERSITY OF TEXAS SOUTHWESTERN MEDICAL CENTER V. NASSAR

Supreme Court of the United States, 2013.
___ U.S. ___, 133 S. Ct. 2517, 186 L.Ed.2d 503.

JUSTICE KENNEDY delivered the opinion of the Court.

When the law grants persons the right to compensation for injury from wrongful conduct, there must be some demonstrated connection, some link, between the injury sustained and the wrong alleged. The requisite relation between prohibited conduct and compensable injury is governed by the principles of causation, a subject most often arising in elaborating the law of torts. This case requires the Court to define those rules in the context of Title VII of the Civil Rights Act of 1964, 42 U. S. C. § 2000e *et seq.*, which provides remedies to employees for injuries related to discriminatory conduct and associated wrongs by employers.

An employee who alleges status-based discrimination under Title VII need not show that the causal link between injury and wrong is so close that the injury would not have occurred but for the act. So-called but-for causation is not the test. It suffices instead to show that the motive to discriminate was one of the employer's motives, even if the employer also had other, lawful motives that were causative in the employer's decision. * * * The question the Court must answer here is whether that lessened causation standard is applicable to claims of unlawful employer retaliation under § 2000e–3(a). Although the Court has not addressed the question of the causation showing required to establish liability for a Title VII retaliation claim, it has addressed the issue of causation in general in a case involving employer discrimination under a separate but related statute, the Age Discrimination in Employment Act of 1967 (ADEA), 29 U.S.C. § 623. See *Gross* v. *FBL Financial Services, Inc.*, 557 U. S. 167, 129 S. Ct. 2343, 174 L. Ed. 2d 119 (2009). In *Gross*, the Court concluded that the ADEA requires proof that the prohibited criterion was the but-for cause of the prohibited conduct. The holding and analysis of that decision are instructive here.

I

Petitioner, the University of Texas Southwestern Medical Center (University), is an academic institution within the University of Texas system. The University specializes in medical education for aspiring physicians, health professionals, and scientists. Over the years, the University has affiliated itself with a number of healthcare facilities including, as relevant in this case, Parkland Memorial Hospital (Hospital). As provided in its affiliation agreement with the University, the Hospital permits the University's students to gain clinical experience working in its facilities. The agreement also requires the Hospital to offer empty staff physician posts to the University's faculty members, see App. 361–362, 366, and, accordingly, most of the staff physician positions at the Hospital are filled by those faculty members.

Respondent is a medical doctor of Middle Eastern descent who specializes in internal medicine and infectious diseases. In 1995, he was hired to work both as a member of the University's faculty and a staff physician at the Hospital. He left both positions in 1998 for additional medical education and then returned in 2001 as an assistant professor at the University and, once again, as a physician at the Hospital.

In 2004, Dr. Beth Levine was hired as the University's Chief of Infectious Disease Medicine. In that position Levine became respondent's ultimate (though not direct) superior. Respondent alleged that Levine was biased against him on account of his religion and ethnic heritage, a bias manifested by undeserved scrutiny of his billing practices and productivity, as well as comments that " 'Middle Easterners are lazy.' "

674 F. 3d 448, 450 (CA5 2012). On different occasions during his employment, respondent met with Dr. Gregory Fitz, the University's Chair of Internal Medicine and Levine's supervisor, to complain about Levine's alleged harassment. Despite obtaining a promotion with Levine's assistance in 2006, respondent continued to believe that she was biased against him. So he tried to arrange to continue working at the Hospital without also being on the University's faculty. After preliminary negotiations with the Hospital suggested this might be possible, respondent resigned his teaching post in July 2006 and sent a letter to Dr. Fitz (among others), in which he stated that the reason for his departure was harassment by Levine. That harassment, he asserted, " 'stems from . . . religious, racial and cultural bias against Arabs and Muslims.' " *Id.*, at 451. After reading that letter, Dr. Fitz expressed consternation at respondent's accusations, saying that Levine had been "publicly humiliated by th[e] letter" and that it was "very important that she be publicly exonerated." App. 41.

Meanwhile, the Hospital had offered respondent a job as a staff physician, as it had indicated it would. On learning of that offer, Dr. Fitz protested to the Hospital, asserting that the offer was inconsistent with the affiliation agreement's requirement that all staff physicians also be members of the University faculty. The Hospital then withdrew its offer.

After exhausting his administrative remedies, respondent filed this Title VII suit in the United States District Court for the Northern District of Texas. He alleged two discrete violations of Title VII. The first was a status-based discrimination claim under § 2000e–2(a). Respondent's second claim was that Dr. Fitz's efforts to prevent the Hospital from hiring him were in retaliation for complaining about Dr. Levine's harassment, in violation of § 2000e–3(a). The jury found for respondent on both claims. On appeal, the Court of Appeals for the Fifth Circuit affirmed in part and vacated in part. The court first concluded that respondent had submitted insufficient evidence in support of his constructive-discharge claim, so it vacated that portion of the jury's verdict. The court affirmed as to the retaliation finding, however, on the theory that retaliation claims brought under § 2000e–3(a)—like claims of status-based discrimination under § 2000e–2(a)—require only a showing that retaliation was a motivating factor for the adverse employment action, rather than its but-for cause. See *id.*, at 454, n. 16.

Four judges dissented from the court's decision not to rehear the case en banc, arguing that the Circuit's application of the motivating-factor standard to retaliation cases was "an erroneous interpretation of [Title VII] and controlling caselaw" and should be overruled en banc. 688 F. 3d 211, 213–214 (CA5 2012) (Smith, J., dissenting from denial of rehearing en banc). Certiorari was granted. 568 U. S. ___, 133 S. Ct. 978, 184 L. Ed. 2d 758 (2013).

II

A

This case requires the Court to define the proper standard of causation for Title VII retaliation claims. Causation in fact—*i.e.*, proof that the defendant's conduct did in fact cause the plaintiff's injury—is a standard requirement of any tort claim, see Restatement of Torts § 9 (1934) (definition of "legal cause"); § 431, Comment *a* (same). This includes federal statutory claims of workplace discrimination. *Los Angeles Dept. of Water and Power* v. *Manhart*, 435 U. S. 702, 711, 98 S. Ct. 1370, 55 L. Ed. 2d 657 (1978) (explaining that the "simple test" for determining a discriminatory employment practice is "whether the evidence shows treatment of a person in a manner which but for that person's sex would be different" (internal quotation marks omitted)).

In the usual course, this standard requires the plaintiff to show "that the harm would not have occurred" in the absence of—that is, but for—the defendant's conduct. Restatement of Torts § 431, Comment *a* (negligence) . . . It is thus textbook tort law that an action "is not regarded as a cause of an event if the particular event would have occurred without it." W. Keeton, D. Dobbs, R. Keeton, & D. Owen, Prosser and Keeton on Law of Torts 265 (5th ed. 1984). This, then, is the background against which Congress legislated in enacting Title VII, and these are the default rules it is presumed to have incorporated, absent an indication to the contrary in the statute itself. See *Meyer* v. *Holley*, 537 U. S. 280, 285, 123 S. Ct. 824, 154 L. Ed. 2d 753 (2003).

B

Under the status-based discrimination provision, it is an "unlawful employment practice" for an employer "to discriminate against any individual . . . because of such individual's race, color, religion, sex, or national origin." § 2000e–2(a). In its 1989 decision in *Price Waterhouse*, the Court * * * addressed what it means for an action to be taken "because of" an individual's race, religion, or nationality. Although no opinion in that case commanded a majority, six Justices did agree that a plaintiff could prevail on a claim of status-based discrimination if he or she could show that one of the prohibited traits was a "motivating" or "substantial" factor in the employer's decision. 490 U. S., at 258, 109 S. Ct. 1775, 104 L. Ed. 2d 268 (plurality opinion); *id.*, at 259, 109 S. Ct. 1775, 104 L. Ed. 2d 268 (White, J., concurring in judgment); *id.*, at 276, 109 S. Ct. 1775, 104 L. Ed. 2d 268 (O'Connor, J., concurring in judgment). If the plaintiff made that showing, the burden of persuasion would shift to the employer, which could escape liability if it could prove that it would have taken the same employment action in the absence of all discriminatory animus. *Id.*, at 258, 109 S. Ct. 1775, 104 L. Ed. 2d 268 (plurality opinion); *id.*, at 259–260, 109 S. Ct. 1775, 104 L. Ed. 2d 268 (opinion of White, J.); *id.*, at 276–277, 109 S. Ct. 1775 (opinion of O'Connor, J.). In other words, the employer had to show that a discriminatory motive was not the but-for cause of the adverse employment action.

Two years later, Congress passed the Civil Rights Act of 1991 (1991 Act), 105 Stat. 1071. [The Court then explained that Congress added a new section (§ 2000e–2(m) relating to the mixed-motives framework that: (1) substituted "a motivating factor" for "substantial motivating" factor and (2) changed the liability rules so that an employer could be held liable based on proof that discrimination played a motivating factor with a new affirmative defense precluding damages if employer can prove it would have made the same decision absent the discriminatory motive.]

After *Price Waterhouse* and the 1991 Act, considerable time elapsed before the Court returned again to the meaning of "because" and the problem of causation. This time it arose in the context of a different, yet similar statute, the ADEA, 29 U.S.C. § 623(a). See *Gross*, *supra*.

Concentrating first and foremost on the meaning of the phrase " '*because of* . . . age,' " the Court in *Gross* explained that the ordinary meaning of " 'because of' " is " 'by reason of' " or " 'on account of.' " *Id.*, at 176, 129 S. Ct. 2343, 174 L. Ed. 2d 119 (citing 1 Webster's Third New International Dictionary 194 (1966). Thus, the "requirement that an employer took adverse action 'because of' age [meant] that age was the 'reason' that the employer decided to act," or, in other words, that "age was the 'but-for' cause of the employer's adverse decision." 557 U. S., at 176, 129 S. Ct. 2343, 174 L. Ed. 2d 119.

* * * These principles [from the *Gross* case] do not decide the present case but do inform its analysis, for the issues possess significant parallels.

III

A

As noted, Title VII's antiretaliation provision, which is set forth in § 2000e–3(a), appears in a different section from Title VII's ban on status-based discrimination. The antiretaliation provision states, in relevant part:

> "It shall be an unlawful employment practice for an employer to discriminate against any of his employees . . . because he has opposed any practice made an unlawful employment practice by this subchapter, or because he has made a charge, testified, assisted, or participated in any manner in an investigation, proceeding, or hearing under this subchapter."

This enactment, like the statute at issue in *Gross*, makes it unlawful for an employer to take adverse employment action against an employee "because" of certain criteria. Given the lack of any meaningful textual difference between the text in this statute and the one in *Gross*, the proper conclusion here, as in *Gross*, is that Title VII retaliation claims require proof that the desire to retaliate was the but-for cause of the challenged employment action. See *Gross*, *supra*, at 176, 129 S. Ct. 2343, 174 L. Ed. 2d 119.

B

The proper interpretation and implementation of § 2000e–3(a) and its causation standard have central importance to the fair and responsible allocation of resources in the judicial and litigation systems. This is of particular significance because claims of retaliation are being made with ever-increasing frequency. The number of these claims filed with the Equal Employment Opportunity Commission (EEOC) has nearly doubled in the past 15 years—from just over 16,000 in 1997 to over 31,000 in 2012. EEOC, Charge Statistics FY 1997 Through FY 2012, *http://www.eeoc.gov/eeoc/statistics/enforcement/charges.cfm* (as visited June 20, 2013). Indeed, the number of retaliation claims filed with the EEOC has now outstripped those for every type of status-based discrimination except race. See *ibid.*

In addition lessening the causation standard could also contribute to the filing of frivolous claims, which would siphon resources from efforts by employer, administrative agencies, and courts to combat workplace harassment. Consider in this regard the case of an employee who knows that he or she is about to be fired for poor performance, given a lower pay grade, or even just transferred to a different assignment or location. To forestall that lawful action, he or she might be tempted to make an unfounded charge of racial, sexual, or religious discrimination; then, when the unrelated employment action comes, the employee could allege that it is retaliation. If respondent were to prevail in his argument here, that claim could be established by a lessened causation standard, all in order to prevent the undesired change in employment circumstances. Even if the employer could escape judgment after trial, the lessened causation standard would make it far more difficult to dismiss dubious claims at the summary judgment stage. * * *

The facts of this case also demonstrate the legal and factual distinctions between status-based and retaliation claims, as well as the importance of the correct standard of proof. Respondent raised both claims in the District Court. The alleged wrongdoer differed in each: In respondent's status-based discrimination claim, it was his indirect supervisor, Dr. Levine. In his retaliation claim, it was the Chair of Internal Medicine, Dr. Fitz. The proof required for each claim differed, too. For the status-based claim, respondent was required to show instances of racial slurs, disparate treatment, and other indications of nationality-driven animus by Dr. Levine. Respondent's retaliation claim, by contrast, relied on the theory that Dr. Fitz was committed to exonerating Dr. Levine and wished to punish respondent for besmirching her reputation. * * *

If it were proper to apply the motivating-factor standard to respondent's retaliation claim, the University might well be subject to liability on account of Dr. Fitz's alleged desire to exonerate Dr. Levine, even if it could also be shown that the terms of the affiliation agreement precluded the Hospital's hiring of respondent and that the University would have sought to prevent respondent's hiring in order to honor that agreement in any event. That result would be inconsistent with the both the text and purpose of Title VII. * * *

V

The text, structure, and history of Title VII demonstrate that a plaintiff making a retaliation claim under § 2000e–3(a) must establish that his or her protected activity was a but-for cause of the alleged adverse action by the employer. The University claims that a fair application of this standard, which is more demanding than the motivating-factor standard adopted by the Court of Appeals, entitles it to judgment as a matter of law. It asks the Court to so hold. That question, however, is better suited to resolution by courts closer to the facts of this case. The judgment of the Court of Appeals for the Fifth Circuit is vacated, and the case is remanded for further proceedings consistent with this opinion.

NOTES AND QUESTIONS

1. The *Nassar* case relies heavily on prior decisions in *Desert Palace v. Costa* (this Chapter) and *Gross v. FBL Financial Servs.* (Chapter 13). In connection with the *Gross* case, the Supreme Court has now largely limited the statutory change addressed in *Desert Palace* to Title VII disparate treatment challenges. Does that limitation make sense to you? In the end, does it really matter? Do you think the particular wording of a causation standard will move a jury or other factfinder one way or the other?

2. *Evidence Establishing Causation*: The causation element can be established several ways. One way is through direct evidence of retaliatory animus. *See* Burnell v. Gates Rubber Co., 647 F.3d 704 (7th Cir.2011); Tomanovich v. City of Indianapolis, 457 F.3d 656, 668 (7th Cir.2006); DeCintio v. Westchester County Med. Ctr., 821 F.2d 111, 115 (2d Cir.1987). Another is through proof that other employees who engaged in protected activity were also subjected to adverse employment action. *DeCintio,* 821 F.2d at 115. A third way is with evidence of a close temporal proximity between the adverse action and protected activity in which the plaintiff engaged. *See* Jones v. Walgreen Co., 679 F.3d 9 (1st Cir.2012). Do you think mere temporal proximity is sufficient to show "but-for" causation as required

by *Nassar*? *See* Loudermilk v. Best Pallet Co., 636 F.3d 312, 315 (7th Cir.2011) (one-day gap between complaint and retaliation: "so close on the heels of a protected act that an inference of causation is sensible"). *But see* Donald v. Sybra, Inc., 667 F.3d 757, 763 (6th Cir.2012) (termination on same day plaintiff returned from medical leave, standing alone, not sufficient to show pretext on the basis of temporal proximity).

3. As you have seen in this section, the *Nassar* case broke a string of successful cases brought by plaintiffs alleging retaliation. Indeed, over the last decade, the Supreme Court has been quite protective of retaliation claims. Consider whether *Nassar* signals a change in direction or whether it might be specific to the issues raised in the case. Do you think the Court's decision in *Nassar* is based primarily on statutory interpretation or is something else driving the decision? *See* Sandra F. Sperino & Suja A. Thomas, *Fakers and Floodgates,* 10 Stan. J.C.R. & C.L. 223 (2014) (criticizing majority opinion claims of false and too many retaliation claims in limiting retaliation claims to "but-for" cause); Jeffrey M. Hirsch, *The Supreme Court's 2012–13 Labor and Employment Law Decisions: The Song Remains the Same,* 17 Emp. Rts. & Employ. Pol'y J. 157, 167 (2013) (Court seemed concerned with flood of litigation and frivolous claims); Michael J. Zimmer, *Hiding the Statute in Plain View:* University of Texas Southwestern Medical Center v. Nassar, 14 Nev. L.J. 705 (2014) (*Nassar* a surprise because Court had consistently held for plaintiffs in retaliation cases).

D. STATISTICAL EVIDENCE AND PATTERN-OR-PRACTICE CASES

The often-cited aphorism from *Alabama v. United States,* 304 F.2d 583, 586 (5th Cir.), *aff'd,* 371 U.S. 37, 83 S.Ct. 145, 9 L.Ed.2d 112 (1962), that "statistics often tell much and Courts listen" is equally applicable in employment discrimination litigation. The materials on statistical evidence in this section examine some of the basic, and largely nontechnical, legal rules on the use of statistical evidence in analyzing claims of employment discrimination. Although the material on statistical evidence is included in this chapter on disparate treatment, statistical evidence and the basic principles covered in this section are equally applicable to disparate impact claims. There are some differences for disparate impact claims and those differences will be explored in Chapter 4.

Broadly speaking, the use of statistics is a "scientific" method of drawing inferences from samples; it is a method of attempting to draw valid conclusions from incomplete data. Mathematics is the medium of expression of statistical evidence. Although shrouded in the language of expertise, statistics are merely one form of circumstantial evidence. Statistics in employment discrimination cases are a form of descriptive evidence, because they are offered to describe the factual consequences of employer policies and practices on the employment opportunities of protected classes.

In the following two cases—*Teamsters* and *Hazelwood*—decided in 1977, the Supreme Court broadly endorsed the use of statistical evidence in employment discrimination law. Both cases involved what is known as "pattern or practice" claims brought pursuant to § 707 of Title VII. The cases are also often referred to as systemic discrimination, and, as discussed in the *Teamsters* case, the basic premise is that an employer has engaged in a pattern (or practice) of intentional discrimination and that pattern is primarily demonstrated through the use of statistics. Almost by definition, the cases are class actions, and, as discussed in the notes that follow, there has been a surge in pattern or practice litigation over the past decade.

TEAMSTERS V. UNITED STATES

Supreme Court of the United States, 1977.
431 U.S. 324, 97 S.Ct. 1843, 52 L.Ed.2d 396.

JUSTICE STEWART delivered the opinion of the Court.

This litigation brings here several important questions under Title VII of the Civil Rights Act of 1964. The issues grow out of alleged unlawful employment practices engaged in by an employer and a union. The employer is a common carrier of motor freight with nationwide operations, and the union represents a large group of its employees. The District Court and the Court of Appeals held that the employer had violated Title VII by engaging in a pattern and practice of employment discrimination against Negroes and Spanish-surnamed Americans * * *.

I

The United States brought an action in a Tennessee federal court against the petitioner T.I.M.E.-D.C., Inc. (company), pursuant to § 707(a) of the Civil Rights Act of 1964. The complaint charged that the company had followed discriminatory hiring, assignment, and promotion policies against Negroes at its terminal in Nashville, Tenn. The Government brought a second action against the company almost three years later in a Federal District Court in Texas, charging a pattern and practice of employment discrimination against Negroes and Spanish-surnamed persons throughout the company's transportation system. The petitioner International Brotherhood of Teamsters (union) was joined as a defendant in that suit. * * *

The central claim in both lawsuits was that the company had engaged in a pattern or practice of discriminating against minorities in hiring so-called line drivers. Those Negroes and Spanish-surnamed persons who had been hired, the Government alleged, were given lower paying, less desirable jobs as servicemen or local city drivers, and were thereafter discriminated against with respect to promotions and transfers.[3] * * *

The cases went to trial and the District Court found that the Government had shown "by a preponderance of the evidence that T.I.M.E.-D.C. and its predecessor companies were engaged in a plan and practice of discrimination in violation of Title VII * * * ."

* * * We granted both the company's and the union's petitions for certiorari to consider the significant questions presented under the Civil Rights Act of 1964.

II

In this Court the company and the union contend that their conduct did not violate Title VII in any respect, asserting first that the evidence introduced at trial was insufficient to show that the company engaged in a "pattern or practice" of employment discrimination. * * *

A

We agree with the District Court and the Court of Appeals that the Government carried its burden of proof. As of March 31, 1971, shortly after the Government filed its complaint alleging systemwide discrimination, the company had 6,472 employees. Of these, 314 (5%) were Negroes and 257 (4%) were Spanish-surnamed Americans. Of the 1,828 line drivers, however, there were only 8 (0.4%) Negroes and 5 (0.3%) Spanish-surnamed persons, and all of the Negroes had been hired after the litigation had commenced. With one exception—a man who worked as a line driver at the Chicago terminal from 1950 to 1959—the company and its predecessors *did not employ a Negro on a regular basis as a line driver until 1969*. And, as the Government showed, even in 1971 there were terminals in areas of substantial Negro population where all of the company's line drivers were white. A great majority of the Negroes (83%) and Spanish-surnamed Americans (78%) who did work for the company held the lower paying city operations and serviceman jobs, whereas only 39% of the nonminority employees held jobs in those categories.

The Government bolstered its statistical evidence with the testimony of individuals who recounted over 40 specific instances of discrimination. Upon the basis of this testimony the District Court found that "[numerous] qualified black and Spanish-surnamed American applicants who sought line driving jobs at the company over the years, either had their requests ignored, were given false or misleading information about requirements, opportunities, and application procedures, or were not

[3] *Line drivers*, also known as over-the-road drivers, engage in long-distance hauling between company terminals. * * *

considered and hired on the same basis that whites were considered and hired." Minority employees who wanted to transfer to line-driver jobs met with similar difficulties.

The company's principal response to this evidence is that statistics can never in and of themselves prove the existence of a pattern or practice of discrimination, or even establish a prima facie case shifting to the employer the burden of rebutting the inference raised by the figures. But, as even our brief summary of the evidence shows, this was not a case in which the Government relied on "statistics alone." The individuals who testified about their personal experiences with the company brought the cold numbers convincingly to life.

In any event, our cases make it unmistakably clear that "[s]tatistical analyses have served and will continue to serve an important role" in cases in which the existence of discrimination is a disputed issue. Mayor of Philadelphia v. Educational Equality League, 415 U.S. 605, 620, 94 S.Ct. 1323, 1333, 39 L.Ed.2d 630 (1974). *See also* McDonnell Douglas Corp. v. Green, 411 U.S. 792, 805, 93 S.Ct. 1817, 1825–26, 36 L.Ed.2d 668 (1973). We have repeatedly approved the use of statistical proof, where it reached proportions comparable to those in this case, to establish a prima facie case of racial discrimination in jury selection cases. Statistics are equally competent in proving employment discrimination.[20] We caution only that statistics are not irrefutable; they come in infinite variety and, like any other kind of evidence, they may be rebutted. In short, their usefulness depends on all of the surrounding facts and circumstances.

---

[20] Petitioners argue that statistics, at least those comparing the racial composition of an employer's work force to the composition of the population at large, should never be given decisive weight in a Title VII case because to do so would conflict with § 2000e–2(j). That section provides:

> "Nothing contained in this subchapter shall be interpreted to require any employer * * * to grant preferential treatment to any individual or to any group because of the race * * * or national origin of such individual or group on account of an imbalance which may exist with respect to the total number or percentage of persons of any race * * * or national origin employed by any employer * * * in comparison with the total number or percentage of persons of such race * * * or national origin in any community, State, section, or other area, or in the available work force in any community, State, section, or other area."

The argument fails in this case because the statistical evidence was not offered or used to support an erroneous theory that Title VII requires an employer's work force to be racially balanced. Statistics showing racial or ethnic imbalance are probative in a case such as this one only because such imbalance is often a telltale sign of purposeful discrimination; absent explanation, it is ordinarily to be expected that nondiscriminatory hiring practices will in time result in a work force more or less representative of the racial and ethnic composition of the population in the community from which employees are hired. Evidence of long-lasting and gross disparity between the composition of a work force and that of the general population thus may be significant even though § 703(j) makes clear that Title VII imposes no requirement that a work force mirror the general population. Considerations such as small sample size may, of course, detract from the value of such evidence, and evidence showing that the figures for the general population might not accurately reflect the pool of qualified job applicants would also be relevant. * * *

In addition to its general protest against the use of statistics in Title VII cases, the company claims that in this case the statistics revealing racial imbalance are misleading because they fail to take into account the company's particular business situation as of the effective date of Title VII. The company concedes that its line drivers were virtually all white in July 1965, but it claims that thereafter business conditions were such that its work force dropped. Its argument is that low personnel turnover, rather than post-Act discrimination, accounts for more recent statistical disparities. It points to substantial minority hiring in later years, especially after 1971, as showing that any pre-Act patterns of discrimination were broken.

The argument would be a forceful one if this were an employer who, at the time of suit, had done virtually no new hiring since the effective date of Title VII. But it is not. Although the company's total number of employees apparently dropped somewhat during the late 1960's, the record shows that many line drivers continued to be hired throughout this period, and that almost all of them were white. To be sure, there were improvements in the company's hiring practices. The Court of Appeals commented that "T.I.M.E.-D.C.'s recent minority hiring progress stands as a laudable good faith effort to eradicate the effects of past discrimination in the area of hiring and initial assignment." But the District Court and the Court of Appeals found upon substantial evidence that the company had engaged in a course of discrimination that continued well after the effective date of Title VII. The company's later changes in its hiring and promotion policies could be of little comfort to the victims of the earlier post-Act discrimination, and could not erase its previous illegal conduct or its obligation to afford relief to those who suffered because of it.[23]

The District Court and the Court of Appeals, on the basis of substantial evidence, held that the Government had proved a prima facie case of systematic and purposeful employment discrimination, continuing

[23] The company's narrower attacks upon the statistical evidence—that there was no precise delineation of the areas referred to in the general population statistics, that the Government did not demonstrate that minority populations were located close to terminals or that transportation was available, that the statistics failed to show what portion of the minority populations were located close to terminals or that transportation was available, that the statistics failed to show what portion of the minority population was suited by age, health, or other qualifications to hold trucking jobs, etc.—are equally lacking in force. At best, these attacks go only to the accuracy of the comparison between the composition of the company's work force at various terminals and the general population of the surrounding communities. They detract little from the Government's further showing that Negroes and Spanish-surnamed Americans who were hired were overwhelmingly excluded from line-driver jobs. Such employees were willing to work, had access to the terminal, were healthy and of working age, and often were at least sufficiently qualified to hold city-driver jobs. Yet they became line drivers with far less frequency than whites.

In any event, fine tuning of the statistics could not have obscured the glaring absence of minority line drivers. As the Court of Appeals remarked, the company's inability to rebut the inference of discrimination came not from a misuse of statistics but from "the inexorable zero."

well beyond the effective date of Title VII. The company's attempts to rebut that conclusion were held to be inadequate.[24] For the reasons we have summarized, there is no warrant for this Court to disturb the findings of the District Court and the Court of Appeals on this basic issue. * * *

HAZELWOOD SCHOOL DISTRICT V. UNITED STATES

Supreme Court of the United States, 1977.
433 U.S. 299, 97 S.Ct. 2736, 53 L.Ed.2d 768.

JUSTICE STEWART delivered the opinion of the Court.

The petitioner Hazelwood School District covers 78 square miles in the northern part of St. Louis County, Mo. In 1973 the Attorney General brought this lawsuit against Hazelwood and various of its officials, alleging that they were engaged in a "pattern or practice" of employment discrimination in violation of Title VII of the Civil Rights Act of 1964. * * *

Hazelwood was formed from 13 rural school districts between 1949 and 1951 by a process of annexation. By the 1967–1968 school year, 17,550 students were enrolled in the district, of whom only 59 were Negro; the number of Negro pupils increased to 576 of 25,166 in 1972–1973, a total of just over 2%.

From the beginning, Hazelwood followed relatively unstructured procedures in hiring its teachers. * * * The personnel office did not substantively screen the applicants in determining which of them to send for interviews, other than to ascertain that each applicant, it selected, would be eligible for state certification by the time he began the job. Generally, those who had most recently submitted applications were most likely to be chosen for interviews.

Interviews were conducted by a department chairman, program coordinator, or the principal at the school where the teaching vacancy existed. Although those conducting the interviews did fill out forms rating the applicants in a number of respects, it is undisputed that each school principal possessed virtually unlimited discretion in hiring teachers for his school. The only general guidance given to the principals was to hire the "most competent" person available, and such intangibles as "personality, disposition, appearance, poise, voice, articulation, and ability to deal with people" counted heavily. The principal's choice was

[24] The company's evidence, apart from the showing of recent changes in hiring and promotion policies, consisted mainly of general statements that it hired only the best qualified applicants. But "affirmations of good faith in making individual selections are insufficient to dispel a prima facie case of systematic exclusion." Alexander v. Louisiana, 405 U.S. 625, 632, 92 S.Ct. 1221, 1226, 31 L.Ed.2d 536 (1972). * * *

routinely honored by Hazelwood's Superintendent and the Board of Education.

In the early 1960's Hazelwood found it necessary to recruit new teachers, and for that purpose members of its staff visited a number of colleges and universities in Missouri and bordering States. All the institutions visited were predominantly white, and Hazelwood did not seriously recruit at either of the two predominantly Negro four-year colleges in Missouri. As a buyer's market began to develop for public school teachers, Hazelwood curtailed its recruiting efforts. For the 1971–1972 school year, 3,127 persons applied for only 234 teaching vacancies; for the 1972–1973 school year, there were 2,373 applications for 282 vacancies. A number of the applicants who were not hired were Negroes.

Hazelwood hired its first Negro teacher in 1969. The number of Negro faculty members gradually increased in successive years: 6 of 957 in the 1970 school year; 16 of 1,107 by the end of the 1972 school year; 22 of 1,231 in the 1973 school year. By comparison, according to 1970 census figures, of more than 19,000 teachers employed in that year in the St. Louis area, 15.4% were Negro. That percentage figure included the St. Louis City School District, which in recent years has followed a policy of attempting to maintain a 50% Negro teaching staff. Apart from that school district, 5.7% of the teachers in the county were Negro in 1970.

Drawing upon these historic facts, the Government mounted its "pattern or practice" attack in the District Court upon four different fronts. It adduced evidence of (1) a history of alleged racially discriminatory practices, (2) statistical disparities in hiring, (3) the standardless and largely subjective hiring procedures, and (4) specific instances of alleged discrimination against 55 unsuccessful Negro applicants for teaching jobs. Hazelwood offered virtually no additional evidence in response, relying instead on evidence introduced by the Government, perceived deficiencies in the Government's case, and its own officially promulgated policy "to hire all teachers on the basis of training, preparation and recommendations, regardless of race, color or creed."

The District Court ruled that the Government had failed to establish a pattern or practice of discrimination. * * * The court found nothing illegal or suspect in the teacher-hiring procedures that Hazelwood had followed. * * *

The Court of Appeals for the Eighth Circuit reversed. After suggesting that the District Court had assigned inadequate weight to evidence of discriminatory conduct on the part of Hazelwood before the effective date of Title VII, the Court of Appeals rejected the trial court's analysis of the statistical data as resting on an irrelevant comparison of Negro teachers to Negro pupils in Hazelwood. The proper comparison, in the appellate court's view, was one between Negro teachers in Hazelwood and Negro teachers in the relevant labor market area. Selecting St. Louis County and St. Louis City as the relevant area, the Court of Appeals compared the 1970 census figures, showing that 15.4% of teachers in that area were Negro, to the racial composition of Hazelwood's teaching staff. In the 1972–1973 and 1973–1974 school years, only 1.4% and 1.8%, respectively, of Hazelwood's teachers were Negroes. This statistical disparity, particularly when viewed against the background of the teacher-hiring procedures that Hazelwood had followed, was held to constitute a prima facie case of a pattern or practice or racial discrimination.

In addition, the Court of Appeals reasoned that the trial court had erred in failing to measure the 55 instances in which Negro applicants were denied jobs against the four-part standard for establishing a prima facie case of individual discrimination set out in this Court's opinion in *McDonnell Douglas Corp. v. Green*. Applying that standard, the appellate court found 16 cases of individual discrimination, which "buttressed" the statistical proof. Because Hazelwood had not rebutted the Government's prima facie case of a pattern or practice of racial discrimination, the Court of Appeals directed judgment for the Government and prescribed the remedial order to be entered.

We granted certiorari to consider a substantial question affecting the enforcement of a pervasive federal law.

The petitioners primarily attack the judgment of the Court of Appeals for its reliance on "undifferentiated work force statistics to find an unrebutted prima facie case of employment discrimination." The question they raise, in short, is whether a basic component in the Court of Appeals' finding of a pattern or practice of discrimination—the comparatively small percentage of Negro employees on Hazelwood's teaching staff—was lacking in probative force.

This Court's recent consideration in *Teamsters v. United States* of the role of statistics in pattern-or-practice suits under Title VII provides substantial guidance in evaluating the arguments advanced by the petitioners. * * * We also noted that statistics can be an important source or proof in employment discrimination cases * * *. [The Court here quoted a portion of note 20 from *Teamsters*.] Where gross statistical disparities can be shown, they alone may in a proper case constitute prima facie proof of a pattern or practice of discrimination.

There can be no doubt, in light of the *Teamsters* case, that the District Court's comparison of Hazelwood's teacher work force to its student population fundamentally misconceived the role of statistics in employment discrimination cases. The Court of Appeals was correct in the view that a proper comparison was between the racial composition of Hazelwood's teaching staff and the racial composition of the qualified public school teacher population in the relevant labor market.[13] The percentage of Negroes on Hazelwood's teaching staff in 1972–1973 was 1.4%, and in 1973–1974 it was 1.8%. By contrast, the percentage of qualified Negro teachers in the area was, according to the 1970 census, at least 5.7%.[14] Although these differences were on their face substantial, the Court of Appeals erred in substituting its judgment for that of the District Court and holding that the Government had conclusively proved its "pattern or practice" lawsuit.

The Court of Appeals totally disregarded the possibility that this prima facie statistical proof in the record might at the trial court level be rebutted by statistics dealing with Hazelwood's hiring after it became subject to Title VII. Racial discrimination by public employers was not made illegal under Title VII until March 24, 1972. A public employer who from that date forward made all its employment decisions in a wholly nondiscriminatory way would not violate Title VII even if it had formerly maintained an all-white work force by purposefully excluding Negroes. For this reason, the Court cautioned in the *Teamsters* opinion that once a prima facie case has been established by statistical workforce disparities, the employer must be given an opportunity to show that "the claimed discriminatory pattern is a product of pre-Act hiring rather than unlawful post-Act discrimination." 431 U.S. at 360, 97 S.Ct. at 1867.

---

[13] In *Teamsters*, the comparison between the percentage of Negroes on the employer's work force and the percentage in the general areawide population was highly probative, because the job skill there involved—the ability to drive a truck—is one that many persons possess or can fairly readily acquire. When special qualifications are required to fill particular jobs, comparisons to the general population (rather than to the smaller group of individuals who possess the necessary qualifications) may have little probative value. The comparative statistics introduced by the Government in the District Court, however, were properly limited to public school teachers * * * .

Although the petitioners concede as a general matter the probative force of the comparative work-force statistics, they object to the Court of Appeals' heavy reliance on these data on the ground that applicant-flow data, showing the actual percentage of white and Negro applicants for teaching positions at Hazelwood, would be firmer proof. * * * [T]here was no clear evidence of such statistics. We leave it to the District Court on remand to determine whether competent proof of those data can be adduced. If so, it would, of course, be very relevant.

[14] As is discussed below, the Government contends that a comparative figure of 15.4%, rather than 5.7%, is the appropriate one. But even assuming, *arguendo*, that the 5.7% figure urged by the petitioners is correct, the disparity between that figure and the percentage of Negroes on Hazelwood's teaching staff would be more than fourfold for the 1972–1973 school year, and threefold for the 1973–1974 school year. A precise method of measuring the significance of such statistical disparities was explained in *Castaneda v. Partida*, 430 U.S. 482, 496–97 n. 17, 97 S.Ct. 1272, 1281 n. 17, 51 L.Ed.2d 498 (1977). It involves calculation of the "standard deviation" as a measure of predicted fluctuations from the expected value of a sample. Using the 5.7% figure as the basis for calculating the expected value, the expected number of Negroes on the Hazelwood teaching staff would be roughly 63 in 1972–1973 and 70 in 1973–1974. The observed number in those years was 16 and 22, respectively. The difference between the observed and expected values was more than six standard deviations in 1972–1973 and more than five standard deviations in 1973–1974. The Court in *Castaneda* noted that "[a]s a general rule for such large samples, if the difference between the expected value and the observed number is greater than two or three standard deviations," then the hypothesis that teachers were hired without regard to race would be suspect. 430 U.S. at 496–97 n.17, 97 S.Ct. at 1281 n.17.

The record in this case showed that for the 1972–1973 school year, Hazelwood hired 282 new teachers, 10 of whom (3.5%) were Negroes; for the following school year it hired 123 new teachers, 5 of whom (4.1%) were Negroes. Over the two-year period, Negroes constituted a total of 15 of the 405 new teachers hired (3.7%). Although the Court of Appeals briefly mentioned these data in reciting the facts, it wholly ignored them in discussing whether the Government had shown a pattern or practice of discrimination. And it gave no consideration at all to the possibility that post-Act data as to the number of Negroes hired compared to the total number of Negro applicants might tell a totally different story.

What the hiring figures prove obviously depends upon the figures to which they are compared. The Court of Appeals accepted the Government's argument that the relevant comparison was to the labor market area of St. Louis County and the city of St. Louis, in which, according to the 1970 census, 15.4% of all teachers were Negro. The propriety of that comparison was vigorously disputed by the petitioners, who urged that because the city of St. Louis has made special attempts to maintain a 50% Negro teaching staff, inclusion of that school district in the relevant market area distorts the comparison. Were that argument accepted, the percentage of Negro teachers in the relevant labor market area (St. Louis County alone) as shown in the 1970 census would be 5.7% rather than 15.4%.

The difference between these figures may well be important; the disparity between 3.7% (the percentage of Negro teachers hired by Hazelwood in 1972–1973 and 1973–1974) and 5.7% may be sufficiently small to weaken the Government's other proof, while the disparity between 3.7% and 15.4% may be sufficiently large to reinforce it.[17] In

[17] Indeed, under the statistical methodology explained in *Castaneda v. Partida*, 430 U.S. at 496–97 n.17, 97 S.Ct. at 1281 n.17, involving the calculation of the standard deviation as a measure of predicted fluctuations, the difference between using 15.4% and 5.7% as the areawide figure would be significant. If the 15.4% figure is taken as the basis for comparison, the expected number of Negro teachers hired by Hazelwood in 1972–1973 would be 43 (rather than the actual figure of 10) of a total of 282, a difference of more than five standard deviations; the expected number in 1973–1974 would be 19 (rather than the actual figure 5) of a total of 123, a difference of more than three standard deviations. For the two years combined, the difference between the observed number of 15 Negro teachers hired (of a total of 405) would vary from the expected number of 62 by more than six standard deviations. Because a fluctuation of more than two or three standard deviations would undercut the hypothesis that decisions were being made randomly with respect to race, each of these statistical comparisons would reinforce rather than rebut the Government's other proof. If, however, the 5.7% areawide figure is used, the expected number of Negro teachers hired in 1972–1973 would be roughly 16, less than two standard deviations from the observed number of 10; for 1973–1974, the expected value would be roughly seven, less than one standard deviation from the observed value of 5; and for the two years combined, the expected value of 23 would be less than two standard deviations from the observed total of 15. A more precise method of analyzing these statistics confirms the results of the standard deviation analysis. *See* F. Mosteller, R. Rourke, & G. Thomas, Probability with Statistical Applications 494 (2d ed. 1970).

These observations are not intended to suggest that precise calculations of statistical significance are necessary in employing statistical proof, but merely to highlight the importance of the choice of the relevant labor market area.

determining which of the two figures—or, very possibly, what intermediate figure—provides the most accurate basis for comparison to the hiring figures at Hazelwood, it will be necessary to evaluate such considerations as (i) whether the racially based hiring policies of the St. Louis City School District were in effect as far back as 1970, the year in which the census figures were taken; (ii) to what extent those policies have changed the racial composition of that district's teaching staff from what it would otherwise have been; (iii) to what extent St. Louis' recruitment policies have diverted to the city, teachers who might otherwise have applied to Hazelwood; (iv) to what extent Negro teachers employed by the city would prefer employment in other districts such as Hazelwood; and (v) what the experience in other school districts in St. Louis County indicates about the validity of excluding the City School District from the relevant labor market.

It is thus clear that a determination of the appropriate comparative figures in this case will depend upon further evaluation by the trial court. As this Court admonished in *Teamsters*: "[S]tatistics * * * come in infinite variety. * * * [T]heir usefulness depends on all of the surrounding facts and circumstances." 431 U.S. at 340, 97 S.Ct. at 1856–57. Only the trial court is in a position to make the appropriate determination after further findings. And only after such a determination is made can a foundation be established for deciding whether or not Hazelwood engaged in a pattern or practice of racial discrimination in its employment practices in violation of the law.

We hold, therefore, that the Court of Appeals erred in disregarding the post-Act hiring statistics in the record, and that it should have remanded the case to the District Court for further findings as to the relevant labor market area and for an ultimate determination of whether Hazelwood engaged in a pattern or practice of employment discrimination after March 24, 1972. Accordingly, the judgment is vacated, and the case is remanded to the District Court for further proceedings consistent with this opinion.

[The opinions of JUSTICE BRENNAN and JUSTICE WHITE, concurring, and JUSTICE STEVENS, dissenting, are omitted.]

NOTES AND QUESTIONS

1. Although the *Teamsters* and *Hazelwood* cases might seem dated, they remain the Supreme Court's best discussions of the use of statistical evidence to prove intentional discrimination. The statistical method discussed in these cases, and in the notes that follow, also apply to the disparate impact theory discussed in Chapter 4. The primary difference between the two theories and the use of statistics is that in a disparate treatment pattern-or-practice case, the statistics are relied on to establish an intent to discriminate whereas in a disparate impact case the statistics

establish a prima facie case of discriminatory effect of a particular employment practice, thus shifting to the employer the burden of justifying the practice. In the context of disparate treatment, what is the theory behind the use of statistics to demonstrate an unlawful intent to discriminate? How is it that statistics prove intent?

2. *Statistical Significance and Demonstrating Discrimination*: Pattern-or-practice cases always involve statistical evidence and the prima facie case depends upon the relative quality of the evidence presented by the opposing parties. Much like the *McDonnell Douglas* proof structure, statistical evidence in a pattern-or-practice case is designed to eliminate nondiscriminatory reasons and thereby create an inference of discrimination. Not just any evidence will suffice. Rather, statistical evidence is not probative unless it satisfies the statistical significance rule, that is, unless it supports the inference that a policy or practice has a significant effect on limiting the employment opportunities of a protected class. Statistical significance, which is discussed further below, provides a measure of the probability that a disparity is due to chance; when the disparity is statistically significant, chance has generally been ruled out as the cause of the disparity, at least as a statistical matter. Courts have followed a variety of approaches to assess whether statistics adequately demonstrate discriminatory intent.

a. *Gross disparities*: Gross statistical disparities alone in some—but increasingly rare—cases, may be sufficient to establish a prima facie case of systemic disparate treatment. For example, in *Teamsters*, note 23, the Supreme Court observed that the inability of the employer to rebut the inference of discrimination based on statistical evidence was not the result of the misuse of statistics but from the "inexorable zero," that is, the total absence of blacks and Hispanics from the at-issue jobs. Teamsters v. United States, 431 U.S. 324, 342 n. 23, 97 S.Ct. 1843, 1858 n. 23, 52 L.Ed.2d 396 (1977). In *Hazelwood*, the Court held that "gross statistical disparities * * * alone may in a proper case constitute prima facie evidence of a pattern or practice of discrimination." 433 U.S. at 307–08, 97 S.Ct. at 2741 (citing *Teamsters*). *See also* EEOC v. Am. Nat'l Bank, 652 F.2d 1176, 1190 (4th Cir.1981) (focusing on the underrepresentation of blacks in office, clerical, and management jobs). Statistics, however, must always be probative, and it will rarely be sufficient to demonstrate a gross disparity without also showing, at a minimum, that the group is large enough to warrant drawing an inference of discrimination.

b. *Standard deviation*: One of the most widely accepted statistical methods is application of the standard deviation formula. Standard deviation analysis is a professionally accepted methodology used to determine whether observed differences in an employer's workforce occurred by chance, or whether an explanation other than chance, for example, race or sex, explains the differences. The Supreme Court sanctioned standard deviation analysis for employment discrimination cases in *Hazelwood*, where the Court cited with approval its prior jury discrimination case that applied a standard deviation analysis. *See* Castaneda v. Partida, 430 U.S. 482, 97 S.Ct. 1272, 51

L.Ed.2d 498 (1977). For a fascinating narrative of how statistics came to be so significant in the *Hazelwood* litigation and the Supreme Court's decision see Stewart J. Schwab & Steven L. Willborn, *The Story of Hazelwood: Employment Discrimination by the Numbers*, *in* Employment Discrimination Stories 37 (Joel Wm. Friedman ed., 2006).

The standard deviation is a measure of spread, dispersion, or variability of a group of numbers. In litigation, its primary purpose is to provide a gauge of how the observed statistics differ from what one might expect. We can use the common example of flipping a coin. If you flipped a coin 100 times, you would generally expect that the coin would come up heads 50 times and tails 50 times. If the coin comes up heads 48 times, you probably would think little of it, but if the coin comes up heads 80 times, you might think it has been rigged in some way, and you might seek an explanation. By employing a standard deviation analysis, you can determine how likely the observed result (80 heads) might be considered a chance occurrence compared to what you predicted (50 heads). Generally, the fewer the number of standard deviations that separate an observed from a predicted result, the more likely it is that the observed disparity could be the product of random or chance fluctuation. Conversely, the greater the number of standard deviations, the less likely it is that chance is the cause of any difference between the expected and observed results. A finding of two standard deviations corresponds approximately to a one in twenty—or 5 percent—chance that a disparity is merely a random deviation from the norm, and most social scientists accept two standard deviations as a threshold level of "statistical significance." *See* Cooper v. Univ. of Tex. at Dallas, 482 F.Supp. 187, 194 (N.D.Tex.1979) (citing Norman H. Nie et al., SPSS: Statistical Package for the Social Sciences 222 (2d ed.1975)), *aff'd*, 648 F.2d 1039 (5th Cir.1981) (per curiam). Another way to express the relevance of a standard deviation is that 95 times out of 100 we would expect the results to fall within two standard deviations. As a general matter, when the observed results of an employment process are more than two standard deviations from what one expected, courts will draw an inference that discrimination, not chance, was the likely cause of the disparity.

Perhaps the easiest way to illustrate the way statistics are used in disparate treatment litigation is to look at one of the above cases in detail. For example, in the *Teamsters* case, there were 8 African-American over-the-road drivers, and the question at issue was why that was the case. Since African Americans constituted 5 percent of the workforce, one might expect that at least 5 percent of the drivers would be African Americans. There are reasons why we might expect more or less than 5 percent, but this is the beginning assumption, and based on the 5 percent figure, we would expect that at least 91 of the 1,828 drivers (.05 x 1,828) would be African Americans. From the *Teamsters* case, we know that only 8 of the drivers were African Americans, or 83 fewer than we would expect. The statistical question is then whether that disparity might have been the product of chance—effectively a random occurrence—or might we be able, as a statistical matter, to identify the disparity as a product of discrimination. More accurately, using statistics, could we rule out chance as the cause of the disparity? Alternatively, we could ask, what is the probability that only 8 of the drivers would be African Americans if the hiring process had been nondiscriminatory?

This is where the standard deviation comes in. Under accepted social science methodology, if a disparity is greater than two standard deviations from what would normally be predicted, the law will infer discrimination as the most likely cause of the disparity. The standard deviation can be calculated based on a formula:

$$\sqrt{(n)(p)(q)}$$

n = number of drivers (1828)

p = percent African American (.05)

q = percent not African American (.95)

When the numbers from the *Teamsters* case are entered into the formula, the result is 9.318, which represents one standard deviation. Two standard deviations would be 18.636. As a practical matter, this means that so long as the disparity between what was observed and what was predicted was less than 18—or if there were anywhere between 91 and 73 African-American drivers—chance could not be ruled out as a cause of the disparity. Any number of drivers below 73, however, would raise a question of discrimination since there would be a very low probability—less than 5 percent—that the results were the product of chance. In this particular case, where only 8 drivers were African American, the observed disparity was nearly nine standard deviations from what we would expect in a nondiscriminatory process. We determine this by simply dividing the disparity by the standard deviation:

$$(91-8)/9.318 = 8.91$$

Statistics cannot prove causation; in other words, the fact that the disparity is statistically significant does not mean that discrimination was the cause of that disparity. Rather, courts are willing to accept such proof as evidence of discrimination because, at this stage of the proceedings, no other plausible explanation has been offered. The defendant, however, has an opportunity to dispute the statistical proof; not, as it argued in the *Teamsters* case, to say that statistics are irrelevant to establish intent, but rather to show that the statistics are inaccurate, incomplete, or focused on the wrong measure. Some of these defenses will be discussed in more detail below, but it might be the case that fewer African Americans were qualified for over-the-road driving jobs or that fewer were interested. Once these issues are introduced, the statistical issues become more complicated as discussed in Note 4 below. One important point about these, and all statistical methods of proof, is that it is not sufficient for the defendant to simply raise doubts about the qualifications or interests of the plaintiff class, but instead, it is the burden of the defendant to show that there is a meaningful difference between the African-American and white groups. *See* Bazemore v. Friday, 478 U.S. 385, 390–401, 106 S.Ct. 3000, 3004–09, 92 L.Ed.2d 315 (1986). For example, in the *Teamsters* case, the defendant could not simply assert that fewer African Americans than whites might have had driver's licenses or that African Americans were less interested than whites in being drivers. Rather, the defendant would have to show that there was an actual difference between the two groups—that African Americans, in fact, had fewer drivers' licenses or less interest in the job than whites.

In notes 14 and 17 of the *Hazelwood* opinion, the Supreme Court discusses the statistics and standard deviation at issue in the case. See if you can replicate that analysis and identify what defenses might have been available to the school district.

3. *Relevant Labor Market*: *Hazelwood* introduced the notion that relevant labor market analysis is critical to fine-tuning statistical evidence for determining statistical significance. As a general proposition, the relevant labor market includes both the geographical area from which the employer draws its employees and the population in that area which has the qualifications for the at-issue jobs. Parties often disagree over how the relevant labor market should be defined. What was the relevant labor market for statistical purposes in *Teamsters*? In *Hazelwood? See also* Carpenter v. Boeing, 456 F.3d 1183, 1198 (10th Cir.2006) (in a case challenging differentials in overtime assignments court emphasized the importance of including in the analysis only those "individuals who were equally eligible for overtime assignments").

4. *Multiple Regression Analysis*: The statistical method discussed above works well in cases where limited issues are at stake: if the question is whether a protected group has been hired or passed a test at a differential rate, a basic standard deviation analysis will generally be sufficient. When more issues or variables are at stake, however, more sophisticated statistical analysis is necessary. Multiple regression analysis is a statistical technique designed to estimate the effects of several independent variables on a single dependent variable. In the employment discrimination law context, it is used to measure the effect of factors such as race, sex, age, education, and experience on the outcome of an employment decision, often pay discrimination. The Supreme Court endorsed the use of multiple regression in *Bazemore v. Friday*, 478 U.S. 385, 390–401, 106 S.Ct. 3000, 3004–09, 92 L.Ed.2d 315 (1986), and the methodology has been used extensively in salary discrimination cases, especially cases involving professional positions, in which the claim is that African Americans or women are paid less than similarly situated whites or males. *See, e.g.*, Sobel v. Yeshiva Univ., 839 F.2d 18, 21–22 (2d Cir.1988).

An important aspect of a multiple regression study is determining what variables to include in the study. In a pay discrimination case, for example, it is necessary to determine what factors are relevant to salary determinations and then to control for those factors as variables in the analysis. In a pay discrimination case, in which the plaintiffs contended that United Parcel Service (UPS) paid African-American managers less than their white counterparts, the court explained the purpose and structure of a multiple regression study as follows:

> A multiple regression analysis attempts to reveal relationships between explanatory variables and a dependent variable. Daniel L. Rubinfeld, Reference Guide on Multiple Regression, in Federal Judicial Center, Reference Manual on Scientific Evidence 181 (2d ed. 2000). Explanatory variables are the expected influences on the dependent variable. *Id.* In this case, pay is the dependent variable. The explanatory variables are what bring race into the picture. In effect, the regression controls for the explanatory variables—those factors that one would expect to influence pay—and then compares the wages of white and black employees. * * * Thus, the selection of explanatory variables is quite important. However, even the best regression equation cannot directly show discrimination because it cannot prove causation. The most it can show is a correlation that can give rise to an inference of discrimination. Ramona L. Paetzold & Steven L. Willborn, The Statistics of Discrimination: Using Statistical Evidence in Discrimination Cases § 2.05 (2002). Whether such an inference is reasonable is the legal question we address. * * *
>
> Evaluating the propriety of explanatory variables is a somewhat comparative exercise. When a defendant attacks a plaintiff's regression, he must typically do more than point out the flaws in his opponent's analysis. Instead, the defendant must show that the omission had an impact on the result. * * * But, "there may be a few instances in which the relevance of a factor * * * is so obvious that the defendants, by merely pointing out its omission, can defeat the inference of discrimination created by the plaintiffs' statistics." Palmer v. Shultz, 815 F.2d 84, 101 (D.C.Cir.1987).
>
> Selecting proper explanatory variables is a function of the particular employer's compensation determinations. Under UPS's pay scheme, center-manager pay has two components: base pay and salary increases. A center manager's base pay is determined when he becomes a center manager, subject to later salary increases based on performance. An individual's base pay remains constant during his tenure as a center manager. Center-manager base pay is calculated in part by using the individual's prior pay, generally as a supervisor. * * *
>
> The discrimination alleged in this claim is that black center managers, between 1991 and the time of judgment, were paid less than similarly situated white center managers because they were black. All experts agree that their regressions revealed no racial disparity in terms of center-manager pay raises for the class period.

> So in order for the pay of black class members to be lower than that of white center managers, the discrimination had to occur with regard to center-manager base pay. Because the base pay is set according to past pay, variable(s) representing that factor are important. As UPS points out, both Dr. Weiner and Dr. Stapleton excluded past pay from their regressions. Dr. Stapleton admitted that if past pay was included in the analysis, then no statistically significant disparity between white and black pay existed. Plaintiffs argue that the exclusion was justified under Bazemore v. Friday, 478 U.S. 385, 92 L.Ed.2d 315, 106 S.Ct. 3000 (1986). We disagree.
>
> * * * Plaintiffs correctly note that *Bazemore* means that past discriminatory pay cannot be a legitimate excuse for a later pay disparity. 478 U.S. at 394–96. Regression analyses in discrimination cases attempt to control for the legitimate reasons for pay disparities through the use of explanatory variables. But, illegitimate reasons—reasons themselves representative of the unlawful discrimination at issue—should be excluded from the regression (or otherwise dealt with) to avoid underestimating the significance of a disparity. See Paetzold & Willborn, ante § 6.13 (discussing the problem of tainted variables). Thus, a regression could be probative of discrimination without taking into account past pay if that past pay was set according to race. This is because past discriminatory pay makes current pay disparities actionable. * * *
>
> Plaintiffs appear to justify the omission of past pay by pointing to the class period disparity that their experts found, inferring discrimination, and claiming that a reasonable inference is that past pay disparities were also race based. This argument is circular. The correlation between race and center-manager base pay from 1991 on exists only if past pay is omitted from the regression. Past pay can only be omitted if it is somehow linked to race. Plaintiffs' only evidence of discrimination in past pay is the apparent correlation between race and center-manager base pay during the class period. But that correlation is what Plaintiffs have evidence of only by omitting past pay. They have no evidence, statistical or otherwise, that past pay disparities were racially discriminatory. This sort of bootstrapping cannot create an inference of discrimination with regard to either class-period base pay or past pay.

Morgan v. UPS, 380 F.3d 459, 466–472 (8th Cir.2004). The court went on to note that the variables the plaintiffs did include in their regression analyses did not compensate for the exclusion of past pay. *Id.* at 472. As a result, the court upheld the lower court's grant of summary judgment for the defendant. For a further discussion of multiple regression analysis, see Michael O. Finkelstein, *The Judicial Recognition of Multiple Regression Studies in Race and Sex Discrimination Cases*, 80 Colum.L.Rev. 737 (1980); Franklin M.

Fisher, *Multiple Regression in Legal Proceedings*, 80 Colum.L.Rev. 702 (1980); D. James Grenier, *Causal Inference in Civil Rights Litigation*, 122 Harv.L.Rev. 533 (2008).

5. *Lack of Interest Defense*: The lack of interest defense to a prima facie case of intentional discrimination is based on the argument that a statistically significant disparity in race or sex is not the result of discrimination, but the lack of interest by minorities or women in jobs in which they are underrepresented. A leading case endorsing the lack of interest defense is *EEOC v. Sears, Roebuck & Co.*, 628 F.Supp. 1264 (N.D.Ill.1986), *aff'd*, 839 F.2d 302 (7th Cir.1988). The case was brought on behalf of a class of women who claimed that Sears had discriminated against them by maintaining a sex-stratified sales force, with men dominating the higher paid, commissioned sales jobs for "big ticket" items such as home improvements, major appliances, furnaces, air conditioners, heating, and plumbing systems. Women, on the other hand, were concentrated in lower paid, noncommissioned jobs selling apparel, linens, towels, paint, and cosmetics. Sears convinced the court that the statistical evidence was not probative of sex discrimination because the sexual disparity was attributable to women's own preferences for noncompetitive work. In affirming the lower court's ruling in favor of Sears, the Seventh Circuit set forth the findings of the trial court:

> The [trial] court found that "[t]he most credible and convincing evidence offered at trial regarding women's interest in commission sales at Sears was the detailed, uncontradicted testimony of numerous men and women who were Sears store managers, personnel managers and other officials, regarding their efforts to recruit women into commission sales." These witnesses testified to their only limited success in affirmative action efforts to persuade women to sell on commission, and testified that women were generally more interested in product lines like clothing, jewelry, and cosmetics that were usually sold on a noncommissioned basis, than they were in product lines involving commission selling like automotive, roofing, and furnaces. The contrary applied to men. Women were also less interested in outside sales which often required night calls on customers than were men, with the exception of selling custom draperies. Various reason for women's lack of interest in commission selling included fear or dislike of what they perceived as cut-throat competition, and increased pressure and risk associated with commission sales. Noncommission selling, on the other hand, was associated with more social contact and friendship, less pressure and less risk. This evidence was confirmed by a study of national surveys and polls from the mid-1930's through 1983 regarding the changing status of women in American society, from which Sears' experts made conclusions regarding women's interest in commission selling; morale surveys of Sears employees, which the court found "demonstrate[ ] that

> noncommission saleswomen were generally happier with their present jobs at Sears, and were much less likely than their male counterparts to be interested in other positions, such as commission sales"; a job interest survey taken at Sears in 1976; a survey taken in 1982 of commission and noncommission salespeople at Sears regarding their attitudes, interests, and the personal beliefs and lifestyles of the employees, which the court concluded showed that noncommission salesmen were "far more interested" in commission sales than were noncommission saleswomen; and national labor force data.

Sears, 839 F.2d at 320–21. A detailed examination of the *Sears* case is found in Ruth Milkman, *Women's History and the* Sears *Case*, 12 Feminist Stud. 375 (1986).

Professors Vicki Schultz and Stephen Petterson, in *Race, Gender, Work, and Choice: An Empirical Study of the Lack of Interest Defense in Title VII Cases Challenging Job Segregation*, 59 U.Chi.L.Rev. 1073 (1992), did an analysis of the judicial treatment of the lack of interest defense in race and sex discrimination cases. The authors concluded that *Sears* was not an atypical case. The courts in almost half of the cases they examined concluded that sex segregation was attributable to women's own work preferences. The authors also found that between 1967 and 1977, the ten-year period just after the enactment of Title VII, the courts more often than not rejected the lack of interest defense in race discrimination cases and seemed to assume that racial discrimination was a product of racial inequities in the work place. Since 1977, however, courts have been more apt to attribute racial segregation to the choices of minority workers. *See also* Vicki Schultz, *Telling Stories About Women and Work: Judicial Interpretations of Sex Segregation in the Workplace in Title VII Cases Raising the Lack of Interest Argument*, 103 Harv.L.Rev. 1749 (1990).

a. To what extent might the lack of interest defense be based on stereotypical assumptions about women? About blacks? About other minorities? What are those assumptions?

b. To what extent might systemic unlawful discriminatory practices in the workplace, such as sexual harassment, explain why women may be reluctant to seek jobs in traditionally male-dominated positions? Sexual harassment is covered in Chapter 10.

6. *Expert Witnesses*: The statistical analysis relied on in employment discrimination litigation is invariably conducted by expert witnesses, who may be statisticians, labor economists, industrial psychologists, and others with expertise in employment settings. While attorneys do not conduct the statistical analyses themselves, it is extremely helpful if they understand the basic theories and methodology used by the expert witnesses. Experts, and their reports, are also subject to the evidentiary principles that govern the admissibility of expert testimony. *See* Kumho Tire Co. v. Carmichael, 526

U.S. 137, 119 S.Ct. 1167 143 L.Ed.2d 238 (1999); Daubert v. Merrell Dow Pharms., Inc., 509 U.S. 579, 113 S.Ct. 2786, 125 L.Ed.2d 469 (1993).

7. *The Role of Statistical Evidence in Individual Disparate Treatment Claims*: In *McDonnell Douglas v. Green*, the Court recognized that statistical evidence can be relevant in individual disparate treatment cases. 411 U.S. 792, 804–05, 93 S.Ct. 1817,1825, 36 L.Ed.2d 668 (1973) (instructing on remand that "evidence that may be relevant to any showing of pretext includes * * * petitioner's general policy and practice with respect to minority employment," including "statistics as to petitioner's employment policy and practice [that] may be helpful to a determination of whether petitioner's refusal to rehire respondent in this case conformed to a general pattern of discrimination against blacks"). As a practical matter, however, individual disparate treatment cases generally rely primarily on anecdotal testimony and documentary evidence. As one court noted, "[W]hile statistics may be used to demonstrate that the employer's proferred reason for discharge is pretextual, standing alone they are not likely to establish a case of individual disparate treatment." Rummery v. Ill. Bell Tel., Co., 250 F.3d 553, 559 (7th Cir.2001).

8. A number of class action, pattern-or-practice employment discrimination suits have been resolved through record-breaking settlements. One of the most well-known cases was a racial discrimination lawsuit against Texaco that settled for $176 million after public disclosure of a tape-recorded meeting that allegedly indicated that some managerial agents of Texaco used explicit racial epithets in a discussion about black employees. Other cases include Coca-Cola ($192 million); Home Depot ($104 million); Shoney's ($105 million); and State Farm Insurance ($152 million). These and other class action cases are discussed in Michael Selmi, *The Price of Discrimination: The Nature of Class Action Employment Discrimination and Its Effects*, 81 Tex.L.Rev. 1249 (2003). All of the above cases settled before trial, which is true for the vast majority of pattern-or-practice cases. If such cases were to go to trial, the *Teamsters* case suggests that the issues should be addressed in two separate judicial proceedings. The first part, known as stage one, would involve a liability determination, and if the defendant is found to be liable, the second stage, would involve a remedial phase where the court would determine the appropriate relief for each class member. *See Teamsters*, 431 U.S. at 358–59, 97 S.Ct. at 1865–67.

9. *The Economics of Discrimination*: The persistence of class-wide discrimination poses a particular puzzle for economic theories of discrimination. Economist Gary Becker long ago hypothesized that, in competitive labor markets, employment discrimination should largely be eradicated because it is economically irrational. *See* Gary S. Becker, The Economics of Discrimination (2d ed. 1971). He noted that discrimination based on status injects a characteristic into the employment process that is unrelated to a worker's productivity and should thus impose significant costs on discriminating firms. The particular insight Professor Becker brought to the issue was that firms that do not discriminate should have a significant

advantage in the marketplace because they will have lower labor costs, and ultimately, these lower-cost firms would drive out the discriminating firms. *Id.* at 39–42.

Few, including Professor Becker, would argue that the markets have functioned in this manner, and even those who are most enthusiastic about the market acknowledge that employment discrimination remains a feature of most labor markets. Where disagreements arise is over just how much discrimination remains and why it persists. One theory that has been advanced is that discrimination may not always be irrational; in fact, it has been argued that some discrimination might be rational and this theory is often referred to as rational or statistical discrimination. Discrimination might be rational, it is argued, to the extent groups have different characteristics and employers have a difficult time assessing individual talents or capabilities. *See, e.g.,* Dennis J. Aigner & Glen G. Cain, *Statistical Theories in the Labor Market,* 30 Indus. & Lab.Rel.Rev. 175 (1977); Stewart J. Schwab, *Is Statistical Discrimination Efficient?,* 76 Am.Econ.Rev. 228 (1986). The most common example involves gender discrimination—as a general matter, women are more likely than men to leave their employment for some period of time to have and to care for children. It is certainly not the case that all or even most women will do so, but employers might be reluctant to hire women knowing that as a group they will impose higher costs on the firm than men, and employers may not be able to identify which women are likely to stay in the workforce.

It is quite likely that some employers make these judgments, but it is less clear that they ought to be defined as rational. Whether they should be defined as rational will depend on the costs that women, as a group, may impose on employers and whether the costs of excluding women or limiting their opportunities exceeds the benefits of an inclusionary policy. *See, e.g.,* Michael Selmi, *Family Leave and the Gender Wage Gap,* 78 N.C.L.Rev. 707, 748–50 (2000) (exploring the implications of arguments based on statistical discrimination that are used to justify the gender wage gap). In any event, the notion behind statistical discrimination is that employers make statistical judgments about groups because doing so is more efficient than trying to obtain accurate individual judgments. It is important to emphasize that statistical discrimination, even where it might be rational, clearly violates the dictates of Title VII and it is never a defense for an employer to assert that discrimination is cost effective. *See* L.A. Dep't of Water & Power v. Manhart, 435 U.S. 702, 716–17, 98 S.Ct. 1370, 1379–80, 55 L.Ed.2d 657 (1978) (noting that Title VII contains no "cost-justification defense.").

In addition to the claim that discrimination in certain circumstances might be rational, there are other reasons why labor markets have not eliminated discrimination. One of the most widely recognized arguments is that such markets are not perfectly competitive—employees might not have information sufficient to enable them to gravitate towards nondiscriminating firms, and the labor costs that arise from discrimination may not be sufficiently high to provide a competitive disadvantage for discriminating firms. Others have argued that discrimination in firms is often structural in nature, becoming essentially part of the fabric of the firm that can influence entire industries and be perpetuated by stereotypes that are difficult to eradicate. Many scholars, particularly critical race theorists, find the economic rationale unpersuasive. In commenting upon the different perspective of law and economics scholars and critical race scholars on the subject of racial discrimination, Professor Rachel Moran observed,

> In contrast to law and economics, critical race theory has concerned itself with how race is constructed through unconscious bias and institutional structures. Race scholars do not presume that rational choice is the sine qua non of human behavior. Instead, they try to unpack the reflexive habits and hidden assumptions that guide racial judgments. Rather than worry about whether statistical discrimination is rational, critical race theorists question whether it is just. In analyzing how privilege is perpetuated, race scholars see social networks as only one example of the patterns and practices that entrench inequality.

Rachel F. Moran, *The Elusive Nature of Discrimination*, 55 Stan. L. Rev. 2365, 2367 (2003).

The literature relating to the economics of discrimination is substantial. For a sampling see Ian Ayres, Pervasive Prejudice? Unconventional Evidence of Race and Gender Discrimination (2001); Encyclopedia of Labor and Employment Law and Economics (Kenneth Dau-Schmidt, Seth Harris & Orley Lobel eds., 2008); Devon W. Carbado & Mitu Gulati, *The Law and Economics of Critical Race Theory*, 112 Yale L.J. 1757 (2003); Michael Ashley Stein, *The Law and Economics of Disability Accommodations*, 53 Duke L.J. 79 (2003).

The next case involved a complicated question regarding the appropriate standard for certifying a plaintiff class, and you may have encountered the case in Civil Procedure. The case also provides a contemporary look at the many issues that arise in seeking to prove a claim of systemic discrimination, which is what the excerpt below focuses on.

WAL-MART STORES, INC. V. DUKES

Supreme Court of the United States, 2011.
564 U.S. 338, 131 S.Ct. 2541, 180 L.Ed.2d 374.

JUSTICE SCALIA delivered the opinion of the Court.

We are presented with one of the most expansive class actions ever. The District Court and the Court of Appeals approved the certification of a class comprising about one and a half million plaintiffs, current and former female employees of petitioner Wal-Mart who allege that the discretion exercised by their local supervisors over pay and promotion matters violates Title VII by discriminating against women. In addition to injunctive and declaratory relief, the plaintiffs seek an award of backpay. We consider whether the certification of the plaintiff class was consistent with Federal Rules of Civil Procedure 23(a) and (b)(2).

I

A

Petitioner Wal-Mart is the Nation's largest private employer. * * * In all, Wal-Mart operates approximately 3,400 stores and employs more than one million people.

Pay and promotion decisions at Wal-Mart are generally committed to local managers' broad discretion, which is exercised "in a largely subjective manner." Local store managers may increase the wages of hourly employees (within limits) with only limited corporate oversight. As for salaried employees, such as store managers and their deputies, higher corporate authorities have discretion to set their pay within preestablished ranges.

Promotions work in a similar fashion. Wal-Mart permits store managers to apply their own subjective criteria when selecting candidates as "support managers," which is the first step on the path to management. Admission to Wal-Mart's management training program, however, does require that a candidate meet certain objective criteria, including an above-average performance rating, at least one year's tenure in the applicant's current position, and a willingness to relocate. But except for those requirements, regional and district managers have discretion to use their own judgment when selecting candidates for management training. Promotion to higher office—*e.g.,* assistant manager, co-manager, or store manager—is similarly at the discretion of the employee's superiors after prescribed objective factors are satisfied.

B

The named plaintiffs in this lawsuit, representing the 1.5 million members of the certified class, are three current or former Wal-Mart employees who allege that the company discriminated against them on the basis of their sex by denying them equal pay or promotions, in violation of Title VII of the Civil Rights Act of 1964, 78 Stat. 253, as amended, 42 U.S.C. § 2000e–1 *et seq.*

* * *

These plaintiffs, respondents here, do not allege that Wal-Mart has any express corporate policy against the advancement of women. Rather, they claim that their local managers' discretion over pay and promotions is exercised disproportionately in favor of men, leading to an unlawful disparate impact on female employees, see 42 U.S.C. § 2000e–2(k). And, respondents say, because Wal-Mart is aware of this effect, its refusal to cabin its managers' authority amounts to disparate treatment, see

§ 2000e–2(a). Their complaint seeks injunctive and declaratory relief, punitive damages, and backpay. It does not ask for compensatory damages.

Importantly for our purposes, respondents claim that the discrimination to which they have been subjected is common to *all* Wal-Mart's female employees. The basic theory of their case is that a strong and uniform "corporate culture" permits bias against women to infect, perhaps subconsciously, the discretionary decisionmaking of each one of Wal-Mart's thousands of managers—thereby making every woman at the company the victim of one common discriminatory practice. Respondents therefore wish to litigate the Title VII claims of all female employees at Wal-Mart's stores in a nationwide class action.

C

* * * [R]espondents moved the District Court to certify a plaintiff class consisting of " '[a]ll women employed at any Wal-Mart domestic retail store at any time since December 26, 1998, who have been or may be subjected to Wal-Mart's challenged pay and management track promotions policies and practices.' " As evidence that there were indeed "questions of law or fact common to" all the women of Wal-Mart, as [Federal Rule of Civil Procedure] 23(a)(2) requires, respondents relied chiefly on three forms of proof: statistical evidence about pay and promotion disparities between men and women at the company, anecdotal reports of discrimination from about 120 of Wal-Mart's female employees, and the testimony of a sociologist who conducted a "social framework analysis" of Wal-Mart's "culture" and personnel practices, and concluded that the company was "vulnerable" to gender discrimination. 603 F.3d 571, 601 (CA9 2010) (en banc).

Wal-Mart unsuccessfully moved to strike much of this evidence. It also offered its own countervailing statistical and other proof in an effort to defeat Rule 23(a)'s requirements of commonality, typicality, and adequate representation. Wal-Mart further contended that respondents' monetary claims for backpay could not be certified under Rule 23(b)(2), first because that Rule refers only to injunctive and declaratory relief, and second because the backpay claims could not be manageably tried as a class without depriving Wal-Mart of its right to present certain statutory defenses. [T]he District Court granted respondents' motion and certified their proposed class.

D

A divided en banc Court of Appeals substantially affirmed the District Court's certification order. The majority concluded that respondents' evidence of commonality was sufficient to "raise the common question whether Wal-Mart's female employees nationwide were subjected to a single set of corporate policies (not merely a number of independent discriminatory acts) that may have worked to unlawfully discriminate against them in violation of Title VII." It also agreed with the District Court that the named plaintiffs' claims were sufficiently typical of the class as a whole to satisfy Rule 23(a)(3), and that they could serve as adequate class representatives, see Rule 23(a)(4). With respect to the Rule 23(b)(2) question, the Ninth Circuit held that respondents' backpay claims could be certified as part of a (b)(2) class because they did not "predominat[e]" over the requests for declaratory and injunctive relief, meaning they were not "superior in strength, influence, or authority" to the nonmonetary claims.

Finally, the Court of Appeals determined that the action could be manageably tried as a class action because the District Court could adopt the approach the Ninth Circuit approved in *Hilao v. Estate of Marcos,* 103 F.3d 767, 782–787 (1996). There compensatory damages for some 9,541 class members were calculated by selecting 137 claims at random, referring those claims to a special master for valuation, and then extrapolating the validity and value of the untested claims from the sample set. The Court of Appeals "s[aw] no reason why a similar procedure to that used in *Hilao* could not be employed in this case." It would allow Wal-Mart "to present individual defenses in the randomly selected 'sample cases,' thus revealing the approximate percentage of class members whose unequal pay or nonpromotion was due to something other than gender discrimination." * * *

II

The class action is "an exception to the usual rule that litigation is conducted by and on behalf of the individual named parties only." *Califano v. Yamasaki,* 442 U.S. 682, 700–701, 99 S.Ct. 2545, 61 L.Ed.2d 176 (1979). * * * Rule 23(a) ensures that the named plaintiffs are appropriate representatives of the class whose claims they wish to litigate. The Rule's four requirements—numerosity, commonality, typicality, and adequate representation—"effectively 'limit the class claims to those fairly encompassed by the named plaintiff's claims.'" *General Telephone Co. of Southwest v. Falcon,* 457 U.S. 147, 156, 102 S.Ct. 2364, 72 L.Ed.2d 740 (1982) (quoting *General Telephone Co. of Northwest v. EEOC,* 446 U.S. 318, 330, 100 S.Ct. 1698, 64 L.Ed.2d 319 (1980)).

A

The crux of this case is commonality—the rule requiring a plaintiff to show that "there are questions of law or fact common to the class." Rule 23(a)(2). That language is easy to misread, since "[a]ny competently crafted class complaint literally raises common questions." Nagareda, Class Certification in the Age of Aggregate Proof, 84 N.Y.U.L.Rev. 97, 131–132 (2009). For example: Do all of us plaintiffs indeed work for Wal-

Mart? Do our managers have discretion over pay? Is that an unlawful employment practice? What remedies should we get? Reciting these questions is not sufficient to obtain class certification. Commonality requires the plaintiff to demonstrate that the class members "have suffered the same injury," *Falcon, supra,* at 157, 102 S.Ct. 2364. This does not mean merely that they have all suffered a violation of the same provision of law. Title VII, for example, can be violated in many ways—by intentional discrimination, or by hiring and promotion criteria that result in disparate impact, and by the use of these practices on the part of many different superiors in a single company. * * * Their claims must depend upon a common contention—for example, the assertion of discriminatory bias on the part of the same supervisor. That common contention, moreover, must be of such a nature that it is capable of classwide resolution—which means that determination of its truth or falsity will resolve an issue that is central to the validity of each one of the claims in one stroke. * * *

Rule 23 does not set forth a mere pleading standard. A party seeking class certification must affirmatively demonstrate his compliance with the Rule—that is, he must be prepared to prove that there are *in fact* sufficiently numerous parties, common questions of law or fact, etc. We recognized in *Falcon* that "sometimes it may be necessary for the court to probe behind the pleadings before coming to rest on the certification question," 457 U.S., at 160, 102 S.Ct. 2364, and that certification is proper only if "the trial court is satisfied, after a rigorous analysis, that the prerequisites of Rule 23(a) have been satisfied," *id.,* at 161, 102 S.Ct. 2364. Frequently that "rigorous analysis" will entail some overlap with the merits of the plaintiff's underlying claim.

* * *

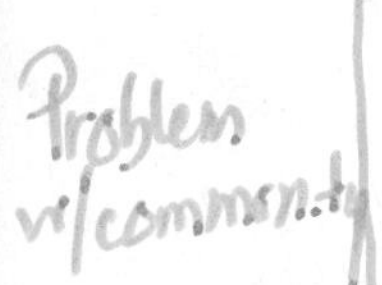

In this case, proof of commonality necessarily overlaps with respondents' merits contention that Wal-Mart engages in a pattern or practice of discrimination. That is so because, in resolving an individual's Title VII claim, the crux of the inquiry is "the reason for a particular employment decision," *Cooper v. Federal Reserve Bank of Richmond,* 467 U.S. 867, 876, 104 S.Ct. 2794, 81 L.Ed.2d 718 (1984). Here respondents wish to sue about literally millions of employment decisions at once. Without some glue holding the alleged *reasons* for all those decisions together, it will be impossible to say that examination of all the class members' claims for relief will produce a common answer to the crucial question why was I disfavored.

B

This Court's opinion in *Falcon* describes how the commonality issue must be approached. There an employee who claimed that he was deliberately denied a promotion on account of race obtained certification of a class comprising all employees wrongfully denied promotions and all applicants wrongfully denied jobs. 457 U.S., at 152, 102 S.Ct. 2364. We rejected that composite class for lack of commonality and typicality, explaining: "Conceptually, there is a wide gap between (a) an individual's claim that he has been denied a promotion [or higher pay] on discriminatory grounds, and his otherwise unsupported allegation that the company has a policy of discrimination, and (b) the existence of a class of persons who have suffered the same injury as that individual, such that the individual's claim and the class claim will share common questions of law or fact * * * ." *Id.*, at 157–158, 102 S.Ct. 2364.

Falcon suggested two ways in which that conceptual gap might be bridged. First, if the employer "used a biased testing procedure to evaluate both applicants for employment and incumbent employees, a class action on behalf of every applicant or employee who might have been prejudiced by the test clearly would satisfy the commonality and typicality requirements of Rule 23(a)." *Id.*, at 159, n. 15, 102 S.Ct. 2364. Second, "[s]ignificant proof that an employer operated under a general policy of discrimination conceivably could justify a class of both applicants and employees if the discrimination manifested itself in hiring and promotion practices in the same general fashion, such as through entirely subjective decisionmaking processes." *Ibid.* We think that statement precisely describes respondents' burden in this case. The first manner of bridging the gap obviously has no application here; Wal-Mart has no testing procedure or other companywide evaluation method that can be charged with bias. The whole point of permitting discretionary decisionmaking is to avoid evaluating employees under a common standard.

The second manner of bridging the gap requires "significant proof" that Wal-Mart "operated under a general policy of discrimination." That is entirely absent here. Wal-Mart's announced policy forbids sex discrimination, and as the District Court recognized the company imposes penalties for denials of equal employment opportunity The only evidence of a "general policy of discrimination" respondents produced was the testimony of Dr. William Bielby, their sociological expert. Relying on "social framework" analysis, Bielby testified that Wal-Mart has a "strong corporate culture," that makes it " 'vulnerable' " to "gender bias." He could not, however, "determine with any specificity how regularly stereotypes play a meaningful role in employment decisions at Wal-Mart. At his deposition . . . Dr. Bielby conceded that he could not calculate whether 0.5 percent or 95 percent of the employment decisions at Wal-Mart might be determined by stereotyped thinking." 222 F.R.D. 189, 192 (N.D.Cal.2004). * * * Bielby's testimony does nothing to advance respondents' case. "[W]hether 0.5 percent or 95 percent of the employment decisions at Wal-Mart might be determined by stereotyped thinking" is the essential question on which respondents' theory of commonality depends. If Bielby admittedly has no answer to that question, we can safely disregard what he has to say. It is worlds away from "significant proof" that Wal-Mart "operated under a general policy of discrimination."

C

The only corporate policy that the plaintiffs' evidence convincingly establishes is Wal-Mart's "policy" of *allowing discretion* by local supervisors over employment matters. On its face, of course, that is just the opposite of a uniform employment practice that would provide the commonality needed for a class action; it is a policy *against having* uniform employment practices. It is also a very common and presumptively reasonable way of doing business—one that we have said "should itself raise no inference of discriminatory conduct," *Watson v. Fort Worth Bank & Trust,* 487 U.S. 977, 990, 108 S.Ct. 2777, 101 L.Ed.2d 827 (1988).

To be sure, we have recognized that, "in appropriate cases," giving discretion to lower-level supervisors can be the basis of Title VII liability under a disparate-impact theory—since "an employer's undisciplined system of subjective decisionmaking [can have] precisely the same effects as a system pervaded by impermissible intentional discrimination." *Id.,* at 990–991, 108 S.Ct. 2777. But the recognition that this type of Title VII claim "can" exist does not lead to the conclusion that every employee in a company using a system of discretion has such a claim in common. To the contrary, left to their own devices most managers in any corporation—and surely most managers in a corporation that forbids sex discrimination—would select sex-neutral, performance-based criteria for hiring and promotion that produce no actionable disparity at all. Others may choose to reward various attributes that produce disparate impact—such as scores on general aptitude tests or educational achievements, see *Griggs v. Duke Power Co.,* 401 U.S. 424, 431–432, 91 S.Ct. 849, 28 L.Ed.2d 158 (1971). And still other managers may be guilty of intentional discrimination that produces a sex-based disparity. In such a company, demonstrating the invalidity of one manager's use of discretion will do nothing to demonstrate the invalidity of another's. A party seeking to certify a nationwide class will be unable to show that all the employees' Title VII claims will in fact depend on the answers to common questions.

Respondents have not identified a common mode of exercising discretion that pervades the entire company—aside from their reliance on Dr. Bielby's social frameworks analysis that we have rejected. In a company of Wal-Mart's size and geographical scope, it is quite unbelievable that all managers would exercise their discretion in a common way without some common direction. Respondents attempt to make that showing by means of statistical and anecdotal evidence, but their evidence falls well short.

The statistical evidence consists primarily of regression analyses performed by Dr. Richard Drogin, a statistician, and Dr. Marc Bendick, a labor economist. Drogin conducted his analysis region-by-region, comparing the number of women promoted into management positions with the percentage of women in the available pool of hourly workers. After considering regional and national data, Drogin concluded that "there are statistically significant disparities between men and women at Wal-Mart . . . [and] these disparities . . . can be explained only by gender discrimination." 603 F.3d, at 604 (internal quotation marks omitted). Bendick compared work-force data from Wal-Mart and competitive retailers and concluded that Wal-Mart "promotes a lower percentage of women than its competitors." *Ibid.*

Even if they are taken at face value, these studies are insufficient to establish that respondents' theory can be proved on a classwide basis. In *Falcon,* we held that one named plaintiff's experience of discrimination was insufficient to infer that "discriminatory treatment is typical of [the employer's employment] practices." 457 U.S., at 158, 102 S.Ct. 2364. A similar failure of inference arises here. As Judge Ikuta observed in her dissent, "[i]nformation about disparities at the regional and national level does not establish the existence of disparities at individual stores, let alone raise the inference that a company-wide policy of discrimination is implemented by discretionary decisions at the store and district level." 603 F.3d, at 637. A regional pay disparity, for example, may be attributable to only a small set of Wal-Mart stores, and cannot by itself establish the uniform, store-by-store disparity upon which the plaintiffs' theory of commonality depends.

There is another, more fundamental, respect in which respondents' statistical proof fails. Even if it established (as it does not) a pay or promotion pattern that differs from the nationwide figures or the regional figures in *all* of Wal-Mart's 3,400 stores, that would still not demonstrate that commonality of issue exists. Some managers will claim that the availability of women, or qualified women, or interested women, in their stores' area does not mirror the national or regional statistics. And almost all of them will claim to have been applying some sex-neutral, performance-based criteria—whose nature and effects will differ from store to store. In the landmark case of ours which held that giving discretion to lower-level supervisors can be the basis of Title VII liability under a disparate-impact theory, the plurality opinion *conditioned* that holding on the corollary that merely proving that the discretionary system has produced a racial or sexual disparity *is not enough.* "[T]he plaintiff must begin by identifying the specific employment practice that is challenged." *Watson,* 487 U.S., at 994, 108 S.Ct. 2777. That is all the more necessary when a class of plaintiffs is sought to be certified. Other than the bare existence of delegated discretion, respondents have identified no "specific employment practice"—much less one that ties all their 1.5 million claims together. Merely showing that Wal-Mart's policy of discretion has produced an overall sex-based disparity does not suffice.

Respondents' anecdotal evidence suffers from the same defects, and in addition is too weak to raise any inference that all the individual, discretionary personnel decisions are discriminatory. In *Teamsters v. United States,* 431 U.S. 324, 97 S.Ct. 1843, 52 L.Ed.2d 396 (1977), in addition to substantial statistical evidence of company-wide discrimination, the Government (as plaintiff) produced about 40 specific accounts of racial discrimination from particular individuals. See *id.,* at 338, 97 S.Ct. 1843. That number was significant because the company involved had only 6,472 employees, of whom 571 were minorities, *id.,* at 337, 97 S.Ct. 1843, and the class itself consisted of around 334 persons, *United States v. T.I.M.E.-D.C., Inc.,* 517 F.2d 299, 308 (C.A.5 1975), overruled on other grounds, *Teamsters, supra.* The 40 anecdotes thus represented roughly one account for every eight members of the class. Moreover, the Court of Appeals noted that the anecdotes came from individuals "spread throughout" the company who "for the most part" worked at the company's operational centers that employed the largest numbers of the class members. 517 F.2d, at 315, and n. 30. Here, by contrast, respondents filed some 120 affidavits reporting experiences of discrimination—about 1 for every 12,500 class members—relating to only some 235 out of Wal-Mart's 3,400 stores. 603 F.3d, at 634 (Ikuta, J., dissenting). More than half of these reports are concentrated in only six States (Alabama, California, Florida, Missouri, Texas, and Wisconsin); half of all States have only one or two anecdotes; and 14 States have no anecdotes about Wal-Mart's operations at all. *Id.,* at 634–635, and n. 10. Even if every single one of these accounts is true, that would not demonstrate that the entire company "operate[s] under a general policy of discrimination," *Falcon, supra,* at 159, n. 15, 102 S.Ct. 2364, which is what respondents must show to certify a companywide class.

The dissent misunderstands the nature of the foregoing analysis. It criticizes our focus on the dissimilarities between the putative class members on the ground that we have "blend[ed]" Rule 23(a)(2)'s commonality requirement with Rule 23(b)(3)'s inquiry into whether common questions "predominate" over individual ones. See *post,* at 2550–2552 (GINSBURG, J., concurring in part and dissenting in part). That is not so. We quite agree that for purposes of Rule 23(a)(2) " '[e]ven a single [common] question' " will do, *post,* at 2556, n.9 (quoting Nagareda, The Preexistence Principle and the Structure of the Class Action, 103 Colum.L.Rev. 149, 176, n.110 (2003)). We consider dissimilarities not in order to determine (as Rule 23(b)(3) requires) whether common questions *predominate,* but in order to determine (as Rule 23(a)(2) requires) whether there *is* "[e]ven a single [common] question." And there is not here. Because respondents provide no convincing proof of a companywide discriminatory pay and promotion policy, we have concluded that they have not established the existence of any common question.

* * *

III

We also conclude that respondents' claims for backpay were improperly certified under Federal Rule of Civil Procedure 23(b)(2). Our opinion in *Ticor Title Ins. Co. v. Brown,* 511 U.S. 117, 121, 114 S.Ct. 1359, 128 L.Ed.2d 33 (1994) *(per curiam)* expressed serious doubt about whether claims for monetary relief may be certified under that provision. We now hold that they may not, at least where (as here) the monetary relief is not incidental to the injunctive or declaratory relief. [The remaining discussion of the proper basis for certification has been deleted.]

* * *

C

* * *

Contrary to the Ninth Circuit's view, Wal-Mart is entitled to individualized determinations of each employee's eligibility for backpay. Title VII includes a detailed remedial scheme. If a plaintiff prevails in showing that an employer has discriminated against him in violation of the statute, the court "may enjoin the respondent from engaging in such unlawful employment practice, and order such affirmative action as may be appropriate, [including] reinstatement or hiring of employees, with or without backpay . . . or any other equitable relief as the court deems appropriate." § 2000e–5(g)(1). But if the employer can show that it took an adverse employment action against an employee for any reason other than discrimination, the court cannot order the "hiring, reinstatement, or promotion of an individual as an employee, or the payment to him of any backpay." § 2000e–5(g)(2)(A).

We have established a procedure for trying pattern-or-practice cases that gives effect to these statutory requirements. When the plaintiff seeks individual relief such as reinstatement or backpay after establishing a pattern or practice of discrimination, "a district court must usually conduct additional proceedings . . . to determine the scope of individual relief." *Teamsters,* 431 U.S., at 361, 97 S.Ct. 1843. At this phase, the burden of proof will shift to the company, but it will have the right to raise any individual affirmative defenses it may have, and to "demonstrate that the individual applicant was denied an employment opportunity for lawful reasons." *Id.*, at 362, 97 S.Ct. 1843.

The Court of Appeals believed that it was possible to replace such proceedings with Trial by Formula. A sample set of the class members would be selected, as to whom liability for sex discrimination and the backpay owing as a result would be determined in depositions supervised by a master. The percentage of claims determined to be valid would then be applied to the entire remaining class, and the number of (presumptively) valid claims thus derived would be multiplied by the average backpay award in the sample set to arrive at the entire class recovery—without further individualized proceedings. We disapprove that novel project. Because the Rules Enabling Act forbids interpreting Rule 23 to "abridge, enlarge or modify any substantive right," 28 U.S.C. § 2072(b)a class cannot be certified on the premise that Wal-Mart will not be entitled to litigate its statutory defenses to individual claims. And because the necessity of that litigation will prevent backpay from being "incidental" to the classwide injunction, respondents' class could not be certified even assuming, *arguendo,* that "incidental" monetary relief can be awarded to a 23(b)(2) class. * * *

The judgment of the Court of Appeals is *Reversed.*

JUSTICE GINSBURG, with whom JUSTICE BREYER, JUSTICE SOTOMAYOR, and JUSTICE KAGAN join, concurring in part and dissenting in part.

The class in this case, I agree with the Court, should not have been certified under Federal Rule of Civil Procedure 23(b)(2). The plaintiffs, alleging discrimination in violation of Title VII, 42 U.S.C. § 2000e *et seq.*, seek monetary relief that is not merely incidental to any injunctive or declaratory relief that might be available. A putative class of this type may be certifiable under Rule 23(b)(3), if the plaintiffs show that common class questions "predominate" over issues affecting individuals—*e.g.*, qualification for, and the amount of, backpay or compensatory damages—and that a class action is "superior" to other modes of adjudication.

Whether the class the plaintiffs describe meets the specific requirements of Rule 23(b)(3) is not before the Court, and I would reserve that matter for consideration and decision on remand. The Court, however, disqualifies the class at the starting gate, holding that the plaintiffs cannot cross the "commonality" line set by Rule 23(a)(2). In so ruling, the Court imports into the Rule 23(a) determination concerns properly addressed in a Rule 23(b)(3) assessment.

I

A

Rule 23(a)(2) establishes a preliminary requirement for maintaining a class action: "[T]here are questions of law or fact common to the class." The Rule "does not require that all questions of law or fact raised in the litigation be common," 1 H. Newberg & A. Conte, Newberg on Class Actions § 3.10, pp. 3–48 to 3–49 (3d ed.1992); indeed, "[e]ven a single question of law or fact common to the members of the class will satisfy the commonality requirement," Nagareda, The Preexistence Principle and the Structure of the Class Action, 103 Colum. L.Rev. 149, 176, n. 110 (2003).

A "question" is ordinarily understood to be "[a] subject or point open to controversy." American Heritage Dictionary 1483 (3d ed.1992). See also Black's Law Dictionary 1366 (9th ed.2009) (defining "question of fact" as "[a] disputed issue to be resolved . . . [at] trial" and "question of law" as "[a]n issue to be decided by the judge"). Thus, a "question" "common to the class" must be a dispute, either of fact or of law, the resolution of which will advance the determination of the class members' claims.

B

The District Court, recognizing that "one significant issue common to the class may be sufficient to warrant certification," 222 F.R.D. 137, 145 (N.D.Cal.2004), found that the plaintiffs easily met that test. Absent an error of law or an abuse of discretion, an appellate tribunal has no warrant to upset the District Court's finding of commonality. See *Califano v. Yamasaki,* 442 U.S. 682, 703, 99 S.Ct. 2545, 61 L.Ed.2d 176 (1979).

The District Court certified a class of "[a]ll women employed at any Wal-Mart domestic retail store at any time since December 26, 1998." The named plaintiffs, led by Betty Dukes, propose to litigate, on behalf of the class, allegations that Wal-Mart discriminates on the basis of gender in pay and promotions. They allege that the company "[r]eli[es] on gender stereotypes in making employment decisions such as . . . promotion[s] [and] pay." Wal-Mart permits those prejudices to infect personnel decisions, the plaintiffs contend, by leaving pay and promotions in the hands of "a nearly all male managerial workforce" using "arbitrary and subjective criteria." Further alleged barriers to the advancement of female employees include the company's requirement, "as a condition of promotion to management jobs, that employees be willing to relocate." Absent instruction otherwise, there is a risk that managers will act on the familiar assumption that women, because of their services to husband and children, are less mobile than men. See Dept. of Labor, Federal Glass Ceiling Commission, Good for Business: Making Full Use of the Nation's Human Capital 151 (1995).

Women fill 70 percent of the hourly jobs in the retailer's stores but make up only "33 percent of management employees." 222 F.R.D., at 146. "[T]he higher one looks in the organization the lower the percentage of women." *Id.*, at 155. The plaintiffs' "largely uncontested descriptive statistics" also show that women working in the company's stores "are paid less than men in every region" and "that the salary gap widens over time even for men and women hired into the same jobs at the same time." *Ibid.*; cf. *Ledbetter v. Goodyear Tire & Rubber Co.*, 550 U.S. 618, 643, 127 S.Ct. 2162, 167 L.Ed.2d 982 (2007) (GINSBURG, J., dissenting).

The District Court identified "systems for . . . promoting in-store employees" that were "sufficiently similar across regions and stores" to conclude that "the manner in which these systems affect the class raises issues that are common to all class members." 222 F.R.D., at 149. The selection of employees for promotion to in-store management "is fairly characterized as a 'tap on the shoulder' process," in which managers have discretion about whose shoulders to tap. *Id.*, at 148. Vacancies are not regularly posted; from among those employees satisfying minimum qualifications, managers choose whom to promote on the basis of their own subjective impressions. *Ibid.*

Wal-Mart's compensation policies also operate uniformly across stores, the District Court found. The retailer leaves open a $2 band for every position's hourly pay rate. Wal-Mart provides no standards or criteria for setting wages within that band, and thus does nothing to counter unconscious bias on the part of supervisors. See *id.*, at 146–147.

Wal-Mart's supervisors do not make their discretionary decisions in a vacuum. The District Court reviewed means Wal-Mart used to maintain a "carefully constructed . . . corporate culture," such as frequent meetings to reinforce the common way of thinking, regular transfers of managers between stores to ensure uniformity throughout the company, monitoring of stores "on a close and constant basis," and "Wal-Mart TV," "broadcas[t] . . . into all stores." *Id.*, at 151–153.

The plaintiffs' evidence, including class members' tales of their own experiences, suggests that gender bias suffused Wal-Mart's company culture. Among illustrations, senior management often refer to female associates as "little Janie Qs." Plaintiffs' Motion for Class Certification in No. 3:01–cv–02252–CRB (ND Cal.), Doc. 99, p. 13. One manager told an employee that "[m]en are here to make a career and women aren't." 222 F.R.D., at 166. A committee of female Wal-Mart executives concluded that "[s]tereotypes limit the opportunities offered to women." Plaintiffs' Motion for Class Certification in No. 3:01–cv–02252–CRB (ND Cal.), Doc. 99, at 16.

Finally, the plaintiffs presented an expert's appraisal to show that the pay and promotions disparities at Wal-Mart "can be explained only by gender discrimination and not by . . . neutral variables." 222 F.R.D., at 155. Using regression analyses, their expert, Richard Drogin, controlled for factors including, *inter alia,* job performance, length of time with the company, and the store where an employee worked. *Id.*, at 159. The results, the District Court found, were sufficient to raise an "inference of discrimination." *Id.*, at 155–160.

C

The District Court's identification of a common question, whether Wal-Mart's pay and promotions policies gave rise to unlawful discrimination, was hardly infirm. The practice of delegating to supervisors large discretion to make personnel decisions, uncontrolled by formal standards, has long been known to have the potential to produce disparate effects. Managers, like all humankind, may be prey to biases of which they are unaware. The risk of discrimination is heightened when those managers are predominantly of one sex, and are steeped in a corporate culture that perpetuates gender stereotypes. * * *

We have held that "discretionary employment practices" can give rise to Title VII claims, not only when such practices are motivated by discriminatory intent but also when they produce discriminatory results. See *Watson v. Fort Worth Bank & Trust,* 487 U.S. 977, 988, 991, 108 S.Ct. 2777, 101 L.Ed.2d 827 (1988). In *Watson,* as here, an employer had given its managers large authority over promotions. An employee sued the bank under Title VII, alleging that the "discretionary promotion system" caused a discriminatory effect based on race. 487 U.S., at 984, 108 S.Ct. 2777 (internal quotation marks omitted). Four different supervisors had declined, on separate occasions, to promote the employee. *Id.,* at 982, 108 S.Ct. 2777. Their reasons were subjective and unknown. The employer, we noted "had not developed precise and formal criteria for evaluating candidates"; "[i]t relied instead on the subjective judgment of supervisors." *Ibid.*

Aware of "the problem of subconscious stereotypes and prejudices," we held that the employer's "undisciplined system of subjective decisionmaking" was an "employment practic[e]" that "may be analyzed under the disparate impact approach." *Id.*, at 990–991, 108 S.Ct. 2777. * * *

The plaintiffs' allegations state claims of gender discrimination in the form of biased decisionmaking in both pay and promotions. The evidence reviewed by the District Court adequately demonstrated that resolving those claims would necessitate examination of particular policies and practices alleged to affect, adversely and globally, women employed at Wal-Mart's stores. Rule 23(a)(2), setting a necessary but not a sufficient criterion for class-action certification, demands nothing further.

II

A

The Court gives no credence to the key dispute common to the class: whether Wal-Mart's discretionary pay and promotion policies are discriminatory. "What matters," the Court asserts, "is not the raising of common 'questions,'" but whether there are "[d]issimilarities within the proposed class" that "have the potential to impede the generation of common answers." * * *

The Court's emphasis on differences between class members mimics the Rule 23(b)(3) inquiry into whether common questions "predominate" over individual issues. And by asking whether the individual differences "impede" common adjudication, the Court duplicates 23(b)(3)'s question whether "a class action is superior" to other modes of adjudication. * * * If courts must conduct a "dissimilarities" analysis at the Rule 23(a)(2) stage, no mission remains for Rule 23(b)(3). * * *

The "dissimilarities" approach leads the Court to train its attention on what distinguishes individual class members, rather than on what unites them. Given the lack of standards for pay and promotions, the majority says, "demonstrating the invalidity of one manager's use of discretion will do nothing to demonstrate the invalidity of another's." Wal-Mart's delegation of discretion over pay and promotions is a policy uniform throughout all stores. The very nature of discretion is that people will exercise it in various ways. A system of delegated discretion, *Watson* held, is a practice actionable under Title VII when it produces discriminatory outcomes. 487 U.S., at 990–991, 108 S.Ct. 2777. A finding that Wal-Mart's pay and promotions practices in fact violate the law would be the first step in the usual order of proof for plaintiffs seeking individual remedies for company-wide discrimination. *Teamsters v. United States,* 431 U.S. 324, 359, 97 S.Ct. 1843, 52 L.Ed.2d 396 (1977). That each individual employee's unique circumstances will ultimately determine whether she is entitled to backpay or damages, § 2000e–5(g)(2)(A) (barring backpay if a plaintiff "was refused . . . advancement . . . for any reason other than discrimination"), should not factor into the Rule 23(a)(2) determination. * * *

The Court errs in importing a "dissimilarities" notion suited to Rule 23(b)(3) into the Rule 23(a) commonality inquiry. I therefore cannot join Part II of the Court's opinion.

NOTES AND QUESTIONS

1. Although the *Wal-Mart* case was decided on a Motion relating to class certification, the Court also discussed the substance of a pattern and practice case. Based on the case, what do you think the Court would require to establish a pattern and practice claim? Do you think the Court's view of

the merits of the underlying claims influenced its decision? If so, is there something in the opinion you can point to that reflects the Court's views?

2. The Supreme Court's decision was expected to make it more difficult to certify class actions but, the early evidence, is not so clear on that point. The Fourth Circuit, for example, reversed a district court's decision denying leave to amend a class action complaint based on the lower court's "erroneous" reading of the *Wal-Mart* decision. *See Scott v. Family Dollar Stores*, 733 F.3d 105 (4th Cir.2014), *cert. denied*, 134 S. Ct. 2871 (2014). A recent study found that although class action filings seem to have decreased, and perhaps substantially, there has not been as significant a shift in class certification decisions, and it appears that courts are certifying cases at about the same rate as they had before the *Wal-Mart* decision. *See* Michael Selmi & Sylvia Tsakos, *Employment Discrimination Class Actions After Wal-Mart v. Dukes*, 48 Akron L. Rev. 803 (2015). It does seem that nationwide class actions, like that brought in *Dukes*, are now more difficult to certify and attorneys are likely to focus on more regional lawsuits. Indeed, the attorneys who represented the plaintiffs in the original litigation have filed a series of smaller regional cases, though to date the class allegations raised in most of the cases have been dismissed. *See Dukes v. Wal-Mart Stores, Inc.*, 964 F. Supp. 2d 1115 (N.D. Cal. 2013) (smaller class dismissed); *Love v. Wal-Mart Stores*, 2013 U.S. Dist. LEXIS 143234 (S.D. Fla. Sept. 23, 2013). The Sixth Circuit, however, recently held that plaintiffs' claims were not time-barred and thus reversed a District Court's dismissal of those claims. *See Phipps v. Wal-Mart Stores*, 792 F.3d 637 (6th Cir.2015).

3. In its decision, the Supreme Court criticized the plaintiff's use of "social framework" evidence. This kind of evidence has been controversial but it has also played an important role in establishing patterns of discrimination that may not be tied to a single actor or even a group of individual actors. In its most basic sense, social framework evidence provides a framework to explain how systemic discrimination permeates institutional organizations and workplaces. For example, in the *Wal-Mart* case, the evidence focused primarily on how subjective employment practices lead to discriminatory decisions that are infused with gender stereotypes, such as the notion that women are traditionally secondary earners or that their childcare responsibilities will interfere with their job performance. The difficulty with applying the evidence to a particular workplace is that the framework itself is generic in nature—it explains research findings but does not involve any analysis or investigation of a particular workplace, other than to say that a workplace, like Wal-Mart's, has the characteristics that can lead to discrimination. This led to the admission by the plaintiff's expert, noted by Justice Scalia, that he was unable to say more than that Wal-Mart's system was "vulnerable" to discrimination and was unable to quantify just how vulnerable it might have been. For a discussion of social framework evidence and its limitations see Melissa Hart & Paul M. Secunda, *A Matter of Social Framework Evidence in Employment Discrimination Class Actions*, 78 Fordham L. Rev. 37 (2009) (discussing importance of social framework

evidence to establishing systemic discrimination) and Gregory Mitchell, Laurens Walker & John Monahan, *Beyond Context: Social Facts as Case-Specific Evidence*, 60 Emory L.J. 1109 (2011) (criticizing introduction of social framework evidence). The Supreme Court's criticism of the social framework evidence offered by the plaintiffs is likely to restrict this kind of evidence in future cases. How else might a plaintiff go about establishing discrimination based on subjective practices across an organization? What about in the case of Wal-Mart, what do you think might have helped persuade the Court that there were common questions to link the class claims?

4. The *Wal-Mart* case was the first class action gender discrimination case to be heard by a Supreme Court that included three female Justices, all of whom were in dissent. What significance might one draw from this fact?

CHAPTER 4

DISPARATE IMPACT

■ ■ ■

A. INTRODUCTION

The courts developed the disparate impact theory during the first decade of enforcement of Title VII. See Alfred W. Blumrosen, *Strangers in Paradise:* Griggs v. Duke Power Co. *and The Concept of Employment Discrimination*, 71 Mich.L.Rev. 59 (1972). The term "disparate impact" refers to "employment practices that are facially neutral in their treatment of different groups but that in fact fall more harshly on one group than another and cannot be justified by business necessity." Teamsters v. United States, 431 U.S. 324, 335 n.15, 97 S.Ct. 1843, 1854 n.15, 52 L.Ed.2d 396 (1977). The theory of disparate impact is sometimes called "adverse impact," "disparate effect," or "unintentional discrimination," with the core element that a disparate impact claim does not require proof of an intent to discriminate. Initially, disparate impact theory was a rather straightforward yet important doctrinal development in employment discrimination law, but over the years it has been transformed into a complex, controversial, and sometimes confusing body of law.

The materials in this chapter are divided into the following three sections: The first section, Section B, traces the evolution of the disparate impact theory from the seminal decision in *Griggs v. Duke Power Co.*, 401 U.S. 424, 91 S.Ct. 849, 28 L.Ed.2d 158 (1971), to the Supreme Court's decision in *Wards Cove Packing Co. v. Atonio*, 490 U.S. 642, 109 S.Ct. 2115, 104 L.Ed.2d 733 (1989), which was seen as a significant reconsideration of the theory. Following the Supreme Court's decision in *Wards Cove*, Congress passed the Civil Rights Act of 1991 to codify and alter the components of the theory. Next, Section C explores the disparate impact theory after the Civil Rights Act of 1991. Finally, Section D includes the Supreme Court's most recent disparate impact case, which involved voluntary efforts to reduce or remedy the disparate impact of a testing program.

As you study the materials in this chapter, keep in mind the questions on the meaning of equality that are raised in Chapter 1. Consider also the following: (1) What conception of equality is embraced by the majority and dissenting opinions in the principal cases in this chapter? (2) Does *Griggs* provide a coherent theoretical underpinning for the disparate impact theory? If not, then do *Watson* and *Wards Cove*? Recall also the discussion of statistical proof of discrimination in section D of Chapter 3, as claims under the disparate impact theory generally rely on the same methods of statistical proof, with one exception noted below.

B. THE THEORY OF DISPARATE IMPACT

1. OBJECTIVE CRITERIA

The disparate impact theory was first articulated in Title VII class action cases brought by black job applicants and employees who alleged that their employment opportunities were limited by the pen and paper tests and educational requirements used by employers in hiring and promotion decisions. Both of these practices were challenged in *Griggs v. Duke Power Co.*, reproduced below. As you read the *Griggs* case, think about the following questions: Why do employers use objective tests? What are they trying to learn from the test? What is the Court's rationale for the standards it establishes with the disparate impact theory? As you read the case, keep in mind that *Griggs* predates *McDonnell Douglas* and was, in fact, the Court's second decision interpreting Title VII.

GRIGGS V. DUKE POWER CO.

Supreme Court of the United States, 1971.
401 U.S. 424, 91 S.Ct. 849, 28 L.Ed.2d 158.

CHIEF JUSTICE BURGER delivered the opinion of the Court.

We granted the writ in this case to resolve the question whether an employer is prohibited by the Civil Rights Act of 1964, Title VII, from requiring a high school education or passing of a standardized general intelligence test as a condition of employment in or transfer to jobs when (a) neither standard is shown to be significantly related to successful job performance, (b) both requirements operate to disqualify Negroes at a substantially higher rate than white applicants, and (c) the jobs in question formerly had been filled only by white employees as part of a longstanding practice of giving preference to whites.

* * * All the petitioners are employed at the Company's Dan River Steam Station, a power generating facility located at Draper, North Carolina. At the time this action was instituted, the Company had 95 employees at the Dan River Station, 14 of whom were Negroes; 13 of these are petitioners here.

The District Court found that prior to July 2, 1965, the effective date of the Civil Rights Act of 1964, the Company openly discriminated on the basis of race in the hiring and assigning of employees at its Dan River plant. The plant was organized into five operating departments: (1) Labor, (2) Coal Handling, (3) Operations, (4) Maintenance, and (5)

Laboratory and Test. Negroes were employed only in the Labor Department where the highest paying jobs paid less than the lowest paying jobs in the other four "operating" departments in which only whites were employed. Promotions were normally made within each department on the basis of job seniority. Transferees into a department usually began in the lowest position.

In 1955 the Company instituted a policy of requiring a high school education for initial assignment to any department except Labor, and for transfer from the Coal Handling to any "inside" department (Operations, Maintenance, or Laboratory). When the Company abandoned its policy of restricting Negroes to the Labor Department in 1965, completion of high school also was made a prerequisite to transfer from Labor to any other department. From the time the high school requirement was instituted to the time of trial, however, white employees hired before the time of the high school education requirement continued to perform satisfactorily and achieve promotions in the "operating" departments. Findings on this score are not challenged.

The Company added a further requirement for new employees on July 2, 1965, the date on which Title VII became effective. To qualify for placement in any but the Labor Department it became necessary to register satisfactory scores on two professionally prepared aptitude tests, as well as to have a high school education. Completion of high school alone continued to render employees eligible for transfer to the four desirable departments from which Negroes had been excluded if the incumbent had been employed prior to the time of the new requirement. In September 1965 the Company began to permit incumbent employees who lacked a high school education to qualify for transfer from Labor or Coal Handling to an "inside" job by passing two tests—the Wonderlic Personnel Test, which purports to measure general intelligence, and the Bennett Mechanical Comprehension Test. Neither was directed or intended to measure the ability to learn to perform a particular job or category of jobs. The requisite scores used for both initial hiring and transfer approximated the national median for high school graduates.[3]

The District Court had found that while the Company previously followed a policy of overt racial discrimination in a period prior to the Act, such conduct had ceased. The District Court also concluded that Title VII was intended to be prospective only and, consequently, the impact of prior inequities was beyond the reach of corrective action authorized by the Act.

The Court of Appeals was confronted with a question of first impression, as are we, concerning the meaning of Title VII. After careful

[3] The test standards are thus more stringent than the high school requirement, since they would screen out approximately half of all high school graduates.

analysis a majority of that court concluded that a subjective test of the employer's intent should govern, particularly in a close case, and that in this case there was no showing of a discriminatory purpose in the adoption of the diploma and test requirements. On this basis, the Court of Appeals concluded there was no violation of the Act.

The Court of Appeals reversed the District Court in part * * * . The Court of Appeals noted, however, that the District Court was correct in its conclusion that there was no showing of a racial purpose or invidious intent in the adoption of the high school diploma requirement or general intelligence test and that these standards had been applied fairly to whites and Negroes alike. It held that, in the absence of a discriminatory purpose, use of such requirements was permitted by the Act. In so doing, the Court of Appeals rejected the claim that because these two requirements operated to render ineligible a markedly disproportionate number of Negroes, they were unlawful under Title VII unless shown to be job related. We granted the writ on these claims.

The objective of Congress in the enactment of Title VII is plain from the language of the statute. It was to achieve equality of employment opportunities and remove barriers that have operated in the past to favor an identifiable group of white employees over other employees. Under the Act, practices, procedures, or tests neutral on their face, and even neutral in terms of intent, cannot be maintained if they operate to "freeze" the status quo of prior discriminatory employment practices.

The Court of Appeals' opinion, and the partial dissent, agreed that, on the record in the present case, "whites register far better on the Company's alternative requirements" than Negroes.[6] This consequence would appear to be directly traceable to race. Basic intelligence must have the means of articulation to manifest itself fairly in a testing process. Because they are Negroes, petitioners have long received inferior education in segregated schools and this Court expressly recognized these differences in *Gaston County v. United States*, 395 U.S. 285, 89 S.Ct. 1720, 23 L.Ed.2d 309 (1969). There, because of the inferior education received by Negroes in North Carolina, this Court barred the institution of a literacy test for voter registration on the ground that the test would abridge the right to vote indirectly on account of race. Congress did not intend by Title VII, however, to guarantee a job to every person regardless of qualifications. In short, the Act does not command that any person be hired simply because he was formerly the subject of

[6] In North Carolina, 1960 census statistics show that, while 34% of white males had completed high school, only 12% of Negro males had done so. U.S. Bureau of the Census, U.S. Census of Population: 1960, Vol. 1 * * * .

Similarly, with respect to standardized tests, the EEOC in one case found that use of a battery of tests, including the Wonderlic and Bennett tests used by the Company in the instant case, resulted in 58% of whites passing the tests, as compared with only 6% of the blacks.

discrimination, or because he is a member of a minority group. Discriminatory preference for any group, minority or majority, is precisely and only what Congress has proscribed. What is required by Congress is the removal of artificial, arbitrary, and unnecessary barriers to employment when the barriers operate invidiously to discriminate on the basis of racial or other impermissible classification.

Congress has now provided that tests or criteria for employment or promotion may not provide equality of opportunity merely in the sense of the fabled offer of milk to the stork and the fox. On the contrary, Congress has now required that the posture and condition of the job-seeker be taken into account. It has—to resort again to the fable—provided that the vessel in which the milk is proffered be one all seekers can use. The Act proscribes not only overt discrimination but also practices that are fair in form, but discriminatory in operation. The touchstone is business necessity. If an employment practice which operates to exclude Negroes cannot be shown to be related to job performance, the practice is prohibited.

On the record before us, neither the high school completion requirement nor the general intelligence test is shown to bear a demonstrable relationship to successful performance of the jobs for which it was used. Both were adopted, as the Court of Appeals noted, without meaningful study of their relationship to job-performance ability. Rather, a vice president of the Company testified, the requirements were instituted on the Company's judgment that they generally would improve the overall quality of the work force.

The evidence, however, shows that employees who have not completed high school or taken the tests have continued to perform satisfactorily and make progress in departments for which the high school and test criteria are now used.[7] The promotion record of present employees who would not be able to meet the new criteria thus suggests the possibility that the requirements may not be needed even for the limited purpose of preserving the avowed policy of advancement within the Company. In the context of this case, it is unnecessary to reach the question whether testing requirements that take into account capability for the next succeeding position or related future promotion might be utilized upon a showing that such long-range requirements fulfill a genuine business need. In the present case the Company has made no such showing.

The Court of Appeals held that the Company had adopted the diploma and test requirements without any "intention to discriminate

---

[7] For example, between July 2, 1965, and November 14, 1966, the percentage of white employees who were promoted but who were not high school graduates was nearly identical to the percentage of nongraduates in the entire white work force.

against Negro employees." We do not suggest that either the District Court or the Court of Appeals erred in examining the employer's intent; but good intent or absence of discriminatory intent does not redeem employment procedures or testing mechanisms that operate as "built-in headwinds" for minority groups and are unrelated to measuring job capability.

The Company's lack of discriminatory intent is suggested by special efforts to help the undereducated employees through Company financing of two-thirds the cost of tuition for high school training. But Congress directed the thrust of the Act to the *consequences* of employment practices, not simply the motivation. More than that, Congress has placed on the employer the burden of showing that any given requirement must have a manifest relationship to the employment in question.

The facts of this case demonstrate the inadequacy of broad and general testing devices as well as the infirmity of using diplomas or degrees as fixed measures of capability. History is filled with examples of men and women who rendered highly effective performance without the conventional badges of accomplishment in terms of certificates, diplomas, or degrees. Diplomas and tests are useful servants, but Congress has mandated the commonsense proposition that they are not to become masters of reality.

The Company contends that its general intelligence tests are specifically permitted by § 703(h) of the Act. That section authorizes the use of "any professionally developed ability test" that is not "designed, intended *or used* to discriminate because of race * * *." (Emphasis added.)

The Equal Employment Opportunity Commission, having enforcement responsibility, has issued guidelines interpreting § 703(h) to permit only the use of job-related tests.[9] The administrative interpretation of the Act by the enforcing agency is entitled to great deference. Since the Act and its legislative history support the Commission's construction, this affords good reason to treat the guidelines as expressing the will of Congress.

Section 703(h) was not contained in the House version of the Civil Rights Act but was added in the Senate during extended debate. For a period, debate revolved around claims that the bill as proposed would

---

[9] EEOC Guidelines on Employment Testing Procedures, issued August 24, 1966, provide[d]:

> The Commission accordingly interprets "professionally developed ability test" to mean a test which fairly measures the knowledge or skills required by the particular job or class of jobs which the applicant seeks, or which fairly affords the employer a chance to measure the applicant's ability to perform a particular job or class of jobs. The fact that a test was prepared by an individual or organization claiming expertise in test preparation does not, without more, justify its use within the meaning of Title VII. * * *

prohibit all testing and force employers to hire unqualified persons simply because they were part of a group formerly subject to job discrimination. Proponents of Title VII sought throughout the debate to assure the critics that the Act would have no effect on job-related tests. Senators Case of New Jersey and Clark of Pennsylvania, comanagers of the bill on the Senate floor, issued a memorandum explaining that the proposed Title VII "expressly protects the employer's right to insist that any prospective applicant, Negro or white, *must meet the applicable job qualifications*. Indeed, the very purpose of Title VII is to promote hiring on the basis of job qualifications, rather than on the basis of race or color." 110 Cong.Rec. 7247. (Emphasis added.) Despite these assurances, Senator Tower of Texas introduced an amendment authorizing "professionally developed ability tests." Proponents of Title VII opposed the amendment because, as written, it would permit an employer to give any test, "whether it was a good test or not, so long as it was professionally designed. Discrimination could actually exist under the guise of compliance with the statute." 110 Cong. Rec. 13504 (remarks of Sen. Case).

The amendment was defeated and two days later Senator Tower offered a substitute amendment which was adopted verbatim and is now the testing provision of § 703(h). Speaking for the supporters of Title VII, Senator Humphrey, who had vigorously opposed the first amendment, endorsed the substitute amendment, stating: "Senators on both sides of the aisle who were deeply interested in title VII have examined the text of this amendment and have found it to be in accord with the intent and purpose of that title." 110 Cong.Rec. 13724. The amendment was then adopted. From the sum of the legislative history relevant in this case, the conclusion is inescapable that the EEOC's construction of § 703(h) to require that employment tests be job related comports with congressional intent.

Nothing in the Act precludes the use of testing or measuring procedures; obviously they are useful. What Congress has forbidden is giving these devices and mechanisms controlling force unless they are demonstrably a reasonable measure of job performance. Congress has not commanded that the less qualified be preferred over the better qualified simply because of minority origins. Far from disparaging job qualifications as such, Congress has made such qualifications the controlling factor, so that race, religion, nationality, and sex become irrelevant. What Congress has commanded is that any tests used must measure the person for the job and not the person in the abstract.

The judgment of the Court of Appeals is, as to that portion of the judgment appealed from, reversed.

JUSTICE BRENNAN took no part in the consideration or decision of this case.

NOTES AND QUESTIONS

1. *Griggs* was the result of a litigation campaign that was patterned, in substantial part, on the litigation strategy that led to *Brown v. Board of Education,* 347 U.S. 483, 74 S.Ct. 686, 98 L.Ed.873 (1954). The strategy involved the filing of large numbers of cases under Title VII and § 1981, a monitoring system—to identify cases, issues, and industries—that suggested a systematic law reform approach, and the use of class actions. *See* Jack Greenberg, Crusaders in the Courts: How a Dedicated Band of Lawyers Fought for the Civil Rights Revolution 412–29 (1994); Robert Belton, *A Comparative Review of Public and Private Enforcement of Title VII of the Civil Rights Act of 1964,* 31 Vand.L.Rev. 905 (1978). *Brown* overturned the "separate but equal" doctrine that had legitimated racial segregation of public schools, and the decision profoundly altered equal protection jurisprudence. The rationale of *Griggs*, too, had a similarly significant impact on civil rights jurisprudence. For recent histories of the development of the doctrine see Robert Belton and Stephen L. Wasby, The Crusade for Equality in the Workplace: The *Griggs v. Duke Power* Story (2014) (Robert Belton was the lead attorney for the plaintiffs in *Griggs*) and Susan D. Carle, *A Social Movement History of Title VII Disparate Impact Analysis*, 63 Fla. L. Rev. 251 (2011) (emphasizing the deliberate and prolonged development of the theory by activists).

2. The *Griggs* disparate impact theory holds that a facially neutral employment practice that has a substantial adverse effect on the employment opportunities of members of a protected class constitutes unlawful employment discrimination unless justified by business necessity. How would you describe the Court's rationale for adopting the theory? Why was the theory considered so important and necessary at the time? Do you believe the theory retains its importance today?

3. The issue that has come to be most closely associated with the *Griggs* case is whether discriminatory intent is an element that is required in all employment discrimination claims brought under Title VII. This was an issue that neither the statute nor the legislative history dealt with definitively. Contrast the language of § 703(a)(2) with § 703(a)(1). The term "discriminate" is used in § 703(a) (1), but not in § 703(a)(2). The Supreme Court did not articulate its reliance on the language of § 703(a)(2) to support the disparate impact theory until eleven years after *Griggs* in *Connecticut v. Teal,* 457 U.S. 440, 102 S.Ct. 2525, 73 L.Ed.2d 130 (1982):

> [Section 703(a)(2)] speaks, not in terms of jobs and promotions, but in terms of *limitations* and *classifications* that would deprive any individual of employment *opportunities*. A disparate impact claim reflects the language of § 703(a)(2) and Congress' basic objectives in enacting that statute: "to achieve equality of employment *opportunities* and remove barriers that have operated in the past to favor an identifiable group of white employees over other employees." When an employer uses a nonjob-related barrier in

> order to deny a minority or woman applicant employment or promotion, and that barrier has a significant adverse effect on minorities or women, then the applicant has been deprived of an employment *opportunity* "because of * * * race, color, religion, sex, or national origin."

Id. at 448, 102 S.Ct. at 2531 (original emphasis) (quoting *Griggs*, 401 U.S. at 429–30, 91 S.Ct. at 852–53).

As pointed out in Chapter 3, an oft-quoted interpretive memorandum entered into the Congressional Record by Senators Case and Clark, the respective Republican and Democratic floor managers of Title VII in the Senate, simply states, for example, that

> [t]o discriminate is to make a distinction, to make a difference in treatment or favor, and those distinctions or differences in treatment or favor which are prohibited by section 703 are those which are based on any five of the forbidden criteria: race, color, religion, sex, and national origin. Any other criterion or qualification for employment is not affected by this title.

110 Cong. Rec. 7213 (1964). However, the legislative history of the 1972 amendments to Title VII cites *Griggs* with approval. The Senate Report states:

> Employment discrimination as viewed today is a * * * complex and pervasive phenomenon. Experts familiar with the subject now generally describe the problem in terms of "systems" and "effects" rather than simply intentional wrongs * * * .

S.Rep.No.92–415, at 5 (1971). In addition, the section-by-section analyses of the 1972 amendments submitted to both Houses explicitly stated that in any area not addressed by the amendments, present case law—which, as Congress had already recognized, included the then recent decision in *Griggs*—was intended to continue to govern. 118 Cong.Rec. 7166, 7564 (1972). Should the favorable discussion of *Griggs* in the 1972 legislative history be deemed congressional approval of the disparate impact theory? Congress ultimately codified the disparate impact theory in the Civil Rights Act of 1991, which is covered later in this chapter.

4. In thinking about the comparison between the disparate impact and disparate treatment theories of discrimination, would you argue that both are necessary to achieve equality in the workplace, or should one theory be given preference over the other? Consider the following excerpt:

> Disparate impact theory presents a monumentally different conceptualization of discrimination than that embraced by traditional disparate treatment jurisprudence. Defining discrimination in terms of consequence rather than purpose or motive, disparate impact theory interprets Title VII to require that members of protected groups not be unnecessarily harmed in employment because of group differences. Under disparate impact

theory, use of employment practices that have a disparate impact on groups with protected characteristics is unlawful unless the employer can show that the practices are job related and justified by business necessity. The employer need not intend to discriminate in these circumstances; it is enough that the employer uses an employment practice that, although facially neutral and neutral in application, disqualifies a disproportionate percentage of a particular group of applicants from consideration. Disparate impact theory marks a significant departure from the purely individualistic conception of discrimination underlying existing disparate treatment doctrine. * * *

As *Griggs* illustrates, the disparate impact theory conceptualizes discrimination in terms of institutional barriers to equal opportunity for women and minorities. Accordingly, disparate impact theory has proven an invaluable tool for reducing employer reliance on job requirements that are unrelated to job performance but that stand in the way of minority progress. Without such a tool, employers would have been free to adopt facially neutral job requirements that maintained the exclusion of blacks and minorities from vast areas of employment. In addition, by recognizing systems as legitimate subjects for legal regulation, the *Griggs* Court opened the door for a structural approach to combating discrimination more broadly. * * * [Disparate impact] recognizes the role that institutional choices, even those that are neutral in design and in application, can play in perpetuating stratification in the workplace.

Tristin K. Green, *Discrimination in the Workplace Dynamics: Toward a Structural Account of Disparate Treatment Theory*, 38 Harv.C.R.–C.L.L.Rev. 91, 136–37 (2003).

5. In addition to providing a theoretical and legal basis for remedying institutional discrimination, does the impact theory also provide a theoretical and legal basis for remedying the effects of societal discrimination (generally defined as discrimination without a single actor that is perpetrated broadly within society)? Along these lines, it is worth considering who was responsible for the disparities in education in the *Griggs* case? In thinking about these questions, it should be noted that the Supreme Court has rejected the argument that societal discrimination can be a compelling state interest sufficient to justify affirmative action under the equal protection clause. *See, e.g.*, Wygant v. Jackson Bd. of Ed., 476 U.S. 267, 276, 106 S.Ct. 1842, 1848, 90 L.Ed.2d 260 (1986) ("Societal discrimination, without more, is too amorphous a basis for imposing a racially classified remedy" because a "court could uphold remedies that are ageless in their reach into the past, and timeless in their ability to affect the future.") (plurality opinion).

6. *Analytical Framework*: The Supreme Court addressed the analytical framework for disparate impact claims in *Albemarle Paper Co. v. Moody*, 422

U.S. 405, 95 S.Ct. 2362, 45 L.Ed.2d 280 (1975). *Albemarle Paper Co.*, like *Griggs*, was a Title VII class action case brought by black employees who challenged the employer's use of professionally developed general ability tests, as well as its high school diploma requirement. The Court relied on professional standards of test validation promulgated by the EEOC to determine that the employer had not met its burden of proving the "job relatedness" of its testing program. In addition, the Court announced the burden of allocation rules for litigating a disparate impact case:

> In *Griggs v. Duke Power Co.*, this Court unanimously held that Title VII forbids the use of employment tests that are discriminatory in effect unless the employer meets "the burden of showing that any given requirement [has] * * * a manifest relationship to the employment in question." This burden arises, of course, only after the complaining party or class has made out a prima facie case of discrimination, *i.e.*, has shown that the tests in question select applicants for hire or promotion in a racial pattern significantly different from that of the pool of applicants. *See* McDonnell Douglas Corp. v. Green, 411 U.S. 792, 802, 93 S.Ct. 1817, 1824, 36 L.Ed.2d 668 (1973). If an employer does then meet the burden of proving that its tests are "job related," it remains open to the complaining party to show that other tests or selection devices, without a similarly undesirable racial effect, would also serve the employer's legitimate interest in "efficient and trustworthy workmanship." *Id.* at 801, 93 S.Ct. at 1823. Such a showing would be evidence that the employer was using its tests merely as a "pretext" for discrimination.

Albemarle Paper Co., 422 U.S. at 425, 95 S.Ct. at 2375. In this third step, what does the Court mean by "pretext"? Does it have the same meaning as in the context of intentional discrimination claims?

7. In *Griggs*, the Supreme Court relied upon the EEOC's 1966 and 1970 testing guidelines. Those guidelines were modified to ensure consistency with other agencies, and the result was the promulgation in 1978 of the *Uniform Guidelines on Employee Selection Procedures*, 29 C.F.R. § 1607 (2009), which today still govern federal administrative enforcement of laws prohibiting employment discrimination by all of the federal agencies.

The *Uniform Guidelines* adopt a broad definition of "selection procedures" that may be subjected to disparate impact analysis:

> Any measure, combination of measures, or procedures used as a basis for any employment decision. Selection procedures include the full range of assessment techniques from traditional paper and pencil tests, performance tests, training programs, or probationary periods and physical, educational, and work experience requirements through informal or casual interviews and unscored application forms.

29 C.F.R. § 1607.16Q. The Guidelines also create an expectation that selection procedures, particularly written tests, will be professionally validated in order to satisfy the Court's business necessity standard, an issue that was discussed in *Albemarle Paper Co.* Although the Supreme Court has never held that a test must be validated in order to satisfy the business necessity standard, test validation has become common and is designed to ensure that the test is providing reliable and useful information.

As a practical matter, there are two types of validation procedures: (1) content and (2) criterion. A content-based validation study seeks to replicate the content of the job; for example, if the job is for a word processor, the test would involve word processing. Some police department examinations have been validated on a content basis, typically for promotions, and these tests attempt to measure the knowledge an officer would need to perform his or her job. A criterion-related validation study involves a statistical procedure that demonstrates a statistically significant correlation between a selection procedure and job performance. There are similarities between the two validation procedures but the primary distinction is that a content validation study seeks to replicate the content of the job while a criterion-related study seeks to demonstrate a statistical correlation between the selection procedure and successful job performance. Consider the Wonderlic test at issue in both *Griggs* and *Albemarle Paper*. The test might measure the actual job duties (content) or it might be that the employer will demonstrate that those who perform better on the test are also the best, or better, employees (criterion). An employer might accomplish this latter task by having incumbent employees take the test and then compare their scores to their performance ratings to determine whether the best existing employees also score the highest on the examination.

A third type of validation is known as construct validation, which seeks to measure constructs such as intelligence, judgment or leadership. This form of validation is both difficult and rare, and effectively combines aspects of content and criterion-related validity. *See* Gulino v. N.Y. State Educ. Dep't, 460 F.3d 361, 384 (2d Cir.2006) (discussing construct validation). Validation studies are commonly invoked in disparate impact cases, particularly those that involve objective criteria, and they invariably involve expert witnesses. What is most important here is that an employer must justify the use of a procedure that has adverse impact, and a validation study is one accepted means of doing so. For helpful discussions of validation studies see Frank J. Landy & Jeffrey M. Conte, Work in the 21st Century: An Introduction to Industrial and Organizational Psychology, 77–80 (2d ed. 2007); Michael Kirkpatrick, *Employment Testing: Trends and Tactics*, 10 Emp.Rts. & Emp. Pol'y J. 623 (2006). It should also be noted that there is a distinction between a professionally developed test and one that is professionally validated. The fact that a test has been professionally developed does not mean that it is necessarily validated for its particular use. Validation studies are occasionally performed prior to (or after) a test administration but more commonly they are conducted in the course of litigation.

8. *The 80-Percent Rule*: An essential part of a disparate impact claim is that an employer's practice must be demonstrated to have a significant disparate effect on a protected group. There are generally two ways to document the disparate impact of a selection procedure. The most common means is to rely on the statistical method of proof outlined in Chapter 3, Section D, where the plaintiff demonstrates that the observed number of hires or promotions was statistically significantly different from what one would expect in a neutral selection process. The other means of proof is specific to the disparate impact theory. Under the Uniform Guidelines, applying what is known as the 80 percent or "four-fifths" rule, a plaintiff may establish adverse impact by showing that the employees in the protected class are hired, or pass a test, at a rate that is below 80 percent of the rate of the most successful group. *See* 29 C.F.R. § 1607.4(D) ("Adverse impact and the 'four-fifths' rule."). For example, if 80 percent of men passed a test administered by an employer while 40 percent of women passed, the pass rate for women compared to men would be 50 percent (40/80), which falls below 80 percent and therefore can be evidence of disparate impact. Although more rigorous statistical proof is typically offered in cases today, the 80 percent rule remains a useful benchmark and in appropriate circumstances can be sufficient to establish the first step in a disparate impact case. For a detailed discussion of the role the 80 percent rule can have in establishing disparate impact see Jones v. City of Boston, 752 F.3d 38, 52 (1st Cir.2014) (court concludes that the rule can serve "as a helpful rule of thumb for employers not wanting to perform more expansive statistical exercises.").

9. Plaintiffs have used the disparate impact theory to challenge a wide range of facially neutral employment practices and policies. *See, e.g.*, N.Y.C. Transit Auth. v. Beazer, 440 U.S. 568, 99 S.Ct. 1355, 59 L.Ed.2d 587 (1979) (disparate impact on minorities of policy limiting employment opportunities of methadone users); Dothard v. Rawlinson, 433 U.S. 321, 97 S.Ct. 2720, 53 L.Ed.2d 786 (1977) (disparate impact on females of height and weight requirements for employment as prison guards); Green v. Mo. Pac. R.R., 549 F.2d 1158 (8th Cir.1977) (disparate impact on African Americans of policies limiting employment opportunities because of prior criminal convictions); Gregory v. Litton Sys., Inc., 316 F.Supp. 401 (C.D.Cal.1970), *aff'd as modified*, 472 F.2d 631 (9th Cir.1972) (disparate impact on blacks of employers' inquiries about arrest records); Local 53, Asbestos Workers v. Vogler, 407 F.2d 1047 (5th Cir.1969) (disparate impact on African Americans of nepotism rules for union membership in an all-white union). In the early years of Title VII, the written examinations used by police and fire departments, for entry-level jobs and promotions, were the most frequent subject of disparate impact lawsuits, in part because the Department of Justice made a concerted effort to diversify those departments. Most large departments, and many smaller ones, were sued. *See, e.g.*, Guardians Ass'n of N.Y.C. v. Civil Serv. Comm'n, 630 F.2d 79 (2d Cir.1980); Firefighters' Inst. for Racial Equal. v. City of St. Louis, 616 F.2d 350 (8th Cir.1980); United States v. Chicago, 549 F.2d 415 (7th Cir.1977); Boston Chapter, NAACP, Inc. v. Beecher, 504 F.2d 1017 (1st Cir.1974). These cases often last many years.

See, e.g., Lewis v. City of Chicago, 702 F.3d 958 (7th Cir.2012) (case arose out of 1995 test administration).

10. The Supreme Court has only occasionally addressed disparate impact cases. One such case involved what has come to be known as "the bottom line" defense. In *Connecticut v. Teal*, 457 U.S. 440, 102 S.Ct. 2525, 73 L.Ed.2d 130 (1982), a promotional examination administered by the State had an adverse impact on black candidates but the State took steps to ensure the actual promotions were made in a way to minimize the test's adverse impact. As a result, while the examination had an adverse effect, the actual promotions did not. A group of employees who were adversely affected by the examination sued alleging that a cognizable injury arose from the examination's adverse impact and that the injury was not remedied by the subsequent efforts to promote African Americans. The Court, in an opinion written by Justice Brennan, agreed, holding that "Title VII guarantees these individual respondents the opportunity to compete equally with white workers on the basis of job-related criteria." *Id.* at 451, 102 S.Ct. at 2533, 73 L.Ed.2d at 139. The Court went on to add, "The principal focus of the statute is the protection of the individual employee, rather than the protection of the minority group as a whole." *Id.* at 453–54, 102 S.Ct. at 2533, 73 L.Ed.2d at 141. The majority decision in *Teal* was written by the liberal Justice William Brennan, and the Court's more conservative Justices dissented. With this in mind, one might view *Teal* as beneficial to employees but, in an extensive analysis of the case, Professor Martha Chamallas suggested caution was in order:

> Despite its apparent interventionist posture on behalf of minority interests, *Teal* ultimately may not prove to be a victory for civil rights advocates. * * * By requiring even "affirmative action" employers to validate their tests or be subject to liability for unintentional discrimination, *Teal* reduces the incentive for employers to engage in affirmative action.

Martha Chamallas, *Evolving Conceptions of Equality Under Title VII: Disparate Impact and the Demise of the Bottom Line Principle*, 31 UCLA L.Rev. 305, 313 (1983). As you read through the remaining cases in this chapter, consider Professor Chamallas's perspective and the fate of employees in light of the *Teal* decision.

11. Several years later, in another case that turned out to be a mixed blessing for employees, the Court took up the question whether subjective employment practices—primarily practices that involve some discretion in their administration—could be challenged under the disparate impact theory. A unanimous Supreme Court, in an opinion authored by Justice O'Connor, held that subjective employment practices could be challenged under the disparate impact theory, and did so, in part, to protect against "subconscious stereotypes and prejudice." Watson v. Fort Worth Bank & Trust, 467 U.S. 977, 990, 108 S.Ct. 2777, 101 L.Ed.2d 827 (1988). Yet, concerned that employers might have a difficult time validating subjective employment

practices and therefore might resort to quotas as a way of avoiding a lawsuit, Justice O'Connor authored an opinion that was joined by three other Justices that tightened the standards for proving a disparate impact claim. Specifically, the plurality opinion emphasized the need to identify a specific employment practice and also suggested the plaintiff had the ultimate burden of proving the practice did not satisfy the business necessity test. These stringent requirements would garner a majority a year later in the controversial case of *Wards Cove Packing Co. v. Atonio*, 490 U.S. 642, 109 S.Ct. 2115, 104 L.Ed.2d 733 (1989), a decision taken up shortly. For a variety of reasons, subjective employment practices are more commonly challenged under an intentional discrimination theory, though occasionally a claim will proceed as a disparate impact challenge. *See* Tabor v. Hilti, Inc., 703 F.3d 1206 (10th Cir.2013) (allowing disparate impact challenge to employer's practice of determining when an employee was ready for promotion); McClain v. Lufkin Indus., Inc., 519 F.3d 264, 276 (5th Cir.2008), *cert. denied*, 555 U.S. 81, 129 S.Ct. 1981, 172 L.Ed.2d 141 (2008) (allowing disparate impact challenge to process that included subjective and objective components).

NOTE: THE LEGITIMACY OF THE DISPARATE IMPACT THEORY

By any standard, *Griggs v. Duke Power Co.* ranks as one of the most important civil rights case since *Brown v. Board of Education*. Like *Brown*, the Court's adoption of the disparate impact theory, however, has generated an on-going debate about the legitimacy of the theory and its underlying rationale. The debate among the Justices of the Supreme Court is reflected in cases such as *Connecticut v. Teal*, 457 U.S. 440, 448, 102 S.Ct. 2525, 2531, 73 L.Ed.2d 130 (1982), *Wards Cove Packing Co. v. Atonio*, 490 U.S. 642, 109 S.Ct. 2115, 104 L.Ed.2d 733 (1989), and *United Steelworkers of America v. Weber*, 443 U.S. 193, 99 S.Ct. 2721, 61 L.Ed.2d 480 (1979). *Wards Cove* is reproduced in this chapter and *Weber* is reproduced in Chapter 15 on affirmative action.

Scholars have criticized the Supreme Court for its failure in *Griggs* to explain the theoretical underpinnings of the disparate impact theory. As one commentator observed,

> Missing from the Burger Court's opinion was a clear explanation of the theory underlying disparate impact law. Was the theory bottomed on the existence of past or present discrimination against minorities? Did the theory—as suggested by the reliance on the "the fabled offer of milk to the stork and the fox"—assume that prerequisites for employment might validly test the qualifications of persons of one race while excluding qualified members of another race? Was the disparate impact test designed to provide equality of results rather than equality of opportunity? Was the test to erode or promote merit systems of employment?

Brian K. Landsberg, *Race and the Rehnquist Court*, 66 Tul.L.Rev. 1267, 1281 (1992).

Another commentator stated that

> [a]lthough *Griggs v. Duke Power Co.*, the seminal disparate impact case, was decided well over a decade ago, there is still disagreement on the underlying theory of the disparate impact model. An acceptable theory must resolve a paradox created by the model: how can an employer who uses only a racially neutral employment criterion be deemed to have made an employment decision based on race? [There are] four approaches to this paradox. The "intent" theory postulates that evidence of adverse impact is evidence of discriminatory intent. Thus, although an employment criterion is facially neutral, its disparate impact exposes race-based decisionmaking. Under the "past discrimination" theory, an employment criterion with a disparate impact on black persons is unlawful if the disparate impact results from past race-based decisionmaking. * * * The "functional equivalence" theory holds that neutral criteria that have an adverse impact on black persons and cannot be justified by any business necessity are the functional equivalents of race and, therefore, should be treated like race. Finally, the "statistical discrimination" theory views the disparate impact model as a mechanism to prohibit discrimination as defined by economic theory.

Steven L. Willborn, *The Disparate Impact Model of Discrimination: Theory and Limits*, 34 Am.U.L.Rev. 799, 804 (1985).

Professor Willborn offers an explanation for and a criticism of each rationale. The intent rationale, he suggests, is structured around the argument that disparate impact is clearly relevant to the issue of discriminatory intent; thus a severe disparate impact may by itself justify a finding of discriminatory motive as the Court held in *Teamsters v. United States*, 431 U.S. 324, 97 S.Ct. 1843, 52 L.Ed.2d 396 (1977). Several Supreme Court Justices have subscribed to the functional equivalency theory. Justice O'Connor, writing for a plurality in *Watson v. Fort Worth Bank & Trust*, 487 U.S. 977, 987, 108 S.Ct. 2777, 2785, 101 L.Ed.2d 827 (1988), argued that "the necessary premise of the disparate impact approach is that some employment practices, adopted without a deliberately discriminatory motive, may in operation be functionally equivalent to intentional discrimination." The statistical discrimination rationale is grounded in an economic analysis of labor markets and assumes that employers take action because they lack sufficient information to make low cost decisions. He argues that the statistical discrimination theory best explains the disparate impact theory. *See* Willborn, *supra*, at 804–26.

Other scholars have advanced other theoretical justifications for the disparate impact theory. Professor Caldwell, a critical race scholar, has argued the disparate impact theory is designed to enhance productivity and efficiency by redistributing employment opportunities. Paulette Caldwell, *Reaffirming the Disproportionate Effects Standard of Liability in Title VII*

Litigation, 46 U.Pitt.L.Rev. 555 (1985). Professor Perry has argued that the theory is designed to prevent the perpetuation of past discrimination. Michael J. Perry, *The Disproportionate Theory of Discrimination*, 125 U.Pa.L.Rev 540 (1977). Professor Rutherglen has argued that the theory is designed to prevent disparate treatment in cases where pretextual discrimination is difficult to prove. George Rutherglen, *Disparate Impact Theory Under Title VII: An Objective Theory of Discrimination*, 73 Va.L.Rev. 1297 (1987). For an argument that *Griggs* was wrongly decided, see Michael Evan Gold, *Griggs' Folly: An Essay on the Theory, Problems, and Origin of the Adverse Impact Definition of Employment Discrimination and a Recommendation for Reform*, 7 Indus.Rel.L.J. 429 (1985).

2. *GRIGGS* REVISITED

The impact of *Griggs* on the development of employment discrimination law, and more generally on the development of civil rights jurisprudence, has been profound. But neither the courts nor Congress has resolved the fundamental policy question about competing theories of equality—equal treatment versus equal opportunity. And in fact, support for both visions of equality can be found in *Griggs*. As the membership on the Supreme Court and lower federal courts began to change in the 1980s, so did the jurisprudence of employment discrimination law.

WARDS COVE PACKING CO. V. ATONIO

Supreme Court of the United States, 1989.
490 U.S. 642, 109 S.Ct. 2115, 104 L.Ed.2d 733.

JUSTICE WHITE delivered the opinion of the Court.

* * *

I

The claims before us are disparate-impact claims, involving the employment practices of petitioners, two companies that operate salmon canneries in remote and widely separated areas of Alaska. The canneries operate only during the salmon runs in the summer months. They are inoperative and vacant for the rest of the year. In May or June of each year, a few weeks before the salmon runs begin, workers arrive and prepare the equipment and facilities for the canning operation. Most of these workers possess a variety of skills. When salmon runs are about to begin, the workers who will operate the cannery lines arrive, remain as long as there are fish to can, and then depart. The canneries are then closed down, winterized, and left vacant until the next spring. During the off-season, the companies employ only a small number of individuals at their headquarters in Seattle and Astoria, Oregon, plus some employees at the winter shipyard in Seattle.

The length and size of salmon runs vary from year to year, and hence the number of employees needed at each cannery also varies. Estimates are made as early in the winter as possible; the necessary employees are hired, and when the time comes, they are transported to the canneries. Salmon must be processed soon after they are caught, and the work during the canning season is therefore intense. For this reason, and because the canneries are located in remote regions, all workers are housed at the canneries and have their meals in company-owned mess halls.

Jobs at the canneries are of two general types: "cannery jobs" on the cannery line, which are unskilled positions; and "noncannery jobs," which fall into a variety of classifications. Most noncannery jobs are classified as skilled positions. Cannery jobs are filled predominantly by nonwhites: Filipinos and Alaska Natives. The Filipinos are hired through, and dispatched by, Local 37 of the International Longshoremen's and Warehousemen's Union pursuant to a hiring hall agreement with the local. The Alaska Natives primarily reside in villages near the remote cannery locations. Noncannery jobs are filled with predominantly white workers, who are hired during the winter months from the companies' offices in Washington and Oregon. Virtually all of the noncannery jobs pay more than cannery positions. The predominantly white noncannery workers and the predominantly nonwhite cannery employees live in separate dormitories and eat in separate mess halls.

In 1974, respondents, a class of nonwhite cannery workers who were (or had been) employed at the canneries, brought this Title VII action against petitioners. Respondents alleged that a variety of petitioners' hiring/promotion practices—*e.g.*, nepotism, a rehire preference, a lack of objective hiring criteria, separate hiring channels, a practice of not promoting from within—were responsible for the racial stratification of the work force and had denied them and other nonwhites employment as noncannery workers on the basis of race. Respondents also complained of petitioners' racially segregated housing and dining facilities. All of respondents' claims were advanced under both the disparate-treatment and disparate-impact theories of Title VII liability.

The District Court held a bench trial, after which it entered 172 findings of fact. It then rejected all of respondents' disparate-treatment claims. It also rejected the disparate-impact challenges * * * .

* * * [The Court of Appeals] held that respondents had made out a prima facie case of disparate impact in hiring for both skilled and unskilled noncannery positions. The panel remanded the case for further proceedings, instructing the District Court that it was the employer's burden to prove that any disparate impact caused by its hiring and employment practices was justified by business necessity. Neither the en

banc court nor the panel disturbed the District Court's rejection of the disparate-treatment claims.

* * * Because some of the issues raised by the decision below were matters on which this Court was evenly divided in *Watson v. Fort Worth Bank & Trust*, 487 U.S. 977, 108 S.Ct. 2777, 101 L.Ed.2d 827 (1988), we granted certiorari, for the purpose of addressing these disputed questions of the proper application of Title VII's disparate-impact theory of liability.

II

In holding that respondents had made out a prima facie case of disparate impact, the Court of Appeals relied solely on respondents' statistics showing a high percentage of nonwhite workers in the cannery jobs and a low percentage of such workers in the noncannery positions. Although statistical proof can alone make out a prima facie case, the Court of Appeals' ruling here misapprehends our precedents and the purposes of Title VII, and we therefore reverse.

"There can be no doubt," as there was when a similar mistaken analysis had been undertaken by the courts below in *Hazelwood School Dist. v. United States*, 433 U.S. 299, 308, 97 S.Ct. 2736, 2741, 53 L.Ed.2d 768 (1977), "that the * * * comparison * * * fundamentally misconceived the role of statistics in employment discrimination cases." The "proper comparison [is] between the racial composition of [the at-issue jobs] and the racial composition of the qualified * * * population in the relevant labor market." *Id.* It is such a comparison—between the racial composition of the qualified persons in the labor market and the persons holding at-issue jobs—that generally forms the proper basis for the initial inquiry in a disparate-impact case. Alternatively, in cases where such labor market statistics will be difficult if not impossible to ascertain, we have recognized that certain other statistics—such as measures indicating the racial composition of "otherwise-qualified applicants" for at-issue jobs—are equally probative for this purpose. *See, e.g.*, New York City Transit Authority v. Beazer, 440 U.S. 568, 585, 99 S.Ct. 1355, 1366, 59 L.Ed.2d 587 (1979).

It is clear to us that the Court of Appeals' acceptance of the comparison between the racial composition of the cannery work force and that of the noncannery work force * * * was flawed for several reasons. Most obviously, with respect to the skilled noncannery jobs at issue here, the cannery work force in no way reflected "the pool of *qualified* job applicants" or the "*qualified* population in the labor force." Measuring alleged discrimination in the selection of accountants, managers, boat captains, electricians, doctors, and engineers—and the long list of other "skilled" noncannery positions found to exist by the District Court, by comparing the number of nonwhites occupying these jobs to the number of nonwhites filling cannery worker positions is nonsensical. If the absence of minorities holding such skilled positions is due to a dearth of qualified nonwhite applicants (for reasons that are not petitioners' fault), petitioners' selection methods or employment practices cannot be said to have had a "disparate impact" on nonwhites.

* * * [U]nder the Court of Appeals' theory, simply because nonwhites comprise 52% of the cannery workers at the cannery in question, respondents would be successful in establishing a prima facie case of racial discrimination under Title VII.

Such a result cannot be squared with our cases or with the goals behind the statute. The Court of Appeals' theory, at the very least, would mean that any employer who had a segment of his work force that was—for some reason—racially imbalanced, could be haled into court and forced to engage in the expensive and time-consuming task of defending the "business necessity" of the methods used to select the other members of his work force. The only practicable option for many employers would be to adopt racial quotas, insuring that no portion of their work forces deviated in racial composition from the other portions thereof; this is a result that Congress expressly rejected in drafting Title VII. *See* 42 U.S.C. § 2000e–2(j); *see also* Watson v. Fort Worth Bank & Trust, 487 U.S. at 992–94 & n.2, 108 S.Ct. at 2787–89 & n.2 (opinion of O'CONNOR, J.). * * *

The Court of Appeals also erred with respect to the unskilled noncannery positions. Racial imbalance in one segment of an employer's work force does not, without more, establish a prima facie case of disparate impact with respect to the selection of workers for the employer's other positions, even where workers for the different positions may have somewhat fungible skills (as is arguably the case for cannery and unskilled noncannery workers). As long as there are no barriers or practices deterring qualified nonwhites from applying for noncannery positions, if the percentage of selected applicants who are nonwhite is not significantly less than the percentage of qualified applicants who are nonwhite, the employer's selection mechanism probably does not operate with a disparate impact on minorities. Where this is the case, the percentage of nonwhite workers found in other positions in the employer's labor force is irrelevant to the question of a prima facie statistical case of disparate impact. * * *

Consequently, we reverse the Court of Appeals' ruling that a comparison between the percentage of cannery workers who are nonwhite and the percentage of noncannery workers who are nonwhite makes out a prima facie case of disparate impact. Of course, this leaves unresolved whether the record made in the District Court will support a conclusion that a prima facie case of disparate impact has been established on some basis other than the racial disparity between cannery and noncannery workers. This is an issue that the Court of Appeals or the District Court should address in the first instance.

III

Since the statistical disparity relied on by the Court of Appeals did not suffice to make out a prima facie case, any inquiry by us into whether the specific challenged employment practices of petitioners caused that disparity is pretermitted, as is any inquiry into whether the disparate impact that any employment practice may have had was justified by business considerations. Because we remand for further proceedings, however * * *, we address two other challenges petitioners have made to the decision of the Court of Appeals.

A

First is the question of causation in a disparate-impact case. The law in this respect was correctly stated by Justice O'Connor's opinion last Term in *Watson v. Fort Worth Bank & Trust*, 487 U.S. at 994, 108 S.Ct. at 2788–89 * * * .

Our disparate-impact cases have always focused on the impact of *particular* hiring practices on employment opportunities for minorities. Just as an employer cannot escape liability under Title VII by demonstrating that, "at the bottom line," his work force is racially balanced (where particular hiring practices may operate to deprive minorities of employment opportunities), *see* Connecticut v. Teal, 457 U.S. at 450, 102 S.Ct. at 2532, a Title VII plaintiff does not make out a case of disparate impact simply by showing that, "at the bottom line," there is racial *imbalance* in the work force. As a general matter, a plaintiff must demonstrate that it is the application of a specific or particular employment practice that has created the disparate impact under attack. Such a showing is an integral part of the plaintiff's prima facie case in a disparate-impact suit under Title VII.

Here, respondents have alleged that several "objective" employment practices (e.g., nepotism, separate hiring channels, rehire preferences), as well as the use of "subjective decision making" to select noncannery workers, have had a disparate impact on nonwhites. Respondents base this claim on statistics that allegedly show a disproportionately low percentage of nonwhites in the at-issue positions. However, even if on remand respondents can show that nonwhites are underrepresented in the at-issue jobs in a manner that is acceptable under the standards set forth in Section II, this alone will *not* suffice to make out a prima facie case of disparate impact. Respondents will also have to demonstrate that the disparity they complain of is the result of one or more of the employment practices that they are attacking here, specifically showing that each challenged practice has a significantly disparate impact on employment opportunities for whites and nonwhites. To hold otherwise would result in employers being potentially liable for "the myriad of innocent causes that may lead to statistical imbalances in the composition of their work forces." *Watson*, 487 U.S. at 992, 108 S.Ct. at 2787.

* * *

B

If, on remand, respondents meet the proof burdens outlined above, and establish a prima facie case of disparate impact with respect to any of petitioners' employment practices, the case will shift to any business justification petitioners offer for their use of these practices. This phase of the disparate-impact case contains two components: first, a consideration of the justifications an employer offers for his use of these practices; and second, the availability of alternative practices to achieve the same business ends, with less racial impact. We consider these two components in turn.

(1)

Though we have phrased the query differently in different cases, it is generally well established that at the justification stage of such a disparate-impact case, the dispositive issue is whether a challenged practice serves, in a significant way, the legitimate employment goals of the employer. The touchstone of this inquiry is a reasoned review of the employer's justification for his use of the challenged practice. * * * A mere insubstantial justification in this regard will not suffice, because such a low standard of review would permit discrimination to be practiced through the use of spurious, seemingly neutral employment practices. At the same time, though, there is no requirement that the challenged practice be "essential" or "indispensable" to the employer's business for it to pass muster: this degree of scrutiny would be almost impossible for most employers to meet, and would result in a host of evils we have identified above.

In this phase, the employer carries the burden of producing evidence of a business justification for his employment practice. * * * We acknowledge that some of our earlier decisions can be read as suggesting otherwise. But to the extent that those cases speak of an employer's "burden of proof" with respect to a legitimate business justification * * * they should have been understood to mean an employer's production—but not persuasion—burden.

(2)

Finally, if on remand the case reaches this point, and respondents cannot persuade the trier of fact on the question of petitioners' business necessity defense, respondents may still be able to prevail. To do so, respondents will have to persuade the factfinder that "other tests or selection devices, without a similarly undesirable racial effect, would also serve the employer's legitimate [hiring] interest[s]"; by so demonstrating, respondents would prove that "[petitioners were] using [their] tests merely as a 'pretext' for discrimination." *Albemarle Paper Co.*, 422 U.S. at 425, 95 S.Ct. at 2375. If respondents, having established a prima facie case, come forward with alternatives to petitioners' hiring practices that reduce the racially disparate impact of practices currently being used, and petitioners refuse to adopt these alternatives, such a refusal would belie a claim by petitioners that their incumbent practices are being employed for nondiscriminatory reasons.

Of course, any alternative practices which respondents offer up in this respect must be equally effective as petitioners' chosen hiring procedures in achieving petitioners' legitimate employment goals. Moreover, "[f]actors such as the cost or other burdens of proposed alternative selection devices are relevant in determining whether they would be equally as effective as the challenged practice in serving the employer's legitimate business goals." *Watson*, 487 U.S. at 998, 108 S.Ct. at 2790. "Courts are generally less competent than employers to restructure business practices," Furnco Constr. Corp. v. Waters, 438 U.S. 567, 578, 98 S.Ct. 2943, 2950, 57 L.Ed.2d 957 (1978); consequently, the judiciary should proceed with care before mandating that an employer must adopt a plaintiff's alternative selection or hiring practice in response to a Title VII suit. * * *

JUSTICE BLACKMUN, with whom JUSTICE BRENNAN and JUSTICE MARSHALL join, dissenting.

* * * The salmon industry as described by this record takes us back to a kind of overt and institutionalized discrimination we have not dealt with in years: a total residential and work environment organized on principles of racial stratification and segregation, which, as Justice Stevens points out, resembles a plantation economy. This industry long has been characterized by a taste for discrimination of the old-fashioned sort: a preference for hiring nonwhites to fill its lowest level positions, on the condition that they stay there. The majority's legal rulings essentially immunize these practices from attack under a Title VII disparate-impact analysis.

Sadly, this comes as no surprise. One wonders whether the majority still believes that race discrimination—or, more accurately, race discrimination against nonwhites—is a problem in our society, or even remembers that it ever was.

JUSTICE STEVENS, with whom JUSTICE BRENNAN, JUSTICE MARSHALL, and JUSTICE BLACKMUN join, dissenting, omitted.

NOTES AND QUESTIONS

1. The views of Justice O'Connor in *Watson v. Fort Worth Bank & Trust* formed the basis for the Court's decision in *Wards Cove*. How would you describe her conception of equality? It seems clear, does it not, that Justice O'Connor was unwilling to endorse a rule of law that would legitimate "quotas"? Why do you think that is, and what might account for the Court's focus on the quota issue? Similarly, consider whether *Wards Cove* resolves the tension in *Griggs* between competing theories of equality? If so, what theory of equality does *Wards Cove* embrace?

2. *The Civil Rights Act of 1991*: The *Wards Cove* case was highly controversial because it was seen as severely restricting the scope of the disparate impact theory. The case also came on the heels of a series of restrictive Supreme Court decisions, and almost immediately following the Court's decision in *Wards Cove*, Congress moved to enact legislation to overturn or modify the cases. The initial legislation, known as the Civil Rights Act of 1990, was vetoed by President George Bush, and the most controversial provision related to the *Wards Cove* case. The following year Congress passed the Civil Rights Act of 1991, which the President signed, and the Act significantly altered the Court's decision in *Wards Cove*. For the first time, Congress codified the theory of disparate impact and also specified the analytical framework as follows:

> (k) Burden of proof in disparate impact cases
>
> (1)(A) An unlawful employment practice based on disparate impact is established under this subchapter only if—
>
> > (i) a complaining party demonstrates that a respondent uses a particular employment practice that causes a disparate impact on the basis of race, color, religion, sex, or national origin and the respondent fails to demonstrate that the challenged practice is job related for the position in question and consistent with business necessity; or
> >
> > (ii) the complaining party makes the demonstration described in subparagraph (C) with respect to an alternative employment practice and the respondent refuses to adopt such alternative employment practice.
>
> (B)(i) With respect to demonstrating that a particular employment practice causes a disparate impact as described in subparagraph (A)(i), the complaining party shall demonstrate that each particular challenged employment practice causes a disparate impact, except that if the complaining party can demonstrate to the court that the elements of a respondent's decisionmaking process are not capable of separation for analysis, the decisionmaking process may be analyzed as one employment practice.

(ii) if the respondent demonstrates that a specific employment practice does not cause the disparate impact, the respondent shall not be required to demonstrate that such practice is required by business necessity.

(C) The demonstration referred to by subparagraph (A)(ii) shall be in accordance with law as it existed on June 4, 1989, with respect to the concept of "alternative employment practices."

Title VII, § 703(k), 42 U.S.C. § 2000e–2(k).

As stated in the Findings and Purposes section of the Civil Rights Act of 1991, Congress acted to codify the theory of discrimination found in *Griggs v. Duke Power* and to respond to a variety of Supreme Court cases, including *Wards Cove*. Civil Rights Act of 1991, Sec. 2 and 3, Pub. L. No. 102–166, 105 Stat. 1071 (1991). More specifically, the statute established that the employer has the burden of proof on the business necessity defense. The statute also restored the meaning of "business necessity" to what it was prior to the Court's decision in *Wards Cove*, though it remains unclear what that meaning was (an issue discussed in the next case). The statute also modified the Court's requirement that the plaintiff identify a specific employment practice; while the plaintiff must identify a specific employment practice, the statute makes an exception to the extent the employer's decisionmaking process is not capable of separation. Would this have mattered to the *Wards Cove* decision?

It is important to emphasize that one part of the *Wards Cove* case was not altered by the Civil Rights Act of 1991. The Court's discussion of the plaintiff's statistical proof, and the need to identify the proper labor market, was not changed by the statute and remains a central part of the plaintiff's statistical burden. As one court explained in a case in which the plaintiffs were challenging the company's provision of overtime, "To establish a prima facie case, it is not enough for plaintiffs to show simply that more overtime assignments go to men than to women, or even that men get a higher percentage of those assignments than their percentage in the work force. They must compare *qualified* men to *qualified* women." Carpenter v. Boeing, 456 F.3d 1183, 1194 (10th Cir.2006) (emphasis in original).

3. *The Aftermath of* Wards Cove: Despite the plaintiffs' loss in the Supreme Court, and a peculiar statutory provision that made the changes legislated in the Civil Rights Act of 1991 inapplicable to the *Wards Cove* case, the plaintiffs carried on with their litigation for another ten years. After further hearings and several decisions, the litigation finally came to an end when the court of appeals affirmed the district court's rulings for the defendant. *See* Atonio v. Wards Cove, 275 F.3d 797 (9th Cir.2001).

4. *The Business Necessity Defense*: A defendant can rebut a prima facie case of disparate impact under the Civil Rights Act of 1991 by meeting the burden of production of evidence and the burden of persuasion with proof that a "challenged practice is job related for the position in question and

consistent with business necessity." 42 U.S.C. § 2000e–2(k) (1) (A). Is the defense as now provided in the 1991 Act more onerous or less onerous than the business necessity test as it existed before *Wards Cove*? Consider the following case:

C. THE CIVIL RIGHTS ACT OF 1991 AND CONTEMPORARY DISPARATE IMPACT DOCTRINE

LANNING V. SOUTHEASTERN PENNSYLVANIA TRANSPORTATION AUTHORITY (LANNING I)

United States Court of Appeals for the Third Circuit, 1999.
181 F.3d 478, *cert. denied*, 528 U.S. 1131, 120 S.Ct. 970, 145 L.Ed.2d 840 (2000).

MANSMANN, CIRCUIT JUDGE.

In this appeal, we must determine the appropriate legal standard to apply when evaluating an employer's business justification in an action challenging an employer's cutoff score on an employment screening exam as discriminatory under a disparate impact theory of liability. We hold today that under the Civil Rights Act of 1991, a discriminatory cutoff score on an entry level employment examination must be shown to measure the minimum qualifications necessary for successful performance of the job in question in order to survive a disparate impact challenge. * * *

I.

* * *

A.

SEPTA is a regional mass transit authority that operates principally in Philadelphia, Pennsylvania. In 1989, in response to a perceived need to upgrade the quality of its transit police force, SEPTA initiated an extensive program designed to improve the department. * * *

In 1991, SEPTA hired Dr. Paul Davis to develop an appropriate physical fitness test for its police officers. * * * Ultimately, Dr. Davis recommended a 1.5 mile run within 12 minutes. * * *

Dr. Davis recommended that SEPTA use the 1.5 mile run as an applicant screening test. Dr. Davis understood that SEPTA officers would not be required to run 1.5 miles within 12 minutes in the course of their duties, but he nevertheless recommended this test as an accurate measure of the aerobic capacity necessary to perform the job of SEPTA transit police officer. Based upon Dr. Davis' recommendation, SEPTA adopted a physical fitness screening test for its applicants, which included a 1.5 mile run within 12 minutes. * * *

* * * [R]esearch studies confirm that a cutoff of 12 minutes on a 1.5 mile run will have a disparately adverse impact on women. SEPTA concedes that its 1.5 mile run has a disparate impact on women.

* * *

II.

* * *

Because SEPTA concedes that its 1.5 mile run has a disparate impact on women, the first prong of the disparate impact analysis is not at issue in this appeal. Rather, this appeal focuses our attention on the proper standard for evaluating whether SEPTA's 1.5 mile run is "job related for the position in question and consistent with business necessity" under the Civil Rights Act of 1991. Because the Act instructs that this standard incorporates only selected segments of prior Supreme Court jurisprudence on the business necessity doctrine, we examine the history of this doctrine in order to resolve this threshold issue.

A.

[The court initially examined the Supreme Court decisions on business necessity, *Griggs*, *Albemarle Paper Co. v. Moody*, *Dothard v. Rawlinson*, and *New York Transit Authority v. Beazer*.]

III.

The Supreme Court has yet to interpret the "job related for the position in question and consistent with business necessity" standard adopted by the Act. In addition, our sister courts of appeals that have applied the Act's standard to a Title VII challenge have done so with little analysis. * * *

Because the Act proscribes resort to legislative history with the exception of one short interpretive memorandum endorsing selective caselaw, our starting point in interpreting the Act's business necessity language must be that interpretive memorandum. The memorandum makes clear that Congress intended to endorse the business necessity standard enunciated in *Griggs* and not the *Wards Cove* interpretation of that standard. By Congress' distinguishing between *Griggs* and *Wards Cove*, we must conclude that Congress viewed *Wards Cove* as a significant departure from *Griggs*. Accordingly, because the Act clearly chooses *Griggs* over *Wards Cove*, the Court's interpretation of the business necessity standard in *Wards Cove* does not survive the Act.

We turn now to articulate the standard for business necessity—one most consistent with *Griggs* and its pre*Wards Cove* progeny. The laudable mission begun by the Court in *Griggs* was the eradication of discrimination through the application of practices fair in form but discriminatory in practice by eliminating *unnecessary* barriers to employment opportunities. In the context of a hiring exam with a cutoff score shown to have a discriminatory effect, the standard that best effectuates this mission is implicit in the Court's application of the business necessity doctrine to the employer in *Griggs, i.e.*, that a discriminatory cutoff score is impermissible unless shown to measure the minimum qualifications necessary for successful performance of the job in question. Only this standard can effectuate the mission begun by the Court in *Griggs*; only by requiring employers to demonstrate that their discriminatory cutoff score measures the minimum qualifications necessary for successful performance of the job in question can we be certain to eliminate the use of excessive cutoff scores that have a disparate impact on minorities as a method of imposing unnecessary barriers to employment opportunities.

* * *

Our conclusion that the Act incorporates this standard is further supported by the business necessity language adopted by the Act. Congress chose the terms "job related for the position in question" *and* "consistent with business necessity." Judicial application of a standard focusing solely on whether the qualities measured by an entry level exam bear some relationship to the job in question would impermissibly write out the business necessity prong of the Act's chosen standard. * * *

In addition, Congress' decision to emphasize the importance of the policies underlying the disparate impact theory of discrimination through its codification supports application of this standard to discriminatory cutoff scores. The disparate impact theory of discrimination combats not intentional, obvious discriminatory policies, but a type of covert discrimination in which facially neutral practices are employed to exclude, unnecessarily and disparately, protected groups from employment opportunities. Inherent in the adoption of this theory of discrimination is the recognition that an employer's job requirements may incorporate societal standards based not upon necessity but rather upon historical, discriminatory biases. A business necessity standard that wholly defers to an employer's judgment as to what is desirable in an employee therefore is completely inadequate in combating covert discrimination based upon societal prejudices. * * *

Accordingly, we hold that the business necessity standard adopted by the Act must be interpreted in accordance with the standards articulated by the Supreme Court in *Griggs* and its pre-*Wards Cove* progeny which demand that a discriminatory cutoff score be shown to measure the minimum qualifications necessary for the successful performance of the job in question in order to survive a disparate impact challenge.[16]

---

[16] Relying upon *Spurlock v. United Airlines, Inc.*, 475 F.2d 216 (10th Cir.1972), and like cases from our sister courts of appeals, the dissent asserts that this standard should not apply to

* * *

WEIS, CIRCUIT JUDGE, dissenting:

The "minimum qualifications" criterion of business justification does not apply to all types of employment. When public safety is at stake, a lighter burden is placed on employers to justify their hiring requirements. Because I believe that the latter standard applies in this case, I would affirm.

* * *

III.

* * *

The Courts of Appeals have explicitly recognized the relevance of safety considerations in a series of decisions beginning with *Spurlock v. United Airlines, Inc.*, 475 F.2d 216 (10th Cir.1972). In that case, an airline required that applicants for flight officer positions have a college degree and a minimum of 500 flight hours. The Court, citing *Griggs*, held that where "the job clearly requires a high degree of skill and the economic and human risks involved in hiring an unqualified applicant are great, the employer bears a correspondingly lighter burden to show his employment criteria are job related." *Id.* at 219. * * *

Another leading case, *Davis v. City of Dallas*, 777 F.2d 205 (5th Cir.1985), applied the *Spurlock* doctrine to criteria for hiring police officers. The City required a specific amount of college education, no history of recent marijuana usage, and a negative history of traffic violations. Despite findings of disparate impact, the Court upheld the requirements. Having reviewed the many cases following *Spurlock*, the Court had "no difficulty * * * equating the position of police officer in a major metropolitan area such as Dallas with other jobs that courts have found to involve the important public interest in safety." *Id.* at 215 (internal quotation marks omitted). The degree of public risk and

---

SEPTA because the job of SEPTA transit officer implicates issues of public safety. Under the Act, however, our interpretation of the business necessity language is limited to "the concepts enunciated by the Supreme Court in *Griggs v. Duke Power Co.*, 401 U.S. 424, 91 S.Ct. 849, 28 L.Ed.2d 158 (1971), and in the other *Supreme Court* decisions prior to *Wards Cove Packing Co. v. Atonio*, 490 U.S. 642, 109 S.Ct. 2115, 104 L.Ed.2d 733 (1989)." *See* 137 Cong. Rec. 28,680 (1991) (emphasis added). Because the Supreme Court never adopted the holding of *Spurlock* prior to *Wards Cove*, its [sic] is clear that, under the Act, we are not to consider *Spurlock* as authoritative. * * *

Furthermore, to the limited extent that the Supreme Court's pre-*Wards Cove* jurisprudence instructs that public safety is a legitimate consideration, application of the business necessity standard to SEPTA is consistent with that jurisprudence because the standard itself takes public safety into consideration. If, for example, SEPTA can show on remand that the inability of a SEPTA transit officer to meet a certain aerobic level would significantly jeopardize public safety, this showing would be relevant to determine if that level is necessary for the successful performance of the job. Clearly a SEPTA officer who poses a significant risk to public safety could not be considered to be performing his job successfully. * * *

responsibility alone "would warrant examination of the job relatedness of the * * * education requirement under the lighter standard imposed under *Spurlock* and its progeny." *Id.* at 215.

* * *

In a similar case, the Court of Appeals for the Eighth Circuit wrote that "the law does not require the city to put the lives of [plaintiff] and his fellow firefighters at risk by taking the chance that he is fit for duty when solid scientific studies indicate that persons with test results similar to his are not." *Smith v. City of Des Moines*, 99 F.3d 1466, 1473 (8th Cir.1996). Other Courts of Appeals have reached similar conclusions in cases involving safety-sensitive positions such as truck drivers, bus drivers, firefighters, and police officers. [Citations omitted.]

IV.

With this in mind, I cannot agree that the majority's standard is the correct one for this case. Reducing standards towards the lowest common denominator is particularly inappropriate for a police force. Undoubtedly, candidates who fail the running test—female or male—may have other qualities of particular value to SEPTA, but they must possess the requisite aerobic capacity as well. No matter how laudable it is to reduce job discrimination, to achieve this goal by lowering important public safety standards presents an unacceptable risk.

Aerobic capacity is an objective, measurable factor which gauges the ability of a human being to perform physical activity. The aerobic demands on the human system are affected by absolutes such as the distance traveled, the speed, the number of steps to be climbed, and similar factors. Governmental agency pronouncements will not shorten distances, reduce the number of steps, or decrease the aerobic capacity of perpetrators to match the reduced standards of officers, male or female. Some males and more females cannot meet the necessary requirements. Based on the facts established at trial, those individuals simply cannot perform the job efficiently. To the extent that they cannot, their hire adversely affects public safety.

* * *

In the *Lanning* decision just discussed, the court resolved the dispute over what the business necessity test, as codified in the Civil Rights Act of 1991, required. The case was remanded for the district court to apply the appropriate standard. On remand, the district court upheld the transit department's standard, and that determination was then appealed.

LANNING V. SOUTHEASTERN PENNSYLVANIA TRANSPORTATION AUTHORITY (LANNING II)

United States Court of Appeals for the Third Circuit, 2002.
308 F.3d 286.

BARRY, CIRCUIT JUDGE.

In *Lanning v. SEPTA,* 181 F.3d 478 (3d Cir.1999) (hereafter *"Lanning I"*), we held that "under the Civil Rights Act of 1991, a discriminatory cutoff score on an entry level employment examination must be shown to measure the minimum qualifications necessary for successful performance of the job in question in order to survive a disparate impact challenge." 181 F.3d at 481. We * * * remanded the appeal for the [District] Court to determine whether the employer, the Southeastern Pennsylvania Transportation Authority ("SEPTA"), had carried its burden of establishing that its 1.5 mile run within twelve minutes measures the minimum aerobic capacity necessary to perform successfully the job of a SEPTA transit police officer. *Id.* * * *

Because we conclude that SEPTA produced more than sufficient competent evidence to support the finding that a pre-hire, pre-academy training aerobic capacity of 42.5 mL/kg/min measures the minimum qualifications necessary for successful performance as a SEPTA transit police officer and has, thus, justified the conceded disparate impact on female candidates by showing business necessity, we will affirm the judgment of the District Court in favor of SEPTA.

* * *

We start by noting that when this case was last before us, we expressed concerns as to certain aspects of the statistical studies upon which the District Court relied, and we "encouraged the District Court to take a critical look at these studies, if necessary, on remand." *Id.* In its second memorandum opinion, the District Court noted that it had "indeed taken a second critical look at these studies as suggested and once again reaffirmed their validity consistent with its prior extensive 160 plus page memorandum opinion." Significantly, after the five-day hearing on remand, the District Court made additional findings of fact that bolster its conclusion. As the following brief discussion demonstrates, it is evident that the District Court's findings regarding the studies in this case were not clearly erroneous.

In *Lanning I,* we were concerned that "the absolute number of arrests or 'arrest rates' [in certain studies did] not necessarily correlate with successful job performance." 181 F.3d at 492 n.21. While we continue to believe that a "SEPTA officer should generally attempt to control a situation without having to make an arrest," id., the District Court found, based upon its review of the extensive body of evidence before it, that "lost arrests have a significant impact on the public safety" in the SEPTA transit system. This finding indicates that arrests do, in fact, correlate to successful performance as a SEPTA transit police officer.

We also questioned whether certain studies overemphasized the role of aerobic capacity in making arrests, and whether other studies placed too much emphasis on arrest rates for "serious crimes" given that, historically, the bulk of SEPTA arrests has been for lesser crimes. While not all SEPTA arrests are aerobic contests, nor are they always effectuated to apprehend "serious" criminals, the District Court found that "an inability to proficiently perform any * * * task[ ] would compromise the effectiveness of the SEPTA transit police." In essence, the Court concluded what, to us, is now evident: a SEPTA transit police officer must be ready and able to apprehend not just the numerous sedentary, petty criminals, but also the fleet-footed few who, from time to time, wreak serious harm on the people of Philadelphia. * * *

And so we move more directly to the critical issue before us—the minimum qualifications necessary in terms of aerobic capacity to successfully perform as a SEPTA transit police officer. * * * SEPTA argued that the run test measures the "minimum qualifications necessary" because the relevant studies indicate that individuals who fail the test will be much less likely to successfully execute critical policing tasks. For example, the District Court credited a study that evaluated the correlation between a successful run time and performance on 12 job standards. The study found that individuals who passed the run test had a success rate on the job standards ranging from 70% to 90%. The success rate of the individuals who failed the run test ranged from 5% to 20%. The District Court found that such a low rate of success was unacceptable for employees who are regularly called upon to protect the public. In so doing, the District Court implicitly defined "minimum qualifications necessary" as meaning "likely to be able to do the job."

Plaintiffs argued, however, that within the group that failed the run test, significant numbers of individuals would still be able to perform at least certain critical job tasks. They argued that as long as some of those failing the run test can do the job, the standard cannot be classified as a "minimum." In essence, plaintiffs proposed that the phrase "minimum qualifications necessary" means "some chance of being able to do the job." * * *

We are not saying * * * that "more is better." While, of course, a higher aerobic capacity will translate into better field performance—at least as to many job tasks which entail physical capability—to set an unnecessarily high cutoff score would contravene *Griggs*. It would clearly be unreasonable to require SEPTA applicants to score so highly on the run test that their predicted rate of success be 100%. It is perfectly reasonable, however, to demand a chance of success that is better than 5% to 20%. In sum, SEPTA transit police officers and the public they serve should not be required to engage in high-stakes gambling when it comes to public safety and law enforcement. SEPTA has demonstrated that the cutoff score it established measures the minimum qualifications necessary for successful performance as a SEPTA officer. * * *

One final note. While it is undisputed that SEPTA's 1.5 mile run test has a disparate impact on women, it is also undisputed that, in addition to those women who could pass the test without training, nearly all the women who trained were able to pass after only a moderate amount of training. It is not, we think, unreasonable to expect that women—and men—who wish to become SEPTA transit officers, and are committed to dealing with issues of public safety on a day-to-day basis, would take this necessary step. Moreover, we do not consider it unreasonable for SEPTA to require applicants, who wish to train to meet the job requirements, to do so before applying in order to demonstrate their commitment to physical fitness. The poor physical condition of SEPTA officers prior to 1989 demonstrates that not every officer is willing to make that commitment once he or she is hired. * * *

The judgment of the District Court will be affirmed.

MCKEE, CIRCUIT JUDGE dissenting.

* * * I cannot stress too strongly that the issue is not now, and never has been, whether SEPTA must jeopardize public safety in order to eliminate the disparate impact that SEPTA concedes * * * . Rather, the issue continues to be whether SEPTA can justify that cutoff under the business necessity test that is incorporated into Title VII by the 1991 Civil Rights Act. * * *

Accordingly, any suggestion that "federal courts" are advocating that diminished public safety is the social price that we must pay to eliminate gender discrimination is as unfortunate as it is inaccurate and misleading. Despite continuing protestations to the contrary, SEPTA has simply not demonstrated the business necessity of its cutoff though it has had several opportunities to do so. The implication that changing SEPTA's cutoff would endanger the public is therefore nothing more than the proverbial red herring.

* * * The District Court's analysis never focused on the fact that the 42.5 mL/kg/min cutoff is enforced when someone applies for the position of a SEPTA police officer, not when an offer of employment is extended or when an applicant graduates from the police academy and actually goes on the job. All of the studies the District Court relied upon purport to correlate success in job-related tasks to fitness level at the time of the task, not at some time prior to hiring and training. However, an offer to hire may be extended as much as two and one-half years after the aerobic

running test is administered and the 42.5 mL/kg/min cutoff applied, and there is absolutely no retest before beginning as a SEPTA officer. Accordingly, there is no way for SEPTA to know if even a male incumbent police officer has the aerobic capacity deemed so necessary to the job when he actually begins patrolling. * * *

Although the requirement of running 1.5 miles in 12 minutes and the corresponding 42.5 mL/kg/min cutoff may not appear that daunting a requirement for someone who exercises regularly and is in fairly good condition, it is nevertheless more than certain branches of the United States military demand of incumbents. I can understand and appreciate SEPTA's argument that its zone system, and its reliance on foot patrols explains why the 42.5 mL/kg/min cutoff is more demanding than the standard set for New York City Police. Differences between what is required of SEPTA police and New York City transit police perhaps rebut the testimony of Former New York City Transit Police Chief, Michael O'Connor, as to the need for SEPTA's aerobic standard. He led a significant reduction of crime in New York City's transit system. When he testified before the District Court as an expert witness in this suit he emphatically rejected the concept of comparing police officers' running ability with that of fleeing felons as a job requirement. SEPTA had argued that its officers must have an aerobic capacity at least equal to that of the "perpetrator" population SEPTA officers may have to chase. Chief O'Connor disagreed. He testified: "how fast you run is not a measure of how good a cop you are. It takes a lot more than just running fast to be a good cop."

SEPTA's own experience confirms this. Crime has been reduced on SEPTA facilities even though SEPTA does not require incumbent officers to achieve the 42.5 ml/kg/min cutoff. This undermines SEPTA's assertion about the relationship between the aerobic cutoff and effective policing, and it corroborates Chief O'Connor's view of the cutoff. * * *

SEPTA's insistence that the 42.5 mL/kg/min cutoff satisfies the business necessity test is undermined by the fact that it does not require its incumbent police officers to meet that standard. Yet, there is nothing to suggest that public safety has been jeopardized. * * *

It is uncontested that, despite SEPTA's claim that officers who cannot meet the 42.5 mL/kg/min standard endanger public safety, SEPTA has promoted officers who failed the running test, and given commendations to others who failed a component of that test. It is also uncontested that SEPTA has never suspended, reassigned, disciplined or demoted any officer "for failing to perform the physical requirements of the job." It has also promoted officers who could not meet the standard. * * *

"Reasonable" though it may be, the question remains, what cutoff is necessary to ensure public safety and effective policing? * * *

The inquiry would be furthered if SEPTA could point to some objective basis for defining a cutoff or aerobic threshold. However, the 42.5 mL/kg/min threshold seems to have been plucked from the air by Dr. Davis after SEPTA contacted him and asked him to assist in improving the quality of transit police officers. Dr. Davis testified that he initially sought the advice of twenty experienced SEPTA officers (designated as "subject matter experts" or "SMEs") to determine the level of physical exertion they thought was required of transit police officers. The SMEs told him that they thought a SEPTA officer should be able to run a mile in full gear in 11.78 minutes. However, Dr. Davis rejected that cutoff because it was too low. He believed nearly anyone in the general public could satisfy that standard. He rejected a standard of 50 mL/kg/min because it was too high. It would have had a "Draconian effect on women applicants." He therefore apparently decided upon a cutoff of 42.5 mL/kg/min because it was not too high, it was not too low; it was just right. But under *Griggs*, it is not permissible to select a discriminatory employment test in the same manner that Goldilocks chooses which bed to sleep in or which bowl of porridge to eat.

* * *

Prior to today's decision, it was established in this Circuit, as it remains established in others, that a job requirement that has a disparate impact based upon gender could only be upheld if the relationship between the discriminatory requirement was so closely related to the essential of a given job that it could be justified as a business necessity. Today, in upholding a discriminatory application process based only upon a colorable claim of business necessity, we retreat from that standard while purporting to apply it. Yet, in enacting the Civil Rights Act of 1991, I believe Congress meant exactly what it said; discrimination in the name of "business necessity" must truly be necessary. No such necessity has been established here.

* * *

NOTES AND QUESTIONS

1. The *Lanning* case provides the most comprehensive analysis of the business necessity defense after the passage of the Civil Rights Act. In *Lanning I*, the court reached two significant conclusions. First, the court held that the Civil Rights Act of 1991 was intended to adopt the standards articulated in *Griggs* and *Albemarle Paper*, while repudiating the standard adopted in *Wards Cove*. Second, the court interpreted that standard as requiring the employer to justify its practice as necessary to ensure employees meet the "minimum qualifications" of the job, as opposed to some

optimal standard. In doing so, the court rejected the employer's argument that a higher standard will provide better officers, what is referred to as the "more is better" standard. What was the court's rationale for adopting the minimal qualifications standard and rejecting the transit authority's approach? Do you believe that the court in *Lanning II* was faithful to its standard or did the court deviate from the standard it had previously adopted, as the dissenting judge suggested?

2. In *Lanning II*, the court explores the employer's justifications for its standard and the various methods of proof. What do you think was the employer's strongest argument? What do you think was the plaintiffs' strongest challenge to the employer's efforts? In this case, SEPTA developed the running test as a means of improving the quality of its force. The test was developed by an expert who observed the job and met with experienced officers to determine what qualities were necessary to be a successful transit officer. As discussed earlier in this chapter, employment practices are often justified through a validation study, and in this case, the department conducted a validation effort after the plaintiffs filed their charges with the EEOC. Although there was some dispute at the trial about the exact nature of the validation study, the employer offered what appeared to be a criterion-related validation study. In essence, the employer sought to determine what qualities made a transit officer successful, and in the context of this challenge, they sought to determine whether aerobic capacity was related to being a successful officer. They did that by documenting arrest records of officers and by testing the aerobic capacity of those officers to determine if there was a connection between aerobic capacity and higher arrest records. As a statistical matter, the question would be whether there was a statistically significant correlation between having a certain aerobic capacity (42 mL/kg/min) and making more arrests. This would not mean that only officers with that aerobic capacity could be successful; rather, it would mean that, on average, those officers who had an aerobic capacity of at least 42mL/kg/min would likely make more arrests than those who were less fit.

The department conducted other tests, including simulations designed to measure the aerobic capacity necessary to catch the average perpetrator. Under the standard established in *Lanning I*, the underlying issue is more complicated since the standard is whether the running test measured the minimum qualifications necessary to be successful as a transit officer. How does that test factor into the court's analysis with respect to the validation efforts, as discussed in *Lanning II*? What is the minimal standard identified by the court that is necessary for successful performance of the job? One issue worth noting is that the department was not arguing that an officer would be expected to run a mile and a half on the job (presumably to chase a suspect), but rather that having the capacity to run that distance within twelve minutes was correlated with successful job performance.

Another complicating factor was the physical condition and advice of incumbent employees, many of whom were unable to pass the running test. Union rules prevented the department from imposing the test on all existing employees, but it was clear that many successful officers were unable to pass the test. How should that information be weighed in the analysis? As an aside, the incumbent officers also suggested that new employees should be able to run a mile in full gear in 11.78 mins, a standard the department's expert rejected as too low. In its opinion, the district court noted that it was not surprising that the incumbent officers would suggest such a low standard since they did not want to establish a standard they could not pass.

3. *Alternative Employment Practices*: Under the Civil Rights Act of 1991, regardless of whether the employer is able to justify its selection procedure under § 703(k)(1)(A)(i), as "job related for the position in question and consistent with business necessity," the plaintiffs have an opportunity to demonstrate that an alternative employment practice would serve the employer's needs while reducing adverse impact. Title VII, § 703(k)(1)(A)(ii), 42 U.S.C. § 2000e–2(k)(1)(A)(ii). The employer is liable for discrimination if the employer "refuses to adopt such alternative employment practice." *Id.* One court has defined this test to mean, "The proposed alternative must be available, equally valid, and less discriminatory." Allen v. City of Chicago, 351 F.3d 306, 312 (7th Cir.2003). What alternatives might have been available in *Lanning*? The dissenting judge emphasized one alternative, which was to require applicants to pass the test after they had been selected for employment rather than at the time of their application. As the court noted, the period from application to employment offer could be as long as two years. Does this suggestion seem plausible? What objection might the department have to such an alternative? A frequent alternative practice is to lower the passing score, in this case perhaps requiring individuals to complete the mile and a half run in thirteen minutes or some other time. Assuming altering the time would reduce adverse impact, what would the plaintiffs need to prove to establish a viable alternative practice?

4. Since the passage of the Civil Rights Act of 1991, the volume of disparate impact litigation has decreased rather dramatically. One reason for this development has already been touched on—because damages are available for disparate treatment claims but not for disparate impact claims, plaintiffs have a clear incentive to proceed under a disparate treatment theory whenever possible. What other reasons might account for the decline in disparate impact cases? Many of the recent cases involve issues that have long been staples of the disparate impact theory. *See, e.g.*, M.O.C.H.A. Soc'y, Inc. v. City of Buffalo, 689 F.23d 263 (2nd Cir.2012) (dismissing challenge to promotional fire examination); Franklin v. Local 2 of the Sheet Metal Workers Int'l Ass'n, 565 F.3d 508, 516–21 (8th Cir.2009) (unsuccessful disparate impact challenge to a union referral policy brought by African-American workers); El v. Se. Penn. Transp. Auth. (SEPTA), 479 F.3d 232 (3d Cir.2007) (unsuccessful disparate impact challenge to defendants' policy of excluding individuals with felony convictions from transit driver positions brought by African-American driver-trainee); Isabel v. City of Memphis, 404 F.3d 404 (6th Cir.2005) (successful disparate impact challenge to police lieutenants' written exam brought by African-American candidates). New job

requirements have also faced challenges under the disparate impact theory. For example, the United States Department of Justice brought a number of cases challenging the residency requirements imposed by suburbs that surrounded large cities. *See, e.g.*, United States v. City of Warren, 138 F.3d 1083 (6th Cir.1998) (successful challenge to residency requirement and recruitment practices of suburb outside Detroit). Similar challenges continue to arise. NAACP v. North Hudson Regional Fire & Rescue, 665 F.3d 464 (3rd Cir.2011) (invalidating City's residency requirement for firefighter applicants). The examination to certify the competency of teachers in New York City was also recently invalidated because the examination failed to emphasize tasks that were important to teaching. *See* Gulino v. Bd. of Educ. of the City Sch. Dist. of NY, 907 F. Supp. 2d 492 (S.D.N.Y. 2012), *aff'd*, 555 Fed. Appx. 37 (2nd Cir.2014). A group of plaintiffs have also challenged the City of Boston's police department's practice of using hair samples to test for drug use, and the First Circuit Court of Appeals recently found that the practice had an adverse impact on African-American officers. *See* Jones v. City of Boston, 752 F.3d 38, 52 (1st Cir.2014). The court did not address whether the practice could be justified under the business necessity test, what would the defendants have to show to satisfy that test? The plaintiffs' contention was not that drug use was irrelevant but that the practice was inaccurate, how does that argument fit within the disparate impact theory? Policies that require workers to speak English on the job have also been the subject of disparate impact challenges, and will be discussed further in Chapter 12.

5. Although private lawsuits based on disparate impact claims have declined substantially, the Equal Employment Opportunity Commission has recently begun a litigation campaign that has challenged various employer policies under the disparate impact theory. The agency has emphasized two areas in particular: (1) credit history checks as part of an application process and (2) employer's policies that prohibit employment of those with felony convictions. There have not been many cases filed and to date the cases have been unsuccessful primarily because of difficulties involving data or establishing the existence of a policy. *See* EEOC v. Kaplan Higher Educ. Corp., 748 F.3d 749 (6th Cir.2014) (upholding exclusion of expert testimony that sought to determine the race of applicants in connection with challenge to employer's use of credit history checks); EEOC v. Peoplemark, 732 F.3d 584 (6th Cir.2013) (upholding attorneys' fee award against the EEOC after it was determined that the employer did not have a company policy that refused to employ individuals with felony convictions); EEOC v. Freeman, 778 F.3d 463 (4th Cir.2015) (granting summary judgment to defendant in EEOC's challenge to credit background checks for failure to establish disparate impact). In order to prove disparate impact on a challenge to an employer's use of credit history, what would a plaintiff need to establish? What about on a criminal conviction policy? Would it matter what the nature of the conviction was?

6. The *Griggs* case, and the disparate impact theory, has been the subject of several comprehensive retrospectives. Professor Robert Belton, one of the co-counsel in the *Griggs* case, has written:

> Aside from *Brown v. Board of Education*, the single most influential civil rights case during the past forty years that has profoundly shaped, and continues to shape, civil rights jurisprudence and the discourse on equality is *Griggs v. Duke Power Co* * * * . * * * Without the *Griggs* disparate impact theory, I doubt seriously whether we could have made the same degree of progress under the disparate treatment theory of discrimination alone, because the observations that the courts made in the early Title VII cases are probably as true today: "[d]efendants of even minimal sophistication will neither admit discriminatory animus nor leave a paper trail demonstrating it" and "unless the employer is a latter-day George Washington, employment discrimination is as difficult to prove as who chopped down the cherry tree."

Robert Belton, *A Brief Look at the Birth, Death, and Resurrection of the Disparate Impact Theory of Discrimination*, 22 Hofstra Lab. & Emp.L.J. 431, 433, 468 (2005) (citations omitted). Professor Belton adds: "A point that is often overlooked and too often overshadowed by the Court's most recent equal protection affirmative action cases is that *Griggs* provides the doctrinal foundations for legitimizing affirmative action in the employment context, particularly in the private sector." *Id.* at 469.

Professor Michael Selmi, while not questioning the importance of the *Griggs* case itself, has questioned the ultimate value of the disparate impact theory. In an article entitled *Was the Disparate Impact Theory a Mistake?*, he suggests that, outside the context of written tests, the disparate impact theory has produced "strikingly limited results," and he contends that many of the gains from the testing cases likely would have arisen from political pressure in the 1970s. He also argues that the theory may have had the unintended effect of restricting our interpretation of intentional discrimination: "As a concept, the disparate impact theory begins where intentional discrimination ends, and seeking an expansive role for the disparate impact theory ultimately has left us with a truncated definition of intentional discrimination." Michael Selmi, *Was the Disparate Impact Theory a Mistake?* 53 UCLA L.Rev. 701, 706 (2006). He concludes, "[T]he disparate impact theory was based on two critical mistakes—that the theory would be easier to prove [than intentional discrimination] and that it was possible to redefine discrimination purely through legal doctrine. At bottom, that is what the theory sought to do—redefine our concept of discrimination to focus on unequal results." *Id.* at 782. To do that, he suggests, a broad social movement focusing on the persistence of discrimination was necessary, a movement that has never materialized. Despite the decline in litigation, a number of scholars continue to emphasize the importance of the disparate impact theory. *See, e.g.*, Lawrence Rosenthal, *Saving Disparate Impact*, 34 Cardozo L. Rev. 2157 (2013).

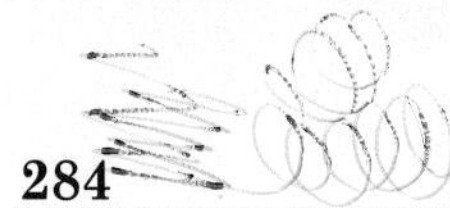

D. REMEDYING THE DISPARATE IMPACT OF SELECTION PROCEDURES

RICCI V. DESTEFANO

Supreme Court of the United States, 2009.
557 U.S. 557, 129 S.Ct. 2658, 174 L.Ed.2d 490.

JUSTICE KENNEDY delivered the opinion of the Court.

In the fire department of New Haven, Connecticut—as in emergency-service agencies throughout the Nation—firefighters prize their promotion to and within the officer ranks. An agency's officers command respect within the department and in the whole community; and, of course, added responsibilities command increased salary and benefits. Aware of the intense competition for promotions, New Haven, like many cities, relies on objective examinations to identify the best qualified candidates.

In 2003, 118 New Haven firefighters took examinations to qualify for promotion to the rank of lieutenant or captain. Promotion examinations in New Haven (or City) were infrequent, so the stakes were high. The results would determine which firefighters would be considered for promotions during the next two years, and the order in which they would be considered. Many firefighters studied for months, at considerable personal and financial cost.

When the examination results showed that white candidates had outperformed minority candidates, the mayor and other local politicians opened a public debate that turned rancorous. Some firefighters argued the tests should be discarded because the results showed the tests to be discriminatory. They threatened a discrimination lawsuit if the City made promotions based on the tests. Other firefighters said the exams were neutral and fair. And they, in turn, threatened a discrimination lawsuit if the City, relying on the statistical racial disparity, ignored the test results and denied promotions to the candidates who had performed well. In the end the City took the side of those who protested the test results. It threw out the examinations.

Certain white and Hispanic firefighters who likely would have been promoted based on their good test performance sued the City and some of its officials. Theirs is the suit now before us. The suit alleges that, by discarding the test results, the City and the named officials discriminated against the plaintiffs based on their race, in violation of both Title VII of the Civil Rights Act of 1964, as amended, 42 U.S.C. § 2000e *et seq.*, and the Equal Protection Clause of the Fourteenth Amendment. The City and the officials defended their actions, arguing that if they had certified the results, they could have faced liability under Title VII for adopting a practice that had a disparate impact on the minority firefighters. The District Court granted summary judgment for the defendants, and the Court of Appeals affirmed.

We conclude that race-based action like the City's in this case is impermissible under Title VII unless the employer can demonstrate a strong basis in evidence that, had it not taken the action, it would have been liable under the disparate-impact statute. The respondents, we further determine, cannot meet that threshold standard. As a result, the City's action in discarding the tests was a violation of Title VII. In light of our ruling under the statutes, we need not reach the question whether respondents' actions may have violated the Equal Protection Clause.

I

This litigation comes to us after the parties' cross-motions for summary judgment, so we set out the facts in some detail. As the District Court noted, although "the parties strenuously dispute the relevance and legal import of, and inferences to be drawn from, many aspects of this case, the underlying facts are largely undisputed."

A

When the City of New Haven undertook to fill vacant lieutenant and captain positions in its fire department (Department), the promotion and hiring process was governed by the city charter, in addition to federal and state law. The charter establishes a merit system. That system requires the City to fill vacancies in the classified civil-service ranks with the most qualified individuals, as determined by job-related examinations. After each examination, the New Haven Civil Service Board (CSB) certifies a ranked list of applicants who passed the test. Under the charter's "rule of three," the relevant hiring authority must fill each vacancy by choosing one candidate from the top three scorers on the list. Certified promotional lists remain valid for two years.

The City's contract with the New Haven firefighters' union specifies additional requirements for the promotion process. Under the contract, applicants for lieutenant and captain positions were to be screened using written and oral examinations, with the written exam accounting for 60 percent and the oral exam 40 percent of an applicant's total score. * * *

After reviewing bids from various consultants, the City hired Industrial/Organizational Solutions, Inc. (IOS) to develop and administer the examinations, at a cost to the City of $100,000. * * * In order to fit the examinations to the New Haven Department, IOS began the test-design process by performing job analyses to identify the tasks, knowledge, skills, and abilities that are essential for the lieutenant and captain positions. IOS representatives interviewed incumbent captains and lieutenants and their supervisors. They rode with and observed other on-duty officers. Using information from those interviews and ride-alongs, IOS wrote job-analysis questionnaires and administered them to most of the incumbent battalion chiefs, captains, and lieutenants in the Department. At every stage of the job analyses, IOS, by deliberate choice, oversampled minority firefighters to ensure that the results—which IOS would use to develop the examinations—would not unintentionally favor white candidates.

With the job-analysis information in hand, IOS developed the written examinations to measure the candidates' job-related knowledge. For each test, IOS compiled a list of training manuals, Department procedures, and other materials to use as sources for the test questions. IOS presented the proposed sources to the New Haven fire chief and assistant fire chief for their approval. Then, using the approved sources, IOS drafted a multiple-choice test for each position. Each test had 100 questions, as required by CSB rules, and was written below a 10th-grade reading level. After IOS prepared the tests, the City opened a 3-month study period. It gave candidates a list that identified the source material for the questions, including the specific chapters from which the questions were taken.

IOS developed the oral examinations as well. These concentrated on job skills and abilities. Using the job-analysis information, IOS wrote hypothetical situations to test incident-command skills, firefighting tactics, interpersonal skills, leadership, and management ability, among other things. Candidates would be presented with these hypotheticals and asked to respond before a panel of three assessors.

IOS assembled a pool of 30 assessors who were superior in rank to the positions being tested. * * * Sixty-six percent of the panelists were minorities, and each of the nine three-member assessment panels contained two minority members. * * *

Candidates took the examinations in November and December 2003. Seventy-seven candidates completed the lieutenant examination—43 whites, 19 blacks, and 15 Hispanics. Of those, 34 candidates passed—25 whites, 6 blacks, and 3 Hispanics. Eight lieutenant positions were vacant at the time of the examination. As the rule of three operated, this meant that the top 10 candidates were eligible for an immediate promotion to lieutenant. All 10 were white. Subsequent vacancies would have allowed at least 3 black candidates to be considered for promotion to lieutenant.

Forty-one candidates completed the captain examination—25 whites, 8 blacks, and 8 Hispanics. Of those, 22 candidates passed—16 whites, 3 blacks, and 3 Hispanics. Seven captain positions were vacant at the time of the examination. Under the rule of three, 9 candidates were eligible for an immediate promotion to captain—7 whites and 2 Hispanics.

B

The City's contract with IOS contemplated that, after the examinations, IOS would prepare a technical report that described the examination processes and methodologies and analyzed the results. But in January 2004, rather than requesting the technical report, City officials, including the City's counsel, Thomas Ude, convened a meeting with IOS Vice President Chad Legel. Based on the test results, the City officials expressed concern that the tests had discriminated against minority candidates. Legel defended the examinations' validity, stating that any numerical disparity between white and minority candidates was likely due to various external factors and was in line with results of the Department's previous promotional examinations. * * *

1

The CSB first met to consider certifying the results on January 22, 2004. Tina Burgett, director of the City's Department of Human Resources, opened the meeting by telling the CSB that "there is a significant disparate impact on these two exams." She distributed lists showing the candidates' races and scores (written, oral, and composite) but not their names. Ude also described the test results as reflecting "a very significant disparate impact," and he outlined possible grounds for the CSB's refusing to certify the results.

Although they did not know whether they had passed or failed, some firefighter-candidates spoke at the first CSB meeting in favor of certifying the test results. Michael Blatchley stated that "[e]very one" of the questions on the written examination "came from the [study] material. * * * [I]f you read the materials and you studied the material, you would have done well on the test." Frank Ricci stated that * * * he had "several learning disabilities," including dyslexia; that he had spent more than $1,000 to purchase the materials and pay his neighbor to read them on tape so he could "give it [his] best shot" and that he had studied "8 to 13 hours a day to prepare" for the test. "I don't even know if I made it," Ricci told the CSB, "[b]ut the people who passed should be promoted. When your life's on the line, second best may not be good enough."

Other firefighters spoke against certifying the test results. They described the test questions as outdated or not relevant to firefighting practices in New Haven. Gary Tinney stated that source materials "came out of New York * * *. Their makeup of their city and everything is totally different than ours." And they criticized the test materials, a full set of which cost about $500, for being too expensive and too long.

* * *

4

At the [fourth] meeting, on March 11, the CSB heard from three witnesses it had selected to "tell us a little bit about their views of the testing, the process, [and] the methodology." The first, Christopher Hornick, spoke to the CSB by telephone. Hornick is an industrial/organizational psychologist from Texas who operates a consulting business that "direct[ly]" competes with IOS. Hornick, who had not "stud[ied] the test at length or in detail" and had not "seen the job analysis data," told the CSB that the scores indicated a "relatively high adverse impact." Hornick stated that the "adverse impact on the written exam was somewhat higher but generally in the range that we've seen professionally."

When asked to explain the New Haven test results, Hornick opined that the collective-bargaining agreement's requirement of using written and oral examinations with a 60/40 composite score might account for the statistical disparity. * * * Hornick suggested that testing candidates at an "assessment center" rather than using written and oral examinations "might serve [the City's] needs better." Hornick stated that assessment centers, where candidates face real-world situations and respond just as they would in the field, allow candidates "to demonstrate how they would address a particular problem as opposed to just verbally saying it or identifying the correct option on a written test."

Hornick * * * described the IOS examinations as "reasonably good test[s]." He stated that the CSB's best option might be to "certify the list as it exists" and work to change the process for future tests, including by "[r]ewriting the Civil Service Rules." Hornick concluded his telephonic remarks by telling the CSB that "for the future," his company "certainly would like to help you if we can." * * *

The final witness was Janet Helms, a professor at Boston College whose "primary area of expertise" is "not with firefighters per se" but in "race and culture as they influence performance on tests and other assessment procedures." Helms expressly declined the CSB's offer to review the examinations. At the outset, she noted that "regardless of what kind of written test we give in this country * * * we can just about predict how many people will pass who are members of under-represented groups. And your data are not that inconsistent with what predictions would say were the case." * * *

5

At the final CSB meeting, on March 18, Ude (the City's counsel) argued against certifying the examination results. * * * Ude offered his "opinion that promotions . . . as a result of these tests would not be consistent with federal law, would not be consistent with the purposes of our Civil Service Rules or our Charter[,] nor is it in the best interests of the firefighters * * * who took the exams." He stated that previous Department exams "have not had this kind of result," and that previous results had not been "challenged as having adverse impact, whereas we are assured that these will be."

* * *

At the close of witness testimony, the CSB voted on a motion to certify the examinations. With one member recused, the CSB deadlocked 2 to 2, resulting in a decision not to certify the results. * * *

C

The CSB's decision not to certify the examination results led to this lawsuit. The plaintiffs—who are the petitioners here—are 17 white firefighters and 1 Hispanic firefighter who passed the examinations but were denied a chance at promotions when the CSB refused to certify the test results. * * *

The parties filed cross-motions for summary judgment. * * * The District Court granted summary judgment for respondents. * * * After full briefing and argument by the parties, the Court of Appeals affirmed in a one-paragraph, unpublished summary order; it later withdrew that order, issuing in its place a nearly identical, one-paragraph *per curiam* opinion adopting the District Court's reasoning.

This action presents two provisions of Title VII to be interpreted and reconciled, with few, if any, precedents in the courts of appeals discussing the issue. Depending on the resolution of the statutory claim, a fundamental constitutional question could also arise. We found it prudent and appropriate to grant certiorari [and w]e now reverse.

II

Petitioners raise a statutory claim, under the disparate-treatment prohibition of Title VII, and a constitutional claim, under the Equal Protection Clause of the Fourteenth Amendment. A decision for petitioners on their statutory claim would provide the relief sought, so we consider it first.

A

* * *

B

Petitioners allege that when the CSB refused to certify the captain and lieutenant exam results based on the race of the successful candidates, it discriminated against them in violation of Title VII's disparate-treatment provision. The City counters that its decision was permissible because the tests "appear[ed] to violate Title VII's disparate-impact provisions."

Our analysis begins with this premise: The City's actions would violate the disparate-treatment prohibition of Title VII absent some valid defense. All the evidence demonstrates that the City chose not to certify the examination results because of the statistical disparity based on race—*i.e.*, how minority candidates had performed when compared to white candidates. * * * Without some other justification, this express, race-based decisionmaking violates Title VII's command that employers cannot take adverse employment actions because of an individual's race. * * *

We consider, therefore, whether the purpose to avoid disparate-impact liability excuses what otherwise would be prohibited disparate-treatment discrimination. Courts often confront cases in which statutes and principles point in different directions. Our task is to provide guidance to employers and courts for situations when these two prohibitions could be in conflict absent a rule to reconcile them. In providing this guidance our decision must be consistent with the important purpose of Title VII—that the workplace be an environment free of discrimination, where race is not a barrier to opportunity. * * *

In searching for a standard that strikes a more appropriate balance, we note that this Court has considered cases similar to this one, albeit in the context of the Equal Protection Clause of the Fourteenth Amendment. The Court has held that certain government actions to remedy past racial discrimination—actions that are themselves based on race—are constitutional only where there is a " 'strong basis in evidence' " that the remedial actions were necessary. *Richmond* v. *J. A. Croson Co.*, 488 U.S. 469, 500, 109 S.Ct. 706, 102 L.Ed.2d 854 (1989) (quoting *Wygant* [v. *Jackson Bd. of Ed.*, 476 U.S. 267, 277, 106 S.Ct. 1842, 90 L.Ed.2d 260 (1986)] (plurality opinion)). This suit does not call on us to consider whether the statutory constraints under Title VII must be parallel in all respects to those under the Constitution. That does not mean the constitutional authorities are irrelevant, however. * * *

Writing for a plurality in *Wygant* and announcing the strong-basis-in-evidence standard, Justice Powell recognized the tension between eliminating segregation and discrimination on the one hand and doing away with all governmentally imposed discrimination based on race on the other. 476 U.S. at 277. The plurality required a strong basis in evidence because "[e]videntiary support for the conclusion that remedial action is warranted becomes crucial when the remedial program is challenged in court by nonminority employees." *Ibid.* * * *

The same interests are at work in the interplay between the disparate-treatment and disparate-impact provisions of Title VII. * * * Applying the strong-basis-in-evidence standard to Title VII gives effect to both the disparate-treatment and disparate-impact provisions, allowing violations of one in the name of compliance with the other only in certain, narrow circumstances. The standard leaves ample room for employers' voluntary compliance efforts, which are essential to the statutory scheme and to Congress's efforts to eradicate workplace discrimination. And the standard appropriately constrains employers' discretion in making race-based decisions: It limits that discretion to cases in which there is a strong basis in evidence of disparate-impact liability, but it is not so restrictive that it allows employers to act only when there is a provable, actual violation.

* * * Examinations like those administered by the City create legitimate expectations on the part of those who took the tests. As is the case with any promotion exam, some of the firefighters here invested substantial time, money, and personal commitment in preparing for the tests. Employment tests can be an important part of a neutral selection system that safeguards against the very racial animosities Title VII was intended to prevent. Here, however, the firefighters saw their efforts invalidated by the City in sole reliance upon race-based statistics.

* * *

Title VII does not prohibit an employer from considering, before administering a test or practice, how to design that test or practice in order to provide a fair opportunity for all individuals, regardless of their race. * * * We hold only that, under Title VII, before an employer can engage in intentional discrimination for the asserted purpose of avoiding or remedying an unintentional disparate impact, the employer must have a strong basis in evidence to believe it will be subject to disparate-impact liability if it fails to take the race-conscious, discriminatory action.

C

The City argues that, even under the strong-basis-in-evidence standard, its decision to discard the examination results was permissible under Title VII. That is incorrect. Even if respondents were motivated as a subjective matter by a desire to avoid committing disparate-impact discrimination, the record makes clear there is no support for the conclusion that respondents had an objective, strong basis in evidence to find the tests inadequate, with some consequent disparate-impact liability in violation of Title VII.

* * *

The racial adverse impact here was significant, and petitioners do not dispute that the City was faced with a prima facie case of disparate-impact liability. On the captain exam, the pass rate for white candidates was 64 percent but was 37.5 percent for both black and Hispanic candidates. On the lieutenant exam, the pass rate for white candidates was 58.1 percent; for black candidates, 31.6 percent; and for Hispanic candidates, 20 percent. The pass rates of minorities, which were approximately one-half the pass rates for white candidates, fall well below the 80-percent standard set by the EEOC to implement the disparate-impact provision of Title VII. See 29 CFR § 1607.4(D) (2008) (selection rate that is less than 80 percent "of the rate for the group with the highest rate will generally be regarded by the Federal enforcement agencies as evidence of adverse impact"). Based on how the passing candidates ranked and an application of the "rule of three," certifying the examinations would have meant that the City could not have considered black candidates for any of the then-vacant lieutenant or captain positions.

Based on the degree of adverse impact reflected in the results, respondents were compelled to take a hard look at the examinations to determine whether certifying the results would have had an impermissible disparate impact. The problem for respondents is that a prima facie case of disparate-impact liability—essentially, a threshold showing of a significant statistical disparity and nothing more—is far from a strong basis in evidence that the City would have been liable under Title VII had it certified the results. That is because the City could be liable for disparate-impact discrimination only if the examinations were not job related and consistent with business necessity, or if there existed an equally valid, less-discriminatory alternative that served the City's needs but that the City refused to adopt. § 2000e–2(k)(1)(A), (C). We conclude there is no strong basis in evidence to establish that the test was deficient in either of these respects. * * *

1

There is no genuine dispute that the examinations were job-related and consistent with business necessity. The CSB heard statements from Chad Legel (the IOS vice president) as well as city officials outlining the detailed steps IOS took to develop and administer the examinations. IOS devised the written examinations, which were the focus of the CSB's inquiry, after painstaking analyses of the captain and lieutenant positions—analyses in which IOS made sure that minorities were overrepresented. And IOS drew the questions from source material approved by the Department. Of the outside witnesses who appeared before the CSB, only one, Vincent Lewis, had reviewed the examinations in any detail, and he was the only one with any firefighting experience. Lewis stated that the "questions were relevant for both exams." * * *

Arguing that the examinations were not job-related, respondents note some candidates' complaints that certain examination questions were contradictory or did not specifically apply to firefighting practices in New Haven. But Legel told the CSB that IOS had addressed those concerns—that it entertained "a handful" of challenges to the validity of particular examination questions, that it "reviewed those challenges and provided feedback [to the City] as to what we thought the best course of action was," and that he could remember at least one question IOS had thrown out ("offer[ing] credit to everybody for that particular question"). * * *

The City, moreover, turned a blind eye to evidence that supported the exams' validity. Although the City's contract with IOS contemplated that IOS would prepare a technical report consistent with EEOC guidelines for examination-validity studies, the City made no request for its report. * * *

2

Respondents also lacked a strong basis in evidence of an equally valid, less-discriminatory testing alternative * * * . Respondents raise three arguments to the contrary, but each argument fails. First, respondents refer to testimony before the CSB that a different composite-score calculation—weighting the written and oral examination scores 30/70—would have allowed the City to consider two black candidates for then-open lieutenant positions and one black candidate for then-open captain positions. But respondents have produced no evidence to show that the 60/40 weighting was indeed arbitrary. In fact, because that formula was the result of a union-negotiated collective-bargaining agreement, we presume the parties negotiated that weighting for a rational reason. Nor does the record contain any evidence that the 30/70 weighting would be an equally valid way to determine whether candidates possess the proper mix of job knowledge and situational skills to earn promotions. Changing the weighting formula, moreover, could well have violated Title VII's prohibition of altering test scores on the basis of race. See § 2000e–2(l).

* * * [F]inally, respondents refer to statements by Hornick in his telephone interview with the CSB regarding alternatives to the written examinations. Hornick stated his "belie[f]" that an "assessment center process," which would have evaluated candidates' behavior in typical job tasks, "would have demonstrated less adverse impact." But Hornick's brief mention of alternative testing methods, standing alone, does not raise a genuine issue of material fact that assessment centers were available to the City at the time of the examinations and that they would have produced less adverse impact. * * *

The record in this litigation documents a process that, at the outset, had the potential to produce a testing procedure that was true to the promise of Title VII: No individual should face workplace discrimination based on race. Respondents thought about promotion qualifications and relevant experience in neutral ways. They were careful to ensure broad racial participation in the design of the test itself and its administration. As we have discussed at length, the process was open and fair.

The problem, of course, is that after the tests were completed, the raw racial results became the predominant rationale for the City's refusal to certify the results. The injury arises in part from the high, and justified, expectations of the candidates who had participated in the testing process on the terms the City had established for the promotional process. Many of the candidates had studied for months, at considerable personal and financial expense, and thus the injury caused by the City's reliance on raw racial statistics at the end of the process was all the more severe. Confronted with arguments both for and against certifying the test results—and threats of a lawsuit either way—the City was required to make a difficult inquiry. But its hearings produced no strong evidence of a disparate-impact violation, and the City was not entitled to disregard the tests based solely on the racial disparity in the results.

Our holding today clarifies how Title VII applies to resolve competing expectations under the disparate-treatment and disparate-impact provisions. If, after it certifies the test results, the City faces a disparate-impact suit, then in light of our holding today it should be clear that the City would avoid disparate-impact liability based on the strong basis in evidence that, had it not certified the results, it would have been subject to disparate-treatment liability.

Petitioners are entitled to summary judgment on their Title VII claim, and we therefore need not decide the underlying constitutional question. The judgment of the Court of Appeals is reversed, and the cases are remanded for further proceedings consistent with this opinion.

[The concurring opinions of JUSTICE SCALIA and JUSTICE ALITO, joined by JUSTICE SCALIA and JUSTICE THOMAS, have been omitted.]

JUSTICE GINSBURG, with whom JUSTICE STEVENS, JUSTICE SOUTER, and JUSTICE BREYER join, dissenting.

In assessing claims of race discrimination, "[c]ontext matters." *Grutter* v. *Bollinger*, 539 U.S. 306, 327, 123 S.Ct. 2325, 156 L.Ed.2d 304 (2003). In 1972, Congress extended Title VII of the Civil Rights Act of 1964 to cover public employment. At that time, municipal fire departments across the country, including New Haven's, pervasively discriminated against minorities. The extension of Title VII to cover jobs in firefighting effected no overnight change. It took decades of persistent effort, advanced by Title VII litigation, to open firefighting posts to members of racial minorities.

The white firefighters who scored high on New Haven's promotional exams understandably attract this Court's sympathy. But they had no vested right to promotion. Nor have other persons received promotions in preference to them. New Haven maintains that it refused to certify the test results because it believed, for good cause, that it would be vulnerable to a Title VII disparate-impact suit if it relied on those results. The Court today holds that New Haven has not demonstrated "a strong basis in evidence" for its plea. In so holding, the Court pretends that "[t]he City rejected the test results solely because the higher scoring candidates were white." That pretension, essential to the Court's disposition, ignores substantial evidence of multiple flaws in the tests New Haven used. The Court similarly fails to acknowledge the better tests used in other cities, which have yielded less racially skewed outcomes.

By order of this Court, New Haven, a city in which African-Americans and Hispanics account for nearly 60 percent of the population, must today be served—as it was in the days of undisguised discrimination—by a fire department in which members of racial and ethnic minorities are rarely seen in command positions. * * * The Court's order and opinion, I anticipate, will not have staying power.

I

A

The Court's recitation of the facts leaves out important parts of the story. Firefighting is a profession in which the legacy of racial discrimination casts an especially long shadow. In extending Title VII to state and local government employers in 1972, Congress took note of a U.S. Commission on Civil Rights (USCCR) report finding racial discrimination in municipal employment even "more pervasive than in the private sector." H.R. Rep. No. 92–238, p. 17 (1971). * * * The USCCR report singled out police and fire departments for having "[b]arriers to equal employment * * * greater * * * than in any other area of State or local government," with African-Americans "hold[ing] almost no positions in the officer ranks." *Ibid.*

The city of New Haven (City) was no exception. In the early 1970's, African-Americans and Hispanics composed 30 percent of New Haven's population, but only 3.6 percent of the City's 502 firefighters. The racial disparity in the officer ranks was even more pronounced: "[O]f the 107 officers in the Department only one was black, and he held the lowest rank above private." *Firebird Soc. of New Haven, Inc.* v. *New Haven Bd. of Fire Comm'rs*, 66 F.R.D. 457, 460 (Conn. 1975).

Following a lawsuit and settlement agreement, the City initiated efforts to increase minority representation in the New Haven Fire Department (Department). Those litigation-induced efforts produced some positive change. New Haven's population includes a greater proportion of minorities today than it did in the 1970's: Nearly 40 percent of the City's residents are African-American and more than 20 percent are Hispanic. Among entry-level firefighters, minorities are still underrepresented, but not starkly so. As of 2003, African-Americans and Hispanics constituted 30 percent and 16 percent of the City's firefighters, respectively. In supervisory positions, however, significant disparities remain. Overall, the senior officer ranks (captain and higher) are nine percent African-American and nine percent Hispanic. Only one of the Department's 21 fire captains is African-American. It is against this backdrop of entrenched inequality that the promotion process at issue in this litigation should be assessed.

B

* * *

Pursuant to New Haven's specifications, IOS developed and administered the oral and written exams. The results showed significant racial disparities. On the lieutenant exam, the pass rate for African-American candidates was about one-half the rate for Caucasian candidates; the pass rate for Hispanic candidates was even lower. * * * More striking still, although nearly half of the 77 lieutenant candidates were African-American or Hispanic, none would have been eligible for promotion to the eight positions then vacant. The highest scoring African-American candidate ranked 13th; the top Hispanic candidate was 26th. As for the seven then-vacant captain positions, two Hispanic candidates would have been eligible, but no African-Americans.

These stark disparities, the Court acknowledges, sufficed to state a prima facie case under Title VII's disparate-impact provision. * * * New Haven thus had cause for concern about the prospect of Title VII litigation and liability. City officials referred the matter to the New Haven Civil Service Board (CSB), the entity responsible for certifying the results of employment exams.

Between January and March 2004, the CSB held five public meetings to consider the proper course. * * * Seeking a range of input on these questions, the CSB heard from test takers, the test designer, subject-matter experts, City officials, union leaders, and community members. Several candidates for promotion, who did not yet know their exam results, spoke at the CSB's first two meetings. Some candidates favored certification. The exams, they emphasized, had closely tracked the assigned study materials. Having invested substantial time and money to prepare themselves for the test, they felt it would be unfair to scrap the results.

Other firefighters had a different view. A number of the exam questions, they pointed out, were not germane to New Haven's practices and procedures. At least two candidates opposed to certification noted unequal access to study materials. Some individuals, they asserted, had the necessary books even before the syllabus was issued. Others had to invest substantial sums to purchase the materials and "wait a month and a half for some of the books because they were on back-order." These disparities, it was suggested, fell at least in part along racial lines. While many Caucasian applicants could obtain materials and assistance from relatives in the fire service, the overwhelming majority of minority applicants were "first-generation firefighters" without such support networks. * * * After giving members of the public a final chance to weigh in, the CSB voted on certification, dividing 2 to 2. By rule, the result was noncertification.

* * *

II

* * *

The Court's decision in this litigation underplays a dominant Title VII theme. This Court has repeatedly emphasized that the statute "should not be read to thwart" efforts at voluntary compliance. *Johnson* [v. *Transportation Agency, Santa Clara Cty.*, 480 U.S. 616, 630, 107 S.Ct. 1442, 94 L.Ed.2d 615 (1987)]. Such compliance, we have explained, is "the preferred means of achieving [Title VII's] objectives." *Firefighters* v. *Cleveland*, 478 U.S. 501, 515, 106 S.Ct. 3063, 92 L.Ed.2d 405 (1986). The strong-basis-in-evidence standard, however, as barely described in general, and cavalierly applied in this case, makes voluntary compliance a hazardous venture.

As a result of today's decision, an employer who discards a dubious selection process can anticipate costly disparate-treatment litigation in which its chances for success—even for surviving a summary-judgment motion—are highly problematic. Concern about exposure to disparate-impact liability, however well grounded, is insufficient to insulate an employer from attack. Instead, the employer must make a "strong" showing that (1) its selection method was "not job related and consistent with business necessity," or (2) that it refused to adopt "an equally valid, less-discriminatory alternative." It is hard to see how these requirements differ from demanding that an employer establish "a provable, actual violation" *against itself*. * * *

3

The Court's additional justifications for announcing a strong-basis-in-evidence standard are unimpressive. First, discarding the results of tests, the Court suggests, calls for a heightened standard because it "upset[s] an employee's legitimate expectation." This rationale puts the cart before the horse. The legitimacy of an employee's expectation depends on the legitimacy of the selection method. If an employer reasonably concludes that an exam fails to identify the most qualified individuals and needlessly shuts out a segment of the applicant pool, Title VII surely does not compel the employer to hire or promote based on the test, however unreliable it may be. * * *

Second, the Court suggests, anything less than a strong-basis-in-evidence standard risks creating "a *de facto* quota system, in which * * * an employer could discard test results * * * with the intent of obtaining the employer's preferred racial balance." Under a reasonableness standard, however, an employer could not cast aside a selection method based on a statistical disparity alone. The employer must have good cause to believe that the method screens out qualified applicants and would be difficult to justify as grounded in business necessity. * * *

III

A

Applying what I view as the proper standard to the record thus far made, I would hold that New Haven had ample cause to believe its selection process was flawed and not justified by business necessity. Judged by that standard, petitioners have not shown that New Haven's failure to certify the exam results violated Title VII's disparate-treatment provision.

The City, all agree, "was faced with a prima facie case of disparate-impact liability." Alerted to this stark disparity, the CSB heard expert and lay testimony, presented at public hearings, in an endeavor to ascertain whether the exams were fair and consistent with business necessity. Its investigation revealed grave cause for concern about the exam process itself and the City's failure to consider alternative selection devices.

Chief among the City's problems was the very nature of the tests for promotion. In choosing to use written and oral exams with a 60/40 weighting, the City simply adhered to the union's preference and apparently gave no consideration to whether the weighting was likely to identify the most qualified fire-officer candidates. There is strong reason to think it was not.

Relying heavily on written tests to select fire officers is a questionable practice, to say the least. Successful fire officers, the City's description of the position makes clear, must have the "[a]bility to lead personnel effectively, maintain discipline, promote harmony, exercise sound judgment, and cooperate with other officials." These qualities are not well measured by written tests. Testifying before the CSB, Christopher Hornick, an exam-design expert with more than two decades of relevant experience, was emphatic on this point: Leadership skills, command presence, and the like "could have been identified and evaluated in a much more appropriate way."

Hornick's commonsense observation is mirrored in case law and in Title VII's administrative guidelines. Courts have long criticized written firefighter promotion exams for being "more probative of the test-taker's ability to recall what a particular text stated on a given topic than of his firefighting or supervisory knowledge and abilities." *Vulcan Pioneers, Inc.* v. *New Jersey Dep't of Civil Serv.*, 625 F.Supp. 527, 539 (NJ 1985). A fire officer's job, courts have observed, "involves complex behaviors, good interpersonal skills, the ability to make decisions under tremendous pressure, and a host of other abilities—none of which is easily measured by a written, multiple choice test." *Firefighters Inst. for Racial Equality* v. *St. Louis*, 616 F.2d 350, 359 (CA8 1980). Interpreting the Uniform Guidelines, EEOC and other federal agencies responsible for enforcing equal opportunity employment laws have similarly recognized that, as measures of "interpersonal relations" or "ability to function under danger (*e.g.*, firefighters)," "[p]encil-and-paper tests * * * generally are not close enough approximations of work behaviors to show content validity." 44 Fed. Reg. 12007 (1979).

Given these unfavorable appraisals, it is unsurprising that most municipal employers do not evaluate their fire-officer candidates as New Haven does. Although comprehensive statistics are scarce, a 1996 study found that nearly two-thirds of surveyed municipalities used assessment centers ("simulations of the real world of work") as part of their promotion processes. P. Lowry, A Survey of the Assessment Center Process in the Public Sector, 25 Public Personnel Management 307, 315 (1996). That figure represented a marked increase over the previous decade, see *ibid.*, so the percentage today may well be even higher. Among municipalities still relying in part on written exams, the median weight assigned to them was 30 percent—half the weight given to New Haven's written exam. *Id.*, at 309.

* * *

In sum, the record solidly establishes that the City had good cause to fear disparate-impact liability. Moreover, the Court supplies no tenable explanation why the evidence of the tests' multiple deficiencies does not create at least a triable issue under a strong-basis-in-evidence standard.

B

It is indeed regrettable that the City's noncertification decision would have required all candidates to go through another selection process. But it would have been more regrettable to rely on flawed exams to shut out candidates who may well have the command presence and other qualities needed to excel as fire officers. Yet that is the choice the Court makes today. It is a choice that breaks the promise of *Griggs* that groups long denied equal opportunity would not be held back by tests "fair in form, but discriminatory in operation." 401 U.S., at 431.

* * *

This case presents an unfortunate situation, one New Haven might well have avoided had it utilized a better selection process in the first place. But what this case does not present is race-based discrimination in violation of Title VII. I dissent from the Court's judgment. * * *

NOTES AND QUESTIONS

1. The *Ricci* case raises important issues regarding how an employer can address the adverse impact of a test or selection procedure, and as the Court noted, there was little precedent to guide the Court's decision. What do you think was most important to the majority in reaching its decision? What do you think accounted for the division on the Court between the majority and dissenting Justices?

2. The Court holds that an employer must have a "strong basis in evidence" that it would be subject to liability under Title VII before it can discard results of an examination process. The dissent contends that this is both an amorphous and stringent standard, noting that it would likely require the City to prove an "actual violation against itself." Does that seem accurate or might a lesser showing suffice? How would the City make such a showing, keeping in mind that in most litigation over tests it is the City, or the employer, that defends the test? If you were advising another municipality that found itself in a similar situation, how would you suggest that it proceed?

3. Following the Supreme Court's decision in *Ricci*, the City certified the test results and made promotions. Michael Briscoe, an African-American firefighter who had taken the Lieutenant's test, then filed a disparate impact challenge to the use of the test, specifically identifying the 60/40 weighting as having caused disparate impact. The District Court initially dismissed the case as foreclosed by the *Ricci* decision but the Second Circuit Court of Appeals reversed, holding instead that the City was required to defend the test against the disparate impact challenge. *See* Briscoe v. City of New Haven, 654 F.3d 200 (2nd Cir.2011), *cert. denied*, 132 S.Ct. 2741 (2012). On remand, the District Court held that the 60/40 weighting, which received considerable attention in the Supreme Court proceeding, was not the cause of the disparate impact—changing the weights would not have altered the number of African Americans who would have been promoted (3 of 16 promotions went to African Americans), though it would have meant that Mr. Briscoe would have been promoted instead of one of the other African-American candidates. The court, however, noted that the disparate impact theory is not concerned with the individual results of the examination but only the disparate effects on a group and therefore dismissed the challenge. *See* Briscoe v. City of New Haven, 967 F. Supp.2d 563 (D. Conn. 2013).

4. One issue raised by the Court's decision is what impact it might have on direct challenges to examination results. As discussed earlier in the

chapter, lower courts have developed an extensive body of law regarding test validation, and the Court in *Ricci* failed to discuss any of that case law. It seems the Supreme Court may have conflated the issue of professional test development with the more important question of test validation. In other words, although the tests used by New Haven had been professionally developed that does not necessarily mean they had been validated under the law. Rather, validation requires more extensive analysis of how the test might predict performance, an issue that was never explored in the various hearings before the Civil Service Board. A validation study would also have sought to justify the 60/40 division between the written and oral examination, as well as the cut-off scores and the validity of using the test for rank order selection. *See, e.g.*, Isabel v. City of Memphis, 404 F.3d 404, 413 (6th Cir.2005) (invalidating promotion examination for failure to validate cut-off score). As the Court noted in its opinion, the test developer offered to provide a technical report, which the City opted not to obtain. Why do you think the City made that decision? Based on the record, it is not clear what that technical report would have included or whether it would have met the standards for test validation. It should also be noted here that test validation is not required to meet the business necessity test, though it has traditionally been the most common means of establishing that a selection procedure satisfies the business necessity standard.

5. The Court—both the majority and dissenting opinions—also discussed potential alternative selection procedures that might have reduced adverse impact while serving the employer's needs. As was true with validation, the record was clearly inadequate to assess possible alternative selection methods. One expert mentioned the possibility of using assessment centers, which are common practices, particularly for promotional positions, that require candidates to perform certain job tasks in simulated settings. Although assessment centers can have less adverse impact, there was no evidence to suggest that an assessment center would have lowered adverse impact in this particular case.

6. The *Ricci* case echoes many of the themes developed in the earlier disparate impact cases. What themes do you see in the case, and how does it fit with the prior case law? Among scholars, the *Ricci* case has generated a substantial amount of criticism. Professor Girardeau Spann, for example, criticized the Court's conclusion that the test was valid, noting, "The only reason that the *Ricci* court was willing to disregard conflicting evidence, and view the non-validated New Haven exam as establishing the appropriate baseline for firefighter promotions, is that whites performed in a way that the Court expected. If racial minorities had outperformed whites in the face of conflicting evidence concerning the exam's validity, the Court would almost certainly have viewed the exam results as suspect." Girardeau A. Spann, *Disparate Impact*, 98 Geo. L.J. 1133, 155 (2010). Do you agree? Professor Michael Selmi criticized the litigation for ignoring what he suggested were two critical questions: the source of the disparate impact and whether the examination succeeded in predicting who would be good officers. See Michael

Selmi, *Indirect Discrimination and the Anti-Discrimination Mandate*, at 265, in Philosophical Foundations of Discrimination Law (D. Hellman & D. Moreau eds., 2014). For additional critiques see Roberto L. Corrada, *Ricci's Dicta: Signaling a New Standard for Affirmative Action Under Title VII?*, 46 Wake Forest L. Rev. 241 (2011); Cheryl I. Harris & Kimberly West Faulcon, *Reading Ricci: Whitening Discrimination, Racing Test Fairness*, 58 UCLA L. Rev. 73 (2010); Michael J. Zimmer, *Ricci's "Color-Blind" Standard in a Race Conscious Society: A Case of Unintended Consequences*? 2010 BYU L. Rev. 1257. In her critique of the case, Professor Melissa Hart made the point that, "Ricci, did not, in fact, eliminate—or even really change—disparate impact law. Employers are still required under Title VII, if their employment practices have an adverse impact, to ensure the practices are job related and consistent with business necessity." Melissa Hart, *From Wards Cove to Ricci: Struggling Against the "Built-In Headwinds" of a Skeptical Court*, 46 Wake Forest L. Rev. 261, 277 (2011). In fact, the *Ricci* decision has rarely been successfully invoked. Recently the city of Buffalo decided to create a new promotional examination for its Police Department, and it used the results of that test to make promotions instead of an earlier examination. An employee who had done well on the prior examination and was awaiting promotion—but who declined to take the new examination—sued alleging that the City's actions ran afoul of the Supreme Court's *Ricci* decision. The Second Circuit disagreed, upholding the City's actions because the City had been concerned about the utility of the prior examination. The City's problem, the Court noted, "was with the test, itself rather than with a particular set of results." Maraschiello v. City of Buffalo Police Dept., 709 F.3d 87 (2nd Cir.), *cert. denied*, 134 S.Ct. 119 (2013). The City's additional concern or desire to achieve a more "racially balanced" officer corps did not invalidate the City's action. *Id. at 96*.

— STOP —

CHAPTER 5

EQUAL PROTECTION AND THE RECONSTRUCTION CIVIL RIGHTS ACTS

■ ■ ■

A. INTRODUCTION: THE LEGACY OF THE RECONSTRUCTION-ERA REFORMS

During Reconstruction, Congress embarked on a program of constitutional and legislative reform to benefit the newly freed slaves that produced three constitutional amendments—the Thirteenth, Fourteenth, and Fifteenth Amendments—and a number of statutory enactments, including civil rights legislation. *See* Eugene Gressman, *The Unhappy History of Civil Rights Legislation*, 50 Mich.L.Rev. 1323 (1952). The Thirteenth Amendment outlaws slavery and involuntary servitude. The Fourteenth Amendment guarantees to all persons the privileges and immunities of United States citizenship, due process of law, and equal protection of the laws. The Fifteenth Amendment prohibits both the federal and state governments from depriving citizens of the right to vote on account of race, color, or previous condition of servitude.

After the Thirteenth Amendment was ratified in 1865, Congress passed the Civil Rights Act of 1866 to carry out the purposes of the amendment. Because of Republican concerns that the Thirteenth Amendment did not provide adequate constitutional authority for the Civil Rights Act of 1866, Congress drafted the Fourteenth Amendment to provide the Act of 1866 with a firmer constitutional foundation. Gressman, *supra*, at 1324–35. Professor Douglas Colbert described the origins of the 1866 Act:

> Although the states ratified the [Thirteenth] Amendment in December 1865, a wave of brutal, racially motivated violence against African Americans swept the South the following year. Local law enforcement officials generally refused to prosecute offenders, and southern states enacted Black Code laws, which were intended to perpetuate African American slavery. * * *
>
> Northern legislators had anticipated southern resistance to the Thirteenth Amendment. While some suggested providing economic reparations to accompany the constitutional guarantee, a strong consensus developed among moderates and conservatives favoring equal protection of the law for all men.

> The debates leading to passage of the 1866 Civil Rights Act reveal legislators' broad and developing vision of what Thirteenth Amendment freedom rights meant * * * .
>
> The Bill's first section guaranteed citizenship to all people, other than Native Americans, who were born in the United States. It specifically identified fundamental rights necessary to make all men equal before the law. These included contract and property rights, access to courts, and equality under the law.

Douglas L. Colbert, *Liberating the Thirteenth Amendment*, 30 Harv.C.R.–C.L.L.Rev. 1, 11–13 (1995) (footnotes omitted). In the Equal Protection Clause, the Fourteenth Amendment embodied the fundamental rights of civil equality under the law as expressed in the 1866 Act. The ratification of the Fourteenth Amendment was followed by the enactment of the Enforcement Act of 1870, which was, in part, a rewording of the Act of 1866 to protect "all persons," instead of "citizens, of every race and color." The language of the 1870 Act is now codified at 42 U.S.C. § 1981(a), and discrimination actions brought under the statute are known as § 1981 claims.

As historian Eric Foner has observed, "[t]he transformation of slaves into free laborers and equal citizens was the most dramatic example of the social and political changes unleashed by the Civil War and emancipation." Eric Foner, Reconstruction: America's Unfinished Revolution, 1863–1877, at xxv (1988). The reform agenda forced Congress to address the meanings of equality, but, as Foner has noted, this was not a simple undertaking.

> [T]he implications of the elusive term "equality" were anything but clear in 1865. At the outset of Reconstruction most Republicans still adhered to a political vocabulary inherited from the antebellum era, which distinguished sharply between natural, civil, political, and social rights. The first could not legitimately be circumscribed by government; slavery had been wrong, fundamentally, because it violated the natural rights—life, liberty, and the pursuit of happiness—common to all humanity. Equality in civil rights—equal treatment by the courts and civil and criminal laws—most Republicans now deemed nearly as essential, for an individual's natural rights could not be secured without it. Although Radicals insisted black suffrage must be part of Reconstruction, the vote was commonly considered a "privilege" rather than a right; requirements varied from state to state, and unequal treatment or even complete exclusion did not compromise one's standing as a citizen. And social relations—the choice of business and personal associates—

most Americans deemed a personal matter, outside the purview of government.

Id. at 231.

In a series of early cases, the Supreme Court substantially eviscerated the civil rights legislation enacted by Congress during Reconstruction. In the *Slaughter-House Cases*, 83 U.S. (16 Wall.) 36, 21 L.Ed.394 (1873), the Court largely gutted the privileges and immunities clause of the Fourteenth Amendment by construing it to protect only those rights incident to national citizenship, such as the right to travel. The Court rejected a construction of the privileges and immunities clause that would offer federal protection to the right to property or the right to freedom of contract. In the *Civil Rights Cases*, 109 U.S. 3, 3 S.Ct. 18, 27 L.Ed.835 (1883), the Court struck down the public accommodations provisions of the Civil Rights Act of 1875 on the ground that Congress lacked the power under either the Thirteenth or Fourteenth Amendment to prohibit private discrimination. And in the 1896 decision of *Plessy v. Ferguson*, 163 U.S. 537, 16 S.Ct. 1138, 41 L.Ed.256 (1896), the Court constitutionalized the "separate but equal" doctrine. As a result of these developments, for nearly one hundred years equal protection doctrine and the early civil rights laws on racial equality had little or no relevance in the context of employment as well as many other areas of civil life.

During the slow and often contentious dismantling of *de jure* racial segregation in the South in the years following *Brown v. Board of Education*, 347 U.S. 483, 74 S.Ct. 686, 98 L.Ed.873 (1954), and the contemporaneous civil rights protests that preceded the passage of the Civil Rights Act of 1964, some federal judges began to examine anew the jurisprudential doctrines underpinning the Reconstruction-era constitutional amendments and laws. With a series of Supreme Court cases beginning in the 1950s and 1960s, both the doctrine of equal protection of the laws embodied in the Fourteenth Amendment and the principles of racial equality promised to African-Americans by the Civil Rights Act of 1866 took on new life.

The Thirteenth and Fourteenth Amendments to the Constitution—and the Reconstruction civil rights statutes enacted to fulfill the purposes of those amendments—have thus raised several questions that the Supreme Court has had to address or readdress over time. Two of the most important are (1) whether any of these constitutional amendments or laws apply to discrimination against individuals or groups other than blacks, and (2) whether any of these constitutional amendments or laws apply to discriminatory conduct by private as well as public entities. The Supreme Court addressed the first question with regard to § 1981 in *St. Francis College v. Al-Khazraji*, 481 U.S. 604, 107 S.Ct. 2022, 95 L.Ed.2d

582 (1987), reproduced in Chapter 2, and both of these questions are among the issues covered in this chapter.

Though they share a common origin and purpose, the Equal Protection Clause of the Fourteenth Amendment and the Civil Rights Act of 1866 have produced distinct bodies of law that now can provide the basis for employment discrimination claims in certain situations. In some circumstances, these are claims that can be brought in addition to or in lieu of Title VII discrimination claims. Section B of this chapter covers employment discrimination claims brought against state and local government employers under the Equal Protection Clause of the Fourteenth Amendment, as well as employment discrimination claims brought against the federal government under the analogous equal protection component of the Fifth Amendment by employees who are not covered by federal antidiscrimination statutes. Section C treats the theory of liability and scope of protection in employment discrimination claims brought under 42 U.S.C. § 1981, the current amended version of the Civil Rights Act of 1866. As you read the following materials, consider the ways in which the courts have defined and redefined the concept of equality and equal protection of the laws.

B. EQUAL PROTECTION: THE FIFTH AND FOURTEENTH AMENDMENTS

The Equal Protection Clause of the Fourteenth Amendment permits state and local government employees to challenge a variety of discriminatory policies and practices of their employers in § 1983 actions brought in federal or state court. *See* the Civil Rights Act of 1871, 42 U.S.C. § 1983. Although most governmental classifications of persons are subject to a test of reasonableness, classifications on the basis of race, national origin, or alienage are considered "inherently suspect" and are subjected to strict scrutiny. City of Cleburne, Tex. v. Cleburne Living Ctr., 473 U.S. 432, 440, 105 S.Ct. 3249, 3254, 87 L.Ed.2d 313 (1985). The Supreme Court has held that under the strict scrutiny test, racial classifications are constitutional only if they are narrowly tailored to further some compelling state interest. *See, e.g.*, Grutter v. Bollinger, 539 U.S. 306, 326–27, 123 S.Ct. 2325, 2337–38, 156 L.Ed.2d 304 (2003). Likewise, the Court has recognized that the equal protection component of the Fifth Amendment is congruent with the Equal Protection Clause of the Fourteenth Amendment; thus, for example, "all racial classifications, imposed by whatever federal, state, or local government actor, must be analyzed by a reviewing court under strict scrutiny." Adarand Constructors, Inc. v. Pena, 515 U.S. 200, 227, 115 S.Ct. 2097, 2113, 132 L.Ed.2d 158 (1995). An intermediate level of review is used for classifications based on sex. *See, e.g.*, Nev. Dept. of Human Res. v. Hibbs, 538 U.S. 721, 728, 123 S.Ct. 1972, 1978, 155 L.Ed.2d 953 (2003); United

States v. Virginia, 518 U.S. 515, 116 S.Ct. 2264, 135 L.Ed.2d 735 (1996). Other governmental classifications, such as those based on age or disability, are subject to rational basis review. Kimel v. Fla. Bd. of Regents, 528 U.S. 62, 83, 120 S.Ct. 631, 646, 145 L.Ed.2d 522 (2000) (age); Bd. of Trs. of Univ. of Ala. v. Garrett, 531 U.S. 356, 367, 121 S.Ct. 955, 964, 148 L.Ed.2d 866 (2001) (disability). Most of the claims brought under these constitutional provisions involve groups and the Supreme Court has rejected an equal protection claim challenging a government employer's irrational conduct against one employee alone. Although the employee sought to prevail on a theory of rational basis, the Court held that a "class of one," as opposed to a class based on race or sex, is not cognizable under the Equal Protection Clause of the Fourteenth Amendment. *See* Engquist v. Or. Dep't of Agric., 553 U.S. 591, 128 S.Ct. 2146, 170 L.Ed.2d 975 (2008).

In the wake of *Brown v. Board of Education*, 347 U.S. 483, 74 S.Ct. 686, 98 L.Ed.873 (1954), public employers began to abandon policies that overtly discriminated on the basis of race. The effects of many years of racial discrimination and segregation, however, left the workforces of many public employers just as stratified in terms of race as was the case in the private sector. For this reason, a number of lower courts approved the use of the *Griggs v. Duke Power Co.* disparate impact analysis in cases challenging, on equal protection grounds, certain employment tests and hiring practices used by public employers. *See, e.g.*, Chance v. Board of Examiners, 458 F.2d 1167, 1176–77 (2d Cir.1972). The following case is the Supreme Court's response to that development.

WASHINGTON V. DAVIS

Supreme Court of the United States, 1976.
426 U.S. 229, 96 S.Ct. 2040, 48 L.Ed.2d 597.

JUSTICE WHITE delivered the opinion of the Court.

This case involves the validity of a qualifying test administered to applicants for positions as police officers in the District of Columbia Metropolitan Police Department. The test was sustained by the District Court but invalidated by the Court of Appeals. We are in agreement with the District Court and hence reverse the judgment of the Court of Appeals.

I

This action began on April 10, 1970, when two Negro police officers filed suit against the then Commissioner of the District of Columbia, the Chief of the District's Metropolitan Police Department, and the Commissioners of the United States Civil Service Commission. An amended complaint * * * alleged that the promotion policies of the Department were racially discriminatory and sought a declaratory judgment and an injunction. The respondents * * * were permitted to intervene, their amended complaint asserting that their applications to become officers in the Department had been rejected, and that the Department's recruiting procedures discriminated on the basis of race against black applicants by a series of practices including, but not limited to, a written personnel test which excluded a disproportionately high number of Negro applicants. These practices were asserted to violate respondents' rights "under the due process clause of the Fifth Amendment to the United States Constitution * * * ." * * *

According to the findings and conclusions of the District Court, to be accepted by the Department and to enter an intensive 17-week training program, the police recruit was required to satisfy certain physical and character standards, to be a high school graduate or its equivalent, and to receive a grade of at least 40 out of 80 on "Test 21," which is "an examination that is used generally throughout the federal service," which "was developed by the Civil Service Commission, not the Police Department," and which was "designed to test verbal ability, vocabulary, reading and comprehension."

The validity of Test 21 was the sole issue before the court on the motions for summary judgment. The District Court noted that there was no claim of "an intentional discrimination or purposeful discriminatory acts" but only a claim that Test 21 bore no relationship to job performance and "has a highly discriminatory impact in screening out black candidates." Respondents' evidence, the District Court said, warranted three conclusions: "(a) The number of black police officers, while substantial, is not proportionate to the population mix of the city. (b) A higher percentage of blacks fail the Test than whites. (c) The Test has not been validated to establish its reliability for measuring subsequent job performance." This showing was deemed sufficient to shift the burden of proof to the defendants in the action, petitioners here; but the court nevertheless concluded that on the undisputed facts respondents were not entitled to relief. The District Court relied on several factors. Since August 1969, 44% of new police force recruits had been black; that figure also represented the proportion of blacks on the total force and was roughly equivalent to 20- to 29-year-old blacks in the 50-mile radius in which the recruiting efforts of the Police Department had been concentrated. It was undisputed that the Department had systematically and affirmatively sought to enroll black officers many of whom passed the test but failed to report for duty. The District Court rejected the assertion that Test 21 was culturally slanted to favor whites and was "satisfied that the undisputable facts prove the test to be reasonably and directly related to the requirements of the police recruit training program and that it is neither so designed nor operates [*sic*] to discriminate against otherwise qualified blacks." * * * The District Court ultimately concluded that "[t]he proof is wholly lacking that a police officer qualifies on the color of his skin rather than ability" and that the Department "should not be required on this showing to lower standards or to abandon efforts to achieve excellence."

Having lost * * * in the District Court, respondents brought the case to the Court of Appeals claiming that their summary judgment motion, which rested on purely constitutional grounds, should have been granted. The tendered constitutional issue was whether the use of Test 21 invidiously discriminated against Negroes and hence denied them due process of law contrary to the commands of the Fifth Amendment. The Court of Appeals, addressing that issue, announced that it would be guided by *Griggs v. Duke Power Co.*, 401 U.S. 424, 91 S.Ct. 849, 28 L.Ed.2d 158 (1971), a case involving the interpretation and application of Title VII of the Civil Rights Act of 1964, and held that the statutory standards elucidated in that case were to govern the due process question tendered in this one. The court went on to declare that lack of discriminatory intent in designing and administering Test 21 was irrelevant; the critical fact was rather that a far greater proportion of blacks—four times as many—failed the test than did whites. This disproportionate impact, standing alone and without regard to whether it indicated a discriminatory purpose, was held sufficient to establish a constitutional violation, absent proof by petitioners that the test was an adequate measure of job performance in addition to being an indicator of probable success in the training program, a burden which the court ruled petitioners had failed to discharge. * * * The Court of Appeals, over a dissent, accordingly reversed the judgment of the District Court and directed that respondents' motion for partial summary judgment be granted. * * *

II

Because the Court of Appeals erroneously applied the legal standards applicable to Title VII cases in resolving the constitutional issue before it, we reverse its judgment in respondents' favor. Although the petition for certiorari did not present this ground for reversal,[8] our Rule 40(1)(d)(2) provides that we "may notice a plain error not presented"; and this is an appropriate occasion to invoke the Rule.

As the Court of Appeals understood Title VII,[10] employees or applicants proceeding under it need not concern themselves with the

[8] Apparently not disputing the applicability of the *Griggs* and Title VII standards in resolving this case, petitioners presented issues going only to whether *Griggs v. Duke Power Co.* had been misapplied by the Court of Appeals.

[10] Although Title VII standards have dominated this case, the statute was not applicable to federal employees when the complaint was filed; and although the 1972 amendments extending the Title to reach Government employees were adopted prior to the District Court's judgment, the complaint was not amended to state a claim under that Title, nor did the case thereafter proceed as a Title VII case. * * *

employer's possibly discriminatory purpose but instead may focus solely on the racially differential impact of the challenged hiring or promotion practices. This is not the constitutional rule. We have never held that the constitutional standard for adjudicating claims of invidious racial discrimination is identical to the standards applicable under Title VII, and we decline to do so today.

The central purpose of the Equal Protection Clause of the Fourteenth Amendment is the prevention of official conduct discriminating on the basis of race. It is also true that the Due Process Clause of the Fifth Amendment contains an equal protection component prohibiting the United States from invidiously discriminating between individuals or groups. But our cases have not embraced the proposition that a law or other official act, without regard to whether it reflects a racially discriminatory purpose, is unconstitutional *solely* because it has a racially disproportionate impact.

Almost 100 years ago, *Strauder v. West Virginia*, 100 U.S. 303, 25 L.Ed.664 (1880), established that the exclusion of Negroes from grand and petit juries in criminal proceedings violated the Equal Protection Clause, but the fact that a particular jury or a series of juries does not statistically reflect the racial composition of the community does not in itself make out an invidious discrimination forbidden by the Clause. "A purpose to discriminate must be present which may be proven by systematic exclusion of eligible jurymen of the proscribed race or by unequal application of the law to such an extent as to show intentional discrimination." Akins v. Texas, 325 U.S. 398, 403–04, 65 S.Ct. 1276, 1279, 89 L.Ed.1692, 1696 (1945). * * *

The rule is the same in other contexts. *Wright v. Rockefeller*, 376 U.S. 52, 84 S.Ct. 603, 11 L.Ed.2d 512 (1964) upheld a New York congressional apportionment statute against claims that district lines had been racially gerrymandered. The challenged districts were made up predominantly of whites or of minority races, and their boundaries were irregularly drawn. The challengers did not prevail because they failed to prove that the New York Legislature "was either motivated by racial considerations or in fact drew the districts on racial lines"; the plaintiffs had not shown that the statute "was the product of a state contrivance to segregate on the basis of race or place of origin." *Id.* at 56, 58, 84 S.Ct. at 605, 11 L.Ed.2d at 515. * * *

The school desegregation cases have also adhered to the basic equal protection principle that the invidious quality of a law claimed to be racially discriminatory must ultimately be traced to a racially discriminatory purpose. That there are both predominantly black and predominantly white schools in a community is not alone violative of the Equal Protection Clause. The essential element of *de jure* segregation is "a current condition of segregation resulting from intentional state action." Keyes v. School Dist. No.1, 413 U.S. 189, 205, 93 S.Ct. 2686, 2696, 37 L.Ed.2d 548 (1973). "The differentiating factor between *de jure* segregation and so-called *de facto* segregation * * * is *purpose* or *intent* to segregate." *Id.* at 208, 93 S.Ct. at 2696. The Court has also recently rejected allegations of racial discrimination based solely on the statistically disproportionate racial impact of various provisions of the Social Security Act because "[t]he acceptance of appellants' constitutional theory would render suspect each difference in treatment among the grant classes, however lacking in racial motivation and however otherwise rational the treatment might be." Jefferson v. Hackney, 406 U.S. 535, 548, 92 S.Ct. 1724, 1732, 32 L.Ed.2d 285, 297 (1972).

This is not to say that the necessary discriminatory racial purpose must be express or appear on the face of the statute, or that a law's disproportionate impact is irrelevant in cases involving Constitution-based claims of racial discrimination. A statute, otherwise neutral on its face, must not be applied so as invidiously to discriminate on the basis of race. Yick Wo v. Hopkins, 118 U.S. 356, 6 S.Ct. 1064, 30 L.Ed.220 (1886). It is also clear from the cases dealing with racial discrimination in the selection of juries that the systematic exclusion of Negroes is itself such an "unequal application of the law * * * as to show intentional discrimination." *Akins*, 325 U.S. at 404, 65 S.Ct. at 1279. A prima facie case of discriminatory purpose may be proved as well by the absence of Negroes on a particular jury combined with the failure of the jury commissioners to be informed of eligible Negro jurors in a community, or with racially non-neutral selection procedures. With a prima facie case made out, "the burden of proof shifts to the State to rebut the presumption of unconstitutional action by showing that permissible racially neutral selection criteria and procedures have produced the monochromatic result." Alexander v. Louisiana, 405 U.S. 625, 632, 92 S.Ct. 1221, 1226, 31 L.Ed.2d 536, 542 (1972).

Necessarily, an invidious discriminatory purpose may often be inferred from the totality of the relevant facts, including the fact, if it is true, that the law bears more heavily on one race than another. It is also not infrequently true that the discriminatory impact—in the jury cases for example, the total or seriously disproportionate exclusion of Negroes from jury venires—may for all practical purposes demonstrate unconstitutionality because in various circumstances the discrimination is very difficult to explain on nonracial grounds. Nevertheless, we have not held that a law, neutral on its face and serving ends otherwise within the power of government to pursue, is invalid under the Equal Protection Clause simply because it may affect a greater proportion of one race than of another. Disproportionate impact is not irrelevant, but it is not the sole touchstone of an invidious racial discrimination forbidden by the

Constitution. Standing alone, it does not trigger the rule that racial classifications are to be subjected to the strictest scrutiny and are justifiable only by the weightiest of considerations.

* * *

As an initial matter, we have difficulty understanding how a law establishing a racially neutral qualification for employment is nevertheless racially discriminatory and denies "any person * * * equal protection of the laws" simply because a greater proportion of Negroes fail to qualify than members of other racial or ethnic groups. Had respondents, along with all others who had failed Test 21, whether white or black, brought an action claiming that the test denied each of them equal protection of the laws as compared with those who had passed with high enough scores to qualify them as police recruits, it is most unlikely that their challenge would have been sustained. Test 21, which is administered generally to prospective Government employees, concededly seeks to ascertain whether those who take it have acquired a particular level of verbal skill; and it is untenable that the Constitution prevents the Government from seeking modestly to upgrade the communicative abilities of its employees rather than to be satisfied with some lower level of competence, particularly where the job requires special ability to communicate orally and in writing. Respondents, as Negroes, could no more successfully claim that the test denied them equal protection than could white applicants who also failed. The conclusion would not be different in the face of proof that more Negroes than whites had been disqualified by Test 21. That other Negroes also failed to score well would, alone, not demonstrate that respondents individually were being denied equal protection of the laws by the application of an otherwise valid qualifying test being administered to prospective police recruits.

Nor on the facts of the case before us would the disproportionate impact of Test 21 warrant the conclusion that it is a purposeful device to discriminate against Negroes and hence an infringement of the constitutional rights of respondents as well as other black applicants. As we have said, the test is neutral on its face and rationally may be said to serve a purpose the Government is constitutionally empowered to pursue. Even agreeing with the District Court that the differential racial effect of Test 21 called for further inquiry, we think the District Court correctly held that the affirmative efforts of the Metropolitan Police Department to recruit black officers, the changing racial composition of the recruit classes and of the force in general, and the relationship of the test to the training program negated any inference that the Department discriminated on the basis of race or that "a police officer qualifies on the color of his skin rather than ability."

Under Title VII, Congress provided that when hiring and promotion practices disqualifying substantially disproportionate numbers of blacks are challenged, discriminatory purpose need not be proved, and that it is an insufficient response to demonstrate some rational basis for the challenged practices. It is necessary, in addition, that they be "validated" in terms of job performance in any one of several ways, perhaps by ascertaining the minimum skill, ability, or potential necessary for the position at issue and determining whether the qualifying tests are appropriate for the selection of qualified applicants for the job in question. However this process proceeds, it involves a more probing judicial review of, and less deference to, the seemingly reasonable acts of administrators and executives than is appropriate under the Constitution where special racial impact, without discriminatory purpose, is claimed. We are not disposed to adopt this more rigorous standard for the purposes of applying the Fifth and the Fourteenth Amendments in cases such as this.

A rule that a statute designed to serve neutral ends is nevertheless invalid, absent compelling justification, if in practice it benefits or burdens one race more than another would be far reaching and would raise serious questions about, and perhaps invalidate, a whole range of tax, welfare, public service, regulatory, and licensing statutes that may be more burdensome to the poor and to the average black than to the more affluent white.[14]

Given that rule, such consequences would perhaps be likely to follow. However, in our view, extension of the rule beyond those areas where it is already applicable by reason of statute, such as in the field of public employment, should await legislative prescription.

* * *

NOTES AND QUESTIONS

1. In note 10 of *Washington v. Davis*, the Court observed that plaintiffs had failed to amend their complaint to state a claim under Title VII, although they could have done so. The plaintiffs, in fact, intended to use their case to test whether the disparate impact theory was applicable to equal protection employment discrimination claims. Suppose the plaintiffs had amended their complaint to include a race discrimination disparate impact claim under Title VII, in addition to their equal protection race discrimination claim. What result? In a portion of the Court's opinion in *Davis* that is not reproduced

[14] Goodman, *De Facto School Segregation: A Constitutional and Empirical Analysis*, 60 Calif.L.Rev. 275, 300 (1972), suggests that disproportionate-impact analysis might invalidate "tests and qualifications for voting, draft deferment, public employment, jury service, and other government-conferred benefits and opportunities * * * ; [s]ales taxes, bail schedules, utility rates, bridge tolls, license fees, and other state-imposed charges." It has also been argued that minimum wage and usury laws as well as professional licensing requirements would require major modifications in light of the unequal-impact rule. Silverman, *Equal Protection, Economic Legislation, and Racial Discrimination*, 25 Vand.L.Rev. 1183 (1972). . . .

here, the Court held that it was not clear error for the district court to conclude, on the basis of Title VII standards, "that Test 21 was directly related to the requirements of the police training program and that a positive relationship between the test and training-course performance was sufficient to validate the former, wholly aside from its possible relationship to actual performance as a police officer." 426 U.S. at 250, 96 S.Ct. at 2052.

2. The equal protection component of the Fifth Amendment has long been recognized as a constitutional bar to discrimination in federal employment on the basis of race or other suspect classifications. Bolling v. Sharpe, 347 U.S. 497, 74 S.Ct. 693, 98 L.Ed.884 (1954). Historically, however, most federal employees primarily relied on the administrative processes of the Civil Service Commission (now the Merit Systems Protection Board) to redress discrimination complaints. When Title VII was amended in 1972 to cover employees of federal, state, and local governments, § 717 was added to provide special procedures for federal employees. Section 717 of Title VII now provides the exclusive judicial remedy for discrimination complaints by federal employees covered by that amendment. Brown v. Gen. Servs. Admin., 425 U.S. 820, 96 S.Ct. 1961, 48 L.Ed.2d 402 (1976). The Civil Rights Act of 1991 extended the antidiscrimination provisions of Title VII to employees of the House of Representatives and the Senate and several other groups of federal employees. Nevertheless, in limited circumstances, federal employees who are not covered under these statutes may pursue equal protection claims under the Fifth Amendment. In *Davis v. Passman*, 442 U.S. 228, 247, 99 S.Ct. 2264, 60 L.Ed.2d 846 (1979), the Court held that its ruling in *Brown v. GSA*, did not foreclose an implied right of action for damages based on the Fifth Amendment when the complainant was expressly unprotected by Title VII. Today, however, such cases are quite rare.

3. In *Village of Arlington Heights v. Metropolitan Housing Development Corp.*, 429 U.S. 252, 97 S.Ct. 555, 50 L.Ed.2d 450 (1977), the Supreme Court upheld a facially neutral zoning board decision that had the foreseeable effect of perpetuating racially segregated housing. The Court provided a useful summary of the types of evidence that might be used to prove the existence of an invidious racially discriminatory purpose under the Equal Protection Clause:

> *Davis* does not require a plaintiff to prove that the challenged action rested solely on racially discriminatory purposes. Rarely can it be said that a legislature or administrative body operating under a broad mandate made a decision motivated solely by a single concern, or even that a particular purpose was the "dominant" or "primary" one. In fact, it is because legislators and administrators are properly concerned with balancing numerous competing considerations that courts refrain from reviewing the merits of their decisions, absent a showing of arbitrariness or irrationality. But racial discrimination is not just another competing consideration. When there is a proof that a discriminatory purpose has been a

motivating factor in the decision, this judicial deference is no longer justified.

Determining whether invidious discriminatory purpose was a motivating factor demands a sensitive inquiry into such circumstantial and direct evidence of intent as may be available. The impact of the official action—whether it "bears more heavily on one race than another," Washington v. Davis, 426 U.S. 229, 246, 96 S.Ct. 2040, 2049, 48 L.Ed.2d 597 (1976)—may provide an important starting point. Sometimes a clear pattern, unexplainable on grounds other than race, emerges from the effect of the state action even when the governing legislation appears neutral on its face. Yick Wo v. Hopkins, 118 U.S. 356, 6 S.Ct. 1064, 30 L.Ed.220 (1886); Gomillion v. Lightfoot, 364 U.S. 339, 81 S.Ct. 125, 5 L.Ed.2d 110 (1960). The evidentiary inquiry is then relatively easy. But such cases are rare. Absent a pattern as stark as that in *Gomillion* or *Yick Wo*, impact alone is not determinative, and the Court must look to other evidence.

The historical background of the decision is one evidentiary source, particularly if it reveals a series of official actions taken for invidious purposes. The specific sequence of events leading up to the challenged decision also may shed some light on the decisionmaker's purposes. * * * Departures from the normal procedural sequence also might afford evidence that improper purposes are playing a role. Substantive departures too may be relevant, particularly if the factors usually considered important by the decisionmaker strongly favor a decision contrary to the one reached.

The legislative or administrative history may be highly relevant, especially where there are contemporary statements by members of the decisionmaking body, minutes of its meetings, or reports. In some extraordinary instances the members might be called to the stand at trial to testify concerning the purpose of the official action, although even then such testimony frequently will be barred by privilege.

429 U.S. at 265–68, 97 S.Ct. at 563–65.

4. In *Personnel Administrator of Massachusetts v. Feeney*, 442 U.S. 256, 99 S.Ct. 2282, 60 L.Ed.2d 870 (1979), the Supreme Court addressed a challenge to the constitutionality of the Massachusetts veterans' preference statute on the ground that it discriminated against women in violation of the Equal Protection Clause of the Fourteenth Amendment. The plaintiff, Helen Feeney, was a female civil service employee of twelve years who had passed a number of open competitive civil service examinations for better jobs. Because of the veterans' preference statute, Feeney, a nonveteran, was ranked in each instance below male veterans who had achieved lower test scores. The statute mandated that all veterans who qualified for state civil service positions had to be considered for appointment ahead of any

qualifying nonveterans. The statutory preference was facially neutral because it applied to all honorably discharged veterans, male or female; nevertheless, it "operate[d] overwhelmingly to the advantage of males." *Id.* at 259, 99 S.Ct. at 2286. The plaintiff claimed that the inevitable effect of the law was to exclude women from consideration for the best state civil service jobs: at the commencement of the suit over 98 percent of the veterans in Massachusetts were male. A three-judge district court declared the statute unconstitutional and enjoined its operation, finding "that the absolute preference afforded by Massachusetts to veterans ha[d] a devastating impact upon the employment opportunities of women." *Id.* at 260, 99 S.Ct. at 2286.

The Supreme Court vacated the judgment and remanded for further consideration in light of *Washington v. Davis*. Massachusetts v. Feeney, 434 U.S. 884, 98 S.Ct. 252, 54 L.Ed.2d 169 (1977). Upon remand, the district court reaffirmed its original judgment, concluding that the absolute veterans' preference was "inherently nonneutral because it favors a class from which women have traditionally been excluded," and that its adverse effects on women's employment opportunities were "too inevitable to have been 'unintended.'" *Feeney*, 442 U.S. at 260–61, 99 S.Ct. at 2286. The Supreme Court reversed a second time:

> The cases of *Washington v. Davis* and *Arlington Heights v. Metropolitan Hous. Dev. Corp.* recognize that when a neutral law has a disparate impact upon a group that has historically been the victim of discrimination, an unconstitutional purpose may still be at work. But those cases signaled no departure from the settled rule that the Fourteenth Amendment guarantees equal laws, not equal results. * * * Those principles apply with equal force to a case involving alleged gender discrimination.
>
> When a statute gender-neutral on its face is challenged on the ground that its effects upon women are disproportionately adverse, a twofold inquiry is thus appropriate. The first question is whether the statutory classification is indeed neutral in the sense that it is not gender-based. If the classification itself, covert or overt, is not based upon gender, the second question is whether the adverse effect reflects invidious gender-based discrimination. In this second inquiry, impact provides an "important starting point," but purposeful discrimination is "the condition that offends the Constitution." Swann v. Charlotte-Mecklenburg Bd. of Educ., 402 U.S. 1, 16, 91 S.Ct. 1267, 1276, 28 L.Ed.2d 554 (1971).
>
> * * * The distinction made by [the Massachusetts veteran's preference statute] is, as it seems to be, quite simply between veterans and nonveterans, not between men and women.
>
> * * * The appellee's ultimate argument rests upon the presumption, common to the criminal and civil law, that a person intends the natural and foreseeable consequences of his voluntary

actions. Her position was well stated in the concurring opinion in the District Court:

> Conceding * * * that the goal here was to benefit the veteran, there is no reason to absolve the legislature from awareness that the means chosen to achieve this goal would freeze women out of all those state jobs actively sought by men. To be sure, the legislature did not wish to harm women. But the cutting-off of women's opportunities was an inevitable concomitant of the chosen scheme—as inevitable as the proposition that if tails is up, heads must be down. Where a law's consequences are *that* inevitable, can they meaningfully be described as unintended?

This rhetorical question implies that a negative answer is obvious, but it is not. The decision to grant a preference to veterans was of course "intentional." So, necessarily, did an adverse impact upon nonveterans follow from that decision. And it cannot seriously be argued that the Legislature of Massachusetts could have been unaware that most veterans are men. It would thus be disingenuous to say that the adverse consequences of this legislation for women were unintended, in the sense that they were not volitional or in the sense that they were not foreseeable.

"Discriminatory purpose," however, implies more than intent as volition or intent as awareness of consequences. It implies that the decisionmaker, in this case a state legislature, selected or reaffirmed a particular course of action at least in part "because of," not merely "in spite of," its adverse effects upon an identifiable group. Yet nothing in the record demonstrates that this preference for veterans was originally devised or subsequently re-enacted because it would accomplish the collateral goal of keeping women in a stereotypic and predefined place in the Massachusetts Civil Service.

To the contrary, the statutory history shows that the benefit of the preference was consistently offered to "any person" who was a veteran. That benefit has been extended to women under a very broad statutory definition of the term veteran. The preference formula itself, which is the focal point of this challenge, was first adopted—so it appears from this record—out of a perceived need to help a small group of older Civil War veterans. It has since been reaffirmed and extended only to cover new veterans. When the totality of legislative actions establishing and extending the Massachusetts veterans' preference are considered, the law remains what it purports to be: a preference for veterans of either sex over nonveterans of either sex, not for men over women.

442 U.S. at 273–74, 278–80, 99 S.Ct. at 2293, 2295–97.

On the issue of foreseeability of the discriminatory consequences of a practice, the Court noted:

> This is not to say that the inevitability or foreseeability of consequences of a neutral rule has no bearing upon the existence of discriminatory intent. Certainly, when the adverse consequences of a law upon an identifiable group are as inevitable as the gender-based consequences of [the Massachusetts veterans' preference statute], a strong inference that the adverse effects were desired can reasonably be drawn. But in this inquiry—made as it is under the Constitution—an inference is a working tool, not a synonym for proof. When, as here, the impact is essentially an unavoidable consequence of a legislative policy that has in itself always been deemed to be legitimate, and when, as here, the statutory history and all of the available evidence affirmatively demonstrate the opposite, the inference simply fails to ripen into proof.

442 U.S. at 279 n.25, 99 S.Ct. at 2296 n.25.

In a later case, the Court, citing *Feeney*, stated that "the law distinguishes between actions taken 'because of' a given end from actions taken 'in spite of' their unintended consequences." Vacco v. Quill, 521 U.S. 793, 802–03, 117 S.Ct. 2293, 138 L.Ed.2d 834 (1997). Although *Feeney* involved a claim of sex discrimination, rather than race discrimination, the *Feeney* refinement of the *Washington v. Davis* purposeful discrimination test is equally applicable to other classifications, such as race and other forms of discrimination. *See, e.g.*, United States v. LULAC, 793 F.2d 636, 646–67 (5th Cir.1986) (race discrimination); Gonzalez v. Connecticut, 151 F.Supp.2d 174 (D.Conn.2001) (race discrimination claim by a Latino employee).

NOTE: THE ANALYTICAL FRAMEWORK AND THE BURDEN OF PROOF IN EQUAL PROTECTION CASES

Employment discrimination claims against state and local government employers brought under the Equal Protection Clause of the Fourteenth Amendment are generally brought pursuant to 42 U.S.C. § 1983. The courts have stated that an action under § 1983 has two essential elements. The first is that the plaintiff must prove that the defendant acted under color of state law. The second is that the plaintiff must prove that, as a result of defendant's action or conduct, the plaintiff suffered a denial of her federal statutory or constitutional rights or privileges. A § 1983 plaintiff is denied the rights guaranteed by the Equal Protection Clause when she proves she has been treated differently from other similarly situated employees because of race, gender, or national origin. *See, e.g.*, Annis v. County of Westchester, 136 F.3d 239, 245 (2d Cir.1998).

Neither *Washington v. Davis*, *Arlington Heights*, nor *Feeney* provides clear guidance on the order and allocation of the burden of proof in Equal Protection Clause cases. Nor does the Court in any of these cases discuss whether the "purposeful discrimination" theory now applicable in Equal

Protection Clause cases is the same as or different from the "intent" theory applicable in Title VII disparate treatment cases. Is the order and allocation of the burdens of proof in Equal Protection Clause and Title VII disparate treatment cases the same or different? Or, how relevant is the *McDonnell Douglas Corp. v. Green* analysis in the Equal Protection employment discrimination cases?

Recall that in *St. Mary's Honor Center v. Hicks*, 509 U.S. 502, 113 S.Ct. 2742, 125 L.Ed.2d 407 (1993), reproduced in Chapter 3, the plaintiff, a black male, brought a racial discrimination claim against his employer, a state agency, under both Title VII and the Equal Protection Clause of the Fourteenth Amendment. His equal protection claim, based on 42 U.S.C. § 1983, permitted him to sue his supervisor, an individual who was a state actor. Without deciding specifically whether the *McDonnell Douglas* framework is applicable to Equal Protection Clause claims, the Court stated:

> The Court of Appeals held that the purposeful discrimination element of respondent's § 1983 claim against petitioner Long [a state employee who was Hick's supervisor and who fired Hicks] is the same as the purposeful-discrimination element of his Title VII claim against petitioner St. Mary's. * * * Neither side challenges that proposition, and we shall assume that the *McDonnell Douglas* framework is fully applicable to racial-discrimination-in-employment claims under 42 U.S.C. § 1983. Cf. Patterson v. McLean Credit Union, 491 U.S. 164, 186, 109 S.Ct. 2363, 2377–78, 105 L.Ed.2d 132 (1989) (applying framework to claims under 42 U.S.C. § 1981).

Id. at 506 n.1, 113 S.Ct. at 2756 n.1.

Based on the Court's dicta in note 1 in *Hicks*, lower courts have generally applied the *McDonnell Douglas* framework to § 1983 employment discrimination cases based on the Equal Protection Clause. *See, e.g.*, Annis v. County of Westchester, 136 F.3d 239, 245 (2d Cir.1998) (sexual harassment case), Boutros v. Canton Reg'l Transit Auth., 997 F.2d 198, 202 (1993) (national origin and racial harassment); Silverman v. City of N.Y., 216 F.Supp.2d 108, 114–115 (E.D.N.Y.2002) (age, race, and religion). Consider the following:

> "To establish a *prima facie* case [of racial discrimination under the fourteenth amendment] a plaintiff must show: 'that he or she is a member of a protected class, that he or she is otherwise similarly situated to members of the unprotected class, and that he or she was treated differently from members of the unprotected class.' " * * * However, * * * a discrimination plaintiff alleging a violation of the equal protection clause bears a heavier burden of proof than a discrimination plaintiff under Title VII: "Under Title VII, the [plaintiff] must prove that she was discriminated against through disparate treatment based on an impermissible factor * * * . In an Equal Protection claim, the [plaintiff] faces the tougher standard of

proving purposeful and intentional acts of discrimination based on her membership in a particular class not just on an individual basis."

Sims v. Mulcahy, 902 F.2d 524, 538 (7th Cir.1990) (brackets in original).

> [T]his Court established that a plaintiff asserting a Fourteenth Amendment equal protection claim under 42 U.S.C. § 1983 must prove the same elements required to establish a disparate treatment claim under Title VII of the Civil Rights Act of 1964. * * * [I]n order to establish a *prima facie* case, the plaintiff must set forth the following elements: "1) he was a member of a protected class; 2) he was subject to an adverse employment action; 3) he was qualified for the job; and 4) for the same or similar conduct, he was treated differently from similarly situated non-minority employees." * * * It should be noted that the plaintiff's race need only be a motivating factor not necessarily the sole factor—in order for the plaintiff to succeed in his claim.

Perry v. McGinnis, 209 F.3d 597 (6th Cir.2000). In a later case, *Weberg v. Franks*, 229 F.3d 514 (6th Cir.2000), the Sixth Circuit noted that because both Title VII and the Equal Protection Clause prohibit racially discriminatory employment practices by public employers, the court will look to Title VII disparate treatment cases for assistance in analyzing § 1983 equal protection claims brought by public employees. *Id.* at 522.

a. In *Texas v. Lesage*, 528 U.S. 18, 120 S.Ct. 467, 145 L.Ed.2d 347 (1999), the Court held that the *Mt. Healthy* same-decision test is equally applicable in a claim based on the Equal Protection Clause. See Chapter 3.B, discussing mixed-motive cases. Thus, under *Lesage*, it is theoretically possible to bring a mixed-motive equal protection employment discrimination case. Note also that in the excerpt from *Arlington Heights* quoted above, the Court said, "When there is a proof that a discriminatory purpose has been *a motivating factor* in the decision, * * * judicial deference is no longer justified." It does not appear that the broader mixed-motives standard from the 1991 Civil Rights Act (as interpreted in the *Costa* decision) has been incorporated into section 1983 claims. *See, e.g.*, Velez-Rivera v. Agosto-Alicea, 437 F.3d 145 (1st Cir.2006) (applying *Mt. Healthy* analysis to employment discrimination claim brought under § 1983).

b. Questions have also arisen whether an employee may pursue a retaliation claim under section 1983 given the statute makes no mention of such claims. In reviewing the Supreme Court's precedent for implying a retaliation claim in statutes, the Second Circuit has recently held that a retaliation claim was cognizable under section 1983. *See* Vega v. Hempstead Union Free Sch. Dist., 801 F.3d 72, 78 (2d Cir.2015).

c. An important difference between Title VII and Equal Protection Clause employment discrimination claims is that individuals can be held personally liable under the Equal Protection Clause if they are found to be state actors. Moreover, they may be liable for damages unless foreclosed by the qualified immunity doctrine (a complicated topic best left to other courses). *See, e.g.*, Johnson v. Martin, 195 F.3d 1208 (10th Cir.1999). *See generally* Cheryl L. Anderson, *"Nothing Personal:" Individual Liability Under 42 U.S.C. § 1983 for Sexual Harassment as an Equal Protection Claim*, 19 Berkeley J.Emp. & Lab.L. 60 (1998). Local government employers are not liable under the theory of respondeat superior; they are liable only if the plaintiff alleges and proves that the alleged discrimination was based on a policy or custom adopted by a policymaker of the government employer. *See* Monell v. N.Y.C. Dep't of Soc. Servs., 436 U.S. 658, 98 S.Ct. 2018, 56 L.Ed.2d 611 (1978). It should be noted that it is rarely the case that a plaintiff would prefer to proceed under a constitutional provision via section 1983 if a traditional statutory claim is available (Title VII, ADEA, ADA etc.). A section 1983 claim will most commonly be brought when the procedural requirements for those statutes have not been met or for a claim that is not covered by the statutes.

d. One advantage of the constitutional equal protection doctrine for plaintiffs is that, unlike the antidiscrimination statutes, it theoretically can reach whatever category of persons the courts deem to be in need of special protection. For example, commentators have urged, and a few lower courts have held, that heightened scrutiny under equal protection should be extended to classifications based on sexual orientation. *See generally* Patricia A. Cain, *Litigating for Lesbian and Gay Rights: A Legal History,* 79 Va.L.Rev. 1551 (1993); Cass R. Sunstein, *Sexual Orientation and the Constitution: A Note on the Relationship Between Due Process and Equal Protection,* 55 U.Chi.L.Rev. 1161 (1988). Recently, the Ninth Circuit provided heightened scrutiny in a constitutional challenge to the exclusion of jurors based on their sexual orientation. *See* SmithKline Beecham Corp. v. Abbott Labs., 740 F.3d 471 (9th Cir.2014).

C. THE CIVIL RIGHTS ACT OF 1866, 42 U.S.C. § 1981

Following the ratification of the Thirteenth Amendment, Congress enacted the Civil Rights Act of 1866, now known as § 1981. In commenting upon the Reconstruction reforms, the Supreme Court observed that "[t]he legislative history of the 1866 Act clearly indicates that Congress intended to protect a limited category of rights, specifically defined in terms of racial equality." General Bldg. Contractors Ass'n v. Pennsylvania, 458 U.S. 375, 386, 102 S.Ct. 3141, 73 L.Ed.2d 835 (1982). As amended in 1870, after the ratification of the Fourteenth Amendment, § 1981 contains three clauses that extend to "[a]ll persons within the jurisdiction of the United States" the same three specific sets of rights as are "enjoyed by white citizens." 42 U.S.C. § 1981(a). The three sets of rights are: (1) the right "to make and enforce contracts," (2) the right "to sue, be parties, [and] give evidence," and (3) the right "to the full and equal benefit of all laws and proceedings for the security of persons and property." *Id.* A final clause provides that all such persons "shall be subject to like punishment, pains, penalties, taxes, licenses, and exactions of every kind, and to no other" as are enjoyed by white citizens. *Id.* The right "to make and enforce contracts" clause of § 1981 is now an integral part of the legal regime prohibiting employment discrimination on the basis of race in both public (except the federal government) and private employment. Yet for almost a century after its enactment, the statute was largely ignored, primarily because the Supreme Court construed most of the major post-Civil War civil rights legislation to apply only to states and state actors. The extension of § 1981 to cover private employment had its genesis in the celebrated case of *Jones v. Alfred H. Mayer Co.*, 392 U.S. 409, 88 S.Ct. 2186, 20 L.Ed.2d 1189 (1968), which held that § 1 of the Civil Rights Act of 1866—now codified at 42 U.S.C. § 1982—"bars *all* racial discrimination, private as well as public, in the sale or rental of property." *Id.* at 413, 88 S.Ct. at 2189 (emphasis in original). Then, in *Johnson v. Railway Express Agency*, 421 U.S. 454, 95 S.Ct. 1716, 44 L.Ed.2d 295 (1975), the Court endorsed the position of the lower courts that the right "to make and enforce contracts" clause of § 1981 prohibits racial discrimination in private employment.

The history of § 1981 is explored in *Runyon v. McCrary*, 427 U.S. 160, 96 S.Ct. 2586, 49 L.Ed.2d 415 (1976), which held that § 1981 prohibits racially discriminatory admission policies at privately operated nonsectarian schools. After oral argument and prior to its decision in *Patterson v. McLean Credit Union*, 491 U.S. 164, 109 S.Ct. 2363, 105 L.Ed.2d 132 (1989), the Supreme Court specifically directed the parties to address the question whether the interpretation of § 1981 adopted in *Runyon*, extending § 1981 to the private sector, should be reconsidered. Patterson v. McLean Credit Union, 485 U.S. 617, 108 S.Ct. 1419, 99 L.Ed.2d 879 (1988). This suggested that the Court might be prepared to overrule *Runyon*, but the Court declined to do so.

1. THEORY OF LIABILITY

GENERAL BUILDING CONTRACTORS ASSOCIATION V. PENNSYLVANIA

Supreme Court of the United States, 1982.
458 U.S. 375, 102 S.Ct. 3141, 73 L.Ed.2d 835.

JUSTICE REHNQUIST delivered the opinion of the Court.

Respondents, the Commonwealth of Pennsylvania and the representatives of a class of racial minorities who are skilled or seek work as operating engineers in the construction industry in Eastern Pennsylvania and Delaware, commenced this action under a variety of federal statutes protecting civil rights, including 42 U.S.C. § 1981. The complaint sought to redress racial discrimination in the operation of an exclusive hiring hall established in contracts between Local 542 of the International Union of Operating Engineers and construction industry employers doing business within the Union's jurisdiction. * * * The question[ ] we resolve [is] whether liability under 42 U.S.C. § 1981 requires proof of discriminatory intent * * * .

II

The District Court held that petitioners had violated 42 U.S.C. § 1981 notwithstanding its finding that, as a class, petitioners did not intentionally discriminate against minority workers and neither knew nor had reason to know of the Union's discriminatory practices. The first question we address, therefore, is whether liability may be imposed under § 1981 without proof of intentional discrimination.

Title 42 U.S.C. § 1981 provides:

> All persons within the jurisdiction of the United States shall have the same right in every State and Territory to make and enforce contracts, to sue, be parties, give evidence, and to the full and equal benefit of all laws and proceedings for the security of persons and property as is enjoyed by white citizens, and shall be subject to like punishment, pains, penalties, taxes, licenses, and exactions of every kind, and to no other.

We have traced the evolution of this statute and its companion, 42 U.S.C. § 1982, on more than one occasion, and we will not repeat the narrative again except in broad outline.

The operative language of both laws apparently originated in § 1 of the Civil Rights Act of 1866, 14 Stat. 27, enacted by Congress shortly after ratification of the Thirteenth Amendment. "The legislative history of the 1866 Act clearly indicates that Congress intended to protect a limited category of rights, specifically defined in terms of racial equality." Georgia v. Rachel, 384 U.S. 780, 791, 86 S.Ct. 1783, 1789, 16 L.Ed.2d 925 (1966). The same Congress also passed the Joint Resolution that was later adopted as the Fourteenth Amendment. As we explained in *Hurd v. Hodge*, 334 U.S. 24, 32–33, 68 S.Ct. 847, 851–52, 92 L.Ed.1187 (1948):

> Frequent references to the Civil Rights Act are to be found in the record of the legislative debates on the adoption of the Amendment. It is clear that in many significant respects the statute and the Amendment were expressions of the same general congressional policy. Indeed, as the legislative debates reveal, one of the primary purposes of many members of Congress in supporting the adoption of the Fourteenth Amendment was to incorporate the guaranties of the Civil Rights Act of 1866 in the organic law of the land. Others supported the adoption of the Amendment in order to eliminate

doubt as to the constitutional validity of the Civil Rights Act as applied to the States.

Following ratification of the Fourteenth Amendment, Congress passed what has come to be known as the Enforcement Act of 1870, 16 Stat. 140, pursuant to the power conferred by § 5 of the Amendment. Section 16 of that Act contains essentially the language that now appears in § 1981. Indeed, the present codification is derived from § 1977 of the Revised Statutes of 1874, which in turn codified verbatim § 16 of the 1870 Act. Section 16 differed from § 1 of the 1866 Act in at least two respects. First, where § 1 of the 1866 Act extended its guarantees to "citizens, of every race and color," § 16 of the 1870 Act—and § 1981—protects "all persons." Second, the 1870 Act omitted language contained in the 1866 Act, and eventually codified as § 1982, guaranteeing property rights equivalent to those enjoyed by white citizens. Thus, "[a]lthough the 1866 Act rested only on the Thirteenth Amendment * * * and, indeed, was enacted before the Fourteenth Amendment was formally proposed, * * * the 1870 Act was passed pursuant to the Fourteenth, and changes in wording may have reflected the language of the Fourteenth Amendment." Tillman v. Wheaton-Haven Recreation Ass'n, 410 U.S. 431, 439–40 n. 11, 93 S.Ct. 1090, 1095 n. 11, 35 L.Ed.2d 403 (1973).

In determining whether § 1981 reaches practices that merely result in a disproportionate impact on a particular class, or instead is limited to conduct motivated by a discriminatory purpose, we must be mindful of the "events and passions of the time" in which the law was forged. United States v. Price, 383 U.S. 787, 803, 86 S.Ct. 1152, 1161, 16 L.Ed.2d 267 (1966). The Civil War had ended in April 1865. The First Session of the Thirty-ninth Congress met on December 4, 1865, some six months after the preceding Congress had sent to the States the Thirteenth Amendment and just two weeks before the Secretary of State certified the Amendment's ratification. On January 5, 1866, Senator Trumbull introduced the bill that would become the 1866 Act.

The principal object of the legislation was to eradicate the Black Codes, laws enacted by Southern legislatures imposing a range of civil disabilities on freedmen. Most of these laws embodied express racial classifications and although others, such as those penalizing vagrancy, were facially neutral, Congress plainly perceived all of them as consciously conceived methods of resurrecting the incidents of slavery. Senator Trumbull summarized the paramount aims of his bill:

> Since the abolition of slavery, the Legislatures which have assembled in the insurrectionary States have passed laws relating to the freedmen, and in nearly all the States they have discriminated against them. They deny them certain rights, subject them to severe penalties, and still impose upon them the

> very restrictions which were imposed upon them in consequence of the existence of slavery, and before it was abolished. The purpose of the bill under consideration is to destroy all these discriminations, and to carry into effect the [Thirteenth] amendment.

Cong.Globe, 39th Cong., 1st Sess., 474 (1866). * * *

Of course, this Court has found in the legislative history of the 1866 Act evidence that Congress sought to accomplish more than the destruction of state-imposed civil disabilities and discriminatory punishments. We have held that both § 1981 and § 1982 "prohibit all racial discrimination, whether or not under color of law, with respect to the rights enumerated therein." Jones v. Alfred H. Mayer Co., 392 U.S. 409, 436, 88 S.Ct. 2186, 2201, 20 L.Ed.2d 1189 (1968). Nevertheless, the fact that the prohibitions of § 1981 encompass private as well as governmental action does not suggest that the statute reaches more than purposeful discrimination, whether public or private. Indeed, the relevant opinions are hostile to such an implication. Thus, although we held in *Jones*, that § 1982 reaches private action, we explained that § 1 of the 1866 Act "was meant to prohibit *all racially motivated* deprivations of the rights enumerated in the statute." 392 U.S. at 426, 88 S.Ct. at 2196 (emphasis on "racially motivated" added). Similarly, in *Runyon v. McCrary*, we stated that § 1981 would be violated "if a private offeror refuses to extend to a Negro, *solely because he is a Negro*, the same opportunity to enter into contracts as he extends to white offerees." 427 U.S. 160, 170–71, 96 S.Ct. 2586, 2594, 49 L.Ed.2d 415 (1976).

The immediate evils with which the Thirty-ninth Congress was concerned simply did not include practices that were "neutral on their face, and even neutral in terms of intent," Griggs v. Duke Power Co., 401 U.S. 424, 430, 91 S.Ct. 849, 853, 28 L.Ed.2d 158 (1971), but that had the incidental effect of disadvantaging blacks to a greater degree than whites. Congress instead acted to protect the freedmen from intentional discrimination by those whose object was "to make their former slaves dependent serfs, victims of unjust laws, and debarred from all progress and elevation by organized social prejudices." Cong.Globe, 39th Cong., 1st Sess., 1839 (1866) (Rep. Clarke). The supporters of the bill repeatedly emphasized that the legislation was designed to eradicate blatant deprivations of civil rights, clearly fashioned with the purpose of oppressing the former slaves. To infer that Congress sought to accomplish more than this would require stronger evidence in the legislative record than we have been able to discern.

Our conclusion that § 1981 reaches only purposeful discrimination is supported by one final observation about its legislative history. As noted earlier, the origins of the law can be traced to both the Civil Rights Act of

1866 and the Enforcement Act of 1870. Both of these laws, in turn, were legislative cousins of the Fourteenth Amendment. The 1866 Act represented Congress' first attempt to ensure equal rights for the freedmen following the formal abolition of slavery effected by the Thirteenth Amendment. As such, it constituted an initial blueprint of the Fourteenth Amendment, which Congress proposed in part as a means of "incorporat[ing] the guaranties of the Civil Rights Act of 1866 in the organic law of the land." Hurd v. Hodge, 334 U.S. at 32, 68 S.Ct. at 851. The 1870 Act, which contained the language that now appears in § 1981, was enacted as a means of enforcing the recently ratified Fourteenth Amendment. In light of the close connection between these Acts and the Amendment, it would be incongruous to construe the principal object of their successor, § 1981, in a manner markedly different from that of the Amendment itself.

With respect to the latter, "official action will not be held unconstitutional solely because it results in a racially disproportionate impact," Arlington Heights v. Metropolitan Housing Dev. Corp., 429 U.S. 252, 264–65, 97 S.Ct. 555, 562–63, 50 L.Ed.2d 450 (1977). "[E]ven if a neutral law has a disproportionately adverse impact upon a racial minority, it is unconstitutional under the Equal Protection Clause only if that impact can be traced to a discriminatory purpose." Personnel Administrator of Mass. v. Feeney, 442 U.S. 256, 272, 99 S.Ct. 2282, 60 L.Ed.2d 870 (1979). The same Congress that proposed the Fourteenth Amendment also passed the Civil Rights Act of 1866, and the ratification of that Amendment paved the way for the Enforcement Act of 1870. These measures were all products of the same milieu and were directed against the same evils. Although Congress might have charted a different course in enacting the predecessors to § 1981 than it did in proposing the Fourteenth Amendment, we have found no convincing evidence that it did so.

We conclude, therefore, that § 1981, like the Equal Protection Clause, can be violated only by purposeful discrimination. * * *

NOTES AND QUESTIONS

1. *Analytical Framework*: In *Patterson v. McLean Credit Union*, 491 U.S. 164, 186, 109 S.Ct. 2363, 2377–78, 105 L.Ed.2d 132 (1989), the Supreme Court held that, in the absence of direct evidence of discrimination, the *McDonnell Douglas/Burdine* circumstantial evidence analytic scheme is applicable in § 1981 cases to prove purposeful or intentional discrimination:

> We have developed, in analogous areas of civil rights law, a carefully designed framework of proof to determine, in the context of disparate treatment, the ultimate issue whether the defendant intentionally discriminated against the plaintiff. *See* Texas Dep't of Community Affairs v. Burdine, 450 U.S. 248, 101 S.Ct. 1089, 67

L.Ed.2d 207 (1981); McDonnell Douglas Corp. v. Green, 411 U.S. 792, 93 S.Ct. 1817, 36 L.Ed.2d 668 (1973). We agree with the Court of Appeals that this scheme of proof * * * should apply to claims of racial discrimination under § 1981.

The analytical models covered in Chapter 3 are generally applicable to § 1981 claims. Courts, however, have been divided over whether the mixed-motive amendments to Title VII, added under the Civil Rights Act of 1991 (§§ 703(m) and 706(g)(2)(B)), apply to mixed-motive cases under § 1981. *Compare* Mabra v. United Food & Commercial Workers, 176 F.3d 1357 (11th Cir.1999) (holding that the law prior to the 1991 Amendments applies to claims filed under § 1981), *with* Metoyer v. Chassman, 504 F.3d 919 (9th Cir.2007) (applying analytical framework from 1991 Amendments to § 1981). In the aftermath of *Gross v. FBL Financial Services,* 557 U.S. 167, 129 S.Ct. 2343, 174 L.Ed.2d 119 (2009) (an ADEA case reproduced in Chapter 14), which both rejected the *Price Waterhouse* framework for ADEA cases and held that the 1991 Amendments to Title VII do not apply to claims brought under the ADEA, lower courts have begun to examine the potential effect of *Gross* on § 1981 mixed-motive claims. For example, in *Brown v. J. Kaz, Inc.*, 581 F.3d 175, 182 (3rd Cir.2009). the Court applied the *Price Waterhouse* standard, which it concluded "made sense in light of section 1981's text." *Id.* at 182 n.5.

2. Unlike Title VII, claims brought under § 1981 are not limited to employees of an employer having fifteen or more employees. *See* Title VII § 701(b), 42 U.S.C. § 2000e(b). Thus, mom-and-pop corner grocery stores are subject to the reach of § 1981. Section 1981 prohibits racial discrimination in contexts other than employment, but the majority of § 1981 claims involve employment discrimination claims. *See* Theodore Eisenberg & Stewart Schwab, *The Importance of Section 1981*, 73 Cornell L.Rev. 596, 601 (1988) (approximately 77% of all § 1981 claims involve employment claims).

3. *Section 1981 Claims Cognizable Under the "To Make and Enforce Contract" Clause*:

a. *Prohibited conduct*: Prior to *Patterson v. McLean Credit Union*, 491 U.S. 164, 109 S.Ct. 2363, 105 L.Ed.2d 132 (1989), lower courts were generally in agreement that § 1981 was co-extensive with the kinds of racial discrimination claims that could be brought under Title VII, e.g., hiring, discharge, denial of promotion, and racial harassment. In *Patterson*, the Supreme Court held that § 1981 prohibits racial discrimination only in the making and enforcement of employment contracts, not in other aspects of the contractual relationship. *Patterson* involved a § 1981 suit by a black female who claimed she was harassed, rejected for promotion, and eventually discharged, all because of her race. The Court held that the plaintiff had no claim under § 1981 for racial harassment because the alleged violation involved not the making of a contract but conduct that occurred after the formation of the contract. The Court's limited interpretation of the scope of claims cognizable in § 1981 actions led to a conflict in the lower courts over what claims—other than cases of racially discriminatory hiring—could be brought under § 1981. *See generally* Caroline R. Fredrickson, *The Misreading of* Patterson v. McLean Credit Union: *The Diminishing Scope of Section 1981*, 91 Colum.L.Rev. 891 (1991).

Patterson was among a number of Supreme Court cases that Congress either overturned or otherwise modified in the Civil Rights Act of 1991. Congress amended § 1981 to overturn *Patterson* by adding, *inter alia,* the following new subsection:

> (b) For purposes of this section, the term "make and enforce contracts" includes the making, performance, modification, and termination of contracts, and the enjoyment of all benefits, privileges, terms, and conditions of the contractual relationship.

105 Stat. 1071, 42 U.S.C. § 1981(b).

b. *Claims by at-will employees*: Employers have advanced the argument that § 1981 does not apply to at-will employees because, by definition, at-will employees do not have formal employment contracts. The 1991 amendments to § 1981, however, were intended to restore the law on claims that could be brought against private employers prior to *Patterson* by overturning the Court's narrow reading of the statute. Since the 1991 Act, the six courts of appeals that have addressed the issue have been unanimous in concluding that an at-will employment relationship is contractual in nature for purposes of a § 1981 claim. *See* Walker v. Abbott Labs., 340 F.3d 471, 477 (7th Cir.2003) (holding that an at-will employee can bring a § 1981 claim and citing as persuasive authority court of appeals decisions from the Second, Fifth, Seventh, Eighth, and Tenth Circuits). As a result, at-will employees can generally pursue racial discrimination claims under § 1981. *See generally* Joanna L. Grossman, *Making a Federal Case Out of It: Section 1981 and At-Will Employment*, 67 Brook.L.Rev. 329 (2001).

c. *Application to white persons*: The Supreme Court has held that § 1981 prohibits racial discrimination in private employment against whites as well as nonwhites, despite the language in § 1981 providing that "[a]ll persons" covered by the statute shall have the same rights as "white citizens." McDonald v. Santa Fe Trail Transp. Co., 427 U.S. 273, 96 S.Ct. 2574, 49 L.Ed.2d 493 (1976). In this respect, the application of § 1981 is analogous to Title VII, the terms of which are not limited to discrimination against members of any particular race. *See* §§ 703(a)(1) & 703(a)(2) of Title VII, 42 U.S.C. §§ 2000e–2(a)(1) & 2000e–2(a)(2).

d. *Discrimination because of national origin*: A plaintiff bringing a discrimination claim under § 1981 against a private employer solely on the basis of national origin is likely to face a motion to dismiss on the authority of *Saint Francis College v. Al-Khazraji*, 481 U.S. 604, 107 S.Ct. 2022, 95 L.Ed.2d 582 (1987), reproduced in Chapter 2. In *Al-Khazraji*, a professor who was a practicing Moslem born in Iraq of Arabian ancestry brought a § 1981 action against a private university claiming discrimination on the basis of "national origin, religion, and/or race." *Id.* at 605, 107 S.Ct. at 2022. The Supreme Court affirmed the Third Circuit's judgment that the plaintiff's § 1981 case could go forward because he had properly alleged racial discrimination on the basis of his Arabian ancestry. The Court, in an opinion by Justice White, made the following distinction between the viability of claims based on race as opposed to national origin or religion:

> Based on the history of § 1981, we have little trouble in concluding that Congress intended to protect from discrimination identifiable classes of persons who are subjected to intentional discrimination solely because of their ancestry or ethnic characteristics. Such discrimination is racial discrimination that Congress intended § 1981 to forbid, whether or not it would be classified as racial in terms of modern scientific theory. * * * If respondent on remand can prove that he was subjected to intentional discrimination based on the fact that he was born an Arab, rather than solely on the place or nation of his origin, or his religion, he will have made out a case under § 1981.

Id. at 613, 107 S.Ct. at 2028.

In a concurring opinion, however, Justice Brennan suggested that the Court's attempt to distinguish between race and national origin claims was problematical:

> Pernicious distinctions among individuals based solely on their ancestry are antithetical to the doctrine of equality upon which this Nation is founded. * * * I write separately only to point out that the line between discrimination based on "ancestry or ethnic characteristics," and discrimination based on "place or nation of * * * origin," is not a bright one. It is true that one's ancestry—the ethnic group from which an individual and his or her ancestors are descended—is not necessarily the same as one's national origin—the country "where a person was *born*, or more broadly, the country from which his or her ancestors *came*." Espinoza v. Farah Manufacturing Co., 414 U.S. 86, 88, 94 S.Ct. 334, 336, 38 L.Ed.2d 287 (1973) (emphasis added). Often, however, the two are identical as a factual matter: one was born in the nation whose primary stock is one's own ethnic group. Moreover, national origin claims have been treated as ancestry or ethnicity claims in some circumstances. For example, in the Title VII context, the terms overlap as a legal matter. * * * I therefore read the Court's opinion to state only that discrimination based on *birthplace alone* is insufficient to state a claim under § 1981.

Id. at 614, 107 S.Ct. at 2028–29. Lower courts have adopted the following rules: claims based on ancestry or ethnic characteristics can be brought under § 1981 but not claims based on national origin. *See, e.g.*, Anderson v. Conboy, 156 F.3d 167, 170 (2d Cir.1998), *cert. dismissed sub nom.* United Bhd. of Carpenters & Joiners of Am. v. Anderson, 527 U.S. 1030, 119 S.Ct. 2418, 144

L.Ed.2d 789 (1999) . In *Magnana v. Northern Mariana Islands*, 107 F.3d 1436, 1446–47 (9th Cir.1997), the court held that although the plaintiff could not pursue a "national origin" claim under § 1981, her claim that she was discriminated against because she was Filipino was permissible as it raised a question of ancestry discrimination. According to the court, a national origin claim would have alleged discrimination because she was from the Philippines, highlighting the fine line between an ancestry and national origin claim. *Id.*

e. *Discrimination because of alienage*: Although Title VII does not prohibit discrimination on the basis of citizenship status, Espinoza v. Farah Mfg. Co., 414 U.S. 86, 94 S.Ct. 334, 38 L.Ed.2d 287 (1973), it is well settled that § 1981 prohibits discrimination on the basis of alienage by state actors. *See* Graham v. Richardson, 403 U.S. 365, 377, 91 S.Ct. 1848, 29 L.Ed.2d 534 (1971) (recognizing that "[t]he protection of [§ 1981] has been held to extend to aliens as well as to citizens," and citing Takahashi v. Fish & Game Comm'n, 334 U.S. 410, 419–20, 68 S.Ct. 1128 (1948)); Sagana v. Tenorio, 384 F.3d 740 (9th Cir.2004) (holding that "§ 1981 prohibits governmental discrimination on the basis of alienage"). This interpretation rests on the text of § 1981, which affords to "all persons within the jurisdiction of the United States" the "same right" to "make and enforce contracts * * * as is enjoyed by white citizens." 42 U.S.C. § 1981(a). *Sagana*, 384 F.3d at 738–39. In addition, since the 1991 amendments to § 1981, it has generally been agreed that the statute also prohibits alienage discrimination by private actors. *See,* Anderson v. Conboy, 156 F.3d 167, 170 (2d Cir.1998) (holding that post-amendment § 1981 prohibits alienage discrimination by private actors in making of contracts); *see also* Duane v. GEICO, 37 F.3d 1036, 1044 (4th Cir.1994) (holding that even pre-amendment § 1981 prohibits alienage discrimination claim by private insurance carrier in making of contracts). The interplay between national origin and alienage discrimination claims under Title VII, § 1981, and the Immigration Reform and Control Act of 1986 (IRCA), 8 U.S.C. 1324a *et seq.*, will be discussed further in Chapter 13. *See, e.g., Anderson*, 156 F.3d at 180 ("If an employer refuses to hire a person because that person is in the country illegally [pursuant to IRCA], that employer is discriminating on the basis not of alienage but of noncompliance with federal law.").

f. *Sex, religion, age, and disability are not protected under § 1981*: The Supreme Court has acknowledged that contract discrimination claims based on sex or religion cannot be brought under § 1981. *See* Runyon v. McCrary, 427 U.S. 160, 167, 96 S.Ct. 2586, 2593, 49 L.Ed.2d 415 (1976) (recognizing, in dictum, that § 1981 does not apply to discrimination based on sex or religion); *see also* Bobo v. ITT, Continental Baking Co., 662 F.2d 340, 342 (5th Cir.1981) (holding that § 1981 does not cover claims of sex discrimination). Likewise, courts have held that § 1981 does not cover discrimination on the basis of age, Kodish v. United Air Lines, 628 F.3d 1301, 1303 (10th Cir.1980), or disability, Aramburu v. Boeing Co., 112 F.3d 1398, 1411 (10th Cir.1997).

2. SECTION 1981 REMEDIES AND PROCEDURAL REQUIREMENTS

Unlike claims brought under Title VII, a claim for race (or alienage) discrimination brought under § 1981 is not subject to a requirement of exhaustion of administrative remedies. In *Johnson v. Railway Express Agency*, 421 U.S. 454, 461, 95 S.Ct. 1716, 1721, 44 L.Ed.2d 295 (1975), the Supreme Court noted that "the remedies available under Title VII and under § 1981, although related, and although directed to most of the same ends, are separate, distinct, and independent." Importantly, under § 1981 compensatory and punitive damages are not subject to the damage caps applicable to Title VII, and § 1981 backpay awards are not limited to two years as provided under Title VII. *Id.* at 460, 95 S.Ct. at 1720. Thus, as a practical matter, discrimination claims based on race or ancestry should be brought under both § 1981 and Title VII—when the Title VII procedural requirements can be satisfied. Plaintiffs bringing Title VII national origin claims should also ascertain whether a § 1981 alienage discrimination claim would be appropriate. If the Title VII procedural requirements cannot be met, plaintiffs should bring such claims under § 1981. Section1981 claims are subject to statutes of limitations as discussed in the following case.

JONES V. R. R. DONNELLEY & SONS

Supreme Court of the United States, 2004.
541 U.S. 369, 124 S.Ct. 1836, 158 L.Ed.2d 645.

JUSTICE STEVENS delivered the opinion for a unanimous Court.

Like many federal statutes, 42 U.S.C. § 1981 does not contain a statute of limitations. We held in *Goodman v. Lukens Steel Co.,* 482 U.S. 656, 660, 107 S.Ct. 2617, 96 L.Ed.2d 572 (1987), that federal courts should apply "the most appropriate or analogous state statute of limitations" to claims based on asserted violations of § 1981. Three years after our decision in *Goodman*, Congress enacted a catchall 4-year statute of limitations for actions arising under federal statutes enacted after December 1, 1990. 28 U.S.C. § 1658. The question in this case is whether petitioners' causes of action, which allege violations of § 1981, as amended by the Civil Rights Act of 1991 (1991 Act) * * * are governed by § 1658 or by the personal injury statute of limitations of the forum State.

I

Petitioners are African-American former employees of respondent's Chicago manufacturing division. On November 26, 1994, petitioners filed this class action alleging violations of their rights under § 1981, as amended by the 1991 Act. Specifically, the three classes of plaintiffs alleged that they were subjected to a racially hostile work environment, given an inferior employee status, and wrongfully terminated or denied a transfer in connection with the closing of the Chicago plant. Respondent sought summary judgment on the ground that petitioners' claims are barred by the applicable Illinois statute of limitations because they arose more than two years before the complaint was filed. Petitioners responded that their claims are governed by § 1658, which provides: "Except as otherwise provided by law, a civil action arising under an Act of Congress enacted after the date of enactment of this section may not be commenced later than 4 years after the cause of action accrues." 28 U.S.C. § 1658(a). * * * Section 1658 was enacted on December 1, 1990. Thus, petitioners' claims are subject to the 4-year statute of limitations if they arose under an Act of Congress enacted after that date.

The original version of the statute * * * was enacted as § 1 of the Civil Rights Act of 1866. It was amended in minor respects in 1870 and recodified in 1874, but its basic coverage did not change prior to 1991. As first enacted, § 1981 provided in relevant part that "all persons [within the jurisdiction of the United States] shall have the same right in every State and Territory to make and enforce contracts * * * as is enjoyed by white citizens." 14 Stat 27. We held in *Patterson v. McLean Credit Union*, 491 U.S. 164, 109 S.Ct. 2363, 105 L.Ed.2d 132 (1989), that the statutory right "to make and enforce contracts" did not protect against harassing conduct that occurred after the formation of the contract. Under that holding, it is clear that petitioners' hostile work environment, wrongful discharge, and refusal to transfer claims do not state violations of the original version of § 1981. In 1991, however, Congress responded to *Patterson* by adding a new subsection to § 1981 that defines the term "make and enforce contacts" to include the "termination of contracts and the enjoyment of all benefits, privileges, terms, and conditions of the contractual relationship." 42 U.S.C. § 1981(b). * * * It is undisputed that petitioners have alleged violations of the amended statute. The critical question, then, is whether petitioners' causes of action "ar[ose] under" the 1991 Act or under § 1981 as originally enacted.

The District Court determined that petitioners' wrongful termination, refusal to discharge, and hostile work environment claims arose under the 1991 Act and therefore are governed by § 1658. [The Court of Appeals reversed, concluding that § 1658 "applies only when an act of Congress creates a wholly new cause of action, one that does not depend on the continued existence of a statutory cause of action previously enacted and kept in force by the amendment." 305 F.3d 717 (7th Cir.2002). The Supreme Court granted certiorari to resolve the circuit split on this issue.]

II

Petitioners * * * argue that reversal is required by the "plain language" of § 1658, which prescribes a 4-year statute of limitations for "civil action[s] arising under an Act of Congress enacted after" December 1, 1990. They point out that the 1991 Act is, by its own terms, an "Act" of Congress that was "enacted" after December 1, 1990. *See* Pub.L. 102–166, 105 Stat. 1071. Moreover, citing our interpretations of the term "arising under" in other federal statutes and in Article III of the Constitution, petitioners maintain that their causes of action arose under the 1991 Act.

Respondent concedes that the 1991 Act qualifies as an "Act of Congress enacted" after 1991, but argues that the meaning of the term "arising under" is not so clear. We agree. Although our expositions of the "arising under" concept in other contexts are helpful in interpreting the term as it is used in § 1658, they do not point the way to one obvious answer. * * * [Precedent] would suggest that petitioners' causes of action arose under the pre-1991 version of § 1981 as well as under the 1991 Act, just as a cause of action may arise under both state and federal law. As the Court of Appeals observed, however, § 1658 does not expressly "address the eventuality when a cause of action 'arises under' two different 'Acts,' one enacted before and one enacted after the effective date of § 1658." 305 F.3d, at 724.

* * *

III

In *Board of Regents of Univ. of State of N. Y. v. Tomanio*, 446 U.S. 478, 483, 100 S.Ct. 1790, 64 L.Ed.2d 440, (1980), we observed that Congress' failure to enact a uniform statute of limitations applicable to federal causes of action created a "void which is commonplace in federal statutory law." Over the years that void has spawned a vast amount of litigation. Prior to the enactment of § 1658, the "settled practice was to adopt a local time limitation as federal law if it [was] not inconsistent with federal law or policy to do so." Wilson v. Garcia, 471 U.S. 261, 266–67, 105 S.Ct. 1938, 85 L.Ed.2d 254 (1985). Such "[l]imitation borrowing" generated a host of issues that required resolution on a statute-by-statute basis. For example, it often was difficult to determine which of the forum State's statutes of limitations was the most appropriate to apply to the federal claim. * * *

The practice of borrowing state statutes of limitation also forced courts to address the "frequently present problem of a conflict of laws in determining which State statute [was] controlling, the law of the forum or that of the situs of the injury." S.Rep.No. 619, 84th Cong., 1st Sess., 4–6 (1955) (discussing problems caused by borrowing state statutes of limitations for antitrust claims). Even when courts were able to identify the appropriate state statute, limitation borrowing resulted in uncertainty for both plaintiffs and defendants, as a plaintiff alleging a federal claim in State A would find herself barred by the local statute of limitations while a plaintiff raising precisely the same claim in State B would be permitted to proceed. Interstate variances of that sort could be especially confounding in class actions because they often posed problems for joint resolution. Courts also were forced to grapple with questions such as whether federal or state law governed when an action was "commenced," or when service of process had to be effectuated. And the absence of a uniform federal limitations period complicated the development of federal law on the question when, or under what circumstances, a statute of limitations could be tolled.

* * *

The Court of Appeals reasoned that § 1658 must be given a narrow scope lest it disrupt litigants' settled expectations. * * * Concerns about settled expectations provide a valid reason to reject an interpretation of § 1658 under which any new amendment to federal law would suffice to trigger the 4-year statute of limitations, regardless of whether the plaintiff's claim would have been available—and subject to a state statute of limitations—prior to December 1, 1990. Such concerns do not, however, carry any weight against the reading of § 1658 adopted by the District Court and urged by petitioners, under which the catchall limitations period applies only to causes of action that *were not available* until after § 1658 was enacted. If a cause of action did not exist prior to 1990, potential litigants could not have formed settled expectations as to the relevant statute of limitations that would then be disrupted by application of § 1658.

We conclude that a cause of action "aris[es] under an Act of Congress enacted" after December 1, 1990—and therefore is governed by § 1658's 4-year statute of limitations—if the plaintiff's claim against the defendant was made possible by a post-1990 enactment. That construction best serves Congress' interest in alleviating the uncertainty inherent in the practice of borrowing state statutes of limitations while at the same time protecting settled interests. It spares federal judges and litigants the need to identify the appropriate state statute of limitations to apply to new claims but leaves in place the "borrowed" limitations periods for preexisting causes of action, with respect to which the difficult work already has been done.

* * *

IV

In this case, petitioners' hostile work environment, wrongful termination, and failure-to-transfer claims "ar[ose] under" the 1991 Act in the sense that petitioners' causes of action were made possible by that Act. *Patterson* held that "racial harassment relating to the conditions of employment is *not actionable* under § 1981." 491 U.S., at 171, 109 S.Ct. 2363, 105 L.Ed.2d 132 (emphasis added). The 1991 Act overturned *Patterson* by defining the key "make and enforce contracts" language in § 1981 to include the "termination of contracts and the enjoyment of all benefits, privileges, terms, and conditions of the contractual relationship." 42 U.S.C. § 1981(b). In *Rivers* v. *Roadway Express, Inc.*, we recognized that the 1991 amendment "enlarged the category of conduct that is subject to § 1981 liability," 511 U.S. 298, 303, 114 S.Ct. 1510, 128 L.Ed.2d 274 (1994), and we therefore held that the amendment does not apply "to a case that arose before it was enacted," *id.*, at 300, 114 S.Ct. 1510. Our reasoning in *Rivers* supports the conclusion that the 1991 Act fully qualifies as "an Act of Congress enacted after [December 1, 1990]" within the meaning of § 1658. Because petitioners' hostile work environment, wrongful termination, and failure-to-transfer claims did not allege a violation of the pre-1990 version of § 1981 but did allege violations of the amended statute, those claims "ar[ose] under" the amendment to § 1981 contained in the 1991 Act. * * *

The judgment of the Court of Appeals is reversed, and the case is remanded for further proceedings consistent with this opinion.

NOTES AND QUESTIONS

1. The *Donnelley* decision clarifies that § 1981 claims relating to racial discrimination that occurs outside of the contract formation stage (i.e., harassment, demotions, and terminations) enjoy the four-year statute of limitations in § 1658. In order to protect "settled interests," however, the Court leaves in place the rule that the statute of limitations for contract *formation* claims must still be determined under the most analogous state statute of limitations. Lower courts that have addressed the issue have found that in cases of racial discrimination in contract formation, the analogous state statute of limitations applies to § 1981 claims. *See* Brown v. Unified Sch. Dist. 501, 465 F.3d 1184, 1188 (10th Cir.2006) (applying Kansas's two-year personal injury statute of limitations); Johnson v. Crown Enters., Inc., 398 F.3d 339, 341 (5th Cir.2005) (applying Louisiana's one-year personal injury statute of limitations).

2. *Section 1981 Claims by Union Members Against Unions*: In *Daniels v. Pipefitters' Association Local Union No. 597*, 945 F.2d 906 (7th Cir.1991), the court found a union liable under § 1981 because it had denied a black employee a referral to a job on the basis of race. Because the union's job referral service was the primary process through which employers hired union members, the discriminatory conduct of the union interfered with the plaintiff's ability to enter into an employment contract. In addition, the union was liable under § 1981 for interfering with the employee's ability to enforce a provision of the collective bargaining agreement that required the union to

refer its members on a nondiscriminatory basis. Union liability for discrimination under Title VII was covered in Chapter 2.

3. *Section 1981 Claims Against State and Local Government Employers*: In *Jett v. Dallas Independent School District*, 491 U.S. 701, 109 S.Ct. 2702, 105 L.Ed.2d 598 (1989), the Supreme Court held that while § 1981 provides certain rights, it does not itself provide a remedy against state actors. The Court concluded that § 1983, 42 U.S.C. § 1983, provides the exclusive federal cause of action for damages for deprivations of rights under § 1981. Consequently, plaintiffs were required to seek enforcement of their § 1981 claims against state and local governmental entities and officials by means of a lawsuit under § 1983. (At the same time, *Jett* reaffirmed that § 1981 provides an implied right of action against private employers because no other statute provides a remedy. 491 U.S. at 731–32, 109 S.Ct. 2721.) Following *Jett*, Congress passed the Civil Rights Act of 1991, amending § 1981 to provide that "[t]he rights protected by this section are protected against impairment by nongovernmental discrimination and impairment under color of state law." 42 U.S.C. § 1981I. Although this was understood to codify the long-recognized § 1981 implied cause of action against private ("nongovernmental") actors, the appellate courts faced the question of whether Congress intended in the 1991 amendments to overrule *Jett* and create an implied cause of action under § 1981 against governmental actors who impaired rights "under color of state law." All but one of the circuit courts that have addressed the question have reaffirmed *Jett's* principle that § 1981 does not create a remedy against state actors. *See* Brown v. Sessoms, 774 F.3d 1016 (D.C. Cir.2014) ("We . . . join our sister circuits (minus the Ninth Circuit) in concluding that the [1991] Act's Amendments to section 1981 did not nullify *Jett*.") The lone holdout is the Ninth Circuit, which held that the 1991 amendments overturned *Jett* and created "an implied cause of action against state actors" under § 1981. *See* Fed'n of Afr. Am. Contractors v. City of Oakland, 96 F.3d 1204, 1214 (9th Cir.1996).

In those circuits that now hold that § 1981 does not provide an independent, private right of action against state actors, plaintiffs—as *Jett* acknowledged—can bring § 1981 race or alienage discrimination claims under § 1983. 42 U.S.C. § 1983. Because § 1983 has somewhat complex procedural and substantive requirements, however, the statute is only occasionally used for employment cases, typically only when a plaintiff has failed to comply with the administrative procedures necessary to pursue one of the other federal statutory discrimination claims such as Title VII, the ADEA, and ADA. (Subject to the principles of sovereign immunity, as discussed in Chapter 2, state and local governmental entities can be sued under federal statutes, like Title VII, that provide for access to the courts and a right to remedies.) As a general matter, to prevail under § 1983, a plaintiff must demonstrate that she has been deprived of federal constitutional or statutory rights under color of state law. For example, public employees alleging retaliation for exercising their First Amendment rights most commonly pursue claims under § 1983. *See, e.g.*, Garcetti v. Cebbalos, 547

U.S. 410, 126 S.Ct. 1951, 164 L.Ed.2d 684 (2005). As discussed in Section B of this chapter, equal protection claims against state actors are brought under § 1983. Although individual governmental defendants acting in their official capacity are entitled to a defense of qualified immunity, if the plaintiff can establish that she was deprived of a right that was "clearly established" at the time of the deprivation, the responsible official can be held liable for money damages. *See* Stafford Unified Sch. Dist. V. Redding, 557 U.S. 364, 129 S.Ct. 2633, 2643–44 (2009); Morgan v. Swanson, 755 F.3d 757 (5th Cir.2014). A detailed examination of the requirements of § 1983 actions is beyond the scope of this book.

4. *Title VII is the Exclusive Remedy for Race Discrimination Claims Against Federal Employers*: Congress extended the protections of Title VII to most federal employees in the Equal Employment Opportunity Act of 1972. *See* Title VII, § 717, 42 U.S.C. § 2000e–16. Subsequently, in *Brown v. General Services Administration,* 425 U.S. 820, 96 S.Ct. 1961, 48 L.Ed.2d 402 (1976), discussed in Section B of this chapter, the Supreme Court ruled that § 717 of Title VII is the exclusive remedy for job-related racial discrimination by covered federal government employers and that federal employees covered by Title VII may not sue federal agencies under § 1981. Section 117 of the Civil Rights Act of 1991 later extended the rights and protections of Title VII to employees of the House of Representatives and employees of agencies of Congress. Title III of the 1991 Act, known as the Government Employee Rights Act of 1991 (GERA), also created an Office of Senate Fair Employment Practices and established procedures to protect Senate employees from discrimination on the basis of race, color, religion, sex, national origin, age, or disability.

CHAPTER 6

EVIDENTIARY FRAMEWORKS FOR STATUS DISCRIMINATION: AN UNDERVIEW

■ ■ ■

The primary challenge for a regulatory framework aimed at rooting out and remedying status discrimination is to create legal structures that efficiently and effectively handle exculpatory and inculpatory evidence. Chapters 3, 4, and 5 have been designed to introduce the various evidentiary frameworks that have developed under Title VII and § 1981. These chapters show you how to identify and analyze particular kinds of evidence of discrimination. They do not, however, attempt to treat these frameworks in a unified fashion. Needless to say, clients' problems regarding discrimination do not come neatly wrapped in packages, each labeled according to the evidentiary framework that is implicated by individual and isolated facts. This "underview" (a term we have coined for this occasion) is intended to allow a discussion regarding how the frameworks fit together, a critical piece of the puzzle for attorneys who need to be able to understand how to use multiple frameworks to advise clients adequately about their options.

SCENARIO 1: THE RESTAURANT

Britney Brown, a 28-year-old Caucasian woman with extensive experience as a food server, recently applied to work at Michael's Shrimp & Lobster, Inc. ("Michael's") in Beach City. Her application was rejected. Michael's is a sixth-generation, family-owned seafood restaurant and Beach City landmark. During the lobster season, which lasts for five months, the restaurant is extremely busy. The restaurant employs 225 employees; of those, approximately 70 are food servers. From 1950 onward, the food servers have been almost exclusively male.

To hire new food servers, Michael's conducts a "roll call" every year. The roll call is widely known throughout the local food server community, and it generally attracts over 100 applicants for a limited number of openings. At a typical roll call, each applicant completes a written application and has an interview with three members of management. In addition, each applicant is required to take and pass a "tray test," which involves lifting and carrying a loaded serving tray. Applicants who are selected for hire then enter a training program in which they shadow experienced servers. After completing their training, the new hires become permanent food servers.

Although for many years most of the owners and managers of Michael's have been women, most of the female employees have worked in low-status, low-paid positions traditionally viewed as "women's jobs," such as cashier or laundry worker. The more desirable—and much more financially rewarding—food server positions have been staffed by men. While Michael's hired female food servers during World War II, most of these positions reverted to men at the conclusion of the war. In justifying, historically, the relative absence of female food servers, the current owner, Andrea Dillon, said that Michael's maintains an "Old World" European tradition, in which the highest level of food service is performed by men in order to create an ambience of "fine dining" for its customers. There is no express policy of excluding women from food server positions. Indeed, Michael's owners and managers have at times been courageous in opposing overt discrimination. For example, Michael's was picketed in the late 1950s when the original owner, Dan Michael, insisted on hiring African-American workers who had been excluded from membership in the Food Service Workers Union because of race. When questioned about the low number of female food servers, Dillon stated, "I cannot explain the predominance of male servers, but perhaps it has to do with the very heavy trays they have to carry, the ambience of the restaurant, and the extremely low turnover in servers." A longtime head waiter with hiring authority asserted that Michael's had a tradition that food server positions were "a male server type of job," but stated also that gender was never mentioned by managers or employees because of "a perception that people didn't even think about—that many fine dining establishments throughout the world have an all-male staff. The restaurant has sought to emulate Old World traditions by creating an ambience in which tuxedo-clad men serve its distinctive menu."

Until this year, the number of female food server applicants at the annual hiring roll calls has been minuscule. While there is little available evidence as to the actual number of female applicants at these roll calls (because Michael's usually does not retain any employment data from its roll calls), no more than two or three women per year (or, at most, 3 percent of the overall applicant class) have attended the roll calls. In the last ten years, about 100 new male food servers were hired while no women were hired.

A nearby restaurant on the beach, Atlantic Seafood has a female waitstaff of 25 percent. Other similar restaurants not on the beach, but in the same neighborhood, have female waitstaffs of 42 percent and 36 percent respectively. The qualified female labor pool for waitstaff is 20 percent based on recent census data for female food servers living and/or working in the Beach City area (and adjusted to meet Michael's general hiring criteria).

Evaluate Britney's potential Title VII claim. What potential defenses could Michael's assert?

SCENARIO 2: THE LAW FIRM

After graduating from Harvard Law School, Larry Monroe worked as an associate in a large Philadelphia firm for several years. When that firm began experiencing financial difficulties, though, it froze associate salaries. At the time, Monroe was making $100,000 per year. A headhunter sent Monroe's resume to Matt Dole, the hiring partner at Cali & Columbus, a nation-wide law firm with offices in San Francisco, Kansas City, and Philadelphia. Accompanying the resume was the headhunter's note pitching Monroe to prospective employers: not only would Monroe bring with him a $250,000 to $500,000 book of business but "he is a minority." (Larry Monroe is African American.)

When he interviewed with Matt Dole at Cali & Columbus's office in Kansas City, Monroe said he was interested in bankruptcy work and was "looking for a law firm with an established bankruptcy practice" because, contrary to the headhunter's note, he didn't "have a book of business of his own." Monroe also said that he wanted to be considered for partnership the following year. Dole, a bankruptcy specialist and the biggest rainmaker at the firm, assured Monroe that he would be "more than busy." Moreover, with the firm's recent addition of John Dunn, a new bankruptcy partner in the Philadelphia office, as well as the possibility of doing work with Cali & Columbus's Finance Department in San Francisco, the future in bankruptcy practice in the firm looked bright. On the spot, Dole offered Monroe a position as a senior associate in the Philadelphia office, with an annual salary of $115,000. As was the firm's policy, Monroe would be considered for partnership the following year.

Before accepting the offer, Monroe met with John Dunn, the only bankruptcy partner in Philadelphia. Dunn told Monroe that there would be "plenty of bankruptcy work in the Philadelphia office" and that he was "hoping to get work from the San Francisco office as well." Monroe accepted the position at Cali & Columbus, contingent on being able to visit the firm's home office in San Francisco, the headquarters of the firm's Finance Department, which supervised all of the firm's bankruptcy work throughout the nation. Monroe visited the San Francisco office and met with the head of the Finance Department, Lisa Golden. He then promptly accepted the firm's offer. At the time he joined the firm, Monroe was one of only three African Americans (and the only associate) out of a total of 200 attorneys firm-wide. Two long-time partners in the San Francisco office are African-American men.

In the beginning of his tenure at Cali & Columbus, Monroe kept busy, receiving his work almost exclusively through Dunn and Dole, with Dunn serving as Monroe's supervisor and mentor. After less than a year, however, Dunn left the firm. Monroe thus wound up as the only bankruptcy attorney in the Philadelphia office. When the time came for Monroe's annual performance review, nothing happened. Monroe maintained a low profile while the firm accepted nominations for partnership. Although there was a buzz in the office about who was being considered for partnership, no partners told Monroe they would sponsor him for partnership. Also that fall, the firm made its compensation decisions. Monroe received an annual bonus, in the amount of $6,000, though the average bonus for attorneys with his seniority was $12,000. His base salary for the next year remained unchanged. The firm's other associates received a 3 percent raise.

Monroe asked the firm's human resources director why he had not received a raise; the director told him to talk to Lisa Golden. Monroe flew to San Francisco to meet with Golden. She presented him with the two performance reviews that partners had prepared, one by Dole and the other by Dunn, who was by then no longer with the firm. Dunn's evaluation was positive overall:

> Much of Larry's time is consumed by routine tasks, such as drafting status letters to our client. Occasionally we receive a challenging assignment from Allied Insurance [a large client], which Larry accomplishes with great skill. Allied is a very difficult client and Larry's ongoing efforts to coordinate with me have made a potentially troublesome situation relatively easy. I do not believe that, for the most part, Allied offers challenging work to Larry. Larry nonetheless accomplishes the tasks for them with a helpful attitude and a willingness to tackle the unique problems this client presents.

Golden explained to Monroe that she considered Dunn's review not as a substantive evaluation of his performance—that is, a description of Monroe's strengths and weaknesses—but as a testament to his affability. Golden also stated that Dunn had not been well respected by the firm's partners and that his opinions would not help Monroe achieve partnership. The second evaluation, from Dole, reported that he was "not in a position to judge the quality of Larry's work," but that Monroe "has always appeared cooperative and willing to get the job done." Golden told Monroe that although he had not been considered for partnership, he would still be eligible the following year.

After the meeting with Golden, the quality of work assigned to Monroe did not improve. He found himself still doing work he believed less-experienced attorneys could have performed. But two months after his meeting with Golden, the firm did raise Monroe's salary to $123,000 a year, bringing him more into line with other firm attorneys with similar experience. Since then, Monroe has received raises at the low end of the range for his level of skill and experience. Despite doing good, solid work for the firm, and mostly for Matt Dole's clients, Monroe has never really been supported for partnership by Dole. When Monroe has asked Dole about his chances for partnership, Dole always just said, "Well, maybe next year." Monroe has remained the only African-American associate at the firm for several years, though the firm has had many African-American summer associates. Offers have been extended to them, but none were accepted. The firm did finally hire an entry-level African-American woman associate who will start next fall in San Francisco. Meanwhile, Monroe was recently passed over for partner yet again and was told he should start looking for another job.

Evaluate Monroe's potential claims against Cali & Columbus under Title VII and § 1981, and describe the firm's potential defenses.

SCENARIO 3: THE CONSTRUCTION SITE

Recently, the ABC Building Company secured a contract to construct a new high school in Chicago, Illinois. It engaged Lima Brothers as the masonry subcontractor. Because the job was publicly funded, contractors and subcontractors were told that they had to conform to specific equal employment opportunity (EEO) rules and to issue weekly EEO summaries documenting the number of hours worked by minority employees.

Sabados Lima, a Portuguese immigrant, owns Lima Brothers. He retained a Brazilian, Leo Souza, as the masonry foreman for the Chicago project. Lima and Souza then hired a number of masons and laborers to work on the job. Those engaged included three masons—Jose Fernandez, a dark-skinned Puerto Rican, and two white males, George Clark and George Manson. These three men worked as a team for several months until Souza laid them off due to weather conditions and lack of heat in the workplace. He assured them that he would recall them when the heating issue had been solved.

After a month, Lima Brothers resumed work on the Chicago project. It recalled some masons but not Fernandez. The following week, Fernandez visited the job site and asked Souza when he would be rehired. Souza responded, "The way things are going now . . . I wouldn't count on it."

Fernandez visited the site the next Saturday. He noticed masons working there and questioned Lima about this circumstance. Lima replied, "We're doing a little fixing up here." Fernandez then asked, "Am I going to get called back?" Lima responded, "We're going to close in," a comment that Fernandez took to mean that the building would be enclosed in order to create a heated space in which the masons could work.

Having heard nothing further, Fernandez checked back two weeks later. He saw that the job site was fully heated and asked Lima, "When am I coming back?" Lima replied cryptically, "Well, I got my men." When Fernandez inquired about what had happened to the plan to recruit residents and minorities, Lima stated, "I don't need no minorities, and I don't need no residents on this job. I got my men. These guys have more experience and do better work than you anyway." Fernandez complained that Lima had "eight new faces" working on the project, but Lima abruptly terminated the conversation.

In point of fact, during the month after restarting work on the project, Lima Brothers recalled a total of twelve workers (masons and laborers) and hired eight new workers (none of whom had previously worked for Lima Brothers). Eighteen of twenty were Caucasian males, and two were Caucasian women. Five of the masons and laborers were of Portuguese extraction. From time to time, Lima Brothers has suggested that these employees should be counted as "minorities." Two of the Caucasian men actually had less experience than Fernandez.

Fernandez returned to the job site on numerous occasions. Each time, Lima told him that there was no work available but to come back again. After several weeks, Fernandez asked Souza why he had not been recalled. Souza replied that Lima Brothers "had only hired a few minorities because of local pressure."

A month later, Lima and a representative of the general contractor met with Fernandez and Lakisha Jones, a civil rights activist, and others from the local community regarding Lima Brothers' compliance with EEO requirements. Jones noted that Lima Brothers had hired more workers, all of whom were white, but that it had no minorities working at the site. She implored Lima to rehire Fernandez because "whatever is going on now will stop if he at least puts one Puerto Rican back to work." Lima said nothing at the time about the quality of Fernandez's work and indicated that he would honor this request.

When Fernandez arrived at the job site the following Monday, he was informed that there was no work available. This experience was repeated several times. Lima Brothers finally restored Fernandez to the payroll, albeit as a laborer rather than as a mason. When Fernandez reported for work, Lima instructed him to get an "F block." Fernandez was unsure what an "F block" was and asked Lima who, as matters turned out, had wanted a standard "half block." After castigating Fernandez for his ignorance, Lima declared that he was "tired of what's going on with you guys," and he voiced the opinion that "you guys are trying to hurt me." He then proclaimed: "I don't have to hire you guys. This is my business. It belongs to me." At that juncture, Lima fired Fernandez.

Evaluate the potential employment discrimination claims of Fernandez and Lima's potential defenses.

QUESTIONS

1. The three scenarios above are based on real cases. With respect to each scenario, what more would an attorney want to know in order to properly evaluate each case for potential liability under Title VII? Explain why any such additional information would be helpful.

2. Do you ultimately believe that the employees highlighted in the three scenarios were discriminated against? If so, what informs your belief? Were any of the evidentiary frameworks discussed in prior chapters useful in helping to evaluate the claims? If so, which ones? Are there evidentiary frameworks that are not implicated by any of the scenarios? Which ones? If you were a plaintiff's attorney considering whether to take one of these cases, which one would you choose? Keeping in mind that plaintiffs are permitted to plead in the alternative, would you nonetheless choose to limit the arguments you would make based on what you have learned about how evidence is developed and presented in employment discrimination litigation?

3. For each scenario, consider how the evidence is evaluated within a particular evidentiary framework. What evidence fits into the plaintiff's prima facie case in each circumstance? Can the plaintiff in each scenario prove a prima facie case?

4. Are the frameworks helpful in allowing decisionmakers to evaluate and compare the quality of evidence used by either the plaintiff or the defendant? If so, how? If not, why are the frameworks of any use? Can a decisionmaker reach the correct result without channeling evidence into a framework?

5. Can statistics be used in any of the scenarios to strengthen or weaken the employee's case? Which statistics in which cases? Where would these statistics be appropriately discussed in the relevant frameworks?

6. What about the defendants—is there sufficient evidence to make out a defense using any of the evidentiary frameworks? Which frameworks? How and when would defensive evidence be presented in each type of case?

PART 3

SPECIFIC CATEGORIES OF DISCRIMINATION

■ ■ ■

CHAPTER 7

DISCRIMINATION BECAUSE OF SEX

■ ■ ■

A. INTRODUCTION AND HISTORICAL OVERVIEW

On February 8, 1964, two days before the House voted on the Civil Rights Bill, Representative Howard W. Smith, a Southern Democrat who opposed the bill, proposed that "sex" be added as a prohibited category to Title VII. Despite the ensuing "humorous debate, later enshrined as 'Ladies Day in the House,' " the amendment was passed that same day by a vote of 168 to 133. Jo Freeman, *How "Sex" Got into Title VII: Persistent Opportunism as a Maker of Public Policy*, 9 Law & Ineq. J. 163, 163 (1991). Most courts and commentators have viewed this sparse legislative history as evidence that "sex" was included in Title VII as a "joke" or a failed eleventh-hour maneuver to defeat the Civil Rights Bill. *See id.* at 164, 176–77; Robert C. Bird, *More Than a Congressional Joke: A Fresh Look at the Legislative History of Sex Discrimination of the 1964 Civil Rights Act*, 3 Wm. & Mary J. Women & L. 137, 137–40 (1997). More recent interpretations of the context of the passage of the "sex" amendment suggest, however, that the "sex discrimination provision was the result of complex political struggles involving racial issues, presidential politics, and competing factions of the women's rights movement." Bird, *supra*, at 138; *see generally* Freeman, *supra*. According to these revisionist accounts, members of the National Women's Party (NWP), who for years had lobbied Congress for an Equal Rights Amendment (ERA), and a handful of women members of the House, who spoke out in favor of the amendment, were instrumental in assuring its passage. By this account

> [t]he civil rights movement, and the various civil rights bills, opened up a window of opportunity of which the activists took advantage. The NWP and women members of Congress lacked the resources to effect major policy changes by themselves; instead they grabbed the coattails of a major social movement which did have these resources. Persistent opportunism forced the federal government to make a major public innovation in an area which it had not previously acknowledged as being very important.

Freeman, *supra*, at 184.

Despite its ambiguous origins, the prohibition of employment discrimination because of sex ultimately has proved to be as significant in many respects as the primary purpose behind Title VII—the elimination and remediation of race-based employment discrimination. While Title VII has certainly not eliminated discriminatory employment practices or inequality between the sexes, the thousands of meritorious statutory claims brought by women who were the victims of unlawful employment discrimination have undoubtedly altered the way employers and employees think about sex discrimination in the workplace. Today few would question the wisdom or necessity of including "sex" as a prohibited basis for employment discrimination.

Of course, while Title VII and other state and federal laws promise women equal opportunity in the labor market, they can neither eradicate fundamental attitudes about women and work nor alter the underlying structure of the labor market. In 1979, Professor Catharine MacKinnon presented evidence that sex discrimination in employment is, in some respects, an even more intractable and harmful social and economic problem than race discrimination. Catharine A. MacKinnon, Sexual Harassment of Working Women: A Case of Sex Discrimination 14 (1979). And it is true that change for women in the workplace has been slow.

In 1965, shortly after both Title VII and the 1963 Equal Pay Act were passed, median annual earnings for women working full-time were only 59.9 percent of men's earnings. Institute for Women's Policy Research, The Gender Wage Gap: 2012, 1–2 (September 2013), available at *http://www.iwpr.org/publications/pubs/the-gender-wage-gap-2012-1.* While sex-based wage disparity has decreased in the last fifty years, significant differences remain. Earnings data from the Current Population Survey (CPS) conducted by the U.S. Census Bureau indicates that in 2013 the median weekly earnings of women who worked full-time was $706, which was about 82 percent of the $860 median earnings of male full-time workers. U.S. Dep't of Labor, Bureau of Labor Statistics, Highlights of Women's Earnings in 2013, Rep. No. 1051, at 1 (December 2014), available at *http://www.bls.gov/opub/reports/cps/highlights-of-womens-earnings-in-2013.pdf.*

The disparity between the average wages of men and women has always been related to a separate phenomenon—the sex-segregation of jobs. Indeed, pay inequality and the sex-segregation of work have been described as "the twin pillars of women's subordination in the workplace." Ruth Milkman, Gender at Work: The Dynamics of Job Segregation by Sex During World War II, at 153 (1987). Although workplaces are more integrated today than they were in 1963, de facto sex-segregation of many occupations persists.

> The gender wage gap and occupational segregation—men primarily working in occupations done by men, and women primarily working with other women—are persistent features of the U.S. labor market. Only four of the 20 most common occupations for men and the 20 most common occupations for women overlap. Four of ten women (39.5 percent) work in traditionally female occupations and between four and five of ten male workers (44.5 percent) work in traditionally male occupations; only 5.8 percent of women work in traditionally male occupations and only 4.6 percent of men in traditionally female occupations.

Institute for Women's Policy Research, Fact Sheet, The Gender Wage Gap by Occupation 1 (April 2012) (IWPR Publication #C350a), *http://www.iwpr.org/publications/pubs/the-gender-wage-gap-by-occupation-1/*. Women are more than two times as likely to work in jobs with poverty wages. *Id.* at 4. Moreover, even in jobs that are held predominantly by women—for example, secretaries, teachers, and nurses—men who work in these positions often earn more than women. *Id. See also* The Wage Gap in the 20 Most Common Occupations for Women (Full-Time Workers Only), 2011, Table 1.

Explanations for the continued wage gap, job segregation, and other differences in the experiences of men and women at work are varied. Economic and social conditions, and individual education, ability, and personality, all help determine the job opportunities of both women and men. *See generally* Mitra Toossi, *A Century of Change: The U.S. Labor Force, 1950–2050*, Monthly Lab.Rev., May 2002, at 15. Geography plays a role, too. The gender wage gap in 2013 continued to vary depending on a worker's place of residence, with a female-to-male earnings ratio of 68.6 percent in Wyoming and 91.3 percent in Vermont. Highlights of Women's Earnings at 25 tbl 3. These geographic differences are in part explained by the different occupations and industries found in different states and by the age of the working population in different communities. *Id.* at 5. Race and ethnicity also make a considerable difference. The CPS data shows that

> When adjusted for inflation, women's earnings since 1979 have increased considerably across the major race and Hispanic ethnicity categories. Earnings growth has been greatest for White women, outpacing that of their Black and Hispanic counterparts. Between 1979 and 2013, inflation-adjusted earnings (also called constant-dollar earnings) rose by 31 percent for White women, compared with an increase of 20 percent for Black women and 15 percent for Hispanic women.

Id. at 3.

Women's personal choices about education and occupations, as well as decisions to leave the labor market for childbirth, parenting, and other family responsibilities, can also affect wage-earning potential and job opportunities. For example, one survey of the wage gap reports that "[m]others are more likely than fathers (or other women) to work part time, take leave, or take a break from the work force—factors that negatively affect wages." Judy Goldberg Dey & Catherine Hill, AAUW Educational Foundation, Behind the Pay Gap 2 (2007), available at *http://www.aauw.org/files/2013/02/Behind-the-Pay-Gap.pdf*. But such decisions do not fully explain the wage gap. Consider the following data comparing earnings of male and female college graduates:

> One year out of college, women working full time earn only 80 percent as much as their male colleagues earn. Ten years after graduation, women fall farther behind, earning only 69 percent as much as men earn. Controlling for hours, occupation, parenthood, and other factors normally associated with pay, college-educated women still earn less than their male peers earn.

Id. Even women who earn their baccalaureate degree in the same college major as men experience a wage gap within the first year after they graduate. *Id.* Another study found that "[a]fter accounting for college major, occupation, economic sector, hours worked, months unemployed since graduation, GPA, type of undergraduate institution, institution selectivity, age, geographical region, and marital status . . . a 7 percent difference in the earnings of male and female college graduates one year after graduation was still unexplained." American Association of University Women, The Simple Truth About the Gender Pay Gap 6 (2015 Edition), available at *http://www.aauw.org/files/2015/02/The-Simple-Truth_Spring-2015.pdf*.

Despite both state and federal laws prohibiting gender discrimination, sex often continues to play a role, directly or indirectly, in the availability of job opportunities. Moreover, "workplace inequity * * * is often structurally embedded in the norms and cultural practices of an institution." Susan Sturm, *Lawyers and the Practice of Workplace Equity*, 2002 Wis.L.Rev. 277, 281. Other institutional actors, besides employers, can also affect the culture and practices of the workplace. The courts, for example, have significant responsibility for filling in the details in any outline of legislative reform—for determining in many individual cases how capacious or narrow the legislative vision of statutes like Title VII will ultimately prove to be. Are courts partly responsible for perpetuating workplace sex discrimination when they fail to challenge underlying assumptions about gender and work? Professor Vicki Schultz wrote:

> Title VII promised working women change. But, consciously or unconsciously, courts have interpreted the statute with some of the same assumptions that have historically legitimated women's economic disadvantage. Most centrally, courts have assumed that women's aspirations and identities as workers are shaped exclusively in private realms that are independent of and prior to the work world. By assuming that women form stable job aspirations before they begin working, courts have missed the ways in which employers contribute to creating women workers in their images of who "women" are supposed to be. Judges have placed beyond the law's reach the structural features of the workplace that gender jobs and people, and disempower women from aspiring to higher-paying nontraditional employment.

Vicki Schultz, *Telling Stories About Women and Work: Judicial Interpretations of Sex Segregation in the Workplace in Title VII Cases Raising the Lack of Interest Argument*, 103 Harv.L.Rev. 1749, 1756 (1990).

As you read the cases and materials in this chapter, evaluate them as a basis for developing your own ideas about the relationship of legislative reform and judicial decision making to social change. Is the existing framework of civil rights statutes and judge-made law adequate now to address the problems of sex discrimination in employment? What, exactly, are the problems of sex discrimination? Will the nature of discrimination vary significantly depending on the work context? For example, a growing number of women work in jobs like construction or firefighting that nevertheless continue to be highly sex-segregated. Some jobs may have physical requirements that few women can satisfy without additional training. *See, e.g.*, Lanning v. Southeastern Pennsylvania Transp. Auth. (SEPTA), 308 F.3d 286 (3d Cir.2002) (*Lanning II*) (upholding an aerobic test for applicants to a transit police training program that disqualifies 90% of female applicants), discussed in Chapter 4. Other jobs, such as nursing or the legal profession, may have more subtle barriers to entry by individuals—both men and women—who do not match the gender roles historically associated with those careers. Sex discrimination may appear different as well over the course of a person's life and career. Mothers and fathers face a different set of workplace challenges and employer assumptions than do nonparents. And the problems faced by women seeking positions in the executive and partnership ranks may be quite different than those of the applicant for her first job. *See generally* Sheryl Sandberg, Women, Work, and the Will to Lead (2013) (discussing the unique challenges that women seeking leadership roles face in the workplace).

Consider your own career aspirations. Most law students are by now familiar with the case of *Bradwell v. Illinois*, 83 U.S. (16 Wall.) 130, 21

L.Ed.442 (1873), in which the Supreme Court upheld the decision of the Illinois Supreme Court denying Myra Bradwell admittance to the bar solely because she was a woman. Justice Bradley concurred in the opinion, observing that the Court's ruling was justified because women's "natural and proper timidity and delicacy" and their "paramount destiny and mission * * * to fulfill the noble and benign offices of wife and mother" made them inherently unsuited for the demands of the legal profession. *Id.* at 141. Looking at the gender composition of your law school class, you might conclude that the gender bias and stereotyping typified by Justice Bradley's concurrence in *Bradwell* is a relic of ancient history. For the past decade the number of women entering law school each year has been very close to equal the number of men. Among the students who started law school in 2011, 46.8 percent were women. *See* First Year and Total J.D. Enrollment by Gender, 1947–2011, available at *http://www.americanbar.org/content/dam/aba/administrative/legal_education_and_admissions_to_the_bar/statistics/jd_enrollment_1yr_total_gender.authcheckdam.pdf.*

As law students, you can examine your own assumptions about whether or to what extent gender discrimination is still a problem in the workplace generally or in the workplace you are about to enter—the legal profession. The American Bar Association reported in 2014 that 34 percent of lawyers in the United States were women. A Current Glance at Women in the Law 2 (July 2014), available at *http://www.americanbar.org/content/dam/aba/marketing/women/current_glance_statistics_july2014.authcheckdam.pdf.* But the data also reveal that women continue to be underrepresented at the highest levels of the legal profession. For example, women made up only 17 percent of equity partners in law firms, only 4 percent of managing partners at the largest law firms, and only 21 percent of Fortune 500 general counsel. *Id.* at 2–3. Within the federal judiciary, the number of women hovered around 24 percent, and on state courts, about 27 percent of judges were women. *Id.* at 5. On average, the median weekly earnings of women lawyers in 2013 was about 79 percent that of their male cohort. *Id. See also* Marina Angel, *Women Lawyers of All Colors Steered to Contingent Positions in Law Schools and Law Firms,* 26 Chicana/o-Latina/o L.Rev. 169 (2006).

If sex discrimination continues to limit women's employment opportunities (even in the legal profession), what is the explanation? *See* Federal Glass Ceiling Commission, Good for Business: Making Full Use of the Nation's Human Capital 26–27 (1995); *see also* Ramona L. Paetzold & Rafael Gely, *Through the Looking Glass: Can Title VII Help Women and Minorities Shatter the Glass Ceiling?*, 31 Hous.L.Rev. 1517, 1520 (1995) (arguing that "[t]he courts' interpretation of Title VII has not been sufficiently sensitive to the subtle ways in which women and minorities come to be excluded from mid-level and upper level positions within organizations—ways so subtle that employers themselves are not always aware of them"). Are the theories of liability developed under Title VII adequate to explain these persistent disparities in employment opportunities for men and women? How can we know for sure whether the disparities are caused by unlawful discrimination or by other factors? *See* Christine Jolls, *Is There a Glass Ceiling?,* 25 Harv.Women's L.J. 1 (2002) (arguing that the "glass ceiling" exists and is significantly explained by unlawful sex discrimination).

This chapter focuses on several selected topics and cases that raise concerns that are unique in sex discrimination cases. Section B will consider the meaning of discrimination "because of sex" under Title VII. Section C will discuss the Equal Pay Act of 1963 (EPA) and the interplay between Title VII and the EPA. Section D explores the sex-based bona fide occupational qualification (BFOQ) defense. Section E discusses how the theories of liability and defenses developed in sex discrimination cases have been applied in the context of challenges to sex-based dress, grooming, and appearance requirements. Finally, Section F will examine systemic claims challenging employer policies and practices that operate as a glass ceiling for women seeking advancement and financial equality. Discrimination on the basis of pregnancy, parenting, and other caregiving responsibilities are the focus of Chapter 8. Chapter 9 will consider how the law deals with discrimination on the basis of sexual orientation and gender identity. Sexual harassment—as well as racial harassment—will be covered in Chapter 10.

B. WHAT IS DISCRIMINATION "BECAUSE OF SEX"?

Title VII has proved to be remarkably adaptable in addressing a range of difficult questions about the meaning of discrimination. As Professor Kathryn Abrams commented, "[t]his flexibility is particularly evident with respect to women." Kathryn Abrams, *Title VII and the Complex Female Subject*, 92 Mich.L.Rev. 2479, 2497 (1994). Over the course of more than four decades, the courts have accepted several distinct theories of liability in gender discrimination cases. Professor Abrams described three of these theories:

> The most recurrent, and most influential, theory has been an "equality" or "sameness" theory of discrimination. This theory describes women as substantially similar to men in most respects germane to employment; it describes discrimination as the prejudiced or erroneous failure to recognize this similarity, resulting in treatment of women as inferior, unable, or otherwise different from the paradigmatic male denizens of the workplace. A second theory, which has surfaced in cases involving

> pregnancy or gender-role expectations, highlights ways in which women differ from men. It notes that women's participation in the workforce is shaped by biological differences related to gestation and childbirth and by gender-role expectations that affect behavior in the workplace and require the integration of conflicting responsibilities of work and family. According to the "difference" theory, discrimination results from the failure to recognize these differences, to anticipate the devaluative light in which employers may view them, or to accommodate them in structuring the demands of workplaces. A third theory, which has been particularly influential in cases involving sexual harassment, characterizes discrimination as the devaluative sexualization or derogation of women in the workplace. Whether employers are expressing overt hostility or manifesting "sex role spillover," harassment characterizes women primarily as sexual objects, or as objects of sex-based derision, rather than as competent workers.

Id. at 2479–80 (citations omitted).

While scholars see different theories of discrimination come and go in judicial decisions, it is evident that courts continue to struggle with precisely what it means to discriminate "because of sex." In the three cases that follow, one can see the Supreme Court wrestling with how best to guide the lower courts in recognizing and defining sex discrimination. The cases arise in very different factual contexts—the first a challenge by women to a sex-based pension contribution system at a public utility, the second a suit over the failure of an accounting firm to promote a woman to partnership, and the third a man's claim of sexual harassment by his male co-workers and supervisors on an oil rig. The cases also span three decades in the development of sex discrimination law. Together, they offer a snapshot of some of the most important questions that have arisen as courts, lawyers, and academics work to understand both what sex discrimination is and how it can be proven in litigation.

CITY OF LOS ANGELES DEPARTMENT OF WATER & POWER V. MANHART

Supreme Court of the United States, 1978.
435 U.S. 702, 717, 98 S.Ct. 1370, 1380, 55 L.Ed.2d 657.

JUSTICE STEVENS delivered the opinion of the Court.

As a class, women live longer than men. For this reason, the Los Angeles Department of Water and Power required its female employees to make larger contributions to its pension fund than its male employees. We granted certiorari to decide whether this practice discriminated against individual female employees because of their sex in violation of § 703(a)(1) of the Civil Rights Act of 1964, as amended.

For many years the Department has administered retirement, disability, and death-benefit programs for its employees. Upon retirement each employee is eligible for a monthly retirement benefit computed as a fraction of his or her salary multiplied by years of service. The monthly benefits for men and women of the same age, seniority, and salary are equal. * * *

Based on a study of mortality tables and its own experience, the Department determined that its 2,000 female employees, on the average, will live a few years longer than its 10,000 male employees. The cost of a pension for the average retired female is greater than for the average male retiree because more monthly payments must be made to the average woman. The Department therefore required female employees to make monthly contributions to the fund which were 14.84% higher than the contributions required of comparable male employees. Because employee contributions were withheld from paychecks, a female employee took home less pay than a male employee earning the same salary.

[In 1973, plaintiffs sued the Department on behalf of a class of female employees and former employees, seeking injunctive relief and a refund of their excess contributions. The district court granted summary judgment for the plaintiffs, and the Ninth Circuit affirmed.]

* * *

There are both real and fictional differences between women and men. It is true that the average man is taller than the average woman; it is not true that the average woman driver is more accident prone than the average man. Before the Civil Rights Act of 1964 was enacted, an employer could fashion his personnel policies on the basis of assumptions about the differences between men and women, whether or not the assumptions were valid.

It is now well recognized that employment decisions cannot be predicated on mere "stereotyped" impressions about the characteristics of males or females. Myths and purely habitual assumptions about a woman's inability to perform certain kinds of work are no longer acceptable reasons for refusing to employ qualified individuals, or for paying them less. This case does not, however, involve a fictional difference between men and women. It involves a generalization that the parties accept as unquestionably true: Women, as a class, do live longer than men. The Department treated its women employees differently from its men employees because the two classes are in fact different. It is equally true, however, that all individuals in the respective classes do not share the characteristic that differentiates the average class representatives. Many women do not live as long as the average man and many men outlive the average woman. The question, therefore, is whether the existence or nonexistence of "discrimination" is to be determined by comparison of class characteristics or individual characteristics. A "stereotyped" answer to that question may not be the same as the answer that the language and purpose of the statute command.

The statute makes it unlawful "to discriminate against any *individual* with respect to his compensation, terms, conditions, or privileges of employment, because of such *individual's* race, color, religion, sex, or national origin." 42 U.S.C. § 2000e–2(a)(1) (emphasis added). The statute's focus on the individual is unambiguous. It precludes treatment of individuals as simply components of a racial, religious, sexual, or national class. If height is required for a job, a tall woman may not be refused employment merely because, on the average, women are too short. Even a true generalization about the class is an insufficient reason for disqualifying an individual to whom the generalization does not apply.

That proposition is of critical importance in this case because there is no assurance that any individual woman working for the Department will actually fit the generalization on which the Department's policy is based. Many of those individuals will not live as long as the average man. While they were working, those individuals received smaller paychecks because of their sex, but they will receive no compensating advantage when they retire.

It is true, of course, that while contributions are being collected from the employees, the Department cannot know which individuals will predecease the average woman. Therefore, unless women as a class are assessed an extra charge, they will be subsidized, to some extent, by the class of male employees. It follows, according to the Department, that fairness to its class of male employees justifies the extra assessment against all of its female employees.

But the question of fairness to various classes affected by the statute is essentially a matter of policy for the legislature to address. Congress has decided that classifications based on sex, like those based on national origin or race, are unlawful. Actuarial studies could unquestionably identify differences in life expectancy based on race or national origin, as well as sex. But a statute that was designed to make race irrelevant in the employment market, could not reasonably be construed to permit a take-home-pay differential based on a racial classification.

Even if the statutory language were less clear, the basic policy of the statute requires that we focus on fairness to individuals rather than fairness to classes. Practices that classify employees in terms of religion, race, or sex tend to preserve traditional assumptions about groups rather than thoughtful scrutiny of individuals. The generalization involved in this case illustrates the point. Separate mortality tables are easily interpreted as reflecting innate differences between the sexes; but a significant part of the longevity differential may be explained by the social fact that men are heavier smokers than women.

Finally, there is no reason to believe that Congress intended a special definition of discrimination in the context of employee group insurance coverage. It is true that insurance is concerned with events that are individually unpredictable, but that is characteristic of many employment decisions. Individual risks, like individual performance, may not be predicted by resort to classifications proscribed by Title VII. Indeed, the fact that this case involves a group insurance program highlights a basic flaw in the Department's fairness argument. For when insurance risks are grouped, the better risks always subsidize the poorer risks. Healthy persons subsidize medical benefits for the less healthy; unmarried workers subsidize the pensions of married workers; persons who eat, drink, or smoke to excess may subsidize pension benefits for persons whose habits are more temperate. Treating different classes of risks as though they were the same for purposes of group insurance is a common practice that has never been considered inherently unfair. To insure the flabby and the fit as though they were equivalent risks may be more common than treating men and women alike; but nothing more than habit makes one "subsidy" seem less fair than the other.

An employment practice that requires 2,000 individuals to contribute more money into a fund than 10,000 other employees simply because each of them is a woman, rather than a man, is in direct conflict with both the language and the policy of the Act. Such a practice does not pass the simple test of whether the evidence shows "treatment of a person in a manner which but for that person's sex would be different." It constitutes discrimination and is unlawful unless exempted by the Equal Pay Act of 1963 or some other affirmative justification. [The Court's discussion rejecting the Equal Pay Act affirmative defense in *Manhart* is covered in Chapter 11.]

* * *

[JUSTICE BLACKMAN concurred in part and concurred in the judgment. CHIEF JUSTICE BURGER, joined by JUSTICE REHNQUIST, concurred in part and dissented in part. JUSTICE MARSHALL concurred in the parts of the Court's opinion reprinted here and dissented in an omitted part regarding relief. JUSTICE BRENNAN took no part in the consideration or decision of this case.]

NOTES AND QUESTIONS

1. In *Arizona Governing Committee v. Norris*, 463 U.S. 1073, 103 S.Ct. 3492, 77 L.Ed.2d 1236 (1983), the Court extended the reach of *Manhart*'s prohibition of using sex-based actuarial tables to determine employees' fringe benefits. The Court held that an employer violates Title VII when its deferred compensation plan provides employees the option of purchasing—from one of several participating private insurance companies—retirement annuities that pay a woman lower benefits than a man who has contributed the same amount in deferred compensation.

2. During the 1980s, *Manhart* and *Norris* provoked a "highly polarized" debate about the use of sex-based statistical differences in employment benefits as well as in the insurance industry generally. Jill Gaulding, Note, *Race, Sex, and Genetic Discrimination in Insurance: What's Fair?*, 80 Cornell L.Rev. 1646, 1661 (1995). On one side of the debate, scholars utilized efficiency arguments to "demonstrate that employee pension, annuity, and life insurance plans that do not use sex-distinct mortality tables in fact violate the Equal Pay Act and Title VII." George J. Benston, *The Economics of Gender Discrimination in Employee Fringe Benefits*: Manhart *Revisited*, 49 U.Chi.L.Rev. 489, 492–93 (1982); *see generally* Spencer Kimball, *Reverse Sex Discrimination*: Manhart, 1979 Am.B.Found.Res.J. 83. On the other side, scholars argued that an employer's use of sex-based actuarial tables in providing fringe benefits violates Title VII because the purpose of the statute is to assure equal treatment of individuals, not groups. *See generally* Lea Brilmayer, Richard W. Hekeler, Douglas Laycock & Teresa A. Sullivan, *Sex Discrimination in Employer-Sponsored Insurance Plans: A Legal and Demographic Analysis*, 47 U.Chi.L.Rev. 505 (1980).

3. Prior to the enactment of the Patient Protection and Affordable Care Act ("ACA") in 2010, individuals who purchased insurance or annuities on the "open market"—not through their employers—would very likely discover that their premium or contribution rates and benefits were calculated using sex-based actuarial tables. When Congress considered the ACA, the overwhelming majority of states permitted significant "gender-rating" of plans. In 95 percent of surveyed best-selling plans, a 40-year-old woman was charged more than a 40-year-old man for identical coverage. *What Women Want: Equal Benefits for Equal Premiums*, Hearing before the Senate Comm. on Health, Education, Labor and Pensions, 111th Congress (Oct. 15, 2009) (testimony of Marcia D. Greenberger, President, National Women's Law Center), available at *http://help.senate.gov/imo/media/doc/Greenberger.pdf*. Almost none of these plans included maternity coverage, and thus costs associated with pregnancy and childbirth did not explain this difference. *Id.* Rather, the differences in premiums were highly variable. In Arkansas, premiums among the ten best-selling plans ranged from 13 to 63 percent more for women. Lisa Codispoti et al., *Nowhere to Turn: How the Individual Health Insurance Market Fails Women*, National Women's Law Center, 10 (June 9, 2008), available at *http://www.nwlc.org/resource/no*

where-turn-how-individual-health-insurance-market-fails-women-1. An insurer in Missouri charged 40-year-old women 140 percent more than men of the same age. *Id.* One small employer with a predominantly female workforce estimated that she paid $2,000 more per employee for health coverage due to her company's gender makeup. Jenny Gold, *Fight Erupts Over Health Insurance Rates for Businesses with More Women*, Kaiser Health News (October 25, 2009), available at *http://www.kaiserhealthnews.org/Stories/2009/October/23/gender-discrimination-health-insurance.aspx.* Ending gender rating was an important purpose of the ACA, which makes gender-rating illegal in every state—as applied to both individuals and small employers. *See* Pub. L. No. 111–148, § 1201.

4. The Court in *Manhart* dismisses the argument that "fairness to its class of male employees justifies the extra assessment against all of its female employees." What could an employer do if it wanted to avoid the possibility that its male employees were subsidizing the pension benefits paid to its female employees?

5. How can a descriptive statement about longevity of women be both a fact and a stereotype? Professor Ramona Paetzold wrote that "[i]t is through *Manhart* that one learns that 'fact' or 'statistical truths' can still be the basis for illegal stereotypes when their use disadvantages a protected class, as when all women are asked to pay higher pension premiums because as a class, women tend to live longer than men." Ramona L. Paetzold, *Commentary: Feminism and Business Law: The Essential Interconnection*, 31 Am.Bus.L.J. 699, 710 (1994). What if a "statistical truth" is used to advantage a protected class? Would that make it a "legal" stereotype? Wouldn't providing special advantages to one class of employees inevitably impose disadvantages on other classes of employees? As you read the next case, *Price Waterhouse v. Hopkins*, also reproduced, in part, in Chapter 3, consider whether the harms caused by the kind of "stereotype" at issue in *Manhart* are the same as those that infected the decision making process in Ann Hopkins' partnership evaluation.

PRICE WATERHOUSE V. HOPKINS

Supreme Court of the United States, 1989.
490 U.S. 228, 109 S.Ct. 1775, 104 L.Ed.2d 268.

JUSTICE BRENNAN announced the judgment of the Court and delivered an opinion, in which JUSTICE MARSHALL, JUSTICE BLACKMUN, and JUSTICE STEVENS join.

Ann Hopkins was a senior manager in an office of Price Waterhouse when she was proposed for partnership in 1982. She was neither offered nor denied admission to the partnership; instead, her candidacy was held for reconsideration the following year. When the partners in her office later refused to repropose her for partnership, she sued Price Waterhouse under Title VII * * * .

Ann Hopkins had worked at Price Waterhouse's Office of Government Services in Washington, D. C., for five years when the partners in that office proposed her as a candidate for partnership. Of the 662 partners at the firm at that time, 7 were women. Of the 88 persons proposed for partnership that year, only 1—Hopkins—was a woman. Forty-seven of these candidates were admitted to the partnership, 21 were rejected, and 20—including Hopkins—were "held" for reconsideration the following year. Thirteen of the 32 partners who had submitted comments on Hopkins supported her bid for partnership. Three partners recommended that her candidacy be placed on hold, eight stated that they did not have an informed opinion about her, and eight recommended that she be denied partnership.

In a jointly prepared statement supporting her candidacy, the partners in Hopkins' office showcased her successful 2-year effort to secure a $25 million contract with the Department of State, labeling it "an outstanding performance" and one that Hopkins carried out "virtually at the partner level." Despite Price Waterhouse's attempt at trial to minimize her contribution to this project, Judge Gesell specifically found that Hopkins had "played a key role in Price Waterhouse's successful effort to win a multi-million dollar contract with the Department of State." [618 F. Supp. 1109, 1112 (D.D.C. 1985).] Indeed, he went on, "[n]one of the other partnership candidates at Price Waterhouse that year had a comparable record in terms of successfully securing major contracts for the partnership." *Ibid.*

The partners in Hopkins' office praised her character as well as her accomplishments, describing her * * * as "an outstanding professional" who had a "deft touch," a "strong character, independence and integrity." Clients appear to have agreed with these assessments. At trial, one official from the State Department described her as "extremely competent, intelligent," "strong and forthright, very productive, energetic and creative." * * *

On too many occasions, however, Hopkins' aggressiveness apparently spilled over into abrasiveness. Staff members seem to have borne the brunt of Hopkins' brusqueness. Long before her bid for partnership, partners evaluating her work had counseled her to improve her relations with staff members. Although later evaluations indicate an improvement, Hopkins' perceived shortcomings in this important area eventually doomed her bid for partnership. Virtually all of the partners' negative remarks about Hopkins—even those of partners supporting her—had to do with her "inter-personal skills." Both "[s]upporters and opponents of her candidacy," stressed Judge Gesell, "indicated that she was sometimes overly aggressive, unduly harsh, difficult to work with and impatient with staff." *Id.*, at 1113.

There were clear signs, though, that some of the partners reacted negatively to Hopkins' personality because she was a woman. One partner described her as "macho"; another suggested that she "overcompensated for being a woman"; a third advised her to take "a course at charm school." Several partners criticized her use of profanity; in response, one partner suggested that those partners objected to her swearing only "because it's a lady using foul language." Another supporter explained that Hopkins "ha[d] matured from a tough-talking somewhat masculine hard-nosed mgr to an authoritative, formidable, but much more appealing lady ptr candidate." But it was the man who, as Judge Gesell found, bore responsibility for explaining to Hopkins the reasons for the Policy Board's decision to place her candidacy on hold who delivered the *coup de grace*: in order to improve her chances for partnership, Thomas Beyer advised, Hopkins should "walk more femininely, talk more femininely, dress more femininely, wear make-up, have her hair styled, and wear jewelry." 618 F. Supp., at 1117.

Dr. Susan Fiske, a social psychologist and Associate Professor of Psychology at Carnegie-Mellon University, testified at trial that the partnership selection process at Price Waterhouse was likely influenced by sex stereotyping. Her testimony focused not only on the overtly sex-based comments of partners but also on gender-neutral remarks, made by partners who knew Hopkins only slightly, that were intensely critical of her. One partner, for example, baldly stated that Hopkins was "universally disliked" by staff, and another described her as "consistently annoying and irritating"; yet these were people who had had very little contact with Hopkins. According to Fiske, Hopkins' uniqueness (as the only woman in the pool of candidates) and the subjectivity of the evaluations made it likely that sharply critical remarks such as these were the product of sex stereotyping—although Fiske admitted that she could not say with certainty whether any particular comment was the result of stereotyping.

* * *

Judge Gesell found that Price Waterhouse legitimately emphasized interpersonal skills in its partnership decisions, and also found that the firm had not fabricated its complaints about Hopkins' interpersonal skills as a pretext for discrimination. Moreover, he concluded, the firm did not give decisive emphasis to such traits only because Hopkins was a woman; although there were male candidates who lacked these skills but who were admitted to partnership, the judge found that these candidates possessed other, positive traits that Hopkins lacked.

The judge went on to decide, however, that some of the partners' remarks about Hopkins stemmed from an impermissibly cabined view of the proper behavior of women, and that Price Waterhouse had done nothing to disavow reliance on such comments. He held that Price Waterhouse had unlawfully discriminated against Hopkins on the basis of sex by consciously giving credence and effect to partners' comments that resulted from sex stereotyping.

[The district court further concluded that Price Waterhouse had not made the requisite showing that it would have reached the same decision even absent the discrimination. The court of appeals affirmed, though it disagreed with the district court's approach to the "same decision" defense.]

* * *

Congress' intent to forbid employers to take gender into account in making employment decisions appears on the face of the statute. In now-familiar language, the statute forbids an employer to "fail or refuse to hire or to discharge any individual, or otherwise to discriminate with respect to his compensation, terms, conditions, or privileges of employment, * * * *because of* such individual's * * * sex." 42 U.S.C. §§ 2000e–2(a)(1), (2) (emphasis added). We take these words to mean that gender must be irrelevant to employment decisions. To construe the words "because of" as colloquial shorthand for "but-for causation," as does Price Waterhouse, is to misunderstand them.

* * * The critical inquiry, the one commanded by the words of § 703(a)(1), is whether gender was a factor in the employment decision *at the moment it was made*. Moreover, since we know that the words "because of" do not mean "*solely* because of," we also know that Title VII meant to condemn even those decisions based on a mixture of legitimate and illegitimate considerations. When, therefore, an employer considers both gender and legitimate factors at the time of making a decision, that decision was "because of" sex and the other, legitimate considerations—even if we may say later, in the context of litigation, that the decision would have been the same if gender had not been taken into account.

* * *

To say that an employer may not take gender into account is not, however, the end of the matter, for that describes only one aspect of Title VII. The other important aspect of the statute is its preservation of an employer's remaining freedom of choice. We conclude that the preservation of this freedom means that an employer shall not be liable if it can prove that, even if it had not taken gender into account, it would have come to the same decision regarding a particular person. * * *

* * * The central point is this: while an employer may not take gender into account in making an employment decision (except in those very narrow circumstances in which gender is a BFOQ), it is free to decide against a woman for other reasons. We think these principles

require that, once a plaintiff in a Title VII case shows that gender played a motivating part in an employment decision, the defendant may avoid a finding of liability only by proving that it would have made the same decision even if it had not allowed gender to play such a role. This balance of burdens is the direct result of Title VII's balance of rights.

* * *

In saying that gender played a motivating part in an employment decision, we mean that, if we asked the employer at the moment of the decision what its reasons were and if we received a truthful response, one of those reasons would be that the applicant or employee was a woman. In the specific context of sex stereotyping, an employer who acts on the basis of a belief that a woman cannot be aggressive, or that she must not be, has acted on the basis of gender.

* * * As for the legal relevance of sex stereotyping, we are beyond the day when an employer could evaluate employees by assuming or insisting that they matched the stereotype associated with their group, for " '[i]n forbidding employers to discriminate against individuals because of their sex, Congress intended to strike at the entire spectrum of disparate treatment of men and women resulting from sex stereotypes.' " *Los Angeles Dept. of Water and Power* v. *Manhart*, 435 U.S. 702, 707, n.13, 98 S.Ct. 1370, n.13, 55 L.Ed.2d 657 (1978), quoting *Sprogis* v. *United Air Lines, Inc.*, 444 F.2d 1194, 1198 (CA7 1971). An employer who objects to aggressiveness in women but whose positions require this trait places women in an intolerable and impermissible catch 22: out of a job if they behave aggressively and out of a job if they do not. Title VII lifts women out of this bind.

Remarks at work that are based on sex stereotypes do not inevitably prove that gender played a part in a particular employment decision. The plaintiff must show that the employer actually relied on her gender in making its decision. In making this showing, stereotyped remarks can certainly be *evidence* that gender played a part. In any event, the stereotyping in this case did not simply consist of stray remarks. On the contrary, Hopkins proved that Price Waterhouse invited partners to submit comments; that some of the comments stemmed from sex stereotypes; that an important part of the Policy Board's decision on Hopkins was an assessment of the submitted comments; and that Price Waterhouse in no way disclaimed reliance on the sex-linked evaluations. This is not, as Price Waterhouse suggests, "discrimination in the air"; rather, it is, as Hopkins puts it, "discrimination brought to ground and visited upon" an employee. Brief for Respondent 30. * * *

* * *

[JUSTICE WHITE concurred in the judgment; JUSTICE O'CONNOR concurred in the judgment; JUSTICE KENNEDY, with whom THE CHIEF JUSTICE and JUSTICE SCALIA join, dissented.]

NOTES AND QUESTIONS

1. *Price Waterhouse* was one of twelve cases that Congress responded to in passing the Civil Rights Act of 1991. *See* Deborah Widiss, *Shadow Precedents and the Separation of Powers: Statutory Interpretation of Congressional Overrides*, 84 Notre Dame L.Rev. 511, 539 (2009). The legislative disagreement with the Supreme Court's *Price Waterhouse* decision centered on burdens of proof, both for a plaintiff seeking to show that an employer had "mixed motives" for a decision and for the affirmative defense that the same decision would have been made even absent consideration of the illegitimate factor. This aspect of *Price Waterhouse* and its aftermath is discussed in Chapter 3.B.

2. Ann Hopkins had substantial evidence of the stereotypes that partners at Price Waterhouse applied in evaluating her candidacy because of the overtly gendered statements some of them made. Plaintiffs are not usually so fortunate. Absent direct statements by decision makers, how would a plaintiff prove that stereotyping played a role in a workplace decision? Hopkins hired a social psychologist to offer expert testimony to the court about the way stereotyping operates in workplace decisions. Should a plaintiff be required to offer such expert testimony? Alternatively, are sex stereotypes so widely understood that such testimony should be excluded because it will not be helpful to the fact finder as required by Federal Rule of Evidence 703? For an argument that social science experts don't help plaintiffs significantly see Andrea Doneff, *Social Framework Studies Such as* Women Don't Ask *and* It Does Hurt to Ask *Show us the Next Step Toward Achieving Gender Equality—Eliminating the Long-Term Effects of Implicit Bias—But Are Not Likely to Get Cases Past Summary Judgment*, 20 Wm. & Mary J. of Women & the Law 573 (2014). The use of social psychologists as experts in litigation has generated considerable debate, both in the courts and among academics. *See, e.g.,* David L. Faigman, Nilanjana Dasgupta & Cecilia L. Ridgeway, *A Matter of Fit: The Law of Discrimination and the Science of Implicit Bias*, 59 Hastings L.J. 1389 (2008); Melissa Hart & Paul Secunda, *A Matter of Context: Social Framework Evidence in Employment Discrimination Class Actions*, 78 Fordham L.Rev. 101 (2009); John Monahan, Laurens Walker & Gregory Mitchell, *Contextual Evidence of Gender Discrimination: The Ascendance of "Social Frameworks,"* 94 Va.L.Rev. 1715 (2008).

3. In *Wal-Mart Stores, Inc. v. Dukes*, 564 U.S. 338, 131 S.Ct. 2541, 180 L.Ed.2d. 374 (2011) (reprinted in Chapter 3), the Supreme Court rejected evidence presented by a social scientist in support of class certification, concluding that the expert's testimony about stereotyping generally offered

no proof of which specific decisions had been influenced by stereotypes. As Justice Scalia explained:

> The only evidence of a "general policy of discrimination" respondents produced was the testimony of Dr. William Bielby, their sociological expert. Relying on "social framework" analysis, Bielby testified that Wal-Mart has a "strong corporate culture," that makes it " 'vulnerable' " to "gender bias." He could not, however, "determine with any specificity how regularly stereotypes play a meaningful role in employment decisions" at Wal-Mart. At his deposition . . . Dr. Bielby conceded that he could not calculate "whether 0.5 percent or 95 percent of the employment decisions at Wal-Mart might be determined by stereotyped thinking." * * * Bielby's testimony does nothing to advance respondents' case. "[W]hether 0.5 percent or 95 percent of the employment decisions at Wal-Mart might be determined by stereotyped thinking" is the essential question on which respondents' theory of commonality depends. If Bielby admittedly has no answer to that question, we can safely disregard what he has to say.

Does *Wal-Mart*'s treatment of evidence about stereotyping call the Court's *Price Waterhouse* decision into question, is it a straightforward application of *Price Waterhouse*, or do the cases present two distinct approaches to the use of evidence about stereotyping? For a discussion about the differences between the two cases' use of stereotyping to support their claims, see Michael Selmi, *Theorizing Systemic Disparate Treatment Law After* Wal-Mart v. Dukes, 32 Berkeley J. Emp. & Lab. L. 477, 506–07 (2011).

4. Professor Mary F. Radford's article, *Sex Stereotyping and the Promotion of Women to Positions of Power*, 41 Hastings L.J. 471, 494–96 (1990), contains an excellent discussion of the stereotyping of women in the workplace. Radford surveyed the literature on sex stereotyping at that time, noting that

> [i]n what has been referred to as the "definitive work on sex-role stereotypes," Broverman [Inge K. Broverman et al., *Sex-Role Stereotypes: A Current Appraisal*, 28:2 J.Soc. Issues 59 (1972)] measured the degree to which various personality traits were perceived as typical of men or women. Adjectives that consistently were viewed as describing "male" traits included the following: aggressive, independent, unemotional, objective, not easily influenced, dominant, calm, active, competitive, logical, worldly, skilled in business, direct, adventurous, self-confident, ambitious. Adjectives representing "female" traits included: talkative, does not use harsh language, tactful, gentle, aware of other's feelings, religious, neat, quiet, easily expresses tender feelings, very strong need for security. * * *
>
> * * * As these adjectives indicate, and as numerous studies have confirmed, the "masculine" traits generally are associated

> more strongly in our society with good mental health. Consequently, these traits are viewed (by both males and females) as being those to which a mature adult should aspire. * * * Despite the numerous criticisms that may be leveled against the sex stereotyping of personality traits, an important phenomenon is that the "masculine" traits are correlated strongly with success in the workplace.

Id. While Radford was writing 25 years ago (and Broverman 20 years before that), not much has changed with regard to the stereotypical personality traits associated with men and women and the challenges those stereotypes can present for women at work. *See, e.g.*, Kenji Yoshino, *Covering*, 111 Yale L. J. 769, 905–24 (2002) ("To succeed as a woman, one must have the correctly titrated balance of masculine and feminine traits. One must be 'authoritative' and 'formidable,' but remain an 'appealing lady.' "); Andrea Macerollo, *The Power of Masculinity in the Legal Profession: Women Lawyers and Identity Formation*, 25 Windsor Rev. Legal & Soc. Issues 121, 13–37 (2008).

5. Another set of stereotypes attaches when women become mothers. Professor Joan Williams has written extensively about the phenomenon of the "maternal wall" and the substantial body of social scientific research that has identified the stereotypes at play for working mothers and fathers. *See, e.g.*, Joan C. Williams, UnBending Gender: Why Family and Work Conflict and What to Do About It (2000). Williams and her co-author, Stephanie Bornstein, observed:

> Social scientists have documented an underlying schema that assumes a lack of competence and commitment when women are viewed through the lens of motherhood and housework. Earlier studies document that, although "businesswomen" are considered highly competent, similar to "businessmen," "housewives" are rated as extremely low in competence, alongside such highly stigmatized groups as the elderly, blind, "retarded," and "disabled" (to quote the words tested by researchers).

Joan C. Williams & Stephanie Bornstein, *The Evolution of "FReD": Family Responsibilities Discrimination and Developments in the Law of Stereotyping and Implicit Bias*, 59 Hastings L.J. 1311, 1327 (2008). In cases challenging the maternal wall and discrimination because of family responsibilities, litigators are increasingly presenting courts with evidence of these kinds of stereotyping and the role they play in workplace decisions. Pregnancy and family responsibility discrimination are discussed in Chapter 8.

6. If a female plaintiff presents evidence that decision makers in her workplace use sex stereotypes when referring to female employees, under what circumstances should that evidence relieve her of the obligation to point to a similarly situated male comparator for purposes of proving that she suffered an adverse employment action "because of sex"?

7. The *Price Waterhouse* decision stresses that stereotyping itself is not actionable conduct. Rather, the Court says "stereotyped remarks can certainly be *evidence* that gender played a part" in an employment decision. The case that follows raises the question of what other avenues a plaintiff might take to prove that workplace conduct occurred "because of sex." It does so in the context of a sexual harassment claim. Sexual harassment policy and doctrine is discussed in more detail in Chapter 10. The focus of this case is on the specific question of how a plaintiff can demonstrate that harassment at work occurred "because of sex."

ONCALE V. SUNDOWNER OFFSHORE SERVICES, INC.

Supreme Court of the United States, 1998.
523 U.S. 75, 118 S.Ct. 998, 140 L.Ed.2d 201.

JUSTICE SCALIA delivered the opinion of the Court.

This case presents the question whether workplace harassment can violate Title VII's prohibition against "discriminat[ion] * * * because of * * * sex," 42 U.S.C. § 2000e–2(a)(1), when the harasser and the harassed employee are of the same sex.

I

The District Court having granted summary judgment for respondent, we must assume the facts to be as alleged by petitioner Joseph Oncale. The precise details are irrelevant to the legal point we must decide, and in the interest of both brevity and dignity we shall describe them only generally. In late October 1991, Oncale was working for respondent Sundowner Offshore Services on a Chevron U.S.A., Inc., oil platform in the Gulf of Mexico. He was employed as a roustabout on an eight-man crew which included respondents John Lyons, Danny Pippen, and Brandon Johnson. Lyons, the crane operator, and Pippen, the driller, had supervisory authority. On several occasions, Oncale was forcibly subjected to sex-related, humiliating actions against him by Lyons, Pippen and Johnson in the presence of the rest of the crew. Pippen and Lyons also physically assaulted Oncale in a sexual manner, and Lyons threatened him with rape.

Oncale's complaints to supervisory personnel produced no remedial action; in fact, the company's Safety Compliance Clerk, Valent Hohen, told Oncale that Lyons and Pippen "picked [on] him all the time too," and called him a name suggesting homosexuality. Oncale eventually quit—asking that his pink slip reflect that he "voluntarily left due to sexual harassment and verbal abuse." When asked at his deposition why he left Sundowner, Oncale stated "I felt that if I didn't leave my job, that I would be raped or forced to have sex."

Oncale filed a complaint against Sundowner * * * alleging that he was discriminated against in his employment because of his sex. * * *

[T]he district court held that "Mr. Oncale, a male, has no cause of action under Title VII for harassment by male co-workers." [The Fifth Circuit affirmed.]

II

* * *

Title VII's prohibition of discrimination "because of * * * sex" protects men as well as women, and in the related context of racial discrimination in the workplace we have rejected any conclusive presumption that an employer will not discriminate against members of his own race. "Because of the many facets of human motivation, it would be unwise to presume as a matter of law that human beings of one definable group will not discriminate against other members of that group." Castaneda v. Partida, 430 U.S. 482, 499, 97 S.Ct. 1272, 1282, 51 L.Ed.2d 498 (1977). In *Johnson v. Transportation Agency, Santa Clara Cty.*, 480 U.S. 616, 107 S.Ct. 1442, 94 L.Ed.2d 615 (1987), a male employee claimed that his employer discriminated against him because of his sex when it preferred a female employee for promotion. Although we ultimately rejected the claim on other grounds, we did not consider it significant that the supervisor who made that decision was also a man. If our precedents leave any doubt on the question, we hold today that nothing in Title VII necessarily bars a claim of discrimination "because of * * * sex" merely because the plaintiff and the defendant (or the person charged with acting on behalf of the defendant) are of the same sex.

Courts have had little trouble with that principle in cases like *Johnson*, where an employee claims to have been passed over for a job or promotion. But when the issue arises in the context of a "hostile environment" sexual harassment claim, the state and federal courts have taken a bewildering variety of stances. Some, like the Fifth Circuit in this case, have held that same-sex sexual harassment claims are never cognizable under Title VII. Other decisions say that such claims are actionable only if the plaintiff can prove that the harasser is homosexual (and thus presumably motivated by sexual desire). *Compare* McWilliams v. Fairfax County Board of Supervisors, 72 F.3d 1191 (4th Cir.1996), *with* Wrightson v. Pizza Hut of America, 99 F.3d 138 (4th Cir.1996). Still others suggest that workplace harassment that is sexual in content is always actionable, regardless of the harasser's sex, sexual orientation, or motivations. *See* Doe v. Belleville, 119 F.3d 563 (7th Cir.1997).

We see no justification in the statutory language or our precedents for a categorical rule excluding same-sex harassment claims from the coverage of Title VII. As some courts have observed, male-on-male sexual harassment in the workplace was assuredly not the principal evil Congress was concerned with when it enacted Title VII. But statutory prohibitions often go beyond the principal evil to cover reasonably comparable evils, and it is ultimately the provisions of our laws rather than the principal concerns of our legislators by which we are governed. Title VII prohibits "discriminat[ion] * * * because of * * * sex" in the "terms" or "conditions" of employment. Our holding that this includes sexual harassment must extend to sexual harassment of any kind that meets the statutory requirements.

Respondents and their *amici* contend that recognizing liability for same-sex harassment will transform Title VII into a general civility code for the American workplace. But that risk is no greater for same-sex than for opposite-sex harassment, and is adequately met by careful attention to the requirements of the statute. Title VII does not prohibit all verbal or physical harassment in the workplace; it is directed only at "*discriminat[ion]* * * * because of * * * sex." We have never held that workplace harassment, even harassment between men and women, is automatically discrimination because of sex merely because the words used have sexual content or connotations. "The critical issue, Title VII's text indicates, is whether members of one sex are exposed to disadvantageous terms or conditions of employment to which members of the other sex are not exposed." *Harris*, 510 U.S. at 25, 114 S.Ct. at 372 (Ginsburg, J., concurring).

Courts and juries have found the inference of discrimination easy to draw in most male-female sexual harassment situations, because the challenged conduct typically involves explicit or implicit proposals of sexual activity; it is reasonable to assume those proposals would not have been made to someone of the same sex. The same chain of inference would be available to a plaintiff alleging same-sex harassment, if there were credible evidence that the harasser was homosexual. But harassing conduct need not be motivated by sexual desire to support an inference of discrimination on the basis of sex. A trier of fact might reasonably find such discrimination, for example, if a female victim is harassed in such sex-specific and derogatory terms by another woman as to make it clear that the harasser is motivated by general hostility to the presence of women in the workplace. A same-sex harassment plaintiff may also, of course, offer direct comparative evidence about how the alleged harasser treated members of both sexes in a mixed-sex workplace. Whatever evidentiary route the plaintiff chooses to follow, he or she must always prove that the conduct at issue was not merely tinged with offensive sexual connotations, but actually constituted "*discrimina[tion]* * * * because of * * * sex."

[Two paragraphs of the *Oncale* opinion are omitted here and reproduced in Chapter 10, where the topic of sexual harassment is explored in further detail.]

III

Because we conclude that sex discrimination consisting of same-sex sexual harassment is actionable under Title VII, the judgment of the Court of Appeals for the Fifth Circuit is reversed, and the case is remanded for further proceedings consistent with this opinion.

NOTES AND QUESTIONS

1. *Evidence of Discrimination "Because of Sex"*: Justice Scalia suggested three possible "evidentiary route[s]" or "chain[s] of inference" that a plaintiff might follow to show that same-sex sexual harassment constitutes discrimination "because of sex." What are they? Oncale did not allege that his harassers were homosexuals acting out of sexual desire, and the drilling rig where Oncale worked was a single-sex, not a mixed-sex, workplace. Thus, Oncale would not be able to establish discrimination because of sex through either the first or third evidentiary route suggested by Justice Scalia. Would Oncale's claim fit into Justice Scalia's second suggested evidentiary paradigm? If not, how would you suggest that Oncale attempt to prove that he was a victim of discrimination "because of sex"? *See* David S. Schwartz, *When Is Sex Because of Sex? The Causation Problem in Sexual Harassment Law*, 150 U.Pa.L.Rev. 1697, 1734–36 (2002) (discussing the outcome of the remand in *Oncale*).

2. *Harassment That Is "Sexual" in Nature*: Before *Oncale*, some scholars had argued that same-sex harassing conduct that is "sexual" in nature should violate Title VII regardless of the sex of the perpetrator and victim. For example, Professor Ramona Paetzold had proposed that "sexual conduct—sexualized language, sexual innuendo, sexual touchings, sexual displays—in same-sex cases should always be actionable under Title VII, to the same extent that it is in male-female cases. Further, * * * the same presumptions and inferences should apply in same-sex cases as in male-female harassment cases." Ramona L. Paetzold, *Same-Sex Sexual Harassment: Can It Be Sex-Related for Purposes of Title VII?*, 1 Emp.Rts. & Emp. Pol'y J. 25, 47 (1997). In *Oncale*, the Court appeared to reject the argument, which had been adopted in one case in the Seventh Circuit, that "workplace harassment that is sexual in content is always actionable, regardless of the harasser's sex, sexual orientation, or motivations." *Oncale*, 523 U.S. at 29 (discussing Doe v. Belleville, 119 F.3d 563 (7th Cir.1997), *cert. granted, judgment vacated*, 523 U.S. 1001, 118 S.Ct. 1183 140 L.Ed.2d 313 (1998)).

Since *Oncale* was decided, courts have rejected same-sex harassment claims, even where the harassment was explicitly sexual in nature, when the victim had no evidence that the conduct was specifically motivated by sex or gender. *See, e.g.,* Davis v. Coastal Int'l Sec., 275 F.3d 1119, 1123 (D.C.Cir.2002) (finding that same-sex harassment that is sexual in nature is not actionable under Title VII where conduct of harassers was motivated by a grudge against the plaintiff and was not related to his sex or gender); EEOC

v. Harbert-Yeargin, Inc., 266 F.3d 498, 520 (6th Cir.2001) (Guy, Circuit Judge, concurring in part and dissenting in part, for a majority of the court) (observing, in a same-sex harassment case, that "if the environment is just sexually hostile without an element of gender discrimination, it is not actionable"). If the harasser and victim are of the opposite sex, is harassment necessarily "because of sex" when the harassing behavior and language is sexual in nature? *See, e.g.,* Brown v. Henderson, 257 F.3d 246, 255–56 (2d Cir.2001) (finding that harassment with sexual content is not sex-based harassment where both men and women are harassed and female plaintiff was targeted because of a dispute with her union).

3. *Harassment Based on Gender Animus*: After *Oncale,* is a hostile work environment "because of sex" established if female employees repeatedly taunt their female co-worker, calling her "bitch" and, in effect, accusing her of being sexually promiscuous? *See* Bailey v. Henderson, 94 F.Supp.2d 68, 70 (D.D.C.2000). In *Passananti v. Cook County*, the Seventh Circuit reversed a district court's conclusion that "[t]he mere fact that a defendant used a pejorative term that is more likely to be directed toward a female than a male does not alone establish unwelcome sexual conduct." 689 F.3d 655, 665–65 (7th Cir.2012). The appellate court distinguished its earlier decision in *Galloway v. General Motors Serv. Parts Operations*, 78 F.3d 1164 (7th Cir.1996), in which an employer had been granted summary judgment in a dispute also involving a supervisor's use of the pejorative "bitch." The difference, the court explained, was the context surrounding what it characterized as an "ambiguous term." In *Galloway*, the supervisor and the plaintiff had a failed relationship, and the court concluded that the negative treatment was more likely the result of personal animus than sexism. In *Passananti*, by contrast, "there was no contextual evidence * * * that undermined the reasonable interpretation that * * * repeated and hostile use of 'bitch' to address and demean [an employee] was based on her sex." *Passananti*, 689 F.3d at 665. Can "context" ever eliminate the gendered nature of words like "bitch"? Other courts have concluded that it cannot. *See, e.g.*, Reeves v. C.H. Robinson Worldwide, Inc., 594 F.3d 798, 813 (11th Cir.2010) ("It is undeniable that the terms 'bitch' and 'whore' have gender-specific meanings."); Forrest v. Brinker Int'l Payroll Co., 511 F.3d 225, 229–30 (1st Cir.2007) ("A raft of case law * * * establishes that the use of sexually degrading, gender-specific epithets * * * has been consistently held to constitute harassment based upon sex."). In the absence of this kind of gender-specific language, how should courts determine when misconduct at work is just a workplace personality conflict and not a hostile work environment "because of sex"? What if male computer programmers ostracize a female co-worker and refuse to provide her with the system passwords and other information that she needs to perform her job? *See* O'Shea v. Yellow Tech. Servs., 185 F.3d 1093 (10th Cir.1999).

4. *Intersectional and Sex-Plus Claims*: Some cases present evidence that points to discrimination occurring not only because of the plaintiff's sex, but because of both sex and some other characteristic of the particular

plaintiff. Intersectional claims, discussed in Chapter 2, rely on the intersection of two or more prohibited categories, such as sex and race (e.g., black women, Asian women, black men) or sex and age (e.g., women over forty). *See, e.g.*, Shazor v. Professional Transit Management, Ltd., 744 F.3d 948, 958 (6th Cir.2014) (sex and race); Lam v. Univ. of Haw., 40 F.3d 1551, 1562 (9th Cir.1994) (sex and race); Arnett v. Aspin, 846 F.Supp. 1234, 1239–41 (E.D.Pa.1994) (sex and age). *See generally* Kimberlé Crenshaw, *Demarginalizing the Intersection of Race and Sex: A Black Feminist Critique of Antidiscrimination Doctrine, Feminist Theory and Antiracist Politics*, 1989 U.Chi. Legal F. 139; Minna J. Kotkin, *Diversity and Discrimination: A Look at Complex Bias*, 50 Wm. & Mary L.Rev. 1439 (2009). Sex-plus claims, by contrast, involve allegations that sex is combined with some non-protected characteristic, "such as weight or marital or parental status." Kathryn Abrams, *Title VII and the Complex Female Subject*, 92 Mich.L.Rev. 2479, 2495 (1994).

The Supreme Court's first case to address sex discrimination recognized the viability of a "sex-plus" claim. In *Phillips v. Martin Marietta Corp.*, 400 U.S. 542, 91 S.Ct. 496, 27 L.Ed.2d 613 (1971), the Court held that an employer's rule that prohibited mothers of preschool-aged children from holding certain positions was a prima facie violation of Title VII. Because mothers of very young children were treated differently from fathers of young children, the company policy discriminated on the basis of sex. *See also* Coleman v. B-G Maint. Mgmt. of Colo., Inc., 108 F.3d 1199, 1203–04 (10th Cir.1997) (holding that to prevail on sex-plus-marriage discrimination claim, plaintiff must prove that the subclass of married women was treated differently from the corresponding subclass of married men); Sprogis v. United Air Lines, 444 F.2d 1194 (7th Cir.1971) (holding that a rule excluding married women from positions as airline flight attendants violates Title VII). Moreover, a plaintiff can be in a subclass characterized as raising a combination of "intersectional" and "sex-plus" claims. *See, e.g.,* Chambers v. Omaha Girls Club, 834 F.2d 697 (8th Cir.1987) (single black pregnant women); Fisher v. Vassar Coll., 114 F.3d 1332 (2d Cir.1997) (en banc) (older married women).

5. *Distinguishing Disparate Treatment and Disparate Impact Claims*: Both disparate treatment and disparate impact analysis can be applied to sex discrimination claims. Consider how these paradigms might be applied to the following problems:

a. Lynch, a woman, was hired by a construction company as a carpenter's apprentice. All construction workers were required to use the same portable toilets. The toilets were dirty, had no running water or sanitary napkins, and often had no toilet paper or the paper was soiled. The employer owned a building near the construction site that had fully equipped restroom facilities for men and women. Company policy, however, prohibited construction workers from using these indoor restrooms. After she developed several urinary tract infections as a result of using the unsanitary portable toilets, Lynch began to use the company's indoor women's restroom. When she continued to use this restroom despite a warning from her employer, Lynch was discharged for violating a company rule. Does Lynch have a claim under Title VII for sex discrimination if the evidence shows that none of the male construction workers had ever used the company's indoor restroom facilities? If so, under what theory? *See* Lynch v. Freeman, 817 F.2d 380 (6th Cir.1987). *Compare* DeClue v. Cent. Ill. Light Co., 223 F.3d 434 (7th Cir.2000), *with id.* at 437 (Rovner, J., dissenting). For a discussion of the elements of a disparate treatment sex discrimination claim brought by a woman working at an all-male construction site, see *Davis v. Team Electric Co.,* 520 F.3d 1080, 1093 (9th Cir.2008) (holding, inter alia, that plaintiff could go to trial on issue of employer's "motive in assigning her a disproportionate amount of dangerous and strenuous work").

b. Sal and Robin, husband and wife, worked for the same bank branch—Sal as the manager and Robin as an assistant cashier. Sal was discharged after he pleaded guilty to federal bank fraud charges for misappropriating a substantial amount of money belonging to an elderly client. The bank also discharged Robin because the officers and directors feared that customers would question Robin's credibility because of her husband's criminal conduct. Robin sues under Title VII alleging sex discrimination on the theory that she is a victim of a sexual stereotype that a woman's character mirrors her husband's. Does Robin have a viable sex discrimination claim? *See* Panis v. Mission Hills Bank, 60 F.3d 1486 (10th Cir.1995).

c. Sarah was employed as a dispatcher for United Parcel Service. She was denied a promotion to the position of dispatcher supervisor, and the position was later filled by a male. The division manager told her she was not recommended for the position "because of her inability to handle confrontational situations" that were likely to arise in the job. In particular, her immediate supervisor said he was "scared that [she] might cry if [she] got into a confrontation * * * with a driver" or "if [she] ever got a good ass chewing." Does Sarah have a claim for sex discrimination? *See* Crone v. United Parcel Serv., Inc., 301 F.3d 942 (8th Cir.2002). What if the facts involved John, a male substitute teacher in a public school system who is told he will not be called to substitute again. At a meeting with the school principal, she told him he was "too macho." Is this statement evidence of actionable sex discrimination under Title VII? What else would you want to know? *See* Lautermilch v. Findlay City Sch., 314 F.3d 271 (6th Cir.2003).

C. SEX-BASED WAGE DISCRIMINATION

The sexual division of labor—and the hierarchical assumptions about gender roles and work that have provided the rationale for sex-based dual wage scales—have long been a feature of American society. In the colonial economy, although many agrarian and commodity production tasks were shared by men and women, the religious and social customs and legal rules defining relations in the patriarchal family encouraged a division of labor along gender lines. These gender divisions persisted as women entered the market for wage labor. Between 1820 and 1860, as America developed from a pre-industrial to an industrial society, economic and social changes, as well as attitudes about women's roles, reinforced the gender divisions of wage work.

During and after the Civil War, a number of traditional male jobs were "feminized." For example, wartime labor shortages created new opportunities for women to work as schoolteachers, secretaries, bookkeepers, clerks, and retail sales clerks—jobs that had formerly been almost exclusively male occupations. Notably, during the Civil War, the United States Treasury began to employ women as clerks, assigning them to low-level tasks previously performed by men. *See* Margery W. Davies, Woman's Place Is at the Typewriter: Office Work and Office Workers, 1870–1930, at 51–52 (1982). At the time, Congress imposed a statutory sex-based dual wage scale by setting maximum annual salaries for female clerks. *See* Act of Mar. 14, 1864, ch. 30, § 6, 13 Stat. 22 (1864) ($600 maximum); Act of July 23, 1866, ch. 208, §§ 6–7, 14 Stat. 191 (1866) ($900 maximum).

The Senate first considered the merits of a proposal for equal pay for women in the federal service in 1870. A compromise bill was enacted that gave the heads of federal government departments the authority "to appoint female clerks, who may be found to be competent and worthy, to any of the grades of clerkship known to the law * * * with the compensation belonging to the class to which they may be appointed * * * ." Act of July 12, 1870, ch. 251, § 2, 16 Stat. 230 (1870), *quoted in* Cathryn L. Claussen, *Gendered Merit: Women and the Merit Concept in Federal Employment, 1864–1944*, 40 Am.J. Legal Hist. 229, 233 (1996). With this legislation, statutory wage ceilings for female clerks in the federal civil service were formally abandoned, but the discretionary authority of department heads, in effect, permitted informal dual wage scales and ultimately led to the sex-segregation of many government jobs.

During World War I, "women poured into jobs vacated by men, as well as many of the 100,000 newly created war preparation jobs," and "by the war's end, overwhelming occupational segregation had evolved, and wage disparities between the sexes persisted." *Id.* at 239–40. *See generally* Valerie Jean Conner, The National War Labor Board: Stability, Social Justice, and the Voluntary State in World War I, at 142–57 (1983); Maurine Weiner Greenwald, Women, War, and Work: The Impact of World War I on Women Workers in the United States 3–45 (1980).

Formal recognition of the concept of equal pay for equal work followed women's suffrage and active reform efforts by women's organizations. Claussen, *supra*, at 241. By 1919, two states—Michigan and Montana—had adopted equal pay statutes that reached private employers. *See* Carin Ann Clauss, *Comparable Worth—The Theory, Its Legal Foundation, and the Feasibility of Implementation*, 20 U.Mich.J.L.Ref. 7, 12 (1986). In 1923, Congress enacted legislation that classified jobs and pay scales in the federal civil service and acknowledged the merit principle by mandating equal pay for equal work. *Id.* (discussing the Classification Act of 1923, ch. 265, 42 Stat. 954 (repealed 1949)). The 1923 Act provided that "[i]n determining the rate of compensation which an employee shall receive, the principle of equal compensation for equal work irrespective of sex shall be followed." Classification Act of 1923, § 4, 42 Stat. 1488. "[A]lthough [the Act] theoretically ended the practice of sex-typing of jobs, by the time of its enactment, occupational segregation and the corollary wage disparities had become entrenched in the federal workplace, with over ninety percent of all women in clerical positions." Claussen, *supra*, at 242.

While World War I had "primarily occasioned a shift within the female labor force, rather than a movement of non-wage earning women into categories of paid labor," during World War II, the number of women in the workforce grew by six million, a 50 percent increase. Greenwald, *supra*, at 13. In her study of the electrical and automobile industries during the second world war, Professor Milkman commented:

> Wartime mobilization swept aside the traditional sexual division of labor, and women entered "men's jobs" in basic industry on a massive scale. Women showed that they were fully capable of performing such work. Yet after the war, they were forced back into traditionally female occupations, or out of the labor market altogether.

Ruth Milkman, Gender at Work: The Dynamics of Job Segregation by Sex During World War II, at 1 (1987).

During World War II, the goal of equal pay was significant for some unions concerned with "protecting the wages of 'men's jobs' in the face of wartime female substitution." *Id.* at 9. In 1942, in carrying out its function to stabilize wages and avert labor strife, the National War Labor Board—concerned with the effects of pay disparities based on both race and gender—formally adopted the principle that " '[i]ncreases which equalize the wage or salary rates paid to females with the rates paid to males for comparable quality and quantity of work on the same or similar operations * * * may be made without approval of the National War Labor Board * * * .' " National War Labor Board, General Order No. 16, Nov. 24, 1942, *quoted in* Clauss, *supra*, at 13. *See also* James B. Atleson, Labor and the Wartime State: Labor Relations and Law During World War II, at 164–69 (1998) (discussing wartime sex-based pay discrimination). The experiences of the War Labor Board with setting wartime wage ceilings and adjusting private wage disputes prompted Congress to propose the first federal equal pay law in 1945. S. 1178, 79th Cong., 1st Sess. (1945); *see* Clauss, *supra*, at 13–14.

1. THE EQUAL PAY ACT

Equal pay bills were introduced in every session of Congress for the eighteen years from 1945 to 1963. Finally, in 1963, after changing the language of the bill from "work of *comparable* character on jobs the performance of which requires *comparable* skills" to "*equal* work on jobs the performance of which requires *equal* skills," Congress approved the Equal Pay Act (EPA), 29 U.S.C. § 206(d). *See* Clauss, *supra*, at 14 (emphasis added). President Kennedy signed the Act on June 10, 1963. Equal Pay Act of 1963, Pub. L. No. 88–38, 77 Stat. 56. Shortly after the Equal Pay Act went into effect on June 11, 1964, Congress enacted Title VII, including language in § 703(h)—the Bennett Amendment—that refers to the Equal Pay Act. The two statutes now offer alternative, but complementary, bases for challenging sex-based disparities in employers' compensation schemes.

The Equal Pay Act (EPA), passed as an amendment to the Fair Labor Standards Act, provides:

> (1) No employer having employees subject to any provisions of this section shall discriminate, within any establishment in which such employees are employed, between employees on the basis of sex by paying wages to employees in such establishment at a rate less than the rate at which he pays wages to employees of the opposite sex in such establishment for equal work on jobs the performance of which requires equal skill, effort, and responsibility, and which are performed under similar working conditions, except where such payment is made pursuant to (i) a seniority system; (ii) a merit system; (iii) a system which measures earnings by quantity or quality of production; or (iv) a differential based on any other factor other than sex: *Provided*, That an employer who is paying a wage rate differential in violation of this subsection shall not, in order to comply with the provisions of this subsection, reduce the wage rate of any employee.

29 U.S.C. § 206(d)(1).

To make out a prima facie EPA case against a covered employer, a plaintiff must establish that (1) in the same establishment, (2) the employer pays different wages to employees of the opposite sex, (3) who perform equal work on jobs requiring equal skill, effort, and responsibility, and (4) the jobs are performed under similar working conditions. Unlike a Title VII case of disparate treatment, "proof of discriminatory intent is not required to establish a prima facie case under the Equal Pay Act." Peters v. City of Shreveport, 818 F.2d 1148, 1153 (5th Cir.1987), *cert. dismissed*, 485 U.S. 930, 108 S.Ct. 1101, 99 L.Ed.2d 264 (1988).

1. *The "Establishment" Requirement*: The term "establishment" is not defined in the Fair Labor Standards Act (FLSA), but in an early case construing the FLSA, the Supreme Court held that the term means what it "normally [means] in business and government"—"a distinct physical place of business." A. H. Phillips, Inc. v. Walling, 324 U.S. 490, 496, 65 S.Ct. 807, 810, 89 L.Ed.1095 (1945). Under the Equal Pay Act, however, courts have tended to construe broadly the requirement that the EPA violation occur "within any establishment." Thus, where the employer maintains centralized control and administration of separate job sites, it will generally be deemed a single establishment under the EPA. *See* Mulhall v. Advance Sec., Inc., 19 F.3d 586, 591–92 & 591 n.11 (11th Cir.1994) (collecting cases); Marshall v. Dallas Indep. Sch. Dist., 605 F.2d 191, 194 (5th Cir.1979) (holding that, for purposes of an EPA claim, all the schools in a school district are a single establishment). Unless the plaintiff presents evidence of "unusual circumstances," however, the EEOC presumes that the term "establishment" means "a distinct physical place of business rather than * * * an entire business or 'enterprise' which may include several separate places of business." 29 C.F.R. § 1620.9(a). The EEOC Interpretive Guidelines continue:

> (b) Unusual circumstances may call for two or more distinct physical portions of a business enterprise being treated as a single establishment. For example, a central administrative unit may hire all employees, set wages, and assign the location of employment; employees may frequently interchange work location; and daily duties may be virtually identical and performed under similar working conditions.

29 C.F.R. § 1620.9(b). A broad reading of "establishment" may enable a plaintiff who works in a small branch office of a larger enterprise to find in another branch office an appropriate opposite-sex comparator who receives higher wages.

2. *Equal Work*: To establish a prima facie case under the Equal Pay Act, a female plaintiff does not need to demonstrate that the job she performs is identical to a higher paid job held by a male comparator in the same establishment. Rather, she has to establish only that the two jobs are "substantially equal." *See, e.g.*, Lavin-McEleny v. Marist Coll., 239 F.3d 476, 480 (2d Cir.2001) (noting that the EPA requires the plaintiff's job to be "substantially equal" but not "identical" to the comparator's job, and ruling that whether the jobs at issue were "substantially equal" was question of fact); Sprague v. Thorn Americas, Inc., 129 F.3d 1355, 1364 (10th Cir.1997) (agreeing that the jobs being

compared must be "substantially equal," but noting that "[c]ourts do not construe the 'equal work' requirement broadly, and 'failure to furnish equal pay for "comparable work" or "like jobs" is not actionable' "). Courts consider the duties actually performed in each job, not the title or job description used by the employer. Cullen v. Ind. Univ. Bd. of Trs., 338 F.3d 693, 700 (7th Cir.2003). In determining whether two jobs are substantially equal, courts generally will make an "overall comparison of the work" rather than examining the "individual segments." Buntin v. Breathitt County Bd. of Educ., 134 F.3d 796, 799 (6th Cir.1998). Should the level of scrutiny that a court uses in making the equal work comparison depend on the nature of the job? Would you expect courts to be more exacting or less exacting in comparing jobs in professional occupations as opposed to semi-skilled or technical jobs? As Deborah Eisenberg has noted "plaintiffs in non-standardized jobs have a difficult time showing that they can even compare themselves to their peers." Deborah Thompson Eisenberg, *Shattering the Equal Pay Act's Glass Ceiling*, 63 SMU L. Rev. 17, 31 (2010). Are there any special concerns that courts should consider in Equal Pay Act cases involving academic institutions as employers? A 2010 study found that of the twenty-three federal appellate EPA cases involving university professors, the plaintiffs lost 65 percent of the time at summary judgment. *Id.* at 33. Professor Melissa Hart has argued that the explanation for this may in part be the substantial deference that courts afford academic institutions. Melissa Hart *Missing the Forest for the Trees: Gender Pay Discrimination in Academia*, 91 Denver L. Rev. 873 886 (2015).

3. *The Opposite-Sex Comparator(s)*: Selecting an appropriate opposite-sex comparator (or comparators) is an important part of a plaintiff's prima facie case under the Equal Pay Act. Although some courts have held that an individual plaintiff can meet this element of a prima facie EPA case with evidence that a single opposite-sex comparator earns more than the plaintiff, *see, e.g.,* Mitchell v. Jefferson County Bd. of Educ., 936 F.2d 539, 547 (11th Cir.1991), other courts have held that the plaintiff does not meet her prima facie burden if there is evidence that she is paid the same as or more than some male comparators, *see, e.g.,* Sowell v. Alumina Ceramics, Inc., 251 F.3d 678, 684 (8th Cir.2001). *But see* Hutchins v. Int'l Bhd. of Teamsters, 177 F.3d 1076, 1081 (8th Cir.1999) (holding that district court did not err in finding the plaintiff met her prima facie case when evidence showed she earned less than the comparators she selected but more than others she failed to include). What if a female employee is paid half as much as nine male employees performing "equal work," but a tenth male employee earns the same as or less than she does? Can she make out a prima facie case on these facts? *See* Hennick v. Schwans Sales Enters., 168 F.Supp.2d 938, 947–50 (N.D.Iowa 2001) (discussing this hypothetical in light of conflicting intra-circuit rulings).

If there are no appropriate opposite-sex comparators currently employed in the same establishment, a plaintiff cannot create a "hypothetical" or "composite" opposite-sex comparator. Strag v. Bd. of Trs., Craven Cmty. Coll., 55 F.3d 943, 948 (4th Cir.1995). But a number of courts have held that a plaintiff can use evidence that an opposite-sex predecessor or successor in the at-issue job received higher wages. *See, e.g.*, Buntin v. Breathitt County Bd. of Educ., 134 F.3d 796, 799 (6th Cir.1998) (predecessor is appropriate comparator); Lawrence v. CNF Transp., Inc., 340 F.3d 486, 492 (8th Cir.2003) (immediate successor is appropriate comparator). One district court permitted the plaintiff's case to go forward with a comparator that was "a combination of the three particular, identifiable persons who succeeded her." Emswiler v. Great Eastern Resort Corp., 602 F.Supp.2d 737, 746 (W.D.Va.2009). Is this a "hypothetical composite" comparator? Or a recognition that it may be difficult in some work situations to identify a "perfect" individual successor as a comparator? *See id.* Class comparisons may also be made based on the sex-based wage differentials of groups of employees who perform the same job. In these cases, "perfect diversity" of the sexes between the two groups is not necessary. *See* Beck-Wilson v. Principi, 441 F.3d 353, 362 (6th Cir.2006).

4. *Defining Unequal Pay*: "Compensation," of course, is a much broader concept than just wages and would include fringe benefits such as insurance and pensions. Moreover, a plaintiff's prima facie case requires only proof of an unequal *rate* of pay, not unequal *total remuneration*. Bence v. Detroit Health Corp., 712 F.2d 1024 (6th Cir.1983). Consistent with regulations and judicial decisions interpreting the term "wages" under the Fair Labor Standards Act, courts have similarly interpreted "wages" under the Equal Pay Act to include the value of goods or services that employees receive, such as uniforms or lodging that are not provided "primarily for the benefit or convenience of the employer." Laffey v. Northwest Airlines, 642 F.2d 578, 588 (D.C.Cir.1980). Should the concept of compensation also include the value of job security—such as academic tenure—or status within the company hierarchy? Should the "intrinsic rewards" of a job such as "a sense of accomplishment attained from the job, its challenge, variety, and degree of autonomy" be valued as part of an employee's compensation? Nicholas J. Mathys & Laura B. Pincus, *Is Pay Equity Equitable? A Perspective that Looks Beyond Pay*, 44 Lab.L.J. 351, 352 (1993).

5. *Similar Working Conditions*: In *Corning Glass Works v. Brennan,* 417 U.S. 188, 94 S.Ct. 2223, 41 L.Ed.2d. 1 (1974), the only Supreme Court decision addressing a claim brought solely under the EPA, the Court adopted a narrow definition of "working conditions" based on the technical "language of industrial relations" that Congress utilized in drafting the Equal Pay Act. *Id.* at 202. Under this interpretation, the

concept of working conditions covers only "surroundings" and "hazards," both of which are focused on physical hazards faced by the employees. *Id.* Should Congress amend the Act to include psychological, social, and physiological impacts as well as physical "surroundings" and "hazards" within the definition of "working conditions"? Does the *Corning* definition accurately account for the significant similarities and differences between the working conditions of many jobs in post-industrial society?

6. *The Equal Pay Act's Affirmative Defenses*: The Equal Pay Act allows an employer to pay employees of the opposite sex unequal wages "pursuant to (i) a seniority system; (ii) a merit system; (iii) a system which measures earnings by quantity or quality of production; or (iv) a differential based on any other factor other than sex * * * ." 29 U.S.C. § 206(d). Of these four defenses, the most often litigated are the defenses of "merit system" and "any factor other than sex."

a. *The "Merit System" Defense*: How can an employer insure that "merit" raises are actually based on merit and not on factors unrelated to merit, such as nepotism or sex? When would an employer rely on the "merit system" defense instead of arguing that a pay differential is based on "any other factor other than sex"? Courts generally define a merit system that meets the EPA affirmative defense as being known to employees, and employing "an organized and structured procedure whereby employees are evaluated systematically according to predetermined criteria." EEOC v. Aetna Ins. Co., 616 F.2d 719, 725 (4th Cir.1980). *See also* Price v. Northern States Power Co., 664 F.3d 1186 1193 (8th Cir.2011); Ryduchowski v. Port Auth. of N.Y. & N.J., 203 F.3d 135, 142–43 (2d Cir.2000) (collecting cases that rely on the "merit system" defense).

b. *"Any Other Factor Other Than Sex"*: The "catch-all" fourth affirmative defense under the Equal Pay Act, "any other factor other than sex," is susceptible to varying interpretations, and the courts have found it difficult to develop appropriate standards for the defense. For discussion of the developments in the case law, see Ellen M. Bowden, *Closing the Pay Gap: Redefining the Equal Pay Act's Fourth Affirmative Defense*, 27 Colum.J.L. & Soc.Probs. 225 (1994) and Peter Avery, Note, *The Diluted Equal Pay Act: How It Was Broken? How It Can Be Fixed?*, 56 Rutgers L.Rev. 849, 863–68 (2004). The Supreme Court has dealt with the defense in two cases other than *Corning Glass*, but has yet to articulate a comprehensive theory of the defense. In *City of Los Angeles Department of Water & Power v. Manhart*, 435 U.S. 702, 98 S.Ct. 1370, 55 L.Ed.2d 657 (1978), reproduced earlier in this chapter, at 356, the Court indicated that the relative average greater costs of employing one sex would not qualify as a factor other than sex. In *County of Washington v. Gunther*, 452 U.S. 161, 101 S.Ct. 2242, 68 L.Ed.2d 751 (1981), discussed below, the Court held that the Equal Pay Act defenses are applicable to a sex-based wage discrimination claim brought solely under Title VII. In a footnote in *Smith v. City of Jackson*, 544 U.S. 228, 239 n.11, 125 S.Ct. 1536, 1544 n.11, 161 L.Ed.2d 410 (2005), a plurality of the Court indicated that the EPA's "any other factor other than sex" means *any* factor—whether it is "reasonable or unreasonable." *See* William E. Doyle Jr., *Implications of* Smith v. City of Jackson *on Equal Pay Act Claims and Sex-Based Pay Discrimination Claims Under Title VII,* 21 Lab. Law. 183, 183–87 (2005) (discussing footnote 11 of the *Smith* case and noting the continuing circuit split after *Smith* on the meaning of the fourth affirmative defense).

7. *Salary Policies as a "Factor Other Than Sex"*: The federal courts have developed conflicting approaches to the EPA's fourth affirmative defense in cases involving sex-based pay disparities resulting from prior salary or salary retention policies.

a. *Prior Salary and Market Demand*: Can an employer set its starting wages for newly hired employees at the level of their prior wages with their last employer even if it results in unequal pay for equal work by men and women? Are prior wages a "factor other than sex"? What if use of prior wages perpetuates sex-based wage discrimination? The courts of appeals are in conflict regarding whether an employer must have an "acceptable business reason" to set an employee's starting pay based on prior salary. *See* Wernsing v. Dep't of Human Servs., 427 F.3d 466, 468 (7th Cir.2005) (collecting cases).

In *Kouba v. Allstate Insurance Co.*, 691 F.2d 873 (9th Cir.1982), the employer used the "ability, education, experience, and prior salary" of new employees to determine their minimum wage guarantee. *Id.* at 874. This minimum salary was the only compensation paid until a training period was completed. Then new agents earned the minimum guaranteed wage or sales commissions, whichever was greater. The court found that, because of this compensation scheme, female sales agents were paid less, on average, than male agents. In remanding the case to determine whether the employer satisfied its "factor other than sex" defense, the court observed that "[w]hile Congress fashioned the Equal Pay Act to help cure long-standing societal ills, it also intended to exempt factors such as training and experience that may reflect opportunities denied to women in the past." *Id.* The court articulated a theory of the EPA's fourth affirmative defense that is analogous to a business necessity defense under Title VII:

> The Equal Pay Act concerns business practices. It would be nonsensical to sanction the use of a factor that rests on some consideration unrelated to business. An employer thus cannot use a factor which causes a wage differential between male and female employees absent an acceptable business reason.

> Conversely, a factor used to effectuate some business policy is not prohibited simply because a wage differential results.

Id. at 876. *See also* Aldrich v. Randolph Cent. Sch. Dist., 963 F.2d 520, 525 (2d Cir.1992) (holding that gender-neutral job classification systems "may qualify under the factor-other-than-sex defense only when they are based on legitimate business-related considerations").

One business reason advanced by the employer in *Kouba* was that "an individual with a higher prior salary can demand more in the marketplace." *Kouba*, 691 F.2d at 877 n.7. Is this an "acceptable" or "legitimate" business reason? For example, can a university defend its decision to pay a higher salary to a female chemistry professor than to a similarly qualified male chemistry professor using a market demand argument that because of the shortage of qualified female chemistry Ph.D.'s they are able to command premium pay in the market? *See* Univ. & Comty. Coll. Sys. of Nev. v. Farmer, 113 Nev. 90, 930 P.2d 730, 737 (Nev. 1997). *See also* Brinkley v. Harbour Recreation Club, 180 F.3d 598, 619 (4th Cir.1999) (Motz, J., dissenting) (noting that the "fact that a woman has less bargaining power to demand a higher salary than a man does not constitute a valid factor 'other than sex' under the Equal Pay Act," and collecting cases rejecting market defense as a "factor other than sex"); Drum v. Leeson Elec. Corp., 565 F.3d 1071, 1073 (8th Cir.2009) (rejecting employer's attempt to defend female manager's lower wages under a "market force theory" that they were consistent with her prior below-market salaries). Do men generally bargain harder for higher wages? If so, is such hard bargaining a "factor other than sex"? *See* Charles B. Craver, *If Women Don't Ask: Implications for Bargaining Encounters, The Equal Pay Act, and Title VII*, 102 Mich.L.Rev. 1104 (2004) (reviewing Linda Babcock & Sara Laschever, Women Don't Ask: Negotiation and the Gender Divide (2003)); Christine Elzer, *Wheeling, Dealing, and the Glass Ceiling: Why the Gender Difference in Salary Negotiation Is Not a "Factor Other Than Sex" Under the Equal Pay Act*, 10 Geo.J. Gender & L. 1 (2009).

The approach adopted in *Kouba*, and followed in the Second, Sixth, and Eleventh Circuits, has been rejected in the Seventh and Eighth Circuits. *See* Wernsing v. Dep't of Human Servs., 427 F.3d 466, 468 (7th Cir.2005). For example, in *Wernsing*, Judge Easterbrook observed that "[s]ection 206(d) does not authorize federal courts to set their own standards of 'acceptable' business practices. The statute asks whether the employer has a reason other than sex—not whether it has a 'good' reason." *Id. Wernsing* criticized *Kouba* for treating the EPA's fourth affirmative defense "as if the Equal Pay Act worked like the disparate-impact theory under Title VII," when the EPA "deals exclusively with disparate treatment" and "does not have a disparate-impact component." *Id.* at 469. Moreover, the Seventh Circuit would not prohibit employer reliance on competitive markets to set salaries. Judge Easterbrook asserted that "[t]he Equal Pay Act forbids sex discrimination, an intentional wrong, while markets are impersonal and have no intent." *Id.* Which approach to the EPA's fourth affirmative defense—*Kouba*'s or *Wernsing*'s—is best supported by the language and purpose of the Act? *See* Nicole Buonocore Porter and Jessica R. Vartanian, *Debunking the Market Myth in Pay Discrimination Cases*, 12 Geo.J. Gender & L. 159 (2011) (exploring the flaws with relying on the "market" to excuse gender-based pay differentials).

b. *Salary Retention or "Red Circling"*: Under a salary retention or "red circling" policy, an employer transfers an employee from a higher-paid skilled job to a less demanding position but continues to pay the employee his same salary. An employer might red circle an employee for economic reasons—to keep him available if his particular services are needed in the future or to keep him from going to work for a competitor—or for more altruistic reasons, such as a desire to retain a loyal older or disabled worker in a less demanding job. Because the employee retains his former salary, he may earn more than a woman whose job is substantially equal to his new job. Courts have found employer reliance on a salary retention policy to be a legitimate affirmative defense under the Equal Pay Act. *See, e.g.*, Taylor v. White, 321 F.3d 710, 717–20 (8th Cir.2003) (analyzing cases and legislative history on salary retention policies); Mulhall v. Advance Sec., Inc., 19 F.3d 586, 595–96 (11th Cir.1994) (collecting cases). Can you explain why red circling might be upheld as an affirmative defense but a pay disparity based on prior salary with another employer might be considered suspect?

8. *Equal Pay Act Claims Against State Employers and Sovereign Immunity*. When initially enacted in 1963, the Equal Pay Act covered only private employers, but in 1974 the Act was amended to cover state and local government employees. See Fair Labor Standards Amendments of 1974, Pub.L. No. 93–259, § 6, 88 Stat. 55, 58–62. All the federal courts of appeals that have addressed the question of Eleventh Amendment immunity under the Equal Pay Act since the Supreme Court's decision in *Kimel v. Florida Board of Regents*, 528 U.S. 62, 120 S.Ct. 631, 145 L.Ed.2d 522 (2000), have held that the Eleventh Amendment does not bar state employees from suing their employers in federal court under the Equal Pay Act. *See, e.g.*, Hundertmark v. Fla. Dep't of Transp., 205 F.3d 1272 (11th Cir.2000). *See also* Siler-Khodr v. Univ. of Tex. Health Sci. Ctr. San Antonio, 261 F.3d 542, 550 (5th Cir.2001) (collecting post-*Kimel* cases). These developments are discussed in Chapter 2. In *Nevada Department of Human Resources v. Hibbs*, 538 U.S. 721, 123 S.Ct. 1972, 155 L.Ed.2d 953 (2003), discussed in Chapter 8, the Supreme Court held that state employees may recover money damages from state employers that violate the family-care leave provisions of the Family and Medical

Leave Act. In light of the rationale and holding of *Hibbs*, how do you think the Supreme Court would rule on the issue of Eleventh Amendment immunity to Equal Pay Act claims brought against state employers? *See generally* Deborah L. Brake, *What Counts as "Discrimination" in* Ledbetter *and the Implications for Sex Equality Law,* 59 S.C.L.Rev. 657, 664–71 (2008) (discussing constitutional challenges to sex equality statutes).

2. THE BENNETT AMENDMENT TO TITLE VII

During its consideration of the proposal to add "sex" as a prohibited category to Title VII, the Senate approved the following amendment proposed by Senator Bennett:

> It shall not be an unlawful employment practice under [Title VII] for any employer to differentiate upon the basis of sex in determining the amount of the wages or compensation paid or to be paid to employees of such employer if such differentiation is authorized by the provisions of section 6(d) of the [Equal Pay Act].

Title VII, § 703(h), 42 U.S.C. § 2000e–2(h). The intent of the so-called Bennett Amendment was to incorporate the four affirmative defenses of the Equal Pay Act into Title VII's prohibition of sex discrimination. For the first decade after the passage of Title VII, the EPA was still used as the exclusive basis for lawsuits challenging sex-based wage disparities. *See* Carin Ann Clauss, *Comparable Worth—The Theory, Its Legal Foundation, and the Feasibility of Implementation*, 20 U.Mich.J.L.Ref. 7, 16 (1986). There were several reasons why the EPA was used during this decade instead of Title VII: the EPA contains fewer procedural hurdles for plaintiffs and the EEOC had issued guidelines in 1965 (that were later withdrawn in 1972) requiring Title VII sex-based wage claims to satisfy the substantive standards under the EPA of "equal pay for equal work." *Id.* at 16 & nn.44–45, 46 n.167. Moreover, as Professor Clauss observed:

> the Equal Pay Act no matter how broadly the courts construed the phrase "equal work," did not apply to jobs that were dissimilar from any of those performed by men. * * * Because the great majority of women were employed in female jobs, the Equal Pay Act had very little effect on the discriminatory undervaluation of women's work.

Id. at 16.

By the mid-1970s, after the withdrawal of the EEOC's restrictive interpretation of Title VII, women began to use the broader substantive provisions of Title VII to challenge wage differentials in jobs of "comparable" worth, as well as sex-based discriminatory practices in the hiring, promotion, and compensation of women. *Id.* Plaintiffs' attempts to use Title VII to articulate a theory of liability for sex-based discriminatory compensation that was broader than the Equal Pay Act's "equivalence" requirement forced the courts to interpret the meaning of the Bennett Amendment. By the end of the 1970s, a conflict had developed in the circuits over whether the Bennett Amendment imposed the "equal work" requirement of the Equal Pay Act in Title VII sex-based wage claims. *See* Clauss, *supra*, at 16, 7 n.2 (collecting cases).

The Supreme Court addressed the effect of the Bennett Amendment in *County of Washington v. Gunther*, 452 U.S. 161, 101 S.Ct. 2242, 68 L.Ed.2d 751 (1981). In *Gunther*, four women brought a Title VII sex discrimination claim against a county in Oregon that paid female guards in the women's section of the county jail substantially less than the male guards in the men's section. The plaintiffs

> alleged that they were paid unequal wages for work substantially equal to that performed by male guards, and in the alternative, that part of the pay differential was attributable to intentional sex discrimination * * * because * * * the county set the pay scale for female guards, but not for male guards, at a level lower than that warranted by its own survey of outside markets and the worth of the jobs.

Id. at 164–65, 101 S.Ct. at 2245. Under Oregon law, only females were permitted to guard women prisoners, and, at the time, no women were employed to guard male inmates. *See id.* at 164 n.2, 101 S.Ct. at 2245 n.2. The plaintiffs conceded that "gender is a bona fide occupation qualification for some of the female guard positions." *Id.* Because the Equal Pay Act did not apply to municipal employees until the enactment of the Fair Labor Standards Amendments of 1974, the plaintiffs had to base their claim solely on Title VII, which had covered municipal employees since 1972. *See id.* at 164 n.3, 101 S.Ct. at 2245 n.3.

The trial court in *Gunther* held that the female guard jobs were not "substantially equal" to the jobs of the male guards because "male guards supervised more than 10 times as many prisoners per guard as did the female guards, and * * * the females devoted much of their time to less valuable clerical duties." *Id.* at 165, 101 S.Ct. at 2245. In addition, the district court refused to permit evidence regarding the plaintiffs' claim that the sex-based disparities in the pay scale were the result of intentional sex discrimination. In dismissing the case, the district court held that "a sex-based wage discrimination claim cannot be brought under Title VII unless it would satisfy the equal work standard of the Equal Pay Act of 1963." *Id.* at 165, 101 S.Ct. at 2246. The Court of Appeals reversed and the Supreme Court affirmed in an opinion by Justice Brennan.

The Court held that a Title VII plaintiff is not required to satisfy the Equal Pay Act's standard of "equal or substantially equal work" in order to proceed with a claim of sex-based wage discrimination under Title VII and then proceeded to interpret the Bennett Amendment:

> The language of the Bennett Amendment suggests an intention to incorporate only the affirmative defenses of the Equal Pay Act into Title VII. The Amendment bars sex-based wage discrimination claims under Title VII where the pay differential is "authorized" by the Equal Pay Act. * * * The question, then, is what wage practices have been affirmatively authorized by the Equal Pay Act.
>
> The Equal Pay Act is divided into two parts: a definition of the violation, followed by four affirmative defenses. The first part can hardly be said to "authorize" anything at all: it is purely prohibitory. The second part, however, in essence "authorizes" employers to differentiate in pay on the basis of seniority, merit, quantity or quality of production, or any other factor other than sex, even though such differentiation might otherwise violate the Act. It is to these provisions, therefore, that the Bennett Amendment must refer.
>
> * * * The Bennett Amendment was offered as a "technical amendment" designed to resolve any potential conflicts between Title VII and the Equal Pay Act. Thus, with respect to the first three defenses, the Bennett Amendment has the effect of guaranteeing that courts and administrative agencies adopt a consistent interpretation of like provisions in both statutes. Otherwise, they might develop inconsistent bodies of case law interpreting two sets of nearly identical language.
>
> More importantly, incorporation of the fourth affirmative defense could have significant consequences for Title VII litigation. Title VII's prohibition of discriminatory employment practices was intended to be broadly inclusive, proscribing "not only overt discrimination but also practices that are fair in form, but discriminatory in operation." Griggs v. Duke Power Co., 401 U.S. 424, 431, 91 S.Ct. 849, 853, 28 L.Ed.2d 158 (1971). The structure of Title VII litigation, including presumptions, burdens of proof, and defenses, has been designed to reflect this approach. The fourth affirmative defense of the Equal Pay Act, however, was designed differently, to confine the application of the Act to wage differentials attributable to sex discrimination. * * * Although we do not decide in this case how sex-based wage discrimination litigation under Title VII should be structured to accommodate the fourth affirmative defense of the Equal Pay

Act, we consider it clear that the Bennett Amendment, under this interpretation, is not rendered superfluous.

We therefore conclude that only differentials attributable to the four affirmative defenses of the Equal Pay Act are "authorized" by that Act within the meaning of § 703 (h) of Title VII. * * *

Under petitioners' reading of the Bennett Amendment, only those sex-based wage discrimination claims that satisfy the "equal work" standard of the Equal Pay Act could be brought under Title VII. In practical terms, this means that a woman who is discriminatorily underpaid could obtain no relief—no matter how egregious the discrimination might be—unless her employer also employed a man in an equal job in the same establishment, at a higher rate of pay. * * *

Moreover, petitioners' interpretation would have other far-reaching consequences. Since it rests on the proposition that any wage differentials not prohibited by the Equal Pay Act are "authorized" by it, petitioners' interpretation would lead to the conclusion that discriminatory compensation by employers not covered by the Fair Labor Standards Act is "authorized"—since not prohibited—by the Equal Pay Act. Thus it would deny Title VII protection against sex-based wage discrimination by those employers not subject to the Fair Labor Standards Act but covered by Title VII. There is no persuasive evidence that Congress intended such a result, and the EEOC has rejected it since at least 1965. *See* 29 C.F.R. § 1604.7 (1966). * * *

Id. at 167–80, 101 S.Ct. at 2247–53.

NOTES AND QUESTIONS

1. *Proving "Similar" Work Under Title VII*: If *Gunther* requires only proof of similar—not "substantially equal"—work to make out a prima facie case of wage discrimination under Title VII, what is the difference between the two standards? *See* Sprague v. Thorn Americas, Inc., 129 F.3d 1355, 1363 (10th Cir.1997) (because the pay disparity between a female plaintiff and male assistant product managers was "consistent with the different levels of importance, value, and depth of responsibility between the respective departments," the plaintiff failed to make out a prima facie case under either Title VII or the Equal Pay Act).

2. *The Role of Intent*: The courts have consistently held that discriminatory intent is not an element of the plaintiff's prima facie case under the Equal Pay Act. *See* Fallon v. Ill., 882 F.2d 1206, 1217 (7th Cir.1989) (collecting cases). But intent is an element of a Title VII disparate treatment case of sex-based wage discrimination. If a plaintiff challenges a

sex-based pay disparity under both the EPA and Title VII, will her evidence supporting a prima facie EPA case necessarily support a prima facie Title VII case?

The EEOC has adopted the view that a finding of a violation of the Equal Pay Act is sufficient to establish a violation of Title VII. 29 C.F.R. § 1620.27. The courts are divided on this issue, and only a minority of courts disregard the differences between the elements and the proof schemes of the two statutes and hold that liability under the Equal Pay Act automatically establishes Title VII liability. *See* Belfi v. Prendergast, 191 F.3d 129, 137 (2d Cir.1999) (recognizing that, "[u]nder the EPA, proof of the employer's discriminatory intent is not necessary for the plaintiff to prevail on her claim," and finding that plaintiff failed to prove discriminatory intent under her Title VII disparate treatment claim); Meeks v. Computer Assocs. Int'l, 15 F.3d 1013, 1019–20 (11th Cir.1994) (discussing conflicting cases). Which approach makes the most sense to you?

3. *Statute of Limitations, Procedural Requirements, and Remedies*: Title VII and the Equal Pay Act have different statutes of limitations, procedural requirements, and remedies. Unlike Title VII, the Equal Pay Act does not require administrative exhaustion before filing an action in court. The Equal Pay Act also provides a much longer statute of limitations than Title VII. As discussed in Chapter 2, before bringing a lawsuit, a Title VII plaintiff must first file a charge with the EEOC within 180 days or 300 days after the unlawful employment practice occurred, depending on whether the state has a state fair employment agency. Under the Equal Pay Act, a plaintiff has two years to file an action, which is extended to three years in cases of "willful" violations. 29 U.S.C. § 255(a). Remedies for the two statutes are explored further in Chapter 2, but a significant difference is that as a remedy for willful violations the Equal Pay Act provides for liquidated damages, which are an additional amount equal to the amount of wages lost. Title VII, on the other hand, allows recovery of punitive damages, subject to statutory caps, when the defendant acts "with malice or reckless indifference to the federally protected rights" of the plaintiff. 42 U.S.C. § 1981a(b)(1). Both statutes permit equitable relief such as back pay and reinstatement.

4. *The Lilly Ledbetter Fair Pay Act of 2009*: Wage payments that are discriminatory under the Equal Pay Act trigger the statute of limitations regardless of whether the unlawful wage payment is a single, discrete event or a continuing violation. *See, e.g.,* Mitchell v. Jefferson County Bd. of Ed., 936 F.2d 539, 548 (11th Cir.1991) ("The theory of continuing violations has been applied consistently to actions under the Equal Pay Act."). Before the Supreme Court decision in *Ledbetter v. Goodyear Tire & Rubber Co.,* 550 U.S. 618, 127 S.Ct. 2162, 167 L.Ed.2d 982 (2007), reproduced in Chapter 2, most courts had held that discriminatory wage payments are "continuing violations of Title VII, regardless of whether the plaintiff challenged a single act of wage discrimination or a discriminatory wage policy." Inglis v. Buena Vista Univ., 235 F.Supp.2d 1009, 1021 (N.D.Iowa 2002). *Ledbetter* distinguished between (1) wage payments that are individual, "discrete" acts,

which trigger the EEOC charging period at the time the discriminatory pay decision is made and communicated to the employee, and (2) wage payments that are part of a discriminatory pay structure and result in a continuing violation with payment of each paycheck. 550 U.S. at 628, 634, 127 S.Ct. at 2169, 2173. Because Lily Ledbetter did not have evidence that she was the victim of a pay structure that was adopted with discriminatory animus and she filed her claim too late to challenge any "discrete" discriminatory pay decision, the Supreme Court denied her Title VII wage claim entirely. The Court acknowledged that if she had not abandoned the wage claim that she had brought under the Equal Pay Act, which had been dismissed by the district court, her lawsuit would not have been time-barred. *Id.* at 650, 127 S.Ct. at 2176. Congress responded to the Court's interpretation of Title VII in the *Ledbetter* case by enacting the Lilly Ledbetter Fair pay Act of 2009, Pub. L. No. 111–2, 123 Stat. 5 (2009). For purposes of determining whether an allegedly discriminatory sex-based wage payment triggers the statute of limitations, there is now essentially no distinction between claims brought under the EPA and Title VII. The Lilly Ledbetter Fair Pay Act of 2009 is covered in Chapter 2.

5. *Sex-Plus-Race Claims of Wage Discrimination*: Plaintiff, a black woman, claims that her employer is discriminating against her on the basis of sex and race by paying her less than certain other employees who perform substantially the same work. She sues her employer under the Equal Pay Act, Title VII, and § 1981. Plaintiff's evidence shows that one white female, three white males, and three black males are paid more than she is, although one black male is paid the same salary and one white female is paid less. The employer concedes that the positions of all ten employees are essentially identical, but has evidence that salary decisions are determined on the basis of each employee's experience and longevity of service, which vary. Given these facts, how would the plaintiff's and the defendant's evidentiary burdens be satisfied under each of these three statutes? The litigation structure of a wage discrimination suit brought by a black woman requires that the plaintiff disaggregate sex and race and, in effect, treat them as separate statuses for purposes of claims under the Equal Pay Act, Title VII, and § 1981. Only under Title VII have some courts permitted a plaintiff to make out a prima facie case of disparate treatment based on the "sex-plus-race" paradigm. *See* Jefferies v. Harris County Cmty. Action Ass'n, 615 F.2d 1025, 1032–35 (1980), which is discussed in the note on intersectionality in Chapter 2.

D. THE BONA FIDE OCCUPATIONAL QUALIFICATION DEFENSE TO SEX DISCRIMINATION

Should we permit an employer to defend an employment policy that explicitly treats women differently from men if it can establish that the policy is based on a biological difference? What if the policy is required to "protect" women or third parties? Or if the policy is designed to accommodate privacy concerns of customers? What if an employer adopts sex-based policies to satisfy the sexual or cultural preferences or tastes of its customers? Title VII contains a statutory loophole that, to varying degrees and depending on the particular workplace context, may permit each of these justifications for explicitly sex-based workplace practices. Section 703(e)(1) of Title VII, the "bona fide occupational qualification" or BFOQ defense provides:

> Notwithstanding any other provision of this title * * * it shall not be an unlawful employment practice for an employer to hire and employ employees * * * on the basis of religion, sex, or national origin in those certain instances where religion, sex, or national origin is a bona fide occupational qualification reasonably necessary to the normal operation of that particular business or enterprise * * * .

42 U.S.C. § 2000e–2(e)(1). Note that "race" and "color" are not included in § 703(e)(1). Can you think of reasons why Congress determined that employment decisions based on race or color could not be defended as a BFOQ?

The question whether particular policies constitute true job qualifications or whether they are merely paternalistic or stereotype-driven sex discrimination has occupied many courts. The first BFOQ cases focused particularly on determining under what circumstances protectionist policies—which deny women freedom of choice of employment opportunities—do or do not constitute unlawful sex discrimination. The debate in the courts mirrors a tension that has long resided at the core of efforts to define and achieve sex equality. Professor Calloway has observed:

> Feminists have long struggled with the problem of developing a legal theory capable of promoting employment opportunities for women, without either ignoring women's inherent biological differences or demanding special treatment or accommodation for those differences. The early vision of equality for women, based on equal treatment, has been criticized for failing to acknowledge that women's differences place them at a disadvantage when the law requires only that women be treated the same as men. The strict equality approach fails to question the assumptions underlying gender-neutral social institutions that severely disadvantage women and fails to protect women when they are victimized by those institutions. On the other hand, achieving employment opportunities for women by requiring special treatment or accommodation for women's differences has its own dangers. Highlighting

> differences stereotypes gender roles and provides a justification for imposing harmful limitations on women. The history of gender discrimination in the United States is littered with cases of "protective" legislation and policies that, in reality, served primarily to limit the rights and opportunities of women.

Deborah A. Calloway, *Accommodating Pregnancy in the Workplace*, 25 Stetson L.Rev. 1, 22 (1995). *See generally* Mary E. Becker, *From* Muller v. Oregon *to Fetal Vulnerability Policies*, 53 U.Chi.L.Rev. 1219 (1986).

In the 1970s, the Supreme Court had two occasions to discuss the merits of employer "benevolent" paternalism versus employee autonomy in the context of sex discrimination cases that raised BFOQ defenses. First, in *Phillips v. Martin Marietta Corp.*, 400 U.S. 542, 91 S.Ct. 496, 27 L.Ed.2d 613 (1971) (per curiam), discussed in Section B of this chapter, the Court discussed whether a BFOQ defense arguably could insulate an employer's practice of denying certain jobs to mothers—but not fathers—of preschool-aged children. The issue on appeal in *Martin Marietta* was whether the plaintiff had made out a prima facie case of sex discrimination under that particular set of facts. Deciding in the affirmative and remanding the case, the Court was not required to reach the substantive merits of the employer's BFOQ defense. Nevertheless, the Court's opinion included speculation about the possibility that a sex-based BFOQ defense might be satisfied with proof that "[t]he existence of such conflicting family obligations" are "demonstrably more relevant to job performance for a woman than for a man." *Id.* at 544, 91 S.Ct. at 498. Justice Marshall, in dissent, objected to the Court's discussion of the BFOQ issue:

> I fear that in this case, where the issue is not squarely before us, the Court has fallen into the trap of assuming the Act permits ancient canards about the proper role of women to be a basis for discrimination. Congress, however, sought just the opposite result.
>
> * * * Even characterizations of the proper domestic roles of the sexes were not to serve as predicates for restricting employment opportunity. The exception for a "bona fide occupational qualification" was not intended to swallow the rule.

Id. at 545, 91 S.Ct. at 498.

Six years later, in *Dothard v. Rawlinson*, 433 U.S. 321, 97 S.Ct. 2720, 53 L.Ed.2d 786 (1977), the Court directly confronted the merits of a sex-based BFOQ defense. In *Dothard*, a female plaintiff claimed that Alabama's height and weight requirements for correctional counselors in the state's prison system violated Title VII because of their disparate impact on women. The Court upheld the district court's finding of a prima facie case based on disparate impact analysis and ruled that Alabama had failed to present any evidence that its height/weight requirements were job-related. In the portion of the *Dothard* opinion reproduced below, the Court considered the plaintiff's challenge to Regulation 204 which required that guards who worked with inmates in the state's sex-segregated correctional facilities had to be the same gender as the inmates. Alabama defended its sex-based job classification as a bona fide occupational qualification under § 703(e) of Title VII. The Supreme Court concluded "that the District Court erred in rejecting the State's contention that Regulation 204 falls within the narrow ambit of the bfoq exception." *Id.* at 334, 97 S.Ct. at 2729. The Court continued:

> The environment in Alabama's penitentiaries is a peculiarly inhospitable one for human beings of whatever sex. Indeed, a Federal District Court has held that the conditions of confinement in the prisons of the State, characterized by "rampant violence" and a "jungle atmosphere," are constitutionally intolerable. Pugh v. Locke, 406 F.Supp. 318, 325 (M.D.Ala.1976). * * *
>
> In this environment of violence and disorganization, it would be an oversimplification to characterize Regulation 204 as an exercise in "romantic paternalism." In the usual case, the argument that a particular job is too dangerous for women may appropriately be met by the rejoinder that it is the purpose of Title VII to allow the individual woman to make that choice for herself. More is at stake in this case, however, than an individual woman's decision to weigh and accept the risks of employment in a "contact" position in a maximum-security male prison.
>
> The essence of a correctional counselor's job is to maintain prison security. A woman's relative ability to maintain order in a male, maximum-security, unclassified penitentiary of the type Alabama now runs could be directly reduced by her womanhood. There is a basis in fact for expecting that sex offenders who have criminally assaulted women in the past would be moved to do so again if access to women were established within the prison. There would also be a real risk that other inmates, deprived of a normal heterosexual environment, would assault women guards because they were women. In a prison system where violence is the order of the day, where inmate access to guards is facilitated by dormitory living arrangements, where every institution is understaffed, and where a substantial portion of the inmate population is composed of sex offenders mixed at random with other prisoners, there are few visible deterrents to inmate assaults on women custodians.

> * * * The likelihood that inmates would assault a woman because she was a woman would pose a real threat not only to the victim of the assault but also to the basic control of the penitentiary and protection of its inmates and the other security personnel. The employee's very womanhood would thus directly undermine her capacity to provide the security that is the essence of a correctional counselor's responsibility.

Id. at 334–36, 97 S.Ct. at 2729–30.

Justices Marshall and Brennan concurred in the Court's conclusion "that the bfoq exception was in fact meant to be an extremely narrow exception to the general prohibition of discrimination on the basis of sex." Their objection was that the Court improperly concluded that the BFOQ exception applied to the facts of this case. Justice Marshall wrote in partial dissent:

> It appears that the real disqualifying factor in the Court's view is "[t]he employee's very womanhood." * * * In short, the fundamental justification for the Court's decision is that women as guards will generate sexual assaults. With all respect, this rationale regrettably perpetuates one of the most insidious of the old myths about women—that women, wittingly or not, are seductive sexual objects. The effect of the decision, made I am sure with the best of intentions, is to punish women because their very presence might provoke sexual assaults. It is women who are made to pay the price in lost job opportunities for the threat of depraved conduct by prison inmates. Once again, "[t]he pedestal upon which women have been placed has * * *, upon closer inspection, been revealed as a cage." Sail'er Inn, Inc. v. Kirby, 5 Cal.3d 1, 20, 95 Cal.Rptr. 329, 485 P.2d 529, 541 (1971). It is particularly ironic that the cage is erected here in response to feared misbehavior by imprisoned criminals.
>
> * * *
>
> The proper response to inevitable attacks on both female and male guards is not to limit the employment opportunities of law-abiding women who wish to contribute to their community, but to take swift and sure punitive action against the inmate offenders. Presumably, one of the goals of the Alabama prison system is the eradication of inmates' antisocial behavior patterns so that prisoners will be able to live one day in free society. Sex offenders can begin this process by learning to relate to women guards in a socially acceptable manner. To deprive women of job opportunities because of the threatened behavior of convicted criminals is to turn our social priorities upside down.

Id. at 345–46, 97 S.Ct. at 2734–35 (Marshall, J., dissenting).

Underlying the asserted BFOQ defenses in both *Martin Marietta* and *Dothard* were assumptions about women's nature—their reproductive functions and their sexuality. Although *Dothard* purported to adopt a "narrow ambit" constraining an employer's safety justification for its BFOQ defense, the Court's rationale provided limited guidance for lower courts. In later cases involving challenges to restrictions on female employment in male prison facilities, lower courts have distinguished the specific factual context of *Dothard* and have generally not been persuaded by BFOQ arguments. *See, e.g.,* Gunther v. Iowa State Men's Reformatory, 612 F.2d 1079 (1980). *See generally* Suzanne Wilhelm, *Perpetuating Stereotypical Views of Women: The Bona Fide Occupational Qualification Defense in Gender Discrimination Under Title VII*, 28 Women's Rts.L.Rep. 73, 85–90 (2007) (discussing BFOQ arguments in prison facilities).

In a subsequent case, brought under the Age Discrimination in Employment Act (ADEA), the Court refined its test for establishing a BFOQ defense by relying on a safety rationale. In *Western Air Lines, Inc. v. Criswell*, 472 U.S. 400, 105 S.Ct. 2743, 86 L.Ed.2d 321 (1985), discussed in Chapter 14, the Court considered whether an airline's policy of imposing mandatory retirement on flight engineers at age sixty could be justified as an age-based BFOQ. The *Criswell* test emphasized the importance of making employment decisions based on the actual capabilities of individual employees rather than on stereotyped assumptions about the workers in the protected class. In the following case, *Johnson Controls*, the Court had the opportunity to evaluate a sex-based BFOQ defense to a claim of sex discrimination brought under Title VII and the PDA. As you read the case, evaluate carefully the Court's rationale for the procedural and substantive choices that it made. The Court relies on *Dothard* and *Criswell* for its BFOQ analysis in *Johnson Controls*, but does Justice Blackmun's majority opinion implicitly draw some of its central insights about women and work from Justice Marshall's dissent in *Dothard*?

INTERNATIONAL UNION, UNITED AUTOMOBILE WORKERS V. JOHNSON CONTROLS

Supreme Court of the United States, 1991.
499 U.S. 187, 111 S.Ct. 1196, 113 L.Ed.2d 158.

JUSTICE BLACKMUN delivered the opinion of the Court.

In this case we are concerned with an employer's gender-based fetal-protection policy. May an employer exclude a fertile female employee from certain jobs because of its concern for the health of the fetus the woman might conceive?

I

Respondent Johnson Controls, Inc., manufactures batteries. In the manufacturing process, the element lead is a primary ingredient. Occupational exposure to lead entails health risks, including the risk of harm to any fetus carried by a female employee.

Before the Civil Rights Act of 1964 became law, Johnson Controls did not employ any woman in a battery-manufacturing job. In June 1977, however, it announced its first official policy concerning its employment of women in lead-exposure work:

> [P]rotection of the health of the unborn child is the immediate and direct responsibility of the prospective parents. While the medical profession and the company can support them in the exercise of this responsibility, it cannot assume it for them without simultaneously infringing their rights as persons.
>
> * * * Since not all women who can become mothers wish to become mothers (or will become mothers), it would appear to be illegal discrimination to treat all who are capable of pregnancy as though they will become pregnant.

Consistent with that view, Johnson Controls "stopped short of excluding women capable of bearing children from lead exposure," but emphasized that a woman who expected to have a child should not choose a job in which she would have such exposure. The company also required a woman who wished to be considered for employment to sign a statement that she had been advised of the risk of having a child while she was exposed to lead. The statement informed the woman that although there was evidence "that women exposed to lead have a higher rate of abortion," this evidence was "not as clear * * * as the relationship between cigarette smoking and cancer," but that it was, "medically speaking, just good sense not to run that risk if you want children and do not want to expose the unborn child to risk, however small. * * * "

Five years later, in 1982, Johnson Controls shifted from a policy of warning to a policy of exclusion. Between 1979 and 1983, eight employees became pregnant while maintaining blood lead levels in excess of 30 micrograms per deciliter. This appeared to be the critical level noted by the Occupational Safety and Health Administration (OSHA) for a worker who was planning to have a family. *See* 29 C.F.R. § 1910.1025 (1989). The company responded by announcing a broad exclusion of women from jobs that exposed them to lead:

> [I]t is [Johnson Controls'] policy that women who are pregnant or who are capable of bearing children will not be placed into jobs involving lead exposure or which could expose them to lead

through the exercise of job bidding, bumping, transfer or promotion rights.

The policy defined "women * * * capable of bearing children" as "all women except those whose inability to bear children is medically documented." It further stated that an unacceptable work station was one where, "over the past year," an employee had recorded a blood lead level of more than 30 micrograms per deciliter or the work site had yielded an air sample containing a lead level in excess of 30 micrograms per cubic meter.

II

In April 1984, petitioners filed * * * a class action challenging Johnson Controls' fetal-protection policy as sex discrimination that violated Title VII of the Civil Rights Act of 1964. Among the individual plaintiffs were petitioners Mary Craig, who had chosen to be sterilized in order to avoid losing her job, Elsie Nason, a 50-year-old divorcee, who had suffered a loss in compensation when she was transferred out of a job where she was exposed to lead, and Donald Penney, who had been denied a request for a leave of absence for the purpose of lowering his lead level because he intended to become a father. * * *

The District Court granted summary judgment for * * * Johnson Controls[,] [a]pplying a three-part business necessity defense * * *.

The Court of Appeals for the Seventh Circuit, sitting *en banc*, affirmed the summary judgment by a 7-to-4 vote. The majority held that the proper standard for evaluating the fetal-protection policy was the defense of business necessity; that Johnson Controls was entitled to summary judgment under that defense; and that even if the proper standard was a BFOQ, Johnson Controls still was entitled to summary judgment.

* * *

III

The bias in Johnson Controls' policy is obvious. Fertile men, but not fertile women, are given a choice as to whether they wish to risk their reproductive health for a particular job. Section 703(a) of the Civil Rights Act of 1964 prohibits sex-based classifications in terms and conditions of employment, in hiring and discharging decisions, and in other employment decisions that adversely affect an employee's status. Respondent's fetal-protection policy explicitly discriminates against women on the basis of their sex. The policy excludes women with childbearing capacity from lead-exposed jobs and so creates a facial classification based on gender. Respondent assumes as much in its brief before this Court.

Nevertheless, the Court of Appeals assumed, as did the two appellate courts that already had confronted the issue, that sex-specific fetal-protection policies do not involve facial discrimination. These courts analyzed the policies as though they were facially neutral and had only a discriminatory effect upon the employment opportunities of women. Consequently, the courts looked to see if each employer in question had established that its policy was justified as a business necessity. The business necessity standard is more lenient for the employer than the statutory BFOQ defense. The Court of Appeals * * * assumed that because the asserted reason for the sex-based exclusion (protecting women's unconceived offspring) was ostensibly benign, the policy was not sex-based discrimination. That assumption, however, was incorrect.

First, Johnson Controls' policy classifies on the basis of gender and childbearing capacity, rather than fertility alone. Respondent does not seek to protect the unconceived children of all its employees. Despite evidence in the record about the debilitating effect of lead exposure on the male reproductive system, Johnson Controls is concerned only with the harms that may befall the unborn offspring of its female employees. * * * This Court faced a conceptually similar situation in *Phillips v. Martin Marietta Corp.*, 400 U.S. 542, 91 S.Ct. 496, 27 L.Ed.2d 613 (1971), and found sex discrimination because the policy established "one hiring policy for women and another for men—each having pre-school-age children." *Id.* at 544, 91 S.Ct. at 498. Johnson Controls' policy is facially discriminatory because it requires only a female employee to produce proof that she is not capable of reproducing. * * *

[T]he absence of a malevolent motive does not convert a facially discriminatory policy into a neutral policy with a discriminatory effect. Whether an employment practice involves disparate treatment through explicit facial discrimination does not depend on why the employer discriminates but rather on the explicit terms of the discrimination. In *Martin Marietta*, the motives underlying the employers' express exclusion of women did not alter the intentionally discriminatory character of the policy. Nor did the arguably benign motives lead to consideration of a business necessity defense. The question in that case was whether the discrimination in question could be justified under § 703(e) as a BFOQ. The beneficence of an employer's purpose does not undermine the conclusion that an explicit gender-based policy is sex discrimination under § 703(a) and thus may be defended only as a BFOQ.

* * *

IV

Under § 703(e)(1) of Title VII, an employer may discriminate on the basis of "religion, sex, or national origin in those certain instances where religion, sex, or national origin is a bona fide occupational qualification reasonably necessary to the normal operation of that particular business or enterprise." We therefore turn to the question whether Johnson Controls' fetal-protection policy is one of those "certain instances" that come within the BFOQ exception.

The BFOQ defense is written narrowly, and this Court has read it narrowly. *See, e.g.*, Dothard v. Rawlinson, 433 U.S. 321, 332–37, 97 S.Ct. 2720, 2728–30, 53 L.Ed.2d 786 (1977); Trans World Airlines, Inc. v. Thurston, 469 U.S. 111, 122–25, 105 S.Ct. 613, 622–23, 83 L.Ed.2d 523 (1985). We have read the BFOQ language of § 4(f) of the Age Discrimination in Employment Act of 1967 (ADEA), 29 U.S.C. § 623(f)(1), which tracks the BFOQ provision in Title VII, just as narrowly. *See* Western Air Lines, Inc. v. Criswell, 472 U.S. 400, 105 S.Ct. 2743, 86 L.Ed.2d 321 (1985). Our emphasis on the restrictive scope of the BFOQ defense is grounded on both the language and the legislative history of § 703.

The wording of the BFOQ defense contains several terms of restriction that indicate that the exception reaches only special situations. The statute thus limits the situations in which discrimination is permissible to "certain instances" where sex discrimination is "reasonably necessary" to the "normal operation" of the "particular" business. Each one of these terms—certain, normal, particular—prevents the use of general subjective standards and favors an objective, verifiable requirement. But the most telling term is "occupational"; this indicates that these objective, verifiable requirements must concern job-related skills and aptitudes.

Justice White [in concurrence] defines "occupational" as meaning related to a job. According to Justice White, any discriminatory requirement imposed by an employer is "job-related" simply because the employer has chosen to make the requirement a condition of employment. In effect, Justice White argues that sterility may be an occupational qualification for women because Johnson Controls has chosen to require it. This reading of "occupational" renders the word mere surplusage. "Qualification" by itself would encompass an employer's idiosyncratic requirements. By modifying "qualification" with "occupational," Congress narrowed the term to qualifications that affect an employee's ability to do the job.

Johnson Controls argues that its fetal-protection policy falls within the so-called safety exception to the BFOQ. Our cases have stressed that discrimination on the basis of sex because of safety concerns is allowed only in narrow circumstances. In *Dothard v. Rawlinson*, 433 U.S. 321, 97 S.Ct. 2730, 53 L.Ed.2d 786 (1997), this Court indicated that danger to a woman herself does not justify discrimination. We there allowed the employer to hire only male guards in contact areas of maximum-security male penitentiaries only because more was at stake than the "individual woman's decision to weigh and accept the risks of employment." We found sex to be a BFOQ inasmuch as the employment of a female guard would create real risks of safety to others if violence broke out because the guard was a woman. Sex discrimination was tolerated because sex was related to the guard's ability to do the job—maintaining prison security. We also required in *Dothard* a high correlation between sex and ability to perform job functions and refused to allow employers to use sex as a proxy for strength although it might be a fairly accurate one.

Similarly, some courts have approved airlines' layoffs of pregnant flight attendants at different points during the first five months of pregnancy on the ground that the employer's policy was necessary to ensure the safety of passengers. [*See, e.g.,*] Burwell v. Eastern Air Lines, Inc., 633 F.2d 361 (4th Cir.1980), *cert. denied*, 450 U.S. 965, 101 S.Ct. 1480, 67 L.Ed.2d 613 (1981). In two * * * cases, the courts pointedly indicated that fetal, as opposed to passenger, safety was best left to the mother.

We considered safety to third parties in *Western Airlines, Inc. v. Criswell*, in the context of the ADEA. We focused upon "the nature of the flight engineer's tasks," and the "actual capabilities of persons over age 60" in relation to those tasks. Our safety concerns were not independent of the individual's ability to perform the assigned tasks, but rather involved the possibility that, because of age-connected debility, a flight engineer might not properly assist the pilot, and might thereby cause a safety emergency. Furthermore, although we considered the safety of third parties in *Dothard* and *Criswell*, those third parties were indispensable to the particular business at issue. In *Dothard*, the third parties were the inmates; in *Criswell*, the third parties were the passengers on the plane. We stressed that in order to qualify as a BFOQ, a job qualification must relate to the " 'essence' " or to the "central mission of the employer's business."

Justice White [in concurrence] ignores the "essence of the business" test and so concludes that "protecting fetal safety while carrying out the duties of battery manufacturing is as much a legitimate concern as is safety to third parties in guarding prisons (*Dothard*) or flying airplanes (*Criswell*)." By limiting its discussion to cost and safety concerns and rejecting the "essence of the business" test that our case law has established, he seeks to expand what is now the narrow BFOQ defense. Third-party safety considerations properly entered into the BFOQ analysis in *Dothard* and *Criswell* because they went to the core of the employee's job performance. Moreover, that performance involved the central purpose of the enterprise. Justice White attempts to transform this case into one of customer safety. The unconceived fetuses of Johnson Controls' female employees, however, are neither customers nor third parties whose safety is essential to the business of battery manufacturing. No one can disregard the possibility of injury to future children; the BFOQ, however, is not so broad that it transforms this deep social concern into an essential aspect of battery making.

Our case law, therefore, makes clear that the safety exception is limited to instances in which sex or pregnancy actually interferes with the employee's ability to perform the job. * * * We reiterate our holdings in *Criswell* and *Dothard* that an employer must direct its concerns about a woman's ability to perform her job safely and efficiently to those aspects of the woman's job-related activities that fall within the "essence" of the particular business.[4]

V

We have no difficulty concluding that Johnson Controls cannot establish a BFOQ. Fertile women, as far as appears in the record, participate in the manufacture of batteries as efficiently as anyone else. Johnson Controls' professed moral and ethical concerns about the welfare of the next generation do not suffice to establish a BFOQ of female sterility. Decisions about the welfare of future children must be left to the parents who conceive, bear, support, and raise them rather than to the employers who hire those parents. Congress has mandated this choice through Title VII, as amended by the PDA. Johnson Controls has attempted to exclude women because of their reproductive capacity. Title VII and the PDA simply do not allow a woman's dismissal because of her failure to submit to sterilization.

Nor can concerns about the welfare of the next generation be considered a part of the "essence" of Johnson Controls' business. Judge Easterbrook in this case pertinently observed: "It is word play to say that 'the job' at Johnson [Controls] is to make batteries without risk to fetuses in the same way 'the job' at Western Air Lines is to fly planes without crashing."

Johnson Controls argues that it must exclude all fertile women because it is impossible to tell which women will become pregnant while working with lead. This argument is somewhat academic in light of our conclusion that the company may not exclude fertile women at all; it perhaps is worth noting, however, that Johnson Controls has shown no "factual basis for believing that all or substantially all women would be

[4] Justice White predicts that our reaffirmation of the narrowness of the BFOQ defense will preclude considerations of privacy as a basis for sex-based discrimination. We have never addressed privacy-based sex discrimination and shall not do so here because the sex-based discrimination at issue today does not involve the privacy interests of Johnson Controls' customers. Nothing in our discussion of the "essence of the business test," however, suggests that sex could not constitute a BFOQ when privacy interests are implicated. *See, e.g.*, Backus v. Baptist Medical Center, 510 F.Supp. 1191 (E.D.Ark.1981) (essence of obstetrics nurse's business is to provide sensitive care for patient's intimate and private concerns), *vacated as moot*, 671 F.2d 1100 (8th Cir.1982).

unable to perform safely and efficiently the duties of the job involved." Weeks v. Southern Bell Tel. & Tel. Co., 408 F.2d 228, 235 (5th Cir.1969), quoted with approval in *Dothard*. Even on this sparse record, it is apparent that Johnson Controls is concerned about only a small minority of women. Of the eight pregnancies reported among the female employees, it has not been shown that any of the babies have birth defects or other abnormalities. The record does not reveal the birth rate for Johnson Controls' female workers, but national statistics show that approximately nine percent of all fertile women become pregnant each year. The birthrate drops to two percent for blue collar workers over age 30. Johnson Controls' fear of prenatal injury, no matter how sincere, does not begin to show that substantially all of its fertile women employees are incapable of doing their jobs.

VI

A word about tort liability and the increased cost of fertile women in the workplace is perhaps necessary. One of the dissenting judges in this case expressed concern about an employer's tort liability and concluded that liability for a potential injury to a fetus is a social cost that Title VII does not require a company to ignore. It is correct to say that Title VII does not prevent the employer from having a conscience. The statute, however, does prevent sex-specific fetal-protection policies. These two aspects of Title VII do not conflict.

More than 40 States currently recognize a right to recover for a prenatal injury based either on negligence or on wrongful death. According to Johnson Controls, however, the company complies with the lead standard developed by OSHA and warns its female employees about the damaging effects of lead. It is worth noting that OSHA gave the problem of lead lengthy consideration and concluded that "there is no basis whatsoever for the claim that women of childbearing age should be excluded from the workplace in order to protect the fetus or the course of pregnancy." 43 Fed. Reg. 52952, 52966 (1978). Instead, OSHA established a series of mandatory protections which, taken together, "should effectively minimize any risk to the fetus and newborn child." *Id.* at 52966. *See* 29 C.F.R. § 1910.1025(k)(ii) (1990). Without negligence, it would be difficult for a court to find liability on the part of the employer. If, under general tort principles, Title VII bans sex-specific fetal-protection policies, the employer fully informs the woman of the risk, and the employer has not acted negligently, the basis for holding an employer liable seems remote at best.

Although the issue is not before us, Justice White observes that "it is far from clear that compliance with Title VII will pre-empt state tort liability." The cases relied upon by him to support his prediction, however, are inapposite. For example, in *California Federal Savings and*

Loan Assn. v. Guerra, 479 U.S. 272, 107 S.Ct. 683, 93 L.Ed.2d 613 (1987), we considered a California statute that expanded upon the requirements of the PDA and concluded that the statute was not pre-empted by Title VII because it was not inconsistent with the purposes of the federal statute and did not require an act that was unlawful under Title VII. Here, in contrast, the tort liability that Justice White fears will punish employers for complying with Title VII's clear command. When it is impossible for an employer to comply with both state and federal requirements, this Court has ruled that federal law pre-empts that of the States.

* * *

If state tort law furthers discrimination in the workplace and prevents employers from hiring women who are capable of manufacturing the product as efficiently as men, then it will impede the accomplishment of Congress' goals in enacting Title VII. Because Johnson Controls has not argued that it faces any costs from tort liability, not to mention crippling ones, the pre-emption question is not before us. * * *

The tort-liability argument reduces to two equally unpersuasive propositions. First, Johnson Controls attempts to solve the problem of reproductive health hazards by resorting to an exclusionary policy. Title VII plainly forbids illegal sex discrimination as a method of diverting attention from an employer's obligation to police the workplace. Second, the specter of an award of damages reflects a fear that hiring fertile women will cost more. The extra cost of employing members of one sex, however, does not provide an affirmative Title VII defense for a discriminatory refusal to hire members of that gender. *See Manhart*. Indeed, in passing the PDA, Congress considered at length the considerable cost of providing equal treatment of pregnancy and related conditions, but made the "decision to forbid special treatment of pregnancy despite the social costs associated therewith." Arizona Governing Comm. for Tax Deferred Annuity and Deferred Compensation Plans v. Norris, 463 U.S. 1073, 1085 n. 14, 103 S.Ct. 3492, 3499 n. 14, 77 L.Ed.2d 1236 (1983).

We, of course, are not presented with, nor do we decide, a case in which costs would be so prohibitive as to threaten the survival of the employer's business. We merely reiterate our prior holdings that the incremental cost of hiring women cannot justify discriminating against them.

VII

Our holding today that Title VII, as so amended, forbids sex-specific fetal-protection policies is neither remarkable nor unprecedented. Concern for a woman's existing or potential offspring historically has been the excuse for denying women equal employment opportunities. *See, e.g.*, Muller v. Oregon, 208 U.S. 412 (1908). Congress in the PDA prohibited discrimination on the basis of a woman's ability to become pregnant. We do no more than hold that the PDA means what it says.

It is no more appropriate for the courts than it is for individual employers to decide whether a woman's reproductive role is more important to herself and her family than her economic role. Congress has left this choice to the woman as hers to make.

Holding

The judgment of the Court of Appeals is reversed, and the case is remanded for further proceedings consistent with this opinion.

[JUSTICE WHITE, concurred, joined by THE CHIEF JUSTICE and JUSTICE KENNEDY; JUSTICE SCALIA concurred.]

NOTES AND QUESTIONS

1. Fetal protection policies were developed because of the well-known fact that exposure to toxins in the workplace can adversely affect the reproductive health of employees. According to one report, there are fifteen to twenty million jobs in the United States that may expose workers to toxins in the workplace that cause reproductive harm. Bureau of National Affairs, Special Report, Pregnancy and Employment: The Complete Handbook on Discrimination, Maternity Leave, and Health and Safety 57 (1987). According to a 1979 estimate, at least 100,000 jobs in the United States excluded women because of potential exposure to toxins that might affect reproductivity. *See* Wendy W. Williams, *Firing the Woman to Protect the Fetus: The Reconciliation of Fetal Protection with Employment Opportunity Goals Under Title VII*, 69 Geo.L.J. 641, 647 n.30 (1981).

Even though *Johnson Controls* addresses employers' sex discrimination on the basis of toxins in the workplace, does it leave unresolved the problem of reproductive harms that such toxins may cause? One commentator observed:

> The controversy surrounding fetal protection policies touches on political and philosophical questions regarding the very definitions of gender equality and gender difference. Feminists are faced with a paradox: To ignore difference is to risk placing women in a workplace designed by and for men, with all of its hazards and lack of concern for the preservation of health and life. On the other hand, to treat women differently from men in the workplace is to reinforce those assumptions and economic structures which form the foundation of women's inequality.

Cynthia R. Daniels, At Women's Expense: State Power and the Politics of Fetal Rights 93 (1993). In requiring that employers treat fertile men and women the same, does the Court in *Johnson Controls* ignore the risks of "placing women in a workplace designed by and for men"? Is there any way to resolve the paradox? Does the Family and Medical Leave Act (FMLA), discussed in Chapter 8, provide a solution or just create another paradox?

2. The primary reason that courts had adopted the disparate impact/business necessity analytic scheme for the fetal protection polices before *Johnson Controls* was because they accepted the view that the policies served an important social purpose of protecting unborn fetuses and they did not consider this laudable result to be achievable under a direct evidence/BFOQ analytic scheme. Until 1990, the EEOC had endorsed the disparate impact/business necessity approach to fetal protection policies. Then, in response to the Seventh Circuit's 7–4 en banc decision in *International Union, UAW v. Johnson Controls*, 886 F.2d 871 (7th Cir.1989), the EEOC issued a new Policy Guidance that adopted the direct evidence/BFOQ approach. *See Johnson Controls*, 499 U.S. at 200, 111 S.Ct. at 1204. What is the difference, if any, between the business necessity and bona fide occupational qualification defenses? See Chambers v. Omaha Girls Club, Inc., 834 F.2d 697 (8th Cir.1987) ("This court has noted that the analysis of a bfoq is similar to and overlaps with the judicially created 'business necessity' test.") (internal quotation and citation omitted); Harriss v. Pan Am. World Airways, Inc., 649 F.2d 670, 674–75 (9th Cir.1980) (discussing distinction between BFOQ and business necessity). Between the BFOQ and the legitimate, nondiscriminatory reason defense?

3. If a pregnant doctor or nurse works in the radiology department of a hospital that offers no special accommodations to pregnant employees, such as temporary transfer to another department during the pregnancy, what are her options after *Johnson Controls* if she wants to avoid exposing her fetus to radiation? *See* Duncan v. Children's Nat'l Med. Ctr., 702 A.2d 207 (D.C.1997) (rejecting pregnant plaintiffs' state law tort and contract claims and finding no public policy entitlement to transfer). *See generally* Suzanne U. Samuels, *The Fetal Protection Debate Revisited: The Impact of* U.A.W. v. Johnson Controls *on the Federal and State Courts*, 17 Women's Rts.L.Rep. 209 (1996); Suzanne U. Samuels, *The Lasting Legacy of* International Union, U.A.W. v. Johnson Controls: *Equal Employment and Workplace Health and Safety Five Years Later*, 12 Wis. Women's L.J. 1 (1997).

4. What options are open to the employer in a *Johnson Controls*-type case now that the Supreme Court has rejected all of its defenses to the fetal protection plan? *See generally* Mary Becker, *Reproductive Hazards After* Johnson Controls, 31 Hous.L.Rev. 43 (1994); Elaine Draper, *Reproductive Hazards and Fetal Exclusion Policies After* Johnson Controls, 12 Stan. L. & Pol'y Rev. 117 (2001); Susan S. Grover, *Employer's Fetal Injury Quandary After* Johnson Controls, 81 Ky.L.J. 639 (1993). *See also* Asad v. Continental Airlines, 328 F.Supp.2d 772, 790 (N.D. Ohio 2004) (reviewing possible transfer and job relief plans that employers might consider). Could an employer protect itself from future tort claims by requesting a signed waiver of liability from pregnant employees whose jobs place their fetuses at risk? *See* Peralta v. Chromium Plating & Polishing Corp., 2000 WL 34633645, at *7 (E.D.N.Y.2000) (noting that employee might waive her own tort claims but

probably cannot waive future claims by her child for exposure to toxins as a fetus).

5. *The Safety Element of the BFOQ*: In formulating its test of BFOQ, the Supreme Court in *Johnson Controls* relied heavily on its decisions in *Dothard v. Rawlinson* and *Western Air Lines, Inc. v. Criswell.* Should the concern for the health of fetuses be just as strong if not stronger than the concern for inmates in *Dothard* and airline passengers in *Criswell*? Are you persuaded by the distinctions that the Court makes between safety of fetuses and safety of inmates or passengers? In order to establish the safety-based defense under either the BFOQ or the business necessity defense, the defendant must present convincing expert testimony demonstrating that the challenged practice is required to protect employees or third parties from documented hazards. *See e.g.*, Fitzpatrick v. City of Atlanta, 2 F.3d 1112, 1119–20 (11th Cir.1993) (discussing expert testimony offered by the employer to support its business necessity defense in challenge to policy prohibiting firefighters from maintaining facial hair); Stewart v. City of Houston, No. H–07–4021, 2009 WL 2849728, at *11 (S.D.Tex. Sep. 3, 2009) (same); EEOC v. Exxon Mobil Corp. 560 Fed.Appx. 282, 289 (5th Cir.2014) (discussing expert testimony offered to support an age-based BFOQ for company pilots).

6. *"Role-Modeling" as an Element of the BFOQ*: The EEOC recognizes that "the psychological needs of an employer's clients or customers can make sex a BFOQ." EEOC Compl. Ma. (BNA) § 625.8(a)(2) at 625:0017 (April 1982). Some courts have interpreted this provision as permitting a "role-model" BFOQ. In *Healey v. Southwood Psychiatric Hospital*, 78 F.3d 128, 130 (3d. Cir.1996), for example, a female child-care specialist sued her employer when she was assigned the night shift because she was female. The hospital argued that it was necessary to have a female on shift to care for the sexually abused female patients. The Third Circuit agreed that role-modeling was an essential part of the job and that caretakers of the same gender made better role models. *Id.* at 134. The court explained that "children who have been sexually abused will disclose their problems more easily to a member of a certain sex, depending on their sex and the sex of the abuser." *Id.* at 133. The Seventh Circuit took a different approach in a similar case, concluding that same-gender mentoring was "necessary to achieve [a juvenile facility's] mission of rehabilitation," but that the facility had not offered factual support for the claim that this purpose required a same-gender staff member on the night shift, when juvenile inmates would be sleeping. Henry v. Milwaukee County, 539 F.3d 573, 583 (7th Cir.2008). Should courts making these kinds of determinations rely on expert testimony? *See* Katie Manley, *The BFOQ Defense: Title VII's Concession to Gender Discrimination*, 16 Duke J. Gender L. & Pol'y 169, 178 (2009).

Consider the following: Crystal Chambers, an adult, single black female, was employed as an arts and crafts instructor at the Omaha Girls Club, a private, nonprofit corporation. The Club offered young girls from eight to eighteen years old a number of activities, including programs aimed at preventing pregnancies. At the facility where Chambers worked, 90 percent of the members were black, and all of the instructors were black. The Club encouraged close relationships between the girls and the adult staff members who were "trained and expected to act as role models for the girls, with the intent that the girls [would] seek to emulate their behavior." The Club adopted a rule against employing single women who are pregnant because of its view that such women would be negative role models to teenage girls and would frustrate one of the Club's goals—preventing teenage pregnancies. After Chambers became pregnant and informed her supervisor, the Club discharged her pursuant to its policy against single-parent pregnancies. Chambers then filed a claim under Title VII alleging discrimination on the basis of sex. The primary issue before the court of appeals was whether the Club's "role-model" rule was justifiable as a business necessity or a bona fide occupational qualification. The court in *Chambers v. Omaha Girls Club, Inc.*, 834 F.2d 697, 704–05 (8th Cir.1987), found the rule was justifiable under both defenses: the rule's disparate impact on black females was justified as a business necessity, and the rule's disparate treatment of Chambers because of her pregnancy was justified as a BFOQ.

Professor Regina Austin, in *Sapphire Bound!*, 1989 Wis.L.Rev. 539, argued that the judges and the employer in *Chambers* imposed their own personal perspectives on morality—"white, male, and middle class"—on a group of inner-city, black teenage girls, without justifying that perspective or determining the perspective of the black teenage members of the Club. *Id.* at 555. Professor Austin, a critical race scholar, also challenged the assumptions of decision makers that affect their ability to deal with individuals of different genders, ethnicities, and social status. How would you critique Professor Austin's argument? For an interesting discussion of the ways that the state interacts with poor women in and through pregnancy, see Khiara M. Bridges, *Pregnancy, Medicaid, State Regulation, and the Production of Unruly Bodies*, 3 Nw. J.L. & Soc. Pol'y 62 (2008).

7. *The Cost Justification Defense*: *Johnson Controls* rejects a cost justification defense—tort liability, reducing workers' compensation claims, or decreasing insurance costs—for the fetal protection policy. Is the Court's analysis consistent with the court's treatment of the cost justification defense in *Wards Cove*, discussed in Chapter 4? Note that the Court leaves open the possibility that cost may be a defense in a case in which costs are so prohibitive as to threaten the survival of the business. Consider the following case:

Wilson v. Southwest Airlines, 517 F.Supp. 292 (N.D.Tex.1981), raised a cost justification defense as a rationale for hiring only women as flight attendants and airline ticket agents. By 1971, when its first planes finally began to fly, the fledgling Southwest Airlines had barely survived the four years of litigation that it had taken to obtain permission from the Texas Aeronautics Commission to enter the short-haul airline commuter market of Texas. Facing financial ruin and hoping to gain a competitive advantage quickly in the intrastate market, Southwest adopted a "catchy" advertising campaign based on "an image of feminine spirit, fun and sex appeal" that it believed would appeal to "its predominantly male, business passengers." *Id.* at 294. For example, in its television commercials, "while an alluring feminine voice promise[d] inflight love," attractive female attendants in skimpy outfits served male passengers " 'love bites' (toasted almonds) and 'love potions' (cocktails.) Even [its] ticketing system feature[d] a 'quickie machine' to provide 'instant gratification.' " *Id.* at 294 n.3. Southwest's "Love" campaign was extremely successful, but it entailed hiring only women for its flight attendant and ticket agent positions even though courts and the EEOC had found by then that female-only hiring policies in the airline industry violate Title VII. *See, e.g.*, Diaz v. Pan Am. World Airways, Inc., 442 F.2d 385 (5th Cir.); EEOC Opinion, "Flight Cabin Attendant," 33 Fed.Reg. 3361 (1968).

When Gregory Wilson brought a class action sex discrimination lawsuit challenging Southwest's female-only hiring policy, the company defended it as a BFOQ that was "crucial to the airline's continued financial success." *Wilson*, 517 F.Supp. at 293. Southwest argued that the central mission of its business was to make a profit and that its "Love" campaign was an essential marketing tool used to increase profits. How would this argument fare under the Court's analysis in *Johnson Controls*? Consider how the district court responded in *Wilson*:

> [T]he fact that a vibrant marketing campaign was necessary to distinguish Southwest in its early years does not lead to the conclusion that sex discrimination was then, or is now, a business necessity. * * *
>
> * * * [S]ex does not become a BFOQ merely because an employer chooses to exploit female sexuality as a marketing tool, or to better insure profitability.

Id. at 303.

8. *Customer Preferences*: The courts have consistently held that customer preferences do not satisfy the BFOQ. In *Diaz v. Pan American World Airways, Inc.*, 442 F.2d 385 (5th Cir.1971), the district court had concluded that being female was a BFOQ for the position of airline attendant because it found that women were better than men at "providing reassurance to anxious passengers, giving courteous personalized service and, in general, making flights as pleasurable as possible within the limitations imposed by aircraft operations." *Id.* at 387 (citing *Diaz*, 311 F.Supp. 559, 563 (S.D.Fla.1970)). The Fifth Circuit reversed, without disturbing the lower court's findings, on the ground that ministering to the psychological needs of passengers was "tangential" to the airline's "primary function" of safely transporting passengers. *Id.* at 388. The court observed:

> While a pleasant environment, enhanced by the obvious cosmetic effect that female stewardesses provide as well as, according to the findings of the trial court, their apparent ability to perform the non-mechanical functions of the job in a more effective manner than most men, may all be important, they are tangential to the essence

> of the business involved. No one has suggested that having male stewards will so seriously affect the operation of the airline as to jeopardize or even minimize its ability to provide safe transportation from one place to another.

Id.

The court in *Wilson v. Southwest Airlines*, discussed above, acknowledged the "very narrow standard for weighing customer preference" that courts following *Diaz* had adopted. 517 F.Supp. at 302 n.24. Furthermore, the court acknowledged the EEOC's "authenticity and genuineness" exception to this narrow standard. *Id.* at 301 & 301 n.20 (citing C.F.R. § 1604.2(a)(2) as amended by 45 Fed.Reg. 74676). Where "the primary function of the position, its essence, is to fulfill the audience's expectation and desire for a particular role, characterized by particular physical or emotional traits," the EEOC's regulation would permit male actors to fill male roles. *Id.* at 301. Also, where "sex or vicarious sexual recreation is the primary service provided" such that "the employee's sex and the service provided are inseparable," the regulation would permit employment of a female as "a social escort or topless dancer." *Id.* Can you think of any other jobs that would fit into the EEOC's "authenticity and genuineness" exception? In *Wilson*, the court ruled that Southwest Airlines "is not a business where vicarious sex entertainment is the primary service provided." *Id.* at 302. *See generally* Kimberly A. Yuracko, *Private Nurses and Playboy Bunnies: Explaining Permissible Sex Discrimination*, 92 Cal.L.Rev. 147 (2004) (describing how courts apply the "essence of the business" test in cases involving sexual titillation and comparing the results in these cases to those involving privacy concerns).

Some business clients have pushed the law firms they hire to employ a more diverse range of lawyers. *See* Karen Donovan, *Pushed by Clients, Law Firms Step up Diversity Efforts*, New York Times, July 21, 2006, available at *http://www.nytimes.com/2006/07/21/business/21legal.html.* Some clients will require a commitment from the firm that matters for that client will be staffed by attorneys of different races and genders. *Id.* Should law firms be permitted to defend against claims of gender discrimination by pointing to this client demand? *See generally* Ernest F. Lidge III, *Law Firm Employment Discrimination in Case Assignments at the Client's Insistence: A Bona Fide Occupational Qualification*, 38 Conn.L.Rev. 159 (2005).

9. *Customs of Foreign Nations*: Can an American company rely on the customs of a foreign country to justify a sex-based BFOQ for jobs that its employees—who are United States citizens—perform in that country? Title VII clearly covers such employees. *See* § 701(f), 42 U.S.C. § 2000e(f). Thus, explicit sex-based hiring and promotion decisions regarding such employees could only be defended as a BFOQ. Should the courts adopt a broader BFOQ analysis for American corporations doing business in foreign countries in which the prevailing social customs and practices discriminate on the basis of gender?

In *Fernandez v. Wynn Oil Co.*, 653 F.2d 1273 (9th Cir.1981), the employer initially asserted an alternative defense to its failure to promote the female plaintiff to Director of International Operations—that being male was a BFOQ for a job that involved spending time in South American countries, cultivating new clients and doing business with its customers there. The company claimed that the customs and mores of its South American clientele would make it impossible for a woman to succeed in the position. For example, at trial, the employer argued that, because of their attitudes about "the proper roles of men and women," South Americans would be "offended" if a woman held meetings with business clients in her hotel room. *Fernandez*, No. CV–78–0160–RJK, 1979 WL 290, at *2 (C.D.Cal. July 30, 1979). Applying the *Diaz* BFOQ analysis (discussed *supra* Note 7), the district court found that employing a man for the position went to the "essence" of the business since hiring a female as Director of International Operations "would have totally subverted any business [the company] hoped to accomplish in those areas of the world." *Id.* at *4. The district court entered judgment for the employer on several grounds, including the BFOQ defense.

When the plaintiff appealed to the Ninth Circuit, the employer disavowed reliance on the district court's BFOQ analysis, and the plaintiff lost on grounds unrelated to her challenge of the employer's BFOQ defense. *See Fernandez*, 653 F.2d at 1275–76. Nevertheless, the Ninth Circuit, in dictum, rejected the district court's factual findings and legal conclusions pertaining to the employer's BFOQ defense. *Id.* at 1276. The court noted that no evidence was presented that the plaintiff would be required to conduct business from her hotel room in South America and no evidence supported the district court's conclusion that hiring a female for the job would " 'destroy the essence' of the [employer's] business or 'create serious safety and efficacy problems.' " *Id.* The court of appeals stressed that neither "stereotypic impressions of male and female roles" nor "stereotyped customer preference[s]" can make gender a BFOQ. *Id.* at 1276–77.

10. *The Privacy-Based BFOQ*: Courts do recognize a distinction between "customer preference" and privacy in evaluating employer claims that sex is a BFOQ for a particular position. The notion that a BFOQ could be based on the privacy interests of clients or customers was raised in the floor debates on the Civil Rights Act of 1964. The House of Representatives briefly considered the BFOQ exception to Title VII on the last day of debate on the bill. Because "sex" had been proposed as a prohibited category under Title VII, Representative Goodell suggested why it should also be included under the BFOQ exception:

> There are so many instances where the matter of sex is a bona fide occupational qualification. For instance, I think of an elderly woman who wants a female nurse. There are many things of this nature which are bona fide occupational qualifications, and it seems to me they would be properly considered here as an exception.

110 Cong.Rec. 2718 (1964).

Courts, before and after *Johnson Controls*, have recognized sex as a BFOQ where health care providers have defended hiring employees of only one sex on the basis of the privacy interests of their patients. These cases have relied on preferences of patients for sexual privacy—as well as assumptions by courts and employers about patient preferences—in situations where the patients have to undress, bathe, or perform toileting functions in the presence of employees. *See, e.g.*, Jennings v. N.Y. State Office of Mental Health, 786 F.Supp. 376 (S.D.N.Y.) (holding that sex is a BFOQ for aides who feed, clothe, and bathe patients in a psychiatric hospital), *aff'd per curiam*, 977 F.2d 731 (2d Cir.1992); EEOC v. Mercy Health Ctr., 29 Fair Empl.Prac.Cas. (BNA) 159 (W.D.Okla.1982) (relying, in part, on patient surveys to uphold the exclusion of male nurses from a maternity center); Fesel v. Masonic Home of Del., Inc., 447 F.Supp. 1346 (D.Del.1978) (relying on affidavits of female patients to uphold the exclusion of male nurses and aides in a nursing home), *aff'd mem.*, 591 F.2d 1334 (3d Cir.1979). *See also* Emily Gold Waldman, *The Case of the Male Ob-Gyn: A Proposal for Expansion of the Privacy BFOQ in the Healthcare Context*, 6 U.Pa.J.Lab. & Emp.L. 357 (2004). Did the Supreme Court in *Johnson Controls* implicitly recognize that privacy concerns could justify sex as a BFOQ in certain circumstances? *See Johnson Controls*, *supra* at n.4.

A number of commentators have criticized the privacy-based BFOQ, arguing that it rests on stereotyped assumptions about the need to separate the sexes and that it essentially permits customer preference to justify discrimination. *See, e.g.*, Katherine T. Bartlett, *Only Girls Wear Barrettes: Dress and Appearance Standards, Community Norms, and Workplace Equality*, 92 Mich.L.Rev. 2541, 2542 & n.8 (1994); Suzanne Wilhelm, *Perpetuating Stereotypical Views of Women: The Bona Fide Occupational Qualification Defense in Gender Discrimination Under Title VII*, 28 Women's Rts.L.Rep. 73, 79–83 (2007) (discussing cases involving nursing staff).

11. *The Privacy BFOQ in Correctional Facilities*: Arguments for a privacy-based BFOQ are also made in some cases challenging gender-regulated prison staffing. In *Torres v. Wisconsin Department of Health & Social Services*, 859 F.2d 1523 (7th Cir.1988) (en banc), plaintiffs, male prison guards at a maximum security prison for women, brought a sex discrimination claim challenging a prison policy providing that correctional officer positions in the prison's living quarters would be staffed only by female correctional officers. As a result, the male officers who had worked in the living quarters were required to accept lower-grade positions. The superintendent of the prison, a female, promulgated the policy based only on her "professional judgment" that removing men from the area was "necessary to foster the goal of rehabilitation" and on the fact that sixty percent of the inmates had been abused by males at some point in their lives. *Id.* at 1530. The parties and the trial court agreed that empirical studies that might validate the policy did not exist. The district court found that the prison failed to satisfy the BFOQ because it "offered no objective evidence, either from empirical studies or otherwise" that supported the policy. *Id.* at 1531.

An en banc decision of the Seventh Circuit reversed and remanded, emphasizing that the unique nature of the "business" at issue—administering a prison for female inmates—meant that "the defendants, of necessity, had to innovate." *Id.* at 1532. Their efforts, the court concluded, ought to be given some deference and "are entitled to substantial weight when they are the product of a reasoned decision making process, based on available information and experience." *Id.* This standard did not require the objective studies supporting the prison administrator's judgment that rehabilitation goals made gender a BFOQ for correctional officers in this particular facility. The appellate court emphasized that "it would be a mistake to read our decision today as a signal that we are willing to allow employers to elude Title VII's requirements simply by arguing that they are 'innovating.'" *Id.* In subsequent cases, however, *Torres* has been cited to explain the special deference due to prison administrators in their judgment about when gender is a BFOQ for particular positions within a correctional facility. *See, e.g.,* Everson v. Mich. Dep't of Corr., 391 F.3d 737 (6th Cir.2004) (reversing district court to conclude that the proffered explanation for requiring female guards was reasonable); Teamsters Local Union No. 117 v. Washington Dept. of Corrections, 789 F.3d 979, 991–93 (9th Cir.2015) (deferring to prison administrators about the need for female-only guards to protect prisoner privacy, increase prison safety, and prevent sexual assault). *But see* Ambat v. City and County of San Francisco, 757 F.3d 1017 (9th Cir.2014) (concluding that city had not offered sufficient evidence that its gender-specific deputy assignments were necessary to achieve essential goals). *See generally* Suzanne Wilhelm, *Perpetuating Stereotypical Views of Women: The Bona Fide Occupational Qualification Defense in Gender Discrimination Under Title VII*, 28 Women's Rts.L.Rep. 73, 83–90 (2007) (discussing discrimination cases challenging sex-based hiring in correctional facilities).

While suits challenging gender-specific policies in correctional facilities tend to be framed in terms of the prison officials' entitlement to deference in their judgments about prison policy, courts also recognize that there is another interest at play—that of the inmates. In *Robino v. Iranon*, 145 F.3d 1109 (9th Cir.1998), the court upheld a BFOQ defense of the policy of a women's correctional facility which designated six guard positions as female-only. The court held that "these six female-only posts are a reasonable response to the [defendants'] concerns about inmate privacy and allegations of abuse by male [corrections officers]." *Id.* at 1111. The court observed that the plaintiffs—male corrections officers—

> contend a BFOQ defense cannot be based on the privacy rights of the inmates and they correctly note that inmates' privacy rights are limited. However, a person's interest in not being viewed unclothed by members of the opposite sex survives incarceration. Whether or not the inmates could successfully assert their own right to privacy is immaterial in this case. We are concerned here with a considered

prison policy that takes into account security, rehabilitation, and morale.

Id.

E. SEX-BASED DRESS, GROOMING, AND APPEARANCE REQUIREMENTS

Once on the job, many employees accept without question the legitimacy of employer rules regarding workplace dress, grooming, and appearance. Indeed, the pressure to conform to informal "dress codes" in some workplaces—such as corporate offices, law offices, or courtrooms—may obviate the need for formal rules. Even when casual dress is permitted in some workplaces, there may be unspoken rules about acceptable attire. But what if an employer's formal rules impose greater burdens on women than on men or, for that matter, on members of a particular race or religion? In deciding whether an employee is suited for a particular job, does an employer violate Title VII when it relies on gender-based assumptions about how men and women should appear? Professor Katharine Bartlett has observed:

> [e]mployers have traditionally assumed substantial prerogatives with respect to the dress and appearance of their employees, imposing burdens on women that are different from those imposed on men. For example, women may be required to wear skirts of a certain length or high-heeled shoes, to conform to different weight criteria than men, or to wear makeup. They may be fired if they have unladylike facial hair or if they wear their hair in a style that may offend customers. They may be required to have sexually alluring figures or to wear sexually provocative clothing, or they may be made to downplay their sexuality. Men, in turn, may be required to wear ties or to keep their hair cut short, or may be prohibited from wearing "women's" jewelry. These requirements pose a special challenge to conventional equality concepts and illustrate especially well the difficulties of rooting out workplace rules and practices that are based on well-settled community norms.

Katharine T. Bartlett, *Only Girls Wear Barrettes: Dress and Appearance Standards, Community Norms, and Workplace Equality*, 92 Mich.L.Rev. 2541, 2543–44 (1994) (citations omitted).

Although the EEOC was initially receptive to the argument that gender-based dress and grooming codes constitute sex discrimination in violation of Title VII, the courts, with a few limited exceptions, have consistently rejected challenges to employer rules and informal practices regarding employee workplace attire, grooming standards, and personal appearance. *See, e.g.*, Bartlett, *supra*, at 2556 n.70 (citing EEOC administrative decisions from the early 1970s that "invalidated hair-length requirements or no-beard rules, which applied to men but not women"); *see generally id.* at 2556–68 (discussing the rationales that courts have adopted to deny Title VII claims based on sex-based dress and grooming requirements). The EEOC Compliance Manual now expressly permits different dress codes for men and women, requiring only that the employers impose "equivalent" standards or burdens on both male and female employees. EEOC Compliance Manual § 619.4(d).

In the early Title VII cases upholding employer dress and grooming codes that are explicitly based on gender, the courts adopted several rationales. First was that these types of policies, which do no more than reflect reasonable community norms of appearance, have only a trivial or de minimus impact on employees' working condition. *See, e.g.*, Dodge v. Giant Food, Inc., 488 F.2d 1333, 1337 (D.C.Cir.1973) ("Title VII was never intended to encompass sexual classifications having only an insignificant effect on employment opportunities"). Second, many courts considered dress and grooming codes to be outside the legitimate scope of Title VII's statutory objectives and firmly within the lawful prerogatives of the employer:

> Equal employment *opportunity* may be secured only when employers are barred from discriminating against employees on the basis of immutable characteristics, such as race and national origin. Similarly, an employer cannot have one hiring policy for men and another for women *if* the distinction is based on some fundamental right. But a hiring policy that distinguishes on some other ground, such as grooming codes or length of hair, is related more closely to the employer's choice of how to run a business than to equality of employment opportunity.

Willingham v. Macon Tel. Publ'g Co., 507 F.2d 1084, 1092 (5th Cir.1975) (en banc). The employer's business interests seemed particularly strong in frontline service occupations and the television and entertainment industries, where courts allowed employers to condition certain types of jobs on an employee's conformity with gender-based, stereotypical appearance standards. *See, e.g.*, Craft v. Metromedia, Inc., 766 F.2d 1205, 1215 (8th Cir.1985) ("Courts have recognized that the appearance of a company's employees may contribute greatly to the company's image and success with the public and thus that a reasonable dress or grooming code is a proper management prerogative."). *But see* Lewis v. Heartland of America, L.L.C., 591 F.3d 1033 (8th Cir.2010) (reversing summary judgment for the employer when supervisor for a group of hotels fired a front desk employee allegedly because she lacked the "Midwestern girl look"). Finally, some courts accepted the argument that the only way to treat men and women equally with regard to appearance is to adopt disparate rules that reflect community norms and expectations about appropriate appearance and attire for men and women. *See, e.g.*, Fagan v. Nat'l Cash Register Co., 481 F.2d 1115, 1117 n.3 (D.C.Cir.1973) (taking "judicial notice that reasonable regulations prescribing good grooming standards are not at all uncommon in the business world, indeed, taking account of basic differences in male and female physiques and common differences in customary dress of male and female employees, it is not usually thought that there is unlawful discrimination 'because of sex' "). As you read the following case, consider how the judges in the majority and dissenting opinions treat these rationales.

JESPERSEN V. HARRAH'S OPERATING COMPANY, INC.

United States Court of Appeals for the Ninth Circuit, 2006 (en banc).
444 F.3d 1104.

SCHROEDER, CHIEF JUDGE.

* * * The plaintiff, Darlene Jespersen, was terminated from her position as a bartender at the sports bar in Harrah's Reno casino not long after Harrah's began to enforce its comprehensive uniform, appearance and grooming standards for all bartenders. The standards required all bartenders, men and women, to wear the same uniform of black pants and white shirts, a bow tie, and comfortable black shoes. The standards also included grooming requirements that differed to some extent for men and women, requiring women to wear some facial makeup and not permitting men to wear any. Jespersen refused to comply with the makeup requirement and was effectively terminated for that reason.

* * *

I. INTRODUCTION

Plaintiff Darlene Jespersen worked successfully as a bartender at Harrah's for twenty years and compiled what by all accounts was an exemplary record. During Jespersen's entire tenure with Harrah's, the company maintained a policy encouraging female beverage servers to wear makeup. The parties agree, however, that the policy was not enforced until 2000. In February 2000, Harrah's implemented a "Beverage Department Image Transformation" program at twenty Harrah's locations, including its casino in Reno. Part of the program consisted of new grooming and appearance standards, called the "Personal Best" program. The program contained certain appearance standards that applied equally to both sexes, including a standard uniform of black pants, white shirt, black vest, and black bow tie. Jespersen has never objected to any of these policies. The program also contained some sex-differentiated appearance requirements as to hair, nails, and makeup.

In April 2000, Harrah's amended that policy to require that women wear makeup. Jespersen's only objection here is to the makeup requirement. The amended policy provided in relevant part:

> All Beverage Service Personnel, in addition to being friendly, polite, courteous and responsive to our customer's needs, must possess the ability to physically perform the essential factors of the job as set forth in the standard job descriptions. They must be well groomed, appealing to the eye, be firm and body toned, and be comfortable with maintaining this look while wearing the specified uniform. Additional factors to be considered include, but are not limited to, hair styles, overall body contour, and degree of comfort the employee projects while wearing the uniform.

* * *

Beverage Bartenders and Barbacks will adhere to these additional guidelines:

- Overall Guidelines (applied equally to male/female):
  - Appearance: Must maintain Personal Best image portrayed at time of hire.
  - Jewelry, if issued, must be worn. Otherwise, tasteful and simple jewelry is permitted; no large chokers, chains or bracelets.
  - No faddish hairstyles or unnatural colors are permitted.
- Males:
  - Hair must not extend below top of shirt collar. Ponytails are prohibited.
  - Hands and fingernails must be clean and nails neatly trimmed at all times. No colored polish is permitted.
  - Eye and facial makeup is not permitted.
  - Shoes will be solid black leather or leather type with rubber (non skid) soles.
- Females:
  - Hair must be teased, curled, or styled every day you work. Hair must be worn down at all times, no exceptions.
  - Stockings are to be of nude or natural color consistent with employee's skin tone. No runs.

- Nail polish can be clear, white, pink or red color only. No exotic nail art or length.
- Shoes will be solid black leather or leather type with rubber (non skid) soles.
- *Make up (face powder, blush and mascara) must be worn and applied neatly in complimentary colors. Lip color must be worn at all times. (emphasis added).*

Jespersen did not wear makeup on or off the job, and in her deposition stated that wearing it would conflict with her self-image. It is not disputed that she found the makeup requirement offensive, and felt so uncomfortable wearing makeup that she found it interfered with her ability to perform as a bartender. Unwilling to wear the makeup, and not qualifying for any open positions at the casino with a similar compensation scale, Jespersen left her employment with Harrah's.

* * *

Harrah's moved for summary judgment, supporting its motion with documents giving the history and purpose of the appearance and grooming policies. * * *

In her deposition testimony, attached as a response to [Harrah's] motion for summary judgment, Jespersen described the personal indignity she felt as a result of attempting to comply with the makeup policy. Jespersen testified that when she wore the makeup she "felt very degraded and very demeaned." In addition, Jespersen testified that "it prohibited [her] from doing [her] job" because "[i]t affected [her] self-dignity * * * [and] took away [her] credibility as an individual and as a person." * * * Her response to Harrah's motion for summary judgment relied solely on her own deposition testimony regarding her subjective reaction to the makeup policy, and on favorable customer feedback and employer evaluation forms regarding her work.

The record therefore does not contain any affidavit or other evidence to establish that complying with the "Personal Best" standards caused burdens to fall unequally on men or women, and there is no evidence to suggest Harrah's motivation was to stereotype the women bartenders. Jespersen relied solely on evidence that she had been a good bartender, and that she had personal objections to complying with the policy, in order to support her argument that Harrah's " 'sells' and exploits its women employees." Jespersen contended that as a matter of law she had made a prima facie showing of gender discrimination, sufficient to survive summary judgment on both of her claims.

The district court granted Harrah's motion for summary judgment on all of Jespersen's claims. In this appeal, Jespersen maintains that the record before the district court was sufficient to create triable issues of material fact as to her unlawful discrimination claims of unequal burdens and sex stereotyping. We deal with each in turn.

II. UNEQUAL BURDENS

* * *

In this case, Jespersen argues that the makeup requirement itself establishes a prima facie case of discriminatory intent and must be justified by Harrah's as a bona fide occupational qualification. *See* 42 U.S.C. § 2000e–2(e)(1). Our settled law in this circuit, however, does not support Jespersen's position that a sex-based difference in appearance standards alone, without any further showing of disparate effects, creates a prima facie case.

In *Gerdom v. Cont'l Airlines, Inc.*, 692 F.2d 602 (9th Cir.1982), we considered the Continental Airlines policy that imposed strict weight restrictions on female flight attendants, and held it constituted a violation of Title VII. We did so because the airline imposed no weight restriction whatsoever on a class of male employees who performed the same or similar functions as the flight attendants. Indeed, the policy was touted by the airline as intended to "create the public image of an airline which offered passengers service by thin, attractive women, whom executives referred to as Continental's 'girls.'" *Id.* at 604. In fact, Continental specifically argued that its policy was justified by its "desire to compete [with other airlines] by featuring attractive female cabin attendants[,]" a justification which this court recognized as "discriminatory on its face." *Id.* at 609. The weight restriction was part of an overall program to create a sexual image for the airline. *Id.* at 604.

In contrast, this case involves an appearance policy that applied to both male and female bartenders, and was aimed at creating a professional and very similar look for all of them. All bartenders wore the same uniform. The policy only differentiated as to grooming standards.

In *Frank v. United Airlines, Inc.*, 216 F.3d 845 (9th Cir.2000), we dealt with a weight policy that applied different standards to men and women in a facially unequal way. The women were forced to meet the requirements of a medium body frame standard while men were required to meet only the more generous requirements of a large body frame standard. *Id.* at 854. In that case, we recognized that "[a]n appearance standard that imposes different but essentially equal burdens on men and women is not disparate treatment." *Id.* The United weight policy, however, did not impose equal burdens. On its face, the policy embodied a requirement that categorically " 'applie[d] less favorably to one gender[,]' " and the burdens imposed upon that gender were obvious from the policy itself. *Id.* (quoting *Gerdom*, 692 F.2d at 608 (alteration omitted)).

This case stands in marked contrast, for here we deal with requirements that, on their face, are not more onerous for one gender than the other. Rather, Harrah's "Personal Best" policy contains sex-differentiated requirements regarding each employee's hair, hands, and face. While those individual requirements differ according to gender, none on its face places a greater burden on one gender than the other. Grooming standards that appropriately differentiate between the genders are not facially discriminatory.

We have long recognized that companies may differentiate between men and women in appearance and grooming policies, and so have other circuits. *See, e.g., Fountain v. Safeway Stores, Inc.,* 555 F.2d 753, 755 (9th Cir.1977) [citations from cases from the 1970s from the Second, Fourth, Fifth, Sixth, Eighth, Ninth, and District of Columbia Circuits are omitted]. The material issue under our settled law is not whether the policies are different, but whether the policy imposed on the plaintiff creates an "unequal burden" for the plaintiff's gender. *See Frank; Gerdom; see also Fountain.*

Not every differentiation between the sexes in a grooming and appearance policy creates a "significantly greater burden of compliance[.]" *Gerdom,* 692 F.2d at 606. For example, in *Fountain,* this court upheld Safeway's enforcement of its sex-differentiated appearance standard, including its requirement that male employees wear ties, because the company's actions in enforcing the regulations were not "overly burdensome to its employees [.]" 555 F.2d at 756. Similarly, as the Eighth Circuit has recognized, "[w]here, as here, such [grooming and appearance] policies are reasonable and are imposed in an evenhanded manner on all employees, slight differences in the appearance requirements for males and females have only a negligible effect on employment opportunities." *Knott* [*v. Mo. Pac. R.R. Co.,* 527 F.2d 1249, 1252 (8th Cir.1975)]. Under established equal burdens analysis, when an employer's grooming and appearance policy does not unreasonably burden one gender more than the other, that policy will not violate Title VII.

Jespersen asks us to take judicial notice of the fact that it costs more money and takes more time for a woman to comply with the makeup requirement than it takes for a man to comply with the requirement that he keep his hair short, but these are not matters appropriate for judicial notice. Judicial notice is reserved for matters "generally known within the territorial jurisdiction of the trial court" or "capable of accurate and ready determination by resort to sources whose accuracy cannot reasonably be questioned." Fed.R.Evid. 201. The time and cost of makeup and haircuts is in neither category. The facts that Jespersen would have this court judicially notice are not subject to the requisite "high degree of indisputability" generally required for such judicial notice. Fed.R.Evid. 201 advisory committee's note.

Our rules thus provide that a plaintiff may not cure her failure to present the trial court with facts sufficient to establish the validity of her claim by requesting that this court take judicial notice of such facts. Those rules apply here. Jespersen did not submit any documentation or any evidence of the relative cost and time required to comply with the grooming requirements by men and women. As a result, we would have to speculate about those issues in order to then guess whether the policy creates unequal burdens for women. This would not be appropriate.

Having failed to create a record establishing that the "Personal Best" policies are more burdensome for women than for men, Jespersen did not present any triable issue of fact. The district court correctly granted summary judgment on the record before it with respect to Jespersen's claim that the makeup policy created an unequal burden for women.

III. SEX STEREOTYPING

[Jespersen also argued that Harrah's makeup requirement for female bartenders was discriminatory because the policy was based on a sex stereotype about women's appearance that was unlawful under *Price Waterhouse*, 490 U.S. 228, 109 S.Ct. 1775, 104 L.Ed.2d 268 (1989).]

* * *

The stereotyping in *Price Waterhouse* interfered with Hopkins' ability to perform her work; the advice that she should take "a course at charm school" was intended to discourage her use of the forceful and aggressive techniques that made her successful in the first place. *Id.* at 251, 109 S.Ct. 1775. Impermissible sex stereotyping was clear because the very traits that she was asked to hide were the same traits considered praiseworthy in men.

Harrah's "Personal Best" policy is very different. The policy does not single out Jespersen. It applies to all of the bartenders, male and female. It requires all of the bartenders to wear exactly the same uniforms while interacting with the public in the context of the entertainment industry. It is for the most part unisex, from the black tie to the non-skid shoes. There is no evidence in this record to indicate that the policy was adopted to make women bartenders conform to a commonly-accepted stereotypical image of what women should wear. The record contains nothing to suggest the grooming standards would objectively inhibit a woman's ability to do the job. The only evidence in the record to support the stereotyping claim is Jespersen's own subjective reaction to the makeup requirement.

Judge Pregerson's dissent improperly divides the grooming policy into separate categories of hair, hands, and face, and then focuses exclusively on the makeup requirement to conclude that the policy constitutes sex stereotyping. This parsing, however, conflicts with established grooming standards analysis. *See, e.g., Knott v. Mo. Pac. R. Co.*, 527 F.2d at 1252 ("Defendant's hair length requirement for male employees is *part of a comprehensive personal grooming code* applicable to all employees.") (emphasis added). The requirements must be viewed in the context of the overall policy. The dissent's conclusion that the unequal burdens analysis allows impermissible sex stereotyping to persist if imposed equally on both sexes, is wrong because it ignores the protections of *Price Waterhouse* our decision preserves. If a grooming standard imposed on either sex amounts to impermissible stereotyping, something this record does not establish, a plaintiff of either sex may challenge that requirement under *Price Waterhouse.*

We respect Jespersen's resolve to be true to herself and to the image that she wishes to project to the world. We cannot agree, however, that her objection to the makeup requirement, without more, can give rise to a claim of sex stereotyping under Title VII. If we were to do so, we would come perilously close to holding that every grooming, apparel, or appearance requirement that an individual finds personally offensive, or in conflict with his or her own self-image, can create a triable issue of sex discrimination.

This is not a case where the dress or appearance requirement is intended to be sexually provocative, and tending to stereotype women as sex objects. *See, e.g., EEOC v. Sage Realty Corp.*, 507 F.Supp. 599 (S.D.N.Y.1981). In *Sage Realty,* the plaintiff was a lobby attendant in a hotel that employed only female lobby attendants and required a mandatory uniform. The uniform was an octagon designed with an opening for the attendant's head, to be worn as a poncho, with snaps at the wrists and a tack on each side of the poncho, which was otherwise open. The attendants wore blue dancer pants as part of the uniform but were prohibited from wearing a shirt, blouse, or skirt under the outfit. There, the plaintiff was required to wear a uniform that was "short and revealing on both sides [such that her] thighs and portions of her buttocks were exposed." *Id.* Jespersen, in contrast, was asked only to wear a unisex uniform that covered her entire body and was designed for men and women. The "Personal Best" policy does not, on its face, indicate any discriminatory or sexually stereotypical intent on the part of Harrah's.

Nor is this a case of sexual harassment. *See Rene v. MGM Grand Hotel, Inc.*, 305 F.3d 1061, 1068–69 (9th Cir.2002) (en banc); *Nichols v. Azteca Restaurant Enters., Inc.*, 256 F.3d 864, 874 (9th Cir.2001). Following *Price Waterhouse,* our court has held that sexual harassment of an employee because of that employee's failure to conform to commonly-accepted gender stereotypes is sex discrimination in violation of Title VII. In *Nichols,* a male waiter was systematically abused for failing to act "as a man should act," for walking and carrying his tray "like a woman," and was derided for not having sexual intercourse with a female waitress who was his friend. *Nichols,* 256 F.3d at 874. Applying *Price Waterhouse,* our court concluded that this harassment was actionable discrimination because of the plaintiff's sex. In *Rene,* the homosexual plaintiff stated a Title VII sex stereotyping claim because he endured assaults "of a sexual nature" when Rene's co-workers forced him to look at homosexual pornography, gave him sexually-oriented "joke" gifts and harassed him for behavior that did not conform to commonly-accepted male stereotypes. *Rene,* 305 F.3d at 1064–65. *Nichols* and *Rene* are not grooming standards cases, but provide the framework for this court's analysis of when sex stereotyping rises to the level of sex discrimination for Title VII purposes. Unlike the situation in both *Rene* and *Nichols,* Harrah's actions have not condoned or subjected Jespersen to any form of alleged harassment. It is not alleged that the "Personal Best" policy created a hostile work environment.

Nor is there evidence in this record that Harrah's treated Jespersen any differently than it treated any other bartender, male or female, who did not comply with the written grooming standards applicable to all bartenders. Jespersen's claim here materially differs from Hopkins' claim in *Price Waterhouse* because Harrah's grooming standards do not require Jespersen to conform to a stereotypical image that would objectively impede her ability to perform her job requirements as a bartender.

We emphasize that we do not preclude, as a matter of law, a claim of sex-stereotyping on the basis of dress or appearance codes. Others may well be filed, and any bases for such claims refined as law in this area evolves. This record, however, is devoid of any basis for permitting this particular claim to go forward, as it is limited to the subjective reaction of a single employee, and there is no evidence of a stereotypical motivation on the part of the employer. This case is essentially a challenge to one small part of what is an overall apparel, appearance, and grooming policy that applies largely the same requirements to both men and women. As we said in *Nichols,* in commenting on grooming standards, the touchstone is reasonableness. A makeup requirement must be seen in the context of the overall standards imposed on employees in a given workplace.

Affirmed.

PREGERSON, CIRCUIT JUDGE, with whom JUDGES KOZINSKI, GRABER, and W. FLETCHER join, dissenting:

* * * The majority contends that it is bound to reject Jespersen's sex stereotyping claim because she presented too little evidence—only her "own subjective reaction to the makeup requirement." I disagree. Jespersen's evidence showed that Harrah's fired her because she did not comply with a grooming policy that imposed a facial uniform (full makeup) on only female bartenders. Harrah's stringent "Personal Best"

policy required female beverage servers to wear foundation, blush, mascara, and lip color, and to ensure that lip color was on at all times. Jespersen and her female colleagues were required to meet with professional image consultants who in turn created a facial template for each woman. Jespersen was required not simply to wear makeup; in addition, the consultants dictated where and how the makeup had to be applied.

Quite simply, her termination for failing to comply with a grooming policy that imposed a facial uniform on only female bartenders is discrimination "because of" sex. Such discrimination is clearly and unambiguously impermissible under Title VII, which requires that "gender must be *irrelevant* to employment decisions." *Price Waterhouse v. Hopkins,* 490 U.S. 228, 240, 109 S.Ct. 1775, 104 L.Ed.2d 268 (1989) (plurality opinion) (emphasis added).

Notwithstanding Jespersen's failure to present additional evidence, little is required to make out a sex-stereotyping—as distinct from an undue burden—claim in this situation. In *Price Waterhouse,* the Supreme Court held that an employer may not condition employment on an employee's conformance to a sex stereotype associated with their gender. As the majority recognizes, *Price Waterhouse* allows a Title VII plaintiff to "introduce evidence that the employment decision was made in part because of a sex stereotype." It is not entirely clear exactly what this evidence must be, but nothing in *Price Waterhouse* suggests that a certain type or quantity of evidence is required to prove a prima facie case of discrimination. *Cf. Desert Palace, Inc. v. Costa,* 539 U.S. 90, 98–102, 123 S.Ct. 2148, 156 L.Ed.2d 84 (2003) (holding that a plaintiff may prove discrimination in a Title VII case using either direct or circumstantial evidence and that, to obtain a mixed-motive instruction, the plaintiff need only present evidence sufficient for a reasonable jury to conclude, by a preponderance of the evidence, that sex was a motivating factor for an employment practice).

Moreover, *Price Waterhouse* recognizes that gender discrimination may manifest itself in stereotypical notions as to how women should dress and present themselves, not only as to how they should behave. *See* 490 U.S. at 235, 109 S.Ct. 1775 (noting that the plaintiff was told that her consideration for partnership would be enhanced if, among other things, she "dress[ed] more femininely, [wore] make-up, [had] her hair styled, and [wore] jewelry"); *see also Dawson v. Bumble & Bumble,* 398 F.3d 211, 221 (2d Cir.2005) (recognizing that one can fail to conform to gender stereotypes either through behavior *or* through appearance); *Smith v. City of Salem,* 378 F.3d 566, 574 (6th Cir.2004) ("After *Price Waterhouse,* an employer who discriminates against women because, for instance, they do not wear dresses or makeup, is engaging in sex discrimination because the discrimination would not occur but for the victim's sex."); *Doe v. City of Belleville,* 119 F.3d 563, 582 (7th Cir.1997) (rejecting the defendant's argument that *Price Waterhouse* does not apply to personal appearance standards), *vacated and remanded on other grounds,* 523 U.S. 1001, 118 S.Ct. 1183, 140 L.Ed.2d 313 (1998).

Hopkins, the *Price Waterhouse* plaintiff, offered individualized evidence, describing events in which she was subjected to discriminatory remarks. However, the Court did not state that such evidence was required. * * * The fact that Harrah's required female bartenders to conform to a sex stereotype by wearing full makeup while working is not in dispute, and the policy is described at length in the majority opinion. This policy did not, as the majority suggests, impose a "grooming, apparel, or appearance requirement that an individual finds personally offensive," but rather one that treated Jespersen differently from male bartenders "because of" her sex. I believe that the fact that Harrah's designed and promoted a policy that required women to conform to a sex stereotype by wearing full makeup is sufficient "direct evidence" of discrimination.

The majority contends that Harrah's "Personal Best" appearance policy is very different from the policy at issue in *Price Waterhouse* in that it applies to both men and women. ("[The Personal Best policy] applies to all of the bartenders, male and female. It requires all of the bartenders to wear exactly the same uniforms while interacting with the public in the context of the entertainment industry.") I disagree. As the majority concedes, "Harrah's 'Personal Best' policy contains sex-differentiated requirements regarding each employee's hair, hands, and face." The fact that a policy contains sex-differentiated requirements that affect people of both genders cannot excuse a particular requirement from scrutiny. By refusing to consider the makeup requirement separately, and instead stressing that the policy contained some gender-neutral requirements, such as color of clothing, as well as a variety of gender-differentiated requirements for "hair, hands, and face," the majority's approach would permit otherwise impermissible gender stereotypes to be neutralized by the presence of a stereotype or burden that affects people of the opposite gender, or by some separate non-discriminatory requirement that applies to both men and women. By this logic, it might well have been permissible in *Frank v. United Airlines, Inc.,* 216 F.3d 845 (9th Cir.2000), to require women, but not men, to meet a medium body frame standard *if* that requirement were imposed as part of a "physical appearance" policy that also required men, but not women, to achieve a certain degree of upper body muscle definition. But the fact that employees of both genders are subjected to gender-specific requirements does not necessarily mean that particular requirements are not motivated by gender stereotyping.

Because I believe that we should be careful not to insulate appearance requirements by viewing them in broad categories, such as "hair, hands, and face," I would consider the makeup requirement on its own terms. Viewed in isolation—or, at the very least, as part of a narrower category of requirements affecting employees' faces—the makeup or facial uniform requirement becomes closely analogous to the uniform policy held to constitute impermissible sex stereotyping in *Carroll v. Talman Federal Savings & Loan Ass'n of Chicago,* 604 F.2d 1028, 1029 (7th Cir.1979). In *Carroll,* the defendant bank required women to wear employer-issued uniforms, but permitted men to wear business attire of their own choosing. The Seventh Circuit found this rule discriminatory because it suggested to the public that the uniformed women held a "lesser professional status" and that women could not be trusted to choose appropriate business attire. *Id.* at 1032–33.

Just as the bank in *Carroll* deemed female employees incapable of achieving a professional appearance without assigned uniforms, Harrah's regarded women as unable to achieve a neat, attractive, and professional appearance without the facial uniform designed by a consultant and required by Harrah's. The inescapable message is that women's undoctored faces compare unfavorably to men's, not because of a physical difference between men's and women's faces, but because of a cultural assumption—and gender-based stereotype—that women's faces are incomplete, unattractive, or unprofessional without full makeup. We need not denounce all makeup as inherently offensive, just as there was no need to denounce all uniforms as inherently offensive in *Carroll,* to conclude that *requiring* female bartenders to wear full makeup is an impermissible sex stereotype and is evidence of discrimination because of sex. Therefore, I strongly disagree with the majority's conclusion that there "is no evidence in this record to indicate that the policy was adopted to make women bartenders conform to a commonly-accepted stereotypical image of what women should wear." * * *

KOZINSKI, CIRCUIT JUDGE, with whom JUDGES GRABER and W. FLETCHER join, dissenting:

I agree with Judge Pregerson and join his dissent—subject to one caveat: I believe that Jespersen also presented a triable issue of fact on the question of disparate burden.

The majority is right that "[t]he [makeup] requirements must be viewed in the context of the overall policy." But I find it perfectly clear that Harrah's overall grooming policy is substantially more burdensome for women than for men. Every requirement that forces men to spend time or money on their appearance has a corresponding requirement that is as, or more, burdensome for women: short hair v. "teased, curled, or styled" hair; clean trimmed nails v. nail length and color requirements; black leather shoes v. black leather shoes. The requirement that women spend time and money applying full facial makeup has no corresponding requirement for men, making the "overall policy" more burdensome for the former than for the latter. The only question is how much.

It is true that Jespersen failed to present evidence about what it costs to buy makeup and how long it takes to apply it. But is there any doubt that putting on makeup costs money and takes time? Harrah's policy requires women to apply face powder, blush, mascara and lipstick. You don't need an expert witness to figure out that such items don't grow on trees.

Nor is there any rational doubt that application of makeup is an intricate and painstaking process that requires considerable time and care. Even those of us who don't wear makeup know how long it can take from the hundreds of hours we've spent over the years frantically tapping our toes and pointing to our wrists. It's hard to imagine that a woman could "put on her face," as they say, in the time it would take a man to shave—certainly not if she were to do the careful and thorough job Harrah's expects. Makeup, moreover, must be applied and removed every day; the policy burdens men with no such daily ritual. While a man could jog to the casino, slip into his uniform, and get right to work, a woman must travel to work so as to avoid smearing her makeup, or arrive early to put on her makeup there.

It might have been tidier if Jespersen had introduced evidence as to the time and cost associated with complying with the makeup requirement, but I can understand her failure to do so, as these hardly seem like questions reasonably subject to dispute. We could—and should—take judicial notice of these incontrovertible facts.

Alternatively, Jespersen did introduce evidence that she finds it burdensome to *wear* makeup because doing so is inconsistent with her self-image and interferes with her job performance. My colleagues dismiss this evidence, apparently on the ground that wearing makeup does not, as a matter of law, constitute a substantial burden. This presupposes that Jespersen is unreasonable or idiosyncratic in her discomfort. Why so? Whether to wear cosmetics—literally, the face one presents to the world—is an intensely personal choice. Makeup, moreover, touches delicate parts of the anatomy—the lips, the eyes, the cheeks—and can cause serious discomfort, sometimes even allergic reactions, for someone unaccustomed to wearing it. If you are used to wearing makeup—as most American women are—this may seem like no big deal. But those of us not used to wearing makeup would find a requirement that we do so highly intrusive. Imagine, for example, a rule that all judges wear face powder, blush, mascara and lipstick while on the bench. Like Jespersen, I would find such a regime burdensome and demeaning; it would interfere with my job performance. I suspect many of my colleagues would feel the same way.

Everyone accepts this as a reasonable reaction from a man, but why should it be different for a woman? It is not because of anatomical differences, such as a requirement that women wear bathing suits that cover their breasts. Women's faces, just like those of men, can be perfectly presentable without makeup; it is a cultural artifact that most women raised in the United States learn to put on—and presumably enjoy wearing—cosmetics. But cultural norms change; not so long ago a man wearing an earring was a gypsy, a pirate or an oddity. Today, a man wearing body piercing jewelry is hardly noticed. So, too, a large (and perhaps growing) number of women choose to present themselves to the world without makeup. I see no justification for forcing them to conform to Harrah's quaint notion of what a "real woman" looks like.

Nor do I think it appropriate for a court to dismiss a woman's testimony that she finds wearing makeup degrading and intrusive, as Jespersen clearly does. Not only do we have her sworn statement to that effect, but there can be no doubt about her sincerity or the intensity of her feelings: She quit her job—a job she performed well for two decades—rather than put on the makeup. That is a choice her male colleagues were not forced to make. To me, this states a case of disparate burden, and I would let a jury decide whether an employer can force a woman to make this choice.

Finally, I note with dismay the employer's decision to let go a valued, experienced employee who had gained accolades from her customers, over what, in the end, is a trivial matter. Quality employees are difficult to find in any industry and I would think an employer would long hesitate before forcing a loyal, long-time employee to quit over an honest and heartfelt difference of opinion about a matter of personal significance to her. Having won the legal battle, I hope that Harrah's will now do the generous and decent thing by offering Jespersen her job back, and letting her give it her personal best—without the makeup.

NOTES AND QUESTIONS

1. *Unequal Burdens*: *Jespersen* holds that the "unequal burdens" test is an appropriate test to apply to sex-based grooming standards and that Harrah's makeup requirements did not impose an unequal burden on female bartenders as compared to male bartenders. How did the court reach these conclusions? In evaluating the burden of grooming requirements on each sex, is the appropriate comparison between the makeup rule for women and the no makeup rule for men as Judge Pregerson argued in dissent? Or is the majority more persuasive in ruling that all of the employer's grooming requirements for women should be weighed against all of its grooming requirements for men?

2. *The Reasonableness of Grooming Standards*: Does it matter for purposes of determining that Harrah's sex-based grooming policy is

reasonable—and therefore not discriminatory under Title VII—whether the standards reflect widely accepted community norms about how men and women do or should appear? If so, what community or communities are relevant in considering these questions? The city of Reno where Jespersen worked? The customers of casinos, or of sports bars or bars generally? The image consultants who advise casino owners and other businesses in the entertainment industry? How did the *Jespersen* court reach its conclusion that Harrah's policies are reasonable? Are these questions that should best be left to juries?

3. *Judicial Notice and the Costs of Dress and Grooming Rules*: Writing for the majority in *Jespersen*, Chief Judge Mary Schroeder stated that Darlene Jespersen did not raise a triable issue of fact about the burden of the grooming policy on women because she failed to present any evidence of the time and cost of complying with the rule. In his dissent in *Jespersen,* Judge Alex Kozinski disagreed, arguing that the court should take judicial notice of the "incontrovertible facts" that "putting on makeup costs money and takes time." Do you find the majority or the dissent more persuasive on this issue? Could the fact that the writer of the majority opinion, Chief Judge Schroeder, is a woman and, Judge Kozinski is a man have affected their willingness to take judicial notice of the time and cost of putting on makeup for work every day? Is Judge Kozinski's view of the "incontrovertible facts" about the time women spend putting on makeup itself a stereotype? On the other hand, does the majority, in effect, take judicial notice of the reasonableness of the sex-based appearance norms of the entertainment industry while, at the same time, refusing to take judicial notice of how (and how much) makeup gets applied to the faces of the female employees in that industry? What about the costs of allergies or other adverse medical reactions to makeup, which Judge Kozinski raises? What about other potential health risks of dress and grooming rules? *See, e.g.*, Marc Linder, *Smart Women, Stupid Shoes, and Cynical Employers: The Unlawfulness and Adverse Health Consequences of Sexually Discriminatory Workplace Footwear Requirements for Female Employees*, 22 J.Corp.L. 295, 298 (1997) (discussing the health risks of wearing high-heel shoes for work); Deborah L. Rhode, *The Injustice of Appearance*, 61 Stan.L.Rev. 1033, 1044–48 (2009) (discussing health risks from cosmetics, cosmetic surgery, and dieting). Is it fair to place the burden of producing evidence on the costs of an employer's grooming rule on the plaintiff? Why or why not?

4. *Sex Stereotyping*: The court in *Jespersen* also holds that "appearance standards, including makeup requirements, may well be the subject of a Title VII claim for sexual stereotyping, but * * * on this record Jespersen has failed to create any triable issue of fact that the challenged policy was part of a policy motivated by sex stereotyping." 444 F.3d at 1106. Is it necessary for a plaintiff to prove unlawful intent or motive when a workplace policy is discriminatory on its face? Is a requirement that women wear makeup based on a stereotype about how women should appear or about how they usually do appear? Does a mandatory makeup requirement subordinate women?

yes!

Professor Jennifer Levi argues that sex-stereotyping and anti-subordination analyses of sex-based dress and grooming rules fail to capture their harms under the anti-differentiation principle of discrimination law. She asserts that:

> courts have relied (overly so) upon group anti-subordination equality theory and ignore the "first-order" equality principle that different treatment of individuals is itself harmful even in the absence of demonstrable group-based harm. * * * The harm caused by these dress codes is perceived exclusively as an individualized harm not shared by other members of the affected class. However, Title VII, * * * does not require a showing of group harm. It only requires that an individual be able to demonstrate that he or she has been affected personally on the basis of gender—not that all men or all women are similarly affected by differential treatment.

Jennifer L. Levi, *Misapplying Equality Theories: Dress Codes at Work,* 19 Yale J.L. & Feminism 353, 356–57 (2008). Do you agree? How would this approach have helped Darlene Jespersen?

In any event, does it make sense to use litigation to attempt to alter gendered social norms about makeup, even—or especially—in the workplace? Professor Michael Selmi argued that:

> Jespersen's claim might be seen as a search for * * * authenticity, a desire to be true to one's self in and out of the workplace. But the workplace is not traditionally a place for authenticity: It is a place of uniforms and conformity, a place where we go to be someone else, to perform for someone else, and a legally protectable claim to authenticity threatens to unravel the existing workplace structure.

Michael Selmi, *The Many Faces of Darlene Jespersen,* 14 Duke J. Gender L. & Pol'y 467, 468 (2007) (citation omitted). Would you agree?

5. Price Waterhouse *and Sexual Harassment*: The *Jespersen* court stressed that this grooming case is distinguishable from the court's earlier cases that had applied *Price Waterhouse* gender stereotyping analysis to situations where male employees were sexually harassed by male co-workers because they failed to conform to stereotypical gender norms. *See* Rene v. MGM Grand Hotel, Inc., 305 F.3d 1061, 1068–69 (9th Cir.2002) (en banc), reproduced in Chapter 9; Nichols v. Azteca Rest. Enters., Inc., 256 F.3d 864, 874 (9th Cir.2001). Does the court leave open the possibility of using gender stereotyping in a future grooming case simply because it does not feel comfortable rejecting the theory entirely in light of its reliance on *Price Waterhouse* in the *Rene* and *Nichols* cases? Was there a risk that Jespersen might be harassed by co-workers or customers if she wore makeup in order to appear at her "Personal Best"? If not, what was her concern? For a discussion of Title VII protections from sexual harassment for women who work in sexualized environments, see Ann C. McGinley, *Harassing Girls at the "Hard Rock": Masculinities in Sexualized Environments*, 2007 U.Ill.L.Rev. 1229.

6. *Stereotyping Women as Sex Objects*: The court in *Jespersen* concludes that Harrah's dress and grooming policy for its bartenders was not "intended to be sexually provocative" or "to stereotype women as sex objects," which might, indeed, lead to sexual harassment. Harrah's undoubtedly intends that the grooming and costumes for the show girls and female dancers in its casinos and night clubs will convey a "sexually provocative" image. *See also* McGinley, *Harassing Girls*, *supra*, note 5, at 1239–40 (describing the sexy dress and makeup required for female dealers at the Hard Rock Café in Las Vegas); Ann C. McGinley, *Babes and Beefcake: Exclusive Hiring Arrangements and Sexy Dress Codes*, 14 Duke J. Gender L. & Pol'y 257, 260–61 (2007) (describing sexy dress codes for female cocktail servers in casinos). The court, however, describes Harrah's bartenders' uniform as "unisex" and "designed for men and women." If the uniform is the same for both male and female bartenders and is, arguably, not intended to be "sexually provocative," why does Harrah's have different grooming requirements for male and female bartenders? Why did Darlene Jespersen believe that Harrah's imposition of the makeup requirement treated her as a "sex object"? *See generally* Dianne Avery, *The Great American Makeover: The Sexing Up and Dumbing Down of Women's Work After* Jespersen v. Harrah's Operating Co., Inc., 42 U.S.F. L.Rev. 299 (2007) (critiquing sex-based dress codes and sexualization of women's work).

7. In light of the court's unequal burdens and stereotyping analysis in *Jespersen*, could any employer adopt a policy requiring its female employees to wear makeup to work—and prohibiting male employees from wearing makeup—without violating Title VII? For example, could a law firm require all female associates to wear makeup? Could a law school require all female professors to wear makeup? If a plaintiff could produce evidence that applying makeup is more burdensome in cost and time than not wearing makeup, would that be the end of makeup rules? What if an employer compensates female employees for the additional cost and time of wearing makeup on the job? Wouldn't the cost and time burdens on men and women then be equal? Would that resolve the issue of the burden on women of the stereotype that "women's faces are incomplete, unattractive, or unprofessional without full makeup"? *Jespersen,* 444 F.3d at 1116 (Pregerson, J., dissenting).

8. *Sex-Based Weight Requirements*: Many airlines require applicants for flight attendant positions to meet specified height and weight standards. The maximum weight limits are generally set according to insurance industry charts showing average heights and weights for men and women by age. In general, courts tend to treat an airline's use of dual sex-based weight standards derived from insurance industry data with the same deference they give to sex-based dress and grooming codes that are designed to assure that employees who come in contact with the public have a pleasing, attractive appearance. *See, e.g.*, Jarrell v. Eastern Airlines, 430 F.Supp. 884 (E.D.Va.1977) (rejecting disparate treatment and disparate impact claims in upholding dual sex-based weight maximums for male and female flight

attendants), *aff'd*, 577 F.2d 869 (4th Cir.1978) (per curiam). *See* Pamela Whitesides, Note, *Flight Attendant Weight Policies: A Title VII Wrong Without a Remedy*, 64 S.Cal.L.Rev. 175 (1990) (discussing *Jarrell* case, *id.* at 204–08, and other unsuccessful Title VII challenges to airline weight policies). The court in *Jespersen* discusses the unequal burdens rationale that it relied on in *Frank v. United Airlines, Inc.*, 216 F.3d 845 (9th Cir.2000), to find that the airline's weight policy discriminated against female flight attendants. Explain why the court in *Frank* found the airline's sex-based weight policy unlawful under Title VII. Is the use of sex-based weight charts to screen job applicants unlawful per se? What evidence would be sufficient to make out a "gender-plus-weight" claim? *See* Kate Sablosky, *Probative "Weight": Rethinking Evidentiary Standards in Title VII Sex Discrimination Cases*, 30 N.Y.U.Rev.L. & Soc. Change 325 (2006). Challenges to weight restrictions in employment that are brought under disability law are treated in Chapter 14.

9. *Physical Attractiveness*: There is some evidence that people who are considered good looking earn higher wages than people whose looks are considered below average. *See generally* Daniel S. Hamermesh, Beauty Pays: Why Attractive People are More Successful (2013); Daniel S. Hamermesh & Jeff E. Biddle, *Beauty and the Labor Market*, 84 Am.Econ.Rev. 1174 (1994). Should discrimination based on physical appearance be treated differently from dress and grooming codes because one's appearance is "immutable"? Is it unfair to discriminate against people because of bodily or facial characteristics that they cannot change? Is "lookism"—discrimination on the basis of one's appearance—a phenomenon that harms women in the labor market more than men? If so, would it be unlawful sex discrimination for a male manager to base an employment decision on a female employee's sexual attractiveness? Consider the following: Sandra is employed to sell men's fragrances in a large up-scale department store. In her first year, Sandra's sales record was one of the best of all sales associates for men's fragrances in the store's regional division. At the end of the year, during a tour of the men's fragrance department, Jack, the new manager of the Designer Fragrance Division, observed Sandra working at her counter. He later told Sandra's supervisor, Elysa, that she should fire Sandra because she was "not good looking enough." Jack said, "Get me somebody hot." If Sandra is fired, does she have a claim for sex discrimination? What if Elysa refuses to carry out Jack's order to fire Sandra because she believes that it is discriminatory to fire a female employee simply because she is not sufficiently sexually attractive to a male manager? If she is then fired for refusing to carry out the manager's order would she have a claim for retaliation under Title VII? *See* Yanowitz v. L'Oreal USA, Inc., 116 P.3d 1123, 1132 (Cal. 2005) (holding on these facts that Elysa had engaged in protected opposition conduct under retaliation provision of the state human rights law). Retaliation claims are discussed in Chapter 3.C. *See also* Stacey S. Baron, Note, *(Un)Lawfully Beautiful: The Legal (De)Construction of Female Beauty*, 46 B.C.L.Rev. 359 (2005) (discussing the *Yanowitz* case and the role of the law in challenging "the use of the female body as a consumer artifact," *id.* at 361).

10. *State and Local Laws Prohibiting Appearance Discrimination*: Although Congress has not enacted a statutory prohibition against appearance discrimination in employment, other government entities have passed such laws. For example, the District of Columbia Human Rights Act prohibits discrimination on the basis of "appearance." D.C. Code § 1–2502(22) defines "appearance" as:

> the outward appearance of any person, irrespective of sex, with regard to bodily condition or characteristics, manner or style of dress, and manner or style of personal grooming, including, but not limited to, hair style and beards. It shall not relate, however, to the requirement of * * * prescribed standards * * * when uniformly applied to a class of employees for a reasonable business purpose * * * .

If a female office worker at a lobbying firm in Washington, D.C., is criticized by her supervisor and then discharged because she wears "low cut and tight blouses" and has "disheveled hair," would she have a viable appearance discrimination claim under the D.C. Human Rights Act? *See* Atlantic Richfield Co. v. D.C. Comm'n on Hum. Rights, 515 A.2d 1095, 1100–01 (D.C.1986) (holding that substantial evidence supported Commission's finding that employer discriminated against employee on the basis of her personal appearance where it concluded that her appearance was not different from that of other employees). In 1992, Santa Cruz, California, adopted a controversial appearance ordinance banning discrimination on the basis of height, weight, and appearance. *See* Robert Post, *Prejudicial Appearances: The Logic of American Antidiscrimination Law*, 88 Cal.L.Rev. 1 (2000) (discussing the Santa Cruz ordinance in light of a sociological account of the limits of antidiscrimination laws in regulating appearance); Rhode, *supra*, note 3, at 1081–90 (examining antidiscrimination statutes and ordinances in the United States that regulate appearance of workers, including the Santa Cruz ordinance). *See also* William R. Corbett, *The Ugly Truth About Appearance Discrimination and the Beauty of Our Employment Discrimination Law*, 14 Duke J. Gender L. & Pol'y 153 (2007) (predicting that "federal employment discrimination law will never prohibit appearance-based discrimination, and few if any state discrimination laws will add appearance as a protected characteristic," and that "appearance-based discrimination will continue to be on the periphery, with cases being pulled under existing categories when arguably viable," *id.* at 158).

11. *Intersecting Claims of Sex and Race*: In *Rogers v. American Airlines, Inc.*, 527 F.Supp. 229, 231 (S.D.N.Y.1981), an airline grooming rule prohibited all employees who dealt with the public "from wearing an all-braided hairstyle." A female African-American employee who wanted to wear her hair braided in "corn rows" unsuccessfully challenged the rule under Title VII on the grounds of sex and race discrimination. The court reached the conclusion that there was no discrimination by analyzing the sex and race claims separately. Should the court have treated the plaintiff as member of a protected class consisting of black women? *See generally* Paulette Caldwell, *A*

Hair Piece: Perspectives on the Intersection of Race and Gender, 1991 Duke L.J. 365; Kimberly A. Yuracko, *Trait Discrimination as Race Discrimination: An Argument About Assimilation*, 74 Geo.Wash.L.Rev. 365 (2006) (exploring the nature of workplace discrimination on the basis of culturally linked racial and ethnic traits).

12. For an account of the history of the *Jespersen* litigation from its inception through the 2004 three-judge panel decision, see Devon Carbado, Mitu Gulati & Gowri Ramachandran, *The Jespersen Story: Makeup and Women at Work,* in Employment Discrimination Stories 105 (Joel W. Friedman, ed. 2005). *See also* Avery & Crain, *supra*, Note 9; Selmi, supra, Note 4. Employer dress and grooming rules, whether formal or informal, have been the subject of much scholarly criticism. In addition to the articles cited above in this section, see Mark R. Bandsuch, *Dressing Up Title VII's Analysis of Workplace Appearance Policies*, 40 Colum.Hum.Rts.L.Rev. 287 (2009); Symposium, *Makeup, Identity Performance & Discrimination*, 14 Duke J. Gender Law & Pol'y1 (2007); Catherine L. Fisk, *Privacy, Power, and Humiliation at Work: Re-Examining Appearance Regulation as an Invasion of Privacy*, 66 La.L.Rev. 1111 (2006).

F. SYSTEMIC CLAIMS AND THE GLASS CEILING

During the 1990s and 2000s, many plaintiffs filed class action lawsuits challenging a range of workplace policies that allegedly limited promotion and compensation opportunities for women. *See, e.g.*, Tristin K. Green, *Targeting Workplace Context: Title VII as a Tool for Institutional Reform*, 72 Fordham L.Rev. 659, 660 (2003). While the specific allegations in each of these cases have depended on the policies and practices in place at the particular workplace, all of the cases focused on challenging the aggregate results of practices that, while appearing at first neutral, in fact led to systemic disadvantaging of women in the challenged workplace. The evidence presented in these suits showed, according to the plaintiffs, that women have had fewer promotional opportunities and that their compensation has been consistently lower than their male colleagues, even when the female workers have been performing better or have been with the company longer. These "glass-ceiling" lawsuits have been pursued in industries ranging from financial services to grocery and "big box" stores. *See, e.g.*, Chen-Oster v. Goldman, Sachs & Co., 285 F.R.D. 294 (SDNY 2012); Wal-Mart Stores, Inc. v. Dukes, 564 U.S. 338, 131 S.Ct. 2541 (2011); Ellis v. Costco Wholesale Corp., 240 F.R.D. 627 (N.D.Cal.2007); Butler v. Home Depot, Inc., No. C–94–4335, 1996 WL 421436 (N.D.Cal. Jan. 25, 1996); Stender v. Lucky Stores, Inc., 803 F.Supp. 259 (N.D.Cal.1992).

The Supreme Court's 2011 decision in *Wal-Mart Stores, Inc. v. Dukes* (reproduced in Chapter 3), which reversed the certification of the largest gender discrimination class in U.S. history, called into question the continued viability of these private class action lawsuits. The *Dukes* plaintiffs sought to represent a class of more than one million current and former female employees at Wal-Mart's 3400 stores around the country. The suit challenged Wal-Mart's pay and promotion policies, alleging that in both contexts the company gave local managers too much unguided discretion and that this unguided discretion was used disproportionately and consistently in favor of male employees. The plaintiffs showed that, although women filled 70 percent of the hourly jobs at Wal-Mart, they were only 33 percent of management employees. Further, women were paid less than men in every region and "the salary gap widens over time even for men and women hired into the same jobs at the same time." 564 U.S. 338, 131 S.Ct. 2541, 2563 (Ginsburg, J., dissenting).

The district court certified the class, and that certification decision was upheld by the Ninth Circuit. In reversing the decision to certify, the Supreme Court found that the plaintiffs could not satisfy the Federal Rule of Civil Procedure 23 requirement that their claims encompass common questions. The Court described the class allegations, and explained its reasons for rejecting those reasons, as follows:

> These plaintiffs, respondents here, do not allege that Wal-Mart has any express corporate policy against the advancement of women. Rather, they claim that their local managers' discretion over pay and promotions is exercised disproportionately in favor of men, leading to an unlawful disparate impact on female employees, see 42 U.S.C. § 2000e–2(k). And, respondents say, because Wal-Mart is aware of this effect, its refusal to cabin its managers' authority amounts to disparate treatment, see § 2000e–2(a). * * * Importantly for our purposes, respondents claim that the discrimination to which they have been subjected is common to *all* Wal-Mart's female employees. The basic theory of their case is that a strong and uniform "corporate culture" permits bias against women to infect, perhaps subconsciously, the discretionary decisionmaking of each one of Wal-Mart's thousands of managers—thereby making every woman at the company the victim of one common discriminatory practice. Respondents therefore wish to litigate the Title VII claims of all female employees at Wal-Mart's stores in a nationwide class action. * * *
>
> The only corporate policy that the plaintiffs' evidence convincingly establishes is Wal-Mart's "policy" of *allowing discretion* by local supervisors over employment matters. On its face, of course, that is just the opposite of a uniform employment practice that would provide the commonality needed for a class action; it is a policy *against having* uniform employment practices. It is also a very common and presumptively reasonable

> way of doing business—one that we have said "should itself raise no inference of discriminatory conduct," *Watson v. Fort Worth Bank & Trust,* 487 U.S. 977, 990, 108 S.Ct. 2777, 101 L.Ed.2d 827 (1988). To be sure, we have recognized that, "in appropriate cases," giving discretion to lower-level supervisors can be the basis of Title VII liability under a disparate-impact theory—since "an employer's undisciplined system of subjective decisionmaking [can have] precisely the same effects as a system pervaded by impermissible intentional discrimination." *Id.,* at 990–991, 108 S.Ct. 2777. But the recognition that this type of Title VII claim "can" exist does not lead to the conclusion that every employee in a company using a system of discretion has such a claim in common. To the contrary, left to their own devices most managers in any corporation—and surely most managers in a corporation that forbids sex discrimination—would select sex-neutral, performance-based criteria for hiring and promotion that produce no actionable disparity at all. Others may choose to reward various attributes that produce disparate impact—such as scores on general aptitude tests or educational achievements, see *Griggs v. Duke Power Co.,* 401 U.S. 424, 431–432, 91 S.Ct. 849, 28 L.Ed.2d 158 (1971). And still other managers may be guilty of intentional discrimination that produces a sex-based disparity. In such a company, demonstrating the invalidity of one manager's use of discretion will do nothing to demonstrate the invalidity of another's. A party seeking to certify a nationwide class will be unable to show that all the employees' Title VII claims will in fact depend on the answers to common questions.

Id. at 2548–2554.

Following the Court's decision in *Dukes*, many of the plaintiffs filed smaller, more localized class action suits, alleging the same type of discrimination, but narrowing the claims to focus on particular regions, stores, or decisionmakers. Phipps v. Wal-Mart Stores, Inc., 792 F.3d 637, 641–42 (6th Cir.2015) (describing these follow-on suits). These more limited class action suits have not fared well in the lower courts. In two of the cases, the class claims were dismissed, with the courts concluding that the plaintiffs "have not shown how the class they propose solves any of the problems the Court found in *Dukes*." Ladik v. Wal-Mart Stores, Inc., 291 F.R.D. 263, 265 (W.D. Wis.2013). *See also* Dukes v. Wal-Mart Stores, Inc., 964 F.Supp.2d 1115, 1118 (N.D. Cal. 2013) ("[T]hough they have cut down the raw number of proposed class members significantly, Plaintiffs continue to challenge four different kinds of decisions across hundreds of decisionmakers."). In a third, the court found the claims to be time-barred. Love v. Wal-Mart Stores, Inc., 2013 WL 543565, *1 (S.D. Fl.

Sept. 23, 2013). A fourth follow-on suit is still being litigated. Phipps, 792 F.3d at 640. Even the courts that have denied certification have emphasized that the procedural question of whether plaintiffs' claims can proceed as a class action is distinct from the question of whether an employer should examine and perhaps change workplace policies and practices. As one court expressed it:

> In concluding that the plaintiffs cannot proceed as a class action, I do not mean to question the seriousness of the allegations in the complaint. These allegations paint a disturbing picture about defendant's attitude and treatment of its female employees over the course of many years. If true, they demand immediate and comprehensive action by defendant to investigate and correct the problems. However, even the most serious problems cannot always be resolved by a class action lawsuit.

Ladik, 291 F.R.D. at 265.

The Supreme Court's decision in *Dukes* led some commentators to conclude that employment discrimination class action litigation was a thing of the past. *See, e.g.* Marcia C. McCormick, *Implausible Injuries:* Wal-Mart v. Dukes *and the Future of Class Actions and Employment Discrimination Cases*, 62 Depaul L. Rev. 711, 728 (2013). Others have argued that the decision, while it narrowed the scope of permissible class litigation, left some room for lawsuits challenging specific employer policies that impermissibly burden women's advancement at work. Professor Michael Harper, for example, notes that courts since *Dukes* have continued to certify class claims "where the alleged degree of involvement of central management in the allegedly discriminatory decisions made plausible that every member of the class could have been affected by the same discriminatory intent." Michael C. Harper, *Class-Based Adjudication of Title VII Claims in the Age of the Roberts Court*, B.U. L. Rev. 1112 (2015). Harper further observes that "[t]his ultimately is the unsurprising lesson iterated by the Supreme Court in *Wal-Mart*: class litigation is appropriate only where it will be more efficient because each member of the requested class has a potential Title VII claim that turns on resolution of a common issue—either the existence of discriminatory intent, whether conscious or unconscious, from the same decisionmakers, or the unjustified disparate impact of a specific employment practice applied to all members of the class." *Id.* at 1113. See also Elizabeth Tippett, *Robbing a Barren Vault: The Implications of* Dukes v. Wal-Mart *for Cases Challenging Subjective Employment Practices*, 29 Hofstra Lab. & Emp. L.J. 433, 435 (2012) (arguing that the impact of *Dukes* will be limited for most employers and employees because most litigation encompasses more circumscribed class definitions than that at issue in *Dukes*); Katherine E. Lamm, *Work in Progress: Civil Rights Class Actions After Wal-Mart v. Dukes*, 50 Harv. C.R.–C.L. L. Rev.

153, 155 (2015) (noting that "post-Dukes decisions show that plaintiffs may prevail when they assert focused class allegations supported by a well-developed and tailored factual record").

Professor Michael Selmi has observed that the *Dukes* decision, without explicitly overruling any of the Court's earlier cases, undermined the continuing validity of the 1970s decisions in which the Court accepted relatively unsophisticated statistical models for proving discrimination. *See* Michael Selmi, *The Evolution of Employment Discrimination Law: Changed Doctrine for Changed Social Conditions*, 2014 Wis. L. Rev. 937, 992 (2014). The Court's reluctance to endorse reliance on statistics to the same extent in the 2000s as it had in the 1970s, Selmi argues, may trace to the view that statistical disparities in the early days of Title VII were in fact more likely to be attributable to discrimination. Today, "there is little question that the inferences one can draw from statistical workforce imbalances are now diminished." *Id.* at 993. Do you agree?

Professor Selmi goes on to observe that class actions challenging systemic discrimination are still viable after *Dukes*, but that:

> As a practical matter, this will lead to cases in which the employer either has a demonstrated history of discrimination—much like in the early days of Title VII—or there is clear evidence of a culture of discrimination. This was true in the series of cases involving the securities industry where the plaintiffs were able to demonstrate that the companies treated women differently and disparagingly. Indeed, many of the cases involved graphic and extreme examples of sexist behavior, including trips to strip clubs and the appearance of strippers in the office. These cases also involved statistical presentations, but the anecdotal evidence bolstered the statistical case.

Id. at 994. The securities cases to which Professor Selmi refers are described in some detail in Susan Antilla, Tales from the Boom-Boom Room: Women vs. Wall Street 10 (2002). As Selmi notes "[d]uring the 1990s, many, if not most, of the major securities firms were sued for sex discrimination; however, most of the cases settled and only a few produced written opinions." Selmi, *supra* at 994, n. 246. *See, e.g.*, *Martens v. Smith Barney Inc.*, No. 96 Civ. 3779(CBM), 1998 WL 1661385, at *1 (S.D.N.Y. July 28, 1998); *Cremin v. Merrill Lynch Pierce Fenner & Smith, Inc.*, 957 F. Supp. 1460, 1462–1465 (N.D. Ill. 1997).

Wal-Mart is the largest retailer and the largest private employer in the United States. With the Supreme Court's *Wal-Mart* decision foreclosing class actions with the scope of the *Dukes* lawsuit, how else can employees change company practices, such as subjective decisionmaking, which could account for findings of gender-based disparities in compensation and promotions? Are individual disparate treatment or disparate impact claims—involving a few plaintiffs at a particular store—likely to have much impact on the corporate culture of companies like Wal-Mart even if they are successful?

Importantly, while the *Dukes* decision has impacted the scope of private class actions alleging systemic discrimination, the EEOC is able to pursue systemic claims through its authority to bring pattern or practice challenges independent of Rule 23's commonality requirements. In recent years, the agency has made systemic discrimination a significant enforcement priority. In its 2013 Strategic Enforcement Plan, the agency included systemic gender discrimination within three of its six enforcement priorities. The Plan explained that the EEOC would "target class-based intentional recruitment and hiring practices that adversely impact particular groups" and "compensation systems and practices that discriminate based on gender," and would focus on "systemic enforcement" of sexual harassment claims. U.S. Equal Employment Opportunity Commission, Strategic Enforcement Plan FY 2013–2016, available at *http://www.eeoc.gov/eeoc/plan/upload/sep.pdf.* In 2014, the EEOC conducted 260 investigations of claims of systemic discrimination, obtained 78 settlements and conciliation agreements as a result of those investigations, and filed 17 systemic lawsuits. By the end of the 2014 fiscal year, systemic litigation represented 25 percent of all active merits litigation, the largest proportion since the agency began tracking these numbers in 2006. *See* EEOC Issues FY 2014 Performance Report, available at *http://www.eeoc.gov/eeoc/newsroom/release/11–18–14.cfm. See generally* Margo Schlanger & Pauline Kim, *The Equal Employment Opportunity Commission and Structural Reform of the American Workplace*, 91 Wash. U. L. Rev. 1519 (2014).

— STOP —

CHAPTER 8

DISCRIMINATION BECAUSE OF PREGNANCY AND FAMILY RESPONSIBILITIES

■ ■ ■

A. INTRODUCTION AND HISTORICAL OVERVIEW

Discrimination against pregnant women and women with children has long been among the most serious impediments to gender equality in the workplace. As Congress understood in considering the Pregnancy Discrimination Act in 1977, "[t]he assumption that women will become pregnant and leave the labor force leads to the view of women as marginal workers, and is at the root of the discriminatory practices which keep women in low-paying and dead-end jobs." H.R. Rep. No. 95–948, at 3 (1978). In fact, for centuries before the passage of Title VII, women's capacity to bear children was regularly used to justify restricting their access to certain kinds of work, or to any work at all. When the Supreme Court upheld a law prohibiting women from being lawyers in 1873, Justice Joseph Bradley explained in his concurring opinion: "The natural and proper timidity and delicacy which belongs to the female sex evidently unfits it for many of the occupations of civil life. * * * The paramount destiny and mission of women are to fulfill the noble and benign offices of wife and mother." Bradwell v. Ill., 83 U.S. 130, 141, 21 L.Ed.442 (1873). And in the landmark case of *Muller v. Oregon*, the Court upheld a law establishing maximum hours of work for women, explaining, "that women's physical structure and the performance of maternal functions place her at a disadvantage in the struggle for subsistence is obvious. This is especially true when the burdens of motherhood are upon her." 208 U.S. 412, 421, 28 S.Ct. 324, 326, 52 L.Ed.551 (1907). By the middle of the twentieth century, when the number of women in the workforce was increasing steadily, women were still likely to leave their jobs when they became pregnant. Some left voluntarily, but many left either because they were forced to by their employers or because they knew that it would be only a matter of time before they would be required to leave. *See* Courtni E. Molnar, *Has the Millennium Yet Dawned?: A History of Attitudes Toward Pregnant Workers in America*, 12 Mich. J. Gender & L. 163, 170 (2005).

During the 1940s and 1950s, even the Women's Bureau of the Department of Labor, which was created to advocate for working women, recommended that women stop working six weeks before their due date and remain out of the workplace for at least two months after giving birth. Women's Bureau, Off. of the Sec'y, U.S. Dep't of Labor, Bull. No. 240, Maternity Protection of Employed Women 7 (1952). Many states and employers based mandatory pregnancy leave policies on this and other similar recommendations, with the consequence that women's ability to make their own judgments about when and whether to leave or return to work was essentially eliminated. "Pregnant women were considered unavailable for work for a set period of time before and after childbirth, whether or not they were willing to work." Molnar, *supra*, at 172. Even into the 1960s and 1970s, "many employers continued to refuse to hire pregnant women, to require them to leave before a certain point in their pregnancies, to exclude them from certain jobs, or to deny them fringe benefits like insurance, disability coverage, or leave." Joanna L. Grossman & Gillian L. Thomas, *Making Pregnancy Work: Overcoming the Pregnancy Discrimination Act's Capacity-Based Model*, 21 Yale J.L. & Feminism 15, 23 (2009).

Attitudes toward pregnant workers and working mothers changed considerably during the last several decades of the twentieth century, in part due to the passage of Title VII and the Pregnancy Discrimination Act, which made unlawful the kind of mandatory maternity leave policies that were once common. A study released by the Census Bureau in 2011 showed that, among women who had their first child between 2006 and 2008, 66 percent worked during their pregnancies and of those who worked, 65 percent stayed on the job until within a month of the child's birth. Lynda Laughlin, Maternity Leave and Employment Patterns of First-Time Mothers: 1961–2008, U.S. Census Bureau P70–128, at 6 (Oct. 2011). More than half of women returned to work within six months of the birth of their first child. *Id.* at 15. In 2013, almost 75 percent of women with children under the age of eighteen were working outside the home. Bureau of Labor Statistics, Women in the Labor Force: A Data Book, tbl. 6 (2014).

In spite of these changing demographics, discrimination on the basis of pregnancy is still a significant problem for working women. In fact, between 1997 and 2011, the number of pregnancy discrimination complaints filed with the EEOC and state fair employment agencies increased from about 4000 to about 6000 in a year. EEOC, Pregnancy Discrimination Charges EEOC & FEPAs Combined: FY 1997—FY 2011, available at *http://www.eeoc.gov/eeoc/statistics/enforcement/pregnancy.cfm*. In 2014, 3400 charges of pregnancy discrimination were filed with the EEOC alone. EEOC, Pregnancy Discrimination Charges: FY 2010—FY2014, available at *http://www.eeoc.gov/eeoc/statistics/enforcement/*

pregnancy_new.cfm. Working mothers similarly face continued discrimination. As Chief Justice Rehnquist wrote in 2003, "the faultline between work and family [is] precisely where sex-based overgeneralization has been and remains strongest." Nev. Dep't of Hum. Resources v. Hibbs, 538 U.S. 721, 731, 123 S.Ct. 1972, 155 L.Ed.2d 953 (2003). This "sex-based overgeneralization" can affect both men and women, relying on stereotypes about proper roles to penalize both sexes when the obligations of work and family conflict.

This chapter considers legal protections currently available for pregnancy discrimination and for discrimination against parents and others with family caregiving responsibilities. Section B discusses the Pregnancy Discrimination Act. Section C explores remedies for what has come to be known as "family responsibility discrimination."

B. THE PREGNANCY DISCRIMINATION ACT

With the passage of Title VII in 1964, it might have been reasonable to believe that pregnancy discrimination had been declared unlawful. In 1973, the Equal Employment Opportunity Commission issued formal guidelines expressing the Commission's view that discrimination on the basis of pregnancy was sex discrimination. *See* 29 C.F.R. § 1604.10 (1973). All of the courts of appeals and the vast majority of district courts to consider whether pregnancy discrimination was sex discrimination had similarly concluded that it was. *See* AT&T Corp. v. Hulteen, 129 S.Ct. 1962, 1974 & n.2, 173 L.Ed.2d 898 (2009) (Ginsburg, J., dissenting) (discussing history). The Supreme Court, however, took a different view. In *General Electric Co. v. Gilbert,* 429 U.S. 125, 97 S.Ct. 401, 50 L.Ed.2d 343 (1976), the Court upheld a short-term disability plan that was otherwise comprehensive, but that excluded pregnancy-related conditions from its coverage. The Court concluded that, because not all women are pregnant, discrimination against pregnancy is not sex discrimination. *Id.* at 135. Moreover, the majority held that the plan treated the sexes equally because it offered identical coverage to men and women. *Id.* at 139–40. The dissenting Justices argued that the relevant question was not whether the coverage was identical, but whether it was equally comprehensive for women as it was for men. *Id.* at 152 (Brennan, J., dissenting). They further argued that, since only women can become pregnant, excluding pregnancy from coverage was in fact sex discrimination. *Id.* at 161–62 (Stevens, J., dissenting).

Shortly after the *Gilbert* decision was handed down, Congress began considering the amendment to Title VII that was passed as the Pregnancy Discrimination Act ("PDA") in 1978. The PDA provided a definition of the terms "because of sex" and "on the basis of sex," making clear that they "include, but are not limited to, because of or on the basis of pregnancy, childbirth or related medical conditions, and women affected by pregnancy, childbirth or related medical conditions shall be treated the same for all employment-related purposes * * * as other persons not so affected but similar in their ability or inability to work." 42 U.S.C. § 2000e(k).

Newport News Shipbuilding & Dry Dock Co. v. EEOC, 462 U.S. 669, 103 S.Ct. 2622, 77 L.Ed.2d 89 (1983) presented the Supreme Court with its first opportunity to interpret the PDA. When the Amendment went into effect, Newport News Shipbuilding amended its health insurance offerings so that its female employees received benefits for pregnancy-related conditions to the same extent that they did for other medical needs. The amended plan did not change the coverage offered to the pregnant wives of male employees. The company's male employees challenged the new plan under the PDA and the Supreme Court held that "[u]nder the proper test petitioner's plan is unlawful, because the protection it affords to married male employees is less comprehensive than the protection it affords to married female employees." *Id.* at 675. The Court elaborated, explaining that:

> Section 703(a) makes it an unlawful employment practice for an employer to "discriminate against any individual with respect to his compensation, terms, conditions, or privileges of employment, because of such individual's race, color, religion, sex, or national origin * * * ." Health insurance and other fringe benefits are "compensation, terms, conditions, or privileges of employment." Male as well as female employees are protected against discrimination. Thus, if a private employer were to provide complete health insurance coverage for the dependents of its female employees, and no coverage at all for the dependents of its male employees, it would violate Title VII.[22]
>
> * * * Petitioner's practice is just as unlawful. Its plan provides limited pregnancy-related benefits for employees' wives, and affords more extensive coverage for employees' spouses for all other medical conditions requiring hospitalization. Thus the husbands of female employees receive a specified level of hospitalization coverage for all conditions; the wives of male employees receive such coverage except for pregnancy-related conditions. Although *Gilbert* concluded that an otherwise inclusive plan that singled out pregnancy-related benefits for

[22] Consistently since 1970 the EEOC has considered it unlawful under Title VII for an employer to provide different insurance coverage for spouses of male and female employees. *See* Guidelines On Discrimination Because of Sex, 29 C.F.R. 1604.9(d), * * * .

Similarly, in our Equal Protection Clause cases we have repeatedly held that, if the spouses of female employees receive less favorable treatment in the provision of benefits, the practice discriminates not only against the spouses but also against the female employees on the basis of sex. [*See, e.g.,*] Frontiero v. Richardson, 411 U.S. 677, 688, 93 S.Ct. 1764, 1771, 36 L.Ed.2d 583 (1973) [other citations omitted].

> exclusion was nondiscriminatory on its face, because only women can become pregnant, Congress has unequivocally rejected that reasoning. The 1978 Act makes clear that it is discriminatory to treat pregnancy-related conditions less favorably than other medical conditions. Thus petitioner's plan unlawfully gives married male employees a benefit package for their dependents that is less inclusive than the dependency coverage provided to married female employees.

Id. at 682–84.

While the PDA was a definitive rejection of *Gilbert*, the effects of the *Gilbert* decision were much longer-lived. In *AT&T Corp. v. Hulteen,* 556 U.S. 701, 129 S.Ct. 1962, 173 L.Ed.2d 898 (2009), the Supreme Court rejected the claims of female employees and retirees whose post-PDA pensions were lower than they would have been as a consequence of pre-PDA leave calculations that gave lesser credit to pregnancy leave than to disability leave. In the 1960s and early 1970's, AT&T employees received full seniority-accruing credit for time on disability leave. For personal leave, however, AT&T capped seniority accrual at 30 days. At that time, the company defined pregnancy leave as personal leave. In 1977, AT&T slightly modified its system, shifting pregnancy leave to disability leave with full disability benefits, but with a six-week cap that was not imposed on other disability leaves. In 1979, in response to the passage of the PDA, AT&T altered its system once again, treating pregnancy leave the same as other disability leave for seniority accrual. Years later, women who had worked for AT&T during the 1970s and who had become pregnant and taken leave while employed there began retiring and seeking their pension benefits. In calculating pensions for these women, AT&T used the accrued seniority totals that included the lower credit for pregnancy leaves; the lesser credit award during that leave had a significant impact on their pension payout amounts.

A group of female employees of AT&T whose pensions were lower than they otherwise would have been because of AT&T's treatment of pregnancy leave prior to 1979 brought suit alleging that the calculation of pensions using a rule that disfavored pregnancy violated the PDA. Their complaint was not that AT&T's pre-PDA conduct was currently illegal, but that AT&T illegally discriminated at the moment that it calculated their pensions. The district court and the en banc Ninth Circuit agreed, concluding that Title VII was violated when post-PDA retirement benefit calculations incorporated pre-PDA accrual rules that discriminated on the basis of pregnancy.

The Supreme Court reversed, finding that the matter was controlled by Title VII's exemption for "bona fide seniority systems," which exempts seniority systems that apply different standards of compensation "provided that such differences are not the result of an intention to discriminate." Title VII, § 703(h), 42 U.S.C. § 2000e–2(h). The Court explained that

> AT&T's system must * * * be viewed as bona fide, that is, as a system that has no discriminatory terms, with the consequence that subsection (h) controls the result here * * * . It is true that in this case the pre-April 29, 1979 rule of differential treatment was an element of the seniority system itself; but it did not taint the system under the terms of subsection (h), because this Court held in *Gilbert* that an accrual rule limiting the seniority credit for time taken for pregnancy leave did not unlawfully discriminate on the basis of sex. As a matter of law, at that time, "an exclusion of pregnancy from a disability-benefits plan providing general coverage [was] not a gender based discrimination at all."

Hulteen, 556 U.S. at 710.

In dissent, Justice Ginsburg argued that, in enacting the PDA, Congress meant to "protect women, from and after April 1979, when the Act became fully effective, against repetition or continuation of pregnancy-based disadvantageous treatment." *Id.* at 719. The dissent focused on the history of the PDA's enactment, which evidenced the legislature's strong disapproval of the Court's decision in *Gilbert.* Given this history, the dissent argued, the PDA "calls for an immediate end to any pretense that classification on the basis of pregnancy can be 'facially non-discriminatory.' " *Id.* at 721. On this interpretation of the PDA, Title VII's exemption for "bona fide seniority systems" would not protect AT&T's pension calculation system because the system explicitly relied on differential treatment of pregnancy and thus includes "discriminatory terms" that render it unlawful.

Justice Ginsburg's dissenting opinion details the discrimination that women have historically faced because of pregnancy and motherhood and notes that the Court itself, in its earlier decisions, sometimes "exemplified the once 'prevailing ideology.' " *Id.* at 725. The decision in *Gilbert*, argued the dissent, is an example of the Supreme Court falling prey to stereotypical views about women.

> Congress put the Court back on track in 1978 when it amended Title VII to repudiate *Gilbert*'s holding and reasoning. * * * It is at least reasonable to read the PDA to say, from and after the effective date of the Act, no woman's pension payments are to be diminished by the pretense that pregnancy-based discrimination displays no gender bias.

> I would construe the Act to embrace plaintiffs' complaint, and would explicitly overrule *Gilbert* so that the decision can generate no more mischief.

Id. at 727–28.

Which understanding of the effect of the PDA is more persuasive? Should congressional disapproval of a Supreme Court decision through responsive legislation be treated as "overruling" the decision or does the decision in *Gilbert* render pregnancy-based classifications prior to 1979 facially neutral as a matter of law? Regardless of how it ruled in this specific case, should the Court have overruled *Gilbert* in light of current understandings about pregnancy discrimination as sex discrimination?

The circumstances of the *Hulteen* case were relatively unique. The vast majority of cases under the PDA involve debates over the precise meaning of "discrimination on the basis of pregnancy" or the "related medical conditions" that receive the same protection.

1. THE MEANING OF "DISCRIMINATION ON THE BASIS OF PREGNANCY"

The PDA amended Title VII to ensure that "sex discrimination" was understood to include discrimination on the basis of pregnancy. The law that Congress enacted included two clauses. In its first clause, the PDA makes clear that the terms "because of sex" and "on the basis of sex," must be understood to include, but not be limited to, "because of or on the basis of pregnancy, childbirth or related medical conditions." 42 U.S.C. § 2000e(k). The second clause of the PDA provides that "women affected by pregnancy, childbirth or related medical conditions shall be treated the same for all employment-related purposes * * * as other persons not so affected but similar in their ability or inability to work." *Id.*

Many pregnancy discrimination claims involve allegations that implicate only the first clause of the statute, alleging that an employer took an adverse employment action against an employee because of her pregnancy. In these cases, in order to make out a prima facie case, "a plaintiff must show that (1) she was pregnant, (2) she was qualified for her job, (3) she was subjected to an adverse employment decision; and (4) there is a nexus between her pregnancy and the adverse employment decision." Koch v. Lightning Transp., LLC, 2015 WL 66971, *3 (M.D.Tenn 2015). In many PDA cases, the third prong of the prima facie case involves an allegation that the employer failed to offer a workplace accommodation to a pregnant employee that the employer has offered to other employees in need of accommodation. In those cases, employees have argued that the second clause of the PDA requires employers to accommodate pregnant employees to the same extent that they accommodate any other employee needing a job modification. The

Supreme Court's most recent PDA case gave the Court an opportunity to consider what type of accommodation the PDA requires in these contexts.

YOUNG V. UNITED PARCEL SERVICES

Supreme Court of the United States, 2015.
__ U.S. __, 135 S.Ct. 1338, 191 L.Ed.2d 279.

JUSTICE BREYER delivered the opinion of the Court.

The Pregnancy Discrimination Act makes clear that Title VII's prohibition against sex discrimination applies to discrimination based on pregnancy. It also says that employers must treat "women affected by pregnancy . . . the same for all employment-related purposes . . . as other persons not so affected but similar in their ability or inability to work." We must decide how this latter provision applies in the context of an employer's policy that accommodates many, but not all, workers with nonpregnancy-related disabilities.

In our view, the Act requires courts to consider the extent to which an employer's policy treats pregnant workers less favorably than it treats nonpregnant workers similar in their ability or inability to work. And here—as in all cases in which an individual plaintiff seeks to show disparate treatment through indirect evidence—it requires courts to consider any legitimate, nondiscriminatory, nonpretextual justification for these differences in treatment. See *McDonnell Douglas Corp. v. Green,* 411 U.S. 792, 802, 93 S.Ct. 1817, 36 L.Ed.2d 668 (1973). Ultimately the court must determine whether the nature of the employer's policy and the way in which it burdens pregnant women shows that the employer has engaged in intentional discrimination. * * *

I

A

We begin with a summary of the facts. The petitioner, Peggy Young, worked as a part-time driver for the respondent, United Parcel Service (UPS). Her responsibilities included pickup and delivery of packages that had arrived by air carrier the previous night. In 2006, after suffering several miscarriages, she became pregnant. Her doctor told her that she should not lift more than 20 pounds during the first 20 weeks of her pregnancy or more than 10 pounds thereafter. UPS required drivers like Young to be able to lift parcels weighing up to 70 pounds (and up to 150 pounds with assistance). UPS told Young she could not work while under a lifting restriction. Young consequently stayed home without pay during most of the time she was pregnant and eventually lost her employee medical coverage.

Young subsequently brought this federal lawsuit. We focus here on her claim that UPS acted unlawfully in refusing to accommodate her pregnancy-related lifting restriction. Young said that her co-workers were willing to help her with heavy packages. She also said that UPS accommodated other drivers who were "similar in their * * * inability to work." She accordingly concluded that UPS must accommodate her as well.

UPS responded that the "other persons" whom it had accommodated were (1) drivers who had become disabled on the job, (2) those who had lost their Department of Transportation (DOT) certifications, and (3) those who suffered from a disability covered by the Americans with Disabilities Act of 1990 (ADA). UPS said that, since Young did not fall within any of those categories, it had not discriminated against Young on the basis of pregnancy but had treated her just as it treated all "other" relevant "persons."

* * * Title VII of the Civil Rights Act of 1964 forbids a covered employer to "discriminate against any individual with respect to * * * terms, conditions, or privileges of employment, because of such individual's * * * sex." In 1978, Congress enacted the Pregnancy Discrimination Act, 92 Stat. 2076, which added new language to Title VII's definitions subsection. The first clause of the 1978 Act specifies that Title VII's "ter[m] 'because of sex' * * * include[s] * * * because of or on the basis of pregnancy, childbirth, or related medical conditions." The second clause says that

> "women affected by pregnancy, childbirth, or related medical conditions shall be treated the same for all employment-related purposes * * * as other persons not so affected but similar in their ability or inability to work. * * * " *Ibid.*

This case requires us to consider the application of the second clause to a "disparate-treatment" claim—a claim that an employer intentionally treated a complainant less favorably than employees with the "complainant's qualifications" but outside the complainant's protected class. *McDonnell Douglas, supra,* at 802, 93 S.Ct. 1817. We have said that "[l]iability in a disparate-treatment case depends on whether the protected trait actually motivated the employer's decision." *Raytheon Co. v. Hernandez,* 540 U.S. 44, 52, 124 S.Ct. 513, 157 L.Ed.2d 357 (2003) (ellipsis and internal quotation marks omitted). We have also made clear that a plaintiff can prove disparate treatment either (1) by direct evidence that a workplace policy, practice, or decision relies expressly on a protected characteristic, or (2) by using the burden-shifting framework set forth in *McDonnell Douglas.* See *Trans World Airlines, Inc. v. Thurston,* 469 U.S. 111, 121, 105 S.Ct. 613, 83 L.Ed.2d 523 (1985).

In *McDonnell Douglas,* we considered a claim of discriminatory hiring. We said that, to prove disparate treatment, an individual plaintiff must "carry the initial burden" of "establishing a prima facie case" of discrimination. * * * If a plaintiff makes this showing, then the employer must have an opportunity "to articulate some legitimate, non-discriminatory reason for" treating employees outside the protected class better than employees within the protected class. *Ibid.* If the employer articulates such a reason, the plaintiff then has "an opportunity to prove by a preponderance of the evidence that the legitimate reasons offered by the defendant [*i.e.,* the employer] were not its true reasons, but were a pretext for discrimination." *Texas Dept. of Community Affairs v. Burdine,* 450 U.S. 248, 253, 101 S.Ct. 1089, 67 L.Ed.2d 207 (1981). * * *

In July 2007, Young filed a pregnancy discrimination charge with the Equal Employment Opportunity Commission (EEOC). In September 2008, [she] filed this complaint in Federal District Court. She argued, among other things, that she could show by direct evidence that UPS had intended to discriminate against her because of her pregnancy and that, in any event, she could establish a prima facie case of disparate treatment under the *McDonnell Douglas* framework.

After discovery, UPS filed a motion for summary judgment. In reply, Young pointed to favorable facts that she believed were either undisputed or that, while disputed, she could prove. They include the following:

1. Young worked as a UPS driver, picking up and delivering packages carried by air.

2. Young was pregnant in the fall of 2006.

3. Young's doctor recommended that she "not be required to lift greater than 20 pounds for the first 20 weeks of pregnancy and no greater than 10 pounds thereafter."

4. UPS required drivers such as Young to be able to "[l]ift, lower, push, pull, leverage and manipulate * * * packages weighing up to 70 pounds" and to "[a]ssist in moving packages weighing up to 150 pounds."

5. UPS' occupational health manager, the official "responsible for most issues relating to employee health and ability to work" at Young's UPS facility, told Young that she could not return to work during her pregnancy because she could not satisfy UPS' lifting requirements.

6. The manager also determined that Young did not qualify for a temporary alternative work assignment.

7. UPS, in a collective-bargaining agreement, had promised to provide temporary alternative work assignments to employees "unable to perform their normal work assignments due to an *on-the-job* injury."

8. The collective-bargaining agreement also provided that UPS would "make a good faith effort to comply * * * with requests for a reasonable accommodation because of a permanent disability" under the ADA.

9. The agreement further stated that UPS would give "inside" jobs to drivers who had lost their DOT certifications because of a failed medical exam, a lost driver's license, or involvement in a motor vehicle accident.

10. When Young later asked UPS' Capital Division Manager to accommodate her disability, he replied that, while she was pregnant, she was "too much of a liability" and could "not come back" until she " 'was no longer pregnant.' "

11. Young remained on a leave of absence (without pay) for much of her pregnancy.

12. Young returned to work as a driver in June 2007, about two months after her baby was born.

As direct evidence of intentional discrimination, Young relied, in significant part, on the statement of the Capital Division Manager (10 above). As evidence that she had made out a prima facie case under *McDonnell Douglas,* Young relied, in significant part, on evidence showing that UPS would accommodate workers injured on the job (7), those suffering from ADA disabilities (8), and those who had lost their DOT certifications (9). That evidence, she said, showed that UPS had a light-duty-for-injury policy with respect to numerous "other persons," but not with respect to pregnant workers.

Young introduced further evidence indicating that UPS had accommodated several individuals when they suffered disabilities that created work restrictions similar to hers. UPS contests the correctness of some of these facts and the relevance of others. But because we are at the summary judgment stage, and because there is a genuine dispute as to these facts, we view this evidence in the light most favorable to Young, the nonmoving party.

13. Several employees received accommodations while suffering various similar or more serious disabilities incurred on the job.

14. Several employees received accommodations following injury, where the record is unclear as to whether the injury was incurred on or off the job.

15. Several employees received "inside" jobs after losing their DOT certifications.

16. Some employees were accommodated despite the fact that their disabilities had been incurred off the job.

17. According to a deposition of a UPS shop steward who had worked for UPS for roughly a decade, "the only light duty requested [due to physical] restrictions that became an issue" at UPS "were with women who were pregnant."

The District Court granted UPS' motion for summary judgment. It concluded that Young could not show intentional discrimination through direct evidence. Nor could she make out a prima facie case of discrimination under *McDonnell Douglas*. The court wrote that those with whom Young compared herself—those falling within the on-the-job, DOT, or ADA categories—were too different to qualify as "similarly situated comparator[s]." * * * On appeal, the Fourth Circuit affirmed. * * *

Young filed a petition for certiorari essentially asking us to review the Fourth Circuit's interpretation of the Pregnancy Discrimination Act. In light of lower-court uncertainty about the interpretation of the Act, we granted the petition. Compare *Ensley-Gaines v. Runyon,* 100 F.3d 1220, 1226 (C.A.6 1996), with *Urbano v. Continental Airlines, Inc.,* 138 F.3d 204, 206–208 (C.A.5 1998); *Reeves v. Swift Transp. Co.,* 446 F.3d 637, 640–643 (C.A.6 2006); *Serednyj v. Beverly Healthcare, LLC,* 656 F.3d 540, 547–552 (C.A.7 2011); *Spivey v. Beverly Enterprises, Inc.,* 196 F.3d 1309, 1312–1314 (C.A.11 1999). * * *

II

The parties disagree about the interpretation of the Pregnancy Discrimination Act's second clause. * * * Does this clause mean that courts must compare workers *only* in respect to the work limitations that they suffer? Does it mean that courts must ignore all other similarities or differences between pregnant and nonpregnant workers? Or does it mean that courts, when deciding who the relevant "other persons" are, may consider other similarities and differences as well? If so, which ones? * * *

The parties propose very different answers to this question. Young and the United States believe that the second clause of the Pregnancy Discrimination Act "requires an employer to provide the same accommodations to workplace disabilities caused by pregnancy that it provides to workplace disabilities that have other causes but have a similar effect on the ability to work." * * * UPS takes an almost polar opposite view. It contends that the second clause does no more than define sex discrimination to include pregnancy discrimination. Under this view, courts would compare the accommodations an employer provides to pregnant women with the accommodations it provides to others *within* a facially neutral category (such as those with off-the-job injuries) to determine whether the employer has violated Title VII. * * *

We cannot accept either of these interpretations. * * * The problem with Young's approach is that it proves too much. It seems to say that the statute grants pregnant workers a "most-favored-nation" status. As long as an employer provides one or two workers with an accommodation—say, those with particularly hazardous jobs, or those whose workplace presence is particularly needed, or those who have worked at the company for many years, or those who are over the age of 55—then it must provide similar accommodations to *all* pregnant workers (with comparable physical limitations), irrespective of the nature of their jobs, the employer's need to keep them working, their ages, or any other criteria. * * *

We doubt that Congress intended to grant pregnant workers an unconditional most-favored-nation status. The language of the statute does not require that unqualified reading. The second clause, when referring to nonpregnant persons with similar disabilities, uses the open-ended term "other persons." It does not say that the employer must treat pregnant employees the "same" as "*any* other persons" (who are similar in their ability or inability to work), nor does it otherwise specify *which* other persons Congress had in mind.

Moreover, disparate-treatment law normally permits an employer to implement policies that are not intended to harm members of a protected class, even if their implementation sometimes harms those members, as long as the employer has a legitimate, nondiscriminatory, nonpretextual reason for doing so. * * *

We find it similarly difficult to accept the opposite interpretation of the Act's second clause. UPS says that the second clause simply defines sex discrimination to include pregnancy discrimination. But that cannot be so.

The first clause accomplishes that objective when it expressly amends Title VII's definitional provision to make clear that Title VII's words "because of sex" and "on the basis of sex" "include, but are not limited to, because of or on the basis of pregnancy, childbirth, or related medical conditions." We have long held that " 'a statute ought, upon the whole, to be so construed that, if it can be prevented, no clause' " is rendered " 'superfluous, void, or insignificant.' " *TRW Inc. v. Andrews,* 534 U.S. 19, 31, 122 S.Ct. 441, 151 L.Ed.2d 339 (2001) (quoting *Duncan v. Walker,* 533 U.S. 167, 174, 121 S.Ct. 2120, 150 L.Ed.2d 251 (2001)). But that is what UPS' interpretation of the second clause would do. * * *

Moreover, the interpretation espoused by UPS and the dissent would fail to carry out an important congressional objective. As we have noted, Congress' "unambiguou[s]" intent in passing the Act was to overturn "both the holding and the reasoning of the Court in the *Gilbert* decision." *Newport News Shipbuilding & Dry Dock Co. v. EEOC,* 462 U.S. 669, 678, 103 S.Ct. 2622, 77 L.Ed.2d 89 (1983); see also *post,* at 1364 (recognizing that "the object of the Pregnancy Discrimination Act is to displace this

Court's conclusion in [*Gilbert*]"). In *Gilbert,* the Court considered a company plan that provided "nonoccupational sickness and accident benefits to all employees" without providing "disability-benefit payments for any absence due to pregnancy." 429 U.S., at 128, 129, 97 S.Ct. 401. The Court held that the plan did not violate Title VII; it did not discriminate on the basis of sex because there was "no risk from which men are protected and women are not." *Id.,* at 138, 97 S.Ct. 401 (internal quotation marks omitted). Although pregnancy is "confined to women," the majority believed it was not "comparable in all other respects to [the] diseases or disabilities" that the plan covered. *Id.,* at 136, 97 S.Ct. 401. Specifically, the majority explained that pregnancy "is not a 'disease' at all," nor is it necessarily a result of accident. *Ibid.* Neither did the majority see the distinction the plan drew as "a subterfuge" or a "pretext" for engaging in gender-based discrimination. *Ibid.* In short, the *Gilbert* majority reasoned in part just as the dissent reasons here. The employer did "not distinguish between pregnant women and others of similar ability or inability *because of pregnancy.*" *Post,* at 1362. It distinguished between them on a neutral ground—*i.e.,* it accommodated only sicknesses and accidents, and pregnancy was neither of those.

Simply including pregnancy among Title VII's protected traits (*i.e.,* accepting UPS' interpretation) would not overturn *Gilbert* in full—in particular, it would not respond to *Gilbert*'s determination that an employer can treat pregnancy less favorably than diseases or disabilities resulting in a similar inability to work. * * *

III

The statute lends itself to an interpretation other than those that the parties advocate. * * * Our interpretation minimizes the problems we have discussed, responds directly to *Gilbert,* and is consistent with longstanding interpretations of Title VII.

In our view, an individual pregnant worker who seeks to show disparate treatment through indirect evidence may do so through application of the *McDonnell Douglas* framework. That framework requires a plaintiff to make out a prima facie case of discrimination. But it is "not intended to be an inflexible rule." *Furnco Constr. Corp. v. Waters,* 438 U.S. 567, 575, 98 S.Ct. 2943, 57 L.Ed.2d 957 (1978). Rather, an individual plaintiff may establish a prima facie case by "showing actions taken by the employer from which one can infer, if such actions remain unexplained, that it is more likely than not that such actions were based on a discriminatory criterion illegal under" Title VII. *Id.,* at 576, 98 S.Ct. 2943 (internal quotation marks omitted). The burden of making this showing is "not onerous." *Burdine,* 450 U.S., at 253, 101 S.Ct. 1089. * * *

Thus, a plaintiff alleging that the denial of an accommodation constituted disparate treatment under the Pregnancy Discrimination

Act's second clause may make out a prima facie case by showing, as in *McDonnell Douglas*, that she belongs to the protected class, that she sought accommodation, that the employer did not accommodate her, and that the employer did accommodate others "similar in their ability or inability to work."

The employer may then seek to justify its refusal to accommodate the plaintiff by relying on "legitimate, nondiscriminatory" reasons for denying her accommodation. But, consistent with the Act's basic objective, that reason normally cannot consist simply of a claim that it is more expensive or less convenient to add pregnant women to the category of those ("similar in their ability or inability to work") whom the employer accommodates. After all, the employer in *Gilbert* could in all likelihood have made just such a claim.

If the employer offers an apparently "legitimate, non-discriminatory" reason for its actions, the plaintiff may in turn show that the employer's proffered reasons are in fact pretextual. We believe that the plaintiff may reach a jury on this issue by providing sufficient evidence that the employer's policies impose a significant burden on pregnant workers, and that the employer's "legitimate, nondiscriminatory" reasons are not sufficiently strong to justify the burden, but rather—when considered along with the burden imposed—give rise to an inference of intentional discrimination.

The plaintiff can create a genuine issue of material fact as to whether a significant burden exists by providing evidence that the employer accommodates a large percentage of nonpregnant workers while failing to accommodate a large percentage of pregnant workers. Here, for example, if the facts are as Young says they are, she can show that UPS accommodates most nonpregnant employees with lifting limitations while categorically failing to accommodate pregnant employees with lifting limitations. Young might also add that the fact that UPS has multiple policies that accommodate nonpregnant employees with lifting restrictions suggests that its reasons for failing to accommodate pregnant employees with lifting restrictions are not sufficiently strong—to the point that a jury could find that its reasons for failing to accommodate pregnant employees give rise to an inference of intentional discrimination.

This approach, though limited to the Pregnancy Discrimination Act context, is consistent with our longstanding rule that a plaintiff can use circumstantial proof to rebut an employer's apparently legitimate, nondiscriminatory reasons for treating individuals within a protected class differently than those outside the protected class. * * *

IV

Under this interpretation of the Act, the judgment of the Fourth Circuit must be vacated. A party is entitled to summary judgment if there is "no genuine dispute as to any material fact and the movant is entitled to judgment as a matter of law." We have already outlined the evidence Young introduced. Viewing the record in the light most favorable to Young, there is a genuine dispute as to whether UPS provided more favorable treatment to at least some employees whose situation cannot reasonably be distinguished from Young's. In other words, Young created a genuine dispute of material fact as to the fourth prong of the *McDonnell Douglas* analysis.

Young also introduced evidence that UPS had three separate accommodation policies (on-the-job, ADA, DOT). Taken together, Young argued, these policies significantly burdened pregnant women. The Fourth Circuit did not consider the combined effects of these policies, nor did it consider the strength of UPS' justifications for each when combined. That is, why, when the employer accommodated so many, could it not accommodate pregnant women as well?

We do not determine whether Young created a genuine issue of material fact as to whether UPS' reasons for having treated Young less favorably than it treated these other nonpregnant employees were pretextual. We leave a final determination of that question for the Fourth Circuit to make on remand, in light of the interpretation of the Pregnancy Discrimination Act that we have set out above.

* * *

For the reasons above, we vacate the judgment of the Fourth Circuit and remand the case for further proceedings consistent with this opinion.

[JUSTICE ALITO concurred. JUSTICE SCALIA, with whom JUSTICE KENNEDY and JUSTICE THOMAS joined, dissented.]

NOTES AND QUESTIONS

1. Justice Scalia's sharply worded dissent argued that the Court had conflated disparate treatment and disparate impact analysis in interpreting the second clause of the Pregnancy Discrimination Act. After first concluding that that same-treatment clause requires only that an employer not draw distinctions between pregnant employees and all other employees, the dissent takes the majority to task for creating a disparate treatment test that permits a plaintiff to "establish disparate *treatment* by showing that the *effects* of her employer's policy fall more harshly on pregnant women than on others (the policies "impose a significant burden on pregnant workers") and are inadequately justified (the "reasons are not sufficiently strong to justify the burden")." *Id.* at 1362. Justice Scalia added that Title VII *already* has a

framework that allows judges to home in on a policy's effects and justifications—disparate impact. Under that framework, it is *already* unlawful for an employer to use a practice that has a disparate impact on the basis of a protected trait, unless (among other things) the employer can show that the practice "is job related * * * and consistent with business necessity." § 2000e–2(k)(1)(A)(i). *Id.* at 1366. "The Court," Justice Scalia concluded, "does not explain why we need (never mind how the Act could possibly be read to contain) today's ersatz disparate-impact test, under which the disparate-impact element gives way to the significant-burden criterion and the business-necessity defense gives way to the sufficiently-strong-justification standard. Today's decision can thus serve only one purpose: allowing claims that belong under Title VII's disparate-impact provisions to be brought under its disparate-treatment provisions instead." *Id.* Justice Breyer, on the other hand, argues that this approach to the same-treatment clause of the PDA mirrors the *McDonnell Douglas* burden-shifting framework for disparate treatment analysis. Are you persuaded?

2. As the Court noted in *Young*, cases of individual disparate treatment under the PDA are generally analyzed under the burden-shifting scheme of *McDonnell Douglas-Burdine-Hicks*, which is covered in Chapter 3. While some PDA cases involve requests for accommodation, many are straightforward claims that an employer took an adverse employment action against an employee because of her pregnancy. In those cases, the lower courts have consistently held that "Title VII does not prohibit the termination of employees who are pregnant—it prohibits treating pregnant employees dissimilarly from others." Kucharski v. CORT Furniture Rental, 2009 WL 2524041, at *2 (2d Cir.2009). *See also* Armindo v. Padlocker, Inc., 209 F.3d 1319, 1322 (11th Cir.2000) ("The PDA is not violated by an employer who fires a pregnant employee for excessive absences, unless the employer overlooks the comparable absences of non-pregnant employees."). Is this consistent with the Court's decision in *Young*? Recall that the Court in *Young* was interpreting the second clause of the PDA. Does that make a difference to your analysis?

3. A pair of Seventh Circuit cases highlights one way that arguments about whether an adverse action was taken "because of pregnancy" can play out. In the first case, *Troupe v. May Department Stores*, 20 F.3d 734 (7th Cir.1994), Kimberly Hern Troupe had been employed by Lord & Taylor for about three years before she became pregnant. During her pregnancy, she was chronically late to work because of severe morning sickness. Lord & Taylor terminated her employment the day before her maternity leave, explaining that the termination was a consequence of her chronic lateness. The Seventh Circuit, in an often-cited decision authored by Judge Richard Posner, concluded that Troupe had not made out a claim of pregnancy discrimination. As the court explained:

> Against the inference that Troupe was fired because she was chronically late to arrive at work and chronically early to leave, she has only two facts to offer. The first is the timing of her discharge:

she was fired the day before her maternity leave was to begin. Her morning sickness could not interfere with her work when she was not working because she was on maternity leave, and it could not interfere with her work when she returned to work after her maternity leave because her morning sickness would end at the latest with the birth of her child. Thus her employer fired her one day before the problem that the employer says caused her to be fired was certain to end. If the discharge of an unsatisfactory worker were a purely remedial measure rather than also, or instead, a deterrent one, the inference that Troupe wasn't really fired because of her tardiness would therefore be a powerful one. But that is a big "if." We must remember that after two warnings Troupe had been placed on probation for sixty days and that she had violated the implicit terms of probation by being as tardy during the probationary period as she had been before. If the company did not fire her, its warnings and threats would seem empty. Employees would be encouraged to flout work rules knowing that the only sanction would be a toothless warning or a meaningless period of probation.

Yet this is only an interpretation; and it might appear to be an issue for trial whether it is superior to Troupe's interpretation. But what is Troupe's interpretation? Not (as we understand it) that Lord & Taylor wanted to get back at her for becoming pregnant or having morning sickness. The only significance she asks us to attach to the timing of her discharge is as reinforcement for the inference that she asks us to draw from Rauch's statement about the reason for her termination: that she was terminated because her employer did not expect her to return to work after her maternity leave was up. We must decide whether a termination so motivated is discrimination within the meaning of the pregnancy amendment to Title VII.

Standing alone, it is not. * * * Suppose that Lord & Taylor had an employee named Jones, a black employee scheduled to take a three-month paid sick leave for a kidney transplant; and whether thinking that he would not return to work when his leave was up or not wanting to incur the expense of paying him while he was on sick leave, the company fired him. In doing so it might be breaking its employment contract with Jones, if it had one, or violating a state statute requiring the payment of earned wages. But the company could not be found guilty of racial discrimination unless (in the absence of any of the other types of evidence of discrimination that we have discussed) there was evidence that it failed to exhibit comparable rapacity toward similarly situated employees of the white race. We must imagine a hypothetical Mr. Troupe, who is as tardy as Ms. Troupe was, also because of health problems, and who is about to take a protracted sick leave growing out of those

> problems at an expense to Lord & Taylor equal to that of Ms. Troupe's maternity leave. If Lord & Taylor would have fired our hypothetical Mr. Troupe, this implies that it fired Ms. Troupe not because she was pregnant but because she cost the company more than she was worth to it.
>
> The Pregnancy Discrimination Act does not, despite the urgings of feminist scholars, e.g., Herma Hill Kay, "Equality and Difference: The Case of Pregnancy," 1 Berkeley Women's L.J. 1, 30–31 (1985), require employers to offer maternity leave or take other steps to make it easier for pregnant women to work * * *—to make it as easy, say, as it is for their spouses to continue working during pregnancy. Employers can treat pregnant women as badly as they treat similarly affected but nonpregnant employees * * * .
>
> The plaintiff has made no effort to show that if all the pertinent facts were as they are except for the fact of her pregnancy, she would not have been fired. So in the end she has no evidence from which a rational trier of fact could infer that she was a victim of pregnancy discrimination. * * * The Pregnancy Discrimination Act requires the employer to ignore an employee's pregnancy, but * * * not her absence from work, unless the employer overlooks the comparable absences of nonpregnant employees.

Id. at 737–38. What if an employee does not have a current attendance problem or a record of attendance problems because of pregnancy, but the employer assumes that, because the employee is pregnant, she is likely to be absent in the future? Will the employer violate Title VII if it discharges her in anticipation of her possible future absences? This is the question that the Seventh Circuit confronted in the second case. In this instance, the court observed,

> There might be some limited circumstances in which an employer could be justified in taking anticipatory adverse action against a pregnant employee. Although the PDA was designed to allow individual women to make independent choices about whether to continue to work while pregnant, it was not designed to handcuff employers by forcing them to wait until an employee's pregnancy causes a special economic disadvantage. The PDA does not create such an artificial divide between pregnancy, childbirth and related medical conditions and the secondary effects of a pregnancy which might affect job performance. Pregnancy causes normal inconveniences that might "interrupt the workplace's daily routines," including, for example, the need to take more frequent snack and restroom breaks and the need to take some time off, at the very least, to give birth. Judith G. Greenberg, *The Pregnancy Discrimination Act: Legitimating Discrimination Against Pregnant Women in the Workforce*, 50 Me.L.Rev. 225, 250 (1998); *see also* In re Carnegie Center Associates, 129 F.3d 290, 306 (3d Cir.1997)

> (McKee, J., dissenting) (describing "the absence [from work] endemic to pregnancy"). An employer may, under narrow circumstances * * * project the normal inconveniences of pregnancy and their secondary effects into the future and take actions in accordance with and in proportion to those predictions. Of course, it will rarely be one hundred percent demonstrable that a pregnant woman will be unable to meet a BFOQ sometime in the future. Cases such as *Marshall v. American Hospital Association,* 157 F.3d 520, 522–23 (7th Cir.1998), in which an employee announces that she will be unavailable to work in the future and thus explicitly requests special treatment, are exceptional. It is not merely a question whether the pregnant employee asks for special treatment, however; other evidence might also be probative of the employee's ability to continue to meet the employer's legitimate job expectations. But an employer cannot take anticipatory action unless it has a good faith basis, supported by sufficiently strong evidence, that the normal inconveniences of an employee's pregnancy will require special treatment.

Maldonado v. U.S. Bank, 186 F.3d 759, 767 (7th Cir.1999). *See also* Laxton v. Gap, Inc., 333 F.3d 572, 583–84 (5th Cir.2003) (a jury can infer discriminatory animus when a supervisor makes angry comments that reflect assumptions about the timing and length of maternity leave that the plaintiff will take).

4. Recall that the first element of the prima facie case requires a plaintiff to show that she is a member of a protected class. To prevail in a pregnancy discrimination case, does a plaintiff have to establish as part of her prima facie case that the employer knew that she was pregnant at the time of the adverse employment decision? *See* Serednyj v. Beverly Healthcare, LLC, 656 F.3d 540, 550 (7th Cir.2011) (demonstration that the employer knew of the pregnancy is part of the prima facie case); Prebilich-Holland v. Gaylord Ent'mt Co., 297 F.3d 438 (6th Cir.2002) (same). If this is part of a plaintiff's burden, what is required—evidence of the employer's actual knowledge or evidence that the employer reasonably should have known that she was pregnant?

5. Some plaintiffs are able to establish the fourth element of the prima facie case—that the adverse employment action took place under circumstances suggesting discrimination—by pointing to a similarly situated nonpregnant employee who was treated differently. In other cases, plaintiffs have sought to rely on the timing of the adverse employment action in relation to disclosure of the pregnancy. *See, e.g.,* McCallum v. Archstone Communities, LLC, 2013 WL 5496837, *12 (D. Md. 2013) (plaintiff was fired 15 days after notifying her employer of her pregnancy); Templet v. Hard Rock Constr. Co., 2003 WL 181363, at *2–3 (E.D.La.2003) (demotion occurred eight weeks after plaintiff announced her pregnancy). A plaintiff's evidence of discriminatory intent may also include comments made by supervisors or others in the workplace. Often these cases turn on whether the comments are

interpreted by the judge or jury as reflecting discriminatory animus by the decision maker or as simply "stray remarks." *Compare* Sheehan v. Donlen Corp., 173 F.3d 1039, 1042–43 (7th Cir.1999) (affirming jury verdict for employee who presented evidence that (1) When the plaintiff first returned to work following the birth of her second child, she complained about the volume of work and said, "Maybe I should go home and have another baby." Her supervisor responded, "If you have another baby, I'll invite you to stay home." (2) At the time the plaintiff told her supervisor that she was pregnant again, the supervisor said to the department head, "Oh, my God, she's pregnant again." (3) At the time the plaintiff was fired, her supervisor said, "Hopefully this will give you some time to spend at home with your children."), *with* Wallace v. Methodist Hosp. Sys., 271 F.3d 212, 223–24 (5th Cir.2001) (affirming a district court grant of judgment as a matter of law to the employer, concluding that supervisors' comments that plaintiff was fired because "[f]irst of all, she's been pregnant three times in three years" and that she "needed to choose between work and family" were both insufficient to show invidious intent because one was not made by a direct decision maker and the other was not directly related to an adverse action). For a discussion of the stray remarks doctrine, see Chapter 3.

6. Standing: A husband and wife were employed as vice presidents in the same company. Shortly after the company president learned that the wife was pregnant, he terminated both employees. They filed a lawsuit alleging that they were both discharged because of the wife's pregnancy. Would the husband have standing to sue under Title VII? Under the PDA? On what theory? See Nicol v. Imagematrix, Inc., 773 F.Supp. 802 (E.D.Va.1991) (granting husband standing to sue because only a man can be discharged due to the pregnancy of his spouse). If an employer discharges an employee because it believes that she is pregnant, but it turns out that the employee was not actually pregnant at the time she was fired, can she seek relief under the PDA? See Jolley v. Phillips Educ. Group of Cent. Fla., Inc., 71 Fair Empl.Prac.Cas. (BNA) 916 (M.D.Fla.1996) (yes).

7. What if the employee is not pregnant at the time of the adverse employment decision, but is attempting to become pregnant? See Pacourek v. Inland Steel Co., 858 F.Supp. 1393, 1400–01 (N.D.Ill.1994) (permitting claim where plaintiff was going through in vitro fertilization efforts). Should it matter whether the employee is actively trying to become pregnant or has simply told her employer that she plans to try to become pregnant at some point in the future? *Compare* Barnowe v. Kaiser Found. Health Plan of the Nw., 2005 WL 1113855, at *4 (D.Or.2005) (PDA claim requires that the plaintiff be actively attempting to become pregnant) *and* Hesse v. Dolgencorp of New York, Inc., 2014 WL 1315337 (W.D.N.Y. 2014) (accepting plaintiff's argument that her intention to become pregnant might be enough to make out a prima facie case). The Supreme Court in *International Union, United Automobile Workers* v. Johnson Controls, 499 U.S. 187, 206, 111 S.Ct. 1196, 1207, 113 L.Ed.2d 158 (1991), explained that the PDA prohibits discrimination against a woman "because of her capacity to become

pregnant." Shouldn't that broad prohibition cover a claim that an employer refused to hire a potential employee because she said that she intended to have children in the future? See Kocak v. Cmty. Health Partners of Ohio, Inc., 400 F.3d 466, 469–70 (6th Cir.2005) (yes).

8. Pregnancy and Disparate Impact: Although the vast majority of claims under the PDA are pursued as disparate treatment claims, plaintiffs may pursue disparate impact claims alleging that the burdens of an employer's facially neutral policy falls more heavily on pregnant women. Is there tension between courts' repeated insistence that "the PDA does not require the creation of any special programs for pregnant women; nor does it mandate any special treatment," Dimino v. N.Y.C. Transit Auth., 64 F.Supp.2d. 136, 157–58 (E.D.N.Y. 1999), and the viability of a PDA disparate impact claim? Some courts have concluded that, where the policy being challenged is universally applicable in a workplace—for example a policy that prohibits any medical restricted-duty assignments—a pregnancy-related disparate impact claim is inappropriate because it might force the creation of "special treatment" for pregnancy. *Id.* at 158. By contrast, where an employer has a policy with certain defined exceptions—for example the policy at issue in *Young*, which permitted light duty for on-the-job injury but not for off-duty injury—plaintiffs might successfully challenge the exceptions as having an impermissible disparate impact. *See* Lochren v. County of Suffolk, 2008 WL 2039458, at *1 (E.D.N.Y. 2008). After *Young*, are plaintiffs more likely to challenge these types of policies under a disparate treatment or disparate impact framework? What are the advantages and disadvantages of each approach?

9. While *Young* may increase the likelihood that a pregnant employee will receive accommodation, the framework set out in the decision does not guarantee accommodation. Should employers be required to accommodate pregnant workers who need job modifications in order to continue to work? In *Young*, the Court noted that "statutory changes made after the time of Young's pregnancy may limit the future significance of our interpretation of the Act." 135 S.Ct. at 1348. In particular, the Court noted, the Americans with Disabilities Amendments Act of 2008 clarified that limitations on an employee's ability to "lift, stand, or bend" are ADA-covered disabilities. The EEOC has interpreted the new law to require employers to accommodate employees who have a temporary lifting restriction because of an off-the-job injury. *See id. See also* 29 CFR pt. 1630, App., § 1630.2(j)(1)(ix). This interpretation of the ADA Amendments would ensure that pregnant women in need of on-the-job accommodation would be entitled to that accommodation without having to meet the burdens imposed by the *Young* framework. Some have proposed that the federal government should enact an independent statute that would ensure that pregnant workers receive accommodation. A bipartisan bill is currently pending in Congress to achieve that end. *See* Pregnant Worker's Fairness Act, S. 942, 114th Cong. (2015), H.R. 1975, 114th Cong. (2015). A number of states also have laws designed to ensure that

pregnant employees receive reasonable accommodation. *See, e.g.*, Cal. Govt. Code § 12945 (2012); N.J. Stat. Ann. § 10:5–12(s) (2013).

10. *The Role of EEOC Guidance.* In a section of the *Young* opinion not reproduced above, the Court explains that it does not give even limited deference to the EEOC's interpretation of the same-treatment clause in its decision. The Court's explanation for its lack of deference highlights the fact that agency interpretation may well change from administration to administration.

> Soon after the Act was passed, the EEOC issued guidance [explaining]: "Disabilities caused or contributed to by pregnancy * * * for all job-related purposes, shall be treated the same as disabilities caused or contributed to by other medical conditions." Moreover, the EEOC stated that "[i]f other employees temporarily unable to lift are relieved of these functions, pregnant employees also unable to lift must be temporarily relieved of the function."
>
> This post-Act guidance, however, does not resolve the ambiguity of the term "other persons" in the Act's second clause. Rather, it simply tells employers to treat pregnancy-related disabilities like nonpregnancy-related disabilities, without clarifying how that instruction should be implemented when an employer does not treat all nonpregnancy-related disabilities alike.
>
> More recently—in July 2014—the EEOC promulgated an additional guideline apparently designed to address this ambiguity. That guideline says that "[a]n employer may not refuse to treat a pregnant worker the same as other employees who are similar in their ability or inability to work by relying on a policy that makes distinctions based on the source of an employee's limitations (e.g., a policy of providing light duty only to workers injured on the job)." * * * The EEOC further added that "an employer may not deny light duty to a pregnant employee based on a policy that limits light duty to employees with on-the-job injuries."
>
> The Solicitor General argues that we should give special, if not controlling, weight to this guideline. He points out that we have long held that "the rulings, interpretations and opinions" of an agency charged with the mission of enforcing a particular statute, "while not controlling upon the courts by reason of their authority, do constitute a body of experience and informed judgment to which courts and litigants may properly resort for guidance." *Skidmore v. Swift & Co.,* 323 U.S. 134, 140, 65 S.Ct. 161, 89 L.Ed.124 (1944).
>
> But we have also held that the "weight of such a judgment in a particular case will depend upon the thoroughness evident in its consideration, the validity of its reasoning, its consistency with earlier and later pronouncements, and all those factors that give it power to persuade, if lacking power to control." *Skidmore, supra,* at

> 140, 65 S.Ct. 161. These qualifications are relevant here and severely limit the EEOC's July 2014 guidance's special power to persuade.
>
> We come to this conclusion not because of any agency lack of "experience" or "informed judgment." Rather, the difficulties are those of timing, "consistency," and "thoroughness" of "consideration." The EEOC promulgated its 2014 guidelines only recently, after this Court had granted certiorari in this case. In these circumstances, it is fair to say that the EEOC's current guidelines take a position about which the EEOC's previous guidelines were silent. And that position is inconsistent with positions for which the Government has long advocated. See Brief for Defendant-Appellee in *Ensley-Gaines v. Runyon,* No. 95–1038 (CA6 1996), pp. 26–27 (explaining that a reading of the Act like Young's was "simply incorrect" and "runs counter" to this Court's precedents). See also Brief for United States as *Amicus Curiae* 16, n. 2 ("The Department of Justice, on behalf of the United States Postal Service, has previously taken the position that pregnant employees with work limitations are not similarly situated to employees with similar limitations caused by on-the-job injuries"). Nor does the EEOC explain the basis of its latest guidance. Does it read the statute, for example, as embodying a most-favored-nation status? Why has it now taken a position contrary to the litigation position the Government previously took? Without further explanation, we cannot rely significantly on the EEOC's determination.

Should the Court have deferred to the EEOC then-current position on the meaning of the PDA? What difference does it make? Do you think the Court would have been more willing to defer if the EEOC guidelines reflected a change in position from earlier agency interpretations but they had been enacted before the Court had granted certiorari in *Young?* Following the Court's decision in *Young*, the EEOC revised its guidance to comport with the Court's approach to pregnancy discrimination claims. *See* Equal Empl. Oppt'y Comm'n, *Enforcement Guidance: Pregnancy and Related Issues* (2015), available at *http://www.eeoc.gov/laws/guidance/pregnancy_guidance.cfm.*

NOTE ON THE SCOPE OF "RELATED MEDICAL CONDITIONS" UNDER THE PDA

The PDA defines sex discrimination to include discrimination on the basis of "pregnancy, childbirth, or related medical conditions," but the law does not define "related medical conditions." 42 U.S.C. § 2000e(k). The term has been consistently interpreted to mean at least that an employer must cover pregnancy-related medical conditions to the same extent that it covers other conditions in a health insurance, temporary disability or other benefit plan offered to employees. *See* Newport News Shipbldg. & Dry Dock Co. v.

EEOC, 462 U.S. 669, 682–84, 103 S.Ct. 2622, 2630–31, 77 L.Ed.2d 89 (1983); Equal Emp. Oppt'y Comm'n, Facts About Pregnancy Discrimination, available at *http://www.eeoc.gov/eeoc/publications/fs-preg.cfm*. In recent years, courts have considered numerous PDA challenges to employer policies on issues ranging from abortion to breast-feeding.

Prior to the passage of the Affordable Care Act, which requires employer-provided insurance to include contraceptive coverage, courts considered a number of cases challenging employer-provided health care policies that denied coverage of some or all contraceptives. *See, e.g., EEOC v. United Parcel Service, Inc.,* 141 F.Supp.2d 1216 (D.Minn.2001) (allowing EEOC to proceed with both a disparate impact and a disparate treatment challenge to a policy excluding coverage of oral contraceptives); Cooley v. DaimlerChrysler Corp., 281 F.Supp.2d. 979, 985–86 (E.D.Mo. 2003) (allowing plaintiffs to pursue a disparate impact claim where employer excluded coverage for prescription contraceptives); In re Union Pac. R.R. Emp. Prac. Litig., 479 F.3d 936, 942 (8th Cir.2007) (upholding a comprehensive contraception exclusion permissible on the grounds that it is gender-neutral and that contraception is not "related to" pregnancy under the PDA because "[c]ontraception is not a medical treatment that occurs when or if a woman becomes pregnant; instead, contraception prevents pregnancy from even occurring"). Is contraception of pregnancy "related to" pregnancy under the PDA?

The Affordable Care Act also amended the Fair Labor Standards Act (FLSA) to include provisions requiring employers to provide "reasonable break time" and a private space for nursing mothers to express breast milk. *See* Patient Protection and Affordable Care Act, Pub. L. No. 111–148, 124 Stat. 119 (2010). Prior to passage of the "Break Time for Nursing Mothers" provision, a variety of state laws provided some protection for nursing mothers. These separate laws offered important protection not provided by Title VII because courts had consistently held that even if breastfeeding was a pregnancy-related condition, the PDA did not require employers to provide any special accommodation for nursing mothers. *See, e.g.* EEOC v. Houston Funding II, Ltd., 717 F.3d 425 (5th Cir.2013) (holding that an employer may not punish an employee for lactating, but did not have to provide special accommodations to pump breast milk during the work day). As Deborah Brake and Joanna Grossman have noted, "[s]ome courts have even interpreted the PDA to allow women to be fired for requesting accommodations for lactation, restricting the PDA's protection to those lactating women who suffer in silence." Deborah L. Brake & Joanna L. Grossman, *Unprotected Sex: The Pregnancy Discrimination Act at 35*, 21 Duke J. Gender L. & Pol'y 67, 85 (2013).

Courts have also confronted challenges to policies excluding medical treatments for infertility from employer health plans. Is infertility a medical condition "related" to pregnancy under the PDA? In *Krauel v. Iowa Methodist Medical Center,* 95 F.3d 674, 679 (8th Cir.1996), the court held that infertility treatments are not included in the PDA's definition of "related medical conditions" because infertility is not related to "pregnancy" and "childbirth"—the terms used in the PDA—but to prevention of conception—a term not found in the PDA. *See also* Saks v. Franklin Covey, Co., 316 F.3d 337, 345 (2d Cir.2003) ("Because reproductive capacity is common to both men and women, we do not read the PDA as introducing a completely new classification of prohibited discrimination based solely on reproductive capacity."). The Seventh Circuit distinguished the decisions in *Saks* and *Krauel* when it confronted a case in which the employer terminated the plaintiff because she took time off to undergo in vitro fertilization. *See* Hall v. Nalco, 534 F.3d 644, 648–49 (7th Cir.2008). In this instance, the court reasoned, the adverse action was not gender neutral—as exclusion of all infertility treatments from a health plan might be—but was based on the plaintiff's participation in a surgical process that only women undergo. *Id.* at 648–49. *See also* Herx v. Diocese of Fort Wayne-South Bend, Inc., 48 F.Supp.3d 1168 (N.D.Ind. 2014) (permitting PDA claim where teacher was fired because she underwent in vitro fertilization).

Is abortion a pregnancy-related "medical condition" that affects women? Congress indicated that it is. Following the broad statutory mandate that "women affected by pregnancy, childbirth, or related medical conditions shall be treated the same for all employment-related purposes, including receipt of benefits under fringe benefit programs, as other persons not so affected but similar in their ability or inability to work," the PDA provides the following exclusion and a proviso regarding abortion:

> This subsection shall not require an employer to pay for health insurance benefits for abortion, except where the life of the mother would be endangered if the fetus were carried to term, or except where medical complications have arisen from an abortion: *Provided*, That nothing herein shall preclude an employer from providing abortion benefits or otherwise affect bargaining agreements in regard to abortion.

42 U.S.C. § 2000e(k). The EEOC interprets this statutory language to mean that

> [t]he basic principle of the [PDA] is that women affected by pregnancy and related conditions must be treated the same as other applicants and employees on the basis of their ability or inability to work. A woman is therefore protected against such practices as being fired * * * merely because she is pregnant or has had an abortion.

Questions and Answers on the Pregnancy Discrimination Act, 29 C.F.R. pt. 1604, app. (2009). Finally, the legislative history of § 2000e(k) provides:

> Because [the PDA] applies to all situations in which women are "affected by pregnancy, childbirth, and related medical conditions," its basic language covers women who chose to terminate their pregnancies. Thus, no employer may, for example, fire or refuse to

hire a woman simply because she has exercised her right to have an abortion.

H.R.Conf.Rep. No. 95–1786, 95th Cong., 2d Sess. 4 (1978). Thus, Title VII protects the status of being pregnant and indicates that abortion is a "medical condition" related to pregnancy. The EEOC guidelines and legislative history assert that the PDA protects the status of having had an abortion. *See* Doe v. C.A.R.S. Protection Plus, Inc., 527 F.3d 358, 364 (3d Cir.2008) (holding that the term "related medical conditions" in the PDA includes abortions and "an employer may not discriminate against a woman employee because she has exercised her right to have an abortion").

Consider the applicability of the PDA in the following case: A restaurant employee was a young, unwed mother who discovered that she was pregnant for a second time. Her pregnancy and the fact that she was contemplating having an abortion became a subject of controversy among her co-workers. Ultimately, she decided not to terminate her pregnancy and carried to term. In the meantime, however, her employer discharged her on the ground that the uproar caused by her "contemplated" abortion interfered with her ability to perform her job. Does the employee have a viable claim under Title VII? *See* Turic v. Holland Hospitality, Inc., 85 F.3d 1211 (6th Cir.1996) (holding that, as a matter of law, "[a] woman's right to have an abortion encompasses more than simply the act of having an abortion; it includes the contemplation of an abortion, as well"). Are you persuaded by the reasoning of the court in *Turic* that "[s]ince an employer cannot take adverse employment action against a female employee for her decision to have an abortion, it follows that the same employer also cannot take adverse employment action against a female employee for merely thinking about what she has a right to do." *Id.* at 1214.

The district court in *Turic* found that the employee was discharged because she merely thought about having an abortion. But what about the employer's argument that her thoughts were communicated to her co-workers and disrupted the workplace? Is it ever reasonable for employment decisions to hinge on the subjective responses of fellow employees? Would the employer in *Turic* have a legitimate, nondiscriminatory reason for its action on the basis that it would discharge any employee who disrupts the work environment by discussing his or her private plans for controversial elective medical procedures? For example, can an employee be disciplined for disrupting the workplace by talking about her plans to have liposuction? Or body piercing? What about a man discussing a planned vasectomy or a woman discussing her planned breast implants? *Turic* suggests that employers must treat a female employee's on-the-job "contemplation"—and discussion—of having an abortion with greater deference than her contemplation and discussion of a medical procedure not related to pregnancy. Is this what the PDA requires?

C. DISCRIMINATION AGAINST CAREGIVERS

In the past decade there has been a growing focus on the need for—and possibility of—legal protection for workers who face workplace discrimination because of their family obligations. With changing demographics, it is all but inevitable that most workers today will face some conflict between their employer's demands and their family obligations. In 64 percent of two-parent families with children, both parents were employed outside the home in 2014. Bureau of Labor Statistics, Economic News Release, Families with Own Children: Employment Status of Parents by Age of Youngest Child and Family Type, 2013–2014 Annual Averages, tbl.4, available at *http://www.bls.gov/news.release/famee.t04.htm*. In addition, reports show that about 16 percent of Americans provide unpaid care to an elderly relative or friend each year and that about one-fifth of those providing eldercare are caring for children at the same time. The Council of Economic Advisors, *Nine Facts about American Families and Work* 12 (June 2014), available at *https://www.whitehouse.gov/sites/default/files/docs/nine_facts_about_family_and_work_real_final.pdf*. While the burdens of family responsibility discrimination fall much more heavily on women, there are consequences for both men and women workers. As the EEOC explained in its enforcement guidance on family responsibilities discrimination:

> [W]omen with caregiving responsibilities may be perceived as more committed to caregiving than to their jobs and as less competent than other workers, regardless of how their caregiving responsibilities actually impact their work. Male caregivers may face the mirror image stereotype: that men are poorly suited to caregiving. As a result, men may be denied parental leave or other benefits routinely afforded their female counterparts.

Equal Empl. Oppt'y Comm'n, Enforcement Guidance: Unlawful Disparate Treatment of Workers with Caregiving Responsibilities (2007), available at *http://www.eeoc.gov/policy/docs/caregiving.html* (hereinafter EEOC, Guidance on Caregiving Responsibilities).

Of course, explicit discrimination against mothers as compared to similarly situated fathers has long been recognized as unlawful. In the Supreme Court's first case to consider the meaning of sex discrimination under Title VII, *Phillips v. Martin Marietta Corp.*, 400 U.S. 542, 91 S.Ct. 496, 27 L.Ed.2d 613 (1971), also discussed in Chapter 7, the Court held that an employer's rule that prohibited mothers of preschool-aged children from holding certain positions was a prima facie violation of federal law. Because mothers of very young children were treated differently from fathers of young children, the company policy discriminated on the basis of sex. Notwithstanding that settled principle, social scientists continue to find that motherhood triggers a significant increase in gender stereotyping at work. For example, a Cornell University study asked participants to rate candidates for hire and identified some candidates as mothers and others—with identical qualifications—as nonmothers; while 84 percent of the nonmothers were considered qualified for hire, only 47 percent of mothers received a hiring recommendation. Shelley J. Cornell, Stephen Benard & In Paik, *Getting a Job: Is There a Motherhood Penalty?*, 112 Amer.J.Soc. 1297, 1316 (2007). Further, the candidates identified as mothers were offered an average of $11,000 less in salary for the same position. *Id.* The same study also found that mothers were held to higher standards for both performance and punctuality than nonmothers. *Id.* In contrast, fathers were advantaged over men without children: they were rated as more committed to work, offered higher salaries, and held to lower performance and punctuality standards than men without children. *Id.* at 1317. *See also* Joan C. Williams & Stephanie Bornstein, *The Evolution of "FRED": Family Responsibilities Discrimination and Developments in the Law of Stereotyping and Implicit Bias*, 59 Hastings L.J. 1311, 1326–30 (2008) (describing other sociological studies).

In spite of this evidence of employment discrimination against caregivers, particularly mothers, no federal law explicitly prohibits discrimination on the basis of family responsibilities. The federal law that most directly addresses the need for work-family balance is the Family and Medical Leave Act of 1993, 29 U.S.C. § 2601 *et. seq*, which requires certain larger employers to provide twelve weeks of unpaid leave annually for employees who give birth to or adopt a child, or who are sick or need to care for sick family members. As well, in 2007, the EEOC issued enforcement guidance to explain to Commission investigators, employers, and employees how employer treatment of an employee with a work-family conflict might constitute unlawful gender discrimination under Title VII or disability discrimination under the Americans with Disabilities Act. EEOC, Guidance on Caregiving Responsibilities, *supra*. Recent years have seen a growing number of lawsuits challenging what has come to be known as "family responsibility discrimination" (FRD) under one or more of these federal laws. This section will explore developments in this area.

1. FAMILY RESPONSIBILITIES DISCRIMINATION

CHADWICK V. WELLPOINT, INC.

United States Court of Appeals for the First Circuit, 2009.
561 F.3d 38.

STAHL, CIRCUIT JUDGE.

Laurie Chadwick brought a claim of sex discrimination under Title VII against WellPoint, Inc. and Anthem Health Plans of Maine, Inc. (collectively, "WellPoint"), after she was denied a promotion. She alleged that her employer failed to promote her because of a sex-based stereotype that women who are mothers, particularly of young children, neglect their jobs in favor of their presumed childcare responsibilities. Having carefully reviewed the record, we are convinced that the district court erred in granting summary judgment in favor of WellPoint and therefore reverse and remand for further proceedings. * * *

Chadwick was a long-time employee of WellPoint, an insurance company, in its Maine office. * * * In 2006, encouraged by her supervisor, she applied for a promotion to a management position entitled "Recovery Specialist Lead" or "Team Lead." * * * Because Chadwick was already performing several of the responsibilities of the Team Lead position and based on her supervisor's comments, Chadwick believed she was the frontrunner for the position. In addition, on her most recent performance evaluation in 2005, she had received excellent reviews, scoring a 4.40 out of a possible 5.00 points.

There were two finalists for the Team Lead position, Chadwick and another in-house candidate, Donna Ouelette. While Chadwick had held the Recovery Specialist II position for seven years, Ouelette had only been promoted to that position about a year earlier. In addition, Ouelette had scored lower than Chadwick, though satisfactorily, on her most recent performance review, receiving a 3.84 out of a possible 5.0 points.

Three managers interviewed the two finalists: Linda Brink, who had previously supervised and worked closely with Chadwick; Dawn Leno, the Director of Recovery; and Nanci Miller, Chadwick's immediate supervisor. Nanci Miller was the ultimate decisionmaker for the promotion but she considered input from Brink and Leno in reaching her decision. Based on her own perceptions and those of Brink and Leno, Miller graded Ouelette's interview performance higher than Chadwick's. Miller subsequently offered the promotion to Ouelette over Chadwick.

At the time of the promotion decision, Chadwick was the mother of an eleven-year-old son and six-year-old triplets in kindergarten. There is no allegation, insinuation, or for that matter evidence that Chadwick's work performance was negatively impacted by any childcare responsibilities she may have had. Indeed, Miller, the decisionmaker, did not know that Chadwick was the mother of young triplets until shortly before the promotion decision was made. Apparently, Chadwick's husband, the primary caretaker for the children, stayed home with them during the day while Chadwick worked. He also worked off-hour shifts, presumably nights and weekends, when Chadwick was at home with the children. During the same period, Chadwick was also taking one course a semester at the University of Southern Maine.

Chadwick alleges that WellPoint denied her the promotion based on the sex-based stereotype that mothers, particularly those with young children, neglect their work duties in favor of their presumed childcare obligations. To support this claim, Chadwick points to the fact that she was significantly more qualified[3] for the promotion than was Ouelette, and also highlights three statements made by management around the time of the promotion decision.

First, on May 9, 2006, two months before the decision was reached, Miller, the decisionmaker, found out that Chadwick had three six-year-old children (in addition to an eleven-year-old son). Miller sent an email to Chadwick stating, "Oh my—I did not know you had triplets. Bless you!"

Second, during Chadwick's interview with Brink, her former supervisor, she was asked how she would respond if an associate did not complete a project on time. Unhappy with Chadwick's answer, Brink replied, "Laurie, you are a mother [.] [W]ould you let your kids off the hook that easy if they made a mess in [their] room[?] [W]ould you clean it or hold them accountable?"

Third, and most important, when Miller informed Chadwick that she did not get the promotion, Miller explained:

> It was nothing you did or didn't do. It was just that you're going to school, you have the kids and you just have a lot on your plate right now.

In the same conversation, Miller said that, "if [the three interviewers] were in your position, they would feel overwhelmed." Finally, Miller also told Chadwick that, "there would be something better down the road," and that Chadwick would look back and say "it's a good thing that that opportunity didn't work out because I'm happier with this down the road."

In her deposition, Miller said that she decided not to promote Chadwick because she interviewed poorly, and that she (Miller) only told Chadwick that she had "too much on her plate" in an ill-advised attempt to soften the blow. In addition, in its brief, WellPoint makes much of its

[3] It is a fair inference that Chadwick's qualifications significantly outweighed those of Ouelette. Whether a finder of fact would so conclude is a question for another day.

assertion that Ouelette was apparently the mother of two children, ages nine and fourteen. However, unlike the district court, we do not give weight to this assertion.[4]

d.Ct. ruling

Procedurally, WellPoint moved for summary judgment following discovery. A magistrate judge recommended the motion be granted, and the district court, in a separate opinion, agreed. The district court concluded that Chadwick's claim could not proceed to a jury because "[n]othing in Miller's words show[ed] that" Chadwick was not promoted because of her sex, nor was there a "general atmosphere" of sex-based assumptions in the workplace. Chadwick now appeals. * * *

Title VII of the Civil Rights Act of 1964 prohibits discrimination based on sex. Notably, the Act does not prohibit discrimination based on caregiving responsibility. Chadwick's claim can be characterized as a "sex plus" claim. This denomination refers to the situation where "an employer classifies employees on the basis of sex *plus* another characteristic." 1 Barbara Lindemann & Paul Grossman, *Employment Discrimination Law* 456 (3d ed.1996) (emphasis in original). The terminology may be a bit misleading, however, because the "plus" does not mean that more than simple sex discrimination must be alleged; rather, it describes the case where "not all members of a disfavored class are discriminated against." *Back v. Hastings on Hudson Union Free Sch. Dist.*, 365 F.3d 107, 118 (2d Cir.2004). In other words, "[i]n such cases the employer does not discriminate against the class of men or women as a whole but rather treats differently a subclass of men or women." Lindemann, 456. Here, Chadwick alleges that the subclass being discriminated against based on sex is women with children, particularly young children. Ultimately, regardless of the label given to the claim, the simple question posed by sex discrimination suits is whether the employer took an adverse employment action *at least in part* because of an employee's sex.

The type of discrimination Chadwick alleges involves stereotyping based on sex. * * * The Supreme Court and several circuits, including this one, have had occasion to confirm that the assumption that a woman will perform her job less well due to her presumed family obligations is a form of sex-stereotyping and that adverse job actions on that basis constitute sex discrimination. *See Nevada Dep't of Human Res. v. Hibbs,* 538 U.S. 721, 730, 123 S.Ct. 1972, 155 L.Ed.2d 953 (2003); *Back*, 365 F.3d at 120 (identifying sex-stereotyping where employer stated that a woman could not "be a good mother" and work long hours, and that a woman "would not show the same level of commitment . . . because [she] had little ones

[4] WellPoint's assertion that Ouelette was a mother of two does not receive weight in our assessment of the summary judgment motion for several reasons. * * * [T]he record does not support the inference that WellPoint knew of Ouelette's status as a mother of two children, while it is uncontested that WellPoint knew of Chadwick's children. [As well,] the stereotype that Chadwick complains of would arguably be more strongly held as to a mother of four children, three of whom were only six years old, than as to a mother of two older children.

at home"); *Lust v. Sealy, Inc.*, 383 F.3d 580, 583 (7th Cir.2004) (sex-stereotyping found where decisionmaker admitted he didn't promote plaintiff "because she had children and he didn't think she'd want to relocate her family, though she hadn't told him that"); *Santiago-Ramos v. Centennial P.R. Wireless Corp.*, 217 F.3d 46, 57 (1st Cir.2000) (finding proof of sex-based discriminatory animus where direct supervisor questioned "whether [the plaintiff] would be able to manage her work and family responsibilities"); *Sheehan v. Donlen Corp.*, 173 F.3d 1039, 1045 (7th Cir.1999) (in a Pregnancy Discrimination Act case, finding direct evidence of discrimination where supervisor told employee "that she was being fired so that she could 'spend more time at home with her children'" because statement "invoked widely understood stereotypes the meaning of which is hard to mistake").

In its 2003 decision in *Hibbs*, the Supreme Court took judicial notice of the stereotype that women, not men, are responsible for family caregiving. The Court noted that the Family Medical Leave Act (FMLA) was enacted by Congress because, "stereotype-based beliefs about the allocation of family duties remained firmly rooted [in society]." *Hibbs*, 538 U.S. at 730, 123 S.Ct. 1972. The Court acknowledged the "pervasive sex-role stereotype that caring for family members is women's work." *Id.* at 731, 123 S.Ct. 1972. It explained that Congress created the FMLA's gender-neutral twelve-week leave program in order to "attack the formerly state-sanctioned stereotype that only women are responsible for family caregiving, thereby reducing employers' incentives to engage in discrimination by basing hiring and promotion decisions on stereotypes." *Id.* at 737, 123 S.Ct. 1972.

In the simplest terms, these cases stand for the proposition that unlawful sex discrimination occurs when an employer takes an adverse job action on the assumption that a woman, because she is a woman, will neglect her job responsibilities in favor of her presumed childcare responsibilities. It is undoubtedly true that if the work performance of a woman (or a man, for that matter) actually suffers due to childcare responsibilities (or due to any other personal obligation or interest), an employer is free to respond accordingly, at least without incurring liability under Title VII. However, an employer is not free to assume that a woman, because she is a woman, will necessarily be a poor worker because of family responsibilities. The essence of Title VII in this context is that women have the right to prove their mettle in the work arena without the burden of stereotypes regarding whether they can fulfill their responsibilities. * * *

In the opinion below, the district court acknowledged two important pieces of the puzzle. First, it found that sex-based stereotypes regarding women, families, and work are alive and well in our society. Second, it concluded that the statements made to Chadwick were based on "an assumption or generalization about the demands of continuing education coupled with child rearing responsibilities." Yet the district court granted summary judgment to WellPoint because, as the court explained, Miller did not explicitly say that Chadwick's sex was the basis for her assumption that Chadwick would not be able to handle the demands of work and home. The district court complained that the decisionmaker "[did] not refer explicitly to women," and that "nothing in Miller's words," showed that the decision was based on "a stereotype about female caregivers, not about caregivers generally," Presumably, the district court was looking for Miller to say explicitly that she thought Chadwick would be overwhelmed because she is *a woman* with kids, rather than, as Miller actually said, "you have the kids." But this critique is not an adequate basis upon which to grant summary judgment in this case.

* * * We reject the district court's requirement that Miller's words explicitly indicate that Chadwick's sex was the basis for Miller's assumption about Chadwick's inability to balance work and home. To require such an explicit reference (presumably use of the phrase "because you are a woman," or something similar) to survive summary judgment would undermine the concept of proof by circumstantial evidence, and would make it exceedingly difficult to prove most sex discrimination cases today.

* * * Given what we know about societal stereotypes regarding working women with children, we conclude that a jury could reasonably determine that a sex-based stereotype was behind Miller's explanation to Chadwick that, "It was nothing you did or didn't do. It was just that you're going to school, you have the kids and you just have a lot on your plate right now." Particularly telling is Miller's comment that, "It was nothing you did or didn't do." After all, the essence of employment discrimination is penalizing a worker not for something she did but for something she simply is. A reasonable jury could infer from Miller's explanation that Chadwick wasn't denied the promotion because of her work performance or her interview performance but because Miller and others assumed that as a *woman* with four young children, Chadwick would not give her all to her job.

This inference is supported by several facts. First, the decisionmaker learned of Chadwick's three six-year-olds just two months before she denied Chadwick the promotion. The young age and unusually high number of children would have been more likely to draw the decisionmaker's attention and strengthen any sex-based concern she had that a woman with young children would be a poor worker.

Second, the decisionmaker's reaction upon learning of Chadwick's three small children was, "Bless you!" This statement is susceptible to various interpretations, but a jury could reasonably conclude that Miller meant that she felt badly for Chadwick because her life must have been so difficult as the mother of three young children.[10] This conclusion could be bolstered by Miller's later explanation to Chadwick that the WellPoint interviewers, all female, would feel "overwhelmed" if they were in Chadwick's position.

Third, because a plaintiff alleging discrimination infrequently has direct evidence of bias, the discrimination can "be proven through the elimination of other plausible non-discriminatory reasons until the most plausible reason remaining is discrimination." *Thomas v. Eastman Kodak Co.*, 183 F.3d 38, 61 (1st Cir.1999). *See also Reeves v. Sanderson Plumbing Prods., Inc.*, 530 U.S. 133, 147, 120 S.Ct. 2097, 147 L.Ed.2d 105 (2000) ("Proof that the defendant's explanation is unworthy of credence is simply one form of circumstantial evidence that is probative of intentional discrimination, and it may be quite persuasive."). In Chadwick's case, Miller explained the non-promotion in one way to Chadwick (that she had too much on her plate with her kids and school) and in a very different way in her deposition (that Chadwick had performed poorly in her interviews). A jury could reasonably question the veracity of this second explanation given that Chadwick was an in-house, long-time employee who had worked closely with her interviewers, had received stellar performance reviews, and was already performing some of the key tasks of the Team Lead position. A jury could rightly question whether brief interviews would actually trump Chadwick's apparently weighty qualifications, or whether, given the other circumstantial evidence discussed above, Chadwick was really passed over because of sex-based stereotypes.

In sum, we find that Chadwick has put forth sufficient evidence of discrimination that a reasonable jury could conclude that the promotion denial was more probably than not caused by discrimination. We do not opine on the ultimate balance of the evidence in this case. We only conclude that Chadwick has presented sufficient evidence of sex-based stereotyping to have her day in court. Given the common stereotype about the job performance of women with children and given the surrounding circumstantial evidence presented by Chadwick, we believe that a reasonable jury could find that WellPoint would not have denied a promotion to a similarly qualified man because he had "too much on his plate" and would be "overwhelmed" by the new job, given "the kids" and his schooling. *See Hibbs*, 538 U.S. at 736, 123 S.Ct. 1972 ("Stereotypes about women's domestic roles are reinforced by parallel stereotypes presuming a lack of domestic responsibilities for men.").

---

[10] The district court erred by concluding that the "Bless you!" comment was conclusively "a friendly exclamation." This is a factual conclusion that a judge at summary judgment is not free to make. A jury could agree with Chadwick's view that Miller's comment suggested pity rather than respect. Therefore, at summary judgment, we must draw this inference in Chadwick's favor.

NOTES AND QUESTIONS

1. Professor Joan Williams, one of the originators of the acronym "FRD" to identify this category of cases, defines FRD as:

> employment discrimination against people based on their caregiving responsibilities—whether for children, elderly parents, or ill partners. FRD includes both "maternal wall" discrimination—the equivalent of the glass ceiling for mothers—and discrimination against men who participate in childcare or provide care for other family members. When an employer treats an employee with caregiving responsibilities based on stereotypes about how the employee will or should behave, rather than on that employee's individual interests or performance, it has engaged in FRD.

Joan C. Williams, *Caregivers in the Courtroom: The Growing Trend of Family Responsibilities Discrimination,* 41 U.S.F.L.Rev. 171, 171 (2006). Does this definition create a new category for protection under federal laws, or does it simply expand or refine the definition of the already protected "sex"? When the EEOC released its 2007 enforcement guidance on caregiving responsibilities, the Commission specifically noted that "[t]his document is not intended to create a new protected category, but rather to illustrate circumstances in which stereotyping or other forms of disparate treatment may violate Title VII." Equal Empl. Oppt'y Comm'n, Enforcement Guidance: Unlawful Disparate Treatment of Workers with Caregiving Responsibilities (2007), available at *http://www.eeoc.gov/policy/docs/caregiving.html* (hereinafter EEOC Guidance on Caregiving Responsibilities). *See also* Palomares v. Second Federal Sav. And Loan Ass'n of Chicago, 2011 WL 760088, *3 (N.D. Ill. 2011) (rejecting male employee's claim that he was discriminated against because he was a "primary caregiver" where he offered no evidence to tie the alleged discrimination to his gender).

2. A 2010 report by the Center for Worklife Law identified a 400 percent increase in the number of FRD cases being filed in 1999–2008 compared to the preceding decade, with 444 cases filed between 1989 and 1998 and 2207 cases filed between 1999 and 2008. Cynthia Thomas Calvert, *Family Responsibilities Discrimination: Litigation Update 2010* 9, available at *http://www.worklifelaw.org/pubs/FRDupdate.pdf.* Of the cases identified as FRD in the study, 67 percent involved claims related to pregnancy or maternity leave. *Id.* at 10. Eighty-eight percent of the plaintiffs included in the study were female and about 37 percent of the cases were filed by workers in managerial or professional occupations. *Id.* at 13. Why would the number of FRD cases increase so substantially over time? Possible explanations include an increase in the number of mothers in the workforce, an increase in actual discrimination, an increase in employee awareness of legal rights, and changes in the law—such as the availability of punitive damages after the Civil Rights Act of 1991 or the passage of the FMLA in 1993—that made the suits more viable. *See id.* at 9. Which seems most likely to you? Are there other possible explanations?

3. What evidence should be sufficient to suggest gender discrimination in an FRD case? In *Back v. Hastings on Hudson Union Free School District,* 365 F.3d 107 (2d Cir.2004), a public school psychologist who was denied tenure alleged that her supervisors discriminated against her on the basis of sex in violation of her rights to equal protection under the Fourteenth Amendment. Her evidence of discrimination was based on stereotypical statements that her supervisors made about whether she could "be a good mother" and, at the same time, meet the demands and long hours her job required. The court concluded that, "at least where stereotypes are considered, the notions that mothers are insufficiently devoted to work, and that work and motherhood are incompatible, are properly considered to be, themselves, gender-based. * * * [S]tereotyping of women as caregivers can by itself and without more be evidence of an impermissible, sex-based motive." *Id.* at 121. *See also* Zambrano-Lamhaouhi v. New York City Bd. Of Educ., 866 F.Supp.2d 147, 172 (EDNY 2011) (noting that "courts * * * have taken judicial notice of the real-world prevalence of the stereotype that pregnant women and young mothers will make undesirable employees" and taking "the recognized pervasiveness of such gender stereotypes into account" in denying defendant's summary judgment motion). In a 2008 Title VII case, the EEOC settled a sex discrimination lawsuit with Centenary College of Louisiana for $200,000. The college had fired its women's intercollegiate basketball head coach after her child was born. Allegedly the college's assistant athletic director had repeatedly expressed concerns to the coach about the wisdom of her "life choice" to become a mother and her ability to remain fully committed to her coaching responsibilities. Equal Empl. Oppt'y Comm'n, Press Release, *Centenary College to Pay $200,000 to Settle EEOC Sex Discrimination Suit* (Mar. 28, 2008), available at *http://www.eeoc.gov/press/3-28-08.html.* Are these cases consistent with *Price Waterhouse v. Hopkins*, 490 U.S. 228, 109 S.Ct. 1775, 104 L.Ed.2d 268 (1989), or do they take a more expansive view of the evidentiary value of stereotypical comments?

4. In *Phillips v. Martin Marietta Corp.*, 400 U.S. 542, 91 S.Ct. 496, 27 L.Ed.2d 613 (1971) (per curiam), the Court discussed whether a bona fide occupational qualification (BFOQ) defense arguably could insulate an employer's practice of denying certain jobs to mothers—but not fathers—of preschool-aged children. Although the suit's procedural posture meant the Court was not required to reach the merits of the BFOQ argument, the Court's opinion included speculation about the possibility that a sex-based BFOQ defense might be satisfied with proof that "[t]he existence of such conflicting family obligations" are "demonstrably more relevant to job performance for a woman than for a man." *Id.* at 544, 91 S.Ct. at 498. Justice Marshall, in dissent, expressed "fear that in this case, where the issue is not squarely before us, the Court has fallen into the trap of assuming the Act permits ancient canards about the proper role of women to be a basis for discrimination." *Id.* at 545, 91 S.Ct. at 498. Can you imagine a job in which not being a mother would be an occupational qualification?

5. While a majority of FRD cases are brought by women, the number of cases in which male workers have sought time to care for family members and have faced discriminatory employer responses is significant and growing. The most common scenario faced by men is that a request for leave is denied or the worker is fired for taking leave to participate in caregiving. *See, e.g.*, Knussman v. Md., 272 F.3d 625, 629–30 (4th Cir.2001) (state trooper requested "nurturing leave" to care for infant child after his wife's extremely difficult pregnancy and subsequent illness; supervisor said that men could not be primary caregivers and that he would only receive leave if his wife was "in a coma or dead"); EEOC Guidance on Caregiving Responsibilities (offering two examples of discrimination against male caregivers through the denial of leave and/or part-time work benefits). Reviewing a database of FRD cases, of which approximately 15–20 percent involved male plaintiffs, Joan Williams and Allison Tait observed that "[d]iscrimination against male caregivers takes various forms, including holding men with family responsibilities to higher standards, hyper-scrutinizing their work, interfering with their ability to take leave as guaranteed by the Family and Medical Leave Act (FMLA), or retaliating against men who take FMLA leave (typically via wrongful demotion or termination)." Joan C. Williams & Allison Tait, *"Mancession" or "Momcession"?: Good Providers, A Bad Economy, and Gender Discrimination*, 86 Chi.-Kent L. Rev. 857, 865–66 (2011). *See also* Keith Cunningham-Parmeter, *Men at Work, Fathers at Home: Uncovering the Masculine Face of Caregiver Discrimination*, 24 Colum. J. Gender & L. 253 (2013) (observing that "men remain bound by, and largely conform to, the historical expectation that they will provide for their families, avoid caregiving, and rely on their wives and partners to attend to domestic work").

6. On May 2, 2000, President Clinton signed Executive Order 13152 prohibiting federal employers from discriminating against employees based on their "status as a parent." How does this provision add to existing statutory protections of family care-givers? Should federal laws be amended to prohibited discrimination against parents?

7. For further reading on the topic of work-family conflict, see Joan Williams, Unbending Gender: Why Family and Work Conflict and What to Do About It (1999); Laura T. Kessler, *The Attachment Gap: Employment Discrimination Law, Women's Cultural Caregiving, and the Limits of Economic and Liberal Legal Theory,* 34 U. Mich.J.L.Reform 371 (2001); Peggie R. Smith, *Accommodating Routine Parental Obligations in an Era of Work-Family Conflict: Lessons from Religious Accommodations,* 2001 Wis.L.Rev. 1443; Joan C. Williams & Nancy Segal, *Beyond the Maternal Wall: Relief for Family Caregivers Who Are Discriminated Against on the Job*, 26 Harv. Women's L.J. 77 (2003); Joan C. Williams & Stephanie Bornstein, *The Evolution of "FRED": Family Responsibilities Discrimination and Developments in the Law of Stereotyping and Implicit Bias*, 59 Hastings L.J. 1311, 1326–30 (2008); Kyle Velte, *So You Want to Have a Second Child? Second Child Bias and the Justification-Suppression Model of Prejudice in Family Responsibilities Discrimination*, 61 Buff. L. Rev. 909 (2013).

2. THE FAMILY AND MEDICAL LEAVE ACT

The FMLA guarantees eligible employees at least twelve weeks of leave for childbirth or adoption and related childcare and to attend to serious personal or family health problems. By its ten-year anniversary, over 35 million employees had taken FMLA leaves. *10 Years After It Was Enacted, FMLA Needs Makeover, Advocates Contend*, 21 Hum. Resources Rep. (BNA) No.5, at 117 (Feb. 10, 2003). A report released on the law's 20th anniversary found that 13 percent of all covered workers had taken FMLA leave in the preceding 12 months. *See* Jacob Alex Klerman, Kelly Dailey & Alyssa Pozniak, *Family and Medical Leave in 2012: Technical Report* (2014), available at *http://www.dol.gov/asp/evaluation/fmla/FMLA-2012-Technical-Report.pdf*. The FMLA requires covered employers to provide an eligible employee with up to twelve workweeks of leave during any twelve-month period because of (1) the birth of the employee's child and attendant child care; (2) the placement of a child with the employee for adoption or foster care; (3) a serious health condition of the employee's spouse, son, daughter or parent requiring the employee's care; or (4) a serious health condition that makes the employee unable to perform the functions of the job. 29 U.S.C. § 2612(a). A 2008 amendment to the Act also provides special extended leave of up to 26 weeks in a year for family members of individuals injured on active duty in the Armed Forces where the servicemember needs special care. *See* 29 U.S.C. § 2612(a)(3)–(4).

The FMLA does not necessarily extend leave already provided by an employer. If any employer chooses to provide additional leave beyond the FMLA's twelve weeks, it may, but the employer is also entitled to treat all leave as concurrent. *See* Ragsdale v. Wolverine World Wide, Inc., 535 U.S. 81, 87–88, 122 S.Ct. 1155, 152 L.Ed.2d 167 (2002) (invalidating a Department of Labor regulation that required an employer to specify if non-FMLA leave and FMLA leave were to run concurrently). Similarly, although the FMLA provides for unpaid leave, the employee may elect, or the employer may require, that paid leave already offered by the employer be substituted for all or part of FMLA leave. When two spouses are employed by the same employer, they are entitled to a combined total of twelve weeks of leave for birth or placement of a child or to care for parents with a serious health condition.

An employee taking FMLA leave must provide the employer with thirty days' notice if leave is foreseeable; otherwise the employee must provide such notice as is practicable. The employee's notice does not have to specify that the leave is being taken under the Act, but must provide sufficient information that the employer should know that leave is being requested for an FMLA-covered circumstance. *See, e.g.,* Scobey v. Nucor Steel-Ark., 580 F.3d 781, 786–87 (8th Cir.2009) (employee's phone calls mentioning funeral and saying he was distraught were insufficient to provide notice of FMLA leave entitlement); Tate v. Farmland Indus. Inc., 268 F.3d 989, 997 (10th Cir.2001) (notice does not have to include mention of the statute specifically). *See generally* Timothy Stewart Bland, *The Required Content of Employees' Notice to Employers of the Need for Leave Under the FMLA*, 12 Lab.Law. 235 (1996). Final regulations promulgated by the Department of Labor in 2009 provide detailed timing and notice provisions for employees seeking to take intermittent leave, to work a reduced-hours schedule or to take a temporary transfer to lighter duty in connecting with FMLA leave. *See* Leslie Goff Sanders, *Revised FMLA Regulations: Quagmire or Roadmap?*, 33 Emp.Disc.Rep. (BNA) 489 (Oct. 21, 2009).

An employee on FMLA leave cannot lose benefits accrued prior to the start of leave, and the employer must maintain the employee's benefits under a properly recognized group health plan at the same level and under the same terms as though the employee had continued to work. If the employee does not return to work at the completion of the leave, the employer may recover any health plan premium costs paid during the leave. The general rule, with some exceptions, is that an employee returning from leave is entitled to reinstatement to her former job or an equivalent position if the former job is no longer available.

The FMLA covers employees who have worked for at least one year for an employer who employs at least fifty workers. Legislation to extend coverage to employers with at least 25 employees is regularly proposed in Congress, but has never gained much traction. *See, e.g.,* 31 Emp. Disc. Rep. (BNA) 472 (Oct. 22, 2008) (noting reintroduction of bill to extend coverage to small businesses). Nearly half of all private sector employees are not covered by the FMLA as it is currently written. Extending coverage to smaller employers would bring millions of employees into the law's ambit.

The FMLA is enforced through either a private civil action for damages or equitable relief, or through administrative action by filing a complaint with the Secretary of Labor. The FMLA does not modify or affect any state or federal law prohibiting discrimination, nor does it preempt state or local laws providing greater leave rights than those found in the FMLA. Thus, state laws providing for preferential treatment of workers on the basis of family leave continue to play a significant role in this area. A number of complex issues arise when rights created under the FMLA overlap or conflict with rights provided under state laws dealing with family and medical leave or workers compensation, or with other federal statutes covering these rights or benefits. *See, e.g.,* Martin W. Aron & Richard M. De Aguizio, *The Four-Headed Monster: ADA, FMLA, OSHA and Workers' Compensation*, 46 Lab.L.J. 48 (1995).

NOTES AND QUESTIONS

1. The FMLA begins with several legislative "findings," including the statement that "due to the nature of the roles of men and women in our society, the primary responsibility for family caretaking often falls on women, and such responsibility affects the working lives of women more than it affects the working lives of men." 29 U.S.C. § 2601(a)(5). The Act further includes among its purposes "to promote the goal of equal employment opportunity for women and men." § 2601(b)(5). Is the FMLA an extension of the antidiscrimination principles embodied in Title VII and the PDA? Does the FMLA achieve its goal of increasing equal employment opportunity? Several years before the enactment of the FMLA, Professor Nancy Dowd wrote:

> [I]t is essential that we recognize this fundamental paradox about work and family: that the structure of work and family, and the nature of the conflict between work and family, is not just a women's issue and a gender issue. We must constantly take women and gender into account because they are inseparable from the existing structure and assumptions of family and work. We otherwise risk ignoring, perpetuating or recreating the gendered structure of work and family. At the same time, however, we must get beyond gender, to redefining the relationship between work and family. We must take account of gender in order to transform the workplace, and get beyond gender in order to imagine a world where gender is not a primary determinant of our choices and our vision.

Nancy E. Dowd, *Work and Family: The Gender Paradox and the Limitations of Discrimination Analysis in Restructuring the Workplace*, 24 Harv.C.R.–C.L.L.Rev. 79, 80–81 (1989). To what extent does the FMLA resolve the "paradox" noted by Dowd?

2. Does the FMLA currently create incentives for working men to increase their involvement in family responsibilities? Soon after the passage of the FMLA, Professor Martin Malin observed:

> Largely missing from the debate over maternal work-family conflicts is any discussion of paternal work-family conflicts. The two, however, are linked to a significant extent. Just as the absence of adequate maternal leave policies has been a barrier to women's roles in the workplace, the absence of adequate paternal leave policies has been a barrier to men's roles in the home. Furthermore, as long as parental leave remains de facto maternal leave, work-family conflicts will remain a significant barrier to women's employment and a significant source of discrimination against women.

Martin H. Malin, *Fathers and Parental Leave*, 72 Tex.L.Rev. 1047, 1052 (1994). *See also* Kelli K. Garcia, 20 Duke J. Gender L. & Pol'y 1, 3 (2012) (noting that "men who want to participate fully in family life face discrimination in the workplace, including the denial of leave and potentially greater harm to their careers than women in the same position").

Professor Michael Selmi has argued "that the FMLA [should] be amended so as to create greater incentives for men to take leave around the birth or adoption of a child," because "the disproportionate burden of child rearing that falls on women explains a substantial portion of their labor market inequality." Michael Selmi, *Family Leave and the Gender Wage Gap*, 78 N.C.L.Rev. 707, 712, 713 (2000). Selmi explores a range of incentives, "from forcing men to take six weeks of paid leave to the less drastic measure of creating a governmental contract set-aside program aimed at rewarding employers who succeed in encouraging their employees to take family leave." *Id.* at 712–13. Would you support or oppose such amendments to the FMLA? *See also* Michael Selmi, *The Work-Family Conflict: An Essay on Employers, Men and Responsibility,* 4 U.St. Thomas L.J. 573, 576 (2007) (exploring the question: "why should the public expect employers to change their practices to accommodate the demands of family life when men fail to do so?").

3. In *Nevada Department of Human Resources v. Hibbs*, 538 U.S. 721, 123 S.Ct. 1972, 155 L.Ed.2d 953 (2003), the Supreme Court considered whether the FMLA had been passed pursuant to a valid exercise of congressional authority under § 5 of the Fourteenth Amendment and therefore constituted a valid abrogation of the states' immunity from money damages in suits brought by private individuals. (This issue is discussed more generally in Chapter 2.) To make this determination, the Court considered whether the FMLA exhibited "congruence and proportionality between the injury to be prevented or remedied and the means adopted to that end." City of Boerne v. Flores, 521 U.S. 507, 520, 117 S.Ct. 2157, 2164, 138 L.Ed.2d 624 (1997). Chief Justice Rehnquist's opinion for the Court explained with passion the ongoing discrimination that justified congressional action under the Fourteenth Amendment:

> The FMLA aims to protect the right to be free from gender-based discrimination in the workplace. We have held that statutory classifications that distinguish between males and females are subject to heightened scrutiny. See, *e.g., Craig v. Boren,* 429 U.S. 190, 197–199, 97 S.Ct. 451, 50 L.Ed.2d 397 (1976). For a gender-based classification to withstand such scrutiny, it must "serv[e] important governmental objectives," and "the discriminatory means employed [must be] substantially related to the achievement of those objectives." *United States v. Virginia,* 518 U.S. 515, 533, 116 S.Ct. 2264, 135 L.Ed.2d 735 (1996) (citations and internal quotation marks omitted). The State's justification for such a classification "must not rely on overbroad generalizations about the different talents, capacities, or preferences of males and females." *Ibid.* We now inquire whether Congress had evidence of a pattern of constitutional violations on the part of the States in this area.

The history of the many state laws limiting women's employment opportunities is chronicled in—and, until relatively recently, was sanctioned by—this Court's own opinions. For example, in *Bradwell v. State,* 16 Wall. 130, 21 L.Ed.442 (1873) (Illinois), and *Goesaert v. Cleary,* 335 U.S. 464, 466, 69 S.Ct. 198, 93 L.Ed.163 (1948) (Michigan), the Court upheld state laws prohibiting women from practicing law and tending bar, respectively. State laws frequently subjected women to distinctive restrictions, terms, conditions, and benefits for those jobs they could take. In Muller v. Oregon, 208 U.S. 412, 419, n. 1, 28 S.Ct. 324, 52 L.Ed.551 (1908), for example, this Court approved a state law limiting the hours that women could work for wages, and observed that 19 States had such laws at the time. Such laws were based on the related beliefs that (1) woman is, and should remain, "the center of home and family life," *Hoyt v. Florida,* 368 U.S. 57, 62, 82 S.Ct. 159, 7 L.Ed.2d 118 (1961), and (2) "a proper discharge of [a woman's] maternal functions—having in view not merely her own health, but the well-being of the race—justif[ies] legislation to protect her from the greed as well as the passion of man," Muller, supra, at 422, 28 S.Ct. 324. Until our decision in Reed v. Reed, 404 U.S. 71, 92 S.Ct. 251, 30 L.Ed.2d 225 (1971), "it remained the prevailing doctrine that government, both federal and state, could withhold from women opportunities accorded men so long as any 'basis in reason' "—such as the above beliefs—"could be conceived for the discrimination." *Virginia, supra,* at 531, 116 S.Ct. 2264 (quoting *Goesaert, supra,* at 467, 69 S.Ct. 198).

As the FMLA's legislative record reflects, a 1990 Bureau of Labor Statistics (BLS) survey stated that 37 percent of surveyed private-sector employees were covered by maternity leave policies, while only 18 percent were covered by paternity leave policies. S.Rep. No. 103–3, pp. 14–15 (1993), U.S.Code Cong. & Admin.News 1993, p. 3. The corresponding numbers from a similar BLS survey the previous year were 33 percent and 16 percent, respectively. *Ibid.* While these data show an increase in the percentage of employees eligible for such leave, they also show a widening of the gender gap during the same period. Thus, stereotype-based beliefs about the allocation of family duties remained firmly rooted, and employers' reliance on them in establishing discriminatory leave policies remained widespread.

Congress also heard testimony that "[p]arental leave for fathers * * * is rare. Even * * * [w]here child-care leave policies do exist, men, *both in the public and private sectors,* receive notoriously discriminatory treatment in their requests for such leave." *Id.,* at 147 (Washington Council of Lawyers) (emphasis added). Many States offered women extended "maternity" leave that far exceeded the typical 4- to 8-week period of physical disability due to pregnancy and childbirth, but very few States granted men a parallel benefit: Fifteen States provided women up to one year of extended maternity leave, while only four provided men with the same. M. Lord & M. King, The State Reference Guide to Work-Family Programs for State Employees 30 (1991). This and other differential leave policies were not attributable to any differential physical needs of men and women, but rather to the pervasive sex-role stereotype that caring for family members is women's work.

* * * The impact of the discrimination targeted by the FMLA is significant. Congress determined:

> Historically, denial or curtailment of women's employment opportunities has been traceable directly to the pervasive presumption that women are mothers first, and workers second. This prevailing ideology about women's roles has in turn justified discrimination against women when they are mothers or mothers-to-be.

Joint Hearing 100. Stereotypes about women's domestic roles are reinforced by parallel stereotypes presuming a lack of domestic responsibilities for men. Because employers continued to regard the family as the woman's domain, they often denied men similar accommodations or discouraged them from taking leave. These mutually reinforcing stereotypes created a self-fulfilling cycle of discrimination that forced women to continue to assume the role of primary family caregiver, and fostered employers' stereotypical views about women's commitment to work and their value as employees. Those perceptions, in turn, Congress reasoned, lead to subtle discrimination that may be difficult to detect on a case-by-case basis. * * *

By creating an across-the-board, routine employment benefit for all eligible employees, Congress sought to ensure that family-care leave would no longer be stigmatized as an inordinate drain on the workplace caused by female employees, and that employers could not evade leave obligations simply by hiring men. By setting a minimum standard of family leave for *all* eligible employees, irrespective of gender, the FMLA attacks the formerly state-sanctioned stereotype that only women are responsible for family caregiving, thereby reducing employers' incentives to engage in discrimination by basing hiring and promotion decisions on stereotypes.

* * * [T]he FMLA is narrowly targeted at the fault line between work and family—precisely where sex-based overgeneralization has been and remains strongest * * * .

538 U.S. at 728–39, 123 S.Ct. 1978–83. Are you persuaded by this narrative of the FMLA as an anti-discrimination law? Would it affect your opinion to

know that most leave taken under the FMLA is not family leave, but personal sick leave? *See* Jane Waldfogel, *Family and Medical Leave: Evidence from the 2000 Surveys*, 20 Monthly Lab.Rev. (Sept. 2001), *available at http://www.bls.gov/opub/mlr/2001/09/art2full.pdf*. In *Coleman v. Court of Appeals of Maryland,* 132 S.Ct. 1327 (2012), the Supreme Court considered whether the provisions of the FMLA that provided for personal care, rather than family care, had been validly enacted under the Fourteenth Amendment. The Court concluded that they had not been, explaining that "what the family-care provisions have to support them, the self-care provision lacks, namely evidence of a pattern of state constitutional violations accompanied by a remedy drawn in narrow terms to address or prevent those violations." *Id.* at 1334.

4. The dissenters in *Hibbs* argued that the FMLA is not an anti-discrimination statute like Title VII, but a "social benefits regime" providing "substantive entitlements." 538 U.S. at 755–56, 123 S.Ct. 1972, 1992 (Kennedy, J., dissenting). *See also* Diaz v. Fort Wayne Foundry Corp., 131 F.3d 711, 712 (7th Cir.1997) (distinguishing the FMLA from Title VII by noting that "claims under the FLMA do not depend on discrimination" and comparing the FMLA to the NLRA, FLSA, and ERISA). Nevertheless, the FMLA complements and reinforces Title VII's prohibition against discrimination on the basis of pregnancy, childbirth, and related medical conditions by assuring that many women who seek or take leaves for these reasons have legal protections for their jobs and employee benefits. But do the PDA and the FMLA go far enough toward these goals?

5. Who are the primary beneficiaries of the FMLA? Professor Marion Crain observed that

> [t]he hard-won Family and Medical Leave Act * * * is limited to the protection of workers' jobs and maintenance of existing health benefits (if any) during an unpaid leave of up to twelve weeks to accommodate the birth or adoption of a child, or for care of a seriously ill child, spouse, or parent. The absence of wage replacement in the Act continues the assumption of female dependence on a male breadwinner. Notwithstanding the statute's gender-neutral language, only those who share expenses with a wage earner whose income is sufficient to support the family will be able to take advantage of the limited right to job security that the Act affords. From the perspective of single mothers and working class women whose wages are an essential part of the family income, the Act confers a hollow right. Most working class women will not be able to afford to take unpaid leave, whether or not they are part of a two-earner household, and many have no health benefits to extend during the leave. Moreover, part-time and temporary employees, who are disproportionately female, are not covered by the statute. Finally, the lack of wage replacement ensures that the statutory right is skewed disproportionately towards white women. Women of color are both more likely to be

> functioning as single heads-of-households and likely to derive a lesser economic benefit (relative to white women) from their associations with men because of the wage disparities between white men and men of color.

Marion Crain, *Confronting the Structural Character of Working Women's Economic Subordination: Collective Action vs. Individual Rights Strategies*, 3–Spring Kan.J.L. & Pub.Pol'y 26, 27–28 (1994). *See also* Nicole Buonocore Porter, *Synergistic Solutions: An Integrated Approach to Solving the Caregiver Conundrum for "Real" Workers*, 39 Stetson L. Rev. 777, 789–90 (2010) (noting that lack of financial resources makes FMLA leave and other necessary family supports, such as daycare, unattainable for many workers). The Healthy Families Act, a proposed law requiring employers with fifteen or more employees to provide workers with paid family leave, has been repeatedly introduced in both the House and the Senate. *See, e.g,* S. 1152, 111th Cong., 1st Sess. (2009); H.R. 2460, 111th Cong., 1st Sess. (2009); S. 497, 114th Cong., 1st Sess. (2015); H.R. 932, 114th Cong. 1st Sess. (2015). Provision of paid leave would answer some of Professor Crain's critiques of the FMLA. Would it address them all? Professor Arnow-Richman has suggested that discrimination against caregivers might be more effectively countered by a system that encourages employers and employees to seek internal workplace processes for resolving conflicts. Rachel Arnow-Richman, *Public Law and Private Process: Toward an Incentivized Organizational Justice Model of Equal Employment Quality for Caregivers,* 2007 Utah L. Rev. 25.

6. *Pregnancy and the Interplay Between Title VII, the PDA, the FMLA, and the ADA*: The FMLA requires employers to provide unpaid leave for employees with serious medical conditions; Title VII, as amended by the PDA, requires employers to treat pregnant employees the same as other employees who are similar in their ability or inability to perform the job (including the provision of accommodations where similar accommodations are made to other employees); and the Americans with Disabilities Act of 1991 (ADA), covered in Chapter 14, requires employers to make reasonable accommodations for employees with disabilities who are otherwise qualified to do the job. Often these statutes will address very different situations, but occasions will arise where the provisions of the statutes and agency regulations may provide overlapping, conflicting, or alternative theories of employee rights and employer liability. *See, e.g.*, Smith v. Diffee Ford-Lincoln-Mercury, Inc., 298 F.3d 955 (10th Cir.2002) (finding that an FMLA leave is a reasonable accommodation under the ADA); Navarro v. Pfizer Corp., 261 F.3d 90 (1st Cir.2001) (holding that EEOC's interpretation of a regulation issued under the ADA is not entitled to deference in interpreting the identical regulation adopted by the Secretary of Labor under the FMLA). For example, if a pregnant employee who experiences persistent, disabling morning sickness is denied part-time leave and then is fired when she cannot perform her job adequately due to recurrent bouts of nausea, does she have a viable claim under Title VII, the PDA, the FMLA, the ADA, or under all of

them? *See generally* Deborah A. Calloway, *Accommodating Pregnancy in the Workplace*, 25 Stetson L. Rev. 1 (1995).

Recently enacted EEOC regulations interpreting the ADA Amendments Act (ADAAA) explain that "although pregnancy itself is not an impairment, and therefore is not a disability, a pregnancy-related impairment that substantially limits a major life activity is a disability . . ." 29 C.F.R. § 1630.2(h) app. (2011). These regulations replaced the agency's former position that "conditions, such as pregnancy, that are not the result of a physiological disorder are not impairments." 29 C.F.R. § 1630.2(h)(1) app. (1996). The change in the EEOC's interpretation of the ADA may have been a result of the strong message of the ADAAA in favor of broad coverage. See 42 U.S.C. § 12101 (2013). They may also have been responsive to extensive criticism of the earlier, narrower interpretation. *See, e.g.*, Calloway, *supra*, at 28–29; Collette G. Matzzie, *Substantive Equality and Antidiscrimination: Accommodating Pregnancy Under the Americans with Disabilities Act*, 82 Geo.L.J. 193 (1993); Laura Schlictmann, *Accommodation of Pregnancy-Related Disabilities on the Job*, 15 Berkeley J.Emp. & Lab.L. 335 (1994).

The Labor Department regulations interpreting the FMLA clearly permit FMLA leave for pregnancy-related health conditions. *See* 29 C.F.R. § 825.120(a)(4) (providing that a woman "is entitled to FMLA leave for incapacity due to pregnancy, [or] for prenatal care"). However, the burden of proving "incapacity" may bar many pregnancy-related FMLA claims. For example, in *Gudenkauf v. Stauffer Commc'ns, Inc.*, 922 F.Supp. 465, 475–76 (D.Kan. 1996), the plaintiff's FMLA claim failed because there was insufficient evidence that her "pregnancy and related conditions kept her from performing the functions of her job for more than one-half day."

How would you advise an employer who has received a request for part-time leave from a pregnant employee who is experiencing severe morning sickness? Or from an employee who has requested to be assigned no overtime work solely because she is pregnant? *See* Whitaker v. Bosch Braking Sys., 180 F.Supp.2d 922, 926–31 (2001).

7. *Timing of Pregnancy-Related FMLA Leaves*: Can an employer unilaterally determine the timing of a twelve-week FMLA leave for a pregnant employee once the conditions for such a leave have been satisfied? Consider the following scenario: An employee whose job as a laboratory technician involves working with toxic chemicals learns that she is pregnant. Hoping to be given an alternative working assignment for the duration of her pregnancy, she submits to her employer a letter from her doctor stating that she should not be exposed to certain chemicals in the lab while she is pregnant. At the time, she is in her second month of pregnancy. The employer, who has no alternative positions available, immediately places the employee on a twelve-week leave that it designates as FMLA leave. In addition, the employer notifies the employee that if she is unable to return to her position as a lab technician at the end of the twelve-week period, she will be deemed to have voluntarily quit her job. When the FMLA leave ends, the

employee—who is then almost six months pregnant—chooses not to return to work at that time, and the employer terminates her employment. Does the employee have a viable claim that the employer violated the FMLA by unilaterally placing her on FMLA leave, at a time when she did not request such a leave, but only sought an alternative job assignment? *See* Harvender v. Norton Co., No. 96–CV–653 (LEK/RWS), 1997 WL 793085, at *7 (N.D.N.Y. 1997) (noting that "[n]owhere in the [FMLA] does it provide that FMLA leave must be granted only when the employee wishes it to be granted"). If the employer has not violated the FMLA, has it violated the Pregnancy Discrimination Act? *See* Carney v. Martin Luther Home, Inc., 824 F.2d 643 (8th Cir.1987) (holding that an employer violated the PDA when it required a pregnant employee to take an unpaid medical leave). Can the purposes of the FMLA and PDA be reconciled if employers are free to determine the timing of FMLA leaves?

8. *FMLA Retaliation and Association Discrimination Claims*: The FMLA has an anti-retaliation provision as well as a nondiscrimination provision. *See* 29 U.S.C. § 2615(b). The FMLA anti-retaliation language, however, is somewhat different from the corresponding anti-retaliation provisions in Title VII, § 704(a), the ADEA, § 623(d), and the ADA, § 503(a). Compare the statutory sections in the Statutory Supplement. How might these differences in statutory language affect the rights of claimants seeking relief under the FMLA as opposed to the other three antidiscrimination statutes? While it is clear that an employee who is fired for exercising her rights under the FMLA has a valid retaliation claim under § 2615(b), can her spouse who works for the same employer bring a third-party derivative claim based on the fact that he has suffered an adverse employment action simply because he silently supported his wife's protected activity and was prepared to testify on her behalf in any proceedings? A number of courts have considered this question, particularly in light of the Supreme Court's decision in *Thompson v. North American Stainless, LP,* 562 U.S. 170 (2011), holding that Title VII does permit suits for third-party retaliation. *See, e.g.,* Kastor v. Cash Express of Tennessee, LLC, 77 F.Supp.3d 605 (W.D. Ky. 2015); Lopez v. Four Dee, Inc., 2012 WL 2339389 (E.D.N.Y. 2012); Gilbert v. St. Rita's Professional Services, LLC, 2012 WL 2344583 (N.D. Ohio 2012); Elsensohn v. St. Tammany Parish Sheriff's Off., 530 F.3d 368 (5th Cir.2008) (per curiam). These courts have reached varying conclusions. *Compare* Kastor, 77 F.Supp.3d at 610 (concluding that the FMLA does permit third-party retaliation claims) *and Lopez*, 2012 WL 2339389, at *2 (concluding that the FMLA's retaliation provision is sufficiently expansive to encompass third-party claims) *with Gilbert*, 2012 WL 2344583, at *6 (noting that "although it is true that the FMLA often borrows from Title VII jurisprudence, there are limitations" and concluding that the FMLA's language did not permit third-party claims) *and Elsensohn*, 530 F.3d at 374 (denying the plaintiff/husband's third-party association discrimination claim on these facts and concluding that "the protections afforded under the ADEA are actually greater than the protections afforded under the FMLA because § 623(d) protects an individual who participates in an investigation, proceeding or litigation *in any manner,*

whereas § 2615(b) is limited to specific enumerated activities"). Does it make sense that a statute designed to accommodate workers' family responsibilities could be interpreted to permit an employer to discharge the co-worker spouse (or brother or mother) of any employee who has asserted his or her rights under the statute? For a discussion of third-party retaliation more generally, see Chapter 3.

9. *Comparative Perspectives on Family and Medical Leave Policies*: The United States has long been criticized for lagging behind other industrialized nations in the provision of family leave. *See, e.g.,* Linda A. White, *The United States in Comparative Perspective: Maternity and Parental Leave and Child Care Benefits Trends in Liberal Welfare States*, 21 Yale J.L. & Feminism 185 (2009) (discussing and evaluating long history of critical comparison); Saul Levmore, *Parental Leave and American Exceptionalism*, 58 Case W.Res.L.Rev. 203, 204 (2007) ("Outside of the United States, paid parental leave is nearly universal, though it comes in different forms."). A 2007 study of 173 countries found that 168 provided some form of paid leave to women in connection with childbirth. Jody Heymann, Alison Earle & Jeffrey Hayes, *The Work, Family and Equity Index: How Does the United States Measure Up?* 1–2 (2007) (noting that the United States, Lesotho, Liberia, Papua New Guinea, and Swaziland were the only countries with no paid maternity leave guarantee). The same study found that 66 countries offer some form of paid paternity leave. *Id.* at 2. Guaranteed leave that permits employees to address family needs and other personal matters has long been the right of employees in most European countries. The prevailing European model for treating maternity leave goes much further than either the PDA or the FMLA:

> [A]ll women in the European Community nations receive at least seventy-five percent of their salary, save those in Portugal and Britain.
>
> * * * [I]n all European countries that provide pregnancy benefits, with the partial exception of Britain, the prime source of payment is out of general revenues or general social insurance funds. In other words, society as a whole rather than the individual employer assumes the burden for pregnancy leave.
>
> The rejection of the antidiscrimination model for pregnancy-related workplace matters and the direct confrontation with the cost of accommodation establish the critical disparities between European and American law in this area.

Samuel Issacharoff & Elyse Rosenblum, *Women and the Workplace: Accommodating the Demands of Pregnancy*, 94 Colum.L.Rev. 2154, 2213–14 (1994).

10. In 2002, California became the first state to enact legislation that provides paid family leave. The California law, which went into effect in 2004, increases employee contributions to the State Disability Insurance

(SDI) fund; employees who take family leave under the California Family Rights Act (CFRA) are eligible for a weekly benefit based on California's workers compensation benefits. *See* Cal. Unemp. Ins. Code § 3301 ("Paid Family Leave"). Washington, Rhode Island, and New Jersey have since enacted similar plans. *See* National Partnership for Women & Families, *State Paid Family Leave Insurance Laws* (2015), available at *http://www.nationalpartnership.org/research-library/work-family/paid-leave/state-paid-family-leave-laws.pdf*. In California and Rhode Island, the paid leave is funded by contributions from employees only. *See id.* at 3. Does the fact that these paid family leave programs are funded by employees reduce employers' incentives to discriminate against employees who take family leave or are likely to request family leave? Does it make more sense to address family leave policies at the state or federal level?

CHAPTER 9

DISCRIMINATION BECAUSE OF SEXUAL ORIENTATION, GENDER EXPRESSION, AND GENDER IDENTITY

■ ■ ■

A. INTRODUCTION

Few areas of the law have seen as much change in the 21st century as the range of laws surrounding discrimination on the basis of sexual orientation, gender expression, and gender identity. In June 2015, the Supreme Court held that the Due Process Clause of the Fourteenth Amendment guarantees same-sex couples the right to marry and that state laws refusing to license or recognize same-sex marriages are unconstitutional. Obergefell v. Hodges, 576 U.S. ___, 135 S.Ct. 2017 (2015). In July 2015, the "Equality Act" was introduced in both the House and the Senate that would amend numerous federal statutes to make discrimination on the basis of sexual orientation and gender identity unlawful not only in employment, but also in public accommodations, housing, and education. *See* S. 1858, 114th Cong. (2015–2016); H.R. 3185, 114th Cong. (2015–2016). That same month, the Equal Employment Opportunity Commission declared that it interpreted Title VII to prohibit discrimination on the basis of sexual orientation, ruling that "allegations on the basis of sexual orientation necessarily state a claim of discrimination on the basis of sex." Baldwin v. Foxx, EEOC Appeal No. 0120133080 (July 15, 2015), available at *http://www.eeoc.gov/decisions/0120133080.pdf.*

These events undeniably suggest significant progress toward preventing and remedying discrimination on the basis of sexual orientation and gender identity. The reality, however, remains that there is still no federal law that explicitly outlaws employment discrimination on the basis of sexual orientation. The EEOC's July 2015 ruling was a clear break from the current interpretation of Title VII by the federal courts and from the agency's own previous position. And almost half of the gay, lesbian, bisexual, and transgender (LGBT) community in the U.S. lives in a state or locality with no prohibition on sexual orientation discrimination. *See* Movement Advancement Project, *LGBT Policy Spotlight: Local Employment Nondiscrimination Ordinances* (Oct. 2015), available at *http://lgbtmap.org/file/policy-spotlight-local-NDOs.pdf.*

Nevertheless, an increasing number of state and local governments include sexual orientation, as well as gender identity and gender expression, as protected statuses in their civil rights laws and ordinances. In addition, executive orders prohibit discrimination on the basis of sexual orientation, gender identity, and/or gender expression in many state and federal government jobs. A growing number of federal cases have challenged the distinctions between "sex," "gender," "gender identity," and "sexual orientation" in Title VII jurisprudence, and a few federal courts have found that workplace discrimination against transsexual individuals is "sex" discrimination under Title VII. In addition, some gender nonconforming employees have brought successful Title VII claims for workplace sexual harassment.

This chapter will consider the settled and developing law in this area. Section B will define some important terminology. Section C discusses the current debate over Title VII's applicability to claims of employment discrimination based on sexual orientation and gender identity. This Section also explores sexual harassment claims brought under Title VII by employees who either are or are perceived to be lesbian, gay, bisexual, or transgender. Finally, Section D addresses alternative sources of workplace protections against discrimination for lesbian, gay, bisexual and transgender employees, including recent proposals to enact federal legislation that explicitly prohibits discrimination against sexual minorities.

B. DEFINITIONS

The size of the lesbian, gay, bisexual, and transgender (LGBT) population in the United States is difficult to quantify because of the imprecise nature of data collection. *See* Gary J. Gates, *How many people are lesbian, gay, bisexual, and transgender?* 2 (April 2011), available at *http://williamsinstitute.law.ucla.edu/wp-content/uploads/Gates-How-Many-People-LGBT-Apr-2011.pdf.* According to a 2011 study that used the results of nine surveys conducted between 2004 and 2011, the adult LGBT population in the United States is about 9 million, or just under 4 percent of the adult population. *Id.* at 1. The 2013 National Health Interview Survey found that 1.6 percent of U.S. adults identified as gay or lesbian and .7 percent identified as bisexual. Brian W. Ward et al, Sexual Orientation and Health Among U.S. Adults: National Health Interview Survey, 2013 (2014), available at *http://www.cdc.gov/nchs/data/nhsr/nhsr077.pdf.* It is similarly difficult to estimate the number of LGBT employees in the American workforce, but a 2013 study estimated that about 5.4 million workers in the U.S identify as LGBT. *See* Movement Advancement Project, *A Broken Bargain: Discrimination, Fewer Benefits and More Taxes for LGBT Workers* 5 (June 2013), available at *http://www.lgbtmap.org/file/a-broken-bargain-full-report.pdf.* Moreover, "[a]s the Millennial generation increasingly enters the workforce, employers can expect to see greater numbers of openly LGBT workers. According to a 2012 Gallup survey, 6.4% of adults between the ages of 18 and 29 self-identify as LGBT; this is three times the percentage of adults age 65+ who do so (1.9%)." *Id.*

Accurate survey data on the extent of workplace discrimination against LGBT individuals is also hard to obtain for a variety of reasons, including the reliance on self-reporting. In a 2008 survey, 42 percent of LGBT-identified respondents said they had experienced employment discrimination because of their sexual orientation. Brad Sears & Christy Mallory, *Documented Evidence of Employment Discrimination & Its Effects on LGBT People* 4 (July 2011), available at *http://williamsinstitute.law.ucla.edu/wp-content/uploads/Sears-Mallory-Discrimination-July-2011.pdf.* The most common form of discrimination reported was harassment, which 35 percent of respondents had faced. *Id.* at 5. A 2013 survey found that 21 percent of LGBT respondents reported facing unfair treatment in hiring, pay or promotions. Pew Research Center, *A Survey of LGBT Americans: Attitudes, Experiences and Values in Changing Times* 1 (June 2013), available at *http://www.pewsocialtrends.org/files/2013/06/SDT_LGBT-Americans_06-2013.pdf.*

Developing case law on LGBT workplace rights, as well as statutes and proposed legislation at the federal, state, and local level, emphasizes the need for greater clarity about terminology. Defining terms is essential, but also complicated because the terms change, and certain labels, once popular, may come to be viewed as pejorative in the LGBT community. Following are some definitions of a few terms, drawn in part from Human Rights Campaign, *Transgender Inclusion in the Workplace* 2–3 (2d ed. 2008) [hereinafter *Transgender Inclusion*], available at *http://www.hrc.org/issues/transgender/transgender_inclusion_workplace.htm.*

Sex and *Gender.* Title VII law on sex discrimination has developed based on the assumption that "sex" is a binary concept—that there are two sexes based on anatomical, biological characteristics—male and female—and that "gender"—masculine or feminine—follows from sex. *See* Ann McGinley, *Erasing Boundaries: Masculinities, Sexual Minorities and Employment Discrimination*, 43 Univ. Mich. J. L. Reform 713, 715 (2010). Gender refers to external behavior—including dress, grooming, and mannerisms—that are viewed as being socially or culturally linked either to men or to women.

Sexual Orientation. The term sexual orientation has been defined as "a person's enduring physical, romantic, emotional and/or spiritual attraction to another person." *Transgender Inclusion*, *supra*, at 2. It is often assumed that individuals can be categorized as heterosexual, homosexual (gay or lesbian), bisexual, or asexual depending on how they manifest or express their sexuality.

Gender identity and gender expression. Gender identity "refers to a person's innate, deeply felt psychological sense of gender, which may or may not correspond to the person's body or designated sex at birth." *Transgender Inclusion, supra* at 2. Gender expression describes the ways that people, regardless of biological sex, outwardly display traits, behaviors, and styles of dress and grooming that are socially and culturally assumed to be masculine or feminine.

Transgender. The term "transgender" today is "an umbrella term to denote transsexuals, transvestites, crossdressers, and anyone else whose gender identity or gender expression varies from the dimorphic norm." Jillian Todd Weiss, *Transgender Identity, Textualism, and the Supreme Court: What Is the "Plain Meaning" of "Sex" in Title VII of the Civil Rights Act of 1964*, 18 Temp.Pol. & Civ.Rts.L.Rev. 573, 589 (2009).

Transsexual. A "transsexual" is "a person who has changed, or is in the process of changing, his or her physical sex to conform to his or her internal sense of gender identity." *Transgender Inclusion, supra,* at 3. Transsexual persons who experience severe discomfort from the mismatch between their biological sex and their gender identity may be diagnosed as having "gender identity disorder" (GID), sometimes called "gender dysphoria," which is a mental disorder recognized by the American Psychiatric Association. *Id.* The term "transsexual" also includes "people who, without undergoing medical treatment, identify and live their lives full-time as a member of the gender different from their designated sex at birth."

Intersex. Even biological sex based on the presence or absence of sex-based anatomical features, external genitalia, internal reproductive organs, chromosomes, and hormones is not necessarily binary. "Intersex" individuals—a very small minority of the population—are born with a mixture of both male and female biological characteristics. *See generally* Alice Domurat Dreger, Hermaphrodites and the Medical Invention of Sex (2000); Anne Fausto-Sterling, Sexing the Body: Gender Politics and the Construction of Sexuality (2000); Sharon Preves, Intersex and Identity, the Contested Self (2003); Julie A. Greenberg, *Defining Male or Female: Intersexuality and the Collision Between Law and Biology*, 41 Ariz.L.Rev. 265 (1999). Usage of the term intersex is now preferred over the word "hermaphrodite," which is considered "outdated and offensive to the people it once described." Ariel Levy, *Either/Or*, New Yorker, Nov. 30, 2009, at 53. The acronym "LGBTQI" is now sometimes used to label a class that expressly includes both queer and intersex individuals. Levy, *supra,* at 54. In this chapter, the more common term LGBT will be used to refer to all sexual minorities.

C. THE APPLICABILITY OF TITLE VII TO DISCRIMINATION AGAINST LGBT EMPLOYEES

1. DISCRIMINATION ON THE BASIS OF SEXUAL ORIENTATION

In 1979, the Court of Appeals for the Ninth Circuit held that discrimination against employees on the basis of their sexual orientation is not discrimination on the basis of "sex" under Title VII. DeSantis v. Pac. Tel. & Tel. Co., 608 F.2d 327 (9th Cir.1979), *abrogated in part by* Nichols v. Azteca Rest. Enters, Inc., 256 F.3d 864, 874–75 (9th Cir.2001). Addressing three cases consolidated on appeal, *DeSantis* rejected the Title VII claims of (1) a male nursery school teacher who was fired for wearing a small, gold earring, (2) a class of openly gay men who were either harassed by their supervisors and co-workers at a telephone company or were not hired at all because of a company policy not to hire gay men, and (3) two female telephone company employees who were harassed and then fired when their lesbian relationship became known at work. The plaintiffs in *DeSantis* asserted several theories: (1) that "sex" in Title VII should be interpreted broadly to include sexual orientation, *id.* at 329; (2) that "discrimination against homosexuals disproportionately affects men both because of the greater incidence of homosexuality in the male population and because of the greater likelihood of an employer's discovering male homosexuals compared to female homosexuals," *id.* at 330; (3) that "if a male employee prefers males as sexual partners, her will be treated differently from a female who prefers male partners," *id.* at 331; (4) that "discrimination because of the sex of the employees' sexual partner should constitute discrimination based on sex," *id.*; and (5) that an employer's "reliance on a stereotype—that a male should have a virile rather than an effeminate appearance—violates Title VII," *id.* The court rejected all of these attempts to "bootstrap" sexual orientation claims on to Title VII. Nearly a quarter of a century after *DeSantis*, a judge on the Ninth Circuit Court of Appeals observed: "While societal attitudes toward homosexuality have undergone some changes since *DeSantis* was decided, Title VII has not been amended to prohibit discrimination based on sexual orientation; this aspect of *DeSantis* remains good law and has been followed in other circuits." Rene v. MGM Grand Hotel, 305 F.3d 1061, 1075–76 (9th Cir.2002) (en banc) (Hug, J., dissenting). *See also* Brian Soucek, *Perceived Homosexuals: Looking Gay Enough for Title VII,* 63 Am. U. L. Rev. 715, 722, & n.34 (2014) (collecting cases and noting that "every other circuit to address the issue has agreed" with *DeSantis*).

Nevertheless, much of the rationale of *DeSantis* has been undercut by developments in sex discrimination law, sexual harassment law, and other laws regarding gender nonconforming conduct. In July 2015, the

EEOC issued a ruling that overturned the Agency's previous position (which had been consistent with *DeSantis*) and concluded that Title VII is appropriately interpreted to protect against discrimination on the basis of sexual orientation.

BALDWIN V. FOXX

EEOC Appeal No. 0120133080 (July 15, 2015).

[David Baldwin worked as a Supervisory Air Traffic Control Specialist at the Miami International Airport. When he was not selected for a position as a Front Line Manager (FLM), he filed a complaint of discrimination with the Equal Employment Opportunity Commission (EEOC), alleging that he was not selected because he is gay. Baldwin alleged that his supervisor, who was involved in the selection process, made several negative comments about his sexual orientation. For example, Baldwin alleged that when he mentioned at work that he and his partner had attended Mardi Gras in New Orleans, the supervisor said, "We don't need to hear about that gay stuff." Baldwin also alleged that the supervisor told him on a number of occasions that he was "a distraction in the radar room" when his participation in conversations included mention of his male partner.]

Title VII's prohibition of sex discrimination means that employers may not "rel[y] upon sex-based considerations" or take gender into account when making employment decisions. *See* Price Waterhouse v. Hopkins, 490 U.S. 228, 239, 241–42 (1989).[4] This applies equally in claims brought by lesbian, gay, and bisexual individuals under Title VII.

When an employee raises a claim of sexual orientation discrimination as sex discrimination under Title VII, the question is not whether sexual orientation is explicitly listed in Title VII as a prohibited basis for employment actions. It is not. Rather, the question for purposes of Title VII coverage of a sexual orientation claim is the same as any other Title VII case involving allegations of sex discrimination—whether the agency has "relied on sex-based considerations" or "take[n] gender into account" when taking the challenged employment action.

In the case before us, we conclude that Complainant's claim of sexual orientation discrimination alleges that the Agency relied on sex-based considerations and took his sex into account in its employment decision regarding the permanent FLM position. Complainant, therefore, has stated a claim of sex discrimination. Indeed, we conclude that sexual

[4] As used in Title VII, the term "sex" "encompasses both sex—that is, the biological differences between men and women—and gender." *See* Schwenk v. Hartford, 204 F.3d 1187, 1202 (9th Cir. 2000); *see also* Smith v. City of Salem, 378 F.3d 566, 572 (6th Cir. 2004) ("The Supreme Court made clear that in the context of Title VII, discrimination because of 'sex' includes gender discrimination."). * * *

orientation is inherently a "sex-based consideration," and an allegation of discrimination based on sexual orientation is necessarily an allegation of sex discrimination under Title VII. A complainant alleging that an agency took his or her sexual orientation into account in an employment action necessarily alleges that the agency took his or her sex into account.

Discrimination on the basis of sexual orientation is premised on sex-based preferences, assumptions, expectations, stereotypes, or norms. "Sexual orientation" as a concept cannot be defined or understood without reference to sex. A man is referred to as "gay" if he is physically and/or emotionally attracted to other men. A woman is referred to as "lesbian" if she is physically and/or emotionally attracted to other women. Someone is referred to as "heterosexual" or "straight" if he or she is physically and/or emotionally attracted to someone of the opposite-sex. *See, e.g.,* American Psychological Ass'n, "Definition of Terms: Sex, Gender, Gender Identity, Sexual Orientation" (Feb. 2011), *available at http://www.apa.org/pi/lgbt/resources/sexuality-definitions.pdf.* It follows, then, that sexual orientation is inseparable from and inescapably linked to sex and, therefore, that allegations of sexual orientation discrimination involve sex-based considerations. One can describe this inescapable link between allegations of sexual orientation discrimination and sex discrimination in a number of ways.

Sexual orientation discrimination is sex discrimination because it necessarily entails treating an employee less favorably because of the employee's sex. For example, assume that an employer suspends a lesbian employee for displaying a photo of her female spouse on her desk, but does not suspend a male employee for displaying a photo of his female spouse on his desk. The lesbian employee in that example can allege that her employer took an adverse action against her that the employer would not have taken had she been male. That is a legitimate claim under Title VII that sex was unlawfully taken into account in the adverse employment action. The same result holds true if the person discriminated against is straight. Assume a woman is suspended because she has placed a picture of her husband on her desk but her gay colleague is not suspended after he places a picture of his husband on his desk. The straight female employee could bring a cognizable Title VII claim of disparate treatment because of sex.

The court in *Hall v. BNSF Ry. Co.*, No. 13–2160, 2014 WL 4719007 (W.D. Wash., Sept. 22 2014) adopted this analysis of Title VII. In that case, the court found that the plaintiff, a male who was married to another male, alleged sex discrimination under Title VII when he stated that he "experienced adverse employment action in the denial of the spousal health benefit, due to sex, where similarly situated females [married to males] were treated more favorably by getting the benefit." *Id.* at *2. The court recognized that the sexual orientation discrimination alleged by the plaintiff constituted an allegation that the employer was treating female employees with male partners more favorably than male employees with male partners simply because of the employee's sex. * * *

Sexual orientation discrimination is also sex discrimination because it is associational discrimination on the basis of sex. That is, an employee alleging discrimination on the basis of sexual orientation is alleging that his or her employer took his or her sex into account by treating him or her differently for associating with a person of the same sex. For example, a gay man who alleges that his employer took an adverse employment action against him because he associated with or dated men states a claim of sex discrimination under Title VII; the fact that the employee is a man instead of a woman motivated the employer's discrimination against him. Similarly, a heterosexual man who alleges a gay supervisor denied him a promotion because he dates women instead of men states an actionable Title VII claim of discrimination because of his sex.

In applying Title VII's prohibition of race discrimination, courts and the Commission have consistently concluded that the statute prohibits discrimination based on an employee's association with a person of another race, such as an interracial marriage or friendship. *See, e.g.,* Floyd v. Amite County School Dist., 581 F.3d 244, 249 (5th Cir.2009) ("This court has recognized that . . . Title VII prohibit[s] discrimination against an employee on the basis of a personal relationship between the employee and a person of a different race."); Holcomb v. Iona Coll., 521 F.3d 130, 138 (2d Cir.2008) ("We . . . hold that an employer may violate Title VII if it takes action against an employee because of the employee's association with a person of another race."). This is because an employment action based on an employee's relationship with a person of another race necessarily involves considerations of the employee's race, and thus constitutes discrimination because of the employee's race.

This analysis is not limited to the context of race discrimination. Title VII "on its face treats each of the enumerated categories"—race, color, religion, sex, and national origin—"exactly the same." *Price Waterhouse*, 490 U.S. at 243 n.9 ("[O]ur specific references to gender throughout this opinion, and the principles we announce, apply with equal force to discrimination based on race, religion, or national origin."); *see also* Whidbee v. Garzarelli Food Specialties, Inc., 223 F.3d 62, 69 n.6 (2d Cir.2000) ("[T]he same standards apply to both race-based and sex-based hostile environment claims."); Williams v. Owens-Illinois, Inc., 665 F.2d 918, 929 (9th Cir.1982) ("[T]he standard for proving sex discrimination and race discrimination is the same."). * * *

Therefore, Title VII similarly prohibits employers from treating an employee or applicant differently than other employees or applicants based on the fact that such individuals are in a same-sex marriage or because the employee has a personal association with someone of a particular sex. Adverse action on that basis is, "by definition," discrimination because of the employee or applicant's sex. * * *

Sexual orientation discrimination also is sex discrimination because it necessarily involves discrimination based on gender stereotypes. In *Price Waterhouse*, the Court reaffirmed that Congress intended Title VII to "strike at the entire spectrum of disparate treatment of men and women resulting from sex stereotypes." 490 U.S. at 251 (quoting Los Angeles Dep't of Water & Power v. Manhart, 435 U.S. 702, 707 n.13 (1978)). In the wake of *Price Waterhouse*, courts and the Commission have recognized that lesbian, gay, and bisexual individuals can bring claims of gender stereotyping under Title VII if such individuals demonstrate that they were treated adversely because they were viewed—based on their appearance, mannerisms, or conduct—as insufficiently "masculine" or "feminine." But as the Commission and a number of federal courts have concluded in cases dating from 2002 onwards, discrimination against people who are lesbian, gay, or bisexual on the basis of gender stereotypes often involves far more than assumptions about overt masculine or feminine behavior.

Sexual orientation discrimination and harassment "[are] often, if not always, motivated by a desire to enforce heterosexually defined gender norms." Centola v. Potter, 183 F. Supp. 2d 403, 410 (D. Mass. 2002). The *Centola* court continued:

> In fact, stereotypes about homosexuality are directly related to our stereotypes about the proper roles of men and women. While one paradigmatic form of stereotyping occurs when co-workers single out an effeminate man for scorn, in fact, the issue is far more complex. The harasser may discriminate against an openly gay co-worker, or a co-worker that he perceives to be gay, whether effeminate or not, because he thinks, "real" men should date women, and not other men.

Id.

* * *

In the past, courts have often failed to view claims of discrimination by lesbian, gay, and bisexual employees in the straightforward manner described above. Indeed, many courts have gone to great lengths to distinguish adverse employment actions based on "sex" from adverse employment actions based on "sexual orientation." The stated justification for such intricate parsing of language has been the bare conclusion that "Title VII does not prohibit . . . discrimination because of sexual orientation." Dawson v. Bumble & Bumble, 398 F.3d 211, 217 (2d Cir.2005) (*quoting* Simonton v. Runyon, 232 F.3d 33, 35 (2d Cir.2000)).

For that reason, courts have attempted to distinguish discrimination based on sexual orientation from discrimination based on sex, even while noting that the "borders [between the two classes] are . . . imprecise." *Id.* (alteration in original). * * *

Some of these decisions reason that Congress in 1964 did not intend Title VII to apply to sexual orientation and, therefore, Title VII could not be interpreted to prohibit such discrimination. *See, e.g.,* DeSantis v. Pacific Telephone & Telegraph Co., 608 F.2d 327, 329 (9th Cir.1979) ("Congress had only the traditional notions of 'sex' in mind" when it passed Title VII and those "traditional notions" did not include sexual orientation or sexual preference.) *abrogated by* Nichols v. Azteca Restaurant Enterprises, Inc., 256 F.3d 864, 875 (9th Cir.2001).

Congress may not have envisioned the application of Title VII to these situations. But as a unanimous Court stated in *Oncale v. Sundowner Offshore Services, Inc.*, "statutory prohibitions often go beyond the principal evil [they were passed to combat] to cover reasonably comparable evils, and it is ultimately the provisions of our laws rather than the principal concerns of our legislators by which we are governed." 523 U.S. 75, 79, 78–80 [118 S.Ct. 998, 140 L.Ed.2d 201] (1998) (holding that same-sex harassment is actionable under Title VII). Interpreting the sex discrimination prohibition of Title VII to exclude coverage of lesbian, gay or bisexual individuals who have experienced discrimination on the basis of sex inserts a limitation into the text that Congress has not included. Nothing in the text of Title VII "suggests that Congress intended to confine the benefits of [the] statute to heterosexual employees alone." Heller v. Columbia Edgewater Country Club, 195 F.Supp.2d. 1212, 1222 (D.Or.2002).

Some courts have also relied on the fact that Congress has debated but not yet passed legislation explicitly providing protections for sexual orientation. *See* Bibby v. Phila. Coca Cola Bottling Co., 260 F.3d 257, 261 (3d Cir.2001) ("Congress has repeatedly rejected legislation that would extend Title VII to cover sexual orientation."). But the Supreme Court has ruled that "[c]ongressional inaction lacks persuasive significance because several equally tenable inferences may be drawn from such inaction, including the inference that the existing legislation already incorporated the offered change." Pension Benefit Guar. Corp. v. LTV Corp., 496 U.S. 633, 650 (1990) (citation omitted) (internal quotation marks omitted).

The idea that congressional action is required (and inaction is therefore instructive in part) rests on the notion that protection against sexual orientation discrimination under Title VII would create a new class of covered persons. But analogous case law confirms this is not true. When courts held that Title VII protected persons who were discriminated against because of their relationships with persons of another race, the courts did not thereby create a new protected class of "people in interracial relationships." *See, e.g.*, Deffenbaugh-Williams v. Wal-Mart Stores, Inc., 156 F.3d 581, 588–89 (5th Cir.1998), *reinstated in relevant part*, Williams v. Wal-Mart Stores, Inc., 182 F.3d 333 (5th Cir.1999) (en banc). And when the Supreme Court decided that Title VII protected persons discriminated against because of gender stereotypes held by an employer, it did not thereby create a new protected class of "masculine women." *See Price Waterhouse*, 490 U.S. at 239–40 (plurality opinion). Similarly, when ruling under Title VII that discrimination against an employee because he lacks religious beliefs is religious discrimination, the courts did not thereby create a new Title VII basis of "non-believers." *See, e.g.*, EEOC v. Townley Eng'g & Mfg. Co., 859 F.2d. 610, 621 (9th Cir.1988). These courts simply applied existing Title VII principles on race, sex, and religious discrimination to these situations. Further, the Supreme Court was not dissuaded by the absence of the word "mothers" in Title VII when it decided that the statute does not permit an employer to have one hiring policy for women with pre-school children and another for men with pre-school children. *See* Phillips v. Martin-Mn on the basis of sex. We further conclude that allegations of discrimination on the basis of sexual orientation necessarily state a claim of discrimination on the basis of sex. An employee could show that the sexual orientation discrimination he or she experienced was sex discrimination because it involved treatment that would not have occurred but for the individual's sex; because it was based on the sex of the person(s) the individual associates with; and/or because it was premised on the fundamental sex stereotype, norm, or expectation that individuals should be attracted only to those of the opposite sex. * * *

NOTES AND QUESTIONS

1. As an EEOC ruling, *Baldwin* is not controlling on the federal courts. *See* Skidmore v. Swift & Co., 323 U.S. 134, 140 (1944). Courts might, however, defer to the Agency's interpretation. *Id.* In its most recent decision considering whether to defer to the EEOC, however, the Supreme Court declined deference because of concerns about "timing, consistency, and thoroughness of consideration" reflected in the Agency's guidelines interpreting the Pregnancy Discrimination Act. Young v. United Parcel Service, 575 U.S. ___, 135 S.Ct. 1338 (2015) (internal quotations omitted). For a discussion of the Court's view of the EEOC's PDA guidelines, *see supra*, Chapter 8, Section 1. Given that *Baldwin* represents a fundamental change in the EEOC's position on the proper interpretation of Title VII, is it likely to face skepticism in the courts? Are you persuaded by the opinion? In Isaacs v. Felder Services, LLC, ___ F.Supp.3d ___, 2015 WL 6560655, at *3 (M.D.Ala. 2015), the court agreed with the EEOC's view that "claims of sexual orientation are cognizable under Title VII," though the particular plaintiff had failed to present sufficient evidence to support his claim. One

commentator has argued that *Baldwin* should not be seen as "a watershed moment for advocates of LGBT workplace equality," because it is not likely to receive deference in the courts. Ryan H. Nelson, *Sexual Orientation Discrimination Under Title VII after Baldwin v. Foxx*, 72 Wash. & Lee L. Rev. Online 255, 276–77 (2015).

2. While the federal courts have consistently resisted the argument that sexual orientation discrimination is sex discrimination, scholars and advocates have been arguing that the two are formally equivalent for decades. *See* Keith Cunningham-Parmeter, *Marriage Equality, Workplace Inequality: The Next Gay Rights Battle*, 67 Fla. L. Rev. 1099, 1134 (2015). As Professor Andrew Koppelman has explained, "[t]he basic sex-discrimination argument is simple. Any action that singles out homosexuals facially classifies on the basis of sex. If a business fires Ricky, or if the state prosecutes him, because of his sexual activities with Fred, whereas similar adverse actions would not be taken against Lucy if she did exactly the same things with Fred, then Ricky is being discriminated against on the basis of his sex." Andrew Koppelman, *Response: Sexual Disorientation*, 100 Geo. L.J. 1083, 1087 (2012). This argument is not a claim that Congress intended Title VII to cover sexual orientation discrimination. "Rather, the theory asserts that discrimination against sexual minorities constitutes both sex discrimination and sexual orientation discrimination, and that Congress obviously intended to prohibit the former type of discrimination." Cunningham-Parmeter, *supra* at 1146.

3. In *Hall v. BNSF Ry. Co.*, No. C13–2160 RSM, 2014 WL 4719007, at *2 (W.D. Wash. Sept. 22, 2014), the plaintiff alleged that he was "a male properly performing his job, who experienced adverse employment action in the denial of the spousal health benefit, due to his sex, where similarly situated females were treated more favorably by getting the benefit. If Michael Hall were female, the benefit would be provided; BNSF provides it to female employees who are married to males but denied it to Hall who is married to a male." The defendant filed a motion to dismiss, arguing that the claim was really one of sexual orientation discrimination, and thus was not cognizable under Title VII. The court denied the motion to dismiss, explaining:

> While acknowledging that it is often difficult to distinguish sex discrimination claims made by people identifying as homosexual from those claims based solely on alleged sexual orientation discrimination, the Court disagrees with Defendant's interpretation of the instant claims.
>
> As an initial matter, Mr. Hall's Amended Complaint sets forth, *inter alia,* the following factual allegations, which clearly frame his Title VII claim as one based on sex:
>
> > 7. Michael Hall and Elijah Uber (also known as Elijah Hall and referred to herein as Elijah Hall) are males residing in

Pierce County, Washington who legally married in Washington State on January 21, 2013. * * *

22. BNSF pays spousal health coverage throughout its enterprise where a male employee is married to a female spouse and where a female employee is married to a male spouse.

23. Starting in early 2013, Michael Hall repeatedly requested that BNSF cover Elijah's health care costs.

24. Michael Hall has provided documentation of marriage required by BNSF or its authorized agent for health care benefits, United Healthcare.

25. BNSF has failed and refused to cover the health care costs of Michael Hall's legal spouse, Elijah Hall.

26. This failure to pay is based solely on the fact Michael is male.

27. If Michael Hall were female, married to a male, BNSF would pay him the spousal health coverage benefits as it does to all employees who are female married to male spouses, or males married to female spouses.

28. BNSF pays in its enterprise many female employees the health care benefits concerning their male spouses, including many locomotive engineers who are female.

29. BNSF has directly and through its apparent and authorized agent United Healthcare stated its reason for not covering Elijah is it has a "policy" that "marriage is one man, one woman"; although Michael Hall and Elijah Hall have explained many times this definition of marriage is not the law in Washington state, and Elijah is the spouse and husband of Michael Hall, factually, and legally.

30. The one man/one woman definition of spouse used by BNSF to limit its liability to cover spousal health benefits amounts to a BNSF policy to discriminate against Michael Hall simply because he is male; under this policy, if he were a female married to Elijah, the benefit would be paid.

Defendant tries desperately to cast these allegations solely in terms of sexual orientation, emphasizing that Plaintiffs are comparing "only *homosexual* men to *heterosexual* women (and vice versa)." (emphasis in original). This reading not only ignores the plain language of the Amended Complaint, it improperly restricts the class of employees affected by the policy at issue in which Plaintiff Michael Hall is a member. But a careful reading of the Amended Complaint, construed in favor of the Plaintiff as the non-moving party, demonstrates that Plaintiff alleges disparate treatment based

> on his sex, not his sexual orientation, specifically that he (as a male who married a male) was treated differently in comparison to his female coworkers who also married males.

Id. at *2–*3. In light of the Supreme Court's decision in *Obergefell v. Hodges*, 576 U.S. ___, 135 S.Ct. 2017 (2015), that states must permit same-sex couples to marry, will claims like Hall's become more common? *See, e.g.*, Koren v. Ohio Bell Telephone Co., 894 F.Supp.2d 1032, 1038 (N.D. Ohio 2012) (denying defendant's motion for summary judgment where plaintiff alleged discrimination against him because he is married to a man and took his husband's last name, the court concluded that plaintiff had a cognizable claim of sex discrimination). Does the reasoning in *Hall* suggest that the court would be receptive to a claim that sexual orientation discrimination is covered by Title VII? Or does the opinion simply recognize that "[t]he presence of one type of bias that Title VII does not cover (sexual orientation discrimination) does not preclude the coexistence of another type of bias that Title VII prohibits (sex discrimination)." Cunningham-Parmeter, *supra*, at 1146.

4. A growing number of courts have permitted LGBT plaintiffs to bring sex discrimination claims on a sex-stereotyping theory. What evidence beyond the fact of a plaintiff's sexual orientation should be sufficient to survive a motion to dismiss? In *Terveer v. Billington*, 34 F.Supp.3d 100 (D.D.C. 2014), the court denied defendant's motion to dismiss, rejecting the argument that plaintiffs alleging sex-stereotyping should be required "to set forth specific allegations regarding the particular ways in which an employee failed to conform to such stereotypes" and that the plaintiff in this instance had not suggested that his supervisor's conduct was a result of his "behavior, demeanor or appearance." *Id.* at 115. Instead, the court concluded that the plaintiff's allegation that "his orientation as homosexual had removed him from [his supervisor's] preconceived definition of male" was sufficient to survive a motion to dismiss. *Id.* at 116. *See also* Heller v. Columbia Edgewater Country Club, 195 F.Supp.2d 1212, 1224 (D.Or. 2002) ("[A] jury could find that Cagle [discharged] Heller because Heller did not conform to Cagle's stereotype of how a woman ought to behave. Heller is attracted to and dates other women, whereas Cagle believes that a woman should be attracted to and date only men."). *But see* Simonton v. Runyon, 232 F.3d 33, 38 (2d Cir.2000) ("We do not have sufficient allegations before us to decide Simonton's claims based on stereotyping because we have no basis in the record to surmise that Simonton behaved in a stereotypically feminine manner and that the harassment he endured was, in fact, based on his non-conformity with gender norms instead of his sexual orientation."). If the non-conforming behavior of a plaintiff claiming sex discrimination can be the fact of his "orientation as homosexual," will sexual orientation discrimination always be sex discrimination?

5. In *Dawson v. Bumble & Bumble*, 398 F.3d 211 (2d Cir.2005), a lesbian hairdresser sued her former employer under Title VII for failure to promote and wrongful discharge because of sex, gender, sexual stereotypes,

and sexual orientation. The court ruled that her claim that the employer discriminated against her because of her "manner of dress" was not supported by substantial evidence. In any event, the court considered her gender stereotyping claim to be problematic because she was a lesbian; the court observed:

> When utilized by an avowedly homosexual plaintiff, however, gender stereotyping claims can easily present problems for an adjudicator. This is for the simple reason that "[s]tereotypical notions about how men and women should behave will often necessarily blur into ideas about heterosexuality and homosexuality." Like other courts, we have therefore recognized that a gender stereotyping claim should not be used to "bootstrap protection for sexual orientation into Title VII."

Id. at 218 (citations omitted). Do you agree that claims based on evidence of gender stereotyping can or should be limited in this way?

6. *Race or Sex Plus Sexual Orientation*: If a gay black man sues his employer under Title VII on the basis of circumstantial evidence of a racially motivated discharge, can the employer successfully rebut a prima facie case of race discrimination with evidence that the discharge was based solely on the employee's sexual orientation? In other words, is aversion to gay men a "legitimate, nondiscriminatory reason" for an employer's adverse employment action? Or could this be analyzed under a mixed-motive framework? What evidence would a gay black male need in order to prove that he was treated differently, at least in part, because of his race (a violation of Title VII) rather than solely because of his sexual orientation (not a violation of Title VII)? *See* Williamson v. A.G. Edwards & Sons, Inc., 876 F.2d 69, 70 (8th Cir.1989) (per curiam) (to survive summary judgment, plaintiff, a gay black male, would have to allege facts adequate to show that "similarly situated" gay white male employees were treated more favorably). For an exploration of these issues, see Mary Eaton, *At the Intersection of Gender and Sexual Orientation: Toward Lesbian Jurisprudence*, 3 S.Cal.Rev.L. & Women's Stud. 183 (1994); Francisco Valdes, *Sex and Race in Queer Legal Culture: Ruminations on Identities & Inter-connectivities*, 5 S.Cal.Rev.L. & Women's Stud. 25 (1995).

2. DISCRIMINATION ON THE BASIS OF GENDER IDENTITY

In *Ulane v. Eastern Airlines, Inc.*, 742 F.2d 1081 (7th Cir.1984), the court held that Title VII does not protect employees from being discriminated against because they are transsexual. A former Army pilot decorated for combat service in Vietnam, Kenneth Ulane worked for Eastern Airlines for over a decade before undergoing psychiatric counseling, hormone treatments, and finally sex reassignment surgery in order to become a female named Karen Frances Ulane. When Eastern discovered the "sex" change, it fired Ulane. The district court ruled that Eastern had violated Title VII, but the Seventh Circuit reversed, holding that "Title VII does not protect transsexuals * * * ." *Id.* at 1084. Because "the operation would not create a biological female in the sense that Ulane would 'have a uterus and ovaries and be able to bear babies[,]' " and because "Ulane's chromosomes * * * are unaffected by the hormones and surgery[,]" *id.* at 1083, the court rejected the argument that Ulane was discriminated against on the basis of "sex." Agreeing with rulings of two other circuits, the court concluded that "if the term 'sex' as it is used in Title VII is to mean more than biological male or biological female, the new definition must come from Congress." *Id.* at 1087; *see also id.* at 1087 n.12 (citing cases).

In response to the argument that Ulane was discriminated against because she is now a female, the court observed:

> Ulane is entitled to any personal belief about her sexual identity she desires. After the surgery, hormones, appearance changes, and a new Illinois birth certificate and FAA pilot's certificate, it may be that society, as the trial judge found, considers Ulane to be female. But even if one believes that a woman can be so easily created from what remains of a man, that does not decide this case. If Eastern had considered Ulane to be female and had discriminated against her because she was female * * * , then the argument might be made that Title VII applied, but that is not this case. It is clear from the evidence that if Eastern did discriminate against Ulane, it was not because she is female, but because Ulane is a transsexual—a biological male who takes female hormones, cross-dresses, and has surgically altered parts of her body to make it appear to be female.

Id. at 1087.

Although most federal courts that have considered claims of sex discrimination brought by transsexual employees under Title VII have, until recently, agreed with *Ulane*, some courts construing state or local antidiscrimination laws have rejected the approach in *Ulane*. Consider the Sixth Circuit's analysis of the Title VII claim of a transsexual woman in the following case:

SMITH V. CITY OF SALEM, OHIO

United States Court of Appeals for the Sixth Circuit, 2004.
378 F.3d 566.

COLE, CIRCUIT JUDGE.

* * *

[Jimmie L.] Smith is—and has been, at all times relevant to this action—employed by the city of Salem, Ohio, as a lieutenant in the Salem

Fire Department (the "Fire Department"). Prior to the events surrounding this action, Smith worked for the Fire Department for seven years without any negative incidents. Smith—biologically and by birth a male—is a transsexual and has been diagnosed with Gender Identity Disorder ("GID"), which the American Psychiatric Association characterizes as a disjunction between an individual's sexual organs and sexual identity. American Psychiatric Association, Diagnostic and Statistical Manual of Mental Disorders 576–582 (4th ed.2000). After being diagnosed with GID, Smith began "expressing a more feminine appearance on a full-time basis"—including at work—in accordance with international medical protocols for treating GID. Soon thereafter, Smith's co-workers began questioning him about his appearance and commenting that his appearance and mannerisms were not "masculine enough." As a result, Smith notified his immediate supervisor, Defendant Thomas Eastek, about his GID diagnosis and treatment. He also informed Eastek of the likelihood that his treatment would eventually include complete physical transformation from male to female. Smith had approached Eastek in order to answer any questions Eastek might have concerning his appearance and manner and so that Eastek could address Smith's co-workers' comments and inquiries. Smith specifically asked Eastek, and Eastek promised, not to divulge the substance of their conversation to any of his superiors, particularly to Defendant Walter Greenamyer, Chief of the Fire Department. In short order, however, Eastek told Greenamyer about Smith's behavior and his GID.

Greenamyer then met with Defendant C. Brooke Zellers, the Law Director for the City of Salem, with the intention of using Smith's transsexualism and its manifestations as a basis for terminating his employment. On April 18, 2001, Greenamyer and Zellers arranged a meeting of the City's executive body to discuss Smith and devise a plan for terminating his employment. The executive body included Defendants Larry D. DeJane, Salem's mayor; James A. Armeni, Salem's auditor; and Joseph S. Julian, Salem's service director. Also present was Salem Safety Director Henry L. Willard, now deceased, who was never a named defendant in this action.

* * *

During the meeting, Greenamyer, DeJane, and Zellers agreed to arrange for the Salem Civil Service Commission to require Smith to undergo three separate psychological evaluations with physicians of the City's choosing. They hoped that Smith would either resign or refuse to comply. If he refused to comply, Defendants reasoned, they could terminate Smith's employment on the ground of insubordination. Willard, who remained silent during the meeting, telephoned Smith afterwards to inform him of the plan, calling Defendants' scheme a "witch hunt."

Two days after the meeting, on April 20, 2001, Smith's counsel telephoned DeJane to advise him of Smith's legal representation and the potential legal ramifications for the City if it followed through on the plan devised by Defendants during the April 18 meeting. On April 22, 2001, Smith received his "right to sue" letter from the U.S. Equal Employment Opportunity Commission ("EEOC"). * * *

Smith then filed suit in the federal district court. In his complaint, he asserted Title VII claims of sex discrimination and retaliation * * * . [The facts alleged regarding Smith's retaliation claim have been omitted.] [T]he district court dismissed the federal claims and granted judgment on the pleadings to Defendants pursuant to Federal Rule of Civil Procedure. * * *

On appeal, Smith contends that the district court erred in holding that: (1) he failed to state a claim of sex stereotyping; [and] (2) Title VII protection is unavailable to transsexuals * * * .

In his complaint, Smith asserts Title VII claims of retaliation and employment discrimination "because of * * * sex." The district court dismissed Smith's Title VII claims on the ground that he failed to state a claim for sex stereotyping pursuant to *Price Waterhouse v. Hopkins,* 490 U.S. 228, 109 S.Ct. 1775, 104 L.Ed.2d 268 (1989). The district court implied that Smith's claim was disingenuous, stating that he merely "invokes the term-of-art created by *Price Waterhouse,* that is, 'sex-stereotyping,'" as an end run around his "real" claim, which, the district court stated, was "based upon his transsexuality." The district court then held that "Title VII does not prohibit discrimination based on an individual's transsexualism."

Relying on *Price Waterhouse*—which held that Title VII's prohibition of discrimination "because of * * * sex" bars gender discrimination, including discrimination based on sex stereotypes—Smith contends on appeal that he was a victim of discrimination "because of * * * sex" both because of his gender non-conforming conduct and, more generally, because of his identification as a transsexual.

We first address whether Smith has stated a claim for relief, pursuant to *Price Waterhouse*'s prohibition of sex stereotyping, based on his gender non-conforming behavior and appearance. In *Price Waterhouse,* the plaintiff, a female senior manager in an accounting firm, was denied partnership in the firm, in part, because she was considered "macho." She was advised that she could improve her chances for partnership if she were to take "a course at charm school," "walk more femininely, talk more femininely, dress more femininely, wear make-up, have her hair styled, and wear jewelry." Six members of the Court agreed that such comments bespoke gender discrimination, holding that Title VII barred not just discrimination because Hopkins was a woman, but also sex stereotyping—that is, discrimination because she failed to *act* like a woman. As Judge Posner has pointed out, the term "gender" is one "borrowed from grammar to designate the sexes as viewed as social rather than biological classes." Richard A. Posner, Sex and Reason, 24–25 (1992). The Supreme Court made clear that in the context of Title VII, discrimination because of "sex" includes gender discrimination: "In the context of sex stereotyping, an employer who acts on the basis of a belief that a woman cannot be aggressive, or that she must not be, has acted on the basis of gender." *Price Waterhouse,* 490 U.S. at 250, 109 S.Ct. 1775. The Court emphasized that "we are beyond the day when an employer could evaluate employees by assuming or insisting that they matched the stereotype associated with their group." *Id.* at 251, 109 S.Ct. 1775.

Smith contends that the same theory of sex stereotyping applies here. His complaint sets forth the conduct and mannerisms which, he alleges, did not conform with his employers' and co-workers' sex stereotypes of how a man should look and behave. Smith's complaint states that, after being diagnosed with GID, he began to express a more feminine appearance and manner on a regular basis, including at work. The complaint states that his co-workers began commenting on his appearance and mannerisms as not being masculine enough; and that his supervisors at the Fire Department and other municipal agents knew about this allegedly unmasculine conduct and appearance. The complaint then describes a high-level meeting among Smith's supervisors and other municipal officials regarding his employment. Defendants allegedly schemed to compel Smith's resignation by forcing him to undergo multiple psychological evaluations of his gender non-conforming behavior. The complaint makes clear that these meetings took place soon after Smith assumed a more feminine appearance and manner and after his conversation about this with Eastek. In addition, the complaint alleges that Smith was suspended for twenty-four hours for allegedly violating an unenacted municipal policy, and that the suspension was ordered in retaliation for his pursuing legal remedies after he had been informed about Defendants' plan to intimidate him into resigning. In short, Smith claims that the discrimination he experienced was based on his failure to conform to sex stereotypes by expressing less masculine, and more feminine mannerisms and appearance.

Having alleged that his failure to conform to sex stereotypes concerning how a man should look and behave was the driving force behind Defendants' actions, Smith has sufficiently pleaded claims of sex stereotyping and gender discrimination.

In so holding, we find that the district court erred in relying on a series of pre-*Price Waterhouse* cases from other federal appellate courts holding that transsexuals, as a class, are not entitled to Title VII protection because "Congress had a narrow view of sex in mind" and "never considered nor intended that [Title VII] apply to anything other than the traditional concept of sex." *Ulane v. Eastern Airlines, Inc.*, 742 F.2d 1081, 1085, 1086 (7th Cir.1984); *see also Holloway v. Arthur Andersen & Co.,* 566 F.2d 659, 661–63 (9th Cir.1977) (refusing to extend protection of Title VII to transsexuals because discrimination against transsexuals is based on "gender" rather than "sex"). It is true that, in the past, federal appellate courts regarded Title VII as barring discrimination based only on "sex" (referring to an individual's anatomical and biological characteristics), but not on "gender" (referring to socially-constructed norms associated with a person's sex). * * * In this earlier jurisprudence, male-to-female transsexuals (who were the plaintiffs in *Ulane, Sommers,* and *Holloway*)—as biological males whose outward behavior and emotional identity did not conform to socially-prescribed expectations of masculinity—were denied Title VII protection by courts because they were considered victims of "gender" rather than "sex" discrimination.

However, the approach in *Holloway, Sommers,* and *Ulane*—and by the district court in this case—has been eviscerated by *Price Waterhouse.* * * * By holding that Title VII protected a woman who failed to conform to social expectations concerning how a woman should look and behave, the Supreme Court established that Title VII's reference to "sex" encompasses both the biological differences between men and women, and gender discrimination, that is, discrimination based on a failure to conform to stereotypical gender norms. * * *

After *Price Waterhouse,* an employer who discriminates against women because, for instance, they do not wear dresses or makeup, is engaging in sex discrimination because the discrimination would not occur but for the victim's sex. It follows that employers who discriminate against men because they *do* wear dresses and makeup, or otherwise act femininely, are also engaging in sex discrimination, because the discrimination would not occur but for the victim's sex. * * * Yet some courts have held that this latter form of discrimination is of a different and somehow more permissible kind. For instance, the man who acts in ways typically associated with women is not described as engaging in the same activity as a woman who acts in ways typically associated with women, but is instead described as engaging in the different activity of being a transsexual (or in some instances, a homosexual or transvestite). Discrimination against the transsexual is then found not to be discrimination "because of * * * sex," but rather, discrimination against the plaintiff's unprotected status or mode of self-identification. In other words, these courts superimpose classifications such as "transsexual" on a plaintiff, and then legitimize discrimination based on the plaintiff's gender non-conformity by formalizing the non-conformity into an ostensibly unprotected classification. Such was the case here: despite the fact that Smith alleges that Defendants' discrimination was motivated by his appearance and mannerisms, which Defendants felt were inappropriate for his perceived sex, the district court expressly declined to discuss the applicability of *Price Waterhouse.* The district court therefore gave insufficient consideration to Smith's well-pleaded claims concerning his contra-gender behavior, but rather accounted for that behavior only insofar as it confirmed for the court Smith's status as a transsexual, which the district court held precluded Smith from Title VII protection.

Such analyses cannot be reconciled with *Price Waterhouse,* which does not make Title VII protection against sex stereotyping conditional or provide any reason to exclude Title VII coverage for non sex-stereotypical behavior simply because the person is a transsexual. As such, discrimination against a plaintiff who is a transsexual—and therefore fails to act and/or identify with his or her gender—is no different from the discrimination directed against Ann Hopkins in *Price Waterhouse,* who, in sex-stereotypical terms, did not act like a woman. Sex stereotyping based on a person's gender non-conforming behavior is impermissible discrimination, irrespective of the cause of that behavior; a label, such as "transsexual," is not fatal to a sex discrimination claim where the victim has suffered discrimination because of his or her gender non-conformity. Accordingly, we hold that Smith has stated a claim for relief pursuant to Title VII's prohibition of sex discrimination.

Finally, we note that, in its opinion, the district court repeatedly places the term "sex stereotyping" in quotation marks and refers to it as a "term of art" used by Smith to disingenuously plead discrimination because of transsexualism. Similarly, Defendants refer to sex stereotyping as "the *Price Waterhouse* loophole." These characterizations are almost identical to the treatment that Price Waterhouse itself gave sex stereotyping in its briefs to the U.S. Supreme Court. As we do now, the Supreme Court noted the practice with disfavor, stating:

> In the specific context of sex stereotyping, an employer who acts on the basis of a belief that a woman cannot be aggressive, or that she must not be, has acted on the basis of gender. Although the parties do not overtly dispute this last proposition, the placement by Price Waterhouse of "sex stereotyping" in quotation marks throughout its brief seems to us an insinuation either that such stereotyping was not present in this case or that it lacks legal relevance. We reject both possibilities.

Price Waterhouse, 490 U.S. at 250, 109 S.Ct. 1775.

* * *

Because Smith has successfully stated claims for relief pursuant to * * * Title VII * * * , the judgment of the district court is REVERSED and this case is REMANDED to the district court for further proceedings consistent with this opinion.

NOTES AND QUESTIONS

1. Was Jimmie Smith discriminated against because he was a man, because he was a man who looked and acted like a woman, or because he was a transsexual? If a job applicant has been diagnosed with GID and plans to undergo sex reassignment surgery, does she have an affirmative duty to inform the prospective employer of her GID and her biological sex if sex is not a bona fide occupational qualification for the job? *See* Lopez v. River Oaks Imaging & Diagnostic Group, Inc., 542 F.Supp.2d 653, 664 (S.D.Tex.2008) (refusing to recognize such a duty).

2. Ulane *Revisited*: In *Schroer v. Billington,* 424 F.Suppp.2d 203 (D.D.C.2006), Judge Robertson held that a male-to-female transsexual stated a claim for discrimination "because of sex" under Title VII when the Library of Congress refused to hire her "solely because of her sexual identity." *Id.* at 213. Although he rejected a sex-stereotyping theory based on *Price Waterhouse, id* at 209, and agreed that Title VII does not cover sexual orientation or sexual preference, *id.* at 208, Judge Robertson revisited the district court decision of Judge Grady in *Ulane,* which was reversed by the Seventh Circuit on appeal, to find a rationale that broadens the definition of "sex" in Title VII to include "sexual identity." Judge Robertson wrote:

> All the courts that have treated *Price Waterhouse* as irrelevant to transsexual cases, have looked back to the Seventh Circuit's decision in *Ulane,* and from that vantage point have determined that transsexuals are not a protected class. * * * [Judge Grady] determined that [Ulane] had been fired because she was a transsexual and ruled that discrimination against transsexuals violates Title VII. * * *
>
> * * * Judge Grady determined that "sex is not a cut-and-dried matter of chromosomes." *Ulane v. Eastern Airlines, Inc.,* 581 F.Supp. 821, 825 (N.D.Ill.1983) (*Ulane I*). Rather, it encompasses "sexual identity," which "is in part a psychological question—a question of self-perception; and in part a social matter—a question of how society perceives the individual." *Ulane,* 742 F.2d at 1084. The court distinguished "sexual identity" from "sexual preference," holding that "sex" under Title VII comprehends the former but not the latter. Accordingly, the district court held that the term "sex" "literally and * * * scientifically" applies to transsexuals, but not to homosexuals or transvestites. *Id.* * * *
>
> Without good reasons to oppose it, and with numerous courts now joining its conclusion—albeit under the *Price Waterhouse* framework—it may be time to revisit Judge Grady's conclusion in *Ulane I* that discrimination against transsexuals *because they are transsexuals* is "literally" discrimination "because of * * * sex." That

> approach strikes me as a straightforward way to deal with the factual complexities that underlie human sexual identity. These complexities stem from real variations in how the different components of biological sexuality—chromosomal, gonadal, hormonal, and neurological—interact with each other, and in turn, with social, psychological, and legal conceptions of gender.
>
> Dealing with transsexuality straightforwardly, and applying Title VII to it (if at all) as discrimination "because of * * * sex," preserves the outcomes of the post-*Price Waterhouse* case law without colliding with the sexual orientation and grooming code lines of cases. Twenty-plus years after *Ulane I,* scientific observation may well confirm Judge Grady's conclusion that "sex is not a cut-and-dried matter of chromosomes."

Id. at 211–13. Compare the court's treatment of discrimination against transsexual employees using Title VII's phrase "because of * * * sex" in *Ulane*, *Smith*, and *Schroer*. Which approach do you find most persuasive? *Smith* has been followed in the Sixth and the Eleventh Circuits. *See* Barnes v. City of Cincinnati, 401 F.3d 729, 737 (6th Cir.2005); Glenn v. Brumby, 663 F.3d 1312, 1317 (11th Cir.2011).

3. *The Americans with Disabilities Act*: Congress explicitly excluded homosexuality and bisexuality, as well as transsexuality and transvestitism, from the definitions of a "disability" under the Americans with Disabilities Act. Are these statutory exclusions from the ADA relevant to the question of whether the prohibition of "sex" discrimination in Title VII includes discrimination on the basis of sexual orientation, gender identity, or gender expression? *See* 42 U.S.C. § 12211(a) (providing that "homosexuality and bisexuality are not impairments and as such are not disabilities under [the ADA]"); 42 U.S.C § 12211(b)(1) (providing that "under [the ADA], the term 'disability' shall not include—transvestism, transsexualism, * * * gender disorders not resulting from physical impairments, or other sexual behavior disorders; * * * "); 42 U.S.C. § 12208 (providing that "[f]or the purposes [of the ADA], the term 'disabled' or 'disability' shall not apply to an individual solely because that individual is a transvestite").

4. *Access to Restroom Facilities for Transsexual or Transgender Employees.* An estimated 1,000 to 2,000 Americans have sex-change operations each year and many of these transsexuals try to continue working for the same employer while going through the transition. *When Harry Becomes Sally: Transgender Issues Increasingly Confront Employers,* 19 Hum. Resources Rep. (BNA) No. 48, at 1321 (Dec. 10, 2001) (citing Janis Walworth, Transsexual Workers: An Employer's Guide (1998)). This phenomenon has presented employers, employees, and the courts with some unique questions. For example, when workplace restrooms are designated as men's or women's, which restroom should a transsexual use while at work? Does it matter if the employee has completed the transsexual surgery or is just preparing for the operation—by taking hormones and dressing like the

opposite sex? *See* Etsitty v. Utah Transit Auth., 502 F.3d 1215 (10th Cir.2007) (upholding termination of pre-operative male-to-female transsexual bus driver who was fired because she expressed her intent to use the women's public restrooms along her bus route while wearing her uniform). What if the employee is not a transsexual (either pre- or post-operative) but just chooses to cross-dress for work?

If the employer designates restrooms according to biological sex, can a formerly male transsexual claim that she was discriminated against when she was not permitted to use the women's restroom? *See* Goins v. West Group, 635 N.W.2d 717 (Minn.2001) (holding that a post-operative male-to-female transsexual denied use of women's restroom at work had no cause of action under state law prohibiting sexual orientation discrimination); Kastl v. Maricopa County Community College Dist., 325 Fed.Appx. 492 (9th Cir.2009) (affirming grant of summary judgment where employer refused to allow a transsexual employee to use the women's restroom until she had completed reassignment surgery); Johnson v. University of Pittsburgh, 97 F.Supp.3d 657, 680–81 (W.D.Pa.2015) (rejecting claim that refusal to allow plaintiff to use the bathroom "consistent with his gender identity rather than his birth sex" constituted impermissible stereotyping). If the employer permits a formerly male transsexual to use the women's restroom at work, do female employees using the same restroom have any basis to complain under discrimination laws? *See* Cruzan v. Special Sch. Dist. #1, 294 F.3d 981 (8th Cir.2002) (holding that a female employee who objected to sharing the employer's women's restroom with a formerly male transsexual had no claim under Title VII for sexual harassment based on a hostile work environment). For an exploration of these issues, see Terry S. Kogan, *Sex-Separation in Public Restrooms: Law, Architecture, and Gender*, 14 Mich.J. Gender & L. 1 (2007) (discussing the history of sex-segregated public bathrooms from the perspective of critical architectural theory); Terry S. Kogan, *Transsexuals in Public Restrooms: Law, Cultural Geography and* Etsitty V. Utah Transit Authority, 18 Temp.Pol. & Civ.Rts.L.Rev. 673 (2009); *Richard* F. Storrow, *Gender Typing in Stereo: The Transgender Dilemma in Employment Discrimination*, 55 Me.L.Rev. 117, 151–53 (2003) (discussing *Goins* and *Cruzan*).

5. For scholarship on rights of transsexual and transgender individuals, see Joanne Meyerowitz, How Sex Changed: A History of Transsexuality in the United States (2002); Richard Green, *Spelling "Relief" for Transsexuals: Employment Discrimination and the Criteria of Sex*, 4 Yale L. & Pol'y Rev. 125 (1985); L. Camille Hébert, *Transforming Transsexual and Transgender Rights*, 15 Wm. & Mary J. Women & L. 535 (2009); Anna Kirkland, *Victorious Transsexuals in the Courtroom: A Challenge for Feminist Legal Theory*, 28 L. & Soc. Inquiry 1 (2003); Jillian Todd Weiss, *Transgender Identity, Textualism, and the Supreme Court: What Is the "Plain Meaning" of "Sex" in Title VII of the Civil Rights Act of 1964*, 18 Temp.Pol. & Civ.Rts.L.Rev. 573, 589 (2009).

3. SEXUAL HARASSMENT OF SEXUAL MINORITIES

Some in the LGBT community believed that Oncale v. Sundowner Offshore Services, Inc., 523 U.S. 75, 118 S.Ct. 998, 140 L.Ed.2d 201 (1998), might change the legal landscape for same-sex harassment claims brought by gay and lesbian plaintiffs. *Oncale* is reproduced in Chapter 7. Nevertheless, following Oncale, the federal courts uniformly held that Title VII does not prohibit workplace harassment because of sexual orientation. *See, e.g.,* Bibby v. Phila. Coca Cola Bottling Co., 260 F.3d 257, 261 (3d Cir.2001) (holding that Title VII does not prohibit discrimination on the basis of sexual orientation); Simonton v. Runyon, 232 F.3d 33, 35 (2d Cir.2000) (same). In light of these developments, consider the following case:

RENE V. MGM GRAND HOTEL, INC.

United States Court of Appeals for the Ninth Circuit, 2002 (en banc).
305 F.3d 1061, *cert. denied,* 538 U.S. 922, 123 S.Ct. 1573, 155 L.Ed.2d 313 (2003).

WILLIAM A. FLETCHER, CIRCUIT JUDGE.

This case presents the question of whether an employee who alleges that he was subjected to severe, pervasive, and unwelcome "physical conduct of a sexual nature" in the workplace asserts a viable claim of discrimination based on sex under Title VII of the 1964 Civil Rights Act, even if that employee also alleges that the motivation for that discrimination was his sexual orientation. We would hold that an employee's sexual orientation is irrelevant for purposes of Title VII. It neither provides nor precludes a cause of action for sexual harassment. That the harasser is, or may be, motivated by hostility based on sexual orientation is similarly irrelevant, and neither provides nor precludes a cause of action. It is enough that the harasser have [sic] engaged in severe or pervasive unwelcome physical conduct of a sexual nature. We therefore would hold that the plaintiff in this case has stated a cause of action under Title VII.

I

Medina Rene, an openly gay man, appeals from the district court's grant of summary judgment in favor of his employer MGM Grand Hotel in his Title VII action alleging sexual harassment by his male coworkers and supervisor. The relevant facts are not in dispute. Rene worked for the hotel, located in Las Vegas, Nevada, from December 1993 until his termination in June 1996. He worked as a butler on the 29th floor, where his duties involved responding to the requests of the wealthy, high-profile and famous guests for whom that floor was reserved. All of the other butlers on the floor, as well as their supervisor, were also male.

Rene provided extensive evidence that, over the course of a two-year period, his supervisor and several of his fellow butlers subjected him to a hostile work environment on almost a daily basis. The harassers' conduct included whistling and blowing kisses at Rene, calling him "sweetheart" and "muñeca" (Spanish for "doll"), telling crude jokes and giving sexually oriented "joke" gifts, and forcing Rene to look at pictures of naked men having sex. On "more times than [Rene said he] could possibly count," the harassment involved offensive physical conduct of a sexual nature. Rene gave deposition testimony that he was caressed and hugged and that his coworkers would "touch [his] body like they would to a woman." On numerous occasions, he said, they grabbed him in the crotch and poked their fingers in his anus through his clothing. When asked what he believed was the motivation behind this harassing behavior, Rene responded that the behavior occurred because he is gay.

[After exhausting his administrative remedies, Rene sued MGM Grand in federal district court. In response to MGM Grand's motion for summary judgment, the district court "concluded that 'Title VII's prohibition of "sex" discrimination applies only [to] discrimination on the basis of gender and is not extended to include discrimination based on sexual preference.' "]

* * *

III

Title VII of the 1964 Civil Rights Act, provides that "[i]t shall be an unlawful employment practice * * * to discriminate against any individual with respect to his compensation, terms, conditions, or privileges of employment because of * * * sex[.]" The Supreme Court made clear, more than 15 years ago, in *Mentor Savings Bank v. Vinson*, 477 U.S. 57, 64, 106 S.Ct. 2399, 91 L.Ed.29 49 (1986), that sexual harassment violates Title VII. Rene alleged that he was sexually harassed by his male supervisor and male coworkers under the hostile work environment theory of sexual harassment.

In describing the kinds of sexual harassment that can create a hostile work environment, the Court in *Meritor* explicitly included "physical conduct of a sexual nature." *Meritor,* 477 U.S. at 65, 106 S.Ct. 2399 (quoting EEOC Guidelines, 29 C.F.R. § 1604.11(a) (1985)). We have applied this holding on numerous occasions, "explain[ing] that a hostile environment exists when an employee can show (1) that he or she was subjected to * * * physical conduct of a sexual nature, (2) that this conduct was unwelcome, and (3) that the conduct was sufficiently severe or pervasive as to alter the conditions of the victim's employment and create an abusive working environment." *Ellison v. Brady,* 924 F.2d 872, 875–76 (9th Cir.1991).

It is clear that Rene has alleged physical conduct that was so severe and pervasive as to constitute an objectively abusive working environment. It is equally clear that the conduct was "of a sexual nature." Rene's tormentors did not grab his elbow or poke their fingers in his eye. They grabbed his crotch and poked their fingers in his anus.

Physical sexual assault has routinely been prohibited as sexual harassment under Title VII. * * * The most extreme form of offensive physical, sexual conduct—rape—clearly violates Title VII.

In granting MGM Grand's motion for summary judgment, the district court did not deny that the sexual assaults alleged by Rene were so objectively offensive that they created a hostile working environment. Rather, it appears to have held that Rene's otherwise viable cause of action was defeated because he believed he was targeted because he is gay. This is not the law. We have surveyed the many cases finding a violation of Title VII based on the offensive touching of the genitalia, buttocks, or breasts of women. In none of those cases has a court denied relief because the victim was, or might have been, a lesbian. The sexual orientation of the victim was simply irrelevant. If sexual orientation is irrelevant for a female victim, we see no reason why it is not also irrelevant for a male victim.

The premise of a sexual touching hostile work environment claim is that the conditions of the work environment have been made hostile "because of * * * sex." The physical attacks to which Rene was subjected, which targeted body parts clearly linked to his sexuality, were "because of * * * sex." Whatever else those attacks may, or may not, have been "because of" has no legal consequence. "[S]o long as the environment itself is hostile to the plaintiff because of [his] sex, why the harassment was perpetrated (sexual interest? misogyny? personal vendetta? misguided humor? boredom?) is beside the point." *Doe*, 119 F.3d at 578.

Our opinion today is guided by the principles established by the Supreme Court in Oncale v. Sundowner Offshore Servs., Inc., 523 U.S. 75, 118 S.Ct. 998, 140 L.Ed.2d 201 (1998). * * * We take two lessons from the Court's decision in Oncale.

First, Title VII forbids severe or pervasive same-sex offensive sexual touching. The Court made clear that a plaintiff's action for sexual harassment under Title VII cannot be defeated by a showing that the perpetrator and the victim of an alleged sexual assault are of the same gender. The Court wrote,

> We see no justification in the statutory language or our precedents for a categorical rule excluding same-sex harassment claims from the coverage of Title VII. As some courts have observed, male-on-male sexual harassment in the workplace was assuredly not the principal evil Congress was concerned with

> when it enacted Title VII. But statutory prohibitions often go beyond the principal evil to cover reasonably comparable evils, and it is ultimately the provisions of our laws rather than the principal concerns of our legislators by which we are governed.

Oncale, 523 U.S. at 79, 118 S.Ct. 998. Thus, Oncale's cause of action could not be defeated based on the fact that he was tormented *by other men.*

Second, offensive sexual touching is actionable discrimination even in a same-sex workforce. The Court in Oncale made clear that "discrimination" is a necessary predicate to every Title VII claim. That is, a defendant's conduct must not merely be "because of * * * sex"; it must be " '*discriminat[ion]* * * * because of * * * sex.' " Oncale, 523 U.S. at 81, 118 S.Ct. 998 (emphasis in original). The Court in Oncale held that "discrimina[tion] * * * because of * * * sex" can occur entirely among men, where some men are subjected to offensive sexual touching and some men are not. There were no women on Oncale's drilling rig; indeed, there were no women on any of his employer's oil rigs. Discrimination is the use of some criterion as a basis for a difference in treatment. In the context of our civil rights laws, including Title VII, discrimination is the use of a *forbidden* criterion as a basis for a *disadvantageous* difference in treatment. "Sex" is the forbidden criterion under Title VII, and discrimination is any disadvantageous difference in treatment "because of * * * sex." The *Oncale* Court's holding that offensive sexual touching in a same-sex workforce is actionable discrimination under Title VII necessarily means that discrimination can take place between members of the same sex, not merely between members of the opposite sex. Thus, Onacle did not need to show that he was treated worse than members of the opposite sex. It was enough to show that he suffered discrimination *in comparison to other men.*

Viewing the facts, as we must, in the light most favorable to the nonmoving party, we are presented with the tale of a man who was repeatedly grabbed in the crotch and poked in the anus, and who was singled out from his other male co-workers for this treatment. It is clear that the offensive conduct was sexual. It is also clear that the offensive conduct was discriminatory. That is, Rene has alleged that he was treated differently—and disadvantageously—based on sex. This is precisely what Title VII forbids: "discriminat[ion] * * * because of * * * sex."

In sum, what we have in this case is a fairly straightforward sexual harassment claim. Title VII prohibits offensive "physical conduct of a sexual nature" when that conduct is sufficiently severe or pervasive. *Meritor,* 477 U.S. at 65, 106 S.Ct. 2399. It prohibits such conduct without regard to whether the perpetrator and the victim are of the same or different genders. *See* Oncale, 523 U.S. at 79, 118 S.Ct. 998. And it prohibits such conduct without regard to the sexual orientation—real or perceived—of the victim.

There will be close cases on the question of what constitutes physical conduct of a sexual nature, for there are some physical assaults that are intended to inflict physical injury, but are not intended to have (and are not interpreted as having) sexual meaning. That is, there will be some cases in which a physical assault, even though directed at a sexually identifiable part of the body, does not give rise to a viable Title VII claim. But this is not such a case. Like the plaintiff in Oncale, Rene has alleged a physical assault of a sexual nature that is sufficient to survive a defense motion for summary judgment.

This opinion is joined by Judges Trott, Thomas, Graber, and Fisher. Judge Pregerson, in a separate opinion joined by Judges Trott and Berzon, reaches the same result but under a different rationale. Taken together, these two opinions are joined by a majority of the en banc panel. Accordingly, the district court's grant of summary judgment to MGM Grand is REVERSED, and the case is REMANDED for further proceedings.

PREGERSON, CIRCUIT JUDGE, with whom TROTT and BERZON, CIRCUIT JUDGES, join, concurring.

I concur in the result of Judge Fletcher's opinion. I write separately to point out that in my view, this is a case of actionable gender stereotyping harassment.

More than a decade ago, the Supreme Court held that gender stereotyping is actionable under Title VII. *See Price Waterhouse v. Hopkins,* 490 U.S. 228, 250–251, 109 S.Ct. 1775, 104 L.Ed.2d 268 (1989). More recently, the Supreme Court held that "same-sex sexual harassment is actionable under Title VII." Oncale v. Sundowner Offshore Services, Inc., 523 U.S. 75, 82, 118 S.Ct. 998, 140 L.Ed.2d 201 (1998). And only last year, we held that same-sex gender stereotyping of the sort suffered by Rene—*i.e.,* gender stereotyping of a male gay employee by his male co-workers—"constituted actionable harassment under * * * Title VII." *Nichols v. Azteca Restaurant Enterprises, Inc.,* 256 F.3d 864, 874–75 (9th Cir.2001).

Rene testified in his deposition that his co-workers teased him about the way he walked and whistled at him "[l]ike a man does to a woman." Rene also testified that his co-workers would "caress my butt, caress my shoulders" and blow kisses at him "the way * * * a man would treat a woman," hugged him from behind "like a man hugs a woman," and would "touch my body like they would to a woman, touch my face." Rene further testified that his co-workers called him "sweetheart" and "muñeca" ("doll"), "a word that Spanish men will say to Spanish women." This conduct occurred "many times." The repeated testimony that his co-workers treated Rene, in a variety of ways, "like a woman" constitutes ample evidence of gender stereotyping.

The conduct suffered by Rene is indistinguishable from the conduct found actionable in *Nichols.* In that case,

> Male co-workers and a supervisor repeatedly referred to [the male gay plaintiff] in Spanish and English as "she" and "her." Male co-workers mocked [him] for walking and carrying his serving tray "like a woman," and taunted him in Spanish and English as, among other things, a "faggot" and a " * * * female whore."

256 F.3d at 870. We concluded in *Nichols* that "[the] rule that bars discrimination on the basis of sex stereotypes" set in *Price Waterhouse* "squarely applies to preclude the harassment here." *Nichols,* 256 F.3d at 874–75. More generally, we held that "this verbal abuse was closely related to gender," "occurred because of sex," and therefore "constituted actionable harassment under * * * Title VII." *Id.*

The similarities between *Nichols* and the present case are striking. In both cases, a male gay employee was "teased" or "mocked" by his male co-workers because he walked "like a woman."[2] And in both cases, a male gay employee was referred to by his male-co-workers in female terms—"she," "her," and "female whore" in *Nichols;* "sweetheart" and "muñeca" ("doll") in the present case—to "remind[ ] [him] that he did not conform to their gender-based stereotypes." *Nichols,* 256 F.3d at 874. For the same reasons that we concluded in *Nichols* that "[the] rule that bars discrimination on the basis of sex stereotypes" set in *Price Waterhouse* "squarely applie[d] to preclude the harassment" at issue there, *Nichols,* 256 F.3d at 874–75, I conclude that this rule also squarely applies to preclude the identical harassment at issue here.[3] Accordingly, this is a case of actionable gender stereotyping harassment.

---

[2] It is not significant that, unlike the male employee in *Nichols,* Rene did not testify that his co-workers teased him for "walking * * * 'like a woman,' " *id.* at 870, but only that his co-workers "teas[ed][him] about the way [he] walk[ed] and * * * whistle[d] at [him] like a woman." There would be no reason for Rene's co-workers to whistle at Rene "like a woman," unless they perceived him to be not enough like a man and too much like a woman. That is gender stereotyping, and that is what Rene meant when he said he was discriminated against because he was *openly* gay. Likewise, contrary to a claim in the dissent, it is not significant that Rene apparently perceived himself to be "masculine." At issue is not what Rene perceived himself to be, but rather what his co-workers perceived him to be, and how they acted upon that perception.

[3] It is also worth noting that the "butlers" that served the Grand Hotel's guests on the 29th floor were, for whatever reason, all male, as the term "butler" connotes. All-male workplaces are common sites for the policing of gender norms and the harassment of men who transgress such norms. *See, e.g.,* Margaret Stockdale, Michelle Visio, and Leena Batra, *The Sexual Harassment of Men: Evidence for a Broader Theory of Harassment and Sex Discrimination,* 5 Psychol.Pub.Pol'y & L. 630, 653–54 (1999) (stating that "Predominantly or exclusively male environments tend to be more sexualized and less professional than gender neutral environments," and finding that data from a Department of Defense sexual harassment survey "support the trend that same-sex sexually harassed men worked in more male-dominated workplaces than did other men"); Vicki

GRABER, CIRCUIT JUDGE, concurring.

I concur in Judge W. Fletcher's opinion because the facts here are materially indistinguishable from the facts in Oncale v. Sundowner Offshore Services, Inc., 523 U.S. 75, 118 S.Ct. 998, 140 L.Ed.2d 201 (1998). If summary judgment in the employer's favor was inappropriate in that case, it is equally so in this one. * * *

[The concurring opinion by JUDGE FISHER is omitted.]

HUG, CIRCUIT JUDGE, with whom SCHROEDER, CHIEF JUDGE, FERNANDEZ, and T.G. NELSON, CIRCUIT JUDGES, join, dissenting.

* * * Judge Fletcher's opinion in effect interprets *Oncale* to mean that if the defendant's conduct was "sexual in nature" the statutory requirements of Title VII are met. The opinion then reasons that because the touching in this case was sexual in nature and was discriminatory, Rene has stated a claim under Title VII. This misinterprets *Oncale.* * * *

Title VII is not an anti-harassment statute; it is an anti-discrimination statute against persons in five specific classifications: race, color, religion, sex, or national origin. * * * There are many types of harassment in the workplace that are very offensive but are not actionable under the federal Title VII law.

While the Court held in *Oncale* that same-sex harassment can be actionable under Title VII, it did not hold that same-sex harassment because of sexual orientation is actionable under Title VII. * * *

Recently, we held in *Nichols*, that harassment of a male waiter by male workers and a supervisor amounted to harassment because of sex stereotyping and thus was discrimination because of gender. * * * This corresponds to the sex stereotyping described in *Price Waterhouse.*

In Rene's case there was no contention before the district court that the harassment Rene experienced was because he acted effeminately on the job, or for any reason other than his sexual orientation. * * *

The degrading and humiliating treatment Rene describes is appalling and deeply disturbing. I agree with the eloquent words of the First Circuit:

> We hold no brief for harassment because of sexual orientation; it is a noxious practice, deserving of censure and opprobrium. But we are called upon here to construe a statute as glossed by the Supreme Court, not to make a moral judgment—and we regard it as settled law that, as drafted and

Schultz, *Reconceptualizing Sexual Harassment,* 107 Yale L.J. 1683, 1755 n.387 (1998) ("[M]any male workers may view not only their jobs, but also the male-dominated composition and masculine identification of their work, as forms of property to which they are entitled."); Oncale, 523 U.S. at 77, 118 S.Ct. 998 (oil rig crew in which harassed male plaintiff worked was all male).

> authoritatively construed, Title VII does not proscribe harassment simply because of sexual orientation.

Higgins [*v. New Balance Athletic Shoe, Inc.*], 194 F.3d [252, 259 (1st Cir.1999)]. * * *

NOTES AND QUESTIONS

1. Is "physical conduct of a sexual nature" always sexual harassment regardless of the sexual orientation and gender identity of the harasser or the victim? Should there be a legal distinction between verbal gay-baiting—verbal taunting of a "sexual nature"—and a physical sexual assault? Should it matter whether the victim is an openly declared lesbian or gay man or is just perceived to be gay? For example, if the victim is openly gay and is subjected to repeated physical abuse from co-workers and supervisors, is the employer liable for hostile work environment under Title VII? Should it matter, as Judge William Fletcher concludes in the *Rene* case, that the nature of the physical abuse was sexual? Should the employer ever be able to defeat a claim like Rene's on the ground that the conduct was because of the victim's sexual orientation, not because of his sex? Is this case the same as or different from *Oncale?* If, unlike the situation in *Oncale* and *Rene,* both men and women were present in the workplace, could the victim successfully argue that he was subjected to working conditions that his female co-workers did not have to endure?

2. In *Doe v. City of Belleville*, 119 F.3d 563 (7th Cir.1997), *cert. granted, judgment vacated,* 523 U.S. 1001, 118 S.Ct. 1183, 140 L.Ed.2d 313 (1998), the employer argued that the evidence showed that the plaintiff was harassed because of his perceived sexual orientation, not his sex. The Seventh Circuit observed:

> The possibility that [the plaintiff's] harassers may have been motivated by more than one type of animus renders this case no different from one in which the employer may have had mixed motives in treating the plaintiff adversely—one motive proscribed by law, another not. The fact that one motive was permissible does not exonerate the employer from liability under Title VII; the employee can still prevail so long as she shows that her sex played a motivating role in the employer's decision. *See* 42 U.S.C. § 2000e–2(m). The same is true here—all that [the plaintiff] need show is that sex was a motivating (not the sole) factor in the harassment. The evidence before us permits that inference, and we cannot just declare that a case is about sexual orientation, rather than sex, simply because homophobia has reared its head along with sexism.

Id. at 594.

3. *"Sex Plus" Discrimination*: In *Higgins v. New Balance Athletic Shoe, Inc.*, 194 F.3d 252 (1st Cir.1999), the plaintiff alleged that his supervisor and co-workers harassed him because of his sexual orientation as a gay man. The

abusive conduct included sexually derogatory remarks and gestures, as well as physical abuse. The plaintiff raised a "sex-plus" theory on appeal, but it was deemed waived because it had not been presented to the court below. The theory was that the employer treated men who were sexually attracted to other men differently from women who were attracted to other women. In the *Hamm* case, Judge Posner observed that "men are more hostile to male homosexuality than they are to lesbianism." Hamm v. Weyauwega Milk Prods., Inc., 332 F.3d 1058, 1067 (7th Cir.2003) (Posner, J., concurring). What evidence would you need to support a viable "sex-plus" claim of sexual harassment under Title VII?

4. *Antigay Epithets and Gestures as a Form of Sexual Harassment*: In *Schmedding v. Tnemec Company, Inc.*, 187 F.3d 862 (8th Cir.1999), the Eighth Circuit Court reversed the dismissal of a same-sex sexual harassment claim brought by a male plaintiff who alleged that he was

> patted on the buttocks; asked to perform sexual acts; given derogatory notes referring to his anatomy; called names such as "homo" and "jerk off"; and was subject to the exhibition of sexually inappropriate behavior by others including unbuttoning of clothing, scratching of crotches and buttocks; and humping the door frame of [his] office.

Id. at 865. The plaintiff argued on appeal that "the harassment [by his coworkers] included rumors that falsely labeled him as homosexual in an effort to debase his masculinity, not that he was harassed because he *is* homosexual or *perceived* as being a homosexual." *Id.* Relying on *Oncale*, the court concluded, "We do not think that, simply because some of the harassment alleged by [the plaintiff] includes taunts of being homosexual or other epithets connoting homosexuality, the complaint is thereby transformed from one alleging harassment based on sex to one alleging harassment based on sexual orientation." *Id.* Is the court in *Schmedding* saying that when straight men harass other straight men using anti-gay epithets and gestures it is harassment because of sex? *See also* E.E.O.C. v. Boh Bros. Const. Co., L.L.C., 731 F.3d 444, 457–58 (5th Cir.2013) (finding that supervisor's use of homophobic terms to denigrate plaintiff were sufficient evidence for jury to conclude that harassment was "because of sex"). *See generally* Jennifer A. Drobac, *The* Oncale *Opinion: A Pansexual Response*, 30 McGeorge L.Rev. 1269 (1999); Toni Lester, *Protecting the Gender Nonconformist from the Gender Police—Why the Harassment of Gays and Other Gender Nonconformists Is a Form of Sex Discrimination in Light of the Supreme Court's Decision in* Oncale v. Sundowner, 92 N.M.L.Rev. 89 (1999).

5. *Gender Stereotyping Claims—Effeminate Men and Masculine Women*: In *Nichols v. Azteca Restaurant Enterprises,* 256 F.3d 864 (9th Cir.2001), discussed in Judge Pregerson's concurring opinion in *Rene*, the court applied the rationale of *Price Waterhouse*, to find that that the male-on-male harassment experienced by the plaintiff was harassment "because of sex"—and thus actionable—since it was based on an assumption that the

plaintiff "did not act as a man should act." *Id.* at 874. The rationale in *Nichols* would appear to provide Title VII protection from workplace harassment to some gay men and lesbians, as well as to straight men and women, who do not conform to culturally acceptable gender stereotypes in their dress and behavior while in the workplace—as in *Price Waterhouse*. For example, in *Prowel v. Wise Business Forms, Inc.*, 579 F.3d 285 (3d Cir.2009), the plaintiff, an openly gay male, was permitted to get to a jury on his Title VII claim of gender stereotyping where the facts were ambiguous whether the co-worker harassment he experienced was motivated by his sexual orientation or his effeminacy or both. The court described Prowel's gender nonconforming appearance and mannerisms and quoted Prowel's own view of how he was different from his male co-workers:

> Prowel identifies himself as an effeminate man and believes that his mannerisms caused him not to "fit in" with the other men at Wise. Prowel described the "genuine stereotypical male" at the plant as follows:
>
> > [B]lue jeans, t-shirt, blue collar worker, very rough around the edges. Most of the guys there hunted. Most of the guys there fished. If they drank, they drank beer, they didn't drink gin and tonic. Just you know, all into football, sports, all that kind of stuff, everything I wasn't.
>
> In stark contrast to the other men at Wise, Prowel testified that he had a high voice and did not curse; was very well-groomed; wore what others would consider dressy clothes; was neat; filed his nails instead of ripping them off with a utility knife; crossed his legs and had a tendency to shake his foot "the way a woman would sit"; walked and carried himself in an effeminate manner; drove a clean car; had a rainbow decal on the trunk of his car; talked about things like art, music, interior design, and decor; and pushed the buttons on the nale encoder with "pizzazz."

Id. at 287.

Is there a distinction between nonconforming sexual *practices* and gender nonconforming *appearance*? Some courts have relied on this distinction to reject the *Price Waterhouse* gender stereotyping theory in sexual harassment claims brought by employees who either are or are perceived to be gay. For example, in *Vickers v. Fairfield Medical Center*, 453 F.3d 757 (6th Cir.2006), the plaintiff alleged that his co-workers wrongly perceived that his "sexual practices * * * did not conform to the traditionally masculine role[,] [r]ather in his supposed sexual practices, he behaved more like a woman." *Id.* at 763. The court concluded that "the theory of sex stereotyping under *Price Waterhouse* is not broad enough to encompass" this situation and "his claim fails because [he] has failed to allege that he did not conform to traditional gender stereotypes in any observable way at work." *Id.* at 764.

6. *"Reverse" Sexual Orientation Discrimination*: After *Oncale*, can a female heterosexual employee prevail in a discrimination claim under Title VII on the theory that she has been harassed by lesbian employees who were motivated by sexual desire? *See* Dick v. Phone Directories Co., 397 F.3d 1256 (10th Cir.2005) (finding genuine issue of material fact on whether female heterosexual plaintiff was harassed "because of sex" where offensive conduct of lesbian co-workers was allegedly motivated by sexual desire). In critiquing *Dick*, Professor Brower argued that "when the schema of lesbians and gay men as sexual predators intersects with desire-based sexual harassment, heterosexual plaintiffs win those cases in which they are harassed by homosexuals—even if the court has to misread a fact pattern to fit it within the desire-based model." Todd Brower, *Social Cognition "At Work": Schema Theory and Lesbian and Gay Identity in Title VII*, 18 L. & Sexuality 1, 76 (2009); *see also id.* at 28–33 (discussing *Dick* case). If a heterosexual female is harassed by her lesbian co-workers because she does not dress and act like a stereotypical lesbian, would she have a claim of sexual harassment under Title VII? *See* Medina v. Income Support Div., State of N.M., 413 F.3d 1131, 1135 (10th Cir.2005) (finding that plaintiff was essentially alleging that she was "discriminated against because she is heterosexual," and "Title VII's protections * * * do not extend to harassment due to a person's sexuality.") Can you distinguish *Dick* and *Medina*? How would the different judges in *Rene* be likely to treat the reverse discrimination claims in the two cases? Professor Kramer would characterize the plaintiff's claim in *Medina* as a "sexual orientation simpliciter claim," which would not be actionable under Title VII because it is based "solely on account of his or her sexual orientation." Zachary A. Kramer, *Heterosexuality and Title VII*, 103 Nw.U.L.Rev. 205, 217 (2009).

What arguments could you make that heterosexual employees should or should not be protected under statutes and ordinances enacted to prohibit discrimination on the basis of "sexual orientation"? Professor Schwartz has written: "There can be no serious question that sexual orientation discrimination falls predominantly upon gays, lesbians, and bisexuals; while the occasional charge of 'reverse' sexual orientation discrimination against heterosexuals is little more than the rare but newsworthy 'man bites dog' story." David S. Schwartz, *When Is Sex Because of Sex? The Causation Problem in Sexual Harassment Law*, 150 U. Pa. L. Rev. 1697, 1077 n.32 (2002). Should it matter that such claims are rare? In a lawsuit brought under the New York City Human Rights Law, the court agreed that a claim for reverse sexual orientation discrimination was actionable; nevertheless, the plaintiff failed to prove that she had experienced a hostile work environment on the basis of her sexual orientation. Brennan v. Metro. Opera Ass'n, 729 N.Y.S.2d 77 (N.Y.App.Div. 2001). The plaintiff, a heterosexual female, had objected to the display of photographs of nude men and the sexual banter among gay male co-workers at the opera house where they worked. The court rejected her hostile work environment claim under the local ordinance, which prohibited discrimination on the basis of sexual orientation, because the offending conduct was neither severe enough to be actionable harassment nor was it based on her sexual orientation as a heterosexual female. The plaintiff had previously failed to prove actionable sexual harassment under Title VII. *See* Brennan v. Metropolitan Opera Ass'n, 192 F.3d 310 (2d Cir.1999).

D. SOURCES OF EMPLOYMENT RIGHTS FOR LGBT INDIVIDUALS BEYOND TITLE VII

1. FEDERAL LEGISLATIVE REFORM PROPOSALS

Since 1975, Congress has considered—but failed to enact—a number of bills that would amend Title VII to prohibit employment discrimination on the basis of "affectional or sexual orientation." Ulane v. Eastern Airlines, Inc., 742 F.2d 1081, 1085 & 1085 n.11 (7th Cir.1984). Indeed, federal courts have often used this fact to support the conclusion that Congress did not intend "sex" in Title VII to include "sexual orientation," *see, e.g.*, DeSantis v. Pac. Tel. & Tel. Co., 608 F.2d 327, 329 (9th Cir.1979), or "transsexualism," *see, e.g.*, *Ulane*, 742 F.2d at 1085.

On November 7, 2007, the House of Representatives, for the first time, passed a version of the Employment Non-Discrimination Act (ENDA) that would protect employees from discrimination on the basis of "actual or perceived sexual orientation," but not on the basis of gender identity. H.R. 3685, 110th Cong., 1st Sess. (2007). In order to gain passage of the bill, House Democrats omitted provisions in an earlier bill, H.R. 2015, 110th Cong., 1st Sess. (2007), that would have covered transsexual and transgender individuals, thus provoking opposition to H.R. 3685 by some LGBT advocates. *See* David M. Herszenhorn, *House Approves Broad Protections for Gay Workers,* N.Y. Times, Nov. 8, 2007. The House bill was placed on the Legislative Calendar in the Senate in November of 2007, where the proposed law stalled.

In 2009, both the House of Representatives and the Senate held hearings on a new version of ENDA—the Employment Non-Discrimination Act of 2009—that include gender identity as well as sexual orientation as protected statuses. *See* H.R. 3017, 111th Cong., 1st Sess. (2009); S. 1584, 111th Cong., 1st Sess. (2009). This version of the proposed law defined "sexual orientation" as "homosexuality, heterosexuality, or bisexuality," § 3(a)(9), and "gender identity" as "the gender-related identity, appearance, or mannerisms or other gender-related characteristics of an individual, with or without regard to the individual's designated sex at birth," § 3(a)(6). For an account of the legislative history of ENDA and a discussion of the significance of including gender identity as a protected status in the bill, see Jill D. Weinberg, *Gender Nonconformity: An Analysis of Perceived Sexual Orientation and Gender Identity Protection Under the Employment Non-Discrimination Act*, 44 U.S.F.L.Rev. 1 (2009).

The 2009 ENDA bill covered employers with fifteen or more employees and offered many protections and remedies that track Title VII. To address concerns of opponents, the bill exempted religious organizations and the armed forces from coverage (§§ 6, 7), prohibited the EEOC from collecting or compelling the collection of statistics "on actual or perceived sexual orientation or gender identity from covered entities" (§ 9), and prohibited preferential treatment or quotas (§ 4(f)). Unlike Title VII, the bill expressly permitted only disparate treatment—not disparate impact—claims (§ 4(g)). In addition to an anti-retaliation provision in § 5, the bill made it unlawful for employers to take an adverse employment action "against an individual based on the actual or perceived sexual orientation or gender identity of a person with whom the individual associates or has associated." ENDA, § 4(e).

ENDA did not make it out of committee in either the House or the Senate in 2009 or when it was reintroduced in substantially the same form in 2011. In 2013, a version of ENDA passed the Senate, *see* S. 815, 113th Cong, 1st Sess. (2013), but that version contained very broad religious exemptions that prompted several prominent LGBT rights organizations to withdraw their support of the law. It was never considered in the House. *See* Keith Cunningham-Parmeter, *Marriage Equality, Workplace Inequality: The Next Gay Rights Battle*, 67 Fla. L. Rev. 1099, 1145 (2015) (describing how LGBT groups withdrew their support of ENDA in 2013); Erik S. Thompson, *Compromising Equality: An Analysis of the Religious Exemption in the Employment Non-Discrimination Act and Its Impact on LGBT Workers*, 35 B.C. J. L. & Soc. Just. 285, 302–308 (2015) (describing the potential consequences of the broad religious exemptions included in the 2013 version of ENDA).

In 2015, the Equality Act was introduced in both the House and the Senate. This proposed legislation would expand Title VII to protect against sexual orientation discrimination in employment and public accommodations and would also amend a variety of other laws to prohibit discrimination in housing, jury selection, and federal contracting. *See* S. 1858, 114th Cong., 1st Sess. (2015); H.R. 3185, 114th Cong., 1st Sess. (2015). The proposed Equality Act does not include any religious exemptions beyond those already provided by the relevant federal laws. *Id.*

2. EXISTING FEDERAL AND STATE PROTECTIONS

In 1973—the year that the American Psychiatric Association formally acknowledged that homosexuality was not a mental disease—the United States Civil Service Commission ruled that homosexuality could not be used as the sole basis for denying a person employment with the federal government. *See* Nan D. Hunter, *Life After* Hardwick, 27 Harv.C.R.–C.L.L.Rev. 531, 539 (1992). On May 28, 1998, President

Clinton amended Executive Order 11478, Equal Employment Opportunity in Federal Government, "to prohibit discrimination based on sexual orientation" in federal employment. Exec. Order No. 13,087, 63 Fed.Reg. 30,097 (1998). On June 23, 2000, President Clinton issued Executive Order 13,160, which prohibits "discrimination on the basis of race, sex, color, national origin, disability, religion, age, sexual orientation, and status as a parent" in "a Federally conducted education or training program or activity." Exec. Order No. 13,160, 65 Fed.Reg. 39,773 (2000). The order excludes members of the armed forces and students in military academies. In July, 2014, President Obama issued Executive Order 13, 672, which amended two earlier Executive Orders. First, it amended Executive Order 11478, Equal Employment Opportunity in Federal Government by adding gender identity to the list of prohibited bases of discrimination in federal employment. (President Clinton's 1998 Executive Order, *supra*, had added only sexual orientation.) Second, Executive Order 13,672 amended Executive Order 11,246, which prohibits discrimination by federal government contractors, to add sexual orientation and gender identity to its list of prohibited bases of discrimination. Exec. Order No. 13,673, 79 Fed.Reg. 42,971 (2014). *See also* U.S. Office of Personnel Management, *Addressing Sexual Orientation and Gender Identity Discrimination in Federal Civilian Employment: A Guide to Employment Rights, Protections, and Responsibilities* (Rev. June 2015).

In addition to these Executive Orders, the EEOC ruled in July 2015 that sex discrimination under Title VII encompasses discrimination based on sexual orientation. *See* Baldwin v. Foxx, EEOC Appeal No. 0120133080 (July 15, 2015), available at *http://www.eeoc.gov/decisions/0120133080.pdf* (reproduced *supra* in Section B). That determination is binding on federal employers. Thus, while the inclusion of sexual orientation under Title VII is not resolved as a matter of judicial determination, until the Supreme Court weighs in on whether to uphold the EEOC's interpretation, federal employees are protected by Title VII from discrimination on the basis of sexual orientation and gender identity.

A growing number of states also explicitly prohibit discrimination on the basis of sexual orientation. As of 2015, twenty-two states and the District of Columbia had statutes prohibiting employment discrimination on the basis of sexual orientation. *See* Movement Advancement Project, Non-Discrimination Laws, available at *http://www.lgbtmap.org/equality-maps/non_discrimination_laws.* The states are California, Colorado, Connecticut, Delaware, Hawaii, Illinois, Iowa, Maine, Maryland, Massachusetts, Minnesota, Nevada, New Hampshire, New Jersey, New Mexico, New York, Oregon, Rhode Island, Utah, Vermont, Washington, and Wisconsin. *Id.* Nineteen of these jurisdictions also prohibit employment discrimination on the basis of gender identity. *Id.* New Hampshire, New York, and Wisconsin did not, as of 2015, include gender identity as a protected status. *Id.* Many of these state statutes are part of comprehensive laws prohibiting discrimination in employment, housing, public accommodations, education, and other essential services. *See generally* Movement Advancement Project, *Equality Maps,* available at *http://www.lgbtmap.org/equality-maps.* By 2015, Indiana, Kentucky, Michigan, Pennsylvania and Virginia had enacted a state administrative order or personnel regulation prohibiting discrimination against public employees based on sexual orientation and gender identity. *See www.hrc.org/state_maps* (map of "Statewide Employment Laws and Policies") (last visited December 14, 2015). Alaska, Arizona, Missouri, and Montana prohibit discrimination on the basis of sexual orientation in public employment only. *Id.* In addition, "[m]ore than two hundred cities and counties have enacted local ordinances prohibiting employment discrimination on the basis of sexual orientation and/or gender identity." Jennifer C. Pizer, Brad Sears, Christy Mallory, Nan D. Hunter, *Evidence of Persistent and Pervasive Workplace Discrimination Against LGBT People: The Need for Federal Legislation Prohibiting Discrimination and Providing for Equal Employment Benefits*, 45 Loy. L.A. L. Rev. 715, 757 (2012). It is important to keep in mind that local antidiscrimination laws may have broader substantive and procedural protections than analogous federal and state statutes. *See, e.g.*, Williams v. N.Y.C. Housing Auth., 872 N.Y.S.2d 27, 31–33 (N.Y.App.Div.2009) (discussing the distinctions between New York City's Civil Rights Restoration Act and its state and federal counterparts).

At the same time that many jurisdictions are adding protections against discrimination on the basis of sexual orientation and gender identity, the Arkansas legislature passed a law in 2015 that prohibits localities from enacting their own laws protecting against sexual orientation discrimination by forbidding local government from adding to the list of protected classes already included in state laws. *See* Arkansas Act 137 (2/24/2015), available at *http://www.arkleg.state.ar.us/assembly/2015/2015R/Acts/Act137.pdf.* The Arkansas law mirrors a similar measure passed in Tennessee in 2011. *See* Tenn.Code Ann. § 7–51–1802 (Supp.2013). Legislatures in West Virginia and Texas have considered similar laws as well. *See* Jeff Guo, *Everything you need to know about the gay discrimination wars in 2015* (Feb. 25, 2015), available at *https://www.washingtonpost.com/blogs/govbeat/wp/2015/02/25/these-states-are-marching-ahead-with-laws-that-would-allow-gay-discrimination/.*

NOTES AND QUESTIONS

1. *Protections Under the United States Constitution*: The Supreme Court has issued several historic decisions acknowledging the constitutional

rights of gay men and lesbians to marry and otherwise to a guarantee of "liberty" that "presumes an autonomy of self that includes freedom of thought, belief, expressions, and certain intimate conduct." Lawrence v. Texas, 539 U.S. 558, 562, 123 S.Ct. 2472, 2475, 156 L.Ed.2d 508 (2003). *See also* Obergefell v. Hodges, 576 U.S. ___, 135 S.Ct. 2017 (2015) (recognizing the right to marry); United States v. Windsor, 570 U.S. ___, 133 SCt. 2675, 186 L.Ed.2d 808 (2013) (concluding that the federal law that restricted the definition of marriage to include only heterosexual unions was unconstitutional). These decisions have had a significant impact on gay civil rights generally, including on attitudes about employment rights. In *Obergefell,* the Court recognized that laws prohibiting same sex couples to marry violated both the Due Process Clause and the Equal Protection Clause. *Obergefell*, 135 S.Ct. at 2604–05. The Court's Equal Protection discussion did not, however, rest on the idea that LGBT individuals are entitled to any kind of heightened protection under the Equal Protection Clause. *Id. See also* Nan D. Hunter, *Interpreting Liberty and Equality Through the Lens of Marriage*, 6 Cal. L. Rev. Circuit 107, 113 (2015) (noting the uncertainty that the *Obergefell* opinion leaves as to how equal protection analysis might apply in a context not involving a fundamental right).

In *Romer v. Evans*, 517 U.S. 620, 116 S.Ct. 1620, 1629, 134 L.Ed.2d 855 (1996), in a 6–3 decision, the Supreme Court struck down, on equal protection grounds, a 1992 Colorado constitutional amendment, adopted by statewide referendum, that "prohibit[ed] all legislative, executive or judicial action at any level of state or local government designed to protect the named class * * * [of] homosexual persons or gays and lesbians." *Id.* at 624, 116 S.Ct. at 1623. Writing for the majority, Justice Kennedy found that the law—Amendment 2—produced a "[s]weeping and comprehensive * * * change in legal status" of homosexuals:

> Homosexuals, by state decree, are put in a solitary class with respect to transactions and relations in both the private and governmental spheres. The amendment withdraws from homosexuals, but no others, specific legal protection from the injuries caused by discrimination, and it forbids reinstatement of these laws and policies.

Id. at 627, 116 S.Ct. at 1625. The Court ruled that "Amendment 2 fails, indeed defies, even [the] conventional inquiry" for upholding a legislative classification under the Equal Protection Clause. *Id.* at 632, 116 S.Ct. at 1627. By relying on rational basis review, however, the Court in *Romer* avoided addressing whether Amendment 2 "burdens a fundamental right [or] targets a suspect class." *Id.*

In 2011, Tennessee enacted a statute that prohibited local governments within the state from including sexual orientation within their local non-discrimination ordinances. *See* Tenn.Code Ann. § 7–51–1802 (Supp.2013). Denying a constitutional challenge to this law, the court distinguished *Romer*, explaining that "[a]though HB600 curtails the authority of local governments to vary from the generally applicable State anti-discrimination laws, it does not impose a structural barrier to Appellants' ability to advocate for political change." Howe v. Haslam, 2014 WL 5698877, at *15 (Tenn.Ct.Ap. 2014).

2. *State Constitutional Protections*: States may interpret their own constitutional guarantees of due process, equal protection, and freedom of association to provide broader rights than are afforded under the United States Constitution. *See, e.g.*, Gay Law Students Ass'n v. Pac. Tel. & Tel. Co., 24 Cal.3d 458, 474–75, 156 Cal.Rptr. 14, 24, 595 P.2d 592, 602 (Cal.1979) (holding that "the California Constitution precludes a public utility's management from automatically excluding all homosexuals from consideration for employment positions"). *See also* In re Marriage Cases, 43 Cal.4th 757, 843, 183 P.3d 384 (Cal.2008) (concluding that "statutes imposing differential treatment on the basis of sexual orientation should be viewed as constitutionally suspect under the California Constitution's equal protection clause"), *superseded on a different issue by constitutional amendment as stated in* Strauss v. Horton, 207 P.3d 48, 62 (Cal. 2009); Varnum v. Brien, 763 N.W.2d 862 (Iowa 2009) (holding that Iowa's ban on same sex marriage violated the state equal protection clause). In addition, some states may have additional protections not found in the federal constitution. For example, the California Constitution has an expansive right of privacy that has been interpreted to bar a private employer from using questions regarding an applicant's sexual orientation on a job screening test. Soroka v. Dayton Hudson Corp., 1 Cal.Rptr.2d 77 (Cal.App.1991), *review dismissed as moot*, 24 Cal.Rptr.2d 587, 862 P.2d 148 (Cal.1993).

3. *Corporate Nondiscrimination Policies*: Since as early as the mid-1970s, some private employers—particularly in white-collar, high-tech industries—have promulgated internal nondiscrimination policies protecting their LGBT employees. *See* James B. Stewart, *Coming Out at Chrysler*, New Yorker, July 21, 1997, at 40. At least among major companies in the United States, the percentage of employers that prohibit discrimination on the basis of sexual orientation and gender identity has continued to increase in recent years. The Human Rights Campaign (HRC) reported that by 2015, 93 percent of Fortune 500 companies prohibited discrimination on the basis of sexual orientation and 75 percent had policies banning discrimination on the basis of gender identity. Human Rights Campaign, Corporate Equality Index 2016: Rating American Workplaces on Lesbian, Gay, Bisexual and Transgender Equality, at 7 (2015), *available at http://www.hrc.org/workplace*.

4. *Collective Bargaining Agreements*: LGBT employees can have broader procedural and substantive protections under collective bargaining agreements than under statutes and ordinances. Collective bargaining agreements and grievance procedures can protect employees from workplace harassment because of sexual orientation and gender identity as well as from adverse discriminatory employment actions. *See, e.g.*, Charter Comm'l Enter. 1, L.P. v. Int'l Bhd. of Elec. Workers, Local 399, 114 Lab.Arb. (BNA) 769 (2000) (Kelly, Arb.) (finding that an employer had just cause in discharging

an employee accused of harassing a gay co-worker in violation of a sexual harassment policy in the company handbook). Major unions in both the public and private sectors have succeeded in obtaining provisions in collective bargaining agreements that go beyond prohibiting discrimination to extend employment benefits to same-sex domestic partners. *See UAW, Automakers Agree on Extending Health Benefits to Domestic Partners*, 18 Hum. Resources Rep. (BNA) No. 23, at 622 (June 12, 2000) (describing the agreement between the UAW and the Big Three automakers to extend coverage of health care benefits to same-sex domestic partners). In many unionized workplaces, LGBT caucuses now play a significant role in union negotiating processes. *See, e.g.*, Ruben J. Garcia, *New Voices at Work: Race and Gender Identity Caucuses in the U.S. Labor Movement*, 54 Hastings L.J. 79 (2002).

5. *Nondiscrimination Policies of Professional and Academic Associations*: Some associations that regulate entry into the professions and accreditation of professional schools have adopted policies barring discrimination on the basis of sexual orientation. For example, in his dissent in *Romer v. Evans*, 517 U.S. 620, 116 S.Ct. 1620, 134 L.Ed.2d 855 (1996), Justice Scalia distinguished "the views and values of the lawyer class from which the Court's Members are drawn" from the "more plebeian attitudes that apparently still prevail in the United States Congress," by observing that

> [h]ow [the lawyer] class feels about homosexuality will be evident to anyone who wishes to interview job applicants at virtually any of the Nation's law schools. The interviewer may refuse to offer a job because the applicant is a Republican; because he is an adulterer; because he went to the wrong prep school or belongs to the wrong country club; because he eats snails; because he is a womanizer; because she wears real-animal fur; or even because he hates the Chicago Cubs. But if the interviewer should wish not to be an associate or partner of an applicant because he disapproves of the applicant's homosexuality, then he will have violated the pledge which the Association of American Law Schools requires all its member-schools to exact from job interviewers: "assurance of the employer's willingness" to hire homosexuals. Bylaws of the Association of American Law Schools, Inc. § 6–4(b); Executive Committee Regulations of the Association of American Law Schools § 6.19, in 1995 Handbook, Association of American Law Schools.

Id. at 652, 116 S.Ct. at 1637. *See also Lawrence v. Texas*, 539 U.S. 558, 602, 123 S.Ct. 2472, 2496, 156 L.Ed.2d 508 (2003) (Scalia, J., dissenting). Do you believe that this policy of the Association of American Law Schools (AALS) provides effective antidiscrimination protection for gay and lesbian law students seeking jobs in the legal profession?

By 2010, the rules of professional conduct for lawyers in many states included some form of prohibition of discrimination on the basis of sexual orientation, some also including gender identity discrimination. *See* William

C. Duncan, *Sexual Orientation Bias: The Substantive Limits of Ethics Rules*, 11 Am.U.J. Gender Soc. Pol'y & L. 85, 88–89 (2002); Sarah Valentine, *When Your Attorney is Your Enemy: Preliminary Thoughts on Ensuring Effective Representation for Queer Youth*, 19 Colum. J. Gender & L. 773, 801 (2010). Canon 2 of the Model Code of Judicial Conduct admonishes judges to avoid "bias or prejudice" on the basis of "sexual orientation" in "the performance of judicial duties." Model Code of Jud. Conduct, Canon 2, Rule 2.3 (2011). For a discussion of how this professional standard might affect judicial decisionmaking as well as how judges treat lawyers, litigants, and staff members, see Jennifer Gerarda Brown, *Sweeping Reform for Small Rules? Anti-Bias Canons as a Substitute for Heightened Scrutiny,* 85 Minn.L.Rev. 363 (2000). For a critique, see Duncan, *supra. See also* Tobin A. Sparling, *Judicial Bias Claims of Homosexual Persons in the Wake of* Lawrence v. Texas, 46 S. Tex. L. Rev. 255 (2004).

6. *Employer First Amendment Defenses to Nondiscrimination Claims*: If an employer refuses to hire a man who is openly gay and the applicant brings a claim under a state civil rights statute that prohibits employment discrimination on the basis of sexual orientation, can the employer defend its decision on First Amendment grounds? Suppose the employer is the sole proprietor of a small business who asserts that homosexuality is morally repugnant to her and she does not wish to associate with lesbians or gay men in her work. Would *Boy Scouts of America v. Dale*, 530 U.S. 640, 120 S.Ct. 2446, 147 L.Ed.2d 554 (2000), provide a potential constitutional argument for the employer? *Dale* held that the application of New Jersey's public accommodation law to require the Boy Scouts to accept a gay activist as a scoutmaster violated the group's First Amendment right of "expressive association." How is an employer's freedom to select its employees different from a private association's freedom to select its members and leaders? Do employment discrimination laws regulate conduct or speech? In *Boy Scouts of America v. Wyman,* 335 F.3d 80, 93 (2d Cir.2003), *cert. denied,* 541 U.S. 903, 1235 S.Ct. 1602, 158 L.Ed.2d 244 (2004), the Second Circuit found that "Connecticut's Gay Rights Law regulates membership and employment policies as conduct, not as expression and, as such, is not obviously viewpoint discriminatory." *Id.* The court concluded that the law "[o]n its face * * * prohibits discriminatory membership and employment policies not because of the viewpoints such policies express, but because of the immediate harms—like denial of concrete economic and social benefits—such discrimination causes homosexuals." *Id. See also* Dale Carpenter, *Expressive Association and Anti-Discrimination Law After* Dale: *A Tripartite Approach*, 85 Minn.L.Rev. 1515 (2001).

7. *Protection of Sexual Orientation and Gender Identity Under International Human Rights Laws*: Outside of the United States, a potential source of anti-discrimination protection for sexual minorities can be found in international human rights laws. Two commentators observed that

> [a]lthough no international human rights treaties expressly mention homosexuality or sexual orientation, human rights

> monitoring institutions, both judicial and political, have recently begun to interpret these treaties to protect certain aspects of lesbian and gay identity and conduct. Similarly, legal scholars and human rights activists have argued with increased frequency that governments may not discriminate on the basis of sexual orientation when upholding individual rights and freedoms.

Laurence R. Helfer & Alice M. Miller, *Sexual Orientation and Human Rights: Toward a United States and Transnational Jurisprudence*, 9 Harv.Hum.Rts.J. 61, 61–62 (1996). *See also* Ronnie Cohen, Shannon O'Byrne & Patricia Maxwell, *Employment Discrimination Based on Sexual Orientation: The American, Canadian and U.K. Responses*, 17 Law & Ineq. 1 (1999); Aaron Xavier Fellmeth, *State Regulation of Sexuality in International Human Rights Law and Theory,* 50 Wm. & Mary L.Rev. 797 (2008); Michael O'Flaherty & John Fisher, *Sexual Orientation, Gender Identity and International Human Rights Law: Contextualising the Yogyakarta Principles,* 8 Hum. Rts. L.Rev. 207 (2008). Is it appropriate or necessary for legislators in the United States to acknowledge these developments in international human rights law when they are considering proposals to extend employment discrimination laws to homosexuals?

In *Lawrence v. Texas*, 539 U.S. 558, 573, 576, 123 S.Ct. 2472, 2481, 2483, 156 L.Ed.2d 508 (2003), the Supreme Court cited cases decided by the European Court of Human Rights as support for overruling *Bowers v. Hardwick*, observing that "[t]he [constitutional] right the petitioners seek in this case has been accepted as an integral part of human freedom in many other countries." *Id.* at 577, 123 S.Ct. at 2483. *But see id.* at 598, 123 S.Ct. at 2494–95 (Scalia, J., dissenting) (arguing that the Court's reliance on "foreign views" to support "[c]onstitutional entitlements" in *Lawrence* is "meaningless dicta"). If you were representing a lesbian plaintiff in an employment discrimination case in a court in the United States, what arguments could you make for or against reliance on principles drawn from international human rights cases or treaties? *See generally* Robert Wintemute, Sexual Orientation and Human Rights: The United States Constitution, The European Convention, and the Canadian Charter (1995).

CHAPTER 10

HARASSMENT

■ ■ ■

A. INTRODUCTION

Employees covered by Title VII, the ADEA, and the ADA have a right to work in an environment free of discriminatory harassment that adversely affects their "terms, conditions, or privileges of employment." But not all workplace harassment is actionable discrimination under these statutes, and, in certain circumstances, employers may have defenses that limit their liability for discriminatory harassment. Because workplace harassment is not expressly addressed by federal antidiscrimination laws, federal courts have articulated the elements of a plaintiff's claim of discriminatory harassment, a defendant's defenses, and the burdens of proof each party bears in litigation.

Although most of the Supreme Court cases dealing with discriminatory workplace harassment have arisen from claims of sexual harassment, the doctrinal foundations of harassment claims under Title VII originated in cases of racial and ethnic harassment dating from the early 1970s. *Rogers v. EEOC*, 454 F.2d 234 (5th Cir.1971), *cert. denied*, 406 U.S. 957, 92 S.Ct. 2058, 32 L.Ed.2d 343 (1972), was the first case to recognize that "a working environment heavily charged with discrimination may constitute an unlawful practice" under Title VII, despite the absence of discrete employment actions such as hiring or firing. *Id.* at 239. *Rogers* held that a doctor's practice of segregating his Hispanic patients from his non-Hispanic patients constituted discrimination in "the terms, conditions, or privileges of employment" of a Spanish-surnamed employee, Josephine Chavez, who worked in his office. In *Rogers*, Judge Goldberg wrote: "Title VII * * * should be accorded a liberal interpretation in order to effectuate the purpose of Congress to eliminate the inconvenience, unfairness, and humiliation of ethnic discrimination." *Id.* at 238.

Following *Rogers,* other federal courts recognized hostile work environment claims based on race, religion, and national origin. The federal courts, however, were initially reluctant to extend the rationale underlying racial harassment claims to women's claims of sexual harassment. Judicial decisions in the decade between 1976 and 1986, changed the face of harassment law, eventually placing sexual harassment law at the forefront in the Supreme Court case of *Meritor*

Savings Bank, FSB v. Vinson, 477 U.S. 57, 106 S.Ct. 2399, 91 L.Ed.2d 49 (1986). Citing the *Rogers* case and its progeny, *id.* at 65–66, 106 S.Ct. at 2405, *Meritor* held that discriminatory sexual harassment that creates a hostile work environment for the complainant violates Title VII.

The Title VII jurisprudence of harassment as a form of employment discrimination has developed largely in the context of sexual harassment, and this topic is the primary focus of this chapter. Section B.1 presents some statistical data on the pervasiveness and estimated costs of workplace sexual harassment. Section B.2 introduces the two theories of actionable sexual harassment: *quid pro quo* and hostile work environment. Section B.3 demonstrates the continuing evolution of sexual harassment doctrine in the Supreme Court's 1998 decision in *Oncale v. Sundowner Offshore Services,* which held that same-sex sexual harassment may be actionable under Title VII. Finally, Section C explores the standards and burdens of proof for employer liability for discriminatory harassment by supervisory employees. In addition, in its 2004 decision, *Pennsylvania State Police v. Suders,* the Court clarified the burdens of proof each party bears in a sexual harassment case involving a constructive discharge. The chapter concludes, in Section D, with an exploration of how racial and ethnic harassment cases have been affected by doctrinal developments in sexual harassment law. Workplace harassment based on other statutorily protected categories is discussed in Chapter 9 (sexual orientation and gender identity), Chapter 11 (religion), Chapter 12 (national origin), Chapter 13 (age), and Chapter 14 (disability).

B. HARASSMENT BECAUSE OF SEX

1. ESTIMATING THE PREVALENCE AND COSTS OF WORKPLACE SEXUAL HARASSMENT

Numerous studies since the 1970s have documented the pervasiveness of sexual harassment in the workplace. *See, e.g.*, B. Glenn George, *The Back Door: Legitimizing Sexual Harassment Claims,* 73 B.U.L.Rev. 1, 2 n.3 (1993) (listing surveys). In one of the first surveys, published in *Redbook* magazine in 1976, 92% of the 9,000 respondents listed sexual harassment as a "serious" problem, and nine out of ten respondents reported personal experiences with sexual harassment in the workplace. Claire Safran, *What Men Do to Women on the Job: A Shocking Look at Sexual Harassment,* Redbook, Nov. 1976, at 149, 149, 217. *See* Catharine A. MacKinnon, Sexual Harassment of Working Women: A Case of Sex Discrimination 25–29 (1979). In 1988, *Working Woman* magazine reported that almost 90% of the Fortune 500 companies surveyed had acknowledged receiving complaints of sexual harassment from employees.

Ronni Sandroff, *Sexual Harassment in the Fortune 500*, Working Woman, Dec. 1988, at 69.

The incidence of workplace sexual harassment remains high. A 2010 study by the Society of Human Resource Management reported that 36 percent of responding employers had received a complaint of sexual harassment within the preceding 24 months. *See* Is Workplace Sexual Harassment on the Rise? SHRM Poll, available at *http://www.shrm.org/research/surveyfindings/articles/pages/sexualharassmentontherise.aspx.* A 2015 survey of 2,235 women found that 1 in 3 women between the ages of 18 and 34 report having been sexually harassed at work. *See* Alanna Vagianos, 1 in 3 Women Has Been Sexually Harassed at Work, According to Survey (Feb 19, 2015), available at *http://www.huffingtonpost.com/2015/02/19/1-in-3-women-sexually-harassed-work-cosmopolitan_n_6713814.html.*

The number of sexual harassment charges filed with the Equal Employment Opportunity Commission declined between 2010 and 2014 from 7,944 to 6,862. *See* EEOC, Charges Alleging Sexual Harassment FY 2010–FY 2014, available at *http://www.eeoc.gov/eeoc/statistics/enforcement/sexual_harassment_new.cfm*. The full extent of sexual harassment in the workplace, however, is difficult to measure because many incidents may never be reported. Professor MacKinnon observed, "Like women who are raped, sexually harassed women feel humiliated, degraded, ashamed, embarrassed, and cheap, as well as angry." MacKinnon, *supra*, at 47. *See generally* Ellen Bravo & Ellen Cassedy, The 9 to 5 Guide to Combatting Sexual Harassment (1992); Louise Fitzgerald et al., *Why Didn't She Just Report Him? The Psychological and Legal Implications of Women's Responses to Sexual Harassment*, 51 J.Soc. Issues 117, 119–21 (1995). Furthermore, the costs to employees of complaining about harassment suggest that underreporting is to be expected, and that even our best statistical measures of the extent and costs of workplace harassment can only roughly approximate reality. *See* Deborah L. Brake & Joanna L. Grossman, *The Failure of Title VII as a Rights-Claiming System*, 86 N.C.L.Rev. 859, 879–84 (2008) (discussing burdens of reporting requirements and the risks of retaliation for employees who report sexual harassment). Of the women surveyed in the 2015 study by Cosmopolitan Magazine, only 29 percent of those who were sexually harassed said that they reported the harassment. Vagianos, *supra*.

2. THE TWO THEORIES OF SEXUAL HARASSMENT: QUID PRO QUO AND HOSTILE WORK ENVIRONMENT

The courts rejected the early Title VII claims of women that sexual harassment constituted sex discrimination "in essence because the acts complained of were not seen to be sufficiently tied to the workplace context." Catharine A. MacKinnon, Sexual Harassment of Working Women: A Case of Sex Discrimination 59 (1979). To the contrary, Professor MacKinnon explained:

> Women's experiences of sexual harassment can be divided into two forms which merge at the edges and in the world. The first I term the *quid pro quo*, in which sexual compliance is exchanged, or proposed to be exchanged, for an employment opportunity. The second arises when sexual harassment is a persistent *condition of work*.

MacKinnon, *supra*, at 32. By the late 1970s and early 1980s, the federal courts and the EEOC had begun to adopt the framework—and often the terminology—that Professor MacKinnon had used for analyzing sexual harassment cases. *See, e.g.*, Henson v. Dundee, 682 F.2d 897, 908, 909 n.18 (11th Cir.1982). Two cases from the D.C. Circuit—*Williams v. Saxbe*, 413 F.Supp. 654 (D.D.C. 1976), *vacated*, *Williams v. Bell*, 587 F.2d 1240 (D.C.Cir.1978) and *Barnes v. Costle*, 561 F.2d 983 (D.C.Cir.1977)—are recognized as the earliest examples of the quid pro quo paradigm, which is discussed *infra,* in Section B.1. *Bundy v. Jackson*, 641 F.2d 934 (D.C.Cir.1981), is considered the first case to endorse the hostile work environment theory of sexual harassment, which is discussed *infra*, in Section B.2. For an analysis of these early sexual harassment cases, see Catharine A. MacKinnon, *The Logic of Experience: Reflections on the Development of Sexual Harassment Law,* 90 Geo.L.J. 813 (2002).

In 1980, the EEOC promulgated guidelines on "Sexual Harassment," 29 C.F.R. § 1604.11, as part of its *Guidelines on Discrimination Because of Sex*. The 1980 Guidelines specifically recognized sexual harassment as a violation of Title VII and adopted the two judicially developed theories of sexual harassment: quid pro quo and hostile work environment.

> Harassment on the basis of sex is a violation of Sec. 703 of Title VII. Unwelcome sexual advances, requests for sexual favors, and other verbal or physical conduct of a sexual nature constitute sexual harassment when (1) submission to such conduct is made either explicitly or impliedly a term or condition of an individual's employment, (2) submission to or rejection of such conduct by an individual is used as the basis for employment decisions affecting such individual, or (3) such conduct has the purpose or effect of unreasonably interfering with an individual's work performance or creating an intimidating, hostile, or offensive environment.

29 C.F.R. § 1604.11(a). In 1986, the Supreme Court for the first time used the terms "quid pro quo" and "hostile work environment" to describe the two categories of sexual harassment actionable under Title VII. *See*

Meritor Savings Bank, FSB v. Vinson, 477 U.S. 57, 65, 106 S.Ct. 2399, 2404–05, 91 L.Ed.2d 49 (1986).

a. Quid Pro Quo Sexual Harassment: The Prima Facie Case

In *Nichols v. Frank*, 42 F.3d 503 (9th Cir.1994), a paradigmatic quid pro quo case, the Ninth Circuit relied on the 1980 EEOC Guidelines on Sexual Harassment to find that a supervisor's conduct constituted sexual harassment under Title VII. The plaintiff was a deaf-mute female who read at a fifth-grade level and could communicate only through writing and sign language. While she was employed as a mail sorter at a United States postal facility, her night shift supervisor repeatedly demanded that she perform oral sex on him. He was the highest ranking manager on her shift and the only supervisor who could use sign language. All of his requests for sexual favors occurred at the work site in the context of discussions about her sick leave, attendance record, job evaluations, and requests for leaves-of-absence. Because the plaintiff feared she would lose her job or job benefits if she refused the supervisor's sexual demands, she "repeatedly but unwillingly performed oral sex on him over a period of approximately six months." *Id.* at 506. After these sex acts, the supervisor would grant the plaintiff certain job benefits. Although she did not report the supervisor's harassing conduct at the time, she subsequently reported the harassment and filed complaints with the Postal Service, the EEOC, and her union, and then brought a Title VII action against the Postal Service. On appeal, the Ninth Circuit held that "quid pro quo sexual harassment occurs whenever an individual explicitly or implicitly conditions a job, a job benefit, or the absence of a job detriment upon an employee's acceptance of sexual conduct." *Id.* at 511.

Using the facts and holding in *Nichols v. Frank* for guidance, can you articulate the elements of a prima facie case of quid pro quo sexual harassment? Which part or parts of the 1980 EEOC Guidelines on Sexual Harassment, reproduced above, were violated by the supervisor's conduct in *Nichols*? Would the plaintiff's claim for Title VII relief in *Nichols* have been less compelling if she had not been physically impaired? If she had had a high school education? Should she have complained sooner? Will Title VII "chill the incidence of legitimate romance" in the workplace? *Nichols,* 42 F.3d at 510. Was the supervisor in *Nichols* interested in a romantic relationship with the plaintiff? Or was he using sex and his position of authority to humiliate her? Does it matter what his intentions were if his sexual advances were not welcomed by the plaintiff?

When alleged harassment potentially falls into a quid pro quo paradigm, the evidentiary challenge of establishing causation is demonstrated in the following series of hypotheticals:

> [D]ifficult factual and legal questions will almost always arise whenever either the conditioning of benefits (or absence of

> detriment) or the request for favors is not explicit, but is instead *implicit* in the harasser's communications or dealings with his prey. For example, *quid pro quo* harassment is clear if a manager explicitly tells his subordinate "I will fire you unless you sleep with me." However, it is much less clear whether a violation has occurred if a manager simply asks the subordinate whether she would like to have a drink after work to talk about a possible promotion and then sometime after she refuses, awards the position to another employee. It is even less clear if the manager merely invites the employee out for a drink on one or more occasions but does not suggest that he wishes to discuss work-related matters; if the manager is spurned and subsequently withholds anticipated benefits, it may set off alarm bells, but further evidence would be required before a charge of sexual harassment could be sustained.

Nichols, 42 F.3d at 512.

The topic of quid pro quo sexual harassment will be explored further in Section C, Employer Liability for Harassment. It is important to note here, however, that defining conduct as quid pro quo or hostile work environment harassment does not provide an automatic answer to the question of whether the employer will be liable for the conduct. That question requires a separate inquiry. Consequently, as the Supreme Court observed many years after it had endorsed the distinction between these two types of actionable sexual harassment, "[t]he terms *quid pro quo* and hostile work environment are helpful, perhaps, in making a rough demarcation between cases in which threats are carried out and those where they are not or are absent altogether, but beyond this are of limited utility." Burlington Industries, Inc. v. Ellerth, 524 U.S. 742, 751, 118 S.Ct. 2257, 2265, 141 L.Ed.2d 633 (1998). While "the terms are relevant when there is a threshold question whether a plaintiff can prove discrimination in violation of Title VII," *id.* at 753, 118 S.Ct. at 2265, defining harassment as quid pro quo or hostile work environment is only the first step in a sexual harassment suit.

b. Hostile Work Environment: The Prima Facie Case

The Supreme Court first recognized the viability of the hostile work environment theory of sexual harassment in *Meritor Savings Bank, FSB v. Vinson*, 477 U.S. 57, 106 S.Ct. 2399, 91 L.Ed.2d 49 (1986). In reaching its conclusion, the Court explained:

> Without question, when a supervisor sexually harasses a subordinate because of the subordinate's sex, that supervisor "discriminate[s]" on the basis of sex. Petitioner apparently does not challenge this proposition. It contends instead that in prohibiting discrimination with respect to "compensation, terms,

> conditions, or privileges" of employment, Congress was concerned with what petitioner describes as "tangible loss" of "an economic character," not "purely psychological aspects of the workplace environment." In support of this claim petitioner observes that in both the legislative history of Title VII and this Court's Title VII decisions, the focus has been on tangible, economic barriers erected by discrimination.
>
> We reject petitioner's view. First, the language of Title VII is not limited to "economic" or "tangible" discrimination. The phrase "terms, conditions, or privileges of employment" evinces a congressional intent " 'to strike at the entire spectrum of disparate treatment of men and women' " in employment. Los Angeles Dept. of Water and Power v. Manhart, 435 U.S. 702, 707 n.13, 98 S.Ct. 1370, 1375 n.13, 55 L.Ed.2d 657 (1978). Petitioner has pointed to nothing in the Act to suggest that Congress contemplated the limitation urged here.
>
> Second, in 1980 the EEOC issued Guidelines specifying that "sexual harassment," as there defined, is a form of sex discrimination prohibited by Title VII. As an "administrative interpretation of the Act by the enforcing agency," Griggs v. Duke Power Co., 401 U.S. 424, 433–34, 91 S.Ct. 849, 855, 28 L.Ed.2d 158 (1971), these Guidelines, " 'while not controlling upon the courts by reason of their authority, do constitute a body of experience and informed judgment to which courts and litigants may properly resort for guidance.' " General Electric Co. v. Gilbert, 429 U.S. 125, 141–42, 97 S.Ct. 401, 411, 50 L.Ed.2d 343 (1976). The EEOC Guidelines fully support the view that harassment leading to noneconomic injury can violate Title VII.
>
> * * *
>
> Of course * * * not all workplace conduct that may be described as "harassment" affects a "term, condition, or privilege" of employment within the meaning of Title VII. For sexual harassment to be actionable, it must be sufficiently severe or pervasive "to alter the conditions of [the victim's] employment and create an abusive working environment."

Meritor, 477 U.S. at 64–67, 106 S.Ct. at 2404–05 (citations omitted). The Court went on to explain that explain that, in addition to being "severe or pervasive," to be actionable, the alleged misconduct had to be "unwelcome." Significantly, the Court distinguished between conduct that was "involuntary" and advances that were "unwelcome," explaining that:

> the fact that sex-related conduct was "voluntary," in the sense that the complainant was not forced to participate against her

> will, is not a defense to a sexual harassment suit brought under Title VII. The gravamen of any sexual harassment claim is that the alleged sexual advances were "unwelcome." 29 C.F.R. § 1604.11(a) (1985). While the question whether particular conduct was indeed unwelcome presents difficult problems of proof and turns largely on credibility determinations committed to the trier of fact, the District Court in this case erroneously focused on the "voluntariness" of respondent's participation in the claimed sexual episodes. The correct inquiry is whether respondent by her conduct indicated that the alleged sexual advances were unwelcome, not whether her actual participation in sexual intercourse was voluntary.

Id. at 68, 106 S.Ct. at 2406. While the Court's opinion in *Meritor* established the basic elements of a prima facie case of hostile work environment sexual harassment, a conflict quickly developed among the lower courts as to whether harassment had to cause a tangible psychological injury in order to be actionable under Title VII. The Court addressed this question in the following case.

HARRIS V. FORKLIFT SYSTEMS, INC.

Supreme Court of the United States, 1993.
510 U.S. 17, 114 S.Ct. 367, 126 L.Ed.2d 295.

JUSTICE O'CONNOR delivered the opinion of the Court.

* * *

I

Teresa Harris worked as a manager at Forklift Systems, Inc., an equipment rental company, from April 1985 until October 1987. Charles Hardy was Forklift's president.

The Magistrate found that, throughout Harris' time at Forklift, Hardy often insulted her because of her gender and often made her the target of unwanted sexual innuendos. Hardy told Harris on several occasions, in the presence of other employees, "You're a woman, what do you know" and "We need a man as the rental manager"; at least once, he told her she was "a dumb ass woman." Again in front of others, he suggested that the two of them "go to the Holiday Inn to negotiate [Harris'] raise." Hardy occasionally asked Harris and other female employees to get coins from his front pants pocket. He threw objects on the ground in front of Harris and other women, and asked them to pick the objects up. He made sexual innuendos about Harris' and other women's clothing.

In mid-August 1987, Harris complained to Hardy about his conduct. Hardy said he was surprised that Harris was offended, claimed he was only joking, and apologized. He also promised he would stop, and based on this assurance Harris stayed on the job. But in early September, Hardy began anew: While Harris was arranging a deal with one of Forklift's customers, he asked her, again in front of other employees, "What did you do, promise the guy * * * some [sex] Saturday night?" On October 1, Harris collected her paycheck and quit.

Harris then sued Forklift, claiming that Hardy's conduct had created an abusive work environment for her because of her gender. The [district court] * * * found this to be "a close case," but held that Hardy's conduct did not create an abusive environment. The court found that some of Hardy's comments "offended [Harris], and would offend the reasonable woman," but that they were not

> so severe as to be expected to seriously affect [Harris'] psychological well-being. A reasonable woman manager under like circumstances would have been offended by Hardy, but his conduct would not have risen to the level of interfering with that person's work performance.
>
> Neither do I believe that [Harris] was subjectively so offended that she suffered injury * * * . Although Hardy may at times have genuinely offended [Harris], I do not believe that he created a working environment so poisoned as to be intimidating or abusive to [Harris]. * * *
>
> [The Court of Appeals affirmed, and the Supreme Court] granted certiorari, to resolve a conflict among the Circuits on whether conduct, to be actionable as "abusive work environment" harassment (no *quid pro quo* harassment issue is present here), must "seriously affect [an employee's] psychological well-being" or lead the plaintiff to "suffe[r] injury."

II

* * * When the workplace is permeated with "discriminatory intimidation, ridicule, and insult," that is "sufficiently severe or pervasive to alter the conditions of the victim's employment and create an abusive working environment," Title VII is violated.

This standard, which we reaffirm today, takes a middle path between making actionable any conduct that is merely offensive and requiring the conduct to cause a tangible psychological injury. As we pointed out in *Meritor*, "mere utterance of an * * * epithet which engenders offensive feelings in a [sic] employee," does not sufficiently affect the conditions of employment to implicate Title VII. Conduct that is not severe or pervasive enough to create an objectively hostile or abusive work environment—an environment that a reasonable person would find hostile or abusive—is beyond Title VII's purview. Likewise, if the victim does not subjectively perceive the environment to be abusive, the conduct has not actually altered the conditions of the victim's employment, and there is no Title VII violation.

But Title VII comes into play before the harassing conduct leads to a nervous breakdown. A discriminatorily abusive work environment, even one that does not seriously affect employees' psychological well-being, can and often will detract from employees' job performance, discourage employees from remaining on the job, or keep them from advancing in their careers. Moreover, even without regard to these tangible effects, the very fact that the discriminatory conduct was so severe or pervasive that it created a work environment abusive to employees because of their race, gender, religion, or national origin offends Title VII's broad rule of workplace equality. * * *

We therefore believe the District Court erred in relying on whether the conduct "seriously affected plaintiff's psychological well-being" or led her to "suffe[r] injury." Such an inquiry may needlessly focus the factfinder's attention on concrete psychological harm, an element Title VII does not require. Certainly Title VII bars conduct that would seriously affect a reasonable person's psychological well-being, but the statute is not limited to such conduct. So long as the environment would reasonably be perceived, and is perceived, as hostile or abusive, there is no need for it also to be psychologically injurious.

This is not, and by its nature cannot be, a mathematically precise test. We need not answer today all the potential questions it raises, nor specifically address the [EEOC's] new regulations on this subject. But we can say that whether an environment is "hostile" or "abusive" can be determined only by looking at all the circumstances. These may include the frequency of the discriminatory conduct; its severity; whether it is physically threatening or humiliating, or a mere offensive utterance; and whether it unreasonably interferes with an employee's work performance. The effect on the employee's psychological well-being is, of course, relevant to determining whether the plaintiff actually found the environment abusive. But while psychological harm, like any other relevant factor, may be taken into account, no single factor is required.

III

Forklift, while conceding that a requirement that the conduct seriously affect psychological well-being is unfounded, argues that the District Court nonetheless correctly applied the *Meritor* standard. We disagree. Though the District Court did conclude that the work environment was not "intimidating or abusive to [Harris]," it did so only after finding that the conduct was not "so severe as to be expected to seriously affect plaintiff's psychological well-being," and that Harris was not "subjectively so offended that she suffered injury." The District

Court's application of these incorrect standards may well have influenced its ultimate conclusion, especially given that the court found this to be a "close case."

We therefore reverse the judgment of the Court of Appeals, and remand the case for further proceedings consistent with this opinion.

JUSTICE SCALIA, concurring.

* * * "Abusive" (or "hostile," which in this context I take to mean the same thing) does not seem to me a very clear standard—and I do not think clarity is at all increased by adding the adverb "objectively" or by appealing to a "reasonable person['s]" notion of what the vague word means. Today's opinion does list a number of factors that contribute to abusiveness, but since it neither says how much of each is necessary (an impossible task) nor identifies any single factor as determinative, it thereby adds little certitude. As a practical matter, today's holding lets virtually unguided juries decide whether sex-related conduct engaged in (or permitted by) an employer is egregious enough to warrant an award of damages. One might say that what constitutes "negligence" (a traditional jury question) is not much more clear and certain than what constitutes "abusiveness." Perhaps so. But the class of plaintiffs seeking to recover for negligence is limited to those who have suffered harm, whereas under this statute "abusiveness" is to be the test of whether legal harm has been suffered, opening more expansive vistas of litigation.

Be that as it may, I know of no alternative to the course the Court today has taken. One of the factors mentioned in the Court's nonexhaustive list—whether the conduct unreasonably interferes with an employee's work performance—would, if it were made an absolute test, provide greater guidance to juries and employers. But I see no basis for such a limitation in the language of the statute. Accepting *Meritor*'s interpretation of the term "conditions of employment" as the law, the test is not whether work has been impaired, but whether working conditions have been discriminatorily altered. I know of no test more faithful to the inherently vague statutory language than the one the Court today adopts. For these reasons, I join the opinion of the Court.

JUSTICE GINSBURG, concurring.

Today the Court reaffirms the holding of *Meritor Savings Bank v. Vinson*: "[A] plaintiff may establish a violation of Title VII by proving that discrimination based on sex has created a hostile or abusive work environment." The critical issue, Title VII's text indicates, is whether members of one sex are exposed to disadvantageous terms or conditions of employment to which members of the other sex are not exposed. As the Equal Employment Opportunity Commission emphasized, the adjudicator's inquiry should center, dominantly, on whether the discriminatory conduct has unreasonably interfered with the plaintiff's work performance. To show such interference, "the plaintiff need not prove that his or her tangible productivity has declined as a result of the harassment." Davis v. Monsanto Chemical Co., 858 F.2d 345, 349 (6th Cir.1988). It suffices to prove that a reasonable person subjected to the discriminatory conduct would find, as the plaintiff did, that the harassment so altered working conditions as to "ma[k]e it more difficult to do the job." *See id. Davis* concerned race-based discrimination, but that difference does not alter the analysis; except in the rare case in which a bona fide occupational qualification is shown, Title VII declares discriminatory practices based on race, gender, religion, or national origin equally unlawful. * * *

NOTES AND QUESTIONS

1. *The Prima Facie Case*: To make out a prima facie hostile work environment case, the plaintiff must demonstrate: (1) that she belongs to a protected class; (2) that she was subjected to unwelcome sexual harassment; (3) that the harassment was based on sex; (4) that the harassment was sufficiently severe or pervasive to alter the terms and conditions of employment; and (5) that there is a basis for holding the employer liable for the misconduct. *See, e.g.,* Stewart v. Rise, Inc., 791 F.3d 849, 859–60 (8th Cir.2015); Mendoza v. Borden, Inc., 195 F.3d 1238, 1245 (11th Cir.1999) (en banc); Henson v. City of Dundee, 682 F.2d 897, 902 (11th Cir.1982).

2. *Proving Unwelcomeness*: What purpose does the "unwelcomeness" requirement serve, and what obligations does it impose on the plaintiff? How did Teresa Harris satisfy this element in *Harris*? In its amicus brief in *Meritor*, the EEOC argued for inclusion of this element on the ground that it was needed to "ensure that sexual harassment charges do not become the tool by which one party to a consensual relationship may punish the other." Brief for the United States and the EEOC as Amici Curiae [Supporting Petitioner], Meritor Sav. Bank, FSB v. Vinson, 477 U.S. 57 (No. 84–1979), 1985 WL 670162, at *15. Is this concern consistent with the *Harris* "totality of the circumstances" test?

Professor Henry Chambers offers the following "working theory" of the requirement of proof of "unwelcomeness" in sexual harassment cases: "[U]nwelcomeness stems from the notions that welcome conduct does not tend to cause harm and that harassers and employers need affirmative notice that conduct is harassing before the employer is deemed responsible for subsequent similar conduct." Professor Henry L. Chambers, Jr., *(Un)Welcome Conduct and the Sexually Hostile Environment*, 53 Ala.L.Rev. 733, 750 (2002). Should plaintiffs be required to "express" unwelcomeness? If so, how? Should a simple request to "stop" be sufficient? Or necessary? Is this too much of a burden? As you read the sexual harassment materials in this chapter, consider whether you would agree with Professor Chambers' conclusion that "[t]he unwelcomeness requirement should be eliminated because it no longer serves any useful purpose that is not already served by another feature of sexual harassment law and is at odds with Title VII's goals." *Id.* at 787. *See also* Grace S Ho, *Not Quite Rights: How the Unwelcomeness Element in Sexual Harassment Law Undermines Title VII's Transformative Potential*, 20 Yale J.L. & Feminism 131, 155, 156 (2008) (proposing that the defendant should bear the burden of showing that an alleged harasser's conduct was welcome); Casey J. Wood, *"Inviting Sexual Harassment": The Absurdity of the Welcomeness Requirement in Sexual Harassment Law,* 38 Brandeis L.J. 423, 430 (1999–2000) (arguing that "a separate finding of welcomeness by the court is an unneeded and redundant step in sexual harassment cases").

a. *The plaintiff's provocative speech and dress*: In *Meritor*, the Court explained that although " 'voluntariness' in the sense of consent is not a defense to [a harassment] claim, it does not follow that a complainant's sexually provocative speech or dress is irrelevant as a matter of law in determining whether he or she found particular sexual advances unwelcome." To the contrary, such evidence is obviously relevant." *Meritor*, 477 U.S. at 69, 106 S.Ct. at 2406. One commentator criticizing this "welcomed conduct" defense argued that the *Meritor* evidentiary standard (1) "implies that the primary motivation for sexual harassment is sexual attraction" and "ignores that harassment is often a manifestation of power"; (2) "mischaracterizes female sexuality" by "categoriz[ing] female sexual conduct according to conventional, passive sex roles"; and (3) "is reminiscent of defense tactics in rape cases that attempt to blame the victim for the crime." Christina A. Bull, Comment, *The Implications of Admitting Evidence of a Sexual Harassment Plaintiff's Speech and Dress in the Aftermath of* Meritor Savings Bank v. Vinson, 41 UCLA L.Rev. 117, 119 (1993). Are these valid criticisms? When is harassment ever "welcome"?

b. *Employer policies on appearance and behavior*: Some management attorneys recommend that employers adopt policies on personal appearance and behavior. For example, two commentators suggested the following policy:

> Please avoid extremes in dress and behavior. Flashy, skimpy, or revealing outfits and other non-business-like clothing are unacceptable. Likewise, unprofessional behavior in the workplace, such as sexually related conversations, inappropriate touching (*i.e.*, kissing, hugging, massaging, sitting on laps) of another employee, and any other behavior of a sexual nature is prohibited. Employees who fail to observe these standards will be subject to disciplinary action, up to and including termination.

James J. McDonald, Jr. & Daniel S. Fellner, *A Plaintiff's Obligation to "Avoid Harm Otherwise": New Life for the Welcomeness Defense*, 25 Employee Rel.L.J. 17, 32 (1999). What are the advantages for an employer in adopting and implementing such a policy? What are the disadvantages for employees? *See generally* Vicki Schultz, *The Sanitized Workplace*, 112 Yale L.J. 2061 (2003).

c. *The plaintiff's use of vulgar language*: If a female subordinate uses vulgar language in the workplace, will she be able to demonstrate that a male supervisor's use of similar offensive and vulgar language was unwelcome? *See* Hocevar v. Purdue Frederick Co., 223 F.3d 721, 736–37 (8th Cir.2000) (no). What if the language being used by male co-workers is not simply crude, but is sexually degrading? In Carr v. Allison Gas Turbine Div., 32 F.3d 1007, 1011–12 (7th Cir.1994), the Seventh Circuit reversed a district court's conclusion that plaintiff "invited" extremely degrading language and conduct because she tried to be "one of the boys," noting that the profanity used by the plaintiff at work was markedly different from the sexually charged and hostile language used by her male co-workers.

d. *The adolescent plaintiff*: Are there special concerns about the "welcomeness" of sexual advances when the victim of workplace harassment is an adolescent? Can a 16-year-old have a truly "consensual" sexual relationship with an older co-worker? With a supervisor? Does that depend on their relative ages and status in the workplace? In *Doe v. Oberweiss Dairy*, 456 F.3d 704, 713 (7th Cir.2006), the court held that an adolescent female plaintiff who was below the age of consent under the statutory rape laws in the state where she worked was incapable, as a matter of law, of "welcoming" sexual advances from an older man who was her supervisor. *See generally* Anastasia M. Boles, *Centering the Teenage "Siren": Adolescent Workers, Sexual Harassment, and the Legal Construction of Race and Gender*, 22 Mich. J. Gender & L. 1 (2015); Jennifer Ann Drobac, *I Can't to I Kant: The Sexual Harassment of Working Adolescents, Competing Theories, and Ethical Dilemmas*, 70 Alb.L.Rev. 675 (2007); Seymour Moskowitz, *Adolescent Workers and Sexual Harassment,* 51 Lab.L.J., Fall 2000, at 78.

3. *Severity or Pervasiveness*: *Harris v. Forklift* requires a plaintiff to satisfy both an objective and a subjective test in proving that sexual harassment was sufficiently "severe or pervasive" to affect "the conditions of the victim's employment." This is often a difficult burden to meet. *See, e.g.*, Ponte v. Steelcase Inc., 741 F.3d 310, 320–21 (1st Cir.2014) (denying a hostile work environment claim and collecting cases that, in contrast to the allegations here, included conduct that was severe enough to cross the threshold into actionable misconduct); Mendoza v. Borden, 195 F.3d 1238, 1246–49 (11th Cir.1999) (en banc) (denying a hostile work environment claim and collecting other cases where courts have found the conduct does not satisfy the "severe or pervasive" element of the prima facie case).What is the difference, if any, between proving that conduct was severe or pervasive, according to both objective and subjective perspectives, and proving that it was "unwelcome" to the plaintiff? How can employees distinguish between lawful flirtation or teasing and unlawful harassment? *See generally* Richard L. Wiener & Linda E. Hurt, *Social Sexual Conduct at Work: How Do Workers Know When It Is Harassment and When It Is Not?*, 34 Cal.W. L.Rev. 53 (1997).

In his concurrence in *Harris v. Forklift*, Justice Scalia expresses concern that the terms "abusive" or "hostile" do not provide "a very clear standard" and that "virtually unguided juries" will decide whether conduct is "egregious enough to warrant an award of damages." In fact, many sexual harassment claims result in dismissal or summary judgment for the defendant, so the plaintiff never reaches either a bench trial or a jury trial. *See* Ann Juliano & Stewart J. Schwab, *The Sweep of Sexual Harassment Cases*, 86 Cornell L.Rev. 548, 568 (2001) (reporting on the significant increase in the percentage of sexual harassment cases resulting in dismissal or summary judgment from 1986 to 1995). Following the Civil Rights Act of 1991, which granted the right to a jury trial in these cases, even when a hostile work environment case goes to a jury trial, a jury verdict based on a finding of "severe or pervasive" conduct may be overturned by the district court in response to a motion for a judgment n.o.v. or on appeal. *See, e.g.*, Duncan v. Gen. Motors Corp., 300 F.3d 928, 935 (8th Cir.2002) (2–1 decision reversing a $1 million jury verdict on the ground that "as a matter of law * * * [the plaintiff] did not show a sexually harassing hostile environment sufficiently severe or pervasive so as to alter the conditions of her employment"). Is the real concern that judges will improperly substitute their view of the facts for the jury's findings? *See id.* at 936, 938 (Arnold, J., dissenting). *See generally* Elisabeth A. Keller & Judith B. Tracy, *Hidden in Plain Sight: Achieving More Just Results in Hostile Work Environment Sexual Harassment Cases By Re-Examining Supreme Court Precedent*, 15 Duke J. Gender L. & Pol'y 247 (2008) (arguing that lower courts have read Supreme Court cases too narrowly and have thus ruled against plaintiffs with legitimate sexual harassment claims); Theresa M. Beiner, *Let the Jury Decide: The Gap Between What Judges and Reasonable People Believe Is Sexually Harassing*, 75 S.Cal.L.Rev. 791 (2002) (reviewing social science research on what conduct is perceived as "severe or pervasive" sexual harassment); M. Isabel Medina, *A Matter of Fact: Hostile Environments and Summary Judgments*, 8 S.Cal.Rev.L. & Women's Stud. 311 (1999) (arguing that courts are usurping the role of the jury in sexual harassment cases).

a. *What is "severe"?* Can a single incident of harassment, such as a sexual assault, violate Title VII? *See* Ferris v. Delta Air Lines, Inc., 277 F.3d 128, 136 (2d Cir.2001), (finding that a single act of rape is "sufficiently egregious"); Little v. Windermere Relocation, Inc., 301 F.3d 958 (9th Cir.2002) (finding that multiple rapes of an employee in one night was "severe"). When should one or two incidents of forcible sexual touching be considered "severe"? *Compare* Hostetler v. Quality Dining, Inc., 218 F.3d 798, 809 (7th Cir.2000) (finding that plaintiff's allegations that her male coworker forced his tongue down her throat one day and the next day tried to unfasten her bra were sufficiently severe to support a jury finding of a hostile work environment), *with* Brooks v. City of San Mateo, 229 F.3d 917 (9th Cir.2000) (finding that, where a male co-worker forcibly fondled the breast of a female dispatcher, the single incident was not sufficiently severe to impose liability on the employer for hostile work environment).

What if a physical assault is not sexual? *See* Morris v. City of Colorado Springs, 666 F.3d 654, 665–66 (10th Cir.2012) (upholding district court's conclusion that a supervisor twice hitting an employee in the head was not sufficiently severe or pervasive to support a claim); Smith v. Sheahan, 189 F.3d 529, 533 (7th Cir.1999) (holding that an assault based on "sex-based animus" rather than "misdirected sexual desire" is actionable). What about unwelcome touching that is not clearly sexual? *See* Meriwether v. Caraustar Packaging Co., 326 F.3d 990 (8th Cir.2003) (finding that a single incident where a co-worker squeezed the plaintiff's buttocks followed by an encounter where the co-worker "joked about the incident" was not severe or pervasive). What if there is no physical touching, but only a single verbal attack? *See* Howley v. Town of Stratford, 217 F.3d 141, 154 (2d Cir.2000) (finding that "an extended barrage of obscene verbal abuse" of the plaintiff, delivered "at length, loudly, and in a large group in which the [plaintiff] was the only female and many of the men were her subordinates," was severe enough to support a jury finding of hostile work environment); Boyer-Liberto v. Fontainebleau Corp., 786 F.3d 264 (4th Cir.2015) (finding that "an isolated incident of harassment, if extremely serious, can create a hostile work environment," and reversing a grant of summary judgment where plaintiff's supervisor referred to her as a "porch money" several times in a single twenty-four hour period).

Is a single sexual proposition from a high-ranking manager "severe"? Or does a sexual proposition become "severe" only after the subordinate has made it clear that sexual relations would be "unwelcome" and the sexual proposition is repeated? *See* Quantock v. Shared Mkg. Servs., Inc., 312 F.3d 899, 904 (7th Cir.2002) (finding that when a company president made three propositions for sex to his subordinate in a single business meeting the conduct was sufficiently severe to be actionable).

b. *What is "pervasive"?* Can a "pervasive" series of offensive incidents—no one of which taken alone could reasonably be considered "severe" sexual harassment—violate Title VII? Because the terms "severe or pervasive" appear in the disjunctive, the plaintiff should be able to satisfy this element of a sexual harassment case by evidence that the harassing conduct is either severe or pervasive or both. *Compare* Smith v. First Union Nat'l Bank, 202 F.3d 234, 242–43 (4th Cir.2000) ("repeated remarks that belittled [the plaintiff] because she was a woman," along with physical threats, are "severe or pervasive"), *with* Shepherd v. Comptroller of Pub. Accounts of Tex., 168 F.3d 871, 874–75 (5th Cir.1999) (finding that co-worker's "boorish and offensive" comments, staring, and touching plaintiff's arm, which occurred "intermittently for a period of time" were "not severe" and did not "undermine" the plaintiff's "workplace competence"). *See also* Schiano v. Quality Payroll Sys., Inc., 445 F.3d 597, 608 (2d Cir.2006) (finding frequent conduct, its context, and the "physical nature of some of acts complained of," met threshold of "severe or pervasive"). How do courts determine when, as a matter of law, repeated conduct is sufficiently frequent to be actionable? Compare the majority and dissenting opinions in *Burnett v. Tyco Corp.*, 203 F.3d 980, 984, 986–87 (6th Cir.2000) (disagreeing on whether the effects of less severe harassment can be aggregated).

4. *The Problem of Perspective*: *Harris* requires courts to evaluate the severity or pervasiveness of sexual harassment both subjectively and objectively. When making an objective evaluation of the defendant's conduct, how should courts define the "reasonable person" whose objective perspective properly frames the analysis? In *Ellison v. Brady*, 924 F.2d 872 (1991), the Ninth Circuit famously used an analytic approach to hostile environment claims that is based on the victim's perspective, explaining that "[i]f we only examined whether a reasonable person would engage in allegedly harassing conduct, we would run the risk of reinforcing the prevailing level of discrimination." *Id.* at 878. Instead, the court explained, it "prefer[ed] to analyze harassment from the victim's perspective. A complete understanding of the victim's view requires, among other things, an analysis of the different perspectives of men and women. Conduct that many men consider unobjectionable may offend many women." *Id.* The Ninth Circuit concluded that the perspective of a "reasonable woman" would avoid the problem of the hyper-sensitive plaintiff while also acknowledging the unique experiences of women, particularly with regard to sexual abuse and workplace harassment. The use of a "reasonable woman" standard distinct from the "reasonable person" standard generated a great deal of academic controversy. Caroline A. Forell & Donna M. Matthews, A Law of Her Own: The Reasonable Woman as a Measure of Man 21–120 (2000); Ann Juliano & Stewart J. Schwab, *The Sweep of Sexual Harassment Cases*, 86 Cornell L.Rev. 548, 582–85 & 583 n.140 (2001) (citing commentary on the standard). A survey of all federal sexual harassment cases between 1986 and 1995 reports that they "found more articles discussing the reasonable woman standard than courts adopting the standard"—only 25 opinions out of 502 used the "reasonable woman" standard. *Id. at* 584. While the Supreme Court has never explicitly accepted or rejected the "reasonable woman" standard, the Court in *Oncale v. Sundowner Offshore Services, Inc.*, 523 U.S. 75, 118 S.Ct. 998, 140 L.Ed.2d 201 (1998), which is reproduced in Chapter 7, and discussed in more detail below, held that the appropriate standard is that of "a reasonable person in the plaintiff's position, considering 'all the circumstances.'" Is this an endorsement of a more nuanced "reasonable person" standard? Would the following jury instruction be consistent with *Oncale*? "[W]hen you're considering whether the conduct was severe or pervasive, you are to consider * * * the view of * * * an objectively reasonable woman of lesbian orientation." *See* Muzzy v. Cahillane Motors, Inc., 434 Mass. 409, 749 N.E.2d 691, 696–97 (2001).

5. *The "Reasonableness" of Employees' Beliefs—The* Breeden *Retaliation Case*: Recall that in *Clark County School District v. Breeden,* 532 U.S. 268, 121 S.Ct. 1508, 149 L.Ed.2d 509 (2001) (per curiam), reproduced *supra*, Chapter 3, the Supreme Court held that, because an employee's belief that her supervisor's explicit sexual comment was "sexual harassment" was not reasonable, her Title VII claim that her employer had retaliated against her for complaining about the comment was not actionable. The Supreme Court held that even if the plaintiff "had a reasonable, good faith belief that the incident involving the sexually explicit remark constituted unlawful

harassment, * * * no one could reasonably believe that the incident [she] recounted * * * violated Title VII." *Id.* at 270, 121 S.Ct. at 1509. Although *Breeden* is a retaliation case, its discussion of the objective standard for determining whether harassing conduct is sufficiently severe to be actionable under Title VII has implications for hostile work environment cases generally. Relying on language in *Harris v. Forklift*, the Court emphasized that "[a] recurring point in [our] opinions is that simple teasing, offhand comments, and isolated incidents (unless extremely serious) will not amount to discriminatory changes in the 'terms and conditions of employment.'" *Id.* at 271, 121 S.Ct. at 1510 (citation omitted). Does *Breeden* add clarity to the requirements of a prima facie case of hostile work environment?

6. *Claims for Psychological or Mental Distress*: *Harris v. Forklift* rejected the view that psychological harm is an indispensable element of a hostile work environment claim. A plaintiff may nevertheless seek damages for mental anguish or emotional distress caused by sexual harassment. Testimony from a physician or psychologist about the physical or psychological effects of harassment is not required, Farafaras v. Citizens Bank & Trust, 433 F.3d 558, 566 (7th Cir.2006), and plaintiff's own testimony about her feelings of stress, humiliation, embarrassment, and about physical effects, such as nausea, weight loss, and insomnia, may be sufficient to support compensatory damages, Betts v. Costco Wholesale Corp., 558 F.3d 461, 472–74 (6th Cir.2009). If a plaintiff alleges that sexual harassment caused psychological, emotional, or mental distress, should the defendant be allowed, through discovery, to compel the plaintiff to submit to psychological testing or other mental examinations? Discovery requests for such evidence are controlled by a "good cause" provision in Rule 35 of the Federal Rules of Civil Procedure. As a general rule, discovery of psychological evidence is likely to be allowed only when a plaintiff places her mental or emotional condition in controversy. *See* Schlagenhauf v. Holder, 379 U.S. 104, 85 S.Ct. 234, 13 L.Ed.2d 152 (1964); Schoffstall v. Henderson, 223 F.3d 818, 823 (8th Cir.2000) (holding that because the plaintiff had placed her mental state in issue, she had waived the psychotherapist-patient privilege).

7. *Bystander or Nontargeted Harassment*: The lower courts have adopted conflicting views on whether employees can sue under Title VII based on the claim that they have been harmed by harassment that is targeted at co-workers who are in the same protected class—conduct that is sometimes referred to as "bystander," "ambient," or "second-hand" harassment. Some courts have held that harassing comments that the plaintiff overhears, but that are not directed at her, may be considered in assessing the "totality of the circumstances" to determine whether there is an actionable hostile work environment. *See, e.g.*, Ladd v. Grand Trunk W. R.R., 552 F.3d 495, 500–01 (6th Cir.2009); EEOC v. Cent. Wholesalers, Inc., 578 F.3d 167 (4th Cir.2009). For example, the Tenth Circuit held: "We have never held, nor would we, that to be subjected to a hostile work environment the discriminatory conduct must be both directed at the victim and intended to be received by the victim." EEOC v. PVNF, L.L.C., 487 F.3d 790, 798 (10th

Cir.2007). Other courts, however, require the plaintiff to be the target or "within the target area" in order for the harassing conduct to be actionable. *See* Yuknis v. First Student, Inc., 481 F.3d 552, 554 (7th Cir.2007) ("The fact that one's coworkers do or say things that offend one, however deeply, does not amount to harassment if one is not within the target area of the offending conduct * * * ."). Some courts have considered the question as one of standing, particularly when the plaintiff is not in the same protected class as the targets of harassment. For example, in *Childress v. City of Richmond*, 134 F.3d 1205 (4th Cir.1998) (en banc), the court affirmed a district court ruling that seven white male police officers did not have standing to bring a Title VII hostile work environment claim based on racial and sexual harassment directed at black and female officers by their immediate supervisor. *See also id.* at 1208 (Luttig, J. concurring) (discussing standing requirements under Title VII). The EEOC Guidance on Sexual Favoritism, discussed previously, suggests the following framework for analyzing bystander harassment "in a situation in which supervisors in an office regularly make racial, ethnic or sexual jokes": "Even if the targets of the humor 'play along' and in no way display that they object, co-workers of any race, national origin or sex can claim that this conduct, which communicates a bias against protected class members, creates a hostile work environment for them." U.S. Equal Empl. Oppt'y Comm'n, Policy Guidance on Employer Liability Under Title VII for Sexual Favoritism, No. N–915.048, 2 EEOC Compliance Manual § 615 (Jan. 12, 1990), *available at http://www.eeoc.gov/policy/docs/sexualfavor.html* (page last modified June 21, 1999). *See generally* Kelly Cahill Timmons, *Sexual Harassment and Disparate Impact: Should Non-Targeted Workplace Sexual Conduct be Actionable Under Title VII?*, 81 Neb.L.Rev. 1152 (2003); Noah D. Zatz, *Beyond the Zero-Sum Game: Toward Title VII Protection for Intergroup Solidarity*, 77 Ind.L.J. 63 (2002).

8. *Class Actions and Pattern-or-Practice Cases*: Class actions brought by individual plaintiffs under Rule 23 of the Federal Rules of Civil Procedure and pattern-or-practice cases brought by the EEOC under § 707 of Title VII, 42 U.S.C. § 2000e–6, can in theory play an important role in challenging sexual harassment in the workplace. But these types of lawsuits have their limitations. *See* Michael Selmi, *The Price of Discrimination: The Nature of Class Action Employment Discrimination and Its Effects*, 81 Tex.L.Rev. 1249, 1249–50 (2003) (calling into question "whether [class action] lawsuits produce substantial benefits to the plaintiff class, prompt any changes in corporate culture, or exact costs sufficient to serve as an adequate deterrent against discrimination"). Consider the case of *Jenson v. Eveleth Mines*, the first Title VII hostile environment class action case: In 1984, Lois Jenson filed a class action hostile work environment suit against her employer, Eveleth Mines. The class was certified by the district court in 1991. Jenson v. Eveleth Taconite Co., 139 F.R.D. 657 (D.Minn.1991) ("Jenson I"). In 1993, the district court ruled that Eveleth was liable to the class of plaintiffs for claims of hostile work environment. Jenson v. Eveleth Taconite Co., 824 F.Supp. 847 (D.Minn.1993) ("Jenson II") (finding that "a sexualized, male-oriented, and anti-female atmosphere" prevailed at two of the company's mines, *id.* at 880).

Subsequently, in the remedial phase of the trial, the district court denied punitive damages and awarded compensatory damages for mental anguish to some members of the plaintiffs' class, and the Eighth Circuit affirmed in part and vacated and remanded for a new trial on damages. Jenson v. Eveleth Taconite Co., 130 F.3d 1287 (8th Cir.1997) ("Jenson III"), *cert. denied sub nom.* Oglebay Norton Co. v. Jenson, 524 U.S. 953, 118 S.Ct. 2370, 141 L.Ed.2d 738 (1998) . In early 1999, eleven years after the case was filed, the parties reached a settlement. In light of this history, would you encourage plaintiffs to pursue private class action lawsuits to remedy hostile environment sexual harassment? For a detailed account of the *Jenson v. Eveleth* litigation from the perspective of the plaintiffs and their lawyers, see Clara Bingham & Laura Leedy Gansler, Class Action: The Story of Lois Jenson and the Landmark Case that Changed Sexual Harassment Law (2002). *See also* Melissa Hart, *Litigation Narratives: Why* Jenson v. Eveleth *Didn't Change Sexual Harassment Law, But Still Has a Story Worth Telling*, 18 Berkeley Women's L.J. 282 (2003) (reviewing *Class Action*). The story of the Eveleth Mines litigation also became the basis for a feature film: North Country (Warner Bros. Pictures 2005). The potential for private class action litigation of sexual harassment claims is significantly limited by the Supreme Court's decision in Dukes v. Wal-Mart, 131 S.Ct. 2541 (2011), reproduced *supra*, Chapter 3.

On the other hand, consider also the potential impact of a major pattern-or-practice case based on allegations of widespread sexual harassment, *EEOC v. Mitsubishi Motor Manufacturing*, 990 F.Supp. 1059 (C.D.Ill.1998). In June of 1998, Mitsubishi Motor Manufacturing of America agreed to pay $34 million to a class of 350 current and former female employees in order to settle the lawsuit that the EEOC filed in 1996. Michael Bologna, *Mitsubishi Settles EEOC Suit for $34 Million; Agency Says Class and Amount Largest Ever*, Legal News, 66 U.S.L.W. 2781, 2782 (June 23, 1998). In the EEOC lawsuit,

> the EEOC charged that between 1988 and 1993 Mitsubishi had tolerated boorish, even terrifying behavior by some 400 men who resented the women's presence. Men allegedly used air guns to shoot painful blasts at women's chests and crotches. Others frequently grabbed women by their breasts, simulated masturbation or exposed themselves. One worker allegedly forced a woman's legs apart and threatened to sodomize her. The EEOC said the company had "discouraged complaints and permitted retaliation against women who dared to complain." Among the most chilling allegations: as supervisors idly listened, one man said he would force a woman to have sex with him—before he killed her.

Peter Annin & John McCormick, *More Than a Tune-Up: Tough Going in a Fight Against Sexual Harassment*, Newsweek, Nov. 24, 1997, at 50, 50–51. For a discussion of the role of the EEOC, the company, and the union in the *Mitsubishi* case, *see* Marion Crain & Ken Matheny, *"Labor's Divided Ranks": Privilege and the United Front Ideology*, 84 Cornell L.Rev. 1542, 1545–53,

1602–05 (1999); for a discussion of sexual harassment class action lawsuits, including the *Jenson* and *Mitsubishi* cases, see Michael Selmi, *Sex Discrimination in the Nineties, Seventies Style: Case Studies in the Preservation of Male Workplace Norms*, 9 Emp.Rts. & Emp. Pol'y J. 1 (2005).

9. *Defenses*: Typically a first-line defense to any claim of sexual harassment (whether quid pro quo or hostile work environment) is the alleged harasser's assertion that "I didn't do it." The defendant can attack evidence supporting any elements of the plaintiff's prima facie case. *Meritor* and *Harris* clearly endorse the defense to hostile work environment claims that the conduct at issue was either isolated or generally trivial. From a litigation perspective, what are the differences between a defense that the alleged harassing conduct did not occur and a defense that, even if the conduct did occur as alleged, it did not constitute severe or pervasive sexual harassment?

a. *Discovery and admissibility of evidence of plaintiff's prior sexual history*: Defendants in Title VII cases sometimes seek discovery of a plaintiff's prior sexual behavior either to show that a plaintiff welcomed the alleged sexually harassing conduct or to show that she was not subjectively offended by the conduct. In 1994, Congress amended the rules of evidence to extend the protections of the "rape shield law," which was developed for criminal cases, to limit the admissibility at trial of evidence of "alleged sexual misconduct," "other sexual behavior" or "sexual pre-disposition" in civil cases. Violent Crime Control and Law Enforcement Act of 1994, Pub. L. No. 103–322, 108 Stat. 1919. With respect to civil proceedings, Rule 412 of the Federal Rules of Evidence now provides that such evidence "offered to prove the sexual behavior or sexual predisposition" of an alleged victim "is admissible if it is otherwise admissible under [the Federal Rules of Evidence] and its probative value substantially outweighs the danger of harm to any victim and of unfair prejudice to any party." Fed.R.Evid. Rule 412(a)–(b)(2). Furthermore, evidence of "[a]n alleged victim's reputation is admissible only if it has been placed in controversy by the alleged victim." Fed.R.Evid. Rule 412(b)(2).

The courts have recognized that Rule 412 extends to sexual harassment cases. *See* B.K.B. v. Maui Police Dep't, 276 F.3d 1091, 1104 (9th Cir.2002) (collecting cases and citing Fed.R.Evid. 412, Advisory Committee Notes to 1994 Amendments). For example, in *Wolak v. Spucci*, 217 F.3d 157, 159–60 (2d Cir.2000), the court held that Rule 412 applies to the admissibility of evidence of a plaintiff's sexual behavior in a sexual harassment lawsuit. The court observed that "[w]hether a sexual advance was welcome, or whether an alleged victim in fact perceived an environment to be sexually offensive does not turn on the private sexual behavior of the alleged victim, because a woman's expectations about her work environment cannot be said to change depending upon her sexual sophistication." *Id.* at 160.

Discovery is governed by the Federal Rules of Civil Procedure, Fed.R.Civ.Pro. Rule 26(b), which permits a broad scope of discovery.

Although Rule 412 does not control the scope of permissible discovery, courts may limit discovery of the past sexual history of sexual harassment claimants because Rule 412 will limit or bar its admissibility. *See* Ogden v. All-State Career School, 299 F.R.D. 446, 450 (W.D. Pa. 2014) (discussing effect of Rule 412 on scope of discovery in sexual harassment cases and analyzing case law); Macklin v. Mendenhall, 257 F.R.D. 596, 600–04 (E.D. Cal.2009) (same). For a discussion of Rule 412 and the circumstances under which evidence of a plaintiff's sexual behavior and sexual predisposition might be admissible in sexual harassment claims, Paul Nicholas Monnin, *Proving Welcomeness: The Admissibility of Evidence of Sexual History in Sexual Harassment Claims Under the 1994 Amendments to Federal Rule of Evidence 412*, in Special Project: Current Issues in Sexual Harassment Law, 48 Vand.L.Rev. 1155 (1995). For a critique of the role of discretion in judges' application of Rule 412 and a proposal for reforming the rule, see Jane H. Aiken, *Protecting Plaintiff's Sexual Pasts: Coping with Preconceptions Through Discretion*, 51 Emory L.J. 559 (2002).

b. Which of the following should be considered relevant evidence in defending a claim of hostile work environment brought by a female plaintiff?

i. Plaintiff posed nude for *Playboy* magazine on her own time after working hours. She became the subject of sexual harassment after a male co-worker saw the *Playboy* issue and brought it into the workplace. *See* Burns v. McGregor Elec. Indus., 989 F.2d 959 (8th Cir.1993). Should it make a difference if the plaintiff brought the magazine to the workplace and showed it to her co-workers?

ii. In response to crude and provocative sexual teasing, and sexually oriented crude jokes, plaintiff responds in kind. *See* Loftin-Boggs v. City of Meridian, 633 F.Supp. 1323 (S.D.Miss.1986), *aff'd*, 824 F.2d 971 (1987).

iii. Plaintiff wrote her boss at least one personal, affectionate letter, often ate lunch with him, and participated in mutual kissing and petting with him. *See* Kresko v. Rulli, 432 N.W.2d 764 (Minn.Ct.App.1988).

iv. Plaintiff presents credible evidence that she is hypersensitive to conduct of a sexual nature. *See* Ellison v. Brady, 924 F.2d 872, 879–80 (9th Cir.1991).

c. *Free speech*: The defense of constitutionally protected free speech has been raised in some sexual harassment cases, particularly where the nature of the offensive conduct was primarily verbal or where pornographic pictures were prevalent in the workplace. A leading case rejecting the free speech defense is *Robinson v. Jacksonville Shipyards, Inc.*, 760 F.Supp. 1486 (M.D.Fla.1991). The court held that injunctive relief limiting discriminatory workplace speech did not violate the First Amendment because (1) the employer did not intend "to express itself" by allowing workplace displays of sexually explicit pictures or employee use of sexually offensive language, and the employer could ban such displays and language without violating the employees' rights of free speech; (2) the offensive pictures and language were not protected speech, but "discriminatory conduct" that caused a hostile work environment—a harm distinguishable from the "communicative impact" of the speech; (3) the court's order limiting discriminatory speech was "nothing more than a time, place, and manner regulation of speech"; (4) the female workers at the shipyard were a "captive audience" subjected to the discriminatory speech, and the First Amendment "admits great latitude in protecting captive audiences from offensive speech"; (5) even if the discriminatory speech were protected speech, any governmental infringement must be analyzed under a balancing approach, and "the governmental interest in cleansing the workplace of impediments to the equality of women" is a "compelling interest" and "the regulation is narrowly drawn to serve this interest"; and (6) by analogy to public employee free speech cases—which balance "the interests of the employee in commenting on protected matters * * * against the employer's interests in maintaining discipline and order in the workplace"—the courts may "without violating the first amendment, require that a private employer curtail the free expression in the workplace of some employees in order to remedy the demonstrated harm inflicted on other employees." *Id.* at 1534–36.

Can you think of any circumstances where an employer might intend "to express itself" through sexually offensive language and pictures? What type of "narrowly drawn" injunction regulating speech would you want (or expect) for a shipyard? What about a poultry factory or an insurance office? Why should the women in any particular workplace be considered a "captive audience"? Don't employees always have the freedom to leave undesirable jobs? Is it realistic to expect that courts will be able to alter deeply entrenched workplace cultures through the use of injunctions that restrain employee speech? If not, what other remedies would serve the goals of Title VII? In any event, is it fair to say that employees in some work settings should just expect that part of the job includes exposure to offensive language, crude jokes, and displays of pornographic material?

The free speech defense has generated a lively debate among legal scholars. In *Title VII as Censorship: Hostile-Environment Harassment and the First Amendment*, 52 Ohio St.L.J. 481 (1991), Kingsley R. Browne, a strong supporter of the defense, argued that Title VII fails to protect core "political" speech in the workplace. *See also* Kingsley R. Browne, *Workplace Censorship: A Response to Professor Sangree*, 47 Rutgers L.Rev. 579, 580–82 (1995); Eugene Volokh, *What Does "Hostile Work Environment" Harassment Law Restrict?*, 85 Geo.L.J. 627 (1997). For some opposing views, see Mary Becker, *How Free Is Speech at Work?*, 29 U.C. Davis L.Rev. 815 (1996); Cynthia L. Estlund, *The Architecture of the First Amendment and the Case of Workplace Harassment*, 75 Notre Dame L.Rev. 1361 (1997); Cynthia L. Estlund, *Freedom of Expression in the Workplace and the Problem of Discriminatory Harassment*, 75 Tex.L.Rev. 687 (1997).

d. *First Amendment Freedom of Religion and the Ministerial Exception to Title VII*: A novice alleges that he was sexually harassed by priests while he was being trained for the priesthood. He has brought a sexual harassment claim under Title VII. The order of priests has defended on the grounds that the "ministerial exception" to Title VII permits it the freedom to make its own employment decisions about its ministerial employees. Should religious entities be able to avoid sexual harassment liability on the basis of the ministerial exception? *See* Bollard v. Cal. Province of the Soc'y of Jesus, 196 F.3d 940 (9th Cir.1999). For discussion of the "ministerial exception" to Title VII, see Chapter 11.

e. *Off-Site, After-Hours Harassment*: Can an employer defend against a sexual harassment claim on the grounds that the alleged conduct occurred off-site and after working hours? How can an employer control or monitor the behavior of employees who are not at work? Where is the workplace anyway? *See* Moring v. Ark. Dep't of Corrs., 243 F.3d 452 (8th Cir.2001) (holding employer liable for supervisor's unwelcome sexual advances toward a subordinate which occurred in a hotel room during a business trip). If an employee is raped by the employer's client following a business dinner, should the employer be liable for sexual harassment under Title VII? Does your answer depend on what the employer does when it learns about the sexual assault? *See* Little v. Windermere Relocation, Inc., 301 F.3d 958 (9th Cir.2002) (finding that summary judgment was improperly granted where plaintiff alleged her pay was substantially reduced and she was then discharged after she was allegedly raped by the employer's client). If a female flight attendant is raped by a male airline pilot at a hotel where flight crews are booked for stopovers between flights, should the airline be liable for sexual harassment if it immediately fires the pilot? What if the pilot had a reputation for making unwanted sexual advances toward female flight attendants? *See* Ferris v. Delta Air Lines, Inc., 277 F.3d 128 (2d Cir.2001).

NOTE: THE IMPACT OF ONCALE *ON SEXUAL HARASSMENT LAW*

By the 1980s, employees began to bring Title VII claims alleging that they had been sexually harassed in the workplace by persons of the same sex. Because these claims did not fit the paradigm of sexual harassment cases—a male harassing a female—the courts adopted a variety of approaches, from denying all same-sex claims, to permitting them only if the harasser was a homosexual, to permitting them only if the conduct was sexual in nature. In *Oncale v. Sundowner Offshore Services, Inc.*, 523 U.S. 75, 118 S.Ct. 998, 140 L.Ed.2d 201 (1998), which is reproduced in Chapter 7, the Supreme Court firmly rejected these approaches and held: "Nothing in Title VII necessarily bars a claim of discrimination "because of * * * sex" merely because the plaintiff and the defendant (or the person charged with acting on behalf of the defendant) are of the same sex." *Id.* at 79, 118 S.Ct. at 1001–02.

In *Oncale*, Justice Scalia provided examples of three "evidentiary route[s]" to proving that the same-sex harassment was discrimination "because of sex": (1) "if there were credible evidence that the harasser was homosexual," (2) "if a female victim is harassed in such sex-specific and derogatory terms by another woman as to make it clear that the harasser is motivated by general hostility to the presence of women in the workplace," and (3) "comparative evidence about how the alleged harasser treated members of both sexes in a mixed-sex workplace." *Id.* at 80–81, 118 S.Ct. at 1002. In a portion of the opinion that was not reproduced in Chapter 7, the Court addressed the concern of "respondents and their *amici* * * * that recognizing liability for same-sex harassment will transform Title VII into a general civility code for the American workplace" by noting that "Title VII does not prohibit all verbal or physical harassment in the workplace; it is directed only at "*discriminat[ion]* * * * because of * * * sex." *Id.* at 80, 118 S.Ct. at 1002. The Court continued:

> [T]here is another requirement that prevents Title VII from expanding into a general civility code: As we emphasized in *Meritor* and *Harris*, the statute does not reach genuine but innocuous differences in the ways men and women routinely interact with members of the same sex and of the opposite sex. The prohibition of harassment on the basis of sex requires neither asexuality nor androgyny in the workplace; it forbids only behavior so objectively offensive as to alter the "conditions" of the victim's employment. "Conduct that is not severe or pervasive enough to create an objectively hostile or abusive work environment—an environment that a reasonable person would find hostile or abusive—is beyond Title VII's purview." *Harris*, 510 U.S. at 21, 114 S.Ct. at 370, *citing Meritor*, 477 U.S. at 67, 106 S.Ct. at 2405–06. We have always regarded that requirement as crucial, and as sufficient to ensure that courts and juries do not mistake ordinary socializing in the workplace—such as male-on-male horseplay or intersexual flirtation—for discriminatory "conditions of employment."
>
> We have emphasized, moreover, that the objective severity of harassment should be judged from the perspective of a reasonable person in the plaintiff's position, considering "all the circumstances." *Harris*, 510 U.S. at 23, 114 S.Ct. at 371. In same-sex (as in all) harassment cases, that inquiry requires careful consideration of the social context in which particular behavior occurs and is experienced by its target. A professional football player's working environment is not severely or pervasively abusive, for example, if the coach smacks him on the buttocks as he heads onto the field—even if the same behavior would reasonably be experienced as abusive by the coach's secretary (male or female) back at the office. The real social impact of workplace behavior often depends on a constellation of surrounding circumstances, expectations, and relationships which are not fully captured by a simple recitation of the words used or the physical acts performed. Common sense, and an appropriate sensitivity to social context, will enable courts and juries to distinguish between simple teasing or roughhousing among members of the same sex, and conduct which a

> reasonable person in the plaintiff's position would find severely hostile or abusive.

Id. at 81–82, 118 S.Ct. at 1002–03.

While *Oncale*'s facts present an instance of same-sex sexual harassment, the case has had a significant impact on harassment law more generally. One of the important points that the Court clearly rejected in *Oncale* was any notion—held by many lower courts before *Oncale*— that "workplace harassment that is sexual in content is always actionable, regardless of the harasser's sex, sexual orientation, or motivations." 490 U.S. at 79, 118 S.Ct. at 1002. While we tend to use the term "sexual harassment" rather than "sex-based" harassment, the Court in *Oncale* emphasized that the relevant question is not the sexualized nature of the conduct but the sex-based motivation for the conduct.

Several courts since *Oncale* have recognized the "equal opportunity harasser" or "bisexual harasser" defense. For example, in *Holman v. Indiana*, 211 F.3d 399 (7th Cir.2000), the court held that when a male supervisor solicited sex from two employees, a married couple, the harassment was not "because of sex." Relying on *Oncale*, the court ruled that "Title VII does not cover the 'equal opportunity' or 'bisexual' harasser * * * because such person is not *discriminating* on the basis of sex. He is not treating one sex better (or worse) than the other; he is treating both sexes the same (albeit badly)." *Id.* at 403. *See also* Reine v. Honeywell Intern. Inc., 362 Fed.Appx. 395, 397 (5th Cir.2010) ("When the conduct is equally harsh toward men and women, there is no hostile work environment based on sex."); Lack v. Wal-Mart Stores, Inc., 240 F.3d 255, 262 (4th Cir.2001) (concluding that that there could be no sexual harassment when the alleged harasser was "just an indiscriminately vulgar and offensive supervisor, obnoxious to men and women alike"). The court in *Brown v. Henderson*, 257 F.3d 246, 256 (2d Cir.2001), however, held that "there is no *per se* bar to maintaining a claim of sex discrimination where a person of another sex has been similarly treated." *See also* Steiner v. Showboat Operating Co., 25 F.3d 1459, 1463–64 (9th Cir.1995) (rejecting equal opportunity harasser defense). Which approach do you think is best? *See generally* David R. Cleveland, Discrimination Law's Dirty Secret: The Equal Opportunity Sexual Harasser Loophole, 58 How. L.J. 5 (2014); Charles R. Calleros, *The Meaning of "Sex": Homosexual and Bisexual Harassment Under Title VII*, 20 Vt. L. Rev. 55 (1995); Steven S. Locke, *The Equal Opportunity Harasser as a Paradigm for Recognizing Sexual Harassment of Homosexuals Under Title VII*, 27 Rutgers L.J. 383, 406 (1996).

At the same time that *Oncale* concluded that not all sexualized behavior is actionable harassment, the decision also recognized that harassment does not have to involve sexualized behavior in order to be unlawful sexual harassment. Instead, the Court expressly recognized one hostile work environment theory of discrimination that would apply where, for example, either a male or a female harasser uses "sex-specific and derogatory terms" that clearly demonstrate "general hostility to the presence of women in the workplace." 490 U.S. at 80, 118 S.Ct. at 1002. If a woman frequently calls a female co-worker a "bitch," could that be actionable sexual harassment? *See* Bailey v. Henderson, 94 F.Supp.2d 68, 70 (D.D.C.2000). What if men call women "bitches"? *See* Passananti v. Cook County, 689 F.3d 655 (7th Cir.2012) (reinstating a jury verdict for plaintiff where her supervisor repeatedly referred to her as a "bitch" in front of co-workers). *See generally* Yvonne A. Tamayo, *Rhymes with Rich: Power, Law, and the Bitch*, 21 St. Thomas L. Rev. 281, 288–97 (2009) (discussing the use of the epithet "bitch" in the workplace).

Regardless of whether conduct must be sexualized in order to be actionable, plaintiffs whose claims include sexualized behavior may be more persuasive to judges and juries. In a study of all sexual harassment cases that resulted in reported opinions from federal district and appellate courts between 1986 and 1995, Professors Juliano and Schwab found that

> [p]laintiffs alleging "harassment as sexualized behavior" have significantly higher win rates than other sexual harassment plaintiffs. Plaintiffs who alleged harassment based on comments of a sexual or physical nature were more successful than plaintiffs who alleged comments that devalued women as women (such as "honey" or "babe"). Further, harassment claims premised upon physical contact of a sexual nature met greater success than physical conduct of a nonsexual nature.

Ann Juliano & Stewart J. Schwab, *The Sweep of Sexual Harassment Cases,* 86 Cornell L. Rev. 548, 580–81 (2001).

Oncale was also an important case for its focus on the "social context" of harassment and its emphasis on the need to consider "the totality of the circumstances" in assessing whether conduct was actionable harassment. How did the "social context" in *Oncale* affect the question of whether Joseph Oncale experienced "simple teasing or roughhousing among members of the same sex" or an actionable hostile work environment? What is the "social context" of work in an all-male crew that is isolated for long periods of time on a drilling rig in the Gulf of Mexico? *See generally* Hilary S. Axam & Deborah Zalesne, *Simulated Sodomy and Other Forms of Heterosexual "Horseplay": Same Sex Sexual Harassment, Workplace Gender Hierarchies, and the Myth of the Gender Monolith Before and After* Oncale, 11 Yale J.L. & Feminism 155 (1999).

After *Oncale,* if a female plaintiff works in a factory, where the work is strenuous, noisy, and dirty, does the "inhospitable" physical work environment prevent her from asserting a sexual harassment claim for a hostile work environment? *See* Conner v. Schrader-Bridgeport Int'l, Inc., 227 F.3d 179, 194 (4th Cir.2000). If a woman starts a job at a small factory where her all-male co-workers and supervisors continue their practice of exchanging vulgar sexual banter throughout the work day, can she prevail on a complaint that their language, which she finds offensive, constitutes sexual harassment? *See* Ocheltree v. Scollon Prods., Inc., 335 F.3d 325 (4th Cir.2003) (en banc). For exploration of the political, social, and cultural complexity of challenging male workplace norms through sexual harassment law, see Nancy S. Ehrenreich, *Pluralist Myths and Powerless Men: The Ideology of Reasonableness in Sexual Harassment Law*, 99 Yale L.J. 1177, 1193–1214 (1990); Tristin K. Green, *Work Culture and Discrimination*, 93 Cal.L.Rev. 623 (2005); Rebecca K. Lee, *Pink, White, Blue: Class Assumptions in the Judicial Interpretations of Title VII Hostile Environment Sexual Harassment*, 70 Brooklyn L.Rev. 677 (2005).

How is the "totality of the circumstances" different from the "social context" in which workplace behavior occurs? In *Oncale*, Justice Scalia reaffirmed the significance of viewing the harasser's conduct in light of the "surrounding circumstances, expectations, and relationships." Since *Oncale*, the lower courts have adopted differing approaches to assessing the "totality of circumstances." *Compare* Redd v. New York Div. of Parole, 678 F.3d 166, 180 (2d Cir.2012) (holding that the district court had failed to consider "the record as a whole" because it had viewed each individual incident of unwanted touching in isolation) and Williams v. Gen. Motors, Corp., 187 F.3d 553, 562 (6th Cir.1999) (holding that the district court had failed to consider properly the "totality of circumstances" when it divided the allegedly harassing conduct into four types and considered each separately); *with* Penry v. Fed. Home Loan Bank of Topeka, 155 F.3d 1257, 1262–63 (10th Cir.1998) (concluding that the supervisor's "gender-neutral antics" over a four year period made the plaintiffs' work environment merely "unpleasant," and the "gender-based" incidents were "too few and far between" to meet the threshold of "severe or pervasive" sexual harassment) and Mendoza v. Borden, 195 F.3d 1238, 1246 (11th Cir.1999) (en banc) (holding that, considered "in context, not as isolated acts," a supervisor's conduct, which included constantly following and staring at employee, was not severe or pervasive under Title VII).

In *Oncale,* the Court made it clear that recognizing that same-sex harassment claims may be actionable did not "transform Title VII into a general civility code for the American workplace." A 2014 survey conducted by the Workplace Bullying Institute found that, in the United States, more than a quarter of employees interviewed reported past or current bullying at work. 2014 WBI U.S. Workplace Bullying Study, *available at http://www.workplacebullying.org/multi/pdf/WBI-2014-US-Survey.pdf.* In light of the fact that bullying is so common in American workplaces, how can courts distinguish between harassment that is actionable on the basis of a protected status such as sex or race and bullying that is not actionable? In other words, how can courts and juries tell whether a bully is targeting his or her victim "because of sex" or because of "personal animosity" or just because that is how the bully treats everyone? *See, e.g.,* Bowman v. Shawnee St. Univ., 220 F.3d 456, 464 (6th Cir.2000) (finding that female dean's "intimidation, ridicule, and mistreatment" of male physical education instructor was not actionable sexual harassment where her conduct was not of a "sexual" nature and her comments were not "anti-male").

Do we need a new legal theory and a new statute to protect employees against bullies as well as against sexual harassers? *See* David C. Yamada, *Crafting a Legislative Response to Workplace Bullying*, 8 Emp.Rts. & Emp. Pol'y J. 475, 498–509 (2004) (proposing a statutory cause of action to redress the harms of workplace bullying); Catherine L. Fisk, *Humiliation at Work,* 8 Wm. & Mary J. Women & L. 73, 75 (2001) (pointing to the need for a broader understanding of the causes and consequences of humiliation in the workplace as a first step to developing an employment law that balances the sometimes competing concerns of employers and employees). The past decade has seen the development of status-blind anti-bullying laws in many other countries and a model law—the Healthy Workplace Bill—has been proposed (ultimately unsuccessfully) in over 30 state legislatures. *See* Susan Harthill, *Bullying in the Workplace: Lessons from the United Kingdom*, 17 Minn.J. Int'l L. 247, 249–50 (2008) (discussing both state-level and international efforts to address workplace bullying). *See also* Yamada, *supra* at 476–77, 509–14 (same).

NOTE: CLAIMS ARISING OUT OF PARAMOUR PREFERENTIAL TREATMENT AND THE TERMINATION OF CONSENSUAL SEXUAL RELATIONSHIPS

Plaintiffs have brought "reverse discrimination" or "paramour preference" claims under Title VII based on one employee's allegations that a supervisor has given preferential treatment to another employee with whom he has a sexual relationship. For example, in *DeCintio v. Westchester County Medical Center*, 807 F.2d 304, 307 (2d Cir.1986), several male plaintiffs claimed that their employer had violated Title VII when they were passed over for a promotion that was awarded to the girlfriend of the supervisor who made the employment decision. The federal courts have consistently held that employment preferences for lovers are not unlawful discrimination, but instead are forms of favoritism that fall within the scope of employer prerogative. *See, e.g.* Tenge v. Phillips Modern Ag Co., 446 F.3d 903, 908 (8th Cir.2006) (collecting cases); Preston v. Wis. Health Fund, 397 F.3d 539 (7th Cir.2005) (same).

The EEOC's position on "isolated instances of preferential treatment based on consensual romantic relationships" is consistent with these court decisions. *See* U.S. Equal Empl. Oppt'y Comm'n, Policy Guidance on Employer Liability Under Title VII for Sexual Favoritism, No. N–915.048, 2 EEOC Compliance Manual § 615 (Jan. 12, 1990), *available at http://www.eeoc.gov/policy/docs/sexualfavor.html* (page last modified June 21, 1999). The agency's policy guidance draws a distinction among three categories of sexual favoritism: isolated instances of preferential treatment; favoritism based on coerced sexual relations, which may constitute quid pro quo harassment; and widespread favoritism, which may create a hostile work environment. *Id.* In *Miller v. Department of Corrections,* 36 Cal.Rptr.3d 797, 115 P.3d 77 (Cal.2005), the Supreme Court of California drew on this distinction in considering a sexual harassment claim brought under the

California Fair Employment and Housing Act (FEHA). Two female corrections department employees complained about their treatment by their supervisor, the prison warden, who had consensual sexual affairs with three other female subordinates at the same time. The plaintiffs presented evidence that the warden "promised and granted unwarranted and unfair employment benefits to the three women." *Id.* at 814, 115 P.3d at 90. The Supreme Court of California held that

> although an isolated instance of favoritism on the part of a supervisor toward a female employee with whom the supervisor is conducting a consensual sexual affair ordinarily would not constitute sexual harassment, when such sexual favoritism in a workplace is sufficiently widespread it may create an actionable hostile work environment in which the demeaning message is conveyed to female employees that they are viewed by management as "sexual playthings" or that the way required for women to get ahead in the workplace is by engaging in sexual conduct with their supervisors or the management.

Id. at 801–02, 115 P.3d at 79.

How can employers, or courts, determine whether consensual sexual affairs in the workplace cross the line into "widespread sexual favoritism" that constitutes actionable sexual harassment? In its analysis of the favoritism issue, the *Miller* court noted,

> [D]efendants warn that plaintiff's position, if adopted, would inject the courts into relationships that are private and consensual and that occur within a major locus of individual social life for both men and women—the workplace. According to defendants, social policy favors rather than disfavors such relationships, and the issue of personal privacy should give courts pause before allowing claims such as those advance by plaintiffs to proceed.

Id. at 818, 115 P.3d at 94. Do you agree with the concerns raised by the defendants? The court responded that "it is not the relationship, but its effect on the workplace, that is relevant under the applicable legal standard." *Id.* Is this a meaningful distinction?

For an examination of the implications of the *Miller* decision for Title VII sexual harassment law, see Cheryl L. Howard, *Romeo and Juliets: A Modern Workplace Tragedy,* 9 U. Pa. J. Lab. & Emp. L. 805 (2007). For a proposal to treat workplace sexual favoritism as actionable sexual harassment under Title VII, see Joan E. Van Tol, *Eros Gone Awry: Liability Under Title VII for Workplace Sexual Favoritism,* 13 Indus.Rel.L.J. 153 (1992). *See also* Mary Kate Sheridan, Note, *Just Because It's Sex Doesn't Mean It's Because of Sex: The Need for New Legislation to Target Sexual Favoritism,* 40 Colum. J.L. & Soc. Probs. 379, 379 (2007) (arguing that "new legislation should be formulated to specifically target third-party claims for widespread and isolated instances of sexual favoritism").

The Consequences of the Termination of Consensual Relationships: What if the plaintiff had previously been involved in a consensual sexual relationship with her alleged harasser? In *Nichols v. Frank*, 42 F.3d 503 (9th Cir.1994), the quid pro quo case discussed in Section B.1 of this chapter, Judge Reinhardt observed:

> [C]ourts are understandably reluctant to chill the incidence of legitimate romance. People who work closely together and share common interests often find that sexual attraction ensues. It is not surprising that those feelings arise even when one of the persons is a superior and the other a subordinate. As our workforce grows, and more and more of us find it necessary, or desirable, to earn our own living, we spend an increasing amount of our time at work. Sexual barriers to employment have lessened. We tend these days, far more than in earlier times, to find our friends, lovers, and even mates in the workplace. We spend longer hours at the office or traveling for job-related purposes, and often discover that our interests and values are closer to those of our colleagues or fellow employees than to those of people we meet in connection with other activities. In short, increased proximity breeds increased volitional sexual activity.

Id. at 510.

Although courts and the EEOC may be reluctant to interfere with "legitimate" office romance, employers may not be so restrained. Because workplace romances that end may cause disruptions in working relationships or lead to sexual harassment claims, many employers have adopted nonfraternization and love contract policies that apply to sexual relationships between co-workers, as well as to the potentially more troublesome relationships between supervisors and their subordinates. *See generally* Ian J. Silverbrand, *Workplace Romance and the Economic Duress of Love Contract Policies*, 54 Vill.L.Rev. 155 (2009) (critiquing nonfraternization and love contract policies).

How should courts treat claims of sexual harassment brought by one party to a former consensual relationship complaining of misconduct by the other? Some courts assume that hostile treatment in such a case is not "because of sex" but because of disappointment or contempt resulting from the failed relationship. *See, e.g.,* Succar v. Dade County Sch. Bd., 229 F.3d 1343, 1345 (11th Cir.2000). Consider, however, the following analysis in a case where the plaintiff alleged that her co-worker and former paramour was sexually harassing her:

> In cases involving a prior failed relationship between an accused harasser and alleged victim, reasoning that the harassment could not have been motivated by the victim's sex because it was instead motivated by a romantic relationship gone sour establishes a false dichotomy. Presumably the prior relationship would never have occurred if the victim were not a member of the sex preferred

> by the harasser, and thus the victim's sex is inextricably linked to the harasser's decision to harass. To interpret sexual harassment perpetrated by a jilted lover in all cases not as gender discrimination, but rather as discrimination " 'on the basis of the failed interpersonal relationship' * * * is as flawed a proposition under Title VII as the corollary that 'ordinary' sexual harassment does not violate Title VII when the [ ] asserted purpose is the establishment of a 'new interpersonal relationship.' "

Forrest v. Brinker Int'l Payroll Co., 511 F.3d 225, 229 (1st Cir.2007).

NOTE: ALTERNATIVE THEORIES OF LIABILITY FOR SEXUAL HARASSMENT

Sexual and racial harassment in the workplace became actionable "only because of Title VII," since historically such conduct "was not a tort at common law." Griggs v. Nat'l R.R. Passenger Corp., 900 F.2d 74, 75 (6th Cir.1990). As the federal law of sexual harassment developed, however, courts began to uphold a number of common law claims that plaintiffs asserted in order to obtain effective remedies for workplace sexual harassment. Victims of workplace sexual harassment may now sue their employers and harassers under state tort law in addition to bringing claims under state or federal antidiscrimination statutes. Tort theories asserted in sexual harassment cases include assault, battery, intentional or negligent infliction of emotional distress, defamation, invasion of privacy, loss of consortium, negligent hiring and retention, and failure to provide a safe workplace. *See, e.g.*, Myers v. Cent. Fla. Inv., Inc., 592 F.3d 1201, 1205 (11th Cir.2010) (upholding jury award for over $1.5 million in compensatory and punitive damages for battery although plaintiff lost sexual harassment claims under Title VII and state law); Maksimovic v. Tsogalis, 177 Ill.2d 511, 227 Ill.Dec. 98, 687 N.E.2d 21 (1997) (permitting claims of assault, battery, and false imprisonment to go forward in case involving co-worker sexual harassment); Kanzler v. Renner, 937 P.2d 1337 (Wyo.1997) (recognizing a cause of action for intentional infliction of emotional distress on the basis of workplace sexual harassment). In *Gallagher v. C.H. Robinson Worldwide, Inc.*, 567 F.3d 263, 277–78 (6th Cir.2009), the court permitted a pendent state claim for "failing to provide a safe work environment free from sexual harassment" to go trial based on facts alleged in a Title VII hostile work environment case.

In many jurisdictions, however, tort claims based on sexual harassment will be preempted by state civil rights laws. *See, e.g.,* Jansen v. Packaging Corp. of America, 123 F.3d 490 (7th Cir.1997) (en banc) (holding that a tort claim of intentional infliction of emotional distress was preempted by Illinois Human Rights Act), *cert. denied sub nom.* Ellerth v. Burlington Indus., 524 U.S. 951, 118 S.Ct. 2365, 141 L.Ed.2d 734 (1998) ; Thomas v. L'Eggs Prods., Inc., 13 F.Supp.2d 806 (C.D.Ill.1998) (holding that a tort claim of negligent retention was preempted by the Illinois Human Rights Act). See Martha S.

Davis, *Rape in the Workplace*, 41 S.D.L.Rev. 411 (1996) (comparing the treatment of rape under workers' compensations systems, Title VII, and common law tort actions); Pamela J. White & Susan R. Matluck, *Conduct Unbecoming a Lawyer: Expanding Tort Remedies for Sexual Harassment*, Brief, Summer 1995, at 16 (discussing the use of tort law to remedy sexual harassment in law firms).

Other possible tort claims for sexual harassment include breach of the implied covenant of good faith and fair dealing and wrongful discharge in violation of public policy. *See, e.g.*, Schuster v. Derocili, 775 A.2d 1029, 1036 (Del.2001) (recognizing a claim for breach of the implied covenant of good faith and fair dealing where the plaintiff alleged that she was discharged for refusing to submit to the sexual advances of her supervisor). Generally a public policy discharge suit based on sexual harassment will be preempted by a state antidiscrimination statute or other state law that prohibits the same conduct and provides its own remedies, although there are exceptions. *Compare* Makovi v. Sherwin-Williams Co., 316 Md. 603, 561 A.2d 179 (1989) (finding preemption), *with* Insignia Residential Corp. v. Ashton, 359 Md. 560, 755 A.2d 1080, 1087 (2000) (ruling that the plaintiff could bring a common law wrongful discharge suit based on the allegation that her supervisor solicited sexual favors from her in violation of a state law prohibiting prostitution, which lacked a remedial scheme), *and* Rojo v. Kliger, 52 Cal.3d 65, 276 Cal.Rptr. 130, 801 P.2d 373 (1990) (holding that California antidiscrimination statute does not preclude common law actions arising out of employment discrimination and that workplace sexual harassment can support a claim for wrongful discharge in violation of public policy).

Many tort suits against employers based on theories of negligence will be also be barred by the exclusivity provisions of state workers' compensation laws. *See, e.g.*, Chatman v. Gentle Dental Center of Waltham, 973 F.Supp. 228 (D.Mass.1997). Victims of workplace harassment who seek recovery of medical expenses and lost wages may choose to file a workers' compensation claim; however, such a claim may bar a subsequent lawsuit for the same injuries under state antidiscrimination law. *See, e.g.*, Jefferson v. Cal. Dep't of Youth Auth., 48 P.3d 423 (Cal.2002).

From the perspective of a victim of workplace sexual harassment, what are some of the advantages and disadvantages of tort law as compared to discrimination law? What about the employer's perspective? Consider the following: (1) tort law can impose liability on small employers, regardless of their size, whereas Title VII coverage is limited to employers of fifteen or more employees; (2) there is no statutory limit on tort damages, whereas Title VII imposes statutory caps on damages depending on the size of the employer; and (3) a plaintiff can sue an employer's agent in his individual capacity under tort law, whereas the majority of courts do not recognize individual liability of agents under Title VII. For an example of tort remedies, see *Hoffman-La Roche, Inc. v. Zeltwanger*, 69 S.W.3d 634 (Tex.App.2002) (upholding a jury award of $8 million in exemplary damages and $1 million in compensatory damages for mental anguish in a sexual harassment case).

Can you think of other substantive or procedural advantages or disadvantages for plaintiffs or defendants? For an argument that tort suits against harassers would remedy and deter sexual harassment in the workplace better than discrimination suits against employers, see Mark McLaughlin Hager, *Harassment as a Tort: Why Title VII Hostile Environment Liability Should Be Curtailed*, 30 Conn.L.Rev. 375 (1998). *See also* Rosa Ehrenreich, *Dignity and Discrimination: Toward a Pluralistic Understanding of Workplace Harassment,* 88 Geo.L.J. 1 (1999) (arguing that common law tort actions are a good way to deal with the dignitary harms of "classic" cases of male-on-female sexual harassment).

The lower federal courts have ruled that intentional sexual harassment of employees by government officials acting "under color of state law" is actionable under § 1983 as a violation of equal protection or substantive due process under the Fourteenth Amendment. *See, e.g.,* Jones v. Clinton, 990 F.Supp. 657, 668 (E.D.Ark.1998) (collecting sexual harassment cases brought under Equal Protection Clause); Hawkins v. Holloway, 316 F.3d 777, 785 (8th Cir.2003) (finding that a male sheriff's repeated unwelcome sexual touching of his female subordinate constituted "a violation of her bodily integrity sufficient to support a substantive due process claim" under § 1983). Section 1983 claims are discussed in Chapter 5. In general, the courts will look to Title VII cases to determine whether the conduct was "unwelcome" and "severe or pervasive." *See* Cross v. Ala., 49 F.3d 1490 (11th Cir.1995) (holding that the elements of a Title VII and equal protection claim are identical); *Jones*, 990 F.Supp.2d at 668–69 (comparing sexual harassment claims brought under Title VII and § 1983). Because a public official sued in his or her individual capacity under § 1983 can assert a defense of qualified immunity, the threshold of actionable harassment in a substantive due process claim has been held to be "whether conduct amounts to an abuse of governmental power that is so brutal and offensive that it was conscience shocking." *Hawkins,* 316 F.3d at 784 (internal quotation marks omitted). In a § 1983 sexual harassment suit against a municipality, the plaintiff must establish that the municipality had a custom or policy that tolerated or condoned sexual harassment. *See* Kramer v. Wasatch County Sherrif's Office, 743 F.3d 726, 759 (2014). *See generally* Mark M. Hager, *Harassment and Constitutional Tort: The Other Jurisprudence*, 16 Hofstra Lab. & Emp.L.J. 279 (1999).

C. EMPLOYER LIABILITY FOR DISCRIMINATORY HARASSMENT

Although the Supreme Court in *Meritor* held that "workplace sexual harassment is illegal," the Court "le[ft] open the circumstances in which an employer is responsible under Title VII for such conduct." 477 U.S. 57, 74, 106 S.Ct. 2399, 2409, 91 L.Ed.2d 49 (1986) (Marshall, J., concurring). After reviewing the conflicting standards for employer liability that had been raised by the parties and *amici* in *Meritor*, the Court concluded that

> Congress' decision to define "employer" to include any "agent" of an employer, 42 U.S.C. § 2000e(b), surely evinces an intent to place some limits on the acts of employees for which employers under Title VII are to be held responsible. For this reason, we hold that the Court of Appeals erred in concluding that employers are always automatically liable for sexual harassment by their supervisors. For the same reason, absence of notice to an employer does not necessarily insulate that employer from liability.
>
> * * * [W]e reject petitioner's view that the mere existence of a grievance procedure and a policy against discrimination, coupled with respondent's failure to invoke that procedure, must insulate petitioner from liability. While those facts are plainly relevant, the situation before us demonstrates why they are not necessarily dispositive. Petitioner's general nondiscrimination policy did not address sexual harassment in particular, and thus did not alert employees to their employer's interest in correcting that form of discrimination. Moreover, the bank's grievance procedure apparently required an employee to complain first to her supervisor, in this case Taylor. Since Taylor was the alleged perpetrator, it is not altogether surprising that respondent failed to invoke the procedure and report her grievance to him. Petitioner's contention that respondent's failure should insulate it from liability might be substantially stronger if its procedures were better calculated to encourage victims of harassment to come forward.

Meritor, 477 U.S. at 72–73, 106 S.Ct. at 2408. The 1980 EEOC Guidelines, which were rejected in *Meritor*, had provided that an employer "is responsible for its acts and those of its agents and supervisory employees with respect to sexual harassment regardless of whether the specific acts complained of were authorized or even forbidden by the employer and regardless of whether the employer knew or should have known of their occurrence." 29 C.F.R. § 1604.11(c) (1997).

After *Meritor*, the courts of appeals adopted several different standards for imposing liability on employers for the sexual harassment of their supervisors. *See* Frederick J. Lewis & Thomas L. Henderson, *Employer Liability for "Hostile Work Environment" Sexual Harassment Created by Supervisors: The Search for an Appropriate Standard*, 25 U.Mem.L.Rev. 667, 673–86 (1995) (collecting and analyzing the post-*Meritor* cases). In 1998, the Supreme Court resolved the conflicting approaches of the circuit courts and the EEOC to the issue of employer liability for supervisory sexual harassment.

1. VICARIOUS LIABILITY: HARASSMENT BY SUPERVISORS

BURLINGTON INDUSTRIES, INC. V. ELLERTH

Supreme Court of the United States, 1998.
524 U.S. 742, 118 S.Ct. 2257, 141 L.Ed.2d 633.

JUSTICE KENNEDY delivered the opinion of the Court.

We decide whether, under Title VII of the Civil Rights Act of 1964, an employee who refuses the unwelcome and threatening sexual advances of a supervisor, yet suffers no adverse, tangible job consequences, can recover against the employer without showing the employer is negligent or otherwise at fault for the supervisor's actions.

I

Summary judgment was granted for the employer, so we must take the facts alleged by the employee to be true. The employer is Burlington Industries, the petitioner. The employee is Kimberly Ellerth, the respondent. From March 1993 until May 1994, Ellerth worked as a salesperson in one of Burlington's divisions in Chicago, Illinois. During her employment, she alleges, she was subjected to constant sexual harassment by her supervisor, one Ted Slowik.

In the hierarchy of Burlington's management structure, Slowik was a mid-level manager. Burlington has eight divisions, employing more than 22,000 people in some 50 plants around the United States. Slowik was a vice president in one of five business units within one of the divisions. He had authority to make hiring and promotion decisions subject to the approval of his supervisor, who signed the paperwork. According to Slowik's supervisor, his position was "not considered an upper-level management position," and he was "not amongst the decision-making or policy-making hierarchy." Slowik was not Ellerth's immediate supervisor. Ellerth worked in a two-person office in Chicago, and she answered to her office colleague, who in turn answered to Slowik in New York.

Against a background of repeated boorish and offensive remarks and gestures which Slowik allegedly made, Ellerth places particular emphasis on three alleged incidents where Slowik's comments could be construed as threats to deny her tangible job benefits. In the summer of 1993, while on a business trip, Slowik invited Ellerth to the hotel lounge, an invitation Ellerth felt compelled to accept because Slowik was her boss. When Ellerth gave no encouragement to remarks Slowik made about her breasts, he told her to "loosen up" and warned, "[y]ou know, Kim, I could make your life very hard or very easy at Burlington."

In March 1994, when Ellerth was being considered for a promotion, Slowik expressed reservations during the promotion interview because she was not "loose enough." The comment was followed by his reaching over and rubbing her knee. Ellerth did receive the promotion; but when Slowik called to announce it, he told Ellerth, "you're gonna be out there with men who work in factories, and they certainly like women with pretty butts/legs."

In May 1994, Ellerth called Slowik, asking permission to insert a customer's logo into a fabric sample. Slowik responded, "I don't have time for you right now, Kim—unless you want to tell me what you're wearing." Ellerth told Slowik she had to go and ended the call. A day or two later, Ellerth called Slowik to ask permission again. This time he denied her request, but added something along the lines of, "are you wearing shorter skirts yet, Kim, because it would make your job a whole heck of a lot easier."

A short time later, Ellerth's immediate supervisor cautioned her about returning telephone calls to customers in a prompt fashion. In response, Ellerth quit. She faxed a letter giving reasons unrelated to the alleged sexual harassment we have described. About three weeks later, however, she sent a letter explaining she quit because of Slowik's behavior.

During her tenure at Burlington, Ellerth did not inform anyone in authority about Slowik's conduct, despite knowing Burlington had a policy against sexual harassment. In fact, she chose not to inform her immediate supervisor (not Slowik) because " 'it would be his duty as my supervisor to report any incidents of sexual harassment.' " On one occasion, she told Slowik a comment he made was inappropriate.

In October 1994, * * * Ellerth filed suit * * * alleging Burlington engaged in sexual harassment and forced her constructive discharge, in violation of Title VII. The District Court granted summary judgment to Burlington. The Court found Slowik's behavior, as described by Ellerth, severe and pervasive enough to create a hostile work environment, but found Burlington neither knew nor should have known about the conduct. * * *

The Court of Appeals en banc reversed in a decision which produced eight separate opinions and no consensus for a controlling rationale. * * * The disagreement revealed in the careful opinions of the judges of the Court of Appeals reflects the fact that Congress has left it to the courts to determine controlling agency law principles in a new and difficult area of federal law. We granted certiorari to assist in defining the relevant standards of employer liability.

II

At the outset, we assume an important proposition yet to be established before a trier of fact. It is a premise assumed as well, in explicit or implicit terms, in the various opinions by the judges of the Court of Appeals. The premise is: a trier of fact could find in Slowik's remarks numerous threats to retaliate against Ellerth if she denied some sexual liberties. The threats, however, were not carried out or fulfilled. Cases based on threats which are carried out are referred to often as *quid pro quo* cases, as distinct from bothersome attentions or sexual remarks that are sufficiently severe or pervasive to create a hostile work environment. The terms *quid pro quo* and hostile work environment are helpful, perhaps, in making a rough demarcation between cases in which threats are carried out and those where they are not or are absent altogether, but beyond this are of limited utility.

Section 703(a) of Title VII forbids "an employer—

> (1) to fail or refuse to hire or to discharge any individual, or otherwise to discriminate against any individual with respect to his compensation, terms, conditions or privileges of employment, because of such individual's * * * sex." 42 U.S.C. § 2000e–2(a)(1).

"*Quid pro quo*" and "hostile work environment" do not appear in the statutory text. The terms appeared first in the academic literature, see C. MacKinnon, Sexual Harassment of Working Women (1979); found their way into decisions of the Courts of Appeals; and were mentioned in this Court's decision in *Meritor*. See generally E. Scalia, The Strange Career of *Quid Pro Quo* Sexual Harassment, 21 Harv. J.L. & Pub. Policy 307 (1998).

In *Meritor*, the terms served a specific and limited purpose. There we considered whether the conduct in question constituted discrimination in the terms or conditions of employment in violation of Title VII. We assumed, and with adequate reason, that if an employer demanded sexual favors from an employee in return for a job benefit, discrimination with respect to terms or conditions of employment was explicit. Less obvious was whether an employer's sexually demeaning behavior altered terms or conditions of employment in violation of Title VII. We distinguished between *quid pro quo* claims and hostile environment claims, and said both were cognizable under Title VII, though the latter requires harassment that is severe or pervasive. The principal significance of the distinction is to instruct that Title VII is violated by either explicit or constructive alterations in the terms or conditions of employment and to explain the latter must be severe or pervasive. The distinction was not discussed for its bearing upon an employer's liability for an employee's discrimination. On this question *Meritor* held, with no further specifics, that agency principles controlled.

Nevertheless, as use of the terms grew in the wake of *Meritor*, they acquired their own significance. The standard of employer responsibility turned on which type of harassment occurred. If the plaintiff established a *quid pro quo* claim, the Courts of Appeals held, the employer was subject to vicarious liability. [Citations omitted.] The rule encouraged Title VII plaintiffs to state their claims as *quid pro quo* claims, which in turn put expansive pressure on the definition. The equivalence of the *quid pro quo* label and vicarious liability is illustrated by this case. The question presented on certiorari is whether Ellerth can state a claim of *quid pro quo* harassment, but the issue of real concern to the parties is whether Burlington has vicarious liability for Slowik's alleged misconduct, rather than liability limited to its own negligence. The question presented for certiorari asks:

> "Whether a claim of *quid pro quo* sexual harassment may be stated under Title VII * * * where the plaintiff employee has neither submitted to the sexual advances of the alleged harasser nor suffered any tangible effects on the compensation, terms, conditions or privileges of employment as a consequence of a refusal to submit to those advances?"

We do not suggest the terms *quid pro quo* and hostile work environment are irrelevant to Title VII litigation. To the extent they illustrate the distinction between cases involving a threat which is carried out and offensive conduct in general, the terms are relevant when there is a threshold question whether a plaintiff can prove discrimination in violation of Title VII. When a plaintiff proves that a tangible employment action resulted from a refusal to submit to a supervisor's sexual demands, he or she establishes that the employment decision itself constitutes a change in the terms and conditions of employment that is actionable under Title VII. For any sexual harassment preceding the employment decision to be actionable, however, the conduct must be severe or pervasive. Because Ellerth's claim involves only unfulfilled threats, it should be categorized as a hostile work environment claim which requires a showing of severe or pervasive conduct. For purposes of this case, we accept the District Court's finding that the alleged conduct was severe or pervasive. The case before us involves numerous alleged threats, and we express no opinion as to whether a single unfulfilled threat is sufficient to constitute discrimination in the terms or conditions of employment.

When we assume discrimination can be proved, however, the factors we discuss below, and not the categories *quid pro quo* and hostile work environment, will be controlling on the issue of vicarious liability. That is the question we must resolve.

III

We must decide, then, whether an employer has vicarious liability when a supervisor creates a hostile work environment by making explicit threats to alter a subordinate's terms or conditions of employment, based on sex, but does not fulfill the threat. We turn to principles of agency law, for the term "employer" is defined under Title VII to include "agents." 42 U.S.C. § 2000e(b). * * *

As *Meritor* acknowledged, the Restatement (Second) of Agency (1957) (hereinafter Restatement), is a useful beginning point for a discussion of general agency principles. * * *

A

Section 219(1) of the Restatement sets out a central principle of agency law:

> A master is subject to liability for the torts of his servants committed while acting in the scope of their employment.

An employer may be liable for both negligent and intentional torts committed by an employee within the scope of his or her employment. Sexual harassment under Title VII presupposes intentional conduct. While early decisions absolved employers of liability for the intentional torts of their employees, the law now imposes liability where the employee's "purpose, however misguided, is wholly or in part to further the master's business." W. Keeton, D. Dobbs, R. Keeton, & D. Owen, Prosser and Keeton on Law of Torts § 70, at 505 (5th ed.1984). * * *

As Courts of Appeals have recognized, a supervisor acting out of gender-based animus or a desire to fulfill sexual urges may not be actuated by a purpose to serve the employer. The harassing supervisor often acts for personal motives, motives unrelated and even antithetical to the objectives of the employer. There are instances, of course, where a supervisor engages in unlawful discrimination with the purpose, mistaken or otherwise, to serve the employer.

* * *

The general rule is that sexual harassment by a supervisor is not conduct within the scope of employment.

B

Scope of employment does not define the only basis for employer liability under agency principles. In limited circumstances, agency principles impose liability on employers even where employees commit torts outside the scope of employment. The principles are set forth in the much-cited § 219(2) of the Restatement:

> (2) A master is not subject to liability for the torts of his servants acting outside the scope of their employment, unless:
>
> (a) the master intended the conduct or the consequences, or
>
> (b) the master was negligent or reckless, or

(c) the conduct violated a non-delegable duty of the master, or

(d) the servant purported to act or to speak on behalf of the principal and there was reliance upon apparent authority, or he was aided in accomplishing the tort by the existence of the agency relation.

Subsection (a) addresses direct liability, where the employer acts with tortious intent, and indirect liability, where the agent's high rank in the company makes him or her the employer's alter ego. None of the parties contend Slowik's rank imputes liability under this principle. There is no contention, furthermore, that a nondelegable duty is involved. *See* § 219(2)(c). So, for our purposes here, subsections (a) and (c) can be put aside.

Subsections (b) and (d) are possible grounds for imposing employer liability on account of a supervisor's acts and must be considered. Under subsection (b), an employer is liable when the tort is attributable to the employer's own negligence. § 219(2)(b). Thus, although a supervisor's sexual harassment is outside the scope of employment because the conduct was for personal motives, an employer can be liable, nonetheless, where its own negligence is a cause of the harassment. An employer is negligent with respect to sexual harassment if it knew or should have known about the conduct and failed to stop it. Negligence sets a minimum standard for employer liability under Title VII; but Ellerth seeks to invoke the more stringent standard of vicarious liability.

Subsection 219(2)(d) concerns vicarious liability for intentional torts committed by an employee when the employee uses apparent authority (the apparent authority standard), or when the employee "was aided in accomplishing the tort by the existence of the agency relation" (the aided in the agency relation standard). As other federal decisions have done in discussing vicarious liability for supervisor harassment, we begin with § 219(2)(d).

C

As a general rule, apparent authority is relevant where the agent purports to exercise a power which he or she does not have, as distinct from where the agent threatens to misuse actual power. In the usual case, a supervisor's harassment involves misuse of actual power, not the false impression of its existence. Apparent authority analysis therefore is inappropriate in this context. If, in the unusual case, it is alleged there is a false impression that the actor was a supervisor, when he in fact was not, the victim's mistaken conclusion must be a reasonable one. When a party seeks to impose vicarious liability based on an agent's misuse of delegated authority, the Restatement's aided in the agency relation rule, rather than the apparent authority rule, appears to be the appropriate form of analysis.

D

We turn to the aided in the agency relation standard. In a sense, most workplace tortfeasors are aided in accomplishing their objective by the existence of the agency relation: Proximity and regular contact may afford a captive pool of potential victims. Were this to satisfy the aided in the agency relation standard, an employer would be subject to vicarious liability not only for all supervisor harassment, but also for all co-worker harassment, a result enforced by neither the EEOC nor any court of appeals to have considered the issue. The aided in the agency relation standard, therefore, requires the existence of something more than the employment relation itself.

At the outset, we can identify a class of cases where, beyond question, more than the mere existence of the employment relation aids in commission of the harassment: when a supervisor takes a tangible employment action against the subordinate. Every Federal Court of Appeals to have considered the question has found vicarious liability when a discriminatory act results in a tangible employment action. In *Meritor*, we acknowledged this consensus. Although few courts have elaborated how agency principles support this rule, we think it reflects a correct application of the aided in the agency relation standard.

In the context of this case, a tangible employment action would have taken the form of a denial of a raise or a promotion. The concept of a tangible employment action appears in numerous cases in the Courts of Appeals discussing claims involving race, age, and national origin discrimination, as well as sex discrimination. Without endorsing the specific results of those decisions, we think it prudent to import the concept of a tangible employment action for resolution of the vicarious liability issue we consider here. A tangible employment action constitutes a significant change in employment status, such as hiring, firing, failing to promote, reassignment with significantly different responsibilities, or a decision causing a significant change in benefits. *Compare* Crady v. Liberty Nat. Bank & Trust Co. of Ind., 993 F.2d 132, 136 (7th Cir.1993) ("A materially adverse change might be indicated by a termination of employment, a demotion evidenced by a decrease in wage or salary, a less distinguished title, a material loss of benefits, significantly diminished material responsibilities, or other indices that might be unique to a particular situation"), *with* Flaherty v. Gas Research Institute, 31 F.3d 451, 456 (7th Cir.1994) (a "bruised ego" is not enough); Kocsis v. Multi-Care Management, Inc., 97 F.3d 876, 887 (6th Cir.1996) (demotion without change in pay, benefits, duties, or prestige insufficient) and Harlston v. McDonnell Douglas Corp., 37 F.3d 379, 382 (8th Cir.1994) (reassignment to more inconvenient job insufficient).

When a supervisor makes a tangible employment decision, there is assurance the injury could not have been inflicted absent the agency relation. A tangible employment action in most cases inflicts direct economic harm. As a general proposition, only a supervisor, or other person acting with the authority of the company, can cause this sort of injury. A co-worker can break a co-worker's arm as easily as a supervisor, and anyone who has regular contact with an employee can inflict psychological injuries by his or her offensive conduct. But one co-worker (absent some elaborate scheme) cannot dock another's pay, nor can one co-worker demote another. Tangible employment actions fall within the special province of the supervisor. The supervisor has been empowered by the company as a distinct class of agent to make economic decisions affecting other employees under his or her control.

Tangible employment actions are the means by which the supervisor brings the official power of the enterprise to bear on subordinates. A tangible employment decision requires an official act of the enterprise, a company act. The decision in most cases is documented in official company records, and may be subject to review by higher level supervisors. *E.g., Shager v. Upjohn Co.,* 913 F.2d 398, 405 (C.A.7 1990) (noting that the supervisor did not fire plaintiff; rather, the Career Path Committee did, but the employer was still liable because the committee functioned as the supervisor's "cat's-paw"). The supervisor often must obtain the imprimatur of the enterprise and use its internal processes. See *Kotcher v. Rosa & Sullivan Appliance Center, Inc.,* 957 F.2d 59, 62 (C.A.2 1992) ("From the perspective of the employee, the supervisor and the employer merge into a single entity").

For these reasons, a tangible employment action taken by the supervisor becomes for Title VII purposes the act of the employer. Whatever the exact contours of the aided in the agency relation standard, its requirements will always be met when a supervisor takes a tangible employment action against a subordinate. In that instance, it would be implausible to interpret agency principles to allow an employer to escape liability, as *Meritor* itself appeared to acknowledge.

Whether the agency relation aids in commission of supervisor harassment which does not culminate in a tangible employment action is less obvious. Application of the standard is made difficult by its malleable terminology, which can be read to either expand or limit liability in the context of supervisor harassment. On the one hand, a supervisor's power and authority invests his or her harassing conduct with a particular threatening character, and in this sense, a supervisor always is aided by the agency relation. *See Meritor*, 477 U.S. at 77, 106 S.Ct. at 2410–11 (Marshall, J., concurring in judgment) ("[I]t is precisely because the supervisor is understood to be clothed with the employer's authority that he is able to impose unwelcome sexual conduct on subordinates"). On the other hand, there are acts of harassment a supervisor might commit which might be the same acts a co-employee would commit, and there may be some circumstances where the supervisor's status makes little difference.

It is this tension which, we think, has caused so much confusion among the Courts of Appeals which have sought to apply the aided in the agency relation standard to Title VII cases. The aided in the agency relation standard, however, is a developing feature of agency law, and we hesitate to render a definitive explanation of our understanding of the standard in an area where other important considerations must affect our judgment. In particular, we are bound by our holding in *Meritor* that agency principles constrain the imposition of vicarious liability in cases of supervisory harassment. Congress has not altered *Meritor's* rule even though it has made significant amendments to Title VII in the interim.

Although *Meritor* suggested the limitation on employer liability stemmed from agency principles, the Court acknowledged other considerations might be relevant as well. For example, Title VII is designed to encourage the creation of antiharassment policies and effective grievance mechanisms. Were employer liability to depend in part on an employer's effort to create such procedures, it would effect Congress' intention to promote conciliation rather than litigation in the Title VII context and the EEOC's policy of encouraging the development of grievance procedures. *See* 29 C.F.R. § 1604.11(f) (1997); EEOC Policy Guidance on Sexual Harassment, 8 BNA F.E.P. Manual 405:6699 (Mar. 19, 1990). To the extent limiting employer liability could encourage employees to report harassing conduct before it becomes severe or pervasive, it would also serve Title VII's deterrent purpose. As we have observed, Title VII borrows from tort law the avoidable consequences doctrine, and the considerations which animate that doctrine would also support the limitation of employer liability in certain circumstances.

In order to accommodate the agency principles of vicarious liability for harm caused by misuse of supervisory authority, as well as Title VII's equally basic policies of encouraging forethought by employers and saving action by objecting employees, we adopt the following holding in this case and in *Faragher v. Boca Raton*, 524 U.S. 775, 118 S.Ct. 2275, 141 L.Ed.2d 662 (1998), also decided today. An employer is subject to vicarious liability to a victimized employee for an actionable hostile environment created by a supervisor with immediate (or successively higher) authority over the employee. When no tangible employment action is taken, a defending employer may raise an affirmative defense to liability or damages, subject to proof by a preponderance of the evidence, *see* Fed.Rule Civ.Proc. 8(c). The defense comprises two necessary elements: (a) that the employer exercised reasonable care to prevent and correct promptly any sexually harassing behavior, and (b) that the plaintiff employee unreasonably failed to take advantage of any preventive or corrective opportunities provided by the employer or to avoid harm otherwise. While proof that an employer had promulgated an anti-harassment policy with complaint procedure is not necessary in every instance as a matter of law, the need for a stated policy suitable to the employment circumstances may appropriately be addressed in any case when litigating the first element of the defense. And while proof that an employee failed to fulfill the corresponding obligation of reasonable care to avoid harm is not limited to showing any unreasonable failure to use any complaint procedure provided by the employer, a demonstration of such failure will normally suffice to satisfy the employer's burden under the second element of the defense. No affirmative defense is available, however, when the supervisor's harassment culminates in a tangible employment action, such as discharge, demotion, or undesirable reassignment.

IV

Relying on existing case law which held out the promise of vicarious liability for all *quid pro quo* claims, Ellerth focused all her attention in the Court of Appeals on proving her claim fit within that category. Given our explanation that the labels *quid pro quo* and hostile work environment are not controlling for purposes of establishing employer liability, Ellerth should have an adequate opportunity to prove she has a claim for which Burlington is liable.

Although Ellerth has not alleged she suffered a tangible employment action at the hands of Slowik, which would deprive Burlington of the availability of the affirmative defense, this is not dispositive. In light of our decision, Burlington is still subject to vicarious liability for Slowik's activity, but Burlington should have an opportunity to assert and prove the affirmative defense to liability. * * * [The Court affirmed the judgment of the Court of Appeals, reversing the grant of summary judgment against Ellerth, and remanded.]

[JUSTICE GINSBURG concurred in the judgment of the Court. JUSTICE THOMAS, joined by JUSTICE SCALIA dissented.]

VANCE V. BALL STATE UNIVERSITY

Supreme Court of the United States, 2013.
___ U.S. ___, 133 S.Ct. 2434, 186 L.Ed.2d 565.

JUSTICE ALITO delivered the opinion of the Court.

In this case, we decide a question left open in *Burlington Industries, Inc. v. Ellerth,* 524 U.S. 742 (1998), and *Faragher v. Boca Raton,* 524 U.S. 775 (1998), namely, who qualifies as a "supervisor" in a case in which an employee asserts a Title VII claim for workplace harassment?

Under Title VII, an employer's liability for such harassment may depend on the status of the harasser. If the harassing employee is the victim's co-worker, the employer is liable only if it was negligent in controlling working conditions. In cases in which the harasser is a "supervisor," however, different rules apply. If the supervisor's harassment culminates in a tangible employment action, the employer is strictly liable. But if no tangible employment action is taken, the employer may escape liability by establishing, as an affirmative defense, that (1) the employer exercised reasonable care to prevent and correct any harassing behavior and (2) that the plaintiff unreasonably failed to take advantage of the preventive or corrective opportunities that the employer provided. Under this framework, therefore, it matters whether a harasser is a "supervisor" or simply a co-worker.

We hold that an employee is a "supervisor" for purposes of vicarious liability under Title VII if he or she is empowered by the employer to take tangible employment actions against the victim, and we therefore affirm the judgment of the Seventh Circuit.

I

Maetta Vance, an African-American woman, began working for Ball State University (BSU) in 1989 as a substitute server in the University Banquet and Catering division of Dining Services. In 1991, BSU promoted Vance to a part-time catering assistant position, and in 2007 she applied and was selected for a position as a full-time catering assistant.

* * *

During the time in question, [Sandra] Davis, a white woman, was employed as a catering specialist in the Banquet and Catering division. The parties vigorously dispute the precise nature and scope of Davis' duties, but they agree that Davis did not have the power to hire, fire, demote, promote, transfer, or discipline Vance.

In late 2005 and early 2006, Vance filed internal complaints with BSU and charges with the Equal Employment Opportunity Commission (EEOC), alleging racial harassment and discrimination, and many of these complaints and charges pertained to Davis.

Vance filed this lawsuit in 2006 in the United States District Court for the Southern District of Indiana, claiming, among other things, that she had been subjected to a racially hostile work environment in violation of Title VII. In her complaint, she alleged that Davis was her supervisor and that BSU was liable for Davis' creation of a racially hostile work environment.

Both parties moved for summary judgment, and the District Court entered summary judgment in favor of BSU. The court explained that

BSU could not be held vicariously liable for Davis' alleged racial harassment because Davis could not " 'hire, fire, demote, promote, transfer, or discipline' " Vance and, as a result, was not Vance's supervisor under the Seventh Circuit's interpretation of that concept. The court further held that BSU could not be liable in negligence because it responded reasonably to the incidents of which it was aware.

* * *

II

C

Under *Ellerth* and *Faragher,* it is obviously important whether an alleged harasser is a "supervisor" or merely a co-worker, and the lower courts have disagreed about the meaning of the concept of a supervisor in this context. Some courts, including the Seventh Circuit below, have held that an employee is not a supervisor unless he or she has the power to hire, fire, demote, promote, transfer, or discipline the victim. *E.g.,* 646 F.3d, at 470; *Noviello v. Boston,* 398 F.3d 76, 96 (C.A.1 2005); *Weyers v. Lear Operations Corp.,* 359 F.3d 1049, 1057 (C.A.8 2004). Other courts have substantially followed the more open-ended approach advocated by the EEOC's Enforcement Guidance, which ties supervisor status to the ability to exercise significant direction over another's daily work. See, *e.g., Mack v. Otis Elevator Co.,* 326 F.3d 116, 126–127 (C.A.2 2003); *Whitten v. Fred's, Inc.,* 601 F.3d 231, 245–247 (C.A.4 2010); EEOC, Enforcement Guidance: Vicarious Employer Liability for Unlawful Harassment by Supervisors (1999), 1999 WL 33305874, at *3 (hereinafter EEOC Guidance).

III

We hold that an employer may be vicariously liable for an employee's unlawful harassment only when the employer has empowered that employee to take tangible employment actions against the victim, *i.e.,* to effect a "significant change in employment status, such as hiring, firing, failing to promote, reassignment with significantly different responsibilities, or a decision causing a significant change in benefits." *Ellerth, supra,* at 761. We reject the nebulous definition of a "supervisor" advocated in the EEOC Guidance and substantially adopted by several courts of appeals. Petitioner's reliance on colloquial uses of the term "supervisor" is misplaced, and her contention that our cases require the EEOC's abstract definition is simply wrong.

As we will explain, the framework set out in *Ellerth* and *Faragher* presupposes a clear distinction between supervisors and co-workers. Those decisions contemplate a unitary category of supervisors, *i.e.,* those employees with the authority to make tangible employment decisions. There is no hint in either decision that the Court had in mind two categories of supervisors: first, those who have such authority and, second, those who, although lacking this power, nevertheless have the ability to direct a co-worker's labor to some ill-defined degree. On the contrary, the *Ellerth/Faragher* framework is one under which supervisory status can usually be readily determined, generally by written documentation. The approach recommended by the EEOC Guidance, by contrast, would make the determination of supervisor status depend on a highly case-specific evaluation of numerous factors.

A

Petitioner contends that her expansive understanding of the concept of a "supervisor" is supported by the meaning of the word in general usage and in other legal contexts, but this argument is both incorrect on its own terms and, in any event, misguided.

In general usage, the term "supervisor" lacks a sufficiently specific meaning to be helpful for present purposes. Petitioner is certainly right that the term is often used to refer to a person who has the authority to direct another's work. But the term is also often closely tied to the authority to take what *Ellerth* and *Faragher* referred to as a "tangible employment action." * * *

If we look beyond general usage to the meaning of the term in other legal contexts, we find much the same situation. Sometimes the term is reserved for those in the upper echelons of the management hierarchy. But sometimes the term is used to refer to lower ranking individuals. * * *

In sum, the term "supervisor" has varying meanings both in colloquial usage and in the law. And for this reason, petitioner's argument, taken on its own terms, is unsuccessful.

More important, petitioner is misguided in suggesting that we should approach the question presented here as if "supervisor" were a statutory term. "Supervisor" is not a term used by Congress in Title VII. Rather, the term was adopted by this Court in *Ellerth* and *Faragher* as a label for the class of employees whose misconduct may give rise to vicarious employer liability. Accordingly, the way to understand the meaning of the term "supervisor" for present purposes is to consider the interpretation that best fits within the highly structured framework that those cases adopted.

B

* * *

The dissent acknowledges that our prior cases do "not squarely resolve whether an employee without power to take tangible employment actions may nonetheless qualify as a supervisor," but accuses us of ignoring the "all-too-plain reality" that employees with authority to control their subordinates' daily work are aided by that authority in perpetuating a discriminatory work environment. As *Ellerth* recognized, however, "most workplace tortfeasors are aided in accomplishing their tortious objective by the existence of the agency relation," and consequently "something more" is required in order to warrant vicarious liability. 524 U.S., at 760. The ability to direct another employee's tasks is simply not sufficient. Employees with such powers are certainly capable of creating intolerable work environments, but so are many other co-workers. Negligence provides the better framework for evaluating an employer's liability when a harassing employee lacks the power to take tangible employment actions.

C

* * *

Under the definition of "supervisor" that we adopt today, the question of supervisor status, when contested, can very often be resolved as a matter of law before trial. The elimination of this issue from the trial will focus the efforts of the parties, who will be able to present their cases in a way that conforms to the framework that the jury will apply. The plaintiff will know whether he or she must prove that the employer was negligent or whether the employer will have the burden of proving the elements of the *Ellerth/Faragher* affirmative defense. Perhaps even more important, the work of the jury, which is inevitably complicated in employment discrimination cases, will be simplified. The jurors can be given preliminary instructions that allow them to understand, as the evidence comes in, how each item of proof fits into the framework that they will ultimately be required to apply. And even where the issue of supervisor status cannot be eliminated from the trial (because there are genuine factual disputes about an alleged harasser's authority to take tangible employment actions), this preliminary question is relatively straightforward.

The alternative approach advocated by petitioner and the United States would make matters far more complicated and difficult. The complexity of the standard they favor would impede the resolution of the issue before trial. With the issue still open when trial commences, the parties would be compelled to present evidence and argument on supervisor status, the affirmative defense, and the question of negligence, and the jury would have to grapple with all those issues as well. In addition, it would often be necessary for the jury to be instructed about two very different paths of analysis, *i.e.*, what to do if the alleged harasser was found to be a supervisor and what to do if the alleged harasser was found to be merely a co-worker.

Courts and commentators alike have opined on the need for reasonably clear jury instructions in employment discrimination cases. And the danger of juror confusion is particularly high where the jury is faced with instructions on alternative theories of liability under which different parties bear the burden of proof. By simplifying the process of determining who is a supervisor (and by extension, which liability rules apply to a given set of facts), the approach that we take will help to ensure that juries return verdicts that reflect the application of the correct legal rules to the facts.

D

The dissent argues that the definition of a supervisor that we now adopt is out of touch with the realities of the workplace, where individuals with the power to assign daily tasks are often regarded by other employees as supervisors. But in reality it is the alternative that is out of touch. Particularly in modern organizations that have abandoned a highly hierarchical management structure, it is common for employees to have overlapping authority with respect to the assignment of work tasks. Members of a team may each have the responsibility for taking the lead with respect to a particular aspect of the work and thus may have the responsibility to direct each other in that area of responsibility.

Finally, petitioner argues that tying supervisor status to the authority to take tangible employment actions will encourage employers to attempt to insulate themselves from liability for workplace harassment by empowering only a handful of individuals to take tangible employment actions. But a broad definition of "supervisor" is not necessary to guard against this concern.

As an initial matter, an employer will always be liable when its negligence leads to the creation or continuation of a hostile work environment. And even if an employer concentrates all decisionmaking authority in a few individuals, it likely will not isolate itself from heightened liability under *Faragher* and *Ellerth*. If an employer does attempt to confine decisionmaking power to a small number of individuals, those individuals will have a limited ability to exercise independent discretion when making decisions and will likely rely on other workers who actually interact with the affected employee. Under those circumstances, the employer may be held to have effectively delegated the power to take tangible employment actions to the employees on whose recommendations it relies.

* * *

We hold that an employee is a "supervisor" for purposes of vicarious liability under Title VII if he or she is empowered by the employer to take tangible employment actions against the victim. Because there is no evidence that BSU empowered Davis to take any tangible employment actions against Vance, the judgment of the Seventh Circuit is affirmed.

JUSTICE GINSBURG, with whom JUSTICE BREYER, JUSTICE SOTOMAYOR, and JUSTICE KAGAN join, dissenting.

* * * The Court today strikes from the supervisory category employees who control the day-to-day schedules and assignments of others, confining the category to those formally empowered to take tangible employment actions. The limitation the Court decrees diminishes the force of *Faragher* and *Ellerth,* ignores the conditions under which members of the work force labor, and disserves the objective of Title VII to prevent discrimination from infecting the Nation's workplaces. I would follow the EEOC's Guidance and hold that the authority to direct an employee's daily activities establishes supervisory status under Title VII.

I

* * *

B

The distinction *Faragher* and *Ellerth* drew between supervisors and co-workers corresponds to the realities of the workplace. Exposed to a fellow employee's harassment, one can walk away or tell the offender to "buzz off." A supervisor's slings and arrows, however, are not so easily avoided. An employee who confronts her harassing supervisor risks, for example, receiving an undesirable or unsafe work assignment or an unwanted transfer. She may be saddled with an excessive workload or with placement on a shift spanning hours disruptive of her family life. And she may be demoted or fired. Facing such dangers, she may be reluctant to blow the whistle on her superior, whose "power and authority invests his or her harassing conduct with a particular threatening character." *Ellerth,* 524 U.S., at 763. See also *Faragher,* 524 U.S., at 803. In short, as *Faragher* and *Ellerth* recognized, harassment by supervisors is more likely to cause palpable harm and to persist unabated than similar conduct by fellow employees.

* * *

II

B

Workplace realities fortify my conclusion that harassment by an employee with power to direct subordinates' day-to-day work activities should trigger vicarious employer liability. The following illustrations, none of them hypothetical, involve in-charge employees of the kind the Court today excludes from supervisory status.

Yasharay Mack: Yasharay Mack, an African-American woman, worked for the Otis Elevator Company as an elevator mechanic's helper at the Metropolitan Life Building in New York City. James Connolly, the "mechanic in charge" and the senior employee at the site, targeted Mack for abuse. He commented frequently on her "fantastic ass," "luscious lips," and "beautiful eyes," and, using deplorable racial epithets, opined that minorities and women did not "belong in the business." Once, he pulled her on his lap, touched her buttocks, and tried to kiss her while others looked on. Connolly lacked authority to take tangible employment actions against mechanic's helpers, but he did assign their work, control their schedules, and direct the particulars of their workdays. When he became angry with Mack, for example, he denied her overtime hours. And when she complained about the mistreatment, he scoffed, "I get away with everything." See *Mack,* 326 F.3d, at 120–121, 125–126 (internal quotation marks omitted).

Donna Rhodes: Donna Rhodes, a seasonal highway maintainer for the Illinois Department of Transportation, was responsible for plowing snow during winter months. Michael Poladian was a "Lead Lead Worker" and Matt Mara, a "Technician" at the maintenance yard where Rhodes worked. Both men assembled plow crews and managed the work assignments of employees in Rhodes's position, but neither had authority to hire, fire, promote, demote, transfer, or discipline employees. In her third season working at the yard, Rhodes was verbally assaulted with sex-based invectives and a pornographic image was taped to her locker. Poladian forced her to wash her truck in sub-zero temperatures, assigned her undesirable yard work instead of road crew work, and prohibited another employee from fixing the malfunctioning heating system in her truck. Conceding that Rhodes had been subjected to a sex-based hostile work environment, the Department of Transportation argued successfully in the District Court and Court of Appeals that Poladian and Mara were not Rhodes's supervisors because they lacked authority to take tangible employment actions against her. See *Rhodes v. Illinois Dept. of Transp.,* 359 F.3d 498, 501–503, 506–507 (C.A.7 2004).

Clara Whitten: Clara Whitten worked at a discount retail store in Belton, South Carolina. On Whitten's first day of work, the manager, Matt Green, told her to "give [him] what [he] want[ed]" in order to obtain approval for long weekends off from work. Later, fearing what might transpire, Whitten ignored Green's order to join him in an isolated storeroom. Angered, Green instructed Whitten to stay late and clean the store. He demanded that she work over the weekend despite her scheduled day off. Dismissing her as "dumb and stupid," Green threatened to make her life a "living hell." Green lacked authority to fire, promote, demote, or otherwise make decisions affecting Whitten's pocketbook. But he directed her activities, gave her tasks to accomplish, burdened her with undesirable work assignments, and controlled her schedule. He was usually the highest ranking employee in the store, and both Whitten and Green considered him the supervisor. See *Whitten,* 601 F.3d, at 236, 244–247 (internal quotation marks omitted).

Monika Starke: CRST Van Expedited, Inc., an interstate transit company, ran a training program for newly hired truckdrivers requiring a 28-day on-the-road trip. Monika Starke participated in the program. Trainees like Starke were paired in a truck cabin with a single "lead driver" who lacked authority to hire, fire, promote, or demote, but who exercised control over the work environment for the duration of the trip. Lead drivers were responsible for providing instruction on CRST's driving method, assigning specific tasks, and scheduling rest stops. At the end of the trip, lead drivers evaluated trainees' performance with a nonbinding pass or fail recommendation that could lead to full driver status. Over the course of Starke's training trip, her first lead driver, Bob Smith, filled the cabin with vulgar sexual remarks, commenting on her breast size and comparing the gear stick to genitalia. A second lead driver, David Goodman, later forced her into unwanted sex with him, an outrage to which she submitted, believing it necessary to gain a passing grade. See *EEOC v. CRST Van Expedited, Inc.,* 679 F.3d 657, 665–666, 684–685 (C.A.8 2012).

In each of these cases, a person vested with authority to control the conditions of a subordinate's daily work life used his position to aid his harassment. But in none of them would the Court's severely confined definition of supervisor yield vicarious liability for the employer. The senior elevator mechanic in charge, the Court today tells us, was Mack's co-worker, not her supervisor. So was the store manager who punished Whitten with long hours for refusing to give him what he wanted. So were the lead drivers who controlled all aspects of Starke's working environment, and the yard worker who kept other employees from helping Rhodes to control the heat in her truck.

As anyone with work experience would immediately grasp, James Connolly, Michael Poladian, Matt Mara, Matt Green, Bob Smith, and David Goodman wielded employer-conferred supervisory authority over their victims. Each man's discriminatory harassment derived force from, and was facilitated by, the control reins he held.

C

Within a year after the Court's decisions in *Faragher* and *Ellerth,* the EEOC defined "supervisor" to include any employee with "authority to undertake or recommend tangible employment decisions," *or* with "authority to direct [another] employee's daily work activities." EEOC Guidance 405:7654. That definition should garner "respect proportional to its 'power to persuade.'" *United States v. Mead Corp.*, 533 U.S. 218 (2001) (quoting *Skidmore v. Swift & Co.*, 323 U.S. 134, 140 (1944)).

The EEOC's definition of supervisor reflects the agency's "informed judgment" and "body of experience" in enforcing Title VII. For 14 years, in enforcement actions and litigation, the EEOC has firmly adhered to its definition.

In developing its definition of supervisor, the EEOC paid close attention to the *Faragher* and *Ellerth* framework. An employer is vicariously liable only when the authority it has delegated enables actionable harassment, the EEOC recognized. EEOC Guidance 405:7654. For that reason, a supervisor's authority must be "of a sufficient magnitude so as to assist the harasser . . . in carrying out the harassment." *Ibid.* Determining whether an employee wields sufficient authority is not a mechanical inquiry, the EEOC explained; instead, specific facts about the employee's job function are critical. *Id.*, at 405:7653 to 405:7654. Thus, an employee with authority to increase another's workload or assign undesirable tasks may rank as a supervisor, for those powers can enable harassment. *Id.*, at 405:7654. On the other hand, an employee "who directs only a limited number of tasks or assignments" ordinarily would not qualify as a supervisor, for her harassing conduct is not likely to be aided materially by the agency relationship. *Id.*, at 405:7655.

In my view, the EEOC's definition, which the Court puts down as "a study in ambiguity," has the ring of truth and, therefore, powerfully persuasive force. As a precondition to vicarious employer liability, the EEOC explained, the harassing supervisor must wield authority of sufficient magnitude to enable the harassment. In other words, the aided-in-accomplishment standard requires "something more than the employment relation itself." *Ellerth*, 524 U.S., at 760. Furthermore, as the EEOC perceived, in assessing an employee's qualification as a supervisor, context is often key. I would accord the agency's judgment due respect.

III

* * *

B

* * *

Inevitably, the Court's definition of supervisor will hinder efforts to stamp out discrimination in the workplace. Because supervisors are comparatively few, and employees are many, "the employer has a greater opportunity to guard against misconduct by supervisors than by common workers," and a greater incentive to "screen [supervisors], train them, and monitor their performance." *Faragher*, 524 U.S., at 803. Vicarious liability for employers serves this end. When employers know they will be answerable for the injuries a harassing jobsite boss inflicts, their incentive to provide preventative instruction is heightened. If vicarious liability is confined to supervisors formally empowered to take tangible employment actions, however, employers will have a diminished incentive to train those who control their subordinates' work activities and schedules, *i.e.,* the supervisors who "actually interact" with employees.

* * *

NOTES AND QUESTIONS

1. *The EEOC's 1999 Enforcement Guidance on Vicarious Employer Liability*: After the Supreme Court issued its opinions in *Ellerth* and the companion case, *Faragher v. City of Boca Raton*, 524 U.S. 775, 118 S.Ct. 2275, 141 L.Ed.2d 662 (1998), the EEOC rescinded 29 C.F.R. § 1604.11(c)—the standard for employer liability for supervisory sexual harassment found in the EEOC's 1980 Guidelines on Sexual Harassment—and issued a new policy entitled Enforcement Guidance: Vicarious Employer Liability for Unlawful Harassment by Supervisors (6/18/99), EEOC Compliance Manual (BNA) [hereinafter *EEOC Guidance on Vicarious Employer Liability*], available at *http://www.eeoc.gov/policy/docs/harassment.html.* This 1999 Enforcement Guidance, which is reproduced, in part, in the Statutory Supplement, was partially invalidated by the Court's decision in *Vance*, which rejected the EEOC's more expansive definition of "supervisor" in favor of a definition of supervisor that includes only those with the power to take tangible employment actions against the complaining employee. Were you more persuaded by the majority or the dissenting opinion in *Vance*?

2. Although *Vance* purported to establish an easy-to-apply rule for determining who qualifies as a supervisor for purposes of assessing employer liability for sexual harassment, the opinion did leave open the possibility that an employer can be said to have "effectively delegated the power to take tangible employment actions to the employees on whose recommendations it relies." Opinions following *Vance* have taken slightly different approaches to when that circumstance obtains. *See, e.g.,* Boyer-Liberto v. Fontainebleau Corp., 786 F.3d 264 (4th Cir.2015) (noting that "[t]o be considered a supervisor, the employee need not have the final say as to the tangible employment action") with Velazquez-Perez v. Developers Diversified Realty Corp., 753 F.3d 265, 272 (1st Cir.2014) ("There is nothing in *Vance,* though, to warrant ignoring the difference between providing advice and feedback to one who has independent sources of information and truly makes the decision, and providing a recommendation to one whose acceptance of the recommendation is pro forma.").

3. *The Definition and Relevance of a "Tangible Employment Action"*: For purposes of establishing employer liability, the key distinction between sexual harassment claims based on the conduct of a supervisor is not the label—quid pro quo or hostile work environment—that the plaintiff applies to the claim, but the presence or absence of a tangible employment action. *See*

Lutkewitte v. Gonzales, 436 F.3d 248, 260–61 (D.C.Cir.2006) (Brown, J., concurring) (noting *Ellerth's* clarification of the irrelevance of the terms "*quid pro quo*" and "hostile work environment" for purposes of determining whether a "tangible employment action" has occurred). Thus, in all sexual harassment cases involving conduct of certain supervisors, the plaintiff's ability to prove (or the employer's ability to disprove or discount) evidence of a tangible employment action will be critical in establishing employer liability and in determining whether the defendant is entitled to present an affirmative defense. *Ellerth* defines a "tangible employment action" as "a significant change in employment status, such as hiring, firing, failing to promote, reassignment with significantly different responsibilities, or a decision causing a significant change in benefits." 524 U.S. at 761, 118 S.Ct. at 2268. Would a tenured professor's loss of an administrative title be a tangible employment action? *See* Bryson v. Chi. State Univ., 96 F.3d 912 (7th Cir.1996). What about being assigned extra work? *See* Reinhold v. Virginia, 151 F.3d 172, 175 (4th Cir.1998). For a critique of how lower courts have applied *Ellerth's* analysis of a tangible employment action, see Susan Grover, *After* Ellerth: *the Tangible Employment Action in Sexual Harassment Analysis*, 35 U.Mich.J.L. Reform 809 (2002).

a. *Fulfilled promises of job benefits*: Suppose a supervisor promises a subordinate a job benefit, such as a promotion, if she complies with his sexual demands. The employee complies, and the promise is fulfilled—she is promoted. On these facts, is the employer vicariously liable for sexual harassment? Will the employer be permitted to present an affirmative defense? What if a supervisor grants benefits that are not expressly linked to sexual demands? How can a plaintiff establish a nexus between the sexual advances and the job benefits if the benefits were routine, expected, or earned? *See* Matvia v. Bald Head Island Mgmt., Inc., 259 F.3d 261, 267 (4th Cir.2001). *See also* Lutkewitte v. Gonzales, 436 F.3d 248, 262–64 (D.C.Cir.2006) (Brown, J., concurring) (arguing that under the reasoning of *Ellerth* only adverse employment actions—not benefits—can be considered "tangible employment actions" for purposes of triggering strict liability).

b. *Unfulfilled promises of job benefits*: Suppose a supervisor orally (and privately) promised an employee a job benefit, such as a promotion, and subsequently made a sexual advance toward the employee that was implicitly linked to fulfillment of the promised promotion. Then, when the employee refused to comply with the sexual demand, the supervisor failed to promote the employee. Does the supervisor's failure to act under these circumstances constitute a "tangible employment action"? If the supervisor's promise does not appear on the company records—as a "company act"—and was not witnessed by any other employees, and the employee's status has not changed, how can the employee prove there has been a "tangible employment action" consisting of a failure to promote? For a discussion of the functional significance of a "company act," see generally Michael C. Harper, *Employer Liability for Harassment Under Title VII: A Functional Rationale for* Faragher *and* Ellerth, 36 San Diego L.Rev. 41 (1999).

c. *Unfulfilled threats of adverse job consequences—rejection cases*: What if the plaintiff did not acquiesce in her supervisor's implicit demands for sex in exchange for keeping her job, and the implied threat was not fulfilled? She cannot make out a claim of quid pro quo harassment with a tangible employment action on these facts. But if she is able to prove the demands were severe or pervasive, she may be able to establish a hostile work environment claim. *See* Craig v. M & O Agencies, Inc., 496 F.3d 1047, 1054–55 (9th Cir.2007).

d. *Unfulfilled threats of adverse job consequences—submission cases*: Is the definition of "tangible employment action" necessarily limited to economic harm? The Court of Appeals for the Second Circuit held that an employee had suffered a tangible employment action when her supervisor forced her to submit to his sexual demands as a condition of keeping her job. Jin v. Metro. Life Ins., 310 F.3d 84 (2d Cir.2002). *Jin* held that "[r]equiring an employee to engage in unwanted sex acts is one of the most pernicious and oppressive forms of sexual harassment that can occur in the workplace" and "this type of conduct—a classic quid pro quo for which courts have traditionally held employers liable—fits squarely within the definition of 'tangible employment action.'" *Id.* at 94. Is this holding consistent with *Ellerth*? *See also* Holly D. v. California Inst. of Tech., 339 F.3d 1158, 1170–72 (9th Cir.2003) (following *Jin* and the *EEOC Guidance on Vicarious Employer Liability, supra*).

In *Lutkewitte v. Gonzales,* 436 F.3d 248, 251 (D.C.Cir.2006) (per curiam), the court held that an employee's fear of losing her job if she did not submit to her supervisor's sexual demands did not constitute evidence that "her submission itself [was] a tangible employment action" in the absence of evidence that he "implicitly or explicitly conditioned her continued employment on her acquiescence to his sexual overtures." In a concurring opinion in *Lutkewitte,* Judge Brown disagreed with the reasoning in the *Jin* and *Holly* cases, and expressed the view that, as a matter of law, an employee's submission to sexual acts in response to threats of unfulfilled adverse job consequences is not a "tangible employment action" for purposes of determining whether the employer is strictly liable or may assert the *Ellerth/Faragher* affirmative defense. Judge Brown argued:

> [T]angibility should be determined from the employer's perspective. If a supervisor threatens an employee, and she submits in order to avoid adverse consequences, the supervisor has not committed an "official act" but merely threatened to do so. The employer has no way of knowing that its delegated authority has been brandished in such a way as to coerce sexual submission.

Id. at 270 (Brown, J., concurring). Which view on so-called submission cases—*Jin* or *Lutkewitte*—do you find is more consistent with the Court's definition of a "tangible employment action" in *Ellerth?* Does an employee suffer an injury by complying with a supervisor's unwanted sexual demand, regardless of whether the supervisor's economic threat is eventually fulfilled? Are supervisors able to condition sexual demands on credible threats of economic harm in a way no co-worker can? Shortly before *Ellerth* and *Faragher* were decided, Eugene Scalia wrote: "Treating the submission case as actionable quid pro quo harassment is consistent with the term's original definition." Eugene Scalia, *The Strange Career of Quid Pro Quo Sexual Harassment,* 21 Harv.J.L. & Pub. Pol'y 307, 314 (1998). Do you agree?

In *Santiero v. Denny's Rest. Store,* 786 F. Supp. 2d 1228, 1234 (S.D. Tex. 2011), the court concluded that this question had been effectively answered by the Supreme Court's decision in *Pa. State Police v. Suders,* 542 U.S. 129, 148–49, 124 S.Ct. 2342, 159 L.Ed.2d 204 (2004). The *Santiero* court found that *Suders*

> stands for the proposition that an employer is entitled to the *Ellerth/Faragher* defense where there is "uncertainty" concerning how the power granted to the supervisor by the employer was a contributing factor in the harassment. In order to be consistent with this understanding of the affirmative defense, where a supervisor seeks sexual encounters with an employee but no official action is taken, and regardless of whether the demand is acceded to or rebuffed, then the *Ellerth/Faragher* affirmative defense should apply. This is the case because there is no "official act of the enterprise" to show that the supervisor used his power to the employee's disadvantage.

Santiero, 786 F.Supp.2d. at 1234. Do you agree that a "tangible employment action" must be an "official act" of the employer?

e. *A single unfulfilled threat*: The Supreme Court accepted the district court's ruling for purposes of summary judgment that the "numerous alleged threats" of Ellerth's supervisor were "severe or pervasive" sexual harassment. But, the Court "express[ed] no opinion as to whether a single unfulfilled threat is sufficient to constitute discrimination in the terms or conditions of employment." *Ellerth*, 524 U.S. at 754, 118 S.Ct. at 2265. How would you resolve the question that the Supreme Court has left open in *Ellerth*?

f. *Aggregating job detriments*: After *Ellerth*, can a plaintiff establish that she suffered a tangible employment action by aggregating evidence of a series of minor job detriments, none of which, standing alone, would be considered a "tangible job detriment" or "ultimate employment decision"? *See* Reinhold v. Virginia, 151 F.3d 172, 175 (4th Cir.1998) (holding that plaintiff's evidence that "she was assigned extra work and suffered other harm as a result of her rejection of [her supervisor's] sexual advances" does not establish that she suffered a "tangible employment action"). For a discussion of the role of judicial decisions and doctrines like "tangible employment action" in determining the scope of Title VII's regulation of workplace harms, see Rebecca Hanner White, *De Minimis Discrimination*, 47 Emory L.J. 1121 (1998).

4. *Imputed Liability—The High-Ranking Harasser as a "Proxy" or "Alter Ego" for the Employer*: Why was employer liability not an issue in

Harris v. Forklift? Recall that in *Ellerth*, the alleged harasser, Slowik, was not Ellerth's immediate supervisor, but a corporate officer higher in the corporate hierarchy—the supervisor of Ellerth's supervisor. Why was Slowik not considered a proxy for the employer? In concluding that state court judges were not "alter egos" of the state, the Tenth Circuit explained that "an official must be high enough in the management hierarchy that his actions "speak" for the employer before he may be considered the employer's alter ego." *Helm v. Kansas*, 656 F.3d 1277, 1286 (10th Cir.2011). *See* VI. Harassment by "Alter Ego" of Employer, in *EEOC Guidance on Vicarious Employer Liability*, *supra*, and in the Statutory Supplement.

5. *The First Prong of the Employer's Affirmative Defense to Vicarious Liability*: In cases of employer vicarious liability for supervisory harassment that does not involve a tangible employment action, the employer will have an opportunity to establish its affirmative defense under *Ellerth* and *Faragher*. In considering whether an employer has met its burden of proving the first prong of its affirmative defense—that it "exercised reasonable care to prevent and correct promptly any sexually harassing behavior"—a number of factors may be relevant.

a. *Antiharassment policies*: Courts generally agree that "distribution of a valid antiharassment policy provides compelling proof that an employer exercised reasonable care to prevent and correct promptly harassing behavior." *Crawford v. BNSF Ry. Co.*, 665 F.3d 978, 983 (8th Cir.2012). Is it possible to devise a one-size-fits-all, generic anti-harassment policy and grievance procedure that will—without fail—satisfy the first element of an employer's affirmative defense? In *EEOC v. V & J Foods, Inc.*, 507 F.3d 575 (7th Cir.2007), the court held that the reasonableness of a complaint mechanism depends on "the employment circumstances," including "known vulnerabilitie[s]" and "capabilities of the class of employees in question." *Id.* at 578. The court found that, where the employer's business plan is "to employ teenagers [who are] part-time workers often working for the first time," the employer is "obligated to suit its procedures to the understanding of the average teenager." *Id.* Can you imagine any circumstances when an informal policy and procedures would suffice to meet the first element of an employer's affirmative defense under *Ellerth* and *Faragher*?

While *Ellerth* and *Faragher* create incentives for employers to adopt sexual harassment policies, they also have made it clear that, as a matter of law, Title VII does not actually require employers to have formal sexual harassment policies. *See, e.g.,* Hall v. Bodine Elec. Co., 276 F.3d 345, 356 (7th Cir.2002) (finding that an employer with no formal policy was not liable where it had other channels for reporting sexual harassment by a co-worker). On the other hand, even if the employer has instituted a formal sexual harassment policy, it will not automatically meet its burden on this part of its affirmative defense. Frederick v. Sprint/United Mgmt. Co., 246 F.3d 1305, 1313 (11th Cir.2001). Employer practices in disseminating and implementing the policy may be determinative. For example, what if the employer keeps the written policy in the human resources department where potential complainants can go to get a copy? *See id.* What if the employer posted its employment policies in a "shack" on the work site? *See E.E.O.C. v. Boh Bros. Const. Co.*, 731 F.3d 444, 464 (5th Cir.2013). Would it be sufficient if the employer kept the written policy in unmarked binders in public areas in each branch office, which were readily accessible to all employees? Compare the majority and dissenting opinions in *Hill v. American General Finance, Inc.*, 218 F.3d 639, 644–45, 646 (7th Cir.2000). If an employer's practice is to distribute its formal policy to each employee, can it meet its burden on this portion of its defense if the employee claims never to have received it and the company has no record that it was distributed to her? *See* Montero v. Agco Corp., 192 F.3d 856 (9th Cir.1999). *See also* Gordon v. Shafer Contracting Co., 469 F.3d 1191, 1195 (8th Cir.2006) (holding that distributing policy to all employees at beginning of construction season meets first prong). In *Faragher*, the Supreme Court held that the City of Boca Raton was unreasonable, as a matter of law, in not disseminating its antiharassment policy to its lifeguards at the City beach. 524 U.S. at 809, 118 S.Ct. at 2293.

b. *Delegating authority for handling complaints*: Which individuals in a company should be delegated the authority—and given the responsibility—to report incidents of sexual harassment that come to their attention? The Sixth Circuit has held: "An employer is deemed to have notice of harassment reported to any supervisor or department head who has been authorized—or is reasonably believed by a complaining employee to have been authorized—to receive and respond to or forward such complaints to management." Gallagher v. C. H. Robinson Worldwide, Inc., 567 F.3d 263, 277 (6th Cir.2009). *Compare* Clark v. United Parcel Serv., Inc., 400 F.3d 341, 350 (6th Cir.2005) (finding imputed knowledge when company placed duty on all supervisors and managers to report harassment), *with* Chalout v. Interstate Brands Corp., 540 F.3d 64, 76 (1st Cir.2008) (finding no imputed knowledge).

c. *Employer responses to complaints*: Once an employer receives a complaint of a hostile work environment created by a supervisor, it must take affirmative steps to investigate and, if necessary, take corrective action in order to avoid liability. *See* Haugerud v. Amery Sch. Dist., 259 F.3d 678, 700 (7th Cir.2001) (holding that school district was not entitled to affirmative defense to hostile work environment claim when it "simply did not act" in response to custodian's complaints about supervisor's conduct).

i. Investigation. How quickly does an investigation have to occur to constitute appropriate corrective action? On the other hand, even if the employer takes corrective action, a jury or court may second-guess the promptness and effectiveness of its decisions. *See* EEOC v. Management Hospitality of Racine, Inc., 666 F.3d 422, 436 (7th Cir.2012) (finding that a nearly three-month time lapse between the report of sexual harassment and the investigation was too long to constitute effective corrective action).

In *Crawford v. Metropolitan Government of Nashville & Davidson County, Tennessee,* 555 U.S. 271, 129 S.Ct. 846, 172 L.Ed.2d 650 (2009), the Supreme Court held that a worker who is discharged for cooperating with her employer's internal investigation of sexual harassment is protected under Title VII's anti-retaliation provision, § 704(a). The topic of retaliation was covered in Chapter 3. Vicky Crawford, a long-time school district employee, was questioned by a human resources administrator about her supervisor's conduct after the school district had initiated an investigation in response to concerns that several employees had raised about possible sexual harassment. In response to the interviewer's questions, Crawford reported that her supervisor had sexually harassed her and had also harassed other employees. Shortly thereafter, Crawford was fired along with two other employees who worked under the same supervisor and who told about similar harassing conduct when they were questioned in their investigatory interviews. Crawford filed a charge with the EEOC and then sued, alleging that she was fired in retaliation for cooperating in the investigation, although she had been accused of what she claimed to be trumped up charges of embezzlement and drug use. The Sixth Circuit, in a *per curiam* decision, affirmed the district court's grant of summary judgment for the employer, and the Supreme Court reversed.

At issue in the case was whether Crawford's conduct in cooperating with her employer's internal investigation was protected against employer reprisal under either (or both) the "opposition" clause or the "participation" clause of § 704(a) of Title VII, 42 U.S.C. § 2000e–3(a). The Court held that the conduct was protected under the "opposition" clause. Although the *Crawford* case is important for antidiscrimination law generally, it has particular salience for sexual harassment claims, especially claims brought under a hostile work environment theory. If employees feel that they may be vulnerable to retaliation if they respond honestly and candidly to questions in internal investigations of sexual harassment regarding co-workers or supervisors, are they likely to cooperate at all? And if employees do not cooperate, or are not truthful, how can employers protect themselves against liability for sexual harassment?

ii. Discipline. When is discipline short of discharge appropriate in cases of supervisory sexual harassment? *See* Beard v. Flying J., Inc., 266 F.3d 792, 799 (8th Cir.2001) (finding that it was a jury question whether a written warning and suspension without pay were sufficient to establish an affirmative defense to a restaurant manager's sexual harassment of his assistant manager). Is it sufficient if the employer transfers the employee who brings the complaint and tells the alleged harasser to leave the complaining employee alone? What if the transfer is to a different department? A different shift? Another division of the company in a different location? Should the alleged harasser be moved instead? Would your analysis be any different if the harasser were a co-worker instead of a supervisor? *See* Skidmore v. Precision Printing & Pkg., Inc., 188 F.3d 606 (5th Cir.1999). If the employer transfers an alleged harasser to a different facility in another city in response to complaints, is the employer required to notify supervisors in the new location about any past history of sexual harassment complaints regarding the employee? *See* Press Release, EEOC, Dillard's to Pay Half

Million to Settle EEOC Class Sexual Harassment Suit (Apr. 1, 2008), available at *http://www.eeoc.gov/press/4–1–08.html.*

d. *Sexual harassment training programs*: Employer concerns about sexual harassment lawsuits have "spawned a multi-billion dollar sexual harassment training industry staffed by attorneys, consultants, and human resource professionals who offer programs aimed at litigation prevention." Susan Bisom-Rapp, *Fixing Watches with Sledgehammers: The Questionable Embrace of Employee Sexual Harassment Training by the Legal Profession*, 24 T.Jefferson L.Rev. 125, 126 (2002). Professor Bisom-Rapp argues that, although there is "absolutely no empirical support" for the efficacy of such training, the federal courts consider the existence of training programs "as favorable evidence for employers that reasonable steps had been taken to prevent or correct harassment" and to limit liability for punitive damages. *Id.* at 126–27. *See also* Joanna L. Grossman, *The Culture of Compliance: The Final Triumph of Form over Substance in Sexual Harassment Law*, 26 Harv. Women's L.J. 3, 27–49 (2003) (analyzing social science research on preventative measures such as sexual harassment policies and procedures and training programs and concluding that "current preventative efforts employers take may help, but are not sufficient to effect a meaningful reduction in the level of harassment," *id.* at 49); Anne Lawton, *The Bad Apple Theory in Sexual Harassment Law*, 13 George Mason L.Rev. 817 (2005) (critiquing the "individual model" of employer liability under *Ellerth* and *Faragher*, which places the burden of complaining on the victim of harassment while ignoring workplace organizational structures that cause harassment).

6. *The Second Prong of the Employer's Affirmative Defense to Vicarious Liability*: Consider the employer's burden of proof on the second prong of its affirmative defense: "that the plaintiff employee unreasonably failed to take advantage of any preventive or corrective opportunities provided by the employer or to avoid harm otherwise."

a. *Failure to use the employer's complaint procedure*: In *Faragher,* the Court observed that the employee's unreasonable failure to use the employer's complaint procedure "will normally suffice to satisfy the employer's burden under the second element of the defense." 524 U.S. at 808, 118 S.Ct. at 2293. Under what circumstances would a plaintiff's failure to use a complaint procedure be "reasonable"? In *Faragher*, the Court noted that "the City's policy did not include any assurance that the harassing supervisors could be bypassed in registering complaints." *Id.* Is it always reasonable for an employee to forego using a policy that requires complaints to be lodged with the harassing supervisor? What if the employee fears retaliation if she reports harassment? Fear of retaliation will not generally excuse an employee from an obligation to report harassment; courts have concluded that the proper approach is to report the misconduct and then, if necessary, bring a complaint for retaliation. *See* Alvarez v. Des Moines Bolt Supply, Inc., 626 F.3d 410, 422 (8th Cir.2010) (collecting cases). Could a complaint procedure be so cumbersome or intimidating that it would be reasonable not to use it? Is it unreasonable for an employee to complain about harassment by using the grievance procedure provided under the union's collective bargaining agreement instead of the employer's internal reporting procedures? *See* Watts v. Kroger Co., 170 F.3d 505, 511 (5th Cir.1999) (no). What if the victim complains to the union steward and then fails to follow the steward's advice to report to the employer? What if the employee's complaints to the union steward do not mention the sexual nature of the harassing conduct? *See* Casiano v. AT&T, Corp., 213 F.3d 278 (5th Cir.2000).

b. *Failure to take advantage of "corrective opportunities" or "to avoid harm otherwise"*: When is it reasonable for an employee to fail to "take advantage of * * * corrective opportunities provided by the employer"? What if the employer offers to transfer the victim to a different department in order to keep her out of daily contact with her harasser? When would it be reasonable to refuse such an offer? How can an employer prove that a plaintiff has unreasonably failed "to avoid harm otherwise"? *See generally* Margaret Johnson, *"Avoiding Harm Otherwise": Reframing Women Employees' Responses to the Harms of Sexual Harassment,* 80 Temp.L.Rev. 743 (2007); James J. McDonald, Jr. & Daniel S. Fellner, *A Plaintiff's Obligation to "Avoid Harm Otherwise": New Life for the Welcomeness Defense*, 25 Employee Rel.L.J. 17 (1999). Consider the following:

i. A female employee, on an out-of-town business trip with her male supervisor, was working on a project in his hotel room late at night when he made sexual advances toward her. She successfully rebuffed him, left his room immediately, and reported the incident to the company the next day. The supervisor was reprimanded and no other incidents occurred until another business trip six months later. At this time, following a day of conference meetings, the employee accepted her supervisor's invitation to go "bar-hopping." Afterwards, around midnight, he invited her to his room to talk and assured her that his intentions were innocent. She agreed on those terms, but once she was in his room, he sexually assaulted her. She managed to flee the room and subsequently filed a Title VII claim against the employer. Assuming that the employer can satisfy the first prong of its affirmative defense, can it satisfy the second prong? Has the plaintiff unreasonably "failed to avoid harm otherwise"? *See* Brown v. Perry 184 F.3d 388 (4th Cir.1999) (yes).

ii. A male supervisor in a restaurant made several isolated but unwelcome and offensive sexual remarks to a female employee. She told him that his comments were offensive, but she failed to report his conduct to her employer, despite the existence of a widely disseminated anti-harassment policy with effective procedures. The offensive conduct ceased for eight months. Then the supervisor allegedly exposed his genitals to the employee, and she immediately reported the incident to her employer. The employer promptly confronted the supervisor, who then resigned. In response to the employee's Title VII claim of vicarious liability for sexual harassment, can the employer satisfy the second prong of its affirmative defense? *See* Corcoran v. Shoney's Colonial, Inc., 24 F.Supp.2d 601 (W.D.Va.1998) (no).

c. *Delay in complaining*: Assume that an employer has a widely disseminated policy against sexual harassment that (1) defines sexual harassment, (2) identifies employees with authority to deal with harassment complaints, (3) describes the discipline that the company may impose on harassers, and (4) prohibits retaliation for making harassment complaints. The plaintiff, a female employee, who received a copy of the anti-harassment policy when she began her employment, was subjected to harassment by her immediate supervisors for over two years before she reported the conduct to the company's Human Resources Department. Within eleven days of receiving her complaint, the company investigated the allegations and terminated the managers. The plaintiff alleges that she worked in an isolated environment and that the harassing supervisors were the only managers that she reported to in her state. Assuming that the employer has satisfied the first prong of its affirmative defense on these facts, has it also satisfied the second prong? *See* Montero v. AGCO Corp., 192 F.3d 856, 863–64 (9th Cir.1999) (yes). While an employee's limited delay in complaining might be justified, courts have found that even as little as three months' delay is unreasonable. *Compare* Craig v. M & O Agencies, Inc., 496 F.3d 1047, 1057–58 (9th Cir.2007) (nineteen-day delay was not unreasonable where "an employee in [plaintiff's] position may have hoped the situation would resolve itself without the need of filing a formal complaint") with Matvia v. Bald Head Island Mgmt., Inc., 259 F.3d 261, 269–70 (4th Cir.2001) (three-month delay unreasonable); Terry v. Laurel Oaks Behavioral Health Center, Inc., 1 F.Supp.3d 1250, 1275 (M.D.Ala. 2014) (six month delay unreasonable); Taylor v. Solis, 571 F.3d 1313, 1318–20 (D.C.Cir.2009) (same); Gawley v. Ind. Univ., 276 F.3d 301, 312 (7th Cir.2001) (seven-month delay unreasonable). An employee may be excused for a delay in reporting harassment, however, "if the employee can demonstrate a truly credible threat of retaliation." *See* Alvarez v. Des Moines Bolt Supply, Inc., 626 F.3d 410, 422 (8th Cir.2010) (internal quotation omitted). What evidence does the employee have to present to demonstrate a credible threat of retaliation?

d. *Futility of complaining*: An employee who was subjected to hostile environment sexual harassment by her supervisor failed to report the conduct because she believed the following: (1) that her employer has been unresponsive to complaints of sexual harassment brought by other employees, (2) that employees who complained were subjected to subtle forms of workplace retaliation by their supervisors, and (3) that her supervisor is a close friend of several high-level managers in the company. Assuming that the employer can meet the first prong of its affirmative defense, could it satisfy the second prong? Would the plaintiff's failure to report be unreasonable? Would it have been "futile" for her to report the harassing conduct when it began? *See* Monteagudo v. Asociacion de Empleados del Estado Libre Asociado de P.R., 554 F.3d 164, 171–72 (1st Cir.2009) (upholding jury finding that plaintiff was not unreasonable in failing to complain about harassment where all the managers appeared to be friends with the harassing supervisor and ruling that employer failed to meet second prong of *Ellerth/Faragher* defense); Barrett v. Applied Radiant Energy Corp.,

240 F.3d 262, 268 (4th Cir.2001) ("We cannot accept the argument that reporting sexual harassment is rendered futile merely because members of the management team happen to be friends.").

7. A conflict has developed among the courts of appeals on the question of what an employer must prove in order to satisfy the requirements of the *Ellerth/Faragher* affirmative defense, particularly in circumstances that involve a single severe instance of supervisory harassment and a swift, effective employer response to a complaint about that harassment. *Compare* Frederick v. Sprint/United Mgmt. Co., 246 F.3d 1305, 1313 (11th Cir.2001) ("Both elements must be satisfied for the defendant-employer to avoid liability, and the defendant bears the burden of proof on both elements."), *with* McCurdy v. Ark. State Police, 375 F.3d 762, 771–74 (8th Cir.2004) (applying only the first prong of the affirmative defense in a case involving a single instance of harassment which the employer responded to promptly). As one district court succinctly described the argument being made by defendant-employers in these cases:

> In the pending motion, [the defendant] contends—for the first time—that it is not required to satisfy *Ellerth/Faragher's* second prong, despite the Supreme Court's clear directive that both prongs are necessary elements of the defense. Specifically, [the defendant] argues that where, as here, the sexual harassment at issue is a single isolated incident, the employer is entitled to a modified *Ellerth/Faragher* defense, which drops the second prong's requirement that the plaintiff "unreasonably failed to take advantage" of corrective or preventative opportunities. Under this proposed modification, [the defendant's] prompt and effective response to [the] complaint would suffice to avoid liability, notwithstanding [the defendant's] inability to meet the second prong.

Alalade v. AWS Assistance Corp., 796 F. Supp. 2d 936, 938 (N.D. Ind. 2011). Should an employer be liable for a single act of harassment if it takes prompt and effective steps to address the harassment? Will effective corrective action in response to a prompt complaint generally mean that a plaintiff will be unable to show that the harassment was "severe or pervasive"? Will prompt corrective action limit the damages available to the employee? *See supra* Note 8 on punitive damages. *See* Joanna L. Grossman, *Moving Forward, Looking Back: A Retrospective on Sexual Harassment Law*, 95 B.U. L. Rev. 1029, 1044–45 (2015) (criticizing the courts that have ignored the requirement that an employer satisfy both prongs of the affirmative defense); Martha S. West, *Preventing Sexual Harassment: The Federal Courts' Wake-up Call for Women*, 68 Brook.L.Rev. 457 (2002) (same).

8. *Liability for Punitive Damages—The* Kolstad *Case*: In *Kolstad v. American Dental Association*, 527 U.S. 526, 119 S.Ct. 2118, 144 L.Ed.2d 494 (1999), discussed in Chapter 2, the Supreme Court relied on the Civil Rights Act of 1991, 42 U.S.C. § 1981a(b)(1), and agency principles to determine when

liability for punitive damages should be imputed to the employer. Section 1981a(b)(1) permits awards of punitive damages when the employer acts "with malice or with reckless indifference to the federally protected rights of an aggrieved individual." *See Kolstad*, 527 U.S. at 530, 119 S.Ct. at 2121. Relying on the Restatement (Second) of Agency § 217(C)(c), the *Kolstad* Court ruled that an employer may be held liable for punitive damages where an agent is acting in a "managerial capacity" and is "acting in the scope of employment." *Id.* at 543, 119 S.Ct. at 2128. For example, in *Deters v. Equifax Credit Information Services, Inc.*, 202 F.3d 1262 (10th Cir.2000), the court applied *Kolstad* to uphold an award of punitive damages in a sexual harassment case. The court in *Deters* concluded that "recklessness and malice are to be inferred when a manager responsible for setting or enforcing policy in the area of discrimination does not respond to complaints, despite knowledge of serious harassment." *Id.* at 1269.

Kolstad also recognized that employers could not be vicariously liable for the manager's unlawful discrimination that is "contrary to the employer's 'good faith efforts to comply with Title VII.' " 527 U.S. at 545, 119 S. Ct. at 2129. For example, an employer was permitted to assert a good-faith defense to liability for punitive damages under *Kolstad* where the employer was not aware that its restaurant manager was harassing his subordinate, a bartender, and it had made a "good faith attempt" to establish and enforce an antidiscrimination policy. Cooke v. Stefani Mgmt. Serv., Inc., 250 F.3d 564, 568 (7th Cir.2001). *See also* Harsco Corp. v. Renner, 475 F.3d 1179, 1189 (10th Cir.2007) (affirming denial of punitive damages where plaintiff "did not submit sufficient evidence that the company, as opposed to its managerial employees, failed to make good-faith efforts to comply with Title VII"). Simply having an antidiscrimination policy is not enough to avoid punitive damages. "The trend among the Circuits is to focus on the implementation rather than the mere existence" of a policy. West v. Tyson Foods, Inc., 374 Fed. Appx. 624, 639 (6th Cir.2010). *See also* E.E.O.C. v. New Breed Logistics, 783 F.3d 1057, 1073–74 (6th Cir.2015) (employer who failed to distribute its policy to 80 percent of employees was not engaging in good faith efforts to comply with Title VII).

Kolstad also cited the Restatement (Second) of Agency § 217(C)(a): "Punitive damages can properly be awarded against a master or other principal * * * , if (a) the principal authorized the doing and manner of the act * * * ." 527 U.S. at 542, 119 S.Ct. at 2128. After *Kolstad*, if the harassing manager is a high-level employee who can be considered a proxy for the company, can the employer defend against punitive damages regardless of its good faith efforts to comply with Title VII? *See* Passantino v. Johnson & Johnson Consumer Prods., Inc., 212 F.3d 493, 517 (9th Cir.2000) (ordering a new trial for a determination whether the harassers held "positions sufficiently high up" within the employer, in which case "they would be [the employer's] proxies, which would bar [the employer] from asserting a vicarious liability defense to punitive damages"). *See generally* Joseph A. Seiner, *The Failure of Punitive Damages in Employment Discrimination*

Cases: A Call for Change, 50 Wm. & Mary L.Rev. 735 (2008) (critiquing the law on punitive damages after *Kolstad* in light of a survey of all reported district court decisions addressing punitive damages during 2004 and 2005).

9. *Individual Liability of Agents for Harassment*: The majority of the courts of appeals have held that supervisors are not individually liable under either Title VII or the ADEA. *See* Dearth v. Collins, 441 F.3d 931, 933 (11th Cir.2006); Wathen v. Gen. Elec. Co., 115 F.3d 400, 404 (6th Cir.1997) (collecting cases from the Second, Fifth, Seventh, Eighth, Tenth, and D.C. Circuits). Individual liability of agents was covered in Chapter 2. What arguments would you make that imposing individual liability on agents of employers, particularly in the sexual harassment cases, would further the objectives of eliminating discrimination in the workplace? Are employer's agents generally individually liable for their workplace torts? A number of state courts, interpreting state human rights statutes, have held that supervisors can be found personally liable for their own acts of sexual harassment. *See, e.g.*, Brown v. Scott Paper Worldwide Co., 20 P.3d 921, 926 (Wash. 2001); Vivian v. Madison, 601 N.W.2d 872 (Iowa 1999). In addition, professionals who sexually harass their subordinates may risk discipline from licensing bodies. *See Chicago Attorney Loses License to Practice for One Year in Wake of Harassment Verdict*, 21 Hum. Resources Rep. 21 (BNA) No.11, at 301 (Mar. 24, 2003) (citing *In re: Gerald Fishman*, Ill. ARDC, No. 01 CH 109, 2/24/03).

10. *Rights of Alleged Harassers*: Employers may hesitate to discipline or discharge alleged harassers because of concerns about their legal rights to fair treatment. For example, high-level professional employees may be protected by individual contracts, unionized employees may be covered by just cause protections in a collective bargaining agreement, college and university teachers may have academic tenure, and public school teachers may have statutory tenure. Public sector employees may have civil service protections or constitutional rights to due process. *See, e.g.* McDonald v. Wise, 769 F.3d 1202, 1213–14 (10th Cir.2014) (city employee fired for sexual harassment was denied due process when he was discharged without any hearing). At-will employees may have common law or statutory protections against wrongful discharge. *See generally* Hannah Katherine Vorwerk, *The Forgotten Interest Group: Reforming Title VII to Address the Concerns of Workers While Eliminating Sexual Harassment*, 48 Vand.L.Rev. 1019 (1995).

Unionized employees who are discharged for sexual harassment may seek reinstatement by filing a grievance under their collective bargaining agreement. Courts take different views as to whether reinstatement of an employee discharged for sexual harassment is a violation of public policy. *Compare* Chrysler Motors Corp. v. Int'l Union Allied Indus. Workers of Am., 959 F.2d 685 (7th Cir.1992) (upholding arbitration award of reinstatement for grievant who was terminated for sexually assaulting a female worker), *with* Newsday, Inc. v. Long Island Typographical Union, 915 F.2d 840 (2d Cir.1990) (vacating labor arbitrator's award of reinstatement of alleged harasser as contrary to public policy). *See generally* Judith Stilz Ogden, *Do*

Public Policy Grounds Still Exist for Vacating Arbitration Awards?, 20 Hofstra Lab. & Emp.L.J. 87, 113–15 (2002).

At-will employees accused of harassment may have rights to fair procedures under common law theories of implied contract or the implied-in-law obligation of good faith and fair dealing. *See* Cotran v. Rollins Hudig Hall Int'l, Inc., 17 Cal.4th 93, 69 Cal.Rptr.2d 900, 948 P.2d 412 (1998) (holding that, when an employee under an implied contract of employment is discharged for sexual harassment, the employer has an obligation to conduct a reasonable investigation and provide the employee with notice of the alleged misconduct and an opportunity to respond). *But see* McCullough v. Univ. of Ark. 559 F.3d 855, 861 (8th Cir.2009) (holding that employer's good faith belief that employee was guilty of conduct was sufficient to justify discharge). Moreover, employees who are discharged for sexual harassment may bring claims against their employers for torts such as defamation, Meloff v. New York Life Ins. Co., 240 F.3d 138 (2d Cir.2001), and intentional or negligent infliction of mental distress, Malik v. Carrier Corp., 202 F.3d 97 (2d Cir.2000). An employee who is fired for sexual harassment may also have a cause of action against his former co-workers who reported his conduct to the employer during its investigation. Theories of liability might include intentional infliction of mental distress, invasion of privacy, defamation, and interference with advantageous economic relations. *See, e.g.,* Cole v. Chandler, 752 A.2d 1189 (Me.2000).

11. How does the Supreme Court's analysis in *Ellerth* and *Faragher* relate to its per curiam decision in *Clark County School District v. Breeden*, 532 U.S. 268, 121 S.Ct. 1508, 149 L.Ed.2d 509 (2001)? (*Breeden* is discussed *supra,* Section B.2, Note 5, following *Harris v. Forklift.*) In light of *Breeden,* how would you advise an *employee* who tells you that she is uncomfortable with her supervisor's occasional sexual jokes or comments, which she sincerely perceives to be offensive and embarrassing? At what point is it reasonable for your client to complain about her supervisor's conduct? If your client complains too early, after only one or two incidents, she may be disciplined for being a "complainer." If, under *Breeden,* no reasonable person would believe that the conduct was severe or pervasive under Title VII, she cannot succeed on a retaliation claim if her employer disciplines or discharges her for her subjectively sincere but objectively unreasonable complaint about her supervisor's conduct. If she waits to complain, how long should she wait? If the employer has an adequate complaint procedure, which she unreasonably delays in using, the employer should be able to prevail on both prongs of its *Ellerth/Faragher* affirmative defense. Employees, unskilled in the intricacies of sexual harassment law, may lose the protections of Title VII if they misjudge the objective severity of the conduct and "unreasonably" complain too early or too late.

How would you advise an *employer* after *Breeden?* When an employee complains about a supervisor's sexually harassing conduct, how can the employer determine whether the employee's perceptions are sincere or reasonable? If the employer determines after an investigation that the employee's beliefs were sincere but unreasonable under *Breeden* and, therefore, chooses not to take corrective action, what are the possible consequences? The supervisor may continue his offensive behavior, and the employee may file a charge of discrimination and then bring a Title VII action. If a judge or jury then determines that the supervisor's conduct was "severe or pervasive" from the perspective of a reasonable person, the employer will not be able to establish either prong of its affirmative defense under *Ellerth* and *Faragher*. Employers, unskilled in the intricacies of sexual harassment law, may lose their defenses under Title VII if they misjudge the objective severity of their supervisor's conduct.

Breeden demonstrates the importance for both plaintiffs and defendants of correctly assessing whether language or conduct is objectively "severe or pervasive" harassment. Does *Breeden* create incentives for employers to discipline or discharge an employee the first time that he or she complains about isolated and trivial harassment, rather than to attempt to respond to the complaint? Do *Ellerth* and *Faragher* similarly create incentives for employers to discipline or discharge alleged harassers, even for complaints of isolated trivial harassment, just to avoid the costs of investigation and the potential of misjudging the reasonableness of the complaint?

12. *The Impact of* Ellerth *and* Faragher *on Supervisory Harassment on the Basis of Other Protected Statuses*: The lower federal courts have assumed that the vicarious liability principles and affirmative defenses for supervisory sexual harassment apply to cases of supervisory harassment based on race, national origin, religion, age, and disability. *See, e.g.*, Cerros v. Steel Tech., Inc., 288 F.3d 1040, 1048 (7th Cir.2002) (race and national origin); Abrahmson v. William Patterson Coll. of N.J., 260 F.3d 265, 280–81 (3d Cir.2001) (religion); Weyers v. Lear Ops. Corp., 359 F.3d 1049, 1056–57 (8th Cir.2004) (age); Arrieta-Colon v. Wal-Mart P.R., Inc., 434 F.3d 75, 85–86 (1st Cir.2006) (disability). *Vance*, ___ U.S. ___, 133 S.Ct. 2434, 186 L.Ed.2d 565 (2013), involved a hostile work environment claim of racial harassment. In deciding the case, the Supreme Court noted that "[s]everal federal courts of appeals have held that *Faragher* and *Ellerth* apply to other types of hostile environment claims, including race based claims." *Id.* at 2442 n. 3. The question of whether the affirmative defense is available in race-based claims was not raised by either party and the Court "assume[d] that the framework announced in *Faragher* and *Ellerth* applies to cases such as this one." *Id.*

13. *State Antidiscrimination Laws and Title VII*: In the aftermath of the 1998 Supreme Court cases of *Oncale, Ellerth,* and *Faragher,* state courts have been addressing the question of whether and how these decisions interpreting federal law affect state antidiscrimination laws. For example, in *Hampel v. Food Ingredients Specialties, Inc.,* 89 Ohio St.3d 169, 729 N.E.2d 726, 733–34 (2000), the Supreme Court of Ohio relied on *Oncale* to find that same-sex sexual harassment is actionable under the state civil rights law. In a diversity case, a federal district court subsequently interpreted *Hampel* as having adopted the *Ellerth/Faragher* standard for imposing vicarious liability on employers in cases of sexual harassment by supervisors.

McCormick v. Kmart Distrib. Ctr., 163 F.Supp.2d 807, 825 (N.D.Ohio 2001). The Michigan Supreme Court has rejected the approach taken in *Ellerth* and *Faragher* for sexual harassment claims brought under the Michigan Civil Rights Act. Chambers v. Trettco, Inc., 463 Mich. 297, 614 N.W.2d 910, 915–16 (Mich.2000) (holding that employers are liable for harassment by supervisors only if they are aware of the conduct and fail to take prompt, effective corrective action). The California Supreme Court held that employers are strictly liable under the Fair Employment and Housing Act (FEHA) for sexual harassment by supervisors, but that the "avoidable consequences doctrine" may limit the damages that a plaintiff can recover under a FEHA claim. State Dep't of Health Servs. v. Superior Court, 31 Cal.4th 1026, 6 Cal.Rptr.3d 441, 79 P.3d 556 (2003). Thus, for assessing damages, California has adopted the reasoning of the *Ellerth/Faragher* affirmative defense, which "encourages preventive action by both the employer and employee." 79 P.3d at 564. *Ellerth/Faragher* holding, however, the California rule affects only damages and does not limit liability. *Id.* at 565. Illinois holds employers strictly liable for a supervisor's harassment of an employee, even in the absence of a tangible employment action. Sangamon County Sheriff's Dep't v. Ill. Hum. Rights Comm'n, 908 N.E.2d 39, 46 (Ill.2009) (finding "the federal case law to be unhelpful in interpreting" § 2–102(D) of the Illinois Human Right Act,). What are the advantages and disadvantages of having different rules of liability for sexual harassment under state and federal antidiscrimination law?

PENNSYLVANIA STATE POLICE V. SUDERS

Supreme Court of the United States, 2004.
542 U.S. 129, 124 S.Ct. 2342, 159 L.Ed.2d 204.

JUSTICE GINSBURG delivered the opinion of the Court.

Plaintiff-respondent Nancy Drew Suders alleged sexually harassing conduct by her supervisors, officers of the Pennsylvania State Police (PSP), of such severity she was forced to resign. The question presented concerns the proof burdens parties bear when a sexual harassment/constructive discharge claim of that character is asserted under Title VII of the Civil Rights Act of 1964.

To establish hostile work environment, plaintiffs * * * must show harassing behavior "sufficiently severe or pervasive to alter the conditions of [their] employment." *Meritor Savings Bank, FSB v. Vinson*, 477 U.S. 57, 67, 106 S.Ct. 2399, 91 L.Ed.2d (1986) * * * . Beyond that, we hold, to establish "constructive discharge," the plaintiff must make a further showing: She must show that the abusive working environment became so intolerable that her resignation qualified as a fitting response. An employer may defend against such a claim by showing both (1) that it had installed a readily accessible and effective policy for reporting and resolving complaints of sexual harassment, and (2) that the plaintiff unreasonably failed to avail herself of that employer-provided preventive or remedial apparatus. This affirmative defense will not be available to the employer, however, if the plaintiff quits in reasonable response to an employer-sanctioned adverse action officially changing her employment status or situation, for example, a humiliating demotion, extreme cut in pay, or transfer to a position in which she would face unbearable working conditions. In so ruling today, we follow the path marked by our 1998 decisions in *Burlington Industries, Inc. v. Ellerth*, 524 U.S. 742, 118 S.Ct. 2257, 141 L.Ed.2d 633, and *Faragher v. Boca Raton*, 524 U.S. 775, 118 S.Ct. 2275, 141 L.Ed.2d 662.

I

Because this case was decided against Suders in the District Court on the PSP's motion for summary judgment, we recite the facts, as summarized by the Court of Appeals, in the light most favorable to Suders. In March 1998, the PSP hired Suders as a police communications operator for the McConnellsburg barracks. Suders' supervisors were Sergeant Eric D. Easton, Station Commander at the McConnellsburg barracks, Patrol Corporal William D. Baker, and Corporal Eric B. Prendergast. Those three supervisors subjected Suders to a continuous barrage of sexual harassment that ceased only when she resigned from the force.

Easton "would bring up [the subject of] people having sex with animals" each time Suders entered his office. He told Prendergast, in front of Suders, that young girls should be given instruction in how to gratify men with oral sex. Easton also would sit down near Suders, wearing spandex shorts, and spread his legs apart. Apparently imitating a move popularized by television wrestling, Baker repeatedly made an obscene gesture in Suders' presence by grabbing his genitals and shouting out a vulgar comment inviting oral sex. Baker made this gesture as many as five-to-ten times per night throughout Suders' employment at the barracks. Suders once told Baker she " 'd[id]n't think [he] should be doing this' "; Baker responded by jumping on a chair and again performing the gesture, with the accompanying vulgarity. Further, Baker would "rub his rear end in front of her and remark 'I have a nice ass, don't I?' " Prendergast told Suders " 'the village idiot could do her job' "; wearing black gloves, he would pound on furniture to intimidate her.

In June 1998, Prendergast accused Suders of taking a missing accident file home with her. After that incident, Suders approached the PSP's Equal Employment Opportunity Officer, Virginia Smith-Elliott, and told her she "might need some help." Smith-Elliott gave Suders her telephone number, but neither woman followed up on the conversation. On August 18, 1998, Suders contacted Smith-Elliott again, this time stating that she was being harassed and was afraid. Smith-Elliott told

Suders to file a complaint, but did not tell her how to obtain the necessary form. Smith-Elliott's response and the manner in which it was conveyed appeared to Suders insensitive and unhelpful.

Two days later, Suders' supervisors arrested her for theft, and Suders resigned from the force. The theft arrest occurred in the following circumstances. Suders had several times taken a computer-skills exam to satisfy a PSP job requirement. Each time, Suders' supervisors told her that she had failed. Suders one day came upon her exams in a set of drawers in the women's locker room. She concluded that her supervisors had never forwarded the tests for grading and that their reports of her failures were false. Regarding the tests as her property, Suders removed them from the locker room. Upon finding that the exams had been removed, Suders' supervisors devised a plan to arrest her for theft. The officers dusted the drawer in which the exams had been stored with a theft-detection powder that turns hands blue when touched. As anticipated by Easton, Baker, and Prendergast, Suders attempted to return the tests to the drawer, whereupon her hands turned telltale blue. The supervisors then apprehended and handcuffed her, photographed her blue hands, and commenced to question her. Suders had previously prepared a written resignation, which she tendered soon after the supervisors detained her. Nevertheless, the supervisors initially refused to release her. Instead, they brought her to an interrogation room, gave her warnings under *Miranda v. Arizona,* 384 U.S. 436, 86 S.Ct. 1602, 16 L.Ed.2d 694 (1966), and continued to question her. Suders reiterated that she wanted to resign, and Easton then let her leave. The PSP never brought theft charges against her.

In September 2000, Suders sued the PSP in Federal District Court, alleging, *inter alia,* that she had been subjected to sexual harassment and constructively discharged, in violation of Title VII of the Civil Rights Act of 1964. At the close of discovery, the District Court granted the PSP's motion for summary judgment. Suders' testimony, the District Court recognized, sufficed to permit a trier of fact to conclude that the supervisors had created a hostile work environment. The court nevertheless held that the PSP was not vicariously liable for the supervisors' conduct. * * *

Suders' hostile work environment claim was untenable as a matter of law, the District Court stated, because she "unreasonably failed to avail herself of the PSP's internal procedures for reporting any harassment." Resigning just two days after she first mentioned anything about harassment to Equal Employment Opportunity Officer Smith-Elliott, the court noted, Suders had "never given [the PSP] the opportunity to respond to [her] complaints." The District Court did not address Suders' constructive discharge claim.

The Court of Appeals for the Third Circuit reversed and remanded the case for disposition on the merits. The Third Circuit agreed with the District Court that Suders had presented evidence sufficient for a trier of fact to conclude that the supervisors had engaged in a "pattern of sexual harassment that was pervasive and regular." But the appeals court disagreed with the District Court in two fundamental respects. First, the Court of Appeals held that, even assuming the PSP could assert the affirmative defense described in *Ellerth* and *Faragher*, genuine issues of material fact existed concerning the effectiveness of the PSP's "program * * * to address sexual harassment claims." Second, the appeals court held that the District Court erred in failing to recognize that Suders had stated a claim of constructive discharge due to the hostile work environment.

* * *

The Court of Appeals then made the ruling challenged here: It held that "a constructive discharge, when proved, constitutes a tangible employment action." * * * [T]he Court of Appeals remanded Suders' Title VII claim for trial.

This Court granted certiorari, to resolve the disagreement among the Circuits on the question whether a constructive discharge brought about by supervisor harassment ranks as a tangible employment action and therefore precludes assertion of the affirmative defense articulated in *Ellerth* and *Faragher*. We conclude that an employer does not have recourse to the *Ellerth/Faragher* affirmative defense when a supervisor's official act precipitates the constructive discharge; absent such a "tangible employment action," however, the defense is available to the employer whose supervisors are charged with harassment. We therefore vacate the Third Circuit's judgment and remand the case for further proceedings.

* * *

[In a portion of the *Suders* opinion excerpted in Chapter 3, the Court recognized that constructive discharge doctrine applies in Title VII cases.]

The constructive discharge here at issue stems from, and can be regarded as an aggravated case of, sexual harassment or hostile work environment. For an atmosphere of sexual harassment or hostility to be actionable, we reiterate, the offending behavior "must be sufficiently severe or pervasive to alter the conditions of the victim's employment and create an abusive working environment." *Meritor,* 477 U.S., at 67, 106 S.Ct. 2399. A hostile-environment constructive discharge claim entails something more: A plaintiff who advances such a compound claim must show working conditions so intolerable that a reasonable person would have felt compelled to resign. * * *[8]

[H]arassment so intolerable as to cause a resignation may be effected through co-worker conduct, unofficial supervisory conduct, or official company acts. Unlike an actual termination, which is *always* effected through an official act of the company, a constructive discharge need not be. A constructive discharge involves both an employee's decision to leave and precipitating conduct: The former involves no official action; the latter, like a harassment claim without any constructive discharge assertion, may or may not involve official action.

To be sure, a constructive discharge is functionally the same as an actual termination in damages-enhancing respects. As the Third Circuit observed, both "en[d] the employer-employee relationship," and both "inflic[t] * * * direct economic harm." 325 F.3d, at 460. But when an official act does not underlie the constructive discharge, the *Ellerth* and *Faragher* analysis, we here hold, calls for extension of the affirmative defense to the employer. As those leading decisions indicate, official directions and declarations are the acts most likely to be brought home to the employer, the measures over which the employer can exercise greatest control. Absent "an official act of the enterprise," as the last straw, the employer ordinarily would have no particular reason to suspect that a resignation is not the typical kind daily occurring in the work force. And as *Ellerth* and *Faragher* further point out, an official act reflected in company records—a demotion or a reduction in compensation, for example—shows "beyond question" that the supervisor has used his managerial or controlling position to the employee's disadvantage. See *Ellerth,* 524 U.S., at 760, 118 S.Ct. 2257. Absent such an official act, the extent to which the supervisor's misconduct has been aided by the agency relation, as we earlier recounted, is less certain. That uncertainty, our precedent establishes, justifies affording the employer the chance to establish, through the *Ellerth/Faragher* affirmative defense, that it should not be held vicariously liable.

The Third Circuit drew the line differently. Under its formulation, the affirmative defense would be eliminated in all hostile-environment constructive discharge cases, but retained, as *Ellerth* and *Faragher* require, in "ordinary" hostile work environment cases, *i.e.,* cases involving no tangible employment action. That placement of the line, anomalously, would make the *graver* claim of hostile-environment constructive discharge *easier* to prove than its lesser included component, hostile work environment. * * *

---

8 [A] prevailing constructive discharge plaintiff is entitled to all damages available for formal discharge. The plaintiff may recover postresignation damages, including both backpay and, in fitting circumstances, frontpay, as well as the compensatory and punitive damages now provided for Title VII claims generally.

We agree with the Third Circuit that the case, in its current posture, presents genuine issues of material fact concerning Suders' hostile work environment and constructive discharge claims.[11] We hold, however, that the Court of Appeals erred in declaring the affirmative defense described in *Ellerth* and *Faragher* never available in constructive discharge cases. Accordingly, we vacate the Third Circuit's judgment and remand the case for further proceedings consistent with this opinion.

[The dissenting opinion of JUSTICE THOMAS is omitted.]

NOTES AND QUESTIONS

1. *Constructive Discharge*: The Supreme Court in *Suders* granted certiorari to resolve a Circuit split "on the question of whether a constructive discharge brought about by supervisor harassment ranks as a tangible employment action and therefore precludes * * * the [*Ellerth/Faragher*] affirmative defense." 542 U.S. at 140, 124 S.Ct. at 2350. Although the question of what constitutes "constructive discharge" under Title VII was not directly before the Court, Justice Ginsburg addressed the issue by acknowledging, "We agree with the lower courts and the EEOC that Title VII encompasses employer liability for a constructive discharge." *Id.* at 143, 124 S.Ct. at 2352. Claims for constructive discharge are raised in many Title VII cases, but they are very common in sexual harassment cases. Professor Martha Chamallas notes that "[t]he reason constructive discharge cases are so numerous is that sexual harassment victims so often quit their job in response to their discriminatory treatment." Martha Chamallas, *Title VII's Midlife Crisis: The Case of Constructive Discharge,* 77 S.Cal.L.Rev. 307, 310 & n.14 (2004) (citing various studies indicating that from one-tenth to about one-fourth of identified sexual harassment victims leave work due to resignation or discharge).

2. *Remedies for a Compound Hostile Environment/Constructive Discharge Claim*: How do remedies differ for an employee who prevails on a "compound" hostile environment/constructive discharge claim as opposed to an "ordinary" hostile environment claim? *See generally* Chamallas, *supra* note 1, at 319–21 (discussing the differences in remedies). The Court in *Suders* observes that "a constructive discharge is functionally the same as an actual termination in damages-enhancing respects" because both terminate employment and cause "direct economic harm." 542 U.S. at 148, 124 S.Ct. at 2355 (citations omitted). How and why does the Court in *Suders* treat them differently?

3. *Intolerable or Aggravated Harassment*: In *Suders,* Justice Ginsburg concluded that to prevail on a "compound hostile-environment constructive discharge claim," a plaintiff must establish what amounts to an "*aggravated* case of[ ] sexual harassment or hostile work environment." 542 U.S. at 146,

[11] Although most of the discriminatory behavior Suders alleged involved unofficial conduct, the events surrounding her computer-skills exams were less obviously unofficial.

124 S.Ct. at 2354 (emphasis added). In such a case, the plaintiff "must show working conditions *so intolerable* that a *reasonable person* would have felt *compelled* to resign." *Id.* at 147, 124 S.Ct. at 2354 (emphasis added). Courts have noted that, unlike the test for "severity or pervasiveness," the test for whether conditions were so intolerable that they could support constructive discharge includes only an objective analysis, with no consideration of the plaintiffs' subjective feelings. *See, e.g.,* Bryant v. Jones, 575 F.3d 1281, 1298 (11th Cir.2009). Should this objective analysis take into account the gender of the victim? Professor Camille Hébert argues that "it would be appropriate and helpful for courts to apply a gender-conscious standard of reasonableness in judging women's responses to sexual harassment." L. Camille Hébert, *Why Don't "Reasonable Women" Complain About Sexual Harassment?,* 82 Ind.L.J. 711, 713 (2007). Does the decision in *Suders* support this approach?

4. *Unofficial Supervisory Conduct vs. Official Company Acts*: The Supreme Court in *Suders* notes that "[u]nlike an actual termination, which is *always* effected through an official act of the company, a constructive discharge need not be. A constructive discharge involves both an employee's decision to leave and precipitating conduct: The former involves no official action; the latter, like a harassment claim without any constructive discharge assertion, may or may not involve official action." The Third Circuit below had concluded that a constructive discharge always constituted a "tangible employment action," making the *Ellerth/Faragher* affirmative defense unavailable in constructive discharge cases. The Court rejected that approach, concluding that an employer will be vicariously liable for a hostile environment/constructive discharge case when "an official act" led to the employee's reasonable decision to quit. If the decision to quit was reasonable, but it was prompted by "unofficial" supervisory conduct, the employer is entitled to present the *Ellerth/Faragher* affirmative defense, and thus perhaps to avoid liability. Is the distinction between official and unofficial supervisory acts an easy one to draw? In note 11 of *Suders*, the Court observed that most of the harassing conduct that Suders complained of did not involve "official acts," but that "the events surrounding her computer-skills exams were less obviously unofficial." 542 U.S. at 152 n.11, 124 S.Ct. at 2357 n.11. If you were Suders' counsel on remand, what arguments would you make that any or all of these "events" or any other alleged supervisory acts were "official acts"? *See* Current Events, LeiLani J. Hart, Pennsylvania State Police v. Suders, 124 S.Ct. 2342 (2004), 13 Am.U.J. Gender Soc.Pol'y & L. 219, 231(2005). If none of the supervisory conduct were to be found an "official act," would the defendant be likely to establish the elements of the *Ellerth/Faragher* affirmative defense on the facts in *Suders*? Explain why or why not.

5. *Elements of a Constructive Discharge Claim After* Suders: In his dissent in *Suders* (which has not been reproduced here), Justice Thomas criticized the lax standards that many courts have used for defining the elements of constructive discharge. He noted that "a majority of Courts of Appeals have declined to impose a specific intent or reasonable foreseeability

requirement" in Title VII constructive discharge cases. 542 U.S. at 153, 124 S.Ct. at 2358 (Thomas, J., dissenting). Both before and after *Suders,* however, some courts have explicitly imposed an intent requirement as an element of a claim for constructive discharge. For example, after *Suders,* the Court of Appeals for the Eighth Circuit applied a two-step standard to deny, as a matter of law, a claim for constructive discharge that was brought in conjunction with a hostile work environment claim of co-worker harassment. The court reiterated its longstanding rule that "[t]o prove a case of constructive discharge a plaintiff must show that: (1) 'a reasonable person in her situation would find the working conditions intolerable' and (2) 'the employer * * * intended to force the employee to quit.'" Tatum v. Ark. Dep't of Health, 411 F.3d 955 (8th Cir.2005). *See also* Laster v. City of Kalamazoo, 746 F.3d 714, 727 (6th Cir.2014). *Suders* quite clearly supports the objective prong of this two-step approach. Does the decision support a requirement that the plaintiff prove the employer had a specific intent to force a resignation? Or a requirement that the employer reasonably foresee that an employee would be likely to resign in response to the acts of supervisors or co-workers? *See* Lisdahl v. Mayo Foundation, 633 F.3d 712, 718 (8th Cir.2011) (finding that "an intent requirement is implicit in the *Suders* test"). *See* Stephen F. Befort & Sarah J. Gorajski, *When Quitting Is Fitting: The Need for a Reformulated Sexual/Harassment Constructive Discharge Standard in the Wake of* Pennsylvania State Police v. Suders, 67 Ohio St.L.J. 593 (2006) (proposing a "Unitary Standard" of liability for constructive discharge in harassment cases that would incorporate elements of both strict liability and negligence).

6. *Constructive Discharge vs. Retaliatory Discharge*: Can you explain why many women who are victims of sexual harassment might be likely to resign in response to severe or pervasive harassment rather than to report the harassment and wait for a remedy? Professor Deborah Brake notes, "Social science literature on sexual harassment abounds with findings showing that sexually harassed women most often choose coping strategies of avoidance or denial and that the least likely response is to report the harassment to someone in a position of authority." Deborah L. Brake, *Retaliation,* 90 Minn.L.Rev. 18, 28 & n.24 (2005); Hébert, *supra* note 2, at 736–41. Is resignation generally a reasonable means of avoidance of "intolerable" harassment? Is the harassment victim sometimes "between a rock and a hard place"—afraid to endure continuing harassment by remaining an employee and afraid to report the harassment because of concerns about employer retaliation? To answer these questions, do we need better or clearer empirical data measuring the incidence of and reasons for women's reporting, failing to report, or quitting in sexual harassment cases? Professor Brake concludes that "[f]ears of retaliation turn out to be well-founded. Retaliation occurs with sufficient frequency to justify perceptions of the high cost of reporting discrimination and support the rationality of decisions not to do so." Brake, *supra, at* 38 & n.59 (citing studies of the incidence of retaliation in sexual harassment cases). If a plaintiff complains about hostile work environment and is fired, will she have a retaliation claim

in addition to her hostile work environment claim? What will her remedies be if she prevails on both of these claims? What harms has she suffered in each case? Before *Suders* was decided by the Supreme Court, Professor Chamallas questioned whether "constructive discharges are sufficiently similar to retaliatory discharges that they should also be regarded as disparate treatment rather than harassment." Chamallas, *supra* note 1, at 343.

2. LIABILITY FOR NEGLIGENCE: HARASSMENT BY CO-WORKERS AND NONEMPLOYEES

Proof of employer negligence is required in order to establish employer liability in Title VII cases dealing with harassment by nonsupervisory employees or supervisors who do not have the authority to take tangible employment actions against the plaintiff. Subsection 219(2)(b) of the Restatement (Second) of Agency imposes tort liability on employers for their own negligence. The Court in *Ellerth* acknowledged that this is the general standard for employer liability in sexual harassment cases: "Negligence sets a minimum standard for employer liability under Title VII"; therefore, "[a]n employer is negligent with respect to sexual harassment if it knew or should have known about the conduct and failed to stop it." *Ellerth*, 524 U.S. at 758, 118 S.Ct. at 2267. *See also* I. Introduction, in *EEOC Guidance on Vicarious Employer Liability,* reproduced in the Statutory Supplement:

> The Commission's long-standing guidance on employer liability for harassment by co-workers remains in effect—an employer is liable if it knew or should have known of the misconduct, unless it can show that it took immediate and appropriate corrective action. The standard is the same in the case of non-employees, but the employer's control over such individuals' misconduct is considered.

EEOC Enforcement Guidance: Vicarious Employment Liability for Unlawful Harassment by Supervisors, EEOC Compliance Manual (CCH) ¶ 3116 (June 18, 1999). *See also* EEOC Guidelines on Sexual Harassment, 29 C.F.R. § 1604.11(d)–(e).

Professor Oppenheimer summarized the relevant principles of employer liability for co-worker harassment from the common law of agency:

> Properly applied, agency law should impose direct liability when an employer: (1) unreasonably fails to instruct its employees to refrain from sexual harassment; (2) unreasonably fails to adopt rules, policies, and regulations designed to prevent harassment from occurring; (3) unreasonably employs people it knows or should know to be engaged in sexual harassment of other employees; (4) fails to properly supervise its employees to

> prevent harassment from occurring; (5) stands by and does nothing when it knows, or should know, that harassment is occurring; or (6) fails to prevent harassment that it could have reasonably prevented. In such cases, the law of master and servant holds the employer directly liable for the harm caused by the employer's breach of duty. Moreover, when an employer ratifies an act of harassment, it adopts the act as its own. Thus, when an employer fails to disapprove of harassment in an appropriate manner, it may be held directly liable.

David Benjamin Oppenheimer, *Exacerbating the Exasperating: Title VII Liability of Employers for Sexual Harassment Committed by Their Supervisors*, 81 Cornell L.Rev. 66, 98 (1995).

Notice plays an important role in claims of co-worker harassment. Employers are held liable for co-worker sexual harassment that they knew or should have known was occurring and failed to stop. But exactly what is constructive notice? One court defined it as "where an employee provides management level personnel with enough information to raise a probability of sexual harassment in the mind of a reasonable employer, or where the harassment is so pervasive and open that a reasonable employer would have had to be aware of it." Kunin v. Sears Roebuck & Co., 175 F.3d 289, 294 (3d Cir.1999). *See also* Sandoval v. Am. Bldg. Maint. Indus., Inc., 578 F.3d 787, 801–02 (8th Cir.2009) (analyzing liability for negligence and standard for constructive notice); Breda v. Wolf Camera & Video, 222 F.3d 886, 889–90 (11th Cir.2000) (finding that employer had actual notice of co-worker sexual harassment when employee complained to the manager who was designated by the employer's policy to handle complaints).

Under a negligence standard, an employer will not be liable for co-worker sexual harassment if it responds to the harassment with "immediate and appropriate corrective action." *See, e.g.,* Meriwether v. Caraustar Packaging, Co. 326 F.3d 990, 994 (8th Cir.2008) (finding that an immediate investigation and suspension of alleged co-worker harasser within one week following plaintiff's complaint were sufficiently "prompt and effective" responses as a matter of law). What is "appropriate corrective action"? Although firing an alleged harasser may not always be necessary, where an employer fired an alleged harasser within one month of the plaintiff's formal complaint of severe co-worker harassment, the court found the response sufficient to bar the action. Green v. Franklin Nat'l Bank, 459 F.3d 903, 912 (8th Cir.2006). *See also* Swenson v. Potter, 271 F.3d 1184, 1192 (9th Cir.2001) (finding that the employer took appropriate corrective action where it relocated the alleged harasser to a different work site in its facility pending completion of its investigation of the complaint). As you read the following notes and questions, consider how the burdens of proving and defending negligence liability for co-workers and nonemployee third parties differs from the burdens of proving and defending vicarious liability for supervisory harassment.

NOTES AND QUESTIONS

1. *Co-workers Who Are Serial Harassers*: What is appropriate corrective action in dealing with a serial harasser who is a co-worker? In 1997, three women were awarded a jury verdict of $1.2 million (later reduced to $655,000) based, in part, on evidence that their co-worker sexually harassed eighteen women over a period of twenty years before harassing them. The Court of Appeals for the Seventh Circuit initially vacated the award in 2000 on the grounds that the lower court had improperly excluded evidence regarding the employer's reasons for delaying firing the harasser. EEOC v. Ind. Bell Tel. (Ameritech), 214 F.3d 813 (7th Cir.2000), *reh'g on banc*, 256 F.3d 516 (7th Cir.2001). In her dissent in the now-vacated 2000 opinion, Judge Ilana Diamond Rovner wrote that the employer had "allowed the equivalent of an armed torpedo to wander about the workplace for years wreaking havoc upon its female employees." *Id.* at 825, 827. In the case of a serial harasser who was a co-worker, the Sixth Circuit ruled: "An employer's responsibility to prevent future harassment is heightened where it is dealing with a known serial harasser and is therefore on clear notice that the same employee has engaged in inappropriate behavior in the past." Hawkins v. Anheuser-Busch, Inc., 517 F.3d 321, 341 (6th Cir.2008). In *Ferris v. Delta Air Lines, Inc.*, 277 F.3d 128, 136–37 (2d Cir.2001), the Second Circuit held that a reasonable fact-finder could conclude that the airline was negligent in failing to prevent a male flight attendant's off-site rape of a female flight attendant when it had actual notice of his "proclivity to rape co-workers." Is anything short of discharge appropriate discipline for a "repeat offender"? In light of these cases, how would you advise an employer who just suspects on the basis of office gossip that it may be dealing with a co-worker—or a supervisor—who is a serial harasser?

2. *Employer Liability for Subordinates Harassing Supervisors*: Instances of subordinates harassing their supervisors at work, though relatively rarely reported, have begun to appear in decisions by federal courts and agencies, and the issue has prompted new scholarship on the topic of "contra-power harassment." *See* Ann Carey Juliano, *Harassing Women with Power: The Case for Including Contra-Power Harassment Within Title VII,* 87 Boston U. L. Rev. 491 (2007). In her article, Professor Juliano reviews the legal and social science scholarship on contra-power harassment claims, examines the existing empirical data, including reported cases, and sets out a theoretical framework for resolving such claims under Title VII. *Id.* She writes:

> Harassing a female supervisor inherently smacks of the desire to drive her from her job so as to retain the workplace for men, and to remind her of her rightful place lower in the hierarchy. Female

> supervisors may have organizational power but be powerless in terms of societal power and organizational dynamics.

Id. at 515. How would a supervisor who is being harassed by a subordinate in the workplace satisfy the elements of a prima facie case of sexual harassment? *See id.* at 523–40. What about racial harassment? Juliano concludes that the appropriate standard under Title VII for employer liability for contra-power harassment is the negligence standard. *Id.* at 555. In *Lyles v. District of Columbia*, 17 F.Supp.3d 59, 70 (D.D.C. 2014), the court concluded that a modified negligence standard should apply to cases in which a subordinate harasses a supervisor. The court held, in a case of first impression, that "an employer will not be liable for the sexual harassment of a supervisor by a subordinate where the supervisor-plaintiff had the ability to stop the harassment and failed to do so." *Id.* Should contra-power harassment claims be recognized at all?

3. *Liability for Harassment by Customers and Other Third Parties*: When can an employer be found liable for the actionable harassment caused by third parties such as clients or customers? The EEOC Guidelines on Sexual Harassment provide that an

> employer may also be responsible for the acts of non-employees, with respect to sexual harassment of employees in the workplace, where the employer (or its agents or supervisory employees) knows or should have known of the conduct and fails to take immediate and appropriate corrective action.

29 C.F.R. § 1604.11(e); *see also EEOC Guidance on Vicarious Employer Liability, supra.* The First, Fourth, Seventh, Eighth, Ninth, and Tenth Circuits have followed these EEOC Guidelines in cases of sexual harassment of employees by nonemployees. *See* Freeman v. Dal-Tile Corp., 750 F.3d 413, 422–23 (4th Cir.2014); Bernier v. Morningstar, Inc., 495 F.3d 369 (7th Cir.2007); Lockard v. Pizza Hut, Inc., 162 F.3d 1062 (10th Cir.1998); Rodriguez-Hernandez v. Miranda-Velez, 132 F.3d 848 (1st Cir.1998); Crist v. Focus Homes, Inc., 122 F.3d 1107 (8th Cir.1997); Folkerson v. Circus Circus Enter., Inc., 107 F.3d 754 (9th Cir.1997). The courts have applied a negligence theory of liability in these cases because hostile work environment sexual harassment by clients, customers, or suppliers is considered "more analogous to harassment by co-workers than by supervisors." *Lockard*, 162 F.3d at 1074. What should employers do to avoid employees' claims of harassment by customers? What about independent contractors or leased employees? *See, e.g.*, Dunn v. Wash. County Hosp., 429 F.3d 689 (7th Cir.2005) (finding hospital potentially liable under negligence theory for alleged sexual harassment of nurse by doctor who had staff privileges but was not an employee, where hospital knew or should have known of risk of harassment and failed to protect its employees). For an article exploring anomalies in the Title VII law on third-party harassment and proposing a new theory of employment discrimination law, see Noah Zatz, *Managing the*

Macaw: Third-Party Harassers, Accommodation, and the Disaggregation of Discriminatory Intent, 109 Colum.L.Rev. 1357 (2009).

Should sexual harassment of prison guards by inmates be treated the same as sexual harassment of employees by customers? As one court noted: "Prisoners, by definition, have breached prevailing societal norms in fundamentally corrosive ways. By choosing to work in a prison, corrections personnel have acknowledged and accepted the probability that they will face inappropriate and socially deviant behavior." Vajdl v. Mesabi Acad. of Kidspeace, Inc., 484 F3d 546, 551 (8th Cir.2007) (quoting and citing Slayton v. Ohio Dep't of Youth Serv., 206 F.3d 669, 677 (6th Cir.2000). Would it make a difference if the guard's co-workers or supervisors either ignored, condoned, encouraged, or instigated the inmates' offensive conduct? *See, e.g.*, Randolph v. Ohio Dep't of Youth Serv., 453 F.3d 724, 734 (6th Cir.2006) (yes); *Slayton*, 206 F.3d at 677–78 (yes). Can employees who are sexually harassed by their mentally or developmentally disabled clients or patients sue their employers under Title VII? *Compare* Turnbull v. Topeka State Hosp., 255 F.3d 1238 (10th Cir.2001) (finding that a mental hospital could be held liable for a hostile work environment under Title VII for a patient's sexual assault of a staff psychologist), *with* Cain v. Blackwell, 246 F.3d 758 (5th Cir.2001) (rejecting the hostile environment claim brought by a female home health nurse who was sexually harassed by an elderly male patient who suffered from Alzheimer's).

NOTE: TIMELY FILING OF HARASSMENT CHARGES—THE MORGAN *CASE*

If an employee files a charge with the EEOC alleging she was subjected to a hostile work environment in violation of Title VII, at what point has the "unlawful employment practice" occurred for purposes of determining whether the charge is timely? The Supreme Court addressed this question in *National Railroad Passenger Corp. v. Morgan,* 536 U.S. 101, 122 S.Ct. 2061, 153 L.Ed.2d 106 (2002), which is discussed in the *Ledbetter* case in Chapter 2. *Morgan* involved, *inter alia*, a claim of a racially hostile work environment brought against AmTrak by a black male employee. Writing for the Court, Justice Thomas concluded:

> Hostile environment claims are different in kind from discrete acts. Their very nature involves repeated conduct. * * * The "unlawful employment practice" therefore cannot be said to occur on any particular day. It occurs over a series of days or perhaps years and, in direct contrast to discrete acts, a single act of harassment may not be actionable on its own. * * * Such claims are based on the cumulative affect [sic] of individual acts. * * *
>
> In determining whether an actionable hostile work environment claim exists, we look to "all the circumstances," including "the frequency of the discriminatory conduct; its severity; whether it is physically threatening or humiliating, or a mere

offensive utterance; and whether it unreasonably interferes with an employee's work performance." *Harris.* To assess whether a court may, for the purposes of determining liability, review all such conduct, including those acts that occur outside the filing period, we again look to the statute. It provides that a charge must be filed within 180 or 300 days "after the alleged unlawful employment practice occurred." A hostile work environment claim is comprised of a series of separate acts that collectively constitute one "unlawful employment practice." 42 U.S.C. § 2000e–5(e)(1). The timely filing provision only requires that a Title VII plaintiff file a charge within a certain number of days after the unlawful practice happened. It does not matter, for purposes of the statute, that some of the component acts of the hostile work environment fall outside the statutory time period. Provided that an act contributing to the claim occurs within the filing period, the entire time period of the hostile environment may be considered by a court for the purposes of determining liability.

* * * Given, therefore, that the incidents comprising a hostile work environment are part of one unlawful employment practice, the employer may be liable for all acts that are part of this single claim. In order for the charge to be timely, the employee need only file a charge within 180 or 300 days of any act that is part of the hostile work environment. * * *

Our holding does not leave employers defenseless against employees who bring hostile work environment claims that extend over long periods of time. Employers have recourse when a plaintiff unreasonably delays filing a charge. * * * [T]he filing period is not a jurisdictional prerequisite to filing a Title VII suit. Rather, it is a requirement subject to waiver, estoppel, and equitable tolling "when equity so requires."

536 U.S. at 115–21, 122 S.Ct. at 2073–76.

Does *Morgan,* along with the doctrines of waiver, equitable estoppel, and equitable tolling, provide a workable rule on timely filing of an EEOC charge of hostile work environment? Suppose an employee has a colorable claim that her supervisor has created a hostile work environment. The employee pursues relief under the employer's sexual harassment policy. After some time passes, the employee believes she has not obtained appropriate relief under the employer's policy. Is the employee required to bring an EEOC charge within 180 or 300 days of the date of the last act of actionable harassment or the date when it is reasonable to believe that the employer has failed to take appropriate action? *See* Frazier v. Delco Elec. Corp., 263 F.3d 663, 666 (7th Cir.2001) (the latter). If an employee complains about harassment by a co-worker and the employer takes effective corrective action to stop that co-worker's misconduct, but other employees later begin harassing the same employee, can the plaintiff treat all of the harassment as one "unlawful employment practice"? *See* Watson v. Blue Circle, Inc., 324 F.3d 1252, 1258–59 (11th Cir.2003) (no). The D.C. Circuit, however, held that an employee's physical absence from work is not, *per se*, a bar to considering, as part of the actionable hostile environment, conduct before the employee left work or incidents that occurred during the employee's absence. *See* Greer v. Paulson F.3d 1306, 1313–15 (D.C.Cir.2007) (discussing *Morgan* and collecting cases, *id.* at 1314 n.3). If an employer tells an employee not to talk to anyone other than managers about her allegations of sexual harassment, is it reasonable for her not to talk to a lawyer or file a complaint with the EEOC? *See* Beckel v. Wal-Mart Assocs., 301 F.3d 621 (7th Cir.2002).

D. HARASSMENT BECAUSE OF RACE

HARRIS V. INTERNATIONAL PAPER CO.

United States District Court for the District of Maine, 1991.
765 F.Supp. 1509, *vacated in part*, 765 F.Supp. 1529.

CARTER, CHIEF JUDGE.

[Plaintiff Isom Harris was one of three black men who alleged that International Paper Company had permitted supervisors and co-workers to subject the plaintiffs to a racially hostile work environment in violation of the Maine Human Rights Act (MHRA). The elements of a prima facie case of racial hostile work environment under MHRA are essentially the same as under Title VII, requiring proof that the conduct was "unwelcome" and "severe or pervasive."]

* * * The first question which must be answered * * * is what standard is applied by a fact finder to assess whether particular conduct or speech is "unwelcome," and whether that harassment is sufficiently severe and pervasive to violate antidiscrimination law. * * *

In *Lipsett v. University of Puerto Rico*, 864 F.2d 881 (1st Cir.1988), the First Circuit recognized that there may be two different perspectives on the questions of unwelcomeness and pervasiveness: the perpetrator's perspective and the victim's perspective. When considering allegations of sexual harassment, therefore, "the fact finder keeps both the man's and woman's perspective in mind" so that defendants and courts will not " 'sustain ingrained notions of reasonable behavior fashioned by the offenders.' " *Id.* at 898 (quoting Rabidue v. Osceola Refining Co., 805 F.2d 611, 626 (6th Cir.1986) (Keith, J., dissenting)).

* * *

Black Americans are regularly faced with negative racial attitudes, many unconsciously held and acted upon, which are the natural consequences of a society ingrained with cultural stereotypes and race-based beliefs and preferences. *See generally* Charles H. Lawrence, *The Id, the Ego, and Equal Protection: Reckoning with Unconscious Racism*, 39 Stan.L.Rev. 317 (1987).[11] As a result, instances of racial violence or threatened violence which might appear to white observers as mere "pranks" are, to black observers, evidence of threatening, pervasive attitudes closely associated with racial jokes, comments or nonviolent conduct which white observers are also more likely to dismiss as non-threatening isolated incidents. Mari Matsuda, *Public Response to Racist Speech: Considering the Victim's Story*, 87 Mich.L.Rev. 2320, 2326–35 (1989). The omnipresence of race-based attitudes and experiences in the lives of black Americans causes even nonviolent events to be interpreted as degrading, threatening, and offensive. *See, e.g.*, D. Bell, And We Are Not Saved (1987) 181–85 (describing a fictional encounter with a state trooper); Patricia Williams, *Alchemical Notes: Reconstructing Ideals from Deconstructed Rights*, 22 Harv.C.R.–C.L.L.Rev. 401, 406–13 (1987) (explaining why black and white apartment-seekers assume different perspectives on the formalities of renting an apartment). Even an inadvertent racial slight unnoticed either by its white speaker or white bystanders will reverberate in the memory of its black victim. Lawrence, *supra* at 339–41. Since the concern of Title VII and the MHRA is to redress the effects of conduct and speech on their victims, the fact finder must "walk a mile in the victim's shoes" to understand those effects and how they should be remedied. In sum, the appropriate standard to be applied in this hostile environment racial harassment case is that of a "reasonable black person."[12]

* * * Plaintiff Harris was forced to run a gauntlet of racial abuse from the time of his arrival at the Jay mill. Harris's principal harassers were Dwight Goff, a "loaned supervisor" brought to Maine from one of Defendant's southern mills to assist during the strike, and Birchard and Kip Brooks, who were permanent replacement workers. Goff's racist views, including the use of epithets like "lazy nigger" and "black son-of-a-bitch," were well known to other workers in the mill. Goff regularly expressed his hatred of black people in Harris's presence, and sabotaged Harris's work. * * *

---

[11] Because these racial beliefs and stereotypes pervade our society, employing a "reasonable person" standard would permit discriminatory conduct and speech constructed on the foundation of these beliefs and stereotypes to stand unremedied. *See Lipsett*, 864 F.2d at 898 (quoting *Rabidue*, 805 F.2d at 626 (Keith, J. dissenting)).

[12] The Court does not mean to imply that there is unanimity of perspective among black Americans. *See, e.g.*, Judy Scales-Trent, *Black Women and the Constitution: Finding Our Place, Asserting Our Rights, 24 Harv.C.R.–C.L.L.Rev. 9 (1989)* (discussing how black women suffer discrimination of a different form, quality, and intensity than that experienced either by black men or white women). The appropriate standard to be applied in hostile environment harassment cases is that of a reasonable person from the protected group of which the alleged victim is a member. In this instance, because Plaintiffs are black, the appropriate standard is that of a reasonable black person, as that can be best understood and given meaning by a white judge.

Harris's problems with the Brooks brothers were even more serious. Birchard and Kip Brooks were equally free with racially derogatory comments aimed at Harris, and complained about Harris's work performance in racial terms. Their racist views were also widely known. One notable incident of public harassment involved the Brooks brothers donning white suits and white hats, ordinarily used while cleaning the paper machines but on this occasion clearly intended to recall the Ku Klux Klan, and "prancing" around Harris at his work station. This incident occurred in the presence of Foreman Parker, who considered it to be merely a joke. On another occasion, Birchard and Kip Brooks threatened to fight with Harris and warned him to get the other black workers who had accompanied Harris from Mobile to Jay for the fight. Even after Harris notified Foreman Richard Parker of the problem, Birchard Brooks continued to threaten Harris.

As a matter of course, Birchard Brooks ignored work directives from Harris, even though he was subordinate to Harris on the Number 2 machine, and he attempted to get others to join in his racist insubordination. This conduct was known to Foreman Parker, who spoke with Brooks at one point. But Birchard Brooks did not limit his racial attacks to Harris. White co-workers considered by Brooks to be too friendly with Harris were titled "nigger lovers," and were physically harassed.

Harris was also subjected to epithets from other workers and supervisors like "black nigger," "goddamn nigger," "black ass," "watermelon man," and "Buckwheat." These incidents were known, in most cases, to supervisors and foremen. "KKK" appeared on rolls of paper with which Harris worked, on a steel support near Harris's work station, and on a picture of a former employee posted in the mill who had himself engaged in racist name-calling.[20] While there may not have been a means by which a supervisor could have seen the graffiti on the paper rolls, the graffiti on the steel support and on the picture was large, enduring, and occurred in an area supervisors visited daily; thus, a supervisor could have and should have seen it. There was also racist graffiti, such as "nigger go back south," in the bathrooms used by workers and supervisors alike. Harris also felt that he was ignored by supervisors who would not even respond to Harris's normal and polite greetings in the morning. He classified his relationships with all the supervisors as "very negative."

Finally, a picture postcard from the "Our Gang" television series was posted next to the time clock with an added caption reading: "The new generation of papermakers." The postcard was posted within one week of

[20] There was testimony that Harris did not himself remove this cartoon from the bulletin board, even though he had the opportunity. The Court notes that there is no affirmative duty on the part of an employee to act to remove unwelcome racial speech or conduct from the workplace. That burden rests squarely with the employer.

Harris's arrival at the Jay Mill, and depicted the "Little Rascals" in confusion attempting to wash a dog. The character "Buckwheat" was set apart from the other, white children. Harris testified that he perceived this postcard to be racially derogatory and directed at him. When taken in tandem with the use of "Buckwheat" as a racist epithet in the mill, the Court finds that this postcard could be viewed by a reasonable black person to be an unwelcome racial statement.[22]

The Court finds that the quality and quantity of the racial speech and conduct described above and experienced by Plaintiff Harris rises to the level of racial harassment by creating an intimidating, hostile and offensive work environment so severe and pervasive that it substantially altered Harris's working conditions. The Court also finds that there is abundant evidence that Defendant's agents, supervisors, and foremen had actual knowledge of this racial harassment in most circumstances, and in the remaining instances would have had knowledge of the harassment being suffered by Harris had Defendant exercised reasonable care. The Court holds that Plaintiff Harris satisfied his burden of establishing a *prima facie* case of hostile environment racial harassment.

* * *

NOTES AND QUESTIONS

1. Should the courts treat racial and sexual hostile work environment claims the same? Are the elements of a prima facie case the same, as Chief Judge Carter says in *International Paper*? Are there any significant differences between the two types of claims? How is race as a protected status different from sex? Can you think of a case in which a quid pro quo claim of racial or ethnic harassment could be made? Relatively little scholarship has focused on racial harassment as opposed to sexual harassment. Professor Pat Chew has done significant research exploring some distinctions between sexual harassment and racial harassment and analyzing empirical data on racial harassment cases, see Pat K. Chew, *Freeing Racial Harassment from the Sexual Harassment Model,* 85 Or. L. Rev. 615 (2006); Pat K. Chew & Robert E. Kelley, *Unwrapping Racial Harassment Law,* 27 Berkeley J. Emp. & Lab. L. 49 (2006); Pat K. Chew & Robert E. Kelley, *Myth of the Color-Blind Judge: An Empirical Analysis of Racial Harassment Cases*, 86 Wash.U.L.Rev. 1117 (2009).

2. *Unwelcomeness*: Should proof of "unwelcomeness" be an element of a hostile work environment claim based on race or national origin? In its amicus brief in *Meritor*, the EEOC observed that "[w]hereas racial slurs are intrinsically offensive and presumptively unwelcome, sexual advances and innuendos are ambiguous: depending on their context, they may be intended

[22] There was testimony that the person who posted the postcard on the bulletin board did not intend a racial slight, however, as the Court has already noted, the intent of the speaker is not relevant to the question of the unwelcomeness of the speech.

by the initiator, and perceived by the recipient, as denigrating or complimentary, as threatening or welcome, as malevolent or innocuous." Brief for the United States and the Equal Employment Opportunity Commission as Amici Curiae, at E–6, Meritor Sav. Bank, FSB v. Vinson, 477 U.S. 57 (1986), (No. 84–1979). *See* Theresa M. Beiner & John M. A. DiPippa, *Hostile Environments and the Religious Employee*, 19 U. Ark. Little Rock L.J. 577, 585 & 585 n.57 (1997) (noting that "commentators have observed that the unwelcome nature of harassment is presumed where it is based on racial grounds"). How did Chief Judge Carter in *International Paper* treat this issue?

3. *The Victim's Perspective*: Does *International Paper* support a variety of "reasonable victim" standards, for example, "reasonable Asian American," "reasonable Rastafarian," "reasonable Muslim," "reasonable nonadherent"? *See, e.g.*, Torres v. Pisano, 116 F.3d 625, 632–33 (2d Cir.1997) ("a reasonable Puerto Rican would find a workplace in which her boss repeatedly called her a 'dumb spic' and told her that she should stay home, go on welfare, and collect food stamps like the rest of the 'spics' to be hostile"). Can a white judge in a bench trial understand the perspective of a "reasonable black person"? See footnote 12 of *International Paper.* Would the Supreme Court endorse a "reasonable black person perspective"? Or is the victim's perspective as an African American reflected in consideration of the "reasonable person" and the "totality of the circumstances" standards articulated in *Harris* and *Oncale*? *See* McGinest v. GTE Serv. Corp., 360 F.3d 1103 (9th Cir.2004) (stating that "allegations of a racially hostile workplace must be assessed from the perspective of a reasonable person belonging to the racial or ethnic group of the plaintiff," *id.* at 1115, and that "in *Oncale*, the Supreme Court recharacterized the *Harris* statement [on perspective], making it clear that it is proper to use an individualized standard based upon the characteristics of the plaintiff," *id.* at 1115 n.8).

4. *The Totality of Circumstances*: *Oncale* held that the severity or pervasiveness of a hostile work environment is evaluated in light of the "totality of circumstances." How would you evaluate the workplace environment in *International Paper*? How might the workplace context have been affected by the fact that a bitter strike was ongoing? *See* Julius Getman, The Betrayal of Local 14: Paperworkers, Politics, and Permanent Replacements (1998) (describing the sixteen-month strike at the International Paper Mill). If the "entire context" of the workplace is relevant, can an employee who is a member of a racial minority recover for workplace racial harassment targeted at other members of the plaintiff's protected class or at other racial minorities? *See* Cruz v. Coach Stores, 202 F.3d 560, 570 (2d Cir.2000) ("Remarks targeting members of other minorities * * * may contribute to the overall hostility of the working environment for a minority employee.") Can employees recover for incidents of racially harassing language and conduct that occur when they are not at work and which they hear about second-hand? *Compare* Whidbee v. Garzarelli Food Specialties,

Inc., 223 F.3d 62, 71–72 (2d Cir.2000) (yes), *with* McCann v. Tillman, 562 F.3d 1370, 1878–79 (11th Cir.2009) (no).

5. *Racial Animus*: *International Paper* involved language and conduct that is explicitly racial. After *Oncale,* is "racial" language or conduct essential to establishing a claim of racial harassment? What about the Supreme Court's admonition in *Ash v. Tyson Foods, Inc.*, 546 U.S. 454, 456, 126 S.Ct. 1195, 1197, 163 L.Ed.2d 1053, 1057 (2006) about the use of the word "boy" in referring to African-American males? The Court cautioned: "The speaker's meaning may depend on various factors including context, inflection, tone of voice, local custom, and historical usage." *Id.* at 456, 126 S.Ct. at 1197. Some courts have adopted an approach to defining racial and national origin harassment that is similar to the "gender animus" or "gender hostility" approach to defining sexual harassment that was adopted in *O'Shea v. Yellow Technology Services, Inc.*, 185 F.3d 1093 (10th Cir.1999). *See, e.g.*, Landrau-Romero v. Banco Popular De P.R., 212 F.3d 607, 614 (1st Cir.2000) ("Alleged conduct that is not explicitly racial in nature may, in appropriate circumstances, be considered along with more overtly discriminatory conduct in assessing a Title VII harassment claim."). *See also* Cerros v. Steel Tech., Inc., 288 F.3d 1040, 1047 (7th Cir.2002) ("While there is no 'magic number' of slurs that indicate a hostile work environment, we have recognized before that an unambiguously racial epithet falls on the 'more severe' end of the spectrum."); Herrera v. Lufkin Indus., Inc., 474 F.3d 675, 683 (10th Cir.2007) (permitting plaintiff to go to trial where it was a "close question" on the issue of pervasiveness, where the plaintiff "presented evidence of racially derogatory treatment, well beyond being sworn at and joked with, that was specifically directed at [him] because of his national origin").

6. *Liability for Facially Neutral Language—"Code Words"*: In light of *Ash v. Tyson Foods*, discussed *supra,* Note 5, consider the following: Plaintiff, a black woman, alleged that she was subjected to a racially hostile work environment on the basis of the following facts: White supervisors and white co-workers repeatedly referred to the plaintiff and other black workers as "another one," "one of them," and "poor people." In addition, while discussing a personnel dispute about another black worker, a manager told the plaintiff that "if this continues we're going to have to come up there and get rid of all of you." When the plaintiff asked the manager what he meant by "all of you," he refused to elaborate. Plaintiff perceived the comments to be racially motivated. Would such comments be considered "hostile" or "abusive" under *Harris v. Forklift Systems*? Would they be considered discriminatory "because of race" under *Oncale*? On these facts, in *Aman v. Cort Furniture Rental Corp.*, 85 F.3d 1074 (1996), the Court of Appeals for the Third Circuit reversed the district court's finding that such "racially-neutral" language "demonstrated only rudeness, and not racial animus." *Id.* at 1080 & n.2. The court observed,

> Anti-discrimination laws and lawsuits have "educated" would-be violators such that extreme manifestations of discrimination are thankfully rare. Though they still happen, the instances in which

employers and employees openly use derogatory epithets to refer to fellow employees appear to be declining. Regrettably, however, this in no way suggests that discrimination based upon an individual's race, gender, or age is near an end. Discrimination continues to pollute the social and economic mainstream of American life, and is often simply masked in more subtle forms. It has become easier to coat various forms of discrimination with the appearance of propriety, or to ascribe some other less odious intention to what is in reality discriminatory behavior. In other words, while discriminatory conduct persists, violators have learned not to leave the proverbial "smoking gun" behind. As one court has recognized, "defendants of even minimal sophistication will neither admit discriminatory animus nor leave a paper trail demonstrating it." Riordan v. Kempiners, 831 F.2d 690, 697 (7th Cir.1987). But regardless of the form that discrimination takes, the impermissible impact remains the same, and the law's prohibition remains unchanged. "Title VII tolerates no racial discrimination, subtle or otherwise." McDonnell Douglas Corp. v. Green, 411 U.S. 792, 801, 93 S.Ct. 1817, 36 L.Ed.2d 668 (1973).

* * * [T]he use of "code words" can, under circumstances such as we encounter here, violate Title VII. Indeed, a reasonable jury could conclude that the intent to discriminate is implicit in these comments. There are no talismanic expressions which must be invoked as a condition-precedent to the application of laws designed to protect against discrimination. The words themselves are only relevant for what they reveal—the intent of the speaker. A reasonable jury could find that statements like the ones allegedly made in this case send a clear message and carry the distinct tone of racial motivations and implications. They could be seen as conveying the message that members of a particular race are disfavored and that members of that race are, therefore, not full and equal members of the workplace. * * * [T]he pervasive use of derogatory and insulting terms directed at members of a protected class generally, and addressed to those employees personally, may serve as evidence of a hostile environment.

Aman, 85 F.3d at 1081, 1083. *See also* Jones v. UPS Ground Freight, 683 F.3d 1283, 1297–98 (11th Cir.2012) (finding that use of the term "monkey" and placement of bananas on plaintiff's truck created a triable issue of fact on the question of racial hostility); Johnson v. Riverside Healthcare Sys., LP, 534 F.3d 1116, 1123 (9th Cir.2008) (recognizing Ninth Circuit rule that "a coworker's use of a "code word or phrase" can, under certain circumstances, contribute to a hostile work environment," and collecting cases); Diaz v. Swift-Eckrich, Inc., 318 F.3d 796, 799 (8th Cir.2003) (statements that "Hispanics should be cleaning" and Hispanics are "stupid" combined with "rude noises," laughter, and general derogatory comments directed at plaintiff are sufficient to show a hostile work environment based on national origin). Will potential Title VII liability for facially neutral "code words" chill speech between workers of different races in the workplace? On the other hand, if such verbal harassment is not actionable, is there a risk that the harmful effects of racial hostility in the workplace will go unremedied more often than not?

7. *Intersectionality*: Hostile work environment cases often involve the intersection of two or more protected statuses. Professor Tanya Hernandez collected statistics from the 1990s showing that "sexual harassers target White women as victims at disproportionately lower rates than women of color." Tanya Katerí Hernández, *Sexual Harassment and Racial Disparity: The Mutual Construction of Gender and Race*, 4 J. Gender Race & Just. 183, 187 (2001). How should the courts treat hostile environment claims based on the intersection of race and gender? Are those "intersecting" claims any different from claims based solely on either racial harassment or sexual harassment? On June 2, 2008, the EEOC announced that the Tavern on the Green, a landmark restaurant in Central Park in New York City, agreed to pay $2.2 million to settle an EEOC charge that it had

> engaged in severe and pervasive sexual, racial, and national origin harassment of female, black, and Hispanic employees. The sexual harassment included graphic comments and demands for various sex acts, as well as groping of women's buttocks and breasts. The racial and national origin harassment included epithets toward black and Hispanic employees and ridiculing Hispanics for their accents.

Press Release, EEOC, Tavern on the Green to Pay $2.2 Million for Harassment of Females, Blacks, Hispanics (June 2, 2008), available at *http://www.eeoc.gov/press/6-2-08.html.* Could some of these claims have been based on "intersectionality"? If a black female employee is receiving demands for sex acts and being "groped" by a supervisor, is this sexual harassment or racial harassment, or both at once—racialized sexual harassment? *Compare* EEOC v. Cent. Wholesalers, 573 F.3d 167, 175 (4th Cir.2009) (analyzing separately whether African-American female was subjected to sex-based harassment and to race-based harassment), *with* Hicks v. Gates Rubber Co., 833 F.2d 1406, 1416–17 (10th Cir.1987) (permitting district court to "aggregate evidence of racial hostility with evidence of sexual hostility"). See the discussion of intersectionality in Chapter 2. For an exploration of some of these issues, see L. Camille Hébert, *Analogizing Race and Sex in Workplace Harassment Claims*, 58 Ohio St.L.J. 819 (1997); Sumi K. Cho, *Converging Stereotypes in Racialized Sexual Harassment: Where the Model Minority Meets Suzie Wong*, 1 J. Gender Race & Just. 177 (1997); Tanya Katerí Hernández, *The Next Challenge in Sexual Harassment Reform: Racial Disparity*, 23 Women's Rts. L. Rep. 227 (2002); Maria L. Ontiveros, *Three Perspectives on Workplace Harassment of Women of Color*, 23 Golden Gate U.L.Rev. 817 (1993).

8. *Section 1981 Claims of Racial Harassment*: Since the enactment of the Civil Rights Act of 1991, employees have been able to bring race-based hostile work environment claims under § 1981, 42 U.S.C. § 1981. *See* Manatt v. Bank of Am., NA, 339 F.3d 792, 797 (9th Cir.2003) (finding racial hostile work environment claim actionable under § 1981 and collecting cases, *id.* at 797 n.4); Johnson v. Riverside Healthcare Sys., LP, 534 F.3d 1116, 1122 (9th Cir.2008) (same). Recall that, unlike discrimination claims brought under Title VII, § 1981 claims are not subject to administrative exhaustion, and there is no cap on damages. For discussion of § 1981 claims generally, see Chapter 5, Section C. In *Danco, Inc. v. Wal-Mart Stores, Inc.*, 178 F.3d 8 (1st Cir.1999), the court held that independent contractors could also bring claims of hostile work environment racial harassment under § 1981.

9. *Same-Race Harassment*: In *Ross v. Douglas County, Nebraska*, 234 F.3d 391, 396 (8th Cir.2000), the court relied on *Oncale* to recognize a same-race hostile work environment claim brought by a black correctional officer who alleged that his black supervisor had called him "black boy" and "nigger." Is it the same for a black supervisor to call a black subordinate racial epithets as for a white supervisor to do so? *See* Randall Kennedy, Nigger: The Strange Career of a Troublesome Word (2002). What if the harasser directs racial epithets at members of his own race and as well as at workers of a different race? In *McGinest v. GTE Serv. Corp.*, 360 F.3d 1103, 1118 (9th Cir.2004), the court rejected what was essentially an "equal opportunity harasser" defense when it held that "[u]se of racially charged words to goad both black and white employees makes [such] conduct more outrageous, not less so."

10. *Reverse Racial Harassment*: What kind of evidence would a white plaintiff need to prevail on a claim that a black supervisor or co-worker has created a racially hostile work environment? *See, e.g.,* Bowen v. Mo. Dep't of Soc. Servs., 311 F.3d 878, 884 (8th Cir.2002) (ruling that evidence presented by white employee whose supervisor called her "white bitch" and other epithets that "carried clear racial overtones" is sufficient to defeat a summary judgment motion).

11. *Racist Symbols—Nooses in the Workplace*: Racial harassment charges brought to the EEOC more than doubled between 1991 and 2007, when they reached almost 7,000 for fiscal year 2007, and the Commission "investigat[ed] and voluntarily resolv[ed] tens of thousands of racial discrimination cases out of court." *See* EEOC, Press Release, Conectiv and Subcontractors to Pay $1.65 Million to Black Workers Who Were Racially Harassed (May 5, 2008), available at *http://www.eeoc.gov/press/5-5-08.html*. By 2007, the EEOC had brought more than thirty racial harassment lawsuits involving hangman's nooses over the preceding decade. *Id.* In addition, a number of courts have found employers liable for a racially hostile work environment when nooses were hung in the workplace. *See, e.g.,* Turley v. ISG Lackawanna, Inc., 774 F.3d 140 (2d Cir.2014) (egregious hostile work environment, including a noose hanging from plaintiff's rear view mirror, supported award of punitive damages); Porter v. Erie Foods Int'l, Inc., 576

F.3d 629, 635–36 (7th Cir.2009) (discussing the noose as a symbol of terror for African-Americans); Brown v. Nucor Corp., 576 F.3d 149 (7th Cir.2009) (reversing the district court's denial of class certification in a case alleging plant-wide racial harassment, including broadcast of racial epithets, displays of the Confederate flag, and depictions of nooses in e-mails sent to employees); Tademy v. Union Pac. Corp. 520 F.3d 1149, 1162 (10th Cir.2008) (finding actionable hostile work environment where plaintiff alleged "a series of acts of harassment, 'culminating in the life-sized lynching noose[,]' an incident that affected him so profoundly that he did not return to work"); *Id.* (collecting racial harassment cases involving nooses). *See* Jerome R. Watson & Richard W. Warren, *"I Heard It Through the Grapevine": Evidentiary Challenges I Racially Hostile Work Environment Litigation*, 19 Lab. Law. 381, 382–89 (2004) (discussing the noose as evidence of a racially hostile work environment and analyzing cases involving nooses).

In response to several highly publicized incidents involving display of nooses, New York has enacted an "anti-noose" law. *See Law Makes Noose Display a Felony,* N.Y. Times, May 16, 2008. As of November 1, 2008, a person in New York state will be guilty of the felony of aggravated harassment if he or she "places or displays a noose, commonly exhibited as a symbol of racism and intimidation," on public or private property "with intent to harass, annoy, threaten or alarm another person, because of * * * race, color, national origin, ancestry, gender, religion, religious practice, age, disability or sexual orientation." N.Y. Penal L. § 240.31(5). New York already bans burning crosses "in public view" and placing swastikas on any building without the express consent of the owner. N.Y. Penal L. § 240.31(3), (4). *See* Jeannine Bell, *The Hangman's Noose and the Lynch Mob: Hate Speech and the Jena Six,* 44 Harv. C.R.–C.L. L. Rev. 329, 350–53 (2009) (discussing the variety of legal responses to highly publicized noose displays). Should employers adopt a "zero-tolerance" approach to workplace displays of racist symbols like nooses and swastikas? *See* Stephen Plass, *Reinforcing Title VII with Zero Tolerance Rules, 39 Suffolk U. L. Rev. 127, 128–29 (2005)* (examining "zero tolerance rules as a complement to Title VII" and arguing that "such work rules have helped establish workplace culture on issues such as stealing, drug and alcohol abuse, fighting or violence, and sleeping on the job").

–STOP–

CHAPTER 11

DISCRIMINATION BECAUSE OF RELIGION

■ ■ ■

A. INTRODUCTION: STATUTORY OVERVIEW

The legislative history of Title VII provides little insight into the reason that Congress included religion among the prohibited criteria in § 703(a); 42 U.S.C. § 2000e–2(a). Nonetheless, prohibiting employment discrimination on the basis of religion is clearly consistent with the basic concept of religious freedom that is embodied in the First Amendment to the Constitution: in a democratic society people should tolerate the religious beliefs and practices of others. Unlike a person's race, color, sex, national origin, or age, however, an individual's religious beliefs and practices are based on matters of choice rather than on an immutable characteristic or status.

As enacted in 1964, Title VII prohibited discrimination on the basis of religion, but imposed no affirmative obligation on employers to accommodate the religious beliefs of their employees. Without congressional guidance on the scope of the employer's duty not to discriminate, the courts and the EEOC adopted different interpretations of the statute. In its first guidelines on religious discrimination, issued in 1966, the EEOC took the view that Title VII required a covered employer to accommodate the religious practices of its employees or prospective employees unless doing so would create a "serious inconvenience to the conduct of the business." 29 C.F.R. § 1605.1(a)(2) (effective June 15, 1966). Subsection (3)(b)(3) of the guidelines, however, permitted the employer to disregard the religious needs of particular employees when establishing requirements for workweek and overtime schedules, as long as the schedules were adopted in a neutral manner, without an intent to discriminate on the basis of religion. *Id.* § 1605.1(a)(3)(b)(3).

After receiving numerous objections from Sabbatarians, the EEOC revised its guidelines in 1967 by omitting subsection (3)(b)(3) and rewording (and renumbering) subsection (2) to provide that

> the duty not to discriminate on religious grounds * * * includes an obligation on the part of the employer to make reasonable accommodations to the religious needs of employees * * * where such accommodations can be made without undue hardship on the conduct of the employer's business. Such undue hardship, for

> example, may exist where the employee's needed work cannot be performed by another employee of substantially similar qualifications during the period of absence of the Sabbath observer.

29 C.F.R. § 1605.1(b) (effective July 10, 1967). *See* Appendix A to EEOC, Guidelines on Discrimination Because of Religion, 29 C.F.R. § 1605.1(b) (1997). Initially some employers defended religious discrimination claims by challenging the validity of the 1967 guidelines on the ground that they were unconstitutional or were inconsistent with Title VII. Consequently, some courts narrowly construed the EEOC guidelines because of concern that compelling employers to accommodate the religious beliefs and practices of all their employees would violate the Establishment Clause of the First Amendment, which requires governmental neutrality in matters of religion. A narrow construction also avoided confronting whether the EEOC exceeded its rulemaking authority in issuing the guidelines.

For example, in *Dewey v. Reynolds Metals Co.*, 429 F.2d 324 (6th Cir.1970), *aff'd by an equally divided Court*, 402 U.S. 689, 91 S.Ct. 2186, 29 L.Ed.2d 267 (1971), the Sixth Circuit, in a divided opinion, held that an employer made a reasonable accommodation of an employee's religious practices by permitting him to arrange for his own replacement on Saturdays, despite his religious belief that it would be a sin for him to induce other employees to work on his Sabbath. *Dewey* thus avoided addressing the "grave constitutional questions" that the court believed would have been raised by adopting the EEOC's interpretation of Title VII. *Id.* at 334. In addition, the court expressed doubt whether the 1967 guidelines were consistent with the statute. *Id.*

In 1972, Congress confirmed the EEOC's authority to interpret Title VII according to the 1967 guidelines. Acting largely in response to *Dewey*, Congress added § 701(j), 42 U.S.C. § 2000e(j), in the 1972 amendments to Title VII. *See* 118 Cong.Rec., §§ 227–53 (1972); *see also* Cooper v. Gen. Dynamics, 533 F.2d 163, 167–68 & 168 n.9 (5th Cir.1976) (discussing legislative history of § 701(j)). Section 701(j) essentially codified the "reasonable accommodation" and "undue hardship" language found in the EEOC's 1966 and 1967 guidelines:

> The term "religion" includes all aspects of religious observance and practice, as well as belief, unless an employer demonstrates that he is unable to reasonably accommodate to an employee's or prospective employee's religious observance or practice without undue hardship on the conduct of the employer's business.

Title VII, § 701(j), 42 U.S.C. § 2000e(j). For more discussion about the legislative history and congressional intent behind the 1972 amendment, see Roberto L. Corrada, *Toward an Integrated Disparate Treatment and*

Accommodation Framework for Title VII Religion Cases, 77 U.Cin.L.Rev. 1411, 1427–31 (2009).

Any doubts that the EEOC had the authority from Congress to issue its 1967 guidelines on religion were resolved by the 1972 amendment. *See, e.g.*, Reid v. Memphis Publ'g Co., 468 F.2d 346 (6th Cir.1972) (holding that the 1967 EEOC guidelines were consistent with pre-1972 Title VII). But doubts about the constitutionality of the "reasonable accommodation" law persisted. Following the enactment of § 701(j), the Sixth Circuit revisited the constitutionality of Title VII's prohibition against religious discrimination in employment in *Cummins v. Parker Seal Co.*, 516 F.2d 544 (6th Cir.1975), *aff'd by an equally divided Court*, 429 U.S. 65, 97 S.Ct. 342, 50 L.Ed.2d 223 (1976), *vacated on other grounds unrelated to constitutionality and remanded for reconsideration*, 433 U.S. 903, 97 S.Ct. 2965, 53 L.Ed.2d 1087 (1977), *decided on remand*, 561 F.2d 658 (6th Cir.1977). After joining the World Wide Church of God, the plaintiff in *Cummins* refused to work on his church's Sabbath—from Friday sundown to Saturday sundown—or on certain holy days. He was discharged following complaints by other supervisors who had to cover his shift on Saturdays. The employer defended its conduct on the ground that it had reasonably accommodated the plaintiff's religious practices under Title VII and that, in any event, the requirement under § 701(j) of accommodating the religious observances and practices of employees violates the Establishment Clause of the First Amendment because it "fosters religion by requiring private employers to defer to their employee's religious idiosyncrasies." 516 F.2d at 551.

This time the Sixth Circuit, in a divided opinion, rejected the constitutional challenge to § 701(j), as well as to its precursor EEOC regulation—29 C.F.R. § 1605.1. Applying the three standards established by the Supreme Court in *Committee for Public Education v. Nyquist*, 413 U.S. 756, 93 S.Ct. 2955, 37 L.Ed.2d 948 (1973), the circuit court concluded that the statute and regulation passed constitutional muster; they "(1) '* * * reflect a clearly secular legislative purpose,' (2) '* * * have a primary effect that neither advances nor inhibits religion,' and (3) '* * * avoid excessive government entanglement with religion.'" *Cummins*, 516 F.2d at 551–52 (quoting *Nyquist*, 413 U.S. at 772–73, 93 S.Ct. at 2965). Other courts followed *Cummins* in upholding the constitutionality of § 701(j) and the EEOC guidelines from which the amendment to Title VII was derived. *See* McDaniel v. Essex Int'l, Inc., 696 F.2d 34, 37 (6th Cir.1982) (discussing *Cummins* and collecting cases affirming the constitutionality of § 701(j)); EEOC v. Ithaca Indus., Inc., 849 F.2d 116, 119 (4th Cir.1988) (collecting cases).

At first blush § 701(j), when construed in conjunction with § 703(a), 42 U.S.C. § 2000e–2(a), seems to be a straightforward application of a widely recognized and time-honored policy imperative embodied in the

First Amendment. But many difficult questions are raised in attempting to implement this policy of tolerance of religious diversity. For example, what constitutes a religious belief or practice that is entitled to some protection? How should a balance be struck of tolerance for protected religious practices or beliefs that conflict with other deeply held societal values? Some religious discrimination cases involve interests, dynamics, and problems not found in race and sex discrimination cases. For example, the implementation of the equality principle is a major goal of laws prohibiting discrimination on the basis of race and sex in the workplace, but prohibiting discrimination because of religion seeks to preserve diversity, albeit of religious beliefs and practices. What deference, if any, should be given to an employer's religious beliefs and practices when they conflict with those of an employee's on topics such as abortion? If the prohibition against religious discrimination is intended to preserve diversity of religious beliefs and practices, does it mean that the *Griggs* disparate impact theory (see Chapter 4) should not be applied in the religious discrimination cases? In addition, government employers are subject to both the Free Exercise and Establishment Clauses of the First Amendment, as well as to Title VII's prohibition against religious discrimination. What accommodation, if any, should be made between the First Amendment and Title VII in cases against governmental employers?

The materials in this chapter explore some of these questions. Section B treats the meaning of "religion." Section C covers the religious entity exceptions. Section D covers the prima facie case of religious discrimination and includes a note on the applicability of the bona fide occupational qualification defense to religious discrimination claims. Section E examines the statutory obligation of the employer to "reasonably accommodate" the religious beliefs and practices of employees and applicants unless "undue hardship" is shown and includes notes on the charity substitution rule for unionized workplaces, sexual orientation discrimination, religious harassment, and disparate impact. Finally, Section F explores religious discrimination claims against government employers.

B. THE MEANING OF "RELIGION"

Congress did not define the meaning of the term "religion" in Title VII, as originally enacted in 1964. The 1972 amendments, adding "religion" to Title VII definitions in § 701(j), fails to adequately address the meaning of "religion" as well because the offered attempt at a definition is circular: "The term *'religion'* includes all aspects of *religious* observance and practice, as well as belief, * * * ." (Emphasis added.) The courts thus generally have relied upon definitions of religion adopted by the Supreme Court and the EEOC. The Supreme Court has stated that "[a]lthough a determination of what is a 'religious' belief or practice entitled to constitutional protection may present a most delicate question, the very concept of ordered liberty precludes allowing every person to make his own standards on matters of conduct in which society as a whole has important interests." Wisconsin v. Yoder, 406 U.S. 205, 215–16, 92 S.Ct. 1526, 1533, 32 L.Ed.2d 15 (1972). The Court has also observed that a religious belief or practice, unlike "a matter of personal preference," is characterized by a "deep religious conviction, shared by an organized group, and intimately related to daily living." *Id.* at 216, 92 S.Ct. at 1533. But in *Frazee v. Illinois Department of Employment Security*, 489 U.S. 829, 833, 109 S.Ct. 1514, 1517–18, 103 L.Ed.2d 914 (1989), the Court rejected the view that "to claim the protection of the Free Exercise Clause [of the First Amendment], one must be responding to the commands of a particular religious organization." After Frazee had rejected a temporary retail job that would have required him to violate his personal religious beliefs by working on Sundays, the state of Illinois denied him unemployment benefits. Although he did not belong to any particular Christian denomination, Frazee claimed that he was a Christian. The Court accepted the finding of the lower court that Frazee's refusal to work on Sundays was based on a sincerely held "personal professed religious belief," *id.* at 833, 109 S.Ct. at 1517, and held that his beliefs were protected under the First Amendment.

A number of courts have endorsed or deferred to the definition of "religious practices or beliefs" the EEOC has adopted in its *Guidelines on Discrimination Because of Religion*, 29 C.F.R. § 1605.1 (2009):

> In most cases whether or not a practice or belief is religious is not at issue. However, in those cases in which the issue does exist, the [EEOC] will define religious practices to include moral or ethical beliefs as to what is right or wrong which are sincerely held with the strength of traditional religious views. This standard was developed in *United States v. Seeger*, 380 U.S. 163, 85 S.Ct. 850, 13 L.Ed.2d 733 (1965), and *Welsh v. United States*, 398 U.S. 333, 90 S.Ct. 1792, 26 L.Ed.2d 308 (1970). * * * The fact that no religious group espouses such beliefs or the fact that the religious group to which the individual professes to belong may not accept such belief will not determine whether the belief is a religious belief of the employee or prospective employee. The phrase "religious practice" as used in these Guidelines includes both religious observances and practices, as stated in Section 701(j), 42 U.S.C. § 2000e(j).

Courts have, however, continued to struggle with the expansiveness of the *Seeger/Welsh* definition. *See* Rebecca Redwood French, *From* Yoder *to Yoda: Models of Traditional, Modern, and Postmodern Religion in U.S. Constitutional Law,* 41 Ariz.L.Rev. 49 (1999) (analyzing inconsistency and diversity of approaches to defining religion after *Seeger* and *Welsh*). As a result, judicial approaches to the definition of religion have been inconsistent and other tests have emerged. For example, a number of circuit courts have adopted a test taken from Judge Arlin Adams's concurring opinion in a constitutional case, *Malnak v. Yogi*, 592 F.2d 197, 198 (3d Cir.1979) (per curiam). *See, e.g.*, DeHart v. Horn, 227 F.3d 47 (3d Cir.2000); Love v. Reed, 216 F.3d 682 (8th Cir.2000); United States v. Meyers, 95 F.3d 1475 (10th Cir.1996); Alvarado v. City of San Jose, 94 F.3d 1223 (9th Cir.1996). Judge Adams proposed defining religion using three indicia: first, examine "the nature of the ideas in question"—not to examine truth or orthodoxy, but to determine whether the subject matter is consistent with religion; second, examine the comprehensiveness of the religious belief—a religion does not answer only one question, it has a broader scope; third, examine whether the ideas comprising the religious belief have "any formal, external, or surface signs that may be analogized to accepted religions," including "formal services, ceremonial functions, the existence of clergy, structure and organization, efforts at propagation, observation of holidays," etc. *Malnak*, 592 F.2d at 208–09. The last criterion is not determinative, but can lend support to a claim of religion. *See also* Friedman v. S. Cal. Permanente Med. Group, 125 Cal.Rptr.2d 663, 677–79, 682–85 (Cal.Ct.App. 2002) (adopting Judge Adams's test and criticizing the expansiveness of the EEOC definition).

NOTES AND QUESTIONS

Consider whether any of the following would or should qualify as religious observances, practices, or beliefs:

1. An employee was discharged after his employer learned that he claims he has a "personal religious creed" that he must ingest Kozy Kitten Cat Food because it "contribute[s] significantly to his state of well being." Brown v. Pena, 441 F.Supp. 1382, 1384 (S.D.Fla.1977) (quoting plaintiff's E.E.O.C. affidavit), *aff'd without opinion*, 589 F.2d 1113 (5th Cir.1979) (table).

2. A counseling employee of the Centers for Disease Control & Prevention is terminated after refusing, based on religious grounds, to advise homosexual employees in the agency's employee assistance program. Walden v. Centers for Disease Control & Prevention, 669 F.3d 1277 (11th Cir.2012).

3. An employee was dismissed from employment because of his membership in the Ku Klux Klan (KKK). He alleges that the Klan is a religion because its meetings are full of "religious pomp and ceremony." *See* Bellamy v. Mason's Stores, Inc., 508 F.2d 504, 505 (4th Cir.1974), *aff'g*, 368 F.Supp. 1025, 1026 (E.D.Va.1973) ("[T]he proclaimed racist and anti-semitic ideology of the organization to which [plaintiff] belongs takes on * * * a narrow, temporal and political character inconsistent with the meaning of 'religion' as used in [Title VII]."). The history and purpose of the KKK are reviewed extensively in EEOC Dec. No. 79–6, EEOC Dec. P6737 (Oct. 6,

1978), 1978 WL 5828 (E.E.O.C.) (ruling that the KKK is not a religion for purposes of Title VII). What if an employee is dismissed for being a member and minister of a church that promulgates a belief in white supremacy, including the belief that people of color are "savage," that African Americans are subhuman and should be "ship[ped] back to Africa," that Jews control the nation and have instigated the wars in this century and should be driven from power and that the Holocaust never occurred, and also requiring allegiance to the "White Race" and to the "White Man's Bible"? *See* Peterson v. Wilmur Commc'ns, Inc., 205 F.Supp.2d 1014, 1015, 1022 (E.D.Wis.2002) ("Creativity" is a religion despite its white supremacist tenets; the fact that a religious belief is not subjectively moral or ethical does not mean it fails under the EEOC definition of religion). For a discussion of the expansiveness of the definition of religion under Title VII and its meaning, see Jane M. Ritter, *The Legal Definition of Religion: From Eating Cat Food to White Supremacy,* 20 Touro L.Rev. 751 (2004).

4. Ali X is a member of Nation of Islam, otherwise known as the Black Muslims. His employer refuses to permit him to wear the traditional Muslim "Kuffi"—a small skull cap—at work. *See* Calloway v. Gimbel Bros., 19 Fair Empl.Prac.Cas. (BNA) 705 (E.D.Pa.1979); Ali v. Southeast Neighborhood House, 519 F.Supp. 489 (D.D.C.1981).

5. An employer has a workplace dress code that requires all employees to wear pants as part of a uniform. Lois Lane, a female, applied for and was offered a job. She told her employer that her religion prohibits females from wearing pants and asked that she be permitted to substitute a dress or skirt for the uniform. The employer refused her request and then withdrew its offer of employment. *See* Reid v. Kraft Gen. Foods, Inc., 67 Fair Empl.Prac.Cas. (BNA) 1367 (E.D.Pa.1995); Holly M. Bastian, Comment, *Religious Garb Statutes and Title VII: An Uneasy Coexistence*, 80 Geo.L.J. 211 (1991).

6. Employer, a trucking firm, refuses to hire drivers who have used illegal drugs during the previous two years. To implement this policy, the company requires all applicants for truck driving jobs to take a polygraph test to evaluate their responses to questions about their use of illegal drugs. Plaintiff, a Native American who is a member of the Native American Church, applied for a truck driving job. Upon learning the purpose of the polygraph test, he told the interviewer that several times in previous months he had used peyote as a part of his church's religious ceremonies. For this reason, he was denied employment. Use of peyote, a cactus that contains the hallucinogen mescaline, is unlawful under the criminal law of the state in which the employer does business. However, sacramental use of peyote is considered "the central and most sacred practice of the Native American church." Toledo v. Nobel-Sysco, Inc., 892 F.2d 1481, 1484 (10th Cir.1989); *see also* 21 C.F.R. § 1307.31 (2009); Emp. Div., Dep't of Hum. Resources v. Smith, 485 U.S. 660, 672 n.15, 108 S.Ct. 1444, 1451 n.15, 99 L.Ed.2d 753 (1988).

7. An employee is required, as a condition of employment, to attend monthly staff meetings at which business matters pertaining to her job are discussed. All employees are paid to attend these mandatory meetings. A local minister always begins the meetings with a "theological appetizer" consisting of a brief religious message and a prayer. The employee, who is an Atheist, claims that the requirement that she attend these meetings amounts to constructive discharge. *See* Young v. Sw. Sav. & Loan Ass'n, 509 F.2d 140 (5th Cir.1975); *see also* Kolodziej v. Smith, 425 Mass. 518, 682 N.E.2d 604.

8. Would an Atheist have a claim for religious discrimination where her employer gave employees a day off on Good Friday as a spring holiday? Good Friday makes it easier for some Christians to observe their religious beliefs and practices. Is a policy of giving employees Good Friday off as a holiday different from giving employees time off for Thanksgiving? *See* Bridenbaugh v. O'Bannon, 185 F.3d 796 (7th Cir.1999).

9. Plaintiff, a lesbian, is a member of the Reconstructionist Movement of Judaism. The Movement views same-sex marriages as acceptable and desirable in preference to couples living together without benefit of marriage. When the plaintiff advised her prospective employer that she intended to marry her female partner in a religious ceremony, the employer withdrew its job offer. *See* Shahar v. Bowers, 114 F.3d 1097 (11th Cir.1997) (en banc).

C. THE RELIGIOUS ENTITY EXEMPTIONS

Title VII provides two broad exemptions for religious employers. The first exemption is found in § 702(a), 42 U.S.C. § 2000e–1(a). The original version of § 702(a) provided only that Title VII does not apply to "a religious corporation, association, or society with respect to the employment of individuals of a particular religion to perform work connected with the carrying on by such corporation, association, or society of its *religious activities* * * * ." 42 U.S.C. § 2000e–1 (1970) (emphasis added.) Section 702(a), as amended in 1972, now provides that Title VII

> shall not apply to * * * a religious corporation, association, educational institution, or society with respect to the employment of individuals of a particular religion to perform work connected with the carrying on by such corporation, association, educational institution, or society of its *activities*.

42 U.S.C. § 2000e–1(a) (emphasis added). The 1972 amendment removed the "religious" qualifier on "activities" that was included in the original version.

The second exemption, found in § 703(e)(2), 42 U.S.C. § 2000e–2(e)(2), applies only to religious educational institutions. Section 703(e)(2) provides, in relevant part, that

> it shall not be an unlawful employment practice for a school, college, university, or other educational institution or institution

> of learning to hire and employ employees of a particular religion if such [institution] is, in whole or in substantial part, owned, supported, controlled, or managed by a particular religion or by a particular religious corporation, association, or society, or if the curriculum of such [institution] is directed toward the propagation of a particular religion.

For "religious education institutions" or educational institutions that are "owned, supported, controlled or managed" by a "religious association," there is an obvious overlap between §§ 702(a) and 703(e)(2). For this reason religious schools typically invoke both provisions. For example, in *Little v. Wuerl*, 929 F.2d 944 (3d Cir.1991), the court held that both exemptions to Title VII covered a Catholic school's decision not to rehire a Protestant teacher for conduct that violated Catholic canon law. *See also*, Killinger v. Samford Univ., 113 F.3d 196 (11th Cir.1997) (applying the two exemptions to Title VII to deny the religious discrimination claim of a professor who was removed from his position at the divinity school of a Baptist university). The courts, however, are split over how broadly or narrowly the exemptions for religious employers should be construed in light of the constitutional protection afforded by the Free Exercise and Establishment Clauses of the First Amendment. *See* Vigars v. Valley Christian Ctr. of Dublin, Cal., 805 F.Supp. 802, 807 n.3 (N.D.Cal.1992). The problem is compounded further by the fact that neither the 1964 nor 1972 version of § 702(a), nor § 703(e)(2), contains an express exemption for discrimination on the basis of race or sex.

Corporation of the Presiding Bishop v. Amos, 483 U.S. 327, 107 S.Ct. 2862, 97 L.Ed.2d 273 (1987), is the leading Supreme Court case interpreting § 702. (Section 702 is now codified as § 702(a), 42 U.S.C. § 2000e–1(a)). The issue in *Amos* was whether it was unconstitutional under the Establishment Clause of the First Amendment to apply the § 702 exemption to the secular nonprofit activities of a religious organization. The Church of Jesus Christ of Latter-day Saints, an unincorporated religious association sometimes referred to as the Mormon or LDS Church, operated a nonprofit gymnasium in Salt Lake City, Utah, that was open to the public. Plaintiff Mayson had worked at the gym as a building engineer for sixteen years when the church discharged him because he did not qualify for a "temple recommend"—a certificate showing that, as a member of the church in full compliance with its standards and practices, the holder is eligible to enter its temples. Mayson and other class plaintiffs argued that if Title VII were construed to permit religious employers to discriminate on religious grounds in obviously nonreligious, secular jobs, then § 702 would violate the Establishment Clause of the First Amendment. The church argued that it was completely exempt from Title VII under § 702. The Supreme Court ruled in favor of the church.

The *Amos* decision turned largely on the application of the three-part test the Supreme Court enunciated in *Lemon v. Kurtzman*, 403 U.S. 602, 91 S.Ct. 2105, 29 L.Ed.2d 745 (1971), to evaluate alleged violations of the Establishment Clause. First, the law must have been enacted for a "secular legislative purpose"; second, the regulation's "principal or primary effect" must be one that "neither advances nor inhibits religion"; and third, the regulation must not involve the government in undue entanglement with religion. *See Amos*, 483 U.S. at 335–39, 107 S.Ct. at 2868–70 (quoting from *Lemon* and applying the *Lemon* test to the facts in *Amos*). Concluding that § 702 did not satisfy the second prong of the *Lemon* test because it had a primary effect of benefitting religious entities, the lower court in *Amos* had ruled in favor of the plaintiff. The Supreme Court reversed, holding that § 702 passed all three parts of the *Lemon* test. The *Amos* decision can also be viewed as an "accommodation" case in that § 702 serves to lift a burden on religious entities imposed by the general requirements of Title VII. It has been suggested that the Supreme Court applies the *Lemon* test less rigidly when the governmental provision at issue seeks to lift a governmental burden, like § 702 does (easing the burden imposed by Title VII's religious nondiscrimination requirement), and *Amos* has been cited as supporting such a view. *See, e.g.*, Roberto L. Corrada, *Religious Accommodation and the National Labor Relations Act,* 17 Berkeley J.Emp. & Lab.L. 185, 254–63 (1996); Michael W. McConnell, *Accommodation of Religion: An Update and Response to Critics,* 60 Geo.Wash.L.Rev. 685, 696 (1992); Mark Tushnet, *The Emerging Principle of Accommodation of Religion (Dubitante),* 76 Geo.L.J. 1691, 1704 (1988).

Further, the *Amos* Court rejected the appellees' equal protection challenge, holding that "as applied to the nonprofit activities of religious employers, § 702 is rationally related to the legitimate purpose of alleviating significant governmental interference with the ability of religious organizations to define and carry out their religious missions." *Amos,* 483 U.S. at 339, 107 S.Ct. at 2870. Under *Amos*, nonprofit enterprises operated by religious organizations may discriminate on the basis of religion in making employment decisions. However, the Supreme Court left open the issue whether for-profit enterprises operated by religious organizations are similarly exempt from Title VII. Should for-profit operations of religious institutions be exempt from the mandate of Title VII?

QUESTIONS

What arguments can you make for or against applying the religious entity exemptions under Title VII in the following cases?

1. Christian School requires all of its employees to be "born-again believers living a consistent and practical Christian life." Dana Ross, a

female, worked at the school as a librarian, where she dealt with students on a daily basis. On occasion she taught physical education or worked as a teacher's aide, but she had no responsibility for the school's religious or secular courses. Before Ross's annulment of her marriage to her first husband was formalized, she conceived a child with the man who later became her second husband. After learning that she was pregnant, the school fired Ross. At the time of the discharge, the school informed Ross that she was being terminated because of her "sin" of being "pregnant without benefit of marriage." Later, however, the school sought to defend the discharge in court on the sole ground that Ross had committed adultery by having "sexual relations with her 'new' husband before she was divorced from her 'old' husband." *See* Vigars v. Valley Christian Ctr. of Dublin, Cal., 805 F.Supp. 802, 804–05 (N.D.Cal.1992).

2. A church-operated school has a policy that limits health insurance coverage to teachers who are "heads of the household." The school sincerely believes that only males can be heads of households, so female teachers similarly situated to male teachers are denied health insurance coverage. *See* EEOC v. Fremont Christian Sch., 781 F.2d 1362 (9th Cir.1986).

3. A female secretary to a male pastor of a church claims that the pastor subjected her to hostile work environment sexual harassment. She wants to sue the church and pastor under Title VII. Should she be allowed to go forward with her claim against the church? What if the plaintiff is an associate pastor? *See* Black v. Snyder, 471 N.W.2d 715, 721 (Minn.App.1991) (permitting the sexual harassment claim of an associate pastor to go forward "presents no greater conflict with the church's disciplinary authority than that presented in cases enforcing child abuse laws"). Should a sex discrimination claim be treated any differently than a sexual harassment claim? *See* Geary v. Visitation of the Blessed Virgin Mary Parish Sch., 7 F.3d 324, 331 (3d Cir.1993) (age discrimination claim brought by a lay teacher at a parochial school can proceed "[b]ecause application of the ADEA does not present a significant risk of government entanglement in religion"). *But see* Curay-Cramer v. Ursuline Acad., 450 F.3d 130 (3d Cir.2006) (Title VII claim brought by teacher who was fired for pro-choice activism barred because of religious institutions' interest in employing individuals faithful to its doctrinal practices).

NOTE: THE "MINISTERIAL EXCEPTION" TO TITLE VII DISCRIMINATION CLAIMS AGAINST RELIGIOUS INSTITUTIONS

Courts have interpreted Title VII and the ADEA to bar discrimination by religious employers on the basis of race, color, sex, national origin, and age. *See* Geary v. Visitation of the Blessed Virgin Mary Parish Sch., 7 F.3d 324, 331 (3d Cir.1993). They were divided, however, over how broadly or narrowly the exceptions in §§ 702(a) and 703(e)(2) should be construed in sex and race discrimination claims brought against religious employers. *See generally*

Treaver Hodson, Comment, *The Religious Employer Exemption Under Title VII: Should a Church Define Its Own Activities?*, 1994 B.Y.U.L.Rev. 571.

The Fifth Circuit carved out a "ministerial exception" to Title VII in *McClure v. Salvation Army*, 460 F.2d 553, *cert. denied*, 409 U.S. 896, 92 S.Ct. 132, 34 L.Ed.2d 153 (1972). Plaintiff, a female minister, brought a Title VII sex discrimination claim alleging that she received lower wages than similarly situated male ministers. Limiting its decision solely to the relationships between a church and its ministers, the court found that the Free Exercise Clause would preclude judicial review of decisions by religious entities concerning the terms and conditions of employment of their ministers because "[t]he relationship between an organized church and its ministers is its lifeblood." *Id.* at 558. In order to avoid reaching this constitutional question, however, *McClure* held that "Congress did not intend, through the nonspecific wording of the applicable provisions of Title VII, to regulate the employment relationship between church and minister." *Id.* at 560. The ministerial exception is grounded in two constitutional rationales. The first is that the imposition of secular standards on a church's employment of its ministers will burden the free exercise of religion; the second is that "the state's interest in eliminating employment discrimination" is outweighed by the church's constitutional right of autonomy in its own domain. Hodson, *supra*, at 599. *See* EEOC v. Catholic Univ. of Am., 83 F.3d 455, 467 (D.C.Cir.1996). For a treatment of sex discrimination experienced by clergywomen, *see* Elisabeth S. Wendorff, *Employment Discrimination and Clergywomen: Where the Law Has Feared to Tread*, 3 S.Cal.Rev.L. & Women's Stud. 136 (1993).

More than forty years after the Fifth Circuit's decision in *McClure*, the United States Supreme Court officially recognized and sanctioned the ministerial exception. In *Hosanna-Tabor Evangelical Lutheran Church & School v. EEOC*, ___ U.S. ___, 132 S.Ct. 694, 181 L.Ed.2d 650 (2013), the court considered a religious organization's ability to terminate an employee without incurring liability for retaliation under the ADA. The plaintiff in *Hosanna-Tabor* was a teacher in the Church's elementary school. Though a teacher and not a minister, the Church considered her a "called" as opposed to a "lay" employee, one whose educational vocation was a "call" from God. To be a "called" teacher, one must complete a course of theological study in addition to academic courses. "Called" teachers at the Church School received the title, "Minister of Religion, Commissioned." *Id.* at 699. After being diagnosed with narcolepsy, the plaintiff teacher was forced to take medical leave for several months. *Id.* at 700. Once cleared by her physician, the plaintiff informed the school of her intention to return to work, the school resisted and eventually revoked the plaintiff's "called" status. *Id.* The plaintiff then informed the school of her intention to file suit under the Americans with Disabilities Act and was subsequently fired. *Id.*

In a unanimous decision, the Supreme Court held that the defendant school, as a religious organization, could not be held legally liable for the internal decisions made by it regarding its ministerial employees. *Id.* at 709–

10. The Court recognized the ministerial exception as being firmly rooted in the First Amendment under both the Establishment Clause and Free Exercise Clause. *Id.* at 702. In its decision, the Court spent much of its time illustrating how the plaintiff fell into the category of ministerial employee. The Court reasoned that because the plaintiff conveyed the church's message and carried out its mission, her role would be considered ministerial in nature, therefore triggering the exception *Id.* at 707–08. The plaintiff's argument in large part relied on the Court's previous decision in *Employment Division, Department of Human Resources of Oregon v. Smith,* 494 U.S. 872, 110 S.Ct. 1595, 108 L.Ed.2d 876 (1990), discussed in Section F of this chapter. The plaintiff argued that *Smith* foreclosed the applicability of the ministerial exception. *Hosanna-Tabor,* 132 S.Ct. at 697. The court rejected this contention however. Distinguishing *Smith,* all nine justices agreed that because *Hosanna-Tabor* concerned a purely internal decision made by a religious organization and not outward physical acts, the ministerial exception would still apply. *Id.* Although the Supreme Court's decision in *Hosanna-Tabor* does seem to grant extreme discretion to religious organizations concerning internal employment decisions, in a footnote, the court concluded that the ministerial exception would not act as a jurisdictional bar to other similar claims, but only as an affirmative defense, maintaining a plaintiff's ability to have its claim heard before the court. *Id.* at 714 n. 4. For an in-depth treatment of the "ministerial exception" post *Hosanna-Tabor,* see Blair A. Crunk, *New Wine in an Old Chalice: The Ministerial Exception's Humble Roots,* 73 La. L. Rev. 1081 (2013); Michael A. Helfand, *Religion's Footnote Four: Church Autonomy As Arbitration,* 97 Minn. L. Rev. 1891, 1893 (2013); Leslie C. Griffin, *The Sins of Hosanna-Tabor,* 88 Ind. L.J. 981 (2013).

The Court's expansive approach to the definition of "minister" has already resulted in a decision extending the exception to a church's "music director," based on testimony from clergy that "music in the liturgy is sacred and has . . . spiritual dimensions." *See* Cannatta v. Catholic Diocese of Austin, 700 F.3d 169, 177 (5th Cir.2012).

D. ESTABLISHING A PRIMA FACIE CASE

EEOC V. ABERCROMBIE & FITCH STORES, INC.

United States District Court for the Eastern District of Missouri, 2009.
No.4:08CV1470 JCH, 2009 WL 3517584 (Oct. 26, 2009).

MEMORANDUM AND ORDER

JEAN C. HAMILTON, DISTRICT JUDGE.

This matter is before the Court on Defendants' Motion for Summary Judgment * * * .

BACKGROUND

On November 26, 2006, Lakettra Bennett ("Bennett") was hired by Defendants to work as a sales person or "model" in their Abercrombie & Fitch store in Fairview Heights, Illinois. In early June, 2007, Bennett was promoted into a Manager in Training (MIT) position, and transferred to Defendants' Hollister store in the Galleria Mall in St. Louis. At the time of her promotion, Bennett adhered to the Hollister "Look Policy," which directs that associates are expected to wear clothes that are similar to the Hollister brand. During the time Bennett was employed, the Hollister style consisted of "ripped-up jeans, a little revealing, sporty, California beach style, laid back," and was sexy, form-fitting, and designed to show off body contours and draw attention to the wearer. Bennett described the length of skirts and dresses sold by Hollister during the relevant time frame as falling just below the buttocks.

While attending a church service on September 16, 2007, Bennett converted to the Apostolic religion, and began to adhere to its regulations regarding dress. Accordingly, as of September 16, 2007, Bennett could wear only skirts that fell below the knee, and shirts with sleeves that came to the forearm. Bennett was not permitted to wear low-necked shirts, or those that revealed any cleavage.

On September 18, 2007, Bennett arrived to work at Hollister wearing an ankle-length denim skirt. The garment admittedly was inconsistent with the Hollister style, as until that time Hollister had never sold ankle-length skirts of the type worn by Bennett. Bennett explained to Store Manager Jamie Mateer that she was wearing the long skirt in order to adhere to her religious beliefs.

Bennett had several discussions with Mateer, District Manager Leslie Abel, and Human Resources Manager Erin Chura, and they eventually offered that Bennett could: wear jeans instead of skirts; wear short skirts with leggings underneath to cover her legs; or look in other stores for skirts that would both meet her religious requirements and be consistent with the Hollister style. After consultation with her father, Bennett responded that none of the options was acceptable, and reiterated her request that she be permitted to wear skirts that fell at or below the knee. Defendants refused, and Bennett was given two weeks' time to decide whether to continue her employment with Hollister and comply with the Look Policy, or resign. Bennett ultimately elected to submit her notice of resignation.

Plaintiff Equal Employment Opportunity Commission filed this lawsuit on Bennett's behalf on September *25,* 2008. In its Complaint, Plaintiff alleges Defendants violated the religious accommodation requirement of Title VII of the Civil Rights Act of 1964, by making no effort reasonably to accommodate Bennett's request to wear longer skirts in observance of her religious beliefs.

* * *

DISCUSSION

Title VII makes it unlawful, "to fail or refuse to hire or to discharge any individual, or otherwise to discriminate against any individual with respect to [her] compensation, terms, conditions, or privileges of employment, because of such individual's * * * religion." 42 U.S.C. § 2000e–2(a)(1). The statute broadly defines religion as, "all aspects of religious observance and practice, as well as belief, unless an employer demonstrates that he is unable to reasonably accommodate to an employee's * * * religious observance or practice without undue hardship on the conduct of the employer's business." 42 U.S.C. § 2000e(j).

In order to establish a prima facie case of religious discrimination under Title VII, Plaintiff must show that Bennett had a bona fide religious belief that conflicted with an employment requirement; that Bennett informed Defendants of this belief; and that Bennett was disciplined for failing to comply with the conflicting requirement of employment. Jones v. TEK Industries, Inc., 319 F.3d 355, 359 (8th Cir.2003) (citations omitted). If Plaintiff succeeds in establishing its prima facie case, Defendants, "must provide a reasonable accommodation to an employee's religion, unless the employer demonstrates that he is unable to reasonably accommodate to an employee's * * * religious observance or practice without undue hardship on the conduct of the employer's business." *E.E.O.C. v. Chemsico, Inc.*, 216 F.Supp.2d 940, 949 (E.D. Mo. 2002) (internal quotations and citation omitted). *See also Brown v. Polk County, Iowa*, 61 F.3d 650, 654 (8th Cir.1995), *cert. denied*, 516 U.S. 1158 (1996) (because Defendants made no attempt to accommodate Plaintiff's religious activities, they can prevail only by demonstrating that allowing the activities could not be accomplished without undue hardship).

In the instant case, Defendants concede a genuine issue of material fact remains with respect to whether Bennett possessed a sincere religious belief precluding compliance with the Look Policy.* The Court

* *Ed. Note:* The issue regarding Bennett's sincerity of belief arose because she appeared for her deposition in the case wearing a shirt she admitted was "formfitting." Under questioning in her deposition, Bennett admitted that the shirt was "body conscious." *See Court Sends Religious Bias Case to Trial; Employee Quit Over Retailer's "Look Policy,"* 211 Daily Lab.Rep. A–5 (Oct. 27, 2009). In a separate Memorandum and Order, the district judge denied partial summary judgment for the EEOC after finding that "a genuine dispute remains with respect to whether Bennett possessed a sincere religious belief precluding compliance with the Look policy," based on the defendant's "evidence that Bennett appeared for her deposition in this very case wearing clothing that was potentially inconsistent with her alleged faith." EEOC v. Abercrombie & Fitch Stores, Inc., No. 4:08CV1470 JCH, 2009 WL 3517578, at *3 (E.D.Mo. Oct. 26, 2009).

thus turns to a discussion of whether Defendants made a good faith effort reasonably to accommodate Bennett's religious belief, and/or whether granting Bennett's request for a blanket exemption from the Look Policy would have caused Defendants undue hardship.

I. REASONABLE ACCOMMODATION

As stated above, under Title VII an employer must "reasonably accommodate" an employee's religious beliefs, unless doing so would cause an "undue hardship." 42 U.S.C. § 2000e(j). Title VII does not define what constitutes a reasonable accommodation. *E.E.O.C. v. Aldi, Inc.*, 2008 WL 859249 at *7 (W.D. Pa. Mar. 28, 2008). Rather, "[t]he determination of when the reasonable accommodation requirement has been met * * * must be made in the particular factual context of each case." *Chemsico*, 216 F.Supp.2d at 952 (internal quotations and citations omitted). Further, under Eighth Circuit law, while a reasonable accommodation need not always eliminate the religion-work conflict, "there may be many situations in which the only reasonable accommodation is to eliminate the religious conflict altogether." *Sturgill v. United Parcel Service, Inc.*, 512 F.3d 1024, 1032–1033 (8th Cir.2008). Thus, "in close cases, [whether the only reasonable accommodation is to eliminate the religious conflict altogether] is a question for the jury because it turns on fact-intensive issues such as work demands, the strength and nature of the employee's religious conviction, * * * and the contractual rights and workplace attitudes of co-workers." Id. at 1033.

In the instant case, it is undisputed that upon learning of Bennett's alleged religious conflict, Defendants immediately engaged in an interactive process designed to understand and attempt to accommodate Bennett's religious beliefs. Upon consideration, however, the Court finds the question of whether any of Defendants' three proposed solutions, i.e., permitting Bennett to wear jeans instead of skirts, to wear short skirts with leggings underneath to cover her legs, or to look in other stores for skirts that would both meet her religious requirements and be consistent with the Hollister style,[4] constituted a *reasonable* accommodation, remains an issue of fact for the jury. In other words, the Court finds a genuine issue remains as to whether Defendants' offers to compromise effectively eliminated Bennett's religious conflict, sufficient to trigger her, "correlative duty to make a good faith attempt to satisfy her needs through means offered by the employer." *Mann v. Frank*, 795 F.Supp. 1438, 1450 (W.D. Mo. 1992) (citations omitted). *See also E.E.O.C. v. Alamo Rent-A-Car, LLC*, 432 F.Supp.2d 1006, 1013 (D. Ariz. 2006) (Alamo's proposal failed to accommodate the religious conflict, and thus

---

[4] While the Court finds it troubling that Bennett failed to investigate the third option before rejecting it as inconsistent with her religious needs, it declines to grant judgment as a matter of law on this basis.

was not a reasonable accommodation). This portion of Defendants' Motion for Summary Judgment must therefore be denied.

II. UNDUE HARDSHIP

In their Motion for Summary Judgment, Defendants next assert they are entitled to judgment as a matter of law, because the accommodation sought by Bennett would have posed an undue hardship. As stated above, in order to escape liability Defendants must show they made a good faith effort to accommodate Bennett's religious belief, or that employing such an accommodation would have worked an undue hardship on Defendants and their business. *Chemsico*, 216 F.Supp.2d at 952. Undue hardship is not defined within the language of Title VII, and thus "the circumstances under which a particular accommodation may cause undue hardship, must be made in the particular factual context of each case." *Id.* (internal quotations and citations omitted).

To require [an employer] to bear more than a *de minimis* cost * * * is an undue hardship. * * * *De minimis* cost, moreover, entails not only monetary concerns, but also the employer's burden in conducting its business. *Brown*, 61 F.3d at 655 (internal quotations and citations omitted).

In support of their claim of undue hardship, Defendants contend that exempting Bennett from the Look Policy would require Hollister to eliminate an essential function of her MIT position, interfere with enforcement of the Policy, and damage the Hollister brand and thereby damage the Company. Defendants support these assertions with citations to both expert and lay testimony. However, the Court concludes that Defendants have failed to meet their burden of demonstrating that, as a matter of law, they would have suffered more than a *de minimis* hardship had they further accommodated Bennett. *Chemsico*, 216 F.Supp.2d at 954. *See also Brown*, 61 F.3d at 655 (internal quotations and citations omitted) ("Any hardship asserted, furthermore, must be real rather than speculative, merely conceivable, or hypothetical."). The question thus remains one for the jury, and so this portion of Defendants' Motion for Summary Judgment must be denied.

NOTES AND QUESTIONS

1. Should an employer be allowed to challenge the veracity of a plaintiff's asserted "religious" belief or practice that is alleged to conflict with an employer's job requirement? An inquiry into veracity focuses on whether an asserted religious practice or belief falls within the statutory meaning of "religion" under Title VII.

2. Should an employer be permitted to challenge the bona fides or sincerity of a plaintiff's religious beliefs or practices? What is the response of the court in *Abercrombie & Fitch* to this question? In *Philbrook v. Ansonia*

Board of Education, 757 F.2d 476, 481–82 (2d Cir.1985), *rev'd on other grounds*, 479 U.S. 60, 107 S.Ct. 367, 93 L.Ed.2d 305 (1986), the Second Circuit made a distinction between inquiries into the verity—or the veracity—and the sincerity of a plaintiff's asserted beliefs or practices.

> We acknowledge that it is entirely appropriate, indeed necessary for a court to engage in analysis of the sincerity—as opposed, of course, to verity—of someone's religious beliefs in both the free exercise context and the Title VII context. We see no reason for not regarding the standard for sincerity under Title VII as that used in Free Exercise cases. * * * This court has recently held that a sincerity analysis is necessary in order to "differentiat[e] between those beliefs that are held as a matter of conscience and those that are animated by motives of deception and fraud." *Patrick*, [v. LeFevre, 745 F.2d 153, 157 (2d Cir.1984)].

3. If an inquiry into sincerity is appropriate, should an objective or subjective test control? In *Smith v. Pyro Mining Co.*, 827 F.2d 1081, 1086 (6th Cir.1987), the majority adopted a subjective test of sincerity, i.e., what the employee actually believed was required by his religious beliefs. The majority's apparent rejection of an objective test was consistent with the Supreme Court's admonishment in *Fowler v. Rhode Island*, 345 U.S. 67, 70, 73 S.Ct. 526, 527, 97 L.Ed.828 (1953), that "it is no business of courts to say that what is a religious practice or activity for one group is not religion under the protections of the First Amendment." The dissent in *Pyro Mining* argued for the adoption of an objective test on the ground that it would ferret out "purely personal" preferences that are not entitled to constitutional protection. *See id.* at 1096–97 (Krupansky, J., dissenting). Which is the better view? *See* EEOC v. READS, Inc., 759 F.Supp. 1150 (E.D. Pa. 1991) (head covering request by Muslim employee, though not required by religion, protected anyway based on personal religious belief).

4. An employee claims that his religious beliefs and observances require that he should not work on Saturdays but should instead engage in religious activities on that day. The employer hires a private investigator to "tail" the employee for a couple of weeks. The private investigator discovers that the employee regularly plays golf at the local golf course on Saturdays. Should the employer be allowed to introduce the facts uncovered by the private investigator to challenge both the veracity and sincerity of the employee's religious beliefs? What if the employee's adherence to the religious practice or belief is inconsistent? *See* EEOC v. Ilona of Hungary, Inc., 108 F.3d 1569, 1575 (7th Cir.1997) (en banc) (upholding district court finding that plaintiff's request for time off for observance of Yom Kippur was based on a sincere religious belief although she had inconsistently observed Jewish religious holidays in the past). While an employer investigation into the sincerity of an employee's religious beliefs may be troublesome, what if the question of sincerity is put into question by the plaintiff when the employer is present, as Bennett apparently did in *Abercrombie & Fitch* by showing up to her deposition in a "body conscious" shirt?

5. Suppose that an employee's religious beliefs conflict with some legitimate work rule of the employer, but the employee has not notified the employer of the conflict. If the employer nevertheless has actual knowledge of the employee's belief and the conflict, is the employer required to attempt to make an accommodation to resolve the conflict? Should knowledge of the employee's religious beliefs ever be imputed to the employer in order to satisfy the notice requirement of a prima facie case? If so, what facts should be sufficient to be considered constructive notice? The Supreme Court recently shed light on the question. In EEOC v. Abercrombie and Fitch Stores, Inc., 575 U.S. ___, 135 S.Ct. 2028, 192 L.Ed.2d 35 (2015), the Supreme Court held that an applicant only need show that his or her need for an accommodation was a motivating factor in the employer's decision, not that the employer had knowledge of the need for accommodation. In reversing the Tenth Circuit's grant of summary judgment on the issue, the Court stated that Title VII prohibits certain motives, and the applicant only needed to show that the employer failed to hire her because of her religion. Since the employer failed to hire applicant because it knew her headscarf was worn for religious reasons and that her headscarf violated its "look policy," the employer's motivation can be unlawful even if it did not know of any request for accommodation. *Id.* The Court did concede that knowledge requisite for motive may be an issue if the employer does not know that the conflicting requirement is a religious practice. *Id.* at n. 3. The Court also made clear that it is not enough that an employer's policy is neutral, applying equally to religious and nonreligious practice, because Title VII gives religion favored treatment by affirmatively requiring accommodation of religious practice.

6. *Reverse Religious Discrimination Claims*: What must an employee prove to establish a prima facie case when he claims that he was discharged not because of his own religious beliefs but because he did not hold the same religious views as his supervisor? In *Shapolia v. Los Alamos National Laboratory*, 992 F.2d 1033 (10th Cir.1993), plaintiff alleged that he received negative performance evaluations from his supervisor because he was not of the same religious faith as his supervisor, who was a bishop in the Church of Jesus Christ of Latter Day Saints ("Mormon" Church). The negative evaluation eventually led to the plaintiff's discharge. *Shapolia* held that to establish a prima facie case where the plaintiff alleges that he was discriminated against because he did not share his supervisor's religious beliefs, the plaintiff must show "(1) that he was subjected to some adverse employment action; (2) that, at the time the employment action was taken, the employee's job performance was satisfactory; and (3) some additional evidence to support the inference that the employment actions were taken because of a discriminatory motive based upon the employee's failure to hold or follow his or her employer's religious beliefs." *Id.* at 1038. If these elements are satisfied, only then is the plaintiff "entitled to the benefit of the *McDonnell* burden-shifting scheme and its presumption." *Id.* The Tenth Circuit considered this class of cases to be analogous to affirmative action or "reverse discrimination" cases. *Id.* at 1038 n.6. *See also* Venters v. City of Delphi, 123 F.3d 956, 972 (7th Cir.1997) (citing *Shapolia* with approval for

the proposition that a prima facie case of religious discrimination is satisfied when a plaintiff's claim is "not that the [employer] refused to accommodate her religious practices in some way, but that she was discharged because she did not measure up to the * * * religious expectations" of her supervisor, a born-again Christian who wanted to "save her soul"). Harassment against so-called nonadherents—employees who do not adhere to the same religion as a supervisor—is discussed *infra* Section E, in Note: Harassment Because of Religion.

NOTE: THE BONA FIDE OCCUPATIONAL QUALIFICATION DEFENSE

Section 703(e) of Title VII, 42 U.S.C. § 2000e–2(e), provides that it is not an unlawful employment practice for an employer to discriminate "on the basis of * * * religion * * * in those certain instances where religion * * * is a bona fide occupational qualification [BFOQ] reasonably necessary to the normal operation of that particular business or enterprise * * * ." The classic cases in which the BFOQ defense applies are those in which a religious institution limits employment to individuals who are members of the religious order. Most of these cases can be decided under either the religious entity exception or the BFOQ provision. *See, e.g.*, Pime v. Loyola Univ. of Chi., 803 F.2d 351 (7th Cir.1986) (upholding a university's decision to deny a tenure track position to a Jewish professor who was not a Jesuit, on the ground that being a Jesuit was a BFOQ for the available position in the Philosophy Department, even though the district court had rejected the employer's defense that it qualified for the religious employer exemption under § 703(e)(2), because it was not "supported, controlled or managed" by the Society of Jesus). But *EEOC v. Kamehameha Schools/Bishop Estate*, 990 F.2d 458 (9th Cir.1993), suggests that courts are willing to examine critically whether employment must be limited to persons of the same religious order. In *Kamehameha*, the court found that "adherence to the Protestant faith" was not a BFOQ for a teaching position at private schools that were not controlled or supported by a religious organization even though the will creating the schools required that all teachers be Protestant in order to create a "Protestant presence" at the schools. *Id.* at 465–67, 465 n.15.

Consider the following:

1. Pursuant to state law, a school district provides bus service to students living in the district who attend either public or private schools. A number of male students in the district attend an all-male private religious school operated by a sect of Hasidic Jews. Because religious tenets of the Hasidim prohibit any social interactions between the sexes, Hasidic parents object to having their male children ride on school buses driven by female bus drivers. In response to demands of the Hasidic community, the school board has adopted a policy that bars female bus drivers from driving bus routes on which male Hasidic Jewish students live. All female bus drivers are thus denied the opportunity to bid for these routes, even if they would be entitled

to them under seniority rules in the collective bargaining agreement. A group of female school bus drivers brings a class action suit against the school board challenging its policy under Title VII. Is this a case of disparate treatment or disparate impact? In *Bollenbach v. Board of Education of Monroe-Woodbury Central School District*, 659 F.Supp. 1450, 1472 (S.D.N.Y.1987), the court first relied upon the *McDonnell Douglas* circumstantial evidence paradigm of disparate treatment analysis to find that the plaintiffs had made out a prima facie case of sex discrimination; then, adopting the disparate impact paradigm, the court rejected the defendant's asserted business necessity defense on the ground that its policy was not neutral. Should this case more properly have been analyzed as a direct evidence disparate treatment case rather than an amalgam of a circumstantial evidence and disparate impact case? And if it were analyzed as a direct evidence case, could the school board's policy have been justified as a BFOQ?

2. Baylor College of Medicine, in cooperation with the government of Saudi Arabia, has a rotation program that sends surgical teams from its prestigious cardiovascular unit in Houston, Texas, to King Faisal Specialist Hospital and Research Hospital in Riyadh, Saudi Arabia. The surgeons who participate in the program receive twice the salary of the surgeons at Baylor's Texas facility. Even though Baylor has never had an express agreement with the Saudi government that it would not send Jewish doctors, the college has never permitted any of its Jewish doctors to participate in the program because it believes that the Saudi government would not grant them entry visas. In addition, the college has expressed concerns for the safety of its Jewish doctors if they were allowed to go. *See Abrams v. Baylor Coll. of Med.*, 581 F.Supp. 1570 (S.D.Tex.1984) (finding on these facts that plaintiffs had met their burden of proving religious discrimination, and rejecting the employer's business necessity and BFOQ defenses), *aff'd in relevant part*, 805 F.2d 528 (5th Cir.1986). In *Kern v. Dynalectron Corp.*, 577 F.Supp. 1196 (N.D.Tex.1983), *aff'd*, 746 F.2d 810 (5th Cir.1984) (mem.), the district court found that being Moslem was a BFOQ for a position as a pilot who would be required to fly helicopters in Saudi Arabia from Jeddah to the holy area, Mecca. Under Saudi Arabian law, which is based on Islamic principles, any non-Moslem who enters Mecca must be beheaded. What rationale might explain the different outcomes in these two cases?

3. The Supreme Court's acknowledgment, in *UAW v. Johnson Controls*, 499 U.S. 187, 111 S.Ct. 1196, 113 L.Ed.2d 158 (1991), reproduced in Chapter 7, that safety concerns can, in limited circumstances, provide a rationale for a BFOQ defense in sex discrimination cases may also be relevant in the religious discrimination cases. *See id.* at 201, 111 S.Ct. at 1204 ("Our cases have stressed that discrimination on the basis of sex because of safety concerns is allowed only in narrow circumstances."). For example, in *Bhatia v. Chevron USA, Inc.*, 734 F.2d 1382 (9th Cir.1984), the court upheld an employer's rule that any employee whose job as a machinist might involve exposure to toxic gases was required to shave any facial hair that might interfere with the gas-tight seals on respirators worn as a safety

measure to comply with OSHA standards. Plaintiff was a member of the Sikh religion which prohibits its followers from shaving any body hair. *Bhatia* found that although the plaintiff had made out a prima facie case of religious discrimination, the employer could not retain him without undue hardship on the operation of its business. Under *Johnson Controls* and the rationale of *Bhatia* and *Kern*, could an employer adopt a policy, defensible as a BFOQ, prohibiting Sikhs from working as machinists?

E. REASONABLE ACCOMMODATION AND UNDUE HARDSHIP

TRANS WORLD AIRLINES, INC. V. HARDISON

Supreme Court of the United States, 1977.
432 U.S. 63, 97 S.Ct. 2264, 53 L.Ed.2d 113.

JUSTICE WHITE delivered the opinion of the Court.

* * * The issue in this case is the extent of the employer's obligation under Title VII to accommodate an employee whose religious beliefs prohibit him from working on Saturdays.

I

* * *

Petitioner Trans World Airlines (TWA) operates a large maintenance and overhaul base in Kansas City, Mo. On June 5, 1967, respondent Larry G. Hardison was hired by TWA to work as a clerk in the Stores Department at its Kansas City base. Because of its essential role in the Kansas City operation, the Stores Department must operate 24 hours per day, 365 days per year, and whenever an employee's job in that department is not filled, an employee must be shifted from another department, or a supervisor must cover the job, even if the work in other areas may suffer.

Hardison, like other employees at the Kansas City base, was subject to a seniority system contained in a collective-bargaining agreement that TWA maintains with petitioner International Association of Machinists and Aerospace Workers (IAM). The seniority system is implemented by the union steward through a system of bidding by employees for particular shift assignments as they become available. The most senior employees have first choice for job and shift assignments, and the most junior employees are required to work when the union steward is unable to find enough people willing to work at a particular time or in a particular job to fill TWA's needs.

In the spring of 1968 Hardison began to study the religion known as the Worldwide Church of God. One of the tenets of that religion is that one must observe the Sabbath by refraining from performing any work from sunset on Friday until sunset on Saturday. The religion also proscribes work on certain specified religious holidays.

When Hardison informed Everett Kussman, the manager of the Stores Department, of his religious conviction regarding observance of the Sabbath, Kussman agreed that the union steward should seek a job swap for Hardison or a change of days off; that Hardison would have his religious holidays off whenever possible if Hardison agreed to work the traditional holidays when asked; and that Kussman would try to find Hardison another job that would be more compatible with his religious beliefs. The problem was temporarily solved when Hardison transferred to the 11 p.m.–7 a.m. shift. Working this shift permitted Hardison to observe his Sabbath.

The problem soon reappeared when Hardison bid for and received a transfer from Building 1, where he had been employed, to Building 2, where he would work the day shift. The two buildings had entirely separate seniority lists; and while in Building 1 Hardison had sufficient seniority to observe the Sabbath regularly, he was second from the bottom on the Building 2 seniority list.

In Building 2 Hardison was asked to work Saturdays when a fellow employee went on vacation. TWA agreed to permit the union to seek a change of work assignments for Hardison, but the union was not willing to violate the seniority provisions set out in the collective-bargaining contract, and Hardison had insufficient seniority to bid for a shift having Saturdays off.

A proposal that Hardison work only four days a week was rejected by the company. Hardison's job was essential, and on weekends he was the only available person on his shift to perform it. To leave the position empty would have impaired supply shop functions, which were critical to airline operations; to fill Hardison's position with a supervisor or an employee from another area would simply have undermanned another operation; and to employ someone not regularly assigned to work Saturdays would have required TWA to pay premium wages.

When an accommodation was not reached, Hardison refused to report for work on Saturdays. A transfer to the twilight shift proved unavailing since that schedule still required Hardison to work past sundown on Fridays. After a hearing, Hardison was discharged on grounds of insubordination for refusing to work during his designated shift.

Hardison * * * brought this action * * * against TWA and IAM, claiming that his discharge by TWA constituted religious discrimination in violation of Title VII. * * *

[After a bench trial, the district court ruled in favor of TWA and the union. The Eighth Circuit affirmed the judgment for the union, but reversed the judgment for TWA.]

* * *

III

The Court of Appeals held that TWA had not made reasonable efforts to accommodate Hardison's religious needs under the 1967 EEOC guidelines in effect at the time the relevant events occurred. In its view, TWA had rejected three reasonable alternatives, any one of which would have satisfied its obligation without undue hardship. * * *

We disagree with the Court of Appeals in all relevant respects. It is our view that TWA made reasonable efforts to accommodate and that each of the Court of Appeals' suggested alternatives would have been an undue hardship within the meaning of the statute as construed by the EEOC guidelines.

A

It might be inferred from the Court of Appeals' opinion and from the brief of the EEOC in this Court that TWA's efforts to accommodate were no more than negligible. The findings of the District Court, supported by the record, are to the contrary. In summarizing its more detailed findings, the District Court observed:

> TWA established as a matter of fact that it did take appropriate action to accommodate as required by Title VII. It held several meetings with plaintiff at which it attempted to find a solution to plaintiff's problems. It did accommodate plaintiff's observance of his special religious holidays. It authorized the union steward to search for someone who would swap shifts, which apparently was normal procedure.

It is also true that TWA itself attempted without success to find Hardison another job. The District Court's view was that TWA had done all that could reasonably be expected within the bounds of the seniority system.

* * *

We shall say more about the seniority system, but at this juncture it appears to us that the system itself represented a significant accommodation to the needs, both religious and secular, of all of TWA's employees. As will become apparent, the seniority system represents a neutral way of minimizing the number of occasions when an employee must work on a day that he would prefer to have off. Additionally, recognizing that weekend work schedules are the least popular, the company made further accommodation by reducing its work force to a bare minimum on those days.

B

We are also convinced, contrary to the Court of Appeals, that TWA itself cannot be faulted for having failed to work out a shift or job swap for Hardison. Both the union and TWA had agreed to the seniority system; the union was unwilling to entertain a variance over the objections of men senior to Hardison; and for TWA to have arranged unilaterally for a swap would have amounted to a breach of the collective-bargaining agreement.

(1)

Hardison and the EEOC insist that the statutory obligation to accommodate religious needs takes precedence over both the collective-bargaining contract and the seniority rights of TWA's other employees. We agree that neither a collective-bargaining contract nor a seniority system may be employed to violate the statute, but we do not believe that the duty to accommodate requires TWA to take steps inconsistent with the otherwise valid agreement. Collective bargaining, aimed at effecting workable and enforceable agreements between management and labor, lies at the core of our national labor policy, and seniority provisions are universally included in these contracts. Without a clear and express indication from Congress, we cannot agree with Hardison and the EEOC that an agreed-upon seniority system must give way when necessary to accommodate religious observances. The issue is important and warrants some discussion.

Any employer who, like TWA, conducts an around-the-clock operation is presented with the choice of allocating work schedules either in accordance with the preferences of its employees or by involuntary assignment. Insofar as the varying shift preferences of its employees complement each other, TWA could meet its manpower needs through voluntary work scheduling. In the present case, for example, Hardison's supervisor foresaw little difficulty in giving Hardison his religious holidays off since they fell on days that most other employees preferred to work, while Hardison was willing to work on the traditional holidays that most other employees preferred to have off.

Whenever there are not enough employees who choose to work a particular shift, however, some employees must be assigned to that shift even though it is not their first choice. Such was evidently the case with regard to Saturday work; even though TWA cut back its weekend work force to a skeleton crew, not enough employees chose those days off to staff the Stores Department through voluntary scheduling. In these circumstances, TWA and IAM agreed to give first preference to employees who had worked in a particular department the longest.

Had TWA nevertheless circumvented the seniority system by relieving Hardison of Saturday work and ordering a senior employee to replace him, it would have denied the latter his shift preference so that Hardison could be given his. The senior employee would also have been deprived of his contractual rights under the collective-bargaining agreement.

It was essential to TWA's business to require Saturday and Sunday work from at least a few employees even though most employees preferred those days off. Allocating the burdens of weekend work was a matter for collective bargaining. In considering criteria to govern this allocation, TWA and the union had two alternatives: adopt a neutral system, such as seniority, a lottery, or rotating shifts; or allocate days off in accordance with the religious needs of its employees. TWA would have had to adopt the latter in order to assure Hardison and others like him of getting the days off necessary for strict observance of their religion, but it could have done so only at the expense of others who had strong, but perhaps nonreligious, reasons for not working on weekends. There were no volunteers to relieve Hardison on Saturdays, and to give Hardison Saturdays off, TWA would have had to deprive another employee of his shift preference at least in part because he did not adhere to a religion that observed the Saturday Sabbath.

Title VII does not contemplate such unequal treatment. The repeated, unequivocal emphasis of both the language and the legislative history of Title VII is on eliminating discrimination in employment, and such discrimination is proscribed when it is directed against majorities as well as minorities. Indeed, the foundation of Hardison's claim is that TWA and IAM engaged in religious *discrimination* in violation of § 703(a)(1) when they failed to arrange for him to have Saturdays off. It would be anomalous to conclude that by "reasonable accommodation" Congress meant that an employer must deny the shift and job preference of some employees, as well as deprive them of their contractual rights, in order to accommodate or prefer the religious needs of others, and we conclude that Title VII does not require an employer to go that far.

(2)

Our conclusion is supported by the fact that seniority systems are afforded special treatment under Title VII itself. Section 703(h) provides in pertinent part:

> Notwithstanding any other provision of this subchapter, it shall not be an unlawful employment practice for an employer to apply different standards of compensation, or different terms, conditions, or privileges of employment pursuant to a bona fide seniority or merit system * * * provided that such differences are

not the result of an intention to discriminate because of race, color, religion, sex, or national origin. * * *

"[T]he unmistakable purpose of § 703(h) was to make clear that the routine application of a bona fide seniority system would not be unlawful under Title VII." Teamsters v. United States, 431 U.S. 324, 352, 97 S.Ct. 1843, 1863, 52 L.Ed.2d 396 (1977). Section 703(h) is "a definitional provision; as with the other provisions of § 703, subsection (h) delineates which employment practices are illegal and thereby prohibited and which are not." Franks v. Bowman Transp. Co., 424 U.S. 747, 758, 96 S.Ct. 1251, 1261, 47 L.Ed.2d 444 (1976). Thus, absent a discriminatory purpose, the operation of a seniority system cannot be an unlawful employment practice even if the system has some discriminatory consequences.

There has been no suggestion of discriminatory intent in this case. "The seniority system was not designed with the intention to discriminate against religion nor did it act to lock members of any religion into a pattern wherein their freedom to exercise their religion was limited. It was coincidental that in plaintiff's case the seniority system acted to compound his problems in exercising his religion." The Court of Appeals' conclusion that TWA was not limited by the terms of its seniority system was in substance nothing more than a ruling that operation of the seniority system was itself an unlawful employment practice even though no discriminatory purpose had been shown. That ruling is plainly inconsistent with the dictates of § 703(h), both on its face and as interpreted in the recent decisions of this Court.

As we have said, TWA was not required by Title VII to carve out a special exception to its seniority system in order to help Hardison to meet his religious obligations.

C

The Court of Appeals also suggested that TWA could have permitted Hardison to work a four-day week if necessary in order to avoid working on his Sabbath. Recognizing that this might have left TWA short-handed on the one shift each week that Hardison did not work, the court still concluded that TWA would suffer no undue hardship if it were required to replace Hardison either with supervisory personnel or with qualified personnel from other departments. Alternatively, the Court of Appeals suggested that TWA could have replaced Hardison on his Saturday shift with other available employees through the payment of premium wages. Both of these alternatives would involve costs to TWA, either in the form of lost efficiency in other jobs or higher wages.

To require TWA to bear more than a *de minimis* cost in order to give Hardison Saturdays off is an undue hardship.[15] Like abandonment of the seniority system, to require TWA to bear additional costs when no such costs are incurred to give other employees the days off that they want would involve unequal treatment of employees on the basis of their religion. By suggesting that TWA should incur certain costs in order to give Hardison Saturdays off the Court of Appeals would in effect require TWA to finance an additional Saturday off and then to choose the employee who will enjoy it on the basis of his religious beliefs. While incurring extra costs to secure a replacement for Hardison might remove the necessity of compelling another employee to work involuntarily in Hardison's place, it would not change the fact that the privilege of having Saturdays off would be allocated according to religious beliefs.

As we have seen, the paramount concern of Congress in enacting Title VII was the elimination of discrimination in employment. In the absence of clear statutory language or legislative history to the contrary, we will not readily construe the statute to require an employer to discriminate against some employees in order to enable others to observe their Sabbath.

JUSTICE MARSHALL, with whom JUSTICE BRENNAN joins, dissenting.

* * *

Today's decision deals a fatal blow to all efforts under Title VII to accommodate work requirements to religious practices. The Court holds, in essence, that although the EEOC regulations and the Act state that an employer must make reasonable adjustments in his work demands to take account of religious observances, the regulation and Act do not really mean what they say. An employer, the Court concludes, need not grant even the most minor special privilege to religious observers to enable them to follow their faith. As a question of social policy, this result is deeply troubling, for a society that truly values religious pluralism cannot compel adherents of minority religions to make the cruel choice of surrendering their religion or their job. And as a matter of law today's result is intolerable, for the Court adopts the very position that Congress expressly rejected in 1972, as if we were free to disregard congressional choices that a majority of this Court thinks unwise. I therefore dissent.

With respect to each of the proposed accommodations to respondent Hardison's religious observances that the Court discusses, it ultimately notes that the accommodation would have required "unequal treatment,"

---

[15] The dissent argues that "the costs to TWA of either paying overtime or not replacing respondent would [not] have been more than *de minimis*." This ignores, however, the express finding of the District Court that "[b]oth of these solutions would have created an undue burden on the conduct of TWA's business" and it fails to take account of the likelihood that a company as large as TWA may have many employees whose religious observances, like Hardison's, prohibit them from working on Saturdays or Sundays.

in favor of the religious observer. That is quite true. But if an accommodation can be rejected simply because it involves preferential treatment, then the regulation and the statute, while brimming with "sound and fury," ultimately "signif[y] nothing."

* * *

What makes today's decision most tragic, however, is not that respondent Hardison has been needlessly deprived of his livelihood simply because he chose to follow the dictates of his conscience. Nor is the tragedy exhausted by the impact it will have on thousands of Americans like Hardison who could be forced to live on welfare as the price they must pay for worshiping their God. The ultimate tragedy is that despite Congress' best efforts, one of this Nation's pillars of strength—our hospitality to religious diversity—has been seriously eroded. All Americans will be a little poorer until today's decision is erased.

ANSONIA BOARD OF EDUCATION V. PHILBROOK

Supreme Court of the United States, 1986.
479 U.S. 60, 107 S.Ct. 367, 93 L.Ed.2d 305.

CHIEF JUSTICE REHNQUIST delivered the opinion of the Court.

Petitioner Ansonia Board of Education has employed respondent Ronald Philbrook since 1962 to teach high school business and typing classes in Ansonia, Connecticut. In 1968, Philbrook was baptized into the Worldwide Church of God. The tenets of the church require members to refrain from secular employment during designated holy days, a practice that has caused respondent to miss approximately six schooldays each year. We are asked to determine whether the employer's efforts to adjust respondent's work schedule in light of his belief fulfill its obligation under § 701(j) of the Civil Rights Act of 1964, 42 U.S.C. § 2000e(j), to "reasonably accommodate to an employee's * * * religious observance or practice without undue hardship on the conduct of the employer's business."

Since the 1967–1968 school year, the school board's collective-bargaining agreements with the Ansonia Federation of Teachers have granted to each teacher 18 days of leave per year for illness, cumulative to 150 and later to 180 days. Accumulated leave may be used for purposes other than illness as specified in the agreement. A teacher may accordingly use five days' leave for a death in the immediate family, one day for attendance at a wedding, three days per year for attendance as an official delegate to a national veterans organization, and the like. With the exception of the agreement covering the 1967–1968 school year, each contract has specifically provided three days' annual leave for observance of mandatory religious holidays, as defined in the contract. Unlike other categories for which leave is permitted, absences for religious holidays are not charged against the teacher's annual or accumulated leave.

The school board has also agreed that teachers may use up to three days of accumulated leave each school year for "necessary personal business." Recent contracts limited permissible personal leave to those uses not otherwise specified in the contract. This limitation dictated, for example, that an employee who wanted more than three leave days to attend the convention of a national veterans organization could not use personal leave to gain extra days for that purpose. Likewise, an employee already absent three days for mandatory religious observances could not later use personal leave for "[a]ny religious activity," or "[a]ny religious observance." Since the 1978–1979 school year, teachers have been allowed to take one of the three personal days without prior approval; use of the remaining two days requires advance approval by the school principal.

The limitations on the use of personal business leave spawned this litigation. Until the 1976–1977 year, Philbrook observed mandatory holy days by using the three days granted in the contract and then taking unauthorized leave. His pay was reduced accordingly. In 1976, however, respondent stopped taking unauthorized leave for religious reasons, and began scheduling required hospital visits on church holy days. He also worked on several holy days. Dissatisfied with this arrangement, Philbrook repeatedly asked the school board to adopt one of two alternatives. His preferred alternative would allow use of personal business leave for religious observance, effectively giving him three additional days of paid leave for that purpose. Short of this arrangement, respondent suggested that he pay the cost of a substitute and receive full pay for additional days off for religious observances.[3] Petitioner has consistently rejected both proposals.

* * *

[After a bench trial, the district court found that Philbrook had failed to prove his claim of religious discrimination against the school board and the union. The Second Circuit reversed and remanded.]

We granted certiorari to consider the important questions of federal law presented by the decision of the Court of Appeals. Specifically, we are asked to address whether the Court of Appeals erred in finding that Philbrook established a prima facie case of religious discrimination and in opining that an employer must accept the employee's preferred accommodation absent proof of undue hardship. We find little support in the statute for the approach adopted by the Court of Appeals, but we agree that the ultimate issue of reasonable accommodation cannot be

[3] The suggested accommodation would reduce the financial costs to Philbrook of unauthorized absences. In 1984, for example, a substitute cost $30 per day, and respondent's loss in pay from an unauthorized absence was over $130.

resolved without further factual inquiry. We accordingly affirm the judgment of the Court of Appeals remanding the case to the District Court for additional findings.

* * *

* * * [T]he Court of Appeals assumed that the employer had offered a reasonable accommodation of Philbrook's religious beliefs. This alone, however, was insufficient in that court's view to allow resolution of the dispute. The court observed that the duty to accommodate "cannot be defined without reference to undue hardship." It accordingly determined that the accommodation obligation includes a duty to accept "the proposal the employee prefers unless that accommodation causes undue hardship on the employer's conduct of his business." * * *

We find no basis in either the statute or its legislative history for requiring an employer to choose any particular reasonable accommodation. By its very terms the statute directs that any reasonable accommodation by the employer is sufficient to meet its accommodation obligation. The employer violates the statute unless it "demonstrates that [it] is unable to reasonably accommodate * * * an employee's * * * religious observance or practice without undue hardship on the conduct of the employer's business." 42 U.S.C. § 2000e(j). Thus, where the employer has already reasonably accommodated the employee's religious needs, the statutory inquiry is at an end. The employer need not further show that each of the employee's alternative accommodations would result in undue hardship. * * * [T]he extent of undue hardship on the employer's business is at issue only where the employer claims that it is unable to offer any reasonable accommodation without such hardship. Once the Court of Appeals assumed that the school board had offered to Philbrook a reasonable alternative, it erred by requiring the Board to nonetheless demonstrate the hardship of Philbrook's alternatives.

The legislative history of § 701(j) * * * is of little help in defining the employer's accommodation obligation. To the extent it provides any indication of congressional intent, however, we think that the history supports our conclusion. Senator Randolph, the sponsor of the amendment that became § 701(j), expressed his hope that accommodation would be made with "flexibility" and "a desire to achieve an adjustment." 118 Cong. Rec. 706 (1972). Consistent with these goals, courts have noted that "bilateral cooperation is appropriate in the search for an acceptable reconciliation of the needs of the employee's religion and the exigencies of the employer's business." Brener v. Diagnostic Center Hosp., 671 F.2d 141, 145–46 (5th Cir.1982). Under the approach articulated by the Court of Appeals, however, the employee is given every incentive to hold out for the most beneficial accommodation, despite the fact that an employer offers a reasonable resolution of the conflict. This approach, we think, conflicts with both the language of the statute and the views that led to its enactment. We accordingly hold that an employer has met its obligation under § 701(j) when it demonstrates that it has offered a reasonable accommodation to the employee.[6]

The remaining issue in the case is whether the school board's leave policy constitutes a reasonable accommodation of Philbrook's religious beliefs. * * * We think that the school board's policy in this case, requiring respondent to take unpaid leave for holy day observance that exceeded the amount allowed by the collective-bargaining agreement, would generally be a reasonable one. In enacting § 701(j), Congress was understandably motivated by a desire to assure the individual additional opportunity to observe religious practices, but it did not impose a duty on the employer to accommodate at all costs. The provision of unpaid leave eliminates the conflict between employment requirements and religious practices by allowing the individual to observe fully religious holy days and requires him only to give up compensation for a day that he did not in fact work. Generally speaking, "[t]he direct effect of [unpaid leave] is merely a loss of income for the period the employee is not at work; such an exclusion has no direct effect upon either employment opportunities or job status." Nashville Gas Co. v. Satty, 434 U.S. 136, 145, 98 S.Ct. 347, 353, 54 L.Ed.2d 356 (1977).

But unpaid leave is not a reasonable accommodation when paid leave is provided for all purposes *except* religious ones. A provision for paid leave "that is part and parcel of the employment relationship may not be doled out in a discriminatory fashion, even if the employer would be free * * * not to provide the benefit at all." Hishon v. King & Spalding, 467 U.S. 69, 75, 104 S.Ct. 2229, 2233–34, 81 L.Ed.2d 59 (1984). Such an arrangement would display a discrimination against religious practices that is the antithesis of reasonableness. Whether the policy here violates this teaching turns on factual inquiry into past and present administration of the personal business leave provisions of the collective-bargaining agreement. The school board contends that the necessary personal business category in the agreement, like other leave provisions, defines a limited purpose leave. Philbrook, on the other hand, asserts that the necessary personal leave category is not so limited, operating as an open-ended leave provision that may be used for a wide range of secular purposes in addition to those specifically provided for in the contract, but not for similar religious purposes. We do not think that the record is sufficiently clear on this point for us to make the necessary factual findings, and we therefore affirm the judgment of the Court of Appeals

[6] The Court of Appeals found support for its decision in the EEOC's guidelines on religious discrimination. * * * To the extent that the guideline, like the approach of the Court of Appeals, requires the employer to accept any alternative favored by the employee short of undue hardship, we find the guideline simply inconsistent with the plain meaning of the statute. * * *

remanding the case to the District Court. The latter court on remand should make the necessary findings as to past and existing practice in the administration of the collective-bargaining agreements.

[JUSTICES MARSHALL and STEVENS separately concurred in part and dissented in part. A portion of JUSTICE MARSHALL's dissent follows.]

* * *

The Court's analysis in *Trans World Airlines, Inc. v. Hardison*, 432 U.S. 63, 97 S.Ct. 2264, 53 L.Ed.2d 113 (1977), is difficult to reconcile with its holding today. In *Hardison*, the Court held that the employer's chosen work schedule was a reasonable accommodation but nonetheless went on to consider and reject each of the alternative suggested accommodations. The course followed in *Hardison* should have been adopted here as well. "Once it is determined that the duty to accommodate sometimes requires that an employee be exempted from an otherwise valid work requirement, the only remaining question is * * * : Did [the employer] prove that *it exhausted all reasonable accommodations*, and that the *only remaining alternatives would have caused undue hardship* on [the employer's] business?" *Id.*, at 91, 97 S.Ct. at 2280 (Marshall, J., dissenting) (emphasis added).

NOTES AND QUESTIONS

1. *Hardison* suggests a two-step analysis on the defense of inability to reasonably accommodate without undue hardship. Does *Philbrook* modify the *Hardison* analysis? If so, how?

2. Do *Hardison* and *Philbrook* endorse a per se rule that provisions in a collective bargaining agreement dealing with competing interests of the employees whom the union represents constitute reasonable accommodations? The Supreme Court, in an ADA case involving a non-collectively bargained seniority system, found that while ordinarily a disabled employee will not be entitled to an accommodation that places the employee above the requirements of a seniority system, an employee may show special circumstances that make just such an accommodation reasonable. *See* US Airways v. Barnett, 535 U.S. 391, 122 S.Ct. 1516, 152 L.E.2d 589 (2002). Similarly, in *Balint v. Carson City, Nevada,* 180 F.3d 1047 (9th Cir.1999) (en banc), the Ninth Circuit held that a bona fide seniority system does not relieve an employer of the duty to attempt to reasonably accommodate an employee's religious beliefs and practices if an accommodation can be accomplished without violating the seniority rights of other employees. Should it matter for accommodation whether a seniority system arises out of a collective bargaining agreement? *Compare* Beadle v. Hillsborough County Sheriff's Dep't, 29 F.3d 589, 593 (11th Cir.1994) ("While we recognize that *Hardison* specifically concerned the sufficiency of a seniority system under Title VII to determine employee eligibility for weekends off, we are not persuaded that the Court intended its holding apply only to those systems."),

with Opuku-Boateng v. State of Cal., 95 F.3d 1461, 1470 (9th Cir.1996) ("In *Hardison,* the proposed accommodation would have conflicted with the contractually-established seniority system * * * . By contrast, in this case, the scheduling of shifts was not governed by any collective bargaining agreement, and the proposed accommodation would not have deprived any employee of any contractually-established seniority rights or privileges, or indeed of any contractually-established rights or privileges of any kind.").

3. If an employee simply refuses to engage in "bilateral cooperation" with the employer in order to arrange an accommodation for her religious beliefs and practices, should the employer nevertheless be required to propose an accommodation for the employee? *See* EEOC v. Ithaca Indus., Inc., 849 F.2d 116 (4th Cir.1988) (en banc) (where an employee absolutely refuses to work on his Sabbath, the burden is on the employer to attempt to accommodate the employee's religious beliefs by offering alternatives); Smith v. Pyro Mining Co., 827 F.2d 1081, 1085 (6th Cir.1987) ("Although the burden is on the employer to accommodate the employee's religious needs, the employee must make some effort to cooperate with an employer's attempt at accommodation.").

4. In the following situations, what accommodations, if any, could an employer offer to make in order to satisfy its burden under Title VII?

a. An evangelical Christian employee believes that she should share the gospel with her co-workers. Pursuant to her beliefs, she sends letters to the homes of two employees. First, because she believes that her supervisor has engaged in un-Christian conduct in managing the employer's business, she sends him a letter urging him to confess his "sins" to God. His wife reads the letter and mistakenly believes her husband is having an adulterous affair with someone at work. The employee then sends a letter to a co-worker who has just had a child out-of-wedlock and is convalescing at home with an unspecified illness. The letter states that God "doesn't like when people commit adultery" and insinuates that her illness is God's punishment for her adultery. The recipient of the letter finds it "cruel." *See* Chalmers v. Tulon Co. of Richmond, 101 F.3d 1012 (4th Cir.1996), *cert. denied,* 522 U.S. 813, 118 S.Ct. 58, 139 L.Ed.2d 21 (1997).

b. Employees of a fast food establishment tell their employer that, according to their "sincerely held Christian religious beliefs," they feel compelled to greet customers with phrases such as "God bless you" and "Praise the Lord." Not all of the customers find the greetings to be "positive, uplifting, and inspirational," and some co-workers tell the employer that they consider the greetings to be "inappropriate for the workplace." *See* Banks v. Serv. Am. Corp., 952 F.Supp. 703 (D.Kan.1996).

c. Employee, a police officer, objects on religious grounds to being assigned to police duties at abortion clinics. *Compare* Parrott v. District of Columbia, 58 Empl.Prac.Dec. (CCH) ¶ 41,369, 1991 WL 126020, at *3 (D.D.C.1991) (Title VII's guarantee of reasonable accommodation does not require a police department to exempt a police officer from an assignment that requires policing abortion "rescues," because he has a "duty as a law enforcement officer to protect individuals inside abortion clinics from others' interference with their legally protected rights"), *with* Rodriguez v. Chicago, 69 Fair Empl.Prac.Cas. (BNA) 993 (N.D.Ill.1996) (city's refusal to excuse a Roman Catholic police officer from duty assignments at abortion clinics, despite his strong religious objections, is actionable under Title VII).

d. Employer proposes that an employee who objects to working on her Sabbath, which is Saturday, first use all of her accrued vacation days before alternative accommodations are considered. *See* Cooper v. Oak Rubber Co., 15 F.3d 1375 (6th Cir.1994).

e. A female employee has made a private religious vow to wear an anti-abortion button at all times until a national policy is adopted banning all abortions. The button has a color photograph of an aborted fetus and the words "Stop Abortion." Some of her co-workers object to her wearing the pin in the workplace because of the disruption it causes; others do not object because they agree with the button's message. *See* Wilson v. U.S. West Commc'ns, 58 F.3d 1337 (8th Cir.1995). *See also* Nantiya Ruan, *Accommodating Respectful Religious Expression in the Workplace,* 92 Marq.L.Rev. 1 (2008) (arguing that religious accommodation should be more expansive than Title VII currently allows).

f. A Jewish salesman informs his company that his religion requires that he must live in an area with an active synagogue. The community he chooses is outside of his sales territory. The company responds that its salespeople must live in communities within their sales area. The salesman tells the company that he is willing to pay all costs related to commuting from and living within his new community. *See* Vetter v. Farmland Indus., 901 F.Supp. 1446 (N.D.Iowa 1995), *rev'd on other grounds,* 120 F.3d 749 (8th Cir.1997).

g. A pharmacist refuses to dispense emergency contraceptives (e.g., the "Plan B" pill) because of his religious beliefs against contraception. Does it matter that the refusal is with respect to emergency versus nonemergency contraceptives? What accommodations might be reasonable? Is it reasonable to ask another pharmacist to fill the prescription? Is it an undue hardship for the employer to have customers referred to another source of Plan B contraceptives? What if the State Board of Pharmacy issued a regulation prohibiting pharmacists from refusing to dispense emergency contraceptives? *See* Stormans, Inc. v. Selecky, 524 F.Supp.2d 1245 (W.D. Wash.2007), *rev'd and remanded,* 586 F.3d 960 (9th Cir.2009).

5. Noting that the "precise reach" of the employer's duty to accommodate its employees' religious beliefs is not clear, the court in *Brown v. Polk*, 61 F.3d 650, 655 (8th Cir.1995), discussed in Section F of this Chapter, concluded that the issue must be resolved on a case-by-case basis. The court summarized some of the rules on undue hardship that the courts have articulated: (1) "[t]he cost of hiring an additional worker or the loss of production that results from not replacing a worker who is unavailable due to

a religious conflict can amount to undue hardship"; (2) "*[d]e minimis* cost * * * entails not only monetary concerns, but also the employer's burden in conducting its business"; (3) asserted hardships must be "real" rather than "speculative," "merely conceivable," or "hypothetical"; (4) an employer "stands on weak ground when advancing hypothetical hardships in a factual vacuum"; (5) "[u]ndue hardship cannot be proved by assumptions nor by opinions based on hypothetical facts"; (6) "[u]ndue hardship requires more than proof of some fellow-worker's grumbling," and "[a]n employer * * * would have to show * * * actual imposition on co-workers or disruption of the work routine." *Id.* (citations omitted). Based on these guidelines, which of the following, if any, constitutes an undue hardship:

a. Lynn Weber, a truck driver, is a Jehovah's Witness whose religious beliefs prevent him from accepting long-haul overnight runs with a female partner who is not his wife. The company assigns two-person overnight runs on a seniority basis and informs Weber that "working with women is a part of the job and that he would have to work with women or would not receive any driving assignment." *See* Weber v. Roadway Exp., Inc., 199 F.3d 270, 272 (5th Cir.2000).

b. Brenda Enlow, a member of the Conservative Holiness faith, applies to work in a factory manufacturing metal parts. The factory's safety policy includes a requirement that all employees are prohibited from wearing sleeveless shirts and thin-soled shoes, and must wear pants. The policy is intended to reduce exposure of skin to sharp metal parts and the risk of loose clothing becoming stuck on parts and machinery. The policy applies to all employees given that everyone is required to be able to operate all the machines of the plant due to changing production demands on customer orders. According to Brenda, however, her faith has a dress code requiring women and girls to wear dresses that extend below the knee. Brenda also cites the Bible, Deuteronomy 22:5, as the source of her belief that "a woman shall not wear anything that pertains to a man." *See* EEOC v. Oak-Rite Mfg. Corp., 88 Fair Empl.Prac.Cas. (BNA) 126, 2001 WL 1168156, at *6 (S.D.Ind.2001).

6. Employee files a charge with the EEOC alleging that he was discharged because the employer failed to accommodate his religious beliefs and practices. If the employer makes a settlement offer while the claim is pending before the EEOC, does the offer cure the alleged violation? *See* Toledo v. Nobel-Sysco, Inc., 892 F.2d 1481 (10th Cir.1989).

7. An employee claims that he was discharged because he refused to remove religious items from his desk although another employee was not disciplined for keeping a Bible on her desk. The employer claims the employee was discharged based on a reduction in force and that he was the lowest ranked employee in the jobs in which the reduction took place. Should this case be analyzed as a circumstantial evidence case in which the defense of a legitimate, nondiscriminatory reason could be raised? *See* Arvin-Thornton v. Philip Morris Prods., Inc., 64 F.3d 655 (4th Cir.1995)

(unpublished table decision). For a discussion of the difficulty of accurately classifying some disparate treatment religious claims within Title VII evidentiary frameworks, see Roberto L. Corrada, *Toward An Integrated Disparate Treatment and Accommodation Framework for Title VII Religion Cases,* 77 U.Cin.L.Rev. 1411 (2009).

8. *How much of the religious objector's belief or practice must be accommodated?* For many years, courts had widely held that an accommodation does not qualify as reasonable unless the employee's religious belief or practice is completely accommodated. *See* Baker v. Home Depot, 445 F.3d 541, 547–48 (2d Cir.2006) (holding that an employer does not fulfill its obligation when it offers to accommodate only one of two objections); EEOC v. Ilona of Hungary, Inc., 108 F.3d 1569, 1576 (7th Cir.1996) (same); Cooper v. Oak Rubber Co., 15 F.3d 1375, 1379 (6th Cir.1994) (same). Recently, two courts of appeals found that accommodations could be reasonable even if they are incomplete. In *EEOC v. Firestone Fibers & Textiles Co.,* 515 F.3d 307 (4th Cir.2008), the court found that the employer had met its obligation to reasonably accommodate when it allowed the employee to use all of his allotted paid and unpaid leave and some extra half-leave days to cover his religious obligations. Although the employee argued that an employer's only defense after failing to fully accommodate his religious practice is undue hardship, the court disagreed stating that the word "reasonably," not "fully," modifies accommodation. *Id.* at 313–14. In *Sturgill v. United Parcel Serv., Inc.,* 512 F.3d 1024 (8th Cir.2008), the court of appeals partially sustained a jury verdict against the employer for disparate treatment based on its refusal to accommodate the employee's need to stop working after sundown on Friday. The court maintained, however, that neither *Hardison* nor *Ansonia* require that to be reasonable an accommodation must entirely eliminate a religious conflict. Thus, the court overturned the district court's jury instruction that an accommodation must eliminate a conflict to be reasonable. The court concluded that the issue is a jury question because whether an accommodation is reasonable turns on fact-specific evidence. In overturning the jury's award of punitive damages but sustaining other damages against the employer, the court ruled that the erroneous jury instruction on reasonable accommodation had had limited effect on the verdict. *See also* Sanchez-Rodriguez v. AT&T Mobility Puerto Rico, Inc., 673 F.3d 1, 13 (1st Cir.2012) (holding that a series of attempts to accommodate the religious needs of an employee would not be considered in isolation; employer's multiple attempts to accommodate adequate to rebut discrimination claim).

9. In 1997, the Senate Committee on Labor and Human Resources held hearings on a bill, the Workplace Religious Freedom Act, to amend Title VII to provide that undue hardship shall mean "significant difficulty and expense," reversing *Hardison's de minimus* standard, and to provide that general leave shall always be available for religious observance, reversing *Ansonia.* The bill would require employers to weigh "significant difficulty and expense" in the context of 1) the essential functions of a job, 2) the

identifiable cost of accommodation, 3) the impact of an accommodation precedent on a particular workplace, and 4) the size of and geographic distance between the employer's business and facilities. Should *Hardison* and *Ansonia* be reversed? What are the pro's and con's of such a measure? Would such an amendment violate the Constitution's Establishment Clause? *See generally* The Workplace Religious Freedom Act of 1997: Hearings on S. 1124, Senate Committee on Labor and Human Resources, 105th Cong., 1st Sess. 31–57 (statements of Richard Foltin, Lawrence Lorber, Roberto Corrada) (Oct. 21,1997). The bill has been considered by Congress various times since 1997. *See also* Robert Capel, *Note, A Struggle of Biblical Proportions: The Campaign to Enact the Workplace Religious Freedom Act of 2003,* 16 U.Fla.J.L. & Pub.Pol'y 579 (2005).

NOTE: UNIONS, RELIGIOUS DISCRIMINATION CLAIMS, AND THE CHARITY SUBSTITUTION RULE

The liability of labor unions for unlawful discrimination, both as employers and as labor organizations, is covered in Chapter 2. Section 701(j) of Title VII, 42 U.S.C. § 2000e(j), specifically imposes an obligation on employers to reasonably accommodate the religious beliefs and practices of employees unless undue hardship on the conduct of the employer's business is shown. Although § 701(j) is silent with respect to a labor union's obligation to reasonably accommodate the religious beliefs and practices of its members, the courts have nevertheless held that § 701(j) is equally applicable to unions. *See, e.g.*, Tooley v. Martin-Marietta Corp., 648 F.2d 1239 (9th Cir.1981).

The National Labor Relations Act (NLRA) and the Railway Labor Act (RLA) both authorize union security agreements. 29 U.S.C. § 158(a)(3); 45 U.S.C. § 152, Eleventh. Generally a security agreement imposes an obligation on members of a bargaining unit to pay the union a fee that is equivalent to the union's initiation fee and dues even if they choose not to become union members and even if they are ideologically opposed to unionism. Under a typical agreement containing a dues "check-off" provision, every member of the bargaining unit is asked to sign a card authorizing the employer to deduct dues and initiation fees from her wages and forward the money to the union. The funds collected go into the union's treasury and are used for a variety of activities such as the negotiation and administration of collective bargaining agreements, grievance and arbitration proceedings, strike funds, and pension funds. Also, some of the funds may be used for other activities such as political activities, lobbying for labor-related legislation, and contributions to charities. *See generally* Norman L. Cantor, *Uses and Abuses of the Agency Shop*, 59 Notre Dame L.Rev. 61 (1983). One of the rationales for union security clauses is avoidance of the "free rider" situation, that is, allowing nonunion members of a bargaining union to reap the benefits of a collective bargaining agreement without contributing to the operating costs of the union.

Some employees have relied upon the reasonable accommodation provision of § 701(j) of Title VII to challenge union security provisions when they have religious scruples against joining unions or paying union dues. A typical situation in which this issue arises is when an employee objects, on religious grounds, to joining the union or paying union dues. In response, the union seeks, pursuant to the union security provision in the collective bargaining agreement, to have the employee discharged for the nonpayment of union dues or their equivalent in mandatory fees. Relying in substantial part on *Trans World Airlines, Inc. v. Hardison*, 432 U.S. 63, 97 S.Ct. 2264, 53 L.Ed.2d 113 (1977), in Section E of this chapter, courts have endorsed the "substitute charity contribution rule" in an attempt to reconcile the tension between a union's legitimate interest in having all of its member participate in the financial costs of collective bargaining, an employee's religious objections to paying union dues, and a union's obligation to reasonably accommodate the religious objections of an employee to the mandatory payment of union dues. The substitute charity contribution rule allows a religious objector to pay to a charity the equivalent amount that is paid to the union by other employees in the bargaining unit who do not have religious objections to paying union dues. In explaining the substitute charitable contribution rule, the court in *Tooley v. Martin-Marietta Corp.* stated that

> [t]he substituted charity contribution is consistent with the balancing of interests promoted by section 701(j). Under this accommodation, the union is entitled to enjoy the benefits of the union agreement while the [employees] are entitled to practice in accordance with their religious convictions. To the extent that the substituted charity accommodation effects this balance, it is reasonable under section 701(j).

648 F.2d at 1242. In rejecting the union's argument that under *Hardison* the loss of dues imposes an undue hardship on the union, *Tooley* held that

> [a] "wide-spread refusal to pay union dues" is sufficient to establish undue hardship, but that is not the contention here. The [union has] not established that the "substituted charity" accommodation, as applied here, will deprive the union of monies necessary for its maintenance or operation.

Id. at 1243–44 (citation omitted).

Prior to 1980, the courts were more sympathetic to unions in cases in which employees had religious objections to paying union dues. Although employing the same balancing test generally used in Title VII cases, the courts were more likely to tip the balance in favor of unions in the enforcement of union security clauses. *See* Steven C. Schwab, *Union Security Agreements and Title VII: The Scope and Effect of the New Section 19 of the National Labor Relations Act*, 17 Gonz.L.Rev. 329 (1981); Charleston C.K. Wang, Comment, *Religious Accommodation Versus Union Security: A Tale of Two Statutes*, 9 N.Ky.L.Rev. 331 (1982). In 1980 Congress enacted § 19 of the NLRA, 29 U.S.C. § 169, in an attempt to reconcile the inconsistency between

§ 701(j) of Title VII and the NLRA. The scope of the charity substitution rule under § 19 of the NLRA, however, is much narrower than under Title VII. Section 19 affords protection only to "employees who are members of a bona fide religion, body, or sect which has historically held conscientious objections to joining or financially supporting labor organizations." In *International Association of Machinists & Aerospace Workers, Lodge 751 v. Boeing Co.*, 833 F.2d 165, 169 (9th Cir.1987), the union argued that the more recent specific protection of § 19 supersedes and limits the broader protection of § 701(j). The Ninth Circuit rejected this statutory construction argument on the ground that the two statutes are not irreconcilable because they "serve independent and separate purposes." *Id.* The Sixth Circuit found § 19 to be unconstitutional in *Wilson v. National Labor Relations Board*, 920 F.2d 1282 (6th Cir.1990). For a more extensive discussion of the balance between union security and religious freedom, see Roberto L. Corrada, *Religious Accommodation and the National Labor Relations Act,* 17 Berkeley J.Emp. & Lab.L. 185 (1996).

NOTE: RELIGIOUS FREEDOM AND LAWS PROHIBITING DISCRIMINATION ON THE BASIS OF SEXUAL ORIENTATION AND GENDER IDENTITY

Legislation and executive orders at the federal, state, and local level that prohibit workplace discrimination against lesbian, gay, bisexual, and transgender (LGBT) employees and the laws prohibiting discrimination in employment because of religion raise complex issues for employers. *See, e.g.*, Judith Moldover, *When Religious Expression and Gay Rights Conflict*, N.Y.L.J., Oct. 18, 2007, at 24. The rules enunciated by the Supreme Court on employer liability for supervisory harassment in *Ellerth* and *Faragher* (Chapter 10), on liability for same-sex sexual harassment in *Oncale* (covered in Chapters 7, 9, and 10), and on the availability of punitive damages in *Kolstad* (Chapters 2 and 10), impose some obligation on employers to educate their employees about the prohibition against unlawful discrimination in the workplace. *See* Susan Bisom-Rapp, *An Ounce of Prevention Is a Poor Substitute for a Pound of Cure: Confronting the Developing Jurisprudence of Education and Prevention in Employment Discrimination Law*, 22 Berkeley J.Emp. & Lab.L. 1, 15–24 (2001) (describing anti-discrimination and diversity training programs developed in response to changing laws on workplace sexual harassment). As was discussed in Chapter 9, many state and local governments now prohibit employment discrimination on the basis of sexual orientation and gender identity or expression, and, therefore, education about discrimination against LGBT employees is often included in employer diversity training or education programs. Moreover, an increasing number of private employers now include discussion about sexual orientation and gender identity in their diversity awareness programs, raising concerns for employees who hold strong religious beliefs regarding homosexuality. For contrasting perspectives on accommodating the clash in American society between religious freedom and LGBT civil rights, see Chai R. Feldblum,

Moral Conflict and Liberty: Gay Rights and Religion, 72 Brooklyn L.Rev. 61 (2006), and George W. Dent, Jr., *Civil Rights for Whom? Gay Rights Versus Religious Freedom*, 95 Ky.L.J. 553 (2005–2006).

The tension between laws prohibiting employment discrimination because of religion and employers' efforts to protect LGBT employees from employment discrimination is illustrated in *Altman v. Minnesota Department of Corrections*, 251 F.3d 1199 (8th Cir.2001). There, the plaintiffs—three public employees—were directed to participate in a mandatory diversity training program on workplace discrimination against gay and lesbian employees. The plaintiffs alleged that the materials presented at the program caused them discomfort because of their religious beliefs. They attended the session, but read silently from their Bibles at various points. As a result, the employer issued each a written reprimand and one of the plaintiffs was denied a promotion as a result of the reprimand. The reprimands were issued pursuant to an employer policy, and there was no evidence that the employer singled out the plaintiffs solely because of their Bible-reading conduct. The plaintiffs sued their employer alleging violations of their rights Title VII, as well as under the Free Speech and Free Exercise Clauses of the First Amendment. Analyzing the case solely on Title VII grounds, what arguments would you make in favor of the plaintiffs? What defenses would you advance in support of the employer's action? For discussion of these issues, see Laura M. Johnson, Note, *Whether to Accommodate Religious Expression That Conflicts with Employer Anti-Discrimination and Diversity Policies Designed to Safeguard Homosexual Rights: A Multi-Factor Approach for the Courts*, 38 Conn.L.Rev. 295 (2004).

NOTE: HARASSMENT BECAUSE OF RELIGION

Compston v. Borden, Inc., 424 F.Supp. 157 (S.D.Ohio 1976), is one of the earliest cases to recognize that harassment on the basis of religion is actionable under Title VII. *Compston* held that "[w]hen a person vested with managerial responsibilities embarks upon a course of conduct calculated to demean an employee before his fellows because of the employee's professed religious views, such activity necessarily will have the effect of altering the conditions of his employment." *Id.* at 160–61. The Supreme Court approvingly cited *Compston* in its landmark sexual harassment case of *Meritor Savings Bank v. Vinson*, 477 U.S. 57, 66, 106 S.Ct. 2399, 2405, 91 L.Ed.2d 49 (1986), discussed in Chapter 10. The courts generally have applied the analytical framework, burden-shifting, and other rules developed in the sexual harassment cases to claims of religious harassment. *See, e.g.*, Kennedy v. St. Joseph's Ministries, Inc., 657 F.3d 189, 198 (4th Cir.2011) (holding that plaintiff must demonstrate that "the harassment was (1) unwelcome, (2) because of religion, (3) sufficiently severe or pervasive to alter the conditions of employment and create an abusive atmosphere, and (4) imputable to [the employer]"); Dediol v. Best Chevrolet, Inc., 655 F.3d 435, 443 (5th Cir.2011) ("plaintiff must produce evidence that (1) he belongs to a protected class; (2) he was subject to unwelcome harassment; (3) the harassment was based on religion; (4) the harassment affected a term, condition, or privilege of employment; and (5) the employer knew or should have known of the harassment and failed to take prompt remedial action"). Is the *Harris v. Forklift* "reasonable person" standard applicable in the religious harassment cases? How would a court apply a "reasonable religious person" standard? *See* Nantiya Ruan, *Accommodating Respectful Religious Expression in the Workplace,* 92 Marq.L.Rev. 1 (2008) (arguing that religious harassment law should follow sexual harassment law's "unwelcomeness" standard).

Another type of religious harassment claim—the "nonadherent" case—raises the question whether the plaintiff is a member of the "protected class" under Title VII, as well as whether the conduct is "unwelcome." Typically these are cases where the plaintiff alleges that a co-worker or supervisor is proselytizing the plaintiff to participate in the harasser's religious beliefs or practices. The "protected class" issue has arisen in so-called reverse religious discrimination cases where an employee has suffered an adverse employment action because he or she did not belong to the supervisor's religion. (*See, e.g.*, Noyes v. Kelley Servs., 488 F.3d 1163, 1168–69 (9th Cir.2007); Venters v. City of Delphi, 123 v. F.3d 956, 974–77 (7th Cir.1997); Shapolia v. Los Alamos Nat'l Lab., 992 F.2d 1033, 1036 (10th Cir.1993). *See also* Winspear v. Comty. Devel., Inc., 574 F.3d 604, 609 n. 2 (8th Cir.2009) (Smith, J., dissenting) (discussing reverse religious discrimination—or "nonadherence"—cases). Noting that an employer "has no legal obligation to suppress any and all religious expression merely because it annoys a single employee," the court in *Powell v. Yellow Book USA, Inc.,* concluded that a co-worker's posting of religious messages in her own cubicle, which the plaintiff found "inappropriate and distracting," was not actionable religious harassment. 445 F.3d 1074, 1078 (8th Cir.2006). On the other hand, one court of appeals concluded that quid pro quo harassment "is not limited to gender discrimination" and that an employer could be found liable for a supervisor's attempt to require that an employee engage in particular religious practices as a condition of keeping her job. *Venters,* 123 F.3d at 976–77. In public employment, religious harassment claims can be based on the First Amendment's free expression and establishment clauses as well as Title VII, as discussed in Section F of this chapter. *See generally id.* The tension between Title VII's prohibition of harassment because of religion and the First Amendment's protection of religious freedom in light of *Ellerth* and *Faragher* is explored in Kimball E. Gilmer & Jeffrey M. Anderson, *Zero Tolerance for God? Religious Expression in the Workplace After* Ellerth *and* Faragher, 42 How.L.J. 327 (1999).

The EEOC issued proposed guidelines on harassment in 1993, attempting to clarify the line between protected religious speech and unlawful harassment in the workplace. 29 C.F.R. § 1609 (proposed Oct. 1, 1993). Religious groups, in particular, expressed concerns that some employees and employers might rely on the guidelines to justify suppressing religious expression in the workplace. Because of opposition to the proposed guidelines, the EEOC withdrew them in 1994. 59 Fed. Reg. 58,312 (1994). In 2008, the EEOC issued a new compliance manual for Title VII claims of religious discrimination, which includes a discussion of the scope of prohibited religious harassment and the bases for finding employers liable. *See EEOC Questions and Answers: Religious Discrimination in the Workplace* (July 22, 2008), available at *http://www.eeoc.gov/policy/docs/qanda_religion.html* (last modified January 31, 2011). *See also EEOC Best Practices for Eradicating Religious Discrimination in the Workplace* available at *http://eeoc.gov/policy/docs/best_practices_religion.html* (last modified July 23, 2008).

NOTE: DISPARATE IMPACT RELIGIOUS DISCRIMINATION CLAIMS UNDER TITLE VII

Most religious discrimination claims are brought under the disparate treatment theory. When plaintiffs have asserted disparate impact claims, the courts have tended to reject them; for example, in *EEOC v. Sambo's of Georgia*, 530 F.Supp. 86, 92–93 (N.D.Ga.1981), the court held that the disparate impact theory is unavailable to challenge a practice allegedly burdening individuals because of their religious beliefs and practices. Some courts, however, have entertained disparate impact religious discrimination claims without questioning whether these cases are even amenable to disparate impact analysis. *See, e.g.*, Tagatz v. Marquette Univ., 681 F.Supp. 1344, 1357–58 (E.D.Wis.1988) (holding that plaintiff's evidence of salary disparities between Catholic and non-Catholic professors failed to establish a prima facie case of disparate impact based on his religion), *aff'd on other grounds*, 861 F.2d 1040 (7th Cir.1988). The Seventh Circuit has questioned whether the disparate impact theory is appropriate in religious discrimination cases. In *EEOC v. United Parcel Serv.*, 94 F.3d 314 (7th Cir.1996), the employer had a rule that required employees holding jobs that involved contact with the public to be clean-shaven. Plaintiff, a member of an Islamic sect that forbids men from shaving, was denied a job that required contact with the public or customers of the employer. The Seventh Circuit acknowledged that the clean-shaven rule was facially neutral but suggested that the religious discrimination cases "differ from the traditional disparate impact claims in that the discriminatory effect can often be alleviated by some reasonable accommodation of the employment requirement to the employee's particular religious needs," as required by § 701(j) of Title VII. *Id.* at 317 n.3. More recently, a district court denied an employer's motion to dismiss a disparate impact religious discrimination, observing that *EEOC v. Sambo's of Georgia* "long predated [the Civil Rights Act of 1992], which explicitly includes religion in the part of the statute discussing the burden of proof for disparate impact claims." Jenkins v. N.Y.C. Transit Auth., 646 F.Supp.2d 464, 471 (S.D.N.Y.2009). The New York City Transit Authority in *Jenkins* fired the plaintiff, a member of the American Pentecostal religion, because she wanted to wear a skirt for religious reasons and refused to wear the uniform pants required for all bus operators. If disparate impact analysis is appropriate in some religious discrimination cases, should business necessity or reasonable accommodation be the appropriate defense?

F. CLAIMS AGAINST GOVERNMENT EMPLOYERS

BROWN V. POLK COUNTY, IOWA

United States Court of Appeals for the Eighth Circuit, 1995 (en banc).
61 F.3d 650, *cert. denied*, 516 U.S. 1158, 116 S.Ct. 1042, 134 L.Ed.2d 189 (1996).

MORRIS SHEPPARD ARNOLD, CIRCUIT JUDGE.

In mid-1986, Isaiah Brown, a black man who identifies himself as a born-again Christian, became the director of the information services (data processing) department for Polk County, Iowa. He reported directly to the county administrator and supervised approximately 50 employees.

In mid-1990, an internal investigation into religious activities conducted on government time by employees in Mr. Brown's department revealed that Mr. Brown had directed a secretary to type Bible study notes for him, that several employees had said prayers in Mr. Brown's office before the beginning of some workdays, that several employees had said prayers in Mr. Brown's office in department meetings held during the day, and that in addressing one meeting of employees, Mr. Brown had affirmed his Christianity and had referred to Bible passages related to slothfulness and "work ethics." Subsequently, the county administrator reprimanded Mr. Brown in writing for a "lack of judgment pertaining to his personal participation in and/or his knowledge of employees participating in activities that could be construed as the direct support of or the promotion of a religious organization or religious activities utilizing the resources of Polk County Government." The reprimand directed Mr. Brown "immediately [to] cease any activities that could be considered to be religious proselytizing, witnessing, or counseling and * * * further [to] cease to utilize County resources that in any way could be perceived as to be supporting a religious activity or religious organization." * * * Subsequently, on a separate occasion, the county administrator directed Mr. Brown to remove from his office all items with a religious connotation, including a Bible in his desk.

In late 1990, the county administrator again reprimanded Mr. Brown in writing, on that occasion for a "lack of judgment" related to financial constraints in the county's budget. Two weeks later, after an internal investigation into personal use of county computers by employees in Mr. Brown's department, the county administrator asked Mr. Brown to resign; when he refused, the county administrator fired him.

In late 1991, Mr. Brown sued the county, its board of supervisors, and the county administrator. Mr. Brown alleged, under 42 U.S.C. § 1983, that the first reprimand and the order to remove from his office all items with a religious connotation violated constitutional guarantees of free exercise of religion, free speech, and equal protection. He also alleged, under * * * [Title VII] * * * that he was fired because of his * * * religion.

* * *

After a five-day bench trial, the district court found for the defendants in all respects. * * * On rehearing *en banc*, however, we affirm in part and reverse in part.

* * *

II

* * *

The district court made the factual finding that religious animus played no part in the decision to fire Mr. Brown. The district court found, instead, that the reason for Mr. Brown's discharge was inadequate performance, specifically, the inability to supervise and administer his department. Because we find that religious activities played a part in the decision to fire Mr. Brown, and that the proof was inadequate to show that Mr. Brown would have been fired if those activities had not been considered, we reverse the district court judgment with respect to the statutory religious discrimination claims.

In most of the cases alleging religious discrimination under Title VII, the employer is a private entity rather than a government, and the First Amendment to the Constitution is therefore not applicable to the employment relationship. In cases such as this one, however, where a government is the employer, we must consider both the First Amendment and Title VII in determining the legitimacy of the county administrator's action. The First Amendment is, of course, applicable to state-created government units by virtue of the Fourteenth Amendment.

With specific reference to the Free Exercise Clause, we hold that in the governmental employment context, the First Amendment protects at least as much religious activity as Title VII does. *See, e.g.*, United States v. Board of Educ., 911 F.2d 882, 890 (3d Cir.1990) ("at the very least, undue hardship is a lower standard than compelling state interest"). Another way of framing that holding is to say that any religious activities of employees that can be accommodated without undue hardship to the governmental employer are also protected by the First Amendment. In other words, if a governmental employer has violated Title VII, it has also violated the guarantees of the First Amendment. We turn, then, to a more detailed examination of the requirements of Title VII.

III

The county administrator testified that he fired Mr. Brown "because of [a] culmination of incidents" that led him to conclude that Mr. Brown "had lost control of his department and was no longer in a position to manage effectively." The county administrator also testified, moreover, that the reprimand for "religious activities" was "a factor" in the decision to fire Mr. Brown. The labor relations manager for the county testified as well that, in asking for Mr. Brown's resignation and then firing him, the county administrator told Mr. Brown that the first reprimand was among the "concerns" prompting his discharge. Finally, Mr. Brown himself testified that the reasons given for his discharge by the county administrator were "the problems that [had] centered around [Mr. Brown's] department for [the] last two years, primarily religion." Unfortunately, none of the witnesses specified with any more particularity the exact actions to which the county administrator was alluding. We must, therefore, consider what activities were covered by the first reprimand and which, if any, of those activities were protected by Title VII.

* * *

It is undisputed that the defendants made no attempt to accommodate any of Mr. Brown's religious activities. In those circumstances, the defendants may prevail only if they can show that allowing those activities "could not be accomplished without undue hardship." United States v. Board of Educ., 911 F.2d 882, 887 (3d Cir.1990). * * *

* * *

The first reprimand to Mr. Brown was precipitated by the internal investigation into religious activities conducted in mid-1990. The investigation revealed four actions attributed to him—directing a secretary to type his Bible study notes, allowing prayers in his office before the start of the workday, allowing prayers in his office during department meetings, and affirming his Christianity and referring to Bible passages about slothfulness and "work ethics" during one department meeting. We consider each of those activities in light of the commands of Title VII.

The defendants argue that allowing Mr. Brown to direct a county employee to type his Bible study notes would amount to an undue hardship on the conduct of county business, since the work that that employee would otherwise be doing would have to be postponed, done by another employee, or not done at all. We agree that such an activity creates more than a *de minimis* cost to the defendants. We conclude, therefore, that the defendants may not be held liable under Title VII for their actions in relation to that activity.

Nor, by the way, do we believe that the defendants' actions with respect to that activity violate the Free Exercise Clause. That is because we do not consider precluding Mr. Brown from directing a county employee to type his Bible study notes to be a "substantial[ ] burden" upon his religious practices. Employment Div. v. Smith, 494 U.S. 872, 883, 110 S.Ct. 1595, 1602–03, 108 L.Ed.2d 876 (1990). We would be surprised if directing a county employee to type Bible study notes is "conduct mandated by religious belief," Thomas v. Review Bd., 450 U.S. 707, 718, 101 S.Ct. 1425, 1432, 67 L.Ed.2d 624 (1981), and, indeed, Mr. Brown does not so contend. We conclude, therefore, that Mr. Brown's directing a county employee to type his Bible study notes was not an activity protected at all under the law in this case and, accordingly, that the defendants may not be held liable for their actions with respect to that activity.

With respect to Mr. Brown's allowing prayers in his office before the start of the workday, nothing in Title VII requires that an employer open its premises for use before the start of the workday. Nor, incidentally, would the First Amendment so require in this case, since no proof was offered that Mr. Brown's office was a public forum or a limited public forum or that the defendants allowed employees to use their offices for personal purposes before the start of the workday (indeed, the defendants' position was that once an employee arrived at the office, the workday began, regardless of the actual time, and the defendants' policy manual directed that no personal use of county resources was permitted). We conclude, therefore, that Mr. Brown's allowing prayers in his office before the start of the workday was not an activity protected at all under the law in this case and, accordingly, that the defendants may not be held liable for their actions in relation to that activity.

Mr. Brown also allowed prayers in his office during several department meetings and affirmed his Christianity and referred to Bible passages related to slothfulness and "work ethics" during one department meeting. All of the testimony was that the prayers were entirely voluntary and "spontaneous," "did not occur regularly," and dealt with "matters related to Polk County business," and that Mr. Brown's affirmation of Christianity and reference to Bible passages on slothfulness and "work ethics" occurred during only one meeting. Given their context, all of those actions may well have been impolitic on Mr. Brown's part, but we think that they were inconsequential as a legal matter, especially since they were apparently spontaneous and infrequent.

* * *

In our view, the defendants' examples of the burden that they would have to bear by tolerating trifling instances such as those complained of are insufficiently "real" and too "hypothetical" to satisfy the standard required to show undue hardship. The defendants showed no "actual imposition on co-workers or disruption of the work routine" Burns v. Southern Pac. Transp. Co., 589 F.2d 403, 407, (9th Cir.1978), *cert. denied*, 439 U.S. 1072, 99 S.Ct. 843, 59 L.Ed.2d 38 (1979), generated by occasional spontaneous prayers and isolated references to Christian belief. On this record, we hold that the defendants failed to prove that accommodating such instances as they objected to would lead to undue hardship. The defendants may be held liable, therefore, for firing Mr. Brown on account of those activities unless the defendants can prove that they would have fired him regardless of those activities. *See, e.g.*, Price Waterhouse v. Hopkins, 490 U.S. 228, 242, 244–46, 252–53, 258, 109 S.Ct. 1775, 1786 1787–88, 1791–92, 1794–95, 104 L.Ed.2d 268 (1989) (plurality opinion).

The district court held that Mr. Brown had offered no direct evidence that he was fired on account of his religious activities. We do not understand that conclusion, since, as we have already noted, the county administrator himself testified that the first reprimand, which was based on religious activities, was "a factor" in his decision to fire Mr. Brown. We believe that Mr. Brown presented enough evidence to require the application of a "mixed-motives" analysis instead.

In these circumstances, we could remand to the district court for findings on the question of whether the defendants proved that they would have fired Mr. Brown even if they had not considered his religious activities. In this case, however, we hold that it would be futile to do so, since no reasonable person could conclude from the evidence presented that the defendants proved that they would have fired Mr. Brown anyway. Indeed, when asked specifically at trial if Mr. Brown would have been fired absent the first reprimand, the county administrator responded, "I wouldn't want to speculate on that. * * * I just don't know." * * * We therefore reverse the judgment on the statutory religious discrimination claims and remand the case to the district court for consideration of the appropriate relief on those claims.

IV

We last consider constitutional claims that Mr. Brown did not link to his termination. We reverse the district court with respect to those claims and remand the case for consideration of the appropriate relief.

We are mindful (as the dissenting judges are) that our cases, and First Amendment jurisprudence in general, require that plaintiffs in cases like this must show that the governmental action complained of substantially burdened their religious activities. (We take this to mean that Mr. Brown must show that the burdens placed on him were not inconsiderable.) We have already said as much in a previous section of this opinion. But Mr. Brown has carried that burden. From Mr. Brown's testimony, there can be no doubt that his religious beliefs are extremely important to him and play a central role in his life. He testified that in 1986 or early 1987 he underwent a personal spiritual revival that was "a life-changing experience" for him. He stated, in addition, that prayer was "something that's part of [his] being," that prayer "leads [him] and * * * guides [him]," and that he uses prayer in his life "on a daily basis." He believes, according to his testimony, that prayer "changes things" and, furthermore, that his God expects him to pray "for governments, our nation, our schools, our children, all the pandemic problems inherent in our society." There was no challenge to this testimony then or now, and all of the evidence points to a conclusion that Mr. Brown found the defendants' prohibitions oppressive and vexatious.

In these circumstances, the district court's observation that Mr. Brown did not show "that the removal of religious items from his office inhibited his ability to freely exercise his religion," either proceeds from a misunderstanding of what a substantial burden is, or is a clearly erroneous finding of fact. Our observation above that some of Mr. Brown's religious activities were inconsequential was, of course, meant to indicate that they did not produce even an insignificant external effect in the workplace, not that they were not significant to him.

Mr. Brown first asserts that his First Amendment right to the free exercise of his religion was violated when the county administrator ordered him to "cease any activities that could be considered to be religious proselytizing, witnessing, or counseling" while he was on the job. Although the free exercise of religion is certainly a fundamental constitutional right, we believe that the Supreme Court might well adopt, for Free Exercise cases that arise in the context of public employment, an analysis like the one enunciated in *Pickering v. Board of Education*, 391 U.S. 563, 88 S.Ct. 1731, 20 L.Ed.2d 811 (1968). That case dealt with free speech rather than the Free Exercise of religion, but because the analogy is such a close one, and because we see no essential relevant differences between those rights, we shall endeavor to apply the principles of *Pickering* to the case at hand.

Pickering recognizes a public employee's right to speak on matters that lie at the core of the First Amendment, that is, matters of public concern, so long as "the effective functioning of the public employer's enterprise" is not interfered with. The kind of speech that Polk County prohibited in this case lies right at the core of the Free Exercise Clause. We have, moreover, already indicated at some length our belief that the record reveals no diminution whatever in the effectiveness of governmental functions fairly attributable to anything that Mr. Brown did that is forbidden by the order. The order therefore fails to find any justification under well-settled principles governing the constitutional rights of public employees.

We may concede for the sake of argument that Polk County has a legal right to ensure that its workplace is free from religious activity that harasses or intimidates. But any interference with religious activity that the exercise of that right entails must be reasonably related to the exercise of that right and must be narrowly tailored to its achievement. Here, there was not the least attempt to confine the prohibition to harassing or intimidating speech. Instead, Polk County baldly directed Mr. Brown to "cease any activities that *could be considered* to be religious proselytizing, witnessing, or counseling" (emphasis supplied). That order exhibited a hostility to religion that our Constitution simply prohibits. It would seem to require no argument that to forbid speech "that could be considered" religious is not narrowly tailored to the aim of prohibiting harassment, although it is certainly capable of doing that. If Mr. Brown asked someone to attend his church, for instance, we suppose that that "could be considered" proselytizing, but its prohibition runs afoul of the Free Exercise Clause. Similarly, a statement to the effect that one's religion was important in one's life "could be considered" witnessing, yet for the government to forbid it would be unconstitutional.

The defendants would have us hold that their "interest" in avoiding a claim against them that they have violated the Establishment Clause allows them to prohibit religious expression altogether in their workplaces. Such a position is too extravagant to maintain, for it gives a dominance to the Establishment Clause that it does not have and that would allow it to trump the Free Exercise Clause. One might just as well justify erecting a cross and a creche on county property at Christmas as a means of avoiding a claim that employees had been denied their Free Exercise rights. The clauses cannot, in the nature of things, make conflicting demands on a government, and government is charged with making sure that its activities are confined to the ample and well-defined space that separates them.

Mr. Brown also complains about the directive to remove from his office all items with a religious connotation, including a Bible that was in his desk. It is here, perhaps, that the zealotry of the county administrator is most clearly revealed. Mr. Brown had to remove a plaque containing the serenity prayer ("God, grant me the serenity to accept the things I cannot change, the courage to change the things I can, and the wisdom to know the difference"), another that said, "God be in my life and in my commitment," and a third containing the Lord's Prayer. Most intrusive of all was the order to take down a poster that proclaimed some non-religious inspirational commonplaces that were deemed inappropriate because their author, although he occupied no religious office, had "Cardinal" in his name. Mr. Brown testified that he was told that these items had to go because they might be considered "offensive to employees." Our observations above with reference to the application of the principles of *Pickering* apply with equal force to this second portion of Mr. Brown's claim. There was no showing of disruption of work or any interference with the efficient performance of governmental functions sufficient to allow for this extraordinary action on the part of Polk County. We emphasize, moreover, that even if employees found Mr. Brown's displays "offensive," Polk County could not legally remove them if their "offensiveness" was based on the content of their message. In that case, the county would be taking sides in a religious dispute, which, of course, it cannot do under either the Establishment Clause or the Equal protection Clause. If the "offensive" character of the display ran to a well-grounded apprehension among employees of discriminatory treatment by Mr. Brown, then this case might be entirely different. But the evidence will not support such a finding here. We emphasize, too, that fear alone, even fear of discrimination or other illegal activity, is not enough to justify such a mobilization of governmental force against Mr. Brown. The fear must be substantial and, above all, objectively reasonable. A phobia of religion, for instance, no matter how real subjectively, will not do. As Justice Brandeis has said, rather starkly, "Men feared witches and burnt women." Whitney v. California, 274 U.S. 357, 376, 47 S.Ct. 641, 71 L.Ed.1095 (1927) (Brandeis, J., concurring).

V

For the reasons indicated, we affirm the judgment of the district court in part, we reverse it in part, and we remand for further proceedings consistent with this opinion.

FAGG, CIRCUIT JUDGE, dissenting, joined by LOKEN, HANSEN, and MURPHY, CIRCUIT JUDGES.

* * *

Although the Court recognizes the substantial burden requirement, the Court ignores Brown's failure to show the County's actions rose to the level of a substantial burden on his religious practices. The record lacks any evidence that Brown's born-again Christianity required him to display religious items in his office or to engage in the religious activities restricted by the reprimand. Indeed, the district court found Brown did not prove the removal of the items from his office inhibited his ability to exercise his religion freely. * * * The district court's finding is not clearly erroneous anyway. As for the religious activity restrictions, the Court recognizes the prayers at departmental meetings were spontaneous, infrequent, and inconsequential. The evidence about the change in Brown's religious practices after the reprimand shows the restrictions merely inconvenienced Brown. Rather than engaging in group prayers during work, Brown simply went across the street to the library at lunchtime to read his Bible and pray with others. The reprimand did not restrict Brown's private prayers. Brown has not shown any substantial, concrete harm to his religious practice resulted from Polk County's actions. The Court misplaces reliance on evidence that Brown's "religious beliefs are extremely important to him and play a central role in his life." The fact that Brown sincerely held his religious beliefs does not mean the County's actions substantially burdened Brown's exercise of those beliefs. Because Brown failed to show the County's actions substantially burdened his religious practices, the Court should not even reach the *Pickering* analysis on Brown's Free Exercise claim. * * * I would hold the balance of interests tips in the County's favor in this case, primarily given Brown's status as a supervisor of fifty employees.

* * *

NOTES AND QUESTIONS

1. The court in *Brown v. Polk County* applies the *Pickering* free speech balancing test to the employee's claim of religious freedom. Is free speech just like free exercise of religion? In addition to the governmental interest, freedom of religion must be weighed with a constitutional prohibition against establishment of religion. Is this distinction sufficient to make *Pickering* analysis inapplicable? *See* Berry v. Dep't of Social Servs,, 447 F.3d 642 (9th Cir.2006) (government's need to avoid Establishment Clause violation outweighs employee's free speech and free exercise claims). The court in *Brown* also considers the employee's Title VII claim coequally with his Free Exercise claim. Yet, the Supreme Court often refuses to create constitutional precedents when claims can be decided on nonconstitutional grounds. *See, e.g.,* NLRB v. Catholic Bishop of Chi., 440 U.S. 490, 507, 99 S.Ct. 1313, 59 L.E.2d 533 (1979). Should the *Brown* court decide the constitutional claim when it can rule in the employee's favor based on Title VII's religious discrimination provision?

2. *The Religious Freedom Restoration Act*: The *Brown* court found that the governmental employer's actions substantially burdened the employee's religion, yet in *Employment Division, Department of Human Resources of Oregon v. Smith*, 494 U.S. 872, 110 S.Ct. 1595, 108 L.Ed.2d 876 (1990), the Supreme Court ruled that the Free Exercise Clause permits Oregon to include the sacramental use of peyote within the reach of the state's general criminal law prohibiting the use of certain proscribed drugs. The Court upheld the state statute on the ground that the right of free exercise of religion does not relieve an individual of the general obligation of a citizen to comply with a valid and neutral law of general applicability simply because the law proscribes conduct that his religion sanctions. Prior to *Smith*, the Court had adopted a balancing test set forth in *Sherbert v. Verner*, 374 U.S. 398, 83 S.Ct. 1790, 10 L.Ed.2d 965 (1963), to decide Free Exercise Clause claims. The balancing test requires a court to determine first whether a challenged practice substantially burdens a religious practice or belief, and if it does, then to determine whether the burden is justified by a compelling state interest. The *Smith* Court refused to apply the *Sherbert v. Verner*

balancing test in the context of an "across-the-board criminal prohibition on a particular form of conduct." *Smith*, 494 U.S. at 873, 110 S.Ct. at 1597. Should Title VII be viewed as a statute of general applicability for purposes of using the *Smith* case to limit employee Free Exercise protection? How does the *Brown* court rule on this question? Note that Title VII has been viewed as a general antidiscrimination law for purposes of surviving Establishment Clause challenges. *See, e.g.*, Estate of Thornton v. Caldor, 472 U.S. 703, 712, 105 S.Ct. 2914, 86 L.Ed.2d 557 (1985). If the *Smith* case serves to weaken Free Exercise protection should the court's ruling in *Brown* be reconsidered?

In response to *Smith,* Congress enacted the Religious Freedom Restoration Act (RFRA), 42 U.S.C. § 2000bb, to overturn *Smith* and to restore the compelling interest test. The RFRA provided that the "[g]overnment may substantially burden a person's exercise of religion only if it demonstrates that the application of the burden is in furtherance of a compelling governmental interest." In *City of Boerne v. Flores*, 521 U.S. 507, 117 S.Ct. 2157, 138 L.Ed.2d 624 (1997), in a 6–3 decision written by Justice Kennedy, the Supreme Court struck down RFRA on the ground that, in enacting RFRA, Congress had exceeded the scope of its enforcement authority under § 5 of the Fourteenth Amendment. The Court held that the statute violated the separation of powers doctrine and offended the principles of federalism. Under *Boerne v. Flores*, RFRA claims or defenses are now generally unavailable to either employees or employers, but RFRA has survived *City of Boerne* for employees of the federal government, *see* Young v. Crystal Evangelical Free Church, 141 F.3d 854 (8th Cir.1998) (holding that RFRA is constitutional as applied to federal employers), and against actions of the federal government generally. *See* Gonzales v. O Centro Espirita Beneficente, 546 U.S. 418 (2006).

Recently, in *Burwell v. Hobby Lobby Stores, Inc.*, ___ U.S. ___, 134 S.Ct. 2751, 189 L.Ed.2d 675 (2014), the Supreme Court analyzed whether the RFRA prevented the U.S. government from requiring that closely held corporations provide health insurance coverage for contraception in violation of the sincerely held religious beliefs of the corporations' owners. The Court found that the regulations burdened Hobby Lobby's owner's religious beliefs because they forced the company to provide insurance for contraception (violating sincerely held belief that life begins at conception) or face a substantial economic penalty. The Court assumed that the government had a compelling state interest in promulgating the health insurance regulations, but found that the government had not used the least restrictive means because there were other less burdensome ways to ensure cost-free contraception for women. For example, the government had made accommodations for religious nonprofits under the regulations that could easily be extended to closely held corporations. For further discussion on the issue of the Affordable Care Act as it relates to religious freedom, see James M. Oleske, Jr., *Obamacare, RFRA, and the Perils of Legislative History*, 67 Vand. L. Rev. En Banc 77 (2014).

3. *Guidelines on Religious Exercise and Religious Expression in the Federal Workplace*: On August 14, 1997, President Clinton issued guidelines designed to protect religious expression in the workplace for federal civilian employees. *See* 1997 WL 464857 (White House). Under the guidelines,

> [f]ederal employees may keep Bibles or Korans on their desks, tell colleagues how important religion is in their lives and put wreaths on office doors at Christmas time.
>
> They can argue about religion at the water cooler (just as they can argue about baseball or politics), or they can proclaim their atheism if they so choose. They can try to convert co-workers to their religion, but must cease and desist upon request.

David Stout, *Religion and Federal Workers: What Thou Shalt and Shalt Not Do*, N.Y. Times, Aug. 14, 1997, at A14. The guidelines were drafted by a committee representing several religious and civil liberties groups who were responding, in part, to the controversy surrounding the EEOC's failed 1993 effort to adopt guidelines on religious harassment in the workplace. In addition, to avoid potential constitutional challenges, the drafters took into account the reasons that the Supreme Court, in *Boerne v. Flores*, had found the Religious Freedom Restoration Act to be unconstitutional. *See* Susan McInerney, *President Clinton Unveils Religion Guidelines on Expression, Exercise in Federal Workplace*, Legal News, 66 U.S.L.W. 2120, 2121 (Aug. 26, 1997). The guidelines continue to be followed by the federal government. Some observers predict that state and local governments, as well as private employers, will ultimately use the federal guidelines as a model for dealing with issues involving religion in the workplace. *Id.*

4. *Religious Harassment in Public Employment*: In *Venters v. City of Delphi*, 123 F.3d 956 (7th Cir.1997), the plaintiff, Jennifer Venters, claimed that her supervisor, Police Chief Larry Ives, a born-again Christian, subjected her to both quid pro quo and hostile environment religious harassment. The Seventh Circuit reversed a summary judgment in favor of the employer, and remanded for a trial on Venter's Title VII claims, noting that, according to the plaintiff,

> Ives repeatedly subjected her to lectures (at work, during working hours) about her prospects for salvation, made highly personal inquiries into her private life (whether there was truth to purported rumors that she entertained guests in her home with pornography, for example), and ultimately went so far as to tell her that she led a sinful life, that he was certain she had had sex with family members and possibly animals, that she had sacrificed animals in Satan's name, and that committing suicide would be preferable to the life he believed Venters was living. * * * Ives' remarks were uninvited, were intrusive, touched upon the most private aspects of her life, were delivered in an intimidating manner, in some cases were on their face scandalous, and were unrelenting throughout the entire period post-dating [Ives']

> appointment as chief of police, continuing even after she had informed him that his comments to her were inappropriate.

Id. at 976.

With regard to the quid pro quo claim, the court observed that "this type of harassment is not limited to gender discrimination." *Id.* The court continued,

> Ives did not, by Venters' account, simply share his religious beliefs with her, but instead he made it clear to her that if she did [not] conform to those views, she would be discharged. * * * Ives told Venters that in order to be a good employee, one had to be spiritually whole, and to meet that criterion one had to be "saved"; he described the police station as "God's house," and warned her that he would "trade" her if she did not play by "God's rules," if she did not embrace "God's way" over "Satan's"; * * * eventually Ives concluded that an "evil spirit had taken [her] soul," and he admonished her that he would not allow that "evil spirit" to reside in the police department.

Id. at 976–77.

Venters demonstrates the potential conflicts between rights arising under Title VII and the First Amendment that may occur in government employment when one employee attempts to communicate deeply held religious beliefs to another employee who wishes "to be left alone to exercise her own thoughts on the subject of religion in private, free of interference from her governmental employer." *Id.* at 977. The 1997 Guidelines on Religious Exercise and Religious Expression in the Federal Workplace, discussed *supra,* Note 3, deal with this dilemma by permitting the speaker's communication on religious topics, until the listener asks him to stop, at which time his First Amendment protections cease. In light of the facts alleged in *Venters*, would such a rule in the City of Delphi have effectively protected the constitutional and statutory rights of all parties?

5. *Federal Employees*: By virtue of congressional enactment, federal agencies are subject to Title VII, age, disability, and equal pay laws, just as are state and government employers and private employers. However, there are some meaningful differences in the way that these laws are applied to federal employees. Section 717 of Title VII provides the basis for federal employee Title VII claims, which can be handled through the Merit Systems Protection Board or through the separate EEO processes of the various federal agencies and then the EEOC. Importantly, in *Brown v. General Services Administration,* 425 U.S. 820, 835, 96 S.Ct. 1961, 1969, 48 L.Ed.2d 402, 413 (1976), the Supreme Court held that § 717 of Title VII was the exclusive remedy for discrimination by a federal agency. As a result, federal employees may not proceed under § 1981 or the Constitution for discrimination on claims that are otherwise covered by Title VII. If the *Polk County* case had been brought by a federal employee against a federal

agency, the Title VII religious discrimination claim would likely have superseded the constitutional challenge under the *Brown v. GSA* mandate.

CHAPTER 12

DISCRIMINATION BECAUSE OF NATIONAL ORIGIN

■ ■ ■

A. INTRODUCTION

When Congress enacted Title VII, it provided a scanty record of its reasons for including a prohibition against national origin discrimination. *See* U.S. Equal Employment Opportunity Commission, Legislative History of Titles VII and IX, at 3179–81 (1968). Professor Juan F. Perea has offered the following explanation of the history behind the inclusion of national origin in Title VII:

> Prior to the enactment of the Civil Rights Act of 1964, the phrase "national origin" long had been the subject of federal executive and legislative action. In the immigration laws, national origin had been the explicit basis for discrimination because of country of origin by the federal government for approximately four decades, until 1965. With respect to fair employment practices, the phrase appears to have become part of the standard "boilerplate" language of executive orders prohibiting discrimination in employment. This context gave the term its basic meaning, country of birth, at the time of the passage of the Civil Rights Act of 1964.
>
> In 1924 * * * Congress passed * * * legislation creating national origin quotas for immigration. These quotas, defined by the countries of origin of prospective immigrants, attempted to limit immigration so that the demographic composition of immigrants matched the predominantly white, northern European composition of the extant American population. As a result of these quotas, the federal government discriminated explicitly against prospective immigrants based on their countries of birth.

Juan F. Perea, *Ethnicity and Prejudice: Reevaluating "National Origin" Discrimination Under Title VII*, 35 Wm. & Mary L.Rev. 805, 810–12 (1994). Congress amended the Immigration and Nationality Act, 8 U.S.C. § 1151, in 1965 to replace the national origin quotas with new standards for admission to citizenship in the United States.

In studying and analyzing national origin discrimination claims, it is essential to recognize the historical fact that the United States is essentially a nation of immigrants. Except for the descendants of Native Americans who inhabited North America before it was "discovered" by Europeans and the descendants of slaves who were forcibly brought here, every citizen of the United States is either an immigrant or has descended from immigrants. At the beginning of the current century, about 10 percent of the population of the United States was foreign born. EEOC Compliance Manual Section 13–I (2002). Regardless of where they were born, about 13 percent of the United States population identified as Hispanic and over 4 percent identified as Asian. *Id.* As of July 1 2013, Hispanics accounted for about 17 percent of the U.S. population, and the group accounted for one-half of the nation's growth in population. *See* Press Release, Facts for Features, U.S. Census Bureau, Hispanic Heritage Month 2014: Sept. 15–Oct. 15 (Sept. 8, 2014), available at *http://www.census.gov/newsroom/facts-for-features/2014/cb14-ff22.html*. *See generally* U.S. Census Bureau, Hispanic Population of the United States, available at *http://www.census.gov/population/hispanic/*. Even though the United States is a nation of immigrants, nativism, that is, an intense opposition to immigrants, has been deeply embedded in the American character from the early days of the country. Since 2004, about 11 percent of all charges filed with the EEOC included a claim for discrimination based on National Origin, up from 8 percent in 1997. *See* U.S. Equal Empl. Oppt'y Comm'n, Charge Statistics: FY 1997 Through FY 2014, available at *http://www.eeoc.gov/eeoc/statistics/enforcement/charges.cfm*.

In *Paths to Belonging: The Constitution and Cultural Identity*, 64 N.C.L.Rev. 303, 311 (1986), Professor Kenneth L. Karst stated that

> [i]n America hostility among cultural groups * * * is properly seen as a threat to [national unity] * * *. Those who react to cultural differences with fear or anger generally espouse nativist policies designed to repress the differences by excluding the "others" from the country, by forcing them to conform to the norms of the dominant culture, or by relegating them to a subordinate status in society.

Examples of nativism include the Chinese Exclusion Act of 1881, 22 Stat. 58, which suspended Chinese immigration into the United States for ten years; the national origin quotas in immigration laws that favored Anglo-European individuals; the internment of Japanese-American citizens during World War II; and the "No Irish Need Apply" and "No Japs Wanted" employment policies that some employers adopted in the past. *See, e.g.*, President's Committee on Civil Rights, To Secure These Rights 78 (1947). In 1994, California voters approved Proposition 187, a ballot initiative that prohibited undocumented aliens from receiving public education, social welfare benefits, and nonemergency health services. *See* Nancy Cervantes, Sasha Khokha & Bobbie Murray, *Hate Unleashed: Los Angeles in the Aftermath of Proposition 187*, 17 Chicano-Latino L.Rev. 1 (1995) (documenting complaints about the discriminatory impact of Proposition 187 on the Latino community in Los Angeles). In 2010, the state of Arizona passed S.B. 1070, a state anti-immigrant law, that was upheld by the United States Supreme Court in *Arizona v. U.S.*, ___ U.S. ___, 132 S.Ct. 2492, 183 L.Ed.2nd 351 (2012). Other states have passed similar laws, and contemporary debates over the rights to be granted to immigrants, especially undocumented immigrants, continue today.

One scholar has identified four common themes that nativists have expressed throughout the history of the United States:

> One common complaint is that certain "races" are intellectually and culturally inferior and should not be allowed into the [United States], at least not in substantial numbers. Nativists have often regarded immigrant groups as racial "others" quite different from the Euro-American majority. A second and related theme views those who have immigrated from racially and culturally inferior groups as problematical in terms of their complete assimilation to the dominant Anglo culture. A third theme, articulated most often in troubled economic times, is that "inferior" immigrants are taking the jobs and disrupting the economic conditions of native-born Americans. A fourth notion, also heard most often in times of fiscal crisis, is that immigrants are creating serious government crises, such as by corrupting the voting system or overloading school and welfare systems.

Joe R. Feagin, *Old Poison in New Bottles: The Deep Roots of Modern Nativism*, *in* Immigrants Out! The New Nativism and the Anti-Immigrant Impulse in the United States 13–14 (Juan F. Perea ed., 1997). *See generally* Berta Esperanza Hernández-Truyol, *Natives, Newcomers and Nativism: A Human Rights Model for the Twenty-First Century*, 23 Fordham Urb.L.J. 1075 (1996).

A fifth theme has emerged during wartime—a fear that "foreigners" pose a threat to national security. During World War II, for example, Japanese Americans were imprisoned in internment camps and German immigrants were targeted as well. Since the terrorist attacks on New York City and Washington, D.C., on September 11, 2001, concerns about terrorism have been raised predominantly with respect to people with Middle Eastern ancestry. *See* Mary Ann Weston & Marda Dunsky, *One Culture, Two Frameworks: U.S. Media Coverage of Arabs at Home and Abroad*, 7 J. Islamic L. & Culture 129, 133 (2002) (noting that Arabs and Arab-Americans are often stereotyped as terrorists); Lori Sachs, *September 11, 2001: The Constitution During Crisis: A New Perspective*,

29 Fordham Urb.L.J. 1715, 1736–37 (2002) (reporting that the public favors racial profiling of terrorists, mainly targeted at Arab-Americans, to increase security); Susan M. Akram & Kevin R. Johnson, *Race, Civil Rights, and Immigration Law After September 11, 2001: The Targeting of Arabs and Muslims*, 58 N.Y.U. Ann.Surv.Am.L. 295, 311–13, 348–49 (2002) (observing that antiterrorism fear leads to hostility and discrimination against a variety of ethnic groups).

Discriminatory policies and practices because of national origin are not as open and flagrant today as they have been in past years. Nowadays, national origin discrimination is

> more likely to occur against persons because of the perceptible manifestations of ethnic distinction, ethnic traits, than because of the often imperceptible fact of national origin. As Professor Allport wrote, "perceptible differences are of basic importance in distinguishing between out-group and in-group members." The perceptible differences that mark out-groups include, among others, skin color, cast of features, gestures, prevalent facial expression, speech or accent, dress, mannerisms, religious practices, food habits, names, place of residence, and insignia.

Juan F. Perea, *Ethnicity and the Constitution: Beyond the Black and White Binary Constitution*, 36 Wm. & Mary L.Rev. 571, 576 (1995) (quoting Gordon Allport, The Nature of Prejudice 131–32 (2d ed.1988)).

As a general rule, the theories, defenses, and analyses discussed under the disparate treatment and disparate impact models are equally applicable to national origin discrimination claims. *See, e.g.*, Odima v. Westin Tucson Hotel, 53 F.3d 1484 (9th Cir.1995) (disparate treatment); Assoc. of Mexican-American Educators v. Cal., 231 F. 3d 572 (9th Cir.2000) (disparate impact). The materials in this chapter focus on selected issues involving national origin discrimination in the workplace. The meaning of national origin is covered in Section B, which also includes notes on the BFOQ defense and national origin harassment. Section C discusses the relationship between discrimination based on citizenship status and discrimination based on national origin. Language discrimination is treated in Section D.

B. THE MEANING OF "NATIONAL ORIGIN"

In the legislative debates on Title VII, Congressman Roosevelt stated: "May I just make very clear that 'national origin' means national. It means the country from which your forebears came. You may be from Poland, Czechoslovakia, England, France or any other country." 110 Cong.Rec. 2549 (1964). An earlier version of Title VII included "ancestry" as one of the prohibited criteria. H.R.Rep. N. 914, 88th Cong., 1st Sess. 87 (1963), but Congress excluded it from the final version. Does the exclusion of "ancestry" from the statute suggest that Congress thought that "national origin" included "ancestry" or that "ancestry" was a broader concept?

The EEOC has adopted a very expansive definition of national origin:

> The [EEOC] defines national origin discrimination broadly as including, but not limited to, the denial of equal employment opportunity because of an individual's, or his or her ancestor's, place of origin; or because an individual has the physical, cultural or linguistic characteristics of a national origin group. The [EEOC] will examine with particular concern charges alleging that individuals within the jurisdiction of the [EEOC] have been denied equal employment opportunity for reasons which are grounded in national origin considerations, such as (a) marriage to or association with persons of a national origin group; (b) membership in, or association with an organization identified with or seeking to promote the interests of national origin groups; (c) attendance or participation in schools, churches, temples, or mosques, generally used by persons of a national origin group; and (d) because an individual's name or spouse's name is associated with a national origin group. In examining these charges for unlawful national origin discrimination, the [EEOC] will apply general title VII principles, such as disparate treatment and adverse impact.

EEOC, Guidelines on Discrimination Because of National Origin, 29 C.F.R. § 1606.1 (2009) (adopted Dec. 29, 1980).

DAWAVENDEWA V. SALT RIVER PROJECT AGRICULTURAL IMPROVEMENT & POWER DIST.

United States Court of Appeals for the Ninth Circuit, 1998.
154 F.3d 1117, *cert. denied*, 528 U.S. 1098, 120 S.Ct. 843, 145 L.Ed.2d 708 (2000).

REINHARDT, CIRCUIT JUDGE.

Harold Dawavendewa, a Native American, alleges that because he is a Hopi and not a Navajo, he was not considered for a position with a private employer operating a facility on the Navajo reservation. He contends that the employer's conduct constitutes unlawful employment discrimination under Title VII of the Civil Rights Act of 1964. To determine whether Dawavendewa's Title VII complaint may proceed, we address, first, whether discrimination based on tribal affiliation constitutes "national origin" discrimination, and, second, whether such discrimination is permitted under a Title VII provision that allows preferential treatment of Indians in certain specified circumstances.[1] [The portion of the opinion addressing the second issue is omitted.]

Salt River Project Agricultural Improvement and Power District ("Salt River"), an Arizona corporation, entered into a lease agreement with the Navajo Nation in 1969. The agreement allows Salt River to operate a generating station on Navajo land provided that it, among other things, grants employment preferences to members of the Navajo tribe living on the reservation, or, if none are available, to other members of the Navajo tribe.[2] This preference policy is consistent with Navajo tribal law. *See* 15 Navajo Nation Code § 604 (1995).

Dawavendewa, a member of the Hopi tribe, lives in Arizona less than three miles from the Navajo Reservation. In 1991 he unsuccessfully applied for one of seven Operator Trainee positions at the Salt River generating station. He then filed a complaint alleging that Salt River was engaging in national origin discrimination in violation of Title VII. The complaint alleges that he took and passed a test for the position, ranking ninth out of the top twenty applicants, but was neither interviewed nor considered further for it because he was not a member of, or married to a member of, the Navajo Nation.

Salt River moved to dismiss the complaint on the grounds that discrimination on the basis of tribal membership (as opposed to discrimination on the basis of status as a Native American) does not constitute "national origin" discrimination and that Title VII expressly exempts tribal preferences under § 703(i), 42 U.S.C. § 2000e–2 (i) (the "Indian Preferences exemption"). The district court granted the motion to dismiss. It held that Title VII exempts tribal preference policies, and therefore found it unnecessary to decide whether discrimination on the basis of tribal membership constitutes national origin discrimination under Title VII. Dawavendewa appeals.

---

1 We use the terms Indian and Native American interchangeably throughout this opinion. While it is generally desirable for language to retain a fixed meaning, and while unnecessary changes in terminology exacerbate the problems we ordinarily have in understanding each other and in avoiding legal disputes, we recognize that the term Native American has become a part of the common parlance. Nevertheless, the statutes and opinions we examine use the term Indian, which was the appropriate word not so long ago.

2 The employment provision reads as follows:

> Lessees agree to give preference in employment to qualified local Navajos, it being understood that "local Navajos" means members of the Navajo Tribe living on land within the jurisdiction of the Navajo Tribe. All unskilled labor shall be employed from "local Navajos," if available, providing that applicants for employment as unskilled laborers meet the general employment qualifications established by Lessees. Qualified semi-skilled and skilled labor shall be recruited and employed from among "local Navajos." In the event sufficient qualified unskilled, semi-skilled and skilled local Navajo labor is not available, or the quality of work of available skilled or semi-skilled workmen is not acceptable to Lessees, Lessees may then employ, in order of preference, first qualified non-local Navajos, and second, non-Navajos.

I

We first address the issue whether discrimination on the basis of tribal membership constitutes "national origin" discrimination for purposes of Title VII. Title VII prohibits employers from discriminating on the basis of "race, color, religion, sex, or national origin." Civil Rights Act of 1964, § 703 (a), 42 U.S.C. § 2000e–2 (a).[4] Although Title VII fails to define "national origin," we have observed that "the legislative history and the Supreme Court both recognize that 'national origin' includes the country of one's ancestors." *Pejic v. Hughes Helicopters, Inc.*, 840 F.2d 667, 673 (9th Cir.1988); *see Espinoza v. Farah Mfg. Co.*, 414 U.S. 86, 88, 38 L.Ed.2d 287, 94 S.Ct. 334 (1973). Further, the regulations implementing Title VII provide that discrimination on the basis of one's ancestor's "place of origin" not nation of origin is sufficient to come within the scope of the statute. *See* 29 C.F.R. § 1606.1. Accordingly, a claim arises when discriminatory practices are based on the place in which one's ancestors lived.

Consistent with the regulations, we have held that the current political status of the nation or "place" at issue makes no difference for Title VII purposes. In *Pejic v. Hughes Helicopters, Inc.,* we considered the issue whether discrimination against Serbians constituted "national origin" discrimination. 840 F.2d 667, 673 (9th Cir.1988). The employer in *Pejic* contended that a Serbian employee could not bring a discrimination claim because Serbia as a nation had long been extinct. We rejected this argument and held that Serbians were a protected class:

> Unless historical reality is ignored, the term "national origin" must include countries no longer in existence * * * . Given world history, Title VII cannot be read to limit "countries" to those with modern boundaries, or to require their existence for a certain time length before it will prohibit discrimination. Animus based on national origin can persist long after new political structures and boundaries are established.

Id.; *see Roach v. Dresser Indus. Valve & Instr. Div.*, 494 F.Supp. 215, 218 (W.D.La.1980) (recognizing discrimination against "Cajuns" as national origin discrimination under Title VII although colony of Acadia no longer exists).

Under the principles set forth in *Pejic* and the Code of Federal Regulations, we have no trouble concluding that discrimination against Hopis constitutes national origin discrimination under Title VII. The status of Indian tribes among the international community and in

[4] We note that claims of discrimination on the basis of one's status as a Native American are often brought as race discrimination claims, *see, e.g.,* Weahkee v. Perry, 190 U.S.App.D.C. 359, 587 F.2d 1256 (D.C.Cir.1978), although they have also been brought as national origin claims, *see* Perkins v. Lake County Dep't of Utilities, 860 F.Supp. 1262 (N.D.Ohio 1994).

relation to the United States has, of course, a complicated history that cannot be summarized briefly, and we will not attempt to do so. It is elementary, however, that the different tribes were at one time considered to be nations by the both the colonizing countries and later the United States. *See* William C. Canby, Jr., *American Indian Law* 68 (1998). In 1832 Chief Justice Marshall wrote:

> The Indian nations had always been considered as distinct, independent, political communities, retaining their original natural rights, as the undisputed possessors of the soil, from time immemorial. * * *
>
> The Cherokee nation, then is a distinct community, occupying its own territory, with boundaries accurately described. * * *

Worcester v. State of Georgia, 1832, 31 U.S. (6 Pet.) 515, 559–61, 8 L.Ed.483. The Court has in more recent times recognized the erosion of the Indian tribes' "nation" status. *See Organized Village of Kake v. Egan,* 369 U.S. 60, 72, 7 L.Ed.2d 573, 82 S.Ct. 562 (1962) (Frankfurter, J.) (noting that "by 1880 the Court no longer viewed reservations as distinct nations"). Currently, the different Indian tribes are generally treated as domestic dependent nations that retain limited powers of sovereignty. *See* William C. Canby, *American Indian Law* 72–87 (1998).

Because the different Indian tribes were at one time considered nations, and indeed still are to a certain extent, discrimination on the basis of tribal affiliation can give rise to a "national origin" claim under Title VII. The fact that "new political structures and boundaries" now exist has no significance. Further, even if the various tribes never enjoyed formal "nation" status, Section 1606.1 of the regulations makes clear that discrimination based on one's ancestor's "place of origin" is sufficient to state a cause of action. Accordingly, under the case law and the regulations interpreting Title VII, tribal affiliation easily falls within the definition of "national origin."

Salt River does not contend that the different Indian tribes are not "nations" for Title VII purposes. Rather, it relies on *Morton v. Mancari,* 417 U.S. 535, 552 554, 41 L.Ed.2d 290, 94 S.Ct. 2474 (1974), for the proposition that employment preferences based on tribal affiliation are based on *political affiliation* rather than national origin and are thus outside the realm of Title VII. *Morton* involved a Due Process challenge to the Bureau of Indian Affair's policy hiring Indian applicants over non-Indian applicants. The Court found that the policy did not constitute an impermissible racial classification because it was "reasonably designed to further the cause of Indian self-government and to make the BIA more responsive to the needs of its constituent groups." *Id.* at 554. However, *Morton* did not involve a claim of discrimination on the basis of membership in a particular tribe. In fact, in *Morton* no claim was made of any violation of Title VII. *Morton* simply held that the employment preference at issue, though based on a racial classification, did not violate the Due Process clause because there was a legitimate non-racial purpose underlying the preference: the unique interest the Bureau of Indian Affairs had in employing Native Americans, or more generally, Native Americans' interests in self-governance interests not present in this case. For these reasons, *Morton* does not affect our conclusion that discrimination in employment on the basis of membership in a particular tribe constitutes national origin discrimination. We therefore conclude that differential employment treatment based on tribal affiliation is actionable as "national origin" discrimination under Title VII.

* * *

NOTES AND QUESTIONS

1. As the *Dawavendewa* court notes in footnote 4, Title VII claims of discrimination against Native Americans have been brought as either race or national origin claims. Does the expansive definition of race for § 1981 claims that was adopted by the Supreme Court in *St. Francis College v. Al-Khazraji*, 481 U.S. 604, 107 S.Ct. 2022, 95 L.Ed.2d 582 (1987), reproduced in Chapter 2, blur the distinction between race, national origin, ancestry, and ethnicity? One professor argued, with regard to Latinos, that

> discrimination based on race and ethnicity may substantively mean two different things. For example, racial discrimination against Latino-Americans may mean discriminatory reactions to Latino-Americans who have Mestizo or Afro-Latino features. On the other hand, ethnic discrimination may mean discriminatory reactions to evidence of Latino-American culture, including language, accent, behavior and clothing.

Yxta Maya Murray, *The Latino-American Crisis of Citizenship*, 31 U.C. Davis L.Rev. 503, 575 (1998). Is that a sound distinction? *See also* Enriquez v. Honeywell, Inc., 431 F.Supp. 901, 904 (E.D.Okla.1977) (observing that "the line between discrimination on account of race and discrimination on account of national origin may be so thin as to be indiscernible").

In what ways does it matter whether the claim is characterized as based on race or national origin? *See* Gloria Sandrino-Glasser, *Los Confundidos: De-Conflating Latino/as' Race and Ethnicity*, 19 Chicano-Latino L.Rev. 69, 142–57 (1998) (arguing that conflation of race and national origin obscures the unique nature of national origin discrimination suffered by Latina/os.); john a. powell, *Legal Implications of the Census: A Minority-Majority Nation: Racing the Population in the Twenty-First Century*, 29 Fordham Urb.L.J. 1395, 1412 (2002) (asserting that treating Latina/o's as "white" for racial purposes separates them from blacks in the civil rights movement and forces them to prove national origin discrimination, which is factually harder to prove than racial discrimination).

2. What is the distinction between national origin, ancestry, and ethnicity under Title VII? Consider the following analysis of these terms:

> National origin is the most simply defined and most easily understood. * * * "National origin" under Title VII means both one's national origin and the national origin characteristic of one's ancestry.
>
> Ancestry may be defined as "family descent or lineage." Ancestry, therefore, is a somewhat broader concept than national origin, since it may encompass more than one ancestor and more than one national origin. Although ancestry overlaps with national origin, one's ancestors may not have a single or a strict national origin. Acadians, for example, have a specific ancestry, but no national origin, since Acadia has never been a nation. Gypsies, too, have specific ancestry, but claim no particular national origin.
>
> Ancestry may also be distinct from national origin. Consider the situation of a Cuban-born member of a Chinese community in Cuba who emigrates to the United States. Suppose this person becomes a victim of discrimination because he looks Chinese, speaks Chinese, and speaks English with an obvious Chinese accent. While this example may involve discrimination because of ancestry (his Chinese parents and other ancestors) and because of race and ethnic traits (Chinese physical features, color, language, accent), there is no discrimination because of national origin (Cuban birthplace).
>
> Of the three concepts, ethnicity is the most complex and the most difficult to define because it is a varying mix of different traits. Under a broad definition, ethnicity refers to physical and cultural characteristics that make a social group distinctive, either in group members' eyes or in the view of outsiders. Thus ethnicity consists of a set of ethnic traits that may include, but are not limited to: race, national origin, ancestry, language, religion, shared history, traditions, values, and symbols, all of which contribute to a sense of distinctiveness among members of the group. These traits also may engender a perception of group distinctiveness in persons who are not members of that group. It is the perception of difference, often based on ethnic traits, that results in discrimination.

Juan F. Perea, *Ethnicity and Prejudice: Reevaluating "National Origin" Discrimination Under Title VII*, 35 Wm. & Mary L.Rev. 805, 832–34 (1994). Would a prohibition of discrimination because of ethnicity rather than national origin be more compatible with the goals of Title VII? *See* Eugenio Abellera Cruz, *Unprotected Identities: Recognizing Cultural Ethnic Divergence in Interpreting Title VII's "National Origin" Classification*, 9

Hastings Women's L.J. 161, 186 (1998) (critiquing strictly geographic approach to defining national origin as ignoring the true nature of ethnicity.)

3. The term to be applied to different ethnic groups is also a contested area. For example, there appears to be a general preference for the nomenclature "Latino" over "Hispanic." The Supreme Court has used the term "Latino." *See* Hernandez v. New York, 500 U.S. 352, 355, 111 S.Ct. 1859, 1864, 114 L.Ed.2d 395 (1991). " 'Latino' is an abbreviated version of the Spanish word *latinoamericano*, or Latin American. 'Hispanic' is the English translation of *hispano*, a word commonly used to describe all peoples of Spanish-speaking origin." Manuel Peréz-Rivas, *Hispanic, Latino: Which?*, N.Y. Newsday, Oct. 13, 1991, at 6, 6. Although the two terms are roughly synonymous, many prefer the word "Latino" because "Hispanic" is thought to have colonial and assimilative overtones. *See* Paul Brest & Miranda Oshige, *Affirmative Action for Whom?*, 47 Stan.L.Rev. 855, 883 n.148 (1995). The term "Latino" is also suggestive of Latin America's indigenous culture apart from its Spanish origins. Deborah Ramirez, *Multiculture Empowerment: It's Not Just Black and White Anymore*, 47 Stan.L.Rev. 957, 959 n.9 (1995). To be more inclusive of women, some commentators use the term "Latino/a" generally—or just "Latina" to refer specifically to women of Hispanic origin—because in the Spanish language the "a" ending indicates the feminine form of a noun or adjective. The term "Chicano"—or "Chicana"—is primarily used by descendants of Mexican immigrants and often used to suggest a political, in addition to geographic, identity. How does this affect the basis for a claim?

4. Beginning in 1977, individuals filling out federal forms, particularly census questionnaires, had been required to identify themselves as belonging to one of four racial groups: (1) white, (2) black, (3) American Indian, Eskimo, Aleut or (4) Asian or Pacific Islander. The Census Bureau included the term "other" for those persons who did not want to check one of these four categories. In the 1990 Census, almost ten million individuals checked off "other" to describe their identity. *See* Barbara Vobejda, *Census Expands Options for Multiracial Families; After Long Debate, Americans Can Choose More Than One Category on Federal Forms*, Wash. Post, Oct. 30, 1997, at A11. But racial self-identification is problematic for multiracial individuals:

> In the situation in which the mother is white and the father is some other race, compared to all the other groups, blacks have a much higher retention of being black—69.1% of the children are black. Another 8% are reported "other" and 22% are reported as white. In contrast 50% of the offspring of white mothers and Native American fathers are reported to be white, 43% of Japanese-white children are reported as white, 35% of Chinese-white children are reported white and 58% of Korean-white children are reported by their parents to be white. In sharp contrast, when the father is Asian Indian and the mother is white only 20% of the children stay Asian Indian. A much lower percentage of children of Japanese, Chinese and Filipino fathers married to white mothers remain identified with their father's Asian origins. While these Asian groups do show a large

> proportion of the children as "other" race (11.56% for children of Japanese fathers, 15.25% for children of Chinese fathers, and 10.53% for children of Korean fathers), even if one ignores those high percentages, there still are far more children identifying with their white mother's race.

Testimony of Professor Mary C. Waters, Department of Sociology, Harvard University, Before the Subcommittee on Government Management, Information and Technology of the House Committee on Government Reform and Oversight, *reprinted* in Federal News Service, May 22, 1997 (reported in LEXIS, Legis Library, CNGTST file). Professor Waters concluded that "[t]here is no socially meaningful group now that is 'multiracial' in terms of having a culture, a phenotype, a residential or occupational profile, or even of being subject to discrimination." *Id.*

On October 29, 1997, the Census Bureau announced a new federal policy that permits Americans filling out census and other federal forms to select multiple racial categories to describe their racial identity. As one journalist reported,

> In the 2000 census, * * * people can check off as many categories as they like, yielding a much more complex picture of diversity across the American population, but also creating a somewhat unwieldy combination of numbers.
>
> Ultimately * * * the government would publish population totals for each category and for every possible combination. The Census Bureau, for example, would release the number of Americans identifying themselves as white only, a separate number of those considering themselves both white and black and a third tally of those checking white, black and Asian.

Vobejda, *supra*, at A11. The 2010 census also included the multiple race option. Between 2000 and 2010, the number of people reporting more than one race increased by one-third (from 6.8 million people or 2.4% of the population to 9 million people or 2.9% of the population). About 92% of those who reported multiple races chose just two races, and the most common dual race response was White and Black. See U.S. Census Bureau, The Two or More Races Population: 2010, *available at https://www.census.gov/prod/cen2010/briefs/c2010br-13.pdf*.

What are the implications for the enforcement of laws such as Title VII and § 1981—that prohibit discrimination in employment on the basis of race and national origin—of this change in federal census policy? Vobejda reported that the "preliminary analysis" of the acting assistant attorney general for civil rights was that "Americans would be covered by anti-discrimination laws if they considered themselves wholly or partly a member of the protected group." *Id.* In light of this, can you anticipate any particular new problems that employers might face in terms of compliance with antidiscrimination laws? For further discussion of the movement to adopt a multiracial category in the decennial census and its potential effects on discrimination law, see Tanya Katerí Hernández, *"Multiracial" Discourse: Racial Classifications in an Era of Color-Blind Jurisprudence*, 57 Md.L.Rev. 97 (1998).

5. National origin may also overlap with religion, especially when a particular religion is closely associated with a particular national origin. The analysis for discrimination based on religion varies from the analytical model used in other Title VII categories because the statute prohibits discrimination against religious *practice* and requires an employer to accommodate religious practices in certain circumstances. These issues may be particularly acute for Muslims, Arabs, South Asians, and Sikhs. The EEOC has noted a significant increase in claims brought by these groups since September 11, 2001, alleging discrimination based on religious and/or national origin. *See* U.S. Equal Empl. Oppt'y Comm'n, Questions and Answers About the Workplace Rights of Muslims, Arabs, South Asians, and Sikhs Under the Equal Employment Opportunity Laws, available at *http://www.eeoc.gov/eeoc/publications/backlash-employee.cfm* (discussing questions and answers for these groups); U.S. Equal Empl. Oppt'y Comm'n, Questions and Answers About Employer Responsibilities Concerning the Employment of Muslims, Arabs, South Asians, and Sikhs, available at *http://www.eeoc.gov/eeoc/publications/backlash-employer.cfm* (discussing employer responsibilities with respect to these groups).

NOTES: NATIVE AMERICANS

1. Native Americans are not a class specifically protected by Title VII. As a group, however, they have suffered a variety of different types of discrimination and harm. As illustrated by *Morton v. Mancari,* discussed in *Dawavendewa,* Native American status is not considered racial for Equal Protection Clause analysis. Instead, Native Americans tribes have been considered sovereign states, subject by conquest to the legislative power of the United States, while retaining powers of self-government. *See* Felix S. Cohen, Handbook of Federal Indian Law 122–23 (1945). *See* Rodolfo Acuna, Occupied America: A History of Chicanos (3d ed.1988). In *Rice v. Cayetano*, 528 U.S. 495, 120 S.Ct. 1044, 145 L.Ed.2d 1007 (2000), a voting rights case, the Supreme Court distinguished the Native American experience from that of Native Hawaiians in finding that the latter group, consisting of "any descendant of the aboriginal peoples inhabiting the Hawaiian Islands, which exercised sovereignty and subsisted in the Hawaiian Islands in 1778, and which people thereafter have continued to reside in Hawaii," was a "proxy for race." 528 U.S. at 120 S.Ct. at 1055–56. How does this distinguish Native Americans from other groups we have studied? Are Native Americans comparable to Latinos in the Southwest, whose land was occupied and annexed from Mexico in the nineteenth century?

2. As the *Dawavendewa* court noted, Title VII specifically exempts "Indian tribes" from the scope of the definition of employer as used in the statute, 42 U.S.C. § 2000e(b). Courts have construed this exemption broadly,

to include entities in addition to tribes. In *Pink v. Modoc Indian Health Project, Inc.,* 157 F.3d 1185 (9th Cir.1998), the court considered whether to grant an exemption to "a nonprofit corporation created and controlled by the Alturas and Cedarville Rancherias, both federally recognized tribes." *Id.* at 1187. The tribes organized Modoc for "charitable, educational, and scientific purposes" in order to deliver health services to their members. The court concluded:

> Although the Ninth Circuit has not specifically addressed whether a nonprofit organization incorporated by two Indian tribes is a "tribe" for purposes of Title VII exemption, the Tenth Circuit has addressed a similar question. In *Dille v. Council of Energy Resource Tribes,* 801 F.2d 373 (10th Cir.1986), the court held that a council comprised of thirty-nine Indian tribes that had joined together to collectively manage energy resources was a "tribe" within the scope of Title VII's Indian tribe exemption. The *Dille* Court held that Congress intended to exempt individual Indian tribes as well as collective efforts by Indian tribes. The court reasoned that the purpose of the tribal exemption, like the purpose of sovereign immunity itself, was to promote the ability of Indian tribes to control their own enterprises. * * *
>
> Here, Modoc served as an arm of the sovereign tribes, acting as more than a mere business. Modoc's board of directors consisted of two representatives from each Rancheria tribal government. Like the collection of tribes in *Dille,* Modoc was organized to control a collective enterprise and therefore falls within the scope of the Indian Tribe exemption of Title VII.

Id. at 1188. *See also* Allen v. Gold Country Casino, 464 F.3d 1044, 1046 (9th Cir.2006) (tribal casino); Thomas v. Choctaw Mgmt./Servs. Enter., 313 F.3d 910 (5th Cir.2002) (tribal-owned business venture).

3. One commentator has critiqued the *Dawavendewa* opinion as follows:

> It seems that in this era of Indian affairs, many in power have sought ways to erode tribal sovereignty. Any benefit or advantage that a tribe may have is subject to attack. With this case, the Ninth Circuit has found a way to chip away at what little power remains with the Navajo Nation.
>
> This case also opens avenues of attack that no reasonable person would accept. If an Oklahoman denies employment to a Texan, Texas having been a sovereign nation, the Texan would have a "national origin" claim. This would also be true for other citizens of states that were formally nations such as California and Hawaii.

Recent Developments, 23 Am. Indian L.Rev 459, 461 (1998–99).

4. The implications of Title VII's exemption for Indian tribal employers have gained attention as the Indian tribal casino industry has rapidly grown

nationwide. In 2009, tribal gaming generated an estimated 26.2 billion dollars of revenue and created 628,000 jobs for tribes. Jonathan Guss, *Gaming Sovereignty? A Plea for Protecting Worker's Rights While Preserving Tribal Sovereignty*, 102 Cal. L. Rev. 1623, 1625 (2014). This surge in jobs, however, has not stimulated a change in federal antidiscrimination laws as applied to Indian tribes. As a result, casino-employee plaintiffs have begun to pursue their Title VII claims against the private management corporations with whom the tribal casinos contract. Shivani Sutaria, *Employment Discrimination in Indian-Owned Casinos: Strategies to Providing Rights and Remedies to Tribal Casino Employees*, 8 J.L. & Soc. Challenges 132, 145–50 (2006). In such cases, the main issue is whether the management corporation or the Indian tribe is the plaintiff's "employer" for purposes of Title VII. This finding generally hinges on the degree of control the management company asserted over the employee. *Id.* (discussing Hines v. Grand Casino of Louisiana, 140 F.Supp.2d 701 (W.D.La.2001); Vance v. Boyd Miss., Inc., 923 F.Supp. 905 (S.D.Miss.1996)). Assuming that such control was exercised, courts have held that Title VII applies to management companies operating under contract with an Indian tribe. *Id.* In addition, the federal government has authorized states to regulate Indian Tribes through a system of negotiated gaming compacts. Indian Gaming Regulatory Act, 25 U.S.C. §§ 2701–21 (West 2010).

NOTE: NATIONAL ORIGIN AND THE BONA FIDE OCCUPATIONAL QUALIFICATION DEFENSE

Neither race nor color is included in Title VII, § 703(e)(1), 42 U.S.C. § 2000e–2(e)(1), which permits discrimination "where religion, sex, or national origin is a bona fide occupational qualification reasonably necessary to the normal operation of that particular business or enterprise." The legislative history suggests that this provision should be liberally construed. For example, Senators Clark and Case, the floor managers of the Civil Rights Act of 1964, submitted an "Interpretive Memorandum" to the Senate which stated, in part,

> This exception [to Title VII] is a limited right to discriminate on the basis of religion, sex, or national origin where the reason for the discrimination is a bona fide occupational qualification. Examples of such legitimate discrimination would be the preference of a French restaurant for a French cook, the preference of a professional baseball team for male players, and the preference of a business which seeks the patronage of members of particular religious groups for a salesman of that religion.

110 Cong. Rec. 7212, 7213 (1964). During the debate in the House of Representatives, Representative Rodino suggested that the owner of a pizzeria "would probably seek as a chef a person of Italian origin. He would do this because pizza pie is something he believes * * * people of Italian national origin are able to make better than others—and is reasonably

necessary to the operation of his particular business." 110 Cong. Rec. 2549 (1964). What is the purpose in treating national origin differently than race?

The Supreme Court in *International Union, UAW v. Johnson Controls*, 499 U.S. 187, 111 S.Ct. 1196, 113 L.Ed.2d 158 (1991) adopted a very narrow interpretation of § 703(e)(1) in a sex discrimination case involving the BFOQ exception. Should courts similarly apply *Johnson Controls'* narrow interpretation of the BFOQ defense in national origin discrimination cases, or should they adopt a more liberal interpretation as suggested by the legislative history of Title VII?

NOTE: HARASSMENT BECAUSE OF NATIONAL ORIGIN

Harassment cases such as *Meritor Savings Bank v. Vinson*, 477 U.S. 57, 106 S.Ct. 2399, 91 L.Ed.2d 49 (1986), and *Harris v. Forklift Systems*, 510 U.S. 17, 114 S.Ct. 367, 126 L.Ed.2d 295 (1993), are equally applicable in the Title VII national origin cases. *See, e.g.*, Stewart v. Rise, 791 F.3d 849 (8th Cir.2015); Cerros v. Steel Tech., Inc., 288 F.3d 1040 (7th Cir.2002); Miller v. Kenworth of Dothan, Inc., 277 F.3d 1269 (11th Cir.2002); Amirmokri v. Baltimore Gas & Elec. Co., 60 F.3d 1126 (4th Cir.1995). *Rogers v. EEOC*, 454 F.2d 234 (5th Cir.1971), *cert. denied*, 406 U.S. 957, 92, S.Ct. 2058, 32 L.Ed.2d 343 (1972), a national origin harassment case cited with approval by the Supreme Court in *Meritor*, was the first case to recognize a Title VII claim of hostile work environment discrimination.

The EEOC guidelines on harassment because of national origin incorporate the hostile work environment doctrine. *See* EEOC Guidelines on Discrimination Because of National Origin: Harassment, 29 C.F.R § 1606.8 (2009). They define harassment to include "ethnic slurs and other verbal or physical conduct relating to an individual's national origin" when the conduct has "the purpose or effect of creating an intimidating, hostile or offensive working environment," "unreasonably interfering with an individual's work performance," or "[o]therwise adversely affects an individual's employment opportunities." *Id.* § 1606.8(b). The guidelines state that an employer is responsible for harassing conduct of fellow employees and non-employees in the workplace "when the employer, its agents or supervisory employees, knows or should have known of the conduct," unless the employer can show that it took "immediate and appropriate corrective action." *Id.* § 1606.8(d)–(e). In its 1999 Enforcement Guidance: Vicarious Employer Liability for Unlawful Harassment by Supervisors, the EEOC stated that the *Ellerth* and *Faragher* rule of vicarious liability applies to harassment by supervisors on the basis of national origin, as well as all other bases covered by Title VII. 29 C.F.R. § 1604.11 app. A, available at *http://www.eeoc.gov/policy/docs/harassment.html*. *See, e.g.*, *Cerros*, 288 F.3d at 1048 (remanding to permit employer to present *Ellerth/Faragher* affirmative defense to vicarious liability).

In the course of an extended discussion of the nature and effect of ethnic epithets, the court in *Howard v. National Cash Register Co.*, 388 F.Supp. 603, 605–06 (S.D.Ohio 1975), stated:

> It is a fact of life that social, ethnic, religious and racial distinctions are frequently drawn. There are Irish who dislike English; English who dislike French; French who despise Germans, Germans who hate Poles; and Poles who loathe Russians. For almost 100 years as waves of immigration have settled this country, there has been a succession of jokes regarding immigrants and classical comic characters poking fun at national groups. "Pat and Mike" jokes were as derogatory of Irish 100 years ago as "Polack" jokes are today. Stupid German comedians were long a staple of vaudeville, and the sly, grasping, money-hungry Jew has been a classic figure of historical literature. To this number was added the ignorant, lazy, shiftless, caricature of a Black, as portrayed by Stephan Fetchit, Amos and Andy, and Eddie "Rochester" Anderson. That these portrayals were degrading, humiliating, and offensive to the ethnic groups they purported to represent has only recently been recognized. The damage, however, to persons of sensitivity was nonetheless deep, nonetheless real.
>
> The language of the factory and the language of the street have long included words such as "Greaser", "Dago", and "Spick", and "Kike" and "Chink" as well as "Nigger." In the past three years we have even adopted as a part of our folk lore a character who is prejudiced and biased against all persons other than of his own neighborhood, religion and nationality. We refer to such people now as "Archie Bunkers" [after a character in the 1970's television show "All in the Family"]. The Archie Bunkers of this world, within limitations, still may assert their biased view. We have not yet reached the point where we have taken from individuals the right to be prejudiced, so long as such prejudice did not evidence itself in discrimination. This Court will secure plaintiff against discrimination; no court can secure him against prejudice.

If, as the court in *National Cash Register* observed, harassing conduct in the workplace (as in society at large) is the natural historical consequence of a society ingrained with negative attitudes and stereotypes of groups of different national origins, then is the *Harris v. Forklift* "reasonable person" standard likely to be meaningful in "securing" to victims of unlawful harassment freedom from national origin discrimination? *Compare* Richard Delgado, *Words That Wound: A Tort Action for Racial Insults, Epithets, and Name-Calling*, 17 Harv.C.R.–C.L.L.Rev 133 (1982) (advocating civil tort remedy for racial insults as a means of protecting citizens' rights to equality), *with* Kingsley R. Browne, *Title VII as Censorship: Hostile-Environment Harassment and the First Amendment*, 52 Ohio St.L.J. 481 (1991) (arguing that all speech in the workplace is inherently free speech and should be protected).

To what extent should the perspective of the victim in national origin cases be taken into account in determining whether the conduct is deemed to be severe or pervasive under the *Harris v. Forklift* standard? *See generally* Mari J. Matsuda, *Public Response to Racist Speech: Considering the Victim's Story*, 87 Mich.L.Rev. 2320 (1989). Should the reasonableness standard be adapted depending upon the national origin or ethnicity of the plaintiff?

C. CITIZENSHIP AND IMMIGRATION STATUS

Individuals within the United States generally fit into one of four categories:

1. A citizen (a person born here or "naturalized" through a legal process);
2. A noncitizen, legal entrant with authorization to work here;
3. A noncitizen, legal entrant who does not have authorization to work here; or
4. A noncitizen, unauthorized entrant who lacks the legal right to be here or work here.

This section explores the extent to which an employer is discriminating on the basis of national origin when it bases an employment decision on membership in any of these categories.

1. CITIZENSHIP REQUIREMENTS

ESPINOZA V. FARAH MANUFACTURING COMPANY, INC.

Supreme Court of the United States, 1973.
414 U.S. 86, 94 S.Ct. 334, 38 L.Ed.2d 287.

JUSTICE MARSHALL delivered the opinion of the Court.

This case involves interpretation of the phrase "national origin" in Tit. VII of the Civil Rights Act of 1964. Petitioner Cecilia Espinoza is a lawfully admitted resident alien who was born in and remains a citizen of Mexico. She resides in San Antonio, Texas, with her husband, Rudolfo Espinoza, a United States citizen. In July 1969, Mrs. Espinoza sought employment as a seamstress at the San Antonio division of respondent Farah Manufacturing Co. Her employment application was rejected on the basis of a longstanding company policy against the employment of aliens. After exhausting their administrative remedies with the Equal Employment Opportunity Commission, petitioners commenced this suit in the District Court alleging that respondent had discriminated against Mrs. Espinoza because of her "national origin" in violation of § 703 of Tit. VII, 42 U.S.C. § 2000e–2(a)(1). The District Court granted petitioners' motion for summary judgment, holding that a refusal to hire because of lack of citizenship constitutes discrimination on the basis of "national origin." The Court of Appeals reversed, concluding that the statutory phrase "national origin" did not embrace citizenship. We granted the writ to resolve this question of statutory construction, and now affirm.

Section 703 makes it "an unlawful employment practice for an employer * * * to fail or refuse to hire * * * any individual * * * because of such individual's race, color, religion, sex, or national origin." Certainly the plain language of the statute supports the result reached by the Court of Appeals. The term "national origin" on its face refers to the country where a person was born, or, more broadly, the country from which his or her ancestors came. * * *

The statute's legislative history, though quite meager in this respect, fully supports this construction. The only direct definition given the phrase "national origin" is the following remark made on the floor of the House of Representatives by Congressman Roosevelt, Chairman of the House Subcommittee which reported the bill: "It means the country from which you or your forebears came. * * * You may come from Poland, Czechoslovakia, England, France, or any other country." 110 Cong.Rec. 2549 (1964). * * *

Moreover, § 701(b) of Tit. VII, in language closely paralleling § 703, makes it "the policy of the United States to insure equal employment opportunities for Federal employees without discrimination because of * * * national origin * * * ." The legislative history of that section reveals no mention of any intent on Congress' part to reverse the longstanding practice of requiring federal employees to be United States citizens. To the contrary, there is every indication that no such reversal was intended. Congress itself has on several occasions since 1964 enacted statutes barring aliens from federal employment. * * *

To interpret the term "national origin" to embrace citizenship requirements would require us to conclude that Congress itself has repeatedly flouted its own declaration of policy. This Court cannot lightly find such a breach of faith. * * *

Petitioners have suggested that the statutes and regulations discriminating against noncitizens in federal employment are unconstitutional under the Due Process Clause of the Fifth Amendment. We need not address that question here * * * .

The District Court drew primary support for its holding from an interpretative guideline issued by the Equal Employment Opportunity Commission which provides:

> "Because discrimination on the basis of citizenship has the effect of discriminating on the basis of national origin, a lawfully immigrated alien who is domiciled or residing in this country

may not be discriminated against on the basis of his citizenship * * * ." 29 C.F.R § 1606.1(d) (1972).

Like the Court of Appeals, we have no occasion here to question the general validity of this guideline insofar as it can be read as an expression of the Commission's belief that there may be many situations where discrimination on the basis of citizenship would have the effect of discriminating on the basis of national origin. In some instances, for example, a citizenship requirement might be but one part of a wider scheme of unlawful national-origin discrimination. In other cases, an employer might use a citizenship test as a pretext to disguise what is in fact national-origin discrimination. Certainly Tit. VII prohibits discrimination on the basis of citizenship whenever it has the purpose or effect of discriminating on the basis of national origin. "The Act proscribes not only overt discrimination but also practices that are fair in form, but discriminatory in operation." *Griggs v. Duke Power Co.*, 401 U.S. 424, 431, 91 S.Ct. 849, 853, 28 L.Ed.2d 158 (1971).

It is equally clear, however, that these principles lend no support to petitioners in this case. There is no indication in the record that Farah's policy against employment of aliens had the purpose or effect of discriminating against persons of Mexican national origin.[5] It is conceded that Farah accepts employees of Mexican origin, provided the individual concerned has become an American citizen. Indeed, the District Court found that persons of Mexican ancestry make up more than 96% of the employees at the company's San Antonio division, and 97% of those doing the work for which Mrs. Espinoza applied. While statistics such as these do not automatically shield an employer from a charge of unlawful discrimination, the plain fact of the matter is that Farah does not discriminate against persons of Mexican national origin with respect to employment in the job Mrs. Espinoza sought. She was denied employment, not because of the country of her origin, but because she had not yet achieved United States citizenship. In fact, the record shows that the worker hired in place of Mrs. Espinoza was a citizen with a Spanish surname.

The Commission's guideline may have significance for a wide range of situations, but not for a case such as this where its very premise—that discrimination on the basis of citizenship has the effect of discrimination on the basis of national origin—is not borne out.[6] * * *

---

[5] There is no suggestion, for example, that the company refused to hire aliens of Mexican or Spanish-speaking background while hiring those of other national origins. * * * While the company asks job applicants whether they are United States citizens, it makes no inquiry as to their national origin.

[6] It is suggested that a refusal to hire an alien always disadvantages that person because of the country of his birth. A person born in the United States, the argument goes, automatically obtains citizenship at birth, while those born elsewhere can acquire citizenship only through a long and sometimes difficult process. See 8 U.S.C. §§ 1423(1), 1423(2), 1427(a), and 1430. The

Finally, petitioners seek to draw support from the fact that Tit. VII protects all individuals from unlawful discrimination, whether or not they are citizens of the United States. We agree that aliens are protected from discrimination under the Act. That result may be derived not only from the use of the term "any individual" in § 703, but also as a negative inference from the exemption in § 702, which provides that Tit. VII "shall not apply to an employer with respect to the employment of aliens outside any State * * * ." 42 U.S.C. § 2000e–1. Title VII was clearly intended to apply with respect to the employment of aliens inside any State.[8]

The question posed in the present case, however, is not whether aliens are protected from illegal discrimination under the Act, but what kinds of discrimination the Act makes illegal. Certainly it would be unlawful for an employer to discriminate against aliens because of race, color, religion, sex, or national origin—for example, by hiring aliens of Anglo-Saxon background but refusing to hire those of Mexican or Spanish ancestry. Aliens are protected from illegal discrimination under the Act, but nothing in the Act makes it illegal to discriminate on the basis of citizenship or alienage.

We agree with the Court of Appeals that neither the language of the Act, nor its history, nor the specific facts of this case indicate that respondent has engaged in unlawful discrimination because of national origin. * * *

JUSTICE DOUGLAS, dissenting.

It is odd that the Court which holds that a State may not bar an alien from the practice of law or deny employment to aliens can read a federal statute that prohibits discrimination in employment on account of "national origin" so as to permit discrimination against aliens. [Citations omitted.]

Alienage results from one condition only: being born outside the United States. Those born within the country are citizens from birth. It could not be more clear that Farah's policy of excluding aliens is de facto a policy of preferring those who were born in this country. Therefore the construction placed upon the "national origin" provision is inconsistent

---

answer to this argument is that it is not the employer who places the burdens of naturalization on those born outside the country, but Congress itself, through laws enacted pursuant to its constitutional power "(t)o establish an uniform Rule of Naturalization." U.S.Const., Art. 1, § 8, cl. 4. Petitioners' reliance on *Phillips v. Martin Marietta Corp.*, 400 U.S. 542, 91 S.Ct. 496, 27 L.Ed.2d 613 (1971), is misplaced for similar reasons. In *Phillips* we held it unlawful under § 703 to have "one hiring policy for women and another for men * * * ." Id. at 544, 91 S.Ct. at 498. Farah, however, does not have a different policy for the foreign born than for those born in the United States. It requires of all that they be citizens of the United States.

[8] "Title VII of the Civil Rights Act of 1964 protects all individuals, both citizens and noncitizens, domiciled or residing in the United States, against discrimination on the basis of race, color, religion, sex, or national origin." 29 C.F.R § 1606.1(c) (1972).

with the construction this Court has placed upon the same Act's protections for persons denied employment on account of race or sex.

In connection with racial discrimination we have said that the Act prohibits "practices, procedures, or tests neutral on their face, and even neutral in terms of intent," if they create "artificial, arbitrary, and unnecessary barriers to employment when the barriers operate invidiously to discriminate on the basis of racial *or other impermissible classification.*" *Griggs v. Duke Power Co.*, 401 U.S. 424, 430–431, 91 S.Ct. 849, 28 L.Ed.2d 158 (1971) (emphasis added). There we found that the employer could not use test or diploma requirements which on their face were racially neutral, when in fact those requirements had a de facto discriminatory result and the employer was unable to justify them as related to job performance. The tests involved in *Griggs* did not eliminate all blacks seeking employment, just as the citizenship requirement here does not eliminate all applicants of foreign origin. Respondent here explicitly conceded that the citizenship requirement is imposed without regard to the alien's qualifications for the job.

These petitioners against whom discrimination is charged are Chicanos. But whether brown, yellow, black, or white, the thrust of the Act is clear: alienage is no barrier to employment here. *Griggs*, as I understood it until today, extends its protective principles to all, not to blacks alone. Our cases on sex discrimination under the Act yield the same result as *Griggs*. See *Phillips v. Martin Marietta Corp.*, 400 U.S. 542, 91 S.Ct. 496, 27 L.Ed.2d 613 (1971).

The construction placed upon the statute in the majority opinion is an extraordinary departure from prior cases, and it is opposed by the Equal Employment Opportunity Commission, the agency provided by law with the responsibility of enforcing the Act's protections. The Commission takes the only permissible position: that discrimination on the basis of alienage always has the effect of discrimination on the basis of national origin. Refusing to hire an individual because he is an alien "is discrimination based on birth outside the United States and is thus discrimination based on national origin in violation of Title VII." Brief for Commission as Amicus Curiae. The Commission's interpretation of the statute is entitled to great weight.

* * *

Mrs. Espinoza is a permanent resident alien, married to an American citizen, and her children will be native-born American citizens. But that first generation has the greatest adjustments to make to their new country. Their unfamiliarity with America makes them the most vulnerable to exploitation and discriminatory treatment. They, of course, have the same obligation as American citizens to pay taxes, and they are subject to the draft on the same basis. But they have never received equal treatment in the job market. Writing of the immigrants of the late 1800's, Oscar Handlin has said:

> "For want of alternative, the immigrants took the lowest places in the ranks of industry. They suffered in consequence from the poor pay and miserable working conditions characteristic of the sweat-shops and the homework in the garment trades and in cigar making. But they were undoubtedly better off than the Irish and Germans of the 1840's for whom there had been no place at all." The Newcomers 24 (1959).

The majority decides today that in passing sweeping legislation guaranteeing equal job opportunities, the Congress intended to help only the immigrant's children, excluding those "for whom there (is) no place at all." I cannot impute that niggardly an intent to Congress.

NOTES AND QUESTIONS

1. Is *Espinoza* analytically and doctrinally consistent with the Title VII jurisprudence on race and sex discrimination that you have learned? How convincing do you find the dissent's argument that Farrah's policy is prohibited by the disparate impact theory developed in *Griggs* or the sex-plus theory developed in *Phillips* v. *Martin Marietta*? Is there an argument that the employer is using the bottom-line defense prohibited in *Teal*?

2. To what extent should Title VII's prohibition on discrimination based on national origin cover discrimination based on citizenship or migrant status? Articulate the difference in what an employer is seeking to accomplish in citizenship discrimination that is different from what it is seeking to accomplish when discriminating on the basis of national origin and on the basis of race. Although *Espinoza* has created a bright line rule that discrimination based on citizenship status is not prohibited, it can be difficult to tell whether employers are discriminating based on national origin or citizenship status. In *Chellen v. John Pickle Co.,* 446 F.Supp.2d 1247 (N.D.Okla.2006), for example, the employer was charged with abusing more than fifty employees working under H–1B visas. Although the Title VII allegations focused on the employer's use of slurs based on the employees' Indian national origin and/or race, their exploitation was clearly affected by their immigration status. For instance, the employer stated, "These are my Indian animals I brought from India to work." *Id.* at 1265. If the employer had never referred to their country of origin, should they have been left unprotected under Title VII? *See also* EEOC v. Technocrest Sys., Inc., 448 F.3d 1035 (8th Cir.2006), where the EEOC brought a case alleging national origin discrimination on behalf of Filipino H–1B visa workers, and the employer argued that immigration records were not discoverable because any discrimination based on immigration status or citizenship is irrelevant.

3. *Preferences for Noncitizen Employees*: Workers who are United States citizens have brought cases alleging that employers who prefer to hire

foreign nationals with temporary work visas—rather than hire workers whose national origin is the United States—are engaging in national origin discrimination. For example, in *Scott v. Omega Protein, Inc.*, 989 So.2d 827 (La.App.2008), the majority found in favor of the defendants who had hired fishermen from Mexico who had H–1B visas and refused to rehire local fishermen who were United States nationals. The court relied, in part, on the rationale of *Espinoza* to deny the national origin discrimination claim. The dissent, however, argued that the claim should be upheld because it was analytically distinct from the plaintiff's claim in *Espinoza.* Which is the better view? *See also* Rachel Bloomekatz, Comment, *Rethinking Immigration Status Discrimination and Exploitation in the Low-Wage Workplace,* 54 UCLA L.Rev. 1963 (2007) (arguing that Title VII should protect native-born United States citizens and that this will help all low-wage workers).

4. *Constitutionality of Citizenship Requirements*: Although the majority in *Espinoza* did not reach the issue of the constitutionality of a citizenship requirement for federal employment, in his dissenting opinion, Justice Douglas referred to two cases in which the Supreme Court has overturned citizenship restrictions for practicing law or for state employment: In re Griffiths, 413 U.S. 717, 93 S.Ct. 2851, 37 L.Ed.2d 910 (1973); Sugarman v. Dougall, 413 U.S. 634, 93 S.Ct. 2842, 37 L.Ed.2d 853 (1973). Following the terrorist attacks on New York City and Washington, D.C., on September 11, 2001, Congress enacted the Aviation and Transportation Security Act (ATSA), 49 U.S.C. § 40101, which required that all airport security screening personnel be United States citizens. On behalf of a group of plaintiffs—lawful permanent residents and a United States national—who had previously been employed as airport screeners, the American Civil Liberties Union and the Service Employees International Union filed a lawsuit challenging the ATSA citizenship requirement. Gebin v. Mineta, 231 F.Supp.2d 971 (C.D.Cal.2002). The complaint alleged that, at many major airports, a large number of the screeners are legal residents but not citizens (80 percent of the screeners at San Francisco; 40 percent at Los Angeles; 70 percent at Miami; and 80 percent at Dulles). The complaint further alleged that the citizenship requirement served no rational purpose because thousands of other employees (pilots, flight attendants, baggage handlers, mechanics, etc.) have access to secure areas and are not required to be citizens; because noncitizens serve in the National Guard, which performed security duties at screening stations; that the best qualified, most experienced screeners will be fired and replaced by inexperienced screeners; and because no government report has ever identified the citizenship or nationality of screeners as having any connection to the ongoing problems with security. The court found that this categorical exclusion of noncitizens could only be upheld if the government could prove it is a narrowly tailored measure that furthers a compelling governmental interest. *Id.* at 976, *see also* Gebin v. Mineta, 239 F.Supp.2d 967 (C.D.Cal.2002) (granting preliminary injunction), *order vacated*, 328 F.3d 1211 (9th Cir.2003). What interests are served by the citizenship requirement? How are they related to discrimination based on national origin? Congress later amended Section III of the ATSA to allow foreign

nationals to serve as screeners. Homeland Security Act of 2002, Pub.L. No. 107–296, § 1603, 116 Stat. 2135 (2002).

5. *The Immigration Reform and Control Act (IRCA)*: Section 1324B of the Immigration Reform and Control Act of 1986 (IRCA) prohibits four types of unfair immigration-related employment practices for employers with four or more employees: national origin discrimination, citizenship discrimination, document abuse, and intimidation or retaliation. 8 U.S.C.§ 1324B(a). This provision of IRCA has some overlap with Title VII's protections against national origin discrimination. For example, IRCA makes it an unlawful employment practice for some employers not covered by Title VII—that is, employers with four to fourteen employees—to discriminate on the basis of national origin in decisions to hire, discharge, or recruit employees or to refer employees for a fee. 8 U.S.C. § 1324b(1)(A). The provisions, however, reach fewer employer actions than those reached by Title VII. *See generally* Sarah M. Kendall, Comment, *America's Minorities Are Shown the "Back Door" * * * Again: The Discriminatory Impact of the Immigration Reform and Control Act*, 18 Hous. J. Int'l L. 899 (1996). With respect to citizenship status, IRCA prohibits a covered employer from discriminating against United States citizens or other protected individuals (excluding unauthorized workers) on the basis of citizenship in hiring, discharging, or recruiting, or in referring for a fee. *Id.* § 1324b(1)(B). *See* Lucas Guttentag, *Immigration-Related Employment Discrimination: IRCA's Prohibitions, Procedures and Remedies*, 37 Fed.B. News & J. 29 (1990). For an argument about the limitations of IRCA in prohibiting citizenship discrimination, see Rachel Bloomekatz, Comment, *Rethinking Immigration Status Discrimination and Exploitation in the Low-Wage Workplace,* 54 UCLA L.Rev. 1963, 1986–1993 (2007). IRCA also prohibits the employment of certain workers, and the effect of this is discussed below in Section B.2.

6. From a comparative perspective, the laws of many other countries and international treaties (including those signed by the United States) prohibit discrimination based on migrant status. These often include protection for both authorized and unauthorized immigrants. *See* Connie de la Vega & Conchita Lozano-Batista, *Advocates Should Use Applicable International Standards to Address Violations of Undocumented Migrant Workers' Rights in the United States,* 3 Hastings Race & Poverty L. J. 35, 36–39 (2005); Beth Lyon, *Tipping the Balance: Why Courts Should Look to International and Foreign Law on Unauthorized Immigrant Workers,* 29 U.Penn.J. Int'l Law 169, 195–97 (2007); Rebecca Smith, *Human Rights at Home: Human Rights as an Organizing and Legal Tool in Low-Wage Worker Communities,* 3 Stan.J.C.R. & C.L. 285, 302–06 (2007); David Weissbrodt, *Remedies for Undocumented Noncitizens in the Workplace: Using International Law to Narrow the Holding of Hoffman Plastic Compounds, Inc. v. NLRB,* 92 Minn.L.Rev. 1424, 1430–31 (2008).

2. UNDOCUMENTED WORKERS AND TITLE VII

In 1986, Congress enacted the Immigration Reform and Control Act (IRCA), 8 U.S.C. § 1324(b)(a)(1), an amendment to the Immigration and Nationality Act of 1952, 8 U.S.C. § 1101 *et seq.* The goals of IRCA are to curtail the large number of undocumented immigrants entering the United States by reducing the opportunities for employment and to secure national borders. To achieve these goals, Congress, for the first time, subjected employers to sanctions for knowingly hiring, recruiting, or employing unauthorized aliens. An "unauthorized alien" is defined as an alien who, at the time of employment, has not been admitted for permanent residence in the United States or who lacks authorization for employment from IRCA or the Attorney General. 8 U.S.C. § 1324a(h)(3). In order to comply with the law, an employer must have new employees complete an I–9 form that confirm the individual's identity and his or her legal ability to work in the United States. *See generally* U.S. Citizenship and Immigration Services, I–9 Central, available at *http://www.uscis.gov/i-9-central.* Many employers use an electronic verification system called e-verify. *See generally* U.S. Citizenship and Immigration Services, E-Verify, available at *http://www.uscis.gov/e-verify.*

IRCA's prohibition on the employment of undocumented workers raises two questions for Title VII plaintiffs: coverage and remedies. *Espinoza* held that aliens, like citizens, are protected from employment discrimination under Title VII on the basis of all the grounds prohibited under the statute. Does IRCA affect this outcome? In *Egbuna v. Time-Life Libraries, Inc.*, 153 F.3d 184 (4th Cir.1998) (en banc), the issue was whether a Title VII plaintiff must prove that he is eligible to work in the United States under IRCA in order to establish a prima facie case of disparate treatment under Title VII. The district court dismissed plaintiff's claim on the ground that because he lacked a "green card," that is, INS authorization to work in the United States, he could not show that he was qualified for the position. A panel of the Fourth Circuit reversed, holding that undocumented aliens are protected under Title VII despite the provisions of IRCA, and that, to make out a prima facie case under Title VII, a plaintiff need not prove his or her eligibility under IRCA to work in the United States. The panel adopted the reasoning of the only other court that had faced the issue, *EEOC v. Tortilleria "La Mejor"*, 758 F.Supp. 585 (E.D.Cal.1991). *Tortilleria* held that Congress did not intend for IRCA to amend or repeal any of the previous legislated protection of federal labor and employment laws accorded to aliens, documented or undocumented, including the protection under Title VII. The panel in *Egbuna* expressed its concern that a contrary ruling would provide an incentive for employers to hire undocumented aliens, mistreat them, and then argue that the worker has no remedy because of his unauthorized status.

In a 9–4 en banc decision, the Fourth Circuit reversed the panel's decision and affirmed the decision of the district court. *Egbuna*, 153 F.3d 184. The en banc court held that an undocumented alien has no claim under Title VII "because his undocumented status render[s] him ineligible both for the remedies he seeks and for employment within the United States." *Id.* at 186. The Fourth Circuit relied upon the following reasons in support of its decision: First, "[w]hen the applicant is an alien, being 'qualified' for the position is not determined by the applicant's capacity to perform the job—rather, it is determined by whether the applicant was an alien authorized for employment in the United States at the time in question." *Id.* at 187. Second, "IRCA effected a monumental change in our country's immigration policy by criminalizing the hiring of unauthorized aliens." *Id.* at 188. Third, "to order [an employer] to hire an undocumented alien would nullify IRCA, which declares it illegal to hire or to continue to employ unauthorized aliens." *Id.*

In deciding a claim brought under a different federal statute, the Supreme Court in *Hoffman Plastic Compounds, Inc. v. National Labor Relations Board*, 535 U.S. 137, 122 S.Ct. 1275, 152 L.Ed.2d 271 (2002), reviewed the ability of the National Labor Relations Board to award reinstatement, back pay, and other remedies to undocumented workers who were fired in violation of the National Labor Relations Act. In a 5–4 decision, the Court found that such relief is foreclosed by the policies underlying IRCA's statutory scheme. The Court did find that undocumented workers were still covered by the NLRA, even though IRCA limited their remedies. *Id.* at 122 S.Ct. 1275, 1283 n.4. The Court concluded that the Board's authority to select remedies for employer unfair labor practices was necessarily circumscribed by federal immigration policy. The Court stated:

> Under the IRCA regime, it is impossible for an undocumented alien to obtain employment in the United States without some party directly contravening explicit congressional policies. Either the undocumented alien tenders fraudulent identification, which subverts the cornerstone of IRCA's enforcement mechanism, or the employer knowingly hires the undocumented alien in direct contradiction of its IRCA obligations. The Board asks that we overlook this fact and allow it to award backpay to an illegal alien for years of work not performed, for wages that could not lawfully have been earned, and for a job obtained in the first instance by a criminal fraud. We find, however, that awarding backpay to illegal aliens runs counter to policies underlying IRCA, policies the Board has no authority to enforce or administer. Therefore, as we have consistently held in like circumstances, the award lies beyond the bounds of the Board's remedial discretion.

* * *

> Lack of authority to award backpay does not mean that the employer gets off scot-free. The Board here has already imposed other significant sanctions against Hoffman—sanctions Hoffman does not challenge. These include orders that Hoffman cease and desist its violations of the NLRA, and that it conspicuously post a notice to employees setting forth their rights under the NLRA and detailing its prior unfair practices. * * * We have deemed such "traditional remedies" sufficient to effectuate national labor policy * * * .

Id. at 152, 122 S.Ct. at 1283, 1285. After *Hoffman,* courts have generally not limited back pay remedies for undocumented immigrants bringing wage and hour claims because the remedies relate to work already performed. Lamonica v. Safe Hurricane Shutters, Inc., 711 F.3d 1299, 1306 (11th Cir.2013); Lucas v. Jerusalem Cafe, 721 F.3d 927, 935 (8th Cir.2013).

Following *Hoffman*, the EEOC issued a statement that "Federal law makes it illegal to discriminate against any worker in the United States, regardless of immigration status. In response to *Hoffman*, the EEOC recently directed its field offices that claims for all forms of relief, other than reinstatement and back pay for periods after discharge or failure to hire, should be processed in accord with existing standards, without regard to an individual's immigration status." EEOC, EEOC Reaffirms Commitment to Protecting Undocumented Workers from Discrimination, *available at http://www.eeoc.gov/eeoc/newsroom/release/6–28–02.cfm.*

D. NATIONAL ORIGIN DISCRIMINATION BASED ON LANGUAGE AND ACCENT

The number of non-English-speaking and accented employees in the United States workforce has grown due to recent increases in the number of immigrants entering the country from non-English-speaking countries. In 2000, almost 20 percent of the United States population (45 million people) spoke a language other than English at home, and over 4 percent (10.3 million people) spoke little or no English at all. EEOC Compliance Manual, § 13V: National Origin Discrimination (2002). This number has remained fairly stable at the 2010 census date. See Camille Ryan, U.S. Census Bureau, Language Use in the United States: 2011 (Aug. 2013), available at *https://www.census.gov/prod/2013pubs/acs-22.pdf.* The employment of these individuals has given rise to three different claims based on national origin discrimination: challenges to English proficiency as a job qualification; challenges to policies that require bilingual employees to speak only English at the workplace; and lawsuits alleging discrimination based on an accent.

1. ENGLISH PROFICIENCY AS A JOB REQUIREMENT

An employer that requires its employees to be able to speak English well as a condition of employment may face a claim of discrimination based on national origin. If the requirement is applied to a non-English-speaking employee as opposed to a bilingual employee, most courts suggest applying a disparate impact model because the requirement will have a disparate impact based on national origin. *See* Garcia v. Spun Steak Co., 998 F.2d 1480 (9th Cir.1993); Garcia v. Gloor, 618 F.2d 264, 270 (5th Cir.1980); EEOC v. Synchro-Start Prods., Inc., 29 F.Supp.2d 911 (N.D.Ill.1999). *But see* Chavez v. Hydril Co., 2003 WL 22075740 (N.D.Tex.2003) (utilizing circumstantial disparate treatment model); Dercach v. Ind. Dep't of Highways, 1987 WL 46837 (N.D.Ind.1987) (same). Recall that under a disparate impact model, in order to prevail the employer must prove that the language requirement is job related for the position in question and consistent with business necessity. *See* Edward M. Chen, *Speech: Labor Law and Language Discrimination*, 6 Asian L.J. 223, 228–29 (1999). *See generally* EEOC Compliance Manual, § 13V: National Origin Discrimination (2002), *available at http://www.eeoc.gov/policy/docs/national-origin.html.*

At least one commentator has argued that the federal courts have "set up a false dichotomy by distinguishing 'fully' bilingual from monolingual national origin minorities, including in the latter group those plaintiffs with limited English-language proficiency." Mark Colon, *Line Drawing, Code Switching, and Spanish as Second-Hand Smoke: English-Only Workplace Rules and Bilingual Employees*, 20 Yale L. & Pol'y Rev. 227, 229 (2002). What arguments can be made that a disparate impact model should apply to both monolingual and bilingual employees confronting an English language requirement?

2. ENGLISH-ONLY REQUIREMENT FOR BILINGUAL EMPLOYEES

Plaintiffs have utilized both the disparate treatment and disparate impact models to challenge English-only policies.

PACHECO V. NEW YORK PRESBYTERIAN HOSPITAL

United States District Court for the Southern District of New York, 2009.
593 F.Supp.2d 599.

KARAS, DISTRICT COURT JUDGE.

Plaintiff, Jose Pacheco ("Plaintiff"), initiated this action on November 26, 2002, alleging that Defendant, New York Presbyterian Hospital ("Defendant" or the "Hospital"), discriminated against him and a class of Hispanic employees by maintaining an "English-only" policy in violation of Title VII of the Civil Rights Act of 1964, 42 U.S.C. § 2000e *et seq.* ("Title VII"), Title VI of the Civil Rights Act of 1964, 42 U.S.C. § 2000d ("Title VI"), 42 U.S.C. § 1981a, and New York State and New York City human rights laws ("NYSHRL" and "NYCHRL," respectively).

The Hospital now moves for summary judgment. For the reasons stated herein, the Hospital's motion is granted.

* * *

Plaintiff, a United States citizen, was born and raised in Puerto Rico. Plaintiff identifies himself as Hispanic by national origin, and is fully bilingual in English and Spanish. Plaintiff has worked for the Hospital since August 5, 1994. In 2000, Plaintiff was employed as a Patient Representative in the Associates in Internal Medicine ("AIM") Clinic of the Hospital. On approximately May 8, 2000, Plaintiff sought and obtained a transfer within the Hospital to the position of Patient Representative within the Ambulatory Referral Registration Area ("ARRA"), a unit of the Hospital's Patient Financial Services Department, the registration desks of which are located on the first floor of the Hospital. * * *

During the period that Plaintiff worked in the ARRA unit, several patients complained to [Pacheco's supervisor] [Patricia] Votta [Manager of Patient Financial Services, Outpatient Registration] that they believed they were being talked about or ridiculed by ARRA employees who were speaking about them in a language other than English and were laughing at them. Plaintiff was warned by Votta [who does not speak Spanish] on three occasions, that while he was in the vicinity of patients at the ARRA, he was to refrain from speaking in a language other than English in the course of performing his responsibilities.) The exception to this request was that Plaintiff was instructed (without objection) on multiple occasions by Votta and other supervisors, that he could, and should assist Spanish-speaking patients by talking to them in Spanish. Moreover, in the approximately ten weeks Plaintiff worked in the ARRA unit, he was never prohibited from speaking Spanish while not on-duty. Over half the employees and one supervisor in the ARRA unit are of Hispanic descent. There is no evidence that any other ARRA employee complained about Votta or any other supervisor limiting their ability to speak Spanish while performing their jobs. Further, Plaintiff acknowledges that no disparaging remarks were directed at his national origin by any Hospital representative while he was employed in the ARRA unit.

Plaintiff objected to Votta about her request that he speak only English while performing his job duties, and he alleges that in response to his complaint, Votta retaliated against him by varying his job duties and assignments. * * *

II. DISCUSSION

* * *

B. TITLE VII CLAIMS

Plaintiff claims that the Hospital discriminated against him on the basis of his national origin, in violation of Title VII. * * * [T]he thrust of Plaintiff's claim is that he was barred from speaking Spanish at certain times while in the ARRA unit, and that Defendant retaliated against him when he challenged Defendant's language practices in the ARRA unit.

1. Disparate Treatment

The first component of Plaintiff's Title VII claim is that Defendant's limited English-only practice constituted disparate treatment of Plaintiff because of his race and national origin. Indeed, as noted, Title VII bars employers from discriminating against an employee because of that employee's race, color, religion, gender, or national origin. *See Gomez-Perez v. Potter,* 553 U.S. 474, 128 S.Ct. 1931, 1940, 170 L.Ed.2d 887 (2008) (noting that Title VII contains "a broad prohibition of 'discrimination,' rather than a list of specific prohibited practices," all based on "race, color, religion, sex, or national origin"). To prevail on such a claim in the absence of direct evidence of discrimination, a plaintiff usually must satisfy the *McDonnell Douglas* three-part burden-shifting test. *See McDonnell Douglas Corp. v. Green,* 411 U.S. 792, 802–04, 93 S.Ct. 1817, 36 L.Ed.2d 668 (1973).

* * *

"As part of a disparate treatment claim," Plaintiff "must establish that [Defendant] acted with the intent to discriminate" on the basis of race, ethnic origin, gender, or religion. *Hayden v. County of Nassau,* 180 F.3d 42, 52 (2d Cir.1999). As Defendant notes, many courts, including the Second Circuit, have recognized that Title VII does not expressly identify language as a protected class. *See Soberal-Perez v. Heckler,* 717 F.2d 36, 41 (2d Cir.1983) (stating that "[l]anguage, by itself, does not identify members of a suspect class"); *Brewster v. City of Poughkeepsie,* 447 F.Supp.2d 342, 351 (S.D.N.Y.2006) (noting that Title VII "does not protect against discrimination on the basis of language"); *Betances v. Prestige Decorating & Wallcovering, Inc.,* No. 05–CV–4485, 2006 WL 963877, at *2 (S.D.N.Y. Apr. 13, 2006) (holding that "non-English speakers * * * are not a protected class under Title VII"); *Velasquez v. Goldwater Mem'l Hosp.,* 88 F.Supp.2d 257, 262 (S.D.N.Y.2000) (noting that termination from employment for failure to comply with English-only policy did not establish Title VII discrimination claim); *Long v. First Union Corp.,* 894 F.Supp. 933, 941 (E.D.Va.1995), *aff'd,* 86 F.3d 1151 (4th Cir.1996) ("There is nothing in Title VII which protects or provides that an employee has a right to speak his or her native tongue while on the job.").

However, the Supreme Court has observed that "[j]ust as shared language can serve to foster community, language differences can be a source of division." *Hernandez v. New York,* 500 U.S. 352, 371, 111 S.Ct. 1859, 114 L.Ed.2d 395 (1991). As the Supreme Court has put it, language "elicits a response from others, ranging from admiration and respect, to distance and alienation, to ridicule and scorn," which "all too often result from or initiate racial hostility." *Id.* Thus, for example, the Supreme Court has suggested that the striking of potential jurors on the basis of language, could, in certain circumstances, be a "pretext for racial discrimination." *Id.* at 371–72, 111 S.Ct. 1859; *accord Garcia v. Gloor,* 618 F.2d 264, 270 (5th Cir.1980) (noting that "[l]anguage may be used as a covert basis for national origin discrimination"). Consistent with this notion, courts have recognized that an employer's English-only policy can, in certain circumstances, support a Title VII claim of racial discrimination. *See, e.g., Maldonado v. City of Altus,* 433 F.3d 1294, 1304 (10th Cir.2006) (noting that "English-only policies are not always permissible; each case turns on its facts"), *overruled on other grounds by Burlington N. & Santa Fe Ry. Co. v. White,* 548 U.S. 53, 126 S.Ct. 2405, 165 L.Ed.2d 345 (2006); *Garcia v. Spun Steak Co.,* 998 F.2d 1480, 1489 (9th Cir.1993) (refusing to "foreclose the prospect that in some circumstances English-only rules can exacerbate existing tensions, or, when combined with other discriminatory behavior, contribute to an overall environment of discrimination"); *Roman v. Cornell Univ.,* 53 F.Supp.2d 223, 236 (N.D.N.Y.1999) ("A speak-English instruction may form the basis for an inference of national origin discrimination.").

Critical to evaluating the propriety of a language-restriction policy under a disparate treatment theory, as in any such employment discrimination case, is whether the employer's practices reflect an intent to discriminate on the basis of the classifications protected by Title VII, including race and national origin. In conducting this analysis, the courts consider, among other facts, whether there is evidence that the employer, in addition to adopting an English-only policy, has exhibited other forms of racial or ethnic hostility. *See, e.g., Spun Steak,* 998 F.2d at 1489 (noting that English-only policies in conjunction with other discriminatory conduct can "contribute[ ] to an overall environment of discrimination"); *Brewster,* 447 F.Supp.2d at 351 (holding that there was sufficient evidence of discrimination where employer made comments, such as, "Speak English. Go back to your own country if you want to speak Spanish. You're in our country."); *Velasquez,* 88 F.Supp.2d at 262–63 (noting that a "no-Spanish" policy "could be used to disguise a discriminatory motive"). Courts also have distinguished between various types of language-restriction polices, being more forgiving of those that apply only to work-related communication and to bilingual employees. *See, e.g., Montes v. Vail Clinic, Inc.,* 497 F.3d 1160, 1170–71 (10th Cir.2007) (upholding policy prohibiting employees from speaking Spanish while on the job and during job-related discussions, but permitting Spanish conversations during breaks or during non-job related discussions); *Maldonado,* 433 F.3d at 1307–08 (suggesting that an English-only policy, if applied at all times to all employees regardless of activity, could be discriminatory); *Gloor,* 618 F.2d at 270 (noting that "[t]o a person who speaks only one tongue or to a person who has difficulty using another language than the one spoken in his home, language might well be an immutable characteristic like skin color, sex or place of birth. However, the language a person who is multi-lingual elects to speak at a particular time is by definition a matter of choice").

Thus, the strength of Plaintiff's case is not evaluated on a broad analysis of English-only policies in the workplace. The EEOC, for example, "presumes, subject to rebuttal," that English-only policies "blithely enforced at all times [and] places in the work environment" violate Title VII. *Montes,* 497 F.3d at 1171 (citing 29 C.F.R. § 1606.7(a)). But, the EEOC guidelines also provide that "[a]n employer may have a rule requiring that employees speak only in English at certain times where the employer can show that the rule is justified by business necessity." 29 C.F.R. § 1606.7(b); *see also Cosme v. Salvation Army,* 284 F.Supp.2d 229, 239 (D.Mass.2003) (applying § 1606.7(b)); *Prado v. L. Luria & Son, Inc.,* 975 F.Supp. 1349, 1357 (S.D.Fla.1997) (upholding English-only policy as being consistent with EEOC guidelines where employer established business necessity). Given the EEOC's position, it should not be surprising that Plaintiff has failed to identify a single case in which a court upheld a Title VII claim in the face of a summary judgment motion where the language policy involved work-related communications by bilingual employees and the policy was found to further a legitimate business purpose. *See Roman,* 53 F.Supp.2d at 237 ("All decisions of which this Court is aware have held that English-only rules are not discriminatory as applied to bilingual employees where there is a legitimate business justification for implementing such a rule.").

In this case, even if the Court assumes Plaintiff has made out a prima facie case, Plaintiff's case fails because he has not offered enough evidence to dispute Defendant's legitimate, non-discriminatory reason for the English-only practice ARRA followed.[7] To begin, the Court notes that

[7] Aside from the EEOC guidelines, Plaintiff relies on the "preliminary report" of Dr. Susan Berk-Seligson as evidence that the English-only practice at ARRA was discriminatory. According to Dr. Berk-Seligson, an English-only policy can be humiliating and frustrating to native Spanish speakers. Among other sources of frustration, Dr. Berk-Seligson claims that bilingual persons, such as Plaintiff, engage in what is known as "code-switching," which means that they will inevitably speak some Spanish to other Spanish-speaking individuals. According to Dr. Berk-Seligson, "[p]rohibiting a Hispanic employee from speaking a combination of Spanish and English is in effect creating an atmosphere of inferiority, isolation and intimidation." Whatever the merits of Dr. Berk-Seligson's theory, and the Court takes no view on this, it is enough for the Court to assume that Plaintiff has made out a prima facie case for purposes of this motion based on this report.

the practice at issue was not a blanket prohibition against any non-English conversations by employees in the ARRA unit. Instead, the undisputed evidence is that Votta, who does not speak Spanish, asked Plaintiff, who is fully bilingual, on several occasions to speak English when in hearing range of patients. There is no evidence that Plaintiff, or any other ARRA employee, was barred from speaking Spanish during breaks or when not near patients. In fact, Plaintiff admits that he spoke Spanish to his colleagues every day while at the ARRA, and, on occasion, was asked to help communicate with Spanish-speaking patients. This undercuts any claim of bias against Hispanic employees. *See Long,* 894 F.Supp. at 942 (noting that the fact that employees were encouraged to speak Spanish when necessary makes "even more credible" the justification for a limited English-only rule). Moreover, there is no evidence that Votta or any Hospital supervisor or employee made any discriminatory comments, or that Votta (or any other supervisor) selectively enforced the practice of speaking English near patients, either among the employees or on the basis of any particular language. And, notably, Plaintiff was not disciplined in any way for any limited number of instances in which he spoke Spanish while on the job.

On the other hand, Defendant has offered ample evidence that demonstrates a valid business reason for the practice. First, Defendant notes, and Plaintiff does not dispute, that several patients had complained about feeling ridiculed by ARRA employees who were not speaking English in their presence. Thus, Defendant contends that the practice of requiring employees to speak English to and around patients was consistent with Defendant's goal of treating all patients with respect. Second, Defendant notes that it was far easier for Votta and other supervisors in the ARRA, who did not speak Spanish, to properly supervise and evaluate Plaintiff if he spoke English around and to them. Plaintiff does not contest the factual predicate for these claims; nor does he offer any evidence that Votta and other supervisors allowed other employees to speak any languages other than English under similar circumstances. Given this undisputed record, the case law supports Defendant's claim of business necessity. For example, a number of courts have upheld limited English-only policies for bilingual employees as a means of facilitating customer relations. *See, e.g., Gonzalo v. All Island Transp.,* No. 04–CV–3452, 2007 WL 642959, at *2 (E.D.N.Y. Feb. 26, 2007) (noting that English-only policy in dispatch office of transport carrier was justified); *EEOC v. Sephora USA, LLC,* 419 F.Supp.2d 408, 417 (S.D.N.Y.2005) (holding that English-only policy of retailer was justified as a means of improving communication with customers and noting that "promoting politeness to customers is a valid business necessity for requiring sales employees to speak English in their presence"); *Kania v. Archdiocese of Philadelphia,* 14 F.Supp.2d 730, 736 (E.D.Pa.1998) (finding that English-only rule was reasonably necessary to, *inter alia,* improve relations among church members). Furthermore, courts regularly have upheld limited English-only policies for bilingual employees to promote communication among employees and supervisors. *See, e.g., Montes,* 497 F.3d at 1171 (upholding limited English-only policy where it was "undisputed that clear and precise communication between the cleaning staff and the medical staff was essential in the operating rooms" of a hospital); *Sephora,* 419 F.Supp.2d at 415 (noting that courts have found limited English-only practices "permissible when they are justified by a need to stem hostility between bilingual employees speaking a foreign language and employees who do not speak that language, as well as when English-speaking supervisors need to understand what is being said in a work area"); *Roman,* 53 F.Supp.2d at 237 ("Defendants' purported goals of avoiding or lessening interpersonal conflicts, preventing non-foreign language speaking individuals from feeling left out of conversations, and preventing non-foreign language speaking individuals from feeling that they are being talked about in a language they do not understand, are legitimate business reasons justifying [the employer's] English-only rule."); *Long,* 894 F.Supp. at 942 (finding business necessity in limited English-only rule to promote communication among employees and to ensure that the business "runs smoothly and efficiently").

* * *

3. Hostile Work Environment

Plaintiff alleges that Defendant's English-only policy created a hostile work environment. He rests this claim on the conclusory argument that an English-only policy "can induce native speakers of Spanish to experience a work environment as hostile."

" 'When the workplace is permeated with discriminatory intimidation, ridicule, and insult that is sufficiently severe or pervasive to alter the conditions of the victim's employment and create an abusive working environment, Title VII is violated.' " *Oncale v. Sundowner Offshore Servs., Inc.,* 523 U.S. 75, 78, 118 S.Ct. 998, 140 L.Ed.2d 201 (1998) (quoting *Harris v. Forklift Sys., Inc.,* 510 U.S. 17, 21, 114 S.Ct. 367, 126 L.Ed.2d 295 (1993)). To prevail on a hostile work environment claim under Title VII, a plaintiff must show "misconduct" that is "severe or pervasive enough to create an objectively hostile or abusive work environment, and the victim must also subjectively perceive that environment to be abusive." *Terry v. Ashcroft,* 336 F.3d 128, 148 (2d Cir.2003) (internal quotation marks omitted). * * *

Plaintiff asserts that the English-only practice was especially burdensome for employees like him, "who can not avoid the use of Spanish in their interaction with other employees." The alleged difficulty Plaintiff had in not lapsing into Spanish is belied by Plaintiff's testimony that he is fully bilingual in English and Spanish. Plaintiff's allegation of a hostile work environment is further undercut by his acknowledgment that no disparaging remarks of any sort were directed at his national origin by any Hospital representative while he was employed in the ARRA unit. *See Brewster,* 447 F.Supp.2d at 351 (holding that language policy was only actionable because it was accompanied by evidence of ethnically-hostile statements to the plaintiff). In addition, no other ARRA employees, some of whom have been Spanish-speakers, complained about the limited English-only practice, and in fact, some stated that they thought it was a good idea.

Plaintiff also relies on the views of the aforementioned Dr. Susan Berk-Seligson, who holds a Ph.D. in linguistics, to explain how an English-only policy might hurt Plaintiff's ability to perform his job duties. Even if Dr. Berk-Seligson's report were admissible under *Daubert v. Merrell Dow Pharm., Inc.,* 509 U.S. 579, 113 S.Ct. 2786, 125 L.Ed.2d 469 (1993), her largely abstract report adds nothing in the way of evidentiary support for the claim that Plaintiff suffered from an actionable hostile work environment. *See CL-Alexanders Laing & Cruickshank v. Goldfeld,* 739 F.Supp. 158, 164 (S.D.N.Y.1990) ("[W]hile expert opinion may be helpful, summary judgment can be defeated only by the allegation of specific facts. A particular set of facts 'cannot be established by mere speculation or idiosyncratic opinion, even if th[e] opinion [about the facts] is held by one who qualifies as an expert.' " (quoting *In re Agent Orange Prod. Liab. Litig.,* 818 F.2d 187, 193 (2d Cir.1987))). In fact, Dr. Berk-Seligson's conclusion borders on being an improperly legal one that Plaintiff was subject to an unlawfully hostile work environment based on "his Hispanic ethnicity." *See Densberger v. United Tech. Corp.,* 297 F.3d 66, 74 (2d Cir.2002) ("It is a well-established rule in this Circuit that experts are not permitted to present testimony in the form of legal conclusions." (quoting *United States v. Articles of Banned Hazardous Substances,* 34 F.3d 91, 96 (2d Cir.1994))).

It bears noting that Dr. Berk-Seligson reached her conclusion without interviewing Votta or any other Hospital employees (other than Plaintiff) to account for the rationale for the language practice in the ARRA, or what effect the practice had on other Spanish-speaking and/or bilingual employees. Indeed, eleven of the thirteen pages of the expert report reflect upon academic research and theories of "code switching" (the use of more than one language in the course of a single communication) leaving only two pages to facts arguably involving Plaintiff. Taken to its logical limit, the expert report is a broad critique of any language restrictions in the workplace on the premise that many Spanish-speaking people will invariably and inadvertently sprinkle Spanish words when having conversations in English. Of course, the record is barren of any claim that Plaintiff was warned against "code switching." On the contrary, Plaintiff was asked not to engage in work-related conversations in Spanish for the above-described business reasons, and he offers not a single example to the contrary. Thus, whatever difficulties Dr. Berk-Seligson believes that some bilingual persons may have in avoiding code switching, difficulties, again, that the Court is willing to accept for purposes of this motion, the report does not establish that Plaintiff has made out a claim that he was subject to a hostile work environment because of his ethnicity, race, or even the fact that Spanish is his native language.[14] Thus, the Court finds that Plaintiff has failed to raise a genuine issue of material fact that the conditions of Plaintiff's employment were sufficiently severe or pervasive to create an objectively hostile or abusive work environment.

* * *

In recent challenges to English-only policies brought under a disparate impact theory, courts have wrestled with whether to follow the EEOC Guideline, 29 C.F.R. § 1606.7, that an employer's English-only policy establishes the plaintiff's prima facie case. Cases in which courts have agreed to follow the Guideline include *EEOC v. Premier Operator Services,* 113 F.Supp.2d 1066 (N.D.Tex.2000) (following Guideline because of deference due to EEOC Guidelines and significance of expert testimony that the phenomenon known as "code-switching" means that for many "bi-lingual" employees, speaking Spanish is more than just a preference), and *EEOC v. Synchro-Start Products,* Inc., 29 F.Supp.2d 911 (N.D.Ill.1999) (viewing Guideline as properly creating an evidentiary tie-breaker because English-only rules unarguably impact people from certain countries more heavily than others). Cases in which courts have declined to follow the Guideline include *Reyes v. Pharma Chemie, Inc.,* 890 F.Supp.2d 1147 (2012) (rejecting Guideline as contrary to language of Title VII); *Kania v. Archdiocese of Philadelphia,* 14 F.Supp.2d 730 (E.D.Pa.1998) (deciding in retaliation case that Guideline conflicts with statute); *Long v. First Union Corp.,* 894 F.Supp. 933 (E.D.Va.1995) (refusing to follow Guideline because it is agency-created policy that is not consistent with statute). If a court refuses to adopt the rule

---

[14] The Court is aware of two reported cases in which Dr. Berk-Seligson's opinions regarding code-switching were proffered in support of Title VII claims involving English-only policies. In *Premier Operator Services,* the court considered Dr. Berk-Seligson's expert opinion, along with a plethora of other evidence, to find that a blanket English-only policy violated Title VII. *See* 113 F.Supp.2d at 1069–72. Specifically, in *Premier Operator Services,* the court found that the defendant had discriminated against a class of plaintiffs where (i) the English-only policy applied to casual conversations between employees during lunch, (ii) the employees faced termination even for inadvertent use of Spanish, (iii) Hispanic employees were terminated and replaced by non-Hispanic employees, (iv) racially offensive comments were made to the Spanish-speaking employees (where some employers referred to plaintiffs as "wetbacks"), and (v) the employer failed to demonstrate the business necessity for the policy. *See id.* at 1070–73. None of these critical facts, which had nothing to do with Dr. Berk-Seligson's expert opinion, exists in this case.

articulated in the EEOC Guideline, a plaintiff may still make out a prima face case by showing that the English-only policy does have a significant adverse impact on a protected group. *Garcia v. Spun Steak,* 998 F.2d 1480, 1486 (9th Cir.1993).

Once the plaintiff has established a prima face case of disparate impact, the burden of proof will shift to the defendant to establish that the policy is justified by business necessity. The following case considers this step in the analysis:

EEOC v. SEPHORA U.S.A., LLC

United States District Court for the Southern District of New York, 2005.
419 F.Supp.2d 408.

BUCHWALD, DISTRICT COURT JUDGE.

* * *

BACKGROUND

Sephora operates retail cosmetics stores throughout the United States. During the relevant times discussed herein, Sephora operated stores in the New York Metropolitan area. Each Sephora store is managed by a store director, who reports to a regional manager. Stores employ assistant managers and first-level supervisors. Within a store, sales personnel, referred to as "consultants," may be assigned to different departments. Sephora refers to the sales floor staff as the "cast" and the sales floor as the "stage." In addition to sales employees, Sephora stores employ maintenance and stock department employees, referred to as "quality" employees.

This case centers on Sephora's store in Rockefeller Center, which opened in late 1999 and closed in August 2002. The plaintiffs-intervenors are all former employees of Sephora who worked in the Rockefeller Center store as either consultants or cashiers. The plaintiffs-intervenors are all bilingual in Spanish and English. The individual defendants worked at various times as managers in the Rockefeller Center store and at other New York area stores.

In or about August 2002, the plaintiffs-intervenors filed charges with the Equal Opportunity Employment Commission ("EEOC"), complaining of an allegedly discriminatory English-only rule, as well as alleging that defendants discriminated against them on the basis of their national origin.

* * * In September 2002 [Sephora distributed a policy "recap" addressing its expectations with respect to English in the workplace.] * * *

The relevant section of the Recap is as follows:

6. *English in the Workplace*

- Sephora does not have, and has never had, an "English-only" policy.
- Generally, cast members may speak whatever language they choose.
- However, Sephora expects cast members who are on stage during business hours to speak English whenever clients are present.
- Of course, cast members are encouraged to communicate with clients in other languages, if the client wishes to do so.
- Before opening and after closing, as well as times when no clients are in the store, cast members are free to speak any language they choose.
- Cast members may speak any language they choose when off stage—for example, in a break room or office.
- Cast members may speak any language they choose when not on Sephora time—on a break or after a shift.
- Cast members may be asked to speak English in other situations if there is a business need—for example, where safety is an issue (when working on a ladder, changing out shelving, retrofits, etc.)
- While Sephora encourages the spirit of teamwork amongst all cast members, it does not expect cast members to speak English except in the limited circumstances described above.

According to Sephora, each of the plaintiffs-intervenors is fluent in English and capable of complying with Sephora's expectations concerning speaking English while on stage. It is undisputed that Sephora encourages bilingual cast members to speak in a foreign language (including Spanish) to a customer who prefers to speak in that language, and that the plaintiffs-intervenors were sometimes called upon to translate for customers who did not speak English. While plaintiffs do not directly contradict Sephora's characterization of plaintiffs-intervenors' English as fluent, they allege that some of the plaintiffs-intervenors "experience difficulty expressing themselves in English," and therefore "spoke Spanish at work when they were unable to express themselves in English." Plaintiffs further assert that "[a]s a result of a phenomenon known as code-switching—an unconscious tendency to begin to speak in Spanish, to respond in Spanish when addressed in that language, and to continue speaking in Spanish with native Spanish-speakers like themselves * * * the Plaintiffs-Intervenors were not 'capable of complying' with Sephora's 'expectations.'" Plaintiffs further suggest that "[b]ecause [the plaintiffs-intervenors] code-switch as a matter of involuntary habit, they are triggered to speak Spanish not as a matter of 'personal preference and convenience' but as a matter of necessity." Plaintiffs also allege that the plaintiffs-intervenors were disciplined for speaking Spanish in the workplace, including in the break room and during their lunch hour, and for other instances of speaking Spanish that were clearly permissible under the policy outlined in the Recap. In addition to complaints about being disciplined for speaking Spanish in circumstances that would be clearly permissible under the policy outlined in the Recap and complaints about other discrimination on the basis of national origin, plaintiffs also argue that the policy embodied in the Recap violates Title VII.

Defendants moved for summary judgment in the hope of narrowing the issues in the case. Sephora maintains that the English-speaking policy it outlined in the Recap does not violate Title VII and moves for summary judgment on that issue. * * * For the following reasons, we agree with Sephora, and grant summary judgment on that issue.

* * *

DISCUSSION

* * *

II. Disparate Impact Under Title VII

* * *

1. Plaintiffs Have Presumptively Established a Prima Facie Case of Disparate Impact

We begin our discussion by referencing the relevant EEOC guideline which provides that "[a]n employer may have a rule requiring that employees speak only in English at certain times where the employer can show that the rule is justified by business necessity." 29 C.F.R. § 1606.7(b). The "certain times" guideline set out in § 1606.7(b) essentially assumes that the existence of such a rule satisfies an employee's burden of establishing a prima facie showing of disparate impact and advances the inquiry to the second step of the burden-shifting framework. We decline to decide whether that aspect of the guidelines is a proper interpretation of Title VII, and instead follow the example of *Fierro v. Saks Fifth Avenue,* 13 F.Supp.2d 481, 488 (S.D.N.Y.1998) and "proceed[ ] directly to the real issues presented by * * * plaintiff[s'] claims, by simply conceding in the abstract the existence of a *prima facie* case." *See also Roman v. Cornell Univ.,* 53 F.Supp.2d. 223, 235 (N.D.N.Y.1999).

We therefore assume, for the purposes of this motion, that plaintiffs have satisfied the first stage of the three-stage burden-shifting framework by making a prima facie showing of disparate impact.

2. Defendants Have Demonstrated a Business Necessity

As we noted earlier, at the second stage the burden shifts to the defendants to demonstrate that the policy is "job related for the position in question and consistent with business necessity." 42 U.S.C. § 2000e–2(k)(1)(A)(I). Business necessity is also incorporated in the EEOC guidelines, which permit a "certain times" English rule "where the employer can show that the rule is justified by business necessity." 29 C.F.R. § 1606.7(b).

* * *

With this legal framework we will address the specific business justifications Sephora has proposed in defense of the Recap policy. At the outset of this discussion, we will clarify the context in which Sephora asserts it can apply the policy set out in the Recap. Sephora created written job descriptions for the consultant and cashier positions. The written job descriptions include an ability to clearly communicate, which in this context, the midtown Rockefeller Center location, required English proficiency. We note that, consistent with the printed job descriptions, all the plaintiffs-intervenors can communicate in English. * * *

Plaintiffs do not assert that it is illegal for Sephora to require proficiency in English as a condition of employability for consultants and cashiers, but rather argue that a business necessity is needed to require those employees to speak English on stage during business hours when clients are present. Defendants maintain that speaking English in the presence of customers is job related for sales staff and consistent with its business needs of politeness and approachability as components of customer service. Defendants explain that "because client service is the core of Sephora's business, the Company * * * expects employees who are hired and trained specifically to serve clients to speak English while on the sales floor out of respect for the client and in order to remain approachable to clients at all times," and characterize their policy as a "common sense rule against offending customers." (quoting *Rivera v. Baccarat,* 10 F.Supp.2d 318, 324 (S.D.N.Y.1998)). Skinner and Marie-Christine Marchives, who was Regional Director of the Manhattan Region, provided the same rationale for the Sephora English language policy.

* * *

Plaintiffs also argue that Sephora's asserted business necessity justification is impermissible because "customer preference is not a valid defense to discrimination against employees." * * * *Gerdom v. Continental*

Airlines, Inc., 692 F.2d 602, 609 (9th Cir.1982)). Plaintiffs' reliance on *Bradley* and *Gerdom* is misplaced. *Bradley* rejected customers' preference for clean-shaven deliverymen as a defense to a requirement that had a disparate impact on African American men, a large percentage of whom cannot shave because of a skin condition. *Gerdom* rejected customers' preference for slim female flight attendants as a defense to a weight requirement that applied only to women. The courts in *Bradley* and *Gerdom,* however, rejected those preferences as defenses to discrimination because the preferences were unrelated to job performance. If a customer preference is sufficiently related to job performance then it qualifies as a "business necessity." *Gerdom,* 692 F.2d at 609 (quoting *Diaz v. Pan American World Airways, Inc.,* 442 F.2d 385, 389 (5th Cir.1971)) ("customer preference may be taken into account only when it is based on the company's inability to perform the primary function or service it offers"). The requirement that a customer preference relate to job performance prevents employers from using customers' intolerance as a business necessity justification for a policy that has a disparate impact on a protected class. *Id.* Helpfulness, politeness and approachability, however, are central to the job of a sales employee at a retail establishment, and are distinct from customers' prejudices.

When salespeople speak in a language customers do not understand, the effects on helpfulness, politeness and approachability are real and are not a matter of abstract preference. Furthermore, just as courts have upheld a business necessity for a rule mandating that bilingual employees speak English in the workplace to stem hostility between employees, promoting politeness to customers is a valid business necessity for requiring sales employees to speak English in their presence. *See Roman,* 53 F.Supp.2d. at 237; *Kania,* 14 F.Supp.2d at 736; *Prado,* 975 F.Supp. at 1357; *Long,* 894 F.Supp. at 941; *Gonzalez,* 1991 WL 11009376, at *3.

Plaintiffs argue that customers do not actually find it rude when someone speaks a foreign language in front of them, and instead find rules mandating English offensive. In support of their argument, they mention a recent local news story in which a donut shop manager removed an "English Only" sign after customers objected on behalf of the shop's employees. The EEOC relies on a hearsay news story in an endeavor to undercut Sephora's rationale for believing customers "feel welcome" when its employees speak English in their presence. *Id.* Apart from the prohibition on reliance in the summary judgment context on inadmissible hearsay, as we explained above we do not believe Sephora's justifications rest on customer preference. Furthermore, Sephora need not demonstrate that a particular percentage of customers' opinions corroborate its business judgment that certain behavior is impolite and unhelpful. We "do[ ] not sit as a super-personnel department that reexamines an entity's business decisions." *Scaria v. Rubin,* 117 F.3d 652, 655 (2d Cir.1997) (quoting *Dale v. Chicago Tribune Co.,* 797 F.2d 458, 464 (7th Cir.1986)).

Furthermore, the business necessities Sephora describes are similar to those the EEOC itself has suggested are proper. The EEOC's Compliance Manual provides that "situations in which business necessity would justify an English-only rule" include "communications with customers, coworkers, or supervisors who only speak English," "situations in which workers must speak a common language to promote safety," "cooperative work assignments in which the English-only rule is needed to promote efficiency," and "[t]o enable a supervisor who only speaks English to monitor the performance of an employee whose job duties require communication with coworkers or customers." Sephora's own business justifications overlap and are consistent with those suggested by the Compliance Manual.

We agree with the EEOC that "[i]t is common for individuals whose primary language is not English to inadvertently change from speaking English to speaking their primary language," and with its recommendation that an employer should therefore "inform its employees of the general circumstances when speaking only in English is required and of the consequences of violating the rule." 29 C.F.R. § 1606.7(c). Speaking English is undoubtedly less comfortable for some bilingual people than speaking another language, and the EEOC therefore makes the eminently reasonable suggestion that employers evaluating whether to adopt a rule consider the "English proficiency of workers affected by the rule." EEOC Compliance Manual at 13–24. But plaintiffs rely on the extreme views of Dr. Susan Berk-Seligson, who holds a Ph.D in linguistics, about the supposed inability of bilingual Hispanics to refrain from speaking Spanish. Setting aside the issue of the admissibility of Dr. Berk-Seligson's declaration under *Daubert v. Merrell Dow Pharmaceuticals, Inc.,* 509 U.S. 579, 113 S.Ct. 2786, 125 L.Ed.2d 469 (1993), we point out that the EEOC's litigation adoption of Dr. Berk-Seligson's views is inconsistent with its statements in the Compliance Manual. While the Compliance Manual contemplates the circumstances that are appropriate for an English-only rule, Dr. Berk-Seligson claims that Hispanic bilinguals will speak Spanish unless they are "threatened with *corporal* punishment or actually * * * punished." * * * Moreover, there is no suggestion that this case is about instances of reversion to one's native tongue for a single word or phrase.

We therefore conclude that the English language policy set forth in the Recap is job related for Sephora consultants and cashiers, and is consistent with business necessity.

* * *

CONCLUSION

For the foregoing reasons, we find the policy on the use of English outlined in the Recap is legally permissible and therefore grant defendants' motion for partial summary judgment on that issue.

NOTES AND QUESTIONS

1. Compare the procedural posture and the court's analysis of the evidentiary burdens in *Pacheco* and *Sephora*. Which analytical framework better fits the type of discrimination alleged in English-only cases: disparate treatment or disparate impact? In evaluating the discriminatory harm alleged by plaintiffs in the cases, do you find the arguments about the difficulty of code-switching or the stigmatizing effect of these policies convincing? Are there other bases to find discrimination?

In *Garcia v. Spun Steak*, 998 F.3d 1480 (9th Cir.1993), one of the earliest English-only cases, the denial of a motion for en banc reconsideration evoked a powerful dissent from Judge Reinhardt who argued, in part:

> Language is intimately tied to national origin and cultural identity; its discriminatory suppression cannot be dismissed as an "inconvenience" to the affected employees, as *Spun Steak* asserts. Even when an individual learns English and becomes assimilated into American society, his native language remains an important manifestation of his ethnic identity and a means of affirming links to his original culture. English-only rules not only symbolize a rejection of the excluded language and the culture it embodies, but also a denial of that side of an individual's personality.
>
> Thus, the *Spun Steak* majority's emphasis on the *practical* effects of English-only rules is misplaced. Whether or not an individual is, in practice, capable of speaking only English is not the important consideration here by any means. What is far more important is the impact of the prohibition itself. As the EEOC correctly determined, being forbidden under penalty of perjury to speak one's native tongue generally has a pernicious effect on national origin minorities.

Garcia, 13 F.3d 296, 298–99 (9th Cir.1993) (Reinhardt, J., dissenting from denial of rehearing en banc). Do you find Judge Reinhardt's argument convincing?

A number of sociologists and legal scholars argue that language is an important aspect of national origin or ethnicity because it sets a cultural group apart from others. *See, e.g.*, Christopher David Ruiz Cameron, *How the Garcia Cousins Lost Their Accents: Understanding the Language of Title VII Decisions Approving English-Only Rules as the Product of Racial Dualism, Latino Invisibility, and Legal Indeterminacy*, 85 Cal.L.Rev. 1347, 1353 (1997); Mark Colon, *Line Drawing, Code Switching, and Spanish as Second-Hand Smoke: English-Only Workplace Rules and Bilingual Employees*, 20

Yale L. & Pol'y Rev. 227, 246–50 (2002); Juan F. Perea, *Demography and Distrust: An Essay on American Languages, Cultural Pluralism, and Official English*, 77 Minn.L.Rev. 269, 276–79 (1992); Bill Piatt, *Toward Domestic Recognition of a Human Right to Language*, 23 Hous.L.Rev. 885, 896 (1986). Assuming that language is an important aspect of national origin, is it an immutable characteristic like race or sex, or is it a mutable characteristic like the grooming standards which courts generally have held are not protected under Title VII? *See* Colon, *supra*, at 250–57 (discussing the dynamics of "code-switching," the unconscious alternation of two languages in one conversation). Should it make a difference whether it is immutable or mutable? *See, e.g.*, Willingham v. Macon Tel. Publ'g Co., 507 F.2d 1084, 1091 (5th Cir.1975) (holding that a rule regulating hair length for males is not prohibited sex discrimination under Title VII because hair length is not an immutable characteristic).

2. Do you agree with the *Pacheco*'s court evaluation of the hospital's English-only policy as a legitimate, nondiscriminatory reason? How about the *Sephora* court's analysis of business necessity? Are these analyses consistent with Title VII jurisprudence?

In *Spun Steak*, the Ninth Circuit refused to follow its previous decision in *Gutierrez v. Municipal Court*, 838 F.2d 1031 (9th Cir.1988), *vacated as moot*, 490 U.S. 1016, 109 S.Ct. 1736, 104 L.Ed.2d 174 (1989). In *Gutierrez*, the first court of appeals to consider the legality of an employer's English-only rule in light of the EEOC Guidelines struck down an employer's rule that prohibited employees from speaking any language other than English, except when translating official business or during lunch breaks. *Gutierrez* held that an English-only rule in the workplace generally has an adverse impact on non-English speaking employees and for that reason constitutes a discriminatory condition of employment because it has "a direct effect on the general atmosphere and environment of the work place." *Id.* at 1041. *Gutierrez* also held that an employee's ability to comply with an English-only rule was not relevant and could not preclude a finding of disparate impact discrimination. Adopting business necessity as the appropriate defense, *Gutierrez* rejected each of the justifications proffered by the defendant. The employer argued that (1) the rule was necessary because the United States is an English-speaking country and California is an English-speaking state; (2) the use of Spanish is disruptive and creates a "Tower of Babel"; (3) the rule promotes racial harmony; and (4) the rule is required for effective supervision because supervisors do not speak Spanish. *Id.* at 1042–43. *Spun Steak* rejected *Gutierrez* as binding precedent because *Gutierrez* had been vacated as moot by the Supreme Court.

3. In July, 2009, the EEOC issued revised guidelines on English-only policies:

> Sec. 1606.7 *Speak-English-only rules.*
>
> (a) *When applied at all times.* A rule requiring employees to speak only English at all times in the workplace is a burdensome term and

condition of employment. The primary language of an individual is often an essential national origin characteristic. Prohibiting employees at all times, in the workplace, from speaking their primary language or the language they speak most comfortably, disadvantages an individual's employment opportunities on the basis of national origin. It may also create an atmosphere of inferiority, isolation and intimidation based on national origin which could result in a discriminatory working environment. Therefore, the [EEOC] will presume that such a rule violates title VII and will closely scrutinize it.

(b) *When applied only at certain times.* An employer may have a rule requiring that employees speak only in English at certain times where the employer can show that the rule is justified by business necessity.

(c) *Notice of the rule.* It is common for individuals whose primary language is not English to inadvertently change from speaking English to speaking their primary language. Therefore, if an employer believes it has a business necessity for a speak-English-only rule at certain times, the employer should inform its employees of the general circumstances when speaking only in English is required and of the consequences of violating the rule. If an employer fails to effectively notify its employees of the rule and makes an adverse employment decision against an individual based on a violation of the rule, the [EEOC] will consider the employer's application of the rule as evidence of discrimination on the basis of national origin.

EEOC Guidelines on Discrimination Because of National Origin, 29 C.F.R § 1606.7 (2009). If these guidelines had been in effect at the time *Pacheco* and *Sephora* were decided, would they have changed the outcome of any of the cases?

4. A police department has a policy that requires bilingual Spanish-speaking police officers and employees to use their Spanish-speaking skills when necessary to carry out the duties of the police department. They do not receive additional compensation when called upon to speak Spanish in the course of doing their work. Statistics show that more Latino/Latina employees than non-Latino/Latina employees are affected by this policy. Would the Spanish-speaking employees have an argument that the policy violates Title VII prohibition against discrimination because of national origin? Should these be analyzed as disparate impact or disparate treatment claims? *See* Cota v. Tucson Police Dep't, 783 F.Supp. 458 (D.Ariz.1992); Morales v. Human Rights Div., 878 F.Supp. 653 (S.D.N.Y.1995).

5. *Reverse English-Only Claims*: In *McNeil v. Aguilos*, 831 F.Supp. 1079 (S.D.N.Y.1993), the plaintiff, a black female, brought a pro se claim under Title VII and § 1981 alleging that Filipino nurses, including her supervisor, spoke Tagalog on the job in order to isolate and harass her.

Tagalog is the main language of the Philippines. The plaintiff also alleged that the use of Tagalog by her co-workers impeded her ability to perform her job effectively and that, as a result, she was not promoted. Plaintiff cited as a specific example of her difficulty the fact that her supervisor gave the unit report in Tagalog and that, when she asked the supervisor a specific question, her supervisor failed to respond. What argument would you make in support of plaintiff's claim? What defense on behalf of the employer? The trial court dismissed the case on the ground that the plaintiff willfully disregarded discovery orders and failed to prosecute her claim. McNeil v. Aguilos, 1996 WL 219637 (S.D.N.Y.1996), *aff'd*, 107 F.3d 3 (2d Cir.1996) (unpublished table decision).

One example of sentiment against the use of foreign language can be found in the so-called "English Only" movement, which included a number of states attempting to establish English as the official language. For example, in *Arizonans for Official English v. Arizona*, 520 U.S. 43, 117 S.Ct. 1055, 137 L.Ed.2d 170 (1997), the Supreme Court was asked to consider the constitutionality of an Arizona state constitutional provision, adopted by a state referendum, that generally prohibited state employees from using any language other than English in conducting state business. The plaintiffs challenged the Arizona law on the ground that it violated the employees' federal constitutional free speech rights and was facially overbroad. The district court agreed with the plaintiffs' First Amendment free speech challenge and struck down the law. The Ninth Circuit affirmed. The Supreme Court did not reach the merits of the issue on the grounds of standing and mootness. Briefs submitted in the Supreme Court indicated that at least twenty-one states have adopted similar English-only provisions. *See generally* Mark L. Adams, *Fear of Foreigners: Nativism and Workplace Language Restrictions*, 74 Ore.L.Rev. 849, 864–76 (1995); Juan F. Perea, *Demography and Distrust: An Essay on American Languages, Cultural Pluralism, and Official English*, 77 Minn.L.Rev. 269 (1992).

6. For additional analysis supporting English-only policies, *see* Natalie Prescott, *English Only at Work, Por Favor*, 9 U.Pa.J.Lab. & Emp.L 445 (2007) (arguing that language is neither immutable nor a part of the narrow definition of national origin intended by Congress, and that assimilation is preferable to accommodation). For a contrary position, see L. Darnell Weeden, *The Less than Fair Employment Practice of an English-Only Rule in the Workplace*, 7 Nev.L.J. 947 (2007). For a discussion of the Canadian experience in recognizing language rights of its French-and English-speaking citizens and Canada's commitment to equal rights, *see* Terrence Meyerhoff, Note & Comment, *Multiculturalism and Language Rights in Canada: Problems and Prospects for Equality and Unity*, 9 Am.U.J. Int'l L. & Pol'y 913 (1994).

3. ACCENT DISCRIMINATION AS NATIONAL ORIGIN DISCRIMINATION

Another class of cases involving language discrimination arises out of accent discrimination claims. The courts have recognized that discrimination on the basis of a foreign accent can violate the prohibition against national origin discrimination under Title VII. In *Carino v. University of Oklahoma*, 750 F.2d 815 (10th Cir.1984), plaintiff brought an action alleging that he had been demoted from his position as a dental laboratory supervisor because of his Filipino accent. The court of appeals affirmed a decision in favor of the plaintiff and established the basic rule that other courts have followed: "A foreign accent that does not interfere with a Title VII claimant's ability to perform duties of the position he has been denied is not a legitimate justification for adverse employment decisions." *Id.* at 819. *See also* Berke v. Ohio Dep't of Pub. Welfare, 628 F.2d 980 (6th Cir.1980) (finding national origin discrimination against an employee demoted because of his Filipino accent). Courts have approached the issue in a variety of ways.

IN RE RODRIGUEZ

United States Court of Appeals for the Sixth Circuit, 2007.
487 F.3d 1001.

MOORE, CIRCUIT COURT JUDGE.

* * *

I. BACKGROUND

Rodriguez began working for American Freightways ("American") as a truck driver in 1999, under the supervision of Regional Human Resource Manager Rodney Adkinson ("Adkinson"). * * *

In June 2002, Rodriguez told Adkinson that he (Rodriguez) was interested in becoming a FedEx supervisor. Adkinson recommended that Rodriguez take FedEx's Leadership Apprentice Course ("LAC"), and Rodriguez subsequently enrolled in that program. While Rodriguez was taking LAC classes, three supervisory positions became vacant. According to then-Customer Service Manager Jon McKibbon ("McKibbon"), Rodriguez applied and was twice interviewed for at least one of those positions. McKibbon found Rodriguez to be qualified for the position and claims that he would have hired Rodriguez but for Adkinson's stated concern that Rodriguez's accent and speech pattern would adversely impact Rodriguez's ability to rise through the company ranks. Former FedEx Manager Dale Williams ("Williams") similarly avers that, when he asked Adkinson why Rodriguez had not been selected for promotion, Adkinson replied with disparaging remarks concerning Rodriguez's "language" and "how he speaks" and stated that Rodriguez was difficult to understand.

According to Rodriguez, both McKibbon and Williams told him of Adkinson's derogatory remarks about Rodriguez's accent and ethnicity and statements to the effect that Adkinson "would not allow [Rodriguez] to become a supervisor at FedEx because of [Rodriguez's] Hispanic speech pattern and accent." Rodriguez asserts that he complained to various FedEx managers as well as to Adkinson's direct supervisor, John Ravenille ("Ravenille"), about this discrimination, but that no corrective action was taken. FedEx employee Kelly Scrimenti overheard Rodriguez complain to Ravenille on one occasion.

* * *

On July 30, 2003, Rodriguez resigned from his employment with FedEx, citing FedEx's "refus[al] to address [his] numerous complaints of being discriminated against because of [his] race as an Hispanic-American." He subsequently filed suit in Michigan state court, alleging racial discrimination and retaliation in violation of the ELCRA [Michigan's Elliott-Larsen Civil Rights Act]. FedEx removed the case to federal court on the basis of the parties' diversity of citizenship and moved for summary judgment. * * *

* * *

III. ANALYSIS

* * *

B. Rodriguez's Discrimination Claims

1. Failure to Promote

"Cases brought pursuant to the ELCRA are analyzed under the same evidentiary framework used in Title VII cases." *Humenny v. Genex Corp.*, 390 F.3d 901, 906 (6th Cir.2004). * * *

FedEx * * * contends that Rodriguez's evidence does not establish each required element of the prima facie case. The district court, applying the *McDonnell Douglas* framework, concluded that Rodriguez's prima facie case failed because he had not shown that he applied and was qualified for a promotion or that a similarly-situated non-Hispanic employee had received preferential treatment. Before reviewing that ruling, we first consider whether Rodriguez's evidence concerning Adkinson's remarks is properly characterized as direct or circumstantial.

Our precedents, though admittedly not perfectly clear concerning this issue, suggest that the evidence is direct. In *Ang v. Procter & Gamble Co.*, 932 F.2d 540 (6th Cir.1991), we stated that "accent and national origin are inextricably intertwined." *Id.* at 549 * * * citing *Fragante v. City &*

County of Honolulu, 888 F.2d 591 (9th Cir.1989), *cert. denied,* 494 U.S. 1081, 110 S.Ct. 1811, 108 L.Ed.2d 942 (1990)). We also noted that "[t]he [Equal Employment Opportunity Commission ("EEOC")] recognizes linguistic discrimination as national origin discrimination" and that our earlier opinion in *Berke v. Ohio Dep't of Pub. Welfare,* 628 F.2d 980, 981 (6th Cir.1980), "also recognized that discrimination based on manner of speaking can be national origin discrimination." 932 F.2d at 549 (citing 29 C.F.R. § 1606). More recently, in *Momah v. Dominguez,* 175 Fed.Appx. 11 (6th Cir.2006), *vacated & remanded on other grounds,* 127 S.Ct. 933 (2007), we rejected the plaintiff's argument that "comments * * * regarding his African accent and his poor command of the English language" constituted direct evidence, but only "because neither [of the individuals who made the comments was] responsible for the allegedly discriminatory employment action." *Id.* at 19.

Our characterization of Adkinson's comments concerning Rodriguez's accent as direct evidence of national-origin discrimination is consistent with the Supreme Court's statements on the subject. *See Hernandez v. New York,* 500 U.S. 352, 371, 111 S.Ct. 1859, 114 L.Ed.2d 395 (1991) ("It may well be, for certain ethnic groups and in some communities, that proficiency in a particular language, like skin color, should be treated as a surrogate for race under an equal protection analysis."); *Espinoza v. Farah Mfg. Co.,* 414 U.S. 86, 92–93 & n.5, 94 S.Ct. 334, 38 L.Ed.2d 287 (1973) (finding no evidence of national-origin discrimination where there was "no suggestion, for example, that the company refused to hire aliens of Mexican or Spanish-speaking background while hiring those of other national origins"), *abrogated on other grounds by* 8 U.S.C. § 1324(b). It also comports with the holdings of our sister circuits. *See Akouri v. Florida Dep't of Transp.,* 408 F.3d 1338, 1347–48 (11th Cir.2005) (holding that a supervisor's statement that the plaintiff had not been promoted because his fellow employees "are all white and they are not going to take orders from you, especially if you have an accent" constituted direct evidence, "because the statement relates directly to the [employer's] decision * * * and blatantly states that the reason [that the plaintiff] was passed over for the promotion was his ethnicity"); *Ghosh v. Getto,* 146 Fed.Appx. 840, 846 (7th Cir.2005) (rejecting the plaintiff's argument that a co-worker's statement that "people are biased and prejudiced against you if you're not white, if you speak with an accent" constituted direct evidence only because the statement did "not belie a prejudicial mind set on the part of the *decision maker,* but rather observations of how *third parties* might be prejudiced" (internal quotation marks omitted)); *Bhella v. England,* 91 Fed.Appx. 835, 846 (4th Cir.2004) (holding that evidence that fellow employees had mocked the plaintiff's Indian accent was "not sufficiently connected to the actions taken against [the plaintiff] to carry [her] burden of proving that the actions were motivated by discriminatory animus"); *but see Amro v. Boeing Co.,* No. 97–3049, 1998 WL 380510, at

*2 n.3 (10th Cir.1998) (unpublished order) ("We construe comments about foreign accent to constitute indirect evidence of national origin discrimination.").

The question, then, is whether FedEx has borne its burden by demonstrating that it would have refused to promote Rodriguez even absent a discriminatory motive. FedEx argues that Rodriguez's failure to complete the LAC, combined with FedEx's claimed policy against promoting drivers directly into supervisory positions, satisfy that burden. Because it is for the district court to make this determination, applying the appropriate standard, in the first instance, *see Thaddeus-X v. Blatter,* 175 F.3d 378, 399 (6th Cir.1999) (en banc), we vacate the grant of summary judgment in favor of FedEx on Rodriguez's failure-to-promote claim and remand that claim for further proceedings. * * *

ALICE M. BATCHELDER, CIRCUIT COURT JUDGE, concurring.

* * * [W]hile I agree with the lead opinion that we should reverse the district court's grant of summary judgment and remand the case for further proceedings, I disagree with its reasoning in reaching this result. The lead opinion concludes that Rodriguez has produced direct evidence that FedEx failed to promote him based on his national origin. I, however, do not think Rodriguez had presented direct evidence to establish his claim of unlawful employment discrimination, and instead would apply the *McDonnell Douglas* burden-shifting approach. *See McDonnell Douglas Corp. v. Green,* 411 U.S. 792, 802–04, 93 S.Ct. 1817, 36 L.Ed.2d 668 (1973).

"[D]irect evidence is that evidence which, if believed, requires the conclusion that unlawful discrimination was at least a motivating factor in the employer's actions." *Amini v. Oberlin College,* 440 F.3d 350, 359 (6th Cir.2006) (citation omitted). Critically, direct evidence "proves the existence of a fact without any inferences or presumptions." *Abbott v. Crown Motor Co.,* 348 F.3d 537, 542 (6th Cir.2003) (quoting *Norbuta v. Loctite Corp.,* 181 F.3d 102 (6th Cir.1999)). "Such evidence would take the form, for example, of an employer telling an employee, 'I fired you because you are disabled,'" *Smith v. Chrysler Corp.,* 155 F.3d 799, 805 (6th Cir.1998), or, for our purposes, "I did not promote you because of your Hispanic origin." Our circuit has acknowledged that "[r]arely will there be direct evidence from the lips of the defendant proclaiming his or her [discriminatory] animus," *Robinson v. Runyon,* 149 F.3d 507, 513 (6th Cir.1998), and I find that Rodriguez has not presented such evidence here.

The lead opinion cites the affidavits of McKibbon and Williams as direct evidence of FedEx's national origin discrimination. Williams averred that he had a conversation with Adkinson about Rodriguez, during a weekly management meeting. At that time, FedEx was short a supervisor and Adkinson indicated that he had conducted interviews, including existing FedEx employees, to fill the position, but he had not found a qualified candidate. Williams suggested Rodriguez as a possible candidate. In response, Adkinson stated that "Jose is a good worker and could some day move into management." Williams then asked, in that case, why not consider Rodriguez as a candidate for the opening. Adkinson responded, "because of Jose's 'language' and 'how he speaks,' people would have a hard time understanding him." When Williams asked Adkinson if that was his only reason for not choosing Rodriguez for the position, Adkinson responded "pretty much."

McKibbon stated that a supervisor position came open and it was FedEx's practice to promote internally if there was a qualified employee. Rodriguez applied for the supervisor position. McKibbon interviewed Rodriguez two times for that position and concluded that Rodriguez was qualified for the position. McKibbon stated that he "did not hire [Rodriguez] for the supervisor position because * * * Adkinson said he was concerned about [Rodriguez's] accent, speech pattern, and capability to move up in the company." McKibbon declared that Adkinson had made these statements to him on several occasions in McKibbon's office.

While "discrimination based on manner of speaking *can* be national origin discrimination," *Ang v. Procter & Gamble Co.,* 932 F.2d 540, 549 (6th Cir.1991) (emphasis added), I do not agree that McKibbon's and Williams's affidavits constitute direct evidence of national origin discrimination here. One must infer that Adkinson's concern for Rodriguez's "accent," "speech pattern," "language," and "how he speaks" was based on Rodriguez's national origin—and not, for instance, a speech impediment or Rodriguez's ability to successfully fulfill a supervisory position.

As the Ninth Circuit pointed out many years ago,

> Accent and national origin are obviously inextricably intertwined *in many cases.* It would therefore be an easy refuge in this context for an employer unlawfully discriminating against someone based on national origin to state falsely that it was not the person's national origin that caused the employment or promotion problem, but the candidate's inability to measure up to the communications skills demanded by the job.

Fragante v. Honolulu, 888 F.2d 591, 596 (9th Cir.1989) (emphasis added).

To be sure, Williams's and McKibbon's affidavits provide circumstantial evidence that FedEx's proffered reason for failing to promote Rodriguez may well have been pretextual. Accordingly, I find that Rodriguez has provided enough circumstantial evidence to withstand FedEx's motion for summary judgment, and agree with the lead opinion, that this case should be remanded for further proceedings. But I simply do not find that Rodriguez presented *any* direct evidence to establish his claim.

NOTES AND QUESTIONS

1. What are the implications of the majority's conclusion in *Rodriguez* that derogatory comments about an accent are direct evidence of discrimination? In rejecting that view, one court reasoned:

> The Court recognizes that there surely may be cases where comments about a person's accent may be probative of discriminatory intent, *see e.g. Rivera v. Baccarat,* 10 F.Supp.2d 318, 324 (S.D.N.Y.1998), *rev'd on other grounds,* 205 F.3d 1324 (2d Cir.2000), but this is not such a case. There is simply nothing in the September 24, 2001 evaluation—which was the foundation for Thelsuma's complaints to his evaluators and his OEO charge—that contains any racially discriminatory comments about Thelusma's accent. To hold otherwise would mean that any comment by an evaluator about a minority teacher's difficulty in communicating with students could expose the evaluator to a retaliation claim should that teacher thereafter be the subject of an adverse employment action. *See Manessis v. New York City Dept. of Transp.,* 2003 WL 289969, at *8 (S.D.N.Y. Feb, 10, 2003) (citing *Watt v. New York Botanical Garden,* 2000 WL 193626, at *7 (S.D.N.Y. Feb. 16, 2000) ("it would be an inferential leap to infer that a comment about an employee's accent suggests an underlying bias against persons of that national origin."). The Court will not place such a chill on a supervisor's responsibility to render an honest evaluation of a teacher's classroom performance.
>
> * * * Even if Mejia recommended that Thelusma take "accent reduction classes," such advice would be consistent with a beneficent design to afford him the opportunity to improve his communication skills, an absolute prerequisite for adequate job performance by a teacher, rather than evidence of a discriminatory intent. *See also Meng v. Ipanema Shoe Corp.,* 73 F.Supp.2d 392 (S.D.N.Y.1999) (Asian customer service representative's accent properly considered in her termination because it interfered with her job performance) (quoting *Fragante v. City and County of Honolulu,* 888 F.2d 591, 596–597 (9th Cir.1989)); *see also Mejia v. New York Sheraton Hotel,* 459 F.Supp. 375, 377 (S.D.N.Y.1978) (Dominican chambermaid properly denied a promotion to front desk because of her "inability to articulate clearly or coherently and to make herself adequately understood in * * * English"). That a prior evaluator, such as Pike, did not discern a communication problem during a previous evaluation cannot suffice to transform the subject evaluation into one evidencing racial animus.

Thelusma v. New York City Bd. of Educ., No. 02–CV–4446(FB), 2006 WL 2620396, at *3 (E.D.N.Y. Sept. 13, 2006).

2. Some courts have focused on an employer's use of "accent" as the basis for an adverse employment decision as pretext for national origin discrimination because of the close connection between linguistic characteristics and national origin. This is particularly true when there is no evidence that the plaintiff's accent has actually interfered with job performance. Most of these cases have proceeded based on a circumstantial evidence approach, and this evidence is admitted in the third step of the *McDonnell Douglas* framework to help establish pretext. For example, in *Raad v. Fairbanks North Star Borough School District*, 323 F.3d 1185 (9th Cir.2003), the court said:

> The close relationship between language and national origin led the EEOC to classify discrimination based on "linguistic characteristics" as unlawful under Title VII. *See* 29 C.F.R. § 1606.1 (2003); *cf. id.* § 1606.7(a) (noting, in the context of speak-English-only rules, that "[t]he primary language of an individual is often an essential national origin characteristic"). "Accent and national origin are obviously inextricably intertwined in many cases." *Fragante v. City & County of Honolulu,* 888 F.2d 591, 596 (9th Cir.1989). To be sure, we have held that adverse employment decisions may be predicated upon an individual's accent, but only if it interferes with the individual's job performance. *Id.* at 596–97; *see also Carino v. Univ. of Okla. Bd. of Regents,* 750 F.2d 815, 819 (10th Cir.1984) ("A foreign accent that does not interfere with a Title VII claimant's ability to perform duties of the position he has been denied is not a legitimate justification for adverse employment decisions."). Here, the summary judgment record contains evidence that Raad's accent did not impair her performance as a teacher (and therefore was not job-related), including recommendations written by her graduate school instructors, requests for her as a substitute by other teachers employed by the District, and the District's own continued employment of her as a substitute. Based on this evidence, it would be reasonable for a finder of fact to infer that the District used her accent as a pretext to deny her a full-time position because of her national origin.

Id. at 1195. *See also* Fonseca v. Sysco Food Servs. of Ariz., 374 F.3d 840 (9th Cir.2004); Hasham v. Cal. St. Bd. of Equalization, 200 F.3d 1035 (7th Cir.2000) (ruling that comments regarding accent were admissible to show pretext); Altman v. N.Y.C. Dep't of Educ., No. 06 CV 6319(HB), 2007 WL 1290599 (S.D.N.Y. May 1, 2007).

3. Some courts grant summary judgment to an employer when the stated reason for termination is communication skills, even when the basis for the plaintiff's discrimination claim is based on a foreign accent. *See* Meng v. Ipanema Shoe Corp., 73 F.Supp.2d 392, 399 (S.D.N.Y.1999) (granting

summary judgment to defendant that terminated Chinese customer service representative based on fact that "some of her customers had trouble understanding her"); *Thelusma*, 2006 WL 2620396, at * 8–9 (granting summary judgment to defendant that terminated Haitian public school teacher even though defendant recommended that plaintiff take "accent reduction classes").

In *Fragante v. City & County of Honolulu,* 888 F.2d 591 (9th Cir.1989), the plaintiff, Manuel Fragante, had received the highest score for a clerk's position out of over 700 applicants who had taken the test for that position. After a brief interview, which was part of the screening process, he was rejected because of a perceived deficiency in oral communication skills caused by his heavy Filipino accent. The district court ruled for the employer, finding that the decision to deny Fragante the job was justified based on the BFOQ defense, even though the interview lacked formality such as standards, instructions, guidelines, or criteria, and the rating sheet for interviews was inadequate. The Ninth Circuit, in its original decision, affirmed on the basis of the BFOQ defense. In a later amended opinion, the court disregarded its original decision grounded in the BFOQ defense, but nevertheless again ruled in favor of the employer. 888 F.2d 591 (9th Cir.1989). The court then reaffirmed its ruling in favor of the employer on the ground that the employer had articulated a legitimate, nondiscriminatory reason for its rejection of Fragante, namely, that those selected had communication skills superior to Fragante's and that Fragante had failed to show that the employer's explanation was pretext for invidious discrimination on the basis of national origin. *Id.* at 596–99.

4. *The* Fragante *Case and Critical Race Theory*: Several critical race scholars have criticized the *Fragante* decision on the ground that the equality principle on which Title VII is based is conceptually flawed because it requires plaintiffs to introduce direct evidence of discriminatory bias or intent by an employer when in fact discrimination is often based on unconscious bias. For example, Professor Mari Matsuda characterized the defense that the court accepted as the "can't understand" defense. She argued that the courts have failed to address the question whether an employer should be free to choose the "best" accent in view of the fact that everyone has an accent. Mari J. Matsuda, *Voices of America: Accent, Antidiscrimination Law, and a Jurisprudence for the Last Reconstruction*, 100 Yale L.J. 1329, 1333–40, 1350 (1991). She wrote:

> A major complicating factor in applying Title VII to accent cases is the difficulty in sorting out accents that actually impede job performance from accents that are simply different from some preferred norm imposed, whether consciously or subconsciously, by the employer. The reality that accent discrimination is often unconscious, renders the judicial search for pretext pointless. Pretext by definition involves a conscious choice to discriminate.

Id. at 1352. Professor Matsuda relies on the influential article by Professor Charles R. Lawrence, *The Id, the Ego, and Equal Protection: Reckoning with Unconscious Racism*, 39 Stan.L.Rev. 317 (1987), in developing her argument that unconscious bias, "prejudice and status are tied inextricably to speech evaluation" in the accent discrimination cases. Matsuda, *supra*, at 1332. She advocates a four-part inquiry for analyzing accent discrimination cases:

> 1. What level of communication is required for the job?
>
> 2. Was the candidate's speech fairly evaluated?
>
> 3. Is the candidate intelligible to the pool of relevant, nonprejudiced listeners, such that job performance is not unreasonably impeded?
>
> 4. What accommodations are reasonable given the job and any limitations in intelligibility?

Id. at 1368. For another critical race analysis of *Fragante*, see Roy L. Brooks & Mary Jo Newborn, *Critical Race Theory and Classical-Liberal Civil Rights Scholarship: A Distinction Without a Difference?*, 82 Cal.L.Rev. 787, 824–32 (1994).

5. Recent scholarship on accent discrimination has built on the framework developed by critical race scholars. For example, Professor Kimberly Yuracko described three different types of bias which may influence an employer with respect to accents: accent-job link (employers may misjudge the link between accent and job performance, assuming the accent will impair performance, when it will not); accent-comprehension stability (employers may not recognize the ability of accented speakers to become more understandable); and bias-comprehension link (a visual cue for a "foreign speaker" causes listening comprehension problems against non-Caucasian speakers). Kimberly A. Yuracko, *Trait Discrimination as Race Discrimination: An Argument About Assimilation*, 74 Geo. Wash. L. Rev. 365, 392–402 (2006). With respect to the bias-comprehension link, in a study performed by Donald Rubin, sixty-two undergraduates listened to a four minute taped speech. *Id.* at 400 (citing Donald L. Rubin, *Nonlanguage Factors Affecting Undergraduates' Judgments of Nonnative English-Speaking Teaching Assistants*, 33 Res. Higher Educ. 511, 514–18 (1992)). The tapes were all recorded by the same speaker—a native English speaker from Ohio. The study participants were shown a picture of the "speaker" while listening to the tape. Those students shown a picture of an Asian woman comprehended less of what was said and more often reported hearing a foreign accent than students shown a picture of a Caucasian woman. Yuracko concludes,

> Participants not only "heard" a foreign accent when presented with the picture of the Asian instructor, they actually understood less of what she said as a result. These results suggest a need for skepticism anytime customers face non-Caucasian employees and report difficulties understanding their speech. The lack of

> comprehension may be real, but it may not be the speaker's accent that is the problem."

Id. See also Gerrit B. Smith, *I Want to Speak Like a Native Speaker: The Case for Lowering the Plaintiff's Burden of Proof in Title VII Accent Discrimination Cases,* 66 Ohio St. L. J. 231 (2005).

CHAPTER 13

DISCRIMINATION BECAUSE OF AGE

■ ■ ■

A. INTRODUCTION

The Age Discrimination in Employment Act of 1967 (ADEA), 29 U.S.C. § 621–634, protects workers who are at least forty years old against discrimination because of their age. A number of the substantive provisions of the ADEA are patterned after or are similar to provisions in Title VII. As the Supreme Court noted in *McKennon v. Nashville Banner Publishing Co.*, 513 U.S. 352, 358, 115 S.Ct. 879, 884, 130 L.Ed.2d 852 (1995), "[t]he ADEA and Title VII share common substantive features and also a common purpose: 'the elimination of discrimination in the workplace' " (citing Oscar Mayer & Co. v. Evans, 441 U.S. 750, 756, 99 S.Ct. 2066, 2071, 60 L.Ed.2d 609 (1979)). For this reason, courts have relied upon or borrowed from the Title VII jurisprudence in deciding ADEA claims. *See, e.g.*, Madel v. FCI Mktg., Inc., 116 F.3d 1247, 1251 n.2 (8th Cir.1997); Tyler v. Bethlehem Steel Corp., 958 F.2d 1176 (2d Cir.1992); King v. Gen. Elec. Co., 960 F.2d 617 (7th Cir.1992). Recently, however, the Supreme Court has noted differences between the two statutes, specifically in mixed-motive situations and for disparate impact claims. *See, e.g.*, Gross v. FBL Fin. Servs., 557 U.S. 167, 129 S.Ct. 2343, 174 L.Ed.2d 119 (2009); Smith v. City of Jackson, Miss., 554 U.S. 228, 125 S.Ct. 1536, 161 L.Ed.2d 410 (2005).

According to the Equal Employment Opportunity Commission, almost one out every four charges filed with the Commission in recent years contained a claim of discrimination based on age. *See* EEOC, Charge Statistics: FY 1997 Through FY 2009, *available at http://www.eeoc.gov/eeoc/statistics/enforcement/charges.cfm*. The number of charges filed for fiscal year 2012 (22,857) is a sizeable increase from fiscal year 1997 (15,785). This increase has probably been affected by the aging of the workforce. According to the Bureau of Labor Statistics (BLS), the number of workers over the age of 65 increased 101% between 1977 and 2007, compared with a 59% increase in total employment during that time period. U.S. Dep't of Labor, BLS, *Older Workers: Are There More Older People in the Workplace?* (July 2008). In addition, "From 1992 to 2002, the share of the labor force for those aged 55 and over increased from 11.8 percent to 14.3 percent. In 2012, their share of the labor force increased to 20.9 percent and is now projected to increase to 25.6 percent by 2022." U.S. Dep't of Labor, BLS, *Share of Labor Force Projected to Rise for People 55 and Older and Fall for Younger Age Groups* (January 2014), available at *http://www.bls.gov/opub/ted/2014/ted_20140124.htm*. The effect of economic downturns also affect the number of age discrimination claims, as discussed below in the note on Reductions-in-Force and Downsizing in Section C.

The profile of the "typical" age discrimination plaintiff may also influence the number of age discrimination claims. In his 1995 study, Professor George Rutherglen evaluated the empirical differences between ADEA and Title VII plaintiffs. ADEA claims are brought predominantly by white males who have been discharged from relatively high-status, high-paying jobs. Their claims result in recovery of monetary judgments several times higher than claims of discrimination under Title VII. George Rutherglen, *From Race to Age: The Expanding Scope of Employment Discrimination Law,* 24 J. Legal Stud. 491 (1995). A 2003 study conducted by a group of Colorado State University professors, who sought to profile the typical ADEA plaintiff, made similar findings. Peter H. Wingate, et al., *Organizational Downsizing and Age Discrimination Litigation: The Influence of Personnel Practices and Statistical Evidence on Litigation Outcomes*, 27 Law & Hum.Behav. 87 (2003). Based upon 115 ADEA-related cases filed in federal courts between 1993 and 1998, the authors concluded that: the average age of an ADEA plaintiff was 54 years old; the plaintiffs released in connection with an reduction in force ("RIF") program had served with their company for an average of 17 years; 76 percent of the plaintiffs were male; and more than half (58 percent) of the plaintiffs were either categorized as "professionals" or "managers." *Id.* at 98. What reasons might explain this typical profile of the ADEA plaintiff? For a review of the first thirty years of enforcement under the ADEA, see Howard C. Eglit, *The Age Discrimination in Employment Act at Thirty: Where It's Been, Where It Is Today, Where It's Going*, 31 U.Rich.L.Rev. 579 (1997). The note on Sex-Plus-Age claims in Section B, below, examines cases brought by older women.

NOTE: ADEA CLAIMS AGAINST STATES

In *Kimel v. Florida Board of Regents*, 528 U.S. 62, 120 S.Ct. 631, 145 L.Ed.2d 522 (2000), the Supreme Court held that the Eleventh Amendment bars state employees from bringing private actions for monetary damages against nonconsenting states for violations of the ADEA.

B. DISPARATE TREATMENT

Most of the ADEA cases are brought under the disparate treatment theory of discrimination. In *Hazen Paper Co. v. Biggins*, 507 U.S. 604, 609, 113 S.Ct. 1701, 1706, 123 L.Ed.2d 338 (1993), the Supreme Court stated that "[t]he disparate treatment theory is of course available under the ADEA, as the language of that statute makes clear. 'It shall be unlawful for an employer * * * to fail or refuse to hire or to discharge any individual or otherwise discriminate against any individual with respect to his compensation, terms, conditions, or privileges of employment *because of such individual's age.*' 29 U.S.C. § 623(a)(1) (emphasis added)." The Supreme Court has not directly decided whether the analytical scheme of *McDonnell Douglas Corp. v. Green*, 411 U.S. 792, 93 S.Ct. 1817, 36 L.Ed.2d 668 (1973), *Texas Department of Community Affairs v. Burdine*, 450 U.S. 248, 101 S.Ct. 1089, 67 L.Ed.2d 207 (1981), and *St. Mary's Honor Center v. Hicks*, 509 U.S. 502, 113 S.Ct. 2742, 125 L.Ed.2d 407 (1993), is equally applicable to ADEA claims. For example, the Supreme Court observed in *Reeves v. Sanderson Plumbing Products, Inc.*, 530 U.S. 133, 142, 120 S.Ct. 2097, 2105, 147 L.Ed.2d 105, 116 (2000) that "this Court has not squarely addressed whether the *McDonnell Douglas* framework * * * also applies to ADEA actions. Because the parties do not dispute the issue, we shall assume, *arguendo*, that the *McDonnell Douglas* framework is fully applicable here." *See also* O'Connor v. Consol. Coin Caterers Corp., 571 U.S. 308, 311, 116 S.Ct. 1307, 1310, 134 L.Ed.2d 433 (1996); Gross v. FBL Fin. Servs., 557 U.S. 167, 129 S.Ct. 2343, 2349 n.2, 174 L.Ed.2d 119 (2009).

The lower courts have consistently applied some variant of the *McDonnell Douglas-Burdine-Hicks* analytical framework to ADEA cases. A typical formulation of the analytical framework the lower courts have adopted for ADEA cases, based on the Title VII disparate treatment cases, requires a plaintiff to establish a prima facie case. To establish a prima facie case, the plaintiff must show that (1) he is within the age group protected under the ADEA; (2) he suffered an adverse employment action or disposition; (3) he was qualified for the position either lost or not gained; and (4) a person younger than the plaintiff was selected for the position over the plaintiff. If the plaintiff establishes a prima facie case, the burden of production of evidence shifts to the employer to present evidence of a legitimate, nondiscriminatory reason for the adverse action taken. If the employer carries its burden of production on a legitimate, nondiscriminatory reason, the burdens of production and persuasion return to the plaintiff to produce sufficient evidence from which a jury could find that an employer had intentionally discriminated against the plaintiff in violation of the ADEA. *See, e.g.* Filar v. Bd. of Educ. of City of Chi., 526 F.3d 1054, 1059–60 (7th Cir.2008); Roeben v. BG Excelsior Ltd. P'ship, 545 F.3d 639, 642–43 (8th Cir.2008) (citing Mayer v. Nextel W. Corp., 318 F.3d 803, 806–07 (8th Cir.2003)); Mitchell v. Vanderbilt Univ., 389 F.3d 177 (6th Cir.2004); Abdu-Brisson v. Delta Air Lines, 239 F.3d 456 (2d Cir.2001); Russell v. McKinney Hosp. Venture, 235 F.3d 219 (5th Cir.2000); Greene v. Safeway Stores, Inc., 98 F.3d 554, 557–58 (10th Cir.1996).

GROSS V. FBL FINANCIAL SERVICES, INC.

Supreme Court of the United States, 2009.
557 U.S. 167, 129 S.Ct. 2343, 174 L.Ed.2d 119.

JUSTICE THOMAS delivered the opinion of the Court.

The question presented by the petitioner in this case is whether a plaintiff must present direct evidence of age discrimination in order to obtain a mixed-motives jury instruction in a suit brought under the Age Discrimination in Employment Act of 1967 (ADEA). Because we hold that such a jury instruction is never proper in an ADEA case, we vacate the decision below.

I

Petitioner Jack Gross began working for respondent FBL Financial Group, Inc. (FBL), in 1971. As of 2001, Gross held the position of claims administration director. But in 2003, when he was 54 years old, Gross was reassigned to the position of claims project coordinator. [Gross considered the reassignment a demotion. In 2004, Gross sued FBL alleging that his reassignment violated the ADEA.]

The case proceeded to trial, where Gross introduced evidence suggesting that his reassignment was based at least in part on his age. * * *

At the close of trial, and over FBL's objections, the District Court instructed the jury that it must return a verdict for Gross if he proved, by a preponderance of the evidence, that FBL "demoted [him] to claims projec[t] coordinator" and that his "age was a motivating factor" in FBL's decision to demote him. The jury was further instructed that Gross' age would qualify as a " 'motivating factor,' if [it] played a part or a role in [FBL]'s decision to demote [him]." The jury was also instructed regarding FBL's burden of proof. According to the District Court, the "verdict must be for [FBL] * * * if it has been proved by the preponderance of the evidence that [FBL] would have demoted [Gross] regardless of his age. The jury returned a verdict for Gross, awarding him $46,945 in lost compensation.

FBL challenged the jury instructions on appeal. The United States Court of Appeals for the Eighth Circuit reversed and remanded for a new trial, holding that the jury had been incorrectly instructed under the standard established in *Price Waterhouse v. Hopkins*, 490 U.S. 228, 109 S.Ct. 1775, 104 L.Ed.2d 268 (1989). In *Price Waterhouse*, this Court addressed the proper allocation of the burden of persuasion in cases brought under Title VII of the Civil Rights Act of 1964, when an employee alleges that he suffered an adverse employment action because of both permissible and impermissible considerations—i.e., a "mixed-motives" case. * * * Six Justices ultimately agreed that if a Title VII plaintiff shows that discrimination was a "motivating" or a " 'substantial' " factor in the employer's action, the burden of persuasion should shift to the employer to show that it would have taken the same action regardless of that impermissible consideration. Justice O'Connor further found that to shift the burden of persuasion to the employer, the employee must present "direct evidence that an illegitimate criterion was a substantial factor in the [employment] decision."

In accordance with Circuit precedent, the Court of Appeals identified Justice O'Connor's opinion as controlling. Applying that standard, the Court of Appeals found that Gross needed to present "[d]irect evidence * * * sufficient to support a finding by a reasonable fact finder that an illegitimate criterion actually motivated the adverse employment action." * * * Only upon a presentation of such evidence, the Court of Appeals held, should the burden shift to the employer " 'to convince the trier of fact that it is more likely than not that the decision would have been the same absent consideration of the illegitimate factor.' "

The Court of Appeals thus concluded that the District Court's jury instructions were flawed because they allowed the burden to shift to FBL upon a presentation of a preponderance of any category of evidence showing that age was a motivating factor—not just "direct evidence" related to FBL's alleged consideration of age. * * *

We granted certiorari and now vacate the decision of the Court of Appeals.

II

The parties have asked us to decide whether a plaintiff must "present direct evidence of discrimination in order to obtain a mixed-motive instruction in a non-Title VII discrimination case." Before reaching this question, however, we must first determine whether the burden of persuasion ever shifts to the party defending an alleged mixed-motives discrimination claim brought under the ADEA. We hold that it does not.

A

Petitioner relies on this Court's decisions construing Title VII for his interpretation of the ADEA. Because Title VII is materially different with respect to the relevant burden of persuasion, however, these decisions do not control our construction of the ADEA.

* * * Congress has since amended Title VII by explicitly authorizing discrimination claims in which an improper consideration was "a motivating factor" for an adverse employment decision. See 42 U.S.C. § 2000e–2(m) (providing that "an unlawful employment practice is established when the complaining party demonstrates that race, color, religion, sex, or national origin was *a motivating factor* for any employment practice, even though other factors also motivated the

practice" (emphasis added)); § 2000e–5(g)(2)(B) (restricting the remedies available to plaintiffs proving violations of § 2000e–2(m)).

This Court has never held that this burden-shifting framework applies to ADEA claims. And, we decline to do so now. When conducting statutory interpretation, we "must be careful not to apply rules applicable under one statute to a different statute without careful and critical examination." *Federal Express Corp. v. Holowecki*, 128 S.Ct. 1147, 1153, 170 L.Ed.2d 10 (2008). Unlike Title VII, the ADEA's text does not provide that a plaintiff may establish discrimination by showing that age was simply a motivating factor. Moreover, Congress neglected to add such a provision to the ADEA when it amended Title VII to add § § 2000e–2(m) and 2000e–5(g)(2)(B), even though it contemporaneously amended the ADEA in several ways, see Civil Rights Act of 1991, § 115, 105 Stat. 1079; id., § 302, at 1088.

* * * As a result, the Court's interpretation of the ADEA is not governed by Title VII decisions such as *Desert Palace* and *Price Waterhouse*.[2]

B

Our inquiry therefore must focus on the text of the ADEA to decide whether it authorizes a mixed-motives age discrimination claim. It does not. * * * The ADEA provides, in relevant part, that "[i]t shall be unlawful for an employer * * * to fail or refuse to hire or to discharge any individual or otherwise discriminate against any individual with respect to his compensation, terms, conditions, or privileges of employment, *because of* such individual's age." 29 U.S.C. § 623(a)(1) (emphasis added).

The words "because of" mean "by reason of: on account of." 1 Webster's Third New International Dictionary 194 (1966); see also 1 Oxford English Dictionary 746 (1933) (defining "because of" to mean "By reason *of*, on account *of*" (italics in original)); The Random House Dictionary of the English Language 132 (1966) (defining "because" to mean "by reason; on account"). Thus, the ordinary meaning of the ADEA's

---

[2] Justice STEVENS argues that the Court must incorporate its past interpretations of Title VII into the ADEA because "the substantive provisions of the ADEA were derived *in haec verba* from Title VII" and because the Court has frequently applied its interpretations of Title VII to the ADEA. But the Court's approach to interpreting the ADEA in light of Title VII has not been uniform. In *General Dynamics Land Systems, Inc. v. Cline*, 540 U.S. 581, 124 S.Ct. 1236, 157 L.Ed.2d 1094 (2004) for example, the Court declined to interpret the phrase "because of * * * age" in 29 U.S.C. § 623(a) to bar discrimination against people of all ages, even though the Court had previously interpreted "because of * * * race [or] sex" in Title VII to bar discrimination against people of all races and both sexes. And the Court has not definitively decided whether the evidentiary framework of *McDonnell Douglas Corp. v. Green*, utilized in Title VII cases is appropriate in the ADEA context. See *Reeves v. Sanderson Plumbing Products, Inc.*, 530 U.S. 133, 142,120 S.Ct. 2097, 147 L.Ed.2d 105 (2000); *O'Connor v. Consolidated Coin Caterers Corp.*, 517 U.S. 308, 311, 116 S.Ct. 1307, 134 L.Ed.2d 433 (1996). In this instance, it is the textual differences between Title VII and the ADEA that prevent us from applying *Price Waterhouse* and *Desert Palace* [*v. Costa*, 539 U.S. 90, 123 S.Ct. 2148, 156 L.Ed.2d 84 (2003)], to federal age discrimination claims.

requirement that an employer took adverse action "because of" age is that age was the "reason" that the employer decided to act. See *Hazen Paper Co. v. Biggins*, 507 U.S. 604, 610, 113 S.Ct. 1701, 123 L.Ed.2d 338 (1993) (explaining that the claim "cannot succeed unless the employee's protected trait actually played a role in [the employer's decisionmaking] process *and had a determinative influence on the outcome*" (emphasis added)). To establish a disparate-treatment claim under the plain language of the ADEA, therefore, a plaintiff must prove that age was the "but-for" cause of the employer's adverse decision. See *Bridge v. Phoenix Bond & Indemnity Co.*, 553 U.S. ___, ___, 128 S.Ct. 2131, 2141–2142, 170 L.Ed.2d 1012 (2008) (recognizing that the phrase, "by reason of," requires at least a showing of "but for" causation (internal quotation marks omitted)); *Safeco Ins. Co. of America v. Burr*, 551 U.S. 47, 63–64, and n.14, 127 S.Ct. 2201, 167 L.Ed.2d 1045 (2007) (observing that "[i]n common talk, the phrase 'based on' indicates a but-for causal relationship and thus a necessary logical condition" and that the statutory phrase, "based on," has the same meaning as the phrase, "because of" (internal quotation marks omitted)); cf. W. Keeton, D. Dobbs, R. Keeton, & D. Owen, Prosser and Keeton on Law of Torts 265 (5th ed. 1984) ("An act or omission is not regarded as a cause of an event if the particular event would have occurred without it").

It follows, then, that under § 623(a)(1), the plaintiff retains the burden of persuasion to establish that age was the "but-for" cause of the employer's adverse action. Indeed, we have previously held that the burden is allocated in this manner in ADEA cases. And nothing in the statute's text indicates that Congress has carved out an exception to that rule for a subset of ADEA cases. Where the statutory text is "silent on the allocation of the burden of persuasion," we "begin with the ordinary default rule that plaintiffs bear the risk of failing to prove their claims." We have no warrant to depart from the general rule in this setting.

Hence, the burden of persuasion necessary to establish employer liability is the same in alleged mixed-motives cases as in any other ADEA disparate-treatment action. A plaintiff must prove by a preponderance of the evidence (which may be direct or circumstantial), that age was the "but-for" cause of the challenged employer decision.

III

Finally, we reject petitioner's contention that our interpretation of the ADEA is controlled by *Price Waterhouse*, which initially established that the burden of persuasion shifted in alleged mixed-motives Title VII claims.[5] * * *

---

[5] Justice Stevens also contends that we must apply *Price Waterhouse* under the reasoning of *Smith v. City of Jackson*, 544 U.S. 228, 125 S.Ct. 1536, 161 L.Ed.2d 410 (2005). In *Smith*, the Court applied to the ADEA its pre-1991 interpretation of Title VII with respect to disparate-

IV

We hold that a plaintiff bringing a disparate-treatment claim pursuant to the ADEA must prove, by a preponderance of the evidence, that age was the "but-for" cause of the challenged adverse employment action. The burden of persuasion does not shift to the employer to show that it would have taken the action regardless of age, even when a plaintiff has produced some evidence that age was one motivating factor in that decision. * * *

JUSTICE STEVENS, with whom JUSTICE SOUTER, JUSTICE GINSBURG, and JUSTICE BREYER join, dissenting.

The Age Discrimination in Employment Act of 1967 (ADEA), 29 U.S.C. § 621 et seq., makes it unlawful for an employer to discriminate against any employee "because of" that individual's age, § 623(a). The most natural reading of this statutory text prohibits adverse employment actions motivated in whole or in part by the age of the employee. The "but-for" causation standard endorsed by the Court today was advanced in Justice Kennedy's dissenting opinion in *Price Waterhouse v. Hopkins*, a case construing identical language in Title VII of the Civil Rights Act of 1964, 42 U.S.C. § 2000e–2(a)(1). Not only did the Court reject the but-for standard in that case, but so too did Congress when it amended Title VII in 1991. Given this unambiguous history, it is particularly inappropriate for the Court, on its own initiative, to adopt an interpretation of the causation requirement in the ADEA that differs from the established reading of Title VII. I disagree not only with the Court's interpretation of the statute, but also with its decision to engage in unnecessary lawmaking. * * *

I

* * * As we recognized in *Price Waterhouse* when we construed the identical "because of" language of Title VII, * * * the most natural reading of the text proscribes adverse employment actions motivated in whole or in part by the age of the employee.

In *Price Waterhouse*, we concluded that the words " 'because of' such individual's * * * sex * * * mean that gender must be irrelevant to employment decisions." To establish a violation of Title VII, we therefore held, a plaintiff had to prove that her sex was a motivating factor in an

impact claims despite Congress' 1991 amendment adding disparate-impact claims to Title VII but not the ADEA. But the amendments made by Congress in this same legislation, which added the "motivating factor" language to Title VII, undermine Justice Stevens' argument. Congress not only explicitly added "motivating factor" liability to Title VII, but it also partially abrogated *Price Waterhouse*'s holding by eliminating an employer's complete affirmative defense to "motivating factor" claims, see 42 U.S.C. § 2000e–5(g)(2)(B). If such "motivating factor" claims were already part of Title VII, the addition of § 2000e–5(g)(2)(B) alone would have been sufficient. Congress' careful tailoring of the "motivating factor" claim in Title VII, as well as the absence of a provision parallel to § 2000e–2(m) in the ADEA, confirms that we cannot transfer the *Price Waterhouse* burden-shifting framework into the ADEA.

adverse employment decision. We recognized that the employer had an affirmative defense: It could avoid a finding of liability by proving that it would have made the same decision even if it had not taken the plaintiff's sex into account. But this affirmative defense did not alter the meaning of "because of." As we made clear, when "an employer considers both gender and legitimate factors at the time of making a decision, that decision was 'because of' sex." We readily rejected the dissent's contrary assertion. "To construe the words 'because of' as colloquial shorthand for 'but-for' causation," we said, "is to misunderstand them."

Today, however, the Court interprets the words "because of" in the ADEA "as colloquial shorthand for 'but-for' causation." That the Court is construing the ADEA rather than Title VII does not justify this departure from precedent. The relevant language in the two statutes is identical, and we have long recognized that our interpretations of Title VII's language apply "with equal force in the context of age discrimination, for the substantive provisions of the ADEA 'were derived *in haec verba* from Title VII.'" For this reason, Justice Kennedy's dissent in *Price Waterhouse* assumed the plurality's mixed-motives framework extended to the ADEA, and the Courts of Appeals to have considered the issue unanimously have applied Price Waterhouse to ADEA claims. * * *

II

The conclusion that "because of" an individual's age means that age was a motivating factor in an employment decision is bolstered by Congress' reaction to *Price Waterhouse* in the 1991 Civil Rights Act. As part of its response to "a number of recent decisions by the United States Supreme Court that sharply cut back on the scope and effectiveness of [civil rights] laws," Congress eliminated the affirmative defense to liability that *Price Waterhouse* had furnished employers and provided instead that an employer's same-decision showing would limit only a plaintiff's remedies. See § 2000e–5(g)(2)(B). Importantly, however, Congress ratified *Price Waterhouse*'s interpretation of the plaintiff's burden of proof, rejecting the dissent's suggestion in that case that but-for causation was the proper standard. See § 2000e–2(m) ("[A]n unlawful employment practice is established when the complaining party demonstrates that race, color, religion, sex, or national origin was a motivating factor for any employment practice, even though other factors also motivated the practice").

Because the 1991 Act amended only Title VII and not the ADEA with respect to mixed-motives claims, the Court reasonably declines to apply the amended provisions to the ADEA.[6] But it proceeds to ignore the

[6] There is, however, some evidence that Congress intended the 1991 mixed-motives amendments to apply to the ADEA as well. See H.R. Rep., pt. 2, at 4 (noting that a "number of other laws banning discrimination, including * * * the Age Discrimination in Employment Act (ADEA), 29 U.S.C. § 621, et seq., are modeled after and have been interpreted in a manner

conclusion compelled by this interpretation of the Act: *Price Waterhouse*'s construction of "because of" remains the governing law for ADEA claims.

Our recent decision in *Smith v. City of Jackson*, 544 U.S. 228, 240, 125 S.Ct. 1536, 161 L.Ed.2d 410 (2005), is precisely on point, as we considered in that case the effect of Congress' failure to amend the disparate-impact provisions of the ADEA when it amended the corresponding Title VII provisions in the 1991 Act. Noting that "the relevant 1991 amendments expanded the coverage of Title VII [but] did not amend the ADEA or speak to the subject of age discrimination," we held that "*Ward's Cove's* pre-1991 interpretation of Title VII's identical language remains applicable to the ADEA." 544 U.S. at 240, 125 S.Ct. 1536 (discussing *Wards Cove Packing Co. v. Atonio*, 490 U.S. 642, 109 S.Ct. 2115, 104 L.Ed.2d 733 (1989)). If the *Wards Cove* disparate-impact framework that Congress flatly repudiated in the Title VII context continues to apply to ADEA claims, the mixed-motives framework that Congress substantially endorsed surely applies.

* * * Were the Court truly worried about difficulties faced by trial courts and juries, moreover, it would not reach today's decision, which will further complicate every case in which a plaintiff raises both ADEA and Title VII claims. * * *

JUSTICE BREYER, with whom JUSTICE SOUTER and JUSTICE GINSBURG join, dissenting.

* * * The words "because of" do not inherently require a showing of "but-for" causation, and I see no reason to read them to require such a showing.

It is one thing to require a typical tort plaintiff to show "but-for" causation. In that context, reasonably objective scientific or commonsense theories of physical causation make the concept of "but-for" causation comparatively easy to understand and relatively easy to apply. But it is an entirely different matter to determine a "but-for" relation when we consider, not physical forces, but the mind-related characterizations that constitute motive. Sometimes we speak of *determining* or *discovering* motives, but more often we *ascribe* motives, after an event, to an individual in light of the individual's thoughts and other circumstances present at the time of decision. In a case where we characterize an employer's actions as having been taken out of multiple motives, say, both because the employee was old and because he wore loud clothing, to apply "but-for" causation is to engage in a hypothetical inquiry about what would have happened if the employer's thoughts and other circumstances had been different. The answer to this hypothetical inquiry will often be

---

consistent with Title VII," and that "these other laws modeled after Title VII [should] be interpreted consistently in a manner consistent with Title VII as amended by this Act," including the mixed-motives provisions).

far from obvious, and, since the employee likely knows less than does the employer about what the employer was thinking at the time, the employer will often be in a stronger position than the employee to provide the answer.

All that a plaintiff can know for certain in such a context is that the forbidden motive did play a role in the employer's decision. And the fact that a jury has found that age did play a role in the decision justifies the use of the word "because," i.e., the employer dismissed the employee because of his age (and other things). I therefore would see nothing wrong in concluding that the plaintiff has established a violation of the statute.

But the law need not automatically assess liability in these circumstances. In *Price Waterhouse*, the plurality recognized an affirmative defense where the defendant could show that the employee would have been dismissed regardless. The law permits the employer this defense, not because the forbidden motive, age, had no role in the *actual* decision, but because the employer can show that he would have dismissed the employee anyway in the *hypothetical* circumstance in which his age-related motive was absent. And it makes sense that this would be an affirmative defense, rather than part of the showing of a violation, precisely because the defendant is in a better position than the plaintiff to establish how he would have acted in this hypothetical situation. I can see nothing unfair or impractical about allocating the burdens of proof in this way. * * *

For these reasons as well as for those set forth by Justice STEVENS, I respectfully dissent.

NOTES AND QUESTIONS

1. In *Gross,* how persuasive is the majority's argument in support of a "but for" evidentiary framework in ADEA mixed-motive cases? If the same language on causation appears in the ADEA, 29 U.S.C. § 623(a), and in Title VII, § 703(a), 42, U.S.C. § 2000e–2(a), what is the basis for the distinction the Court makes between the meaning of the phrase "because of" in the two statutes? Does the affirmative defense of a "reasonable factor other than age," which is found in the ADEA but not in Title VII, play any role in the Court's analysis? *See* 29 U.S.C. § 623(f)(1).

2. The Supreme Court in note 2 in *Gross* acknowledged that it has "not definitively decided whether the evidentiary framework of *McDonnell Douglass* * * * is appropriate in the ADEA context." 129 S.Ct. at 2349 n.2. In one of the first post-*Gross* cases decided by a Circuit Court, the Sixth Circuit found that *Gross* did not prohibit ADEA plaintiffs from proceeding under the circumstantial evidence framework developed in *McDonnell Douglas*. Geiger v. Tower Auto., 579 F.3d 614, 622–23 (6th Cir.2009). Is this the correct outcome? Other courts of appeals have continued to apply the *McDonnell Douglas* framework to ADEA claim after *Gross. See, e.g.*, Velez v. Thermo

King de P.R., 585 F.3d 441, 446–47 (1st Cir.2009); Leibowitz v. Cornell Univ., 584 F.3d 487, 503–04 (2d Cir.2009); Baker v. Silver Oak Senior Living Mgmt. Co., 581 F.3d 684, 688 (8th Cir.2009).

3. In October 2009, members of the House and Senate introduced identical versions of the Protecting Older Workers Against Discrimination Act. H.R. 3721, 111th Cong. (2009); S. 1756, 111th Cong. (2009). If enacted, the bill would amend the ADEA to provide that it is to be "interpreted consistently with the judicial interpretations of [T]itle VII of the Civil Rights Act of 1964 * * * [and that] [t]he Supreme Court's decision in Gross v. FBL Financial Services * * * has eroded this long-held understanding of consistent interpretation and circumvented well-established precedents." *Id.* at § 2(a)(3). More specifically, the Act would amend the ADEA by adopting the burdens of proof and remedial scheme for mixed-motive cases that is found in Title VII, as amended by the Civil Rights Act of 1991. Similar bills have been introduced in subsequent sessions, including the Protecting Older Workers Against Discrimination Act, H.R. 2852, 113th Cong. (2013).

Defining what constitutes "age" has been a particularly difficult issue for the courts. Consider the following cases.

HAZEN PAPER CO. V. BIGGINS

Supreme Court of the United States, 1993.
507 U.S. 604, 113 S.Ct. 1701, 123 L.Ed.2d 338.

JUSTICE O'CONNOR delivered the opinion of the Court.

In this case we clarify the standards for liability and liquidated damages under the Age Discrimination in Employment Act of 1967 (ADEA).

I

Petitioner Hazen Paper Company manufactures coated, laminated, and printed paper and paperboard. The company is owned and operated by two cousins, petitioners Robert Hazen and Thomas N. Hazen. Hazen hired respondent Walter F. Biggins as their technical director in 1977. They fired him in 1986, when he was 62 years old.

Respondent brought suit against petitioners in the United States District Court for the District of Massachusetts, alleging a violation of the ADEA. He claimed that age had been a determinative factor in petitioners' decision to fire him. Petitioners contested this claim, asserting instead that respondent had been fired for doing business with competitors of Hazen Paper. The case was tried before a jury, which rendered a verdict for respondent on his ADEA claim and also found violations of the Employee Retirement Income Security Act of 1974 (ERISA), 29 U.S.C. § 1140, and state law.

* * *

II

A

The courts of appeals repeatedly have faced the question whether an employer violates the ADEA by acting on the basis of a factor, such as an employee's pension status or seniority, that is empirically correlated with age. *Compare* White v. Westinghouse Electric Co., 862 F.2d 56, 62 (3d Cir.1988) (firing of older employee to prevent vesting of pension benefits violates ADEA); Metz v. Transit Mix, Inc., 828 F.2d 1202 (7th Cir.1987) (firing of older employee to save salary costs resulting from seniority violates ADEA) *with* Williams v. General Motors Corp., 656 F.2d 120, 130, n. 17 (5th Cir.1981) ("Seniority and age discrimination are unrelated. * * * We state without equivocation that the seniority a given plaintiff has accumulated entitles him to no better or worse treatment in an age discrimination suit."), *cert. denied*, 455 U.S. 943, 71 L.Ed.2d 655, 102 S.Ct. 1439 (1982); EEOC v. Clay Printing Co., 955 F.2d 936, 942 (4th Cir.1992) (emphasizing distinction between employee's age and years of service). We now clarify that there is no disparate treatment under the ADEA when the factor motivating the employer is some feature other than the employee's age.

We long have distinguished between "disparate treatment" and "disparate impact" theories of employment discrimination. * * * The disparate treatment theory is of course available under the ADEA, as the language of that statute makes clear. "It shall be unlawful for an employer * * * to fail or refuse to hire or to discharge any individual or otherwise discriminate against any individual with respect to his compensation, terms, conditions, or privileges of employment, *because of such individual's age*." 29 U.S.C. § 623(a)(1) (emphasis added). By contrast, we have never decided whether a disparate impact theory of liability is available under the ADEA, *see* Markham v. Geller, 451 U.S. 945, 68 L.Ed.2d 332, 101 S.Ct. 2028 (1981) (Rehnquist, J., dissenting from denial of certiorari), and we need not do so here. Respondent claims only that he received disparate treatment.

In a disparate treatment case, liability depends on whether the protected trait (under the ADEA, age) actually motivated the employer's decision. The employer may have relied upon a formal, facially discriminatory policy requiring adverse treatment of employees with that trait. Or the employer may have been motivated by the protected trait on an ad hoc, informal basis. Whatever the employer's decisionmaking process, a disparate treatment claim cannot succeed unless the employee's protected trait actually played a role in that process and had a determinative influence on the outcome.

Disparate treatment, thus defined, captures the essence of what Congress sought to prohibit in the ADEA. It is the very essence of age discrimination for an older employee to be fired because the employer believes that productivity and competence decline with old age. As we explained in *EEOC v. Wyoming*, 460 U.S. 226, 75 L.Ed.2d 18, 103 S.Ct. 1054 (1983), Congress' promulgation of the ADEA was prompted by its concern that older workers were being deprived of employment on the basis of inaccurate and stigmatizing stereotypes.

> Although age discrimination rarely was based on the sort of animus motivating some other forms of discrimination, it was based in large part on stereotypes unsupported by objective fact * * * . Moreover, the available empirical evidence demonstrated that arbitrary age lines were in fact generally unfounded and that, as an overall matter, the performance of older workers was at least as good as that of younger workers.

Id. at 231, 103 S.Ct. at 1057–1058. Thus the ADEA commands that "employers are to evaluate [older] employees * * * on their merits and not their age." Western Air Lines, Inc. v. Criswell, 472 U.S. 400, 422, 105 S.Ct. 2743, 2756, 86 L.Ed.2d 321 (1985). The employer cannot rely on age as a proxy for an employee's remaining characteristics, such as productivity, but must instead focus on those factors directly.

When the employer's decision *is* wholly motivated by factors other than age, the problem of inaccurate and stigmatizing stereotypes disappears. This is true even if the motivating factor is correlated with age, as pension status typically is. Pension plans typically provide that an employee's accrued benefits will become nonforfeitable, or "vested," once the employee completes a certain number of years of service with the employer. On average, an older employee has had more years in the work force than a younger employee, and thus may well have accumulated more years of service with a particular employer. Yet an employee's age is analytically distinct from his years of service. An employee who is younger than 40, and therefore outside the class of older workers as defined by the ADEA, *see* 29 U.S.C. § 631(a), may have worked for a particular employer his entire career, while an older worker may have been newly hired. Because age and years of service are analytically distinct, an employer can take account of one while ignoring the other, and thus it is incorrect to say that a decision based on years of service is necessarily "age-based."

The instant case is illustrative. Under the Hazen Paper pension plan, as construed by the Court of Appeals, an employee's pension benefits vest after the employee completes 10 years of service with the company. Perhaps it is true that older employees of Hazen Paper are more likely to be "close to vesting" than younger employees. Yet a decision by the company to fire an older employee solely because he has nine-plus years of service and therefore is "close to vesting" would not constitute discriminatory treatment on the basis of age. The prohibited stereotype ("Older employees are likely to be ___") would not have figured in this decision, and the attendant stigma would not ensue. The decision would not be the result of an inaccurate and denigrating generalization about age, but would rather represent an *accurate* judgment about the employee—that he indeed is "close to vesting."

We do not mean to suggest that an employer *lawfully* could fire an employee in order to prevent his pension benefits from vesting. Such conduct is actionable under § 510 of ERISA, as the Court of Appeals rightly found in affirming judgment for respondent under that statute. But it would not, without more, violate the ADEA. That law requires the employer to ignore an employee's age (absent a statutory exemption or defense); it does not specify *further* characteristics that an employer must also ignore. Although some language in our prior decisions might be read to mean that an employer violates the ADEA whenever its reason for firing an employee is improper *in any respect*, *see* McDonnell Douglas Corp. v. Green, 411 U.S. 792, 802, 36 L.Ed.2d 668, 93 S.Ct. 1817 (1973) (creating proof framework applicable to ADEA) (employer must have "legitimate, nondiscriminatory reason" for action against employee), this reading is obviously incorrect. For example, it cannot be true that an employer who fires an older black worker because the worker is black thereby violates the ADEA. The employee's race is an improper reason, but it is improper under Title VII, not the ADEA.

We do not preclude the possibility that an employer who targets employees with a particular pension status on the assumption that these employees are likely to be older thereby engages in age discrimination. Pension status may be a proxy for age, not in the sense that the ADEA makes the two factors equivalent, *cf. Metz*, 828 F.2d at 1208 (using "proxy" to mean statutory equivalence), but in the sense that the employer may suppose a correlation between the two factors and act accordingly. Nor do we rule out the possibility of dual liability under ERISA and the ADEA where the decision to fire the employee was motivated both by the employee's age and by his pension status. Finally, we do not consider the special case where an employee is about to vest in pension benefits as a result of his *age*, rather than years of service, and the employer fires the employee in order to prevent vesting. That case is not presented here. Our holding is simply that an employer does not violate the ADEA just by interfering with an older employee's pension benefits that would have vested by virtue of the employee's years of service.

NOTES AND QUESTIONS

1. *The Age-Proxy Theory*: The Supreme Court granted certiorari in *Hazen Paper* to resolve what it deemed to be a conflict in the lower courts on

the age-proxy theory. As explained by one commentator who questioned whether there was a genuine conflict about the age-proxy theory:

> "Age-proxy theory" refers to a method of proof that permits a finding of age discrimination to be based on an employer's reliance on an age-related factor. As so defined, the proxy theory is a device for proving a disparate treatment claim. There may be cases where an employer's reliance on an age-related factor has an adverse effect on older workers. These cases, however, are properly analyzed under a disparate impact analysis, not a proxy theory. The thrust of the proxy theory is that the age-related factor is a stand-in for age itself.

Robert J. Gregory, *There Is Life in That Old (I Mean, More "Senior") Dog Yet: The Age-Proxy Theory After* Hazen Paper Co. v. Biggins, 11 Hofstra Lab.L.J. 391, 393 n.14 (1994). What, if anything, remains of the age-proxy theory after *Hazen Paper*? Is there a difference between the age-proxy theory in ADEA cases and pretext analysis in the Title VII disparate treatment circumstantial evidence cases, if age-proxy evidence is deemed to be the equivalent of a "disguised reliance on age"? *See id.* at 396 (citing Howard C. Elgit, 2 Age Discrimination § 16.03A at 2S–97 to 2S–98 (Supp.1992)). Consider also the *Sperling* case, which follows these notes.

2. *Overlap Between the ADEA and the Employee Retirement Income Security Act (ERISA)*: *Hazen Paper* held that the conduct at issue is actionable under the Employee Retirement Income Security Act of 1974, 29 U.S.C. §§ 1001–1461, but it would not, without more, violate the ADEA. ERISA is the primary law that governs employees benefits, including private pension plans and fringe benefits. ERISA does not require employers to provide fringe benefits, nor does it specify any level of benefits that must be granted even if the employer chooses to offer them. What ERISA does is to establish minimum standards to protect employees from breaches of benefit promises made by the employer. ERISA is beyond the scope of this book, but it is not unusual for employees who are protected by the ADEA to add an ERISA claim in cases involving benefits, as the plaintiff did in *Hazen Paper*. For a treatment of the potential dual liability under the ADEA and ERISA and related problems, *see* Louis Maslow II, Comment, *Dual Liability: The Growing Overlap of the Age Discrimination in Employment Act and Section 510 of the Employee Retirement Income Security Act*, 58 Alb.L.Rev. 509 (1994).

3. For an account of the *Hazen Paper* litigation up to 1995, see Paul Barrett, *A Case of Old Age, in* A Year in the Life of the Supreme Court 33 (Rodney A. Smolla ed., 1995). Following the Supreme Court decision in 1993, Biggins turned down a settlement offer from Hazen Paper of about $450,000. *Id.* at 58. On remand, the First Circuit initially upheld the jury verdict on Biggins's ADEA claim, which by the fall of 1993 was worth approximately $1.2 million with interest. *Id.* Hazens Paper sought a rehearing, and the First Circuit remanded the case for a new trial. *See* Biggins v. Hazen Paper, 899

F.Supp. 809 (D.Mass.1995) (denying crossmotions for summary judgment). Following a two-week jury trial of the ADEA claim, Hazen Paper won. *See Hazen Paper*, 111 F.3d 205, 208 (1st Cir.1997), *cert. denied*, 522 U.S. 952, 118 S.Ct 373, 139 L.Ed.2d 290 (1997). District Judge Ponsor, following the retrial, observed: "This case makes *Jarndyce* look like a slip and fall at the corner Dairy Mart." 932 F.Supp. 382, 383 (D.Mass.1996). Circuit Judge Boudin called it a "Flying Dutchman of a case." *Hazen Paper*, 111 F.3d at 206.

SPERLING V. HOFFMANN-LA ROCHE, INC.

United States District Court for the District of New Jersey, 1996.
924 F.Supp. 1396.

ACKERMAN, DISTRICT COURT JUDGE.

[In February 1984, Hoffmann-La Roche discharged or demoted approximately 1,100 employees pursuant to a reduction-in-force, or RIF, known as Operation Turnabout. The plaintiff, Sperling, brought an ADEA class action on behalf of 476 of the affected employees alleging that the discharges or demotions violated their rights under the ADEA. After the Supreme Court decided *Hazen Paper*, and based on plaintiffs' answers to specific interrogatories, Hoffmann La-Roche, relying on the "analytically distinct" doctrine of *Hazen Paper*, filed a motion to dismiss the claims of sixty class members.]

* * *

A. The Individual Claims

Roche argues that the individual disparate treatment claims of sixty plaintiffs must be dismissed because the allegations on which they base their claims of age discrimination, as embodied in their answers to the contention interrogatories, do not state claims of age discrimination after *Hazen Paper*.

* * * [P]laintiffs' answers to the contention interrogatories identified nine factors which Roche allegedly considered in determining who would be fired in Operation Turnabout. Those factors are:

(1) Relatively high salary and/or relatively high salary grade;

(2) Replaced by younger person;

(3) Ample retirement benefits;

(4) Age-related disability;

(5) Proximity to voluntary retirement;

(6) Perceived as less productive and/or less creative;

(7) Perceived as having limited skills and/or ability to acquire skills;

(8) Perceived as over-qualified or over-experienced; and

(9) Perceived as no longer fitting into the organization.

* * * First, it must be determined whether any of the factors that plaintiffs listed in their answers to the contention interrogatories no longer amount to a cause of action under the ADEA after *Hazen Paper* * * * .

1. *Plaintiffs' Contentions and* Hazen Paper

* * *

Factor 1—High Salary: A number of the plaintiffs allege that they were terminated because of their relatively high salary or relatively high salary grade.

* * *

Several courts have noted that high salary is similar to years of service in that while, on average, those workers with the highest salaries are older workers, high salary and age are nonetheless analytically distinct, and therefore, termination decisions based on the employee's level of compensation are not violative of the ADEA. Thomure v. Phillips Furniture Company, 30 F.3d 1020, 1024 (8th Cir.1994) (stating that the defendant could " 'take account of one [salary] while ignoring the other [age]' * * * even though there happened to be a correlation between the two in several cases"), *cert. denied*, 115 S.Ct. 1255, 131 L.Ed.2d 135 (1995); Anderson v. Baxter Healthcare Corp., 13 F.3d 1120, 1125–26 (7th Cir.1994) (after noting that the Supreme Court stated in *Hazen Paper* that the ADEA was enacted by Congress because of "its concern that older workers were being deprived of employment on the basis of inaccurate and stigmatizing stereotypes" * * * , and that the Supreme Court held that "when the employer's decision is wholly motivated by factors other than age, the problem of inaccurate and stigmatizing stereotypes disappears * * * [and that] this is true even if the motivating factor is correlated with age, as pension status typically is[,]", the Court of Appeals held that "this rationale applies with equal force to cases where workers are discharged because of salary considerations"); Chiano v. Dimension Molding Corporation, 1993 WL 326687, at *2 n. 3 (N.D.Ill.1993) (stating that "applying the rationale of *Hazen*, if an older worker's salary is based on years of service and not age, the employer does not violate the ADEA by replacing the worker only because of her high salary"); Bornstad v. Sun Company Inc., 1993 WL 257310, at *2 (E.D.Pa.1993) (citing *Hazen Paper* for the proposition that plaintiff's deposition testimony "equating alleged seniority cost-saving motivation with age discrimination" is an approach that is "no longer viable"), *aff'd*, 19 F.3d 642 (3d Cir.1994) (Table). * * *

Therefore, Roche is correct in arguing that a claim made by a plaintiff that Roche fired him because of his high salary, as defined in any of the alternative ways discussed above, does not state a cause of action for which relief can be granted under the ADEA.

As stated above, Roche is not challenging factor 2. Therefore, I will move on to factor 3.

Factor 3—Ample Retirement Benefits: Next, some plaintiffs allege that they were terminated because they had "ample retirement benefits." * * *

Plaintiffs argue that consideration of this factor violates the ADEA because at Roche an employee's eligibility for retirement benefits is a function of the employee's age. * * *

Roche is correct in arguing that reliance on the existence of "ample retirement benefits" in firing a plaintiff is not violative of the ADEA. This is because reliance on this factor does not involve "the problem of inaccurate and stigmatizing stereotypes" "that productivity and competence decline with old age." *See id.* at 611, 113 S.Ct. at 1706. Plaintiffs' definition states that this factor applies where "Roche perceived or presumed that ample retirement benefits providing a 'financial cushion' were then available to said plaintiff." Thus, under this factor, plaintiffs are not alleging that they were fired based on a perception that older workers were less competent or less productive. Rather, plaintiffs are alleging that Roche fired employees who would be better able to absorb the effects of unemployment because of they had "ample retirement benefits." * * *

That the definition of "ample retirement benefits" also requires that the plaintiff must be at least 50 years old does not detract from this conclusion. First it should be noted that the Supreme Court specifically stated in *Hazen Paper* that it was not "considering the special case where an employee is about to vest in pension benefits as a result of his age, rather than years of service, * * * , and the employer fires the employee in order to prevent vesting." *Hazen Paper*, 507 U.S. at 613, 113 S.Ct. at 1707. Plaintiffs in effect argue that this is such a "special case" because part of the definition of ample retirement benefits is that the employee had to be at least 50 years old and that it should be held that the ADEA is violated in such special cases.

This argument fails because the Supreme Court in *Hazen Paper* clearly stated that "*[i]t is the very essence of age discrimination* for an older employee to be fired because the employer believes that productivity and competence decline with old age," and that "when the employer's decision is wholly motivated by factors other than age, the problem of inaccurate and stigmatizing stereotypes disappear"—even where the motivating factor is correlated with age. *Hazen Paper*, 507 U.S. at 611, 113 S.Ct. at 1706 (emphasis added). Therefore, in this case, even though "ample retirement benefits" clearly is correlated with age, consideration of this factor is not violative of the ADEA because plaintiffs are alleging that Roche fired these plaintiffs because Roche perceived that they had a financial cushion and not because Roche perceived that they were less competent or less productive. Therefore, consideration of this factor would not be within the definition of "the very essence of age discrimination" (*i.e.*, firing someone based on the belief "that productivity and competence decline with old age").

* * *

Factor 4—Age-Related Disability: Next, some plaintiffs claim that they were terminated because they had an "age-related disability." * * *

Thus, the question is whether or not a disability that is "associated" with age is analytically distinct from age.

The Court of Appeals for the Eighth Circuit addressed a similar issue in *Beith v. Nitrogen Products, Inc.*, 7 F.3d 701 (8th Cir.1993). * * * In affirming the judgment for the defendant, the Court of Appeals stated that

> " 'Congress made plain that the age statute was not meant to prohibit employment decisions based on factors sometimes accompanying advancing age, such as declining health or diminished vigor and competence.' " * * * Upon our review of the record, we could discern no evidence that the decision to terminate Beith was other than for his back condition. Because back conditions may be more prevalent in older workers does not alone make the decision an age-based decision.

Id. at 703.

In the case now before the court, the allegation that Roche terminated certain employees due to a disability that was "associated" with age is similarly not violative of the ADEA. Therefore, a claim by a plaintiff that Roche fired her because she had an "age-related disability" does not state a cause of action for which relief can be granted under the ADEA.

Factor 5—Proximity to Retirement: Next, some plaintiffs allege that they were terminated because of their "proximity to retirement." * * *

The analysis with respect to "proximity to retirement" is the same as for "ample retirement benefits." * * *

Factor 6—Perceived as Less Productive and/or Less Creative: Next, some plaintiffs allege that they were terminated because they were perceived as "less productive and/or less creative." * * *

Roche argues that consideration of this factor is not violative of the ADEA because "terminating an employee because he is perceived to be 'less productive or less energetic' (even if the perception is incorrect) is clearly analytically distinct from assuming that the employee is 'less productive or less energetic' because of his advancing age." Thus, Roche argues that consideration of this factor does not violate the ADEA because the plaintiffs did not tack on the words "because of age" after the allegation that they were terminated because they were perceived to be less energetic and productive.

Roche's argument lacks merit given that Roche's motion is in essence a motion to dismiss. Therefore, I must view plaintiffs allegations liberally and give plaintiffs the benefit of all inferences which may be drawn therefrom. Viewing factor 6 liberally, I conclude that a claim that a plaintiff was terminated because Roche believed that the plaintiff was less productive or less energetic states a cause of action under the ADEA. This is because consideration of stereotypes such as these in making employment decisions is precisely what the ADEA was intended to eradicate. *See Hazen Paper*, 507 U.S. at 609–13, 113 S.Ct. at 1706–07.

Factor 7—Perceived to Have Limited Skills and/or Ability to Acquire Skills: Next, some plaintiffs allege that they were terminated because they were perceived as having limited skills and/or a limited ability to acquire skills. * * *

As in the case of factor 6, viewing factor 7 liberally, I conclude that a claim that a plaintiff was terminated because Roche believed that the plaintiff had limited skills or a limited ability to acquire new skills states a cause of action under the ADEA. Consideration of factors such as these are also the types of stereotypes the ADEA was intended to eradicate from the employment decisionmaking process. *See Hazen Paper*, 507 U.S. at 609–13, 113 S.Ct. at 1706–07.

Factor 8—Perceived as Over-Qualified/Over-Experienced: Next, some plaintiffs allege that they were terminated because * * * they were perceived as being over-qualified and/or over-experienced. * * *

This factor is arguably correlated with age because it is reasonable to assume that persons holding supervisory or managerial positions are older, and also because the years-of-service prong of the definition correlates with age. However, *Hazen Paper* teaches that mere correlation with age is not enough. *Hazen Paper*, 507 U.S. at 609–11, 113 S.Ct. at 1706 ("When an employer's decision is wholly motivated by factors other than age, the problem of inaccurate and stigmatizing stereotypes disappears. This is true even if the motivating factor is correlated with age, as pension status typically is."). Furthermore, being perceived as over-qualified and/or over-experienced is not the equivalent of the denigrating stereotype that competence and productivity decline with age. For these reasons, I find that a claim that Roche made an employment decision based solely on the perception that an employee was over-qualified and/or over-experienced does not state a cause of action under the ADEA. *See* Bay v. Times Mirror Magazines, Inc., 936 F.2d 112, 118 (2d Cir.1991) (pre-*Hazen Paper* decision stating that the ADEA does not forbid "employers from declining to place employees in positions for which they are overqualified on the ground that overqualification may affect performance negatively").

Factor 9—"No Longer Fits into Organization": Next, some plaintiffs allege that they were terminated because Roche believed that they no longer fit into the organization. * * *

Roche argues "[t]hat a plaintiff was considered 'to have been around too long' fails for the same reason * * * factors 6 and 7 fail * * *—because mere statements that somebody is 'less productive' [factor 6] or 'has limited skills' [factor 7] or 'has been around too long' are not actionable unless the reason for that belief is the age of the plaintiff." Roche's argument fails for the same reason it did with respect to factors 6 and 7. This is in effect a motion to dismiss. Therefore, I must view the allegation liberally. After doing so, I conclude that a claim that Roche considered subpart c of factor 9 in terminating a plaintiff states a cause of action under the ADEA.

* * *

NOTES AND QUESTIONS

1. Does *Hazen Paper* provide useful guidelines on determining what factors are helpful in applying the "analytically distinct" test? If not, does *Sperling v. Hoffmann-La Roche*? Does the decision in *Sperling* adequately reflect the Act's stated goals? See the ADEA's statement of Findings and Purpose at 29 U.S.C. § 621.

2. Should *Hazen Paper*'s "analytically distinct" doctrine be equally applicable in analyzing Title VII race discrimination cases? In Title VII sex discrimination cases? If not, why?

3. *The Cost Justification Defense in ADEA Cases*: The defense that a high-salaried employee who is protected by the ADEA was discharged as a cost-saving measure is another illustration of the cost justification defense that employers have raised in a number of employment discrimination cases. *Sperling v. Hoffmann-La Roche* correctly noted that prior to *Hazen Paper*, the courts generally rejected a broad-based cost-justification defense in ADEA cases. One of the leading cases rejecting the defense was *Geller v. Markham*, 635 F.2d 1027 (2d Cir.1980), *cert. denied*, 451 U.S. 945, 101 S.Ct. 2028, 68 L.Ed.2d 332 (1981). A 55-year-old substitute teacher brought an ADEA claim alleging that the school board's policy of hiring only teachers who have less than five years of experience had a disparate impact on teachers over 40 years of age. The Second Circuit rejected the school board's defense that its

policy was justified as a necessary cost-cutting measure in the face of tight budgetary constraints. The court held that

> [t]his cost justification must fail * * * because of the clear rule that a general assertion that the average cost of employing older workers as a group is higher than the average cost of employing younger workers as a group will not be recognized as a differentiation under the terms and provisions of the [ADEA], unless one of the other statutory exceptions applies. * * *

Id. at 1034 (citing 29 C.F.R. § 860.103(h) (1979)). In *Metz v. Transit Mix, Inc.*, 828 F.2d 1202 (7th Cir.1987) (cited approvingly by the Supreme Court in *Hazen Paper*), the Seventh Circuit found an ADEA violation where the employer replaced a high-salaried employee protected by the ADEA with a younger, less-senior, lower-paid employee to save on the salary differential. Relying on *Hazen Paper*, the Seventh Circuit overturned *Metz v. Transit Mix* in *Anderson v. Baxter Healthcare Corp.*, 13 F.3d 1120 (7th Cir.1994):

> [The *Hazen Paper*] rationale applies with equal force to cases where workers are discharged because of salary considerations. Thus, *Hazen Paper Co.* vindicates the dissent in *Metz* which contended that "[w]age discrimination is age discrimination only when wage depends directly on age, so that the use for one is a pretext for the other; high covariance is not sufficient * * * ." *Metz*, 828 F.2d at 1212 (Easterbrook, J., dissenting). Compensation is typically correlated with age, just as pension benefits are. The correlation, however, is not perfect. A younger worker who has spent his entire career with the same employer may earn a higher salary than an older worker who has recently been hired by the same employer. "Because age and * * * [compensation levels] are analytically distinct, an employer can take account of one while ignoring the other, and thus it is incorrect to say that a decision based on * * * compensation level is necessarily 'age-based.' " *Hazen*, 113 S.Ct. at 1707. Consequently, Anderson could not prove age discrimination even if he was fired simply because Baxter desired to reduce its salary costs by discharging him.

13 F.3d at 1125–26.

In distinguishing between the problem of costs in Title VII and ADEA cases, Professor Steven J. Kaminshine stated that

> [f]rom Title VII, we are familiar with the maxim that mere cost savings may not be used to justify discrimination. There is, in other words, a price—a cost—for securing more important remedial and social objectives. To cite but a few examples: employers may not justify discrimination on grounds of customer preference regardless of its profitability; they may not rely on race or gender as crude proxies for performance simply because such proxies may be easy to apply and inexpensive to administer; they may not rely solely on the

cheapness of neutral proxies if they operate to target protected groups and are not sufficiently job related; and they must provide women equal pay for equal work even if the market would place a lower value on female labor. These examples illustrate the costs of compliance—employers must forfeit the profits derived from discrimination. But assuming compliance and merit-based selection, blacks and women are not, by their race or gender, uniquely costlier to compensate.

The same cannot be said as easily of workers covered under the ADEA. Seniority and longevity often influence salary and fringe benefit levels. Because these factors correlate with age, older workers can become more costly to compensate than their younger counterparts. This disparity creates significant tension during times of economic stress when employers look to maximize savings by laying off or replacing their costliest workers. The tension exists because the use of salary costs as a criterion for layoffs appears to be both economically rational yet peculiarly burdensome to the older segment of the work force. To the extent that the ADEA prohibits discriminatory discharges out of concern that displaced older workers face unique obstacles in finding employment late in their careers, seniority-related cost comparisons can frustrate that objective. On the other hand, to require employers to ignore such costs as part of an economic cutback may equally frustrate the need for sensible cost-cutting policies.

Steven J. Kaminshine, *The Cost of Older Workers, Disparate Impact, and the Age Discrimination in Employment Act*, 42 Fla.L.Rev. 229, 231–33 (1990). Is a defense based on costs more defensible in ADEA cases than in Title VII race and sex cases? Does *Hazen Paper*, as construed by the courts in *Sperling v. Hoffmann-La Roche* and *Baxter Healthcare*, legitimate a broad-based cost justification defense in ADEA cases? What are the arguments for and against treating a cost-based defense as a reasonable factor other than age (RFOA) under § 623(f)(1) of the ADEA, 29 U.S.C. § 623(f)(1)?

4. As noted in *Hazen Paper,* the ADEA provides for the award of liquidated damages—an amount equal to the amount of unpaid back wages awarded—when the plaintiff proves a willful violation of the statute. 29 U.S.C. § 626(b). "A violation is considered 'willful' if 'the employer knew or showed reckless disregard for the matter of whether its conduct was prohibited by the ADEA.'" Mathis v. Phillips Chevrolet, Inc., 269 F.3d 771, 777 (7th Cir.2001) (citing *Hazen Paper*, 507 U.S. at 614). The Seventh Circuit clarified the distinction between negligent and reckless mistakes: "A defendant's negligent mistake concerning the lawfulness of her conduct does not suffice to make that conduct 'willful,' but a reckless mistake, in the criminal law sense of indifference to whether the conduct violates the law, does." *Id.* Would it be simple negligence or recklessness for a manager with hiring authority not to know that it is illegal to discriminate against applicants on the basis of age? *See id.* at 778.

5. *Fringe Benefits*: Consistent with *Hazen Paper*, may an employer reduce the fringe benefits package only of employees who are protected by the ADEA? Consider the pre-*Hazen* case of *Finnegan v. Trans World Airlines, Inc.*, 967 F.2d 1161 (7th Cir.1992). In an effort to avoid bankruptcy, TWA cut the wages of its nonunion employees by fourteen percent and reduced some of the employees' benefits, including vacation leave. Vacation leave was capped at four weeks per year, although employees who had sixteen or more years of service previously had been entitled to even more paid vacation. The brunt of the vacation cap thus fell on employees who were protected by the ADEA. In holding that the plaintiffs were not entitled to relief under the ADEA, Judge Richard Posner reasoned:

> Across-the-board cuts in wages and fringe benefits necessitated by business downturns or setbacks are a far cry from the situations that brought the [disparate impact] theory into being. These cuts are not a legacy of deliberate discrimination on grounds of age; they are not the product of inertia or insensitivity. They are an unavoidable response to adversity. Their adverse impact on older workers is unavoidable too, because it is impossible to reduce the costs of fringe benefits without making deeper cuts in the benefits of older workers, simply because, by virtue of being older, they have greater benefits. In this situation no inference of discrimination, whether deliberate or merely inadvertent (but avoidable), can be drawn from the greater impact of curtailing employees' benefits on older workers. Otherwise every time a company tried to reduce its labor costs the federal courts would be dragged in and asked to redesign the reduction so as to shift the burden to some unprotected class of workers—a shift that might incidentally be impossible to accomplish, as it might drive all the younger workers out of the company (the 6-days-a-year vacation problem).

Id. at 1164–65.

6. Local 350, a union, operates a hiring hall for its members. A policy of Local 350 provides that retirees who are receiving a pension are not entitled to referral work; retirees who do not receive a pension are eligible for referrals. Assume that members of Local 350 must be fifty-five years old to be eligible to receive a pension. A retiree of the union who is fifty-seven years of age and is receiving a pension is denied a job referral because of the policy. Are retirees who are over forty protected by the ADEA under the reasoning of *Robinson v. Shell Oil Co.*, 519 U.S. 337, 117 S.Ct. 843, 136 L.Ed.2d 808 (1997) (former employees are protected under Title VII)? *See* EEOC v. Local 350, Plumbers & Pipefitters, 998 F.2d 641 (9th Cir.1992); McKeever v. Ironworkers' Dist. Council, 1997 WL 109569, 73 Fair Empl.Prac.Cas. (BNA) 1000 (E.D.Pa.1997).

7. A substantial amount of the scholarly literature on the ADEA has been grounded in law and economics analysis. *See* Richard A. Posner, Aging and Old Age (1995) (an economic analysis of the impact of aging on human

capital theory and an exploration of the implications of stereotypes about age and aging for law and the elderly); Paul H. Brietzke & Linda S. Whitton, *An Old(er) Master Stands on the Shoulders of Ageism to Stake Another Claim for Law and Economics,* 31 Val.U.L.Rev. 89 (1996) (book review of Posner's Age and Old Age). *See also* Samuel Issacharoff & Erica Worth Harris, *Is Age Discrimination Really Age Discrimination?: The ADEA's Unnatural Solution,* 72 N.Y.U.L.Rev. 780 (1997); Christine Jolls, *Hands-Tying and the Age Discrimination in Employment Act*, 74 Tex.L.Rev. 1813 (1996). Arguably, law and economics analysis has had greater influence on the development of ADEA jurisprudence than on the development of Title VII jurisprudence. Richard Posner and Frank Easterbrook, two well-known scholars of law and economics, were formerly law professors at the University of Chicago School of Law and are now judges on the United States Court of Appeals for the Seventh Circuit.

NOTE: KENTUCKY RETIREMENT SYSTEMS V. EEOC

Relying on *Hazen Paper,* the Supreme Court in 2008 held that a state retirement plan for disabled workers does not discriminate on the basis of age even though eligibility for the plan is dependent on an employee's age-based pension status. In *Kentucky Retirement Systems v. EEOC,* 554 U.S. 135, 128 S.Ct. 2361, 171 L.Ed.2d 322 (2008), the EEOC brought an ADEA lawsuit challenging Kentucky's dual retirement plan for state and county workers in "hazardous" jobs. The plan, in effect, provides a bonus to younger workers who retire because of a disability. Employees are eligible for "normal retirement" if they work for 20 years or reach the age of 55 after having worked for at least 5 years. Retirement pay under this plan is a multiple of years actually worked. Alternatively, if an employee retires because of a disability, he or she receives retirement pay based on the number of years of actual service plus bonus years—the number of years he or she would have had to work in order to become eligible for normal retirement. The number of imputed bonus years is capped at a figure equal to the number of years of actual service.

Charles Lickteig, a county sheriff's department employee who worked in a hazardous position, reached his normal retirement age of 55, but continued to work until the age of 61 when he retired because he became disabled. His retirement pay was based on his 18 years of actual service, with no additional credit imputed for years not worked up to 20 years. Lickteig brought an age discrimination complaint to the EEOC, which then filed suit against Kentucky Retirement Systems. The EEOC claimed that Kentucky "failed to impute years solely because Lickteig became disabled after he reached the age of 55." 128 S.Ct. at 2365.

The district court granted summary judgment to the defendant; but the Sixth Circuit, sitting en banc, reversed, ruling that Kentucky's disability retirement plan violates the ADEA. In a 5-to-4 decision, the Supreme Court reversed the judgment of the Sixth Circuit, holding that Kentucky does not discriminate on the basis of age when it denies a special bonus credit for retirement due to disability to employees who become disabled after reaching the age when they would normally become eligible for retirement on the basis of age alone.

Writing for the majority, Justice Breyer discussed the Court's analysis of the ADEA claim in *Hazen Paper* and concluded:

> *Hazen Paper* indicated that discrimination on the basis of pension status could *sometimes* be unlawful under the ADEA, in particular where pension status served as a "proxy for age." Suppose, for example, an employer "target[ed] employees with a particular pension status on the assumption that these employees are likely to be older." In such a case, *Hazen Paper* suggested, age, not pension status, would have "actually motivated" the employer's decisionmaking. *Hazen Paper* also left open "the special case where an employee is about to vest in pension benefits as a result of his *age,* rather than years of service." We here consider a variation on this "special case" theme.
>
> Kentucky's Plan turns normal pension eligibility *either* upon the employee's having attained 20 years of service alone *or* upon the employees having attained 5 years of service and reached the age of 55. The ADEA permits an employer to condition pension eligibility upon age. See 29 U.S.C.A. § 623(*l*)(1)(A)(i) (Supp.2007). Thus we must decide whether a plan that (1) lawfully makes age in part a condition of pension eligibility, and (2) treats workers differently in light of their pension status, (3) *automatically* discriminates *because of* age. The Government argues "yes." But, following *Hazen Paper*'s approach, we come to a different conclusion. In particular, the following circumstances, taken together, convince us that, in this particular instance, differences in treatment were not "actually motivated" by age.

Id. at 2366.

Justice Breyer then listed and analyzed the following six "circumstances," which led him to conclude that a discriminatory age-based motive was not present in this case.

> *First,* as a matter of pure logic, age and pension status remain "analytically distinct" concepts. * * *
>
> *Second,* several background circumstances eliminate the possibility that pension status, though analytically distinct from age, nonetheless serves as a "proxy for age" in Kentucky's Plan. We consider not an individual employment decision, but a set of complex systemwide rules. These systemic rules involve, not wages, but pensions—a benefit that the ADEA treats somewhat more flexibly and leniently in respect to age. * * *
>
> *Third,* there is a clear non-age-related rationale for the disparity here at issue. The manner in which Kentucky calculates

disability retirement benefits is in every important respect but one identical to the manner in which Kentucky calculates normal retirement benefits. The one significant difference consists of the fact that the Plan imputes additional years of service to disabled individuals. * * * The disability rules clearly track Kentucky's normal retirement rules. * * * Age factors into the disability calculation only because the normal retirement rules themselves permissibly include age as a consideration. * * *

Fourth, although Kentucky's Plan placed an older worker at a disadvantage in this case, in other cases, it can work to the *advantage* of older workers. Consider, for example, two disabled workers, one of whom is aged 45 with 10 years of service, one of whom is aged 40 with 15 years of service. Under Kentucky's scheme, the older worker would actually get a bigger boost of imputed years than the younger worker (10 years would be imputed to the former, while only 5 years would be imputed to the latter). And that fact helps to confirm that the underlying motive is not an effort to discriminate "because of * * * age." * * *

Fifth, Kentucky's system does not rely on any of the sorts of stereotypical assumptions that the ADEA sought to eradicate. It does not rest on any stereotype about the work capacity of "older" workers *relative to* "younger" workers. * * *

Sixth, the nature of the Plan's eligibility requirements means that, unless Kentucky were severely to cut the benefits given to disabled workers who are not yet pension eligible (which Kentucky claims it will do if its present Plan is unlawful), Kentucky would have to increase the benefits available to disabled, pension-eligible workers, while lacking any clear criteria for determining how many extra years to impute for those pension-eligible workers who already are 55 or older. The difficulty of finding a remedy that can both correct the disparity and achieve the Plan's legitimate objective—providing each disabled worker with a sufficient retirement benefit, namely, the normal retirement benefit that the worker would receive if he were pension eligible at the time of disability—further suggests that this objective and not age "actually motivated" the Plan.

Id. at 2367–69.

In addition, the Court was not persuaded that a finding of age discrimination was supported by: either (1) the Older Workers Benefit Protection Act (OWBPA), § 102, 29 U.S.C. § 630(*l*) (2000 ed.), which "amended the ADEA to make clear that it covered age-based discrimination in respect to all employee benefits," *id.* at 2370; or (2) the EEOC's interpretation of the ADEA in its regulation and compliance manual. *Id.* at 2370–71. The OWBPA is discussed in Section C.

More importantly, Justice Breyer set out the following analytical framework:

> It bears emphasizing that our opinion in no way unsettles the rule that a statute or policy that facially discriminates based on age suffices to show disparate treatment under the ADEA. We are dealing today with the quite special case of differential treatment based on *pension status,* where pension status—with the explicit blessing of the ADEA—itself turns, in part, on age. Further, the rule we adopt today for dealing with this sort of case is clear: Where an employer adopts a pension plan that includes age as a factor, and that employer then treats employees differently based on pension status, a plaintiff, to state a disparate treatment claim under the ADEA, must adduce sufficient evidence to show that the differential treatment was "actually motivated" by *age,* not pension status.

Id. at 2369–70.

Justice Kennedy, in a forceful dissent joined by Justices Scalia, Ginsburg, and Alito, concluded that

> the most straightforward reading of the statute is the correct one: When an employer makes age a factor in an employee benefit plan in a formal, facial, deliberate, and explicit manner, to the detriment of older employees, this is a violation of the Act. Disparate treatment on the basis of age is prohibited unless some exemption or defense provided in the Act applies.

Id. at 2371. (Kennedy, J., dissenting). Significantly, the dissent disagreed with the majority's reading of *Hazen* as it applied to the Kentucky retirement plan. Justice Kennedy observed that "*Hazen Paper* makes quite clear that no additional proof of motive is required in an ADEA case once the employment policy at issue is deemed discriminatory on its face." *Id.* at 2374. The dissenting opinion continued:

> By interpreting *Hazen Paper* to say that a formal, facial, explicit, mandated, age-based differential does not suffice to establish a disparate-treatment violation (subject to statutory defenses and exemptions), it misconstrues the precedent upon which its entire theory of this case is built. The Court was right in *Hazen Paper* and is wrong here.
>
> At a minimum the Court should not cite *Hazen Paper* to support what it now holds. Its conclusion that no disparate-treatment violation has been established here conflicts with the longstanding rule in ADEA cases. The rule * * * is that once the plaintiff establishes that a policy discriminates on its face, no additional proof of a less-than-benign motive for the challenged employment action is required. For if the plan discriminates on its face, it is obvious that decisions made pursuant to the plan are "actually motivated" by age. * * *

Just as the majority misunderstands *Hazen Paper*'s reference to employment practices that are "actually motivated" by age, so too does it overstate what the *Hazen Paper* Court meant when it observed that pension status and age are "analytically distinct." The Court now reads this language as creating a virtual safe harbor for policies that discriminate on the basis of pension status, even when pension status is tied directly to age and then linked to another type of benefit program. The *Hazen Paper* Court did not allow, or support, this result. In *Hazen Paper* pension status and age were "analytically distinct" because the employee's eligibility to receive a pension formally had nothing to do with age; pension status was tied solely to years of service. * * *

The saving feature that was controlling in *Hazen Paper* is absent here. This case is the opposite of *Hazen Paper*. Here the age distinction is active and present, not superseded and absent. Age is a determining factor of pension eligibility for all workers over the age of 55 who have over 5 (but less than 20) years of service; and pension status, in turn, is used to determine eligibility for disability benefits. For these employees, pension status and age are not "analytically distinct" in any meaningful sense; they merge into one category. When it treats these employees differently on the basis of pension eligibility, Kentucky facially discriminates on the basis of age. Were this not the case, there would be no facial age discrimination if an employer divided his employees into two teams based upon age—putting all workers over the age of 65 on "Team A" and all other workers on "Team B"—and then paid Team B members twice the salary of their Team A counterparts, not on the basis of age (the employer would declare) but of team designation. Neither *Hazen Paper* nor the plain text of the ADEA can be read to permit this result.

Id. at 2374–76.

Justice Kennedy acknowledged that "[t]he Court's desire to avoid construing the ADEA in a way that encourages the Commonwealth to eliminate its early retirement program or to reduce benefits to the policemen and firefighters who are covered under the disability plan is understandable." *Id.* at 2378. Nevertheless, this laudable "desire," in his mind, did not permit the "Court to ignore its precedents and the plain text of the statute." *Id.* Can a benign motive save an employer from liability for discriminatory actions?

Which interpretation of *Hazen Paper* is more persuasive—Justice Breyer's or Justice Kennedy's? Why? How would you counter Justice Kennedy's "floodgate" argument that "[i]f the ADEA allows an employer to tie disability benefits to an age-based pension status designation, that same designation can be used to determine wages, hours, heath care benefits, reimbursements, job assignments, promotions, office space, transportation vouchers, parking privileges, and any other conceivable benefit or condition of employment." *Id.* 2376. The Court in *Hazen Paper* wrote that the ADEA "requires the employer to ignore an employee's age (absent a statutory exemption or defense)." After *Kentucky Retirement Systems,* is this still good law? Why or why not?

NOTE: O'CONNOR V. CONSOLIDATED COIN CATERERS CORP.

In *O'Connor v. Consolidated Coin Caterers Corp.*, 517 U.S. 308, 116 S.Ct. 1307, 134 L.Ed.2d 433 (1996), the Supreme Court considered whether an employee who is fired and replaced by an individual who is also within the age group protected by the ADEA, i.e., forty years of age or older, can establish a prima facie case of age discrimination. The plaintiff in *Consolidated Coin* was fifty-six years old at the time of his discharge and his replacement was forty years of age. Both were protected under the ADEA. The Fourth Circuit held that an ADEA plaintiff must prove, as an element of a prima facie case, that he was replaced by an individual of comparable qualifications who is not within the age group that is protected by the ADEA. The Fourth Circuit was the only court of appeals to adopt such a rule.

The Supreme Court reversed. The Court held that the ADEA "does not ban discrimination against employees because they are aged 40 or older; it bans discrimination against employees because of their age, but limits the protected class to those who are 40 or older." 517 U.S. at 312, 116 S.Ct. at 1310. Justice Scalia, writing for a unanimous Court, stated:

> Perhaps some courts have been induced to adopt the principle urged by [the employer] in order to avoid creating a prima facie case on the basis of thin evidence—for example, the replacement of a 68-year-old by a 65-year-old. While the [employer's] principle theoretically permits such thin evidence (consider the example above of a 40-year-old replaced by a 39-year-old), as a practical matter it will rarely do so, since the vast majority of age-discrimination claims come from older employees. In our view, however, the proper solution to the problem lies not in making an utterly irrelevant factor an element of the prima facie case, but rather in recognizing that the prima facie case requires "*evidence adequate to create an inference that an employment decision was based on a[n] [illegal] discriminatory criterion.* * * * " In the age-discrimination context, such an inference can not be drawn from the replacement of one worker with another worker insignificantly younger. Because the ADEA prohibits discrimination on the basis of age and not class membership, the fact that a replacement is substantially younger than the plaintiff is a far more reliable indicator of age discrimination than is the fact that the plaintiff was replaced by someone outside the protected class.

Id. at 312–13, 116 S.Ct. at 1310 (emphasis in original).

The Supreme Court did not elaborate on the obvious question of how much younger than the plaintiff a replacement has to be to satisfy the

Consolidated Coin "substantially younger" standard. Lower courts have responded to this question by adopting differing standards. In *Showalter v. University of Pittsburgh Medical Center,* 190 F.3d 231 (3d Cir.1999), the court noted that there is no "particular age difference that must be shown" but while "[d]ifferent courts have held * * * that a five year difference can be sufficient, * * * a one year difference cannot." *Id.* at 236 (citing Sempier v. Johnson & Higgins, 45 F.3d 724, 729 (3d Cir.1995)). In *Showalter,* the plaintiff was eight years older than one individual who also was protected by the ADEA and sixteen years older than another. The Eighth Circuit has held that a five-year disparity in ages is not substantial enough to support an inference of age discrimination. *See* Schiltz v. Burlington N. R.R., 115 F.3d 1407 (8th Cir.1997). In *Hartley v. Wisconsin Bell, Inc.,* 124 F.3d 887 (7th Cir.1997), the Seventh Circuit adopted a rule that an age disparity of less than ten years is presumptively insubstantial unless the plaintiff "directs the court to evidence that her employer considered age to be significant." *Id.* at 893. Suppose under the Seventh Circuit's rule the employer had at one time made a statement to the plaintiff that he was "getting too old to do the job." Should that be sufficient? If the plaintiff had evidence that the employer considered age to be significant, should it make any difference that the plaintiff was ten years older than his replacement? *See* Cianci v. Pettibone Corp., 152 F.3d 723 (7th Cir.1998). *See also* Grosjean v. First Energy Corp., 349 F.3d 332, 336–40 (6th Cir.2003) (discussing *Consolidated Coin* and collecting cases from different circuits on significance of various age differences).

As a result of *O'Connor v. Consolidated Coin Caterers,* the Second Circuit now articulates the prima facie case for age discrimination as follows: (1) plaintiff is a member of the protected class; (2) plaintiff is qualified for the position; (3) plaintiff has suffered an adverse employment action; and (4) the circumstances surrounding that action give rise to an inference of discrimination. Abdu-Brisson v. Delta Air Lines, 239 F.3d 456, 466 (2d Cir.2001).

Consider the following in light of Justice Scalia's analysis in *Consolidated Coin Caterers*:

1. Robert Greene, an executive with Safeway Stores, first became a store manager with Safeway when he was 26 years old. When he was 52 years old, he was discharged and replaced by John King who was 57 years old. Green has now filed an age discrimination claim against Safeway. Because Greene cannot show that he was replaced by a "substantially younger" employee, should his age discrimination claim be dismissed as a matter of law under *Consolidated Coin*? *See* Greene v. Safeway Stores, Inc., 98 F.3d 554, 557–58 (10th Cir.1996). *See also* Adamson v. Multi Cmt'y Divers. Servs., 514 F.3d 1136, 1146–47 (10th Cir.2008) (distinguishing *Greene*).

2. An employer and its union negotiate a contract where retirees no longer receive full health benefits. They agree, however, that those employees

who are 50 years of age or older as of the date of the contract may still receive full health benefits when they retire. Employees aged 40–49 years object that this is discrimination against them, based on age. *See* Gen. Dynamics Land Sys. v. Cline, 540 U.S. 581, 124 S.Ct. 1236, 157 L.Ed.2d 1094 (2004) (deciding against the younger employees).

NOTE: SEX-PLUS-AGE CLAIMS

Between 2011 and 2050, the number of women who are 55 years or older is projected to grow by 26 million, and their labor force participation is expected to grow from a rate of 59.4% to 66.6% during that period. *See* Women's Bureau Fact Sheet, Older Women and Work, available at *https://www.dol.gov/wb/media/reports/WB_OlderWomen_v10%20WEB.pdf*. As the rate of older women remaining in and entering the workplace has grown, the "sex-plus-age" discrimination theory has developed, albeit at a much slower rate. In 1996, the Women's Legal Defense Fund prepared two studies for the American Association of Retired Persons. The first study, Volume I, *Employment Discrimination Against Midlife and Older Women: How Courts Treat Sex-and-Age Discrimination Cases* (1996) [hereinafter 1 Midlife and Older Women], examined all court cases decided between 1975 and 1995 that involved claims for sex and age discrimination, and concluded that both judges and lawyers generally have failed to recognize or acknowledge that older women face a unique form of discrimination unlike the type of discrimination that older men and younger women face. The study found that

> [m]idlife and older women make up a steadily increasing share of the American workforce. Yet, too often, they continue to face job discrimination based on both sex and age. To date, however, there has been little research that examines the cumulative or synergistic effect of sex and age on midlife and older women's work opportunities, the form such discrimination may take, or how women's complaints of sex-and-age discrimination are treated in the legal system.

Id. at 1. In comparison, courts have been willing, generally, to recognize black women and Asian-American women as a discrete and protected subclass under the theory of either race-plus-sex or national origin-plus-sex. *See, e.g.*, Jefferies v. Harris County Cmty. Action Ass'n, 615 F.2d 1025 (5th Cir.1980) (black women); Lam v. Univ. of Haw., 40 F.3d 1551 (9th Cir.1994) (Asian-American women).

In sex-plus-age cases, however, few courts have recognized sex-plus-age as a compound discrimination claim. *Arnett v. Aspin*, 846 F.Supp. 1234 (E.D.Pa.1994), represents the first time a federal district court recognized a sex-plus-age claim, and it still serves as the seminal case supporting this claim. Plaintiff, a female who was more than forty years of age, had been passed over twice for a promotion. Her evidence of sex-plus-age discrimination was that every woman selected for the position had been younger than forty years of age and every man selected had been over forty.

The employer sought summary judgment on the ground that plaintiff's sex-plus-age claim had to be treated as two separate claims: one for sex discrimination, the other for age discrimination. The employer argued that it was entitled to summary judgment, as a matter of law, because the evidence showed that *both* younger women and older men had been selected for the at-issue positions. The employer attempted to distinguish the "sex-plus" line of cases, such as *Jefferies*, from Arnett's "age-plus-sex" claim on the ground that Arnett was attempting to combine a subclass based upon two different statutes—Title VII and the ADEA. The court rejected the distinction as insignificant:

> [R]ather than adopt the distinctions suggested by the defendants, I find that the current line drawn between viable and nonviable sex-plus claims is adequate—that the "plus" classification be based on either an immutable characteristic or the exercise of a fundamental right. And, although I have uncovered no other case that recognizes a "sex-plus-age" discrimination claim under Title VII, it is clear that age is an immutable characteristic. For purposes of determining whether the defendants' discriminated against Arnett in violation of Title VII, I find she is member of a discrete subclass of "women over forty." Accordingly, I conclude that Arnett has shown a prima facie case under the *McDonnell Douglas* framework because (1) she is a member of the protected subclass, that is women over forty, (2) she was qualified for and applied for the positions in question, (3) despite her qualifications, she was denied the positions, and (4) other employees outside her protected class were selected, in this case two women under forty.

Id. at 1241. Some courts have implicitly followed the hybrid approach from *Arnett* by allowing the fact finder to consider evidence of discrimination under one statute probative of claims of unlawful discrimination under other statutes. *See, e.g.,* Wittenburg v. Am. Express Fin, Advisors, Inc., No. 04–922, 2005 WL 3047785 (D. Minn. 2005), *aff'd*, 464 F.3d 831 (8th Cir.2006), *cert. denied*, 551 U.S. 1113, 127 S.Ct. 2936, 168 L.Ed.2d 262 (2007); Good v. U.S. West Commc'ns, Inc., Civ. No. 93–302–FR, 1995 WL 67672 (D.Or.1995). *See also* 1 Midlife and Older Women 16–22.

The Supreme Court and the federal courts of appeals have yet to recognize a sex-plus-age theory of liability for discrimination. *See, e.g.,* Sherman v. Am. Cyanamid Co., No. 98–4035, 1999 WL 701911, at *5 (6th Cir.1999) (unpublished table decision) (declining the plaintiff's "invitation" to be the first court of appeals to recognize a sex-plus-age claim). Instead, the federal courts of appeals and district courts have continued to treat sex and age claims separately on the theory that because the causes of action must be brought under separate statutes—Title VII and the ADEA—they must be considered separately as well. *See e.g.*, Hill v. Lockheed Martin Logistics Mgmt., Inc., 354 F.3d 277, 283 (4th Cir.2004) (en banc), (finding against plaintiff on her separate claims of sex and age discrimination despite her allegations of being called a "troubled old lady" or "useless old lady" by her superiors). Professor Nicole Porter noted that "[v]ery few other courts [besides *Arnett*] have addressed the issue of whether a plaintiff can allege a sex plus age theory of discrimination. Of the courts that have had the opportunity to address the issue, they have either declined the invitation to decide the issue, or have recognized the cause of action with little or no discussion." Nicole Buonocore Porter, *Sex Plus Age Discrimination: Protecting Older Workers*, 81 Denv.U.L.Rev. 79, 88–89 & 89 nn.83 & 86–87 (2003) (citing Hall v. Mo. Highway & Transp. Comm'n, 995 F. Supp. 1001 (E.D.Mo.1998); O'Regan v. Arbitration Forums, Inc., 121 F.3d 1060 (7th Cir.1997)). For a discussion of how *Gross* may affect the ability of older women to bring intersectional claims, *see* Jourdan Day, *Closing the Loophole—Why Intersectional Claims are Needed to Address Discrimination Against Older Women,* 75 Ohio St. L. J. 447 (2014).

In Volume II of the study, *Employment Discrimination Against Midlife and Older Women: An Analysis of Discrimination Charges Filed With the EEOC* (1997), the Women's Legal Defense Fund examined charges of discrimination filed with the EEOC or cross-filed with the EEOC and a state agency by women and men age forty and older during a six-year period from fiscal year 1990 through 1995 (Oct. 1, 1989, through Sept. 30, 1995). Of the approximately 90,000 charges filed by women forty and older during the study period, 21 percent were for sex discrimination only, 24 percent for age discrimination only, and 10 percent were for both. 2 *id.* at 12. The average age of the charging parties was 53. 2 *id.* at 15. About one-third of the white women forty and older who filed discrimination charges made ADEA claims only, whereas only 7 percent of black women complained only of age discrimination. 2 *id.* at 17. In its attempt to quantify the number of sex-plus-age claims and identify sex-plus-age claim plaintiffs, the Women's Defense League study reported that 52 percent of the plaintiffs in age and sex cases were women in their fifties, and that, of the 81 percent of the "age-plus-sex" claims in which the plaintiff's job was identified, 24 percent involved professional jobs such as professor, teacher, accountant, or nurse, and 21 percent involved executive or managerial positions. 1 Midlife and Older Women 4. Twenty-four percent of the defendants in sex and age cases were government employers. 1 *id.* at 5.

Consider the following issues that may be raised in "age-plus" discrimination cases:

1. In *Arnett v. Aspin*, the court recognized an "age-plus-sex" claim only with respect to plaintiff's claim brought under Title VII and specifically noted that the claim was not recognized under the ADEA. 846 F.Supp. at 1240. Should it make a difference whether an "age-plus-sex" claim is brought under Title VII or the ADEA? In *Kelly v. Drexel University*, 907 F.Supp. 864 (E.D.Pa.1995), *aff'd*, 94 F.3d 102 (3d Cir.1996), the same judge who decided *Arnett* rejected an "age-plus-disability" claim brought under the ADEA. The court in *Luce v. Dalton*, 166 F.R.D. 457 (S.D.Cal.1996), relying, in part, on *Kelly*, also rejected an "age-plus-disability" claim brought under the ADEA. The court in *Luce* reasoned that

> Congress has not drafted one statute to govern all claims of employment discrimination, regardless of * * * race, sex, religion, national origin, age, and disability. The factors which Plaintiff seeks to lump together in this lawsuit under the title of "age-plus" theories of discrimination are contained within four separate and distinct statutes: the Age Discrimination in Employment Act, Title VII, the Americans with Disabilities Act, and the Rehabilitation Act. If Congress had intended to allow plaintiffs to mix and match theories of liability for employment discrimination, regardless of whether such claim was based upon race, sex, religion, national origin, age, or disability, it could have amended Title VII to provide protections to older Americans and Americans with disabilities within the confines of that statute. However, Congress chose to pass entirely separate legislation, providing for an entirely different basis for relief to persons who believe they have been discriminated against in employment based upon their age or disability. To allow Plaintiff here to aggregate claims under four completely different statutes, as an extension of the "sex-plus" theories of discrimination, would amount to judicial legislation. * * * [T]he arguments of the courts based upon the interpretation of Title VII's explicit language as barring discrimination based upon race, sex, national origin, or religion cannot be extended to support "age-plus" theories of discrimination.
>
> In addition, and perhaps more importantly, the "sex-plus" theories of discrimination are based upon a recognition of the unique discriminatory biases against certain subclasses of individuals under Title VII. Unlike African-American or Asian women, there can be no argument that there are unique discriminatory biases against older workers with disabilities or older non-Mormon workers. There is no danger that Plaintiff would be prejudiced by his claims being analyzed according to the unique statutory schemes set up for claims of age discrimination under the ADEA, claims of religious discrimination under Title VII, and claims of disability discrimination under the ADA or Rehabilitation Act.
>
> This Court finds that there does not exist in the law theories of "age-plus-religion" or "age-plus-disability" discrimination under the ADEA as proposed by Plaintiff in this case.

Id. at 461. Does *Hazen Paper Co. v. Biggins*, 507 U.S. 604, 609, 113 S.Ct. 1701, 1706, 123 L.Ed.2d 338 (1993), support the reasoning of the court in *Luce v. Dalton*?

2. To what extent is it likely that the combination of age and sex creates an especially powerful set of stereotypes that potentially limit the employment opportunities of older women? If so, what are some of those stereotypes?

3. In a jurisdiction that endorses the "age-plus-sex" theory of discrimination, how should the jury be instructed on the theory?

4. Employer, Casino Royale, advertises that it is an "upscale gentlemen's club, boasting of providing the finest service, atmosphere, and entertainment. Its facilities include a gourmet restaurant, conference room with office services, a boutique, wide-screen viewing of sports events, and topless dancing." Lindsey, a forty-year old female, was initially hired by the employer as a waitress, but later sought a promotion to a job as a topless dancer. The employer denied her request for the promotion on the ground that she was "too old." Would she have a potential claim under the ADEA? Title VII? Both? *See* Lindsey v. Prive Corp., 987 F.2d 324, 325 (5th Cir.1993).

NOTE: EMPLOYEE BENEFITS

Section 623(a)(1) of the ADEA makes it unlawful to discriminate on the basis of age with respect to "compensation, terms, conditions, or privileges of employment * * * ." 29 U.S.C. § 623(a)(1). And, as originally enacted, § 623(f)(2) provided that it was not unlawful under the ADEA for an employer to "observe the terms of * * * any bona fide employee benefit plan such as retirement, pension, or insurance plan" as long as the plan was not "a subterfuge to evade the purposes of" the ADEA. 29 U.S.C. § 623(f)(2). The administrative regulations interpreting § 623(f)(2)—promulgated by the Department of Labor and later affirmed by the EEOC when enforcement of the ADEA was transferred to it—take the position that age-based distinctions in benefit plans be cost-justified in order to qualify for the shelter of the exclusion. *See* 29 U.S.C. § 1625.10(a). The regulations impose the burden of persuasion on the employer to prove that the disparity in benefits is in accordance with the terms of a "bona fide employee benefit plan" and that the plan is not "a subterfuge to evade the purposes of" the ADEA. *Id.* An employer could satisfy its burden of proof with respect to disparity in benefits by showing that the lesser package of benefits to older workers was justified by age-related cost considerations. *Id.* § 1625.10(d).

The Supreme Court rejected that administrative interpretation of "subterfuge" in *United Air Lines v. McMann*, 434 U.S. 192, 98 S.Ct. 444, 54 L.Ed.2d 402 (1977), as applied to benefit plans in effect before the ADEA was passed. The Court in *McMann* defined subterfuge to mean "a scheme, plan, strategem, or artifice of evasion." *Id.* at 203, 98 S.Ct. at 450. Under this definition of subterfuge, the Court held that an employer who based its decision on a pre-ADEA plan could not have possessed the subjective intent to evade the ADEA. Less than a year after *McMann*, Congress amended the ADEA with the intent of overturning the decision. *See* Age Discrimination in Employment Act of 1978, Pub. L. No. 95–256, 92 Stat. 189 (1978).

About twelve years after *McMann*, the Supreme Court revisited the meaning of "subterfuge" in *Public Employees Retirement System v. Betts*, 492 U.S. 158, 109 S.Ct. 2854, 106 L.Ed.2d 134 (1989), and expanded the safe haven for benefit plans. In *Betts*, Ohio's employee retirement system provided substantially lower benefits for disabled employees over sixty years of age than for disabled employees younger than sixty. The plan provided two levels of compensation: "normal" retirement benefits for employees who retired because of age and who had worked at least five years, and "enhanced" retirement benefits for employees who retired because of a disability. Betts retired because of a deteriorating medical condition. But because she was then sixty-one years of age she could collect only the "normal" retirement package rather than the greater retirement package under the "enhanced" program. She then sued under the ADEA claiming discrimination because her employer refused to grant disability retirement benefits because of her age. The Supreme Court found that Betts had not been the victim of unlawful age discrimination because the ADEA did not cover employee benefits unless the plaintiff proved that the denial of benefits was a subterfuge to evade other provisions of the ADEA, e.g., trying to coerce the employee to retire. The Court interpreted "subterfuge" to mean intentional discrimination.

Congress expressed its disappointment with the *Betts* decision with the enactment of OWBPA because it thought it had overturned an earlier Supreme Court decision on the same issue in *McMann*. Under OWBPA, Congress specifically prohibited age discrimination in employment by eliminating the use of the term "subterfuge" and by endorsing the EEOC's cost-based justification defense. For a discussion of the effect of OWBPA in overturning *Betts* and reaffirming the cost-justification rule, see David A. Niles, *The Older Workers Benefit Protection Act: Painting Age-Discrimination Law with a Watery Brush*, 40 Buff.L.Rev. 869 (1992). *See generally* Mark S. Brodin, *Costs, Profits, and Equal Employment Opportunity*, 62 Notre Dame L.Rev. 318 (1987); Steven J. Kaminshine, *The Cost of Older Workers, Disparate Impact, and the Age Discrimination in Employment Act*, 42 Fla.L.Rev. 229, 231–33 (1990). For two cases analyzing the availability of the safe harbor provision of 29 U.S.C. § 623(f)(2)(B)(i), compare *Erie County Retirees Ass'n v. County of Erie*, 220 F.3d 193 (3d Cir.2000), with *Gutchen v. Board of Governors of Rhode Island*, 148 F.Supp.2d 151 (D.R.I. 2001).

NOTE: HOSTILE WORK ENVIRONMENT CLAIMS UNDER THE ADEA

Some courts of appeals have recognized hostile work environment claims under the ADEA and have adjusted principles established in sexual harassment cases such as *Harris v. Forklift Systems, Inc.*, 510 U.S. 17, 114 S.Ct. 367, 126 L.Ed.2d 295 (1993), for ADEA claims. *See, e.g.*, Dediol v. Best Chevrolet, Inc., 655 F.3d 435 (5th Cir.2011); Kassner v. 2nd Ave. Delicatessen Inc., 496 F.3d 229, 240–41 (2d Cir.2007); Crawford v. Medina Gen. Hosp., 96 F.3d 830 (6th Cir.1996); Spence v. Md. Cas. Co., 995 F.2d 1147 (2d Cir.1993); Sischo-Nownejad v. Merced Cmty. Coll. Dist., 934 F.2d 1104 (9th Cir.1991). *See also* Racicot v. Wal-Mart Stores, Inc., 414 F.3d 675, 678 (7th Cir.2005) (assuming without deciding that hostile work environment claims may be brought under the ADEA). The courts of appeals have also adopted the *Ellerth/Faragher* rules for employer liability for supervisory harassment in cases of age-based hostile work environment. *See, e.g.*, Weyers v. Lear Ops. Corp., 359 F.3d 1049, 1056–57 (8th Cir.2004). Judicial recognition of ADEA hostile work environment claims can provide older workers protection in circumstances where an employer engages in a course of harassing conduct designed to pressure an older worker to quit. If an older worker succumbs to such pressure and quits, he cannot obtain relief, such as back pay or reinstatement, unless he meets the often-difficult burden of proving a claim of constructive discharge. *See, e.g.*, Suarez v. Pueblo Int'l, Inc., 229 F.3d 49, 54–56 (1st Cir.2000). Imposing liability on employers for hostile work environment claims under the ADEA permits older workers to seek relief while they are still employed. *See generally* Debra D. Burke, *Workplace Harassment: A Proposal for a Bright Line Test Consistent with the First Amendment*, 21 Hofstra Lab. & Emp.L.J. 591, 625–28 (2004) (discussing ADEA hostile work environment cases following *Medina*). *See also* Margaret M. Gembala, Note, *ADEA and the Hostile Work Environment Claim: Are the Circuit Courts Dragging Their Feet at the Expense of the Harassed Older Worker?*, 7 Elder L.J. 341, 360–73 (1999) (surveying court of appeals decisions dealing with hostile work environment claims under the ADEA).

NOTE: THE BONA FIDE OCCUPATIONAL QUALIFICATION DEFENSE

The bona fide occupational qualification (BFOQ) defense in the ADEA is patterned after a similar provision in Title VII. Section 623(f)(1) provides that an action otherwise prohibited under the ADEA is not an unlawful employment practice "where age is a bona fide occupational qualification reasonably necessary to the normal operation of the particular business." 29 U.S.C. § 623(f)(1). Most of the cases in which the defense is raised involve jobs in which public safety is of paramount concern. *E.g.*, Murnane v. American Airlines, Inc., 667 F.2d 98 (D.C. Cir.1981) (airline pilots); Usery v. Tamiami Trail Tours, Inc., 531 F.2d 224 (5th Cir.1976) (bus drivers).

Western Air Lines, Inc. v. Criswell, 472 U.S. 400, 105 S.Ct. 2743, 86 L.Ed.2d 321 (1985), is the leading Supreme Court case construing the BFOQ in ADEA cases. *Criswell* involved a challenge to a provision of Western Air Lines' pension plan imposing mandatory retirement on flight engineers at age sixty. A flight engineer is one member of a three-person cockpit team required for the operation of certain aircraft. The flight engineer is responsible for monitoring an instrument panel but does not fly the aircraft unless both the captain and the first officer become incapacitated. *Criswell* rejected Western Air Lines' argument that an employer need only prove a *rational basis in fact* to justify as a BFOQ a facially discriminatory age-based employment policy. Western Airlines' rational basis argument was that the increased risk of psychological and physiological degeneration that occurs with age makes it unsafe to employ older workers as flight engineers.

In rejecting Western Air Lines' argument, the Supreme Court expressly adopted the test of the BFOQ exception that the Fifth Circuit adopted in

Tamiami Trail Tours. At issue in *Tamiami Trail Tours* was a bus company's policy against hiring persons over the age of forty as intercity bus drivers on the basis of safety considerations; the Fifth Circuit upheld the policy based upon the BFOQ defense. The Supreme Court, in *Criswell*, observed also that the *Tamiami Trail Tours* two-pronged objective test had been approved by every circuit confronting the issue, the EEOC, and implicitly by Congress. 472 U.S. at 415–17, 105 S.Ct. at 2752–53. The first prong of the test requires the employer to prove that the age-related job qualification is "reasonably necessary to the essence of [the employer's] business." *Id.* at 413, 105 S.Ct. at 2751. The second prong requires the employer to prove more than that the qualification is "convenient" or "reasonable," but requires the employer to prove that it is "compelled to rely on age as a proxy for the safety-related qualifications." *Id.* at 414, 105 S.Ct. at 2751. The second prong can be satisfied only if the employer proves that it had a factual basis for believing that "all or substantially all" persons over the age limitation would be "unable to perform safely and efficiently the duties of the job involved," or alternatively, that "age was a legitimate proxy for the safety-related job qualifications" because it is "impossible or highly impractical to deal with older employees on an individualized basis." *Id.* at 414, 105 S.Ct. at 2751–52.

Firefighters and Law Enforcement Officers: When Congress amended the ADEA in 1986 to prohibit mandatory retirement for most employees, it included an exemption for state and local public safety officers, such as police and firefighters, and for university professors. The exemption expired on December 31, 1993. In October, 1996, President Clinton signed legislation that permanently reinstates the provision in the ADEA that allows state and local governments the option of establishing mandatory age requirements for hiring and retirement for public safety officers, including police officers and firefighters. The legislation is retroactive to December 31, 1993. Section 119 of the Omnibus Consolidated Appropriations Act of 1997, P.L.No. 104–208, 110 Stat. 3009, amending the ADEA. Could the exemption for public safety employees be justified as a BFOQ under *Criswell*?

C. SEPARATIONS, WAIVERS, AND REDUCTIONS-IN-FORCE

As American businesses contend with unpredictable economic downturns, threatened mergers and acquisitions, costly technological advances, and increased global competition, the challenge of maintaining profit margins is often met through workforce reductions. As one commentator noted,

> The quickest way to bolster a company's financial position is to cut costs, and an easy way to cut is to reduce the work force. The most expedient solution of all is to get rid of older employees who because of their long tenure earn more money, are entitled to substantial pensions, and raise the company's tab for health benefits.

Ellen Simon Sacks, *Corporate Downsizing—Or Age Discrimination?*, 28 Trial 26, 26 (July 1992). In 1986, the ADEA was amended to eliminate mandatory retirement in most occupations. *See* Age Discrimination in Employment Amendments of 1986, Pub. L. No. 99–592, § 2(c), 100 Stat. 3342, at 3342. The ADEA's prohibition of mandatory retirement policies induced employers to look for innovative ways to reduce the ranks of older workers without violating the ADEA. *See generally* Howard Eglit, *Mandatory Retirement,* Murgia, *and Ageism, in* Employment Discrimination Stories 259 (Joel Wm. Friedman ed., 2006); Charles B. Craver, *The Application of the Age Discrimination in Employment Act to Persons Over Seventy*, 58 Geo.Wash.L.Rev. 52 (1989). "Downsizing" or reductions-in-force (RIF) and early retirement incentive plans (ERIPs), either through "buy-outs" or other incentives for early retirement, are several of the methods employers have adopted to try to satisfy the mandate of the ADEA and to remain profitable in the highly competitive domestic and international economic markets. Increasingly, a number of employers are persuading their older workers to retire earlier than they could be required to retire under laws such as the ADEA. But as a condition of granting sometimes generous early retirement incentives, employers are requiring employees to sign a waiver of their rights under the ADEA and other laws. These plans are sometimes referred to as the "golden handshake." The statute contains specific provisions for allowable waivers.

OUBRE V. ENTERGY OPERATIONS, INC.

Supreme Court of the United States, 1998.
522 U.S. 422, 118 S.Ct. 838, 139 L.Ed.2d 849.

JUSTICE KENNEDY delivered the opinion of the Court.

An employee, as part of a termination agreement, signed a release of all claims against her employer. In consideration, she received severance pay in installments. The release, however, did not comply with specific federal statutory requirements for a release of claims under the Age Discrimination in Employment Act of 1967 (ADEA). After receiving the last payment, the employee brought suit under the ADEA. The employer claims the employee ratified and validated the nonconforming release by retaining the monies paid to secure it. The employer also insists the release bars the action unless, as a precondition to filing suit, the employee tenders back the monies received. We disagree and rule that, as the release did not comply with the statute, it cannot bar the ADEA claim.

I

Petitioner Dolores Oubre worked as a scheduler at a power plant in Killona, Louisiana, run by her employer, respondent Entergy Operations,

Inc. In 1994, she received a poor performance rating. Oubre's supervisor met with her on January 17, 1995, and gave her the option of either improving her performance during the coming year or accepting a voluntary arrangement for her severance. She received a packet of information about the severance agreement and had 14 days to consider her options, during which she consulted with attorneys. On January 31, Oubre decided to accept. She signed a release, in which she "agreed to waive, settle, release, and discharge any and all claims, demands, damages, actions, or causes of action * * * that I may have against Entergy * * * ." In exchange, she received six installment payments over the next four months, totaling $6,258.

The Older Workers Benefit Protection Act (OWBPA) imposes specific requirements for releases covering ADEA claims. OWBPA, 29 U.S.C. §§ 626(f)(1)(B), (F), (G). In procuring the release, Entergy did not comply with the OWBPA in at least three respects: (1) Entergy did not give Oubre enough time to consider her options. (2) Entergy did not give Oubre seven days after she signed the release to change her mind. And (3) the release made no specific reference to claims under the ADEA.

* * * [Oubre] filed this suit against Entergy * * * alleging constructive discharge on the basis of her age in violation of the ADEA * * * . Oubre has not offered or tried to return the $6,258 to Entergy, nor is it clear she has the means to do so. Entergy moved for summary judgment, claiming Oubre had ratified the defective release by failing to return or offer to return the monies she had received. The District Court agreed and entered summary judgment for Entergy. The Court of Appeals affirmed, and we granted certiorari.

II

The employer rests its case upon general principles of state contract jurisprudence. As the employer recites the rule, contracts tainted by mistake, duress, or even fraud are voidable at the option of the innocent party. The employer maintains, however, that before the innocent party can elect avoidance, she must first tender back any benefits received under the contract. If she fails to do so within a reasonable time after learning of her rights, the employer contends, she ratifies the contract and so makes it binding. The employer also invokes the doctrine of equitable estoppel. As a rule, equitable estoppel bars a party from shirking the burdens of a voidable transaction for as long as she retains the benefits received under it. Applying these principles, the employer claims the employee ratified the ineffective release (or faces estoppel) by retaining all the sums paid in consideration of it. The employer, then, relies not upon the execution of the release but upon a later, distinct ratification of its terms.

These general rules may not be as unified as the employer asserts. And in equity, a person suing to rescind a contract, as a rule, is not required to restore the consideration at the very outset of the litigation. Even if the employer's statement of the general rule requiring tender back before one files suit were correct, it would be unavailing. The rule cited is based simply on the course of negotiation of the parties and the alleged later ratification. The authorities cited do not consider the question raised by statutory standards for releases and a statutory declaration making non-conforming releases ineffective. It is the latter question we confront here.

In 1990, Congress amended the ADEA by passing the OWBPA. The OWBPA provides: "An individual may not waive any right or claim under [the ADEA] unless the waiver is knowing and voluntary * * * . [A] waiver may not be considered knowing and voluntary unless at a minimum" it satisfies certain enumerated requirements, including the three listed above. 29 U.S.C. § 626(f)(1).

The statutory command is clear: An employee "may not waive" an ADEA claim unless the waiver or release satisfies the OWBPA's requirements. The policy of the Older Workers Benefit Protection Act is likewise clear from its title: It is designed to protect the rights and benefits of older workers. The OWBPA implements Congress' policy via a strict, unqualified statutory stricture on waivers, and we are bound to take Congress at its word. Congress imposed specific duties on employers who seek releases of certain claims created by statute. Congress delineated these duties with precision and without qualification: An employee "may not waive" an ADEA claim unless the employer complies with the statute. Courts cannot with ease presume ratification of that which Congress forbids.

The OWBPA sets up its own regime for assessing the effect of ADEA waivers, separate and apart from contract law. The statute creates a series of prerequisites for knowing and voluntary waivers and imposes affirmative duties of disclosure and waiting periods. The OWBPA governs the effect under federal law of waivers or releases on ADEA claims and incorporates no exceptions or qualifications. The text of the OWBPA forecloses the employer's defense, notwithstanding how general contract principles would apply to non-ADEA claims.

The rule proposed by the employer would frustrate the statute's practical operation as well as its formal command. In many instances a discharged employee likely will have spent the monies received and will lack the means to tender their return. These realities might tempt employers to risk noncompliance with the OWBPA's waiver provisions, knowing it will be difficult to repay the monies and relying on ratification. We ought not to open the door to an evasion of the statute by this device.

* * *

We reverse the judgment of the Court of Appeals and remand for further proceedings consistent with this opinion.

* * *

[JUSTICE SCALIA dissented in a separate opinion on the ground that there was no "tender back."]

JUSTICE THOMAS, with whom CHIEF JUSTICE REHNQUIST joins, dissenting.

* * * [W]ithout so much as acknowledging the long-established principle that a statute "must 'speak directly' to the question addressed by the common law" in order to abrogate it, the Court holds that the OWBPA abrogates both the common-law doctrine of ratification and the doctrine that a party must "tender back" consideration received under a release of legal claims before bringing suit. Because the OWBPA does not address either of these common-law doctrines at all, much less with the clarity necessary to abrogate them, I respectfully dissent.

* * *

NOTES AND QUESTIONS

1. The OWBPA establishes a two-tiered scheme on waivers. The first, illustrated in *Oubre* and the problem above, establishes the statutory floor for waivers involving individuals. The second involves statutory minimum requirements for waivers "requested in connection with an exit incentive or other employment termination program offered to a group or class of employees." 29 U.S.C. § 626(f)(1)(H). Employees subjected to "exit incentive or other employment termination" programs or policies must be given at least forty-five days instead of twenty-one days to consider the agreement containing the waiver. Also, at the commencement of the forty-five day period, the employer must inform each eligible employee in writing "in a manner calculated to be understood" by him, "or by the average individual eligible to participate," as to a description of eligibility factors: the time limits for the exit incentive program, the job titles and ages of all individuals eligible or selected for the program, and the ages of all employees in the same job classifications or organizational units who are not eligible or who were not selected for the program.

The legislative history of OWBPA reflects congressional intent to prevent employers from unfairly obtaining waivers of ADEA rights from older workers involved in large-scale terminations and layoffs, where the individual employee would not have reason to know or suspect that age may have played a role in the employer's decision or that the program or policy was designed to remove older workers from the workforce. *See* S.Rep.No. 101–263, 101st Cong., 2d Sess. 32 (1990), *reprinted in* 1990 U.S.C.C.A.N.

1509, 1537–38. The assumption is that individual employees are in a much better position to understand the nature of the action an employer may take against them and can possibly negotiate individually with the employer, but that employees who are offered a standardized benefit package are not free to negotiate.

2. The OWBPA makes the validity of a waiver an affirmative defense by providing that "the party asserting the validity of a waiver shall have the burden of proving * * * that a waiver was knowing and voluntary" because all of the minimum requirements of the Act have been satisfied. 29 U.S.C. § 626(f)(3). By making the waiver an affirmative defense, Congress sought to relieve employers from the burden of having to "prove a negative" in the absence of evidence of fraud, duress, or coercion. *See* S.Rep.No. 101–263, 101st Cong., 2d Sess. 35 (1990), *reprinted in* 1990 U.S.C.C.A.N. 1509, 1540. Proof by the employer that all of the statutory minimum requirements have been satisfied shifts the burden to the employee to prove that the waiver was not knowing and voluntary. *Id. See, e.g.*, Griffin v. Kraft Gen. Foods, Inc., 62 F.3d 368 (11th Cir.1995).

Are there arguments open to an employee to support a claim that she did not voluntarily and knowingly waive her rights under the ADEA even if the waiver complies with all of the requirements of the OWBPA? Congress expressly provides in the OWBPA that those standards are the "minimum" that is required for a waiver of rights under the ADEA to be considered voluntary and knowing. 29 U.S.C. § 626(f)(1). In *Bennett v. Coors Brewing Co.*, 189 F.3d 1221 (10th Cir.1999), the court held that under general contract principles, it is well established that a contract is void and unenforceable if procured through fraud. *Id.* at 1229 (citing Restatement (Second) Contracts § 164(1)(1981)). Applying contract principles, the court further held that "non-statutory circumstances such as fraud, duress, or mutual mistake may render an ADEA waiver not 'knowing and voluntary' under the OWBPA." *Id.* The court grounded its rule, in part, on the legislative history of the OWBPA, which stated that "[t]he individual [waiving his rights] * * * *must have acted in the absence of fraud, duress, coercion, or mistake of material fact.*" *Id.* (citing S.Rep.No.263, at 31–32 (1990)), *reprinted in* 1990 U.S.C.C.A.N. 1509, 1537 (emphasis of the court).

3. The OWBPA requires that the waiver be "knowing and voluntary." To qualify as "knowing and voluntary," the waiver must be "written in a manner calculated to be understood" by the average employee eligible to participate in the agreement. 29 U.S.C. § 626(f)(1)(A). In *Syverson v. International Business Machines Corp.*, 472 F.3d 1072 (9th Cir.2007), the employer (IBM) offered employees affected by a reduction in force severance pay and certain benefits in exchange for signing an agreement. The agreement included (1) a release (waiver) of all claims, including claims arising under the ADEA; (2) a covenant not to sue the employer for claims relating to employment or termination of employment; (3) a statement that the covenant not to sue "does not apply to actions based solely under the ADEA"; and (4) a statement that the release "does not preclude filing a

charge" with the EEOC. *Id.* at 1081–82. The Ninth Circuit found that, while a technical legal distinction exists between a waiver and a covenant not to sue, merging these seemingly contradictory provisions into the same document did not pass the "manner calculated to be understood" requirement. Why would IBM want a covenant not to sue, in addition to the waiver? Is there a way to achieve this purpose without violating the OWBPA?

4. Congress enacted the OWBPA to overturn the Supreme Court's controversial decision in *Public Employees Retirement System of Ohio v. Betts*, 492 U.S. 158, 109 S.Ct. 2854, 106 L.Ed.2d 134 (1989). Title II of OWBPA on waivers was added later. *See generally* S.Rep.No. 101–263, 101st Cong., 2d Sess. 5 (1990), *reprinted in* 1990 U.S.C.C.A.N. 1509, 1521–22. One of the causes of the controversy over unsupervised waivers in ADEA cases is the Act's hybrid structure. The ADEA is modeled on Title VII, but its enforcement scheme is taken from the Fair Labor Standards Act. Courts have allowed unsupervised waivers of rights under Title VII but have consistently held that unsupervised waivers are prohibited under the FLSA. For a discussion of pre-OWBPA developments on unsupervised waivers under the ADEA in the courts, the EEOC, and Congress, *see* N. Jansen Calamita, Note, *The Older Worker's Benefit Protection Act of 1990: The End of Ratification and Tender Back in ADEA Waiver Cases*, 73 B.U.L.Rev. 639, 641–46 (1993).

5. Because the written disclosure requirements of the OWBPA may provide "free discovery" that allows affected employees to evaluate the strengths and weaknesses of a potential age discrimination claim, are the OWBPA waiver requirements likely to discourage massive layoffs or downsizing? What advice would you give an employer to minimize the potential for employees to use the required disclosure to explore potential ADEA claims?

6. *Oubre* leaves two important questions unanswered. The first is whether an employer who has paid an ADEA claimant money under a waiver agreement that does not comply with the strict requirements of the OWBPA will be allowed to pursue a claim for restitution, recoupment, or set-off in the event that the employee sues the employer under the ADEA. For example, suppose Lois Lane, a sixty-year-old employee of Karo Company, signs a severance package Karo offered to her as part of a downsizing operation. The agreement requires her to waive her rights under the ADEA, but the agreement fails to conform to the requirements of OWBPA. Lane has received a substantial amount of money pursuant to the terms of the agreement. Suppose she sues Karo at a later date under the ADEA and the court allows her to pursue the claim. The case is tried on the merits; the jury rules in her favor and awards her monetary damages. Under the distinction between void and voidable contracts in *Oubre*, should Karo be entitled to a set-off against her damages award equal to the money it paid her under a nonconforming waiver agreement? Should it make a difference whether the damages the jury awards exceed the amount of money that Karo paid Lane under the nonconforming waiver agreement? *See* Long v. Sears Roebuck & Co., 105 F.3d 1529, 1543 (3rd Cir.1997); Oberg v. Allied Van Lines, Inc., 11 F.3d 679,

683–84 (7th Cir.1998); Forbus v. Sears Roebuck & Co., 958 F.2d 1036, 1041 (11th Cir.1992); Rupert v. PPG Indus., Inc., Nos. 07cv705, 08cv0616, 2009 WL 596014, at * 40–41 (W.D.Pa. Feb. 26, 2009). *See also* N. Jansen Calamita, Note, *The Older Worker's Benefit Protection Act of 1990: The End of Ratification and Tender Back in ADEA Waiver Cases*, 73 B.U.L.Rev. 639, 670–72 (1993).

The EEOC issued regulations, effective January 10, 2001, setting out its views on waivers under the ADEA. 29 C.F.R. § 1625.23 (2002). The regulations adopt the Court's decision in *Oubre* that an employee need not tender back the consideration given for the agreement before filing either a suit in court, a charge with the EEOC, or a charge with a state or local fair employment practice agency. Going beyond *Oubre*, the EEOC takes the position that a provision in a waiver agreement that requires the employee to tender back consideration is unlawful. The EEOC also takes the position that restitution, recoupment, or set-off sought by the employer must be limited to the lesser amount of the award to the prevailing plaintiff or the amount of consideration that the employee received for the waiver.

7. The second question *Oubre* leaves unanswered is whether the terms of the agreement that are not related to the OWBPA aspects of the employment relationship survive as enforceable provisions. For example, Lois Lane has potential claims against Karo for sexual harassment under Title VII, age discrimination under the ADEA, race discrimination under § 1981, and intentional infliction of emotional distress under state law. Karo and Lane enter into a settlement agreement, and a provision in the agreement requires Lane to waive any and all rights that she may have against Karo that arose in the course of her employment with Karo. The waiver agreement does not comply with the strict provisions of the OWBPA. *Oubre* would not preclude her from subsequently suing Karo under the ADEA; but is the waiver provision enforceable with respect to her claims under Title VII, § 1981, and state law? In *Bennett v. Coors Brewing Co.,* 189 F.3d 1221 (10th Cir.1999), the court held that a failure to tender back severance benefits acts as a waiver to state law claims even where the failure to do so would not affect an ADEA claim that does not comply with the OWBPA.

In *Tung v. Texaco Inc.*, 150 F.3d 206 (2d Cir.1998), a case involving both race and age claims, the court held that the provisions on waiver under OWBPA are limited to the ADEA and are not applicable to Title VII cases. The court held that the "totality of the circumstances" test is to be applied in determining the validity of the waiver in Title VII cases. Under this test, courts consider factors such (1) plaintiff's education and business experience; (2) the amount of time plaintiff had possession of the agreement before signing it; (3) the role of the plaintiff had in deciding the terms of the agreement; (4) the clarity of the agreement; (5) whether the plaintiff was represented by counsel; and (6) whether the consideration given, in exchange for the waiver of claims, exceeds benefits to which the employee was already entitled by law. *Id.* at 208.

8. Assume that the waiver agreement an employer obtains from an ADEA-protected employee is invalid under OWBPA. Under *Oubre*, the employer is precluded from seeking to enforce the waiver agreement in a judicial forum. But should the courts recognize an independent cause of action under the ADEA against the employer by the employee for violating the waiver provisions, or should the employee be limited to raising the invalid waiver agreement as a defense to any action the employer may initiate to recover the consideration given to the employee for the invalid waiver agreement? The courts are divided on this issue. *See* Commonwealth of Mass. v. Bull HN Info. Sys., Inc., 16 F.Supp.2d 90, 106–07 (D.Mass.1998) (discussing the cases).

9. Phillip Morris laid off a number of employees and offered each of them a severance package. The severance package required employees to release the employer from "any and all employment claims" they have had or might have in the future against Phillip Morris. The agreement also required the employees to waive their rights to demand reemployment or any benefits other than those in the severance package. John Adams, a 55-year-old black male employee, was one of the employees affected by the lay-off who accepted the severance package. Some time after Adams left Phillip Morris and while he was still receiving benefits under the agreement, Phillip Morris hired a 30-year-old white female to perform the same job Adams had performed. Suppose that the waiver of claims provision complies with the requirements of OWBPA with respect to any age discrimination claim Adams might have. Should the waiver provision be construed to bar any race or sex discrimination claim Adams may have against Phillip Morris? *See* Adams v. Philip Morris, Inc., 67 F.3d 580 (6th Cir.1995).

10. OWBPA's focus is on unsupervised waiver of rights under the ADEA. Suppose Kate Martin, an employee who is 55 years of age, employs an attorney to advise her on a severance package that has been offered by the employer. Does *Oubre* preclude her attorney from recommending terms of acceptance that do not comply with the waiver requirements of OWBPA? Are there ethical considerations that should counsel an attorney from recommending that a client accept an agreement in which the strict provisions under OWBPA are not followed?

11. For a defense of ERIPs and a criticism of the impact of OWBPA, *see* Samuel Issacharoff & Erica Worth Harris, *Is Age Discrimination Really Age Discrimination?: The ADEA's Unnatural Solution*, 72 N.Y.U.L.Rev. 780 (1997); Erica Worth, Note, *In Defense of Targeted ERIPs: Understanding the Interaction of Life-Cycle Employment and Early Retirement Incentive Plans*, 74 Tex.L.Rev. 411 (1995). *See also* Judith Droz Keyes & Douglas J. Farmer, *Settlement of Age Discrimination Claims—The Meaning and Impact of the Older Workers Benefit Protection Act*, 12 Lab.Law. 261 (1996) (suggesting that the requirements of the OWBPA are too formalistic and rigid, and recommending an approach similar to the "totality of the circumstances" test adopted by some courts prior to the OWBPA).

12. *The High Policymaker Exemption*: Section 631(c) of the ADEA, 29 U.S.C. § 631(c), permits the compulsory retirement of "any employee who has attained 65 years of age and who, for the 2 year period immediately before retirement, is employed in a bona fide executive or high policymaking position" if such individual is entitled to nonforfeitable retirement benefits which equal at least $44,000. *See* Morrissey v. Boston Five Cents Savings Bank, 54 F.3d 27 (1st Cir.1995). The test determining whether an employee occupies an "executive or high policymaking position" is one of function, and it has been held that whether the employee was highly paid is immaterial. Whittlesey v. Union Carbide, 567 F.Supp. 1320 (S.D.N.Y.1983), *aff'd*, 742 F.2d 724 (2d Cir.1984). The EEOC has defined "high policymakers" as "individuals who have little or no line authority but whose position and responsibility are such that they play a significant role in the development of corporate policy." EEOC, Guidelines on Discrimination Because of Age, 29 C.F.R. § 1625.12(e) (1994) (quoting H.R.Rep. No. 950, 95th Cong., 2d Sess. 10 (1978)).

NOTE: REDUCTION-IN-FORCE OR DOWNSIZING CASES

The use of reduction-in-force (RIF) schemes or "downsizing" by U.S. corporations has become common industry practice for companies looking to meet their bottom line. These schemes however, have an acute effect on older workers, as evidenced by the increasing number of RIF-related employment discrimination claims brought under the ADEA, as well as a federal circuit court split—and the resulting scholarly critiques—regarding the appropriate analytical framework.

During the past several decades, many employers in the United States have systematically reduced their workforces. For example, in every year between 1988 and 1993, at least one-half of the large and mid-size employers in the United States surveyed by the American Management Association reduced their workforce. Ronald Henkoff, *Getting Beyond Downsizing*, Fortune, Jan. 10, 1994, at 58. Corporate "downsizing" has also been characterized as a "euphemism[ ] for cost-cutting and lay-offs." Christopher Farrell, et al., *It Won't Take Your Breath Away, But * * **, Business Week, Jan. 10, 1994, at 60. In *Opportunistic Downsizing of Aging Workers: The 1990s Version of Age and Pension Discrimination in Employment*, 48 Hastings L.J. 511, 511 n.1 (1997) (citations omitted), Professor Gary Minda interpreted downsizing as follows:

> The word "downsize" first appeared during the oil crisis of the early 1970s, when automobile executives used "downsizing" to describe the move toward the design of smaller, gas-efficient automobiles. When applied to workers, the word "downsize" has come to signify reduced expectations and reduced employment opportunity. In the labor relations offices of corporate America, downsizing has become a euphemism to soften the hard edge of words like "fired," "dismissed," and "laid off." In the corporate-speak of the 1990s, employees "are 'downsized,' 'separated,' 'severed,'

> 'unassigned.' [Employees] are told that their jobs 'are not going forward.'" In board rooms and chief executive officer (CEO) offices of corporate America, downsizing is a word that summarizes a host of business survival strategies designed to save the corporation from death in the global marketplace. For most American workers, the word symbolizes the permanent loss of a career job. In the print media, the word "downsize" is used to characterize a fundamental transformation in the workplace; changes which rival those of the Industrial Revolution of the nineteenth century.

Professor Minda further observed that

> [a]lthough downsizing may not affect all workers, older workers as a group are particularly vulnerable. The job displacement rates for older workers are higher than average, considering the length of time between jobs as well as the wage loss due to unemployment. * * *
>
> For older workers, anxiety about job loss has a real factual basis. * * * The cost of losing a job in today's economy is thus both significant and persistent for older workers who have a higher displacement rate. For many of these older displaced workers, a good job with promise of long-term job security is a thing of the past.

Minda, *supra,* at 518–19 citing a 1994 study by Ann Huff Stevens and the National Bureau of Economic Research that reported that "wage loss resulting from displacement is persistent even after re-employment at another job."

Scholars have recognized that the impact of RIF programs on older workers persists today. Research has indicated that "[i]ncreases in age discrimination charges filed with the Equal Employment Opportunity Commission (EEOC) almost always coincide with downturns in the economy, a correlation which suggests that at least some employers use age as a determining factor when making downsizing decisions." Daniel B. Kohrman & Mark Stewart Hayes, *Employers Who Cry 'RIF' and the Courts That Believe Them*, 23 Hofstra Lab. & Emp.L.J. 153, 158–59 (2005). Other scholars have attributed this result to a "wage" as opposed to "age" bias on the part of employers. Kohrman & Hayes, *supra*, at 160–61, *citing* Charles Koeber & David W. Wright, *Wage Bias in Worker Displacement: How Industrial Structure Shapes the Job Loss and Earnings Decline of Older American Workers*, 30 J.Soc.Econ. 343, 346 (2001). According to Kohrman and Hayes

> [u]nder [the wage bias theory], employers are largely motivated by one factor: profit. Since older workers tend to command higher salaries than their younger counterparts, they will not fare as well in situations where an employer institutes [a] RIF as part of a cost-saving strategy, because the "displacement of these older and more highly compensated workers generates greater returns to capital and higher profit margins.

Id. at 160–61.

Unfortunately, there is little empirical data detailing the national job loss statistics directly resulting from reduction-in-force programs. The Bureau of Labor Statistics, a division of the U.S. Department of Labor, tracks the occurrence of mass layoffs nationwide on its Web site, but does not indicate whether those layoffs were the result of a formalized RIF program or other causes. *See e.g.,* U.S. Dep't of Labor, Bureau of Labor Statistics, Extended Mass Layoff Events and Separations, Selected Measures, 2009, *available at http://www.bls.gov/mls/mlmowsumcur.pdf* (last visited Dec. 3, 2009). The Bureau of National Affairs also fails to track RIF-specific layoffs. *See generally* Ethan Lipsig et al., Reductions in Force in Employment Law (Bureau of National Affairs, Inc., 2007). The AARP Public Policy Institute did report, however, that of the forty-three ADEA-based claims that the EEOC litigated in 2006, 65 percent were based upon an unlawful discharge or impermissible layoff theory. David Neumark, AARP Public Policy Inst., Reassessing the Age Discrimination in Employment Act 41 tbl.1 (2008), *available at http://assets.aarp.org/rgcenter/econ/2008_09_adea.pdf* (last visited Dec. 3, 2009).

The dramatic increase in RIF-related age discrimination claims has led to the development of RIF case law. An initial issue in a RIF or downsizing case is whether, in fact, the employee was terminated as a result of a "true" downsizing or RIF. In *Barnes v. GenCorp Inc.*, 896 F.2d 1457, 1465 (6th Cir.1990), the Sixth Circuit stated that "[a] work force reduction situation occurs when business considerations cause an employer to eliminate one or more positions," but "[a]n employee is not eliminated as part of work force reduction when he or she is replaced after his or her discharge." The court also stated that "a person is replaced only when another employee is hired or reassigned to perform the plaintiff's duties," but not "when another employee is assigned to perform the plaintiff's duties in addition to other duties, or when the work is redistributed among other existing employees already performing related work." *Id.* The court distinguished *Barnes* in *Brocklehurst v. PPG Industries, Inc.*, 123 F.3d 890, 895 (6th Cir.1997), when it upheld the discharge of an ADEA plaintiff even though his position was not eliminated. *Brocklehurst* held that *Barnes* does not "stand[ ] for the proposition that a high-level employee may not be found to have been discharged as part of an economically motivated RIF unless that employee's position is eliminated." *Id.*

Courts have built upon the "redistribution" of work theory proposed in *Brocklehurst* by further classifying RIFs into either a traditional RIF (also known as an "elimination-of duties" RIF) or a "mini-RIF" (also known as a "redistribution-of-duties" RIF). Kohrman & Hayes, *supra,* at 168. A traditional RIF is still used to explain when an employee's job is eliminated, whereas a "mini-RIF" describes when the duties of an employee's job are assumed or absorbed by other current workers. Filar v. Bd. of Educ. of City of Chi., 526 F.3d 1054, 1060 (7th Cir.2000). For a mini-RIF claim, courts have revised the *McDonnell Douglas* framework to fit the situation where a position was eliminated because the traditional fourth element, that a younger person was hired in the plaintiff's place, would not apply. Instead, courts have applied a "modified version of the *McDonnell Douglas* framework." Merillat v. Metal Spinners, Inc. 470 F.3d 685, 690 (7th Cir.2006). This analysis requires the plaintiff to demonstrate that: "(1) she is a member of a protected class; (2) she was meeting her employer's legitimate performance expectations; (3) she suffered an adverse employment action; and (4) her duties were absorbed by employees not in the protected classes." *Merillat*, 470 F.3d at 690, *citing* Johal v. Little Lady Foods, Inc., 434 F.3d 943, 946 (7th Cir.2006); Michas v. Health Cost Controls of Ill., 209 F.3d 687, 693 (7th Cir.2000).

Case law has also developed in the traditional RIF area, but courts disagree on the analytical framework to be used for these types of cases. In particular, the courts disagree on the showing required to establish a prima facie case. The problem is that in a true RIF, the terminated employee is usually meeting the legitimate job performance expectations of the employer and is not replaced after being terminated. *See, e.g.*, Mitchell v. Data Gen. Corp., 12 F.3d 1310, 1315 (4th Cir.1993). The courts in *Coburn* and in *Williams* established two different approaches that today serve the basis for a circuit split on this issue.

In *Coburn v. Pan American World Airways, Inc.*, 711 F.2d 339 (D.C.Cir.1983), the employer instituted a RIF as one of several cost-cutting measures to improve its precarious financial situation. The plaintiff, who was terminated pursuant to the RIF, was then forty-three years old and had been employed for seventeen years. He brought an action under the ADEA, and the jury ruled in his favor. But the district court entered judgment for the employer on the ground that the plaintiff's evidence did not support the finding of a prima facie case, and, even if it did, the plaintiff failed to prove pretext.

The Court of Appeals for the District of Columbia affirmed the judgment of the district court but held that a plaintiff can establish a prima facie case with proof that (1) he is a member of the class protected by the ADEA; (2) he was qualified for the job he was doing at the time he was terminated; (3) he was terminated; and (4) the employer retained younger employees whose job responsibilities were substantially the same as that of the plaintiff's former job. The court of appeals rejected the employer's argument that an ADEA plaintiff should be required "to prove something extra to make out a prima facie case" in RIF situations. *Id.* at 343. Because a discharged employee in a RIF case will virtually always be qualified, the employer argued that the plaintiff should be required to prove "direct evidence" of unlawful discrimination. Under *Coburn* the relative qualifications of the plaintiff would not be a factor in deciding whether an inference of unlawful discrimination is established. The court further held that the "exigencies of a reduction-in-force can best be analyzed at the stage where the employer puts on evidence of a nondiscriminatory reason" for the discharge; thus under its analytical approach, courts are to analyze the employer's reason for the RIF on a case-by-case basis. *Id.*

The First, Third, Fourth, Seventh, and Tenth Circuits have generally adopted this framework by "recast[ing] the fourth element to require the plaintiff to merely show that he or she was 'disadvantaged [during the RIF] in favor of a younger person.'" Kohrman & Hayes, *supra*, at 165, *quoting Coburn* 711 F.2d at 342. *See also id.* at 165 n.75 (citing LeBlanc v. Great Am. Ins. Co., 6 F.3d 836, 842 (1st Cir.1993); In re Carnegie Ctr. Assocs., 129 F.3d 290, 295 (3d Cir.1997); Mitchell Data Gen. Corp., 12 F.3d 1310, 1315 (4th Cir.1993); Blistein v. St. John's College, 74 F.3d 1459, 1470 (4th Cir.1996); Oxman v. WLS–TV, 846 F.2d 448, 455 (7th Cir.1988); Beaird v. Seagate Tech., Inc., 145 F.3d 1159, 1167 (10th Cir.1998)). This approach has been recognized as "relatively plaintiff-friendly." Kohrman & Hayes, *supra*, at 166.

The Tenth Circuit described this approach in *Stone v. Autoliv ASP, Inc.*, 210 F.3d 1132 (10th Cir.), *cert. denied*, 531 U.S. 876, 121 S.Ct. 182, 148 L.Ed.2d 125 (2000):

> To establish a prima facie case of age discrimination in the RIF context, a claimant affected by a RIF must prove: (1) the claimant is within the protected age group; (2) he or she was doing satisfactory work; (3) the claimant was discharged despite the adequacy of his or her work; and (4) there is some evidence the employer intended to discriminate against the claimant in reaching its RIF decision. The fourth element may be established "through circumstantial evidence that the plaintiff was treated less favorably than younger employees during the [RIF]."

Id. at 1137 (citations omitted). Once the plaintiff established a prima facie case, the employer may advance a nondiscriminatory reason. In most cases, the RIF serves as the nondiscriminating reason. The burden then shifts to the plaintiff to establish pretext. According to the Tenth Circuit,

> There are three common methods used to demonstrate pretext in the RIF context: (1) evidence that the termination of the employee is inconsistent with the employer's RIF criteria; (2) evidence that the employer's evaluation of the employee was falsified to cause termination; or (3) "evidence that the RIF is more generally pretextual."

Stone, 210 F.3d at 1140 (citation omitted). *See also* Tyler v. Union Oil Co., 304 F.3d 379, 396–92 (5th Cir.2002) (plaintiffs may show pretext by rebutting particularized evidence of nondiscriminatory reasons for discharge and employer's conscious, unexplained departure from its established RIF process).

The Fifth Circuit in *Williams v. General Motors Corp.*, 656 F.2d 120 (5th Cir.1981), *cert. denied*, 455 U.S. 943, 102 S.Ct. 1439, 71 L.Ed.2d 655 (1982), adopted a different standard for establishing a prima facie case in RIF cases. In *Williams*, as in *Coburn*, the plaintiff brought an ADEA action after he had been terminated from his salaried supervisory position in a RIF in which the employer terminated approximately 59 percent of its salaried supervisory staff. *Williams* held that a plaintiff can establish a prima facie ADEA case by showing (1) membership in the protected class; (2) qualification to assume another position at the time of discharge or demotion; (3) circumstantial or direct evidence that the employer intended to discriminate on the basis of age in reaching the employment decision. *Id.* at 129. The court stated that the first two elements have frequently appeared in ADEA cases but the third—which is specifically tailored for RIF cases—is appropriate because the ADEA does not place an affirmative duty on the employer to accord special treatment to workers protected by the ADEA. *Id.* at 129–30. Thus, instead of focusing on whether the employer retained an equally qualified younger employee, the Fifth Circuit considered whether the plaintiff's evidence was sufficient to support an inference that the employer did not treat age neutrally in making its RIF decisions. *Accord* Oxman v. WLS–TV, 12 F.3d 652, 657–58 (7th Cir.1993). This "more defendant-friendly approach to RIF cases * * * has been followed by the Second, Sixth, Eighth, and Eleventh Circuits." Kohrman & Hayes, *supra,* at 166 & n.81 (citing Hollander v. Am. Cyanide Co., 172 F.3d 192, 199 (2d Cir.1999); Barnes v. GenCorp Inc., 896 F.2d 1475, 1465 (6th Cir.1990); Doerhoff v. McDonnell Douglas Corp., 171 F.3d 1177, 1180 (8th Cir.1999); Standard v. A.B.E.L. Servs., Inc., 161 F.3d 1318, 1331 (11th Cir.1998)).

The analytical approach adopted in *Williams* and *Coburn* has been subjected to much criticism. For example, Professor Minda stated that

> [u]nfortunately, the decisions in cases like *Coburn* and *Williams* have exhibited a lack of judicial understanding about the nature and operation of age discrimination in [the RIF and downsizing context] and consequently, the courts have been unable to develop a workable modification of the *McDonnell Douglas* prima facie case. To develop a workable prima facie standard, the courts must first understand the problem of age discrimination as it is practiced by corporate decision-makers in the era of downsizing.

Gary Minda, *Opportunistic Downsizing of Aging Workers: The 1990s Version of Age and Pension Discrimination in Employment*, 48 Hastings L.J. 511, 544–45 (1997). Professor Minda then argued:

> Because the unique nature of downsizing and RIF does not entail the hiring of replacement workers, a modified formulation of the prima facie case is warranted. The prima facie case for ADEA claims in RIF and downsizing cases should be modified to require the plaintiff to prove that: 1) he or she is forty years old or older; * * * 2) he or she was terminated pursuant to a RIF or downsizing decision; 3) he or she is a late-career employee with firm-specific skills; 4) he or she was permanently laid-off for being too expensive or costly to the firm.

Id. at 567. Under this proposed analysis, a plaintiff should be allowed to present circumstantial evidence that salary or pension was a "proxy" for age and, therefore, age was a motivating factor in the employer's decision. *Id.* The burden of production of evidence would then shift to the employer to show that its "cost containment rationale for downsizing was based on age-neutral considerations which were independent of the salary status of the older workers." *Id.* at 568. The employer could meet its burden with evidence of "technological restructuring, or the elimination of jobs as a result of new technology, reduced market demand for the company's product, and outsourcing and lean manufacturing strategies that do not target older workers by using their salary as a proxy for determining termination." *Id.* at 568–69. In the third stage of the analysis, the plaintiff could establish liability by proving either pretext or the availability of reasonable alternatives that would not result in termination. *Id.* at 569.

A frequently cited student Note, Jessica Lind, *The Prima Facie Case of Age Discrimination in Reduction-in-Force Cases*, 94 Mich.L.Rev. 832 (1995), advocates that the *McDonnell Douglas* prima facie case showing should be reformulated for RIF cases to require the plaintiff to introduce evidence that "1) she is a member of the protected class; 2) she was terminated pursuant to a RIF; 3) her duties were reassigned to a younger, similarly situated employee; and 4) that the younger employee was less qualified than the plaintiff." *Id.* at 845. The Note argues that this proposed modification is more faithful to *McDonnell Douglas* because, at least with respect to the fourth proposed element, all employees are presumably qualified and a consideration of relative qualifications is necessary to protect employers from potential ADEA liability "every time it reduces the size of its workforce." *Id.* at 848.

Kohrman and Hayes suggest that the real problem with the current standards, particularly the *Williams* approach, is that courts fail to distinguish between layoffs resulting from an RIF program versus a simple replacement at the outset; as a result, plaintiffs who were victim to a blatant replacement are forced to prove their case under the much higher—an unwarranted—RIF standard. As a solution, Kohrman and Hayes propose that if courts continue to use the stricter *Williams* evidentiary standard, that they

> acknowledge two propositions that follow directly from the notion of a workforce reduction: (1) a position is not eliminated pursuant to an RIF when job duties are only temporarily dispersed to other employees, pending the assignment of a permanent replacement; and (2) a position is not eliminated pursuant to an RIF when the employer reassigns a second employee to perform substantially the same duties and functions that were previously performed by a terminated employee.

Kohrman & Hayes, *supra*, at 177. The authors theorize that applying these "tools to assist [courts] in distinguishing between RIF and replacement cases" could ultimately lead to more litigation victories for ADEA claimants who were simply, and illegally, replaced by younger workers solely on the basis of age. *Id.* at 176–77.

D. DISPARATE IMPACT

SMITH V. CITY OF JACKSON, MISSISSIPPI

Supreme Court of the United States, 2005.
544 U.S. 228, 125 S.Ct. 1536, 161 L.Ed.2d 410.

JUSTICE STEVENS announced the judgment of the Court.

Petitioners, police and public safety officers employed by the city of Jackson, Mississippi (hereinafter City), contend that salary increases received in 1999 violated the Age Discrimination in Employment Act of 1967 (ADEA) because they were less generous to officers over the age of 40 than to younger officers. Their suit raises the question whether the "disparate-impact" theory of recovery announced in Griggs v. Duke Power Co., 401 U.S. 424, 28 L.Ed.2d 158, 91 S.Ct. 849 (1971), for cases brought under Title VII of the Civil Rights Act of 1964, is cognizable under the ADEA. Despite the age of the ADEA, it is a question that we have not yet addressed.

I

On October 1, 1998, the City adopted a pay plan granting raises to all City employees. The stated purpose of the plan was to "attract and retain qualified people, provide incentive for performance, maintain competitiveness with other public sector agencies and ensure equitable compensation to all employees regardless of age, sex, race and/or disability." * * * On May 1, 1999, a revision of the plan, which was motivated, at least in part, by the City's desire to bring the starting salaries of police officers up to the regional average, granted raises to all police officers and police dispatchers. Those who had less than five years of tenure received proportionately greater raises when compared to their former pay than those with more seniority. Although some officers over the age of 40 had less than five years of service, most of the older officers had more.

Petitioners are a group of older officers who filed suit under the ADEA claiming both that the City deliberately discriminated against them because of their age (the "disparate-treatment" claim) and that they were "adversely affected" by the plan because of their age (the "disparate-impact" claim). The District Court granted summary judgment to the City on both claims. The Court of Appeals held that the ruling on the former claim was premature because petitioners were entitled to further discovery on the issue of intent, but it affirmed the dismissal of the disparate-impact claim. * * * Over one judge's dissent, the majority concluded that disparate-impact claims are categorically unavailable under the ADEA. * * *

We granted the officers' petition for certiorari, and now hold that the ADEA does authorize recovery in "disparate-impact" cases comparable to *Griggs*. Because, however, we conclude that petitioners have not set forth a valid disparate-impact claim, we affirm.

II

During the deliberations that preceded the enactment of the Civil Rights Act of 1964, Congress considered and rejected proposed amendments that would have included older workers among the classes protected from employment discrimination. Congress did, however, request the Secretary of Labor to "make a full and complete study of the factors which might tend to result in discrimination in employment because of age and of the consequences of such discrimination on the economy and individuals affected." The Secretary's report, submitted in response to Congress' request, noted that there was little discrimination arising from dislike or intolerance of older people, but that "arbitrary" discrimination did result from certain age limits. Report of the Secretary of Labor, The Older American Worker: Age Discrimination in Employment 22 (June 1965), reprinted in U. S. Equal Employment Opportunity Commission, Legislative History of the Age Discrimination in Employment Act (1981) (hereinafter Wirtz Report). Moreover, the report observed that discriminatory effects resulted from "[i]nstitutional arrangements that indirectly restrict the employment of older workers."

In response to that report Congress directed the Secretary to propose remedial legislation, see Fair Labor Standards Amendments of 1966, Pub. L. No. 89–601, § 606, 80 Stat. 845, and then acted favorably on his proposal. As enacted in 1967, § 4(a)(2) of the ADEA * * * provided that it shall be unlawful for an employer "to limit, segregate, or classify his employees in any way which would deprive or tend to deprive any individual of employment opportunities or otherwise adversely affect his status as an employee, because of such individual's age * * * ." Except for substitution of the word "age" for the words "race, color, religion, sex, or national origin," the language of that provision in the ADEA is identical to that found in § 703(a)(2) of the Civil Rights Act of 1964 (Title VII). Other provisions of the ADEA also parallel the earlier statute. Unlike Title VII, however, § 4(f)(1) of the ADEA, 81 Stat 603, contains language that significantly narrows its coverage by permitting any "otherwise prohibited" action "where the differentiation is based on reasonable factors other than age" (hereinafter RFOA provision).

III

In determining whether the ADEA authorizes disparate-impact claims, we begin with the premise that when Congress uses the same language in two statutes having similar purposes, particularly when one is enacted shortly after the other, it is appropriate to presume that Congress intended that text to have the same meaning in both statutes. We have consistently applied that presumption to language in the ADEA that was "derived *in haec verba* from Title VII." Our unanimous interpretation of § 703(a)(2) of Title VII in *Griggs* is therefore a precedent of compelling importance.

In *Griggs*, a case decided four years after the enactment of the ADEA, we considered whether § 703 of Title VII prohibited an employer "from requiring a high school education or passing of a standardized general intelligence test as a condition of employment in or transfer to jobs when (a) neither standard is shown to be significantly related to successful job performance, (b) both requirements operate to disqualify Negroes at a substantially higher rate than white applicants, and (c) the jobs in question formerly had been filled only by white employees as part of a longstanding practice of giving preference to whites." Accepting the Court of Appeals' conclusion that the employer had adopted the diploma and test requirements without any intent to discriminate, we held that good faith "does not redeem employment procedures or testing mechanisms that operate as 'built-in headwinds' for minority groups and are unrelated to measuring job capability."

We explained that Congress had "directed the thrust of the Act to the *consequences* of employment practices, not simply the motivation." We relied on the fact that history is "filled with examples of men and women who rendered highly effective performance without the conventional badges of accomplishment in terms of certificates, diplomas, or degrees. Diplomas and tests are useful servants, but Congress has mandated the commonsense proposition that they are not to become masters of reality." And we noted that the Equal Employment Opportunity Commission (EEOC), which had enforcement responsibility, had issued guidelines that accorded with our view. We thus squarely held that § 703(a)(2) of Title VII did not require a showing of discriminatory intent.

* * *

Griggs, which interpreted the identical text at issue here, thus strongly suggests that a disparate-impact theory should be cognizable under the ADEA. Indeed, for over two decades after our decision in *Griggs*, the Courts of Appeal uniformly interpreted the ADEA as authorizing recovery on a "disparate-impact" theory in appropriate cases. * * * It was only after our decision in Hazen Paper Co. v. Biggins, 507 U.S. 604, 123 L.Ed.2d 338, 113 S.Ct. 1701 (1993), that some of those courts concluded that the ADEA did not authorize a disparate-impact theory of liability. * * * Our opinion in *Hazen Paper*, however, did not address or comment on the issue we decide today. * * * While we noted that disparate-treatment "captures the essence of what Congress sought to prohibit in the ADEA," id., at 610, 123 L. Ed. 338, 113 S.Ct. 1701, we were careful to explain that we were not deciding "whether a disparate impact theory of liability is available under the ADEA * * * ." In sum, there is nothing in our opinion in *Hazen Paper* that precludes an interpretation of the ADEA that parallels our holding in *Griggs*.

The Court of Appeals' categorical rejection of disparate-impact liability, like Justice O'Connor's, rested primarily on the RFOA provision and the majority's analysis of legislative history. As we have already explained, we think the history of the enactment of the ADEA, with particular reference to the Wirtz Report, supports the pre-*Hazen Paper* consensus concerning disparate-impact liability. And *Hazen Paper* itself contains the response to the concern over the RFOA provision.

The RFOA provision provides that it shall not be unlawful for an employer "to take any action otherwise prohibited under subsectio[n] (a) * * * where the differentiation is based on reasonable factors other than age discrimination * * * ." 81 Stat 603. In most disparate-treatment cases, if an employer in fact acted on a factor other than age, the action would not be prohibited under subsection (a) in the first place. *See* Hazen Paper, 507 U.S., at 609, 123 L.Ed.2d 338, 113 S.Ct. 1701 ("[T]here is no disparate treatment under the ADEA when the factor motivating the employer is some feature other than the employee's age."). In those disparate-treatment cases, such as in *Hazen Paper* itself, the RFOA provision is simply unnecessary to avoid liability under the ADEA, since there was no prohibited action in the first place. The RFOA provision is not, as Justice O'Connor suggests, a "safe harbor from liability," * * * since there would be no liability under § 4(a). *See* Texas Dep't of Community Affairs v. Burdine, 450 U.S. 248, 254, 67 L.Ed.2d 207, 101 S.Ct. 1089 (1981) (noting, in a Title VII case, that an employer can defeat liability by showing that the employee was rejected for "a legitimate, nondiscriminatory reason" without reference to an RFOA provision).

In disparate-impact cases, however, the allegedly "otherwise prohibited" activity is not based on age. * * * It is, accordingly, in cases involving disparate-impact claims that the RFOA provision plays its principal role by precluding liability if the adverse impact was attributable to a nonage factor that was "reasonable." Rather than support an argument that disparate impact is unavailable under the ADEA, the RFOA provision actually supports the contrary conclusion.[11]

---

[11] We note that if Congress intended to prohibit all disparate-impact claims, it certainly could have done so. For instance, in the Equal Pay Act of 1963, 29 U.S.C. § 206(d)(1) [29 USCS § 206(d)(1)], Congress barred recovery if a pay differential was based "on any other factor"—reasonable or unreasonable—"other than sex." The fact that Congress provided that employees could use only *reasonable* factors in defending a suit under the ADEA is therefore instructive.

Finally, we note that both the Department of Labor, which initially drafted the legislation, and the EEOC, which is the agency charged by Congress with responsibility for implementing the statute, * * * have consistently interpreted the ADEA to authorize relief on a disparate-impact theory. The initial regulations, while not mentioning disparate impact by name, nevertheless permitted such claims if the employer relied on a factor that was not related to age. 29 CFR § 860.103(f)(1)(i) (1970) (barring physical fitness requirements that were not "reasonably necessary for the specific work to be performed"). See also § 1625.7 (2004) (setting forth the standards for a disparate-impact claim).

The text of the statute, as interpreted in *Griggs*, the RFOA provision, and the EEOC regulations all support petitioners' view. We therefore conclude that it was error for the Court of Appeals to hold that the disparate-impact theory of liability is categorically unavailable under the ADEA.

IV

Two textual differences between the ADEA and Title VII make it clear that even though both statutes authorize recovery on a disparate-impact theory, the scope of disparate-impact liability under ADEA is narrower than under Title VII. The first is the RFOA provision, which we have already identified. The second is the amendment to Title VII contained in the Civil Rights Act of 1991, 105 Stat 1071. One of the purposes of that amendment was to modify the Court's holding in Wards Cove Packing Co. v. Atonio, 490 U.S. 642, 104 L.Ed.2d 733, 109 S.Ct. 2115 (1989), a case in which we narrowly construed the employer's exposure to liability on a disparate-impact theory. See Civil Rights Act of 1991, § 2, 105 Stat 1071. While the relevant 1991 amendments expanded the coverage of Title VII, they did not amend the ADEA or speak to the subject of age discrimination. Hence, *Wards Cove's* pre-1991 interpretation of Title VII's identical language remains applicable to the ADEA.

Congress' decision to limit the coverage of the ADEA by including the RFOA provision is consistent with the fact that age, unlike race or other classifications protected by Title VII, not uncommonly has relevance to an individual's capacity to engage in certain types of employment. To be sure, Congress recognized that this is not always the case, and that society may perceive those differences to be larger or more consequential than they are in fact. However, as Secretary Wirtz noted in his report, "certain circumstances * * * unquestionably affect older workers more strongly, as a group, than they do younger workers." Wirtz Report 28. Thus, it is not surprising that certain employment criteria that are routinely used may be reasonable despite their adverse impact on older workers as a group. Moreover, intentional discrimination on the basis of age has not occurred at the same levels as discrimination against those protected by Title VII. While the ADEA reflects Congress' intent to give older workers employment opportunities whenever possible, the RFOA provision reflects this historical difference.

Turning to the case before us, we initially note that petitioners have done little more than point out that the pay plan at issue is relatively less generous to older workers than to younger workers. They have not identified any specific test, requirement, or practice within the pay plan that has an adverse impact on older workers. As we held in *Wards Cove*, it is not enough to simply allege that there is a disparate impact on workers, or point to a generalized policy that leads to such an impact. Rather, the employee is " 'responsible for isolating and identifying the *specific* employment practices that are allegedly responsible for any observed statistical disparities.' " 490 U.S., at 656, 104 L.Ed.2d 733, 109 S.Ct. 2115 (emphasis added) (quoting Watson, 487 U.S., at 994, 101 L.Ed.2d 827, 108 S.Ct. 2777). Petitioners have failed to do so. Their failure to identify the specific practice being challenged is the sort of omission that could "result in employers being potentially liable for 'the myriad of innocent causes that may lead to statistical imbalances * * * .' " 490 U.S., at 657, 104 L.Ed.2d 733, 109 S.Ct. 2115. In this case not only did petitioners thus err by failing to identify the relevant practice, but it is also clear from the record that the City's plan was based on reasonable factors other than age.

The plan divided each of five basic positions—police officer, master police officer, police sergeant, police lieutenant, and deputy police chief—into a series of steps and half-steps. The wage for each range was based on a survey of comparable communities in the Southeast. Employees were then assigned a step (or half-step) within their position that corresponded to the lowest step that would still give the individual a 2% raise. Most of the officers were in the three lowest ranks; in each of those ranks there were officers under age 40 and officers over 40. In none did their age affect their compensation. The few officers in the two highest ranks are all over 40. Their raises, though higher in dollar amount than the raises given to junior officers, represented a smaller percentage of their salaries, which of course are higher than the salaries paid to their juniors. They are members of the class complaining of the "disparate impact" of the award.

Petitioners' evidence established two principal facts: First, almost two-thirds (66.2%) of the officers under 40 received raises of more than 10% while less than half (45.3%) of those over 40 did. * * * Second, the average percentage increase for the entire class of officers with less than five years of tenure was somewhat higher than the percentage for those with more seniority. * * * Because older officers tended to occupy more senior positions, on average they received smaller increases when measured as a percentage of their salary. The basic explanation for the differential was the City's perceived need to raise the salaries of junior officers to make them competitive with comparable positions in the market.

Thus, the disparate impact is attributable to the City's decision to give raises based on seniority and position. Reliance on seniority and rank is unquestionably reasonable given the City's goal of raising employees' salaries to match those in surrounding communities. In sum, we hold that the City's decision to grant a larger raise to lower echelon employees for the purpose of bringing salaries in line with that of surrounding police forces was a decision based on a "reasonable factor other than age" that responded to the City's legitimate goal of retaining police officers. While there may have been other reasonable ways for the City to achieve its goals, the one selected was not unreasonable. Unlike the business necessity test, which asks whether there are other ways for the employer to achieve its goals that do not result in a disparate impact on a protected class, the reasonableness inquiry includes no such requirement.

Accordingly, while we do not agree with the Court of Appeals' holding that the disparate-impact theory of recovery is never available under the ADEA, we affirm its judgment.

* * *

THE CHIEF JUSTICE took no part in the decision of this case.

[JUSTICE SCALIA concurred in part and concurred in the judgment, but concluded that the Court should defer to the EEOC's construction of the ADEA.]

JUSTICE O'CONNOR, with whom JUSTICE KENNEDY and JUSTICE THOMAS joined, concurred in the judgment.

"Disparate treatment * * * captures the essence of what Congress sought to prohibit in the [ADEA]. It is the very essence of age discrimination for an older employee to be fired because the employer believes that productivity and competence decline with old age." Hazen Paper Co. v. Biggins, 507 U.S. 604, 610, 123 L.Ed.2d 338, 113 S.Ct. 1701 (1993). In the nearly four decades since the ADEA's enactment, however, we have never read the statute to impose liability upon an employer without proof of discriminatory intent. I decline to join the Court in doing so today.

I would instead affirm the judgment below on the ground that disparate impact claims are not cognizable under the ADEA. The ADEA's text, legislative history, and purposes together make clear that Congress did not intend the statute to authorize such claims. * * *

Although I would not read the ADEA to authorize disparate impact claims, I agree with the Court that, if such claims are allowed, they are strictly circumscribed by the RFOA exemption. * * * That exemption requires only that the challenged employment practice be based on a "reasonable" nonage factor—that is, one that is rationally related to some legitimate business objective. I also agree with the Court, * * * that, if disparate impact claims are to be permitted under the ADEA, they are governed by the standards set forth in our decision in *Wards Cove Packing Co. v. Atonio*, 490 U.S. 642, 104 L.Ed.2d 733, 109 S.Ct. 2115 (1989). That means, as the Court holds, * * * that "a plaintiff must demonstrate that it is the application of a *specific or particular employment practice* that has *created* the disparate impact under attack," *Wards Cove, supra,* at 657, 104 L.Ed.2d 733, 109 S.Ct. 2115 (emphasis added); see also Watson v. Fort Worth Bank & Trust, 487 U.S. 977, 994, 101 L.Ed.2d 827, 108 S.Ct. 2777 (1988) (opinion of O'Connor, J.). It also means that once the employer has produced evidence that its action was based on a reasonable nonage factor, the plaintiff bears the burden of disproving this assertion. Even if petitioners' disparate impact claim were cognizable under the ADEA, that claim clearly would fail in light of these requirements.

NOTES AND QUESTIONS

1. *City of Jackson* was a plurality decision; nevertheless, five justices (Justice Stevens and the three justices who joined his opinion and Justice Scalia in his partial concurrence) recognized the validity of a disparate impact claim under the ADEA. Articulate the ways in which, after *City of Jackson*, an ADEA disparate impact case differs from a Title VII disparate impact case.

2. All the justices in *City of Jackson* seem to agree that the Civil Rights Act of 1991 and its reversal of *Wards Cove,* as well as its express recognition of a Title VII disparate impact cause of action, were not intended to carry over into the ADEA. Do you agree with this analysis? Why would Congress have objected to the Supreme Court's analysis of disparate impact in *Wards Cove* as applied to Title VII but not to the ADEA? For a discussion of the implications of the application of the specific employment practice requirement in *City of Jackson*, see Sandra F. Sperino, *Disparate Impact or Negative Impact?: The Future of Non-Intentional Discrimination Claims Brought by the Elderly*, 13 Elder L.J. 339, 374–77 (2005).

3. What is the likely impact of *City of Jackson* in the workplace? Consider the following perspective:

> [T]he American workforce is getting older and within less than a decade, a majority of all workers will be over the age of forty. A recent report from the BLS indicates that the labor force participation rates of Americans age fifty-five or older has increased

> because uncertainty about retirement income and other issues have kept many of them on the job longer than in the past. The projected growth of this older cohort of workers, and their manifest ambivalence about leaving the labor force, sets the stage for a period of considerable conflict over questions regarding age discrimination in the immediate future. As the American labor force employs a record number of older workers, there can be little doubt that litigation over issues of age discrimination will increase. If the past is any indication, a sizeable number of these cases will entail the question of disparate impact.

Aïda M. Alaka, *Corporate Reorganizations, Job Layoffs, and Age Discrimination: Has* Smith v. City of Jackson *Substantially Expanded the Rights of Older Workers Under the ADEA?,* 70 Albany L.Rev. 143, 174–75 (2006). Another commentator wrote: "[*City of Jackson*] appeared to help employees by recognizing disparate impact claims, but did so by embracing a standard that made pursuing such claims extremely difficult. * * * [T]he limitations that the Court imposed rendered such claims practically unwinnable." Jessica Sturgeon, Note, Smith v. City of Jackson: *Setting an Unreasonable Standard,* 56 Duke L.J. 1377, 1378 (2007).

4. The plurality in *City of Jackson* recognized that the ADEA's Reasonable Factor Other than Age (RFOA) provision plays a role in ADEA disparate impact cases that is different from the role that the business necessity test plays in a Title VII case. How would you characterize the distinction that the Court makes between the reasonableness inquiry and the business necessity test? Following the *City of Jackson* decision, a conflict developed in the circuits over whether the employer or the employee had the burden of persuasion on the RFOA defense. In *Meacham v. Knolls Atomic Power Laboratory*, 554 U.S. 84, 128 S.Ct. 2395, 171 L.Ed.2d 283 (2008), the Supreme Court held that the employer has a burden of production and persuasion to prove the reasonable factor other than age.

5. What would be an example of an *unreasonable* "factor other than age" that would not itself be unlawful? Is *Meacham* likely to constrain customary business practices of U.S. employers?

6. In light of the Court's analysis of ADEA disparate impact claims in *City of Jackson* and *Meacham,* how would you analyze the following hypothetical situation, which is based on an actual case described in Michael J. Myers, *Wal-Mart, ShopKo Cart Gathering: A Case for* Smith v. City of Jackson *ADEA Disparate Impact?,* 8 Marq. Elder's Advisor 91, 91–92 (2006)? In response to concerns about rising health-related costs for its employees, including absenteeism and health benefits, Buy-Smart, a large discount retailer, initiates a new workplace policy that it believes will help reduce the risks of obesity among its workforce. The policy requires that all customer service representatives engage in some physical activity during the workday, including retrieving shopping carts from the parking lot, assisting customers with lifting large items into their shopping carts and transferring them to

their vehicles, and performing certain custodial tasks such as sweeping floors and cleaning windows. A sixty-five-year-old woman who has worked as a cashier at Buy-Smart for ten years is discharged because—due to her age-related arthritis and a heart condition—she is unable to perform the physical activities required under the new policy. Assume that she would not be considered as having a "disability" for purposes of the Americans with Disability Act. Would she have a viable claim under the ADEA that Buy-Smart's physical activity requirement has a disparate impact on older workers? Would Buy-Smart be able to meet its affirmative defense under the RFOA provision of the ADEA?

7. *The Defense Based on Reasonable Factors Other Than Age (RFOA)*: The legislative history is not particularly helpful in illuminating the substantive content of the RFOA defense. The legislative history is discussed in Judith J. Johnson, *Rehabilitate the Age Discrimination in Employment Act: Resuscitate the "Reasonable Factors Other Than Age," Defense and the Disparate Impact Theory,* 55 Hastings L.J. 1399 (2004), *citing* Steven J. Kaminshine, *The Cost of Older Workers, Disparate Impact, and the Age Discrimination in Employment Act,* 42 Fla. L. Rev. 229, 231–32 (1990); Howard Eglit, *The Age Discrimination in Employment Act's Forgotten Affirmative Defense: The Reasonable Factors Other Than Age Exception*, 66 B.U.L.Rev. 155 (1986); and Toni J. Querry, Comment, *A Rose by Any Other Name No Longer Smells as Sweet: Disparate Treatment Discrimination and the Age Proxy Doctrine After Hazen Paper Co. v. Biggins,* 81 Cornell L.Rev. 530 (1996).

CHAPTER 14

DISCRIMINATION BECAUSE OF DISABILITY

■ ■ ■

A. INTRODUCTION

The elimination of discrimination against individuals with disabilities in transportation, housing, public services, public accommodations, and employment is now a significant component of the national commitment to equality. The two most important federal statutes that prohibit discrimination because of disabilities are the Americans with Disabilities Act of 1990 (ADA), as amended by the ADA Amendments Act of 2008 (ADAAA), and the Rehabilitation Act of 1973, 29 U.S.C. §§ 701–797(b). Of these two statutes, the ADA is the most comprehensive. The ADA, which President Bush signed into law on July 26, 1990, provides comprehensive civil rights protection to individuals with disabilities, which is similar to the protection against discrimination because of race, color, sex, national origin, and religion that is provided to individuals under the Civil Rights Act of 1964. Congress enacted the ADAAA in response to several Supreme Court decisions that limited the plaintiff class through the Court's definition of "disability." Pub. L. No. 110–325, 122 Stat. 3553 (codified at 42 U.S.C. § 12101–13). The ADA is divided into five titles. Title I, which is the subject of this chapter, covers discrimination in employment. Codified at ADA §§ 101–108, 42 U.S.C. §§ 12111–12118, Title I covers essentially the same employers, employment agencies, and labor organizations that Title VII covers, and it incorporates Title VII's administrative exhaustion requirements and remedies. ADA § 107, 42 U.S.C. § 12117. Title II extends the prohibition against discrimination on the basis of disabilities to all programs, activities, and services of state and local governments or agencies, regardless of whether these entities receive federal financial assistance. Title II also covers public transportation. Title III prohibits discrimination against individuals with disabilities by privately run places of public accommodation and by public transportation services provided by private entities. Title IV covers telecommunications, and Title V contains several miscellaneous provisions. *See generally* Bureau of Nat'l Affairs, The Americans with Disabilities Act: A Practical and Legal Guide to Impact, Enforcement and Compliance 63–76 (1990) (a section-by-section analysis of the ADA); Peter A. Susser, Disability Discrimination and the Workplace (2005).

Because it so broadly prohibits discrimination in employment, public services, transportation, and public accommodations, the ADA has been heralded as the twentieth century Emancipation Proclamation and the Bill of Rights for an estimated forty-three million individuals with disabilities. *See, e.g.*, H.R.Rep.No. 101–485, pt.3, at 42 (1990), *reprinted in* 1990 U.S.C.C.A.N. 303, 464–66; 135 Cong.Rec. S10, 789 (daily ed. Sept.7, 1989) (statement of Sen. Kennedy). One commentator has stated that:

> [t]he ADA is the most comprehensive piece of disability civil rights legislation ever enacted, and the most important piece of civil rights legislation since the 1964 Civil Rights Act. This legislation will transform the landscape of American society and will have a profound effect on what it means to be disabled. * * *
>
> From a civil rights perspective, a profound shift in disability public policy occurred in the 1970s. The passage of the first piece of cross-disability civil rights legislation, section 504 of the Rehabilitation Act of 1973, challenged traditional ideas about disability. This legislation, in turn, gave rise to a highly visible and active disability rights movement.
>
> Section 504 of the Rehabilitation Act of 1973 transformed disability public policy in several ways. First, it adopted a cross-disability approach, recognizing that people with different disabilities suffered similar problems in employment, education, and access to society. Second, section 504 used the term "discrimination" for the first time to describe the segregation and exclusion of persons with disabilities. This terminology changed the focus away from the limitations imposed by a disability, and turned it toward the limitations posed by society through attitudinal and architectural barriers. Third, section 504 broadly defined disability to protect those with a current disability, those with a history of disability, or those perceived to have a disability. Finally, and most important, section 504 evidenced Congress' recognition that disability discrimination is a federal civil rights issue. In modeling section 504 on earlier race and sex discrimination statutes, Congress placed disability discrimination firmly within the federal civil rights arena.

Arlene Mayerson, *The Americans with Disabilities Act—An Historic Overview*, 7 Lab.Law. 1, 1–2 (1991). *See generally* Joseph P. Shapiro, No Pity: People with Disabilities Forging a New Civil Rights Movement (1993) (providing a detailed history of the disability rights movement); Bureau of Nat'l Affairs, The Americans with Disabilities Act: A Practical and Legal Guide to Impact, Enforcement and Compliance (1990) (providing a social, legal, and legislative history of the ADA). Beginning in the 1970s, Congress rejected the policy of custodialism for individuals with disabilities, opting instead for a policy of nondiscrimination. *See* Timothy M. Cook, *The Americans with Disabilities Act: The Move to Integration*, 64 Temp.L.Rev. 393 (1991).

Congress's factual findings in the ADA emphasize the need for prohibiting discrimination on the basis of disabilities in American society. In the ADA, Congress found that:

> individuals with disabilities are a discrete and insular minority who have been faced with restrictions and limitations, subjected to a history of purposeful unequal treatment, and relegated to a position of political powerlessness in our society, based on characteristics that are beyond the control of such individuals and resulting from stereotypic assumptions not truly indicative of the individual ability of such individuals to participate in, and contribute to, society[.]

ADA § 2(a)(7), 42 U.S.C. § 12101(a)(7) (2008), *amended by* 42 U.S.C.§ 12101 (2009). The characterization of individuals with disabilities as a "discrete and insular minority" arises out of the famous footnote 4 of *United States v. Carolene Products Co.*, 304 U.S. 144, 152–53 n.4, 58 S.Ct. 778, 783–84 n.4, 82 L.Ed.1234 (1938) where the Supreme Court used the phrase to describe minorities who deserve constitutional protection from discriminatory conduct of governmental actors. *See* Michael L. Perlin, Mental Disability Law: Civil and Criminal § 1.03, at 6 (1989). Because the Supreme Court used this phrase to limit the plaintiff class, the ADAAA eliminated the phrase in the codified findings, but the legislative history reaffirmed the underlying principles. H.R. Rep. No. 110–730 (I) (2008). Congress also enacted the ADA to ensure that the federal government plays a central role in enforcing the "national mandate" of the Act. *Id.* § 2(b)(1), (3), 42 U.S.C. § 12101(b)(1), (3).

Claims arising under the ADA and the Rehabilitation Act have raised and continue to raise a host of difficult and complex issues that are, in many respects, unique to disability jurisprudence. Disability law is one of the most rapidly developing fields in employment discrimination law. Because the case law and scholarly commentary on disability discrimination is so voluminous, only a few selected issues can be treated in a broad-based course on employment discrimination law. Three major themes have emerged in our study of discrimination law: the model or framework for proving discrimination; membership in each protected class; and justification for employer decisions or actions that exclude those members. These themes, as well as a few other selected issues are covered in this chapter. The remainder of this section introduces the statutes covering disability discrimination. Section B of this chapter covers the definition of "discrimination" under the ADA. As amended by the ADAAA, Section C explores the definition of disability. Section D focuses on the issues of qualifications, the direct threat defense, and undue hardship. Section E deals briefly with medical inquiries, medical examinations, and medical benefits. As you read through the materials in this chapter, consider whether the ADA has met its initial promise as a transformative piece of civil rights legislation.

The Americans with Disabilities Act of 1990 ("The ADA"). The ADA, as amended, broadly prohibits discrimination in employment on the basis of disability by providing that "[n]o covered entity shall discriminate against a qualified individual on the basis of disability in regard to job application procedures, the hiring, advancement, or discharge of employees, employee compensation, job training, and other terms, conditions, and privileges of employment." ADA § 102(a), 42 U.S.C. § 12112(a). In addition to prohibiting discrimination as defined by disparate treatment or disparate impact, the ADA imposes upon employers the affirmative obligation to "make reasonable accommodations to the known physical or mental limitations of a qualified individual" unless doing so "would impose an undue hardship on the operation of the business of the covered entity." ADA § 102(5)(A), 42 U.S.C. § 12112(5)(A). The duty imposed under the ADA to provide reasonable accommodations to qualified individuals with disabilities is the same affirmative obligation that is imposed upon entities that are covered by the Rehabilitation Act. A "qualified individual" is defined as "an individual who, with or without reasonable accommodation, can perform the essential functions of the employment position that such individual holds or desires." *Id.* § 101(8), 42 U.S.C. § 12111(8). Thus, the concept of reasonable accommodation occurs in both the determination of discrimination and the determination of qualifications.

The ADA Amendments Act of 2008 ("The ADAAA"). After the Supreme Court restricted the definition of disability in a series of ADA cases, Congress passed the ADAAA to broaden coverage of the ADA. In addition to reasserting the original intent of the ADA, the ADAAA clarified that the definition of disability, changed the prohibition from discrimination against an "individual with a disability" to "on the basis of disability," and clarified the prohibition against discrimination on the basis of "being regarded" as having a disability.

The Rehabilitation Act of 1973. Enacted seventeen years before the ADA, the Rehabilitation Act of 1973 was designed to "promote and expand employment opportunities in the public and private sectors for [individuals with disabilities] and place such individuals in employment." 29 U.S.C. § 701(8). *See* Consol. Rail Corp. v. Darrone, 465 U.S. 624, 626, 104 S.Ct. 1248, 1250, 79 L.Ed.2d 568 (1984); *see generally* Bureau of Nat'l Affairs, The Americans with Disabilities Act: A Practical and Legal Guide to Impact, Enforcement and Compliance 10–23 (1990). Section 501 of the Rehabilitation Act covers all departments and agencies of the federal government, including the United States Postal Service, and imposes upon them the obligation to develop and implement affirmative action plans for the hiring, placement, and advancement of individuals with disabilities. 29 U.S.C. § 791. Section 503 also covers entities that contract with federal departments or agencies to provide goods and services of more than $10,000. Section 503, like § 501, requires these federal contractors to take affirmative action to employ and promote individuals with disabilities. 29 U.S.C. § 793. Both §§ 501 and 503 have been interpreted to prohibit discrimination as well. *See* Gardner v. Morris, 752 F.2d 1271 (8th Cir.1985) (§ 501); Moon v. Sec'y, U.S. Dep't of Labor, 747 F.2d 599 (11th Cir.1984) (§ 503), *cert. denied*, 471 U.S. 1055, 105 S.Ct. 2117, 85 L.Ed.2d 481 (1985). Section 504 covers all entities that receive federal funds, as well as all the programs and activities conducted by federal agencies, and it, too, prohibits discrimination because of disabilities. 29 U.S.C. § 794.

As originally enacted in 1973, the Rehabilitation Act used the term "handicap"; however, Congress amended the Rehabilitation Act in 1992 to substitute the term "disability" for "handicap." *See* Pub. L. No. 102–569, 102(p) (32), 106 Stat. 4344, 4360 (1992). The change in terminology was intended to reflect a new sensitivity to the impact of descriptive language. The phrase "individual with a disability" was formulated to "convey the message that people are not disabled, but are merely encumbered with disabilities." Brent Edward Kidwell, *The Americans with Disabilities Act of 1990: Overview and Analysis*, 26 Ind.L.Rev. 707, 708 n.5 (1993); *see* H.R.Rep.No. 101–484(II), 101st Cong., 2d Sess. 1, 50–53, *reprinted in* 1990 U.S.C.C.A.N. 303, 332–35. Section 504 of the Rehabilitation Act, 29 U.S.C. § 794(a), provides that "[n]o otherwise qualified individual with a disability in the United States * * * shall, solely by reason of her or his disability, be excluded from the participation in, be denied the benefits of, or be subjected to discrimination under any program or activity receiving federal financial assistance * * * ."

Relationship Between the ADA and Rehabilitation Act. The primary focus of this chapter is on Title I of the ADA because it is by far the most comprehensive federal legislation providing protection in the private sector to individuals with disabilities. The materials in this chapter, however, include developments under the Rehabilitation Act because the statutory language and legislative history of both the ADA and the 1992 amendments to the Rehabilitation Act clearly indicate that the legal standards for a finding of unlawful disability discrimination are the same under both statutes.

Regulations. Congress directed the EEOC, which has administrative enforcement responsibility over ADA claims, to issue regulations to carry out the mandate of the ADA. ADA § 106, 42 U.S.C. § 12116. In response, the EEOC issued regulations, 29 C.F.R. § 1630, interpretive directives, and guidelines. For a discussion of the EEOC regulations on the ADA, see Elliot H. Shaller & Dean A. Rosen, *A Guide to the EEOC's Final Regulations on the Americans with Disabilities Act*, 17 Empl.Rel.L.J. 405 (1991–1992). In the ADAAA, Congress authorized the EEOC, the Attorney General, and the Secretary of Transportation to issue regulations. ADA § 506, 42 U.S.C.A § 12205a (2009). The regulations to implement the ADAA became effective on May 24, 2011. Regulations to Implement the Equal Employment Provisions of the Americans With Disabilities Act, codified at 29 C.F.R. § 1630, effective May 14, 2011. The Department of Health and Human Services (HHS) has also promulgated administrative regulations to enforce § 504 of the Rehabilitation Act. 45 C.F.R. § 84.3.

NOTES AND QUESTIONS

1. *Covered Entities*: The ADA uses the phrase "covered entity" to define who is subject to Title I. ADA § 101(2), 42 U.S.C. § 12111(2), defines "covered entity" to mean "an employer, employment agency, labor organization, or joint labor-management committee." "Employer" is further defined in a way that parallels the statutory definition of "employer" under Title VII. *Compare id.* § 102(5)(A), 42 U.S.C. § 12111(5)(A), *with* Title VII, § 701(b), 42 U.S.C. § 2000e–1(b). See Chapter 2. As of July 26, 1994, private employers with fifteen or more employees became subject to the ADA. *Id.*

2. *Federal Employers*: The federal government is specifically excluded from coverage under the ADA. ADA § 101(5)(B), 42 U.S.C. § 12111(5)(B). Congress deemed it unnecessary to extend coverage of the ADA to the federal government in view of the fact that the Rehabilitation Act of 1973 currently protects federal employees from discrimination because of disabilities.

3. *State and Municipal Employers*: In *Board of Trustees of University of Alabama v. Garrett*, 531 U.S. 356, 121 S.Ct. 955, 148 L.Ed.2d 866 (2001), the Supreme Court held that the Eleventh Amendment bars private ADA actions brought against unconsenting states for money damages.

4. Individuals filing employment discrimination claims under Title I of the ADA, like individuals filing claims under Title VII of the Civil Rights Act of 1964, must first exhaust administrative remedies before the EEOC. In fact the ADA specifically provides that the "powers, remedies, and procedures" in Title VII are equally applicable in ADA claims. ADA § 107(a), 42 U.S.C. § 12117(a).

5. There is some dispute over whether public employees may rely upon Title II of the ADA to seek relief from discrimination in employment. The definition of "a qualified individual with a disability" in Title II is broader than the definition under Title I. Title II protects individuals who "with or without reasonable modifications to rules, policies, the removal of architectural, communication, or transportation barriers, or the provisions of auxiliary aids and services, meet the essential eligibility requirements for the

receipt of services or the participation in programs or activities provided by a public entity." 42 U.S.C. § 12121(2). Section 802 of the ADA (Title II), 42 U.S.C. § 12132, provides, in pertinent part, that "no qualified individual with a disability shall, by reason of such disability, be excluded from participation in or be denied the benefits of the services, programs, or activities of a public entity, or be subjected to discrimination by any such entity."

"Public entity" is defined to include any state or local government and any department, agency, special purpose district, or other instrumentality of a state or local government. ADA § 801A, 42 U.S.C. § 12131(A)–(B). In *Bledsoe v. Palm Beach County Soil & Water Conservation District*, 133 F.3d 816 (11th Cir.1998), *cert. denied* 525 U.S. 826, 119 S.Ct. 72, 142 L.Ed.2d 57 (1998) the Eleventh Circuit discussed the split of authority on the issue and held that public employees may bring disability-based employment discrimination claims against public entitles as defined in Title II. In *Bledsoe*, the court broadly construed the statutory phrases "services, programs and activities" and "subjected to discrimination by any such entity." In support of its statutory interpretation, the court relied upon the legislative history of the ADA and the Department of Justice regulations promulgated to enforce Title II. The effect of the *Bledsoe* decision is that a public employee who has an ADA employment discrimination claim against a state or local government employer can avoid the administrative exhaustion requirements of Title I and go directly to court to seek relief under Title II. The Fifth Circuit found otherwise in *Taylor v. City of Shreveport*, 798 F.3d 276 (5th Cir.2015); *see also* Zimmerman v. Or. Dep't of Justice, 170 F.3d 1169 (9th Cir.1999), *cert. denied* 531 U.S. 1189, 121 S.Ct. 1186, 149 L.Ed.2d 103 (2001); *see generally* Wendy Wilkinson, *Judicially Crafted Barriers to Bringing Suit Under the Americans with Disabilities Act*, 38 S.Tex.L.Rev. 907, 931–33 (1997).

B. THE MEANING OF "DISCRIMINATION" UNDER THE ADA

The definition of discrimination under the ADA includes both the disparate impact and disparate treatment theories of discrimination. *See* ADA § 102(b)(1), (b)(6), (b)(7), 42 U.S.C. § 12112(b)(1), (b)(6), (b)(7). Moreover, the ADA definition of disability discrimination places an affirmative obligation on covered entities to make reasonable accommodations that will allow qualified individuals with disabilities to perform the essential functions of the job that they hold or desire. *Id.* § 102(b)(5)(A), 42 U.S.C. § 12112(5)(A).

Professor Robert Burgdorf, who drafted the first ADA bill, which was introduced in Congress in 1988, has written that:

> [d]isability nondiscrimination laws, such as the Americans with Disabilities Act of 1990 (ADA), and the disability rights movement which spawned them have, at their core, a central premise that is both simple and profound. That premise is that

> people denominated as "disabled" are just people, not different in any critical way from other people. Paradoxically, commentators, enforcement agencies and the courts, which manifest good intentions, have frequently interpreted and applied these laws in ways that reinforce a diametrically opposite premise—that people with disabilities are significantly different, special and need exceptional status and protection. One is reminded of Justice Brandeis's admonition that citizens should be most on guard "when Government's purposes are beneficent" and that the greatest dangers arise from "encroachment by [people] of zeal, well-meaning but without understanding."

Robert L. Burgdorf, Jr., *"Substantially Limited" Protection from Disability Discrimination: The Special Treatment Model and Misconstructions of the Definition of Disability*, 42 Vill.L.Rev. 409, 411 (1997). As you read the cases and materials in this chapter, evaluate them in light of Professor Burgdorf's critique, as well as the continuing debate about the aims of employment discrimination laws. What should be the purpose of the laws prohibiting employment discrimination because of disability? Equal treatment? Equal opportunity? Special treatment? Consider also that Congress stated in the ADA's "Findings and Purposes" that "the Nation's proper goals regarding individuals with disabilities are to assure equality of opportunity, full participation, independent living, and economic self-sufficiency for such individuals * * * ." ADA § 2(a)(8), 42 U.S.C. § 12101(a)(8). Does the definition of discrimination in the ADA suggest that Congress intended to do more than simply eradicate discrimination against qualified individuals with disabilities? If so, what might explain the need to go beyond just simply eradicating discrimination on the basis of disability?

RAYTHEON, CO. V. HERNANDEZ

Supreme Court of the United States, 2003.
540 U.S. 44, 124 S.Ct. 513, 157 L.Ed.2d 357.

THOMAS, J., delivered the opinion of the Court, in which all other Members joined, except SOUTER, J., who took no part in the decision of the case, and BREYER, J., who took no part in the consideration or decision of the case.

The Americans with Disabilities Act of 1990 (ADA) makes it unlawful for an employer, with respect to hiring, to "discriminate against a qualified individual with a disability because of the disability of such individual." § 12112(a). * * * The United States Court of Appeals for the Ninth Circuit held that an employer's unwritten policy not to rehire employees who left the company for violating personal conduct rules contravenes the ADA, at least as applied to employees who were lawfully forced to resign for illegal drug use but have since been rehabilitated.

Because the Ninth Circuit improperly applied a disparate-impact analysis in a disparate-treatment case in order to reach this holding, we vacate its judgment and remand the case for further proceedings consistent with this opinion. * * *

I

Respondent, Joel Hernandez, worked for Hughes Missile Systems for 25 years. On July 11, 1991, respondent's appearance and behavior at work suggested that he might be under the influence of drugs or alcohol. Pursuant to company policy, respondent took a drug test, which came back positive for cocaine. Respondent subsequently admitted that he had been up late drinking beer and using cocaine the night before the test. Because respondent's behavior violated petitioner's workplace conduct rules, respondent was forced to resign. Respondent's "Employee Separation Summary" indicated as the reason for separation: "discharge for personal conduct (quit in lieu of discharge)."

More than two years later, on January 24, 1994, respondent applied to be rehired by petitioner. Respondent stated on his application that he had previously been employed by petitioner. He also attached two reference letters to the application, one from his pastor, stating that respondent was a "faithful and active member" of the church, and the other from an Alcoholics Anonymous counselor, stating that respondent attends Alcoholics Anonymous meetings regularly and is in recovery.

Joanne Bockmiller, an employee in the company's Labor Relations Department, reviewed respondent's application. Bockmiller testified in her deposition that since respondent's application disclosed his prior employment with the company, she pulled his personnel file and reviewed his employee separation summary. She then rejected respondent's application. Bockmiller insisted that the company had a policy against rehiring employees who were terminated for workplace misconduct. Thus, when she reviewed the employment separation summary and found that respondent had been discharged for violating workplace conduct rules, she rejected respondent's application. She testified, in particular, that she did not know that respondent was a former drug addict when she made the employment decision and did not see anything that would constitute a "record of" addiction.

Respondent subsequently filed a charge with the Equal Employment Opportunity Commission (EEOC). Respondent's charge of discrimination indicated that petitioner did not give him a reason for his nonselection, but that respondent believed he had been discriminated against in violation of the ADA.

Petitioner responded to the charge by submitting a letter to the EEOC, in which George M. Medina, Sr., Manager of Diversity Development, wrote:

> The ADA specifically exempts from protection individuals currently engaging in the illegal use of drugs when the covered entity acts on the basis of that use. Contrary to Complainant's unfounded allegation, his non-selection for rehire is not based on any legitimate disability. Rather, Complainant's application was rejected based on his demonstrated drug use while previously employed and the complete lack of evidence indicating successful drug rehabilitation.
>
> The Company maintains it's [*sic*] right to deny re-employment to employees terminated for violation of Company rules and regulations. * * * Complainant has provided no evidence to alter the Company's position that Complainant's conduct while employed by [petitioner] makes him ineligible for rehire.

This response, together with evidence that the letters submitted with respondent's employment application may have alerted Bockmiller to the reason for respondent's prior termination, led the EEOC to conclude that petitioner may have "rejected [respondent's] application based on his record of past alcohol and drug use." The EEOC thus found that there was "reasonable cause to believe that [respondent] was denied hire to the position of Product Test Specialist because of his disability." The EEOC issued a right-to-sue letter, and respondent subsequently filed this action alleging a violation of the ADA.

Respondent proceeded through discovery on the theory that the company rejected his application because of his record of drug addiction and/or because he was regarded as being a drug addict. See 42 U.S.C. §§ 12102(2)(B)–(C). * * * In response to petitioner's motion for summary judgment, respondent for the first time argued in the alternative that if the company really did apply a neutral no-rehire policy in his case, petitioner still violated the ADA because such a policy has a disparate impact. The District Court granted petitioner's motion for summary judgment with respect to respondent's disparate-treatment claim. However, the District Court refused to consider respondent's disparate-impact claim because respondent had failed to plead or raise the theory in a timely manner.

The Court of Appeals agreed with the District Court that respondent had failed timely to raise his disparate-impact claim. *Hernandez v. Hughes Missile Systems Co.,* 298 F.3d 1030, 1037, n.20 (9th Cir.2002). In addressing respondent's disparate-treatment claim, the Court of Appeals proceeded under the familiar burden-shifting approach first adopted by this Court in *McDonnell Douglas Corp. v. Green,* 411 U.S. 792, 93 S.Ct. 1817, 36 L.Ed.2d 668 (1973). First, the Ninth Circuit found that with respect to respondent's prima facie case of discrimination, there were genuine issues of material fact regarding whether respondent was qualified for the position for which he sought to be rehired, and whether the reason for petitioner's refusal to rehire him was his past record of drug addiction.[4] The Court of Appeals thus held that with respect to respondent's prima facie case of discrimination, respondent had proffered sufficient evidence to preclude a grant of summary judgment. Because petitioner does not challenge this aspect of the Ninth Circuit's decision, we do not address it here.

The Court of Appeals then moved to the next step of *McDonnell Douglas,* where the burden shifts to the defendant to provide a legitimate, nondiscriminatory reason for its employment action. Here, petitioner contends that Bockmiller applied the neutral policy against rehiring employees previously terminated for violating workplace conduct rules and that this neutral company policy constituted a legitimate and nondiscriminatory reason for its decision not to rehire respondent. The Court of Appeals, although admitting that petitioner's no-rehire rule was lawful on its face, held the policy to be unlawful "as applied to former drug addicts whose only work-related offense was testing positive because of their addiction." 298 F.3d, at 1036. The Court of Appeals concluded that petitioner's application of a neutral no-rehire policy was not a legitimate, nondiscriminatory reason for rejecting respondent's application:

> "Maintaining a blanket policy against rehire of *all* former employees who violated company policy not only screens out persons with a record of addiction who have been successfully rehabilitated, but may well result, as [petitioner] contends it did here, in the staff member who makes the employment decision remaining unaware of the "disability" and thus of the fact that she is committing an unlawful act. * * * Additionally, we hold that a policy that serves to bar the reemployment of a drug addict despite his successful rehabilitation violates the ADA." *Id.* at 1036–37.

In other words, while ostensibly evaluating whether petitioner had proffered a legitimate, nondiscriminatory reason for failing to rehire respondent sufficient to rebut respondent's prima facie showing of disparate treatment, the Court of Appeals held that a neutral no-rehire policy could never suffice in a case where the employee was terminated

[4] The Court of Appeals noted that "it is possible that a drug *user* may not be 'disabled' under the ADA if his drug use does not rise to the level of an addiction which substantially limits one or more of his major life activities." 298 F.3d, at 1033–1034, n.9. The parties do not dispute that respondent was "disabled" at the time he quit in lieu of discharge and thus a record of the disability exists. We therefore need not decide in this case whether respondent's employment record constitutes a "record of addiction," which triggers the protections of the ADA. The parties are also not disputing in this Court whether respondent was qualified for the position for which he applied.

for illegal drug use, because such a policy has a disparate impact on recovering drug addicts. In so holding, the Court of Appeals erred by conflating the analytical framework for disparate-impact and disparate-treatment claims. Had the Court of Appeals correctly applied the disparate-treatment framework, it would have been obliged to conclude that a neutral no-rehire policy is, by definition, a legitimate, nondiscriminatory reason under the ADA. * * * And thus the only remaining question would be whether respondent could produce sufficient evidence from which a jury could conclude that "petitioner's stated reason for respondent's rejection was in fact pretext." *McDonnell Douglas, supra,* at 804.

II

This Court has consistently recognized a distinction between claims of discrimination based on disparate treatment and claims of discrimination based on disparate impact. The Court has said that " '[d]isparate treatment' * * * is the most easily understood type of discrimination. The employer simply treats some people less favorably than others because of their race, color, religion, sex, or [other protected characteristic]." *Teamsters v. United States,* 431 U.S. 324, 335, n.15, 97 S.Ct. 1843, 52 L.Ed.2d 396 (1977). See also *Hazen Paper Co. v. Biggins,* 507 U.S. 604, 609, 113 S.Ct. 1701, 123 L.Ed.2d 338 (1993) (discussing disparate-treatment claims in the context of the Age Discrimination in Employment Act of 1967). Liability in a disparate-treatment case "depends on whether the protected trait * * * actually motivated the employer's decision." *Id.,* at 610. By contrast, disparate-impact claims "involve employment practices that are facially neutral in their treatment of different groups but that in fact fall more harshly on one group than another and cannot be justified by business necessity." *Teamsters, supra,* at 335–336, n.15. Under a disparate-impact theory of discrimination, "a facially neutral employment practice may be deemed [illegally discriminatory] without evidence of the employer's subjective intent to discriminate that is required in a 'disparate-treatment' case." *Wards Cove Packing Co. v. Atonio,* 490 U.S. 642, 645–646, 109 S.Ct. 2115, 104 L.Ed.2d 733 (1989), superseded by statute on other grounds, Civil Rights Act of 1991, § 105, 105 Stat. 1074–1075, 42 U.S.C. § 2000e–2(k) (1994 ed.).

Both disparate-treatment and disparate-impact claims are cognizable under the ADA. See 42 U.S.C. § 12112(b) (defining "discriminate" to include "utilizing standards, criteria, or methods of administration * * * that have the effect of discrimination on the basis of disability" and "using qualification standards, employment tests or other selection criteria that screen out or tend to screen out an individual with a disability"). Because "the factual issues, and therefore the character of the evidence presented, differ when the plaintiff claims that a facially neutral employment policy has a discriminatory impact on protected classes," *Texas Dept. of*

Community Affairs v. Burdine, 450 U.S. 248, 252, n.5, 101 S.Ct. 1089, 67 L.Ed.2d 207 (1981), courts must be careful to distinguish between these theories. Here, respondent did not timely pursue a disparate-impact claim. Rather, the District Court concluded, and the Court of Appeals agreed, that respondent's case was limited to a disparate-treatment theory, that the company refused to rehire respondent because it regarded respondent as being disabled and/or because of respondent's record of a disability.

Petitioner's proffer of its neutral no-rehire policy plainly satisfied its obligation under *McDonnell Douglas* to provide a legitimate, nondiscriminatory reason for refusing to rehire respondent. Thus, the only relevant question before the Court of Appeals, after petitioner presented a neutral explanation for its decision not to rehire respondent, was whether there was sufficient evidence from which a jury could conclude that petitioner did make its employment decision based on respondent's status as disabled despite petitioner's proffered explanation. Instead, the Court of Appeals concluded that, as a matter of law, a neutral no-rehire policy was not a legitimate, nondiscriminatory reason sufficient to defeat a prima facie case of discrimination.[6] The Court of Appeals did not even attempt, in the remainder of its opinion, to treat this claim as one involving only disparate treatment. Instead, the Court of Appeals observed that petitioner's policy "screens out persons with a record of addiction," and further noted that the company had not raised a business necessity defense, 298 F.3d, at 1036–1037, and n.19, factors that pertain to disparate-impact claims but not disparate-treatment claims. See, *e.g., Grano v. Department of Development of Columbus,* 637 F.2d 1073, 1081 (6th Cir.1980) ("In a disparate impact situation * * * the issue is whether a neutral selection device * * * screens out disproportionate numbers of [the protected class]"). * * * By improperly focusing on these factors, the Court of Appeals ignored the fact that petitioner's no-rehire policy is a quintessential legitimate, nondiscriminatory reason for refusing to rehire an employee who was terminated for violating workplace conduct rules. If petitioner did indeed apply a neutral, generally applicable no-rehire policy in rejecting respondent's application, petitioner's decision not to rehire respondent can, in no way, be said to have been motivated by respondent's disability.

The Court of Appeals rejected petitioner's legitimate, nondiscriminatory reason for refusing to rehire respondent because it

[6] The Court of Appeals characterized respondent's workplace misconduct as merely "testing positive because of [his] addiction." 298 F.3d, at 1036. To the extent that the court suggested that, because respondent's workplace misconduct is related to his disability, petitioner's refusal to rehire respondent on account of that workplace misconduct violated the ADA, we point out that we have rejected a similar argument in the context of the Age Discrimination in Employment Act. See *Hazen Paper Co. v. Biggins,* 507 U.S. 604, 611, 113 S.Ct. 1701, 123 L.Ed.2d 338 (1993).

"serves to bar the re-employment of a drug addict despite his successful rehabilitation." 298 F.3d, at 1036–1037. We hold that such an analysis is inapplicable to a disparate-treatment claim. Once respondent had made a prima facie showing of discrimination, the next question for the Court of Appeals was whether petitioner offered a legitimate, nondiscriminatory reason for its actions so as to demonstrate that its actions were not motivated by respondent's disability. To the extent that the Court of Appeals strayed from this task by considering not only discriminatory intent but also discriminatory impact, we vacate its judgment and remand the case for further proceedings consistent with this opinion. * * *

US AIRWAYS, INC. V. BARNETT

Supreme Court of the United States, 2002.
535 U.S. 391, 122 S.Ct. 1516, 152 L.Ed.2d 589.

JUSTICE BREYER delivered the opinion of the Court.

The Americans with Disabilities Act of 1990 (ADA or Act) prohibits an employer from discriminating against an "individual with a disability" who, with "reasonable accommodation," can perform the essential functions of the job. § § 12112(a) and (b) (1994 ed.). This case, arising in the context of summary judgment, asks us how the Act resolves a potential conflict between: (1) the interests of a disabled worker who seeks assignment to a particular position as a "reasonable accommodation," and (2) the interests of other workers with superior rights to bid for the job under an employer's seniority system. In such a case, does the accommodation demand trump the seniority system?

In our view, the seniority system will prevail in the run of cases. As we interpret the statute, to show that a requested accommodation conflicts with the rules of a seniority system is ordinarily to show that the accommodation is not "reasonable." Hence such a showing will entitle an employer/defendant to summary judgment on the question—unless there is more. The plaintiff remains free to present evidence of special circumstances that make "reasonable" a seniority rule exception in the particular case. And such a showing will defeat the employer's demand for summary judgment. Fed. Rule Civ. Proc. 56(e).

I

In 1990, Robert Barnett, the plaintiff and respondent here, injured his back while working in a cargo-handling position at petitioner US Airways, Inc. He invoked seniority rights and transferred to a less physically demanding mailroom position. Under US Airways' seniority system, that position, like others, periodically became open to seniority-based employee bidding. In 1992, Barnett learned that at least two employees senior to him intended to bid for the mailroom job. He asked US Airways to accommodate his disability-imposed limitations by making an exception that would allow him to remain in the mailroom. After permitting Barnett to continue his mailroom work for five months while it considered the matter, US Airways eventually decided not to make an exception. And Barnett lost his job.

Barnett then brought this ADA suit claiming, among other things, that he was an "individual with a disability" capable of performing the essential functions of the mailroom job, that the mailroom job amounted to a "reasonable accommodation" of his disability, and that US Airways, in refusing to assign him the job, unlawfully discriminated against him. US Airways moved for summary judgment. It supported its motion with appropriate affidavits contending that its "well-established" seniority system granted other employees the right to obtain the mailroom position.

The District Court found that the undisputed facts about seniority warranted summary judgment in US Airways' favor. * * * The court said:

> * * * it seems clear that the U.S. Air employees were justified in relying upon the [seniority] policy. As such, any significant alteration of that policy would result in undue hardship to both the company and its non-disabled employees.

An en banc panel of the United States Court of Appeals for the Ninth Circuit reversed. It said that the presence of a seniority system is merely "a factor in the undue hardship analysis." And it held that "[a] case-by-case fact intensive analysis is required to determine whether any particular reassignment would constitute an undue hardship to the employer." US Airways petitioned for certiorari, asking us to decide whether "the [ADA] requires an employer to reassign a disabled employee to a position as a 'reasonable accommodation' even though another employee is entitled to hold the position under the employer's bona fide and established seniority system." * * *

II

In answering the question presented, we must consider the following statutory provisions. First, the ADA says that an employer may not "discriminate against a qualified individual with a disability." 42 U.S.C. § 12112(a). Second, the ADA says that a "qualified" individual includes "an individual with a disability who, *with* or without *reasonable accommodation,* can perform the essential functions of" the relevant "employment position." § 12111(8) (emphasis added). Third, the ADA says that "discrimination" includes an employer's "*not making reasonable accommodations* to the known physical or mental limitations of an otherwise qualified * * * employee, *unless* [the employer] can demonstrate that the accommodation would impose an *undue hardship* on the operation of [its] business." § 12112(b)(5)(A) (emphasis added). Fourth, the ADA says that the term " 'reasonable accommodation' may include

* * * reassignment to a vacant position." § 12111(9)(B). The parties interpret this statutory language as applied to seniority systems in radically different ways. In U.S. Airways' view, the fact that an accommodation would violate the rules of a seniority system always shows that the accommodation is not a "reasonable" one. In Barnett's polar opposite view, a seniority system violation never shows that an accommodation sought is not a "reasonable" one. Barnett concedes that a violation of seniority rules might help to show that the accommodation will work "undue" employer "hardship," but that is a matter for an employer to demonstrate case by case. We shall initially consider the parties' main legal arguments in support of these conflicting positions.

A

US Airways' claim that a seniority system virtually always trumps a conflicting accommodation demand rests primarily upon its view of how the Act treats workplace "preferences." Insofar as a requested accommodation violates a disability-neutral workplace rule, such as a seniority rule, it grants the employee with a disability treatment that other workers could not receive. Yet the Act, U.S. Airways says, seeks only "equal" treatment for those with disabilities. See, *e.g.,* 42 U.S.C. § 12101(a)(9). It does not, it contends, require an employer to grant preferential treatment. Cf. H.R.Rep. No. 101–485, pt. 2, p. 66 (1990), U.S.Code Cong. & Admin.News 1990, pp. 303, 348–349; S.Rep. No. 101–116, pp. 26–27 (1989) (employer has no "obligation to prefer *applicants* with disabilities over other *applicants*" (emphasis added)). Hence it does not require the employer to grant a request that, in violating a disability-neutral rule, would provide a preference.

While linguistically logical, this argument fails to recognize what the Act specifies, namely, that preferences will sometimes prove necessary to achieve the Act's basic equal opportunity goal. The Act requires preferences in the form of "reasonable accommodations" that are needed for those with disabilities to obtain the *same* workplace opportunities that those without disabilities automatically enjoy. By definition any special "accommodation" requires the employer to treat an employee with a disability differently, *i.e.,* preferentially. And the fact that the difference in treatment violates an employer's disability-neutral rule cannot by itself place the accommodation beyond the Act's potential reach.

Were that not so, the "reasonable accommodation" provision could not accomplish its intended objective. Neutral office assignment rules would automatically prevent the accommodation of an employee whose disability-imposed limitations require him to work on the ground floor. Neutral "break-from-work" rules would automatically prevent the accommodation of an individual who needs additional breaks from work, perhaps to permit medical visits. Neutral furniture budget rules would automatically prevent the accommodation of an individual who needs a different kind of chair or desk. Many employers will have neutral rules governing the kinds of actions most needed to reasonably accommodate a worker with a disability. See 42 U.S.C. § 12111(9)(b) (setting forth examples such as "job restructuring," "part-time or modified work schedules," "acquisition or modification of equipment or devices," "and other similar accommodations"). Yet Congress, while providing such examples, said nothing suggesting that the presence of such neutral rules would create an automatic exemption. Nor have the lower courts made any such suggestion. Cf. *Garcia-Ayala v. Lederle Parenterals, Inc.*, 212 F.3d 638, 648 (C.A.1 2000) (requiring leave beyond that allowed under the company's own leave policy); *Hendricks-Robinson v. Excel Corp.*, 154 F.3d 685, 699 (C.A.7 1998) (requiring exception to employer's neutral "physical fitness" job requirement).

In sum, the nature of the "reasonable accommodation" requirement, the statutory examples, and the Act's silence about the exempting effect of neutral rules together convince us that the Act does not create any such automatic exemption. The simple fact that an accommodation would provide a "preference"—in the sense that it would permit the worker with a disability to violate a rule that others must obey—cannot, *in and of itself,* automatically show that the accommodation is not "reasonable." As a result, we reject the position taken by U.S. Airways and Justice SCALIA to the contrary.

US Airways also points to the ADA provisions stating that a " 'reasonable accommodation' may include * * * reassignment to a *vacant* position." § 12111(9)(B) (emphasis added). And it claims that the fact that an established seniority system would assign that position to another worker automatically and always means that the position is not a "vacant" one. Nothing in the Act, however, suggests that Congress intended the word "vacant" to have a specialized meaning. And in ordinary English, a seniority system can give employees seniority rights allowing them to bid for a "vacant" position. The position in this case was held, at the time of suit, by Barnett, not by some other worker; and that position, under the U.S. Airways seniority system, became an "open" one. Moreover, U.S. Airways has said that it "reserves the right to change any and all" portions of the seniority system at will. Consequently, we cannot agree with U.S. Airways about the position's vacancy; nor do we agree that the Act would automatically deny Barnett's accommodation request for that reason.

* * *

III

The question in the present case focuses on the relationship between seniority systems and the plaintiff's need to show that an "accommodation" seems reasonable on its face, *i.e.,* ordinarily or in the run of cases. We must assume that the plaintiff, an employee, is an "individual with a disability." He has requested assignment to a mailroom position as a "reasonable accommodation." We also assume that normally such a request would be reasonable within the meaning of the statute, were it not for one circumstance, namely, that the assignment would violate the rules of a seniority system. See § 12111(9) ("reasonable accommodation" may include "reassignment to a vacant position"). Does that circumstance mean that the proposed accommodation is not a "reasonable" one?

In our view, the answer to this question ordinarily is "yes." The statute does not require proof on a case-by-case basis that a seniority system should prevail. That is because it would not be reasonable in the run of cases that the assignment in question trump the rules of a seniority system. To the contrary, it will ordinarily be unreasonable for the assignment to prevail.

A

* * *

For one thing, the typical seniority system provides important employee benefits by creating, and fulfilling, employee expectations of fair, uniform treatment. These benefits include "job security and an opportunity for steady and predictable advancement based on objective standards." * * * They include "an element of due process," limiting "unfairness in personnel decisions." Gersuny, Origins of Seniority Provisions in Collective Bargaining, 33 Lab. L.J. 518, 519 (1982). And they consequently encourage employees to invest in the employing company, accepting "less than their value to the firm early in their careers" in return for greater benefits in later years. J. Baron & D. Kreps, Strategic Human Resources: Frameworks for General Managers 288 (1999).

Most important for present purposes, to require the typical employer to show more than the existence of a seniority system might well undermine the employees' expectations of consistent, uniform treatment—expectations upon which the seniority system's benefits depend. That is because such a rule would substitute a complex case-specific "accommodation" decision made by management for the more uniform, impersonal operation of seniority rules. Such management decisionmaking, with its inevitable discretionary elements, would involve a matter of the greatest importance to employees, namely, layoffs; it would take place outside, as well as inside, the confines of a court case; and it might well take place fairly often. Cf. ADA, 42 U.S.C. § 12101(a)(1), (estimating that some 43 million Americans suffer from physical or mental disabilities). We can find nothing in the statute that suggests

Congress intended to undermine seniority systems in this way. And we consequently conclude that the employer's showing of violation of the rules of a seniority system is by itself ordinarily sufficient.

B

The plaintiff (here the employee) nonetheless remains free to show that special circumstances warrant a finding that, despite the presence of a seniority system (which the ADA may not trump in the run of cases), the requested "accommodation" is "reasonable" on the particular facts. That is because special circumstances might alter the important expectations described above. Cf. *Borkowski,* 63 F.3d, at 137 ("[A]n accommodation that imposed burdens that would be unreasonable for most members of an industry might nevertheless be required of an individual defendant in light of that employer's particular circumstances"). The plaintiff might show, for example, that the employer, having retained the right to change the seniority system unilaterally, exercises that right fairly frequently, reducing employee expectations that the system will be followed—to the point where one more departure, needed to accommodate an individual with a disability, will not likely make a difference. The plaintiff might show that the system already contains exceptions such that, in the circumstances, one further exception is unlikely to matter. We do not mean these examples to exhaust the kinds of showings that a plaintiff might make. But we do mean to say that the plaintiff must bear the burden of showing special circumstances that make an exception from the seniority system reasonable in the particular case. And to do so, the plaintiff must explain why, in the particular case, an exception to the employer's seniority policy can constitute a "reasonable accommodation" even though in the ordinary case it cannot. * * *

JUSTICE SCALIA, with whom JUSTICE THOMAS joins, dissenting.

The principal defect of today's opinion * * * goes well beyond the uncertainty it produces regarding the relationship between the ADA and the infinite variety of seniority systems. The conclusion that any seniority system can ever be overridden is merely one consequence of a mistaken interpretation of the ADA that makes all employment rules and practices—even those which (like a seniority system) pose no *distinctive* obstacle to the disabled—subject to suspension when that is (in a court's view) a "reasonable" means of enabling a disabled employee to keep his job. That is a far cry from what I believe the accommodation provision of the ADA requires: the suspension (within reason) of those employment rules and practices *that the employee's disability prevents him from observing.*

I

The Court begins its analysis by describing the ADA as declaring that an employer may not "discriminate against a qualified individual with a disability." In fact the Act says more: an employer may not "discriminate against a qualified individual with a disability *because of the disability* of such individual." 42 U.S.C. § 12112(a) (emphasis added). It further provides that discrimination includes "not making reasonable accommodations *to the known physical or mental limitations* of an otherwise qualified individual with a disability." § 12112(b)(5)(A) (emphasis added).

Read together, these provisions order employers to modify or remove (within reason) policies and practices that burden a disabled person "because of [his] disability." In other words, the ADA eliminates workplace barriers only if a disability prevents an employee from overcoming them—those barriers that would not be barriers *but for* the employee's disability. These include, for example, work stations that cannot accept the employee's wheelchair, or an assembly-line practice that requires long periods of standing. But they do not include rules and practices that bear no more heavily upon the disabled employee than upon others—even though an exemption from such a rule or practice might in a sense "make up for" the employee's disability. It is not a required accommodation, for example, to pay a disabled employee more than others at his grade level—even if that increment is earmarked for massage or physical therapy that would enable the employee to work with as little physical discomfort as his co-workers. That would be "accommodating" the disabled employee, but it would not be "making * * * accommodatio[n] *to the known physical or mental limitations*" of the employee, § 12112(b)(5)(A), because it would not eliminate any workplace practice that constitutes an obstacle *because of* his disability.

So also with exemption from a seniority system, which burdens the disabled and nondisabled alike. In particular cases, seniority rules may have a harsher effect upon the disabled employee than upon his co-workers. If the disabled employee is physically capable of performing only one task in the workplace, seniority rules may be, for him, the difference between employment and unemployment. But that does not make the seniority system a disability-related obstacle, any more than harsher impact upon the more needy disabled employee renders the salary system a disability-related obstacle. When one departs from this understanding, the ADA's accommodation provision becomes a standardless grab bag—leaving it to the courts to decide which workplace preferences (higher salary, longer vacations, reassignment to positions to which others are entitled) can be deemed "reasonable" to "make up for" the particular employee's disability.

Some courts, including the Ninth Circuit in the present case, have accepted respondent's contention that the ADA demands accommodation even with respect to those obstacles that have nothing to do with the disability. Their principal basis for this position is that the definition of "reasonable accommodation" includes "reassignment to a vacant position." § 12111(9)(B). This accommodation would be meaningless, they contend, if it required only that the disabled employee be *considered* for a vacant position. The ADA already prohibits employers from discriminating against the disabled with respect to "hiring, advancement, or discharge * * * and other terms, conditions, and privileges of employment." § 12112(a). Surely, the argument goes, a disabled employee must be given preference over a nondisabled employee when a vacant position appears.

This argument seems to me quite mistaken. The right to be given a vacant position so long as there are no obstacles to that appointment (including another candidate who is better qualified, if "best qualified" is the workplace rule) is of considerable value. If an employee is hired to fill a position but fails miserably, he will typically be fired. Few employers will search their organization charts for vacancies to which the low-performing employee might be suited. The ADA, however, prohibits an employer from firing a person whose disability is the cause of his poor performance without first seeking to place him in a vacant job where the disability will not affect performance. Such reassignment is an accommodation *to the disability* because it removes an obstacle (the inability to perform the functions of the assigned job) arising solely from the disability.

* * *

Sadly, this analysis is lost on the Court, which mistakenly and inexplicably concludes that my position here is the same as that attributed to U.S. Airways. In rejecting the argument that the ADA creates no "automatic exemption" for neutral workplace rules such as "break-from-work" and furniture budget rules, the Court rejects an argument I have not made. * * *

JUSTICE SOUTER, with whom JUSTICE GINSBURG joins, dissenting.

"[R]eassignment to a vacant position," 42 U.S.C. § 12111(9), is one way an employer may "reasonabl[y] accommodat[e]" disabled employees under the Americans with Disabilities Act of 1990. The Court today holds that a request for reassignment will nonetheless most likely be unreasonable when it would violate the terms of a seniority system imposed by an employer. Although I concur in the Court's appreciation of the value and importance of seniority systems, I do not believe my hand is free to accept the majority's result and therefore respectfully dissent.

Nothing in the ADA insulates seniority rules from the "reasonable accommodation" requirement, in marked contrast to Title VII of the Civil Rights Act of 1964 and the Age Discrimination in Employment Act of 1967, each of which has an explicit protection for seniority. See 42 U.S.C. § 2000e–2(h). ("Notwithstanding any other provision of this subchapter, it shall not be an unlawful employment practice for an employer to [provide different benefits to employees] pursuant to a bona fide seniority * * * system * * * ."); 29 U.S.C. § 623(f) (1994 ed.) ("It shall not be unlawful for an employer * * * to take any action otherwise prohibited [under previous sections] * * * to observe the terms of a bona fide seniority system [except for involuntary retirement] * * * "). Because Congress modeled several of the ADA's provisions on Title VII, its failure to replicate Title VII's exemption for seniority systems leaves the statute ambiguous, albeit with more than a hint that seniority rules do not inevitably carry the day.

In any event, the statute's legislative history resolves the ambiguity. The Committee Reports from both the House of Representatives and the Senate explain that seniority protections contained in a collective-bargaining agreement should not amount to more than "a factor" when it comes to deciding whether some accommodation at odds with the seniority rules is "reasonable" nevertheless. H.R.Rep. No. 101–485, pt. 2, p. 63 (1990), U.S.Code Cong. & Admin.News 1990, pp. 303, 345, (existence of collectively bargained protections for seniority "would not be determinative" on the issue whether an accommodation was reasonable); S.Rep. No. 101–116, p. 32 (1989) (a collective-bargaining agreement assigning jobs based on seniority "may be considered as a factor in determining" whether an accommodation is reasonable). * * * The point in this case, however, is simply to recognize that if Congress considered that sort of agreement no more than a factor in the analysis, surely no greater weight was meant for a seniority scheme like the one before us, unilaterally imposed by the employer, and, unlike collective bargaining agreements, not singled out for protection by any positive federal statute.

This legislative history also specifically rules out the majority's reliance on *Trans World Airlines, Inc. v. Hardison,* a case involving a request for a religious accommodation under Title VII that would have broken the seniority rules of a collective-bargaining agreement. We held that such an accommodation would not be "reasonable," and said that our conclusion was "supported" by Title VII's explicit exemption for seniority systems. The committees of both Houses of Congress dealing with the ADA were aware of this case and expressed a choice against treating it as authority under the ADA, with its lack of any provision for maintaining seniority rules. *E.g.,* H.R.Rep. No. 101–485, pt. 2, at 68, U.S.Code Cong. & Admin.News 1990, pp. 303, 350 ("The Committee wishes to make it clear that the principles enunciated by the Supreme Court in *TWA v. Hardison*

* * * are not applicable to this legislation."); S.Rep. No. 101–116, at 36 (same).[2]

* * * I would therefore affirm the Ninth Circuit.

NOTES AND QUESTIONS

1. Consider two views regarding individuals with disabilities: that they are individuals needing special help to overcome discernable differences from the rest of the population and that they are individuals, like everyone else, confronting systemic discrimination. Which view does the Supreme Court adopt?

2. Note the three different positions staked out by the opinions in *Barnett*. Which position best serves the purposes of the ADA? Who bears the responsibility to make reasonable accommodation—employers or employees?

3. How does the analysis in the majority opinion in *Barnett* compare with the notion of "reasonable accommodation" found in the religious discrimination cases? How do these views compare with the notion of "discrimination" found in the affirmative action cases? Given the difference in the basis for prohibiting discrimination (disability versus race, color, religion, sex, or national origin), do these distinctions make sense? Would you support the incorporation of a "reasonable accommodation" standard into the discrimination model for race or sex discrimination?

4. *The Aftermath of* Barnett: As Professor Bagenstos has written in his narrative of the history of the *Barnett* case:

> US Airways was pleased with the company's win in the Supreme Court. But Barnett's lawyers also regarded the Supreme Court's decision as a victory on a "very significant issue." The decision left Barnett a clear path to success by showing that the US Airways seniority system did not create settled expectations in its employees. Because the company itself had repeatedly declared that its system was not legally binding, such a showing would be quite plausible. And, as Justice Stevens had emphasized, the Supreme Court's decision did not even call into question the Ninth Circuit's *other* grounds for finding a triable issue of an ADA violation.

Samuel R. Bagenstos, US Airways v. Barnett *and the Limits of Disability Accommodation, in* Civil Rights Stories 323, 341 (Myriam Gilles & Risa Goluboff, eds., 2007). Following the Supreme Court decision in *Barnett,*

---

[2] The House Report singles out *Hardison*'s equation of "undue hardship" and anything more than a "de minimus *[sic]* cost" as being inapplicable to the ADA. By contrast, *Hardison* itself addressed seniority systems not only in its analysis of undue hardship, but also in its analysis of reasonable accommodation. *Hardison,* 432 U.S., at 81, 84, 97 S.Ct. 2264. Nonetheless, Congress's disavowal of *Hardison* in light of the "crucial role that reasonable accommodation plays in ensuring meaningful employment opportunities for people with disabilities," H.R.Rep. No. 101–485, pt. 2, at 68, U.S.Code Cong. & Admin.News 1990, pp. 303, 350, renders that case singularly inappropriate to bolster the Court's holding today.

however, US Airways filed for bankruptcy, dimming Barnett's hopes of a trial, and he eventually settled his lawsuit for about $3,500. *Id.*

5. Section 107(a) of the ADA, 42 U.S.C. § 12117(a), provides that

> [t]he powers, remedies, and procedures set forth in sections 705, 706, 707, 709, and 710 of the Civil Rights Act of 1964 * * * shall be the powers, remedies, and procedures this title provides to the Commission, to the Attorney General, or to any person alleging discrimination on the basis of disability in violation of any provisions of this Act, * * * concerning employment.

There is a similar provision in § 505(a) of the Rehabilitation Act. 29 U.S.C. § 794(a). The courts have focused on these provisions in shaping the rules on the allocation of the burden of proof under the ADA and the Rehabilitation Act. *See, e.g.*, Barth v. Gelb, 2 F.3d 1180, 1182–84 (D.C.Cir.1993) (Rehabilitation Act).

Barnett arose in a somewhat unusual setting, but the issue of what constitutes "failure to make a reasonable accommodation" can arise in other ways, as the next case shows.

HUBER V. WAL-MART STORES, INC.

United States Court of Appeals for the Eighth Circuit, 2007.
486 F.3d 480, *cert. granted,* 552 U.S. 1074, 128 S.Ct. 742, 169 L.Ed.2d 579 (2007), *and cert. dismissed,* 552 U.S. 1136, 128 S.Ct. 1116, 169 L.Ed.2d 801 (2008).

RILEY, CIRCUIT JUDGE.

We are faced with an unanswered question: whether an employer who has an established policy to fill vacant job positions with the most qualified applicant is required to reassign a qualified disabled employee to a vacant position, although the disabled employee is not the most qualified applicant for the position. Pam Huber (Huber) brought an action against Wal-Mart Stores, Inc. (Wal-Mart), claiming discrimination under the Americans with Disabilities Act of 1990 (ADA) * * * . * * *

I. BACKGROUND

Huber worked for Wal-Mart as a dry grocery order filler earning $13.00 per hour, including a $0.50 shift differential. While working for Wal-Mart, Huber sustained a permanent injury to her right arm and hand. As a result, she could no longer perform the essential functions of the order filler job. The parties stipulated Huber's injury is a disability under the ADA.

Because of her disability, Huber sought, as a reasonable accommodation, reassignment to a router position, which the parties stipulated was a vacant and equivalent position under the ADA. Wal-

Mart, however, did not agree to reassign Huber automatically to the router position. Instead, pursuant to its policy of hiring the most qualified applicant for the position, Wal-Mart required Huber to apply and compete for the router position with other applicants. Ultimately, Wal-Mart filled the job with a non-disabled applicant and denied Huber the router position. Wal-Mart indicated, although Huber was qualified with or without an accommodation to perform the duties of the router position, she was not the most qualified candidate. The parties stipulated the individual hired for the router position was the most qualified candidate.

Wal-Mart later placed Huber at another facility in a maintenance associate position (janitorial position), which paid $6.20 per hour. Huber continues to work in that position and now earns $7.97 per hour.

* * *

II. DISCUSSION

* * *

Here, the parties do not dispute Huber (1) has a disability under the ADA, (2) suffered an adverse employment action, or (3) possessed the requisite skills for the router position. The parties' only dispute is whether the ADA requires an employer, as a reasonable accommodation, to give a current disabled employee preference in filling a vacant position when the employee is able to perform the job duties, but is not the most qualified candidate.

The ADA states the scope of reasonable accommodation may include:

> [J]ob restructuring, part-time or modified work schedules, *reassignment to a vacant position,* acquisition or modification of equipment or devices, appropriate adjustment or modifications of examinations, training materials or policies, the provision of qualified readers or interpreters, and other similar accommodations for individuals with disabilities.

42 U.S.C. § 12111(9)(B) (emphasis added).

Huber contends Wal-Mart, as a reasonable accommodation, should have automatically reassigned her to the vacant router position without requiring her to compete with other applicants for that position. Wal-Mart disagrees, citing its nondiscriminatory policy to hire the most qualified applicant. Wal-Mart argues that, under the ADA, Huber was not entitled to be reassigned automatically to the router position without first competing with other applicants. This is a question of first impression in our circuit. As the district court noted, other circuits differ with respect to the meaning of the reassignment language under the ADA.

The Tenth Circuit in *Smith v. Midland Brake, Inc.,* 180 F.3d 1154, 1164–65 (10th Cir.1999) (en banc), stated:

> [I]f the reassignment language merely requires employers to consider on an equal basis with all other applicants an otherwise qualified existing employee with a disability for reassignment to a vacant position, that language would add nothing to the obligation not to discriminate, and would thereby be redundant. * * * Thus, the reassignment obligation must mean something more than merely allowing a disabled person to compete equally with the rest of the world for a vacant position.

In the Tenth Circuit, reassignment under the ADA results in automatically awarding a position to a qualified disabled employee regardless whether other better qualified applicants are available, and despite an employer's policy to hire the best applicant.

On the other hand, the Seventh Circuit in *EEOC v. Humiston-Keeling, Inc.,* 227 F.3d 1024, 1027–28 (7th Cir.2000), explained:

> The reassignment provision makes clear that the employer must also consider the feasibility of assigning the worker to a different job in which his disability will not be an impediment to full performance, and if the reassignment is feasible and does not require the employer to turn away a superior applicant, the reassignment is mandatory.

In the Seventh Circuit, ADA reassignment does not require an employer to reassign a qualified disabled employee to a job for which there is a more qualified applicant, if the employer has a policy to hire the most qualified applicant.

Wal-Mart urges this court to adopt the Seventh Circuit's approach and to conclude (1) Huber was not entitled, as a reasonable accommodation, to be reassigned automatically to the router position, and (2) the ADA only requires Wal-Mart to allow Huber to compete for the job, but does not require Wal-Mart to turn away a superior applicant. We find this approach persuasive and in accordance with the purposes of the ADA. As the Seventh Circuit noted in *Humiston-Keeling:*

> The contrary rule would convert a nondiscrimination statute into a mandatory preference statute, a result which would be both inconsistent with the nondiscriminatory aims of the ADA and an unreasonable imposition on the employers and coworkers of disabled employees. A policy of giving the job to the best applicant is legitimate and nondiscriminatory. Decisions on the merits are not discriminatory.

Id. at 1028 (internal quotation omitted). "[T]he [ADA] is not a mandatory preference act." *Id.*

We agree and conclude the ADA is not an affirmative action statute and does not require an employer to reassign a qualified disabled employee to a vacant position when such a reassignment would violate a legitimate nondiscriminatory policy of the employer to hire the most qualified candidate. This conclusion is bolstered by the Supreme Court's decision in *U.S. Airways, Inc. v. Barnett,* 535 U.S. 391, 406, 122 S.Ct. 1516, 152 L.Ed.2d 589 (2002), holding that an employer ordinarily is not required to give a disabled employee a higher seniority status to enable the disabled employee to retain his or her job when another qualified employee invokes an entitlement to that position conferred by the employer's seniority system. We previously have stated in dicta that "an employer is not required to make accommodations that would subvert other, more qualified applicants for the job." *Kellogg v. Union Pac. R.R. Co.,* 233 F.3d 1083, 1089 (8th Cir.2000) (per curiam).

Thus, the ADA does not require Wal-Mart to turn away a superior applicant for the router position in order to give the position to Huber. To conclude otherwise is "affirmative action with a vengeance. That is giving a job to someone solely on the basis of his status as a member of a statutorily protected group." *Humiston-Keeling,* 227 F.3d at 1029.

Here, Wal-Mart did not violate its duty, under the ADA, to provide a reasonable accommodation to Huber. Wal-Mart reasonably accommodated Huber's disability by placing Huber in a maintenance associate position. The maintenance position may not have been a perfect substitute job, or the employee's most preferred alternative job, but an employer is not required to provide a disabled employee with an accommodation that is ideal from the employee's perspective, only an accommodation that is reasonable. *See Cravens v. Blue Cross & Blue Shield of Kan. City,* 214 F.3d 1011, 1019 (8th Cir.2000). In assigning the vacant router position to the most qualified applicant, Wal-Mart did not discriminate against Huber. On the contrary, Huber was treated exactly as all other candidates were treated for the Wal-Mart job opening, no worse and no better. * * *

NOTES AND QUESTIONS

1. *Equal Opportunity or Affirmative Action?*: Because the *Huber v. Wal-Mart* case settled following the Supreme Court's grant of certiorari, the important questions raised in the case will continue to be vigorously debated, no doubt resulting in more conflicting decisions. Which interpretation of the statutory language do you find more persuasive—the Tenth Circuit's view in *Midland Brake* or the Seventh Circuit's position in *Humiston-Keeling?* The court in *Huber* asserts that its conclusion that "the ADA is not an affirmative action statute" is "bolstered" by *Barnett.* Do you agree? What arguments can you make that the reasoning and holding in *Barnett* do not support the court's decision in *Huber?*

2. The EEOC has interpreted the ADA's statutory language defining "reassignment to a vacant position" as a "reasonable accommodation" to provide that "[t]he employee does not need to be the best qualified individual for the position in order to obtain it as a reassignment." 29 C.F.R. § 1630.2(o)(2)(ii). Do Wal-Mart employees have an "expectation" that "the most qualified applicant" will always be hired for any vacant position in accordance with the company's stated policy? If you believe this is the case, would you describe the "expectation" as a legally enforceable right? Does the EEOC's approach in its interpretation of the statute strike an appropriate balance between (1) "automatically" reassigning an employee with a disability to a vacant position for which she is "qualified" (at least minimally) and (2) requiring that she compete with all other candidates for the position and show that she is "the most qualified"?

3. At the summary judgment stage of the *Huber* litigation, the parties had stipulated "that the Plaintiff's back-pay and compensatory damages total $28,000, and she is willing to accept reinstatement or a pay increase in lieu of front pay." Huber v. Wal-Mart Stores, Inc., 2005 WL 3690679, at *2 (W.D.Ark.2005). They also agreed to a maximum of $50,000 for Huber's attorneys' fees and costs. *Id.* At the time, Huber still worked for Wal-Mart in a janitorial position earning $7.97 per hour—nearly sixty percent of her pay in her previous job filling grocery orders. *Huber,* 486 F.3d at 481. In light of the fact that Huber's "disability" was the result of an on-the-job injury, it is understandable that Wal-Mart's counsel would not want this case to go before a jury. But it would also have been fairly inexpensive to settle early on rather than after several years of litigation when the cost of settlement would be higher and Wal-Mart's ongoing payments of its own attorneys' fees would be substantial. What business interests was Wal-Mart protecting? The interest in hiring "the most qualified" candidates? The interest in hiring and firing at will? Or the interest in making unfettered decisions about what positions within the company are suitable for low-skilled employees with disabilities?

NOTE: ASSOCIATION DISCRIMINATION

The ADA section banning "discrimination" on the basis of the disabilities of employees includes a subsection that prohibits employers from "excluding or otherwise denying equal jobs or benefits to a qualified individual because of the known disability of an individual with whom the qualified individual is known to have a relationship or association." ADA § 102(b)(4), 42 U.S.C. § 12112(b)(4). One of the first "association discrimination" cases interpreting this provision noted that:

> [i]t was apparently inspired in part by testimony before House and Senate Subcommittees pertaining to a woman who was fired from her long-held job because her employer found out that the woman's son, who had become ill with AIDS, had moved into her house so she could care for him.

Den Hartog v. Wasatch Acad., 129 F.3d 1076, 1082 (10th Cir.1997) (citing H.R. Rep. No. 101–485, pt. 2 at 30 (1990), *reprinted in* 1990 U.S.C.C.A.N. 303, 312). In *Larimer v. International Business Machines Corp.*, 370 F.3d 698 (7th Cir.2004), the court concluded that "[t]hree types of situation are * * * within the intended scope of the rarely litigated * * * association section." *Id.* at 700. The court described the three types of claims as based on "expense," "disability by association," or "distraction," *id.,* and offered the following illustrations:

> [A]n employee is fired (or suffers some other adverse personnel action) because (1) ("expense") his spouse has a disability that is costly to the employer because the spouse is covered by the company's health plan; (2a) ("disability by association") the employee's homosexual companion is infected with HIV and the employer fears that the employee may also have become infected, through sexual contact with the companion; (2b) (another example of disability by association) one of the employee's blood relatives has a disabling ailment that has a genetic component and the employee is likely to develop the disability as well (maybe the relative is an identical twin); (3) ("distraction") the employee is somewhat inattentive at work because his spouse or child has a disability that requires his attention, yet not so inattentive that to perform to his employer's satisfaction he would need an accommodation, perhaps by being allowed to work shorter hours. The qualification concerning the need for an accommodation (that is, special consideration) is critical because the right to an accommodation, being limited to disabled employees, does not extend to a nondisabled associate of a disabled person.

Id. Should an employer's "distaste" for "the known disability" of a friend or relative of an employee be included in this list?

What should be required for the plaintiff's prima facie case under any one of the three *Larimer* scenarios? In a 2008 case discussing *Larimer's* "expense" category, the Seventh Circuit observed: "The *McDonnell Douglas* test is not easily adaptable to claims under the section of the ADA that permits causes of action for association discrimination. It's a bit like a mean stepsister trying to push her big foot into one of Cinderella's tiny glass slippers." Dewitt v. Proctor Hosp., 517 F.3d 944, 948 (7th Cir.2008). Why does the court see these cases as problematical? Is the court's analogy apt or even appropriate? In *Dewitt,* a nurse was fired, allegedly because of the expenses of her husband's treatment for prostate cancer, which were covered under her health insurance plan. Her employer was self-insured for all expenses up to $250,000, and in one year her husband's medical claims were close to $178,000. The court reversed the summary judgment for the employer, allowing the plaintiff to proceed to trial on her ADA association discrimination claim. In a concurrence, Judge Posner cautioned:

> Now it is true, as we know from the discussion in the *Larimer* case of the "expense" form of association discrimination, that an employer who discriminates against an employee because of the latter's association with a disabled person is liable even if the motivation is purely monetary. But if the disability plays no role in the employer's decision—if he would discriminate against any employee whose spouse or dependent ran up a big medical bill—then there is no *disability* discrimination. It's as if the defendant had simply placed a cap on the medical expenses, for whatever cause incurred, that it would reimburse an employee for.

Id. at 953. Does Judge Posner's analysis threaten to eviscerate all association discrimination claims based on "expense"? The Court of Appeals for the Tenth Circuit applied the *McDonnell Douglas* burden-shifting framework, as modified in *Den Hartog*, 129 F.3d at 1085, to permit an expense-based association discrimination claim to survive summary judgment. *See* Trujillo v. PacifiCorp, 524 F.3d 1149, 1154–56 (10th Cir.2008). *Trujillo* involved a married couple employed by the same employer and covered under its health insurance plan. Their son, Charlie, had a brain tumor that required expensive experimental treatment costing more than $60,000. Shortly after Charlie suffered a relapse, both parents were fired, ostensibly for falsifying their time sheets. Reversing the district court, the Tenth Circuit viewed the facts quite differently from the lower court:

> Against the backdrop of the [company's] concerns about rising healthcare costs and, more specifically, [its] awareness of the high cost of Charlie's healthcare, the temporal proximity between Charlie's relapse and the decision to terminate both Trujillos powerfully demonstrates the necessary reasonable inference that PacifiCorp terminated the Trujillos for an illegal reason.

Id. at 1158. Would Judge Posner agree with this reasoning? In light of the 2008 appellate decisions in *Dewitt* and *Trujillo*, the importance of health care costs to employers, and the significance of employer-provided health insurance to employees, do you think it is likely that association discrimination cases will continue to be "infrequently litigated"? *Dewitt,* 517 F.3d at 947. ADA cases involving adverse employment actions motivated by the expenses of health care costs of dependents with disabilities also may involve claims of employer interference with employee rights to benefits under the Employee Retirement Security Act (ERISA), 29 U.S.C. § 1140. *See Trujillo*, 524 F.3d at 1160–61.

For a treatment of association discrimination and other claims that may be raised by an individual without a disability, *see* Michelle Travis, *Lashing Back at the ADA Backlash: How the Americans With Disabilities Act Benefits Americans Without Disabilities,* 76 Tenn.L.Rev. 311 (2009). For example, Professor Travis discusses successful ADA claims brought by nondisabled employees under the anti-retaliation provision of the ADA, 42 U.S.C. § 12203(a). *Id.* at 374–77. A teacher of students with disabilities, who alleged that she was constructively discharged for complaining about the adequacy of the school's program for her students, was permitted to sue the school district under the anti-retaliation provisions of Title II of the ADA and the 1973 Rehabilitation Act, even though she was not herself a "qualified individual with a disability." *See* Barker v. Riverside Cty. Office of Educ., 584 F.3d 821 (9th Cir.2009).

NOTE: HOSTILE WORK ENVIRONMENT CLAIMS UNDER THE ADA AND THE REHABILITATION ACT

The Fifth Circuit was the first court of appeals to expressly hold that workplace harassment because of disability is cognizable under the ADA. Flowers v. Southern Reg'l Physician Servs., Inc., 247 F.3d 229, 232–35 (5th Cir.2001). In *Flowers*, the plaintiff, a medical assistant to a physician, alleged that she was harassed and then fired seven months after disclosing that she was HIV-positive. The jury found that her disability was not a motivating factor in her termination, but that she was subjected to disability-based harassment that created a hostile work environment. The court based its ruling on the similarity between Title VII and the ADA, and following *Meritor Savings Bank, FSB v. Vinson*, 477 U.S. 57, 106 S.Ct. 2399, 91 L.Ed.2d 49 (1986) held that the phrase "terms, conditions, and privileges of employment" in the ADA should be construed to strike at harassment in the workplace because of disability. The Fourth and Eighth Circuits also have expressly recognized that hostile work environment claims may be brought under the ADA. Fox v. Gen. Motors Corp., 247 F.3d 169, 175–77 (4th Cir.2001); Shaver v. Indep. Stave Co., 350 F.3d 716, 719–20 (8th Cir.2003). Other courts of appeals have assumed, without deciding, that such claims are actionable under the ADA or the Rehabilitation Act. *See, e.g.*, Arrieta-Colon v. Wal-Mart P.R., Inc., 434 F.3d 75, 85 n.6 (1st Cir.2006) (ADA); Quiles-Quiles v. Henderson, 439 F.3d 1, 5 n.1 (1st Cir.2006) (Rehabilitation Act); Silk v. City of Chicago, 194 F.3d 788, 803–04 (7th Cir.1999) (ADA). An important issue that can arise in an ADA harassment case, which is not generally an issue in harassment claims under Title VII, is whether the plaintiff is in the protected class. For example, in *Arrieta-Colon*, the court noted: "Were we forced to squarely confront it, the question of whether [the plaintiff] suffered from a disability or was regarded as having a disability within the meaning of the ADA, as found by the jury, would be a difficult one." 434 F.3d at 87. Because the employer had failed to preserve for appellate review the issue of whether the plaintiff's medical condition, which required a penile implant, was a disability within the meaning of the ADA, the court upheld the jury verdict for the plaintiff on compensatory and punitive damages. *Id.* at 87–88. For exploration of the topic of workplace harassment on the basis of disabilities, see Mark C. Weber, *Workplace Harassment Claims Under the Americans with Disabilities Act: A New Interpretation*, 14 Stan.L. & Pol'y Rev. 241 (2003); Mark C. Weber, *Exile and the Kingdom: Integration, Harassment, and the Americans with Disabilities Act*, 63 Md.L.Rev. 162 (2004). For an in-depth comparison of the elements of

ADA and Title VII harassment claims, see Tory C. Lucas, *Disabling Complexity: The Americans with Disabilities Act of 1990 and Its Interaction with Other Federal Laws*, 38 Creighton L.Rev. 871, 916–42 (2005).

C. THE MEANING OF "DISABILITY"

Under the Americans with Disabilities Act, a "disability" is defined as:

> "(A) a physical or mental impairment that substantially limits one or more of the major life activities of such individual;
>
> "(B) a record of such an impairment; or
>
> "(C) being regarded as having such an impairment." § 12102(2).

A series of cases decided by the United States Supreme Court in 1999–2002 defined these terms in such a way as to severely limit the number of plaintiffs who could bring claims under the statute. In *Sutton v. United Air Lines, Inc.*, 527 U.S. 471, 119 S.Ct. 2139, 144 L.Ed.2d 450 (1999), twin sisters applied to become airline pilots. Although each petitioner's uncorrected vision was 20/200 or worse in her right eye and 20/400 or worse in her left eye, with the use of corrective lenses, each had vision that was 20/20 or better. When they were denied jobs on the basis of the air line's requirement that pilots have uncorrected vision of 20/100 or better, they sued alleging discrimination on the basis of their disability, or because defendant regarded them as having a disability in violation of the ADA. Evaluating the definition of disability as "a physical or mental impairment that substantially limits one or more of the major life activities of an individual", the Court reiterated the EEOC regulations, stating:

> . . . the EEOC regulations define the three elements of disability: (1) "physical or mental impairment," (2) "substantially limits," and (3) "major life activities." *See id.*, at §§ 1630.2(h)–(j). Under the regulations, a "physical impairment" includes "[a]ny physiological disorder, or condition, cosmetic disfigurement, or anatomical loss affecting one or more of the following body systems: neurological, musculoskeletal, special sense organs, respiratory (including speech organs), cardiovascular, reproductive, digestive, genito-urinary, hemic and lymphatic, skin, and endocrine." § 1630.2(h)(1). The term "substantially limits" means, among other things, "[u]nable to perform a major life activity that the average person in the general population can perform;" or "[s]ignificantly restricted as to the condition, manner or duration under which an individual can perform a particular major life activity as compared to the condition, manner, or duration under which the average person in the general population can perform that same major life activity."

> § 1630.2(j). Finally, "[m]ajor [l]ife [a]ctivities means functions such as caring for oneself, performing manual tasks, walking, seeing, hearing, speaking, breathing, learning, and working." § 1630.2(i). Because both parties accept these regulations as valid, and determining their validity is not necessary to decide this case, we have no occasion to consider what deference they are due, if any.

In determining whether the plaintiffs had a disability, the Court said that the key question was whether or not the determination of a disability is made with reference to corrective measures. The Court concluded that "Looking at the Act as a whole, it is apparent that if a person is taking measures to correct for, or mitigate, a physical or mental impairment, the effects of those measures—both positive and negative—must be taken into account when judging whether that person is 'substantially limited' in a major life activity and thus 'disabled' under the Act." They based this conclusion, in part, on the findings enacted as part of the ADA that "some 43,000,000 Americans have one or more physical or mental disabilities." They found this figure to be inconsistent with the a contrary definition of disability presented by plaintiffs because "the 1986 National Council on Disability report estimated that there were over 160 million disabled under the 'health conditions approach.' Indeed, the number of people with vision impairments alone is 100 million. 'It is estimated that more than 28 million Americans have impaired hearing.' And there were approximately 50 million people with high blood pressure (hypertension)."

In evaluating the plaintiffs' claim that they were discriminated against because the air line regarded them as having a disability, the Court held:

> Subsection (C) provides that having a disability includes "being regarded as having," § 12102(2)(C), "a physical or mental impairment that substantially limits one or more of the major life activities of such individual," § 12102(2)(A). There are two apparent ways in which individuals may fall within this statutory definition: (1) a covered entity mistakenly believes that a person has a physical impairment that substantially limits one or more major life activities, or (2) a covered entity mistakenly believes that an actual, nonlimiting impairment substantially limits one or more major life activities. In both cases, it is necessary that a covered entity entertain misperceptions about the individual—it must believe either that one has a substantially limiting impairment that one does not have or that one has a substantially limiting impairment when, in fact, the impairment is not so limiting. These misperceptions often "resul[t] from stereotypic assumptions not truly indicative of * * * individual ability." *See* 42 U.S.C. § 12101(7).

Finally, the Court provided guidance on the meaning of "substantially limits," writing:

> When the major life activity under consideration is that of working, the statutory phrase "substantially limits" requires, at a minimum, that plaintiffs allege they are unable to work in a broad class of jobs. * * * To be substantially limited in the major life activity of working, then, one must be precluded from more than one type of job, a specialized job, or a particular job of choice. If jobs utilizing an individual's skills (but perhaps not his or her unique talents) are available, one is not precluded from a substantial class of jobs. Similarly, if a host of different types of jobs are available, one is not precluded from a broad range of jobs.

In a companion case to *Sutton*, *Murphy v. United Parcel Service, Inc.*, 527 U.S. 516, 119 S.Ct. 2133, 144 L.Ed.2d 484 (1999), the Court also dealt with the question of which corrective measures to consider in assessing the level of an individual's impairment. The plaintiff in *Murphy* used medication to control his severe hypertension caused by high blood pressure. Murphy, the plaintiff, had suffered from high blood pressure since his youth, but his physician had testified at trial that, with medication, Murphy's blood pressure could be controlled so that it did not significantly restrict his activity and, in general, he could function normally and engage in activities that other persons normally could perform. A Department of Transportation's (DOT) regulation required that a driver of a commercial vehicle have no current clinical diagnosis of high blood pressure that would likely interfere with his/her ability to operate a commercial vehicle safely. In a 7–2 decision, the Court ruled against Murphy. Applying its decision in *Sutton*, the Court held that Murphy was not disabled because his high blood pressure could be controlled by medication. The Court also rejected Murphy's claim that he was disabled under the "regarded as" prong of the definition of disability because, at most, the only fact that Murphy could prove was that United Parcel regarded him as being unable to perform as a mechanic when that job required driving a commercial vehicle. In another companion case to *Sutton*, *Albertson's, Inc. v. Kirkingburg*, 527 U.S. 555, 119 S.Ct. 2162, 144 L.Ed.2d 518 (1999), the Court found plaintiff Kirkingburg was not an individual with a disability because his own body system had compensated for his visual disability. In this case, Kirkingburg's brain had developed subconscious mechanisms for coping with his visual impairment (he had monocular vision).

Three years later, the Supreme Court returned to the issue of when an individual is substantially limited in a major life activity. In *Toyota Motor Manufacturing, Kentucky, Inc. v. Williams,* 534 U.S. 184, 122 S.Ct. 681, 151 L.Ed.2d 615 (2002), the Court wrote:

Our consideration of this issue is guided first and foremost by the words of the disability definition itself. "[S]ubstantially" in the phrase "substantially limits" suggests "considerable" or "to a large degree." See Webster's Third New International Dictionary 2280 (1976) (defining "substantially" as "in a substantial manner" and "substantial" as "considerable in amount, value, or worth" and "being that specified to a large degree or in the main"). * * * The word "substantial" thus clearly precludes impairments that interfere in only a minor way with the performance of manual tasks from qualifying as disabilities. * * *

"Major" in the phrase "major life activities" means important. See Webster's, *supra*, at 1363 (defining "major" as "greater in dignity, rank, importance, or interest"). "Major life activities" thus refers to those activities that are of central importance to daily life. In order for performing manual tasks to fit into this category—a category that includes such basic abilities as walking, seeing, and hearing—the manual tasks in question must be central to daily life. If each of the tasks included in the major life activity of performing manual tasks does not independently qualify as a major life activity, then together they must do so.

That these terms need to be interpreted strictly to create a demanding standard for qualifying as disabled is confirmed by the first section of the ADA, which lays out the legislative findings and purposes that motivate the Act. See 42 U.S.C. § 12101. When it enacted the ADA in 1990, Congress found that "some 43,000,000 Americans have one or more physical or mental disabilities." § 12101(a)(1). If Congress intended everyone with a physical impairment that precluded the performance of some isolated, unimportant, or particularly difficult manual task to qualify as disabled, the number of disabled Americans would surely have been much higher. * * *

We therefore hold that to be substantially limited in performing manual tasks, an individual must have an impairment that prevents or severely restricts the individual from doing activities that are of central importance to most people's daily lives. The impairment's impact must also be permanent or long-term. See 29 CFR §§ 1630.2(j)(2)(ii)–(iii) (2001).

It is insufficient for individuals attempting to prove disability status under this test to merely submit evidence of a medical diagnosis of an impairment. Instead, the ADA requires those "claiming the Act's protection * * * to prove a disability by offering evidence that the extent of the limitation [caused by their impairment] in terms of their own experience * * * is substantial." *Albertson's, Inc.* v. *Kirkingburg, supra,* at 567 (holding that monocular vision is not invariably a disability, but must be analyzed on an individual basis, taking into account the individual's ability to compensate for the impairment).

In 2008, Congress passed the ADAAA, which President Bush signed it into law on September 25, 2008. The Amendments were intended to broaden the coverage of the ADA in response to the Supreme Court's interpretations of the Act in *Sutton* and its companion cases, and *Williams.* In addition to reasserting the original intent of the ADA, the ADAAA clarified that the existence of a disability will be evaluated without regard to the ameliorative effects of mitigating measures, changed the prohibition from discrimination against an "individual with a disability" to "on the basis of disability," clarified discrimination on the basis of "being regarded" as having a disability, and instructed the EEOC to issue new regulations to redefine the term "substantially limits" because it has been read too narrowly. *See generally* Chai R. Feldblum, et al., *The ADA Amendments Act of 2008,* 13 Tex.J.C.L. & C.R. 187 (2008); Alex B. Long, *Introducing the New and Improved Americans with Disabilities Act: Assessing the ADA Amendments Act of 2008,* 103 Nw.U.L.Rev. Colloquy 217 (2008).

The substantive portions of the Act are found at 42 U.S.C. § 12102, which contains the following definitions:

(1) DISABILITY—The term "disability" means, with respect to an individual—

(A) a physical or mental impairment that substantially limits one or more major life activities of such individual;

(B) a record of such an impairment; or

(C) being regarded as having such an impairment (as described in paragraph (4)).

(2) MAJOR LIFE ACTIVITIES—

(A) IN GENERAL—For purposes of paragraph (1), major life activities include, but are not limited to, caring for oneself, performing manual tasks, seeing, hearing, eating, sleeping, walking, standing, lifting, bending, speaking, breathing, learning, reading, concentrating, thinking, communicating and working.

(B) MAJOR BODILY FUNCTIONS—For purposes of paragraph (1), a major life activity also includes the operation of a major bodily function, including but not limited to, functions of the immune system, normal cell growth, digestive, bowel, bladder, neurological, brain, respiratory, circulatory, endocrine, and reproductive functions.

(3) REGARDED AS HAVING SUCH AN IMPAIRMENT—For purposes of paragraph (1)(C):

(A) An individual meets the requirement of 'being regarded as having such an impairment' if the individual establishes that he or she has been subjected to an action prohibited under this Act because of an actual or perceived physical or mental impairment whether or not the impairment limits or is perceived to limit a major life activity.

(B) Paragraph (1)(C) shall not apply to impairments that are transitory and minor. A transitory impairment is an impairment with an actual or expected duration of 6 months or less.

(4) RULES OF CONSTRUCTION REGARDING THE DEFINITION OF DISABILITY—The definition of "disability" in paragraph (1) shall be construed in accordance with the following:

(A) The definition of disability in this Act shall be construed in favor of broad coverage of individuals under this Act, to the maximum extent permitted by the terms of this Act.

(B) The term "substantially limits" shall be interpreted consistently with the findings and purposes of the ADA Amendments Act of 2008.

(C) An impairment that substantially limits one major life activity need not limit other major life activities in order to be considered a disability.

(D) An impairment that is episodic or in remission is a disability if it would substantially limit a major life activity when active.

(E)(i) The determination of whether an impairment substantially limits a major life activity shall be made without regard to the ameliorative effects of mitigating measures such as—

(I) medication, medical supplies, equipment, or appliances, low-vision devices (which do not include ordinary eyeglasses or contact lenses), prosthetics including limbs and devices, hearing aids and cochlear implants or other implantable hearing devices, mobility devices, or oxygen therapy equipment and supplies;

(II) use of assistive technology;

(III) reasonable accommodations or auxiliary aids or services; or

(IV) learned behavioral or adaptive neurological modifications.

(ii) The ameliorative effects of the mitigating measures of ordinary eyeglasses or contact lenses shall be considered in determining whether an impairment substantially limits a major life activity.

(iii) As used in this subparagraph—

(I) the term "ordinary eyeglasses or contact lenses" means lenses that are intended to fully correct visual acuity or eliminate refractive error; and

(II) the term "low-vision devices" means devices that magnify, enhance, or otherwise augment a visual image.

The regulations to implement the ADAA became effective on May 24, 2011. Regulations to Implement the Equal Employment Provisions of the Americans With Disabilities Act, codified at 29 C.F.R. § 1630, effective May 14, 2011. The regulations include the following provisions:

(a) when an individual is not challenging the failure of an employer to make a reasonable accommodation or requesting a reasonable accommodation, the plaintiff may proceed under the "regarded" as prong, which does not require a showing of an impairment that substantially limits a major life activity or a record of such impairment. 29 C.F.R. § 1630.2(g)(3).

(b) the term "major," with respect to life activities shall not be interpreted to create a demanding standard and a "major life activity" is not determined by reference to whether it is of central importance to daily life.29 C.F.R. § 1630.2(i)(2).

(c) list several examples of impairments that will consistently meet the definition of "disability," including deafness, blindness, intellectual disability, partially or completely missing limbs, mobility impairments requiring use of a wheelchair, autism, cancer, cerebral palsy, diabetes, epilepsy, HIV/AIDS, multiple sclerosis, muscular dystrophy, major depression, bipolar disorder, post-traumatic stress disorder, obsessive-compulsive disorder, and schizophrenia. 29 C.F.R. § 1630.2(j)(3).

(d) the term "substantially limits" is not meant to be a demanding standard, is to be construed broadly to give expansive coverage, and should be applied to require a degree of functional limitation that is lower than the standard applied prior to the ADAAA. 29 C.F.R. § 1630.2(j)(1).

(e) instruct that an employee may be discriminated against under the "regarded as" prong when the employer takes an action prohibited by the ADA based on an individual's impairment or an impairment which the employer believes the individual has, even if the employer does not believe that the impairment (or perceived impairment) substantially limits the performance of a major life activity. 29 C.F.R. § 1630.2(l).

MAZZEO V. COLOR RESOLUTIONS INT'L, LLC

United States Court of Appeals for the Eleventh Circuit, 2014.
746 F.3d 1264.

JORDAN, CIRCUIT JUDGE:

Anthony Mazzeo sued his former employer, Color Resolutions International, LLC, claiming discrimination under the Americans with Disabilities Act of 1990, 42 U.S.C. § 12101 *et seq.* (the "ADA"), the Age Discrimination in Employment Act of 1967, 29 U.S.C. § 621 *et seq.* (the "ADEA"), and the Florida Civil Rights Act, Fla. Stat. § 760.10 (the "FCRA"). The district court granted summary judgment in favor of CRI. With respect to the disability claims, the district court concluded that Mr. Mazzeo did not present a *prima facie* case because he failed to show that he either suffered from a disability or was regarded by CRI as having a disability. * * *

Mr. Mazzeo's appeal requires us to address the application of certain recent amendments to the ADA. For the reasons which follow, we conclude that, in light of these amendments, Mr. Mazzeo submitted sufficient evidence on his ADA and FCRA disability claims to make out a *prima facie* case. * * * We therefore vacate the summary judgment entered in favor of CRI and remand for further proceedings.

* * *

II

Starting in 2004, CRI employed Mr. Mazzeo to provide technical and sales service to its customers in Florida and southern Georgia. Mr. Mazzeo's employment claims revolve around his termination by CRI in early 2009.

In 2007, Mr. Mazzeo was diagnosed with a herniated disc and torn ligaments in his back. The herniated disc caused pain along Mr. Mazzeo's lower back, which spread down his right leg and intermittently affected his ability to walk, sit, stand, bend, run, and lift objects weighing greater than ten pounds. In October of 2008, Mr. Mazzeo first discussed his condition with his supervisor at CRI, Hixon Boyd, and with the supervisor of human resources at CRI, Phyllis Arellano. Between January and March of 2009, Mr. Mazzeo had at least three discussions with Mr. Boyd regarding his possible back surgery, which would require him to miss two weeks of work and have three to six months of restricted activity. Mr. Boyd is alleged to have remarked, whether in concern for Mr. Mazzeo's well-being or out of a self-serving business interest, that such a surgical procedure would likely require a longer recovery period of six to eight weeks.

On February 25, 2009, Mr. Mazzeo informed Mr. Boyd that his back surgery had been scheduled for the second week of March. The very next day, Mr. Boyd initiated the paperwork for Mr. Mazzeo's termination. According to CRI, the reason for the termination was the declining sales revenue, over a period of several years, in Mr. Mazzeo's Florida territory. Mr. Boyd handed the termination papers to Mr. Mazzeo two days before his scheduled surgery. When CRI terminated him on March 10, 2009, Mr. Mazzeo was 46. * * *

III

We start with the disability claim under the ADA. In part as a reaction to Supreme Court decisions in cases like *Sutton v. United Air Lines, Inc.,* 527 U.S. 471, 482, 119 S.Ct. 2139, 144 L.Ed.2d 450 (1999) (whether an individual is disabled must be determined with reference to corrective measures), and *Toyota Motor Mfg., Ky., Inc. v. Williams,* 534 U.S. 184, 196–97, 122 S.Ct. 681, 151 L.Ed.2d 615 (2002) (interpreting the phrase "substantially limits" to mean limiting to a considerable or large degree, and the phrase "major life activities" to mean activities that are of central importance to daily life), Congress made significant changes to the ADA by enacting the ADA Amendments Act of 2008 (the "ADAAA"), Pub.L. No. 110–325, 122 Stat. 3553, which became effective on January 1, 2009. Because the critical events in this case—Mr. Mazzeo's continued back problems, scheduled surgery, and termination—took place after the ADAAA went into effect, we apply the post-ADAAA version of the ADA. *See, e.g., McElwee v. Cnty. of Orange,* 700 F.3d 635, 642 n. 5 (2d Cir.2012) ("The ADAAA became effective on January 1, 2009, and applies to claims, such as McElwee's, which arose after that date.").

The ADA prohibits discrimination by an employer "against a qualified individual on the basis of a disability" in any of the "terms, conditions, [or] privileges of employment." 42 U.S.C. § 12112(a). A "qualified individual" is "an individual who, with or without reasonable accommodation, can perform the essential functions of the employment position that such individual holds or desires." *Id.* at § 12111(8). To establish a *prima facie* case of employment discrimination under the

ADA, a plaintiff must show that, at the time of the adverse employment action, he had a disability, he was a qualified individual, and he was subjected to unlawful discrimination because of his disability. *See Holly v. Clairson Indus., L.L.C.,* 492 F.3d 1247, 1255–56 (11th Cir.2007).

When it enacted the ADAAA, Congress indicated that one of its purposes was to "convey that the question of whether an individual's impairment is a disability under the ADA should not demand extensive analysis." 42 U.S.C. § 12101 note. The ADA defines the term "disability" as (1) a physical or mental impairment that "substantially limits one or more" of an individual's "major life activities," (2) a "record of such an impairment," or (3) "being regarded as having such an impairment" as described in subsection (1). 42 U.S.C. § 12102(1). Under the ADA, "major life activities include, but are not limited to, . . . sleeping, walking, standing, lifting, . . . [and] bending[.]" *Id.* at § 12102(2)(A).

Dr. Christopher Roberts, Mr. Mazzeo's treating physician, submitted an affidavit stating that degenerative disc disease and a herniated disc impacted Mr. Mazzeo's ability to walk, bend, sleep, and lift more than ten pounds, and that Mr. Mazzeo's pain would increase with prolonged sitting and standing. The district court thought this affidavit was insufficient, conclusory, and did not demonstrate that Mr. Mazzeo was disabled because it "contain[ed] no detailed discussion as to whether [the] back condition affected any of [Mr. Mazzeo's] life activities." D.E. 33 at 9. The district court cited to a pre-ADAAA Eleventh Circuit opinion for the proposition that there could be "no disability based on physician's lifting restrictions where the plaintiff testified she could still work." *Id.* (citing *Hilburn v. Murata Elecs. N. Am., Inc.,* 181 F.3d 1220, 1228 (11th Cir.1999)). The district court also noted that the post-surgery work restrictions Mr. Mazzeo discussed with Mr. Boyd were no more than a transitory impairment and, therefore, insufficient to establish that CRI regarded Mr. Mazzeo as disabled. For several reasons, we disagree with the district court's analysis as to the matter of disability.

First, although the district court relied on one of our pre-ADAAA cases, *Hilburn,* 181 F.3d at 1228, to support its conclusion that Dr. Roberts' affidavit was conclusory, that case is distinguishable. In *Hilburn,* the physician opined, without articulating any specific facts, that the plaintiff was "substantially limited in performing manual tasks." *Id.* Given that the plaintiff herself testified that she could walk, run, sit, stand, sleep, eat, bathe, dress, write, work around the house, cook, and work, we held that the physician's opinion was conclusory and did not create any issue of material fact. *See id.* at 1227–28. Here, by contrast, Dr. Roberts explained that he had been treating Mr. Mazzeo for an extended period of time, that one of Mr. Mazzeo's disc herniation problems was "nerve root involvement caus[ing] radicular symptoms, that is pain radiating from the lumbar spine down Mr. Mazzeo's right leg," and that the limitations he noted (i.e., the impact on Mr. Mazzeo's ability to walk, bend, sleep, and lift more than ten pounds) were "substantial . . . and permanent." That diagnosis was not, in our view, conclusory, as it explained Mr. Mazzeo's medical condition, what specific pain the condition caused, and the limitations on "major life activities" (as that term is broadly defined by the ADA) resulting from the condition and pain. At the summary judgment stage, there was no need for a more "detailed discussion" of the effects of Mr. Mazzeo's back condition.

* * *

Third, in passing the ADAAA, Congress stated that the Supreme Court's interpretation of the phrase "substantially limits," in cases like *Toyota Motor,* had "created an inappropriately high level of limitation necessary to obtain coverage under the ADA," and that "the primary object of attention in cases brought under the ADA should be whether entities covered by the ADA have complied with their obligations[.]" 42 U.S.C. § 12101 note. The ADA, therefore, now provides that the phrase "substantially limits" "shall be interpreted consistently with the findings and purposes of the [ADAAA]," *id.* at § 12102(4)(B), and that "an impairment that is episodic or in remission is a disability if it would substantially limit a major life activity when active," *id.* at § 12102(4)(D). And the EEOC, pursuant to its statutory authority to issue regulations implementing the definition of "disability" in the ADA, *see id.* at § 12205a, has further explained that the phrase "substantially limits" is to be "construed broadly in terms of extensive coverage" and is "not meant to be a demanding standard." 29 C.F.R. § 1630.2(j)(1)(i). The EEOC's regulations also provide that an "impairment need not prevent, or significantly or severely restrict, the individual from performing a major life activity in order to be considered substantially limiting;" the phrase "substantially limits" "shall be interpreted and applied to require a degree of functional limitation that is lower than the standard for 'substantially limits' applied prior to the ADAAA;" (with the exception of glasses or contact lenses) the "determination of whether an impairment substantially limits a major life activity shall be made without regard to the ameliorative effects of mitigating measures;" and an "impairment that is episodic or in remission is a disability if it would substantially limit a major life activity." *Id.* at § 1630.2(j)(1)(ii), (iv), (vi)–(vii).

As noted earlier, the ADA now states that "major life activities include, but are not limited to, . . . sleeping, walking, standing, lifting, . . . [and] bending [,]" 42 U.S.C. § 12102(2)(A), and Dr. Roberts stated in his affidavit that Mr. Mazzeo's disc herniation problems and resulting pain—which had existed for years and were serious enough to require surgery—substantially and permanently limited Mr. Mazzeo's ability to walk, bend, and lift more than ten pounds. Given the new standards and definitions put in place by the ADAAA, that evidence was enough for Mr.

Mazzeo to present a *prima facie* case on his ADA and FCRA disability claims.[4]

NOTES AND QUESTIONS

1. Empirical evidence reveals that the ADAAA seems to have achieved its goal of eliminating an overly restrictive definition of "disability" preventing plaintiffs from bringing claims. In an analysis of all reported federal district court summary judgment decisions in ADA cases from January 1, 2010 to April 30, 2013, Professor Stephen Befort found a 28.5% decrease in employer summary judgment victories on challenges that a plaintiff was an individual with a disability under the ADAAA (employers won 45.9% of cases under the ADAAA on this basis, as compared to 74.4% of cases under the pre-ADAAA law). Stephen F. Befort, *An Empirical Examination of Case Outcomes Under the ADA Amendments Act*, 70 Wash. & Lee L. Rev. 2027, 2050–51, 2057–58 (2013). *See also* Nicole Buonocore Porter, *The New ADA Backlash*, 82 Tenn. L. Rev. 1, 19–47 (2014).

2. Although most post-ADAAA cases have little trouble finding a disability exists, the Ninth Circuit issued a significant opinion rejecting a jury's finding of disability. In *Weaving v. City of Hillsboro*, 763 F.3d 1106 (9th Cir.2014), the court ruled that a police officer suffering from attention deficit hyperactivity disorder failed to show his condition substantially limited him in the major life activity of interacting with others because his interpersonal problems were primarily with peers and subordinates, not supervisors or the general public. A stinging dissent excoriated the majority for ignoring the findings of the jury, circuit precedent, and the text of the ADAAA. A more typical result is found in *Jacobs v. N.C. Administrative Office of the Courts*, 780 F.3d 562 (4th Cir.2015) (Social anxiety disorder found to be a disability that substantially limited plaintiff's ability to interact with others even though she could socialize with people at some times when she showed she endured these situations with intense anxiety). *See* Kevin Barry, *Chasing the Unicorn: Anti-Subordination and the ADAAA*, 14 Conn.Pub.Int. L.J. 207, 217–35 (2015) (gathering cases).

3. While plaintiffs are not losing on summary judgment as often for failure to show a disability, many courts have started to require the plaintiff to show he or she is a "qualified" individual with a disability as part of the prima facie case. According to Befort's study, more employers are challenging the "qualifications" at the summary judgment stage (employers raised a qualification challenge that was resolved at summary judgment in 47.1% ADAAA cases, compared to 28.2% of pre-ADAAA cases). Befort, 70 Wash. &

---

[4] Because we conclude that Mr. Mazzeo presented sufficient evidence that he was suffering from a disability under the ADA, we need not and do not address his alternative argument that CRI regarded him as disabled. We do, however, note that the district court addressed whether Mr. Mazzeo's impairment was "transitory and minor" without CRI raising that specific argument and without giving Mr. Mazzeo notice. Because this was procedurally improper, *see Imaging Bus. Machines, LLC v. BancTec, Inc.*, 459 F.3d 1186, 1191 (11th Cir.2006), Mr. Mazzeo can pursue his "regarded as" theory on remand if he wishes.

Lee L.Rev. at 2055, 2064. Additionally, the employer summary judgment win rate in these cases rose by 21.8% (employers won 69.7% of cases under the ADAAA on this basis, as compared to 47.9% under the pre-ADAAA law). Befort, at 2055. This move is often done when the court conflates the "qualified" requirement with the "essential functions" analysis. For a description of this phenomenon and a collection of cases, *see* Michelle Travis, *Disqualifying Universality Under the Americans with Disabilities Act Amendments Act*, 2015 Mich.St.Law Rev. (*forthcoming* 2015). Cases dealing with essential functions and qualifications standard are discussed in Section D, below.

4. *Obesity as a Disability*: *Cook v. Rhode Island Dep't of Mental Health, Retardation, & Hosps*, 10 F.3d 17 (1st Cir.1993), is one of the earliest leading cases holding that morbid obesity is a physical disability. The *Cook* case arose under the Rehabilitation Act and involved a plaintiff who was 5'2 tall and weighed 320 pounds. The employer rejected her application on the ground that her "morbid obesity compromised her ability to evacuate patients in case of an emergency and put her at a greater risk of developing serious ailments." *Id.* at 21. The First Circuit held that a "jury could plausibly have found that plaintiff had a physical impairment" based on medical evidence "that morbid obesity is a physiological disorder involving a dysfunction of both the metabolic system and the neurological appetite-suppressing signal system," or that, although not disabled, she was regarded as disabled by the employer. *Id.* at 23. Judge Selya, who wrote the court's opinion, observed that "[i]n a society that all too often confuses 'slim' with 'beautiful' or 'good,' morbid obesity can present formidable barriers to employment." *Id.* at 28. Under the ADAAA, courts have been finding that obesity may be considered a disability either when the obesity is a symptom of an underlying physiological disorder or when a person's weight is significantly outside the normal range and affects one or more bodily system. *See, e.g. EEOC v. Res. for Human Dev., Inc.* 827 F.Supp.2d 688, 694 (E.D. La. 2011). The EEOC Compliance Manual also suggests that "severe obesity, which has been defined as body weight more than 100% over the norm, is clearly an impairment." EEOC Compliance Manual § 902.2(c)(5)(ii). For treatment of the topic of obesity as a disability, *see* Camille A. Monahan, Tanya L. Goldman and Debra Oswald, *Establishing a Physical Impairment of Weight Under the ADA/ADAAA: Problems of Bias in the Legal System,"* 29 ABA J.Lab.Emp.L. 537 (2014); Jane Byeff Korn, *Too Fat*, 17 Va.J.Soc.Pol'y & L. 209 (2010); Jane Byeff Korn, *Fat*, 77 B.U.L.Rev. 25 (1997).

5. Specifically excluded from coverage under the ADA are what some might call "sexual behavior disorders" and "gender-identity disorders." *See* ADA §§ 508 (transvestites), 511 (homosexuality and bisexuality), 42 U.S.C. §§ 12208, 12211. Do these exclusions endorse the use of sex-related moral qualifications for employment? For a critical assessment of the exclusions, *see* Kevin M. Barry, *Disabilityqueer: Federal Disability Rights Protection for Transgender People,* 16 Yale Hum.Rts. & Dev.J. 1 (2013); *Adrienne* L. Hiegel, Note, *Sexual Exclusions: The Americans with Disabilities Act as a Moral*

Code, 94 Colum.L.Rev. 1451 (1994). For a description of a lawsuit challenging the constitutionality of this exclusion, *see* Kevin M. Barry, *Chasing the Unicorn: Anti-Subordination and the ADAAA*, 14 Conn. Pub.Int.L.J. 207, 238–40 (2015).

6. Employees who are forty years of age or older, and thus covered under the Age Discrimination in Employment Act (ADEA), may have age-related medical conditions such as arthritis or diabetes, which may be disabling or require a workplace accommodation, or they may be "regarded as" disabled. How should discrimination claims brought under both the ADA and the ADEA be treated? For an exploration of the potential impact of the ADAAA on discrimination claims brought by older workers with disabilities, see Christopher E. Pashler & Brian C. Lambert, *At the Crossroads of Age and Disability: Can Practitioners Rely on the Amended ADA and the ADEA to Provide Adequate Recourse for the Older Disabled Individual?*, 10 Marq. Elder's Advisor 183 (2009).

D. QUALIFICATIONS, DIRECT THREAT, AND UNDUE HARDSHIP

1. ESSENTIAL FUNCTIONS AND QUALIFICATION STANDARDS

The ADA, as amended by the ADAAA, prohibits discrimination "against a qualified individual on the basis of disability in regard to * * * terms conditions, and privileges of employment." 42 U.S.C. § 12112(a) (2009). Section 12111(8) (2009) defines a "qualified individual" as "an individual who, with or without reasonable accommodation, can perform the essential functions of the employment position that such individual holds or desires." The ADA does not define the "essential functions" of a job, but does provide that "the employer's judgment as to what functions of a job are essential" shall be given "consideration," and if a written job description is prepared "before advertising or interviewing applicants for the job," it "shall be considered evidence of the essential functions of the job." ADA § 101(8), 42 U.S.C. § 12111(8) (2009). The term "essential functions," however, is defined generally in the ADA regulations promulgated by the EEOC.

> *Essential functions—*
>
> (1) *In general.* The term essential functions means the fundamental job duties of the employment position the individual with a disability holds or desires. The term "essential functions" does not include the marginal functions of the position.
>
> (2) A job function may be considered essential for any of several reasons, including but not limited to the following:

(i) The function may be essential because the reason the position exists is to perform that function;

(ii) The function may be essential because of the limited number of employees available among whom the performance of that job function can be distributed; and/or

(iii) The function may be highly specialized so that the incumbent in the position is hired for his or her expertise or ability to perform the particular function.

(3) Evidence of whether a particular function is essential includes, but is not limited to:

(i) The employer's judgment as to which functions are essential;

(ii) Written job descriptions prepared before advertising or interviewing applicants for the job;

(iii) The amount of time spent on the job performing the function;

(iv) The consequences of not requiring the incumbent to perform the function;

(v) The terms of a collective bargaining agreement;

(vi) The work experiences of past incumbents in the job; and/or

(vii) The current work experience of incumbents in similar jobs.

29 C.F.R. § 1630.2(n) (2009).

Plainly, the considerations set out in this regulation are fact-intensive. Usually no single listed factor will be dispositive, and the regulations themselves state that the evidentiary examples provided are not meant to be exhaustive. For example, in *Shell v. Smith*, 789 F.3d 715 (7th Cir.2015), a case involving a vision and hearing impaired plaintiff who could not drive, the court found that driving a bus was not necessarily an essential function of the job of day-shift mechanic helper. Even though the written job description included driving buses to field locations as a job duty, the court relied on an EEOC regulations, 29 CFR § 1630.2(n)(3), to find that other factors must also be considered. *See also* Henschel v. Clare Cty. Road Comm'n, 737 F.3d 1017 (6th Cir.2013) (finding that employer's opinion that hauling an excavator was an essential job function was not dispositive and only one factor to consider, especially where the job description and plaintiff's experience did not include hauling the excavator very often).

One widely litigated issue is whether "regular and predictable attendance" at the workplace is an essential function. In one leading case, *EEOC v. Ford Motor Co.*, 782 F.3d 753 (6th Cir.2015), the Sixth Circuit, sitting *en banc*, overruled an earlier panel and found that such attendance was an essential function for a steel resale buyer who sought to have the ability to telecommute "up to four days a week" as an accommodation for her irritable bowel syndrome. The court credited employer testimony that the job required face-to-face interaction and on-site team meetings. It also noted that the plaintiff's previous attempts to telecommute were unsuccessful and that no other resale buyer telecommuted more than one day a week. *But see* Solomon v. Vilsack, 763 F.3d 1 (D.C. Cir.2014) (overruling district court finding that "regular and predictable attendance is an essential function of all jobs" and holding that flexible work hours can be a reasonable accommodation).

In addition, the ADA prohibits those "qualification standards, employment tests or other selection criteria that screen out or tend to screen out an individual with a disability or a class of individuals with disabilities," unless the employer can show they are "job-related for the position in question" and "consistent with business necessity." 42 U.S.C. § 12112(b)(6). Some courts have categorized qualification standards as essential functions and thereby relieved employers of the requirement to prove job-relatedness. *See, e.g.* Knutson v. Schwan's Home Serv., Inc., 711 F.3d 911 (8th Cir.2013) (court categorized requirement to have a Department of Transportation driving certificate as a job function, instead of a qualification standard); Griffin v. Prince William Health Sys., 2011 WL 1597508 (E.D. Va., Apr. 26, 2011) (court categorized a forty-pound lifting requirement as a job function, rather than a qualification standard).

A number of courts have addressed the issue of whether the doctrine of judicial estoppel precludes an individual from claiming that she is an individual eligible for the protection of the ADA when she has sought or received disability benefits from a source other than the ADA. The issue of judicial estoppel arises in disability discrimination law, for example, when an individual seeks benefits under the Social Security Act and later seeks relief also under either the ADA or the Rehabilitation Act. The Social Security Act is designed to provide a guaranteed level of income to individuals with disabilities when it has been determined that they are incapable of gainful employment. *See generally* 42 U.S.C. §§ 1381, 1382(a)(3)(B). Judicial estoppel also can arise in the context of claims brought under workers' compensation statutes, which are designed to provide for prompt and fair settlements of employee claims against employers for occupational injuries and illnesses. *See generally* 1 Arthur Larson, The Law of Workmen's Compensation § 1–1.10 (1994).

The majority of the courts of appeals have ruled that an employee may qualify for disability benefits and still be a qualified individual with a disability for the purposes of the ADA. *See* Johnson v. Oregon, 141 F.3d 1361, 1367 (9th Cir.1998). The Supreme Court, in *Cleveland v. Policy*

Management Systems Corp., 526 U.S. 795, 119 S.Ct. 1597, 143 L.Ed.2d 966 (1999), agreed as well, concluding that "we would not apply a special legal presumption permitting someone who has applied for, or received, SSDI benefits to bring an ADA suit only in 'some limited and highly unusual set of circumstances.'" The reasoning of the Ninth Circuit in *Johnson* is typical:

> It is possible, due to the different definitions of disability employed by various agencies, to qualify for disability benefits and to satisfy the ADA's definition of a qualified person with a disability. The distinct purposes of the ADA, Social Security, and disability insurance inform the different definitions of disability employed. * * *
>
> The ADA requires a highly fact-specific analysis of whether a particular, disabled individual can perform a certain job with (or without) reasonable accommodation. EEOC Enforcement Guidance, EEOC Notice No. 915.002, February 12, 1997, II.A. This accords with the ADA's goals: to prevent discrimination and further work opportunities for those with disabilities. *See* 42 U.S.C. § 12101(b)(1) * * * .

Id. at 1366. *See also* Fredenburg v. Contra Costa Cty. Dep't of Health Servs., 172 F.3d 1176, 1179 (9th Cir.1999) (analyzing effect of receipt of state disability benefits on ADA discrimination claim); Swanks v. Wash. Metro. Area Transit Auth., 116 F.3d 582, 584 (D.C. Cir.1997) (analyzing the effect of Social Security disability determinations on ADA claims). The different standards have led the SSA to conclude: "The ADA and the disability provision of the Social Security Act have different purposes, and have no direct application to one another." *Id.* at 586 (quoting Daniel L. Skoler, Assoc. Comm'r, Soc. Sec. Admin., Disabilities Act Info. Memo at 3 (June 2, 1993) (No. SG3P2)). *See also*, Anne E. Beaumont, Note, *This Estoppel Has Got to Stop: Judicial Estoppel and the Americans with Disabilities Act*, 71 N.Y.U.L.Rev. 1529 (1996).

2. QUALIFICATION STANDARDS AND THE DIRECT THREAT DEFENSE

The ADA provides that "[t]he term 'qualification standards' may include a requirement that an individual shall not pose a direct threat to the health or safety of other individuals in the workplace." ADA § 103(b), 42 U.S.C. § 12113(b). The ADA defines the phrase "direct threat" to mean "a significant risk to the health or safety of others that cannot be eliminated by reasonable accommodation." The EEOC regulations provide:

> The determination that an individual poses a "direct threat" shall be based on an individual's present ability to safely perform

the essential functions of the job. This assessment shall be based on a reasonable medical judgment that relies on the most current medical knowledge and/or on the best available objective evidence. In determining whether an individual would pose a direct threat, the factors to be considered include:

(1) The duration of the risk;

(2) The nature and severity of the potential harm;

(3) The likelihood that the potential harm will occur; and

(4) The imminence of the potential harm.

29 C.F.R. § 1630.2(r). These factors parallel the factors the Supreme Court endorsed in *School Board of Nassau County v. Arline*, 480 U.S. 273, 107 S.Ct. 1123, 94 L.Ed.2d 307 (1987), a case brought under the Rehabilitation Act. The Rehabilitation Act does not have a provision similar to the "direct threat" provision in the ADA, but the courts have endorsed the "direct threat" principle as being applicable in the Rehabilitation Act cases. In *Arline*, the Court held that the issue of the threat to others posed by an employee with a communicable disease was properly analyzed as a question of whether the individual was "otherwise qualified." *Id.* at 287, 107 S.Ct. at 1130. *Arline* held that a person with an infectious disease who poses a significant risk of communicating the disease to others is not "otherwise qualified" to perform his or her job. *Id.* at 287 n.16, 107 S.Ct. at 1131 n.16.

In *Bragdon v. Abbott*, 524 U.S. 624, 118 S.Ct. 2196, 141 L.Ed.2d 540 (1998), the Supreme Court applied the direct threat standard under Title II of the ADA. When plaintiff Sidney Abbot, who was infected with HIV, sought dental care, her dentist refused to fill her cavity. After finding that HIV infection constituted a disability, the Court turned to the dentist's contention that he did not have to treat plaintiff because her infectious condition posed a direct threat to his safety. The Court adopted the analysis of *Arline* and emphasized that, in order to qualify as a defense under the direct threat standard, a risk must be both significant and based on medical or other objective evidence.

In *Osborne v. Baxter Healthcare Corp.*, 798 F.3d 1260 (10th Cir.2015), the court evaluated whether a deaf blood technician posed a direct threat because she might not notice a donor in distress, even with the installation of visual and vibrating alerts and call buttons for donors. The court rejected the employer's direct threat defense because there was only an "infinitesimal risk" (0.0004 percent) of significant adverse reactions among plasma donors. The court concluded that "infinitesimal risk did not come anywhere close to constituting a 'direct threat'." The court also found no undue hardship where the company needed to contact a vendor to modify the plasmapheresis machines to install the visual and vibrating alerts.

NOTES AND QUESTIONS

1. There is a split of authority on which party bears the burden of proof on the existence of a "direct threat" to the health and safety of others in the workplace. *See* Branham v. Snow, 392 F.3d 896, 906 n.5 (7th Cir.2004) (collecting cases on circuit split). Some courts argue that, as a statutory defense, it is an affirmative defense that should impose the burden of proof on the employer; *see* Jarvis v. Potter, 500 F.3d 1113, 1122 (10th Cir.2007) (noting in Rehabilitation Act case that "[c]ourts generally have held that the existence of a direct threat is a defense to be proved by the employer"); Rizzo v. Children's World Learning Ctrs., Inc., 84 F.3d 758, 764 (5th Cir.1996) ("As with all affirmative defenses, the employer bears the burden of proving that the employee is a direct threat."). On the other hand, the question of whether a plaintiff poses a "direct threat" may be intimately related to the element of a prima facie case that requires the plaintiff to prove that she is a qualified individual who can perform the essential functions of the job, with or without reasonable accommodation. *See* EEOC v. Amego, Inc., 110 F.3d 135, 142–44 (1st Cir.1997); Moses v. Am. Nonwovens, Inc., 97 F.3d 446, 447 (11th Cir.1996). In cases where the job duties necessarily involve the safety of others, some courts that would otherwise place the burden on the employer, require the plaintiff to prove she would not be a "direct threat" to others. *See, e.g., Jarvis*, 500 F.3d at 906; McKenzie v. Benton, 388 F.3d 1342, 1355 (10th Cir.2004). Which of the views on the allocation of the burden of proof on "direct threat" do you believe is more consistent with the mandate of the ADA, as amended by the ADAAA, and the Rehabilitation Act?

2. What advice would you give an employer who wishes to assert the direct threat defense on the basis of a good faith belief that an employee poses a "significant risk to the health or safety of others"? *See* 42 U.S.C. § 12182(b)(3).

3. Section 103(d)(1) of the ADA, 42 U.S.C. § 12113(d)(1), requires the Secretary of Health and Human Services to "review" and "publish a list of" all "infectious and communicable diseases which may be transmitted through handling the food supply," to "publish the methods by which such diseases are transmitted," and to "widely disseminate" the information "to the general public." If an individual has an infectious or communicable disease that appears on the list, an employer "may refuse to assign or continue to assign such individual to a job involving food handling" if the disease "cannot be eliminated by reasonable accommodation." ADA § 103(d)(2), 42 U.S.C. § 2113(d)(2). The most recent list published pursuant to § 103(d)(1) by the Centers for Disease Control and Prevention, 68 F.R. 62809–10 42426 (Nov. 6, 2003), does not include AIDS. Consider the following:

Sharp was hired by a grocery store to work in the produce department. Because they use sharp instruments, such as knives, to prune produce for display, produce department employees are subject to bleeding from nicks and cuts to their hands. Several months after his employment began, Sharp informed his employer that he has AIDS. The employer asked Sharp to provide medical information from his own doctor or to submit to a medical examination by a doctor selected by the employer; in either case, the employer agreed to pay for the medical examination. After waiting a reasonable period of time for Sharp to comply with its request, the employer discharged him. Does Sharp have any rights under the ADA?

What if, after learning about his AIDS, the employer had offered Sharp a job in another department of the grocery store, which did not involve working with sharp instruments, but Sharp had insisted on keeping his current job because AIDS was not on the § 103(d) list of infectious and communicable diseases. Suppose that the employer then had discharged Sharp when he refused to accept the alternative job in which he would have received the same pay and worked the same hours. If Sharp had sought your advice on whether to pursue an ADA claim, what advice would you have given him? Why? *See* EEOC v. Prevo's Family Mkt., Inc., 135 F.3d 1089 (6th Cir.1998).

4. *The Special Problem of Health Care Workers*: Franz Polo was employed as an operating room technician until his employer, the Medical Center, received information that Polo has "full blown" AIDS. As part of his duties, Polo occasionally had to place his hands into a patient's body cavities in the presence of sharp instruments. In the past, he had sustained needle sticks and minor lacerations while assisting in surgeries. Upon learning about Polo's HIV-positive status, the Medical Center created a new full-time job for him as a cart/instrument coordinator, with responsibility for ensuring that the appropriate surgical instruments were ready for surgical operations. How would you evaluate Polo's claim for discrimination on the basis of having a disability? Would your evaluation change if Polo instead had been a pharmacist in the Medical Center's pharmacy? *See In re* Westchester County Med. Ctr., [Sept. 1991–May 1994 Transfer Binder] Empl.Prac.Dec. (CCH) ¶ 5340 (Decision & Order of Admin. Law Judge, U.S. Dep't of Health & Human Servs., Departmental Appeals Bd., Apr. 20, 1992).

On facts similar to these, the Sixth Circuit issued a divided decision in *Estate of Mauro v. Borgess Medical Center*, 137 F.3d 398 (6th Cir.1998). The majority found that Mauro's continued employment as a surgical technician posed a direct threat to the health and safety of others, and the court affirmed the ruling of the lower court against Mauro's estate. The dissenting judge found that the case presented a jury issue; thus the lower court should not have granted summary judgment in favor of the Medical Center. *See also* EEOC v. Prevo's Family Market, Inc., 135 F.3d 1089 (6th Cir.1998).

The Centers for Disease Control has reported that occupational transmission of HIV to health care workers is extremely rare, with only 58 confirmed cases in the United States, as of December 31, 2013. Centers for Disease Control, *Occupational HIV Transmission and Prevention Among Health Care Workers,* available at *http://www.cdc.gov/hiv/workplace/*

occupational.html (last visited Nov. 1, 2015). In addition, transmission of HIV from a health-care worker to patients is extremely rare *See* 57 Morbidity & Mortality Weekly Report (January 9, 2009), *available at http://www.cdc.gov/mmwr/PDF/wk/mm5753.pdf* (last visited Nov. 1, 2015). The report states that the risk of transmission of HIV from an infected health care worker to a patient is very small, and it recommends allowing HIV-positive health care workers to continue performing surgical procedures, provided that they follow safety precautions outlined in the report. The report differentiates between two types of invasive procedures, which it labels as "exposure-prone" procedures and "general invasive" procedures. General invasive procedures range from insertions of intravenous lines to most types of surgery. Exposure-prone procedures are those that pose a greater risk of percutananeous (skin-piercing) procedures.

5. For an article on the "direct threat" standard, *see* Steven H. Winterbauer, *The Direct Threat Defense: Striking a Balance Between the Duties to Accommodate and to Provide a Safe Workplace*, 23 Empl.Rel.L.J. 5 (1997). For discussion of the role of subjective perceptions of risk in cases involving HIV-infected workers, see Richard Bales & Katrina Atkins, *HIV and the Direct Threat Defense*, 91 Ky.L.J. 859 (2002–2003).

NOTE: THREATS TO A WORKER'S OWN HEALTH OR SAFETY

The statutory language of the ADA deals with a threat to the health or safety of *others*. The EEOC promulgated a regulation that expanded on this statutory language to permit a qualification standard that requires a covered individual not to pose a direct threat to his or her *own* health or safety, in addition to the health or safety of others. The application of this expanded qualification was challenged in *Chevron U.S.A., Inc. v. Echazabal*, 536 U.S. 73, 122 S.Ct. 2045, 153 L.Ed.2d 82 (2002). Plaintiff Mario Echazabal suffered from liver damage, a result of having Hepatitis C. The employer refused to hire him because exposure to toxins at the refinery would aggravate his condition. "Chevron defended under a regulation of the Equal Employment Opportunity Commission permitting the defense that a worker's disability on the job would pose a 'direct threat' to his health, see 29 CFR § 1630.15(b)(2) (2001)." Echazabal, 536 U.S. at 77, 122 S.Ct. at 2048. The Supreme Court articulated the employer's argument as an affirmative defense:

> Section 102 of the Americans with Disabilities Act of 1990 prohibits "discriminat[ion] against a qualified individual with a disability because of the disability * * * in regard to" a number of actions by an employer, including "hiring." 42 U.S.C. § 12112(a). The statutory definition of "discriminat[ion]" covers a number of things an employer might do to block a disabled person from advancing in the workplace, such as "using qualification standards * * * that screen out or tend to screen out an individual with a disability." § 12112(b)(6). By that same definition as well as by separate provision, § 12113(a), the Act creates an affirmative defense for action under a qualification standard "shown to be job-

> related for the position in question and * * * consistent with business necessity." Such a standard may include "a requirement that an individual shall not pose a direct threat to the health or safety of other individuals in the workplace," § 12113(b), if the individual cannot perform the job safely with reasonable accommodation, § 12113(a). By regulation, the EEOC carries the defense one step further, in allowing an employer to screen out a potential worker with a disability not only for risks that he would pose to others in the workplace but for risks on the job to his own health or safety as well: "The term 'qualification standard' may include a requirement that an individual shall not pose a direct threat to the health or safety of the individual or others in the workplace." 29 CFR § 1630.15(b)(2) (2001).

Echazabal, 536 U.S. at 78–79, 122 S.Ct. at 2048–49.

The Court deferred to the EEOC's discretion in defining legitimate qualifications that are "job-related and consistent with business necessity." *Echazabal*, 536 U.S. at 80, 122 S.Ct. at 2050. In dealing with plaintiff's objection to the reasonableness of the regulation, the Court argued:

> Nor can the EEOC's resolution be fairly called unreasonable as allowing the kind of workplace paternalism the ADA was meant to outlaw. It is true that Congress had paternalism in its sights when it passed the ADA, see § 12101(a)(5) (recognizing "overprotective rules and policies" as a form of discrimination). But the EEOC has taken this to mean that Congress was not aiming at an employer's refusal to place disabled workers at a specifically demonstrated risk, but was trying to get at refusals to give an even break to classes of disabled people, while claiming to act for their own good in reliance on untested and pretextual stereotypes. Its regulation disallows just this sort of sham protection, through demands for a particularized enquiry into the harms the employee would probably face. The direct threat defense must be "based on a reasonable medical judgment that relies on the most current medical knowledge and/or the best available objective evidence," and upon an expressly "individualized assessment of the individual's present ability to safely perform the essential functions of the job," reached after considering, among other things, the imminence of the risk and the severity of the harm portended. 29 CFR § 1630.2(r) (2001). The EEOC was certainly acting within the reasonable zone when it saw a difference between rejecting workplace paternalism and ignoring specific and documented risks to the employee himself, even if the employee would take his chances for the sake of getting a job.

Echazabal, 536 U.S. at 85–86, 122 S.Ct. at 2052–53.

NOTES AND QUESTIONS

1. The Court in *Echazabal* did not consider whether an individual who poses a direct threat to himself can be a "qualified individual" who can perform the "essential functions" of the employment position.

2. Do you agree with the Court that the EEOC regulation does not represent the type of workplace paternalism that the ADA was meant to outlaw? Does the requirement that the direct threat to oneself be significant and based upon an individualized assessment satisfy this concern?

3. Can you reconcile the approach to workplace paternalism taken by the Court in *Echazabal* with its approach in *Dothard v. Rawlinson*, 433 U.S. 321, 97 S.Ct. 2720, 53 L.Ed.2d 786 (1977), and *International Union, United Automobile Workers v. Johnson Controls, Inc.*, 499 U.S. 187, 111 S.Ct. 1196, 113 L.Ed.2d 158 (1991)? Recall that in *Dothard*, the Court indicated that safety risks to a female prison guard herself would not satisfy a BFOQ defense to sex discrimination under Title VII. 433 U.S. at 335, 97 S.Ct. at 2730. In *Johnson Controls*, the Court struck down the employer's gender-based fetal-protection policy, concluding that Title VII's BFOQ provision, as amended by the Pregnancy Discrimination Act, "prohibit[s] an employer from discriminating against a woman because of her capacity to become pregnant unless her reproductive potential prevents her from performing the duties of her job." 499 U.S. at 206, 111 S.Ct. at 1207.

4. What arguments might be available to plaintiffs and employers in the following cases based on the "direct threat" rule?

a. Moses, an employee in a butcher shop, has applied for a vacancy as a butcher. Butchers operate heavy machinery, including very powerful band saws. Moses has epilepsy and is subject to seizures. He is on medication to control his epileptic seizures. Is Moses "qualified" for the job under the ADA? Can the employer refuse to hire him as a butcher? How would your arguments be affected if the evidence showed that, although Moses is an epileptic, he has never suffered a seizure and that he does not regularly take his prescribed medication? *See* Moses v. Am. Nonwovens, Inc., 97 F.3d 446 (11th Cir.1996).

b. Victoria Rizzo is employed by Children's Learning Center as a teacher's aide. The Learning Center is a day care center for children between the ages of three and five. Until recently, her job functions have included driving a van to transport the children on various outings to museums, zoos, and parks. Usually she has driven the van alone because the regular teachers have used other means of transportation for the outings. In addition, sometimes she has been alone in the classroom with children. Rizzo has a hearing impairment that requires the use of hearing aids, and her hearing has continued to deteriorate over time, requiring that she be fitted with more powerful hearing aids. Several parents whose children are enrolled in the Learning Center have complained to the director about Rizzo. They are concerned about Rizzo's ability to hear sirens on emergency vehicles, e.g., fire trucks, ambulances, or police vehicles, and to hear children who may be choking in the rear of the van. The Learning Center has a job available preparing food in the kitchen for the children and staff. Rizzo could easily do the job, but it involves different hours and less pay. The director of the Learning Center would like to transfer Rizzo to this position, and he has asked you for your advice on what he should do. What advice would you give him and why? *See* Rizzo v. Children's World Learning Ctrs., Inc., 84 F.3d 758 (5th Cir.1996).

c. Would the outcome of the analysis in these cases be different if they were analyzed under the "essential functions" test instead of the "direct threat" standard? *See* Palmer v. Circuit Court of Cook County Ill., 117 F.3d 351 (7th Cir.1997).

5. For articles examining a range of issues involving the "direct threat" standard under the ADA, see Samuel R. Bagenstos, *The Americans with Disabilities Act as Risk Regulation*, 101 Colum.L.Rev. 1479 (2001); Ann Hubbard, *Understanding and Implementing the ADA's Direct Threat Defense*, 95 Nw.U.L.Rev. 1279 (2001); Jeffrey A. Van Detta, *"Typhoid Mary" Meets the ADA: A Case Study of the "Direct Threat" Standard Under the Americans with Disabilities Act,* 22 Harv.J.L. & Pub. Pol'y 849 (1999).

3. REASONABLE ACCOMMODATION AND UNDUE HARDSHIP

In what way does the concept of "undue hardship" interact with the "reasonable" portion of "reasonable accommodation?" The following case looks at the requirement of undue hardship in more detail:

VANDE ZANDE V. WISCONSIN DEPARTMENT OF ADMIN.

United States Court of Appeals for the Seventh Circuit, 1995.
44 F.3d 538.

POSNER, CHIEF JUDGE.

* * *

The more problematic [disability] case is that of an individual who has a vocationally relevant disability—an impairment such as blindness or paralysis that limits a major human capability, such as seeing or walking. In the common case in which such an impairment interferes with the individual's ability to perform up to the standards of the workplace, or increases the cost of employing him, hiring and firing decisions based on the impairment are not "discriminatory" in a sense closely analogous to employment discrimination on racial grounds. The draftsmen of the [Americans with Disabilities] Act knew this. But they were unwilling to confine the concept of disability discrimination to cases in which the disability is irrelevant to the performance of the disabled person's job. Instead, they defined "discrimination" to include an employer's "not making reasonable accommodations to the known physical or mental limitations of an otherwise qualified individual with a disability who is an applicant or employee, unless * * * [the employer] can demonstrate that the accommodation would impose an undue hardship on the operation of the * * * [employer's] business." 42 U.S.C. § 12112(b)(5)(A).

The term "reasonable accommodations" is not a legal novelty, even if we ignore its use in the provision of Title VII forbidding religious discrimination in employment. It is one of a number of provisions in the employment subchapter that were borrowed from regulations issued by the Equal Employment Opportunity Commission in implementation of the Rehabilitation Act of 1973, 29 U.S.C. §§ 701 *et seq.* * * * Indeed, to a great extent the employment provisions of the new Act merely generalize to the economy as a whole the duties, including that of reasonable accommodation, that the regulations under the Rehabilitation Act imposed on federal agencies and federal contractors. We can therefore look to the decisions interpreting those regulations for clues to the meaning of the same terms in the new law.

It is plain enough what "accommodation" means. The employer must be willing to consider making changes in its ordinary work rules, facilities, terms, and conditions in order to enable a disabled individual to work. The difficult term is "reasonable." The plaintiff in our case, a paraplegic, argues in effect that the term just means apt or efficacious. An accommodation is reasonable, she believes, when it is tailored to the particular individual's disability. A ramp or lift is thus a reasonable accommodation for a person who like this plaintiff is confined to a wheelchair. Considerations of cost do not enter into the term as the plaintiff would have us construe it. Cost is, she argues, the domain of "undue hardship" (another term borrowed from the regulations under the Rehabilitation Act)—a safe harbor for an employer that can show that it would go broke or suffer other excruciating financial distress were it compelled to make a reasonable accommodation in the sense of one effective in enabling the disabled person to overcome the vocational effects of the disability.

These are questionable interpretations both of "reasonable" and of "undue hardship." To "accommodate" a disability is to make some change that will enable the disabled person to work. An unrelated, inefficacious change would not be an accommodation of the disability at all. So "reasonable" may be intended to qualify (in the sense of weaken) "accommodation," in just the same way that if one requires a "reasonable effort" of someone this means less than the maximum possible effort, or in law that the duty of "reasonable care," the cornerstone of the law of negligence, requires something less than the maximum possible care. It is understood in that law that in deciding what care is reasonable the court considers the cost of increased care. * * * Similar reasoning could be used to flesh out the meaning of the word "reasonable" in the term "reasonable accommodations." It would not follow that the costs and benefits of altering a workplace to enable a disabled person to work would always have to be quantified, or even that an accommodation would have to be deemed unreasonable if the cost exceeded the benefit however slightly. But, at the very least, the cost could not be disproportionate to the benefit. Even if an employer is so large or wealthy—or, like the principal defendant in this case, is a state, which can raise taxes in order to finance any accommodations that it must make to disabled employees—that it may not be able to plead "undue *hardship*," it would not be required to expend enormous sums in order to bring about a trivial improvement in the life of a disabled employee. If the nation's employers have potentially unlimited financial obligations to 43 million disabled persons, the Americans with Disabilities Act will have imposed an indirect tax potentially greater than the national debt. We do not find an intention to bring about such a radical result in either the language of the Act or its history. The preamble actually "markets" the Act as a cost saver, pointing to "billions of dollars in unnecessary expenses resulting from dependency and nonproductivity." The savings will be illusory if employers are required to expend many more billions in accommodation than will be saved by enabling disabled people to work.

The concept of reasonable accommodation is at the heart of this case. The plaintiff sought a number of accommodations to her paraplegia that were turned down. The principal defendant as we have said is a state, which does not argue that the plaintiff's proposals were rejected because accepting them would have imposed undue hardship on the state or because they would not have done her any good. The district judge nevertheless granted summary judgment for the defendants on the ground that the evidence obtained in discovery, construed as favorably to the plaintiff as the record permitted, showed that they had gone as far to accommodate the plaintiff's demands as reasonableness, in a sense distinct from either aptness or hardship—a sense based, rather, on considerations of cost and proportionality—required. On this analysis, the function of the "undue hardship" safe harbor, like the "failing company" defense to antitrust liability is to excuse compliance by a firm that is financially distressed, even though the cost of the accommodation to the firm might be less than the benefit to disabled employees.

This interpretation of "undue hardship" is not inevitable—in fact probably is incorrect. It is a defined term in the Americans with Disabilities Act, and the definition is "an action requiring significant difficulty or expense." The financial condition of the employer is only one consideration in determining whether an accommodation otherwise reasonable would impose an undue hardship. The legislative history equates "undue hardship" to "unduly costly." These are terms of relation. We must ask, "undue" in relation to what? Presumably (given the statutory definition and the legislative history) in relation to the benefits of the accommodation to the disabled worker as well as to the employer's resources.

So it seems that costs enter at two points in the analysis of claims to an accommodation to a disability. The employee must show that the accommodation is reasonable in the sense both of efficacious and of proportional to costs. Even if this prima facie showing is made, the employer has an opportunity to prove that upon more careful consideration the costs are excessive in relation either to the benefits of the accommodation or to the employer's financial survival or health. * * *

Lori Vande Zande, aged 35, is paralyzed from the waist down as a result of a tumor of the spinal cord. Her paralysis makes her prone to develop pressure ulcers, treatment of which often requires that she stay at home for several weeks. * * * We hold that Vande Zande's pressure ulcers are a part of her disability, and therefore a part of what the State of Wisconsin had a duty to accommodate—reasonably.

Vande Zande worked for the housing division of the state's department of administration for three years, beginning in January 1990. * * * In short, her tasks were of a clerical, secretarial, and administrative assistant character. In order to enable her to do this work, the defendants, as she acknowledges, "made numerous accommodations relating to the plaintiff's disability." As examples, in her words, "they paid the landlord to have bathrooms modified and to have a step ramped; they bought special adjustable furniture for the plaintiff; they ordered and paid for one-half of the cost of a cot that the plaintiff needed for daily personal care at work; they sometimes adjusted the plaintiff's schedule to perform backup telephone duties to accommodate the plaintiff's medical appointments; they made changes to the plans for a locker room in the new state office building; and they agreed to provide some of the specific accommodations the plaintiff requested in her October 5 "Reasonable Accommodation Request."

But she complains that the defendants did not go far enough in two principal respects. One concerns a period of eight weeks when a bout of pressure ulcers forced her to stay home. She wanted to work full time at home and believed that she would be able to do so if the division would provide her with a desktop computer at home (though she already had a laptop). * * *

She argues that a jury might have found that a reasonable accommodation required the housing division either to give her the desktop computer or to excuse her from having to dig into her sick leave to get paid for the hours in which, in the absence of the computer, she was unable to do her work at home. No jury, however, could in our view be permitted to stretch the concept of "reasonable accommodation" so far. Most jobs in organizations public or private involve team work under supervision rather than solitary unsupervised work, and team work under supervision generally cannot be performed at home without a substantial reduction in the quality of the employee's performance. This will no doubt change as communications technology advances, but is the situation today. Generally, therefore, an employer is not required to accommodate a disability by allowing the disabled worker to work, by himself, without supervision, at home. This is the majority view, illustrated by *Tyndall v. National Education Centers, Inc.*, 31 F.3d 209, 213–14 (4th Cir.1994), and *Law v. United States Postal Service*, 852 F.2d 1278 (Fed.Cir.1988) (per curiam). The District of Columbia Circuit disagrees. Langon v. Dep't of Health & Human Serv., 959 F.2d 1053, 1060–61 (D.C.Cir.1992); Carr v. Reno, 23 F.3d 525, 530 (D.C.Cir.1994). But we think the majority view is correct. An employer is not required to allow disabled workers to work at home, where their productivity inevitably would be greatly reduced. No doubt to this as to any generalization about so complex and varied an activity as employment there are exceptions, but it would take a very extraordinary case for the employee to be able to create a triable issue of the employer's failure to allow the employee to work at home.

* * * Wisconsin's housing division was not required by the Americans with Disabilities Act to allow Vande Zande to work at home; even more clearly it was not required to install a computer in her home so that she could avoid using up 16.5 hours of sick leave. It is conjectural that she will ever need those 16.5 hours; the expected cost of the loss must, therefore, surely be slight. An accommodation that allows a disabled worker to work at home, at full pay, subject only to a slight loss of sick leave that may never be needed, hence never missed, is, we hold, reasonable as a matter of law.

* * *

Her second complaint has to do with the kitchenettes in the housing division's building, which are for the use of employees during lunch and coffee breaks. Both the sink and the counter in each of the kitchenettes were 36 inches high, which is too high for a person in a wheelchair. The building was under construction, and the kitchenettes not yet built, when the plaintiff complained about this feature of the design. But the defendants refused to alter the design to lower the sink and counter to 34 inches, the height convenient for a person in a wheelchair. Construction of the building had begun before the effective date of the Americans with Disabilities Act, and Vande Zande does not argue that the failure to include 34-inch sinks and counters in the design of the building violated the Act. She could not argue that; the Act is not retroactive. But she argues that once she brought the problem to the attention of her supervisors, they were obliged to lower the sink and counter, at least on the floor on which her office was located but possibly on the other floors in the building as well, since she might be moved to another floor. All that the defendants were willing to do was to install a shelf 34 inches high in the kitchenette area on Vande Zande's floor. That took care of the counter problem. As for the sink, the defendants took the position that since the plumbing was already in place it would be too costly to lower the sink and that the plaintiff could use the bathroom sink, which is 34 inches high.

Apparently it would have cost only about $150 to lower the sink on Vande Zande's floor; to lower it on all the floors might have cost as much as $2,000, though possibly less. Given the proximity of the bathroom sink, Vande Zande can hardly complain that the inaccessibility of the kitchenette sink interfered with her ability to work or with her physical comfort. Her argument rather is that forcing her to use the bathroom sink for activities (such as washing out her coffee cup) for which the other employees could use the kitchenette sink stigmatized her as different and inferior; she seeks an award of compensatory damages for the resulting emotional distress. We may assume without having to decide that emotional as well as physical barriers to the integration of disabled persons into the workforce are relevant in determining the reasonableness of an accommodation. But we do not think an employer has a duty to expend even modest amounts of money to bring about an absolute identity in working conditions between disabled and nondisabled workers. The creation of such a duty would be the inevitable consequence of deeming a failure to achieve identical conditions "stigmatizing." That is merely an epithet. We conclude that access to a particular sink, when access to an equivalent sink, conveniently located, is provided, is not a legal duty of an employer. The duty of reasonable accommodation is satisfied when the employer does what is necessary to enable the disabled worker to work in reasonable comfort. * * *

NOTES AND QUESTIONS

1. Not all of the circuits follow *Vande Zande*. The Second Circuit adopted a similar cost benefit analysis to determine undue hardship, but it applied a different burden shifting mechanism. As part of proving that she is otherwise qualified, the plaintiff must prove that an effective accommodation exists that enables her to perform the job. As for the cost, she must only identify or produce an accommodation, the "costs of which, facially, do not clearly exceed the benefits." Borkowski v. Valley Cent. Sch. Dist., 63 F.3d 131, 139 (2d Cir.1995). The defendant then has the burden of proving that the accommodation entails an undue hardship, based on a cost benefit analysis. The D.C. Circuit places both the burden of production and persuasion on the plaintiff. See Barth v. Gelb, 2 F.3d 1180, 1186 (D.C. Cir.1993). Both the Fifth and the Ninth circuits favor the plaintiff and place

the burden of persuasion on the defendant throughout. Prewitt v. U.S. Postal Serv., 662 F.2d 292 (5th Cir.1981); Mantolete v. Bolger, 767 F.2d 1416,1423–24 (9th Cir.1985).

2. The EEOC regulations promulgated to implement the ADA provide that

> [t]o determine the appropriate reasonable accommodation it may be necessary for the covered entity to initiate an informal, interactive process with the qualified individual with a disability in need of the accommodation. This process should identify the precise limitations resulting from the disability and potential reasonable accommodations that could overcome those limitations.

29 C.F.R. § 1630.2(*o*)(3). The regulations also state that "[t]he appropriate reasonable accommodation is best determined through a flexible, interactive process that involves both the employer and the qualified individual with a disability." 29 C.F.R. pt. 1630 app. § 1630.9.

3. Employees have an obligation to inform employers of the need for a reasonable accommodation and provide sufficient information to the employer to determine the necessary accommodations. This is particularly true when the disability is nonobvious. *See, e.g.,* Reeves v. Jewel Food Stores, Inc., 759 F.3d 698 (7th Cir.2014) (employee did not provide adequate information); Walz v. Ameriprise Fin., Inc., 779 F.3d 842 (8th Cir.2015) (employee never told employer that he suffered from a disability or requested any accommodation). On the other hand, an employer cannot merely assume that an employee with a disability is unable to perform a job without engaging in an individualized assessment and interactive process to identify a reasonable accommodation. *See* Keith v. Oakland Cty., 703 F.3d 918 (6th Cir.2013) (employer failed to engage in interactive process when it assumed that deaf plaintiff could not be a lifeguard with reasonable accommodations).

4. Taylor, a manager for an investment company, told his supervisor, Mick James, that he was suffering from bipolar disorder, a form of mental depression. Taylor also informed James that he was "okay," and the only help he needed was for James to reduce Taylor's work performance objectives and to learn about the symptoms of the disorder in order to facilitate communication with Taylor. James did nothing. Did Taylor's conversation with James trigger an obligation by the employer to initiate an informal investigation into the need for reasonable accommodations for Taylor? *See* Taylor v. Principal Fin. Group, Inc., 93 F.3d 155 (5th Cir.1996).

5. The allocation of the burden of proof in ADA cases is discussed in Kevin W. Williams, Note, *The Reasonable Accommodation Difference: The Effect of Applying the Burden Shifting Frameworks Developed Under Title VII in Disparate Treatment Cases to Claims Brought Under Title I of the Americans with Disabilities Act*, 18 Berkeley J.Emp. & Lab.L. 98 (1997). For a critique of the propriety of applying the *McDonnell Douglas* burden-shifting rule in disability discrimination cases, see Lianne C. Knych, Note, *Assessing*

the Application of McDonnell Douglas *to Employment Discrimination Claims Brought Under the Americans with Disabilities Act*, 79 Minn.L.Rev. 1515 (1995).

6. One of the most common criticisms of the ADA is that its reasonable accommodation requirement will impose substantial costs on employers that will outweigh the benefits, particularly for small businesses. The argument about costs and benefits is cast primarily in law and economics terms. *See, e.g.*, Max Schulz, *Disability Rules Moving in on Smaller Businesses*, Wash. Times, Aug. 28 1994, at B3; Ron A. Vassel, Note, *The Americans with Disabilities Act: The Cost, Uncertainty and Inefficiency*, 13 J.L. & Com. 397 (1994). An early study commissioned by Sears, Roebuck and Co. indicated that 69 percent of the reasonable accommodations provided by Sears cost nothing; that 28 percent cost less than $1,000; and only 3 percent cost more than $1,000. The average cost of accommodations was less than $50 compared to the average costs of $1,800 to $2,400 that Sears incurred for terminating and replacing an employee. Peter David Blanck, *Transcending Title I of the Americans with Disabilities Act: A Report on Sears, Roebuck and Co.*, 20 Mental & Physical Disability Rep. 278 (1996). Similarly, a 1994 report from the President's Committee on Employment of People with Disabilities found that between October, 1992, and September, 1994, 68 percent of the accommodations made for workers with disabilities cost $500 or less. *See* Steven B. Epstein, *In Search of a Bright Line: Determining When an Employer's Financial Hardship Becomes "Undue" Under the Americans with Disabilities Act*, 48 Vand.L.Rev. 391, 394 n.11 (1995). More recent studies find similar results, with half of the accommodations requiring no cost and three-quarters had a first calendar year direct cost of $500 or less. Helen Schartz, Kevin M. Schartz, D.J. Hendricks and Peter Blanck, *Workplace Accommodations: Empirical Study of Current Employees*, 75 Miss.L.J. 917, 937–38 (2006). Employers also report that providing the accommodation benefited the company by allowing it to retain and/or promote qualified employees. *Id.* (direct benefit estimates ranged from $0 to $100,000, with a median reported benefit of $1,800).

7. Individuals who only meet the "regarded as" definition of disability are not entitled to receive reasonable accommodation. Regulations to Implement the Equal Employment Provisions of the Americans With Disabilities Act, codified at 29 C.F.R. § 1630.2(o)(4), 1630.9(e).

8. If a law firm hires as an associate a recent law school graduate who is wheelchair-bound, what accommodations would you expect the firm to make in order to comply with the ADA? What if the new associate is a quadriplegic? *See* Monica Bay, *Attorneys with Disabilities Get Organized,* The Recorder (San Francisco), Oct. 6, 1992, at 17.

9. *Reasonable Accommodation in the Unionized Sector*: Unions fall within the definition of the term "covered entity" under § 101(2) of the ADA, 42 U.S.C. § 12111(2). See the discussion of union liability for discrimination under Title VII in Chapter 2, Section D.5. Thus, like employers, unions are

now statutorily obligated to refrain from discriminating against individuals with disabilities and to make reasonable accommodations for individuals who are within the class protected under the ADA. Many of these issues are explored in Joanne Jocha Ervin, *Reasonable Accommodation and the Collective Bargaining Agreement Under the Americans with Disabilities Act of 1990*, 1991 Det.C.L.Rev. 925; Jerry M. Hunter, *Potential Conflicts Between Obligations Imposed on Employers and Unions by the National Labor Relations Act and the Americans with Disabilities Act*, 13 N.Ill.U.L. Rev. 207 (1993); Mary K. O'Melveny, *The Americans with Disabilities Act and Collective Bargaining Agreements: Reasonable Accommodations or Irreconcilable Conflicts?*, 82 Ky.L.J. 219 (1994); and Robert W. Pritchard, *Avoiding the Inevitable: Resolving the Conflicts Between the ADA and the NLRA*, 11 Lab. Law. 375 (1996). *See also* William McDevitt, *Seniority Systems and the Americans with Disabilities Act: The Fate of "Reasonable Accommodation" After Eckles*, 9 St. Thomas L.Rev. 359 (1997) (discussing a union's responsibility to fairly represent employees with disabilities during bargaining).

E. MEDICAL INQUIRIES, MEDICAL EXAMINATIONS, AND MEDICAL BENEFITS

1. MEDICAL INQUIRIES AND EXAMINATIONS UNDER THE ADA

Prior to the enactment of the ADA, it was a common practice for many employers to include medical examinations and health history questionnaires as part of the employment application. Also, fairly candid discussions between employers and employees about health concerns was the norm. The ADA imposes a series of restrictions on an employer's use of medical examinations and inquiries in three situations: at the application stage ("pre-offer stage"), after individuals have been offered a job ("entering employees" or "post-offer stage"), and for current or "existing employees." ADA § 102(d), 42 U.S.C. § 1211(d). *See* Norman-Bloodsaw v. Lawrence Berkeley Lab., 135 F.3d 1260 (9th Cir.1998); Chai Feldblum, *Medical Examinations and Inquiries Under the Americans with Disabilities Act: A View from the Inside*, 64 Temple L.Rev. 521 (1991) (discussing the legislative history of the provisions on medical examinations and inquiries). The EEOC has issued enforcement guidance to assist employers in understanding and complying with the ADA's limitations on medical inquiries and medical examinations. EEOC, Guidance on Preemployment Disability-Related Inquiries and Medical Examinations Under the Americans with Disabilities Act (Oct. 1995) (Guidance on Preemployment Inquiries), *reprinted* in BNA, Americans with Disabilities Act Manual, at 70:1103. It has also published a Question and Answer document titled Questions and Answers: Enforcement Guidance on Disability-Related Inquiries and Medical Examinations

Under the American with Disabilities Act, *available at http://www.eeoc.gov/policy/docs/qanda-inquiries.html* (last visited Nov. 1, 2015).

Pre-Offer Stage: Section 102(d)(2)(A) of the ADA, 42 U.S.C. § 12112(d)(2)(A), provides that unless otherwise expressly allowed, an employer may not conduct "a medical examination or make inquiries of a job applicant as to whether such applicant is an individual with a disability or as to the nature or severity of such disability." Although screening of applicants generally must be based on nonmedical factors, the ADA permits employers to discuss medical issues with job applicants in three rather narrow situations. The first, found in ADA § 102(d)(2)(B), 42 U.S.C. § 12112(d)(2)(B), allows an employer to "make preemployment inquiries into the ability of an applicant to perform job-related functions," provided the inquiry is made of all applicants for the particular job. Second, an employer may ask an applicant to demonstrate how she or he would perform the essential functions of the job for which the applicant is applying. Third, an employer may ask an applicant with an obvious or a known disability what accommodation is required. For example, an applicant using a wheelchair may be asked how he would perform the essential functions of the job position, but he may not be asked how long he has used a wheelchair or how the disability occurred. *See* EEOC Guidance on Preemployment Inquiries.

Post-Employment Stage—"Entering Employees": An "entering employee" is an individual who has received a job offer but has not yet started to work. As for "entering employees," ADA § 102(d)(2)(B)(3), 42 U.S.C. § 12112(d)(2)(B)(3), provides that an employer "may require a medical examination after an offer of employment has been made to a job applicant and prior to the commencement of the employment duties of such applicant, and may condition an offer of employment on the results of such examination," provided certain conditions are met. The conditions are that (1) all entering employees must have the same medical examination regardless of whether they have a disability; (2) the employer keeps the medical information on separate forms, in separate medical files, and treats it as a "confidential medical record," and (3) the employer uses the results of any examination only to comply with the ADA. *Id.* As to the confidentiality provision, the ADA allows the employer to disclose medical information to supervisors and managers who have a "need to know" of necessary restrictions on the employee's duties and "necessary accommodations," to first aid and safety personnel who "need to know" should emergency treatment of the employee become necessary, and to government officials who need the information to investigate compliance with the ADA. *Id.* Based upon the information obtained in a medical examination, an offer of employment cannot be withdrawn unless it is (1) related to the individual's job and (2) necessary for the conduct of the employer's business. An offer of employment also can be withdrawn if the entering employee's disability would constitute a "direct threat" to the health and safety of the employee and others and no reasonable accommodation is available.

Current or "Existing Employees": The ADA § 102(d)(4), 42 U.S.C. § 12112(d)(4), prohibits an employer from requiring current employees to submit to a "medical examination" or to "make inquiries of an employee as to whether such employee is an individual with a disability or as to the nature or severity of the disability, unless such examination or inquiry is shown to be job-related and consistent with business necessity." The EEOC has construed § 102(d)(4) of the ADA, 42 U.S.C. § 12112(d)(4), to permit an employer "to make inquiries or require medical examinations (fitness for duty exams) when there is a need to determine whether an employee is still able to perform the essential functions of his or her job." 29 C.F.R. pt. 1630, app. § 1630.14(c). The courts generally have deferred to the EEOC's interpretation of § 102(d)(4), because the EEOC has taken the position that if an employee suffers an injury or arguably has a "serious health condition" that appears to affect the employee's ability to perform the essential functions of a job, a medical examination is deemed to be job related and consistent with business necessity. In *Conroy v. N.Y. State Dep't of Corr. Serv.*, 333 F.3d 88, 97–98 (2d Cir.2003), the Second Circuit held that an employer must prove: "(i) 'that the asserted "business necessity" is vital to the business,' (ii) 'that the examination . . . genuinely serves the asserted business necessity,' and (iii) 'that the request is no broader or more intrusive than necessary.' " *See also* Allen v. Baltimore County, Md., 91 F.Supp.3d 722 (D. Md. 2015); Blake v. Baltimore Cnty., Md., 662 F.Supp.2d 417, 422 (D.Md.2009); Tice v. Centre Area Transp. Auth., 247 F.3d 506 (3d Cir.2001).

Drug Testing: Drug testing for illegal drug use is not prohibited under the ADA because the statute provides that the term "qualified individual with a disability" excludes "any employee or applicant who is currently engaging in the illegal use of drugs." ADA § 104(a), 42 U.S.C. § 12114(a). Nevertheless, the ADA provides that nothing in the statute "shall be construed to exclude as a qualified individual with a disability an individual who * * * has successfully completed a supervised drug rehabilitation program and is no longer engaging in" the use of illegal drugs, or has been "successfully" rehabilitated and "is no longer engaging in" the use of illegal drugs. *Id.* § 104(b)(1), 42 U.S.C. § 12114(b)(1). For a discussion of the ability of employers to test for legal drug use, see Patrick J. Schwedler, *Prescription Drugs and Dangerous Jobs: When Can Disclosure be Required for Public Safety under the ADA*, 17 Employee Rts. & Employment Policy J. 93 (2013).

The Ninth Circuit's decision in *Collings v. Longview Fibre Co.*, 63 F.3d 828 (9th Cir.1995), illustrates how most courts interpret the term "currently" in the phrase "currently engaging in the illegal use of drugs."

In *Collings*, eight employees sued under the ADA after they had been discharged for illegal drug use. The employees admitted they had used illegal drugs in the weeks before their termination, but they argued that they were protected under the ADA because, at the time of discharge, they were drug-free and were enrolled in a rehabilitation program. The Ninth Circuit rejected the argument relying, in substantial part, on the EEOC regulations that interpret "currently engaging" in illegal drug use to mean an illegal use of drugs "that has occurred recently enough to indicate that the individual is actively engaged in such conduct." *Id.* at 833 (citing 29 C.F.R. § 1630.3 app.). Other courts have reached a similar conclusion. *See, e.g.*, McDaniel v. Miss. Baptist Med. Ctr., 877 F.Supp. 321, 327 (S.D. Miss. 1994) (Congress contemplated "a drug free period of some considerable length"), *aff'd*, 74 F.3d 1238 (5th Cir.1995) (table decision).

The ADA treats alcohol users differently from users of illegal drugs because alcohol is not a "drug" within the meaning of the statute, *see* ADA § 101(6)(B), 42 U.S.C. § 12111(6)(b), and an alcoholic is not automatically excluded from ADA protection because of "current" alcohol use. *See* Mararri v. WCI Steel, Inc., 130 F.3d 1180 (6th Cir.1997) (although alcoholism is a disability protected under the ADA, the discharge of an alcoholic employee was upheld when he failed to live up to the terms of an agreement to be tested and treated for his alcoholism). If a former alcoholic has been successfully rehabilitated, can he still qualify as an "individual with a disability" under the ADA or the Rehabilitation Act? Is a rehabilitated alcoholic analogous to an individual with a disability that can be corrected or controlled by mediative procedures? If a rehabilitated alcoholic can no longer be considered an "individual with a disability," does it lead to the anomalous result of affording ADA protection to alcoholics who continue to drink alcohol, but not those who are recovering? *See* Burch v. Coca-Cola Co., 119 F.3d 305 (5th Cir.1997) (ADA protection is limited to alcoholic-induced mental or physical impairments that substantially limit major life activities), *cert. denied*, 522 U.S. 1084, 118 S.Ct. 871, 139 L.Ed.2d 768 (1998).

NOTES AND QUESTIONS

1. An employer, Resort, Inc., has adopted the following policy:

> Employees must report, without qualification, all drugs present within their body systems. Further, they must remain free of drugs while on the job. They must not use, possess, conceal, manufacture, distribute, dispense, transport, or sell drugs while on the job, in Resort vehicles or on Resort's properties. Additionally, prescribed drugs may be used only to the extent that they have been reported and approved by an employee supervisor and that they can be taken

by the employee without risk of sensory impairment and/or injury to any person, employee, or customer of Resort.

Is the policy lawful under the ADA? *See* Roe v. Cheyenne Mountain Conference Resort, Inc., 124 F.3d 1221, 1226 (10th Cir.1997).

2. Joseph Casias suffers from inoperable sinus and brain cancer. His doctor has recently prescribed medical marijuana to treat pain that other drugs cannot alleviate. He only uses the marijuana at home and has never come to work under the influence of the drug. After a work place accident, Casias is given a drug test that detects his marijuana use, and he is fired. Does the test or his discharge violate the ADA? *See* James v. City of Costa Mesa, 700 F.3d 394 (9th Cir.2012) (holding that since the ADA defines "illegal drug use" by reference to federal law, and federal law does not authorize the plaintiffs' medical marijuana use, plaintiff's medical marijuana use is not protected by the ADA; however, the ADA would prohibit discrimination against the plaintiff aimed at the plaintiff's underlying medical condition). For commentary on the issue, see Russell Rendall, *Medical Marijuana and the ADA: Removing Barriers to Employment for Disabled Individuals,* 22 Health Matrix 315 (2012); Stacy A. Hickox, *Clearing the Smoke on Medical Marijuana Users in the Workplace*, 29 Quinnipiac L.Rev. 1001 (2011); Ari Lieberman and Aaron Solomon, *A Cruel Choice: Patients Forced to Decide Between Medical Marijuana and Employment*, 26 Hofstra Lab. & Emp.L.J. 619 (2009).

3. An employer has a practice of making offers of employment conditioned upon the applicant agreeing to submit to a medical examination. In the course of the medical examination, each applicant, who has received an offer of employment, completes a detailed medical history questionnaire and is required to provide blood and urine samples. The questionnaire asks, *inter alia,* whether the applicant has any of sixty-one listed medical conditions, including sickle cell anemia, venereal disease, and, in the case of female applicants, menstrual disorders. The blood and urine samples of all applicants are tested for syphilis, sickle cell traits, and genetic traits. The blood and urine samples of women are tested for pregnancy, and the blood samples of men are tested for prostate gland disorders. The tests on blood and urine samples are conducted without any prior or subsequent notice to applicants that these particular tests will be or have been performed. Does the practice of the employer violate the ADA? Title VII? Both? Neither? *See* Norman-Bloodsaw v. Lawrence Berkeley Lab., 135 F.3d 1260 (9th Cir.1998).

2. MEDICAL BENEFITS UNDER THE ADA

The ADA has several provisions that affect health, disability, and other employee benefits. First, § 102 of the ADA, 42 U.S.C. § 12112, broadly prohibits discrimination because of disability. Health insurance and other benefits fall within the meaning of "terms, conditions, and privileges of employment" under § 102. *See* Ford v. Schering-Plough Corp., 145 F.3d 601, 604 (3d Cir.1998); Lewis v. Aetna Life Ins. Co., 982

F.Supp. 1158, 1160–61 (E.D. Va. 1997). The EEOC's regulations also state that the ADA prohibits an employer from discriminating against a qualified individual with a disability in regard to "[f]ringe benefits available by virtue of employment, whether or not administered by the [employer]," 29 C.F.R. § 1630.4(f). Second, § 101, 42 U.S.C. § 12111, contains a statutory cost-justification defense that is not found in other federal employment discrimination statutes. For example, § 101(10)(A)–(B) provides that "[t]he term 'undue hardship' means an action requiring significant difficulty or expense, when considered in light of * * * factors" such as "the nature and cost of the accommodation," "the overall financial resources of the facility," and "the overall financial resources of the covered entity." Third, § 501(c), 42 U.S.C. § 12201(c), frequently referred to as the safe-harbor provision of the ADA, permits insurance companies and benefit managers to continue their risk-assessment practices so long as these practices are not "used as a subterfuge to evade the purposes of [titles] I and III" of the ADA. Fourth, § 102(2), 42 U.S.C. § 12112(b)(2), defines discrimination to include "participating in a contractual or other arrangement or relationship that has the effect of subjecting a covered entity's qualified applicant or employee with a disability to the discrimination prohibited by [the ADA]."

The ADA's broad prohibition against disability discrimination can conflict with the general practice of the insurance industry and self-insured employers to limit coverage or benefits for certain conditions or classes of conditions. One commentator has described the problem as follows:

> Spiraling health care costs and the concomitant increases in the costs of medical and other insurance coverages have led insurers and employers to make great efforts to reduce coverage costs. This is often accomplished by increasing premiums and employee contributions for the cost of coverage, limiting various coverages (such as those for substance abuse and mental health disorders), or eliminating coverages altogether. Additionally, insurance companies providing group and individual coverages not only limit coverage for particular types of treatments (such as cosmetic surgery and experimental treatment), they often underwrite insurance risks as well. For example, based upon a prospective insured's medical history, an insurer may decline to provide the coverage requested, may limit or eliminate coverage for the prospective insured's known medical conditions, or may charge the prospective insured a higher than standard premium for the coverage requested. Insureds and employees have contested these efforts by claiming that the actions of their actual or prospective insurers or of their employers violate the

statutory protections embodied in the Americans with Disabilities Act.

Daniel A. Engel, *The ADA and Life, Health, and Disability Insurance: Where Is the Liability*? 33 Tort & Ins.L.J. 227, 227 (1997). *See also* Susan Nanovic Flannery, *Employer Health-Care Plans: The Feasibility of Disability-Based Distinctions Under ERISA and the Americans with Disabilities Act*, 12 Hofstra Lab.L.J. 211 (1995); Monica E. McFadden, *Insurance Benefits Under the ADA: Discrimination or Business as Usual?*, 28 Tort & Ins.L.J. 480 (1993); Bonnie Poitras Tucker, *Insurance and the ADA*, 46 DePaul L.Rev. 915 (1997).

One of the major categories of cases involving claims of disability-based discrimination with respect to benefits is that in which the employer or its insurance carrier provides less coverage for mental disabilities than for physical disabilities. This category of cases has raised several issues that have divided the courts. The first issue involves standing. Title I protects only individuals with disabilities who, with or without reasonable accommodation, can perform the essential functions of the job. ADA § 101(8), 42 U.S.C. §§ 12111(8). Does an employee who is unable to perform the essential functions of her job have standing under Title I to challenge her employer's policy of providing different benefits coverage for mental and physical impairments? Several courts of appeals have held that individuals who became unable to work because of mental disabilities do not have standing to sue under Title I when their disability benefits are about to terminate. *See* Parker v. Metro. Life Ins. Co., 875 F.Supp. 1321 (W.D. Tenn. 1995), *aff'd in part and rev'd in part*, 99 F.3d 181 (6th Cir.1996) (*Parker I*), *reh'g en banc*, 121 F.3d 1006 (6th Cir.1997) (*Parker II*); EEOC v. CNA Ins. Co., 96 F.3d 1039 (7th Cir.1996); Beauford v. Father Flanagan's Boys' Home, 831 F.2d 768 (8th Cir.1987) (ADA should be interpreted the same as the Rehabilitation Act, which does not provide protection for employees who are no longer able to do their jobs). The Third Circuit, in *Ford v. Schering-Plough Corp.*, 145 F.3d 601 (3d Cir.1998), ruled in favor of standing on the ground that the plaintiff had been "injured in fact" by the denial of benefits. *Id.* 604–05 (citing Simon v. Eastern Ky. Welfare Rights Org., 426 U.S. 26, 38, 96 S.Ct. 1917, 1924, 48 L.Ed.2d 450 (1976)). *See also* Castellano v. City of N.Y., 142 F.3d 58 (2d Cir.1998) (ruling in favor of standing). Jane Byeff Korn, *Crazy (Mental Illness Under the ADA)*, 36 U.Mich.J.L. Reform 585, 627–29 (2003).

A second major issue is whether, under Title I of the ADA, employers may provide more generous long-term benefits for physical disabilities than for mental disabilities. A number of courts of appeals have held that Title I does not bar employers from providing different long-term benefits for mental and physical disabilities. *See* EEOC v. Staten Island Savings Bank, 207 F.3d 144 (2d Cir.2000) (collecting cases). Adopting the reasoning of other courts of appeals, the Second Circuit in *Staten Island*

Savings Bank held that although § 102(b) of Title I, 42 U.S.C. § 12112(b), defines discrimination to include participating in a relationship that has the effect of subjecting a qualified individual with a disability to discrimination, that section does not provide an unambiguous answer as to whether an employer can offer long-term disability plans that provide differing levels of coverage for different disabilities. The court observed that it has long been insurance industry practice to distinguish between physical and mental conditions and that if Congress had intended to prohibit the practice it would have spoken more plainly to effectuate a radical departure from the practice. The court then considered whether the Mental Health Parity Act, codified primarily at 29 U.S.C. § 1185a and 42 U.S.C. § 300gg–5, dictated a different outcome. The Mental Health Parity Act limits the right of health insurance plans to provide lower benefits for mental conditions than they do for physical conditions. Agreeing with other circuits that had considered the issue, the Second Circuit noted that "Congress' passage of the Mental Health Parity Act suggests Congress believed that the ADA neither governs the content of insurance policies nor requires parity between physical and mental conditions." *Id.* at 152, (citing Parker v. Metro. Life Ins. Co., 121 F.3d 1006, 1018 (6th Cir.1997)). The developments on discrimination because of disability in providing different levels of long-term disability for physical and mental conditions are explored and criticized in Christopher R. Wilson, *A Failure to Rehabilitate: Leaving Disability Insurance Out of the Mental Health Parity Debate*, 21 Wash. & Lee J.Civil Rts & Soc.Just. 471, 483–91 (2015); Andrea K. Short, *Eradicating Discrimination Among Individuals with Disabilities in Employer-Provided, Long-Term Disability Benefit Plans,* 56 Wash. & Lee L.Rev. 1341 (1999).

NOTES AND QUESTIONS

Is infertility a disability? Is so, should an employer be permitted to provide less coverage for infertility than for other diseases and impairments under its employee benefits health plan? *See* Krauel v. Iowa Methodist Med. Ctr., 95 F.3d 674 (8th Cir.1996); Saks v. Franklin Covey Co., 117 F. Supp. 2d 318, 320 (S.D.N.Y. 2000); Jessie R. Cardinale, *The Injustice of Infertility Coverage: An Examination of Marital Status Restrictions Under State Law,* 75 Albany L.Rev. 2133 (2011–12); Deborah K. Dallmann, Note, *The Lay View of What "Disability" Means Must Give Way to What Congress Says It Means: Infertility as a "Disability" Under the Americans with Disabilities Act, 38 Wm. & Mary L.Rev. 371 (1996).*

PART 4

IMPLEMENTING EQUALITY

■ ■ ■

CHAPTER 15

AFFIRMATIVE ACTION

■ ■ ■

A. INTRODUCTION

In the efforts of both public and private employers to give effect to the national commitment to equal employment opportunity, perhaps no issue has generated more debate than the appropriateness of affirmative action. As one commentator has explained:

> To its critics, affirmative action is both a euphemism for discrimination against white men and a system that bureaucratizes the entire society at the cost of meritocratic decision making; it is a symbol for all that has gone wrong with American society since the sixties. To its supporters, it is a first step towards remedying the crime of slavery and eliminating the discriminatory preferences that have guaranteed white men the easiest paths to wealth and power; it is a symbol of justice, and a promise of a future of hope.

David Benjamin Oppenheimer, *Distinguishing Five Models of Affirmative Action*, 4 Berkeley Women's L.J. 42, 42 (1988–89).

Debates over affirmative action are often especially intractable because of the many different ways the policy is defined. When some people use the term "affirmative action" they may be referring to quotas; others define affirmative action as any of a range of outreach and recruitment efforts. "The degree to which people in general are in favor of affirmative action largely depends on how that policy is described." James Sterba, Affirmative Action for the Future 31 (2009). Numerous polls and surveys have found that a large majority of people are opposed to quotas or "racial preferences," but that when asked whether they support "affirmative action—without strict quotas" similar majorities respond favorably. *Id.*

Given this range of possible definitions, and the effect a definition has on attitudes about affirmative action, any discussion about the issue should probably be prefaced by some agreement about definition. The United States Commission on Civil Rights defines affirmative action as "any measure, beyond simple termination of a discriminatory practice, adopted to correct or compensate for past or present discrimination or to prevent discrimination from recurring in the future." United States

Commission on Civil Rights, Statement on Affirmative Action 2 (1977). This relatively open-ended definition has been expanded on by numerous commentators. *See, e.g., Sterba, supra*, at 32 (defining affirmative action "as a policy of favoring qualified women, minority, or economically disadvantaged candidates over qualified men, nonminority or economically advantaged candidates respectively with the immediate goals of outreach, remedying discrimination, or achieving diversity."); Michael K. Braswell, Gary A. Moore & Stephen L. Poe, *Affirmative Action: An Assessment of Its Continuing Role in Employment Discrimination Policy*, 57 Alb.L.Rev. 365, 366 (1993). Professor David Oppenheimer has identified five models of affirmative action:

> [S]trict quotas favoring women or minorities (Model I); preference systems in which women or minorities are given some preference over white men (Model II); self-examination plans in which the failure to reach expected goals within expected periods of time triggers self-study, to determine whether discrimination is interfering with a decisionmaking process (Model III); outreach plans in which attempts are made to include more women and minorities within the pool of persons from which selections are made (Model IV); and, affirmative commitments not to discriminate (Model V).

Oppenheimer, *supra*, at 42. As is discussed *infra*, Model I is illegal. The plans most often discussed in judicial opinions are versions of Model II or Model III. Model IV is sometimes referred to as the "pool problem"; its purpose is to eliminate the "good old boy" network—meaning the informal network of white males—as the basis for defining the pool of candidates for a particular job. Which of the models of affirmative action described by Professor Oppenheimer is the most controversial? Which is the least controversial? Why?

Perhaps the primary justification for affirmative action is that it provides a remedy for the past and continuing effects of societal race and sex discrimination in a broad range of activities, including employment. Consider the following observation:

> The affirmative action concept embodies a policy decision that some forms of race-conscious remedies are necessary to improve the social and economic status of blacks in our society. That policy decision, however, cannot be isolated from the history that gave rise to the affirmative action concept. When viewed in light of that history—decades of blatant public and private discrimination against blacks *as a group*—the underlying premise of affirmative action is manifest: If the chasm between "equality" as an abstract proposition and "equality" as a reality is to be bridged, something more is needed than mere

> prohibitions of positive acts of discrimination and the substitution of passive neutrality. That something more, the affirmative action concept dictates, must include race-conscious remedies.

Robert Belton, *Discrimination and Affirmative Action: An Analysis of Competing Theories of Equality and* Weber, 59 N.C.L.Rev. 531, 534 (1981).

The phrase "societal discrimination" is frequently used in the legal literature on affirmative action, but scholars and other commentators rarely attempt to define the concept. On several occasions, the Supreme Court has acknowledged the existence of societal discrimination, without attempting to articulate its precise meaning. For example, in *City of Richmond v. J.A. Croson Co.*, 488 U.S. 469, 109 S.Ct. 706, 102 L.Ed.2d 854 (1989), Justice O'Connor, writing for the plurality, observed that "the sorry history of both private and public discrimination in this country has contributed to a lack of opportunities for black entrepreneurs * * * ." 488 U.S. at 499, 109 S.Ct. at 724. In *Wards Cove Packing Co. v. Atonio*, 490 U.S. 642, 662, 109 S.Ct. 2115, 2127, 104 L.Ed.2d 733 (1989), reproduced in Chapter 4, Justice Blackmun, in dissent, criticized the Court's decision by questioning whether "the majority still believes that race discrimination * * * against nonwhites * * * is a problem in our society." Justice White, who wrote the majority opinion in *Wards Cove*, responded, "Of course, it is unfortunately true that race discrimination exists in our country." *Id.* at 650 n.4, 109 S.Ct. at 2121 n.4. And, in *Adarand Constructors, Inc. v. Pena*, 515 U.S. 200, 237, 115 S.Ct. 2097, 2117, 132 L.Ed.2d 158 (1995), Justice O'Connor, for the majority, observed that "[t]he unhappy persistence of both the practice and lingering effects of racial discrimination against minority groups in this country is an unfortunate reality, and the government is not disqualified from acting in response to it." In *Wygant v. Jackson Board of Education*, 476 U.S. 267, 276, 106 S.Ct. 1842, 1848, 90 L.Ed.2d 260 (1986), the Court also acknowledged the reality of past "societal discrimination," but concluded that the concept was "too amorphous" to justify remediation.

In *Grutter v. Bollinger*, 539 U.S. 306, 123 S.Ct. 2325, 156 L.Ed.2d 304 (2003), the Supreme Court discussed the effect of societal discrimination on the ability of students to be admitted to law school. Justice O'Connor's opinion for the Court stated that, "[b]y virtue of our Nation's struggle with racial inequality, [underrepresented minority students] are both likely to have experiences of particular importance to the Law School's mission, and less likely to be admitted in meaningful numbers on criteria that ignore those experiences." *Id.* at 338, 123 S.Ct. 2325, 2344. Supporting this claim, the opinion explained that the presence of societal discrimination affects a person's viewpoint, thereby making them valuable in creating a diverse student body. ("Just as growing up in a particular region or having particular professional experiences is likely to affect an individual's views, so too is one's own unique experience of being a racial minority in a society, like our own, in which race unfortunately still matters." *Id.* at 333, 123 S.Ct. 2325, 2341.)

Justice O'Connor concluded her opinion with the following sentiment, "It has been 25 years since Justice Powell first approved the use of race to further an interest in student body diversity in the context of public higher education. Since that time, the number of minority applicants with high grades and test scores has indeed increased. * * * We expect that 25 years from now, the use of racial preferences will no longer be necessary to further the interest approved today." *Id.* at 342, 123 S.Ct. 2325, 2346–47. Do you agree with Justice O'Connor's conclusion?

So what is "societal discrimination"? One commentator stated that it is "nothing more than an accumulation of wrongs on the part of governmental and private entities that cannot be identified with particularity at the present time." Robert Allen Sedler, *Beyond* Bakke*: The Constitution and Redressing the Social History of Racism*, 14 Harv.C.R.–C.L.L.Rev. 133, 157 (1979). Another explanation is that

> societal discrimination might be defined as discrimination for which there is no identifiable responsible party, public or private * * * [or] as discrimination that occurred some time in the past with an identifiable party that is no longer legally culpable because the statute of limitations has run or the effects of the discrimination are now too attenuated to trace. * * * The term may also serve as a surrogate for identifiable discrimination in the circumstance where a governmental entity is reluctant to admit or prove its own discrimination. Finally, * * * societal discrimination might best be seen as the cumulative effects of multiple acts and actors—a combination of all the factors identified above * * * .

Michael Selmi, *Remedying Societal Discrimination Through the Spending Power,* 80 N.C.L.Rev. 1576, 1603–04 (2002).

The existence of "societal discrimination" is itself the subject of some disagreement. *See, e.g.,* Sterba, *supra* at 6–7 (discussing the perspective of many white Americans that people of color are as well off or better off than white people in the United States). Consider the following argument by Professor Alan Freeman:

> The concept of "racial discrimination" may be approached from the perspective of either its victim or its perpetrator. From the victim's perspective, racial discrimination describes those conditions of actual social existence as a member of a perpetual underclass. This perspective includes both the objective conditions of life—lack of jobs, lack of money, lack of housing—

and the consciousness associated with those objective conditions—lack of choice and lack of human individuality in being forever perceived as a member of a group rather than as an individual. The perpetrator perspective sees racial discrimination not as conditions, but as actions, or series of actions, inflicted on the victim by the perpetrator. The focus is more on what particular perpetrators have done or are doing to some victims than it is on the overall life situation of the victim's class.

The victim, or "condition," conception of racial discrimination suggests that the problem will not be solved until the conditions associated with it have been eliminated. To remedy the condition of racial discrimination would demand affirmative efforts to change the condition. The remedial dimension of the perpetrator perspective, however, is negative. The task is merely to neutralize the inappropriate conduct of the perpetrator. * * *

The perpetrator perspective presupposes a world composed of atomistic individuals whose actions are outside of and apart from the social fabric and without historical continuity. From this perspective, the law views racial discrimination not as a social phenomenon, but merely as the misguided conduct of particular actors.

Alan David Freeman, *Legitimizing Racial Discrimination Through Antidiscrimination Law: A Critical Review of Supreme Court Doctrine*, 62 Minn.L.Rev. 1049, 1052–54 (1978). *See also* Russell K. Robinson, *Perceptual Segregation*, 108 Colum.L.Rev. 1093, 1117–18 (2008) (describing racially segregated perceptions of both the pervasiveness and the definition of discrimination).

Beyond debates about whether and to what extent societal discrimination continues to affect women, people of color, or other protected classes, fundamental disagreements exist about the appropriateness and legality of affirmative action as a way to remedy discrimination. This chapter explores affirmative action as a means of implementing equality in the workplace. Section B provides a very brief look at the historical evolution of affirmative action. Section C examines the legality of affirmative action under the Fifth and Fourteenth Amendments. Section D explores the relationship between Title VII and affirmative action.

B. THE EVOLUTION OF AFFIRMATIVE ACTION AS A REMEDY

Although affirmative action appears to be a relatively recent remedy for discrimination, its historical roots can be traced back to developments in the immediate aftermath of the ratification of the Thirteen, Fourteenth, and Fifteenth Amendments. After a detailed review of historical materials, Professor Eric Schnapper argued that "[f]rom the closing days of the Civil War until the end of civilian Reconstruction some five years later, Congress adopted a series of social welfare programs whose benefits were expressly limited to blacks." Eric Schnapper, *Affirmative Action and the Legislative History of the Fourteenth Amendment*, 71 Va.L.Rev. 753, 754 (1985). For example, the Freedman's Bureau was established by Congress in 1866 to provide special protection and assistance to newly freed slaves. *Id.* at 755–75. Much of the legislative material on which Professor Schnapper based his argument was included in the NAACP Legal Defense and Educational Fund, Inc., brief submitted in support of the affirmative action program at issue in *Regents of the University of California v. Bakke*, 438 U.S. 265, 98 S.Ct. 2733, 57 L.Ed.2d 750 (1978). Justice Thurgood Marshall relied on some of this historical material in his separate opinion in *Bakke*. *See id.* at 387–402, 98 S.Ct. at 2797–2805. *See also* Schnapper, *supra*, at n.*; James E. Jones, Jr., *The Genesis and Present Status of Affirmative Action in Employment: Economic, Legal, and Political Realities*, 70 Iowa L.Rev. 901, 903–04 (1985).

The use of affirmative action as a remedy for discrimination has also been associated with Presidential Executive Orders. In 1961, President Kennedy issued Executive Order No. 10,925, which required federal contractors to "take affirmative action to ensure that applicants are employed, and that employees are treated during employment, without regard to their race, creed, color or national origin." Executive Order No. 10,925, 3 C.F.R. 448, 450 (1959–1963 Compilation). President Kennedy borrowed the phrase "affirmative action" from the 1935 National Labor Relations Act which delegated to the National Labor Relations Board the authority to remedy unfair labor practices by ordering "such affirmative action" as was necessary to "effectuate the policies" of the statute. *See* Hugh Davis Graham, *The Origins of Affirmative Action: Civil Rights and the Regulatory State*, 523 Annals Am.Acad.Pol. & Soc.Sci., Sept. 1992, at 50, 53–54

In 1965, shortly after the effective date of Title VII, President Johnson replaced President Kennedy's Executive Order 10,925 with Executive Order No. 11,246, which requires federal agencies to establish and maintain affirmative action programs. 3 C.F.R. 339 (1964–65 Comp.). It also requires federal contractors to adopt affirmative action policies for employment decisions regarding applicants and employees. In October 1965, the Office of Contract Compliance (now called the Office of Federal Contract Compliance Programs (OFCCP)) was established in the Department of Justice and delegated the responsibility for administering Executive Order No. 11,246. In 2014, President Barack Obama extended Executive Order No. 11,246 to include sexual orientation and gender identity. *See https://www.whitehouse.gov/blog/2014/07/21/president-obama-signs-new-executive-order-protect-lgbt-workers.* The history of affirmative action under the Executive Orders is discussed in James E. Jones, Jr., *The Genesis and Present Status of Affirmative Action in Employment: Economic, Legal, and Political Realities*, 70 Iowa L.Rev. 901 (1985), and *Twenty-One Years of Affirmative Action: The Maturation of the Administrative Enforcement Process Under the Executive Order 11,246 as amended*, 59 Chi.-Kent L.Rev. 67 (1982).

For the past several decades affirmative action has been employed more often as a voluntary employer policy than as a court-ordered remedy for discrimination. Title VII speaks to both. Several provisions of the 1964 law are directly relevant to the use of affirmative action as a remedy for discrimination. First, § 703(j), 42 U.S.C. § 2000e–2(j), provides that nothing in Title VII

> shall be interpreted to require any employer, employment agency, [or] labor organization * * * to grant preferential treatment to any individual or to any group because of the race, color, religion, sex, or national origin of such individual or group [in order to correct any imbalance between the employer's work force and the relevant labor market].

Section 706(g)(1), 42 U.S.C. § 2000e–5(g)(1), authorizes the courts, in devising remedies for unlawful violations of Title VII, to "order such affirmative action as may be appropriate." In addition to these specific provisions, Title VII's prohibition of employer policies with a disparate impact on women and minorities has long been viewed as supporting affirmative action. *See* Griggs v. Duke Power Co., 401 U.S. 424, 429–30, 91 S.Ct. 849, 852–53, 28 L.Ed.2d 158 (1971) (finding that the legislative purpose of Title VII was to achieve equality of employment "opportunities" and to remove "barriers" to such equality).

The history of affirmative action has been the topic of a number of books, including Terry H. Anderson, The Pursuit of Fairness: A History of Affirmative Action (2005), and Philip F. Rubio, A History of Affirmative Action, 1619–2000 (2001).

C. AFFIRMATIVE ACTION UNDER FEDERAL ANTIDISCRIMINATION STATUTES

1. AFFIRMATIVE ACTION AS REMEDY FOR PRESENT AND PAST DISCRIMINATION

a. Title VII

UNITED STEELWORKERS OF AMERICA V. WEBER

Supreme Court of the United States, 1979.
443 U.S. 193, 99 S.Ct. 2721, 61 L.Ed.2d 480.

JUSTICE BRENNAN delivered the opinion of the Court.

Challenged here is the legality of an affirmative action plan—collectively bargained by an employer and a union—that reserves for black employees 50% of the openings in an in-plant craft-training program until the percentage of black craftworkers in the plant is commensurate with the percentage of blacks in the local labor force. The question for decision is whether Congress, in Title VII left employers and unions in the private sector free to take such race-conscious steps to eliminate manifest racial imbalances in traditionally segregated job categories. We hold that Title VII does not prohibit such race-conscious affirmative action plans.

I

In 1974, petitioner United Steelworkers of America (USWA) and petitioner Kaiser Aluminum & Chemical Corp. (Kaiser) entered into a master collective-bargaining agreement covering terms and conditions of employment at 15 Kaiser plants. The agreement contained, *inter alia*, an affirmative action plan designed to eliminate conspicuous racial imbalances in Kaiser's then almost exclusively white craft-work forces. Black craft-hiring goals were set for each Kaiser plant equal to the percentage of blacks in the respective local labor forces. To enable plants to meet these goals, on-the-job training programs were established to teach unskilled production workers—black and white—the skills necessary to become craftworkers. The plan reserved for black employees 50% of the openings in these newly created in-plant training programs.

This case arose from the operation of the plan at Kaiser's plant in Gramercy, La. Until 1974, Kaiser hired as craftworkers for that plant only persons who had had prior craft experience. Because blacks had long been excluded from craft unions,[1] few were able to present such credentials. As a consequence, prior to 1974 only 1.83% (5 out of 273) of

[1] Judicial findings of exclusion from crafts on racial grounds are so numerous as to make such exclusion a proper subject for judicial notice [Citations omitted.]

the skilled craftworkers at the Gramercy plant were black, even though the work force in the Gramercy area was approximately 39% black.

Pursuant to the national agreement Kaiser altered its craft-hiring practice in the Gramercy plant. Rather than hiring already trained outsiders, Kaiser established a training program to train its production workers to fill craft openings. Selection of craft trainees was made on the basis of seniority, with the proviso that at least 50% of the new trainees were to be black until the percentage of black skilled craftworkers in the Gramercy plant approximated the percentage of blacks in the local labor force.

During 1974, the first year of the operation of the Kaiser-USWA affirmative action plan, 13 craft trainees were selected from Gramercy's production work force. Of these, seven were black and six white. The most senior black selected into the program had less seniority than several white production workers whose bids for admission were rejected. Thereafter one of those white production workers, respondent Brian Weber (hereafter respondent), instituted this class action in the United States District Court for the Eastern District of Louisiana.

The complaint alleged that the filling of craft trainee positions at the Gramercy plant pursuant to the affirmative action program had resulted in junior black employees' receiving training in preference to senior white employees, thus discriminating against respondent and other similarly situated white employees in violation of §§ 703(a) and (d) of Title VII. The District Court held that the plan violated Title VII * * * . A divided panel of the Court of Appeals for the Fifth Circuit affirmed * * * . We granted certiorari. We reverse.

II

* * * The only question before us is the narrow statutory issue of whether Title VII *forbids* private employers and unions from voluntarily agreeing upon bona fide affirmative action plans that accord racial preferences in the manner and for the purpose provided in the Kaiser-USWA plan. * * *

Congress' primary concern in enacting the prohibition against racial discrimination in Title VII of the Civil Rights Act of 1964 was with "the plight of the Negro in our economy." 110 Cong. Rec. 6548 (1964) (remarks of Sen. Humphrey). * * *

[I]t was clear to Congress that "[t]he crux of the problem [was] to open employment opportunities for Negroes in occupations which have been traditionally closed to them," 110 Cong. Rec. 6548 (1964) (remarks of Sen. Humphrey), and it was to this problem that Title VII's prohibition against racial discrimination in employment was primarily addressed.

It plainly appears from the House Report accompanying the Civil Rights Act that Congress did not intend wholly to prohibit private and voluntary affirmative action efforts as one method of solving this problem. The Report provides:

> No bill can or should lay claim to eliminating all of the causes and consequences of racial and other types of discrimination against minorities. There is reason to believe, however, that national leadership provided by the enactment of Federal legislation dealing with the most troublesome problems *will create an atmosphere conducive to voluntary or local resolution of other forms of discrimination.*

H.R.Rep.No. 914, 88th Cong., 1st Sess., pt. 1, p.18 (1963). (Emphasis supplied.)

Given this legislative history, we cannot agree with respondent that Congress intended to prohibit the private sector from taking effective steps to accomplish the goal that Congress designed Title VII to achieve. The very statutory words intended as a spur or catalyst to cause "employers and unions to self-examine and to self-evaluate their employment practices and to endeavor to eliminate, so far as possible, the last vestiges of an unfortunate and ignominious page in this country's history," *Albemarle Paper Co. v. Moody*, 422 U.S. 405, 418, 95 S.Ct. 2362, 2372, 45 L.Ed.2d 280 (1975), cannot be interpreted as an absolute prohibition against all private, voluntary, race-conscious affirmative action efforts to hasten the elimination of such vestiges. It would be ironic indeed if a law triggered by a Nation's concern over centuries of racial injustice and intended to improve the lot of those who had "been excluded from the American dream for so long," 110 Cong. Rec. 6552 (1964) (remarks of Sen. Humphrey), constituted the first legislative prohibition of all voluntary, private, race-conscious efforts to abolish traditional patterns of racial segregation and hierarchy.

Our conclusion is further reinforced by examination of the language and legislative history of § 703(j) of Title VII.[5] Opponents of Title VII raised two related arguments against the bill. First, they argued that the Act would be interpreted to *require* employers with racially imbalanced work forces to grant preferential treatment to racial minorities in order to integrate. Second, they argued that employers with racially imbalanced work forces would grant preferential treatment to racial minorities, even if not required to do so by the Act. *See* 110 Cong. Rec. 8618–8619 (1964) (remarks of Sen. Sparkman). Had Congress meant to prohibit all race-conscious affirmative action, as respondent urges, it easily could have

[5] * * * Section 703(j) speaks to substantive liability under Title VII, but it does not preclude courts from considering racial imbalance as evidence of a Title VII violation. *See Teamsters v. United States*, 431 U.S. 324, 339–340, n. 20, 97 S.Ct. 1843, 1856, 52 L.Ed.2d 396 (1977). Remedies for substantive violations are governed by § 706 (g), 42 U.S.C. § 2000e–5(g).

answered both objections by providing that Title VII would not require or *permit* racially preferential integration efforts. But Congress did not choose such a course. Rather, Congress added § 703(j) which addresses only the first objection. The section provides that nothing contained in Title VII "shall be interpreted to *require* any employer * * * to grant preferential treatment * * * to any group because of the race * * * of such * * * group on account of" a *de facto* racial imbalance in the employer's work force. The section does not state that "nothing in Title VII shall be interpreted to *permit*" voluntary affirmative efforts to correct racial imbalances. The natural inference is that Congress chose not to forbid all voluntary race-conscious affirmative action.

We therefore hold that Title VII's prohibition in §§ 703(a) and (d) against racial discrimination does not condemn all private, voluntary, race-conscious affirmative action plans.

III

We need not today define in detail the line of demarcation between permissible and impermissible affirmative action plans. It suffices to hold that the challenged Kaiser-USWA affirmative action plan falls on the permissible side of the line. The purposes of the plan mirror those of the statute. Both were designed to break down old patterns of racial segregation and hierarchy. Both were structured to "open employment opportunities for Negroes in occupations which have been traditionally closed to them."[8]

At the same time, the plan does not unnecessarily trammel the interests of the white employees. The plan does not require the discharge of white workers and their replacement with new black hirees. Nor does the plan create an absolute bar to the advancement of white employees; half of those trained in the program will be white. Moreover, the plan is a temporary measure; it is not intended to maintain racial balance, but simply to eliminate a manifest racial imbalance. Preferential selection of craft trainees at the Gramercy plant will end as soon as the percentage of black skilled craftworkers in the Gramercy plant approximates the percentage of blacks in the local labor force.

We conclude, therefore, that the adoption of the Kaiser-USWA plan for the Gramercy plant falls within the area of discretion left by Title VII to the private sector voluntarily to adopt affirmative action plans designed to eliminate conspicuous racial imbalance in traditionally segregated job categories. * * *

JUSTICE POWELL and JUSTICE STEVENS took no part in the consideration or decision of these cases.

---

[8] This is not to suggest that the freedom of an employer to undertake race-conscious affirmative action efforts depends on whether or not his effort is motivated by fear of liability under Title VII.

[The concurring opinion of JUSTICE BLACKMUN, which is quoted, in part, in Note 5 below, and the dissenting opinion of CHIEF JUSTICE BURGER have been omitted here.]

JUSTICE REHNQUIST, with whom THE CHIEF JUSTICE joins, dissenting.

* * * The operative sections of Title VII prohibit racial discrimination in employment *simpliciter*. Taken in its normal meaning, and as understood by all Members of Congress who spoke to the issue during the legislative debates, this language prohibits a covered employer from considering race when making an employment decision, whether the race be black or white. Several years ago, however, a United States District Court held that "the dismissal of white employees charged with misappropriating company property while not dismissing a similarly charged Negro employee does not raise a claim upon which Title VII relief may be granted." *McDonald v. Santa Fe Trail Transp. Co.*, 427 U.S. 273, 278, 96 S.Ct. 2574, 2578, 49 L.Ed.2d 493 (1976). This Court unanimously reversed, concluding from the "uncontradicted legislative history" that "[T]itle VII prohibits racial discrimination against the white petitioners in this case upon the same standards as would be applicable were they Negroes * * * ." *Id.* at 280, 96 S.Ct. at 2579.

We have never wavered in our understanding that Title VII "prohibits *all* racial discrimination in employment, without exception for any group of particular employees." *Id.* at 283 (emphasis in original). In *Griggs v. Duke Power Co.*, 401 U.S. 424, 431, 91 S.Ct. 849, 853, 28 L.Ed.2d 158 (1971), our first occasion to interpret Title VII, a unanimous Court observed that "[d]iscriminatory preference, for any group, minority or majority, is precisely and only what Congress has proscribed." And in our most recent discussion of the issue, we uttered words seemingly dispositive of this case: "It is clear beyond cavil that the obligation imposed by Title VII is to provide an equal opportunity for *each* applicant regardless of race, without regard to whether members of the applicant's race are already proportionately represented in the work force." Furnco Construction Corp. v. Waters, 438 U.S. 567, 579, 98 S.Ct. 2943, 2951, 57 L.Ed.2d 957 (1978) (emphasis in original).[1]

* * *

Thus, by a *tour de force* reminiscent not of jurists such as Hale, Holmes, and Hughes, but of escape artists such as Houdini, the Court eludes clear statutory language, "uncontradicted" legislative history, and uniform precedent in concluding that employers are, after all, permitted to consider race in making employment decisions. * * *

---

[1] Our statements in *Griggs* and *Furnco Construction*, patently inconsistent with today's holding, are not even mentioned, much less distinguished, by the Court.

IV

Reading the language of Title VII, as the Court purports to do, "against the background of [its] legislative history * * * and the historical context from which the Act arose," one is led inescapably to the conclusion that Congress fully understood what it was saying and meant precisely what it said. Opponents of the civil rights bill did not argue that employers would be permitted under Title VII voluntarily to grant preferential treatment to minorities to correct racial imbalance. The plain language of the statute too clearly prohibited such racial discrimination to admit of any doubt. They argued, tirelessly, that Title VII would be interpreted by federal agencies and their agents to require unwilling employers to racially balance their work forces by granting preferential treatment to minorities. Supporters of H. R. 7152 responded, equally tirelessly, that the Act would not be so interpreted because not only does it not require preferential treatment of minorities, it also does not *permit* preferential treatment of any race for any reason. It cannot be doubted that the proponents of Title VII understood the meaning of their words, for "[s]eldom has similar legislation been debated with greater consciousness of the need for 'legislative history,' or with greater care in the making thereof, to guide the courts in interpreting and applying the law." Title VII: Legislative History, at 444.

* * *

Our task in this case, like any other case involving the construction of a statute, is to give effect to the intent of Congress. To divine that intent, we traditionally look first to the words of the statute and, if they are unclear, then to the statute's legislative history. Finding the desired result hopelessly foreclosed by these conventional sources, the Court turns to a third source—the "spirit" of the Act. But close examination of what the Court proffers as the spirit of the Act reveals it as the spirit animating the present majority, not the 88th Congress. For if the spirit of the Act eludes the cold words of the statute itself, it rings out with unmistakable clarity in the words of the elected representatives who made the Act law. It is *equality*. * * *

There is perhaps no device more destructive to the notion of equality than the *numerus clausus*—the quota. Whether described as "benign discrimination" or "affirmative action," the racial quota is nonetheless a creator of castes, a two-edged sword that must demean one in order to prefer another. In passing Title VII, Congress outlawed *all* racial discrimination, recognizing that no discrimination based on race is benign, that no action disadvantaging a person because of his color is affirmative. With today's holding, the Court introduces into Title VII a tolerance for the very evil that the law was intended to eradicate, without offering even a clue as to what the limits on that tolerance may be. We are told simply that Kaiser's racially discriminatory admission quota "falls on the permissible side of the line." By going not merely *beyond*, but directly against Title VII's language and legislative history, the Court has sown the wind. Later courts will face the impossible task of reaping the whirlwind.

NOTES AND QUESTIONS

1. The disagreement between Justice Brennan and Justice Rehnquist about the proper construction of § 703(j) is a debate about what vision of equality Congress intended to express in Title VII. This is also the same debate that is at the heart of the controversy over the meaning of equal protection under the Constitution. How would you describe the different visions of workplace equality advocated by Justices Brennan and Rehnquist in *Weber*?

2. *Weber* established a three-pronged test to determine whether a voluntarily adopted affirmative action plan survives a challenge under Title VII. First, the purpose of the plan must be to remedy traditional patterns of discrimination. Second, the plan must not unduly trammel the interests of applicants and employees who are not beneficiaries of the plan. Third, the plan must be temporary, that is, it must be in effect only so long as it is necessary to eradicate traditional patterns of discrimination. In his concurring opinion in *Weber*, 443 U.S. at 209, 99 S.Ct. at 2730, Justice Blackmun questioned whether the Court's three-pronged test might be overly broad because it would legitimate an affirmative action plan under Title VII even when the plan is designed to remedy societal discrimination. He asserted that an "arguable violation" theory would provide a more legitimate justification for a voluntary affirmative action plan under Title VII:

> In his dissent from the decision of the United States Court of Appeals for the Fifth Circuit, Judge Wisdom pointed out that this litigation arises from a practical problem in the administration of Title VII. The broad prohibition against discrimination places the employer and the union on what he accurately described as a "high tightrope without a net beneath them." If Title VII is read literally, on the one hand they face liability for past discrimination against blacks, and on the other they face liability to whites for any voluntary preferences adopted to mitigate the effects of prior discrimination against blacks. * * *
>
> The "arguable violation" theory has a number of advantages. It responds to a practical problem in the administration of Title VII not anticipated by Congress. It draws predictability from the outline of present law and closely effectuates the purpose of the Act. Both Kaiser and the United States urge its adoption here. Because I agree that it is the soundest way to approach this case, my preference would be to resolve this litigation by applying it and holding that Kaiser's craft training program meets the requirement

> that voluntary affirmative action be a reasonable response to an "arguable violation" of Title VII. * * *
>
> The Court, however, declines to consider the narrow "arguable violation" approach and adheres instead to an interpretation of Title VII that permits affirmative action by an employer whenever the job category in question is "traditionally segregated." The sources cited suggest that the Court considers a job category to be "traditionally segregated" when there has been a societal history of purposeful exclusion of blacks from the job category, resulting in a persistent disparity between the proportion of blacks in the labor force and the proportion of blacks among those who hold jobs within the category.
>
> "Traditional segregated job categories," where they exist, sweep more broadly than the class of "arguable violations" of Title VII. The Court's expansive approach is somewhat disturbing for me because, as Mr. Justice Rehnquist points out, the Congress that passed Title VII probably thought it was adopting a principle of nondiscrimination that would apply to blacks and whites alike.

Weber, 443 U.S. at 209–13, 99 S.Ct. at 2730–32 (Blackmun, J., concurring). What options are open to employers and unions that face the kind of "high tightrope without a net beneath them" described by Justice Blackmun? What advice would you give to an employer or union in this situation?

3. Employers were highly critical of the affirmative action remedy prior to *Weber*, but over time many became strong supporters of affirmative action. The response of the business community to affirmative action is discussed in Note, *Rethinking* Weber: *The Business Response to Affirmative Action*, 102 Harv.L.Rev. 658 (1989).

4. *Collateral Attack on Affirmative Action Consent Decrees*: A consent decree is "a settlement agreement among the parties to a lawsuit, signed by the court and entered as a judgment in the case." Maimon Schwarzschild, *Public Law by Private Bargain: Title VII Consent Decrees and the Fairness of Negotiated Institutional Reform*, 1984 Duke L.J. 887, 894. Consent decrees are entered in many cases, including employment discrimination cases, but this is particularly true in class-action employment discrimination cases. Class action cases cannot be settled, however, without court approval. *See* Fed.R.Civ.P. 23. Prior to the Supreme Court's decision in *Martin v. Wilks*, 490 U.S. 755, 109 S.Ct. 2180, 104 L.Ed.2d 835 (1989), the parties in employment discrimination cases frequently entered into consent decrees that contained affirmative action provisions. *Martin v. Wilks* was a race discrimination case involving the Birmingham fire department. The parties—the black firefighters and the employer—settled the case, which had an affirmative action provision for the benefit of the black plaintiffs. After the parties settled the case, white firefighters were invited to participate in the "fairness" hearing that courts generally conduct before entering the consent decree as the judgment. The white plaintiffs refused to participate in the "fairness" hearing; nevertheless, the court eventually approved the consent

decree. Later, the white firefighters brought a collateral attack against the consent decree by filing a separate Title VII lawsuit alleging that the race-specific provisions of the decree discriminated against them because of their race. The issue before the Supreme Court was whether the white firefighters could collaterally attack the consent decree. The Supreme Court held that they could. The effect of *Martin v. Wilks* was to "open the floodgates" for lawsuits by whites or males on every then-extant consent decree that contained an affirmative action provision. *See* William B. Gould, IV, *The Supreme Court and Employment Discrimination Law in 1989: Judicial Retreat and Congressional Response*, 64 Tul.L.Rev. 1485, 1514 n.124 (1990).

Congress overturned *Martin v. Wilks* in the Civil Rights Act of 1991. Title VII § 703(n), 42 U.S.C. § 2000e–2(n). Section 703(n) makes it more difficult for a nonparty to use a collateral attack to challenge a litigated or consent judgment where he or she has had notice of the proposed disposition of the case and a reasonable opportunity to present objections, or where his or her interests were adequately represented by another party in the litigation. For a discussion of *Martin v. Wilks* and Congress' response in the Civil Rights Act of 1991, *see, e.g.*, Andrea Catania & Charles A. Sullivan, *Judging Judgments: The 1991 Civil Rights Act and the Lingering Ghost of* Martin v. Wilks, 57 Brook.L.Rev. 995 (1992); Susan S. Grover, *The Silenced Majority:* Martin v. Wilks *and the Legislative Response*, 1992 U.Ill.L.Rev. 43 (1992).

JOHNSON V. TRANSPORTATION AGENCY OF SANTA CLARA COUNTY

Supreme Court of the United States, 1987.
480 U.S. 616, 107 S.Ct. 1442, 94 L.Ed.2d 615.

JUSTICE BRENNAN delivered the opinion of the Court.

Respondent, Transportation Agency of Santa Clara County, California, unilaterally promulgated an Affirmative Action Plan applicable, *inter alia*, to promotions of employees. In selecting applicants for the promotional position of road dispatcher, the Agency, pursuant to the Plan, passed over petitioner Paul Johnson, a male employee, and promoted a female employee applicant, Diane Joyce. The question for decision is whether in making the promotion the Agency impermissibly took into account the sex of the applicants in violation of Title VII of the Civil Rights Act of 1964. The District Court * * * held that respondent had violated Title VII. The Court of Appeals for the Ninth Circuit reversed. We granted certiorari. We affirm.[2]

[2] No constitutional issue was either raised or addressed in the litigation below. We therefore decide in this case only the issue of the prohibitory scope of Title VII. Of course, where the issue is properly raised, public employers must justify the adoption and implementation of a voluntary affirmative action plan under the Equal Protection Clause. *See* Wygant v. Jackson Board of Education, 476 U.S. 267, 106 S.Ct. 1842, 90 L.Ed.2d 260 (1986).

I

A

In December 1978, the Santa Clara County Transit District Board of Supervisors adopted an Affirmative Action Plan (Plan) for the County Transportation Agency. The Plan implemented a County Affirmative Action Plan, which had been adopted, declared the County, because "mere prohibition of discriminatory practices is not enough to remedy the effects of past practices and to permit attainment of an equitable representation of minorities, women and handicapped persons." Relevant to this case, the Agency Plan provides that, in making promotions to positions within a traditionally segregated job classification in which women have been significantly underrepresented, the Agency is authorized to consider as one factor the sex of a qualified applicant.

In reviewing the composition of its work force, the Agency noted in its Plan that women were represented in numbers far less than their proportion of the County labor force in both the Agency as a whole and in five of seven job categories. Specifically, while women constituted 36.4% of the area labor market, they composed only 22.4% of Agency employees. Furthermore, women working at the Agency were concentrated largely in EEOC job categories traditionally held by women: women made up 76% of Office and Clerical Workers, but only 7.1% of Agency Officials and Administrators, 8.6% of Professionals, 9.7% of Technicians, and 22% of Service and Maintenance Workers. As for the job classification relevant to this case, none of the 238 Skilled Craft Worker positions was held by a woman. The Plan noted that this underrepresentation of women in part reflected the fact that women had not traditionally been employed in these positions, and that they had not been strongly motivated to seek training or employment in them "because of the limited opportunities that have existed in the past for them to work in such classifications." The Plan also observed that, while the proportion of ethnic minorities in the Agency as a whole exceeded the proportion of such minorities in the County work force, a smaller percentage of minority employees held management, professional, and technical positions.[4]

The Agency stated that its Plan was intended to achieve "a statistically measurable yearly improvement in hiring, training and promotion of minorities and women throughout the Agency in all major job classifications where they are underrepresented." As a benchmark by which to evaluate progress, the Agency stated that its long-term goal was to attain a work force whose composition reflected the proportion of minorities and women in the area labor force. Thus, for the Skilled Craft category in which the road dispatcher position at issue here was

[4] While minorities constituted 19.7% of the County labor force, they represented 7.1% of the Agency's Officials and Administrators, 19% of its Professionals, and 16.9% of its Technicians.

classified, the Agency's aspiration was that eventually about 36% of the jobs would be occupied by women.

* * *

The Agency's Plan thus set aside no specific number of positions for minorities or women, but authorized the consideration of ethnicity or sex as a factor when evaluating qualified candidates for jobs in which members of such groups were poorly represented. One such job was the road dispatcher position that is the subject of the dispute in this case.

B

On December 12, 1979, the Agency announced a vacancy for the promotional position of road dispatcher in the Agency's Roads Division. Dispatchers assign road crews, equipment, and materials, and maintain records pertaining to road maintenance jobs. The position requires at minimum four years of dispatch or road maintenance work experience for Santa Clara County. * * *

Twelve County employees applied for the promotion, including Joyce and Johnson. Joyce had worked for the County since 1970, serving as an account clerk until 1975. She had applied for a road dispatcher position in 1974, but was deemed ineligible because she had not served as a road maintenance worker. In 1975, Joyce transferred from a senior account clerk position to a road maintenance worker position, becoming the first woman to fill such a job. During her four years in that position, she occasionally worked out of class as a road dispatcher.

Petitioner Johnson began with the County in 1967 as a road yard clerk, after private employment that included working as a supervisor and dispatcher. He had also unsuccessfully applied for the road dispatcher opening in 1974. In 1977, his clerical position was downgraded, and he sought and received a transfer to the position of road maintenance worker. He also occasionally worked out of class as a dispatcher while performing that job.

Nine of the applicants, including Joyce and Johnson, were deemed qualified for the job, and were interviewed by a two-person board. Seven of the applicants scored above 70 on this interview, which meant that they were certified as eligible for selection by the appointing authority. The scores awarded ranged from 70 to 80. Johnson was tied for second with a score of 75, while Joyce ranked next with a score of 73. A second interview was conducted by three Agency supervisors, who ultimately recommended that Johnson be promoted. * * * At the time, the Agency employed no women in any Skilled Craft position, and had never employed a woman as a road dispatcher. The Coordinator recommended to the Director of the Agency, James Graebner, that Joyce be promoted.

Graebner, authorized to choose any of the seven persons deemed eligible, thus had the benefit of suggestions by the second interview panel and by the Agency Coordinator in arriving at his decision. After deliberation, Graebner concluded that the promotion should be given to Joyce. As he testified: "I tried to look at the whole picture, the combination of her qualifications and Mr. Johnson's qualifications, their test scores, their expertise, their background, affirmative action matters, things like that * * * . I believe it was a combination of all those."

The certification form naming Joyce as the person promoted to the dispatcher position stated that both she and Johnson were rated as well qualified for the job. The evaluation of Joyce read: "Well qualified by virtue of 18 years of past clerical experience including 3 1/2 years at West Yard plus almost 5 years as a [road maintenance worker]." The evaluation of Johnson was as follows: "Well qualified applicant; two years of [road maintenance worker] experience plus 11 years of Road Yard Clerk. Has had previous outside Dispatch experience but was 13 years ago." Graebner testified that he did not regard as significant the fact that Johnson scored 75 and Joyce 73 when interviewed by the two-person board.

Petitioner Johnson filed a complaint with the EEOC alleging that he had been denied promotion on the basis of sex in violation of Title VII. * * *

* * *

II

* * *

The assessment of the legality of the Agency Plan must be guided by our decision in *Weber*.[6] * * *

In reviewing the employment decision at issue in this case, we must first examine whether that decision was made pursuant to a plan prompted by concerns similar to those of the employer in *Weber*. Next, we

6 Justice SCALIA's dissent maintains that the obligations of a public employer under Title VII must be identical to its obligations under the Constitution, and that a public employer's adoption of an affirmative action plan therefore should be governed by *Wygant*. This rests on the following logic: Title VI embodies the same constraints as the Constitution; Title VI and Title VII have the same prohibitory scope; therefore, Title VII and the Constitution are coterminous for purposes of this case. The flaw is with the second step of the analysis, for it advances a proposition that we explicitly considered and rejected in *Weber*. As we noted in that case, Title VI was an exercise of federal power "over a matter in which the Federal Government was already directly involved," since Congress "was legislating to assure federal funds would not be used in an improper manner." 443 U.S. at 206 n.6, 99 S.Ct. at 2729 n.6. "Title VII, by contrast, was enacted pursuant to the commerce power to regulate purely private decisionmaking and was not intended to incorporate and particularize the commands of the Fifth and Fourteenth Amendments. Title VII and Title VI, therefore, cannot be read *in pari materia*." *Ibid*. This point is underscored by Congress' concern that the receipt of any form of financial assistance might render an employer subject to the commands of Title VI rather than Title VII. * * *

must determine whether the effect of the Plan on males and nonminorities is comparable to the effect of the plan in that case.

The first issue is therefore whether consideration of the sex of applicants for Skilled Craft jobs was justified by the existence of a "manifest imbalance" that reflected underrepresentation of women in "traditionally segregated job categories." In determining whether an imbalance exists that would justify taking sex or race into account, a comparison of the percentage of minorities or women in the employer's work force with the percentage in the area labor market or general population is appropriate in analyzing jobs that require no special expertise or training programs designed to provide expertise, *see* Teamsters v. United States, 431 U.S. 324, 97 S.Ct. 1843, 52 L.Ed.2d 396 (1977) (comparison between percentage of blacks in employer's work force and in general population proper in determining extent of imbalance in truck driving positions), or training programs designed to provide experience, *see* Steelworkers v. Weber, 443 U.S. 193, 99 S.Ct. 2721, 61 L.Ed.2d 480 (1979). Where a job requires special training, however, the comparison should be with those in the labor force who possess the relevant qualifications. *See* Hazelwood School District v. United States, 433 U.S. 299, 97 S.Ct. 2736, 53 L.Ed.2d 768 (1977). The requirement that the "manifest imbalance" relate to a "traditionally segregated job category" provides assurance both that sex or race will be taken into account in a manner consistent with Title VII's purpose of eliminating the effects of employment discrimination, and that the interests of those employees not benefiting from the plan will not be unduly infringed.

A manifest imbalance need not be such that it would support a prima facie case against the employer, as suggested in Justice O'Connor's concurrence, since we do not regard as identical the constraints of Title VII and the Federal Constitution on voluntarily adopted affirmative action plans. Application of the "prima facie" standard in Title VII cases would be inconsistent with *Weber's* focus on statistical imbalance,[10] and

[10] The difference between the "manifest imbalance" and "prima facie" standards is illuminated by *Weber*. Had the Court in that case been concerned with past discrimination by the employer, it would have focused on discrimination in hiring skilled, not unskilled, workers, since only the scarcity of the former in Kaiser's work force would have made it vulnerable to a Title VII suit. In order to make out a prima facie case on such a claim, a plaintiff would be required to compare the percentage of black skilled workers in the Kaiser work force with the percentage of black skilled craft workers in the area labor market.

Weber obviously did not make such a comparison. Instead, it focused on the disparity between the percentage of black skilled craft workers in Kaiser's ranks and the percentage of blacks in the area labor force. Such an approach reflected a recognition that the proportion of black craft workers in the local labor force was likely as minuscule as the proportion in Kaiser's work force. The Court realized that the lack of imbalance between these figures would mean that employers in precisely those industries in which discrimination has been most effective would be precluded from adopting training programs to increase the percentage of qualified minorities. Thus, in cases such as *Weber*, where the employment decision at issue involves the selection of unskilled persons for a training program, the "manifest imbalance" standard permits comparison with the general labor force. By contrast, the "prima facie" standard would require comparison

could inappropriately create a significant disincentive for employers to adopt an affirmative action plan. *See Weber*, 443 U.S. at 204, 99 S.Ct. at 2727–28 (Title VII intended as a "catalyst" for employer efforts to eliminate vestiges of discrimination). A corporation concerned with maximizing return on investment, for instance, is hardly likely to adopt a plan if in order to do so it must compile evidence that could be used to subject it to a colorable Title VII suit.[11]

It is clear that the decision to hire Joyce was made pursuant to an Agency plan that directed that sex or race be taken into account for the purpose of remedying underrepresentation. The Agency Plan acknowledged the "limited opportunities that have existed in the past," for women to find employment in certain job classifications "where women have not been traditionally employed in significant numbers." As a result, observed the Plan, women were concentrated in traditionally female jobs in the Agency, and represented a lower percentage in other job classifications than would be expected if such traditional segregation had not occurred. Specifically, 9 of the 10 Para-Professionals and 110 of the 145 Office and Clerical Workers were women. By contrast, women were only 2 of the 28 Officials and Administrators, 5 of the 58 Professionals, 12 of the 124 Technicians, none of the Skilled Craft Workers, and 1—who was Joyce—of the 110 Road Maintenance Workers. The Plan sought to remedy these imbalances through "hiring, training and promotion of * * * women throughout the Agency in all major job classifications where they are underrepresented."

As an initial matter, the Agency adopted as a benchmark for measuring progress in eliminating underrepresentation the long-term goal of a work force that mirrored in its major job classifications the percentage of women in the area labor market.[13] Even as it did so, however, the Agency acknowledged that such a figure could not by itself necessarily justify taking into account the sex of applicants for positions in all job categories. For positions requiring specialized training and experience, the Plan observed that the number of minorities and women "who possess the qualifications required for entry into such job

---

with the percentage of minorities or women qualified for the job for which the trainees are being trained, a standard that would have invalidated the plan in *Weber* itself.

[11] In some cases, of course, the manifest imbalance may be sufficiently egregious to establish a prima facie case. However, as long as there is a manifest imbalance, an employer may adopt a plan even where the disparity is not so striking, without being required to introduce the nonstatistical evidence of past discrimination that would be demanded by the "prima facie" standard. *See, e.g.*, Teamsters v. United States, 431 U.S. 324, 339, 97 S.Ct. 1843, 1856, 52 L.Ed.2d 396 (1977) (statistics in pattern and practice case supplemented by testimony regarding employment practices). Of course, when there is sufficient evidence to meet the more stringent "prima facie" standard, be it statistical, nonstatistical, or a combination of the two, the employer is free to adopt an affirmative action plan.

[13] Because of the employment decision at issue in this case, our discussion henceforth refers primarily to the Plan's provisions to remedy the underrepresentation of women. Our analysis could apply as well, however, to the provisions of the plan pertaining to minorities.

classifications is limited." The Plan therefore directed that annual short-term goals be formulated that would provide a more realistic indication of the degree to which sex should be taken into account in filling particular positions. The Plan stressed that such goals "should not be construed as 'quotas' that must be met," but as reasonable aspirations in correcting the imbalance in the Agency's work force. These goals were to take into account factors such as "turnover, layoffs, lateral transfers, new job openings, retirements and availability of minorities, women and handicapped persons in the area work force who possess the desired qualifications or potential for placement." The Plan specifically directed that, in establishing such goals, the Agency work with the County Planning Department and other sources in attempting to compile data on the percentage of minorities and women in the local labor force that were actually working in the job classifications constituting the Agency work force. From the outset, therefore, the Plan sought annually to develop even more refined measures of the underrepresentation in each job category that required attention.

As the Agency Plan recognized, women were most egregiously underrepresented in the Skilled Craft job category, since none of the 238 positions was occupied by a woman. In mid-1980, when Joyce was selected for the road dispatcher position, the Agency was still in the process of refining its short-term goals for Skilled Craft Workers in accordance with the directive of the Plan. This process did not reach fruition until 1982, when the Agency established a short-term goal for that year of 3 women for the 55 expected openings in that job category—a modest goal of about 6% for that category.

We reject petitioner's argument that, since only the long-term goal was in place for Skilled Craft positions at the time of Joyce's promotion, it was inappropriate for the Director to take into account affirmative action considerations in filling the road dispatcher position. The Agency's Plan emphasized that the long-term goals were not to be taken as guides for actual hiring decisions, but that supervisors were to consider a host of practical factors in seeking to meet affirmative action objectives, including the fact that in some job categories women were not qualified in numbers comparable to their representation in the labor force.

By contrast, had the Plan simply calculated imbalances in all categories according to the proportion of women in the area labor pool, and then directed that hiring be governed solely by those figures, its validity fairly could be called into question. This is because analysis of a more specialized labor pool normally is necessary in determining underrepresentation in some positions. If a plan failed to take distinctions in qualifications into account in providing guidance for actual employment decisions, it would dictate mere blind hiring by the numbers, for it would hold supervisors to "achievement of a particular percentage of minority employment or membership * * * regardless of circumstances such as economic conditions or the number of available qualified minority applicants * * * ." Sheet Metal Workers v. EEOC, 478 U.S. 421, 495, 106 S.Ct. 3019, 3060, 92 L.Ed.2d 344 (1986) (O'Connor, J., concurring in part and dissenting in part).

The Agency's Plan emphatically did *not* authorize such blind hiring. It expressly directed that numerous factors be taken into account in making hiring decisions, including specifically the qualifications of female applicants for particular jobs. Thus, despite the fact that no precise short-term goal was yet in place for the Skilled Craft category in mid-1980, the Agency's management nevertheless had been clearly instructed that they were not to hire solely by reference to statistics. The fact that only the long-term goal had been established for this category posed no danger that personnel decisions would be made by reflexive adherence to a numerical standard.

Furthermore, in considering the candidates for the road dispatcher position in 1980, the Agency hardly needed to rely on a refined short-term goal to realize that it had a significant problem of underrepresentation that required attention. Given the obvious imbalance in the Skilled Craft category, and given the Agency's commitment to eliminating such imbalances, it was plainly not unreasonable for the Agency to determine that it was appropriate to consider as one factor the sex of Ms. Joyce in making its decision.[14] The promotion of Joyce thus satisfies the first requirement enunciated in *Weber*, since it was undertaken to further an affirmative action plan designed to eliminate Agency work force imbalances in traditionally segregated job categories.

We next consider whether the Agency Plan unnecessarily trammeled the rights of male employees or created an absolute bar to their advancement. In contrast to the plan in *Weber*, which provided that 50% of the positions in the craft training program were exclusively for blacks, and to the consent decree upheld last Term in *Firefighters v. Cleveland*, 478 U.S. 501, 106 S.Ct. 3063, 92 L.Ed.2d 405 (1986), which required the promotion of specific numbers of minorities, the Plan sets aside no positions for women. The Plan expressly states that "[t]he 'goals' established for each Division should not be construed as 'quotas' that must be met." Rather, the Plan merely authorizes that consideration be given to affirmative action concerns when evaluating qualified applicants. As the Agency Director testified, the sex of Joyce was but one of numerous factors he took into account in arriving at his decision. The

[14] In addition, the Agency was mindful of the importance of finally hiring a woman in a job category that had formerly been all male. The Director testified that, while the promotion of Joyce "made a small dent, for sure, in the numbers," nonetheless "philosophically it made a larger impact in that it probably has encouraged other females and minorities to look at the possibility of so-called 'non-traditional' jobs as areas where they and the agency both have samples of a success story."

Plan thus resembles the "Harvard Plan" approvingly noted by Justice Powell in *Regents of University of California v. Bakke*, 438 U.S. 265, 316–319, 98 S.Ct. 2733, 2761–63, 57 L.Ed.2d 750 (1978), which considers race along with other criteria in determining admission to the college. As Justice Powell observed: "In such an admissions program, race or ethnic background may be deemed a 'plus' in a particular applicant's file, yet it does not insulate the individual from comparison with all other candidates for the available seats." *Id.* at 317, 98 S.Ct. at 2762. Similarly, the Agency Plan requires women to compete with all other qualified applicants. *No* persons are automatically excluded from consideration; *all* are able to have their qualifications weighed against those of other applicants.

In addition, petitioner had no absolute entitlement to the road dispatcher position. Seven of the applicants were classified as qualified and eligible, and the Agency Director was authorized to promote any of the seven. Thus, denial of the promotion unsettled no legitimate, firmly rooted expectation on the part of petitioner. Furthermore, while petitioner in this case was denied a promotion, he retained his employment with the Agency, at the same salary and with the same seniority, and remained eligible for other promotions.

Finally, the Agency's Plan was intended to *attain* a balanced workforce, not to maintain one. The Plan contains 10 references to the Agency's desire to "attain" such a balance, but no reference whatsoever to a goal of maintaining it. The Director testified that, while the "broader goal" of affirmative action, defined as "the desire to hire, to promote, to give opportunity and training on an equitable, non-discriminatory basis," is something that is "a permanent part" of "the Agency's operating philosophy," that broader goal "is divorced, if you will, from specific numbers or percentages."

The Agency acknowledged the difficulties that it would confront in remedying the imbalance in its work force, and it anticipated only gradual increases in the representation of minorities and women. It is thus unsurprising that the Plan contains no explicit end date, for the Agency's flexible, case-by-case approach was not expected to yield success in a brief period of time. Express assurance that a program is only temporary may be necessary if the program actually sets aside positions according to specific numbers. *See, e.g., Firefighters*, 478 U.S. at 510, 106 S.Ct. at 3069 (4-year duration for consent decree providing for promotion of particular number of minorities); *Weber*, 443 U.S. at 199, 99 S.Ct. at 2725 (plan requiring that blacks constitute 50% of new trainees in effect until percentage of employer work force equal to percentage in local labor force). This is necessary both to minimize the effect of the program on other employees, and to ensure that the plan's goals "[are] not being used simply to achieve and maintain * * * balance, but rather as a benchmark against which" the employer may measure its progress in eliminating the underrepresentation of minorities and women. *Sheet Metal Workers*, 478 U.S. at 477–78, 106 S.Ct. at 3051. In this case, however, substantial evidence shows that the Agency has sought to take a moderate, gradual approach to eliminating the imbalance in its work force, one which establishes realistic guidance for employment decisions, and which visits minimal intrusion on the legitimate expectations of other employees. Given this fact, as well as the Agency's express commitment to "attain" a balanced work force, there is ample assurance that the Agency does not seek to use its Plan to maintain a permanent racial and sexual balance.

III

In evaluating the compliance of an affirmative action plan with Title VII's prohibition on discrimination, we must be mindful of "this Court's and Congress' consistent emphasis on 'the value of voluntary efforts to further the objectives of the law.'" *Wygant*, 476 U.S. at 290, 106 S.Ct. at 1855 (O'Connor J., concurring in part and concurring in judgment) (quoting *Bakke*, 438 U.S. at 364, 98 S.Ct. 2785–86). The Agency in the case before us has undertaken such a voluntary effort, and has done so in full recognition of both the difficulties and the potential for intrusion on males and nonminorities. The Agency has identified a conspicuous imbalance in job categories traditionally segregated by race and sex. It has made clear from the outset, however, that employment decisions may not be justified solely by reference to this imbalance, but must rest on a multitude of practical, realistic factors. It has therefore committed itself to annual adjustment of goals so as to provide a reasonable guide for actual hiring and promotion decisions. The Agency earmarks no positions for anyone; sex is but one of several factors that may be taken into account in evaluating qualified applicants for a position.[17] As both the

---

[17] Justice Scalia's dissent predicts that today's decision will loose a flood of "less qualified" minorities and women upon the work force, as employers seek to forestall possible Title VII liability. The first problem with this projection is that it is by no means certain that employers could in every case necessarily avoid liability for discrimination merely by adopting an affirmative action plan. Indeed, our unwillingness to require an admission of discrimination as the price of adopting a plan has been premised on concern that the potential liability to which such an admission would expose an employer would serve as a disincentive for creating an affirmative action program.

A second, and more fundamental, problem with Justice Scalia's speculation is that he ignores the fact that

> [i]t is a standard tenet of personnel administration that there is rarely a single, "best qualified" person for a job. An effective personnel system will bring before the selecting official several fully-qualified candidates who each may possess different attributes which recommend them for selection. Especially where the job is an unexceptional, middle-level craft position, without the need for unique work experience or educational attainment and for which several well-qualified candidates are available, final determinations as to which candidate is "best qualified" are at best subjective.

Brief for the American Society for Personnel Administration as *Amicus Curiae* 9.

This case provides an example of precisely this point. Any differences in qualifications between Johnson and Joyce were minimal, to say the least. The selection of Joyce thus belies

Plan's language and its manner of operation attest, the Agency has no intention of establishing a work force whose permanent composition is dictated by rigid numerical standards.

We therefore hold that the Agency appropriately took into account as one factor the sex of Diane Joyce in determining that she should be promoted to the road dispatcher position. The decision to do so was made pursuant to an affirmative action plan that represents a moderate, flexible, case-by-case approach to effecting a gradual improvement in the representation of minorities and women in the Agency's work force. Such a plan is fully consistent with Title VII, for it embodies the contribution that voluntary employer action can make in eliminating the vestiges of discrimination in the workplace. * * *

JUSTICE O'CONNOR, concurring in the judgment.

* * * I concur in the judgment of the Court in light of our precedents. I write separately, however, because the Court has chosen to follow an expansive and ill-defined approach to voluntary affirmative action by public employers despite the limitations imposed by the Constitution and by the provisions of Title VII, and because Justice Scalia's dissent rejects the Court's precedents and addresses the question of how Title VII should be interpreted as if the Court were writing on a clean slate. The former course of action gives insufficient guidance to courts and litigants; the latter course of action serves as a useful point of academic discussion, but fails to reckon with the reality of the course that the majority of the Court has determined to follow.

In my view, the proper initial inquiry in evaluating the legality of an affirmative action plan by a public employer under Title VII is no different from that required by the Equal Protection Clause. In either case, consistent with the congressional intent to provide some measure of protection to the interests of the employer's nonminority employees, the employer must have had a firm basis for believing that remedial action was required. An employer would have such a firm basis if it can point to a statistical disparity sufficient to support a prima facie claim under Title VII by the employee beneficiaries of the affirmative action plan of a pattern or practice claim of discrimination.

* * *

The *Weber* view of Congress' resolution of the conflicting concerns of minority and nonminority workers in Title VII appears substantially similar to this Court's resolution of these same concerns in *Wygant v. Jackson Board of Education*, 476 U.S. 267, 106 S.Ct. 1842, 90 L.Ed.2d 260 (1986), which involved the claim that an affirmative action plan by a

Justice Scalia's contention that the beneficiaries of affirmative action programs will be those employees who are merely not "utterly unqualified."

public employer violated the Equal Protection Clause. In *Wygant*, the Court was in agreement that remedying past or present racial discrimination by a state actor is a sufficiently weighty interest to warrant the remedial use of a carefully constructed affirmative action plan. The Court also concluded, however, that "[s]ocietal discrimination, without more, is too amorphous a basis for imposing a racially classified remedy." *Id.* at 276, 106 S.Ct. at 1848. Instead, we determined that affirmative action was valid if it was crafted to remedy past or present discrimination by the employer. Although the employer need not point to any contemporaneous findings of actual discrimination, I concluded in *Wygant* that the employer must point to evidence sufficient to establish a firm basis for believing that remedial action is required, and that a statistical imbalance sufficient for a Title VII prima facie case against the employer would satisfy this firm basis requirement. * * *

The *Wygant* analysis is entirely consistent with *Weber*. * * *

In sum, I agree that respondents' affirmative action plan as implemented in this instance with respect to skilled craft positions satisfies the requirements of *Weber* and of *Wygant*. Accordingly, I concur in the judgment of the Court.

JUSTICE WHITE, dissenting.

* * * My understanding of *Weber* was, and is, that the employer's plan did not violate Title VII because it was designed to remedy the intentional and systematic exclusion of blacks by the employer and the unions from certain job categories. That is how I understood the phrase "traditionally segregated jobs" that we used in that case. The Court now interprets it to mean nothing more than a manifest imbalance between one identifiable group and another in an employer's labor force. As so interpreted, that case, as well as today's decision, * * * is a perversion of Title VII. I would overrule *Weber* and reverse the judgment below.

JUSTICE SCALIA, with whom THE CHIEF JUSTICE joins, and with whom JUSTICE WHITE joins * * * , in parts I and II, dissenting.

* * *

II

The most significant proposition of law established by today's decision is that racial or sexual discrimination is permitted under Title VII when it is intended to overcome the effect, not of the employer's own discrimination, but of societal attitudes that have limited the entry of certain races, or of a particular sex, into certain jobs. Even if the societal attitudes in question consisted exclusively of conscious discrimination by other employers, this holding would contradict a decision of this Court rendered only last Term. *Wygant v. Jackson Board of Education*, 476 U.S. 267, 106 S.Ct. 1842, 90 L.Ed.2d 260 (1986), held that the objective of remedying societal discrimination cannot prevent remedial affirmative action from violating the Equal Protection Clause. While Mr. Johnson does not advance a constitutional claim here, it is most unlikely that Title VII was intended to place a *lesser* restraint on discrimination by public actors than is established by the Constitution. * * *

It is unlikely that today's result will be displeasing to politically elected officials, to whom it provides the means of quickly accommodating the demands of organized groups to achieve concrete, numerical improvement in the economic status of particular constituencies. Nor will it displease the world of corporate and governmental employers (many of whom have filed briefs as *amici* in the present case, all on the side of Santa Clara) for whom the cost of hiring less qualified workers is often substantially less—and infinitely more predictable—than the cost of litigating Title VII cases and of seeking to convince federal agencies by nonnumerical means that no discrimination exists. In fact, the only losers in the process are the Johnsons of the country, for whom Title VII has been not merely repealed but actually inverted. The irony is that these individuals—predominantly unknown, unaffluent, unorganized—suffer this injustice at the hands of a Court fond of thinking itself the champion of the politically impotent. I dissent.

NOTES AND QUESTIONS

1. Justices Brennan and Scalia disagreed about whether the equal protection strict scrutiny test applies to a public employer even when its affirmative action plan is challenged solely under Title VII. Justice Brennan argued that the test is not the same; Justice Scalia argued that it is. Should the standard of review be the same for both public and private employers? *See* George Rutherglen & Daniel R. Ortiz, *Affirmative Action Under the Constitution and Title VII: From Confusion to Convergence*, 35 UCLA L.Rev. 467 (1988). What problems do you envision if Justice Scalia's view prevailed? If Justice Scalia's view were to prevail, would it mean that the Court would have to overturn *Washington v. Davis*, 426 U.S. 229, 96 S.Ct. 2040, 48 L.Ed.2d 597 (1976), where the Court refused to apply Title VII disparate impact analysis to employment discrimination cases brought under the equal protection component of the Fifth Amendment. *Washington v. Davis* is reproduced in Chapter 5.

2. Justice Brennan and Justice O'Connor disagreed about the applicable standard for the first prong of *Weber*. Justice Brennan adopted the "manifest imbalance" standard; Justice O'Connor advocated the "firm basis in fact for believing that remedial action is necessary" test. What do you think is at the bottom of their disagreement? Is it about the meaning of discrimination? Is it about the appropriateness of societal discrimination as a justification for affirmative action? Is it about whether affirmative action plans adopted by government employers should be subject to the same level of scrutiny under both the Constitution and Title VII? Relying on her opinion

in *Wygant*, Justice O'Connor argues that this initial inquiry is the same for a public employer whether the affirmative action plan is challenged under Title VII or the Equal Protection Clause. Is there any substantive difference between these two standards?

It is clear, is it not, that under Justice Brennan's view, an employer could rely upon societal discrimination to satisfy the "manifest imbalance" test? Justice White, who dissented in *Johnson*, would overrule *Weber* because he viewed *Weber*'s first prong—traditionally segregated jobs or manifest imbalance—to mean only intentional discrimination and not societal discrimination. *Johnson*, 480 U.S. at 657, 107 S.Ct. at 1465. Could a public employer satisfy the first prong of *Weber* under Justice O'Connor's view by relying on evidence of societal discrimination? Does her decision in *Weber* suggest that a private employer or union could rely on evidence of societal discrimination to satisfy the first prong of *Weber*? For a discussion of some of the difficulties with the "manifest imbalance" prong, see David D. Meyer, Note, *Finding a "Manifest Imbalance": The Case for a Unified Statistical Test for Voluntary Affirmative Action Under Title VII*, 87 Mich.L.Rev. 1986 (1989).

3. Justice O'Connor apparently did not disagree with Justice Brennan's treatment and analysis of the "unduly trammel" and "temporary nature" prongs of *Weber*.

4. Suppose the plaintiff in *Johnson v. Transportation Agency* had brought his claim solely under the Fourteenth Amendment Equal Protection Clause instead of under Title VII? What is the likelihood that the result would have been different? If the outcome would have been different, does this mean that Title VII and the Equal Protection Clause embrace different visions of workplace equality?

5. Suppose an employer—public or private—voluntarily adopts an affirmative action plan for persons of color and women but fails to follow that plan with respect to individuals in the beneficiary class. For example, suppose the employer in *Johnson v. Transportation Agency* had failed to follow its affirmative action plan, and Paul Johnson, the male, rather than Diane Joyce, the female, had been awarded the job, even though both were equally qualified and all other facts remained the same. Would a member of a beneficiary class under an affirmative action plan, like Diane Joyce, who arguably should have been awarded an employment opportunity pursuant to the plan, have a claim for discrimination if the employer had failed to follow its plan? Should an employer's failure to follow its own affirmative action plan be sufficient, standing alone, to establish a prima facie case of employment discrimination? If not, what would constitute relevant evidence of discriminatory intent? *See* Liao v. Tenn. Valley Auth., 867 F.2d 1366 (11th Cir.1989). If an employer is not obligated to follow its own affirmative action plan, does it mean that only nonbeneficiaries can sue the employer when it adopts such a plan?

6. For a case study of *Johnson*, see Melvin I. Urofsky, Affirmative Action on Trial: Sex Discrimination in *Johnson v. Santa Clara* (1997).

7. In her article, *Civil Rights Perestroika: Intergroup Relations After Affirmative Action*, 86 Cal.L.Rev. 1251 (1998), Professor Linda Hamilton Krieger raises and responds to questions that permeate much of the debate about affirmative action:

> What might we expect if every institution in the nation—every college and university, every corporation, every state and local public agency, and every arm and organ of the federal government—suddenly prohibited its employees from considering the race, sex, or national origin of applicants or employees in hiring, contracting, promotion, or admission to educational programs? What would happen if every employment and admissions decision maker was told simply to "be color-blind," to base his or her decision only on "considerations of merit"? Would they do it? Could they do it? Could we identify those who did not do it, whose decisions were tainted by intergroup bias?
>
> The answers to these questions are, quite simply, "no," "no," and "no." Perhaps constitutions can be colorblind. Perhaps official government or corporate policies can be colorblind. But human beings living in a society in which history, ideology, law, and patterns of social, economic, and political distribution have made race, sex, and ethnicity salient, cannot be colorblind. The "colorblindness" approach to nondiscrimination will prove ineffective because it provides neither a framework for enabling people to recognize the effects of race, gender, or national origin on their perceptions and judgments, nor the tools required to help them counteract those effects. Indeed, a color blindness-centered interpretation of the nondiscrimination principle, coupled with well-meaning people's awareness that they do categorize along racial and ethnic lines, may exacerbate the very intergroup anxiety and ambivalence that lead to what social psychologist refer to as aversive racism.
>
> Furthermore, decision makers cannot base selection decisions only on colorblind considerations of merit for the simple reason that merit has a color. Conceptions of merit are socially and politically constructed and are shaped by the same ingroup preferences that give rise to other subtle forms of intergroup bias. Affirmative action preferences have, in many ways, diverted our attention from the biases inherent in the construction of merit. But if preferences are eliminated, this problem and the inequities it generates will soon rise in sharp relief.
>
> Finally, there is substantial reason to doubt that remaining law enforcement tools, particularly the adjudication of individual disparate treatment cases, will prove effective in identifying and remedying subtle but pervasive forms of intergroup bias. For a variety of reasons, reliance on individual disparate treatment

> adjudication can be expected to result in the serious underidentification of discrimination by judicial decision makers, victims, and private fact finders.

Id. at 1276–77. Do you agree with the responses that Professor Krieger gives to the questions that she raises? If not, how would you respond to the questions?

8. Studies have indicated that, at least in the early years, "white women have benefited the most from affirmative action." Evelyn Hu-DeHart, *Affirmative Action: Some Concluding Thoughts*, 68 U.Colo.L.Rev. 1209, 1212 (1997). *See also* Heidi Hartmann, *Who Has Benefited from Affirmative Action in Employment?*, *in* The Affirmative Action Debate 77 (George E. Curry ed. 1996). Can you explain this result?

9. For the most part, remedial affirmative action plans have focused on discrimination against blacks and women. Should groups other than blacks and women be included in the dialogue on affirmative action? There is a growing body of scholarship that proposes including other groups in the legal and policy debates on affirmative action. *See, e.g.*, Jeffrey S. Byrne, *Affirmative Action for Lesbians and Gay Men: A Proposal for True Equality of Opportunity and Workplace Diversity*, 11 Yale L. & Pol'y Rev. 47 (1993); Laura M. Padilla, *Intersectionality and Positionality: Situating Women of Color in the Affirmative Action Dialogue*, 66 Fordham L.Rev. 843 (1997); John E. Sanchez, *Religious Affirmative Action in Employment: Fearful Symmetry*, 1991 Det.C.L.Rev. 1019; Frank H. Wu, *Neither Black Nor White: Asian Americans and Affirmative Action*, 15 B.C. Third World L.J. 225 (1995); Wayne R. Farnsworth, Note, *Bureau of Indian Affairs Hiring Preferences After* Adarand Constructors, Inc. v. Pena, 1996 B.Y.U.L.Rev. 503; Harvey Gee, Comment, *Changing Landscapes: The Need for Asian Americans to Be Included in the Affirmative Action Debate*, 32 Gonz.L.Rev. 621 (1996–1997); Barry Bennett Kaufman, Note, *Preferential Hiring Policies for Older Workers Under the Age Discrimination in Employment Act*, 56 S.Cal.L.Rev. 825 (1983). The Rehabilitation Act of 1973 expressly requires federal agencies to implement affirmative action plans for the hiring, placement, and advancement of persons with disabilities. 29 U.S.C. § 791(b).

10. A number of studies have compared affirmative action policies in the United States to similar policies in other countries. *See, e.g.*, Kevin A. Burke, *Fair Employment in Northern Ireland: The Role of Affirmative Action*, 28 Colum.J.L. & Soc.Probs. 1 (1994) (discussing religious discrimination in Northern Ireland); M. Varn Chandola, *Affirmative Action in India and the United States: The Untouchable and Black Experience*, 3 Ind. Int'l & Comp.L.Rev. 101 (1992) (comparing compensatory discrimination in India with affirmative action in the United States); Alan M. Katz, *Benign Preferences: An Indian Decision & the* Bakke *Case*, 25 Am.J.Comp.L. 611 (1977) (comparing *Bakke* with an Indian decision); Deidre A. Grossman, Comment, *Voluntary Affirmative Action Plans in Italy and the United States: Differing Notions of Gender Equality*, 14 Comp.Lab.L.J. 185 (1993)

(comparing affirmative action in Italy and the United States). The Canadian constitution explicitly recognizes and protects affirmative action. *See, e.g.*, Ruth Colker, *Hypercapitalism: Affirmative Protections for People With Disabilities, Illness and Parenting Responsibilities Under United States Law*, 9 Yale J.L. & Feminism 213 (1997).

NOTE: AFFIRMATIVE ACTION AND THE CIVIL RIGHTS ACT OF 1991

Congress overturned or modified a number of the Supreme Court employment discrimination decisions that the Court handed down during its 1988 Term because it viewed the Court's decisions as weakening the scope and effectiveness of laws prohibiting discrimination in employment. *See* Mark S. Brodin, *Reflections on the Supreme Court's 1988 Term: Employment Discrimination Decisions and the Abandonment of the Second Reconstruction*, 31 B.C.L.Rev. 1 (1989) (discussing the cases). The *Griggs* disparate impact theory, which is one of the major underpinnings of affirmative action, was the subject of extensive scrutiny during the congressional debates that led to the enactment of the 1991 Civil Rights Act. Ultimately, Congress codified the *Griggs* disparate impact theory in the 1991 Act. Title VII § 703(k)(1)(A), 42 U.S.C. § 2000e–2(k)(1)(A). Although Congress did not directly address in the 1991 Act the status of the Court's affirmative action analysis in *Johnson* and *Weber*, two provisions of the Act raise questions about the continued vitality of *Weber* and *Johnson*. The first is Title VII § 703(m), 42 U.S.C. § 2000e–2(m). Section 703(m), which is discussed in Chapter 3, provides that

> [e]xcept as otherwise provided in this title, an unlawful employment practice is established when the complaining party demonstrates that race, color, religion, sex, or national origin was a motivating factor for any employment practice, even though other factors also motivated the practice.

Some have argued that § 703(m) "sounded the death knell" or was the "killer provision" for affirmative action under Title VII because affirmative action, by definition, specifically considers race or sex as one factor. *See* Fred Barnes, *Last Laugh*, New Republic, Dec. 16, 1991, at 9; *Uncivil Rites*, New Republic, Dec. 16, 1991, at 9. The second provision is § 116, which provides that "[n]othing in the amendments * * * shall be construed to affect court-ordered remedies, affirmative action, or conciliation agreements, that are in accordance with the law." Pub.L. No. 102–166, § 116, 105 Stat. 1071 (1991).

The Ninth Circuit, in *Officers for Justice v. Civil Service Commission*, 979 F.2d 721 (9th Cir.1992), was the first court of appeals to address the impact of the 1991 Civil Rights Act on affirmative action. In rejecting the argument that the 1991 Act sounded the death knell for affirmative action, the Ninth Circuit, construing §§ 703(m) and 116 together, stated:

> The City asserts, and the Union does not dispute, that the savings clause of section [703(m)—"except as otherwise provided by law"] encompasses section 116 of the 1991 Act. * * * The Union

> argues that the phrase "in accordance with law" refers to the law as amended by the 1991 Act and that because section [703(m)] prohibits the use of race as a motivating factor, "even though other factors also motivated the practice," the race conscious promotions at issue in this case are not "in accordance with law."
>
> The Union's reading of the 1991 Act is predicated on an internal inconsistency: that Congress sought to protect affirmative action in section 116 while outlawing it in section [703(m)]. Such an interpretation should be "avoided if alternative interpretations consistent with the legislative purpose are available." The City properly argues that a more natural reading of the phrase "in accordance with law" is that affirmative action programs that were in accordance with law prior to passage of the 1991 Act are unaffected by the amendments. The language of the statute is clear, and the City's interpretation is consistent with that language.

Id. at 725 (citations omitted). The EEOC has taken the position that the 1991 Act does not change the law on affirmative action under Title VII and declared that its 1979 guidelines on affirmative action under Title VII remain in effect. *See* 29 C.F.R. pt. 1608.

Commentators who have addressed the legal status of affirmative action after the 1991 Civil Rights Act have reached conflicting conclusions. Some commentators have argued that the 1991 Civil Rights Act supports the continued legitimacy of the Court's construction of Title VII in *Weber* and *Johnson*. These commentators argue that Congress did not expressly overrule *Johnson* and *Weber* in the 1991 Act as it had done with other Supreme Court decisions; therefore, the phrase, "in accordance with law," could only refer to *Johnson* and *Weber*. *See, e.g.*, Charles R. Lawrence, III & Mari J. Matsuda, We Won't Go Back: Making the Case for Affirmative Action (1997); Alfred W. Blumrosen, *Society in Transition IV: Affirmation of Affirmative Action Under the Civil Rights Act of 1991*, 45 Rutgers L.Rev. 903 (1993); Robert A. Sedler, *Employment Equality, Affirmative Action, and the Constitutional Political Consensus*, 90 Mich.L.Rev. 1315 (1992) (book review). Others have advanced the argument that Congress laid the foundation in the 1991 Civil Rights Act for the Supreme Court to overturn *Johnson* and *Weber*. *See, e.g.*, Nelson Lund, *The Law of Affirmative Action in and After the Civil Rights Act of 1991: Congress Invites Judicial Reform*, 6 Geo.Mason L.Rev. 87 (1997).

b. Equal Protection Clause

The Equal Protection Clause of the Fourteenth Amendment and the equal protection component of the Due Process Clause of the Fifth Amendment require reasonableness in legislative and administrative classifications. With most governmental classifications, the standard equal protection analysis inquires whether laws that treat persons or groups differently serve a legitimate governmental interest. The Supreme Court has adopted three standards of review in equal protection jurisprudence, ranging from deferential to strict. Strict scrutiny applies when a governmental rule, law, or policy creates a suspect classification, such as race, or burdens a fundamental right. *See, e.g.*, Loving v. Virginia, 388 U.S. 1, 11, 87 S.Ct. 1817, 18 L.Ed.2d 1010 (1967) (striking down state law prohibiting interracial marriage); Kramer v. Union Free Sch. Dist. No. 15, 395 U.S. 621, 89 S.Ct. 1886, 23 L.Ed.2d 583 (1969) (applying equal protection to restrictions on the right to vote). Under strict scrutiny, the Court will uphold the law or policy only if it is necessary to achieve some compelling governmental interest. The means to achieve that end must be narrowly tailored and the Court will always consider whether the same purpose can be achieved with less burdensome means. *See, e.g.*, City of Cleburne v. Cleburne Living Ctr., Inc., 473 U.S. 432, 440, 105 S.Ct. 3249, 3254, 87 L.Ed.2d 313 (1985). An intermediate standard applies heightened scrutiny, which requires an exceedingly persuasive justification when the legislation or policy affects a quasi-suspect classification such as gender. To survive judicial review under this intermediate standard, the law or policy must substantially further an important state interest. *See, e.g.*, United States v. Virginia, 518 U.S. 515, 116 S.Ct. 2264, 135 L.Ed.2d 735 (1996) (striking down, under heightened scrutiny, a male-only admission policy at a state-supported institution of higher education). Rational basis scrutiny, the most deferential of the three standards, applies in all other instances when the courts review government laws or policies. Under this level of review, the Court will uphold a law or policy as long as it is rationally related to a legitimate state interest. *See, e.g.*, Schweiker v. Wilson, 450 U.S. 221, 230, 101 S.Ct. 1074, 1080, 67 L.Ed.2d 186 (1981).

Beginning with its 1978 decision in *Regents of the University of California v. Bakke*, 438 U.S. 265, 98 S.Ct. 2733, 57 L.Ed.2d 750 (1978), the Supreme Court has wrestled with two issues involving the constitutionality of the use of affirmative action plans as a remedy for racial discrimination. The first is what standard of review should be applied when these plans are challenged on equal protection grounds. The second is whether the same standard of equal protection review applies to the laws of both federal and state or local governments. In *Adarand Constructors, Inc. v. Pena*, 515 U.S. 200, 115 S.Ct. 2097, 132 L.Ed.2d 158 (1995), the Court considered whether "the Federal Government's practice of giving general contractors on Government projects a financial incentive to hire subcontractors controlled by 'socially and economically disadvantaged individuals,' and in particular, the Government's use of race-based presumptions in identifying such individuals, violate[d] the equal protection component of the Fifth Amendment's Due Process Clause." *Id.* at 204, 115 S.Ct. at 2101. With regard to the standard of review to be used, the Court began by reviewing its prior cases:

Most of the [Equal Protection Clause cases prior to *Bakke*] involved classifications burdening groups that have suffered discrimination in our society. In 1978, the Court confronted the question whether race-based governmental action designed to *benefit* such groups should also be subject to "the most rigid scrutiny." *Regents of University of California v. Bakke*, 438 U.S. 265, 98 S.Ct. 2733, 57 L.Ed.2d 750 (1978), involved an equal protection challenge to a state-run medical school's practice of reserving a number of spaces in its entering class for minority students. The petitioners argued that "strict scrutiny" should apply only to "classifications that disadvantage 'discrete and insular minorities.' " *Id.* at 287–88, 98 S.Ct. at 2747 (opinion of Powell, J.) (citing United States v. Carolene Products Co., 304 U.S. 144, 152 n. 4, 58 S.Ct. 778, 784 n. 4, 82 L.Ed.1234 (1938)). Bakke did not produce an opinion for the Court, but Justice Powell's opinion announcing the Court's judgment rejected the argument. In a passage joined by Justice White, Justice Powell wrote that "[t]he guarantee of equal protection cannot mean one thing when applied to one individual and something else when applied to a person of another color." 438 U.S. at 289–90, 98 S.Ct. at 2748. He concluded that "[r]acial and ethnic distinctions of any sort are inherently suspect and thus call for the most exacting judicial examination." *Id.* at 291, 98 S.Ct. at 2748. On the other hand, four Justices in *Bakke* would have applied a less stringent standard of review to racial classifications "designed to further remedial purposes," *see id.* at 359, 98 S.Ct. at 2783 (Brennan, White, Marshall, and Blackmun, JJ., concurring in judgment in part and dissenting in part). And four Justices thought the case should be decided on statutory grounds. *Id.* at 411–12, 421, 98 S.Ct. at 2809–10, 2815 (Stevens, J., joined by Burger, C.J., and Stewart and Rehnquist, JJ., concurring in judgment in part and dissenting in part). * * *

In *Wygant v. Jackson Board of Education*, 476 U.S. 267, 106 S.Ct. 1842, 90 L.Ed.2d 260 (1986), the Court considered a Fourteenth Amendment challenge to another form of remedial racial classification. The issue in *Wygant* was whether a school board could adopt race-based preferences in determining which teachers to lay off. Justice Powell's plurality opinion observed that "the level of scrutiny does not change merely because the challenged classification operates against a group that historically has not been subject to governmental discrimination," *id.* at 273, 106 S.Ct. at 1846, and stated the two-part inquiry as "whether the layoff provision is supported by a compelling state purpose and whether the means chosen to accomplish that purpose are narrowly tailored." *Id.* at 274, 106

> S.Ct. at 1847. In other words, "racial classifications of any sort must be subjected to 'strict scrutiny.'" *Id.* at 285, 106 S.Ct. at 1852 (O'Connor, J., concurring in part and concurring in judgment). The plurality then concluded that the school board's interest in "providing minority role models for its minority students, as an attempt to alleviate the effects of societal discrimination," *id.* at 274, 106 S.Ct. at 1847, was not a compelling interest that could justify the use of a racial classification. It added that "[s]ocietal discrimination, without more, is too amorphous a basis for imposing a racially classified remedy," *id.* at 276, 106 S.Ct. at 1848, and insisted instead that "a public employer * * * must ensure that, before it embarks on an affirmative-action program, it has convincing evidence that remedial action is warranted. That is, it must have sufficient evidence to justify the conclusion that there has been prior discrimination," *id.* at 277, 106 S.Ct. at 1848–49. Justice White concurred only in the judgment, although he agreed that the school board's asserted interests could not, "singly or together, justify this racially discriminatory layoff policy." *Id.* at 295, 106 S.Ct. at 1858. Four Justices dissented, three of whom again argued for intermediate scrutiny of remedial race-based government action. *Id.* at 301–02, 106 S.Ct. at 1861–62 (Marshall, J., joined by Brennan and Blackmun, JJ., dissenting).
>
> The Court's failure to produce a majority opinion in *Bakke*, *Fullilove* [v. Klutznik, 448 U.S. 448, 100 S.Ct. 2758, 65 L.Ed.2d 902 (1980)], and *Wygant* left unresolved the proper analysis for remedial race-based governmental action. *See* United States v. Paradise, 480 U.S. at 166, 107 S.Ct. at 1063 (plurality opinion of Brennan, J.) ("[A]lthough this Court has consistently held that some elevated level of scrutiny is required when a racial or ethnic distinction is made for remedial purposes, it has yet to reach consensus on the appropriate constitutional analysis"); Sheet Metal Workers v. EEOC, 478 U.S. 421, 480, 106 S.Ct. 3019, 92 L.Ed.2d 344 (1986) (plurality opinion of Brennan, J.). Lower courts found this lack of guidance unsettling. * * *

Adarand, 515 U.S. at 218–21, 115 S.Ct. at 2108–10. After discussing *Richmond v. J.A. Croson Co.,* 488 U.S. 469, 109 S.Ct. 706, 102 L.Ed.2d 854 (1989), the Court concluded as follows:

> Despite lingering uncertainty in the details, however, the Court's cases through *Croson* had established three general propositions with respect to governmental racial classifications. First, skepticism: "'[a]ny preference based on racial or ethnic criteria must necessarily receive a most searching examination,'" *Wygant*, 476 U.S. at 273, 106 S.Ct. at 1847

> (plurality opinion of Powell, J.); *Fullilove*, 448 U.S. at 491, 100 S.Ct. at 2781 (opinion of Burger, C. J.). * * * Second, consistency: "the standard of review under the Equal Protection Clause is not dependent on the race of those burdened or benefited by a particular classification," *Croson*, 488 U.S. at 494, 109 S.Ct. at 722 (plurality opinion); *id.* at 520, 109 S.Ct. at 735 (Scalia, J., concurring in judgment). * * * And third, congruence: "[e]qual protection analysis in the Fifth Amendment area is the same as that under the Fourteenth Amendment," *Buckley v. Valeo*, 424 U.S. at 93, 96 S.Ct. at 670. * * * Taken together, these three propositions lead to the conclusion that any person, of whatever race, has the right to demand that any governmental actor subject to the Constitution justify any racial classification subjecting that person to unequal treatment under the strictest judicial scrutiny. * * *
>
> * * * [W]e hold today that all racial classifications, imposed by whatever federal, state, or local governmental actor, must be analyzed by a reviewing court under strict scrutiny. In other words, such classifications are constitutional only if they are narrowly tailored measures that further compelling governmental interests. To the extent that *Metro Broadcasting* is inconsistent with that holding, it is overruled.
>
> Our action today makes explicit what Justice Powell thought implicit in the *Fullilove* lead opinion: federal racial classifications, like those of a State, must serve a compelling state interest, and must be narrowly tailored to further that interest. *See Fullilove*, 448 U.S. at 496, 100 S.Ct. at 2783–84 (concurring opinion).

Adarand, 515 U.S. at 223–24, 227, 235, 115 S.Ct. at 2111, 2113, 2117.

NOTES AND QUESTIONS

1. The fundamental issue at stake in the Supreme Court's equal protection jurisprudence is how to harmonize a color- or sex-blind theory of equality with the reality of the present and continuing effects of societal discrimination. Does the strict scrutiny test accommodate both of these concerns? *See, e.g.*, Brent E. Simmons, *Reconsidering Strict Scrutiny*, 2 Mich.J. Race & Law, 51 (1996); K.G. Jan Pillai, *Phantom of the Strict Scrutiny*, 31 New Eng.L.Rev. 397 (1997). *See also* Neil Gotanda, *A Critique of "Our Constitution Is Color-Blind,"* 44 Stan.L.Rev. 1, 2 (1991) (arguing that the Supreme Court's use of "color-blind Constitutionalism * * * legitimates and thereby maintains, the social, economic and political advantages that whites hold over other Americans"). Justice Thomas suggested in *Adarand* that the government would never have a compelling reason to enact race-

specific legislation. Adarand Constructors, Inc. v. Pena, 515 U.S. 200, 240–41, 115 S.Ct. 2097, 2119, 132 L.Ed.2d 158 (1995) (Thomas, J., concurring).

2. If a government employer adopted an affirmative action plan in order to remedy the present effects of past racial discrimination, what kind of evidence of a compelling state interest would it have to produce to satisfy the equal protection standard of *Adarand*? Consider the following observation of the Court in *Croson*:

> In *Wygant*, 476 U.S. 267, 106 S.Ct. 1842, 90 L.Ed.2d 260 (1986), four Members of the Court applied heightened scrutiny to a race-based system of employee layoffs. Justice Powell, writing for the plurality, * * * drew a distinction between "societal discrimination" which is an inadequate basis for race-conscious classifications, and the type of identified discrimination that can support and define the scope of race-based relief. The challenged classification in that case tied the layoff of minority teachers to the percentage of minority students enrolled in the school district. The lower court upheld the scheme, based on the theory that minority students were in need of "role models" to alleviate the effects of prior discrimination in society. This Court reversed, with a plurality of four Justices reiterating the view expressed by Justice Powell in *Bakke* that "[s]ocietal discrimination, without more, is too amorphous a basis for imposing a racially classified remedy." *Wygant*, 476 U.S. at 276, 106 S.Ct. at 1848.

City of Richmond v. J.A. Croson Co., 488 U.S. 469, 497, 109 S.Ct. 706, 723–24, 102 L.Ed.2d 854 (1989). The Court in *Croson* stated that allowing a race-based plan on the basis of societal discrimination, without "particularized findings" of unlawful discrimination would allow " 'remedies that are ageless in their reach into the past, and timeless in their ability to affect the future.' " *Id.* at 498, 109 S.Ct. at 724 (citing *Wygant*, 476 U.S. at 276, 106 S.Ct. at 1848). The Court rejected the "role model" argument in *Wygant* because "the statistical disparity between students and teachers had no probative value in demonstrating the kind of prior discrimination in hiring and promotion that would justify race-based relief" and "the role model theory had no relation to some basis for believing that a constitutional or statutory violation had occurred." *Id.* at 497–98, 109 S.Ct. at 724.

In *Shaw v. Hunt*, 517 U.S. 899, 116 S.Ct. 1894, 135 L.Ed.2d 207 (1996), the Court stated that two conditions must be present to satisfy the compelling governmental interest prong of the strict scrutiny test. First, "the discrimination must be 'identified discrimination,' " *Id.* at 1902 (quoting *Croson*, 488 U.S. at 499, 500, 505, 507, 509, 109 S.Ct. at 724–25, 725, 728, 729, 730). Second, the state entity "must have had a 'strong basis in evidence' to conclude that remedial action was necessary '*before* it embarks on an affirmative-action program.' " 517 U.S. at 910, 116 S.Ct. at 1903 (quoting *Wygant*, 476 U.S. at 277, 106 S.Ct. at 1848 (plurality opinion) (emphasis added by *Shaw* Court)).

In *United States v. Brennan,* 650 F.3d 65 (2dCir.2011), the U.S. Court of Appeals for the Second Circuit cautioned that affirmative action plan defenses like those set out in *Weber* and *Santa Clara County* are only applicable once a court has first established that the employer has an affirmative action plan in place, a plan designated to benefit all members of a protected category of people "in a forward-looking manner." *Id.* at 104. In the case before it, the court found no such affirmative action plan where an employer was merely providing benefits to employees it believed were disadvantaged by a selection process that had a disparate impact on them. In that case, the proper defense is whether the employer had a "strong basis in evidence" to believe that its prior practice had a disparate impact. *See supra* Chapter 4.

3. The federal program at issue in *Adarand* benefitted women as well as minorities. The Court, however, did not address whether strict scrutiny should apply to affirmative action plans adopted to benefit women. When laws and policies that have sex-based classifications are challenged on equal protection grounds, the Supreme Court has applied intermediate scrutiny rather than the more stringent standard of strict scrutiny. *See, e.g.*, United States v. Virginia, 518 U.S. 515, 116 S.Ct. 2264, 135 L.Ed.2d 735 (1996). Does this fact support the proposition that gender-based affirmative action policies are more likely to be upheld than race-based affirmative action plans? Justice Stevens raised this possibility in his dissenting opinion in *Adarand*:

> [T]he Court may find that its new "consistency" approach to race-based classifications is difficult to square with its insistence upon rigidly separate categories for discrimination against different classes of individuals. For example, as the law currently stands, the Court will apply "intermediate scrutiny" to cases of invidious gender discrimination and "strict scrutiny" to cases of invidious race discrimination, while applying the same standard for benign classifications as for invidious ones. If this remains the law, then today's lecture about "consistency" will produce the anomalous result that the Government can more easily enact affirmative-action programs to remedy discrimination against women than it can enact affirmative-action programs to remedy discrimination against African-Americans—even though the primary purpose of the Equal Protection Clause was to end discrimination against the former slaves.

515 U.S. at 247, 115 S.Ct. at 2122. Should the same constitutional standard of review apply to race and sex claims?

4. Does strict scrutiny apply to judicial decrees that impose affirmative action as a remedy after a finding of unlawful employment discrimination? In *United States v. Paradise*, 480 U.S. 149, 107 S.Ct. 1053, 94 L.Ed.2d 203 (1987), the lower court entered a judicial decree directing the employer, the Alabama Department of Public Safety, to hire one black trooper for each white trooper until the number of black troopers constituted approximately

25% of the state trooper work force. The lower court entered its affirmative action decree because the employer had failed to comply with an earlier remedial decree that did not have an affirmative action component. The case had been filed under the Equal Protection Clause of the Fourteenth Amendment. The Court, in an opinion written by Justice Brennan, found that the race-specific decree satisfied the "compelling state interest" prong of strict scrutiny. The Court also found that the one-for-one promotion requirement was narrowly tailored to serve a compelling state interest. Justice O'Connor, with whom Chief Justice Rehnquist and Justice Scalia joined, dissented. She agreed that the state had a compelling interest in remedying its own past and present racial discrimination in employment in the department, but she was of the view that the district court had erred in imposing the hiring ratios without first considering the effectiveness of alternative possibilities under the "narrowly tailored" prong of the strict scrutiny test.

5. *State Laws Prohibiting Affirmative Action*: The Equal Protection Clause permits, but does not require, some affirmative action in the public sector. Ballot initiatives have been used to amend the constitutions of California, Michigan and Nebraska, and to amend statutory law in Washington, to prohibit affirmative action in those states. The measures, basically identical in each state, began as a project of the conservative American Civil Rights Institute (ACRI), which sponsored Proposition 209 in California in 1996. The ACRI's initiative provided that "[t]he State shall not discriminate against or grant preferential treatment to any individual or group on the basis of race, sex, color, ethnicity or national origin in the operation of public employment, public education or public contracting." The key language of the measure is the phrase "or grant preferential treatment to," which has been consistently interpreted to eliminate affirmative action. After the measure was adopted in California, the ACRI proposed, and successfully passed, nearly identical ballot initiatives in Washington (1998), Michigan (2002), and Nebraska (2008). The measure was proposed, but defeated, in Colorado in 2008. The consequences of state prohibitions on affirmative action have been particularly stark in public education and contracting, perhaps because of the limits already imposed on affirmative action in employment by the Supreme Court's equal protection jurisprudence. For a discussion of the ACRI initiative more generally, *see* Melissa Hart, *The State-by-State Assault on Equal Opportunity*, 3 Advance 159 (2009).

In *Schuette v. Coalition to Defend Affirmative Action*, ___ U.S. ___, 134 S.Ct. 1623, 188 L.Ed.2d 613 (2014), the U.S. Supreme Court addressed a challenge to the ballot initiative amending the Michigan Constitution prohibiting the use of affirmative action. The Court reversed an en banc Sixth Circuit decision finding Michigan's proposal 2 unconstitutional in violation of the Equal Protection Clause. The circuit court had said the measure was unconstitutional for limiting minority student pathways to seek preferences for admission from colleges and universities. *See Coalition to Defend Affirmative Action v. Regents of the University of Michigan*, 701 F.3d 466 (6th Cir.2012). In reversing, the U.S. Supreme Court held that there was nothing in the Constitution or its prior affirmative action decisions that allowed a court to set aside an amendment to the Michigan Constitution prohibiting affirmative action.

2. AFFIRMATIVE ACTION TO INCREASE DIVERSITY

In *Grutter v. Bollinger*, 539 U.S. 306, 123 S.Ct. 2325, 156 L.Ed.2d 304 (2003), the Supreme Court applied strict scrutiny in reviewing the admissions policy at the University of Michigan Law School, which sought to achieve a diverse student body by, among other things, enrolling a " 'critical mass' of [underrepresented] minority students." *Id.* at 316, 123 S.Ct. at 2332 (brackets in original). The Court stated, "we have never held that the only governmental use of race that can survive strict scrutiny is remedying past discrimination. * * * Today, we hold that the Law School has a compelling interest in attaining a diverse student body." *Id.* at 328, 123 S.Ct. 2339. In finding that diversity can be a compelling governmental interest, it deferred to the Law School's judgment that such diversity is essential to its educational mission. The Law School supported its judgment by putting forth concrete testimony and well-documented studies showing the benefits of critical mass diversity. Several major American businesses and military leaders filed amicus briefs also documenting the real benefits of exposure to widely diverse people, culture, ideas, and viewpoints. In finding that diversity can be a compelling state interest, the Court implicitly overruled *Hopwood v. Texas*, 78 F.3d 932 (5th Cir.1996).

The Court went on to find that the Law School's policy, although "race-conscious," was narrowly tailored to meet its purpose because the program was flexible enough to ensure that each applicant would be "evaluated as an individual" and that an applicant's race or ethnicity would not be "the defining feature of his or her application." *Grutter*, 539 U.S. at 336–37, 123 S.Ct. 2343. The Law School sufficiently considered workable race-neutral alternatives, such as a lottery, and showed that these alternatives would sacrifice academic quality. The Court concluded that "the Law School's race-conscious admissions program does not unduly harm nonminority applicants" because the Law School considers "all pertinent elements of diversity" in addition to race and ethnicity. *Id.* at 341, 123 S.Ct. 2345–46. It noted that the Law School "can (and does) select nonminority applicants who have greater potential to enhance student body diversity over underrepresented minority applicants." *Id.* at 341, 123 S.Ct. 2345.

In a companion case, *Gratz v. Bollinger*, 539 U.S. 244, 123 S.Ct. 2411, 156 L.Ed.2d 257 (2003), the Court found that the admissions policy used by the University of Michigan's College of Literature, Science and Arts (LSA) violated the equal protection clause because it was not narrowly tailored to meet the compelling government interest in diversity. The LSA policy, which awarded twenty points (out of 150 total points) on a selection index to every applicant from an underrepresented minority group, did not provide individualized consideration and had "the effect of making 'the factor of race * * * decisive' for virtually every minimally qualified underrepresented minority applicant." *Id.* at 272, 123 S.Ct. at 2428.

In *Parents Involved in Community Schools v. Seattle School District No. 1*, 551 U.S. 701, 127 S.Ct. 2738, 168 L.Ed.2d 508 (2007), the Supreme Court considered the impact of *Grutter* on race-based student assignment schemes voluntarily adopted by the schools districts in Seattle, Washington and Jefferson County, Kentucky. The case produced several fractured opinions by the Court and no majority opinion. Parts of Chief Justice Roberts' plurality opinion and the parts of that opinion that Justice Kennedy joined in his concurrence serve as the controlling view of the Court. The Court rejected the schools districts' position that their assignment schemes were akin to the admissions program in *Grutter*, holding that the programs lacked narrow tailoring. *Id.* at 723, 127 S.Ct. at 2753–54. *See also id.* at 783–87, 127 S.Ct. at 2789–91 (Kennedy, J., concurring). Unlike *Grutter*, where the Law School implemented a "holistic review" that used race as one of many factors, the school districts predominantly relied on race to "mechanical[ly]" place students at particular schools to reach target racial percentages. *Id.* at 723, 127 S.Ct. at 2753–54. Furthermore, despite the stated goal of these programs, little racial diversity actually resulted from the schemes. *Id.* at 733–35, 127 S.Ct. at 2759–61.

On the compelling interest analysis, Chief Justice Roberts' plurality opinion and Justice Kennedy's concurring opinion diverged, revealing the significant tensions on the Roberts' Court concerning affirmative action. The plurality emphasized that the Supreme Court has historically only recognized two types of compelling interests under strict scrutiny—remedying past intentional discrimination and achieving diversity in higher education. *Id.* at 720–25, 127 S.Ct. at 2751–54. The Chief Justice argued that, according to Supreme Court precedent, the Fourteenth Amendment can only validate affirmative action programs seeking to remedy state-mandated discrimination, not *de facto* segregation. *Id.* at 720–21, 127 S.Ct. at 2751. Roberts' plurality opinion also stressed that *Grutter* was designed for the "unique context of higher education" and could not be applied by analogy to support racial diversity in the primary and secondary education setting, *id.* at 725, 127 S.Ct. at 2754, or to justify any other interest that would result in "racial balancing." *Id.* at 729–31, 736–48, 127 S.Ct. at 2757–78, 2761–68. Justice Kennedy refrained from adopting this position, noting that although *Grutter* may not bind the Court in *Seattle*, its analysis could "help inform" the Court's inquiry. *Id.* at 791, 127 S.Ct. at 2793. Kennedy asserted that the Chief Justice's opinion "impl[ied] an all-too-unyielding insistence that race cannot be a factor in instances when, in my view, it may be taken into account," *id.* at 787, 127 S.Ct. at 2791, and that "[d]iversity, depending on its meaning and definition, is a compelling educational goal a school district may pursue." *Id.* at 783, 127 S.Ct. at 2789. He recommended that instead of race, schools should use "race-conscious measures" to achieve racial diversity, such as "strategic [school] site selection," "targeted" student and faculty recruitment, and "[re]drawing attendance zones [to recognize neighborhood] demographics." *Id.* at 788–89, 127 S.Ct. at 2792.

In *Fisher v. University of Texas at Austin,* ___ U.S. ___, 133 S.Ct. 2411, 186 L.Ed.2d 474 (2013), the U.S. Supreme Court reviewed a challenge to a University of Texas race conscious affirmative action plan. Several years after *Grutter,* the University of Texas implemented a plan adding points for race to the school's "Personal Achievement Index," a calculation added to other scores for college admission. Following the *Grutter* guideline, the university adopted the affirmative action plan in order to achieve a "critical mass" of minority students at the university. *Id.* at 2416. The United States Court of Appeals for the Fifth Circuit, citing *Grutter,* deferred to university decisionmaking and upheld the plan. The U.S. Supreme Court remanded the case back to the Fifth Circuit stating that the court can defer to the university on whether diversity is a compelling state interest, but that no deference should be given to the school on the question of whether the extant plan is narrowly tailored to achieve its purpose. According to the Court, the only relevant inquiry for narrow tailoring is whether the university undertook "serious, good faith consideration of workable race-neutral alternatives." *Id.* at 2420. On remand, the Fifth Circuit affirmed its earlier decision after closely analyzing whether the University of Texas plan was narrowly tailored. *See Fisher v. University of Texas Austin,* 758 F.3d 633 (5th Cir.2014). According to the court, we are "persuaded by UT Austin from this record of its necessary use of race in a holistic process and the want of workable alternatives that would not require even greater use of race. . . ." *Id.* at 660. The U.S. Supreme Court granted certiorari on the Fifth Circuit's more recent decision. *See Fisher v. University of Texas Austin,* 135 S.Ct. 2888, 192 L.Ed.2d 923 (2015).

For a deeper analysis of the implications of the Court's decision in *Fisher,* see Mario L. Barnes, Erwin Chemerinsky & Angela Onwuachi-Willig, *Judging Opportunity Lost: Assessing the Viability of Race Based Affirmative Action After* Fisher v. University of Texas, 62 UCLA L.Rev. 272 (2015); Tanya Washington, *Jurisprudential Ties that Blind: The Means to End Affirmative Action,* 31 Harv.J.Racial & Eth.J.Online 1 (2015); Girardeau A. Spann, *Fisher v. Grutter,* 65 Vand. L. Rev. En Banc 45 (2012).

NOTES AND QUESTIONS

1. Assume the following facts:

The Piscataway School Board decided to lay off one of the teachers in the Business Education Department of the high school. State law required that public schools lay off teachers on the basis of seniority and gave school boards discretion to make lay off decisions only in the case of a tie in seniority. There were only two teachers in the Piscataway high school Business Education Department: one, Debra Williams, is black; the other, Sharon Taxman, is white. Both Williams and Taxman had the same seniority standing because both had started working at the high school on the same day nine years earlier. The Board determined that both were equally qualified in their "classroom performance, evaluations, volunteerism, and certifications."

In previous decisions regarding lay off of employees with equal seniority, none of which had involved employees of different races, the Board had broken the tie through a random process which included drawing numbers out of a container, drawing lots or having a lottery. In deciding whether to lay off Taxman or Williams, the Board made a discretionary decision to rely on its affirmative action policy even though it was not bound to do so. The Board chose to lay off Taxman and to retain Williams. The president of the Board testified that Williams was retained over Taxman in order to provide a role model for students and to promote understanding and tolerance of persons of different backgrounds.

The affirmative action plan had not been adopted to achieve any remedial purpose, i.e., to remedy prior racial discrimination or to correct an imbalance of minorities in the school system. Statistical evidence showed that the percentage of black teachers in the job category that included all teachers exceeded the percentage of blacks in the available work force. The Affirmative Action plan stated, "In all cases, the most qualified candidate will be recommended for appointment. However, when candidates appear to be of equal qualification, candidates meeting the criteria of the affirmative action program will be recommended."

How should a court decide the case? Is the answer different after *Grutter v. Bollinger, supra*? For a pre-*Grutter* opinion, see *Taxman v. Board of Education of Township of Piscataway*, 91 F.3d 1547 (3d Cir.1996) (en banc), *cert. granted,* 521 U.S. 1117, 117 S.Ct. 2506, 138 L.Ed.2d 1010 (1997), *cert. dismissed*, 522 U.S. 1010, 118 S.Ct. 595, 139 L.Ed.2d 431 (1997). Is the rationale supporting "diversity" as a goal of affirmative action equally compelling in the contexts of both education and employment? For analyses of racial diversity as a governmental goal, *see generally* Andy Portinga, *Racial Diversity as a Compelling Governmental Interest*, 75 U.Det. Mercy L.Rev. 73 (1997); Robert J. Donahue, Note, *Racial Diversity as a Compelling Governmental Interest*, 30 Ind.L.Rev. 523 (1997).

2. Post-*Grutter* cases have considered the diversity rationale in the context of public employment. Within these cases, courts debate whether

Grutter helps or hurts the use of the "operational need" defense by cities claiming a unique need for a diverse work force to serve their racially and ethnically diverse communities.

In *Petit v. City of Chicago*, 352 F.3d 1111 (7th Cir.2003), the Court held that the Chicago police department's promotions program satisfied strict scrutiny under the Fourteenth Amendment Equal Protection Clause. The police department's program considered race in the promotion of patrol officers to sergeants by standardizing test scores to account for race and ethnicity, but without adding any fixed number to a candidate's score. In considering whether the program promoted a compelling state interest, the court suggested that the department's need for diverse police force in a "racially and ethnically divided major American city like Chicago" was arguably stronger than the need for diversity in the law school classroom in *Grutter*. *Id.* at 1114. The court also held that the moderate standardization measures used to equalize the candidate test scores were narrowly tailored because minority candidates had historically scored below white candidates on both the subjective and objective portions of the test and standardization equalized this discrepancy. The court explained that instead of giving minority candidates a statistical advantage on the exam, the procedure "eliminate[ed] an advantage [that] white officers had on the test." *Id.* at 1117.

In *Lomack v. City of Newark*, 463 F.3d 303 (3d Cir.2006), the court also applied *Grutter* to a public employer's affirmative action program, but reached an opposite result. In *Lomack*, the court held that the City of Newark's efforts to integrate the city fire department violated the Equal Protection Clause. In Newark, the mayor had sought to diversify the department's "single-race fire companies," which had developed over the years, by mandating that firefighters would be "involuntarily transferred to different companies solely on the basis of their race." *Id.* at 305. Among the program's compelling interests, the city claimed that the program remedied *de facto* segregation in the force and sought to "[secure] the 'educational, sociological, and job performance' benefits of a diverse fire department." *Id.* at 307. The court rejected both arguments. The court found that the city could only act to integrate the force now if the city had previously caused the segregation by intentionally discriminating against minorities. *Id.* at 307–08. The court also rejected the city's second argument, holding that the city could not use the educational diversity justification from *Grutter* because a fire department's mission categorically differs from that of a university, *id.* at 309–10, or even from a police department which may have "operational needs" necessitating racial diversity. *Id.* at 310, n.8, *citing* Petit v. City of Chi., 352 F.3d 1111, 1114 (7th Cir.2004).

NOTE: DIVERSITY AND TITLE VII

Can the goal of diversity justify an affirmative action plan under Title VII? In 2005, not long after the Supreme Court decision in *Grutter,* Professor Cynthia Estlund wrote:

> The next front in the legal battle over affirmative action may well be the workplace, where diversity has become a widely endorsed desideratum of organizational life. That upcoming showdown may have been on the minds of the numerous major American businesses that lined up in support of affirmative action in *Grutter*. Arguing in defense of the elite and integrated institutions from which these firms draw much of their managerial workforces, these business leaders persuaded the Court that the skills needed in today's increasingly global marketplace can only be developed through exposure to widely diverse people, cultures, ideas, and viewpoints. But their briefs may also have planted the seeds for a defense of the corporate amici's own employment policies. Affirmative action, including preferential consideration of women and people of color, undoubtedly plays some role in the hiring and promotional decisions that go into creating the diverse workforces whose virtues these companies tout. A day of reckoning in the courts cannot be far off.

Cynthia L. Estlund, *Putting* Grutter *to Work: Diversity, Integration, and Affirmative Action in the Workplace,* 26 BERKELEY J. EMP. & LAB. L. 1, 2 (2005). Despite Professor Estlund's bold prediction, no such day of reckoning seems to have emerged in the ten years since. Although it seems obvious that private businesses seek diversity in their workforces for a host of reasons, no legal challenge to any such practices have emerged since the *Grutter* case endorsed diversity as a reason that can underpin an affirmative action plan.

Suppose an employer adopts an affirmative action plan designed to establish a racially, sexually, and ethnically diverse management team in order to develop strategies for marketing its products to a racially, sexually, and ethnically diverse clientele? Would the plan survive scrutiny under *Weber* and *Johnson*? Recall that in *Wygant v. Jackson Board of Education,* 476 U.S. 267, 276, 106 S.Ct. 1842, 1848, 90 L.Ed.2d 260 (1986), the Supreme Court rejected the argument that the "role model" rationale was a sufficiently compelling interest to support an affirmative action plan governing teacher layoffs in an educational institution. Would there be support for such a "business diversity" plan in *Grutter,* despite the fact that *Grutter* is a constitutional equal protection case, not a Title VII precedent? According to Estlund, there is plenty of evidence that doctrinal lines between Title VII and equal protection analysis of affirmative action issues are permeable. Estlund, *supra,* at 13. This means that *Grutter* analysis might well be considered by the Supreme Court in a Title VII case. According to Estlund, the arguments against the applicability of *Grutter* include mostly the references throughout *Grutter* to "the particular context of higher education admissions and to the distinct role and prerogatives of universities." *Id.* at 19–20. On the other hand, Estlund argues, there are parts of *Grutter* that are encouraging for the proponents of workplace diversity programs. *Id.* at 20. These include the majority's reliance on the arguments of corporations and retired generals, general support by the majority of affirmative action beyond higher education, and explicit endorsement of the business case for diversity by references to preparing students for an "increasingly diverse workforce and society" and the idea that the skills needed in today's global marketplace can only be developed through exposure to diverse people, cultures, ideas, and viewpoints. *Id.* Despite this, do you think that Title VII is a broad enough statute to endorse diversity as a basis for affirmative action where there is no finding that an individual business ever discriminated on the basis of race or gender in the past?

PART 5

ALTERNATIVE DISPUTE RESOLUTION

■ ■ ■

CHAPTER 16

ARBITRATION OF EMPLOYMENT DISCRIMINATION CLAIMS

■ ■ ■

A. INTRODUCTION

Alternative dispute resolution (ADR) has been defined as "a set of practices and techniques that aim (1) to permit legal disputes to be resolved outside the courts for the benefit of all disputants; (2) to reduce the cost of conventional litigation and the delays to which it is ordinarily subject; or (3) to prevent legal disputes that would otherwise likely be brought to the courts." Jethro K. Lieberman & James F. Henry, *Lessons from the Alternative Dispute Resolution Movement*, 53 U.Chi.L.Rev. 424, 425–26 (1986). Commonly used ADR methodologies include (1) arbitration, (2) mediation, (3) early neutral evaluation, (4) neutral fact-finding, (5) mini-trials, (6) and summary jury trials. *See generally* Laura J. Cooper, Dennis R. Nolan & Richard A. Bales, Alternative Dispute Resolution in the Workplace (2d ed. 2005); Thomas D. Lambros, *The Summary Jury Trial and Other Alternative Methods of Dispute Resolution: A Report to the Judicial Conference of the United States Committee on the Operation of the Jury System*, 103 F.R.D 461 (1984).

Arbitration is one of the most widely used ADR methods, and it is the primary focus of this chapter. For the most part, arbitration resembles an adjudicative process, but there are some significant differences between arbitration and litigation leading to a court trial before a judge or jury. The parties to an arbitration agreement consent to have their disputes resolved by a neutral third-party in a process that, in most circumstances, is less formal, less costly, and less time-consuming than litigation. The parties waive their rights to bring a lawsuit and agree to be bound by the arbitrator's decision—the "arbitral award." Generally the arbitrator makes a final, binding determination, although the parties may agree to a nonbinding award.

In arbitration, to resolve the parties' dispute, the arbitrator will generally hold a hearing to determine the facts and hear arguments from opposing sides. Procedural rules governing the arbitrator's conduct of the hearing can be defined in the arbitration agreement, but the general practice is that there is no, or very limited, prehearing discovery, the rules of evidence will do not apply unless the agreement states otherwise and there may be no record of the proceedings. The parties may be represented by attorneys who prepare witnesses, present arguments, and submit briefs; although non-lawyers, such as union business agents in labor arbitrations, often will represent employees.

Arbitrators are not required to have legal training, and many arbitrators are not lawyers. Arbitrators, however, generally develop considerable expertise in a specialized field of commercial or labor disputes. Although arbitrators essentially function as judges, arbitral awards are not judicial opinions, though they may, at times, resemble such opinions. If the parties require the arbitrator to submit a written opinion, it can be brief with limited analysis. This is primarily because the role of the arbitrator is to resolve the particular dispute between the parties, not to apply external rules of law. Thus, arbitrators are not constrained by stare decisis, but must find the rationale for resolving the dispute within the four corners of the parties' contract, from the past practices and course of dealing between the parties or under applicable law. More recently, courts have enforced arbitration agreements related to legal statutory claims. In those cases, applicable law is considered.

Arbitration awards are binding only on the parties who have agreed to the process and have no precedential effect on the disputes of third parties. Courts are reluctant to overturn arbitral awards, and a party can obtain judicial review of an arbitral award in only very limited circumstances, such as when the arbitrator makes an award that is clearly illegal or is the result of fraud, egregious error, mistake, or misconduct.

In most other ADR methodologies, such as mediation and negotiated settlements, the third-party neutral is a facilitator, not an adjudicator, the parties are free to agree or not, and either party can resort to judicial processes if they cannot reach an agreement. Mediation is commonly used by the EEOC to attempt to resolve employment discrimination charges at an early stage. Between 2008 and 2012, the EEOC conducted over 61,000 mediations, saving those who participated nearly three-quarters of a billion dollars. Benefits of Mediation available at *http://www.eeoc.gov/employees/mediation.cfm*. In 2012, the EEOC resolved over 76% of the claims it mediated in an average of 101 days, which is half the time it would have taken to resolve a claim through the traditional investigative process. *EEOC Mediation Statistics F.Y. 2008–2012* available at *http://www.eeoc.gov/eeoc/mediation/mediation_stats.cfm*. Mediation outside of the EEOC is also used quite often to help resolve legal claims privately.

B. ARBITRATION OF EMPLOYMENT DISCRIMINATION CLAIMS IN NONUNION WORKPLACES

1. ARBITRABILITY

Concern about the "litigation explosion" in the federal courts has helped to fuel the development of a variety of ADR techniques. *See generally* Roberto L. Corrada, *The Arbitral Imperative in Labor and Employment Law,* 47 Cath.U.L.Rev. 919 (1998). In November 1988, in response to increased public and professional concern with the congestion of the federal courts, the delay and expense of litigation, and the expansion of federal rights, Congress created a Federal Courts Study Committee to examine the "litigation explosion." The Committee reported that since 1969 the number of private employment discrimination cases filed in the federal courts had increased by more than 2,000%—from under 400 cases in 1970 to almost 7,500 cases in 1989. The Committee recommended that Congress authorize a five-year test program to allow the EEOC to arbitrate employment discrimination cases with the consent of both parties. *See* Judicial Conference of the U.S., Report of the Federal Courts Study Committee 19, 60–61 (Apr. 1990). This recommendation was not implemented, but the arbitration of employment discrimination claims was soon endorsed by the courts.

CIRCUIT CITY STORES, INC. V. ADAMS

Supreme Court of the United States, 2001.
532 U.S. 105, 121 S.Ct. 1302, 149 L.Ed.2d 234.

JUSTICE KENNEDY delivered the opinion of the Court.

Section 1 of the Federal Arbitration Act (FAA) excludes from the Act's coverage "contracts of employment of seamen, railroad employees, or any other class of workers engaged in foreign or interstate commerce." 9 U.S.C. § 1. All but one of the Courts of Appeals which have addressed the issue interpret this provision as exempting contracts of employment of transportation workers, but not other employment contracts, from the FAA's coverage. A different interpretation has been adopted by the Court of Appeals for the Ninth Circuit, which construes the exemption so that all contracts of employment are beyond the FAA's reach, whether or not the worker is engaged in transportation. * * * We now decide that the better interpretation is to construe the statute, as most of the Courts of Appeals have done, to confine the exemption to transportation workers.

I

In October 1995, respondent Saint Clair Adams applied for a job at petitioner Circuit City Stores, Inc., a national retailer of consumer electronics. Adams signed an employment application which included the following provision:

> "I agree that I will settle any and all previously unasserted claims, disputes or controversies arising out of or relating to my application or candidacy for employment, employment and/or cessation of employment with Circuit City, exclusively by final and binding arbitration before a neutral Arbitrator. By way of example only, such claims include claims under federal, state, and local statutory or common law, such as the Age Discrimination in Employment Act, Title VII of the Civil Rights Act of 1964, as amended, including the amendments of the Civil Rights Act of 1991, the Americans with Disabilities Act, the law of contract and the law of tort."

Adams was hired as a sales counselor in Circuit City's store in Santa Rosa, California.

Two years later, Adams filed an employment discrimination lawsuit against Circuit City in state court, asserting claims under California's Fair Employment and Housing Act * * * and other claims based on general tort theories under California law. Circuit City filed suit in the United States District Court for the Northern District of California, seeking to enjoin the state-court action and to compel arbitration of respondent's claims pursuant to the FAA, 9 U.S.C. §§ 1–16. The District Court entered the requested order. Respondent, the court concluded, was obligated by the arbitration agreement to submit his claims against the employer to binding arbitration. An appeal followed.

* * * [T]he Court of Appeals [for the Ninth Circuit] held the arbitration agreement between Adams and Circuit City was contained in a "contract of employment," and so was not subject to the FAA. Circuit City petitioned this Court, noting that the Ninth Circuit's conclusion that all employment contracts are excluded from the FAA conflicts with every other Court of Appeals to have addressed the question. * * * We granted certiorari to resolve the issue.

II

A

* * * The FAA's coverage provision, § 2, provides that

> [a] written provision in any maritime transaction or a contract evidencing a transaction involving commerce to settle by arbitration a controversy thereafter arising out of such contract or transaction, or the refusal to perform the whole or any part thereof, or an agreement in writing to submit to arbitration an existing controversy arising out of such a contract, transaction, or refusal, shall be valid, irrevocable, and enforceable, save upon

such grounds as exist at law or in equity for the revocation of any contract.

9 U.S.C. § 2.

* * *

The instant case, of course, involves not the basic coverage authorization under § 2 of the Act, but the exemption from coverage under § 1. The exemption clause provides the Act shall not apply "to contracts of employment of seamen, railroad employees, or any other class of workers engaged in foreign or interstate commerce." 9 U.S.C. § 1. * * *

B

Respondent, at the outset, contends that we need not address the meaning of the § 1 exclusion provision to decide the case in his favor. In his view, an employment contract is not a "contract evidencing a transaction involving interstate commerce" at all, since the word "transaction" in § 2 extends only to commercial contracts. This line of reasoning proves too much, for it would make the § 1 exclusion provision superfluous. If all contracts of employment are beyond the scope of the Act under the § 2 coverage provision, the separate exemption for "contracts of employment of seamen, railroad employees, or any other class of workers engaged in * * * interstate commerce" would be pointless. The proffered interpretation of "evidencing a transaction involving commerce," * * * would be inconsistent with *Gilmer v. Interstate/Johnson Lane Corp.*, 500 U.S. 20, 111 S.Ct. 1647, 114 L.Ed.2d 26 (1991), where we held that § 2 required the arbitration of an age discrimination claim based on an agreement in a securities registration application, a dispute that did not arise from a "commercial deal or merchant's sale." * * * If, then, there is an argument to be made that arbitration agreements in employment contracts are not covered by the Act, it must be premised on the language of the § 1 exclusion provision itself.

Respondent, endorsing the reasoning of the Court of Appeals for the Ninth Circuit that the provision excludes all employment contracts, relies on the asserted breadth of the words "contracts of employment of * * * any other class of workers engaged in * * * commerce." Referring to our construction of § 2's coverage provision in *Allied-Bruce* [Terminix Cos. v. Dobson, 513 U.S. 265, 115 S.Ct. 834, 130 L.Ed.2d 753 (1995)]—concluding that the words "involving commerce" evidence the congressional intent to regulate to the full extent of its commerce power—respondent contends § 1's interpretation should have a like reach, thus exempting all employment contracts. The two provisions, it is argued, are coterminous; under this view the "involving commerce" provision brings within the FAA's scope all contracts within the Congress' commerce power, and the "engaged in * * * commerce" language in § 1 in turn exempts from the FAA all employment contracts falling within that authority.

This reading of § 1, however, runs into an immediate and, in our view, insurmountable textual obstacle. Unlike the "involving commerce" language in § 2, the words "any other class of workers engaged in * * * commerce" constitute a residual phrase, following, in the same sentence, explicit reference to "seamen" and "railroad employees." Construing the residual phrase to exclude all employment contracts fails to give independent effect to the statute's enumeration of the specific categories of workers which precedes it; there would be no need for Congress to use the phrases "seamen" and "railroad employees" if those same classes of workers were subsumed within the meaning of the "engaged in * * * commerce" residual clause. The wording of § 1 calls for the application of the maxim *ejusdem generis*, the statutory canon that "[w]here general words follow specific words in a statutory enumeration, the general words are construed to embrace only objects similar in nature to those objects enumerated by the preceding specific words." Under this rule of construction the residual clause should be read to give effect to the terms "seamen" and "railroad employees," and should itself be controlled and defined by reference to the enumerated categories of workers which are recited just before it; the interpretation of the clause pressed by respondent fails to produce these results.

Canons of construction need not be conclusive and are often countered, of course, by some maxim pointing in a different direction. The application of the rule *ejusdem generis* in this case, however, is in full accord with other sound considerations bearing upon the proper interpretation of the clause. For even if the term "engaged in commerce" stood alone in § 1, we would not construe the provision to exclude all contracts of employment from the FAA. Congress uses different modifiers to the word "commerce" in the design and enactment of its statutes. The phrase "affecting commerce" indicates Congress' intent to regulate to the outer limits of its authority under the Commerce Clause. See, *e.g.*, *Allied-Bruce*, 513 U.S., at 277. The "involving commerce" phrase, the operative words for the reach of the basic coverage provision in § 2, was at issue in *Allied-Bruce*. That particular phrase had not been interpreted before by this Court. Considering the usual meaning of the word "involving," and the pro-arbitration purposes of the FAA, *Allied-Bruce* held the "word 'involving,' like 'affecting,' signals an intent to exercise Congress' commerce power to the full." *Ibid.* Unlike those phrases, however, the general words "in commerce" and the specific phrase "engaged in commerce" are understood to have a more limited reach. In *Allied-Bruce* itself the Court said the words "in commerce" are "often-found words of art" that we have not read as expressing congressional intent to regulate to the outer limits of authority under the Commerce Clause. *Id.* at 273.

It is argued that we should assess the meaning of the phrase "engaged in commerce" in a different manner here, because the FAA was enacted when congressional authority to regulate under the commerce power was to a large extent confined by our decisions. When the FAA was enacted in 1925, respondent reasons, the phrase "engaged in commerce" was not a term of art indicating a limited assertion of congressional jurisdiction; to the contrary, it is said, the formulation came close to expressing the outer limits of Congress' power as then understood. Were this mode of interpretation to prevail, we would take into account the scope of the Commerce Clause, as then elaborated by the Court, at the date of the FAA's enactment in order to interpret what the statute means now.

* * *

In sum, the text of the FAA forecloses the construction of § 1 followed by the Court of Appeals in the case under review, a construction which would exclude all employment contracts from the FAA. While the historical arguments respecting Congress' understanding of its power in 1925 are not insubstantial, this fact alone does not give us basis to adopt, "by judicial decision rather than amendatory legislation," *Gulf Oil* [*v. Copp Paving Co.,* 419 U.S. 186, 202, 95 S.Ct. 392, 42 L.Ed.2d 378 (1974)], an expansive construction of the FAA's exclusion provision that goes beyond the meaning of the words Congress used. While it is of course possible to speculate that Congress might have chosen a different jurisdictional formulation had it known that the Court would soon embrace a less restrictive reading of the Commerce Clause, the text of § 1 precludes interpreting the exclusion provision to defeat the language of § 2 as to all employment contracts. Section 1 exempts from the FAA only contracts of employment of transportation workers.

C

As the conclusion we reach today is directed by the text of § 1, we need not assess the legislative history of the exclusion provision. * * *

* * *

III

Various *amici,* including the attorneys general of 22 States, object that the reading of the § 1 exclusion provision adopted today intrudes upon the policies of the separate States. They point out that, by requiring arbitration agreements in most employment contracts to be covered by the FAA, the statute in effect pre-empts those state employment laws which restrict or limit the ability of employees and employers to enter into arbitration agreements. It is argued that States should be permitted, pursuant to their traditional role in regulating employment relationships, to prohibit employees like respondent from contracting away their right to pursue state-law discrimination claims in court.

It is not our holding today which is the proper target of this criticism. The line of argument is relevant instead to the Court's decision in *Southland Corp. v. Keating*, 465 U.S. 1, 104 S.Ct. 852, 79 L.Ed.2d 1 (1984), holding that Congress intended the FAA to apply in state courts, and to pre-empt state antiarbitration laws to the contrary. *See id.*, at 16, 104 S.Ct. 852.

The question of *Southland's* continuing vitality was given explicit consideration in *Allied-Bruce*, and the Court declined to overrule it. 513 U.S., at 272, 115 S.Ct. 834; see also *id.*, at 282, 115 S.Ct. 834 (O'CONNOR, J., concurring). * * * In *Allied-Bruce* the Court noted that Congress had not moved to overturn *Southland*, see 513 U.S., at 272, 115 S.Ct. 834; and we now note that it has not done so in response to *Allied-Bruce* itself.

Furthermore, for parties to employment contracts not involving the specific exempted categories set forth in § 1, it is true here, just as it was for the parties to the contract at issue in *Allied-Bruce,* that there are real benefits to the enforcement of arbitration provisions. We have been clear in rejecting the supposition that the advantages of the arbitration process somehow disappear when transferred to the employment context. See *Gilmer,* 500 U.S., at 30–32, 111 S.Ct. 1647. Arbitration agreements allow parties to avoid the costs of litigation, a benefit that may be of particular importance in employment litigation, which often involves smaller sums of money than disputes concerning commercial contracts. These litigation costs to parties (and the accompanying burden to the Courts) would be compounded by the difficult choice-of-law questions that are often presented in disputes arising from the employment relationship, and the necessity of bifurcation of proceedings in those cases where state law precludes arbitration of certain types of employment claims but not others. The considerable complexity and uncertainty that the construction of § 1 urged by respondent would introduce into the enforceability of arbitration agreements in employment contracts would call into doubt the efficacy of alternative dispute resolution procedures adopted by many of the Nation's employers, in the process undermining the FAA's proarbitration purposes and "breeding litigation from a statute that seeks to avoid it." *Allied-Bruce, supra,* at 275, 115 S.Ct. 834. The Court has been quite specific in holding that arbitration agreements can be enforced under the FAA without contravening the policies of congressional enactments giving employees specific protection against discrimination prohibited by federal law; as we noted in *Gilmer,* " '[b]y agreeing to arbitrate a statutory claim, a party does not forgo the substantive rights afforded by the statute; it only submits to their resolution in an arbitral, rather than a judicial, forum.' " 500 U.S., at 26, 111 S.Ct. 1647 (quoting

Mitsubishi Motors Corp. v. Soler Chrysler-Plymouth, Inc., 473 U.S. 614, 628, 105 S.Ct. 3346, 87 L.Ed.2d 444 (1985)). *Gilmer,* of course, involved a federal statute, while the argument here is that a state statute ought not be denied state judicial enforcement while awaiting the outcome of arbitration. That matter, though, was addressed in *Southland* and *Allied-Bruce,* and we do not revisit the question here.

* * *

For the foregoing reasons, the judgment of the Court of Appeals for the Ninth Circuit is reversed, and the case is remanded for further proceedings consistent with this opinion.

* * *

NOTES AND QUESTIONS

1. The Court in *Circuit City* seems to suggest that employment discrimination claims generally should be treated like "garden variety" tort claims. Recall that the Court stated that "employment litigation * * * often involves smaller sums of money than disputes concerning commercial contracts." Should employment discrimination claims be considered less worthy of judicial resources than commercial claims?

2. There has been a vigorous debate about mandatory employment arbitration since the Supreme Court issued the *Gilmer* decision in 1991. *See, e.g.,* Martin H. Malin, *Privatizing Justice But by How Much? Questions* Gilmer *Did Not Answer,* 16 Ohio St.J. on Disp.Res. 589, 590–600 (2001) [hereinafter Malin, *Privatizing Justice*]; David S. Schwartz, *Mandatory Arbitration and Fairness,* 84 Notre Dame L.Rev. 1247,1253–57 (2009); Theodore J. St. Antoine, *ADR in Labor and Employment Law During the Past Quarter Century*, 25 ABA J. Lab. & Emp. L. 411, 447 (2010). Those who question arbitration's validity point to the concerns addressed in the *Gilmer* case, including the problem of resolving disputes involving public values and rights in a private setting. Private arbitration awards are not generally available to the public, making it difficult to chart developments and the progress of employment discrimination law. Also, arbitral processes do not generally afford the same discovery as the courts, inhibiting access to information that may be critical for vindicating statutory rights. Moreover, the fact that employers are "repeat" players in the arbitral process, whereas an individual employee will use arbitration only once, raises concerns about possible arbitrator bias in favor of employers.

Those who support mandatory arbitration claim that many of the issues surrounding arbitrability can be raised and addressed in the arbitration proceeding itself and that arbitration is more efficient, faster, and less costly than proceeding through court. *See, e.g.,* Mark Berger, *Can Employment Law Arbitration Really Work?*, 61 UMKC L.Rev. 693 (1993); Samuel Estreicher, *Saturns for Rickshaws: The Stakes in the Debate Over Predispute*

Employment Arbitration Agreements, 16 Ohio St.J. on Disp.Resol. 559 (2001); Theodore J. St. Antoine, *Mandatory Arbitration: Why It's Better Than It Looks,* 41 U.Mich.J.L. Reform 783 (2008). Other commentators have explored ways in which arbitration might be molded to achieve the benefits of litigation while avoiding the disadvantages. *See, e.g.,* Roberto L. Corrada, *Claiming Private Law for the Left: Exploring* Gilmer's *Impact and Legacy,* 73 Denv.U.L.Rev. 1051 (1996); Dennis O. Lynch, *Conceptualizing Forum Selection as a "Public Good": A Response to Professor Stone,* 73 Denv.L.Rev. 1071 (1996); Calvin William Sharpe, *Integrity Review of Statutory Arbitration Awards,* 54 Hastings L.J. 311 (2003). All of these claims in support of arbitration, however, have been challenged. *See, e.g.,* Jean Sternlight, *Disarming Employees: How American Employers are Using Mandatory Arbitration to Deprive Workers of Legal Protection,* 80 Brook. L.Rev. 1309 (2015); Alexander J.S. Colvin, *Empirical Research on Employment Arbitration: Clarity Amidst the Sound and Fury?,* 11 Emp.Rts. & Emp. Pol'y J. 405, 412–37 (2007) (reviewing empirical research); Schwartz, *supra* (arguing there is no "fairness" justification for imposing a dispute resolution system through adhesion contracts, and analyzing studies relating to costs and benefits of mandatory arbitration).

3. Subsequent to *Gilmer,* a number of employers adopted mandatory predispute arbitration policies by including such policies in individual contracts of employment, employee handbooks, or other employment-related documents such as application forms and employment brochures. *See, e.g.,* Tillman v. Macy's, Inc., 735 F.3d 453 (6th Cir.2013); ING Fin. Partners v. Johansen, 446 F.3d 777 (8th Cir.2006); Berkley v. Dillard's, Inc., 450 F.3d 775 (8th Cir.2006); Nghiem v. NEC Elec., Inc., 25 F.3d 1437 (9th Cir.1994) (policy found in employment contract and employee handbook). The Supreme Court has acknowledged the strong trend in favor of including mandatory predispute arbitration agreements in employment contracts. *See* EEOC v. Waffle House, 534 U.S. 279, 296 n.11, 122 S.Ct. 754, 765 n. 11, 151 L.Ed.2d 755, 770 (2002) (indicating that a greater percentage of the workforce is becoming subject to arbitration agreements as a condition of employment). Predispute mandatory arbitration agreements are "often boilerplate provisions in employment contracts at Fortune 500 companies and are the norm in industries such as financial services, health care, engineering, and information technology." Christine M. Reilly, *Achieving Knowing and Voluntary Consent in Pre-Dispute Mandatory Arbitration Agreements at the Contracting Stage of Employment,* 90 Cal.L.Rev. 1203, 1208 (2002).

4. Substantial questions still abound regarding the voluntariness of employee agreements to arbitrate, since employers generally have much greater bargaining power. *See, e.g.,* Stephanie Brown, *Alternative Dispute Resolution and Employment Law: How Mandatory Arbitration Perpetuates Disparate Impact In Statutory Disputes,* 8 S. J. Pol'y & Just. L.J. 62 (2014); David E. Feller, *Putting* Gilmer *Where It Belongs: The FAA's Labor Exemption,* 18 Hofstra Lab. & Emp.L.J. 253 (2000). *See also* Linda J. Demaine & Deborah R. Hensler, *"Volunteering" to Arbitrate Through*

Predispute Arbitration Clauses: The Average Consumer's Experience, 67 Law & Contemp. Probs. 55, 73–74 (2004) (due to lack of information and difficult language, most consumers do not knowingly waive right to sue); Christine M. Reilly, *Achieving Knowing and Voluntary Consent in Pre-Dispute Mandatory Arbitration Agreements at the Contracting Stage of Employment,* 90 Cal.L.Rev. 1203, 1225 (2002) (noting that "very few [employees] are aware of what they are waiving"); Kathryn A. Sabbeth & David C. Vladeck, *Contracting (Out) Rights,* 36 Fordham Urb.L.J. 803, 819–20 (2009) ("The evidence overwhelmingly suggests that individuals entering into consumer and employment contracts are generally unaware that they have agreed to waive their right to sue.").

5. The arbitration provisions of most employment agreements can be used by the employer or the employee; however, employees are more likely to want a chance to present their claims to a jury. As a result, the employer is generally the party seeking to enforce an arbitration agreement. Studies examining arbitral disputes involving employment and commercial claims from 1992–1995 have shown that an employer who is a repeat player in an arbitration scheme has a substantially greater chance of prevailing in arbitration than does an employee. *See* Lisa B. Bingham, *Is There a Bias in Arbitration of Nonunion Employment Disputes? An Analysis of Actual Cases and Outcomes,* 6 Intl.J. Conflict Mgmt. 369 (1995); Lisa B. Bingham, *Employment Arbitration: The Repeat Player Effect,* 1 Emp.Rts. & Emp. Pol'y J. 189 (1997); Lisa B. Bingham, *On Repeat Players, Adhesive Contracts, and the Use of Statistics in Judicial Review of Employment Arbitration Awards,* 29 McGeorge L.Rev. 223 (1998). *See also* Schwartz, *Fairness, supra* Note 2, at 1261–74 (questioning studies' claims of fairness for plaintiffs).

6. *Circuit City* involved state employment discrimination claims. Should *Circuit City* serve as a precedent favoring arbitration in other areas of statutory status discrimination like the Americans with Disabilities Act (ADA), § 1981, or Title VII? *See, e.g.,* EEOC v. Waffle House, 534 U.S. 279, 122 S.Ct. 754, 151 L.Ed.2d 755 (2002) (ADA), discussed in Note 8 below; Johnson v. Circuit City Stores, Inc., 148 F.3d 373 (4th Cir.1998), *aff'd,* 203 F.3d 821 (4th Cir.2000); Desiderio v. Nat'l Ass'n of Sec. Dealers, 191 F.3d 198 (2d Cir.1999) (Title VII). Should subsequent amendments to Title VII (the Civil Rights Act of 1991) and to the ADEA (the Older Worker Benefits and Protection Act (OWBPA)) affect the arbitrability analysis? With respect to Title VII and the Civil Rights Act of 1991, every court of appeals that has ruled on the issue has held that § 118 of the Civil Rights Act of 1991, which provides a right to a jury trial, does not evince a congressional intent to preclude predispute arbitration agreements. *See* EEOC v. Luce, Forward, Hamilton & Scripps, 345 F.3d 742, 750–51 (9th Cir.2003) (en banc) (holding that there is no conflict "between the purpose of Title VII and compulsory arbitration of Title VII claim" and collecting circuit court cases in agreement) *See also* Soto-Fonalledas v. Ritz-Carlton San Juan Hotel Spa & Casino, 640 F.3d 471, 476 (1st Cir.2011) (holding that agreement to submit Title VII and ADA claims to arbitration is not a violation of congressional intent).

7. After *Circuit City,* most employment arbitration agreements signed by individuals will be covered by the FAA and, therefore, will be enforceable (subject to the limitations discussed below) because only "transportation workers" are exempt from the FAA under the Court's interpretation of the statute. What are the implications of *Circuit City* for the future development of employment discrimination law in light of the fact that these decisions have the effect of replacing public processes with private ones, and replacing judges and juries with private parties (arbitrators), to resolve employment discrimination claims?

8. *Circuit City* deals with discrimination claims brought by individual employees. Can an arbitration agreement eliminate or modify the EEOC's statutorily authorized right to pursue judicial relief for an individual employee in an employment discrimination case based on Title VII or the ADA? In *EEOC v. Waffle House*, 534 U.S. 279, 122 S.Ct. 754, 151 L.Ed.2d 755 (2002), the Court addressed whether the existence of a predispute arbitration agreement—under which no arbitration process had been initiated—limits the authority of the EEOC to seek victim-specific relief for an employee who has agreed to submit his employment discrimination claim to arbitration. According to the Court:

> In 1972, Congress amended Title VII to authorize the EEOC to bring its own enforcement actions; indeed, we have observed that the 1972 amendments created a system in which the EEOC was intended "to bear the primary burden of litigation." Those amendments authorize the courts to enjoin employers from engaging in unlawful employment practices, and to order appropriate affirmative action, which may include reinstatement, with or without backpay. Moreover, the amendments specify the judicial districts in which such actions may be brought. They do not mention arbitration proceedings.
>
> In 1991, Congress again amended Title VII to allow the recovery of compensatory and punitive damages by a "complaining party." The term includes both private plaintiffs and the EEOC, and the amendments apply to ADA claims as well. As a complaining party, the EEOC may bring suit to enjoin an employer from engaging in unlawful employment practices, and to pursue reinstatement, backpay, and compensatory or punitive damages. Thus, these statutes unambiguously authorize the EEOC to obtain the relief that it seeks in its complaint if it can prove its case against respondent.
>
> * * * Congress expanded the remedies available in EEOC enforcement actions in 1991 to include compensatory and punitive damages. There is no language in the statute or in either of these cases suggesting that the existence of an arbitration agreement between private parties materially changes the EEOC's statutory function or the remedies that are otherwise available.

Id. at 286–88, 122 S.Ct. at 760–61 (citations omitted).

2. THE ARBITRATION AGREEMENT

a. Contract Formation

For an arbitration agreement between an employer and an employee to be enforced, there must first be a contract between the parties. Contract formation requires offer, acceptance, and consideration. Regarding consideration, what exactly does the employee get out of the arbitral agreement? Is there consideration even though there is no benefit to the employee? Does the job itself supply consideration for the agreement? Certainly express language of agreement in a written contract between the parties should be enforceable, but what if there is no express agreement by the employee? Or, what if the express language is buried in the agreement or is otherwise vague and difficult to comprehend? Can a contractual agreement exist even if assent by the employee can only be inferred by her actions? Can agreement be inferred by employee silence?

CIRCUIT CITY STORES, INC. V. NAJD

United States Court of Appeals for the Ninth Circuit, 2002.
294 F.3d 1104.

O'SCANNLAIN, CIRCUIT JUDGE.

* * *

I

Circuit City Stores ("Circuit City") hired Monir Najd as a sales associate in 1985. In 1995, Circuit City instituted the "Associate Issue Resolution Program" at Najd's store of employment. As part of the program, Circuit City distributed a packet of materials to the store's employees, which included a "Dispute Resolution Agreement" (the "DRA"). The DRA provided that "any and all employment-related legal disputes, controversies or claims of an Associate arising out of, or relating to, * * * employment or cessation of employment with Circuit City * * * shall be settled exclusively by final and binding arbitration." The store's current employees were allowed to opt out of the DRA by returning a form to Circuit City's corporate headquarters. Najd acknowledged receipt of the packet in writing and did not exercise his right to opt out.

In February 1997, Alex Khorsand became Najd's supervisor. According to Najd, Khorsand continually harassed him on the basis of his ethnicity, culminating in his termination in February 1998. Najd filed suit against Circuit City and Khorsand in California Superior Court, alleging various common law torts and a violation of California's Fair Employment and Housing Act ("FEHA"), Cal. Gov't Code § 12940(a).

Circuit City responded by filing a petition in federal district court under the Federal Arbitration Act ("FAA"), seeking to stay the state court action and to compel arbitration of Najd's claims.

* * *

VI

Najd also claims that the DRA is not a valid contract because he never assented to it and it lacks consideration. Neither *Ahmed* [*Circuit City Stores v. Ahmed*, 283 F.3d 1198 (9th Cir.2002)] nor *Adams III* [*Circuit City Stores, Inc. v. Adams*, 279 F.3d 889 (9th Cir.2002)] explicitly addressed these issues, and thus we proceed to consider them in turn.

Section 2 of the FAA provides that arbitration agreements "shall be valid, irrevocable, and enforceable, save upon such grounds that exist at law or in equity for the revocation of any contract." 9 U.S.C. § 2. Hence, generally applicable contract defenses, such as lack of consideration and mutual assent, may invalidate an arbitration agreement. * * * The parties agree that we look to California contract law to determine the DRA's validity * * *. Najd argues that the DRA is not supported by adequate consideration because Circuit City is not required to submit any of its claims against employees to arbitration. However, Circuit City's promise to be bound by the arbitration process itself serves as adequate consideration. *See Armendariz* [*v. Found. Health Psychcare Servs., Inc.*, 6 P.3d 669, 692 (Cal.2000)]. * * * In other words, Circuit City's promise to submit to arbitration and to forego the option of a judicial forum for a specified class of claims constitutes sufficient consideration.[3]

Alternatively, Najd claims that he did not assent to the DRA because he did not affirmatively opt in to the program. "As a general rule, silence or inaction does not constitute acceptance of an offer." Golden Eagle Ins. Co. v. Foremost Ins. Co., 20 Cal. App. 4th 1372, 25 Cal. Rptr. 2d 242, 251 (Ct. App. 1993). However, "where circumstances or the previous course of dealing between the parties places the offeree under a duty to act or be bound, his silence or inactivity will constitute his assent." Beatty Safway Scaffold, Inc. v. B.H. Skrable, 180 Cal. App. 2d 650, 4 Cal. Rptr. 543, 546 (Ct. App. 1960).

Najd and Circuit City were not two typical parties contracting at arm's length. Rather, Najd, as employee of Circuit City, acknowledged receipt of the DRA in writing and was asked to review it within the

[3] In *Armendariz*, the California Supreme Court held a similar agreement substantively unconscionable in part because the agreement only required the employee to submit his claims to arbitration. 6 P.3d at 692–94. However, the court also concluded that the employer's promise to be bound by the arbitration process supplied adequate consideration. 6 P.3d at 692.

course of his employment. In other circumstances acceptance by silence may be troubling, and explicit consent indispensable. Here, however, where the import of Najd's silence was as apparent as if he signed his consent, we may infer assent. The acknowledgment form that Najd signed clearly set out in writing the significance of his failure to opt out and described in detail the mechanism by which he could express his disagreement. The explicit opportunity to review the agreement with an attorney highlighted the legal effect of the agreement. Circuit City communicated in detail and in writing the effect of Najd's acceptance on his right to bring claims against his employer. Also, Circuit City made clear that opting out of the agreement would have no effect on the employment relationship. Finally, Najd had thirty days to review the agreement and mull over whether to opt out of it. When, as here, inaction is indistinguishable from overt acceptance, we may conclude that the parties have come to agreement. Thus, the circumstances of this case permit us to infer that Najd assented to the DRA by failing to exercise his right to opt out of the program. * * * In sum, we uphold the validity of the DRA.

* * *

NOTES AND QUESTIONS

1. In the case of waiver of forum for statutory employment discrimination claims, should ordinary contract law principles apply? Should an arbitration clause regarding such claims only be enforced if employee acceptance is "knowing and voluntary"? After all, the Supreme Court established a "clear and unmistakable" standard for a union's waiver of statutory antidiscrimination rights of employees in a collective bargaining unit. *14 Penn Plaza LLC v. Pyett*, 556 U.S. 247, 129 S.Ct. 1456, 173 L.Ed.2d 398 (2009), discussed in Section C of this chapter. Is there a good reason for a distinction between waiver standards in nonunion and unionized settings? For two differing views on the question of waiver standards, *compare* Dennis R. Nolan, *Employment Arbitration After* Circuit City, 41 Brandeis L.J. 853 (2003) (most courts do not require "knowing and voluntary"), and Stephen J. Ware, *Employment Arbitration and Voluntary Consent,* 25 Hofstra L.Rev. 83 (1996) (contract law question regarding assent is whether an agreement is voluntary or coerced), *with* William W. Fick, *Gnawing at* Gilmer: *Giving Teeth to "Consent" in Employment Arbitration Agreements,* 17 Yale L. & Pol'y Rev. 965 (1999) (standard for consent in arbitration of employment discrimination claims should be "knowing and voluntary"). *See also* Coleman v. Donahoe, 667 F.3d 835, 854 (7th Cir.2012) (holding that because collective bargaining agreement did not expressly require Title VII claims be arbitrated, any decision reached by the arbitrator on this issue is non-binding).

2. Can an employee be held to an agreement to arbitrate if she fails to expressly agree, but continues to work and receive a paycheck? Is the action

of continuing to work sufficient to infer assent to terms of an employment agreement, including an agreement to waive a right to a judicial forum for statutory employment discrimination claims? *See, e.g.*, Tillman v. Macy's, Inc., 735 F.3d 453, 461 (6th Cir.2013) (stating that a party's continued employment can act as consideration in contracts to arbitrate); Tinder v. Pinkerton Sec., 305 F.3d 728, 736 (7th Cir.2002) (applying Wisconsin law and holding that employee's continued work past the effective date of the arbitration agreement coupled with employer's promise to be bound by arbitration policy is sufficient consideration for employee's promise to arbitrate claims). *See also* OblixObi, Inc. v. Winiecki, 374 F.3d 488, 491 (7th Cir.2004) (applying California law and holding that employer's nonnegotiable promise to pay plaintiff a specified salary was sufficient consideration for employee's promise to arbitrate); Davis v. Nordstrom, Inc., 12–17403, 2014 WL 2808139 (9th Cir.June 23, 2014) (same). Is there consideration if virtually all of the obligations of the agreement are shouldered by the employee? *Compare* Gibson v. Neighborhood Health Clinics, Inc., 121 F.3d 1126, 1131 (7th Cir.1997) (applying Indiana law and finding insufficient consideration where employer did not make a reciprocal promise to submit its claims against the employee to arbitration), *with* Soto v. State Indus. Products, Inc., 642 F.3d 67, 76 (1st Cir.2011) (holding that equal obligation of an employee and employer to arbitrate disputes is enough to ensure mutuality of obligation and thus constitute consideration). Is an employer's mere promise to consider an applicant's employment application sufficient consideration for the applicant's agreement to arbitrate employment claims? Walker v. Ryan's Family Steak Houses, 400 F.3d 370, 380–81 (6th Cir.2005) (no); Penn v. Ryan's Family Steak Houses, 269 F.3d 753, 760–61 (7th Cir.2001) (no). *See also* Richard A. Bales, *Contract Formation Issues in Employment Arbitration,* 44 Brandeis L.J. 415, 458 (2006) (noting that "consideration issues are easily avoided, either by making the arbitration promises reciprocal or by providing some other type of consideration, such as a pay increase or a term contract").

3. *Contract Defenses*: Once an arbitral agreement has been formed as a contract between the employer and employee, is there any way to have the contract set aside? An exception to the general rule that arbitration agreements are enforceable is found in § 2 of the FAA: arbitration agreements can be challenged on "such grounds as exist at law or in equity for the revocation of any contract." 9 U.S.C. § 2. Because these grounds are matters of state law, the rules will vary from state to state. The grounds on which courts may invalidate a contract include fraud, duress, mistake, and unconscionability. *See, e.g.*, First Options of Chi., Inc. v. Kaplan, 514 U.S. 938, 944, 115 S.Ct. 1920, 1924, 131 L.Ed.2d 985 (1995) (ruling that "[w]hen deciding whether the parties agreed to arbitrate a certain matter * * * courts generally * * * should apply ordinary state-law principles that govern the formation of contracts"); Haskins v. Prudential Ins. Co. of Am., 230 F.3d 231 (6th Cir.2001); Carey v. 24 Hour Fitness, USA, Inc., 669 F.3d 202, 207–09 (5th Cir.2012) (invalidating arbitration agreement found in defendant's employee manual because employer had reserved its right to unilaterally

modify the arbitration provision making the agreement illusory). *Gilmer* recognized that, pursuant to FAA § 2, "fraud or overwhelming economic power" could provide grounds for revocation of an agreement to arbitrate and that such cases should be "left for resolution in specific cases." *Gilmer*, 500 U.S. at 33, 111 S.Ct. at 1656. What circumstances would constitute "fraud or overwhelming economic power" sufficient to provide grounds for revoking an agreement to arbitrate a claim of employment discrimination? What about mistake or unconscionability? The following case of *Circuit City II*, on remand from the Supreme Court, illustrates an approach to unconscionability under the § 2 exception.

CIRCUIT CITY STORES, INC. V. ADAMS

United States Court of Appeals for the Ninth Circuit, 2002.
279 F.3d 889, *cert. denied*, 535 U.S. 1112, 122 S.Ct. 2329, 153 L.Ed.2d 160.

D.W. NELSON, CIRCUIT JUDGE.

* * *

A. *APPLICABLE LAW*

* * *

Adams argues that the DRA [Circuit City's Dispute Resolution Agreement] is an unconscionable contract of adhesion. Because Adams was employed in California, we look to California contract law to determine whether the agreement is valid. *See* Ticknor v. Choice Hotels Int'l, Inc., 265 F.3d 931 (9th Cir.2001) (applying Montana law to decide whether arbitration clause was valid).

Under California law, a contract is unenforceable if it is both procedurally and substantively unconscionable. Armendariz v. Found. Health Psychcare Svcs., Inc., 24 Cal.4th 83, 99 Cal.Rptr.2d 745, 6 P.3d 669, 690 (2000). When assessing procedural unconscionability, we consider the equilibrium of bargaining power between the parties and the extent to which the contract clearly discloses its terms. Stirlen v. Supercuts, Inc., 51 Cal.App.4th 1519, 60 Cal.Rptr.2d 138, 145 (1997). A determination of substantive unconscionability, on the other hand, involves whether the terms of the contract are unduly harsh or oppressive. *Id.*

B. *THE DRA AND UNCONSCIONABILITY*

The DRA is procedurally unconscionable because it is a contract of adhesion: a standard-form contract, drafted by the party with superior bargaining power, which relegates to the other party the option of either adhering to its terms without modification or rejecting the contract entirely. *Id.* at 145–46 (indicating that a contract of adhesion is procedurally unconscionable). Circuit City, which possesses considerably more bargaining power than nearly all of its employees or applicants, drafted the contract and uses it as its standard arbitration agreement for all of its new employees. The agreement is a prerequisite to employment, and job applicants are not permitted to modify the agreement's terms—they must take the contract or leave it. *See Armendariz,* 99 Cal.Rptr.2d 745, 6 P.3d at 690 (noting that few applicants are in a position to refuse a job because of an arbitration agreement).

The California Supreme Court's recent decision in *Armendariz* counsels in favor of finding that the Circuit City arbitration agreement is substantively unconscionable as well. In *Armendariz,* the California court reversed an order compelling arbitration of a FEHA discrimination claim because the arbitration agreement at issue required arbitration only of employees' claims and excluded damages that would otherwise be available under the FEHA. *Armendariz,* 99 Cal.Rptr.2d 745, 6 P.3d at 694. The agreement in *Armendariz* required employees, as a condition of employment, to submit all claims relating to termination of that employment—including any claim that the termination violated the employee's rights—to binding arbitration. *Id.* at 675. The employer, however, was free to bring suit in court or arbitrate any dispute with its employees. In analyzing this asymmetrical arrangement, the court concluded that in order for a mandatory arbitration agreement to be valid, some "modicum of bilaterality" is required. *Id.* at 692. Since the employer was not bound to arbitrate its claims and there was no apparent justification for the lack of mutual obligations, the court reasoned that arbitration appeared to be functioning "less as a forum for neutral dispute resolution and more as a means of maximizing employer advantage." *Id.*

The substantive one-sidedness of the *Armendariz* agreement was compounded by the fact that it did not allow full recovery of damages for which the employees would be eligible under the FEHA. *Id.* at 694. The exclusive remedy was back pay from the date of discharge until the date of the arbitration award, whereas plaintiffs in FEHA suits would be entitled to punitive damages, injunctive relief, front pay, emotional distress damages, and attorneys' fees.

We find the arbitration agreement at issue here virtually indistinguishable from the agreement the California Supreme Court found unconscionable in *Armendariz.* Like the agreement in *Armendariz,* the DRA unilaterally forces employees to arbitrate claims against the employer. The claims subject to arbitration under the DRA include "any and all employment-related legal disputes, controversies or claims *of an Associate* arising out of, or relating to, an Associate's application or candidacy for employment, employment or cessation of employment with Circuit City." (emphasis added). The provision does not require Circuit City to arbitrate its claims against employees. Circuit City has offered no justification for this asymmetry, nor is there any indication that "business realities" warrant the one-sided obligation. This unjustified one-sidedness deprives the DRA of the "modicum of bilaterality" that the California Supreme Court requires for contracts to be enforceable under California law.

And again as in *Armendariz,* the asymmetry is compounded by the fact that the agreement limits the relief available to employees. Under the DRA, the remedies are limited to injunctive relief, up to one year of back pay and up to two years of front pay, compensatory damages, and punitive damages in an amount up to the greater of the amount of back pay and front pay awarded or $5,000. By contrast, a plaintiff in a civil suit for sexual harassment under the FEHA is eligible for all forms of relief that are generally available to civil litigants—including appropriate punitive damages and damages for emotional distress. *See* Commodore Home Sys., Inc. v. Superior Court of San Bernardino County, 32 Cal.3d 211, 185 Cal.Rptr. 270, 649 P.2d 912, 914 (1982). The DRA also requires the employee to split the arbitrator's fees with Circuit City. This fee allocation scheme alone would render an arbitration agreement unenforceable. *Cf.* Cole v. Burns Intern. Security Svcs., 105 F.3d 1465 (D.C.Cir.1997) (holding that it is unlawful to require an employee, through a mandatory arbitration agreement, to share the costs of arbitration). But the DRA goes even further: it also imposes a strict one year statute of limitations on arbitrating claims that would deprive Adams of the benefit of the continuing violation doctrine available in FEHA suits. *See, e.g.,* Richards v. CH2M Hill, Inc., 26 Cal.4th 798, 111 Cal.Rptr.2d 87, 29 P.3d 175, 176 (2001). In short, and just like the agreement invalidated by the California Supreme Court in *Armendariz,* the DRA forces Adams to arbitrate his statutory claims without affording him the benefit of the full range of statutory remedies.

In addition, our decision is entirely consistent with federal law concerning the enforceability of arbitration agreements. The Supreme Court, in *Gilmer v. Interstate/Johnson Lane Corp.,* 500 U.S. 20, 26, 111 S.Ct. 1647, 114 L.Ed.2d 26 (1991), held that "[b]y agreeing to arbitrate a statutory claim, [an employee] does not forgo the substantive rights afforded by the statute; [he] only submits to their resolution in an arbitral, rather than a judicial forum." While the Court in *Gilmer* affirmed that statutory rights can be resolved through arbitration, the decision also recognized that the arbitral forum must allow the employee to adequately pursue statutory rights. *Id.* at 28, 111 S.Ct. 1647.

Courts have since interpreted *Gilmer* to require basic procedural and remedial protections so that claimants can effectively pursue their statutory rights. *See, e.g., Cole,* 105 F.3d at 1482 (listing five basic requirements that an arbitral forum must meet). We note that here, Circuit City's arbitration agreement fails to meet two of *Cole*'s minimum requirements: it fails to provide for all of the types of relief that would otherwise be available in court, or to ensure that employees do not have to pay either unreasonable costs or any arbitrators' fees or expenses as a condition of access to the arbitration forum. *Id.*

Nor does our decision run afoul of the FAA by imposing a heightened burden on arbitration agreements. Because unconscionability is a defense to contracts generally and does not single out arbitration agreements for special scrutiny, it is also a valid reason not to enforce an arbitration agreement under the FAA. Indeed, the Supreme Court has specifically mentioned unconscionability as a "generally applicable contract defense[ ]" that may be raised consistent with § 2 of the FAA. *Doctor's Assocs.*, 517 U.S. at 687, 116 S.Ct. 1652.

Our conclusion here is further buttressed by this Circuit's recent opinion in *Ticknor*. The majority in *Ticknor* looked to Montana law and found an asymmetrical arbitration clause (similar to the one at issue here) unconscionable and unenforceable. *Ticknor,* 265 F.3d at 942. The majority was careful to explain that the FAA did not stand as a bar to the court's holding because the FAA does not preempt state law governing the unconscionability of adhesion contracts. *Id.* at 935; *see also id.* at 941 (overruling, so far as they are inconsistent with that conclusion, *Cohen v. Wedbush, Noble, Cooke, Inc.,* 841 F.2d 282, 286 (9th Cir.1988), and *Bayma v. Smith Barney, Harris Upham & Co.,* 784 F.2d 1023 (9th Cir.1986)). We follow *Ticknor* in concluding that the result we reach today is fully consistent with the FAA.

C. *SEVERABILITY*

Under California law, courts have discretion to sever an unconscionable provision or refuse to enforce the contract in its entirety. *See* Cal. Civ.Code § 1670.5(a). In deciding whether to invalidate the contract,

> [c]ourts are to look to the various purposes of the contract. If the central purpose of the contract is tainted with illegality, then the contract as a whole cannot be enforced. If the illegality is collateral to the main purpose of the contract, and the illegal provision can be extirpated from the contract by means of severance or restriction, then such severance and restriction are appropriate.

Armendariz, 99 Cal.Rptr.2d 745, 6 P.3d at 696.

In this case, as in *Armendariz,* the objectionable provisions pervade the entire contract. In addition to the damages limitation and the fee-sharing scheme, the unilateral aspect of the DRA runs throughout the agreement and defines the scope of the matters that are covered. Removing these provisions would go beyond mere excision to rewriting the contract, which is not the proper role of this Court. *See id.* at 125, 99

Cal.Rptr.2d 745, 6 P.3d 669. Therefore, we find the entire arbitration agreement unenforceable.

* * *

NOTES AND QUESTIONS

1. Does *Circuit City II* set a reasonable standard for challenging arbitration agreements using traditional contractual defenses? Does the case comport with unconscionability doctrine as it is understood in general contract law analysis? Does the court apply unconscionability too broadly? Can an unconscionability claim be made in any arbitration agreement challenge now? *Compare* Macias v. Excel Bldg. Servs. LLC, 767 F. Supp. 2d 1002 (N.D. Cal. 2011) (finding unconscionability), *with In re* Halliburton Co., 80 S.W.3d 566 (Tex.2004) (no unconscionability where employment is at-will). *See* Dennis R. Nolan, *Employment Arbitration After* Circuit City, 41 Brandeis L.J. 853, 856–59 (2003) (discussing the Ninth Circuit's use of contract avoidance principles as a sword (in *Circuit City II*) to void arbitration agreements rather than as a shield (in *Armendariz*) to protect weaker contracting parties). *See generally* Richard A. Bales, *Contract Formation Issues in Employment Arbitration,* 44 Brandeis L.J. 415, 442–61 (2006); Martin H. Malin, *Due Process in Employment Arbitration: The State of the Law and the Need for Self-Regulation,* 11 Emp.Rts. & Emp.Pol'y J. 363, 379–85 (2007); Tanya M. Marcum, J.D., Elizabeth A. Campbell, J.D., *Corpses on the Arbitration Battlegrounds: A War but No Winners*, 25 Midwest L.J. 1, 6 (2011).

2. Suppose a non-English speaking employee had been required as a condition of employment to sign an arbitration agreement. (See the discussion of English language requirements in Chapter 13.) Assume further that this employee now believes that he was discriminated against because of his national origin. Should the employee be allowed to challenge the arbitration agreement on the ground of procedural unconscionability under *Circuit City II* if he proves that the employer neither translated the agreement into Spanish nor explained it to him in Spanish? *See* Prevot v. Phillips Petrol. Co., 133 F.Supp.2d 937, 940–41 (S.D.Tex.2001). What other illustrations of procedural unconscionability can you think of?

3. If only parts of an arbitration agreement are unconscionable, should the entire agreement be unenforceable? If not, under what circumstances may the offending provisions be severed from the remainder of the agreement? In *Circuit City Stores, Inc. v. Adams,* above, the court refuses to sever the unconscionable provisions because they pervade the contract so much as to be essential to the agreement of the parties. *Compare* Ingle v. Circuit City Stores, Inc., 328 F.3d 1165 (9th Cir.2003) (refusing to sever the unconscionable provisions and enforce the remainder due to the "numerous provisions" in the agreement that were found to be unconscionable), and Nino v. Jewelry Exch., Inc., 609 F.3d 191, 196 (3d Cir.2010) (refusing to sever where unconscionable provisions demonstrated pervasive one-sidedness),

with Morrison v. Circuit City Stores, Inc., 317 F.3d 646, 675 (6th Cir.2003) (severing unconscionable provisions and enforcing remainder of arbitration agreement where unconscionable provisions had not been applied in earlier arbitration) and Ragone v. Atl. Video at Manhattan Ctr., 595 F.3d 115 (2d Cir.2010) (applying New York law and stating that unconscionable provisions could be severed, and would not void entire contract).

4. Who decides an issue of unconscionability when it is raised as a challenge to an arbitration agreement? *See* Rent-A-Ctr., W., Inc. v. Jackson, 561 U.S. 63, 71, 130 S. Ct. 2772, 2778, 177 L. Ed. 2d 403 (2010) (reversing the 9th Circuit's decision that mandated judicial intervention when determining unconscionability of an arbitration clause, holding that because the claim related to the agreement as a whole, and not specifically to arbitration, the issue must be left to the arbitrator).

b. Due Process and the Terms of the Arbitral Contract

It seems clear that if statutory employment discrimination claims are arbitrable, arbitration agreements cannot be used to circumvent substantive rights. In the absence of statutory standards, however, what procedures are at least minimally required in order to allow an employee to vindicate a statutory employment discrimination claim? More importantly, how do courts ensure that appropriate procedures are reflected in arbitration agreements? What is the basis for requiring specific procedures in arbitration agreements? Is it the statutes themselves? Is it some notion of minimal fairness or due process?

The Supreme Court emphasized in *Waffle House* that "federal statutory claims may be the subject of an arbitration agreement * * * enforceable pursuant to the FAA because the agreement only determines the choice of forum." EEOC v. Waffle House, Inc., 534 U.S. 279, 295 n.10, 122 S.Ct. 754, 770 n.10, 151 L.Ed.2d 755, 765 n. 10 (2002). The Supreme Court has acknowledged as much in interpreting the FAA in statutory contexts other than Title VII: "By agreeing to arbitrate a statutory claim, a party does not forgo the substantive rights afforded by the statute; it only submits to their resolution in an arbitral, rather than a judicial, forum." Mitsubishi Motors Corp. v. Soler Chrysler-Plymouth, Inc., 473 U.S. 614, 628, 105 S.Ct. 3346, 3355, 87 L.Ed.2d 444, (1985).

What procedural safeguards must an employer provide in an arbitration agreement that covers federal statutory claims to allow an employee to effectively vindicate statutory rights? Chief Judge Harry Edwards of the Court of Appeals for the District of Columbia Circuit, who is a former labor law professor and labor arbitrator, authored one of the leading opinions on this issue in *Cole v. Burns International Security Services*, 105 F.3d 1465 (D.C.Cir.1997). He interpreted relevant Supreme Court precedent as requiring at least the following: (1) a neutral arbitrator; (2) more than minimal discovery; (3) a written award; (4) an opportunity in the arbitration proceeding to obtain all the remedies that would be available if the plaintiff were successful in a court action; and (5) a requirement that the employee must not be obligated to pay either unreasonable costs or any of the arbitrator's fees or expenses. *Id.* at 1482. *See also* Martin H. Malin, *Privatizing Justice But by How Much? Questions* Gilmer *Did Not Answer,* 16 Ohio St.J. on Disp.Res. 589, 601–22 (2001). *See generally* Laura J. Cooper, *Employment Arbitration 2011: A Realist's View,* 87 Ind. L.J. 317, 318 (2012); Richard A. Bales, *The Employment Due Process Protocol at Ten: Twenty Unresolved Issues, and a Focus on Conflicts of Interest,* 21 Ohio St.J. on Disp.Res. 165 (2005).

NOTES AND QUESTIONS

1. May an employer require a shorter statute of limitations in an arbitration agreement than is provided under federal law for initiating a claim of employment discrimination? Under Title VII, for example, a charging party has either 180 or 300 days within which to file a charge with the EEOC. Title VII, § 706(e)(1), 42 U.S.C. § 2000e–5(e)(1). *See, e.g.*, Lewis v. City of Chicago, Ill., 560 U.S. 205, 130 S. Ct. 2191, 176 L. Ed. 2d 967 (2010); Ledbetter v. Goodyear Tire & Rubber Co., Inc., 550 U.S. 618, 127 S.Ct. 2162, 167 L.Ed.2d 982 (2007), reproduced in Chapter 2. Suppose an employer, in an arbitration agreement, requires employees to initiate the mandatory arbitration process for federal employment discrimination claims within four months after the claim occurs? *See, e.g.*, Soltani v. Western & Southern Life Ins. Co., 258 F.3d 1038 (9th Cir.2001) (applying a reasonableness standard in upholding a six-month statute of limitations in an arbitration agreement in a claim for wrongful discharge based on state law even though the state law limitations period for contract claims was longer). *But see* Pokorny v. Quixtar, Inc., 601 F.3d 987, 1001 (9th Cir.2010) (refusing to enforce shortened limitations period for lack of mutuality between parties). What if the employer, in an arbitration agreement, imposes a more generous limitations period than Title VII, say one year, but makes that limit hard and fast so that continuing violations are effectively cutoff at the one-year mark as well? *See* Kristian v. Comcast Corp., 446 F.3d 25 (6th Cir.2006) (finding the issue is ultimately for the arbitrator); Escobar-Noble v. Luxury Hotels Int'l of Puerto Rico, Inc., 680 F.3d 118, 126 (1st Cir.2012) (reserving issue for the arbitrator due to lack of clarity within the applicable law); Circuit City Stores v. Mantor, 335 F.3d 1101 (9th Cir.2003) (finding agreement unconscionable because of limitations period); Ingle v. Circuit City Stores, Inc., 328 F.3d 1165 (9th Cir.2003) (finding agreement substantively unconscionable because a strict one-year limitations rule benefits only the employer); Clark v. Daimler Chrysler Corp., 706 N.W.2d 471 (Mich.App.Ct.2005) (upholding six-month limitations period). *See also* Sanchez v. Nitro-Lift Technologies, L.L.C., 12–7046, 2014 WL 3882543 (10th Cir.Aug. 8, 2014) (remanding the question of whether cost shifting provision rendered arbitration clause unenforceable); Malin, *Due Process, supra,* at 395–96.

2. May an employer, in an arbitration agreement, place caps on compensatory and punitive damages that are lower than the caps available under Title VII and the ADA? *See* Ingle v. Circuit City Stores, Inc., 328 F.3d 1165 (9th Cir.2003); Paladino v. Avnet Computer Techs., Inc., 134 F.3d 1054 (11th Cir.1998); Alcaraz v. Avnet, Inc., 933 F.Supp. 1025 (D.N.M.1996).

3. In addition to the D.C. Circuit in the *Cole* case, several other courts of appeals have held that a compulsory predispute arbitration agreement that requires an employee to pay a portion of an arbitrator's fees is unenforceable under the FAA. Shankle v. B-G Maint. Mgmt. of Colo., 163 F.3d 1230 (10th Cir.1999) (arbitrator charged $250 per hour; $125 per hour for travel time; and $45 per hour for each hour of paralegal time); *Paladino*, 134 F.3d 1054. *See also,* Malin, *Due Process,* at 390–92.

4. In *Green Tree Financial Corp.-Alabama v. Randolph*, 531 U.S. 79, 121 S.Ct. 513, 148 L.Ed.2d 373 (2000), a case not involving employment discrimination law, the Supreme Court addressed the question whether an arbitration agreement is unenforceable when it imposes costs on both parties but does not specify the amount of those costs. The Court recognized that the existence of large arbitration costs could effectively preclude a person from vindicating her federal statutory rights in an arbitral forum. In *Green Tree,* the Court placed the burden on the person alleging excessive arbitration costs to prove the likelihood that the costs would be prohibitively expensive. *See also* Am. Exp. Co. v. Italian Colors Rest., 133 S. Ct. 2304, 2310–11, 186 L. Ed. 2d 417 (2013) (reiterating that prohibitively high arbitration costs can trigger the effective vindication exception to the FAA when costs make access to the forum impracticable). Despite the possibility of challenging arbitration agreements based on 'prohibitively high arbitration costs,' the Court in *American Express,* in fact, held that courts should nonetheless enforce an arbitration agreement even where a class action prohibition effectively prevented small business owners from enforcing their rights. According to one commentator,

> [i]n light of decisions [like *American Express*] it seems quite likely that companies will increasingly use arbitration to block employees from bringing collective or class claims, and that this Supreme Court will uphold such efforts by employers.

Sternlight, *Disarming* Employees, supra p. 8, at 1318–19. The only hope for plaintiffs may be a statutory interpretation by the National Labor Relations Board that National Labor Relations Act Section 7 forbids arbitral prohibition of class actions. The Board's original such finding in *D.R. Horton*, 357 NLRB 184 (2012), was thwarted by the courts on technical grounds, see 737 F.3d 344 (5th Cir.2013), but the Board recently renewed its analysis in another case. *See* Murphy Oil USA, Inc., 361 NLRB No. 72 (2014). Plaintiffs may, however, be entitled to some discovery on the issue of whether costs of arbitration are likely effectively to preclude them from vindicating their federal rights in arbitration. *See* Blair v. Scott Specialty Gases, 283 F.3d 595 (3d Cir.2002).

In *Morrison v. Circuit City Stores, Inc.*, 317 F.3d 646 (6th Cir.2003) (en banc), the Sixth Circuit applied *Green Tree* to employment arbitration agreements that included cost-splitting provisions for arbitration fees and costs. In forging a standard consistent with *Green Tree,* the court focused on the deterrent component of antidiscrimination laws. In order for the deterrent aspect of these laws to work, the court opined, a useful standard must take into account any chilling effect not only on a particular individual but also on other similarly situated individuals prior to arbitration. *Post hoc* judicial review of arbitration cases and the appropriateness of costs and cost-splitting provisions are inadequate when viewed from a deterrent perspective for two reasons. First, judicial review of arbitration awards is narrow and it is not clear whether it can adequately protect statutory rights. *Id.* at 662. Second, allowing *post hoc* judicial review of arbitration awards places plaintiffs in a Catch-22 situation:

> [T]hey cannot claim, in advance of arbitration, that the risk of incurring arbitration costs would deter them from arbitrating their claims because they do not know what the costs will be, but if they arbitrate and actually incur costs, they cannot then argue that the costs deterred them because they have already arbitrated their claims.

Id. at 662–63. In addition, according to the *Morrison* court, if a "cost-splitting provision would deter a substantial number of potential litigants, then that provision undermines the deterrent effect of the anti-discrimination statutes. Thus, in order to protect the statutory rights at issue, the reviewing court must look to more than just the interests and conduct of a particular plaintiff." *Id.* at 663. The remedial function of antidiscrimination laws, on the other hand, is directed more toward the rights of particular wronged individuals.

Combining these two themes, the *Morrison* court held that "potential litigants must be given an opportunity, prior to arbitration on the merits, to demonstrate that the potential costs of arbitration are great enough to deter them *and* similarly situated individuals from seeking to vindicate their federal statutory rights in the arbitral forum." *Id.* (emphasis added).

Might an arbitrator be unduly influenced by the fact that his or her fees are provided solely by the employer, especially if the arbitrator hopes to get repeat business from that employer? *See* Lisa B. Bingham, *On Repeat Players, Adhesive Contracts, and the Use of Statistics in Judicial Review of Employment Awards,* 29 McGeorge L.Rev. 223 (1998). What if the provision on allocation of costs violates due process or is unconscionable? Must the court void the agreement or would an employer's agreement to pay all arbitration costs eliminate the error? *See* Muriithi v. Shuttle Exp., Inc., 712 F.3d 173, 183 (4th Cir.2013) (stating that the plaintiff failed to show that arbitration costs were prohibitively high where employer offered to pay for the entire proceeding); Carter v. Countrywide Credit, 362 F.3d 294 (5th Cir.2004) (issuing order compelling arbitration after employer agreed to pay all arbitration fees despite contrary language in arbitration agreement,); Branco v. Norwest Bank Minn., N.A., 381 F.Supp.2d 1274 (D.Haw.2005). *See also* Reginald Alleyne, *Arbitrators' Fees: The Dagger in the Heart of Mandatory Arbitration for Statutory Discrimination Claims,* 6 U.Pa.J.Lab. & Emp.L. 1 (2003); Malin, *Due Process, supra,* at 390–92.

5. What about attorney's fees? Can an employer require that an employee pay his or her own attorney's fees in arbitration? *See* McCaskill v. SCI Mgmt. Corp., 298 F.3d 677 (7th Cir.2002) (holding that an agreement requiring arbitration of Title VII claims is unenforceable if it limits an employee's ability to recover attorney's fees); Malin, *Due Process,* at 394–95 (noting that since the U.S. Supreme Court decision in *PacifiCare Health Systems v. Book,* 538 U.S. 401, 123 S.Ct. 1531, 155 L.Ed.2d 578 (2003), a RICO case, most courts have found attorneys' fee limits unconscionable and have severed them from the arbitral agreement or, as in *PacifiCare,* have found that the issue is for the arbitrator to decide).

6. Can an arbitration agreement preclude employee class actions seeking to vindicate claims of systemic discrimination against an employer? What if the agreement is silent on the issue of class actions? In Stolt-Nielsen S.A. v. AnimalFeeds Int'l Corp., 559 U.S. 662, 684, 130 S. Ct. 1758, 1775, 176 L. Ed. 2d 605 (2010), the Supreme Court addressed both questions directly. The court held that because the arbitration agreement between the parties contained no language regarding class-wide arbitration, such a term could not be imposed by the arbitrator. Here, the arbitrator had sought to impose class-arbitration based on public policy concerns, despite both parties concurring that an agreement had not been reached on that particular issue. *Id* at 663. The Supreme Court vehemently disagreed with this approach, holding that an arbitrator may not infer class arbitration simply from the parties' agreement to arbitrate. *Id* at 685. Finally, the court stated that "a party may not be compelled under the FAA to submit to class arbitration unless there is a contractual basis for concluding that the party *agreed* to do so." (emphasis original). *Id* at 684. *But see* Oxford Health Plans LLC v. Sutter, 133 S. Ct. 2064, 2069, 186 L. Ed. 2d 113 (2013) (distinguishing *Stolt-Nielsen,* holding that arbitrator's enforcement of a class-wide arbitration agreement was valid because the decision was based on the text of the arbitration agreement itself). Additionally, the general consensus among the circuit courts is that a dispute concerning the existence of a class-arbitration provision should be considered a question of arbitrability, therefore reserving the resolution of the issue for the courts unless both parties clearly express otherwise. *See* Opalinski v. Robert Half Int'l Inc., 12–4444, 2014 WL 3733685 (3d Cir.July 30, 2014) ("the availability of classwide arbitrability is a substantive gateway question rather than a procedural one"). In mid-2011, the Supreme Court decided *AT&T Mobility v. Concepcion,* 563 U.S. 333, 131 S. Ct. 1740, 179 L.Ed.2d 742 (2011), which held that the Federal Arbitration Act (FAA) of 1925, 9 U.S.C. §§ 1–9, preempts California's judicial rule regarding the unconscionability of class arbitration waivers in consumer contracts. The case arose out of a standardized cellular telephone contract

between a consumer couple, the Concepcions, and a nationwide service provider, AT&T. The contract provided for arbitration of all disputes, but did not permit classwide arbitration. After the Concepcions were charged sales tax on the retail value of phones provided free under their service contract, they sued AT&T in federal district court in California. Their suit was consolidated with a class action alleging, *inter alia,* that AT&T had engaged in false advertising and fraud by charging sales tax on "free" phones. The district court denied the company's motion to compel arbitration under the Concepcions' contract. Relying on the California Supreme Court's decision in *Discover Bank v. Superior Court,* 36 Cal. 4th 148 (2005), it found the arbitration provision unconscionable because it disallowed classwide proceedings. The Ninth Circuit affirmed, but the Supreme Court reversed. Writing for a 5 to 4 majority, Justice Scalia explained that Section 2 of the FAA, which makes arbitration agreements "valid, irrevocable, and enforceable, save upon such grounds as exist at law or in equity for the revocation of any contract," preempts California law in this area. California is free to establish standards regarding the enforceability of contracts, but is not free to have different rules for the enforceability of contracts to arbitrate.

3. THE ARBITRAL RESULT

COLE V. BURNS INTERNATIONAL SECURITY SERVICES

United States Court of Appeals for the District of Columbia Circuit, 1997.
105 F.3d 1465.

EDWARDS, CIRCUIT JUDGE.

* * *

The final issue in this case concerns the scope of judicial review of arbitral awards in cases of this sort, where an employee is compelled as a condition of employment to arbitrate statutory claims. Cole has argued that the arbitration agreement is unconscionable, because any arbitrator's rulings, even as to the meaning of public law under Title VII, will not be subject to judicial review. Cole is wrong on this point.

Judicial review of arbitration awards covering statutory claims is necessarily focused, but that does not mean that meaningful review is unavailable. * * *

* * *

The Supreme Court has * * * indicated that arbitration awards can be vacated if they are in "manifest disregard of the law." *See* First Options of Chicago, Inc. v. Kaplan, 514 U.S. 938, 115 S.Ct. 1920, 1923, 131 L.Ed.2d 985 (1995) (citing Wilko v. Swan, 346 U.S. 427, 436–37, 74 S.Ct. 182, 98 L.Ed.168 (1953), *overruled on other grounds in* Rodriguez de Quijas v. Shearson/American Express, Inc., 490 U.S. 477, 109 S.Ct. 1917, 104 L.Ed.2d 526 (1989)). Although this term has not been defined by the

Court, and the circuits have adopted various formulations, we believe that this type of review must be defined by reference to the assumptions underlying the Court's endorsement of arbitration. As discussed above, the strict deference accorded to arbitration decisions in the collective bargaining arena may not be appropriate in statutory cases in which an employee has been forced to resort to arbitration as a condition of employment. Rather, in this statutory context, the "manifest disregard of law" standard must be defined in light of the bases underlying the Court's decisions in *Gilmer*-type cases.

Two assumptions have been central to the Court's decisions in this area. First, the Court has insisted that, " '[b]y agreeing to arbitrate a statutory claim, a party does not forego the substantive rights afforded by the statute; it only submits to their resolution in an arbitral, rather than a judicial, forum.' " *Gilmer*, 500 U.S. at 26, 111 S.Ct. at 1652 (quoting *Mitsubishi*, 473 U.S. at 628, 105 S.Ct. at 3354) (alteration in original). Second, the Court has stated repeatedly that, " 'although judicial scrutiny of arbitration awards necessarily is limited, such review is sufficient to ensure that arbitrators comply with the requirements of the statute' at issue." *Gilmer*, 500 U.S. at 32 n.4, 111 S.Ct. at 1655 n.4 (quoting *McMahon*, 482 U.S. at 232, 107 S.Ct. at 2340). These twin assumptions regarding the arbitration of statutory claims are valid only if judicial review under the "manifest disregard of the law" standard is sufficiently rigorous to ensure that arbitrators have properly interpreted and applied statutory law.

The value and finality of an employer's arbitration system will not be undermined by focused review of arbitral legal determinations. Most employment discrimination claims are entirely factual in nature and involve well-settled legal principles. * * * In fact, one study done in the 1980s found that discrimination cases involve factual claims approximately 84% of the time. *See* Michele Hoyman & Lamont E. Stallworth, *The Arbitration of Discrimination Grievances in the Aftermath of* Gardner-Denver, 39 Arb. J. 49, 53 (Sept. 1984). As a result, in the vast majority of cases, judicial review of legal determinations to ensure compliance with public law should have no adverse impact on the arbitration process.[21] Nonetheless, there will be some cases in which novel or difficult legal issues are presented demanding judicial judgment. In such cases, the courts are empowered to review an arbitrator's award to ensure that its resolution of public law issues is correct. Indeed, at oral argument, Burns conceded the courts' authority to engage in such review. Because meaningful judicial review of public law issues is available,

[21] The Hoyman/Stallworth study of arbitral awards in discrimination cases found that, even in cases where de novo review was available under *Gardner-Denver*, only 1.2% of all discrimination cases were reversed by the courts. *See* Hoyman & Stallworth, 39 Arb. J. at 55.

Cole's agreement to arbitrate is not unconscionable or otherwise unenforceable.

* * *

NOTES AND QUESTIONS

1. The statutory grounds for vacatur of arbitration awards are narrow and strictly construed by the courts. Indeed, they may well be the only grounds for vacatur under the FAA. *See, e.g.,* Hall Street Assocs. v. Mattel, Inc., 552 U.S. 576 (2008) (statutory grounds set out in Section 10 of the FAA are the "exclusive means for vacatur" under the FAA). The FAA provides that awards may be vacated where

> (1) the award was procured by corruption, fraud or undue means.
>
> (2) there was evident partiality or corruption in the arbitrators * * * .
>
> (3) the arbitrators were guilty of misconduct in refusing to postpone the hearing, upon sufficient cause shown, or in refusing to hear evidence pertinent and material to the controversy; or of any other misbehavior by which the rights of any party have been prejudiced.
>
> (4) the arbitrators exceeded their powers, or so imperfectly executed them that a mutual, final, and definite award upon the subject matter submitted was not made.

9 U.S.C. §§ 10(a)(1)–(4). Additionally, the FAA provides that an arbitral award may be corrected or modified where

> (1) there was an evident miscalculation of figures.
>
> (2) the arbitrators have issued an award on an issue not submitted to them.
>
> (3) the award is imperfect in a manner or form not affecting the merits of the controversy.

9 U.S.C. § 11.

The courts have also crafted additional grounds for vacating or modifying arbitration awards. These nonstatutory grounds include (1) the arbitrator's award is in manifest disregard of the law; (2) the award conflicts with a strong public policy; (3) the award is arbitrary and capricious; (4) the award is completely irrational; or (5) the award fails to draw its essence from the underlying contract. *See* Williams v. Cigna Fin. Advisors, Inc., 197 F.3d 752, 757–58 (5th Cir.1999) (citing Gabriel M. Wilner, 1 Domke on Commercial Arbitration § 34:07 at 14 (rev.ed.1998)). For evidence that the FAA itself, along with state law responses to mandatory arbitration, are resulting in increased judicial vacatur and less finality of arbitration awards, see Michael H. LeRoy, *Misguided Fairness? Regulating Arbitration by Statute: Empirical*

Evidence of Declining Award Finality, 83 Notre Dame L.Rev. 551 (2008). For further discussion on the manifest disregard of law test, including the *Cole* decision, *see* Michael H. LeRoy, *Are Arbitrators Above the Law? The "Manifest Disregard of the Law" Standard*, 52 B.C. L. Rev. 137, 168 (2011).

2. The "manifest disregard of the law" test, which is discussed in the *Cole* case above, has been invoked as a basis to vacate arbitral awards in statutory employment discrimination cases. *See, e.g.,* Halligan v. Piper Jaffray, Inc., 148 F.3d 197 (2d Cir.1998). The courts have not, however, developed a uniform analytical framework for applying the "manifest disregard of the law" test, especially in the context of arbitration of statutory employment discrimination claims. Some courts have been somewhat expansive about applying the "manifest disregard of the law" standard in the context of nonunion, *Gilmer*-type, employment discrimination cases however. *See, e.g.,* Williams v. CIGNA Fin. Advisors, 197 F.3d 752 (5th Cir.1999); Cole v. Burns Int'l Sec. Serv., 105 F.3d 1465 (D.C.Cir.1997). *See also* Christopher R. Drahozal, *Codifying Manifest Disregard*, 8 Nev. L.J. 234, 235–38 (2007); Dennis R. Nolan, *Employment Arbitration After* Circuit City, 41 Brandeis L.J. 853, 877–80 (2003) (most courts reaching the "standard of review" question have favored the narrower view of the manifest disregard standard); Michael Scodro, *Deterrence and Implied Limits on Arbitral Power*, 55 Duke L.J. 547 (2005).

Previously, the Supreme Court's decision in *Hall Street Associates, LLC v. Mattel, Inc.*, 552 U.S. 576, 128 S.Ct. 1396, 170 L.Ed.2d 254 (2008), had created some doubt about whether an arbitrator's manifest disregard of the law can be a basis for vacatur of an arbitral award. Some courts have held that *Mattel*'s holding that the statutory bases in § 10 of the FAA are the exclusive means for vacatur of arbitral results under the FAA means that nonstatutory grounds, like manifest disregard, are invalid. *See, e.g.,* Citigroup Global Mkts., Inc. v. Bacon, 562 F.3d 349 (5th Cir.2009); Ramos-Santiago v. United Parcel Serv., 524 F.3d 120 (1st Cir.2008). Other courts had found that "manifest disregard" is consistent with the "exceeded powers" language in § 10(a)(4) and thus was not invalidated by the *Mattel* case. *See, e.g.,* Comedy Club Inc. v. Improv. West Assocs., 553 F.3d 1277 (9th Cir.2009).

In *Stolt-Nielsen S.A. v. AnimalFeeds Int'l Corp.*, the Supreme Court did have an opportunity to rule on the validity of the "manifest disregard of the law" test once and for all. However, the majority opinion in *Stolt-Nielsen* seemed to avoid answering this question directly. There the Supreme Court, in reversing the 2nd Circuit's decision to enforce an arbitration decision to allow class-arbitration between the parties even though the contract made no mention of such agreement, held that because the arbitrator failed to implement the appropriate legal standard based on state and federal maritime law, its decision should be overruled. *Stolt-Nielsen S.A.* 559 U.S. at 684. Although, the court does seem to concede that the "manifest disregard of law" test may still be relevant. See *Id.* at 672 n. 3 ("assuming, *arguendo,* that such a standard applies, we find it satisfied for the reasons that follow"). In the wake of *Stolt-Nielsen,* and perhaps not surprisingly, there has been some confusion among the Federal Circuits regarding the viability of the manifest disregard of law test. *Compare* Jock v. Sterling Jewelers Inc., 646 F.3d 113, 127 (2d Cir.2011) (prior decision regarding Title VII and ADEA claims can *only* be overturned when arbitrator exceeds its authority) (emphasis added), Johnson v. Wells Fargo Home Mortgage, Inc., 635 F.3d 401, 415 (9th Cir.2011) ("[w]e note that the Supreme Court later expressed some doubt as to whether the ' "manifest disregard" [standard] survive[d] [its] decision in *Hall Street*' "), *with* Wachovia Sec., LLC v. Brand, 671 F.3d 472, 483 (4th Cir.2012) ("[t]herefore, we decline to adopt the position of the Fifth and Eleventh Circuits that manifest disregard no longer exists"). For more clarification on this Supreme Court decision and the current state of the "manifest disregard of law" rule see Patrick Sweeney, *Exceeding Their Powers: A Critique of Stolt-Nielsen and Manifest Disregard, and A Proposal for Substantive Arbitral Award Review*, 71 Wash. & Lee L. Rev. 1571, 1604 (2014).

C. ARBITRATION OF EMPLOYMENT DISCRIMINATION CLAIMS IN UNIONIZED WORKPLACES

Employers and unions have long used arbitration to resolve grievances that arise under collective bargaining agreements. Typically, the collective bargaining agreement will provide for a multi-stage grievance procedure that culminates in binding arbitration. The arbitration provisions of the agreement provide a method for selecting a third-party neutral as arbitrator. The grievance process is initiated when an employee files a written grievance. As the exclusive representative of the employees in the bargaining unit, the union is responsible for handling the grievance through all stages, including representing the employee at the arbitration hearing. Many employee grievances are settled at early stages of the grievance process and never go to arbitration. More importantly, the union is not obligated to accept every grievance; as long as the union does not violate its duty of fair representation, it is free to exercise considerable discretion in determining which employee grievances warrant adjustment through the collective bargaining agreement's grievance and arbitration process, though the employee is generally free to adjust his or her grievance with the employer directly if the union chooses not to take up a claim. *See* Vaca v. Sipes, 386 U.S. 171, 87 S.Ct. 903, 17 L.Ed.2d 842 (1967). It should be noted however that a union, by choosing not to take up a member's claim, is not immunized from being subjected to legal action by that member. *See* Green v. Am. Fed'n of Teachers/Illinois Fed'n of Teachers Local 604, 740 F.3d 1104 (7th Cir.2014) (affirming decision allowing black teacher to bring Title VII action against union alleging discrimination and retaliation after it declined to pursue her claim).The duty of fair representation (DFR) is discussed in Chapter 2, Section D.5. For a comprehensive treatment of the arbitration process, see Elkouri and Elkouri: How Arbitration Works (Alan Miles Ruben ed., 6th ed.2003).

The union arbitral process has been used to vindicate employment discrimination claims. Questions have arisen, however, regarding the use of these processes to decide statutory claims of discrimination. In *Alexander v. Gardner-Denver*, 415 U.S. 36, 94 S.Ct. 1011, 39 L.Ed.2d 147(1974), the plaintiff, a black employee, alleged that he had been discharged because of his race. He had filed a grievance contesting his discharge under the grievance-arbitration provision of the collective bargaining agreement and also had filed an action under Title VII in federal court. The union processed the grievance through arbitration. Without discussing plaintiff's claim of racial discrimination, the arbitrator concluded that the plaintiff had been discharged for just cause. Following the arbitration decision, the employer moved for summary judgment on the Title VII claim. The district court granted the motion, and the court of appeals affirmed. On certiorari, the Supreme Court reversed, holding that an employee does not forfeit his rights under Title VII by first pursuing binding arbitration of a union grievance. The Court reasoned that the contractual rights granted unions under a collective bargaining agreement and the individual rights granted to employees under Title VII are "distinctly separate." *Id.* at 50, 94 S.Ct. at 1020.

The Court concluded that Title VII confers individual rights upon employees that "can form no part of the collective-bargaining process since waiver of these rights would defeat the paramount congressional purpose behind Title VII." *Id.* at 51, 94 S.Ct. at 1021. The Court continued:

> [W]e think it clear that there can be no prospective waiver of an employee's rights under Title VII. It is true, of course, that a union may waive certain statutory rights related to collective activity, such as the right to strike. These rights are conferred on employees collectively to foster the processes of bargaining and properly may be exercised or relinquished by the union as collective-bargaining agent to obtain economic benefits for union members. Title VII, on the other hand, stands on plainly different ground; it concerns not majoritarian processes, but an individual's right to equal employment opportunities. Title VII's strictures are absolute and represent a congressional command that each employee be free from discriminatory practices. Of necessity, the rights conferred can form no part of the collective-bargaining process since waiver of these rights would defeat the paramount congressional purpose behind Title VII. In these circumstances, an employee's rights under Title VII are not susceptible of prospective waiver.

Id. at 51–52, 94 S.Ct. at 1021 (citations omitted). The Court drew a clear distinction between employee rights arising from a statute and employee rights arising from a collective bargaining agreement. It noted that where an employee's claim is based on a collective bargaining agreement, courts should defer to the arbitrator's decision. Different considerations apply, however, where a claim is based on a statute like Title VII, which is designed to provide minimum substantive guarantees to employees.

Of more relevance outside of collective bargaining was the Court's articulation of the view that arbitration was inappropriate for resolving Title VII claims. This conclusion rested on four grounds: (1) that labor arbitrators lack the expertise and authority competently to resolve Title VII claims; (2) that arbitral factfinding procedures fail adequately to protect employees' rights under Title VII; (3) that arbitrators are not required to issue written opinions; and (4) that because unions have exclusive control over the manner and extent to which an individual employee's grievance is pursued, unions and employers can discriminate jointly without suffering adverse legal consequences if arbitration is an employee's exclusive remedy.

In *Gilmer v. Interstate/Johnson Lane Corp*, 500 U.S. 20, 111 S.Ct. 1647, 114 L.Ed.2d 26 (1991), the Court held that a claim under the Age Discrimination in Employment Act could be subjected to compulsory arbitration pursuant to an arbitration agreement in a securities registration application of the employee. Prior to *Gilmer*, lower courts widely interpreted *Gardner-Denver* as holding that employees who asserted statutory discrimination claims were entitled to litigate their claims in court, regardless of any predispute agreement to arbitrate. *See, e.g.*, Rosenfeld v. Department of Army, 769 F.2d 237, 239 (4th Cir.1985) ("The plain lesson of *Alexander v. Gardner-Denver Co.* * * * is that Congress entrusted the ultimate resolution of questions of discrimination to the federal judiciary."); Utley v. Goldman Sachs & Co., 883 F.2d 184 (1st Cir.1989); EEOC v. Children's Hosp. Med. Ctr., 719 F.2d 1426 (9th Cir.1983).

The *Gilmer* decision effectively gave a green light to arbitration of statutory discrimination claims and that decision appeared to be in tension with *Gardner-Denver*. Ultimately, the Supreme Court resolved the tension by holding that a collective bargaining agreement can require arbitration of discrimination claims. In *14 Penn Plaza, LLC v. Pyett*, 556 U.S. 247, 129 S.Ct. 247, 173 L.Ed.2d 398 (2009), a group of employees who had failed to obtain relief on their discrimination claims in arbitration sought to file a federal discrimination claim under the theory that the collective bargaining agreement could not require arbitration of their statutory discrimination claims so long as "the collective-bargaining agreement's arbitration provision expressly covers both statutory and contractual discrimination claims." *Id.* at 257. The Court distinguished its

Gardner-Denver decision by noting the arbitration agreement in that case did not clearly include statutory discrimination claims, and further repudiated its criticism of the use of arbitration agreements to resolve discrimination claims. Accordingly, collective bargaining agreements can require arbitration of discrimination claims but the agreement must clearly intend to include such claims.

The conflation in *Penn Plaza* of labor and employment arbitration raises but does not answer a host of other issues. For example: (a) Is the cost of pursuing a complex employment discrimination claim appropriately shared by all employees paying dues? (b) What is the applicable time period for bringing a discrimination claim—the few days typically listed in the contract for bringing grievances or the longer statute of limitations for discrimination claims under statutes? (c) May a collective bargaining agreement restrict the remedies available when statutory rights are arbitrated? May it restrict the ability to bring class claims? (d) How should the parties handle choice-of-law issues that may arise under state antidiscrimination laws when a collective bargaining agreement covers employees in more than one state? For an in-depth discussion on the effects of *Penn Plaza,* as well as the issue of a union's decision not to arbitrate, a question seemingly left open by the court, see F. Ryan Van Pelt, *Union Refusal to Arbitrate: Pyett's Unanswered Question* Kravar v. Triangle Services, Inc., 2010 J. Disp. Resol. 515 (2010).

INDEX

References are to Pages

ABORTION
As pregnancy-related medical condition, 447, 448

ACCENT
Discrimination based on accent as national origin discrimination, 713–731

AFFIRMATIVE ACTION
Generally, 881–921
Civil Rights Act of 1991, 912, 913
Collateral attack on affirmative action consent decree, 895, 896
Definitions, 881, 882
Equal protection challenges, 913–923
Evolution as remedy, 886–887
Executive orders, 886
Five models, 882
Introduction, 881–885
Societal discrimination, 883, 884
State laws prohibiting affirmative action, 920
Title VII
Generally, 886, 887
Affirmative action and Title VII's equality principle, 888–896
Collateral attack on affirmative action consent decree, 895, 896
Evaluating legitimacy of affirmative action under Title VII, 896–913

AGE DISCRIMINATION IN EMPLOYMENT ACT OF 1967 (ADEA)
Generally, 12, 743–798
Age-proxy theory, 757
Benefits. Fringe benefits, below
Cost justification defense, 764–766
Differences between ADEA and Title VII plaintiffs, 744
Disparate impact
Generally, 798–807
Reasonable factors other than age defense, 806
Disparate treatment
Generally, 744–780
Age-proxy theory, 757
BFOQ defense, 781, 782
Cost justification defense, 764–766
ERISA and ADEA overlap, 757
Fringe benefits, 767, 768
Hostile work environment claims, 798
Sex-plus-age claims, 373–374
Downsizing cases, 791–798
Eleventh Amendment immunity, 17
Employer, defined, 57
ERISA and ADEA overlap, 757
Exhaustion of administrative remedies, 20, 38
Fringe benefits, 767, 768, 779, 780
High policymaker exemption, 791
Hostile work environment claims, 798
Introduction, 743, 744
Law and economics analysis, 767
Liquidated damages, 84, 85, 767
Mixed motives, 154, 155
Older Workers Benefit Protection Act and ADEA, 788–791
Reduction-in-force cases, 791–798
Remedies, 68–69
Retaliation provisions, 161
Separations and waivers
Generally, 782–791
High policymaker exemption, 791
Older Workers Benefit Protection Act, 788–791
Sex-plus-age claims, 373–374
States, ADEA claims against, 744
Title VII, 85–87
Union liability, 62–65

AGENTS
Individual liability, agents of employers, 58, 59

ALIENAGE
Discrimination based on, section 1981 claims, 329, 330
National Origin Discrimination, this index

AMERICANS WITH DISABILITIES ACT OF 1990 (ADA)
Generally, 809–878
ADA Amendments Act of 2008 (ADAAA), 809–811
Alcohol users, 874
Association discrimination, 833–836
Attorney's fees, 85–87
Burden of proof, 869
Covered entities, 814
Direct threat defense, 856–858
Disability, meaning of
Generally, 840–851
ADA Amendments Act of 2008 (ADAAA), 809–811

Obesity as disability, 852
Sexual behavior disorders, 852, 853
Discrimination, meaning under ADA, 815–840
Drug testing, 873, 874
EEOC enforcement. EEOC, this index
Eleventh Amendment immunity, 17, 18
Employer, defined, 55
Essential functions, defined, 853, 854
Exhaustion of administrative remedies, 20, 23–25
Federal employers, 814
FMLA and ADA, 874, 875
Genetic testing and Genetic Information Nondiscrimination Act of 2008, 14
Health care workers, special problems, 858, 859
Hostile work environment claims, 839, 840
Interplay between Title VII, PDA, FMLA and ADA, 486–487
Introduction, 809–814
Judicial estoppel doctrine, 855
Legislative history, 809–814
Medical benefits under ADA, 875–878
Medical inquiries and examinations
Generally, 871–874
Alcohol users, 874
Current employees, 873
Drug testing, 873, 874
Entering employees, 872, 873
Existing employees, 873
FMLA and ADA, 874
Post-employment stage, 872, 873
Pre-offer stage, 872
Mental disabilities, 877, 878
Mitigation of damages, victim's duty, 73, 74
Obesity as disability, 852
Qualification standards
Generally, 853–856
Direct threat defense, 856–858
Essential functions, defined, 853, 854
Judicial estoppel doctrine, 855
Reasonable accommodation and undue hardship
Generally, 876
Burden of proof, 869
Costs vs. benefits, 870
Unionized sector, 870–871
Reassignment to vacant position, 833
Rehabilitation Act of 1973, relationship to ADA, 813
Remedies, 68–69
Retaliation provisions, 161
Sexual behavior disorders, 852, 853
Sexual orientation, ADA exclusions, 513–514
Social Security disability benefits, 856
State and municipal employers, 814, 815
Title I, 12
Undue hardship. Reasonable accommodation and undue hardship, above
Union liability, 62–65
Unionized sector, reasonable accommodation, 870
Worker's own health or safety, threats to, 860–861

ANNUITIES
Sex discrimination, 360

APPRENTICESHIP PROGRAMS
Discriminatory, union liability, 67, 68

ARBITRATION OF CLAIMS
Generally, 931–964
Agreement to arbitrate. Nonunion workplaces, below
Arbitrators, 933
Binding nature of awards, 932
Introduction, 931, 932
Nonunion workplaces
Generally, 932–939
Arbitrability, 932–942
Arbitral result
Generally, 957–959
Manifest disregard of law test, 960, 961
Modifying awards, 959, 960
Vacating awards, 959, 960
Arbitration agreement
Generally, 943–957
Attorney's fees, 956
Class actions, 956, 957
Contract defenses, 946
Contract formation, 943
Due process, 952–953
Attorney's fees, 956
Class actions, 956, 957
Mandatory predispute arbitration policies, 940, 941
Modifying awards, 959, 960
Vacating awards, 959, 960
Voluntariness of employee agreements to arbitrate, 941
Unionized workplaces
Generally, 960–964
Statutory claims of discrimination, 962, 963

ATTORNEY AND CLIENT
Perjurious client and lawyer's ethical obligations, 125, 126

ATTORNEY GENERAL
Suits against governmental employers, 42

ATTORNEY'S FEES
Generally, 85–90
Arbitration, 956
Calculating reasonable fee, 88
Entitlement, 85–87
Hourly rate, reasonable, 89
Hours, reasonable number, 88, 89
Lodestar enhancement, 89, 90
Mixed motive cases, 154
Prevailing plaintiff or defendant, 86–87
Standards for fee award, 88–90

Taxation of fee awards, 90

BACK PAY REMEDY
Generally, 73–75

BFOQ DEFENSE
ADEA claims, 781, 782
National origin discrimination, 699
Religious discrimination, 648–650
Sex Discrimination, this index

BREAST FEEDING
State laws promoting, 465

BULLYING IN WORKPLACE
Same-sex harassment claims, 563

BURDEN OF PROOF
ADA cases, 869
Causation, plaintiff's burden of proof on prima facie case, 184
Disparate treatment, burden allocation rules, 102
Equal protection cases, 318–321
Retaliation, burden shifting, 168

CALIFORNIA
Family Rights Act, 489

CAREGIVERS
Family Responsibilities, this index

CAUSATION
Retaliation, this index
Same-sex harassment, but for formulation, 372

CITIZENSHIP
National Origin Discrimination, this index

CIVIL RIGHTS ACT OF 1991
Generally, 12
Affirmative action, 912, 913
Disparate impact, 268–269, 270–274
Mixed motive cases, 144

CLASS ACTIONS
Arbitration agreements, 956, 957
Compensatory and punitive damages, 81, 82
Settlements, pattern-or-practice cases, 226
Sexual harassment, pattern-or-practice cases, 553, 554

COMPARABLE WORTH
Generally, 386–389

CONGRESSIONAL ACCOUNTABILITY ACT OF 1995
Generally, 14

CONSTITUTIONAL LAW
Citizenship requirements, constitutionality, 708, 709
Due process, 15
As bar to civil damages claims against states, 16–19
Ex Parte Young exception, 19
Local governments, 19
Equal Protection, this index
Fifth Amendment, 15
First Amendment, 16
Fourteenth Amendment, 16
LGBT individuals, protections under U.S. and state constitutions, 669
Reconstruction Era legislation, 3
Sexual harassment
Free speech defense, 556, 557
Freedom of religion and Title VII's ministerial exception, 557
Suspect classifications, 16
Thirteenth Amendment, 303, 304

CONTRACEPTIVES
Insurance exclusions, 465–467

CRITICAL RACE THEORY
Generally, 129–133

DAMAGES
Generally, 77–83
ADEA, liquidated damages, 767
Caps on damages, 77, 75
Class actions, 82, 83
Compensatory damages, 69, 78, 79
Governmental entities, exemption from punitive damages, 78
Liquidated damages, 84, 85
Punitive damages
Generally, 71, 79–83
Caps, 77, 75
Class actions, 82, 83
Employer vicarious liability, 82, 600, 601
Governmental entities, exemption from punitive damages, 78
Limitations, 81, 82
Taxation of awards, 84, 85

DEFAMATION
Bad faith action as basis for retaliation claim, 181

DISABILITIES
Americans with Disabilities Act (ADA), this index

DISCOVERY
Pretext, role of liberal discovery rules in proving, 118
Sexual harassment, discovery of plaintiff's prior sexual history, 555–556

DISPARATE IMPACT
Generally, 245–300
Age Discrimination in Employment Act (ADEA), this index
Alternative employment practices, 271
Analytical framework, 220
Business necessity defense, 269
Civil Rights Act of 1991
Generally, 268–270

Contemporary disparate impact doctrine, 270–283
Discriminatory intent element, 252
Eighty percent rule, 257
Griggs revisited, 261–269
Interview process, unstructured, 241
Legitimacy of disparate impact theory, 259–261
Objective criteria
Generally, 246–261
Discriminatory intent element, 252
Pregnancy, 461–464
Religious discrimination claims under Title VII, 671
Remedying disparate impact of selection procedures, 284–301
Sex discrimination claims, 374, 375
Sexual harassment, 566
Uniform Guidelines on Employee Selection Procedures, 254, 255

DISPARATE TREATMENT
Generally, 95–228
Age Discrimination in Employment Act (ADEA), this index
Burden allocation rules, 102
Constructive discharges, 121–123
Critical race theory, 129–133
Defenses
Honest belief defense, pretext and, 121–123
Lack-of-interest defense, 224–226
Legitimate, nondiscriminatory reason defense, 120
Same actor defense, 126–127
Defined, 96
Demotions, 121
Discharges, 121–123
Evidence
Me too evidence, 123
Statistical evidence and pattern-or-practice cases, below
Futile gesture doctrine, 104
Honest belief defense, pretext and, 121–123
Inferences and presumptions, 111
Legitimate, nondiscriminatory reason defense, 120
Litigation strategy, 121
Me too evidence, 123
Meanings and theories of "discrimination," 95–97
Mixed Motive Cases, this index
Pattern-or-practice cases
Settlements, 226
Statistical evidence and pattern-or-practice cases, below
Pregnancy, 461–464
Honest belief defense, pretext and, 121–123
Pretext maybe rule, 117
Pretext only rule, 117
Pretext-plus rule, 117–120
Role of liberal discovery rules in proving pretext, 121
Prima facie case doctrine
Generally, 102
Elements of prima facie case
Generally, 102–104
Application element, 102, 103
Awarding employment opportunity to person outside plaintiff's protected class, 104–106
Futile gesture doctrine, 104
Qualification element, 104
Similarly situated comparators, 106–108
Inferences and presumptions, 111
Similarly situated comparators, 106–108
Promotion cases, 121
Proof by direct or circumstantial evidence, 98
Rebuttable presumptions, 111
Reductions-in-force (RIFs), 110
Retaliation, this index
Reverse discrimination cases, 127, 128
Same actor defense, 126–127
Sex discrimination claims, 374, 375
Sexual harassment, 566
Statistical evidence and pattern-or-practice cases
Generally, 207–228
Expert witnesses, 225
Gross statistical disparities, 218
Individual claims, 226
Lack-of-interest defense, 224–226
Multiple regression analysis, 221
Relevant labor market, 221
Standard deviation, 218–221

ECONOMICS OF DISCRIMINATION
Generally, 226, 227

EEOC
Auditing, 56, 57
Cause determination, 23
Charge of discrimination, 23
Conciliation, 23
Deferral or nondeferral jurisdictions and timely filing, 25, 26
Enforcement authority, 21 et seq.
Exhaustion of administrative remedies, 23–25
Federal suits against states, 19
Guidelines, 22
Procedural regulations, 21, 22
Reasons for delay in filing charges, 36
Right-to-sue letter, 39
Suits by EEOC in its own name, 42
Testers, use of, 56, 57
Generally, 30
Discrete vs. continuing acts, 37
Equitable considerations, 38
Tolling, 38

Timely filing in court, 38–39

EMPLOYEES
Temporary employees, 59
Who is employee, 57–59

EMPLOYERS
Agents of employers, individual liability, 58, 59
Discriminatory harassment, liability for. Harassment, this index
Integrated employer test, 57, 58
Single employer, 57
Temporary employers, 59
Union as employer, 62–65
Who is employer, 57–59

EMPLOYMENT PRACTICE
Defined, 60, 61

ENGLISH LANGUAGE
Bilingual employees, English-only requirement, 713–722
Proficiency as job requirement, 713, 714
Reverse English-only claims, 730

EQUAL PAY ACT OF 1963 (EPA)
Generally, 378–391
Attorney's fees, 85–87
Eleventh Amendment immunity, 18
Enactment, 13
Liquidated damages, 84, 85
Remedies, 68–69
Wage Discrimination, Sex-Based, this index

EQUAL PROTECTION
Generally, 15
Affirmative action, equal protection challenges, 913–923
Analytical framework, 318–321
Burden of proof, 318–321
Fifth and Fourteenth Amendments, 307–312
Reconstruction Civil Rights Acts and equal protection
Generally, 303–337
Fifth and Fourteenth Amendments, 307–312
Legacy of reconstruction-era reforms, 303–305
Section 1981, this index
Section 1983, this index
Thirteenth Amendment, 303, 304

ESTOPPEL
Disability claims, judicial estoppel doctrine, 855

ETHICS
Perjurious client and lawyer's ethical obligations, 125, 126

EVIDENCE
Causation, retaliatory claims, 184
Direct or circumstantial evidence, proof of disparate treatment, 98
Me too evidence, 123
Mixed motive cases, direct evidence, 141, 142, 150
Sexual harassment, admissibility of plaintiff's prior sexual history, 555–556
Statistical evidence. Disparate Treatment, this index
Status discrimination, evidentiary frameworks, 339–345

EXECUTIVE ORDERS
Generally, 15
Affirmative action, 886

EXHAUSTION OF ADMINISTRATIVE REMEDIES
Generally, 20, 22–39
Federal employees, 39

EXPERT WITNESSES
Statistical evidence, 226

EXTRATERRITORIAL APPLICATION
Discrimination laws, 60

FAMILY AND MEDICAL LEAVE ACT OF 1993 (FMLA)
Generally, 13, 479–490
ADA and FMLA, 874, 875
Anti-retaliation provision, 488, 489
Comparative perspective on family and medical leave policies, 489
Covered employees, 480
Eleventh Amendment immunity, 18
Employee benefits, maintaining, 480
Enforcement, 480
Interplay between Title VII, PDA, FMLA and ADA, 486–487
Nondiscrimination provision, 488, 489
Notice to employer, 479, 480
Pregnancy-related FMLA leaves, timing, 487
Reinstatement to former job, 480

FAMILY RESPONSIBILITIES DISCRIMINATION
Generally, 468–480
Evidence sufficient to suggest gender discrimination, 477, 488
Family and Medical Leave Act, this index
Male workers, claims by, 478

FEDERAL EMPLOYEES
Exhaustion of administrative remedies, 39
Religious discrimination, 683
Sexual orientation, federal government employment nondiscrimination policies, 527

FREE SPEECH
Sexual harassment, free speech defense, 556, 557

FRONT PAY
Generally, 76, 77

GENDER DISCRIMINATION
Sex Discrimination, this index

GENDER EXPRESSION OR IDENTITY
Sexual Orientation, this index

GENDER WAGE GAP
Wage Discrimination, Sex-Based, this index

GENETIC INFORMATION NONDISCRIMINATION ACT OF 2008 (GINA)
Generally, 14

GOVERNMENT EMPLOYEES
Federal Employees, this index
Government Employee Rights Act of 1991 (GERA), 337
Religious Discrimination, this index

HARASSMENT
Generally, 535–620
Admissibility of plaintiff's prior sexual history, 555–556
Adolescent plaintiffs, 548
Agents, individual liability for harassment, 601
Aggravated harassment, 609, 610
Appearance and behavior, employer policies, 548
Avoiding harm otherwise, 597, 598
Bisexual harasser defense, 560, 561
Bullying in workplace, 563
Bystander harassment, 552, 553
Class actions and pattern-or-practice cases, 553, 554
Complaint procedure, failure to use, 596
Compound hostile environment/constructive discharge claim, 609
Consensual relationships, consequences of termination, 565, 566
Constructive discharge, 609, 611
Corrective opportunities, failure to take advantage, 597, 598
Customers and other third parties, employer liability for harassment by, 615, 616
Defenses, 556–557
Delay in complaining, 598
Discovery of plaintiff's prior sexual history, 555–556
Employer liability for discriminatory harassment
Generally, 568–617
Aggregating job detriments, 592
Antiharassment policies, 593
Avoiding harm otherwise, 597, 598
Complaint procedure, failure to use, 597
Compound hostile environment/constructive discharge claim, 609
Consensual relationships, consequences of termination, 565, 566
Constructive discharge, 609, 611, 612
Corrective opportunities, failure to take advantage, 597, 598
Customers and other third parties, liability for harassment by, 615, 616
Delay in complaining, 598
Delegating authority for handling complaints, 594, 595
Futility of complaining, 598
Imputed liability, high-ranking harasser as "proxy" or "alter ego" for employer, 592
Individual liability of agents for harassment, 601
Intolerable or aggravated harassment, 609, 610
Negligence liability for harassment by co-workers and nonemployees
Generally, 612–618
Common law of agency, 612
Corrective action, 612, 613
Customers and other third parties, liability for harassment by, 615, 616
EEOC guidance, 612, 613
Notice to employer, 613
Serial harassers, 614
Subordinates harassing supervisors, employer liability, 614, 615
Paramour preferential treatment claims, 563, 564
Punitive damages liability, 559, 560
Responses to complaints, 613
Retaliatory vs. constructive discharge, 610, 611
Rights of alleged harassers, 602
Serial harassers, 614
State antidiscrimination laws and Title VII, 603
Subordinates harassing supervisors, employer liability, 614, 615
Tangible employment action, definition and relevance, 589–592
Training programs, 597
Unofficial supervisory conduct vs. official company acts, 610
Vicarious liability for harassment by supervisors
Generally, 570–608
Affirmative defenses, 593–596
Aggregating job detriments, 592
Antiharassment policies, 593

Avoiding harm otherwise, 597, 598
Complaint procedure, failure to use, 597
Compound hostile environment/constructive discharge claim, 609
Consensual relationships, consequences of termination, 565, 566
Constructive discharge, 609, 611, 612
Corrective opportunities, failure to take advantage, 597, 598
Delay in complaining, 598
Delegating authority for handling complaints, 594, 595
EEOC's 1999 enforcement guidance, 589
Fulfilled promises of job benefits, 590, 591
Futility of complaining, 598
Individual liability of agents for harassment, 601
Intolerable or aggravated harassment, 609, 610
Paramour preferential treatment claims, 563, 564
Punitive damages liability, 599, 601
Responses to complaints, 594
Rights of alleged harassers, 601, 602
Serial harasser, 614
State antidiscrimination laws and Title VII, 603
Tangible employment action, definition and relevance, 589–592
Training programs, 597
Unfulfilled promises of job benefits, 590
Unfulfilled threats of adverse job consequences, 591, 592
Unofficial supervisory conduct vs. official company acts, 610

Equal opportunity defense, 626
Free speech defense, 556, 557
Freedom of religion and Title VII's ministerial exception, 557
Futility of complaining, 598
High-ranking harasser as "proxy" or "alter ego" for employer, 592
Hostile work environment, prima facie case, 540–565
Individual liability of agents for harassment, 601
Intolerable or aggravated harassment, 609, 610
Introduction, 535, 536
Liability. Employer liability for discriminatory harassment, above
National origin, harassment because of, 699–702
Negligence liability for harassment by co-workers and nonemployees. Employer liability for discriminatory harassment, above
Nontargeted harassment, 552, 553
Off-site, after-hours harassment, 558, 559
Paramour preferential treatment claims, 563, 564
Prima facie case
Hostile work environment, 540–565
Quid pro quo harassment, 539, 540
Prior sexual history, discovery and admissibility, 555–556
Provocative speech and dress, plaintiff's, 547
Psychological or mental distress, claims for, 552
Punitive damages liability, 559, 560
Quid pro quo sexual harassment, prima facie case, 539, 540
Racial harassment
Generally, 618–627
Code words, 623, 624
Facially neutral language, liability for, 623, 624
Intersectionality, 625
Nooses in workplace, 626, 627
Racial animus, 623
Reverse racial harassment, 626
Same-race harassment, 626
Section 1981 claims, 626
Symbols, racist, 626, 627
Totality of circumstances, 622
Unwelcomeness, 621
Victim's perspective, 622
Reasonable person standard, 551
Religious-based harassment, 669, 670
Retaliation claims, 180
Retaliatory vs. constructive discharge, 609, 610
Rights of alleged harassers, 602
Serial harasser, 614
Severity or pervasiveness, 548–550
Sexual harassment
Generally, 536–566
Adolescent plaintiffs, 548
Alternative theories of liability, 566–568
Appearance and behavior, employer policies, 547
Bisexual harasser defense, 560, 561
Bullying in workplace, 563
Bystander or nontargeted harassment, 552, 553
Class actions and pattern-or-practice cases, 553, 554

Defenses, 555–558
EEOC guidelines, 538
Equal opportunity defense, 626
Free speech defense, 556, 557
Freedom of religion and Title VII's ministerial exception, 557
Gender animus, harassment based on, 372, 373
Hostile work environment, prima facie case, 540–565
Off-site, after-hours harassment, 558, 559
Prior sexual history, discovery and admissibility, 555–556
Provocative speech and dress, plaintiff's, 547
Psychological or mental distress, claims for, 552
Quid pro quo harassment, prima facie case, 539, 540
Reasonable person standard, 551
Reasonableness of employee's beliefs, 551
Same-sex harassment
Generally, 372, 373, 558–563
Bisexual harasser defense, 560, 561
Bullying in workplace, 563
Categories, male-on-male harassment, 371, 372
Causation, but for formulation, 372
Equal opportunity defense, 626
Gender animus, harassment based on, 372, 373
Sexualized conduct, 372
Social context of harassment, 561, 562
Totality of circumstances, 622
Section 1983 suits, 568
Severity or pervasiveness, 548–550
Sexualized conduct, 372, 373, 372
Social context of harassment, 561, 562
Tort theories of liability, 566–568
Totality of circumstances, 622
Unwelcomeness, proving, 546–548
Vulgar language, plaintiff's use of, 548
Workplace sexual harassment, estimating prevalence and costs, 536–538
Sexual Orientation, this index
Social context of harassment, 561, 562
State antidiscrimination laws and Title VII, 603
Subordinates harassing supervisors, employer liability, 614, 615
Supervisors, employer's vicarious liability. Employer liability for discriminatory harassment, above
Timely filing of charges, 616–618
Tort theories of liability, 566–568
Totality of circumstances, 622
Training programs, 597
Unofficial supervisory conduct vs. official company acts, 610
Unwelcomeness, proving, 546–548
Vicarious liability for harassment by supervisor. Employer liability for discriminatory harassment, above
Vulgar language, plaintiff's use of, 548
Workplace sexual harassment, estimating prevalence and costs, 536–538

HISTORICAL BACKGROUND
Generally, 3–9

HOSTILE WORK ENVIRONMENT
ADA and Rehabilitation Act claims, 839, 840
ADEA claims, 798
Sexual harassment, prima facie case, 540–567

IMMIGRATION REFORM AND CONTROL ACT OF 1986 (IRCA)
Generally, 13–14
Undocumented workers and Title VII, 710–712
Unfair employment practices, 709

IMMIGRATION STATUS
Undocumented workers and Title VII. National Origin Discrimination, this index

INFERENCES AND PRESUMPTIONS
Disparate treatment, 111
Retaliation, rebuttable presumption, 168

INSURANCE
Contraceptives, 465–467
Insuring against discrimination claims, 90, 91
Sex discrimination, 360

INTEREST
Prejudgment interest, 75, 76

INTERSECTIONALITY
Individuals with multiple identities, 49–51
Racial harassment, 625
Sex and race claims, 433
Sex discrimination claims, 373, 374
Sexual orientation, 625

JUDICIAL ESTOPPEL
Disability claims, 855

JUDICIAL NOTICE
Costs of dress and grooming rules, 429, 430

LABOR RELATIONS LAWS
Generally, 20

LACHES
Title VII, judicial enforcement, 40

LANGUAGE
English language requirements. National Origin Discrimination, this index

LGBT
Sexual Orientation, this index

LILY LEDBETTER FAIR PAY ACT OF 2009
Generally, 37, 38, 390, 391

LIQUIDATED DAMAGES
Generally, 83

LOCAL GOVERNMENT
State and Local Governments, this index

MEDICAL INQUIRIES AND EXAMINATIONS
Americans with Disabilities Act (ADA), this index

MEDICAL INTERNS AND RESIDENTS
Who is employee, 56

MEDICAL LEAVE
Family and Medical Leave Act, this index

MENTAL DISTRESS
Sexual harassment, claims for psychological or mental distress, 552

MIXED MOTIVE CASES
Generally, 133–141
Age discrimination claims, 154
Attorney's fees, 153
Cat's paw theory, 154–160
Civil Rights Act of 1991, 144
Direct evidence, 142, 143
Reinstatement remedy, 73
Stray remarks doctrine, 143, 144

NATIONAL LABOR RELATIONS ACT (NLRA)
Title VII and NLRA's exclusivity principle, 66, 67

NATIONAL ORIGIN DISCRIMINATION
Generally, 685–737
Accent discrimination, 713–731
BFOQ defense, national origin and, 699
Census questionnaires, 695, 696
Citizenship requirements
Generally, 702–707
Constitutionality of citizenship requirements, 708, 709
Immigration Reform and Control Act (IRCA), 13–14, 709
Noncitizen employees, preferences for, 708
Distinction between national origin, ancestry and ethnicity, 694, 695
English language requirements
Generally, 712–728
English proficiency as job requirement, 712, 713
English-only requirement for bilingual employees, 713–731
Reverse English-only claims, 730
Harassment because of national origin, 699–701
Immigration Reform and Control Act (IRCA)
Generally, 13–14
Undocumented workers and Title VII, 710–712
Unfair employment practices, 709
Introduction, 685–687
Meaning of "national origin"
Generally, 688–701
Distinction between national origin, ancestry and ethnicity, 694, 695
EEOC definition, 688, 689
Native Americans, 697–699
Nativist themes, 687
Noncitizen employees, preferences for, 708
Religion, overlap with, 697
Section 1981 claims, 329, 330
Undocumented workers and Title VII, 710–712

NATIVE AMERICANS
Generally, 697–699

NEGLIGENCE
Employer liability for harassment by co-workers and nonemployees. Harassment, this index

PATTERN-OR-PRACTICE CASES
Disparate Treatment, this index

PERJURY
Perjurious client and lawyer's ethical obligations, 125, 126

PLEADING
Complaint, what constitutes, 24, 25

PREGNANCY
Generally, 441–490
Abortion as pregnancy-related medical condition, 447, 448
Disparate impact and disparate treatment, 461–464
Family and Medical Leave Act, this index
Family Responsibilities Discrimination, this index
Historical overview, 441–443
Interplay between Title VII, PDA, FMLA and ADA, 486–487
Introduction, 441–443
Pregnancy Discrimination Act
Generally, 443–467
Abortion as pregnancy-related medical condition, 447, 448
Interplay between Title VII, PDA, FMLA and ADA, 486–487

Meaning of "discrimination on basis of pregnancy," 447–467
Prima facie case, 460
Related medical conditions, scope of, 464–467
Standing, 461
Related medical conditions, scope of, 464–467
Standing, pregnancy-related discrimination, 461

PREJUDGMENT INTEREST
Generally, 75, 76

PRESIDENTIAL EXECUTIVE ORDERS
Generally, 15
Affirmative action, 886

PRESUMPTIONS
Inferences and Presumptions, this index

PRETEXT
Disparate Treatment, this index

PRIVACY
BFOQ, privacy-based, 412–414

PUNITIVE DAMAGES
Damages, this index

RACE
Harassment based on race. Harassment, this index
Workplace equality, race and
Generally, 3–9
Gaps in perspectives between racial groups, 7, 8

REHABILITATION ACT OF 1973
Generally, 812, 813
Direct threat defense, 856
Hostile work environment claims, 839, 840
Relationship to ADA, 813

REINSTATEMENT REMEDY
Generally, 71–74
Denial of reinstatement, special or exceptional circumstances, 72
Innocent employee rule, 72
Mixed motive cases, 73
Objectives, 71, 72

RELIGIOUS DISCRIMINATION
Generally, 629–684
BFOQ defense, 648–650
Disparate impact religious discrimination claims under Title VII, 671
Exemptions for religious entities (Title VII), 632–636
Government employers, claims against
Generally, 671–682
Federal employees, 683
Federal workplace, guidelines on religious exercise and religious expression, 682, 683
Religious Freedom Restoration Act, 680, 681
Religious harassment in public employment, 682, 683
Meaning of "religion" for Title VII purposes, 632–634
Ministerial exception to Title VII claims against religious institutions
Generally, 639–641
Sexual harassment, freedom of religion and Title VII's ministerial exception, 557
Prima facie case of religious discrimination, 641–650
Reasonable accommodation and undue hardship
Generally, 659–668
Disparate impact religious discrimination claims under Title VII, 671
Harassment based on religion, 669, 670
Sexual orientation and gender identity, religious freedom and laws prohibiting discrimination on basis of, 668, 669
Unions, religious discrimination claims and charity substitution rule, 666–668
Religious Freedom Restoration Act, 680, 681
Reverse religious discrimination claims, 647, 648
Title VII, statutory overview, 629–632
Undue hardship. Reasonable accommodation and undue hardship, above
Unions, religious discrimination claims and charity substitution rule, 666–668

REMEDIES
Generally, 68–93
Back pay, 73–75
Basic remedial principles, 69, 70
Compensatory principle, 69
Damages, this index
Deterrence principle, 69
Equal Pay Act of 1963, 390
Front pay, 76, 77
Make whole theory of relief, 69
Monetary relief, 70
Prejudgment interest, 75, 76
Presumptive entitlement rule, 69
Reinstatement, 71–73
Rightful place theory of relief, 69
Statutory provisions, 68
Title VII, 390

RETALIATION
Generally, 161–207
Agents' conduct, employer liability, 182
Analytical framework, 168–172
Burden shifting, 168

Causation
Generally, 182–186
Evidence establishing causation, 184
Plaintiff's burden of proof on prima facie case, 184
Temporal proximity, role of, 185–187
Copying and distribution of employer documents, unauthorized, 196
Defamation action filed in bad faith, 181
Defenses
Employer defenses, 181
Disciplinary charges as materially adverse action, 181
Discriminate against, meaning of, 169–255
Employer defenses, 181
Evidence establishing causation, 184
FMLA retaliation, 488, 489
Former employees, 163
Harassment in response to complaints, 180
Litigation, retaliatory, 181
Materially adverse actions, 169–182
Minor annoyances, 180
Misappropriation of employer documents, 196
Mistaken beliefs, 200
Opposition clause, 191–196
Participation clause, 187–188
Petty slights, 180
Prima facie case
Generally, 168
Causation, 184
Rebuttable presumption, 123, 152
Scope of statutorily protected activity
Generally, 186–199
Opposition clause, 191–196
Participation clause, 187–188
Silent opposition to unlawful discrimination, 196
Summary judgment, 180
Ultimate employment decisions, 180

SECTION 1981
Generally, 321–336
Alienage, discrimination based on, 330, 331
At-will employees, claims by, 328
Claims cognizable under "to make and enforce contracts" clause, 327
Eleventh Amendment immunity, 19
Employers covered, 327
Exhaustion of administrative remedies, 20
Historical background, 14
Individual liability, agents of employers, 59
National origin, discrimination based on, 329, 330
Prohibited conduct, 327, 328
Race and color, meaning of, 44–49
Racial harassment claims, 626
Remedies and procedural requirements, 331–338
Retaliation claims, 161, 162
Sex, religion, age and disability, 331
State and local government employers, section 1981 claims against, 337, 38
Theory of liability
Generally, 323–330
Analytical framework, 326, 327
Union member claims against unions, 337
White persons, application to, 324

SECTION 1983
Burden of proof, 318–321
Equal protection claims against state and local government employers, 318
Historical background, 14

SEX DISCRIMINATION
Generally, 349–440
Annuities, 360
Appearance. Dress, grooming and appearance requirements, sex-based, below
Attractiveness, 432
Benevolent paternalism vs. employee autonomy, 393
BFOQ defense
Generally, 391–413
Benevolent paternalism vs. employee autonomy, 393
Cost justification defense, 408, 409
Customer preferences, 409, 410
Dress and grooming requirements, 431, 432
Fetal protection policies, 405–407
Foreign nations, customs of, 410
Privacy-based BFOQ, 411–414
Safety justification, 395, 406
Cost justification defense, 408, 409
Customer preferences, 409, 410
Disparate treatment and disparate impact claims, distinguishing, 374, 375
Dress, grooming and appearance requirements, sex-based
Generally, 414–429
Immutable traits, 432
Judicial notice and costs of dress and grooming rules, 429, 430
Reasonableness of grooming standards, 428, 429
Sex stereotyping, 429, 430
Sexual attractiveness, 433
State and local laws prohibiting appearance discrimination, 433, 444
Unequal burdens test, 428
Weight requirements, sex-based, 431, 432
Equality theory of discrimination, 430
Evidence of discrimination "because of sex," 426
Fetal protection policies, 405–407
Foreign nations, customs of, 410
Glass ceiling, systemic claims and, 434–440
Grooming. Dress, grooming and appearance requirements, sex-based, above

Harassment, sexual. Harassment, this index
Historical overview, 349–355
Immutable traits, 432
Insurance, 360
Intersectional claims, 373, 374, 433
Introduction, 349–355
Privacy-based BFOQ, 411–414
Safety justification, 395, 406
Sameness theory of discrimination, 355
Sex-plus claims, 373, 374
Sexual attractiveness, 433
State and local laws prohibiting appearance discrimination, 433, 444
Stereotyping, 366–369, 429, 430
Systemic claims and glass ceiling, 434–440
Weight requirements, sex-based, 431, 432
What is discrimination "because of sex," 355–359

SEX-BASED WAGE DISCRIMINATION
Wage Discrimination, Sex-Based, this index

SEXUAL ORIENTATION
Generally, 491–534
ADA exclusions, 513–514
Alternative sources of employment rights for LGBT individuals
Collective bargaining agreements, 531
Common law remedies, 531, 532
Corporate nondiscrimination policies, 530
Domestic partner benefits, 530, 531
Hate crimes legislation, 531
International human rights laws, protection of sexual orientation and gender identity, 532
Professional and academic associations, nondiscrimination policies, 531
U.S. and state constitutions, protections under, 529–531
Collective bargaining agreements, 531
Common law remedies, 531, 532
Corporate nondiscrimination policies, 530
Crossdressers, 513–514
Definitions, 492–494
Discrimination because of sexual orientation, 491–534
Domestic partner benefits, 530, 531
Employment Non-Discrimination Act, 526, 527
Federal government employment nondiscrimination policies, 527
Gender expression or identity, discrimination based on, 505–514
Gender identity and gender expression, defined, 494
Harassment of sexual minorities
Generally, 515–521
Antigay epithets and gestures, 523
Gender stereotyping claims, 523
Reverse discrimination, 525
Sex plus discrimination, 523
International human rights laws, protection of sexual orientation and gender identity, 532
Intersex, defined, 494
Introduction, 491–492
Law and economics, 467
Professional and academic associations, nondiscrimination policies, 531
Race or sex plus sexual orientation, 505
Religious freedom and laws prohibiting discrimination on basis of sexual orientation and gender identity, 668, 669
Restroom facilities, access for transsexual or transgender employees, 513, 514
Reverse discrimination, 525
Sex and gender, defined, 493
Sexual orientation, defined, 493
Stereotyping, 366–369, 429, 430
Transgender, defined, 494
Transsexual, defined, 494
U.S. and state constitutions, protections under, 529–531

SOVEREIGN IMMUNITY
Equal Pay Act claims against state employers, 385

STANDING
Pregnancy-related discrimination, 461

STATE AND LOCAL GOVERNMENTS
ADA actions, 814, 815
ADEA claims against states, 744
Appearance discrimination, state and local laws, 433, 444
Eleventh Amendment immunity, 19
Equal Pay Act claims against state employers and sovereign immunity, 385
Section 1981 claims against government employers, 337, 338
Sexual harassment, state antidiscrimination laws and Title VII, 603, 604

STATISTICAL EVIDENCE
Disparate Treatment, this index

SUMMARY JUDGMENT
Retaliation claims, 180

SUPERVISORS
Harassment by, employer's vicarious liability. Harassment, this index

TAXATION
Damages awards, 84, 85
Fee awards, 90

TEMPORARY EMPLOYEES AND EMPLOYERS
Generally, 59

THEORIES OF EQUALITY
Generally, 4–6
Equal opportunity, 5
Equal treatment, 5

TIME LIMITS
EEOC, this index

TITLE IX
Retaliation protection, 161

TITLE VII
Generally, 11, 12
Affirmative Action, this index
Attorney's fees, 85–87
Bennett Amendment, 386–389
Color, meaning of, 49
Complaint, what constitutes, 40, 41
Damages
Compensatory and punitive, 70
Duty to mitigate, 73, 74
Disparate Impact, this index
Disparate Treatment, this index
EEOC enforcement. EEOC, this index
Eleventh Amendment immunity, 18, 19
Employer, defined, 57
Employment practice, defined, 60, 61
Enactment, 4
Equal Pay Act and Title VII, reconciling, 386–389
Exhaustion of administrative remedies, 20, 22–39
Extraterritorial application, 60
Federal employers, Title VII as exclusive remedy, 314, 337
Harassment, this index
Judicial enforcement
Generally, 40–42
Complaint, what constitutes, 41, 42
Laches, 41
Ninety-day filing period, 41
Right-to-sue letter, 41
Timely filing court, 40, 41
Mitigation of damages, victim's duty, 73, 74
Mixed Motive Cases, this index
National Origin Discrimination, this index
NLRA's exclusivity principle, 66, 67
Pregnancy Discrimination Act. Pregnancy, this index
Religious Discrimination, this index
Remedies, 68–69
Retaliation provisions, 168
Sex Discrimination, this index
Sexual Orientation, this index
Undocumented workers and Title VII. National Origin Discrimination, this index
Union liability, 62–65

TRAINING PROGRAMS
Discriminatory, union liability, 66, 68

UNDOCUMENTED WORKERS
National Origin Discrimination, this index

UNIONS
Acquiescence in employer's discriminatory conduct, 65, 66
ADA, reasonable accommodation requirement in unionized sector, 870, 871
Apprenticeship programs, discrimination, 67, 68
Arbitration in unionized workplace. Arbitration, this index
Employer, union as, 62–68
Liability for discrimination
Generally, 61–64
Duty of fair representation, 61
Employer, union as, 62–68
Labor organization, liability as, 62–64
Religious discrimination claims and charity substitution rule, 666–668
Section 1981 claims by union members against unions, 337
Training programs, discrimination, 66, 68

VETERANS' RIGHTS
Generally, 20

VICARIOUS LIABILITY
Harassment by supervisor, employer's vicarious liability. Harassment, this index

VOCATIONAL REHABILITATION ACT OF 1973
Generally, 13

WAGE DISCRIMINATION, SEX-BASED
Generally, 372–386
Bennett Amendment to Title VII
Generally, 386–391
Intent, role of, 389, 390
Procedural requirements, 390
Proving similar work under Title VII, 389, 390
Remedies, 390
Statute of limitations, 390
Equal Pay Act of 1963
Generally, 378–391
Affirmative defenses, 382
Any factor other than sex defense, 382, 383
Catch-all defense, 382, 383
Equal work, 379, 380
Establishment requirement, 379
Intent, role of, 389, 390
Merit system defense, 382
Opposite sex comparator(s), 380, 381
Prima facie case, 378

Prior salary and market demand, 383–385
Procedural requirements, 390
Remedies, 390
Salary policies as "factor other than sex," 383–385
Salary retention or "red circling," 385
Similar working conditions, 381, 382
State employers, claims against, and sovereign immunity, 385
Statute of limitations, 390
Unequal pay, 381
Lily Ledbetter Fair Pay Act of 2009, 37, 38, 390, 391
Sex-plus-race claims of wage discrimination, 391